# BMW 3 Series
## (E90, E91, E92, E93)

## Service Manual

### 325i, 325xi, 328i, 328xi, 330i, 330xi, 335i, 335xi
### 2006, 2007, 2008, 2009, 2010

**B** BentleyPublishers™
.com

**BENTLEY PUBLISHERS**™ | Automotive Reference™

Bentley Publishers, a division of Robert Bentley, Inc.
1734 Massachusetts Avenue
Cambridge, MA 02138 USA
800-423-4595 / 617-547-4170

*Information that makes the difference*®

**BentleyPublishers**
.com

**Technical contact information**
We welcome your feedback. Please submit corrections and additions to our BMW technical discussion forum at:
`http://www.BentleyPublishers.com`

**Updates and corrections**
We will evaluate submissions and post appropriate editorial changes online as updates or tech discussion. Appropriate updates and corrections will be added to the book in future printings. Check for updates and corrections for this book before beginning work on your vehicle. See the following web address for additional information:
`http://www.BentleyPublishers.com/updates/`

*WARNING—Important Safety Notice*

Do not use this manual for repairs unless you are familiar with automotive repair procedures and safe workshop practices. This manual illustrates the workshop procedures for some maintenance and service work. It is not a substitute for full and up-to-date information from the vehicle manufacturer or for proper training as an automotive technician. Note that it is not possible for us to anticipate all of the ways or conditions under which vehicles may be serviced or to provide cautions as to all of the possible hazards that may result.

We have endeavored to ensure the accuracy of the information in this manual. Please note, however, that considering the vast quantity and the complexity of the service information involved, we cannot warrant the accuracy or completeness of the information contained in this manual.

**FOR THESE REASONS, NEITHER THE PUBLISHER NOR THE AUTHOR MAKES ANY WARRANTIES, EXPRESS OR IMPLIED, THAT THE INFORMATION IN THIS MANUAL IS FREE OF ERRORS OR OMISSIONS, AND WE EXPRESSLY DISCLAIM THE IMPLIED WARRANTIES OF MERCHANTABILITY AND OF FITNESS FOR A PARTICULAR PURPOSE, EVEN IF THE PUBLISHER OR AUTHOR HAVE BEEN ADVISED OF A PARTICULAR PURPOSE, AND EVEN IF A PARTICULAR PURPOSE IS INDICATED IN THE MANUAL. THE PUBLISHER AND AUTHOR ALSO DISCLAIM ALL LIABILITY FOR DIRECT, INDIRECT, INCIDENTAL OR CONSEQUENTIAL DAMAGES THAT RESULT FROM ANY USE OF THE EXAMPLES, INSTRUCTIONS OR OTHER INFORMATION IN THIS MANUAL. IN NO EVENT SHALL OUR LIABILITY, WHETHER IN TORT, CONTRACT OR OTHERWISE, EXCEED THE COST OF THIS MANUAL.**

Before attempting any work on your BMW, read **001 Warnings and Cautions** and any **WARNING** or **CAUTION** that accompanies a procedure in the manual. Review the **WARNINGS** and **CAUTIONS** each time you prepare to work on your BMW.

Your common sense and good judgment are crucial to safe and successful service work. Read procedures through before starting them. Think about whether the condition of your car, your level of mechanical skill or your level of reading comprehension might result in or contribute in some way to an occurrence which might cause you injury, damage your car or result in an unsafe repair. If you have doubts for these or other reasons about your ability to perform safe repair work on your car, have the work done at an authorized BMW dealer or other qualified shop.

Part numbers listed in this manual are for identification purposes only, not for ordering. Always check with your authorized BMW dealer to verify part numbers and availability before beginning service work that may require new parts.

Special tools required to perform certain service operations are identified in the manual and are recommended for use. Use of improper tools may be detrimental to the car's safe operation as well as the safety of the person servicing the car.

The vehicle manufacturer will continue to issue service information updates and parts retrofits after the editorial closing of this manual. Some of these updates and retrofits will apply to procedures and specifications in this manual. We regret that we cannot supply updates to purchasers of this manual.

This manual is prepared, published and distributed by Bentley Publishers, 1734 Massachusetts Avenue, Cambridge, Massachusetts 02138. All information contained in this manual is based on the information available to the publisher at the time of editorial closing. BMW has not reviewed and does not vouch for the accuracy or completeness of the technical specifications and work procedures described and given in this manual.

© 2009 Robert Bentley, Inc. Bentley Publishers is a trademark of Robert Bentley, Inc.

**ISBN 978-0-8376-1685-8**     **Bentley Stock No. B310**     Mfg. code: B310-01-1103, editorial closing 07 / 2009.

Library of Congress Cataloging-in-Publication Data for 2009 Edition
BMW 3 series service manual : 325i, 325xi, 328i, 328xi, 330i, 330xi, 335i, 335xi
2006, 2007, 2008, 2009.
    p. cm.
Includes index.
ISBN 978-0-8376-1608-7 (alk. paper)
  1.  BMW 3 series automobiles--Maintenance and repair--Handbooks, manuals, etc.  I.
Robert Bentley, inc.

TL215.B25B557 2005
629.28'722--dc22
                2009027377

# 0 General Data and Maintenance

| | |
|---|---|
| 001 Warnings and Cautions | 003 Symptoms and Field Observations |
| 002 Vehicle Identification and VIN Decoder | 010 Product Familiarization |
| | 020 Maintenance |

# 1 Engine

| | |
|---|---|
| 100 Engine–General | 120 Ignition System |
| 110 Engine Removal and Installation | 121 Battery, Starter, Alternator |
| 113 Cylinder Head Removal and Installation | 130 Fuel Injection |
| 117 Camshaft Timing Chain | 160 Fuel Tank and Fuel Pump |
| 119 Lubrication System | 170 Radiator and Cooling System |
| | 180 Exhaust System |

# 2 Transmission

| | |
|---|---|
| 200 Transmission–General | 250 Gearshift Linkage |
| 210 Clutch | 260 Driveshafts |
| 230 Manual Transmission | 270 Transfer Case |
| 240 Automatic Transmission | |

# 3 Suspension, Steering and Brakes

| | |
|---|---|
| 300 Suspension, Steering and Brakes–General | 320 Steering and Wheel Alignment |
| 310 Front Suspension | 330 Rear Suspension |
| 311 Front Axle Differential | 331 Rear Axle Differential |
| | 340 Brakes |

# 4 Body

| | |
|---|---|
| 400 Body–General | 411 Doors |
| 410 Fenders, Engine Hood | 412 Trunk Lid, Tailgate |

# 5 Body Equipment

| | |
|---|---|
| 510 Exterior Trim, Bumpers | 515 Central Locking and Anti-theft |
| 512 Door Windows | 520 Seats |
| 513 Interior Trim | 541 Convertible Top |

# 6 Electrical System

| | |
|---|---|
| 600 Electrical System–General | 630 Lights |
| 611 Wipers and Washers | 640 Heating and Air-conditioning |
| 612 Switches | 650 Radio |
| 620 Instruments | |

# 7 Equipment and Accessories

| | |
|---|---|
| 720 Seat Belts | |
| 721 Airbag System (SRS) | |

# ECL / ELE / OBD

ECL Electrical Component Locations

ELE Electrical Wiring Diagrams

OBD On-Board Diagnostics

# Foreword

For the BMW owner with basic mechanical skills and for independent auto service professionals, this manual includes many of the specifications and procedures that were available in an authorized BMW dealer service department as this manual went to press. The BMW owner with no intention of working on his or her car will find that owning and referring to this manual will make it possible to be better informed and to more knowledgeably discuss repairs with a professional automotive technician.

For those intending to do maintenance and repair on their BMW, it is essential that safety equipment be used and safety precautions observed when working on the vehicle. A minimum safety equipment list includes hand protection, eye protection and a fire extinguisher. A selection of good quality hand tools is also needed. This includes a torque wrench to ensure that fasteners are tightened in accordance with specifications. In some cases, the text refers to special tools that are recommended or required to accomplish adjustments or repairs. These tools are often identified by their BMW special tool number and illustrated.

---

## Disclaimer

We have endeavored to ensure the accuracy of the information in this manual. When the vast array of data presented in the manual is taken into account, however, no claim to infallibility can be made. We therefore cannot be responsible for the result of any errors that may have crept into the text. Please also read the **WARNING—Important Safety Notice** on the copyright page at the beginning of this book.

Prior to starting a repair procedure, read the procedure, **001 Warnings and Cautions** and the warnings and cautions that accompany the procedure. Reading a procedure before beginning work helps you determine in advance the need for specific skills, identify hazards, prepare for appropriate capture and handling of hazardous materials, and the need for particular tools and replacement parts such as gaskets.

---

Bentley Publishers encourages comments from the readers of this manual with regard to errors, and suggestions for improvement of our product. These communications have been and will be carefully considered in the preparation of this and other manuals. If you identify inconsistencies in the manual, you may have found an error. Please contact the publisher and we will endeavor to post applicable corrections on our website. Posted corrections (errata) should be reviewed before beginning work. Please see the following web address:

http://www.BentleyPublishers.com/errata/

BMW will continue to issue service information and parts retrofits after the editorial closing of this manual. Some of this updated information may apply to procedures and specifications in this manual. For the latest information, please see the following web address:

http://www.bmwtechinfo.com/

BMW offers extensive warranties, especially on components of the fuel delivery and emission control systems. Therefore, before deciding to repair a BMW that may be covered wholly or in part by any warranties issued by BMW of North America, LLC, consult your authorized BMW dealer. You may find that the dealer can make the repair either free or at minimum cost. Regardless of its age, or whether it is under warranty, your BMW is both an easy car to service and an easy car to get serviced. So if at any time a repair is needed that you feel is too difficult to do yourself, a trained BMW technician is ready to do the job for you.

**Bentley Publishers**

# 001 Warnings and Cautions

## PLEASE READ THESE WARNINGS AND CAUTIONS BEFORE PROCEEDING WITH MAINTENANCE AND REPAIR WORK.

### WARNINGS—
*See also* CAUTIONS

- Read the important safety notice on the copyright page at the beginning of the book.

- Some repairs may be beyond your capability. If you lack the skills, tools and equipment or a suitable workplace for any procedure described in this manual, we suggest you leave such repairs to an authorized BMW dealer service department or other qualified shop.

- Thoroughly read each procedure and the **WARNINGS** and **CAUTIONS** that accompany the procedure. Also review posted corrections at www.BentleyPublishers.com/errata/ before beginning work.

- If any procedure, tightening torque, wear limit, specification or data presented in this manual does not appear to be appropriate for a specific application, contact the publisher or the vehicle manufacturer for clarification before using the information in question.

- Do not reuse any fasteners that are worn or deformed. Many fasteners are designed to be used only once and become unreliable and may fail when used a second time. This includes, but is not limited to, nuts, bolts, washers, self-locking nuts or bolts, circlips and cotter pins. Replace these fasteners with new parts.

- Do not work under a lifted car unless it is solidly supported on stands designed for the purpose. Do not support a car on cinder blocks, hollow tiles or other props that may crumble under continuous load. Do not work under a car that is supported solely by a jack. Do not work under the car while the engine is running.

- If you are going to work under a car on the ground, make sure that the ground is level. Block the wheels to keep the car from rolling. Disconnect the battery negative (–) terminal to prevent others from starting the car while you are under it.

- Do not run the engine unless the work area is well ventilated. Carbon monoxide kills.

- Remove rings, bracelets and other jewelry so that they cannot cause electrical shorts, get caught in running machinery, or be crushed by heavy parts.

- Tie long hair behind your head. Do not wear a necktie, a scarf, loose clothing, or a necklace when you work near machine tools or running engines. If your hair, clothing, or jewelry were to get caught in the machinery, severe injury could result.

- Do not attempt to work on your car if you do not feel well. You increase the danger of injury to yourself and others if you are tired, upset or have taken medication or any other substance that may keep you from being fully alert.

- Illuminate your work area adequately but safely. Use a portable safety light for working inside or under the car. Make sure the bulb is enclosed by a wire cage. The hot filament of an accidentally broken bulb can ignite spilled fuel, vapors or oil.

- Catch draining fuel, oil, or brake fluid in suitable containers. Do not use food or beverage containers that might mislead someone into drinking from them. Store flammable fluids away from fire hazards. Wipe up spills at once, but do not store the oily rags, which can ignite and burn spontaneously.

- Observe good workshop practices. Wear goggles when you operate machine tools or work with battery acid. Wear gloves or other protective clothing whenever the job requires working with harmful substances.

- Greases, lubricants and other automotive chemicals contain toxic substances, many of which are absorbed directly through the skin. Read the manufacturer's instructions and warnings carefully. Use hand and eye protection. Avoid direct skin contact.

- Disconnect the battery negative (–) terminal whenever you work on the fuel system or the electrical system. Do not smoke or work near heaters or other fire hazards. Keep an approved fire extinguisher handy.

- Friction materials (such as brake pads and shoes or clutch discs) contain asbestos fibers or other friction materials. Do not create dust by grinding, sanding, or by cleaning with compressed air. Avoid breathing dust. Breathing any friction material dust can lead to serious diseases and may result in death.

- Batteries give off explosive hydrogen gas during charging. Keep sparks, lighted matches and open flame away from the top of the battery. If hydrogen gas escaping from the cap vents is ignited, it may ignite gas trapped in the cells and cause the battery to explode.

- The air-conditioning system is filled with chemical refrigerant, which is hazardous. Make sure the system is serviced only by a trained technician using approved refrigerant recovery/recycling equipment, trained in related safety precautions, and familiar with regulations governing the discharge and disposal of automotive chemical refrigerants.

*Continued on next page*

## WARNINGS (continued)

- Do not expose any part of the A/C system to high temperatures such as open flame. Excessive heat increases system pressure and may cause the system to burst.

- Some aerosol tire inflators are highly flammable. Be extremely cautious when repairing a tire that may have been inflated using an aerosol tire inflator. Keep sparks, open flame or other sources of ignition away from the tire repair area. Inflate and deflate the tire at least four times before breaking the bead from the rim. Completely remove the tire from the rim before attempting any repair.

- Cars covered by this manual are equipped with a supplemental restraint system (SRS) that automatically deploys airbags and pyrotechnic seat belt tensioners in case of a frontal or side impact. These are explosive devices. Handled improperly or without adequate safeguards, they can be accidently activated and cause serious injury.

- The ignition system produces high voltages that can be fatal. Avoid contact with exposed terminals and use extreme care when working on a car with the engine running or the ignition switched ON.

- Place jack stands only at locations specified by the manufacturer. The vehicle lifting jack supplied with the vehicle is intended for tire changes only. Use a heavy duty floor jack to lift vehicle before installing jack stands. See **020 Maintenance**.

- Battery acid (electrolyte) can cause severe burns. Flush contact area with water, then seek medical attention.

- Aerosol cleaners and solvents may contain hazardous or deadly vapors and are highly flammable. Use only in a well ventilated area. Do not use on hot surfaces (engines, brakes, etc.).

- Due to risk of personal injury, be sure the engine is cold before beginning work on the cooling system.

## CAUTIONS—
### *See also* WARNINGS

- If you lack the skills, tools and equipment, or a suitable workshop for any procedure described in this manual, leave such repairs to an authorized BMW dealer or other qualified shop.

- BMW is constantly improving its cars and sometimes these changes, both in parts and specifications, are made applicable to earlier models. Any part numbers listed in this manual are for reference only. Check with your authorized BMW dealer parts department for the latest information.

- Before starting a job, make certain that you have the necessary tools and parts on hand. Read all the instructions thoroughly, and do not attempt shortcuts. Use tools appropriate to the work and use only replacement parts meeting BMW specifications.

- Use pneumatic and electric tools only to loosen threaded parts and fasteners. Do not use these tools to tighten fasteners, especially on light alloy parts. Use a torque wrench to tighten fasteners to the tightening torque specification listed.

- Be mindful of the environment and ecology. Before you drain the crankcase, find out the proper way to dispose of the oil. Do not pour oil onto the ground, down a drain, or into a stream, pond or lake. Dispose of waste in accordance with federal, state and local laws.

- The control module for the anti-lock brake system (ABS) cannot withstand temperatures from a paint-drying booth or a heat lamp in excess of 203°F (95°C). Do not subject to temperatures in excess of 185°F (85°C) for more than two hours.

- Before doing any electrical welding on cars equipped with ABS, disconnect the battery negative (–) terminal (ground strap) and the ABS control module connector.

- Make sure ignition is switched OFF before disconnecting battery.

- Label battery cables before disconnecting. On some models, battery cables are not color coded.

- Disconnecting the battery may erase fault code(s) stored in control module memory. Using special BMW diagnostic equipment, check for fault codes prior to disconnecting the battery cables. If the malfunction indicator light (MIL) is illuminated, see **OBD On-Board Diagnostics** at the back of this manual. (This light may be identified as the Check Engine light or the Service Engine Soon light.) If any other system faults are detected (indicated by an illuminated warning light), see an authorized BMW dealer.

- If a normal or rapid charger is used to charge battery, disconnect the battery remove it from the vehicle in order to avoid damaging the vehicle.

- Do not quick-charge the battery (for boost starting) for longer than one minute. Wait at least one minute before boosting the battery a second time.

- Connect and disconnect a battery charger only with the battery charger switched OFF.

- Sealed or "maintenance free" batteries should be slow-charged only, at an amperage rate that is approximately 10% of the battery's ampere-hour (Ah) rating.

- Do not allow battery charging voltage to exceed 16.5 volts. If the battery begins producing gas or boiling violently, reduce the charging rate. Boosting a sulfated battery at a high charging rate can cause an explosion.

- Do not use steel fasteners on engine components made of aluminum-magnesium alloy. Use aluminum fasteners only. Test fasteners for aluminum composition with magnet.

- Replace aluminum bolts each time they are loosened. Follow torque instructions, including angle of rotation specifications, when installing aluminum fasteners.

# 002 Vehicle Identification and VIN Decoder

Some of the information in this manual applies only to cars of a particular model year or range of years. For example, 2006 refers to the 2006 model year but does not necessarily match the calendar year in which the car was manufactured or sold. To be sure of the model year of a particular car, check the vehicle identification number (VIN) on the car.

The VIN is a unique sequence of 17 characters assigned by BMW to identify each individual car. When decoded, the VIN tells the country and year of manufacture; make, model and serial number; assembly plant and even some equipment specifications.

The BMW VIN is on a plate mounted on the top of the dashboard, on the driver's side where the number can be seen through the windshield. The 10th character is the model year code. Examples: 6 for 2006, 7 for 2007, 8 for 2008, 9 for 2009, etc. The table below explains some of the codes in the VIN for 2006 through 2010 BMW E90, E91, E92, and E93 3 Series covered by this manual.

**Sample VIN:** WBA DC84 0 X J 1 841989

position    1 2 3    4 5 6 7    8 9 10 11    12-17

| VIN position | Description | Decoding information | |
|---|---|---|---|
| 1 - 3 | Country of manufacture | WBA | BMW, AG. Munich, Germany |
| 4 | Line | P | 328i xDrive Sedan (2009) |
| | | U | 328i, xDrive Sports Wagon (2009) |
| | | V | 325i, 325 xi, 330i, 330xi (2006), 328i Sedan, 328xi Sedan and Sports Wagon, 335i, 335xi (2007-2009) |
| | | W | 328i Coupe and Convertible, 328xi Coupe, 335i Convertible (2007-2009) |
| 5 | Series | A | 328i Sedan (2007-2008) |
| | | B | 325i, 330i, Sedan (2006) 328i Coupe (2007-2009), 335i Sedan and Coupe (2007-2008) |
| | | C | 328i Sedan (2007), 328xi Sedan and Coupe (2007-2009) |
| | | D | 325xi Sedan, 330xi Sedan (2006), 335xi Sedan (2007-2008) |
| | | H | 328i Sedan (2009) |
| | | K | 328i xDrive Sedan (2009) |
| | | L | 328i Convertible, 335i Convertible (2007-2008) |
| | | R | 328i Convertible (2007-2009) |
| | | T | 328xi Sports Wagon (2008), 328i Sports Wagon (2009) |
| | | U | 328xi Sports Wagon (2009) |
| | | V | 328i xDrive Coupe (2009) |
| 6 | Engine type | 1 | 3.0 liter 6-cylinder |
| | | 3 | |
| | | 5 | |
| | | 7 | |
| | | 9 | |
| 7 | Vehicle type | 3, 7 | Passenger vehicle (2006-2009) |
| | | A, G | Passenger vehicle (2010) |
| 8 | Restraint system | 5 | Multiple restraint system |
| 9 | Check digit | | 0 - 9 or X, calculated by NHTSA |
| 10 | Model year | 6 | 2006 |
| | | 7 | 2007 |
| | | 8 | 2008 |
| | | 9 | 2009 |
| | | A | 2010 |
| 11 | Assembly plant | A, F, K | Munich, Germany |
| | | N, V | Leipzig, Germany |
| | | E, J, P | Regensburg, Germany |
| 12-17 | Serial number | | Sequential production number for specific vehicle |

# 003 Symptoms and Field Observations

## GENERAL

This repair group includes a list of symptoms, field observations, and suggested fixes for common problems and issues found on 3 Series (E90, E91, E92, and E93) cars.

The information is organized by sections that correspond to the layout of the repair manual. Additional information (when available) can be found in the repair group associated with the specific issue:

- **0** General Data and Maintenance
- **1** Engine
- **2** Transmission
- **3** Suspension, Steering and Brakes
- **4** Body
- **5** Body Equipment
- **6** Electrical System
- **7** Equipment and Accessories

This information was developed from varied sources, ranging from professional BMW technician feedback to manufacturer-issued technical service bulletins (TSBs). The content is intended to complement the repair information found in this repair manual.

> **CAUTION—**
> - *The information contained in this section is inherently dated material. It was applicable and relevant at the time this manual went to press. Always check BMW factory repair information at www.bmwtechinfo.com or the publisher's website at www.bentleypublishers.com for information that may supersede any information included in this section.*

## 0 GENERAL DATA AND MAINTENANCE

| Topic | Notes | Additional information (when available) |
|---|---|---|
| **Exiting a vehicle that is double-locked from the outside**<br> | Never lock a vehicle from outside the car with an someone inside the car!<br><br>In the unlikely that someone gets double-locked inside the car, the person inside the car can exit the vehicle using the following 2-step procedure:<br><br>• Press the central unlock button to disable "double-lock".<br>• Pull the door handle twice to open door.<br><br>   ***NOTE*** —<br>     *• For vehicles with the factory alarm, opening the door will activate the alarm.* | |
| **Service Engine Soon or Check Gas Cap warning Is illuminated: faulty gas cap or software error (up 09/2008 production)**<br> | DME has stored faults for a small leak, micro leak, super fine leak, or large leak in the tank ventilation or evaporative system.<br><br>Remove the fuel cap and inspect the cap seal for damage (torn, worn or curling seal). If any damage is detected, the cap should be replaced. Be sure the cap is properly tightened down.<br><br>If no cap faults can be found, and the fault returns, further DMTL system diagnosis is required (e.g. run DMTL test plan using the BMW diagnostic scan tool).<br><br>   ***NOTE*** —<br>     *• On vehicles produced from July 1st, 2006 up to September 30th, 2008 with the following stored faults: 2A15 - DMTL minor leak, leak greater than 1.0 mm or 2A16 - DMTL micro leak, leak greater than 0.5 mm, there may be a software error for the tank leak diagnostic system. If these faults are present, be sure the software level (I-level vehicle data status) is up to date.* | **OBD** |
| **Cabin filters, changing**<br> | When servicing fresh air micro (cabin) filter, be sure to reinstall the filter lid correctly. Incorrect installation can result in premature blower motor failure due to water intrusion.<br><br>• Check that gap (**A**) between upper microfilter housing and cowl is no more than 1cm. Remove and reposition housing as necessary to reduce the gap. | **020** |

## 0 GENERAL DATA AND MAINTENANCE (CONTINUED)

| Topic | Notes | Additional information (when available) |
|---|---|---|
| **Engine oil, topping up** <br><br> | Oil residue may collect on the cylinder head cover near the oil filler cap a few days after topping up or refilling the engine oil. <br><br> When oil is added, the filler cap is laid partially upside down. In this position, engine oil seeps into the area of the oil cap that is not sealed by the gasket. When the cap is reinstalled, the oil leaks from the unsealed area onto the cylinder head cover surface. <br><br> If investigating an oil leak in this area, confirm that it is not oil from the cap. | **020** |
| **Replacing spark plugs, service tip (N52 / N51 engines)** <br><br> | When servicing spark plugs, a standard socket may fit too tightly into the spark plug bore in the cylinder head. If this is the case, remove the heat shield inside plug hole (**arrow**) before servicing spark plugs. | **020** |
| **Special tool for spark plug removal (N54 engine)** <br><br> | The N54 uses a new design spark plug from Bosch that consists of a 12mm thread (compared to the 14mm design on the N52 / N51) and a 12-point hex. The plug requires a special tool (BMW special tool part no. 83 30 0 495 560). The special socket is a thin-wall design to facilitate access in the confined area of the N54 cylinder head. | **020** |

## 0 GENERAL DATA AND MAINTENANCE (CONTINUED)

| Topic | Notes | Additional information (when available) |
|---|---|---|
| **Check control messages** | On cars without the Central Information Display (CID), check control (CC) messages stored in the instrument cluster can be viewed in the CC display.<br><br>To check the CC messages in the instrument cluster:<br><br>• Switch on ignition (KL-R or KL-15)<br>• Toggle rocker switch on direction indicator switch to bring up "Check Control"<br>• Briefly press the on-board computer button<br>• Select the check control message required with rocker switch (if multiple check controls messages are present)<br>• Press the on-board computer button for longer than 4 seconds<br>• The CC message will appear for approx. 2 seconds: "CC-ID xxx"<br>• Toggle rocker switch to bring up additional stored messages.<br><br>The above check displays the message identification number, but does not define the message. A list of check control messages and their definitions can be found in **020 Maintenance**.<br><br>*NOTE—*<br>• *When using the BMW diagnostic scan tool, up to 72 messages can be accessed along with the vehicle mileage when message was stored.* | **020** |
| **Engine oil level, checking after oil change - dynamic check (engine running)** | Always perform the dynamic oil level measurement (approx. 5 minutes driving time) after an oil change. The oil level could be misinterpreted as the oil level last stored is initially displayed after an oil change.<br><br>*NOTE—*<br>• *There is no oil level initially stored after replacing or reprogramming the engine control unit ("Oil level below min" is displayed). The correct oil level is indicated after running the engine for approx. 5 minutes.*<br><br>- Start engine.<br><br>- Select on-board computer function - **OIL** using rocker switch. Press BC switch in once. Oil level check begins. A clock symbol (arrow) may appear while the level measurement is running.<br><br>*NOTE—*<br>• *The clock symbol appears for up to 50 seconds after starting the engine when there is no measured value or the last stored value is not within the tolerance range of the currently measured oil level.* | **020** |

## 0 GENERAL DATA AND MAINTENANCE (CONTINUED)

| Topic | Notes | Additional information (when available) |
|---|---|---|
| **Intelligent battery sensor (IBS), service precautions** | The Intelligent Battery Sensor (IBS) is an electronic device connected directly to the negative battery terminal. The IBS is very sensitive to mechanical stress and strain. Particular attention should be paid to the following points:<br><br>• Do not make any additional connections at the negative terminal of the battery.<br>• Do not modify the battery ground cable.<br>• Do not make any connections between the IBS and the sensor screw.<br>• Do not use force when disconnecting the ground terminal from the battery.<br>• Never pull on the ground cable.<br>• Do not use the IBS as a pivot point to lever off the ground terminal.<br>• Do not use the connections of the IBS as a lever.<br>• Use only a torque wrench as described in the repair manual during installation.<br>• Do not release or tighten the sensor screw.<br><br>*NOTE*—<br><br>• A replacement IBS includes the ground cable. The ground cable also serves as a heat dissipater for the IBS. | 121 |
| **Battery, replacing** | When fitting a new battery, it must be "registered" to the vehicle to notify the vehicle power management software (engine electronics and intelligent battery sensor) that a new battery was fitted. This operation requires a BMW diagnostic scan tool or equivalent.<br><br>Without new battery registration, various electrical problems as well odd electrical system behavior can occur. | 121 |

## 1 ENGINE

| Topic | Notes | Additional information (when available) |
|---|---|---|
| **Excessive engine movement results in engine accessory belt failure (N54 engine, up 04/2008 production, except xi models)** | Excessive engine movement can lead to engine accessory belt damage. The drive belt may become dislodged from pulleys or broken when traveling over curbs, speed bumps or at a high rate of speed.<br><br>Inspect power steering pulley for chips or cracks indicating contact with front axle carrier. If you find damage to pulley, inspect front axle carrier. If you find marks that show the pulley has made contact, replace the front axle carrier and the left side engine mount with updated parts.<br><br>See BMW Service Bulletin SIB 11 09 08 (dated October 2008) or an authorized BMW dealer for additional information. | 020 |
| **Coolant contact with magnesium components** | During service procedures which involve coolant, such as cylinder head replacement, the bolt holes must be blown dry immediately. To prevent corrosion, do not allow any traces of coolant to remain in holes. | 113 |
| **No crank, no start** | Engine does not crank. Only the SRS (Supplemental Restraint System) and red brake lights show in the instrument cluster with ignition on. FC A111 (ELV voltage supply fault) is stored in the CAS (Car Access System).<br><br>*NOTE—*<br>• *As a result of a change in government requirements, the ELV was deleted on most 2007 and later models. Anti-theft protection continues to be provided by drive-away protection in EWS.*<br><br>Disconnect the IBS connector (3-pin connector with 2 wires) at the negative battery terminal. Follow the white/blue and gray wires from the IBS to locate the connector.<br><br>Now try starting the vehicle. If the vehicle starts, replace the faulty IBS. | 121 |

## 1 ENGINE (CONTINUED)

| Topic | Notes | Additional information (when available) |
|---|---|---|
| **Cylinder-assigned high pressure injectors (N54 engine)** | On N54 engines, mark the cylinder locations on the fuel injectors when removing them.<br><br>As part of injector manufacturing, tolerance ranges for injection quantity are determined and specified in a six-digit number combination. These values are used by the DME to compensate for variations in the individual injectors.<br><br>*NOTE—*<br>• *When replacing an injector, it is essential to carry out an injector adjustment using the BMW diagnostic scan tool.* | 130 |
| **Servicing high pressure fuel injection system - safety precaution (N54 engine)** | Working on the HPI system must only be carried out after the engine has cooled down. Do not attempt to open any fuel lines or connections on the HPI injection system until the coolant temperature is below 40° C (approx. 104°F)<br><br>If the engine is not cool, there is danger of residual fuel pressure spray in the high-pressure system.<br><br>When working on the high-pressure fuel system, take particular care to ensure conditions of absolute cleanliness and follow the work sequences described in the repair instructions. Even the smallest contaminants and/or damage to the threads on the high-pressure lines can cause leaks. | 130 |
| **Ignition coil fuel/ oil contamination** | When working on the fuel system, it is important to ensure that the ignition coils are not fouled by fuel or oil (especially critical for N54 engines). The resistance of the silicone material is significantly reduced by heavy fuel contact. This can cause spark over at the spark plug and misfires.<br><br>Before servicing the fuel system, remove the ignition coils and cover the spark plug hole with a cloth.<br><br>Ignition coils heavily fouled by fuel must be replaced. | 120 |
| **Valvetrain service note** | When diagnosing engine noise, do not rule out worn timing chain components. This is especially applicable to high mileage engines and engines with extended oil change intervals. | 117 |
| **Valve cover gasket leaks** | When replacing valve cover gasket, take extra caution when tightening fasteners and sealing at metal joining points. For example front timing cover to cylinder head. There is a small area where silicone should be applied to seal where the gasket may not. | 113 |
| **VANOS and silicone sealant** | When working around VANOS units keep area clean and free of silicone sealant. Even a small amount of silicone introduced into VANOS actuator or solenoid can cause a fault. | 117 |

# 1 ENGINE (CONTINUED)

| Topic | Notes | Additional information (when available) |
|---|---|---|
| **Sticky VANOS solenoid sets cam position (CMP) sensor codes** | A sticky/jammed VANOS solenoid can set a camshaft position (CMP) sensor fault (tooth error). | 117 |
| | Models with N52, N52KP and N54 engines may be difficult to start, run rough and have the Service Engine Soon lamp illuminated with one or more of the following stored faults: | |
| | • Cam sensor, inlet signal - signal invalid for synchronization<br>• Crankshaft-inlet camshaft, correlation - Value outside reference range<br>• VANOS intake - stiff, jammed mechanically<br>• Cam sensor, exhaust signal - signal invalid for synchronization<br>• Crankshaft - exhaust camshaft, correlation - Value outside reference range<br>• VANOS exhaust - stiff, jammed mechanically | |
| | N52 only: Remove the VANOS solenoid, intake or exhaust, depending on the fault codes stored and, using shop air, gently blow out any visible particles and reinstall. If the fault returns, try swapping the solenoids between banks to see if the fault follows the solenoid. | |
| | Replace the solenoid if the fault cannot be corrected. | |
| **Intermittent lifter noise (N52 engine)** | An occasional ticking or rattling noise from the hydraulic valve adjusters (HVA) elements may occur during cold engine starts or frequent short-distance driving.This condition will not cause any damage to the engine, and usually remedies itself with a longer driving distance or operating times at full operating temperature. | 113 |
| | In this situation, the lifters can bleed down or have trapped air causing ticking/rattling noise and may require bleeding, as described below. The bleed time may take anywhere from two minutes to a maximum of 30 minutes. | |
| | Procedure preconditions: | |
| | • Engine running at operating temperature<br>• Vehicle stationary on a level surface in a properly ventilated area<br>• Engine oil level correct – not underfilled or overfilled | |
| | 1. Bring engine up to an operating speed (no load) of 2000-3000 rpm and maintain this speed for three minutes. | |
| | 2. Let engine idle for 15-30 seconds. Listen for whether the noise is still present:<br>- If engine is quiet, procedure is finished.<br>- If engine noise still present, repeat procedure; perform steps 1 and 2 up to a maximum of 5 times. | |
| | If the noise remains after performing the bleeding procedure 5 times: proceed by performing the procedure for a final time, also at an engine operating speed of 2000-3000 rpm, but for a total time duration of 15 minutes. If noise returns after multiple bleedings, the cylinder head may be faulty and require replacement. | |

## 1 ENGINE (CONTINUED)

| Topic | Notes | Additional information (when available) |
|---|---|---|
| **Engine knock fault codes** | Engine knock fault codes indicate that the engine is knocking. Detonation or knock is an erratic form of combustion that can cause head gasket failure as well as other engine damage. Prolonged or heavy detonation can be very damaging. The hammer-like shock waves created by detonation subject the head gasket, piston, rings, spark plug and rod bearings to severe overloading. As a first remedy, try higher octane high detergent fuel or switch brands. If the faults codes continue to return, contact your authorized BMW dealer. | 120 |
| **High pressure fuel system faults (N54 engine)** | Service Engine Soon light illuminated, engine enters fail-safe mode with reduced power.<br><br>Scan tool data shows fault codes 10737 (P3283, P3284), and/or 10738 (P3003, P3090) – "High fuel pressure system, plausibility" stored in MSD80 (DME) control module. These fault codes all relate to the high pressure fuel system.<br><br>The possible causes are: incorrect adaptation values of the high pressure pump control valve or failure of the high-pressure fuel pump. Begin by resetting adaptations for engine management. If fault codes return immediately after adaptation, the fuel pump may be faulty. | 160 |
| **High pressure fuel injector, replacing replace teflon seal (N54 engine)** | Always replace the teflon o-ring (arrow) when fitting and removing the fuel injector. This also applies to an injector that has just been fitted and has to be removed again after an engine start. A new injector with a new teflon o-ring should be fitted as quickly as possible as the Teflon sealing ring could swell up.<br><br>Also, be sure that the injector is correctly seated when installing. The injector hold-down must rest on both injector tabs, otherwise the necessary force is not applied.<br><br>Do not clean the nozzle-needle tip of the piezo-injector. | 130 |
| **High pressure fuel pump extended warranty coverage (N54 engine)** | On 2007 and 2008 models with N54 engines, BMW emissions warranty of the high pressure fuel pump (HDP) has been extended from 4 years or 50,000 miles to 10 years or 120,000 miles, whichever comes first.<br><br>Vehicles with a faulty fuel pump may have the Service Engine Soon lamp illuminated with various low fuel pressure-related faults stored in the engine control module (DME). Affected vehicles may experience long cranking times or reduced engine performance (engine in failsafe mode) when the HDP malfunctions.<br><br>If the high pressure fuel pump of a MY 2007/2008 exhibits the symptoms listed above, it should be replaced with the improved part (P/N 13 51 7 592 881). | 160 |

# 1 ENGINE (CONTINUED)

| Topic | Notes | Additional information (when available) |
|-------|-------|------------------------------------------|
| **Fuel injector faults (N54 engine)** | On cars with faulty fuel injectors, various fault codes related to fuel injectors may be stored in the DME control module (Service Engine Soon light is illuminated). The engine may lack power, idle erratically, or have poor throttle response. Faults codes such as injector, cylinder 1-6, short circuit or line break, DME internal fault; Injector driver circuit failure bank 1-3; bank 4-6 or Misfiring, several cylinders may indicate a bank of 3 faulty injectors. Consult your authorized dealer regarding injector replacement as it applies to BMW Service Bulletin SIB 12 02 08 (dated October 2008). | **130** |
| **Faulty valvetronic motor linked to DME failure (N52, N51 engines)** | If diagnosing a faulty DME, be sure to check that the valvetronic motor was not the root cause of the damage to DME control unit.<br><br>If a new control unit is installed and the valvetronic motor is bad (excessive current draw), the new DME will be damaged. | **130** |
| **Defective DME control module (N54 engine from 6/10/07 to 8/18/07)** | Engine runs poorly, misfires, and may not start. One or more of the following fault codes is stored in the DME: 30BA, 30BB or 2ACC. Subsequent fault codes like 29CC, 29CD, 29CE, 29CF or 2ACB may be stored in the DME as well. Service Engine Soon Light may be illuminated.<br><br>This is caused by a defective diode in the DME. To correct this problem, the DME will need to be replaced along with a complete vehicle reprogram/recode. | **130** |
| **EML light illuminated, limp home mode, no boost pressure control (N54 engine)** | In the event of a failure, malfunction or an implausible signal from any of the sensors listed below, activation of the wastegate valves is shut down and the valve flaps are fully opened. Turbocharging ceases at this point.<br><br>• High-pressure fuel system<br>• Inlet or exhaust VANOS<br>• Crankshaft position sensor<br>• Camshaft position sensor<br>• Boost-pressure sensor<br>• Knock sensors<br>• Intake-air temperature sensor<br><br>If the ELML light is illuminated, interrogate fault memory and correct any problems found. | |

# 1 ENGINE (CONTINUED)

| Topic | Notes | Additional information (when available) |
|---|---|---|
| **Damaged connector at throttle module** | When connecting throttle module connector, it is possible to twist the connector before plugging it in, causing damage to the harness and the connector. Be sure to install connector carefully to avoid damage. | |
| **Rattle noise from turbocharger area (N54 engine)** | A metallic noise from the exhaust system near the engine or turbocharger area can occur during deceleration from approx. 3,500 RPM or during a high engine speed without a drive gear being engaged.<br><br>In this situation, the wastegate valve does not completely close due to mechanical tolerances of the wastegate actuator and results in the wastegate valve rattling against its seating surface.<br><br>Do not replace the turbocharger or adjust the existing wastegate actuator control rod. Instead reprogram the DME. If after programming, the noise is no longer present, take no further action. If the noise is still present, replace both of the turbocharger wastegate actuators. | **180** |
| **Electric coolant pump precautions** | Particular care must be taken to ensure that the coolant pump does not run dry. When the pump is removed, it should be stored filled with coolant. The pump bearings could seize if the pump is not filled with coolant. A inoperative coolant pump could cause serious engine damage.<br><br>If the pump should ever run dry, the pump impeller should be turned by hand to ensure the pump is not seized before connecting the coolant hoses. The system should then be immediately filled with coolant. | **170** |

## 2 TRANSMISSION

| Topic | Notes | Additional information (when available) |
|---|---|---|
| **ATF service recommendation** | The automatic transmission fluid in the both the ZF and GM units should be changed at service intervals no greater than 100,000 miles. 60 to 80k miles should be considered a more acceptable maximum interval.<br><br>When checking the fluid level, it is critical that the temperature of the fluid be maintained at approximately 30°C (86°F). (The factory specification is 30 - 50°C.) Checking the temperature can be done using an infrared temp gun or a more correctly, with a BMW diagnostic scan tool. | **240** |
| **Delay and jolt when pulling away (from 03/2007 production with 6HP19TU auto. trans.)** | Transmission exhibits a delayed engagement with a harsh jolt when accelerating from a stop. Occurs only during engine warm-up (cold engine) and cannot be reproduced in Sport mode.<br><br>To correct this problem BMW recommends reprogramming and recoding the complete vehicle with current software. Refer to BMW Service Bulletin SIB 24 03 08 (January 2009) for additional information. | **240** |
| **Transmission/transmission control complaints** | Various complaints associated with inoperative transmission controls. At times the vehicle will not start, gear indicator display not present, transmission failsafe light is on, or there is a transmission failsafe message in the check control. During diagnosis with scan tool, EGS cannot be identified.<br><br>The transmission harness connector may have a loose or pushed back pin(s). This condition can cause various complaints and many different faults to be stored.<br><br>Disconnect the battery and check the transmission connector X8500 for loose or pushed back pins. It may be possible when the connector is removed for the pin to move forward, so check that all the pins are tight and locked in place by using a blunt tool like a pick. Look carefully - a pushed in pin may appear as an open slot.<br><br>*NOTE—*<br>• *It may be necessary to remove the exhaust and lower the back of the transmission to properly inspect plug. If this step is necessary be careful to not bend shifter cable bracket otherwise shifter cable operation will be compromised.* | **240** |

## 2 TRANSMISSION (CONTINUED)

| Topic | Notes | Additional information (when available) |
|---|---|---|
| **Transmission in failsafe mode with fault 4F8D stored** **(from 09/2006 to 02/2007 production with 6HP19TU auto. trans.)** *NOTE—* • *This problem is solved beginning with 3/01/07 production.* | This is caused by highly-sensitive EGS software diagnostics. The fault normally sets during a 5-4 downshift in vehicles with a replacement transmission, or after a reset of the adaptation values. If this fault is present, carry out a transmission adaptation as follows: • Warm up transmission to 75°C (167°F). *NOTE—* • *The transmission adaptation occurs only at a transmission fluid temperature of 75°C or higher. If a scan tool is not available to read ATF temp. directly, use an infrared temp gun.* • In drive position D, increase vehicle speed up to 4th gear (approximately 25 mph), but do not allow a shift into 5th gear. • Allow vehicle to then coast to a stop. Keep the vehicle stationary for approximately 15 seconds with the brake pedal applied. • Next, with the vehicle stationary, change from D to N and back to D again. • Repeat steps 1 to 3 approximately 10 times. | 240 |
| **Mechatronic sealing sleeve leaking** **(with ZF 6-speed 6HP19 transmission)** | Transmission fluid can be seen leaking from transmission oil pan, or more specifically from the Mechatronic sealing sleeve. This repair requires replacing the sealing sleeve and the transmission oil pan gasket. Refer to BMW Service Bulletin SIB 24 08 06 (dated February 2009) for parts and repair information, including proper sleeve installation instructions. *NOTE—* • *After installation of the new sleeve, the correct distance between the transmission harness connector and the housing surface should not exceed 3 mm.* | 240 |

## 3 SUSPENSION, STEERING AND BRAKES

| Topic | Notes | Additional information (when available) |
| --- | --- | --- |
| **Heated steering wheel turns off (produced from 9/2008)** | Immediately following a cold start, if the heated steering wheel is switched on in addition to other electrical consumers, it may switch off after 5-10 seconds of operation. This is an intermittent situation. Cycling the key will typically restore function.<br><br>For the first few seconds after start-up, voltage levels may dip momentarily when electrical consumers are switched on. If the supply voltage dips below the threshold for the heated steering wheel, it will be switched off.<br><br>This situation may be present even if the battery is properly charged and no charging system problems are present. At the time of this printing, no repairs were required for this condition. | |
| **Rear coil spring repair procedures** | For repair procedures that require removal of the rear coil springs, the spring seats must be properly cleaned prior to reinstalling the springs. Dirt, pebbles, and debris left on the spring pads can become trapped between the spring pads and the lower coil of the springs, which can damage the protective coating of the springs. If the coating is damaged, rust may form on the spring. Over time, rust formation on the spring combined with vehicle operating conditions may cause the spring to break. | **330** |
| **Noisy, groaning front sway bar bushings** | A groaning noise can be heard when the front axle compresses and/or rebounds. This may be heard particularly over speed bumps. The noise normally occurs at lower outside temperatures and may be less pronounced when the vehicle has warmed up. To correct this noise, replace the front sway bar bushings (arrow) with updated parts.<br><br>*NOTE*—<br>• *Lubricate the new busings only with water to assist in installation.*<br>• *The bushings used for 2WD vehicles are different than the bushings used in AWD vehicles.* | **310** |
| **Difficulty setting front wheel alignment** | If you are having trouble getting the front alignment to come into spec, the struts may be bent. You can check this by loosening the pinch bolt on the wheel bearing housing. Slide strut up a few inches until you can see where the strut inserts into spindle. There will be a small dimple/dent if the strut is bent. | **310** |

# 3 SUSPENSION, STEERING AND BRAKES (CONTINUED)

| Topic | Notes | Additional information (when available) |
|---|---|---|
| **Brake pad wear sensor, use care when installing / removing** | The brake pad wear sensor is easily damage during installation owing to the 90° design. Be careful not to break the sensor when during installation and removal. | 340 |
| **Brake squeal from pad wear sensor** | Under light / moderate brake applications, brake squeal can be caused by contact between the brake pad wear sensor and the brake rotor (front or rear brakes). The geometry of the pad wear sensor, combined with individual driving habits, can result in a wear pattern that causes a squeaking and/or squealing noise when the brakes are applied with light to moderate force. If the noise is coming from the brake system, inspect the brake pad wear sensor of the affected axle. If the sensor is in contact with the rotor/disc, remove the sensor and drive the vehicle. If the noise is eliminated, replace the brake pads and wear sensor of the affected axle. If the noise is not eliminated, further diagnosis is required to determine the cause of the noise. | |
| **Increased brake pedal effort prior to engine start (up to 9/07 production)** | This situation can occur if the vehicle sits for extended periods of time. Although the brake pedal can be depressed, pedal effort is increased. The vacuum check valve at the brake booster (arrow) may leak. Replace the vacuum valve / hose assembly for the brake booster. | |
| **Steering column, service note** | The steering column must always be replaced after an airbag has been deployed or if the steering shaft is replaced. | 320 |
| **Track, resetting (cars with active steering)** | On cars with the optional active steering (option SA 214), track has to be reset after work on the steering. The procedure for adjusting track on a vehicle with active front steering (total steering angle sensor) is not the same as that for a vehicle with a conventional power-assisted steering system. | |

## 3 SUSPENSION, STEERING AND BRAKES (CONTINUED)

| Topic | Notes | Additional information (when available) |
|---|---|---|
| **ELV (Electric Steering Lock) warning shown in the Instrument Cluster (up to 9/2006 with manual trans.) (up to 12/2006 prod. with auto trans.)** | ELV light on with intermittent no-crank, no-start situation or ELV solenoid in locked position. This fault is usually caused by an ELV voltage supply issue (low terminal KL15 / KL15 (wake up) signal voltage from the ignition switch or CAS (Car Access System)).<br><br>*NOTE —*<br>  • *As a result of a change in government requirement, the ELV was deleted on later models. Note that anti-theft protection continues to be provided by drive-away protection in EWS.*<br><br>For basic troubleshooting, the system requires the following conditions for the starter to operate:<br><br>• Must be a valid key.<br>• No road speed.<br>• ELV must be unlocked (and the "unlocked and secured" telegram received by the CAS).<br>• ELV module must be de-energized by the CAS.<br>• Start button must be pressed with the brake applied.<br><br>Check that the key holder locks the key in position, and that the steering lock unlocks (an audible "clunk" can be heard when the key is inserted).<br><br>*NOTE —*<br>  • *Terminal KL15 is not released unless the steering is unlocked, and the CAS has received the "unlocked" telegram.*<br>  • *The ELV makes three attempts to unlock – a whirring sound can be heard at each attempt.*<br><br>Additional troubleshooting should be carried out using the BMW diagnostic scan tool.<br><br>*NOTE —*<br>  • *If terminal KL15 is not switched on, scan tool communication will be inhibited. In this case, start diagnostics by selecting the vehicle manually. Then follow the diagnostics path: Drive / Engine start / Comfort start / button to get into the scan tool test plan.* | 320 |
| **Front wheel bearing wear** | Worn wheel bearings can often produce a knocking sound while driving. Note that special press tools are needed to replace the bearings.<br><br>• Check the front wheel bearings for wear with the vehicle raised. The bearing will feel tight when spinning the wheel.<br>• Put the vehicle on the ground, pull and push on top of wheel / tire to check for looseness in wheel bearing. Initially it may feel tight. Rock steering wheel back and forth to situate the bearing. Bearing will then feel loose when pushing / pulling on top of tire. | 310 |

## 3 SUSPENSION, STEERING AND BRAKES (CONTINUED)

| Topic | Notes | Additional information (when available) |
|---|---|---|
| **Active steering, reinitializing after battery disconnect** | Active steering must be reinitialized after the battery has been disconnected. Reinitialize as follows:<br><br>• Start engine (the "Active Steering Inactive" Check-Control message appears)<br>• Turn steering wheel as far as it will go counter clockwise and then as far as it will go clockwise. | |
| **Active steering warning lamp illuminated (9/07 to 3/08 production)** | Active steering warning lamp illuminates immediately after starting the engine. After cycling the ignition, the active steering operates normally with no warning indicator.<br><br>A brief voltage drop during starting can cause a fault code (6149: combined position, speed monitoring) to be stored in the active steering control module. If this fault is stored, the warning lamp will be illuminated.<br><br>If other control modules have power supply faults, diagnose and test for voltage related faults, including active steering system faults. | |
| **Tire pressure monitor, damaged wheel electronics** | The tire pressure monitor (TPM) system measures the tire pressures at each of the four wheels. The system utilizes a warning lamp, mounted in the instrument cluster to alert the driver of a low tire pressure condition. The TPM system uses separate wheel electronics mounted at the base of each tire valve inside the wheel. Extra care must be taken when changing tires to avoid damaging the wheel electronics. A damaged wheel electronic can cause the tire warning indicator to illuminate.<br><br>When diagnosing an illuminated TPM warning lamp, the tires and wheels should be inspected for damage and/or prior replacement.<br><br>*NOTE*—<br>• *The last four digits of the tire's DOT number indicate the calendar week, followed by the year in which the tire was produced. This information can be used to determine if one or more tires have been recently replaced.* | |
| **Tire pressure monitoring, illuminated warning lamp** | The warning lamp is illuminated when the tire pressure decreases by approximately 25%. Temperature fluctuations can cause changes in tire pressure. For every 10° F change in ambient temperature, the tire pressure can change by 1 psi. Therefore, the tire warning indicator may be illuminated by a large change in temperature combined with a low pressure condition.<br><br>Inspect tires regularly for physical damage and check tire pressures when the tire warning is illuminated. BMW recommends checking tire inflation pressures every two weeks and before long trips.<br><br>*CAUTION*—<br>• *Driving on a significantly under-inflated tire causes the tire to overheat and can lead to tire failure.*<br>• *Under-inflation reduces fuel efficiency and tire tread life, and may affect the vehicle's handling and stopping ability.* | 020 |

## 4 BODY

| Topic | Notes | Additional information (when available) |
|---|---|---|
| **Rear door brake can pull out of B-pillar (up to 8/2007 production)** Reinforcement plate | The door brake mounting nut may pull through the sheet metal on the B-pillar. When this happens, the door will not stay open on its own and has little resistance when opening and closing. <br><br> To correct this, BMW has devised a reinforcement plate (BMW part no. 41 21 7 207 272 - M8 threaded plate) in place of the welded nut. Refer to BMW Service Bulletin SIB 41 01 08 (dated April 2008) for additional installation information. | |
| **Noisy wiper blades, blades chatter** | Wiper blades in good condition may make noise during operation, or may not clean the windshield properly. This may be caused by contaminants on the glass or blades, or by the blades or arms being out of adjustment. <br><br> The first step is to make sure the glass and the blades are clean and free of contaminants. Common contaminants that are not removed by conventional glass cleaners can be removed with BON AMI®, a household cleanser. <br><br> The cleanser should be applied on a wet cloth or sponge and the windshield must be thoroughly and evenly scrubbed. Wipe off the residue with a clean, dry cloth before the cleanser dries on the glass. <br><br> If there is evidence of heavy overspray of waxes or silicones on the glass, a wax and silicone remover can be used to remove them. <br><br> Clean the wiper blades with a clean cloth soaked in rubbing alcohol Once the blades and glass have been cleaned, check the adjustment of the wiper arms. <br><br> *NOTE*— <br> • *To properly adjust the wiper arms, special BMW adjustment gauges and tools are required. See* **611 Wipers and Washers**. | **611** |

## 5 BODY EQUIPMENT

| Topic | Notes | Additional information (when available) |
|---|---|---|
| **Reactivating folding door mirrors through convenient closure (from 08/2006 production)** | On cars with the auto-dimming mirrors (option code 430) the "convenient closure" feature can be used to close the windows, the sunroof, and fold in the door mirrors.<br><br>Although this feature was deactivated as of August 31, 2006 production, the feature can be reactivated using BMW diagnostic equipment.<br><br>*NOTE—*<br>  • *To check if this feature can be reactivated, first confirm that the mirrors fold in using the push button on the mirror adjustment switch.* | |
| **Rear view mirror compass difficult to read in high temperatures**<br><br> | When the rear view mirror reaches very high temperatures, e.g. the vehicle is parked in direct sunlight in hot climates, the compass becomes difficult to read.<br><br>This is normal as the rear view mirror temperature protection feature is active:<br><br>• Above 130°F (55°C), the compass display dims to 50% of its maximum value.<br>• Above 160°F (70°C), the compass display dims to 5% of its maximum value.<br><br>When the mirror cools, normal operation will resume. | |
| **Side areas in luggage compartment - not intended for storage (convertible model)**<br><br> | The side areas of the luggage compartment are not intended for storage. If an object is stored in these areas when the retractable hard top (RHT) is opened, the RHT may not open fully, or damage may occur to either the RHT or the object itself. Observe the warning labels (arrow) in the luggage side areas. | |
| **Top of rear window does not defrost**<br><br> | The top 3 grid lines in the rear defroster grid (arrows) are not heating elements. These lines are the AM aerial antenna wires. This unheated area is wider on the window of the E93, and may therefore be more noticeable than other vehicles. | |

## 5 BODY EQUIPMENT (CONTINUED)

| Topic | Notes | Additional information (when available) |
|---|---|---|
| **Emergency unlock of center console (convertible model)**<br> | The center console storage compartment contains an electric locking actuator motor operated directly by the junction box when central locking is activated. In an emergency (power loss), the storage compartment can be unlocked by means of a pull cable.<br><br>To access the pull cable, the cover must be removed from the rear compartment air outlet, followed by removal of the air outlet duct. The storage compartment can then be released by pulling the loop of the pull cable (arrow). | **515** |
| **Sunroof moves in small steps or interior lights not working** | Proper function of the slide/tilt sunroof requires initialization.<br><br>The motor of the slide/tilt sunroof uses 2 Hall sensors. They are located on the motor shaft and offset by 90 degrees with respect to each other. When the motor is running, this results in two offset Hall signals that are used to register the direction of rotation and for the anti-trapping protection function.<br><br>*NOTE*—<br>• *The control button must remain pressed during the entire initialization procedure. The initialization procedure must be repeated if the button is released.*<br>• *If the power supply is interrupted during initialization the procedure must be repeated.*<br><br>Press and hold sunroof button in the sunroof tilt direction. After approx. 15 seconds, the initialization begins by storing the tilt-position end stop, then the full open end stop position, etc. Initialization takes about 120 seconds.<br><br>Initialization is erased under the following conditions:<br><br>• Removal of the voltage supply to the Roof Function Center (FZD)<br>• Hall sensor fault detected<br>• Sunroof position implausible<br>• Modified/changed vehicle coding or coding data faulty | |
| **Tailgate opens slow at low ambient temperatures (Sports Wagon)** | Tailgate opens slowly or does not fully open under its own power.<br><br>In low ambient temperatures, the gas pressure in the tailgate struts is reduced. The effect of this is a less powerful strut. Conversely, at very high ambient temperatures, the gas pressure is higher, thus allowing the tailgate to open quicker. This is a normal condition and the struts are not faulty.<br><br>However, to ensure that excessive friction is not present in the hinges due to lack of lubrication, all tailgate and gas strut hinges should be lubricated with grease. | |

## 5 BODY EQUIPMENT (CONTINUED)

| Topic | Notes | Additional information (when available) |
|---|---|---|
| **Doors will not unlock using key fob or central locking button** (up to 11/2008 production) | One or more of the doors may not unlock when using the remote key outside the vehicle, or the central locking button inside the car.<br><br>*NOTE*—<br><br>  • *With this fault, the doors can be unlocked using the key in the driver's door lock cylinder or by pulling the door handle on the inside of the car.*<br><br>Typically fault codes (A6D4 and A6D5) are stored in the Junction Box Electronics (JBBF). This is due to a blown fuse in the JBBF caused by either an excessive amp draw by one of the door lock actuators (commonly caused by silicone spray contamination) or by an intermittent amperage spike (above 15A) due to normal variations in the locking system.<br><br>*NOTE*—<br><br>  • *Never spray any silicone products into the latch, as this will lead to premature failure.*<br><br>Inspect fuse 57 (up to 9/07 production) or 73 (from 9/07 production) in the JBE. Replace the blown 15A fuse with a 20A fuse.<br><br>Test the locking function by activating the door locks 10 times in succession via the central locking switch.<br><br>*NOTE*—<br><br>  • *Thermal protection will be activated after about 15 successive activations and does not indicate any damage to the system.*<br><br>Observe the operation of each lock actuator during the test. Damaged/faulty actuators will operate slowly and/or make unusual noises.<br><br>• If either one of the front door lock actuators is determined to be the source of the blown fuse, **both** front door latches (which contain the lock actuators) should be replaced.<br>• If either one of the rear door lock actuators is determined to be the source of the blown fuse, only that **single** faulty latch should be replaced.<br>• If one of the front lock actuators and one of the rear lock actuators appears to be faulty, **both** front latches and the **single** faulty rear latch should be replaced.<br><br>If no faulty lock actuators can be identified, wait 2 minutes and then repeat the successive (10 times) locking test. If no faulty lock actuators can be identified, no further action is required. | |

## 6 ELECTRICAL SYSTEM

| Topic | Notes | Additional information (when available) |
|---|---|---|
| **Changing / setting date format (mm/dd or dd/mm) in the Personal Profile settings (vehicles without Navigation)** | To change Personal Profile settings:<br><br>• Press rocker switch in direction indicator stalk, up or down until "Personal Profile" function (key with a check mark) appears, accompanied by the word SET in the instrument cluster.<br>• Press Board Computer (BC) button on steering column stalk.<br>• Press rocker switch, up or down, until "tt/mm" or "mm/tt" is shown.<br>• Press the BC button.<br>• Use the rocker switch to make the selection/change.<br>• Press the BC button to confirm and accept the selection/change.<br><br>*NOTE —*<br><br>• *This will also change the date format in the radio display.*<br><br>The following display formats and units of measure can be selected/changed in the same way.<br><br>• Fuel consumption (l/100km, mpg, km/l)<br>• Distance (km, mls)<br>• Time format (12h/24h)<br>• Temperature (°C, °F)<br>• Reset of display formats / units of measure (factory/default setting) | |
| **Closed-circuit current (parasitic draw) specification** | Increased closed-circuit currents may occur permanently or intermittently and cause the battery to discharge. The increase in closed-circuit current may be caused by a faulty control unit, or by the installation of a non-approved accessory.<br><br>**E90, E91, E92, E93: 40 mA after 60-70 minutes with TCU (telematics control unit) (30 minutes without TCU)**<br><br>In general, closed-circuit current consistently over 50 mA must be investigated. | **121** |
| **Stabilant 22A electrical contact enhancer**<br><br> | Connectors carrying low current are particularly susceptible to the formation of deposits. These deposits affect the resistance of the circuit and, depending on the sensitivity of the particular circuit, can cause system malfunctions (very often intermittent), and the activation of warning lamps and check control indicators.<br><br>In difficult to solve electrical resistance situations, Stabilant 22A may help to enhance electrical contact. Stabilant 22A evaporates and leaves a thin polymer film which is conductive between the mating surfaces, while staying non-conductive between adjacent pins. At the same time it prevents the formation of any further harmful deposits.<br><br>*NOTE —*<br><br>• *Read and understand any Stabilant 22A safety precautions provided by the manufacturer.*<br>• *Do not use Stabilant 22A on Oxygen sensor or SRS connectors.* | |

## 6 ELECTRICAL SYSTEM (CONTINUED)

| Topic | Notes | Additional information (when available) |
|---|---|---|
| **Check Control message: Vehicle Battery! Increased Battery Discharge** | If the measured off-load current exceeds 80 mA after 68 minutes of the key being off, the engine management system outputs the CC message "Vehicle Battery! Increased Battery Discharge" the next time Terminal 15 is switched on. This happens regardless of the battery state of charge.<br><br>In the event of the above situation, check the vehicle for non-approved electrical equipment installations.<br><br>Retrofitted after-market equipment (e.g., hands-free systems, navigation systems, GPS or entertainment systems) may have been incorrectly connected to Terminal 30, Terminal 30g-f or directly to the battery.<br><br>*NOTE*—<br>• *The intelligent battery sensor (IBS) monitors the battery's discharge current while the vehicle is off. The measures values are transmitted to the DME/DDE through the bit-serial data interface (BSD).*<br>• *Equipment or accessories must only be connected to Terminal 15 or Terminal 30g, unless otherwise specified in the installation instructions of the BMW retrofit kit.* | 121 |
| **No scan tool communication with instrument cluster (up to 08/2006 production)** | The warning lamps in the instrument cluster come on and go out intermittently after turning on ignition (prior to engine start). It is not possible to carry out diagnosis of the instrument cluster using the BMW diagnostic scan tool.<br><br>First, perform a battery reset by disconnecting the negative battery terminal from the battery for at least 2 minutes. It may be necessary to repeat the process a few times. It will then be possible to diagnose the instrument cluster.<br><br>To correct this problem on these early cars, BMW recommends reprogramming the complete vehicle with current software. | |
| **Windshield washer, low or no volume**<br> | Windshield washers spray a very low volume of fluid, or no fluid at all. The strainer (arrow) on the windshield washer fluid pump may become clogged by debris or an algae-like substance.<br><br>The algae-like substance is typically caused by using non-approved washer fluid or straight water in the washer fluid reservoir.<br><br>To replace the strainer:<br>• Remove the washer fluid pump, located in lower part right front wheel well.<br>• Drain existing washer fluid in the reservoir and properly discard.<br>• Replace the strainer, which is installed on the end of the pump. An updated strainer has a larger mesh to avoid future occurrences.<br>• Refill the washer fluid reservoir with BMW washer fluid at the specified concentration. | 611 |

## 6 ELECTRICAL SYSTEM (CONTINUED)

| Topic | Notes | Additional information (when available) |
|---|---|---|
| **Gong warning without visual check control message** | A gong warning sounds approximately 10-15 seconds after the engine is started. There is no check control warning in the instrument cluster and no faults are stored.<br><br>This can be caused by a center door lock button (permanently closed contacts) Test the functionality of the center door lock button and replace as necessary. | **515** |
| **Wipers park out of position (up to 04/2006 production)** | A faulty windshield wiper relay can cause the wipers to park 10 to 15° (2-3 cm) out of position.<br><br>In this situation, replace the blue windshield wiper relay, located behind the fuse box access panel in the glove box, with updated green relay. | |
| **Sunroof, interior lights, and rain sensor are inoperative (up to 03/2009 production)** | The sunroof, interior lights, rain sensor and other functions controlled by the FZD (Roof Functions Center) are inoperative. There is no communication with the FZD when using the BMW diagnostic tester.<br><br>Reset the FZD by removing/installing the FZD-related fuses in the front fuse box:<br><br>• E90, E91 E92 up to 3/2007: **F5** (7.5A), **F12** (20A), **F28** (5A)<br>• E90, E91 and E92 from 3/2007 to 9/2007: **F40** (7.5A), **F12** (20A), **F28** (5A)<br>• E90, E91 and E92 from 9/2007: **F62** (7.5A), **F25** (20A), **F7** (5A)<br>• E93 up to 3/2007 **F5** (7.5A), **F28** (5A)<br>• E93 from 3/2007 to 9/2007: **F40** (7.5A), **F28** (5A)<br>E93 from 9/2007: **F62** (7.5A), **F7** (5A)<br><br>If functionality is restored, BMW recommends reprogramming and recoding the complete vehicle with current software. Refer to BMW Service Bulletin SIB 61 12 08 (April 2008) for additional information.<br><br>*NOTE*—<br>• *Be sure reinitialize sunroof as described earlier after reprogramming.* | |

## 6 ELECTRICAL SYSTEM (CONTINUED)

| Topic | Notes | Additional information (when available) |
|---|---|---|
| **Junction box electronic (JBE) module failure, various electrical issues (with N51 PZEV engine)** <br><br> | JBE module repeated failures due to shorted fuel sender harness, including various electrical system failures while driving: <br><br> • A/C stopped working <br> • Fuel gauge display shows empty <br> • Rear windows "one-touch" function is inoperative <br> • Windshield wipers run without being switched on <br> • Various warning lights illuminated <br><br> Scan tool diagnosis shows several fault codes in the JBE (Junction Box Electronic) module: <br><br> • Fuel sensor signal plausibility (fuel sensor plausibility faults may also be stored in DME and instrument cluster) <br> • A/C refrigerant sensor signal <br> • Rear window Hall sensor signal <br> • Rear stratification potentiometer <br> • JBE module also shows signs of local overheating. <br><br> Additionally, repair history shows multiple repair attempts for the listed complaints or the JBE module was previously replaced. <br><br> In this situation, the right side fuel sending unit ground wire may be intermittently shorted to the B+ terminal of the electric fuel pump inside the fuel tank. <br><br> As a result, battery voltage (via the chaffed fuel sender ground wire) overloads the ground circuits of the JBE, causing failure. Inspect the in-tank fuel pump ground wire (black wire, pin 6, see graphic inset). If the harness is damaged it should be replaced with an updated harness. See BMW Service Bulletin SIB 61 16 08 (dated November 2008) for additional information. | 160 |
| **Power mirrors and/or windows are inoperative (models with Xenon headlights)** <br><br> | The LED on the headlight switch is flashing and there is a check control message for windows / mirrors / headlights. There may also be water in one or both headlights. One of the following fault codes may be stored: <br><br> • Communication with stepper motor box left / right defective (FC 9CBD / 9CBE) <br> • Communication with mirror driver / passenger side defective (FC 9CC1 / 9CC2) <br> • Communication with LIN control defective (FC 9CCF) <br><br> Check that the left and right headlight access covers are installed correctly. If a cover is not installed correctly, water can get into the stepper motor controller (SMC) connector. Inspect the connector at each headlight assembly for corrosion and replace as necessary. Make sure the covers are reinstalled correctly. | 630 |

## 6 ELECTRICAL SYSTEM (CONTINUED)

| Topic | Notes | Additional information (when available) |
|---|---|---|
| **Bulb out display in Check Control** | A bulb out symbol is shown in the Board Computer, but all bulbs appear to work correctly. Additionally fault codes are stored in the FRM (Footwell Module) for "Rear fog light / US: Brake Force Display left / right defective" | 630 |
| | The cause of the warning is a faulty BFD (Brake Force Display) bulb (arrow). If a faulty bulb is found, check the bulb contact and repair as necessary. | |
| | Check the check control ID fault numbers in the instrument cluster for a faulty bulb message. | |
| | • Switch on ignition (KL-R or KL-15)<br>• Toggle rotary switch on direction indicator switch to bring up "Check Control"<br>• Briefly press the on-board computer button<br>• Select the Check-Control message required with the rocker switch<br>• Press the on-board computer button for longer than 4 seconds<br>• The following message will appear in the bottom line of the LCD display for approx. 2 seconds: "CC-ID xxx" | |
| | CC numbers for a faulty BFD bulb are 372 (left) and 373 (right). | |
| | *NOTE —*<br>   • *A full listing of check control messages and their definitions can be found in* **020 Maintenance**. | |
| **Rear light failure displayed in Check Control**<br>**(Coupe (E92), Convertible (E93)**<br>**(08/2006 to 07/2007 production)** | Check for a light bulb failure or loose contact between light bulb and socket. Check also for a fault code(s) stored in the footwell module (FRM): "Brake force display right /left defective". | |
| | *NOTE —*<br>   • *The brake force display bulb and socket are located in the rear lamp housing on the trunk lid (arrow).* | |
| | If faults are stored, remove the brake force display bulbs and sockets. Replace faulty bulb(s), if applicable and install updated bulb sockets. | |
| | • Bulb: BMW part no. 63 21 7 160 788<br>• Bulb socket: BMW part no. 63 21 7 207 528 | |
| **Xenon lamp bulb color after replacement**<br>**(vehicles with xenon headlights)** | New replacement xenon bulb has a yellow-white appearance when compared with the bluish-white of the original bulb on the other side of the vehicle. | |
| | Due to chemical and physical properties, new Xenon bulbs require a burn-in period, which causes a gradual color change from yellow to blue. The greatest color occurs in the first 5 minutes of use, and stabilizes after approximately 100 hours of use. | |
| **Glove box flashlight deleted**<br>**(from 03/2008 production)** | The glove box rechargeable flashlight has been deleted as standard vehicle equipment as of 03/2008. Flashlights can be purchased through and authorized BMW parts department. | |

## 6 ELECTRICAL SYSTEM (CONTINUED)

| Topic | Notes | Additional information (when available) |
|---|---|---|
| **Automatic headlights, adjusting sensitivity** | Headlights switch on too early or too late, even in daylight, with the headlight switch set to the automatic position.<br><br>The factory default for the rain/light sensor is set to "Sensitive". With this setting, the rain/light sensor is set for optimum operation.<br><br>If the preference is to have the sensor setting either more or less sensitive, this can be adjusted using BMW Diagnostic equipment.<br><br>There are three setting options:<br><br>• Normal (reduced sensitivity)<br>• Sensitive (factory default)<br>• Highly sensitive (most sensitive). | |
| **Front LED turn signal not working (E90 / E91 models with Xenon headlights from 07/2008 production)** | This is caused by either a faulty LED front turn signals or a faulty FRM (Footwell Module).<br><br>Two situations are possible:<br><br>• The front left and/or front right LED (Light Emitting Diode) turn signals do not work, either intermittently or permanently.<br>• The LED turn signals on the vehicle side flash at a higher frequency, either intermittently or permanently. In the case of such a fault, the check control message "Turn indicator defective" appears.<br><br>If the LED turn signal does not work, appropriate diagnostics must be carried out using BMW diagnostic equipment.<br><br>If the LED turn signal works, but either intermittently or permanently has double-speed flashing frequency, the LED indicator module (in the headlight) should be replaced.<br><br>If this does not resolve the problem, the footwell module (FRM) should be replaced. Further information can be found in BMW Service Bulletin SIB 63 06 09 (dated May 2009) | |

## 7 EQUIPMENT AND ACCESSORIES

| Topic | Notes | Additional information (when available) |
|---|---|---|
| **Airbag warning light on (E93 convertible)**<br> | Airbag warning light is illuminated with fault code (rollover protection controller internal fault) stored in the ACSM2 (Advanced Crash and Safety Management) control module.<br><br>The roll-over controller (ROC) must be replaced to correct this fault.<br><br>The ROC is behind the rear seat back, driver's side (**arrow**). Access the ROC by folding the rear seat down and removing the bulkhead access panel.<br><br>Be sure to carry out a short test of the controller using the BMW diagnostic equipment after installation. | |
| **Airbag deployment, service note** | The steering column must always be replaced after an airbag has been deployed. | **320** |
| **Airbag warning lamp illuminated for occupant detection seat mat fault (up to 11/2005 production)**<br> | Airbag warning lamp is illuminated, together with the passenger Airbag status lamp. The problem may be intermittent.<br><br>To correct this problem, the passenger occupant detection seat mat (OC3) should be replaced with a revised version. Under the extended warranty program, the occupant detection mat will be replaced at no charge to the customer.<br><br>*NOTE—*<br>*• The primary purpose of the passenger seat occupant detection mat is to detect a child up to an age of approximately one-year who is placed in an appropriate child seat.*<br><br>The BMW warranty coverage for this specific airbag warning lamp issue has been extended to 10 years without mileage limit. A letter was sent to owners of all affected vehicles to advise of this change. | **721** |
| **Both rear belt tensioners deploy in accident**<br> | In the case of an accident that would trigger the rear belt tensioners, both tensioners will deploy, regardless of whether the rear seats are occupied, or not. This a normal condition as the rear belt buckles have no switch.<br><br>*WARNING—*<br>*• Always replace deployed airbag components and confirm MRS operational status using BMW diagnostic equipment.* | **721** |

## 7 EQUIPMENT AND ACCESSORIES (CONTINUED)

| Topic | Notes | Additional information (when available) |
|---|---|---|
| **Seat belt assist (E92 3 Series Coupe)** | While switching on the ignition and seated in the driver's seat, both the left and right side seat belt assistants will extend (intermittently), instead of only on the driver's side. This is a normal condition.<br><br>If the passenger door is opened and closed, such as to place an object in the car, and then the driver enters the car, the assistant will extend on both sides when the ignition is switched on.<br><br>This airbag pre-check is performed each time the ignition is switched on. During this pre-check, the passenger seat OC3 mat cannot determine if a passenger is present. Since the passenger side door latch has been operated, and the OC3 mat hasn't yet determined whether a passenger is present, both seatbelt assistants will operate. After approximately 10 seconds, the passenger side seat belt assistant will retract. | |

# 010 Product Familiarization

## INTRODUCTION

The information found in this section is based on introductory material for 2006 through 2010 BMW 3 Series vehicles sold in the USA and Canada. The content provided here is intended to serve as a product familiarization guide. The information presented is subject to change and should be used as a general reference only.

> **WARNING—**
> • Check the BMW factory repair information at www.bmwtechinfo.com or the publisher's website at www.bentleypublishers.com for information that may supersede any information included in this section.

## Product Overview

The fifth generation 3 Series (E90) was introduced in the US in model year 2006 as a replacement for the 1999 - 2005 3 Series (E46). The E90 is larger, slightly heavier and faster than the previous 3 Series. It has a bolder look, revised suspension and braking, more power and more interior space.

E90 Sedan

B309010001

| 2006 model introduction | |
|---|---|
| E90 4-door Sedan | 325i, 330i, 325xi, 330xi |
| E91 Sports Wagon (October 2005) | 325xi |

E91 Sports Wagon

B309010051

The rear-wheel drive 3 Series E90 4-door Sedan was introduced first, with the E91 Sports Wagon soon after, both as 2006 models. The E92 Coupe and the E93 retractable hard top Convertible became available as 2007 models.

Overall, the dimensions of the all-new 3 Series are significantly greater than the corresponding dimensions of the 325i and 330i it replaced, adding both interior passenger room and wheelbase length.

Compared to the outgoing model, more generous exterior dimensions ensure even greater spaciousness and comfort for all passengers. At 178.0 inches, the length increases by 1.9 inches. The width at 71.5 inches increases by 3.1. Vehicle height is 55.9 inches, an increase of 0.24. The wheelbase is 1.4 inches longer at 108.7.

The E90 features innovations like Valvetronic engine with weight-saving magnesium in the crankcase, a newly developed double-pivot aluminum front suspension, a redesigned five-link rear suspension made of lightweight steel, and a lighter, 25% stiffer body shell.

The E90 3 Series interior is ergonomically designed with more space and more luxury for both driver and passenger compared to its predecessor. The driver's environment is designed to enhance the driving experience. An onboard navigation system is available with BMW's iDrive control system.

**2006 E90 Sedan**

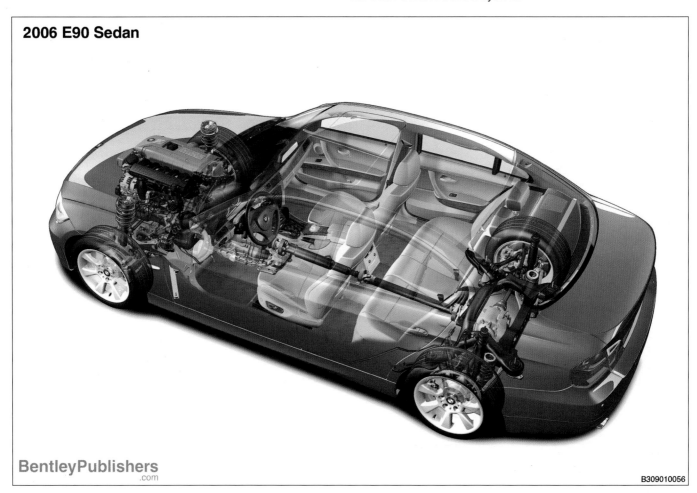

BentleyPublishers
.com

B309010056

## Technical Data

### BMW 3 Series specifications (2006)

| | 325i | 330i |
|---|---|---|
| **Exterior** | | |
| Doors | 4 | 4 |
| Height (A) | 55.9 in (1421 mm) | 55.9 in (1421 mm) |
| Front track (B) | 59.1 in (1500 mm) | 59.1 in (1500 mm) |
| Rear track (C) | 59.6 in (1513 mm) | 59.6 in (1513 mm) |
| Width (E) | 71.5 in (1817 mm) | 71.5 in (1817 mm) |
| Overall width (D) | 79.3 in (2013 mm) | 79.3 in (2013 mm) |
| Wheelbase (F) | 108.7 in (2760 mm) | 108.7 in (2760 mm) |
| Length (G) | 178.2 in (4520 mm) | 178.2 in (4520 mm) |
| | | |
| **Interior** | | |
| Front headroom | 37.4 in | 37.4 in |
| Rear headroom | 37.1 in | 37.1 in |
| Front legroom | 41.5 in | 41.5 in |
| Rear legroom | 34.6 in | 34.6 in |
| EPA passenger compartment vol. | 93.0 cu ft / 2492 liters | 93.0 cu ft / 2492 liters |
| Cargo (trunk) capacity | 12.0 cu ft / 340 liters | 12.0 cu ft / 340 liters |
| | | |
| **Engine** | | |
| Engine configuration, cylinders/valves per cyl. | 3.0 liter In-line 6 / 4 | 3.0 liter in-line 6 / 4 |
| Displacement | 2996 cc (182 cu in) | 2996 cc (182 cu in) |
| Stroke / bore (mm) | 88.0 / 85.0 | 88.0 / 85.0 |
| Rated power | 215 @ 6250 rpm | 255 @ 6600 rpm |
| Max. torque (lb-ft) | 185 @ 2750 rpm | 220 @ 2750rpm |
| Compression | 10.7 : 1 | 10.7 : 1 |
| Fuel requirement | Premium unleaded (91 pump octane) | Premium unleaded (91 pump octane) |
| | | |
| **General** | | |
| Final drive ratio | 3.23 : 1 (MT); 3.73 : 1 (AT) | 3.15 : 1 (MT); 3.64 :1 (AT) |
| Fuel tank capacity | 16.1 US gal | 16.1 US gal |
| Unladen weight (manual) | 3285 lb | 3417 lb |
| Load | 1058 lb | 1058 lb |
| Coefficient of drag (Cd) | 0.30 | 0.30 |
| Max. roof load | 165 lbs. | 165 lbs. |
| Acceleration (0- 60 mph) | 6.7 sec (est) | 6.1 sec (est) |

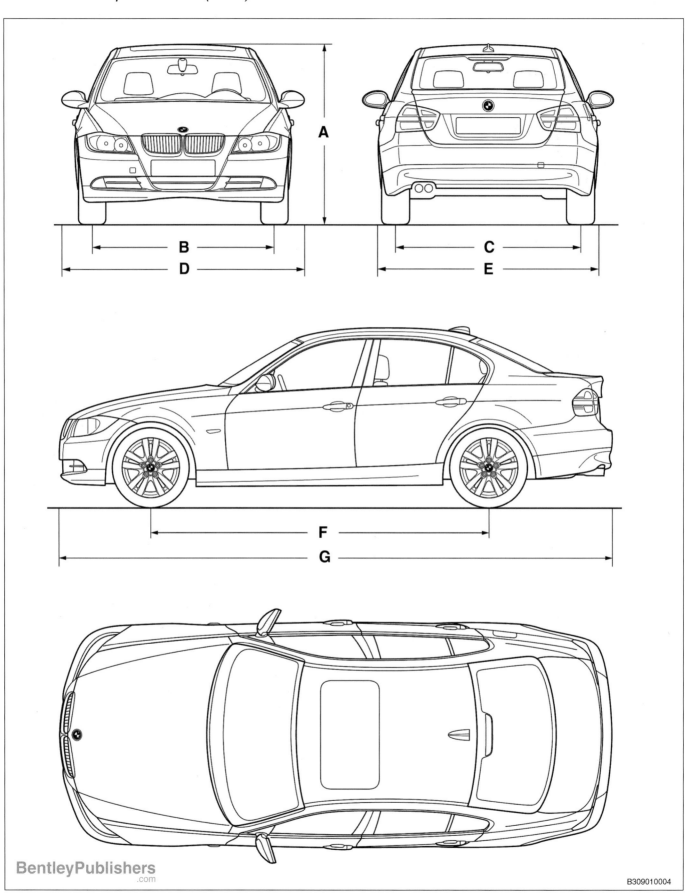

B309010004

## MODEL YEAR HIGHLIGHTS

Below are the 3 Series year-to-year highlights through model year 2010. Major changes are detailed later in this repair group.

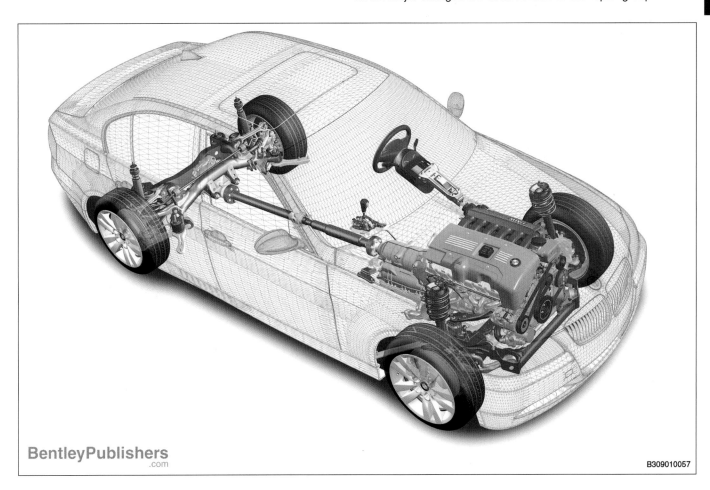

BentleyPublishers
.com

B309010057

### Model year 2006

- First models of the 3 Series for the U.S., the E90 325i and 330i Sedans entered production in March 2005 as 2006 models.

- Optional active steering (RWD models only); varies steering ratio according to vehicle speed and other factors.

- Run-flat tires standard on all models, eliminating the need to carry a spare tire.

- Standard wheels and tires:
  - 325i / xi model with 16-in. wheels, all-season tires.
  - 330i / xi model with 17-in. wheels, all-season tires.

- Flat tire monitor (FTM), standard on all models, monitors tire pressures while the vehicle is being driven. FTM detects any significant loss of pressure in one tire in relation to another and illuminates warning light in Check Control (in instrument cluster).

- 6-speed manual standard, 6-speed Steptronic automatic optional on all models.

- New-generation dynamic stability control (DSC) with many new braking functions.

**6-speed Steptronic transmission**

BentleyPublishers
.com

B309010002

- Fall of 2005, three additional models added:
  - 325xi and 330xi Sedans, featuring BMW's innovative xDrive all-wheel drive system and specific configurations of standard and optional equipment.
  - 325xi Sports Wagon, adding 5-door wagon versatility and xDrive all-weather, any-road capability to the 3 Series.

- New generation 6-cylinder engines, called N52, both with 3.0-liter displacement
  - 325i: 215 hp @ 6250 rpm, 185 lb-ft. torque @ 2750 rpm, single-stage induction system
  - 330i: 255 hp @ 6600 rpm, 220 lb-ft. torque @ 2750 rpm, 3-stage induction system.

- New type differentials (rear and front differential for AWD models).

- Xenon adaptive headlights standard on 330i/xi models, optional on 325i/xi models.

- Adaptive brake lights.

- Ground lighting in door handles.

- Front- and rear-seat head protection system (HPS) airbags.

- Automatic safety-belt tensioners and force limiters standard at rear outboard seating positions (standard on front seats).

- BMW Assist, BMW's system of in-car telematics and customer services, available in Premium Package or as stand-alone option.

## Model year 2007

Model 2007 was a significant change year for the 3 Series.

The Sedans and wagons were upgraded with new engines, a couple of new colors and some minor interior tweaks.

The 325i and 325xi are replaced by the 328i and 328xi. These models received a more powerful version of BMW's 3.0-liter inline six-cylinder engine, generating 230 horsepower and 200 pound-feet of torque, for an increase of 15 hp and 15 lb-ft over the previous models.

In 2007, the 335i and 335 xi replaced the 330i and 330xi, featuring BMW's N54 3.0-liter twin-turbocharged inline 6-cylinder engine producing 300 horsepower and 400 pound-feet of torque. That is an increase of 45 hp and 80 lb-ft for higher end models.

The 3 Series expanded for 2007 with the introduction of a two-door 3 Series Coupe (E92) and a 3 Series Convertible (E93), completing the 3 Series family lineup.

**3 Series family**

B309010012

◀ New for 2007, the 3 Series Coupe.

B309010013

*Model year 2008*

◀ New for 2007, the retractable hardtop Convertible. Made of lightweight steel, the three-piece roof opens in just 22 seconds and folds smoothly into its rear compartment. The new roof structure ensures a lower level of noise even at high speeds while the ultra-stiff platform provides extreme torsional strength for rigidity.

## Model year 2008

V8-powered M3

◀ M3 Sedan and M3 Coupe were introduced in spring 2008. Other models remained essentially unchanged.

There were a few minor enhancements:

- Galvanic silver trim matching the trim around the START/STOP button was applied to the climate control knobs, adding a premium touch to the console. The sport steering wheel, available with the optional Sport Package, was the same as that of the 3 Series Coupe with galvanic accents. Satellite radio preparation was standard.

- A second-generation evolution of the N54 turbocharged engine management system, called MSD81.

Optional paddle shifters

◀ Optional transmission paddle shifters for all models with a 6-speed Steptronic automatic transmission and Sport Package.

## Model year 2009 and 2010

Updates for the 2009 models include:

- Subtle interior and exterior-design freshening for the Sedan and Sports Wagon and refinement of interior design and functions.

- New and revised options.

- New generation iDrive control and display system; expansion of BMW ConnectedDrive functions.

**2009 redesigned interior**

B3090010025

B309010018

The biggest visual change for 2009 was the Sedan and Sports Wagon mid-life update, called Life Cycle Impulse (LCI) by BMW. The exterior design featured a new front end, a more dynamic profile, and a wider appearance at the rear. Headlights and taillights used innovative lighting technology and 3-dimensional effects.

 At the front, width was accented, though actual width was unchanged. The front spoiler / bumper was reshaped with a larger intake air area.

*Model year 2009*

◀ The redesigned headlights were emphasized by chromed tubes.

The luminous rings around the headlights serve as daytime running lights (DRL) on vehicles with xenon adaptive lights (optional on 328i or 328xi models, standard on 335i or 335xi models).

The turn-signal lights received a vertically layered look and use LED technology.

In profile, the side sills and rocker panels set a strong lower accent. Side mirrors had new contours and provided an enlarged visual field for the driver.

◀ At the rear, the bumper, taillights and (on the Sedan) trunk lid were all reshaped. The taillight L-shape was more in evident, and new LED lighting sources illuminate the taillights and turn-signal lamps. An actual increase in rear track adds emphasis to the vehicle's wide stance.

◀ 2009 refinement of interior design and amenities included new colors and materials. Among functional updates were ergonomically enhanced placement of power-window controls for the driver and expanded storage.

◀ BMW iDrive in combination with optional navigation was ergonomically optimized with function selection and activation via turn, push and tilt motions. The redesigned iDrive controller features new direct-select keys and more programmable memory keys.

Included in the navigation option is a hard drive for storage of navigation data (such as destinations) and audio material (such as music). The hard drive allows transfer of material from a CD, MP3 player or a USB stick and can hold up to 8 Gb of music.

With an 8.8-in. high-resolution monitor, the iDrive displays remarkably attractive images.

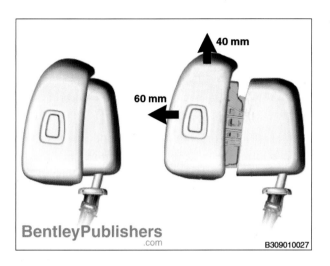

◁ Also for 2009 was active front head restraints, which in a rear-end impact employ pyrotechnics to pivot the restraint forward and upward (up to 60 mm/2.4 in. forward and 40 mm/1.6 in. upward).

The 2010 3 Series models were largely unchanged from the 2009 models. The few notable changes were:

- Automatic high beams became available as a stand-alone option.
- The BMW Professional radio with HD radio reception became standard.
- A new standard wheel style was introduced on 328i and 328i xDrive models Sedan and Sports Wagon models.

## NEW GENERATION (NG) ENGINES

With the E90 chassis came a new generation of engines with advanced concepts and technical sophistication. The primary focus of these engines was the use of Valvetronic, which revolutionized valvetrain technology.

There are 4 variants of the 6-cylinder engines used in the 3 Series. Differences are outlined below.

| Component/System | N52 Engine | N52KP | N51 | N54 |
|---|---|---|---|---|
| Crankcase | Composite magnesium/aluminum | Composite magnesium/aluminum | Composite magnesium/aluminum | All aluminum alloy |
| Cylinder Head | Aluminum | Aluminum (same as N52) | Aluminum - Specific to N51 due to combustion chamber mods | Aluminum - specific to N54 |
| Cylinder Head Gasket | Silicone rubber perimeter to prevent contact corrosion | Same as N52 | Same as N52 | Specific to N54 - multi-layer with no silicone rubber perimeter |
| Cylinder Head Cover | Magnesium | Plastic with integrated crankcase ventilation | Plastic with integrated crankcase ventilation (same as N52KP) | Plastic with integrated crankcase ventilation (specific to N54) |
| Crankcase Ventilation | External crankcase vent valve with cyclone separator. | Crankcase vent valve and labyrinth and cyclone oil separation integrated into cyl. head cover. | Crankcase vent valve and labyrinth and cyclone oil separation integrated into cyl. head cover. | No crankcase vent valve - calibrated orifice with cyclone separation integrated into cyl. head cover. |
| Valvetrain | 5 mm intake and exhaust valve stems (6 mm exhaust valve stem from 6/06) | 5 mm intake and 6 mm exhaust valve stems | 5 mm intake and 6 mm exhaust valve stems | 5 mm intake and 6 mm exhaust valve stems |
| VANOS | Infinitely variable Bi-VANOS | Infinitely variable Bi-VANOS | Infinitely variable Bi-VANOS | Infinitely variable Bi-VANOS |
| Valvetronic | Valvetronic II | Valvetronic II | Valvetronic II | No Valvetronic |
| Intake Manifold | Plastic with 3-stage DISA on high-output version (OL) | Plastic with 3-stage DISA on high-output version (O) | Plastic | Plastic (no DISA) |
| Fuel System | Manifold injection | Manifold injection | Manifold injection | High Precision Injection (HPI) |
| Cooling System | Electric coolant pump - 200 W | 2nd Generation electric coolant pump - 200 W | 2nd generation electric coolant pump - 200 W | 2nd generation electric coolant pump - 400 W |
| Exhaust System | "Near Engine" catalysts | "Near Engine" catalysts with underbody catalysts (ULEV II) | "Near Engine" catalysts with underbody catalysts (ULEV II) | "Near Engine" catalysts with underbody catalysts (ULEV II) |
| Pistons/Comp. Ratio | 10.7 to 1 | 10.7 to 1 | 10 to 1 | 10.2 to 1 |
| Connecting Rods/Crankshaft | Forged Steel with 8 mm bolts "cracked design" (Cast Crank) | Forged Steel (stiffened) with 8mm bolts "cracked design" (cast crankshaft) | Forged steel (stiffened) with 8mm bolts "cracked design" (cast crankshaft) | Forged steel (stiffened) with 8mm bolts "cracked design" (cast crankshaft) |
| HFM | Analog | Digital | Digital | Digital |

B309010026

**N52 3.0 liter Valvetronic engine**

BentleyPublishers.com

B309010030

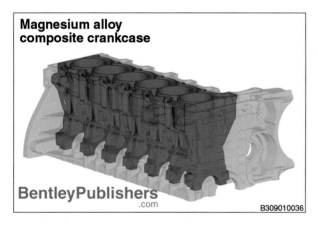

**Magnesium alloy composite crankcase**

BentleyPublishers.com

B309010036

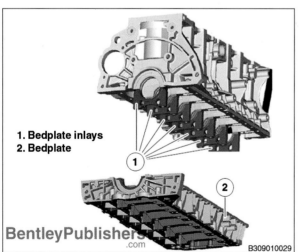

1. Bedplate inlays
2. Bedplate

BentleyPublishers.com

B309010029

## N52 engine (2006)

◄ In 2006, the new generation N52B30 in-line 6-cylinder engine was introduced in the E90 and E91 cars. This engine featured many innovations, including the composite crankcase, Valvetronic system and the 3-stage DISA intake manifold. The oil level dipstick was eliminated.

The same basic engine was shared on the 325i and 330i, with the difference in power ratings being achieved with intake manifold tuning and DME software.

| N52 engine specifications | |
|---|---|
| Displacement (cm3) | 2996 |
| Stroke/bore (mm) | 85.0/88.0 |
| Power output (kW/bhp) @ rpm<br>325i<br>330i | <br>160/215 @ 6250 RPM<br>190/255 @ 6600 RPM |
| Torque (Nm/ft-lb) @ rpm<br>325i<br>330i | <br>185/251 @ 2750<br>220/298 @ 2750 |
| Maximum engine speed | 7000 |
| Compression ratio | 10.7 : 1 |
| Valves/cyl | 4 |
| Engine weight (kg) | 161 kg (355 lb) |
| Engine management | Siemens MSV70 |
| Emission compliancy | ULEV 2 |

◄ The N52 engine weighed 22lbs. less than its predecessor M54 engine. The primary weight savings came from the composite magnesium-aluminum crankcase and the lightweight exhaust manifold.

◄ The magnesium bedplate and cylinder head cover also played a role in overall weight reduction.

The traditional belt driven coolant pump from previous engines was replaced by an electric coolant pump. This allowed for the addition of a single belt drive.

Other N52 engine features included:

- Trapezoidal connecting rods (weight optimized).
- Aluminum silicon (AluSil) cylinder head
- Timing case integrated in crankcase and cylinder head
- Cylinder head gasket with silicon sealing lip
- Weight-optimized double VANOS
- Crankcase ventilation with integrated heater
- Volumetric flow controlled oil pump

The N52 engine features Valvetronic. This advanced technology replaces the conventional throttle butterfly with an electro-mechanical system that controls the amount of lift of the individual intake valves. The Valvetronic engine is able to breathe freely, delivering better performance while using less fuel.

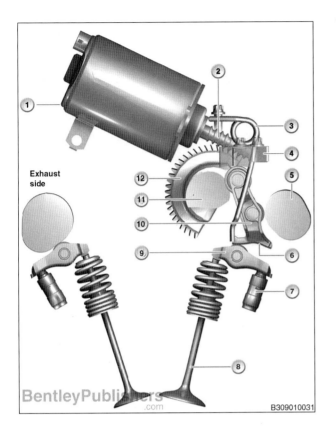

◄ Valvetronic valvetrain uses a stepper motor to control a secondary eccentric shaft fitted with a series of intermediate rocker arms that control the degree of valve lift. The throttle butterfly is no longer needed as a means of controlling the air supply, though for safety reasons it is still fitted as an emergency back-up. Valvetronic improves cold start behavior, lowers exhaust emissions and provides smoother, more immediate power.

1. Actuator
2. Worm shaft
3. Return spring
4. Gate block
5. Intake camshaft
6. Ramp
7. Hydraulic valve adjuster (HVA), intake
8. Intake valve
9. Roller cam follower
10. Intermediate lever
11. Eccentric shaft
12. Worm gear

Exhaust side

B309010031

B309040032

◄ The compact VANOS units use vane-type construction which is less complex and easier to service than previous VANOS designs. The VANOS units have integrated sprockets and are attached to the camshaft via a central bolt.

**NOTE—**

- *Due to the different spread ranges for the intake and exhaust camshaft, the VANOS units cannot be interchanged. Doing so would cause engine damage.*

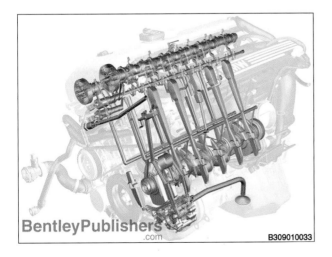

B309010033

◄ To meet the oiling requirements of the N52, a volumetric-flow controlled oil pump is utilized. Systems such as VANOS require a large volume of oil, particularly at low engine speeds.

This pump only delivers as much oil as each operating range of the engine requires. A conventional oil pump would have to be approximately three times the size of that in the N52 engine. A larger oil pump would also consume excess energy and therefore the new pump design allows:

- Increased power output
- Reduced weight
- Optimized fuel consumption
- Reduced exhaust emissions

B309010035

## N52KP engine (2007- )

For 2007, the N52 base engine from the 325i was replaced by the more powerful N52KP engine (230 hp vs. 215 hp). The N52KP engine was an improved and cost-optimized version of the N52 and was first available in the 328i and 328xi Coupe from September 2006.

There are not many changes to the emission systems on this engine. The N52KP continued to use the composite magnesium/aluminum alloy engine block from the existing N52.

The technical highlights of the N52KP include:

- New engine management (MSV80)
- New hot film mass air flow sensor (digital HFM)
- EGAS8 throttle with magnetoresistive position feedback
- Plastic valve cover with integrated crankcase vent valve and oil separation
- Stronger connecting rods
- Exhaust valve stem increased to 6 mm
- Second-generation electric coolant pump
- Lightweight camshafts (hydroformed)

| N52KP engine specifications | |
|---|---:|
| Displacement (cm3) | 2996 |
| Stroke/bore (mm) | 88.0/85.0 |
| Power output (kW/bhp) @ rpm | 172/230 @ 6250 RPM |
| Torque (Nm/ft-lb) @rpm | 200/270 @ 3000 |
| Maximum engine speed | 7000 |
| Compression ratio | 10.7 : 1 |
| Valves/cyl | 4 |
| Engine management | Siemens MSV80 |
| Emission compliancy | ULEV 2 |

## N51 engine (2007 - )

The N51 is variant of the N52 engine, designed to comply with EPA / CARB SULEV 2 emission requirements. There were various measures employed to meet the standards.

***NOTE—***

- *In addition to the 5 existing SULEV states of California, New York, Maine, Massachusetts, and Vermont, four states were added for 2007. These states include, Connecticut, Rhode Island, Oregon and Washington.*

| N51 engine specifications | |
|---|---|
| Displacement (cm3) | 2996 |
| Stroke/bore (mm) | 88.0/85.0 |
| Power output (kW/bhp) @ rpm | 172/230 @ 6250 RPM |
| Torque (Nm/ft-lb) @ rpm | 200/270 @ 3000 |
| Maximum engine speed | 7000 |
| Compression ratio | 10.0 : 1 |
| Valves/cyl | 4 |
| Engine management | Siemens MSV80 |
| Emission compliancy | SULEV 2 |

The N51 engine has a lower compression ratio and the combustion chamber design has been modified to work in conjunction with the N51 piston to achieve the required emission goals.

Some of the SULEV measures for the N51 include:

- Near engine catalyst with additional underbody catalyst
- Secondary air system
- Optimized combustion chamber geometry in cylinder head
- Modified piston crown for lower compression
- Plastic valve cover with integrated crankcase vent valve and separator (from N52KP)
- Stainless steel fuel lines with threaded connections
- Radiator with "Prem-air" coating
- EGAS08 throttle system carried over from N52KP
- Air box with activated carbon filter for EVAP control
- Purge system pipes made from optimized plastic

### N54 engine (2007 - )

The N54 engine is the high-performance top-of-the-range powerplant utilizing twin-turbo technology and high-pressure direct gasoline injection.

The N54 delivers uncompromising response and high torque output in a unit that is about 150 pounds lighter than a V-8 engine. The new technology used in the N54 allows for maximum efficiency and the low exhaust emissions to meet ULEV II guidelines.

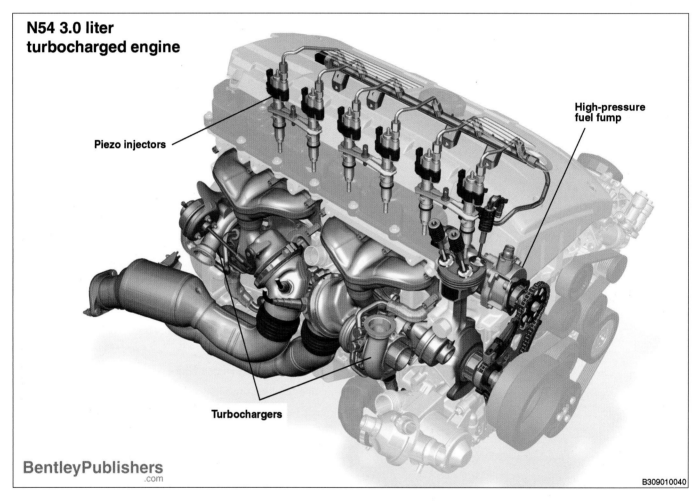

**N54 3.0 liter turbocharged engine**

Piezo injectors

High-pressure fuel fump

Turbochargers

BentleyPublishers.com

B309010040

**N54 engine**

BentleyPublishers.com

B309010034

◁ The N54 is officially referred to as the N54B30O0. The "O" designates the "upper" output range and the "0' indicates the first generation in this series.

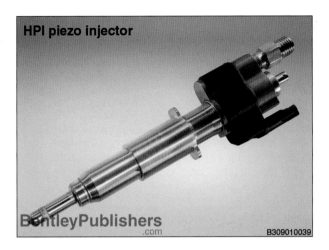

**HPI piezo injector**

B309010039

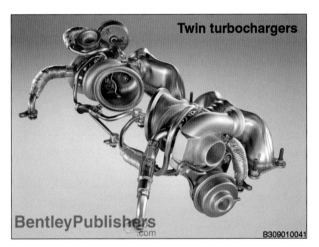

**Twin turbochargers**

B309010041

B309010042

◀ The N54 uses the new HPI injection system, which is capable of pressures of up to 200 bar. This system features piezo injector technology with outward opening injectors.

Developing 300 hp and peak torque of 400 Nm or 295 lb-ft, this new engine offers the highest standard of spontaneous and superior power and performance.

| N54 engine specifications | |
|---|---|
| Displacement (cm3) | 2979 |
| Stroke/bore (mm) | 84/89.6 |
| Power output (kw/bhp) @ rpm | 225/300 @ 5800 RPM |
| Torque (Nm) @rpm | 400 @ 1300 - 5000 |
| Maximum engine speed | 7000 |
| Compression ratio | 10.2 : 1 |
| Valves/cyl | 4 |
| Engine weight (kg) | 187 kg (412 lb) |
| Engine management | MSD80 |
| Emission compliancy | ULEV 2 |
| Injection system type | HPI (DI 2) |

The 3.0 liter N54 engine features the following:

- Exhaust driven twin turbocharger
- Air to air intercooler
- Second generation direct injection (HPI) with piezo injectors
- New engine management (MSD80)
- Bi-VANOS
- All aluminum crankcase with iron cylinder liners
- (similar dimensions to N52)
- External oil cooler
- New high output electric coolant pump (400 W)
- Aluminum cylinder head with plastic valve cover
- Steel crankshaft

## TRANSMISSIONS

All of the 3 Series transmission choices are 6-speed.

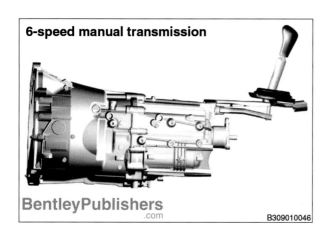

**6-speed manual transmission**

B309010046

## Manual transmissions

◁ The 6-speed manual gearbox, standard on all models, is engineered to provide precise control and a high level of driving pleasure. The manual transmission has a lifetime oil fill. Both Getrag and ZF manufactured units are installed on the 3 Series cars covered by this manual. See 200 Transmission–General for additional application information.

| 6-speed manual transmission applications | |
| --- | --- |
| 325i, 328i | Getrag GS6-17BG (type I) |
| 330i, 325xi, 328xi, 330xi | ZF GS6-37BZ (type H) ZF GS6X-37BZ (type H) |
| 335i 335xi | ZF GS6-53DZ (type G) ZF GS6X-53DZ (type G) |

## Automatic transmissions

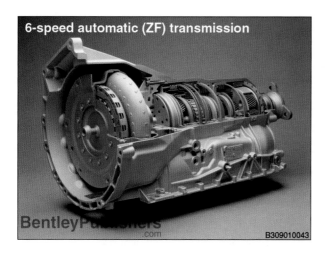

**6-speed automatic (ZF) transmission**

B309010043

◁ A 6-speed automatic transmission is optionally available for all 3 Series cars. Compared to the 5-speed unit it replaces, it is 10% lighter, has a more efficient torque converter and operates with fewer internal clutches.

| 6-speed automatic transmission applications | |
| --- | --- |
| 328i, 328xi | GM GA6L45R (GM6) |
| 325i, 325xi, 330i, 330xi, 335i, 335xi | ZF GA6HP19Z (ZF 6HP19) |

The Steptronic feature offers Normal, Sport and Manual modes. The Sport mode, in which shifts occur at higher engine speeds, is engaged by moving the lever from D; from here, the Manual mode is engaged when the driver manually chooses a gear by tipping the lever forward (for downshifts) or rearward (for upshifts).

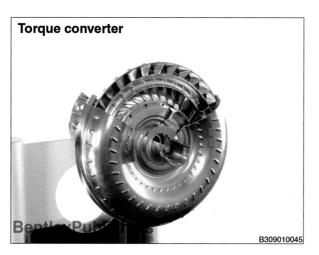

**Torque converter**

B309010045

◁ The torque converter uses an integrated torsion damper which avoids unnecessary slip and power loss. The converter clutch is closed immediately after the vehicle starts off. In this way, it feels similar to a manual transmission, with short response and shift times. With precise control and a low level of converter slip, the 6-speed automatic transmission also improves fuel economy, particularly at highway speeds when 6th gear is in use.

## BMW xDrive

xDrive is BMW's intelligent all-wheel drive system.

### NOTE—

• *2009 and later models with all-wheel drive no longer carry xi on the trunk badge. Instead, there is an xDrive badge on the front fender designating the all-wheel drive configuration.*

xDrive operates as follows:

• Driving torque is always transmitted to the front and rear wheels.

• The portion of torque transmitted to the front wheels is controlled by a multi-disc clutch attached to the transfer box. The torque split between front and rear wheels is steplessly variable.

• Engagement pressure on the multi-disc clutch is directed by an electronic control system in response to actual road and driving conditions.

xDrive doesn't just optimize traction; it also enhances both agility and stability on grippy as well as slippery road surfaces. Via the same type of logic that DSC employs to recognize and correct for excessive over- or understeer, xDrive adjusts the front/rear torque split to avoid these tendencies.

BentleyPublishers.com

B309010047

## SUSPENSION, STEERING AND BRAKES

The front suspension utilizes MacPherson struts. The rear axle is a completely redesigned five-link axle. The steering is an engine-speed-sensitive variable-assist power rack-and-pinion design.

Run-flat tires are standard together with four-wheel ventilated brake rotors and a new-generation dynamic stability control (DSC) system.

## Front suspension

The front suspension utilizes a double pivot spring strut axle with MacPherson struts. The double-pivot concept is a more elaborate system than that of the previous 3 Series, featuring two lower arms (hence the designation double-pivot) that work in concert with the spring / shock-absorber strut.

The system provides:

- Small positive steering offset for best steering feel and control under all road conditions.

- Large steering caster, for outstanding stability in straight-line driving and excellent steering return action coming out of curves.

- Space for large brakes, by virtue of the arrangement of the two lower arms.

**E90 front suspension (RWD)**

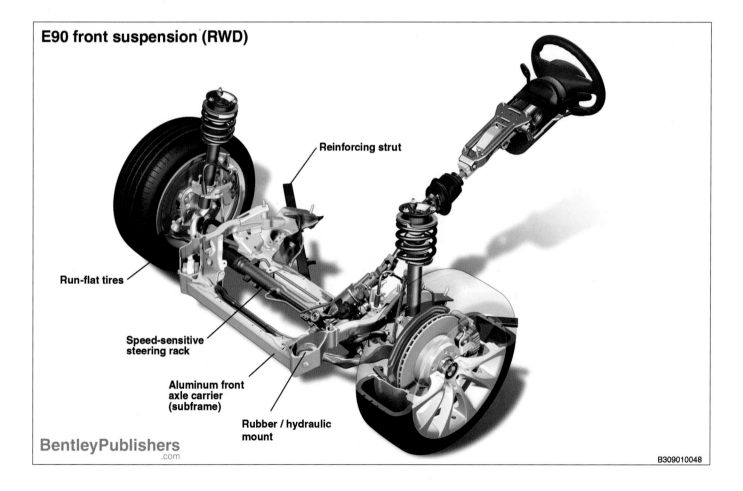

Reinforcing strut

Run-flat tires

Speed-sensitive steering rack

Aluminum front axle carrier (subframe)

Rubber / hydraulic mount

B309010048

Additional front suspension design attributes:

- The trailing (forward) lower arm has a rubber/hydraulic mount for enhanced ride comfort.

- The transverse (rearward) lower arm is cushioned by a finely tuned rubber mount that enables direct and precise steering response in curves and corners.

- Extensive aluminum components in the RWD models for low unsprung weight. This improves suspension response to bumps and other road irregularities and it significantly improves ride comfort and handling on irregular road surfaces.

In addition, the subframe on RWD models is of aluminum, as is the steering rack; these parts are not unsprung, but contribute to overall weight reduction, and a near-50/50 weight distribution. The subframe adds rigidity, enhances steering precision and is also an integral part of energy absorption in a frontal crash.

### NOTE—

- *Because the AWD front suspension handles drive forces as well as those of steering, cornering and braking, AWD (xi) models have mostly steel components in this area.*

## Rear suspension

 The rear suspension is a multi-link independent rear axle with 5 different link arms. Conceptually, this system could be described as a double-A-arm system with an additional lateral thrust rod. The upper and lower A-arms are actually two links each, with their vertical positions differing.

There is a virtual pivot point for each pair of links, similar to the front axle. The result is a system geometry optimized for handling. Also as at the front, the axis connecting these virtual points is configured to ensure that driving, braking and road forces all act effectively on short leverage. The result is very precise handling, especially on rough road surfaces. Under cornering forces, the system controls geometry to ensure predictable, stable handling.

Contributing to this outstanding geometry is the wide and rigid platform the rear tires are planted on. The lateral links are extremely rigid too, as is the subframe.

All suspension links connect to the subframe; no longer does any link pivot directly from the body structure. This further reduces the effects of road irregularities on ride comfort, and improves handling as well.

The large and elaborate subframe enhances energy management in a crash - including the more severe rear-end impact that BMW's new models are designed to withstand.

As always with BMWs, the final drive (differential) is also mounted to the subframe through rubber, creating acoustic decoupling that minimizes the transmission of driveline noises into the body. Widely spread mounts to the body, in an area where the body structure is particularly rigid, further help optimize the combination of precision handling and ride comfort.

The rear suspension system, subframe and brake calipers are all of steel.

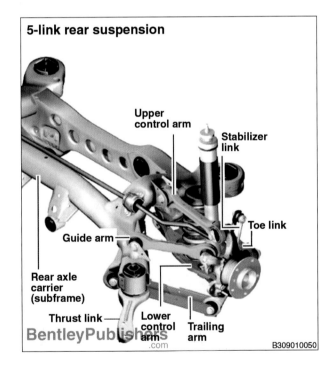

**5-link rear suspension**

Upper control arm

Stabilizer link

Toe link

Guide arm

Rear axle carrier (subframe)

Thrust link

Lower control arm

Trailing arm

B309010050

**E91 (Coupe) rear suspension**

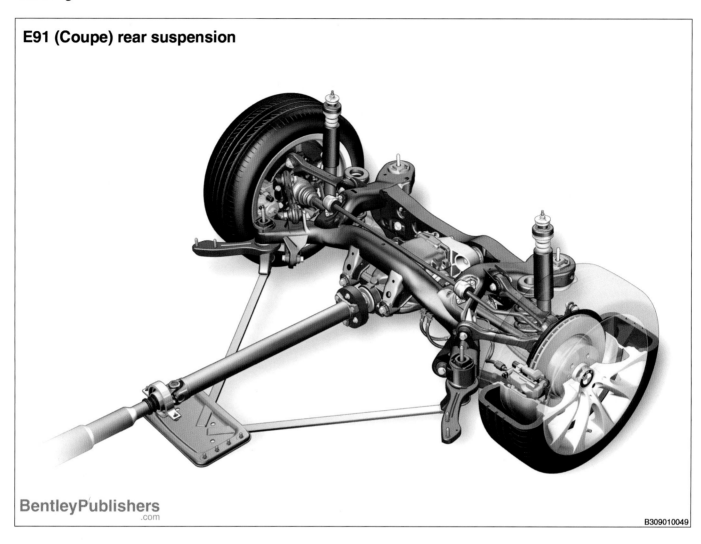

BentleyPublishers.com

B309010049

## Steering

◁ The steering column adjustment range has been extended compared to its predecessor, plus the adjustment unit now supports the airbag and the steering column. An integrated crash element (metal tube) located in the upper area of the steering column are designed as load bearing parts.

The engine-speed-sensitive variable-assist power rack-and-pinion steering system has direct overall ratio of 16.0:1. Together with the redesigned suspension and subframe, the steering reaction to inputs is precise and sharp.

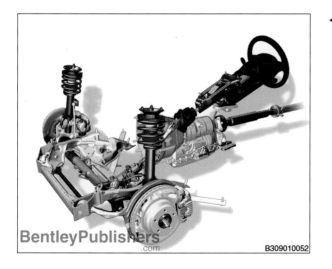

BentleyPublishers.com

B309010052

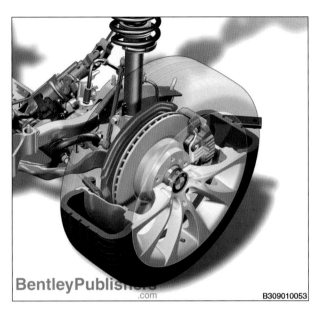

B309010053

## Brakes

 The brakes use ventilated cast-iron rotors all around, and aluminum calipers at the front as a contribution to balanced weight distribution. Braking power is enhanced by large diameter rotors. For example, the 330i front rotors are 330 mm (13.0 in); rear rotors 336 mm (13.2 in).

A new Geomet steel coating eliminates rusting on portions of the rotors not swept by the brake pads. And in the context of condition-based service (CBS), there are separate front and rear wear sensors which allow the mileage remaining on the front and rear pads to be displayed and appropriate service scheduled. See

020 Maintenance for accessing the CBS menu.

## Dynamic stability control (DSC)

The new 3 Series dynamic stability control (DSC) system is referred to as MK60E5 and is manufactured by Continental Teves. Several new functions were introduced, resulting in significantly improved comfort during brake intervention and more precise braking.

Functions introduced with MK60E5:

- Brake fade support
- Braking readiness
- Brake disk drying
- Soft stop
- Start assist
- Electronic control brake actuation (ECBA)
- Yaw moment compensation with AFS

These advanced functions contribute to increased directional stability, optimized comfort, enhanced system availability and response plus reduced braking distance.

### Brake fade support

High brake temperatures (greater than 550°C) can occur when brakes are applied over a long period (i.e. brakes applied while traveling downhill) or as a result of multiple hard brake applications. As the temperature of the brake rotor increases, pads friction decreases, resulting in diminishing brake effect (brake fade).

In order to reduce fade, DSC calculates the temperature of the brake rotors based on:

- Applied brake pressure
- Duration of brake application
- Rate of vehicle deceleration

In case DSC detects brake fade, brake pressure is increased to maintain a constant ratio of brake pedal force to vehicle deceleration. If necessary, pedal travel is increased to compensate for the fading effect.

DSC detects fading as follows:

- DSC compares the current vehicle deceleration with a nominal value based on the current brake pressure.
- DSC increases brake pressure until the nominal deceleration is achieved or until all wheels are subject to ABS control.
- Process is ended when the brake pedal is released.

When this function is activated, a brake warning light appears in the LCD display in the instrument cluster. If the brake rotor temperature increases further, an additional (legally-stipulated) brake warning light is also activated.

## Braking readiness

If the DSC system notices that the accelerator pedal is released quickly, the brakes are immediately pretensioned to shorten the brake apply response time. To accomplish this, DSC control module applies a PWM signal to the DSC hydraulic unit solenoid valves without creating any measurable deceleration of the vehicle. By applying a small amount of brake pressure, the clearance between the brake pads and brake rotors is reduced. If the brakes are not applied within a certain time, brake pressure is reduced. The pre-tensioning of the brakes depends on vehicle speed which must be above 44 mph (70 kph).

## Brake disk drying

Brake disk drying removes moisture on the brake rotors while traveling on wet roads or in the rain. To do this, the DSC control module generates a low brake pressure on the rotors without creating measurable deceleration of the vehicle. Application of the low brake pressure signal is done continually based on:

- Road speed (greater than 44 mph (70 kph).
- Signal from rain sensor indicating continuous wiper operation (stage 1 or 2). The drying action cycle is performed approximately every 200 seconds during stage 1 wiper operation and every 120 seconds during stage 2 operation.

The cycle is altered if the brakes are applied by the driver during these times.

## Soft stop

Soft stop prevents a harsh stop causing the occupants to pitch forward when braking the vehicle to a standstill.

The soft stop function reduces the braking pressure at the rear axle prior to the vehicle reaching a complete stop. DSC calculates the moment that a complete stop can be expected based on the current road speed plus rate of deceleration and reduces braking pressure accordingly.

Activation of function:

- Light brake application, under constant pressure.
- Road speed (under approx. 3 mph (5 kph).

**Start-off assist**

Start-off assist prevents the vehicle from moving unexpectedly on an incline as the driver releases the brake pedal and moves to the accelerator pedal when pulling away on a hill.

Start-off assist functions by applying the brakes based on the degree of incline (determined by the DSC acceleration sensor). Brake pressure is reduced as soon as engine torque is sufficient to move the vehicle or if the accelerator is not depressed within approx. 2 seconds. The function can be activated when driving forward or backwards and is deactivated when the parking brake is applied and can not be activated if the transmission is in neutral.

*NOTE—*

• *After approx. 2 seconds of the brake pedal being released, start-off assist is deactivated.*

## BODY

A new BMW platform always means exciting new technology and innovative, meaningful features. The most noteworthy is the highly sophisticated chassis technology.

The E90 3 Series body incorporated all the trademarks of its predecessors: the double-kidney grille, the power-domed hood, and the Hoffmeister kink in a progressive, sporty, yet elegant design.

**E90 3 Series chassis**

BentleyPublishers
.com

B309010054

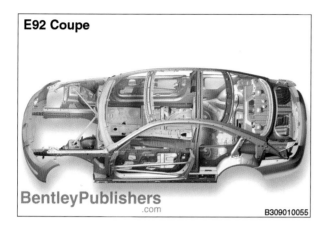

**E92 Coupe**

3 Series Sports Wagon body (Munich plant)

Various engineering structural features include:

- Use of high-strength steels in the large-section structural body sections.

- Targeted application of different types of steel, including multi-phase types, at various points to promote effective energy management.

- Improved structural energy paths for dissipating the immense forces of frontal crash impacts. The engineers concentrated on optimizing the balance between front-end deformation and maintaining an intact passenger compartment.

- Ways to transfer forces onto the other side in the event of a severe offset frontal collision (when one side of the vehicle takes the hit). The high energy absorbing structure is the basis for keeping the passenger compartment intact - and for optimum calibration of passive-safety systems such as safety belts and multiple airbags.

The structure is similarly designed to transfer impact energy to the side opposite the impact in side impacts. Components that help manage this impact energy include:

- Floor structure.

- Doors, including BMW's effective interlocking door anchoring system.

- Reinforced B-pillars.

- Dashboard structure, which functions as much more than just a carrier for instruments, climate control, etc.

- Roof frame.

In rear-end impacts, the deformable area consists of:

- Longitudinal structural members.

- Trunk floor and lid, or tailgate (Sports Wagon).

- Trunk or cargo-area side walls, as integral elements of the overall body-side structures.

- Various additional reinforcements.

The structure is almost completely galvanized, enhancing corrosion resistance and thus helping preserve its strength and energy management over the years.

## Sports Wagon (E91)

As with the Sedan, the body of the new BMW 3 Series Sports Wagon is conventionally manufactured from steel. It is fully galvanized and equipped with a safety passenger cell. All the performance data of the E90 with regard to weight optimization, body stiffness and high safety levels apply to the E91.

Technical highlights of the new 3 Series Sports Wagon body are its two-part rear hatch and a large panorama sunroof.

The rear hatch is set at a much lower level in the interests of a low loading sill. The rear tailgate is comprised of two segments (the rear window can be opened separately). The indentation in the rear bumper reduces the height of the loading sill for easier loading.

The floor assembly does not require any Sports Wagon specific reinforcements.

## Coupe (E92)

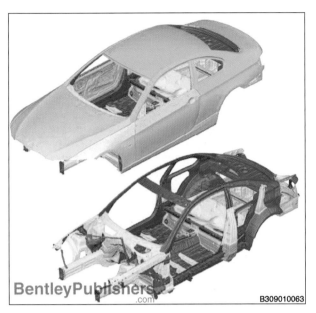

B309010063

◁ A stronger and lighter body is constructed of a combination of different types of materials including many metals of different composition and even plastic. This increases rigidity and provides more structural support where needed without sacrificing weight. The passive safety principle is based on retaining the passenger cell with dynamic deformation zones.

- Carrier structures with a high load bearing capacity
- Optimum utilization of deformation ranges
- Extremely rigid passenger cell
- Effective restraint systems

B309010061

◁ The front fenders and rocker panel covers are fabricated from Thermo-plastic material to promote weight distribution. The use of these plastic components results in a 20 lb reduction of the vehicle body weight, enhancing fuel economy and performance.

The front fenders are made of a special synthetic material and no longer have to be painted separately. Instead, they go through the regular painting process together with the complete body-in-white.

The doors are built of lightweight steel.

## Convertible (E93)

The Convertible bodyshell is light and torsionally stiff. In the E93, BMW's has achieved the highest level of torsional stiffness ever seen in a BMW Convertible.

Unladen weight of the Convertible is approximately 400 lb above the BMW 3 Series Coupe. This extra weight results from the installation of additional support members (struts) in the floor and the electric motors and hydraulic elements required for the retractable hardtop.

◁ A strut concept is employed with the aim of increasing the body rigidity, consisting of:

1. Front end diagonal strut
   Front axle subframe struts
   Bulkhead strut
2. Underbody strut
3. Rollover protection system strut
4. Tension strut

The cross section of the sill (shown in red) has been increased compared to the E92 Coupe. The E93 is also fitted with the innovative plastic front fenders found on the E92 Coupe.

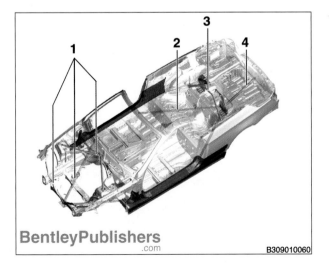

BentleyPublishers
.com

B309010060

## Interior

On the inside, the all-new 3 Series continues the harmonious balance between sportiness and elegance, with an ergonomically designed cockpit for the driver and purposeful materials carefully chosen to please the senses.

This entry-level BMW now receives many of the technological advances of its bigger siblings. Available features include but are not limited to:

- Navigation with voice recognition.
- Stolen vehicle recovery.
- iDrive.
- MOST bus technology.
- Comfort access (from 09 / 2005).
- Active front steering.
- ACC (active cruise control).
- IHKA (automatic climate control).

The E90 was available with basic seats and sports seats. Electrically adjustable versions were also available. The power sports seat include a memory function as well as a backrest width adjustment option. Side airbags are included in the front seats.

**Active front steering**

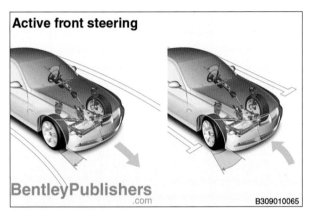

B309010065

**2006 BMW 330i interior**

B309010003

## Multiple restraint system (MRS)

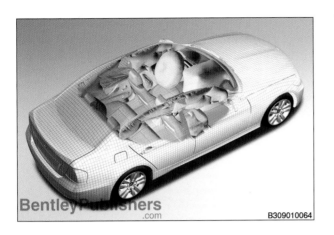

◄ The latest generation of the multiple restraint system (MRS 5) provides enhanced passive protection for vehicle occupants in case of a serious collision. The system is regarded as passive in that it operates automatically. It differs from the previous MRS 4 system in that reaction time is decreased and accuracy increased due to the addition of the door pressure sensors and crash sensors in the engine compartment.

## ELECTRICAL SYSTEM

◄ Multiple control modules are involved in the operation of the vehicle electrical system. BMW calls this the distributed functions approach. There are several systems (i.e. central locking, power windows and interior lighting) whose functions are distributed across multiple control modules. The primary control modules are:

1. Junction box electronics (JBE).
2. Roof functions center (FZD).
3. Car access system (CAS).
4. Footwell module (FRM).

*NOTE—*

• *See 600 Electrical System–General for additional information on control module functions.*

◄ Functions of junction box electronics control module (JBE).

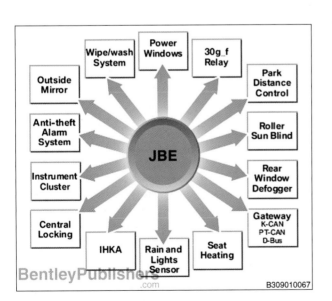

*Multiple restraint system (MRS)*

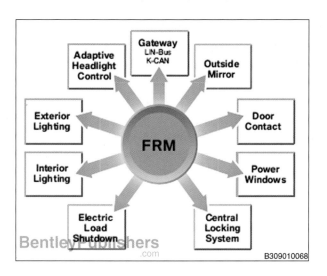

◄ Functions of footwell module (FRM).

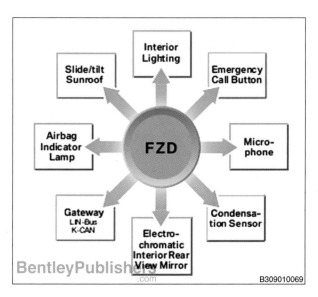

◄ Functions of roof function center (FZD).

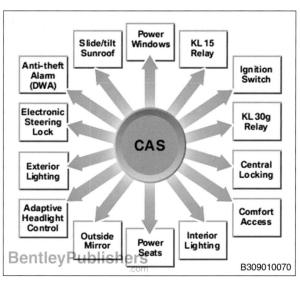

◄ Functions of car access system (CAS).

## Control module locations

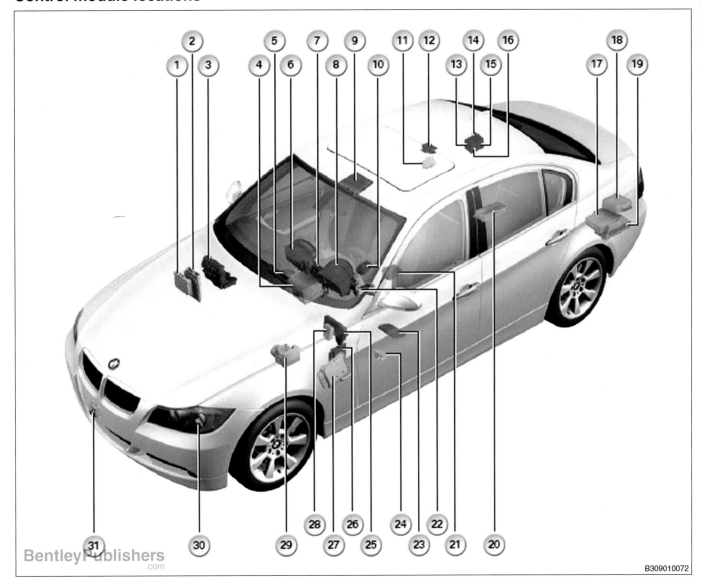

BentleyPublishers
.com

B309010072

1. Sequential manual gearbox (SMG)
2. Digital motor electronics (DME)
3. Junction box (JB)
4. Car communication computer (CCC)
5. Passenger seat module
6. Central information display (CID)
7. Integrated automatic heating and air-conditioning (IHKA)
8. Instrument cluster
9. Roof functions center (FZD)
10. iDrive Controller (CON)
11. Electric fuel pump (EKP)
12. Ultrasonic interior sensor (USIS)
13. Comfort access (CA)
14. Trailer locking module
15. Trailer module (AHM)
16. Park distance control (PDC)

17. Top-HiFi system
18. Video module (VM)
19. CD changer (CDC)
20. Telephone and telematics control unit (TCU)
21. Multiple restraint system (MRS)
22. Steering column switch cluster (SZL)
23. Driver seat module
24. DSC acceleration sensor
25. Comfort access system (CAS)
26. Footwell module (FRM)
27. Active steering (AFS)
28. Longitudinal dynamics management (LDM)
29. Dynamic stability control (DSC)
30. Steering angle sensor
31. Active cruise control (ACC)

## Dashboard and controls overview

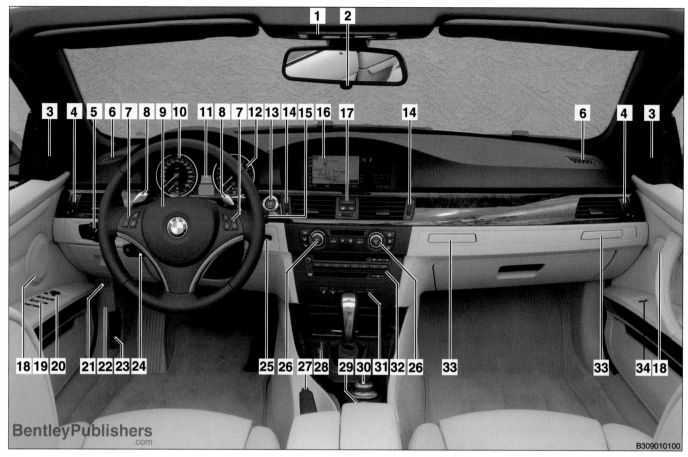

B309010100

1. Roof function center (FZD)
2. Central locking and anti-theft alarm indicator
3. Door mounted tweeter
4. Side air outlet adjuster
5. Light switch
6. Side window defroster outlet
7. Multifunction steering wheel switches
8. Paddle shifter
9. Horn, airbag
10. Speedometer, fuel gauge
11. Instrument cluster LCD screen
12. Tachometer, engine coolant temperature gauge
13. START / STOP switch
14. Center air outlets adjuster
15. Wiper - washer stalk switch
16. Navigation and iDrive display screen
17. Hazard warning and central locking switch
18. Door mounted midrange speaker
19. Driver door window switch cluster
20. Outside mirror control switch
21. Trunk lid or tailgate release button
22. OBD II plug cover
23. Engine hood release

24. Cruise control stalk switch
25. Remote key slot
26. Climate control knobs
27. Parking brake handle
28. Steptronic gear range indicator
29. iDrive main menu button
30. iDrive controller
31. Center console switch cluster
32. Radio and navigation control
33. Cup holder
34. Passenger door window switch

### NOTE—

• *Features and equipment may vary from the illustration.*

# 020 Maintenance

## GENERAL

This repair group explains the structure of this repair manual and details basic information regarding your vehicle and repair procedures for it. Included are service and maintenance procedures.

BMW 3 Series vehicles are equipped with condition based service (CBS) capabilities which monitors many vehicle systems and components and suggests service based on the actual current condition of components. See **Condition Based Service (CBS)** in this repair group. Following the CBS recommended service intervals helps ensure safe and dependable operation of the vehicle.

Aside from keeping your vehicle in the best possible condition, proper maintenance plays a role in maintaining full protection under BMW's new-vehicle warranty coverage. If in doubt about the terms and conditions of your vehicle's warranty, an authorized BMW dealer should be able to explain them.

BMW is constantly updating their recommended maintenance procedures and requirements. The information contained here may not include updates or revisions made by BMW since the publication of the documents supplied with the vehicle. If there is any doubt about what procedures apply to a specific model or model year, or what intervals to follow, consult an authorized BMW dealer.

## How to use this manual

This manual is divided into 11 main sections or partitions:

| | |
|---|---|
| **0** | General Data and Maintenance |
| **1** | Engine |
| **2** | Transmission |
| **3** | Suspension, Steering and Brakes |
| **4** | Body |
| **5** | Body Equipment |
| **6** | Electrical System |
| **7** | Equipment and Accessories |
| **ECL** | Electrical Component Locations |
| **EWD** | Electrical Wiring Diagrams |
| **OBD** | On–Board Diagnostics |

A master listing of the 11 partitions and the corresponding specific repair groups can be found on the inside front cover.

Thumb tabs are used on the first page of each repair group to help locate the groups quickly. Page numbers throughout the manual are organized according to the repair group system. A comprehensive **Index** is at the end of the manual.

020

## Warnings, Cautions and Notes

Throughout this manual, there are numerous paragraphs with the headings **WARNING, CAUTION** or **NOTE**. These headings have different meanings.

*WARNING*—
- *Text under this heading warns of unsafe practices that are very likely to cause injury, either by direct threat to the person(s) doing the work or by increased risk of accident or mechanical failure while driving.*

*CAUTION*—
- *Text under this heading calls attention to important precautions to be observed during the repair work to help prevent accidentally damaging the vehicle or its parts.*

*NOTE*—
- *A note contains information, tips, or pointers which help in doing a better job and completing it more easily.*

Read **WARNING, CAUTION** and **NOTE** headings before you begin repair work. See also **001 Warnings and Cautions**.

## CONDITION BASED SERVICE (CBS)

### CBS basics

The BMW maintenance system, called condition based service (CBS) constantly monitors oil levels and the degree of wear and tear on a limited number of components on the vehicle. CBS uses sensors and special algorithms to monitor vehicle driving conditions, then uses this data to calculate current and future service requirements.

CBS items that are monitored are displayed in the instrument cluster or the iDrive central information display (CID, 2006 - 2010, cars without Navigation option) or car information computer (CIC, 2009 - 2010 with Navigation option). The display shows remaining times or distances for the following maintenance tasks.

- Engine oil and filter change (see **Table a.**)
- Front brake pads replacement (see **Table b**)
- Rear brake pads replacement (see **Table b**)
- Brake fluid change (see **Table b**)
- Cabin microfilter replacement (see **Table b**)

CBS sorts service requirements according to date due and notifies the driver when the vehicle needs a service appointment. Mandatory emissions and safety inspection due dates may also be stored and displayed.

Additional maintenance recommended by BMW is listed in **Table c.** and **Table d**.

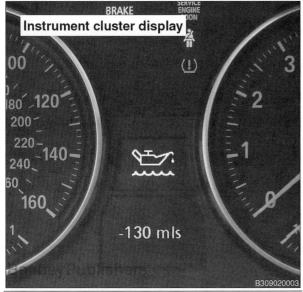

Instrument cluster display

B309020003

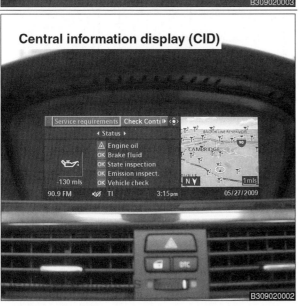

**Central information display (CID)**

B309020002

B309020004

◄ Service requirement information is stored in the remote key while the vehicle is driven. This information can be accessed by an authorized BMW device center at the time of a service appointment.

For CBS to work correctly, make sure correct local date and time are set in vehicle memory.

## Service recognition details

The CBS system recognizes when a service is required using one of the following three methods:

**Adaptive**. Sensor data and algorithms are used to determine the required maintenance interval for a service based on individual user driving style. Examples:

- Oil change interval is determined by engine oil condition sensor (OZS) monitoring oil condition, oil level, and oil temperature; and from additional algorithms using these parameters: engine load, fuel consumption, time and distance since the last oil change.

- Front and rear brake pad replacement intervals are determined from two-stage brake lining wear sensors on left front and right rear brake pads; and from algorithms using these input parameters: travel distance, wheel speed, braking pressure, braking time, and braking frequency.

**Fixed time (months)** determines the required maintenance of the following:

- Brake fluid change
- Mandated safety and emissions inspections

**Fixed distance (miles)** determines the required maintenance of the following:

- Spark plug replacement (dependent on engine)
- Air filter element replacement
- Automatic transmission fluid change
- Microfilter replacement (dependent on vehicle model and CBS version)
- Oxygen sensors replacement
- Vehicle check

020

## Instrument cluster CBS display

— Switch ignition ON.

◀ Center LCD display (between speedometer and tachometer gauges) shows car icon and the word SERVICE.

◀ Use turn signal lever buttons to call up service information:

1. Toggle up or down to scroll through menu items.

2. Press to select menu item.
   Press to enter next menu level.

◀ Center LCD display: Outside temperature reading and time shown if button **2** on turn signal lever is pressed or no entries are made within approx. 15 seconds.

Lower LCD display: Remaining driving distance and date of next scheduled service shown.

⚠ indicates that Check Control messages are stored. See **Check Control** in this repair group.

— Use turn signal lever button **1** to scroll through menu items:

1. Instrument lighting brightness control (when lights are ON). See **630 Lights**.

2. Check Control. See **Check Control** in this repair group.

3. Engine oil level monitoring. See **119 Engine Lubrication**.

4. Set current time using turn signal lever buttons.

5. Set current date using turn signal lever buttons.

6. To retrieve service information, press turn signal lever button **2**. See below.

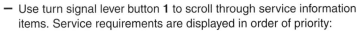

— Use turn signal lever button **1** to scroll through service information items. Service requirements are displayed in order of priority:

1. Vehicle check. See **Table d**.

2. Next oil change due. See **Engine oil service** in this repair group.

3. Next safety inspection and road test due.

4. Next emissions inspection due.

5. Next front brake service due. See **Brake Service** in this repair group. See also **340 Brakes**.

6. Next rear brake service due. See **Brake Service** in this repair group. See also **340 Brakes**.

7. Next brake fluid change due. See **340 Brakes**.

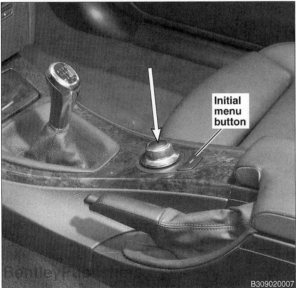

## Central information display (CID)

◄ E90 models with navigation and iDrive are equipped with a liquid crystal display (LCD) known as central information display or CID. The instrument cluster control module communicates service requirements to CID where data can be displayed with graphics and text.

In addition, CID is the graphic display unit for convenience functions and several vehicle functions.

The initial CID screen contains four menu items:
• Communication
• Navigation
• Entertainment
• Climate control

— Switch ignition ON.

◄ Press down iDrive controller (**arrow**) to select **Info sources I Settings** menu.

The button for returning to the initial menu is located behind the controller.

◄ Press down iDrive controller to brings up **Info sources I Settings** menu.

*Central information display (CID)*

◀ Pull back iDrive controller to enter middle screen, then rotate controller to **Service Info**.

◀ Press down controller to enter **Service Info** (or **Service requirements**) submenu.

Service requirements are listed with the most urgent at the top.

– Pull back controller to enter middle screen, then rotate controller to **Engine oil**.

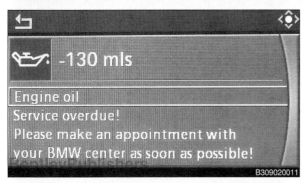

◀ Press down controller to enter **Engine oil** screen.

In this case, engine oil service is overdue by 130 miles.

– Push forward, then down on controller to return to **Service Info** menu.

◀ Use controller to scroll to next service item, in this case **Brake fluid**.

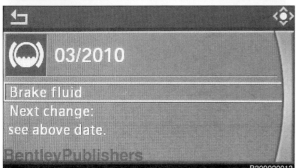

◀ Press down controller to select **Brake fluid** screen.

Brake fluid change is recommended by date.

– Return to **Service Info** menu by pushing controller forward, then down. Scroll through remainder of service items in the same way.

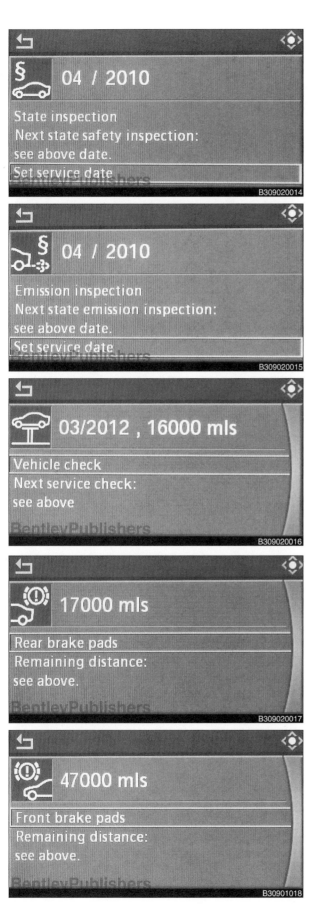

◀ Enter safety inspection date in this screen.

◀ Enter emissions inspection date in this screen.

◀ Next required service due, indicated by date and miles (or kilometers).

For a listing of vehicle check items, see **Table d**.

◀ Next rear brake service due.

◀ Next front brake service due.

*Car information computer (CIC)*

B309020023

## Car information computer (CIC)

 Some 2009 and 2010 models are equipped with a new version of iDrive with multiple menu buttons. The display for this system is known as car information computer (CIC). Functionally, system operations are similar to the older version.

## Resetting service requirements

When one or more service operations are carried out (example: front brake pads are changed) reset these operations to their full service interval.

 Vehicle without iDrive: Reset service requirements in instrument cluster as follows:

• Close all doors. Switch ignition ON.

• Make sure lower displays in cluster show clock and mileage.

• Press and hold trip odometer reset button for about 5 seconds until CBS icons begin to display in cluster. Release button.

• Press turn signal lever BC button (**arrow**) repeatedly to scroll through CBS icons.

• For each icon the word RESET? is displayed. To reset a particular item, press and hold BC button. A small analog clock icon is displayed. When complete, the chosen CBS item is reset.

• To insure that the reset was done, press BC button while looking at CBS reset icon. Acknowledgment of reset is shown with a check mark in a box.

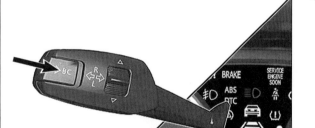

Trip odometer reset button

B309020026

## Recommended maintenance

The publisher of this manual recommends that engine oil and filter be replaced a intervals not greater than 7500 miles or one year, whichever comes first. Oil change service task are shown in **Table a**.

For service prompted by CBS, see **Table b**.

**Table c** lists service and maintenance required at mileage intervals.

**Table d** lists other recommended periodic vehicle inspection tasks.

020

The number in the "additional repair information" column refers to the repair group in this manual where additional information can be found.

| Table a. Engine oil service | Additional repair information |
|---|---|
| Engine oil and oil filter, change. (CBS prompts based on oil condition sensor monitoring. See **119 Lubrication System**.) | 020 |
| Brief diagnostic tests:<br>• Check Control, check messages.<br>• Indicator and warning lights, scan for fault codes using BMW scan tool or equivalent.<br>• CBS display, reset.<br>• Tires, check tread, adjust pressures.<br>• Tire pressure monitor, reset. | 020 |
| Parking brake, check operation, adjust as necessary. | 340 |
| Washer fluid, top off | |

| Table b. CBS prompted service | Additional repair information |
|---|---|
| Front brake pads, replace. (CBS prompts based on pad thickness.) | 340 |
| Rear brake pads, replace. (CBS prompts based on pad thickness.) | 340 |
| Brake fluid, change every 2 years. (CBS prompts based on time elapsed since last change) | 340 |
| Cabin microfilter, change. (CBS prompts based on mileage elapsed.) | 020 |

| Table c. Additional services | Additional repair information |
|---|---|
| **Every 45,000 miles** | |
| Air filter element, replace. Reduce change interval in dusty conditions. | 020 |
| **Every 100,000 miles** | |
| Automatic transmission fluid (ATF), replace. | 240 |
| Spark plugs, replace. | 020 |
| **Every 120,000 miles** | |
| Oxygen sensors, N52, N54 engines, replace. | 180 |
| **Every 150,000 miles** | |
| Oxygen sensors, N51 engine, replace. | 180 |
| *Note:* BMW states that engine coolant, manual transmission fluid, differential fluid and transfer case fluid are life-time fluid and do not require replacement. | |

| Table d. Vehicle check | Additional repair information |
|---|---|
| Horn, headlight flasher, hazard warning flasher, check operation, | |
| Instrument cluster and control lighting, blower, check operation | |
| Lighting system (dome lights, glove compartment light, flashlight, trunk or cargo compartment lights, turn signals, hazard warning flasher, back-up lights, brake lights, license plate lights, check operation. | 630 |
| Safety belts, check condition and function. | 720 |
| Wipers and washers, check. | 611 |
| Body, check for corrosion. | |
| Tires, check tread depth, wear pattern, condition, inflation pressure, correct pressure as necessary. | |
| Run-flat indicator, initialize. | 020 |
| Battery, check state of charge, charge as required. | 121 |
| Power steering fluid, check fluid level. | 020, 320 |
| Airbags, inspect for torn covers, damage or attached stickers. | 721 |
| Mirrors, inspect. | 510 |
| Engine coolant, check level and concentration. | 020, 170 |
| Windshield washer, intensive cleaning system, check protection level, fluid level, top off if necessary. | |
| Brake system connections and lines, check for leaks, damage and correct positioning. | |
| Underbody (transmission, rear axle, fuel lines, exhaust system) check for damage, leaks and corrosion. | |
| Steering components, check for clearance, leaks, damage and wear. | |
| Road test, check for performance, braking, steering, suspension, noises. | |

OBD 2 plug

B309020031

## BASIC SERVICE INFORMATION

### Diagnostic trouble codes (DTCs), accessing

Diagnostic trouble codes (DTCs) that are stored in the engine control module (ECM) or other electronic modules may be accessed as follows:

– Place transmission selector lever in PARK or NEUTRAL. Engage parking brake. Make sure ignition is OFF.

◄ Connect BMW diagnostic scan tool to OBD 2 plug on left door post. (Plug is behind plastic trim.)

– Start engine and let idle.

– Follow scan tool instructions as they appear on scan tool screen.

– For a listing of scan tool suppliers, see **Tools** in this repair group. For additional information, see **OBD On-Board Diagnostics**.

### Non-reusable fasteners

Many fasteners used on the vehicles covered by this manual must be replaced with new ones once they are removed. These include but are not limited to: bolts, nuts (self-locking, nylock, etc.), roll pins,

020

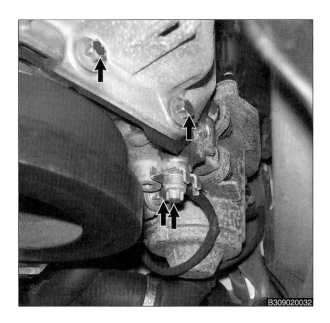

clips and washers. Use genuine BMW replacement parts for this purpose.

Some bolts, known as torque-to-yield fasteners, are designed to stretch during assembly and are permanently altered, rendering them unreliable once removed. Replace these where instructed to do so. Failure to replace these fasteners could cause personal injury or vehicle damage.

◀ Many engine components are assembled using aluminum bolts in order to reduce electrochemical corrosion. Aluminum bolt heads are painted blue (**arrows**) to distinguish them. These fasteners also stretch in use; replace with new during reassembly. Be sure to use aluminum bolts where specified.

See an authorized BMW dealer for applications and ordering information.

## Tightening fasteners

It is good practice to tighten fasteners on a component gradually and evenly to avoid misalignment or over-stressing any one portion of the component. For components sealed with gaskets, this method helps to ensure that the gasket seals correctly.

◀ Where there are several fasteners, tighten them in a sequence alternating between opposite sides of the component. Repeat the sequence until all the fasteners are evenly tightened to the proper specification.

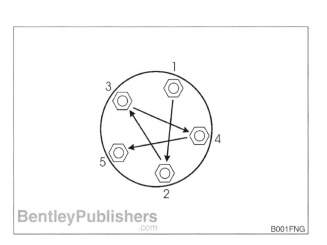

For some repairs a specific tightening sequence is necessary, or particular order of assembly is required. Such special conditions are noted in the text, and the necessary sequence is described or illustrated. Where no specific torque is listed, use **Table e** as a general guide for tightening fasteners.

*NOTE —*
- *Metric bolt classes or grades are marked on the bolt head.*
- *Do not confuse wrench size with bolt diameter.*
- *Values in **Table e** are for reference only.*

| Table e. General bolt tightening torques in Nm (max. permissible) | | | | | | |
|---|---|---|---|---|---|---|
| | **Bolt Class (according to DIN 267)** | | | | | |
| **Bolt diameter** | **5.6** | **5.8** | **6.8** | **8.8** | **10.9** | **12.9** |
| M5 | 2.5 | 3.5 | 4.5 | 6 | 8 | 10 |
| M6 | 4.5 | 6 | 7.5 | 10 | 14 | 17 |
| M8 | 11 | 15 | 18 | 24 | 34 | 40 |
| M10 | 23 | 30 | 36 | 47 | 66 | 79 |
| M12 | 39 | 52 | 62 | 82 | 115 | 140 |
| M14 | 62 | 82 | 98 | 130 | 180 | 220 |
| M16 | 94 | 126 | 150 | 200 | 280 | 340 |
| M18 | 130 | 174 | 210 | 280 | 390 | 470 |

## Buying parts

Many of the maintenance and repair tasks in this manual call for the installation of new parts, or the use of new gaskets and other materials when reinstalling parts. Make sure the parts that are needed are on hand before beginning the job. Read the introductory text and the complete procedure to determine which parts are needed.

For some bigger jobs, partial disassembly and inspection is required to determine a complete parts list. Read the procedure carefully and, if necessary, make other arrangements to get the necessary parts while your vehicle is disassembled.

### Genuine BMW parts

Genuine BMW replacement parts from an authorized BMW dealer are designed and manufactured to the same high standards as the original parts. They are the correct material, manufactured to the same specifications, and guaranteed to fit and work as intended. Most genuine BMW parts carry a limited warranty.

Many independent repair shops make a point of using genuine BMW parts, even though they may at times be more expensive than parts from other sources. They know the value of doing the job right with the right parts. Parts from other sources may be as good as BMW parts, particularly if manufactured by one of BMW's original equipment suppliers, but it is often difficult to know.

BMW is constantly updating and improving their vehicles, often making improvements during a given model year. BMW may recommend a newer, improved part as a replacement, and your authorized dealer's parts department will know about it and provide it. The BMW parts organization is best equipped to deal with your BMW parts needs.

### Non-returnable parts

Some parts cannot be returned, even for credit. The best example is electrical parts, which are almost universally considered non-returnable. Buy electrical parts carefully, and be as sure as possible that a replacement is needed, especially for expensive parts such as electronic control modules. It may be wise to let an authorized BMW dealer or other qualified shop confirm your diagnosis before replacing an expensive non-returnable part.

### Model and model year

When ordering parts it is important that you know the correct model and engine designation for your vehicle. This manual covers 3 Series models with 6-cylinder engines. For information on engine codes and engine applications, see **100 Engine–General**.

Model year is not necessarily the same as date of manufacture or date of sale. A 2007 model may have been manufactured in late 2006, and perhaps not sold until early 2008. It is still a 2007 model. Model years covered by this manual are 2006 to 2010.

## Service

BMW dealers are uniquely qualified to provide service for BMW vehicles. Their authorized relationship with the large BMW service organization means that they have access to special tools and equipment, together with the latest and most accurate repair information.

The BMW dealer's service technicians are highly trained and very capable. Authorized BMW dealers are committed to supporting the BMW product. On the other hand, there are many independent shops that provide quality repair work. Checking with other BMW owners for recommendations on service facilities is good way to learn of reputable BMW shops in your area.

## Tools

Most maintenance can be accomplished with a small selection of tools. Tools range in quality from inexpensive junk, which may break at first use, to very expensive and well-made tools for the professional. The best tools for most do-it-yourself BMW owners lie somewhere in between.

Many reputable tool manufacturers offer good quality, moderately priced tools with a lifetime guarantee. These are your best buy. They cost a little more, but they are good quality tools that will do what is expected of them. Sears' Craftsman® line is one such source of good quality tools.

Some of the repairs covered in this manual require the use of special tools, such as a custom puller or specialized electrical test equipment. These special tools are called out in the text and can be purchased through an authorized BMW dealer. As an alternative, some specialty and scan tools may be purchased from the following tool manufacturers or distributors:

### Specialty tool suppliers

Assenmacher Specialty
Tools, Inc.
800-525-2943
www.asttool.com

Autologic Diagnostics (UK)
44-1865-870050
www.autologic-diagnos.co.uk

Baum Tools Unlimited, Inc.
800-848-6657
www.baumtools.com

Equipment Solutions
800-892-9650

Metalnerd
412-601-4270
www.metalnerd.com

Samstag Sales
615-735-3388
www.samstagsales.com

Shade Tree Software
303-449-1664
www.shadetreesoftware.com

ZDMAK Tools
(877) 938-6657
www.zdmak.com

Zelenda Automotive, Inc.
888-892-8348
www.zelenda.com

Vehicle identification
number (VIN)

B309020035

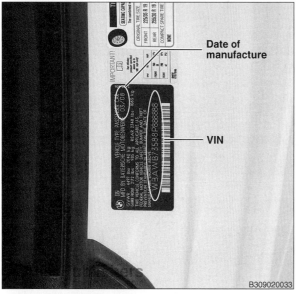

Date of
manufacture

VIN

B309020033

## IDENTIFICATION PLATES AND LABELS

◄ **Vehicle identification number (VIN).** This is a combination of letters and numbers that identify the particular vehicle. The VIN appears on the state registration document, and on the vehicle itself. One location is on the right front strut tower in the engine compartment, another in the lower left corner of the windshield.

For additional information, see **002 Vehicle Identification and VIN Decoder**.

◄ **Date of manufacture.** This information is necessary when ordering replacement parts or determining if any of the warranty recalls are applicable to your vehicle. The VIN plate on the driver door jamb below the door striker also specifies the month and year that the vehicle was built.

**Engine code.** 3 Series vehicles covered in this manual are powered by 6-cylinder engines. For information on engine codes and engine applications, see **100 Engine–General**.

**Transmission code.** The transmission type with its identifying code may be important when buying parts such as seals or gaskets. For information on transmission codes and applications, see **200 Transmission–General**.

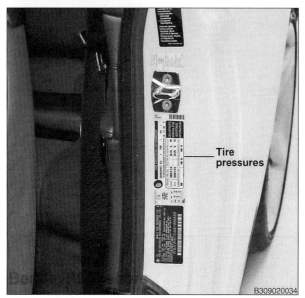

Tire
pressures

B309020034

◄ **Tire pressures.** Recommended tire pressures as well as wheel size, tire size, gross vehicle weight, and carrying capacity are listed on a sticker on the driver door jamb.

020

◁ **Engine serial number** is on left side of engine block behind and under intake manifold.

## RAISING VEHICLE

### Raising vehicle safely using floor jack

> **WARNING—**
> • *When raising the vehicle using a floor jack or hydraulic lift, carefully position the jack pad to prevent damaging the vehicle body.*
> • *Watch the jack closely. Make sure it stays stable and does not shift or tilt.*

◁ For safety and to avoid damaging vehicle, use jack only at four jacking points (**arrows**) just behind front wheels or just in front of rear wheels.

— Park vehicle on flat, level surface.

— If changing a tire, loosen lug bolts before raising vehicle. See **Changing a tire** in this repair group.

— Use wheel chocks to block wheel that is opposite and farthest from jack to prevent vehicle from unexpectedly rolling.

> **WARNING—**
> • *Do not rely on the transmission or the parking brake to keep the vehicle from rolling. They are not a substitute for positively blocking the opposite wheel.*

◁ Place floor jack into position, making sure base of jack is resting on flat, solid surface. Use a board or other support to provide a firm surface for jack, if necessary.

— Raise vehicle slowly while constantly checking position of jack and vehicle.

B309020036

## Raising vehicle using hydraulic lift

◄ Place lifting pads under jacking points (**arrows**) just behind front wheels and just in front of rear wheels. Raise vehicle carefully, checking to make sure that it is solidly balanced on lift.

## Working under vehicle safely

> **WARNING** —
> • A jack is a temporary lifting device. Do not use a jack alone to support the vehicle while you are under it.
> • Do not work under a lifted vehicle unless it is solidly supported on jack stands that are intended for that purpose.
> • Do not use wood, concrete blocks or bricks to support a vehicle. Wood may split. Blocks and bricks, while strong, are not designed for that kind of load and may break or collapse.
> • Use care when removing major (heavy) components from one end of the vehicle. The sudden change in weight and balance can cause vehicle to tip off the lift or jack stands.
> • Do not support vehicle at engine oil pan, transmission, fuel tank, or on front or rear axle. Serious damage may result.

— Disconnect negative (-) cable from battery so that vehicle cannot be started. Let others know what you are doing.

> **CAUTION** —
> • Prior to disconnecting the battery, read the battery disconnection cautions given in **001 Warnings and Cautions**.

— Raise vehicle slowly. See **Raising vehicle safely using floor jack** in this repair group.

◄ Use at least two jack stands to support vehicle. Use jack stands designed for the purpose of supporting a vehicle.

— Place jack stands on firm, solid surface. If necessary, use a flat board or similar solid object to provide a firm footing.

— Lower vehicle slowly until its weight is fully supported by jack stands. Watch to make sure that the jack stands do not tip or lean as the vehicle settles on them.

— Observe jacking precautions again when raising vehicle to remove jack stands.

**Jack stands**

0024408

## EMERGENCIES

The following is a list of emergency procedures and where they are covered in this manual:

- **Alarm** emergency disarming. See **515 Central Locking and Anti-theft**.
- **Convertible center console** opening. See **515 Central Locking and Anti-theft**.
- **Convertible top** manual closing. No procedure given by BMW.
- **Flat tire** warning. See **Flat tire indication** in this repair group.
- **Fuel flap** manual release. See **515 Central Locking and Anti-theft**.
- **Jump start**. See **Jump starting** in this repair group.
- **Sunroof** manual closing. See **Sunroof, emergency closing** in this repair group.
- **Tailgate** emergency opening. See **515 Central Locking and Anti-theft**.
- **Tire** change. See **Tire change** in this repair group.
- **Towing**. See **Towing** in this repair group.
- **Trunk lid** opening. See **515 Central Locking and Anti-theft**.

## Flat tire indication

◀ The air pressure in run-flat tires is automatically checked by the tire pressure monitoring (TPM) system. If a flat tire or substantial loss of tire pressure is detected, warning lights in yellow and red illuminate in the instrument cluster and a tire failure message appears in Check Control display. In addition, an acoustic signal sounds.

---

**WARNING**—

- *In case of run-flat tire failure, drive cautiously and do not exceed a speed of 50 mph or 80 km/h. With tire pressure loss, vehicle handling changes. This includes reduced tracking stability in braking, extended braking distance and altered steering characteristics.*

- *If unusual vibration or loud noises occur while driving on a damaged tire, this may be an indication that the tire has failed completely. Reduce speed and pull over as soon as possible at a suitable location. Otherwise parts of the tire could come loose, resulting in an accident. Do not continue driving.*

---

Avoid sudden braking and steering maneuvers. At the next opportunity, check air pressure in all four tires. Tire pressure specifications are given on a sticker on the driver door jamb.

If all four tires are inflated to the correct pressures, reinitialize TPM. TPM initialization is covered in **300 Suspension, Steering and Brakes–General**.

If warning lights illuminate in yellow and a tire failure message appears in Check Control display, TPM has a malfunction. Have the system checked as soon as possible.

B309020045

## Jump starting

Jump start the vehicle with discharged or dead battery using the good battery from another vehicle. See owner's manual for proper instruction on jump starting.

◄ Attach jumper cables to engine compartment battery B+ terminal and ground lug.

> **WARNING** —
> • Do not jump-start the engine if you suspect that the battery is frozen. Trapped gas may explode. Allow the battery to thaw first.

> **CAUTION** —
> • Do not quick-charge the battery (for boost starting) for longer than one minute, and do not exceed 16.5 volts at the battery with the boosting cables attached. Wait at least one minute before boosting the battery a second time.

## Tire change

3 Series vehicles covered by this manual are equipped with run-flat tires and no spare tire. There is need to change a wheel immediately in case of a puncture. See **Flat tire indication** in this repair group.

The vehicle is also not equipped with tire changing tools. The following details a safe procedure for changing a tire using floor jack and hand tools.

— Chock wheel diagonally opposite to the one being changed.

> **WARNING** —
> • Do not rely on the transmission or the parking brake to keep the vehicle from rolling. They are not a substitute for positively blocking the opposite wheel.

— Loosen lug bolts while vehicle is on ground, but leave them a little snug.

◄ Place jack under jacking point nearest wheel being changed. Use a board to provide a firm footing for jack if ground is soft. Raise vehicle only far enough so that the wheel is fully off ground and then remove lug bolts and wheel.

— Install new wheel. Install lug bolts and tighten hand tight using lug wrench.

◄ Lower vehicle. With all wheels on ground, fully tighten lug bolts in a crisscross pattern. Check inflation pressure of newly installed tire.

| Tightening torque | |
|---|---|
| Wheel to wheel hub | 120 Nm (89 ft-lb) |

B309020075

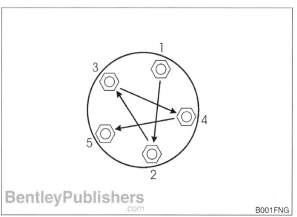

B001FNG

**020**

## Towing

The safest technique for towing vehicles covered by this manual (2-wheel drive or xDrive, manual or automatic transmission) is by using flat bed equipment.

> **WARNING**—
> • Do not tow with rear wheel lifted and front wheels on the ground. There is no steering lock. Vehicle may self-steer and sway dangerously from side to side.

> **CAUTION**—
> • 2-wheel drive model: Do not tow with sling-type equipment. Use a lift bar.
> • 2-wheel drive model: Do not use tow hook to tow faster than 30 mph (50 kph) or for a distance greater than 95 miles (150 km).
> • 2-wheel drive model with automatic transmission: Automatic transmission fluid (ATF) does not circulate when the vehicle is on rear wheels. Severe transmission damage may result. Use flat bed equipment.
> • xDrive model: Do not tow with front or rear axle raised individually. Use flat bed equipment.
> • xDrive model: Do not use tow hook or cable except for very short distances to winch it to a safe place.
> • Winch or tow vehicle with transmission lever in N (neutral).

◁ To access front threaded towing eye socket, press on upper edge of trim (**arrow**) on front bumper and remove trim.

◁ To access rear threaded towing eye socket, press on upper edge of trim (**arrow**) on rear bumper and remove trim.

– Remove towing eye from cargo compartment tool kit and screw into threaded hole in bumper until tight.

– Use towing eye for winching vehicle on flat bed.

B309020076

## Indicator and warning lights

Many vehicle systems are self-monitored for faults while driving. Generally, a red warning light that illuminates while driving should be considered serious. If you cannot immediately determine the seriousness of the warning light, stop the vehicle in a safe place and switch engine OFF as soon as possible. Consult the owner's manual for additional information on the warning light and the recommended action.

 If the malfunction indicator light (MIL) (Service Engine Soon warning light) comes on or flashes, it indicates emissions-related fault in engine management. Faults such as a bad oxygen sensor or a dead fuel injector can cause exhaust or evaporative emissions to exceed a specified limit. When these limits are exceeded, the MIL illuminates. The engine can be safety driven with the light on, but check engine management and emission control systems as soon as possible. See **OBD On–Board Diagnostics** for more information on the MIL and the on-board diagnostic system.

## ENGINE COMPARTMENT

### Engine compartment inspection

Remove upper and lower engine covers as required and check engine compartment for signs of fluid leaks. Fluid leaks attract dust making them easier to spot. Many expensive repairs can be avoided by prompt repair of minor fluid leaks.

Visually inspect for oil and ATF leaks at engine and transmission. Also inspect cooling, fuel, heating and air-conditioning systems for leakage. Visually inspect hoses and hose connections for leaks, worn areas, porosity and brittleness.

Check that fluid levels are between MIN and MAX marks.

The following illustrations show representative engine compartment layouts. There may be minor differences among model years, such as engine cover configuration.

### N51 engine compartment (non-turbo)

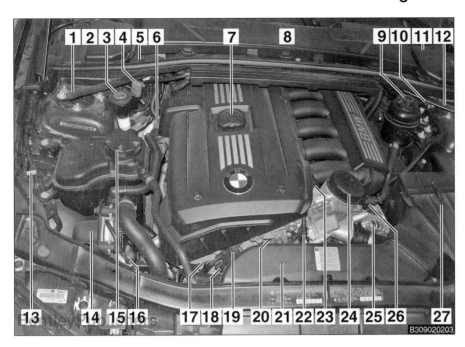

B309020203

1. Right strut tower brace

2. Electronics box (E-box) cover

3. Windshield washer reservoir cap

4. Battery B+ junction

5. Air quality (AUC) sensor

6. Secondary air injection valve

7. Oil filler cap

8. Cabin microfilter (underneath cover)

9. Power steering fluid reservoir

10. A/C refrigerant port

11. Brake fluid reservoir
    (underneath cover)

12. Left strut tower brace

13. Ground lug

14. Secondary air injection pump

15. Coolant reservoir cap

16. A/C refrigerant port

17. Exhaust camshaft sensor

18. Exhaust VANOS solenoid

19. Intake VANOS solenoid

20. Intake camshaft sensor

21. Engine air intake duct

22. Engine coolant temperature sensor

23. Oil pressure switch

24. Oil filter housing

25. Alternator

26. Vacuum motor line connection to brake
    booster

27. Intake air filter housing

## N52 engine compartment (non-turbo)

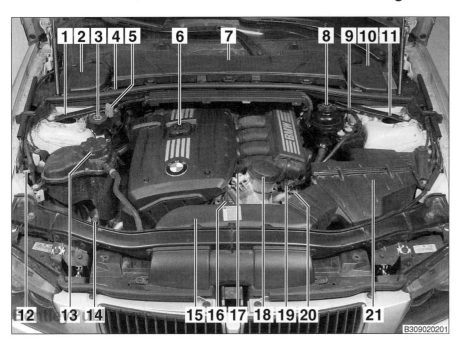

1. Right strut tower brace
2. Electronics box (E-box) cover
3. Windshield washer reservoir cap
4. Air quality (AUC) sensor
5. Battery B+ junction
6. Oil filler cap
7. Cabin microfilter (underneath cover)
8. Power steering fluid reservoir
9. A/C refrigerant port
10. Brake fluid reservoir (underneath cover)
11. Left strut tower brace
12. Ground lug
13. Coolant reservoir cap
14. A/C refrigerant port
15. Engine air intake duct
16. Engine coolant temperature sensor
17. Oil pressure switch
18. Oil filter housing
19. Vacuum motor line connection to brake booster
20. Alternator
21. Intake air filter housing

### N54 engine compartment (turbo)

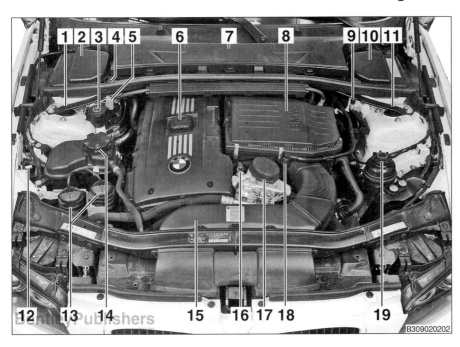

1. Right strut tower brace
2. Electronics box (E-box) cover
3. Windshield washer reservoir cap
4. Air quality (AUC) sensor
5. Battery B+ junction
6. Oil filler cap
7. Cabin microfilter (underneath cover)
8. Intake air filter housing
9. A/C refrigerant port
10. Brake fluid reservoir (underneath cover)
11. Left strut tower brace
12. Ground lug
13. Vacuum reservoirs
14. Coolant reservoir cap
15. Engine air intake duct
16. Oil pressure switch
17. Oil filter housing with oil-coolant heat exchanger
18. Vacuum motor line connection to brake booster
19. Power steering fluid reservoir

### Engine upper cover (ignition coil cover), removing

– Remove upper and lower cabin microfilter housings. See **640 Heating and Air-conditioning**.

◄ N52 engine (metallic cover): Remove cover fasteners (**arrows**) and lift up cover.

◁ N51, N52K, N54 engine (black plastic cover): Remove cover fasteners (**arrows**) and lift up cover.

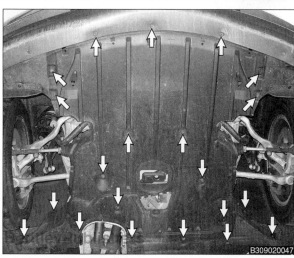

## Engine lower covers (splash shields), removing

◁ Engine splash shield: Unscrew fasteners (**arrows**) and remove cover.

◁ Transmission splash shield: Unscrew fasteners (**arrows**). Rotate cover around lug (**A**) to remove.

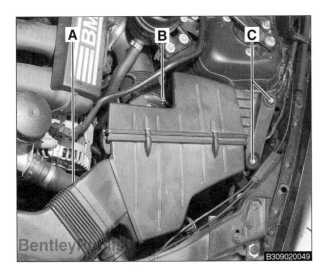

## AIR FILTER SERVICE

### Air filter element, replacing (non-turbo)

◀ Working at air filter housing:

- Detach air intake duct from filter housing (**A**).
- Loosen hose clamp (**B**) at mass air flow sensor.
- Remove filter housing mounting bolts (**C**) and lift housing out of engine compartment.

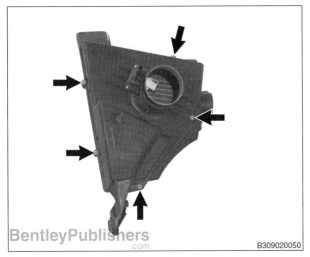

◀ Remove filter housing cover screws (**arrows**) and separate cover.

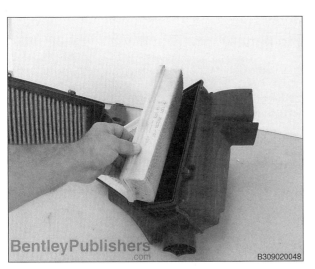

◀ Pull out filter element and replace.

– Installation is reverse of removal.

B309020051

B309020052

## Air filter element, replacing (turbo)

◄ Release air filter cover hold-down clips (**arrows**).

◄ Pull out filter element and replace.

– Installation is reverse of removal.

## BATTERY SERVICE

### Access to battery

The battery is in the right rear of the trunk or cargo compartment.

◄ Working in trunk or cargo compartment, open battery compartment. Twist plastic retainer counterclockwise (**arrow**) and remove right side trim.

B309121012

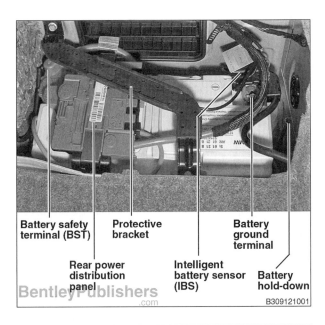

**Battery safety terminal (BST)** — **Protective bracket** — **Battery ground terminal** — **Rear power distribution panel** — **Intelligent battery sensor (IBS)** — **Battery hold-down**

B309121001

◄ Battery is equipped with several devices:

- Battery safety terminal (BST)
- Rear power distribution panel (A46) containing high-amperage fusible links.
- Intelligent battery sensor (IBS)

A bracket spans the top of the battery, protecting the power distribution panel.

The battery is held in place by a hold-down bracket and bolt. A secure battery hold-down is important in order to prevent vibrations and road shock from damaging the battery.

B301121031

## Battery, checking

The original equipment BMW battery is equipped with built-in hydrometer "magic eye".

◄ First remove protective bracket bolts (**arrows**) and lift out bracket.

Magic eye

B309020053

◄ Battery condition is determined by magic eye color:

- Green: Adequate charge
- Black: Inadequate charge, recharge
- Yellow: Defective battery, replace

See **121 Battery, Starter, Alternator** for additional topics:

- Battery removal and installation.
- Replacement battery registration.
- Battery reconnection notes.

> **CAUTION—**
> • *Do not charge battery with conventional charger. Use vehicle power supply device for recharging.*

## BRAKE SERVICE

Routine maintenance of the brake system includes maintaining brake fluid in the reservoir, checking brake pads for wear, checking parking brake function, and inspecting the system for fluid leaks or other damage:

- Check that brake hoses are correctly routed to avoid chafing or kinking.
- Inspect unions and brake calipers for signs of fluid leaks.
- Inspect rigid lines for corrosion, dents, or other damage.
- Inspect flexible hoses for cracking.
- Replace faulty hoses or lines.

> *WARNING —*
> - *Incorrect installation or overtightening of hoses, lines and unions may cause chafing or leakage. This can lead to partial or complete brake system failure.*

Note that brake fluid level and brake pad thickness are monitored and replacement intervals recommended by condition based service (CBS) system. See **Condition Based Service (CBS)** in this repair group.

## Brake fluid level, checking

The brake fluid reservoir is located on the driver's side near the base of the windshield underneath the cabin microfilter side cover.

> *WARNING —*
> - *Brake fluid is poisonous. Do not ingest. Wash thoroughly with soap and water if it comes into contact with skin.*

> *CAUTION—*
> - *Use only new, previously unopened brake fluid conforming to DOT 4.*
> - *Do not let brake fluid come in contact with paint. Wash immediately with soap and water.*
> - *Brake fluid absorbs moisture from the air. Store in an airtight container.*
> - *Do not use DOT 5 (silicone) brake fluid.*
> - *Do not fill brake fluid above* **MAX** *in fluid reservoir.*
> - *Do not mix mineral oil products such as gasoline or engine oil with brake fluid. Mineral oil damages rubber seals in the brake system.*
> - *Dispose brake fluid as a hazardous waste.*

◀ Working near left engine hood hinge, remove cabin microfilter side cover (**inset**) to access brake fluid reservoir.

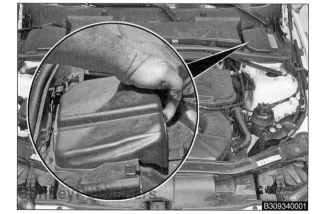

B309340001

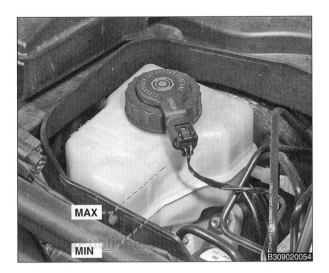

B309020054

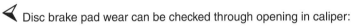

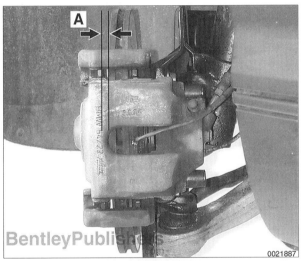

BentleyPublishers.com

0021887

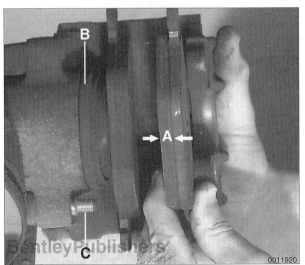

BentleyPublishers.com

0011920

◄ Check that fluid level is between **MIN** and **MAX** marks on brake fluid reservoir. Fluid level drops slightly as brake pad material wears.

| Brake fluid application | |
|---|---|
| BMW preferred fluid | Low viscosity DOT 4 brake fluid |
| *Low viscosity DOT 4 brake fluid may be used in all E90 vehicles. DOT 4 and low viscosity DOT 4 brake fluid can be mixed.* | |

Brake fluid absorbs moisture easily. This affects brake performance and reliability. To eliminate moisture, BMW recommends replacing the brake fluid every two years. When replacing or adding brake fluid, use only new fluid from previously unopened containers. Do not use brake fluid that has been bled from the system, even if it is brand new.

See **340 Brakes** for brake fluid flushing and bleeding.

## Brake pad and rotor wear, checking

Disc brakes are fitted at all four wheels. Although the brakes are equipped with a brake pad warning system, the system only monitors one wheel per axle. Check brake pad thickness whenever wheels are off or brake work is being done.

◄ Disc brake pad wear can be checked through opening in caliper:

- Measure distance (**A**) of brake pad "ear" to brake rotor. Compare to specification below.

◄ Unbolt caliper from steering arm to properly inspect:

- Brake pad thickness (**A**)
- Brake rotor
- Condition of caliper seal (**B**)
- Condition of caliper slider bolts (**C**)

| Brake pad lining minimum thickness | |
|---|---|
| Dimension **A** | 3.0 mm (0.12 in) |

See **340 Brakes** for additional techniques for checking brakes and for brake pad, rotor and caliper replacement procedures.

## Parking brake, checking

The parking brake system is independent of the main braking system and may require periodic adjustment depending on use. Adjust the parking brake if the brake lever can be pulled up more than 8 clicks. Check that the cable moves freely. See **340 Brakes** for parking brake adjustment procedure.

The parking brake may lose some of its effectiveness if it is not used frequently. This is due to rust build-up on the parking brake drum. To remove rust, apply the parking brake just until it begins to grip, then pull the lever up one more stop (click). Drive the vehicle approximately 400 meters (1,300 ft.) and release the brake.

## CABIN AIR MICROFILTER

E90 models are equipped with a cabin air microfilter to filter dust and pollen from incoming air. Filter is located at the base of the windshield under the upper microfilter housing.

### Cabin air microfilter, replacing

– Open engine hood.

◀ Remove upper microfilter housing screws (**arrows**). Lift off housing and microfilter.

B309640035

◀ Unclip filter element from housing and replace.

– Installation is reverse of removal. Make sure filter housing fits snugly over openings in cowl covering in order to keep water out of cabin air intake.

B309020067

020

## COOLING SYSTEM SERVICE

Antifreeze raises the boiling point and lowers the freezing point of coolant. BMW recommends engine coolant that is a 50 / 50 mixture of distilled water and ethylene glycol-based antifreeze.

Routine cooling system maintenance consists of maintaining the coolant level and inspecting hoses.

For additional cooling system information and repair procedures, see **170 Radiator and Cooling System**.

## Coolant level, checking

> **WARNING**—
> • *Allow cooling system to cool before opening or draining the cooling system.*

◀ With engine fully cooled off, carefully open radiator expansion tank cap. Note that when fully closed, **arrows** on cap and tank line up.

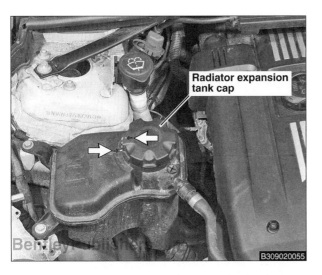

Radiator expansion tank cap

B309020055

◀ Float in expansion tank indicates coolant level when cold.

  • When upper mark on float (**MIN**) is level with top of filler neck, coolant is at minimum allowable level.

  • When lower mark on float (**MAX**) is level with top of filler neck, coolant is at maximum level.

— Top off coolant if necessary.

> **CAUTION**—
> • *Use only BMW approved phosphate-free, nitrite-free and amino-free antifreeze when filling the cooling system.*

MIN - - - - -
MAX - - - - -

B309020056

## Antifreeze concentration, checking

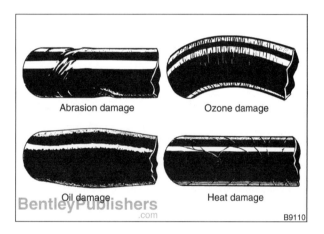

Abrasion damage    Ozone damage

Oil damage    Heat damage

◄ Use a coolant hydrometer to determine antifreeze concentration.

| Coolant mixture recommendations | |
|---|---|
| **Concentration** | **Cold protection** |
| 50% antifreeze | -35°C (-31°F) |
| 60% antifreeze | -40°C (-40°F) |

Do not use a higher concentration of antifreeze than a 60% mixture, as the heat transfer quality of the coolant decreases with higher antifreeze concentrations.

## Cooling system hoses, inspecting

Inspect hoses by first checking that all connections are tight and dry. Coolant seepage indicates that either the hose clamp is loose, hose is damaged, or connection is dirty or corroded. Dried coolant has a chalky appearance.

◄ Check hose condition by a visual and tactile inspection, making sure it is firm and springy. Replace hoses that exhibit conditions noted below. (Illustration courtesy of Gates Rubber Company, Inc.)

- Leakage: Dripping, moisture, or seepage near clamps or connectors.

> **CAUTION—**
> - *When installing or reinstalling coolant hoses, use clamps specified by BMW.*

- Electromechanical degradation: Difficult to see, but detectable by squeezing hose and feeling for cracks, weak areas, and voids.
- Oil damage: Soft and spongy to touch, visible bulges and swelling.
- Abrasion damage: Wear, abrasion, or scuffing, often due to contact with components in engine compartment.
- Heat damage: Internal and external damage, generally due to high under hood temperatures or overheating. Internal heat damage is often indicated by swelling with external damage marked by hardened and cracked areas.
- Ozone damage: Small, parallel cracks in outer layers, but without hardening. Due to exposure to atmospheric conditions.

– As a preventative measure, replace coolant hoses every 4 years.

## ELECTRICAL SERVICE

E90 vehicles are equipped with a complex electrical system. See the following repair groups for detailed information:

- **121 Battery, Starter, Alternator** for engine electrical components
- **600 Electrical System–General** for basic electrical troubleshooting information
- **ECL Electrical Component Locations** for fuse, relay and control module information
- **ELE Electrical Wiring Diagrams** for detailed electrical schematics

## ENGINE ACCESSORY BELT SERVICE

The accessory belt and pulleys transfer power from the engine crankshaft to the alternator, A/C compressor and power steering pump. Note that engine coolant pump and engine cooling fan are both electric.

Inspect belt with engine off. If belt shows signs of wear, cracking, glazing, or missing sections, replace immediately. To reduce the chance of belt failure while driving, replace belt every four years.

When the belt is replaced with a new one, store the old one in the trunk for emergency use.

Note that excessive engine movement due to a defective left side engine mount can lead to accessory belt damage. This is usually caused by contact between the power steering pump pulley and the front axle carrier. The belt may become dislodged from pulleys or broken when traveling over curbs, speed bumps or at a high rate of speed. This is primarily a problem in turbo models.

If accessory belt, power steering pump pulley or front axle carrier are found to be damaged, replace these parts as well as the left engine mount with updated parts.

---

*CAUTION—*

- *To avoid electrochemical corrosion to engine components made of aluminum-magnesium alloy, do not use steel fasteners. Use aluminum fasteners only.*
- *For reliable identification, test fasteners for aluminum composition with magnet.*
- *Replace aluminum bolts each time they are loosened.*
- *Follow torque instructions, including angle of rotation specifications, when installing aluminum fasteners.*

---

### Accessory belt, replacing (non-turbo)

◀ Working above radiator:
  - Remove air intake duct screws (**A**).
  - Pull duct backward to disengage from radiator support crossbar, then detach bellows (**arrow**) from air filter housing.

— Remove electric engine cooling fan and fan cowl. See **170 Radiator and Cooling System**.

— Remove engine splash shield. See **Engine lower covers (splash shields), removing** in this repair group.

— If planning to reinstall old belt, be sure to mark direction of rotation.

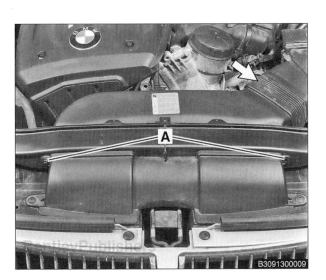

B3091300009

*Accessory belt, replacing (non-turbo)*

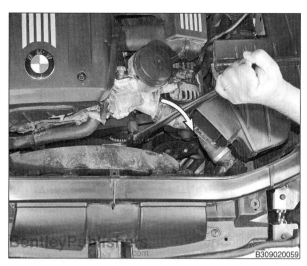

◀ Use Torx socket to rotate belt tensioner clockwise (**arrow**). This releases belt tension.

**11 3 340**

◀ If necessary lock tensioner in released position using awl-shaped tool (BMW special tool 11 3 340).

> **WARNING—**
> • *Observe care when working with tensioner. Personal injury could result if tensioner springs back into position uncontrolled.*

− Work belt off pulleys and remove.

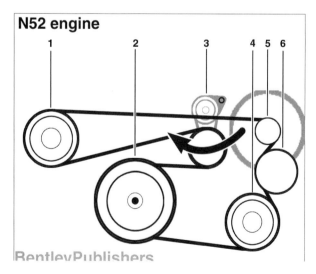

**N52 engine**

◀ Install belt using accompanying diagram as guide. If reinstalling used belt, follow direction-of-rotation mark made previously.

   **1.** A/C compressor pulley

   **2.** Vibration damper (crankshaft pulley)

   **3.** Tensioner pulley

   **4.** Power steering pump pulley

   **5.** Alternator pulley

   **6.** Idler pulley

020

## Accessory belt, replacing (turbo)

◄ Working above radiator:

- Remove air intake duct screws (**A**).

- Pull duct backward to disengage from radiator support crossbar, then detach bellows (**arrow**) from air filter housing.

– Remove electric engine cooling fan and fan cowl. See **170 Radiator and Cooling System**.

– Remove engine splash shield. See **Engine lower covers (splash shields), removing** in this repair group.

– If planning to reinstall old belt, be sure to mark direction of rotation.

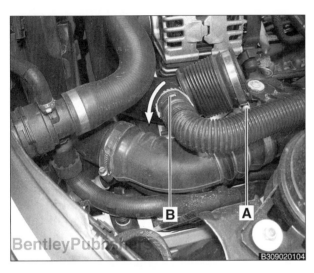

◄ Working at left side of engine compartment:

- Loosen hose clamp **A** and detach air duct from air filter housing.

- Rotate quick-release clamp **B** 90° on boost pressure duct. Separate air ducts.

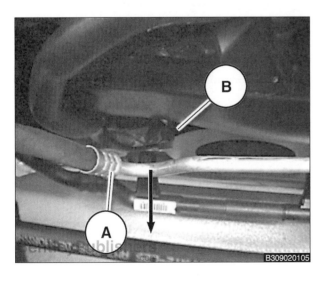

◄ Working underneath radiator, unclip line **A** from clip **B** in direction of **arrow**.

*Accessory belt, replacing (turbo)*

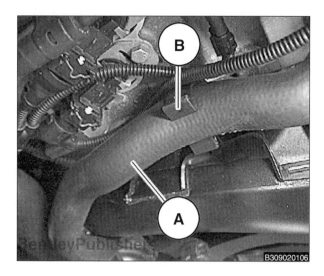

◀ Working at top front of cylinder head, detach coolant hose **A** from bracket **B**.

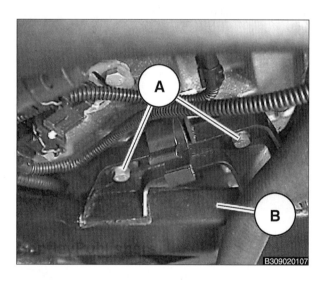

◀ Remove air duct bracket mounting bolts (**A**) at front of engine. Fold air duct (**B**) down without disconnecting or removing.

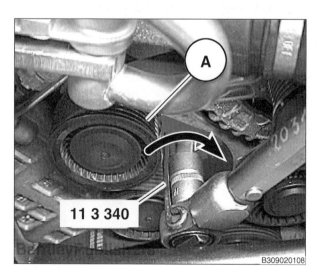

◀ Use Torx socket to rotate belt tensioner (**A**) clockwise (**arrow**). This releases belt tension. Lock tensioner in released position using awl-shaped tool (BMW special tool 11 3 340).

> **WARNING—**
> • *Observe care when working with tensioner. Personal injury could result if tensioner springs back into position uncontrolled.*

− Work belt off pulleys and remove.

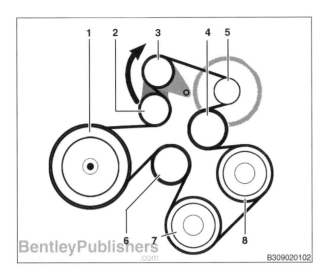

B309020102

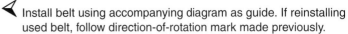 Install belt using accompanying diagram as guide. If reinstalling used belt, follow direction-of-rotation mark made previously.

1. Vibration damper (crankshaft pulley)
2. Tensioner pulley
3. Tensioner-idler pulley
4. Idler pulley
5. Alternator pulley
6. Idler pulley
7. Power steering pump pulley
8. A/C compressor pulley

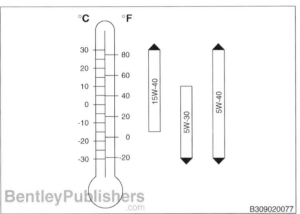

B309020077

## ENGINE OIL SERVICE

---
**CAUTION—**
• *Use BMW specified oil to top off engine between oil changes.*
• *Do not use engine oil additives.*
---

◀ BMW recommends the following engine oils. The recommendation is based on average ambient temperature.

| Engine oil specification | |
|---|---|
| BMW high performance synthetic SAE 5W - 30 or 5W - 40 | API rating SM or higher |

### Engine oil, checking level

There is no engine oil dipstick. Engine oil level and other oil characteristics are monitored electronically by the oil condition sensor (OZS). See **119 Engine Lubrication** for detail of OZS operation.

Monitoring engine oil level electronically ensures that the oil does not reach critically low levels, thus protecting the engine from damage. Overfilling the engine with oil can cause leaks; a corresponding warning is therefore given.

◀ To check oil level:

• Toggle turn signal lever button **1** up or down to scroll through instrument cluster menu items.

• When icon for oil level appears, press button **2** (BC button) to select it.

Oil level is measured in two stages:

• Static oil level measurement while vehicle is stationary.
• Dynamic oil level measurement during vehicle operation.

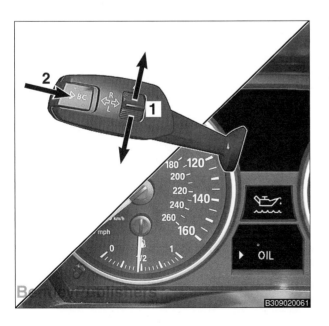

B309020061

### Static oil level

Static oil level measurement (with engine OFF) is only a reference measurement. The oil condition sensor (OZS) is flooded when the engine is OFF and can only detect the minimum oil level.

With vehicle parked on horizontal surface, switch ignition ON and use turn signal lever buttons to activate service information. Static oil level measurement checks whether there is sufficient engine oil for a safe and reliable engine start.

### Dynamic oil level

Oil level is measured correctly only when the engine is running and at operating temperature. Start up engine and drive at least 6.5 miles (10 km). Once oil is fully warmed up, oil level may be displayed while driving or while the vehicle is at a standstill on a level surface with the engine running.

◄ Use turn signal lever buttons to activate service information. When icon for oil level appears, press BC button to select it. Oil level is checked and reading displayed.

1. Oil level OK.

2. Oil level being checked.
   This can take about 3 minutes if vehicle is at a standstill on a level surface, or about 5 minutes if vehicle is on the move.

3. Oil level down to minimum.
   Add 1 US quart or 1 liter of engine oil as soon as possible. See **020 Maintenance**.

4. Oil level too high.
   Too much oil is harmful to engine. Have vehicle checked without delay.

5. Oil level sensor defective.
   Do not add engine oil. Have system checked as soon as possible.

◄ If oil level is low, add oil at oil filler (**arrow**). Use correct viscosity and grade oil.

# Engine oil and filter, changing

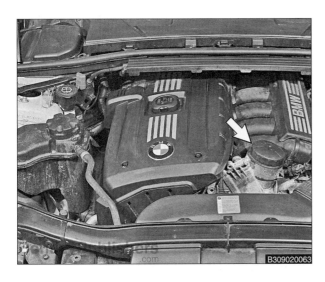

> **CAUTION—**
> - *In the interest of engine longevity, change oil at 7500 mile intervals or once a year, whichever comes first.*
> - *When changing the oil, make sure the engine oil drain plug is started and torqued using hand-tools. Power tools can strip the threads of the plug and the oil pan.*

A complete oil change requires new oil, a new filter insert kit and a new drain plug sealing washer. Run engine for a few minutes to warm engine oil. Switch engine OFF.

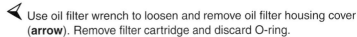 Use oil filter wrench to loosen and remove oil filter housing cover (**arrow**). Remove filter cartridge and discard O-ring.

— Raise vehicle and support safely.

> **WARNING—**
> - *Make sure the vehicle is stable and well supported at all times. Use a professional automotive lift or jack stands designed for the purpose. A floor jack is not adequate support.*

Working underneath engine, open trap door in engine splash shield to expose drain plug (**inset**).

— Place drain pan under oil drain plug. Using a socket or box wrench, loosen drain plug. Remove plug by hand and let oil drain into pan.

> **WARNING—**
> - *Pull the loose plug away from the hole quickly to avoid being scalded by hot oil. It will run out quickly when the plug is removed. If possible, use gloves to protect your hands.*

— When oil flow has diminished to an occasional drip, reinstall drain plug with a new metal sealing washer and torque plug.

| Tightening torque | |
|---|---|
| Engine oil drain plug to oil pan | 25 Nm (18 ft-lb) |

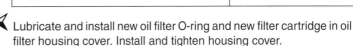 Lubricate and install new oil filter O-ring and new filter cartridge in oil filter housing cover. Install and tighten housing cover.

| Tightening torque | |
|---|---|
| Cover to oil filter housing | 25 Nm (18 ft-lb) |

— Refill crankcase with oil. Approximate oil capacity is listed in **Table f**.

| Table f. Engine oil capacity | |
|---|---|
| **Engine** | **Approx. capacity (incl.oil filter)** |
| 6-cylinder: N51, N52, N54 | 6.5 liters (6.9 US qt) |

— Start engine and check that oil pressure warning light immediately goes out.

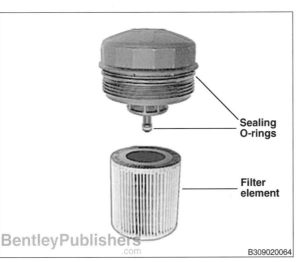

Sealing O-rings

Filter element

— Check for correct oil level:

- Park on horizontal surface.

- Run engine until it reaches operating temperature. Increase engine speed to 1100 rpm and maintain for 3 minutes.

- Read engine oil level using instrument cluster display. See **Engine oil, checking level** in this repair group.

## FUEL FILTER

3 Series models covered by this manual are equipped with a lifetime fuel filter with no specified replacement interval.

## POWER STEERING FLUID SERVICE

### Power steering fluid, checking level

◄ The power steering system is permanently filled with either CHF or ATF hydraulic fluid. Routinely adding fluid is not required unless the system is leaking.

> **CAUTION—**
> • *Power steering reservoir cap is marked with the type of fluid being used— ATF or CHF. Do not mix.*

◄ To check power steering fluid level in fluid reservoir:

- Park vehicle on level ground with engine off.

- Level is correct if it is between **MIN** and **MAX** marks on dipstick.

- If level is below **MIN** mark, add fluid to reservoir to bring level up.

— Hand-tighten reservoir cap.

See **320 Steering and Wheel Alignment** for power steering system bleeding.

B309020071

## SPARK PLUG SERVICE

6-cylinder engines in E90 vehicles (N51, N52, N54) use a coil-over-spark plug configuration, with one ignition coil above each spark plug.

◄ Removal of the turbocharged (N54) engine spark plugs require a special thin-walled 12-point spark plug socket, BMW part no. 83 30 0 495 560.

| Table g. Spark plugs | | |
|---|---|---|
| Manufacturer | Bosch | NGK |
| N51, N52 engine | FR7NPP332 | ILZFR6D11 |
| N54 engine (turbo) | ZGR6STE2 | not available |
| *Check for correct applications with authorized BMW dealer parts department.* | | |

## Spark plugs, replacing

> **WARNING**—
> • *To avoid personal injury, be sure the engine is cold before beginning work in the engine compartment.*

— Remove ignition coil covers. See **Engine upper cover (ignition coil cover), removing** in this repair group.

◄ Unlock (**curved arrow**) ignition coil connector. Pull (**straight arrow**) connector off coil.

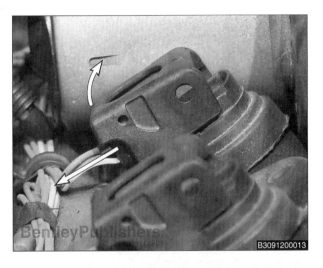

B3091200013

◄ Slide rod-shaped ignition coil straight out of spark plug hole.

> **CAUTION**—
> • *Maintain a high level of cleanliness when servicing ignition coils. Fuel or oil residue can cause a breakdown in the electrical resistance of silicone used in production, resulting in ignition coil failure.*

B3091200014

*Spark plugs, replacing*

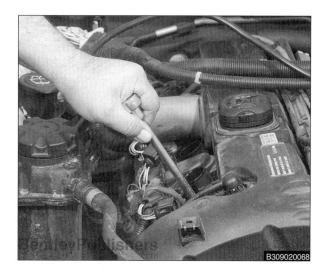

◀ Remove spark plugs:

- Non-turbo engine: Use thin-walled spark plug socket.
- Turbo engine: Use special 12-point spark plug socket.

◀ Non-turbo engine: if thin-walled spark plug socket is not available, carefully remove slotted ignition coil sleeves from cylinder head cover holes, then remove spark plugs.

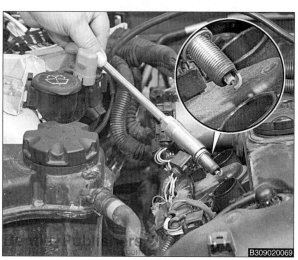

◀ Inspect spark plug electrodes. Light grey indicates normal combustion.

– Installation is reverse of removal, bearing in mind the following:

- Lightly lubricate new spark plug threads with copper-based anti-seize compound.
- Thread plugs into cylinder head by hand to prevent cross-threading.
- Reinsert or replace slotted ignition coil sleeves, if removed.
- Carefully insert ignition coils in spark plug wells and reattach electrical connectors.

| Tightening torque | |
|---|---|
| Spark plug to cylinder head | 23 ± 3 Nm (18 ± 2 ft-lb) |

**020**

## OTHER MECHANICAL MAINTENANCE

### Differential oil level, checking

The E90 front (if applicable) and rear differentials are filled with lifetime oil that ordinarily does not need to be changed. BMW recommends using only a specially formulated synthetic gear oil (SAF-XO) that is available through an authorized BMW dealer parts department. For additional information on this lubricant and any other lubricants that may be compatible, contact an authorized BMW dealer service department.

 Front differential:

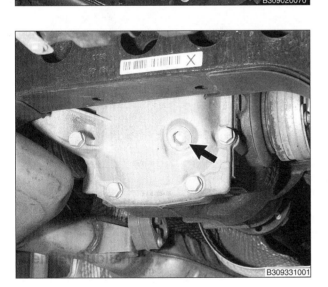

- Remove engine splash shield. See **Engine lower covers (splash shields), removing** in this repair group.
- Remove front reinforcement plate. See **310 Front Suspension**.
- Check oil at filler plug (**arrow**).

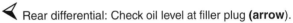 Rear differential: Check oil level at filler plug (**arrow**).

– All: Check lubricant level with vehicle level:

- Use 14 mm or 17 mm Allen socket to remove filler plug.
- Level is correct when fluid just reaches edge of filler hole.
- If necessary, top up fluid.
- Replace filler plug sealing ring.
- Install and tighten oil filler plug when oil level is correct.

| Tightening torque | |
|---|---|
| Filler plug to differential housing (front or rear) | 60 Nm (44 ft-lb) |

See also **311 Front Axle Differential** or **331 Rear Axle Differential**.

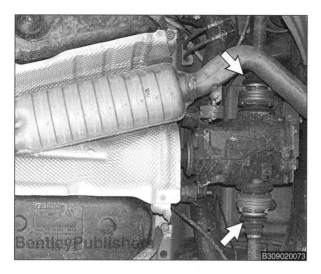

### Drive axle joint (CV joint) boots, inspecting

◀ Inspect CV joint protective boots (**arrows**) for cracks and damage. If the rubber boots fail, water and dirt that enter the joint quickly damage it.

Areas where leaks are most likely to occur are around drive shaft and drive axle mounting flanges.

CV boot replacement is covered in **331 Rear Axle Differential**.

### Exhaust system, inspecting

Exhaust system life varies widely according to driving habits and environmental conditions. If short-distance driving predominates, moisture and condensation in the system does not fully dry out. This leads to early corrosion damage and more frequent replacement.

Scheduled maintenance of the exhaust system is limited to inspection.

◀ Check to see that hangers (**arrow**) are in place and properly supporting the system and that parts of the exhaust system do not contact the body.

– Check for restrictions due to dents or kinks.

– Check for weakness or perforation due to rust.

See **180 Exhaust System**.

### Fuel tank and fuel lines, inspecting

– Inspect fuel tank and fuel lines for damage or leaks.

– Check for fuel leaks in engine compartment or fuel odors in passenger compartment.

– Check for evaporative emissions hoses that may have become disconnected. Check carefully at charcoal canister and leakage diagnosis pump. See **130 Fuel Injection** and **160 Fuel Tank and Fuel Pump** for component locations and additional information.

### Idle speed

Idle speed is electronically adaptive and not adjustable. See **130 Fuel Injection** for more information.

### Oxygen sensors

Replacement of oxygen sensors at specified intervals ensures that the engine and emission control system continue to operate as designed. Extending the replacement interval may void the emission control warranty coverage. Oxygen sensor replacement is covered in **180 Exhaust System**.

## Suspension and steering, inspecting

Check suspension and steering moving parts for wear and excessive play. Inspect ball joint and tie-rod rubber seals and boots for cracks or tears that allow the entry of dirt and water.

See also:

• **310 Front Suspension**.
• **311 Front Axle Differential**
• **320 Steering and Wheel Alignment**
• **330 Rear Suspension**
• **331 Rear Axle Differential**

## Tires, checking inflation pressure

Correct tire pressures are important to handling and stability, fuel economy, and tire wear. Tire pressure changes with temperature. Check tire pressures often during seasonal temperature changes.

 Correct inflation pressures can be found on driver door pillar. Note that tire pressure specifications are higher when the vehicle is more heavily loaded.

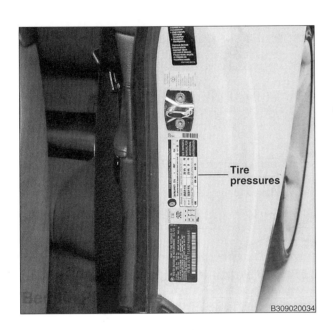

Tire pressures

B309020034

> **WARNING**—
> • *Do not inflate any tire to a pressure higher than maximum inflation pressure listed on the sidewall. Use care when adding air to warm tires. Warm tire pressures can increase as much as 4 psi (0.3 bar) over their cold pressures.*

## Tires, rotating

BMW does not recommend tire rotation. Due to the vehicle's suspension design, the front tires begin to wear first at the outer shoulder and the rear tires begin to wear first at the middle of the tread or inner shoulder. Rotating the tires may adversely affect road handling and tire grip.

## Transmission service

Automatic and manual transmissions in E90 models are provided with lifetime lubrication. No oil change is required for the entire service life of these transmissions. If repairs have to be made to the transmission or transmission oil cooler, use only the approved lifetime lube oil.

### Transmission fluid, automatic

The automatic transmission is not equipped with a dipstick. Checking ATF level is an involved procedure which includes measuring and maintaining a specified ATF temperature during the checking procedure.

For ATF service information, including checking ATF level and ATF filter replacement procedures, see **240 Automatic Transmission**.

### Transmission fluid, manual

Manual transmissions installed in E90 models are filled with a special lifetime fluid. For manual transmission fluid checking and replacement procedures, see **230 Manual Transmission**.

### Wheels, aligning

BMW recommends checking the front and rear alignment once a year and whenever new tires are installed. See **320 Steering and Wheel Alignment**.

## BODY AND INTERIOR MAINTENANCE

### Body, hinges, locks, lubricating

— Lubricate door locks and lock cylinders with an oil that contains graphite.

— Lubricate body and door hinges, hood latch and door check rods with SAE 30 or SAE 40 engine oil.

— Lubricate seat runners with multipurpose grease.

— Lubricate door weather-strips with silicone spray or talcum powder.

— Lubricate engine hood release and hood release cable with spray grease.

> *CAUTION—*
>
> • *Do not apply oil to rubber parts.*
>
> • *Use an absolute minimum of winter lock deicer spray. Alcohol in deicer washes grease out of lock assemblies and may cause locks to corrode internally or to become difficult to operate.*

### Exterior washing

The longer dirt is left on the paint, the greater the risk of damaging the glossy finish, either by scratching or by the chemical effect dirt particles may have on the painted surface.

— Wash with a mixture of lukewarm water and vehicle wash product.

— Rinse using plenty of clear water.

— Wipe body dry with a soft cloth towel or chamois to prevent water-spotting.

> *CAUTION—*
>
> • *Do not wash the vehicle in direct sunlight.*
>
> • *If the engine hood is warm, allow it to cool.*
>
> • *Beads of water not only leave spots when dried rapidly by the sun or heat from the engine, but also can act as small magnifying glasses and burn spots into the finish.*

**020**

## Interior care

— Remove dirt spots on upholstery with lukewarm soapy water or dry foam cleaner.

— Use spot remover for grease and oil spots. Do not pour cleaning liquid directly on carpet or fabric. Dampen clean cloth and rub carefully, starting at edge of the spot and working inward.

> *WARNING—*
> • *Do not use gasoline, naphtha, or other flammable substances.*

## Leather upholstery and trim

— Clean leather upholstery and trim periodically.

— Use slightly damp cotton or wool cloth to get rid of dirt in creases and pores that can cause brittleness and premature aging.

— On heavily soiled areas, use a mild detergent (such as Woolite®) or a specially formulated leather cleaner.

— Dry trim and upholstery completely using a soft cloth. Regular use of a good quality leather conditioner reduces drying and cracking of leather.

## Polishing

— Use paint polish only if finish assumes a dull look after long service.

— Use polish to remove tar spots and tarnish. Afterwards apply coat of wax to protect clean finish.

> *CAUTION—*
> • *Do not use abrasive polish or cleaners on aluminum trim or accessories.*

## Seat belts

Dirt and other abrasive particles damage seat belt webbing.

— To clean seat belts, use a mild soap solution.

> *WARNING—*
> • *Do not clean the seat belt webbing using dry cleaning chemicals, bleach or other strong cleaning agents.*
> • *Allow wet belts to dry before allowing them to retract.*

— Inspect condition of belt webbing and function of retractor mechanisms.

## Special cleaning

— Remove tar and insect spots with a bug and tar remover. Do not use gasoline, kerosene, nail polish remover, or other unsuitable solvents.

A bit of baking soda dissolved in the wash water will facilitate their removal. This method can also be used to remove tree sap spots.

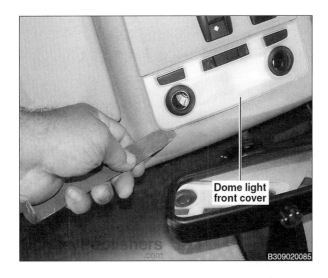

Dome light
front cover

B309020085

## Sunroof, emergency closing

In case of an electrical malfunction, you can close the sunroof manually.

◄ Use plastic prying tool to lever off dome light front plastic cover.

B309020082

◄ Remove roof function center (FZD).

- Retaining clips (**inset**) are aligned with center line of reading lights. Pry carefully (**arrow**) with thin bladed screwdriver

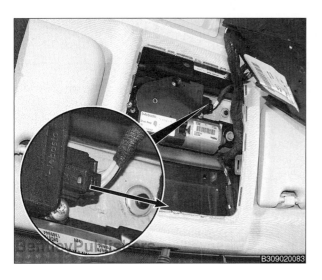

B309020083

◄ Detach sunroof motor electrical connector (**inset**). Considerably less effort is required for manual operation with motor disconnected.

B309020084

◄ Use 4 mm Allen wrench to close sunroof glass. Note that Allen wrench is no longer supplied with vehicle tool kit in trunk.

## Underbody visual inspection

— Inspect the following for leaks or damage:
  - Engine
  - Transmission
  - Fuel system
  - Cooling and heating systems
  - Brake system
  - Exhaust system

A small amount of dampness is considered normal in some cases, especially around axle and pulley seals since the leaking fluid helps the seal work properly. On the other hand, expensive repairs can be avoided by prompt repair of minor fluid leaks. Judgement and experience are required to distinguish among the different kinds of fluid leaks.

— Inspect underside of vehicle for damage caused by normal wear and tear or by driving over road debris. Whenever vehicle is raised on a lift, inspect underbody, wheel wells and sill or rocker panels for damage to underbody sealants and coatings. Also inspect after major repairs to vehicle systems.

— Repair damage or defects found. Only use wax-based or tar-based anti-corrosion compounds as specified. Do not use oil-based anti-corrosion sprays due to possible incompatibility with factory applied protection.

## Washing chassis

— Periodically wash underside of vehicle, especially in winter, to help prevent accumulation of road salt and rust.

The best time to wash the underside is just after the vehicle has been driven in wet conditions. Spray the chassis with a powerful jet of water. Commercial or self-service vehicle washes may not be best for this, as they may recycle the salt-contaminated water.

## Waxing

— For a long-lasting, protective and glossy finish, apply a hard wax after the vehicle has been washed and dried. Use carnauba or synthetic based products.

Waxing is not needed after every washing. You can tell when waxing is required by looking at the finish when it is wet. If the water coats the paint in smooth sheets instead of forming beads that roll off, a new coat of wax is needed. Do not apply wax to black trim pieces, rubber, or other plastic parts.

## Windshield wiper blade maintenance

Common problems with windshield wipers include streaking or sheeting, water drops after wiping, and blade chatter. Streaking is usually caused when wiper blades are coated with road film or vehicle wash wax. Clean the blades using soapy water. If cleaning the blades does not cure the problem, they should be replaced. BMW recommends replacing the wiper blades twice a year, before and after the cold season.

— Check tension spring that forces wiper against glass. Replace wiper arm if spring tension is weak.

— Drops that remain behind after wiping are caused by oil, road film, or diesel exhaust coating the windshield. Use an alcohol or ammonia solution or a nonabrasive cleanser to clean the windshield.

Wiper blade chatter may be caused by dirty or worn blades, by a dirty windshield, or by bent or twisted wiper arms. Clean the blades and windshield as described above. Adjust the wiper arm so that there is even pressure along the blade, and so that the blade is perpendicular to the windshield at rest. Lubricate the wiper linkage with a light oil. The linkage is located under the hood on the driver's side. If the problem persists, the blades are excessively aged or worn and should be replaced.

Wiper blade replacement is covered in **611 Wipers and Washers**.

## CHECK CONTROL

### Check Control codes, instrument cluster

◄ Check Control monitors vehicle functions and alerts the driver to malfunctions using indicator and warning lights in a variety of colors in the instrument cluster. In some circumstances, acoustic signals as well as text messages are given.

⚠ indicates that Check Control messages are stored.

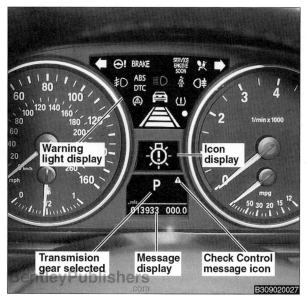

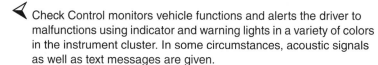

Warning light display

Icon display

Transmission gear selected

Message display

Check Control message icon

B309020027

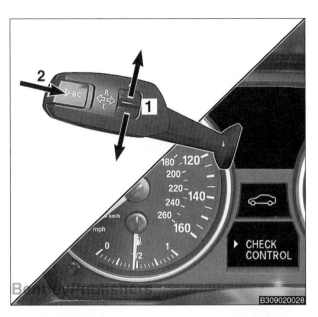

◁ To view Check Control messages in instrument cluster:

- Toggle button **1** in turn signal lever up or down to scroll through instrument cluster menu items.
- When CHECK CONTROL appears in lower display, press button **2** to select it.

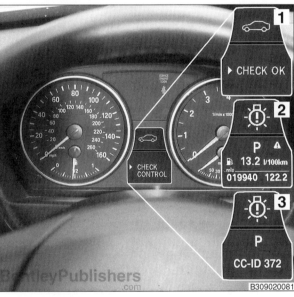

◁ Details of Check Control messages:

1. If CHECK OK appears, there are no Check Control messages.

2. If a message is stored, an icon (light bulb in this case) illuminates in the center cluster display.

3. Press button **2** in turn signal lever and hold for approx. 4 seconds. A numeric message appears in lower display. In this case, Check Control code 372 refers to failed left taillight bulb. See **Table h** for list of Check Control codes (CC-ID).

— Toggle button **1** in turn signal lever to check for other messages.

— Press button **2** to return to outside temperature and clock display.

## Check Control in central information display (CID)

◁ To view Check Control messages in central information display (CID): Press down iDrive controller to brings up **Info sources | Settings** menu.

*Check Control in central information display (CID)*

◤ Pull back iDrive controller to enter middle screen, then rotate controller to **Service Info**.

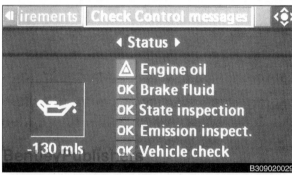

◤ Press down controller to enter **Service Info** (or **Service requirements**) submenu.

– Rotate controller to **Check Control messages**.

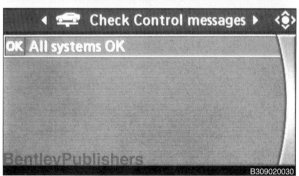

◤ Press down controller to enter **Check Control messages**.

**Table h. Check Control codes (CC-ID)**

| CC-ID | Control module | Message text | Meaning and possible solution |
|---|---|---|---|
| 0 | Instrument cluster (KOMBI) | no faults | |
| 1 * | Longitudinal dynamic management (LDM) | ACC deactivated. Drive with care | Active Cruise Control deactivated due to risk of skidding. Keep your distance and drive with care. Reactivate ACC as needed when driving situation allows. |
| 2 * | Longitudinal dynamic management (LDM) | ACC deactivated. Keep your distance | Active Cruise Control deactivated due to dirty sensor. Keep your distance. Wipe sensor clean, see Owner's Manual. |
| 3 * | Longitudinal dynamic management (LDM) | ACC deactivated. Keep your distance | Active Cruise Control failure Keep your distance. Consult BMW Service. |
| 4 | Trailer module (AHM) | Trailer, parking light, left | |
| 5 | Trailer module (AHM) | Trailer, parking light, right | |
| 6 | Trailer module (AHM) | Trailer, indicator, left | |
| 7 | Trailer module (AHM) | Trailer, indicator, right | |
| 8 | Trailer module (AHM) | Trailer, brake lights | |
| 9 | Trailer module (AHM) | Trailer, fog light | |
| 13 | Instrument cluster (KOMBI) | Radio-control key in lock | |
| 14 | Car Access System (CAS) | Door open. (= front right) | |
| 15 * | Car Access System (CAS) | Door open. (= front left) | |
| 16 * | Car Access System (CAS) | Door open. (= rear left) | |
| 17 * | Car Access System (CAS) | Door open. (= rear right) | |
| 18 * | Car Access System (CAS) | Bonnet open. Stop the vehicle carefully | Engine hood is not locked. Risk of accident. Stop vehicle and close hood. |
| 19 | Car Access System (CAS) or Convertible Top Module (CTM) | Boot open | Trunk lid open. |
| 21 | Car Access System (CAS) | Ignition faulty | Engine can only be started with brake pedal depressed. Contact nearest BMW Service. |
| 22 * | Car Access System (CAS) | Starter motor. Do not stop engine | Not possible to restart engine. Have problem checked by nearest BMW Service. |
| 24 * | Dynamic Stability Control (DSC) | DBC failure. Drive with care | No additional brake support from DBC when emergency braking. Drive with care. Have problem checked by BMW Service as soon as possible. |
| 25 | Digital diesel electronics (DDE) | Preheating. Please wait | |
| 26 | Digital engine electronics (DME), digital diesel electronics (DDE) | Cruise control | Cruise control failure. Possible to continue journey with caution. Have problem checked by nearest BMW Service. |
| 27 | Digital engine electronics (DME), digital diesel electronics (DDE) | Engine oil level. Top up engine oil | Engine oil level at minimum: Add 1 liter of engine oil at next opportunity. Refer to Owner's Manual. |
| 28 | Digital engine electronics (DME), digital diesel electronics (DDE) | Engine oil level. Top up engine oil | Engine oil level below minimum. Add 1 liter of engine oil at next opportunity. Refer to Owner's Manual. |
| 29 | Digital engine electronics (DME), digital diesel electronics (DDE) | Engine fault. Reduced power | Full engine output no longer available. Drive with care. Have problem checked by nearest BMW Service. |

* Stored in instrument cluster

*Check Control in central information display (CID)*

**Table h. Check Control codes (CC-ID)**

| CC-ID | Control module | Message text | Meaning and possible solution |
|---|---|---|---|
| 30 * | Digital engine electronics (DME), digital diesel electronics (DDE) | Engine. Stop the vehicle carefully | Driving on could cause engine damage. Stop vehicle and switch off engine. Contact nearest BMW Service. |
| 31 * | Digital engine electronics (DME), digital diesel electronics (DDE) | Increased emissions | Engine malfunction influencing exhaust emissions. Have problem checked by BMW Service as soon as possible. |
| 32 * | Digital engine electronics (DME), digital diesel electronics (DDE) | Please close filler cap | Fuel or fuel vapors could escape. Check that fuel filler cap is properly closed and engaged. |
| 33 | Digital engine electronics (DME), digital diesel electronics (DDE) | Engine fault. Drive with care | Increased engine load could damage catalytic converter. Drive with moderate engine load. Have problem checked by nearest BMW Service. |
| 35 * | Dynamic Stability Control (DSC) | DSC failure. Drive with care | Driving stability restricted when accelerating and cornering. Drive with care. Have problem checked by BMW Service as soon as possible. |
| 36 | Dynamic Stability Control (DSC) | DSC deactivated | Driving stability restricted when accelerating and cornering. |
| 38 | Car Access System (CAS) | Remote control. Unidentified key | Remote key used is not assigned to this vehicle. |
| 39 * | Digital engine electronics (DME), digital diesel electronics (DDE) | Engine overheated. Stop the vehicle carefully | Stop engine and allow it to cool. Do not open engine hood, risk of scolding. Contact nearest BMW Service. |
| 40 | Car Access System (CAS) | To start engine, press brake pedal | |
| 41 | Instrument cluster (KOMBI) | Service due | Your BMW dealer was unable to be informed automatically. Contact your BMW Service. |
| 42 * | Dynamic Stability Control (DSC) | Control systems. Drive with care | Ground clearance / driving comfort reduced. Avoid high speeds when cornering. Have problem checked by nearest BMW Service. |
| 46 | Multiple restraint system (MRS) | Fasten seat belt | |
| 49 * | Digital diesel electronics (DDE) | Particulate filter malfunction | Possible to continue journey with caution. Have problem checked by nearest BMW Service. |
| 50 * | Dynamic Stability Control (DSC) | Run Flat Indicator failure | Flat tires cannot be detected. Have problem checked by BMW Service as soon as possible. |
| 60 | Instrument cluster (KOMBI) | Speedometer display fault | Speedometer display malfunction. Have problem checked by nearest BMW Service. |
| 62 | Instrument cluster (KOMBI) | Speed limit exceeded. (Gulf states only) | |
| 63 * | Dynamic Stability Control (DSC) | Tire puncture | Journey can be continued for a limited distance at speeds up to max. 50 mph (80 kph). Refer to Owner's Manual. Have problem checked by nearest BMW Service. |
| 65 | Car Access System (CAS) | Charge battery in key / Remote control. Charging | Remote key battery is automatically recharged during lengthy journeys with key in ignition lock. |
| 66 | Car Access System (CAS) | Remote control. No engine start | Remote key not available or faulty. Engine start not possible. Refer to Owner's Manual. |
| 67 | Car Access System (CAS) | Remote control battery discharged | Batteries in remote key discharged. Replace. Refer to Owner's Manual. |
| 68 | Car Access System (CAS) | Bat. remote cont. for stat. funct. | Batteries in remote key discharged. Replace. Refer to Owner's Manual. |

*\* Stored in instrument cluster*

**Table h. Check Control codes (CC-ID)**

| CC-ID | Control module | Message text | Meaning and possible solution |
|---|---|---|---|
| 69 | Longitudinal dynamic management (LDM) | ACC deactivated. Keep your distance | Cruise Control deactivated under approx. 30 km/h (20 mph). Keep your distance. Reactivate ACC as needed. |
| 71 * | Dynamic Stability Control (DSC) | Brake pads. Replace | Brake pads worn. Have them replaced by nearest BMW Service. |
| 73 | Electro-mechanical power steering (EPS) | EPS inoperable (= on-board computer) | |
| 74 * | Dynamic Stability Control (DSC) | Brake fluid. Stop vehicle carefully | Insufficient quantity of brake fluid. Braking effect reduced. Stop vehicle carefully. Contact nearest BMW Service. |
| 75 * | Trailer module (AHM) | Trailer tow bar electrics. | Trailer electrics failed. Trailer lights affected. Have problem checked by nearest BMW Service. |
| 78 | Instrument cluster (KOMBI) | Speed limit exceeded. (= on-board computer) | |
| 79 | Instrument cluster (KOMBI) | Outside temperature (= for northern countries) | |
| 85 * | Longitudinal dynamic management (LDM) | ACC deactivated. Manual braking | Active Cruise Control ACC deactivated due to long downhill drive. Keep your distance. Reactivate ACC as needed. |
| 87 | Footwell module | Rear light, right, failure | Rear right lamp failed. Have problem checked by nearest BMW Service. |
| 88 | Footwell module | Dipped beam, left, failure | Left dipped-beam headlight failed. Have problem checked by nearest BMW Service. |
| 89 | Footwell module | Dipped beam, right, failure | Right dipped-beam headlights failed. Have problem checked by nearest BMW Service. |
| 90 | Trailer module (AHM) | Trailer, reversing light | |
| 91 | Multiple restraint system (MRS) | Fasten seat belt | |
| 92 * | Multiple restraint system (MRS) | Front pass. restraint system faulty | Belt tensioner or belt force limiter malfunction. Fasten seat belt despite malfunction. Have problem checked by nearest BMW Service. |
| 93 * | Multiple restraint system (MRS) | Driver restraint system faulty | Belt tensioner or belt force limiter malfunction. Fasten seat belt despite malfunction. Have problem checked by nearest BMW Service. |
| 94 * | Multiple restraint system (MRS) | Restraint system, rear left, faulty | Belt tensioner malfunction. Fasten seat belt despite malfunction. Have problem checked by nearest BMW Service. |
| 95 * | Multiple restraint system (MRS) | Restraint system, rear right, faulty | Belt tensioner malfunction. Fasten seat belt despite malfunction. Have problem checked by nearest BMW Service. |
| 97 * | Multiple restraint system (MRS) | Restraint systems faulty | Airbags, belt tensioners and belt force limiters malfunction. Fasten belts despite problem. Have problem checked by nearest BMW Service. |
| 103 * | Electronic transmission control (EGS) | Transmission too hot | Transmission too hot. Possible to continue journey with caution. Engine power output reduced. Drive with care. |
| 104 * | Electronic transmission control (EGS) | Transmission fault. Drive with care | Risk of transmission overheating. Shift program with restricted driving active. Avoid high engine loads. |
| 105 * | Electronic transmission control (EGS) | Transmission fault. Stop vehicle carefully | Transmission overheating. Stop vehicle and engage transmission position P. Allow to cool and continue journey with care. In case of repeated overheating, have problem checked by your BMW Service. |
| 108 * | Multiple restraint system (MRS) | Driver airbags faulty | Airbags malfunction. Have problem checked by nearest BMW Service. |

*\* Stored in instrument cluster*

*Check Control in central information display (CID)*

**Table h. Check Control codes (CC-ID)**

| CC-ID | Control module | Message text | Meaning and possible solution |
|---|---|---|---|
| 109 * | Multiple restraint system (MRS) | Front passenger airbags faulty | Airbags malfunction. If possible, do not occupy front-passenger seat. Have problem checked by nearest BMW Service. |
| 111 | Footwell module (FRM) | Number plate light left, failure | Left licence-plate light failed. Have problem checked by nearest BMW Service. |
| 113 | Footwell module (FRM) | Parking lights on | |
| 114 | Footwell module (FRM) | Foglight, rear left, failure | Rear left foglight failed. Have problem checked by nearest BMW Service. |
| 115 | Footwell module (FRM) | Reversing light, right, failure | Right back-up light failed. Have problem checked by nearest BMW Service. |
| 116 | Footwell module (FRM) | Indicator, rear left, failure | Rear left turn signal failed. Have problem checked by nearest BMW Service. |
| 117 | Footwell module (FRM) | Reversing light, left, failure | Left back-up light failed. Have problem checked by nearest BMW Service. |
| 118 | Footwell module (FRM) | Rear light, right, failure | Rear right lamp failed. Have problem checked by nearest BMW Service. |
| 119 | Footwell module (FRM) | Indicator, front right, failure | Front right turn signal failed. Have problem checked by nearest BMW Service. |
| 120 | Footwell module (FRM) | Dipped beam, left, failure | Left dipped-beam headlight failed. Have problem checked by nearest BMW Service. |
| 121 | Footwell module (FRM) | Dipped beam, right, failure | Right dipped-beam headlights failed. Have problem checked by nearest BMW Service. |
| 122 | Footwell module (FRM) | Indicator, front left, failure | Front left turn signal failed. Have problem checked by nearest BMW Service. |
| 123 | Footwell module (FRM) | Rear light, left, failure | Rear left lamps failed. Have problem checked by nearest BMW Service. |
| 124 | Footwell module (FRM) | Side indicator, right, failure | Right side-mounted turn signal failed. Have problem checked by nearest BMW Service. |
| 125 | Footwell module (FRM) | Indicator, rear right, failure | Rear right turn signal failed. Have problem checked by nearest BMW Service. |
| 126 | Footwell module (FRM) | Foglight, front right, failure | Front right foglight failed. Consult BMW Service. |
| 127 | Footwell module (FRM) | Left side-mounted turn signal failed | Left side-mounted turn signal failed. Have problem checked by nearest BMW Service. |
| 128 | Footwell module (FRM) | Full beam headlight left, failure | Left main-beam headlight failed. Consult BMW Service. |
| 129 | Footwell module (FRM) | Foglight, rear right, failure | Right rear foglight failed. Consult BMW Service. |
| 130 | Footwell module (FRM) | Full beam headlight right, failure | Right main-beam headlight failed. Consult BMW Service. |
| 131 | Footwell module (FRM) | Parking light front left, failure | Parking light front left, failure. Have problem checked by nearest BMW Service. |
| 132 | Footwell module (FRM) | Front right side light failed | Front right side light failed. Have problem checked by nearest BMW Service. |
| 133 | Footwell module (FRM) | Rear light, left, failure | Rear left lamps failed. Have problem checked by nearest BMW Service. |
| 134 | Footwell module (FRM) | Brake light right, failure | Right brake light failed. Have problem checked by nearest BMW Service. |
| 135 | Footwell module (FRM) | Third brake light, failure | Centre brake light failed. Have problem checked by nearest BMW Service. |

*\* Stored in instrument cluster*

**Table h. Check Control codes (CC-ID)**

| CC-ID | Control module | Message text | Meaning and possible solution |
|---|---|---|---|
| 136 | Footwell module (FRM) | Brake light left, failure | Left brake light failed. Have problem checked by nearest BMW Service. |
| 137 | Footwell module (FRM) | Number plate light, right, failure | Right licence-plate light failed. Have problem checked by nearest BMW Service. |
| 138 | Footwell module (FRM) | Foglight, front left, failure | Front left foglight failed. Have problem checked by nearest BMW Service. |
| 139 * | Run Flat Indicator (RPA) | Tire puncture front left | Journey can be continued for a limited distance at speeds up to max. 50 mph (80 kph). Refer to Owner's Manual. Have problem checked by nearest BMW Service. |
| 140 * | Run Flat Indicator (RPA) | Tire puncture rear right | Journey can be continued for a limited distance at speeds up to max. 50 mph (80 kph). Refer to Owner's Manual. Have problem checked by nearest BMW Service. |
| 141 * | Run Flat Indicator (RPA) | Tire puncture rear left | Journey can be continued for a limited distance at speeds up to max. 50 mph (80 kph). Refer to Owner's Manual. Have problem checked by nearest BMW Service. |
| 142 | Run Flat Indicator (RPA) | Tire pressure. Check | Tire pressure too low or too high. Check and correct. Refer to Owner's Manual or inflation pressure tag. |
| 143 * | Run Flat Indicator (RPA) | Tire puncture front right | Journey can be continued for a limited distance at speeds up to max. 50 mph (80 kph). Refer to Owner's Manual. Have problem checked by nearest BMW Service. |
| 144 * | Tire pressure control (RDC) | Tire pressure control malfunction | Temporary radio interference in tire pressure control system (RDC) from outside or due to additional RDC wheels inside vehicle. Possible to continue journey with caution. |
| 145 * | Tire pressure control (RDC) | Brake light actuation failed | Brake light failed. Have problem checked by nearest BMW Service. |
| 147 * | Run Flat Indicator (RPA) | Tire puncture | Journey can be continued for a limited distance at speeds up to max. 50 mph (80 kph). Refer to Owner's Manual. Have problem checked by nearest BMW Service. |
| 148 | Digital engine electronics (DME) | Brake light control failure | Brake light failed. Have problem checked by nearest BMW Service. |
| 149 * | Tire pressure control (RDC) | Tire pressure control failed | Tire pressure control (RDC) not available. Burst tires and losses of pressure cannot be detected. Have problem checked by nearest BMW Service. |
| 164 * | Junction box electronics (JBE) | Washer fluid level low | Not enough washer fluid in reservoir. Top up at next opportunity. Refer to Owner's Manual. |
| 165 | Instrument cluster (KOMBI) | Ambient temperature | |
| 166 * | Junction box electronics (JBE) | Coolant level too low | Not enough coolant. Risk of engine damage. Add coolant at next opportunity. Refer to Owner's Manual. Caution: risk of scolding. |
| 167 * | Instrument cluster (KOMBI) | Set time and date | Battery has been disconnected, time and date displays no longer correct. Reset. Refer to Owner's Manual. |
| 171 * | Electronic transmission control (EGS) | Transm. fault. Drive with care | Transmission malfunction. Emergency program active. Transmission positions P, R, N, D possible (forwards only in 3rd and 5th gear). Gear can be engaged without brake. Drive with care. Have problem checked by nearest BMW Service. |
| 172 * | Electronic transmission control (EGS) | Transm. fault. Drive with care | Transmission malfunction. Emergency program active. Reverse gear may not be able to be engaged. Reduced acceleration. Drive with care. Have problem checked by nearest BMW Service. |

*\* Stored in instrument cluster*

**Table h. Check Control codes (CC-ID)**

| CC-ID | Control module | Message text | Meaning and possible solution |
|---|---|---|---|
| 176 * | Longitudinal dynamic management (LDM) | ACC malfunction. Keep your distance | Active cruise control (ACC) sensor possibly dirty. Detection of vehicle in front restricted. Refer to Owner's Manual. Keep your distance. |
| 178 | Electronic transmission control (EGS) | Transmission in N | Transmission position N Vehicle is not secured against rolling. Engage gear or apply parking brake. |
| 179 | Electronic transmission control (EGS) | Transm. fault. Drive with care | Transmission functions and position display may be faulty. Gear can be engaged without applying brake. Have problem checked by nearest BMW Service. |
| 181 | Multiple restraint system (MRS) | (during pre-drive check) | |
| 182 | Digital engine electronics (DME), digital diesel electronics (DDE) | Oil level sensor fault | Oil level sensor malfunction. Have problem checked by BMW Service as soon as possible. |
| 184 | Dynamic Stability Control (DSC) | DTC activated, DSC restricted | Dynamic Traction Control (DTC) increases forward traction on loose surfaces but reduces driving stability. |
| 186 | Car Access System (CAS) | ELV. If possible, do not stop engine | Electric steering wheel lock (ELV) will not be released after engine has been switched OFF. Start not possible. If engine is running, do not switch it OFF. |
| 187 | Car Access System (CAS) | ELV engaged. Move steering wheel | Electric steering wheel lock (ELV) inhibiting engine start. Move steering wheel to allow engine to be started. |
| 192 * | Tire pressure control (RDC) | RDC initialized when driving | RDC is being initialized. RDC is not available for approx. 15 to 30 minutes. Flat tires cannot be detected in this time. System is initialized while vehicle is being driven. |
| 195 * | Park Distance Control (PDC) | PDC failure | No acoustic warning available for Park Distance Control (PDC). Have problem checked by BMW Service as soon as possible. |
| 196 | Footwell module (FRM) | Indicator, front right, failure | Front right turn signal failed. Have problem checked by nearest BMW Service. |
| 197 | Footwell module (FRM) | Indicator, front left, failure | Front left turn signal failed. Have problem checked by nearest BMW Service. |
| 205 | Car Access System (CAS) | Remote control. Do not stop engine | Remote key not in ignition lock. Engine may not be able to be restarted - do not switch off. Have problem checked by nearest BMW Service. |
| 206 | Car Access System (CAS) | Next press of button starts engine | Engine will start with press of START / STOP button, even if clutch and/or brake are not depressed. |
| 207 * | Junction box electronics (JBE) | Electronics malfunction. Stop vehicle carefully | Central vehicle electronics failed. Not possible to continue journey. Contact nearest BMW Service. |
| 208 | Car Access System (CAS) | Comfort Access inactive | Comfort Access deactivated. |
| 209 | Car Access System (CAS) | Remote control inside vehicle | Remote control inside vehicle: Not possible to lock vehicle from outside. Take remote control with you on leaving vehicle |
| 212 * | Digital engine electronics (DME), digital diesel electronics (DDE) | Engine oil pressure. Stop the vehicle carefully | Engine oil pressure too low. Engine damage possible. Switch off engine, do not continue journey. Contact nearest BMW Service. |
| 213 | Digital engine electronics (DME) | Charging fault | Alternator malfunction. Battery not being recharged. Switch off current consumers that are not needed. Have problem checked by nearest BMW Service. |
| 216 * | Electric fuel pump (EKP) | Fuel pump fault. Drive with care | Fuel supply malfunction. Engine output may be reduced. Drive with care. Have problem checked by nearest BMW Service. |

*\* Stored in instrument cluster*

**Table h. Check Control codes (CC-ID)**

| CC-ID | Control module | Message text | Meaning and possible solution |
|---|---|---|---|
| 217 | Car Access System (CAS) | Remote control not present | Remote key not in vicinity of vehicle, therefore not possible to lock vehicle. Keep remote control with you. |
| 220 * | Digital engine electronics (DME), digital diesel electronics (DDE) | High rate of battery discharge | Increased battery discharge when stationary. Engine start may no longer be possible. Switch off current consumers that are not needed. Consult BMW Service. |
| 229 * | Digital engine electronics (DME), digital diesel electronics (DDE) | Battery charge very low | Vehicle battery heavily discharged. Recharge by driving lengthy distance or with external battery charger. Automatic current consumer cutoff soon. |
| 231 | Footwell module (FRM) | Lighting system. Stop the vehicle carefully | Check displays and possibly turn signals, foglights, main-beam headlights and headlight flasher inoperable. Stop vehicle, check and continue journey with care. Have problem checked by nearest BMW Service. |
| 236 * | Dynamic Stability Control (DSC) | Control systems. Drive with care | Stability system failed. Reduced braking and driving stability. If possible, avoid abrupt braking. Have problem check by nearest BMW Service. |
| 237 * | Dynamic Stability Control (DSC) | Drive contr. syst. Drive with care | Driving control system failed. Reduced driving stability when cornering. Drive with care. Have problem checked by nearest BMW Service. |
| 245 * | Electronic height control (DSC) | Level control malfunction | Level control malfunction Driving comfort may be slightly reduced. Have problem checked by nearest BMW Service. |
| 247 * | Digital engine electronics (DME) | Battery monitoring failure | Automatic monitoring of battery charge state failed. Have problem check by your BMW Service. |
| 248 | Electronic transmission control (EGS) | Gear engag. without brake poss. | Apply brake before engaging gear. Switch off engine before leaving vehicle. Risk of accident. Have system checked as soon as possible by your local BMW Service. |
| 250 | Electronic transmission control (EGS) | Gear engag. without brake poss. | Apply brake before engaging a gear. Possible to continue journey with caution. Switch off engine before leaving vehicle. Have problem checked by BMW Service as soon as possible. |
| 254 | Electronic transmission control (EGS) | Transmission fault. Drive with care | Emergency program active. Acceleration may be reduced. Drive with care. Have problem checked by nearest BMW Service. |
| 256 | Footwell module | Headlight range adjustment | Headlight-range adjustment malfunction. Road-surface illumination not optimal. Oncoming traffic may be dazzled. Have problem checked by BMW Service as soon as possible. |
| 257 * | Digital engine electronics (DME), digital diesel electronics (DDE) | Engine too hot. Drive with care | Engine temperature too high. Drive with care to cool. In case of repeated overheating, have problem checked by your BMW Service. |
| 259 | Footwell module | Side window anti-trap function | Power windows anti-trap function inactive. |
| 260 | Roof control panel (FZD) or sliding/tilting sunroof (SHD) | Sliding sunroof anti-trap function | Sliding sunroof anti-trap function inactive. Have problem checked by nearest BMW Service. |
| 261 | Footwell module | Side window anti-trap function | Power windows anti-trap function failure. Have problem checked by nearest BMW Service. |
| 262 | Roof control panel (FZD) or sliding/tilting sunroof (SHD) | Sliding sunroof anti-trap function | Sliding sunroof anti-trap function failure. Have problem checked by nearest BMW Service. |
| 265 * | Run Flat Indicator (RPA) | Tire pressure. Recheck | Left/right pressure difference too high. Recheck tire pressures. Refer to Owner's Manual or inflation pressure tag. |
| 266 | Multiple restraint system (MRS) | Rollover protection malfunction | Rollover protection malfunction. Have problem checked by nearest BMW Service. |

*\* Stored in instrument cluster*

*Check Control in central information display (CID)*

**Table h. Check Control codes (CC-ID)**

| CC-ID | Control module | Message text | Meaning and possible solution |
|---|---|---|---|
| 273 | Active Steering (AL) | Active steering. Exercise care when steering | Steering behavior altered. Steering wheel might be at an angle. Possible to continue journey with caution. Exercise care when steering. Have active steering (AL) checked by nearest BMW Service. |
| 275 | Instrument cluster (KOMBI) | Fuel reserve | |
| 276 | Longitudinal dynamic management (LDM) | Speed Select higher gear | Engine speed too high. Select higher gear if driving situation allows. |
| 277 | Longitudinal dynamic management (LDM) | . | Active cruise control (ACC) deactivated. Gear engaged not appropriate to driving situation. Change gear and reactivate ACC as needed. |
| 278 | Longitudinal dynamic management (LDM) | Speed Select lower gear | Engine speed too low. Select lower gear if driving situation allows. |
| 279 | Instrument cluster (KOMBI) | Driver's seat backrest not locked. | Driver's seat backrest not locked. Increased risk of injury in event of an impact as seat belt cannot work as intended. Engage seat backrest. |
| 280 | Instrument cluster (KOMBI) | Front-passenger seat backrest not locked | Passenger seat backrest not locked. Increased risk of injury in event of an impact as seat belt cannot work as intended. Engage seat backrest. |
| 281 | Instrument cluster (KOMBI) | Service due. (= yellow) | |
| 284 | Instrument cluster (KOMBI) | Service overdue. (= red) | |
| 285 | Instrument cluster (KOMBI) | No service due (= orange) | |
| 286 | Instrument cluster (KOMBI) | Range | |
| 287 | Electronic transmission control (EGS) | Clutch overheating. | Clutch overheating. If possible, stay where you are or pull away quickly. |
| 288 | Electronic transmission control (EGS) | Transm. fault. Drive with care | Transmission malfunction. Emergency program activated. Only transmission positions R, N and 1st to 3rd gear available. Have problem checked by nearest BMW Service. |
| 289 | Electronic transmission control (EGS) | Transm. fault. Drive with care | Transmission malfunction. Emergency program activated. Only transmission positions R, N and 1st to 3rd gear available. Have problem checked by nearest BMW Service. |
| 290 | Electronic transmission control (EGS) | Transm. fault. Drive with care | Transmission malfunction Journey can be continued at moderate speeds. Journey cannot be continued after stopping. Contact nearest BMW Service. |
| 291 | Electronic transmission control (EGS) | Transm. fault. Drive with care | Transmission malfunction. Emergency program activated. Only positions D, N, R available. Have problem checked by nearest BMW Service. |
| 292 | Electronic transmission control (EGS) | Transmission. Engage gear again | Transmission malfunction. Position N automatically engaged when vehicle is stationary. Have problem checked by nearest BMW Service. |
| 293 | Electronic transmission control (EGS) | Start: select pos. N and press brake | Before starting engine, apply brake and move selector lever to position N. |
| 295 | Footwell module | Cornering lights failed. | Adaptive headlights failed. Continue journey with care. Consult BMW Service. |

*\* Stored in instrument cluster*

**Table h. Check Control codes (CC-ID)**

| CC-ID | Control module | Message text | Meaning and possible solution |
|---|---|---|---|
| 296 | Telematics control unit (TCU) | No SOS calls. Mobile phone? | No emergency call possible. Insert mobile phone and switch on. |
| 297 | Telematics control unit (TCU) | Assist SOS calls not enabled | BMW Assist emergency call not possible as not enabled. Refer to your BMW Assist contract and check settings. |
| 298 | Telematics control unit (TCU) | Assist SOS calls not available | BMW Assist emergency call not possible in this country. Consult instructions for BMW Assist roaming. |
| 299 * | Telematics control unit (TCU) | SOS call system failure | Emergency call system functions restricted of failed. Have problem checked by nearest BMW Service. |
| 300 | Telematics control unit (TCU) | Assist SOS calls not available. SIM? | BMW Assist emergency call not available. SIM card not available or not usable. |
| 301 | Instrument cluster (KOMBI) | Seat backrest monitor defective | Seat backrest monitor failed. Engage seat backrest. Have problem checked by nearest BMW Service. |
| 302 | Electronic transmission control (EGS) | Transmission pos. P not engaged | Transmission position P not engaged. Vehicle could roll away. |
| 303 | Car Access System (CAS) | To start engine, depress clutch | |
| 304 * | Digital engine electronics (DME), digital diesel electronics (DDE) | Battery. Check | Battery severely aged. Consult BMW Service. |
| 305 * | Digital engine electronics (DME), digital diesel electronics (DDE) | Battery terminals. Check | Electrical current supply at risk. Have problem checked by nearest BMW Service. |
| 306 * | Digital engine electronics (DME), digital diesel electronics (DDE) | Battery charge very low | Battery heavily discharged. Electric comfort functions deactivated to reduce load on battery. These functions will be reactivated when battery has been recharged. |
| 307 * | Electronic transmission control (EGS) | Transm. fault. Drive with care | Transmission malfunctions possible. Gear can be engaged without brake. Drive with care. Have problem checked by nearest BMW Service. |
| 308 | Instrument cluster (KOMBI) | (= parking brake applied) | |
| 309 * | Electric fuel pump (EKP) | Fuel pump fault | Fuel pump malfunction. Possible to continue journey with caution. Have problem checked by BMW Service as soon as possible. |
| 321 | Active Steering (AL) | Active steering inactive | Active steering inactive. Steering behavior altered. Steering wheel might be at an angle. Possible to continue journey with caution. Exercise care when steering. |
| 322 | Electronic transmission control (EGS) | Transmission. Introduction active | |
| 323 | Electronic transmission control (EGS) | Clutch. Introduction active | |
| 325 | Electronic transmission control (EGS) | Transmission in N | |
| 326 | Electronic transmission control (EGS) | Transmission in drive position | |
| 327 * | Tire pressure control (RDC) | RDC initialized when driving. | RDC is being initialized. RDC is not available for up to 3 minutes. Flat tires cannot be detected in this time. System is initialized while vehicle is being driven. |
| 328 | Dynamic Stability Control (DSC) | Brake pad wear indicator | Sensor malfunction. Fault in brake pad wear sensors. Have problem checked by nearest BMW Service. |

*\* Stored in instrument cluster*

*Check Control in central information display (CID)*

**Table h. Check Control codes (CC-ID)**

| CC-ID | Control module | Message text | Meaning and possible solution |
|---|---|---|---|
| 330 | Dynamic Stability Control (DSC) | HDC not available at present | HDC not available. Automatic brake intervention interrupted for safety reasons to prevent brakes from overheating. Change down a gear and drive carefully to reduce temperature. |
| 331 | Dynamic Stability Control (DSC) | HDC active | |
| 332 | Dynamic Stability Control (DSC) | HDC deactivated | Hill Descent Control (HDC) is deactivated above 60 km/h (37 mph). Reactivation possible below 35 km/h (22 mph). |
| 333 | Dynamic Stability Control (DSC) | HDC not regulating. Drive slower | Regulating range ends at 35 kph (22 mph). To make use of HDC, reduce speed accordingly. |
| 334 | Dynamic Stability Control (DSC) | End of line: Standardize RPA | Standardize Run Flat Indicator. Refer to Owner's Manual. |
| 335 * | Car Access System (CAS) | Ignition switched on | |
| 337 * | Longitudinal dynamic management (LDM) | DCC failed | Dynamic Cruise Control (DCC) failed. Consult BMW Service. |
| 339 * | Longitudinal dynamic management (LDM) | DCC deactivated. Drive with care | Dynamic Cruise Control (DCC) deactivated due to risk of skidding. Drive with care. Reactivate DCC as needed when driving situation allows. |
| 340 * | Longitudinal dynamic management (LDM) | DCC deactivated. Drive with care | Dynamic Cruise Control (DCC) deactivated due to long downhill drive. Reactivate DCC as needed. |
| 341 * | Longitudinal dynamic management (LDM) | DCC deactivated | Dynamic Cruise Control (DCC) deactivated. Gear engaged not appropriate to driving situation. Change gear and reactivate DCC as needed. |
| 342 | Longitudinal dynamic management (LDM) | DCC deactivated | Dynamic Cruise Control (DCC) deactivated under 30 kph (20 mph). Reactivate DCC as needed. |
| 345 | Footwell module (FRM) | Brake/rear light, right, failure | Right-hand lights failed. Have problem checked by nearest BMW Service. |
| 346 | Footwell module (FRM) | Brake/rear light, left, failure | Left-hand lights failed. Have problem checked by nearest BMW Service. |
| 347 * | Car Access System (CAS) | Position R, N, D possibly not avail. | Positions R, N, D may not be possible. If necessary, activate emergency release device for selector lever. Comply with instructions in Owner's Manual. Have problem checked by nearest BMW Service. |
| 348 * | Car Access System (CAS) | Engage pos. P before leaving car | Engage position P before leaving vehicle. Possible malfunction in ignition or transmission / selector lever. Have problem checked by nearest BMW Service. |
| 349 * | Car Access System (CAS) | Ignition off only possible in pos. P | |
| 350 * | Dynamic Stability Control (DSC) | 4x4 system defective. Drive with care | xDrive system defective. Driving stability restricted. Drive with care. Have problem checked by nearest BMW Service. |
| 351 * | Dynamic Stability Control (DSC) | 4x4 system and DSC failed | Driving stability restricted. Drive with care. Have problem checked by nearest BMW Service. |
| 353 * | Dynamic Stability Control (DSC) | Brakes overheated. Allow to cool | Brakes critical temperature exceeded. Braking effect no longer guaranteed. Stop vehicle at next opportunity and allow brakes to cool off significantly |
| 354 * | Dynamic Stability Control (DSC) | Pulling-away assistant inactive | Caution: vehicle may roll back. Have problem checked by your BMW Service at next opportunity. |
| 364 * | Dynamic Stability Control (DSC) | RPA initialization... | |

*\* Stored in instrument cluster*

**Table h. Check Control codes (CC-ID)**

| CC-ID | Control module | Message text | Meaning and possible solution |
|---|---|---|---|
| 367 * | Digital engine electronics (DME), digital diesel electronics (DDE) | Engine too hot. Reduce engine speed | Engine temperature may be too hot. Full engine speed not available. Use high gears. |
| 368 | Electronic transmission control (EGS) | Transmission fault | Transmission malfunction. Possible to continue journey. Have problem checked by nearest BMW Service. |
| 369 * | Dynamic Stability Control (DSC) | 4x4, DSC, ABS and emergency EBV failed | xDrive system, DSC ABS, EBV xDrive system, DSC, ABS and emergency EBV failed. Driving stability restricted. Drive with care. Have problem checked by nearest BMW Service. |
| 370 * | Dynamic Stability Control (DSC) | 4x4 system, DSC and ABS failed | xDrive system, DSC, ABS xDrive system, DSC and ABS failed Driving stability restricted. Drive with care. Have problem checked by nearest BMW Service. |
| 371 | Footwell module | Number plate light failure | Licence-plate light failed. Have problem checked by nearest BMW Service. |
| 372 | Footwell module | Left Brake Force Display faulty | Left-hand Brake Force Display failed. Have problem checked by nearest BMW Service. |
| 373 | Footwell module | Right Brake Force Display faulty | Right 2-stage brake light right failed. Have problem checked by nearest BMW Service. |
| 374 | Main beam assistant (FLA) | Main-beam assistant defective | Main-beam assistant defective Have problem checked by nearest BMW Service. |
| 375 | Main-beam assistant (FLA) | Main-beam assistant not active | Main-beam assistant not active Sensor range covered. Manually switch headlights between main and dipped beam. |
| 377 | Main beam assistant (FLA) | Sensitivity misadjusted | Sensitivity for automatic main-beam headlights set incorrectly. Possible risk of dazzling oncoming vehicles. |
| 378 | Footwell module | Side light and daytime driving light, left, defective | Left-hand side light and daytime driving light failed. Have problem checked by nearest BMW Service. |
| 379 | Footwell module | Turning light left failed | Right-hand side light and daytime driving light failed. Have problem checked by nearest BMW Service. |
| 380 | Footwell module | Turning light right failed | Turning light left failed. Have problem checked by nearest BMW Service. |
| 381 | Footwell module | Side light and daytime driving light, left, defective | Turning light right failed. Have problem checked by nearest BMW Service. |
| 382 | Dynamic Stability Control (DSC) | DSC restricted. Drive with care | Brake pressure sensor failed. Drive with care. Have problem checked by nearest BMW Service. |
| 385 * | Electro-mechanical power steering (EPS) | Steering assistance failed | Steering assistance failed Steering characteristics significantly changed Continue driving with care. Have problem checked by nearest BMW Service. |
| 389 | Multiple restraint system (MRS) | Fasten driver's seat belt | |
| 390 | Multiple restraint system (MRS) | Fasten front-passenger seat belt | |
| 392 | Multiple restraint system (MRS) US version | Fasten driver's seat belt | |
| 401 | Convertible Top Module (CTM) | Roof mechanism function failure | Roof mechanism defective. Have problem checked by nearest BMW Service. |
| 413 * | Car Access System (CAS) | Press START / STOP button | Steering column unlocked Press START / STOP button to lock steering column. |

*\* Stored in instrument cluster*

*Check Control in central information display (CID)*

| CC-ID | Control module | Message text | Meaning and possible solution |
|---|---|---|---|
| 415 * | Junction box electronics (JBE) | Increased battery discharge | Increased battery discharge when stationary. Electrical consumers may be temporarily switched off. It may be necessary to reset date and time. If fault occurs repeatedly, have problem checked by your BMW Service. |
| 416 | Convertible Top Module (CTM) | Luggage compartment partition | Roof drive overheating. Temporarily only closing function available. |
| 419 * | Electronic transmission control (EGS) | Drive malfunction | Drive malfunction. Possible to continue journey with caution. Reduced acceleration. Have problem checked by nearest BMW Service. |
| 420 | Electronic transmission control (EGS) | Transmission fault. Drive with care | Possible to continue journey with caution. Reduced acceleration. Have problem checked by nearest BMW Service. |
| 423 | Trailer module (AHM) | Trailer coupling lock | Trailer coupling folding ball head not securely engaged. Lock ball head again. If fault cannot be rectified, do not drive with a trailer. Have problem checked by your BMW Service. |
| 427 * | Digital engine electronics (DME) | Engine oil pressure. Drive with care | Engine speed limited. Possible to continue journey with caution. Have problem checked as soon as possible by nearest BMW Service. |
| 430 | Junction box electronics (JBE) | Transport mode | Some vehicle systems still deactivated. Have vehicle checked without delay by nearest BMW Service. |
| 431 | Dynamic Stability Control (DSC) | High brake loading | High brake loading. Drive with care. |
| 432 | Convertible Top Module (CTM) | Roof drive overheating | No roof movement possible. Move luggage compartment partition to position required. Refer to Owner's Manual. |
| 437 | Footwell module | Parking light switched on | |
| 445 | Convertible Top Module (CTM) | Vehicle not standing on level surface | Vehicle not standing on level surface. No roof movement possible. |

**Table h. Check Control codes (CC-ID)**

\* *Stored in instrument cluster*

# 100 Engine–General

## GENERAL

This section covers general information on engines and engine components.

For specific repair procedures, refer to:

- **020 Maintenance** for engine compartment views and accessory belt service, oil change and air filter service
- **110 Engine Removal and Installation**
- **113 Cylinder Head Removal and Installation** for cylinder head and cylinder head cover service
- **117 Camshaft Timing Chain** for timing chain and VANOS service
- **119 Lubrication System** for lubrication system description and crankcase seal service
- **120 Ignition System** for ignition coil, cam sensor, crankshaft sensor and knock sensor service
- **130 Fuel Injection** for engine management system description and component replacement
- **170 Radiator and Cooling System** for radiator, coolant pump and coolant service
- **180 Exhaust System** for exhaust manifold, oxygen sensor and turbocharger service

### Engine ID tag

◄ ID tag with engine serial number is on left side of engine block, underneath intake manifold.

Engine serial number

B309020074

# Engine applications

**Table a** gives engine application information and specifications.

**Table a. 3 Series engine applications and specifications**

| Year, model | Engine code, type | Displacement cc (cid) | Bore x stroke mm (in) | Comp. ratio | Horsepower hp @ rpm | Torque lb-ft @ rpm | Engine management |
|---|---|---|---|---|---|---|---|
| **2006** | | | | | | | |
| Sedan: 325i, 325xi<br>Sport Wagon: 325xi | N52 6-cylinder 24-valve | 2996 (183) | 85.0 x 88.0 (3.35 x 3.46) | 10.7 : 1 | 215 @ 6250 | 185 @ 2750 | Siemens MSV70 |
| Sedan: 330i, 330xi | N52 6-cylinder 24-valve | 2996 (183) | 85.0 x 88.0 (3.35 x 3.46) | 10.7 : 1 | 255 @ 6600 | 220 @ 2750 | |
| **2007- 2008** | | | | | | | |
| Sedan, Sport Wagon, Coupe, Convertible: 328i, 328xi | N52KP 6-cylinder 24-valve | 2996 (183) | 85.0 x 88.0 (3.35 x 3.46) | 10.7 : 1 | 230 @ 6500 | 200 @ 2750 | Siemens MSV80 |
| Sedan: 328i, 328xi (automatic transmission)* | N51 6-cylinder 24-valve | 2996 (183) | 85.0 x 88.0 (3.35 x 3.46) | 10 : 1 | 230 @ 6500 | | Siemens MSV80 SULEV II |
| Sedan: 335i, 335xi<br>Coupe: 335i<br>Coupe: 335xi (2008 only)<br>Convertible: 335i | N54 6-cylinder 24-valve twin-turbo | 2979 (182) | 84 x 89.6 (3.31 x 3.53) | 10.2 : 1 | 300 @ 5800 | 300 @ 1400 - 5000 | MSD80 (2007) MSD81 (2008) |
| **2009 - 2010** | | | | | | | |
| Sedan, Coupe: 328i, 328xi<br>Convertible: 328i<br>Sport Wagon: 328i, 328xi | N52KP 6-cylinder 24-valve | 2996 (183) | 85.0 x 88.0 (3.35 x 3.46) | 10.7 : 1 | 230 @ 6500 | 200 @ 2750 | Siemens MSV80 ULEV II |
| Sedan: 328i, 328xi (automatic transmission)* | N51 6-cylinder 24-valve | 2996 (183) | 85.0 x 88.0 (3.35 x 3.46) | 10 : 1 | 230 @ 6500 | | Siemens MSV80 SULEV II |
| Sedan, Coupe: 335i, 335xi<br>Convertible: 335i | N54 6-cylinder 24-valve twin-turbo | 2979 (182) | 84 x 89.6 (3.31 x 3.53) | 10.2 : 1 | 300 @ 5800 | 300 @ 1400 - 5000 | MSD81 ULEV II |

* Starting in 03 / 2007, a super low emission (SULEV II) version of the non-turbo 6-cylinder engine, N51, was sold in California, Connecticut, Maine, Massachusetts, New York, Oregon, Rhode Island, Vermont and Washington (state).

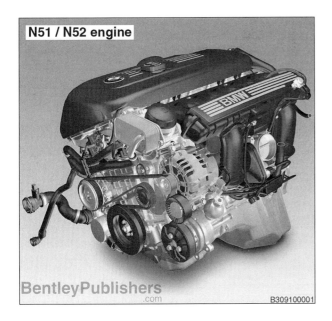

**N51 / N52 engine**

B309100001

## N52 ENGINE OVERVIEW

### N52 engine introduction

◀ 3 Series E90 and E91 (Sedan and Sport Wagon) models were introduced in 2006 in the North American market equipped with the 3-liter in-line 6-cylinder normally-aspirated N52 engine. 2-wheel drive and 4-wheel drive (xDrive) models were offered with two levels of performance:

• Low output engine in 325i or 325xi models

• High output engine in 330i or 330xi models

Beginning with 2007 models, 328i and 328xi models were fitted with the N52KP engine. Some models were equipped with the N51, a modification of the N52 with additional emissions restrictions (SULEV II) including secondary air injection. Vehicles with N51 engine are equipped with automatic transmission.

The N52 engine family features the following:

• 4-valves-per-cylinder friction-optimized components

• Two-piece crankcase

• Composite magnesium-aluminum engine block structure

• Trapezoidal weight-optimized connecting rods

• Aluminum silicon (AluSil) cylinder head

• Timing case integrated in crankcase and cylinder head

• Cylinder head gasket with silicon sealing lip

• Valvetronic system

• Weight-optimized double VANOS system

• Volumetric flow-controlled oil pump

• Electrically controlled coolant pump

• Crankcase ventilation with integrated heater

• 3-stage variable intake manifold or DISA (in 330i / xi models)

The weight reduction in these systems and components, as compared to previous generation 3 Series models, has led to increased power-to-weight ratio, reduced emissions and decreased fuel consumption.

### N52 crankcase components

#### Crankcase

◀ The upper section of the crankcase consists of an aluminum / silicon (AluSil) insert cast in a magnesium alloy. The timing cover is cast as an integral part of the engine block.

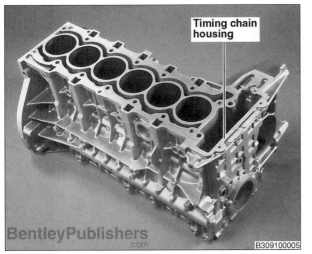

**Timing chain housing**

B309100005

*N52 crankcase components*

◅ The AluSil cylinder bores are not equipped with iron cylinder liners. Therefore, the cylinder bores cannot be machined, but the deck surface may be planed.

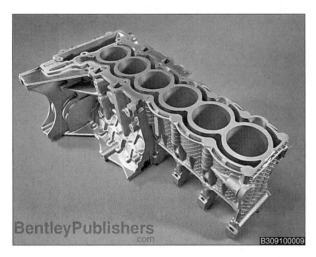

◅ The AluSil insert has threaded bores for transmission, cylinder head and crankshaft main bearing bolts.

The insert provides coolant passages as well. This is to prevent coolant contact with the magnesium portion of the engine block.

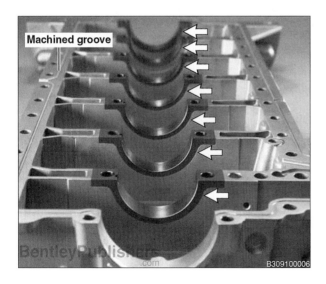

Machined groove

◅ The lower section of the crankcase is a bedplate structure made of magnesium with sintered steel inlays (**arrow**) for main bearing support. The magnesium structure is used to increase crankcase rigidity and the steel inlays take up forces which are not suitable for magnesium alone.

A liquid sealant is injected under high pressure into a machined groove between upper and lower crankcase sections. This detail is critical to understand in service applications. As an example, when the crankcase main seals are replaced, a special sealant is injected into the seal grooves and crankcase seams.

### Crankshaft

◄ The crankshaft is cast iron with 7 main bearing journals. The trigger wheel for the crankshaft sensor is between cylinders 5 and 6. Due to the design of the timing chain housing (one piece with the crankcase), the crankshaft snout is modified to facilitate timing chain module removal and installation during service.

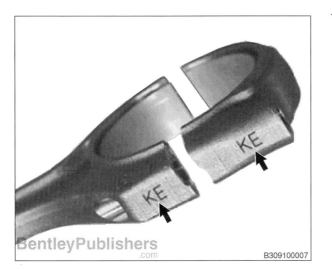

### Connecting rods

◄ The big end of each connecting rod is cracked to allow centering of the bearing cap without the use of dowel pins. This contributes to the overall weight reduction.

Pairing codes (**arrows**) are stamped on each connecting rod to match the correct rod cap to the connecting rod.

The small end of the rod is tapered, reducing weight without affecting strength.

The connecting rods are separated into weight categories and can only be replaced as a set.

### Pistons

The pistons are manufactured from aluminum and have 4 valve reliefs. The undersides of the pistons are cooled with oil spray jets.

## N52 cylinder head and valvetrain

### Cylinder head

◄ The N52 engine uses an AluSil cylinder head with a cast bridge to mount the Valvetronic actuator motor.

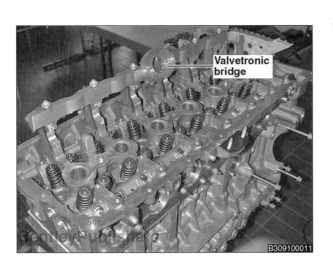

Valvetronic bridge

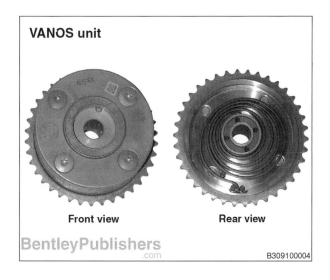

**VANOS unit**

**Front view**          **Rear view**

BentleyPublishers.com

B309100004

### Variable camshaft timing (VANOS)

◄ N52 engines are equipped with compact, infinitely variable vane-type VANOS units for both intake and exhaust camshafts. The VANOS system (from the German words *VAriable NOckenwellen Steuerung*) electrohydraulically adjusts valve timing for enhanced mid-range performance and improved emissions. VANOS is controlled by the engine control module (ECM), using engine speed, engine load and engine coolant temperature as the primary inputs. Engine oil pressure is used for powering camshaft adjustment.

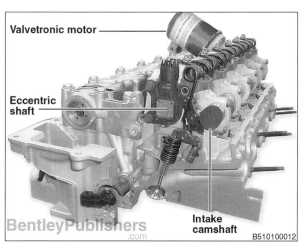

**Valvetronic motor**

**Eccentric shaft**

**Intake camshaft**

BentleyPublishers.com

B510100012

### Valvetronic

◄ N52 engine load is controlled via the valve timing gear. This system, called Valvetronic, varies valve lift rather than throttle valve opening to control engine power and torque. It offers the following:

• Increased engine efficiency.

• Improved emission values.

• Top engine speed to 7,000 rpm.

• Power output of 85 hp / liter displacement.

• Engine torque of 100 Nm / liter displacement over a broad engine speed range.

• Reduced $CO_2$ emissions.

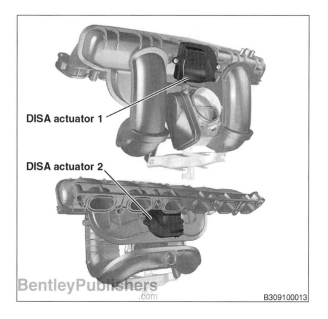

**DISA actuator 1**

**DISA actuator 2**

BentleyPublishers.com

B309100013

## N52 intake manifold

### Variable intake manifold (DISA)

◄ N52 engines in 328i / xi and 330i / xi models are equipped with 3-stage variable intake runners in a system known as DISA.

Valves in the intake manifold are driven by DISA electric motors and gear mechanisms. DISA actuators are driven by pulse width-modulated signals from the engine control module (ECM).

Each valve has only two possible positions: Open or closed.

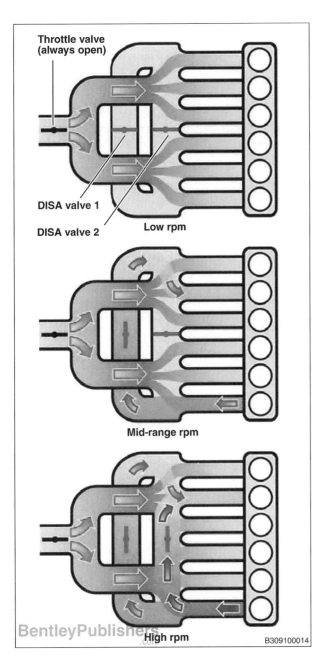

Throttle valve
(always open)

DISA valve 1

DISA valve 2          Low rpm

Mid-range rpm

High rpm          B309100014

◄ Switched-length intake manifold runners help achieve a high torque over the entire engine speed range using two DISA valves and an overflow pipe in the intake.

- **Stage 1**: Idle and low engine speed range. Both DISA valves closed. Intake air flows past throttle valve into resonance pipe. Air flow is split in resonance pipe and is further routed via collector runner and intake resonating runners into individual cylinders. In this way, a relatively large air mass is made available to cylinders.

- **Stage 2**: Medium engine speed range. DISA valve 2 open. (In this example, cylinder 1 intake valves are just closing.) Air flow produces pressure peaks at closing intake valves. This resonates to next cylinder in firing order, thus improving charge of next cylinder.

- **Stage 3**: High engine speed range. Both DISA valves open. (Again, In this example, cylinder 1 intake valves are just closing.) Pressure peaks ahead of closing intake valves are also utilized in this case. Intake air mass is now routed via resonance, overflow and manifold runners.

100

## N52 lubrication, vacuum and cooling systems

### Lubrication and vacuum systems

VANOS requires a large volume of oil, particularly at low engine speeds. To meet the oiling requirements of the engine, a high volume volumetric-flow controlled oil pump is utilized. The pump is designed to provide the high volume when needed, but drop back its flow at higher engine speeds when it is not needed. See **119 Engine Lubrication**.

Valvetronic engine load control requires a wide open throttle under most engine operating conditions, resulting in minimal intake manifold vacuum. In order to operate the brake vacuum booster, an auxiliary vacuum pump is fitted to the engine.

A chain assembly is used to drive the oil pump and brake booster auxiliary vacuum pump sprockets.

1. Auxiliary vacuum pump sprocket bolt
2. Crankshaft sprocket
3. Auxiliary vacuum pump drive sprocket
4. Auxiliary vacuum pump
5. Oil pump sprocket bolt
6. Oil pump drive sprocket
7. Oil pump

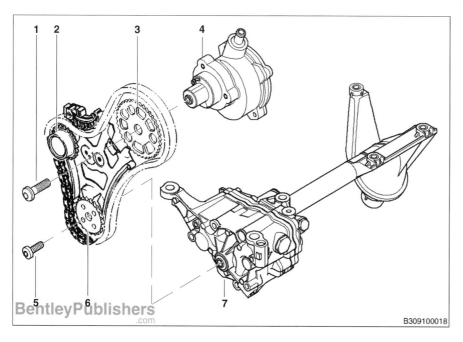

B309100018

### Cooling system

The cooling system utilizes a DME-controlled electric coolant pump which minimizes engine power losses and allows for increased fuel economy by a more efficient method of engine heat management.

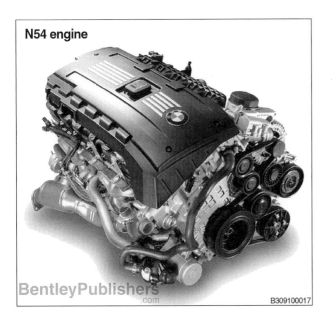

N54 engine

B309100017

## N54 ENGINE OVERVIEW

### N54 engine introduction

◀ The turbocharged in-line 6-cylinder N54 engine was introduced in the 3 Series E92 (Coupe) model. Available as a 3.0 liter engine, it shares the following features with the N52 engine:

- Double VANOS
- High output (400 W) electric coolant pump
- Aluminum cylinder head with plastic cylinder head cover
- Steel crankshaft

The following features are specific to the N54 engine:

- Exhaust driven twin turbochargers (bi-turbo)
- Air to air intercooler
- Direct injection (high pressure injection or HPI) with piezo injectors
- Bosch MSD80 engine management
- External oil cooler
- All aluminum crankcase with iron cylinder liners

### N54 turbochargers

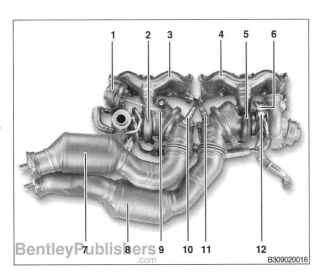

B309020016

1. Wastegate actuator, bank 2
2. Turbocharger, bank 2
3. Exhaust manifold, bank 2
4. Exhaust manifold, bank 1
5. Turbocharger, bank 1
6. Coolant return
7. Catalytic converter, bank 2
8. Catalytic converter, bank 1
9. Wastegate actuating lever
10. Planar broad-band oxygen sensor, bank 2
11. Planar broad-band oxygen sensor, bank 1
12. Coolant supply

### N54 intercooler

◀ The charge air is greatly heated when it is compressed in the turbochargers, making it necessary for the air to be cooled again in an intercooler.

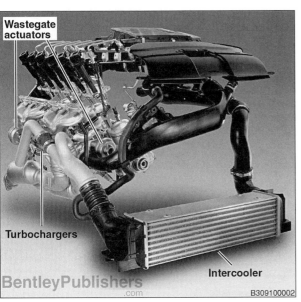

Wastegate actuators

Turbochargers

Intercooler

B309100002

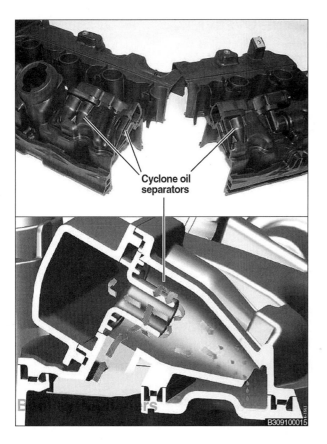

Cyclone oil separators

B309100015

## N54 crankcase breathing

◀ The turbocharged engine crankcase breather valve system is designed so that when the engine is in turbocharged mode, increased manifold pressure does not adversely affect crankcase venting. Instead of a crankcase ventilation valve, the engine breathing system consists of small cyclone separators integrated into the plastic cylinder head cover. The flow of crankcase gases is metered through a series of restrictions which control crankcase pressure.

## N54 engine oil, vacuum and fuel pump drive

As with the non-turbo engine, the turbo engine oil pump and auxiliary vacuum pump are driven by a single chain powered by a sprocket at the front of the crankshaft. In addition, the high pressure fuel pump is tandem mounted to the rear of the vacuum pump.

1. Auxiliary vacuum pump sprocket bolt

2. Crankshaft sprocket

3. Auxiliary vacuum pump-high pressure fuel pump drive sprocket

4. Auxiliary vacuum pump

5. High pressure fuel pump

6. Oil pump sprocket bolt

7. Oil pump drive sprocket

8. Oil pump

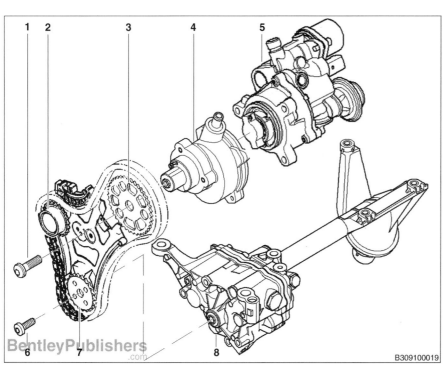

B309100019

# 110 Engine Removal and Installation

**110**

## GENERAL

This repair group includes an overview of non-turbo and turbo engine removal and installation. The procedures have been combined and steps applying to an individual engine have been highlighted.

Transmission removal is required before the engine can be removed.

See also:

- **020 Maintenance** for engine covers removal
- **100 Engine–General** for engine codes and applications
- **121 Battery, Starter, Alternator**
- **170 Radiator and Cooling System**
- **180 Exhaust System**
- **230 Manual Transmission**
- **240 Automatic Transmission**
- **260 Driveshafts**
- **310 Front Suspension**
- **410 Fenders, Engine Hood**

## Warnings and Cautions

> **WARNING—**
> - *The fuel system is designed to retain pressure even when the ignition is OFF. When working with the fuel system, loosen fuel lines slowly to allow residual fuel pressure to dissipate. Avoid spraying fuel.*
> - *Before beginning any work on the fuel system, place a fire extinguisher in the vicinity of the work area.*
> - *Fuel is highly flammable. When working around fuel, do not disconnect any wires that could cause electrical sparks. Do not smoke or work near heaters or other fire hazards.*
> - *Loosen the fuel tank cap to release pressure in the tank before working on the tank or lines.*
> - *When disconnecting a fuel hose, wrap a shop towel around the end of the hose to prevent fuel spray.*
> - *Do not use a work light with an incandescent bulb near any fuel. Fuel may spray on the hot bulb causing a fire.*
> - *Make sure the work area is properly ventilated.*
> - *Steel fasteners may not be used in place of aluminum fasteners due to the threat of corrosion.*
> - *Magnesium crankcase requires aluminum fasteners.*
> - *Replace aluminum fasteners each time they are removed.*
> - *Aluminum fasteners are identified with blue paint marking.*

> **CAUTION—**
> - *If the MIL (malfunction indicator light, also called Check Engine or Service Engine Soon light) is illuminated, see* **OBD On-Board Diagnostics** *for DME fault code information.*
> - *If other system faults are indicated by an illuminated ABS, SRS or DSC warning light, see the appropriate repair group in this manual or an authorized BMW dealer for more information on fault codes.*

## ENGINE REMOVAL AND INSTALLATION

Be sure to cover painted surfaces before beginning the removal procedure. As an aid to installation, label components, wires and hoses before removing them. Do not reuse gaskets, O-rings or seals during reassembly.

> **WARNING—**
> - *Due to risk of personal injury, be sure the engine is cold before beginning the removal procedure.*

## Engine, removing and installing

— Place hood in service position.

— Remove exhaust system. See **180 Exhaust System**.

— Remove transmission. See **230 Manual Transmission** or **240 Automatic Transmission**.

— Drain engine oil.

– Drain engine coolant.

– Disconnect negative (–) cable from battery.

> **CAUTION—**
> • Prior to disconnecting the battery, read the battery disconnection cautions in **001 Warnings and Cautions**.

– Remove air cleaner housing and fresh air ducts. See **130 Fuel Injection**.

– Remove fan cowl with electric cooling fan. See **170 Radiator and Cooling System**.

– Remove radiator. See **170 Radiator and Cooling System**.

– Remove thermostat. See **170 Radiator and Cooling System**.

– Remove all cooling system hoses from vehicle.

– Remove intake manifold. See **130 Fuel Injection**.

– Remove vacuum line from brake booster.

– Disconnect electrical connectors and harness from ignition coils and lay harness aside.

– Disconnect engine electrical harness and lay aside.

– Turbo engine: Remove fuel supply line to high pressure fuel pump. See **160 Fuel Tank and Fuel Pump** for high pressure fuel pump removal and installation.

◀ Remove A/C compressor (**A**) from engine and set on front axle carrier. Do not disconnect A/C lines or discharge system.

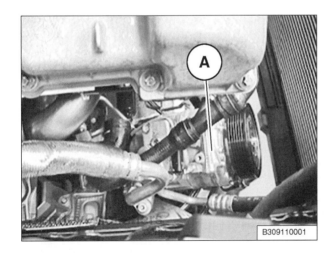

◀ Remove power steering pump (**A**) and set on front axle carrier. Do not disconnect hydraulic lines.

*Engine, removing and installing*

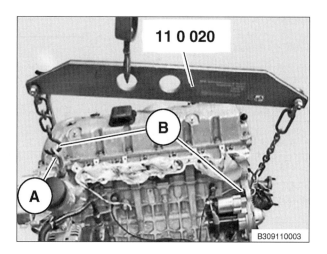

◁ Install engine tow hook (from took kit in trunk) to front of engine (**A**). Attach BMW special tool 11 0 020 to engine using only specified mounting places (**B**).

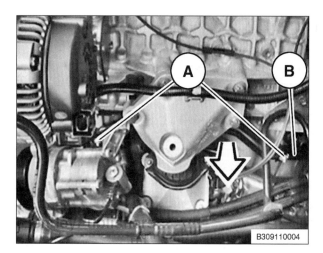

◁ If equipped with automatic transmission: Raise engine 10 cm (4 in) and remove fasteners (**A**) for ATF cooler lines (**B**).

– Remove engine from vehicle using engine hoist attached to BMW special hook 11 0 020.

– Raise engine slowly while watching carefully to make sure no lines, wires or hoses become snagged.

– Installation is reverse of removal. Remember to:
  • Replace aluminum fasteners.
  • Check for fuel leaks.
  • Check for coolant leaks.
  • Check and clear any fault codes using BMW factory scan tool or equivalent.

# 113 Cylinder Head Removal and Installation

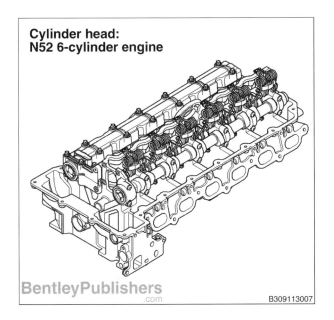

**Cylinder head:
N52 6-cylinder engine**

.com

B309113007

## GENERAL

This repair group provides removal and installation procedures for the cylinder head and associated components.

The cylinder head is equipped with variable camshaft timing (sometimes referred to as VANOS, from the German words *VAriable NOckenwellen Steuerung*). Special tools and procedures are required to remove and install camshaft adjustment units and to time camshafts. Be sure to read each procedure through before starting work.

See also:

- **020 Maintenance**
- **100 Engine–General** for engine code and application information.
- **117 Camshaft Timing Chain** for camshaft timing chain and camshaft adjuster (VANOS) service
- **130 Fuel Injection** for air filter housing and intake manifold removal
- **170 Radiator and Cooling System**

## Engine identification

Engine applications and specifications are detailed in **100 Engine–General**.

In the procedures that follow, non-turbo engine is used to refer to the 6-cylinder 3-liter normally-aspirated engine. There are 3 versions of this engine.

**Table a. Non-turbo engine identification**

| Engine designation | Year, model | Identifying feature |
|---|---|---|
| N51 | 2007 and later 328i, 328ix with automatic transmission (sold in California, Connecticut, Maine, Massachusetts, New York, Oregon, Rhode Island, Vermont, Washington) | Secondary air injection pump<br>Black plastic cylinder head cover<br>Simple, not variable intake manifold |
| N52 | 2006 325i, 325ix, 330i, 330ix | Aluminum-magnesium cylinder head cover |
| N52KP | 2007 and later 328i, 328ix | Black plastic cylinder head cover |

The 6-cylinder turbo engine, N54, is referred to as turbo engine.

Fasteners and fastener torques differ among the versions. Read torque specifications carefully.

## Warnings and Cautions

> **WARNING—**
> • *To avoid personal injury, be sure the engine is cold before beginning work on engine components.*
> • *Use extreme caution when draining and disposing of engine coolant. Coolant is poisonous and lethal to humans and pets. Pets are attracted to coolant because of its sweet smell and taste. Seek medical attention immediately if coolant is ingested.*
> • *The fuel system is designed to retain pressure even when the ignition is OFF. When working with the fuel system, loosen fuel lines slowly to allow residual fuel pressure to dissipate. Avoid spraying fuel. Use shop towels to capture leaking fuel.*
> • *Before beginning work on the fuel system, place a fire extinguisher in the vicinity of the work area.*
> • *Fuel is highly flammable. When working around fuel, do not disconnect wires that could cause electrical sparks. Do not smoke or work near heaters or other fire hazards.*
> • *Wear eye protection and protective clothing to avoid injuries from contact with fuel.*
> • *Unscrew the fuel tank cap to release pressure in the tank before working on fuel lines.*
> • *Do not use a work light with an incandescent bulb near fuel. Fuel may spray on the hot bulb causing a fire.*
> • *Make sure the work area is properly ventilated.*

*Cylinder head cover components (non-turbo)*

> **CAUTION—**
> - To avoid electrochemical corrosion to engine components made of aluminum-magnesium alloy, do not use steel fasteners. Use aluminum fasteners only.
> - The end faces of aluminum fasteners are usually painted blue. For reliable identification, test fasteners for aluminum composition with magnet.
> - Replace aluminum bolts each time they are loosened.
> - Follow torque instructions, including angle of rotation specifications, when installing aluminum fasteners.

## CYLINDER HEAD (NON-TURBO ENGINE)

### Cylinder head cover components (non-turbo)

Cylinder head cover for 2006 N52 engine is made of aluminum-magnesium alloy. Aluminum stretch bolts and fasteners are used. Replace them whenever the cover is removed.

Cylinder head cover for 2007 and later non-turbo engine is made of plastic. Steel fasteners may be used and they can be reused.

1. Valvetronic motor mounting bolt (M6 x 16 mm)
   - Tighten to 10 Nm (7 ft-lb)
2. Valvetronic motor
3. Gasket
4. Cylinder head cover
5. Cylinder head cover fastener
   - N52: M7 aluminum
     Replace with new
     Tighten to 7 Nm (63 in-lb) + 90° additional
   - N52KP or N51: M7, tighten to 9 Nm (7 ft-lb)
6. Bracket (N52 engine only)
7. Cylinder head cover gasket–outer
8. Cylinder head cover gasket–inner (spark plug holes)
9. Crankcase breather hose

### Cylinder head cover, removing and installing (non-turbo)

— Use scan tool to read out and record ECM fault memory.

— Switch ignition OFF and remove key.

— Remove cabin microfilter upper and lower housings. See **640 Heating and Air-conditioning**.

— Remove right strut tower brace.

— Remove ignition coil cover (upper engine cover). See **020 Maintenance**.

— Detach ignition coil connectors. Unclip ignition coil harness from cylinder head cover and lift aside.

— Remove ignition coils. See **120 Ignition System**.

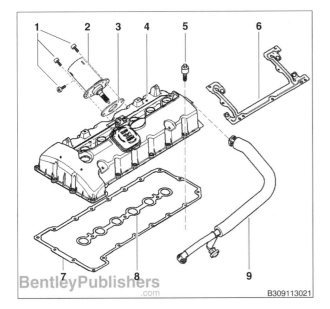

*Cylinder head cover, removing and installing (non-turbo)*

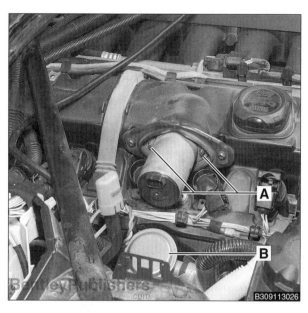

◄ Working at cylinder head cover:

  • Detach crankcase breather hose.

  • If applicable: Pull off metal bracket.

  • Remove valvetronic motor mounting bolts (**A**). To disengage valvetronic motor, see **130 Fuel Injection**.

  • N51 engine: Remove mounting screws and detach secondary air injection valve (**B**) from right side of cylinder head.

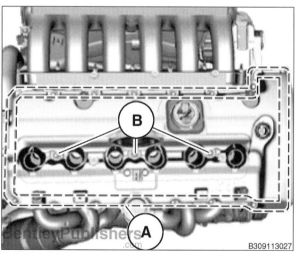

◄ Remove cylinder head cover fasteners (**A**, **B**). Discard if aluminum (blue head).

  • Measure and record lengths and positions of bolts and studs. Different fastener lengths are determined by shapes of bushings.

– Lift off cylinder head cover and discard old gaskets.

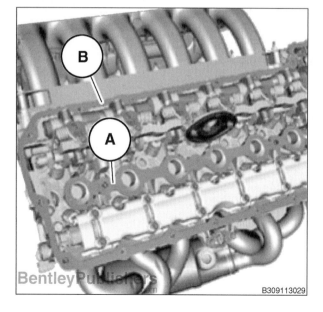

◄ Clean gasket residue from cylinder head and cylinder head cover sealing surfaces (**A**, **B**).

> **CAUTION—**
> • *To avoid gouging the cover, do not use metal scraping tool.*

*Cylinder head cover, removing and installing (non-turbo)*

B309113028

◄ Replace slotted ignition coil sleeves in cylinder head cover.

— Coat cylinder head cover grooves with thin layer of anti-friction compound such as glycerine. Press gaskets in place, making sure they are not stretched at any point.

— Reinstall cylinder head cover.

- Coat cylinder head contact surfaces with thin layer of anti-friction compound such as glycerine.
- Place small quantity of silicone sealant at metal-to-metal seams (such as timing cover to engine block).
- Replace aluminum fasteners. Install in correct locations as noted previously.
- Tighten gradually in crisscross pattern, starting with inside fasteners.

| Tightening torques | |
|---|---|
| N52 engine cylinder head cover to cylinder head (aluminum-magnesium alloy cover, use new aluminum M7 fasteners)<br>• Stage 1<br>• Stage 2 | <br><br><br>7 Nm (63 in-lb)<br>additional 90° |
| N52KP or N51 engine cylinder head cover to cylinder head (plastic cover, steel M7 fasteners) | 9 Nm (7 ft-lb) |

— Reinstall valvetronic servo.

| Tightening torque | |
|---|---|
| Valvetronic motor to cylinder head cover (M6 x 16 mm bolts) | 10 Nm (7 ft-lb) |

— Reinstall secondary air injection valve.

| Tightening torque | |
|---|---|
| Secondary air injection valve to cylinder head (M6 bolts) | 8 Nm (6 ft-lb) |

— Remainder of assembly is reverse of removal. Make sure cabin microfilter housing seals correctly.

| Tightening torques | |
|---|---|
| Ignition coil cover to cylinder head cover (M6) | 4 Nm (35 in-lb) |
| Strut tower brace to bulkhead (replace M12 bolt)<br>• Stage 1<br>• Stage 2 | <br>100 Nm (74 ft-lb)<br>additional 90° |
| Strut tower brace to strut tower (replace M10 bolt)<br>• Stage 1<br>• Stage 2 | <br>40 Nm (30 ft-lb)<br>additional 60° |

113

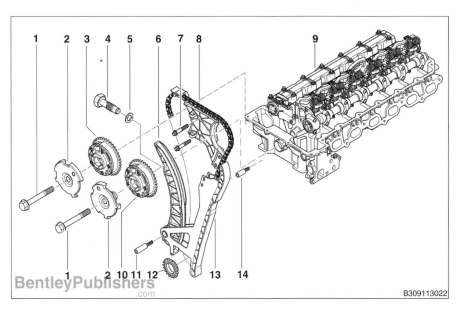

B309113022

## Cylinder head and timing chain (non-turbo)

1. Camshaft adjustment unit mounting bolt (M10 x 94 mm)
   - Replace with new
   - Tighten in 2 stages
     Stage 1: 20 Nm (15 ft-lb)
     Stage 2: Additional 180°

2. Camshaft impulse wheel

3. Exhaust camshaft adjustment unit

4. Chain tensioner (M22 x 1.5)
   - Tighten to 55 Nm (41 ft-lb)

5. Sealing O-ring
   - Install new

6. Chain tensioner rail

7. Chain module mounting bolts (M6 x 35 mm Torx)
   - Tighten to 8.5 Nm (6 ft-lb)

8. Timing chain

9. Cylinder head with camshafts

10. Intake camshaft adjustment unit

11. Chain tensioner rail mounting bolt (M8)
    - Tighten to 20 Nm (15 ft-lb)

12. Crankshaft sprocket

13. Chain guide

14. Chain guide mounting bolt (M7)
    - Tighten to 14 Nm (10 ft-lb)

## Cylinder head, removing and installing (non-turbo)

When removing and installing the cylinder head, special tools and procedures are required to remove and install camshaft adjustment units and valvetronic eccentric shaft and to time camshafts. Read the entire procedure before beginning repairs.

> **CAUTION—**
> - *Disassembly, removal and assembly of camshafts, camshaft adjustment units or cylinder head without special tools poses the risk of damage or breakage: Valves may be bent by contact with the piston crowns.*

**NOTE—**
- *Camshaft timing is covered in* **117 Camshaft Timing Chain***.*

Cylinder head removal and installation procedures are described separately.

If you remove a cylinder head and determine that it requires significant reconditioning work, a remanufactured cylinder head is available from an authorized BMW dealer.

## Cylinder head, removing (non-turbo)

The cylinder head stretch bolts are aluminum. Replace them any time they are removed. Use angle protractor to torque.

> **WARNING—**
> • To avoid personal injury, be sure the engine is cold before beginning the removal procedure.

— Disconnect negative (–) cable from battery.

> **CAUTION—**
> • Prior to disconnecting the battery, read the battery disconnection cautions in **001 Warnings and Cautions**.

— Raise vehicle and support safely.

> **WARNING—**
> • Make sure the vehicle is stable and well supported at all times. Use a professional automotive lift or jack stands designed for the purpose. A floor jack is not adequate support.

— Remove engine compartment splash shield. See **020 Maintenance**.

— With exhaust system fully cooled off, remove exhaust system and both exhaust manifolds. See **180 Exhaust System**.

— Drain engine coolant. See **170 Radiator and Cooling System**.

— Drain engine oil. See **020 Maintenance**.

— Remove ignition coil cover (upper engine cover). See **020 Maintenance**.

— Remove air filter housing, engine air intake ducts and intake manifold. See **130 Fuel Injection**.

> **WARNING—**
> • Unscrew the fuel tank cap to release pressure in the tank before working on fuel lines.

— Remove cylinder head cover. See **Cylinder head cover, removing and installing (non-turbo)** in this repair group.

— Detach coolant hoses from cylinder head.

◄ Using vibration damper bolt, rotate crankshaft to place cylinder 1 in TDC firing position. In this position, cylinder 1 intake camshaft lobe points upward at an angle.

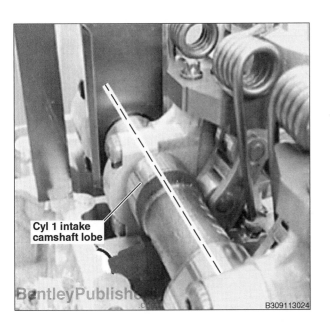

**Cyl 1 intake camshaft lobe**

BentleyPublish

B309113024

*Cylinder head, removing (non-turbo)*

◄ Make sure intake and exhaust camshaft part numbers (**A**) point up.

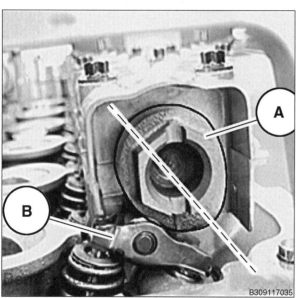

◄ Cylinder 1 in TDC firing position: Cylinder 6 exhaust camshaft lobe (**A**) points downward at an angle (**dashed line**). Cam follower (**B**) is not actuated.

*NOTE —*

• *Use a mirror to check exhaust camshaft lobe position.*

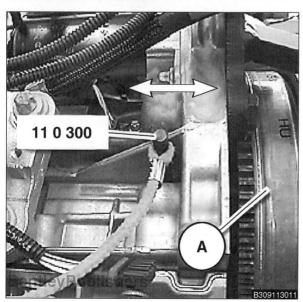

◄ Working underneath engine, slide out protective plug at lower left of engine bell housing flange. Install BMW special tool 11 0 300 (crankshaft locking tool) through bell housing flange port into flywheel (**A**) hole. If necessary, rock flywheel slightly back and forth to line up holes with tool. This locks crankshaft at TDC.

---

*CAUTION—*

• *Automatic transmission model: A short distance before the flywheel special tool bore for TDC position, there is a large bore which can be confused with the special tool bore. If the flywheel is locked using the correct bore, the engine can no longer be rotated at the vibration damper bolt.*

---

*Cylinder head, removing (non-turbo)*

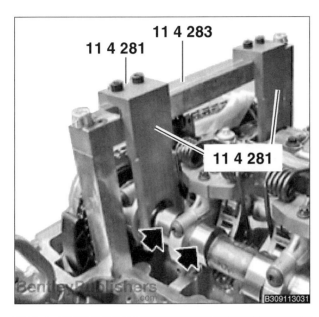

◄ Use BMW special tool set 11 4 280 to lock down camshafts.

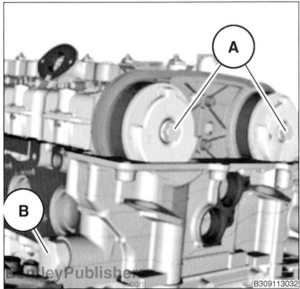

◄ Remove intake and exhaust camshaft adjustment units:

- Loosen and remove adjustment unit mounting bolts (**A**). Discard bolts.
- Remove timing chain tensioner (**B**). Be prepared to catch dripping oil with a shop towel. Do not allow oil to contaminate accessory belt.
- Disengage timing chain from camshaft adjustment unit sprockets. Remove adjustment units and set aside.

*NOTE —*

- *Illustration does not show special tool set 11 4 280 in place.*

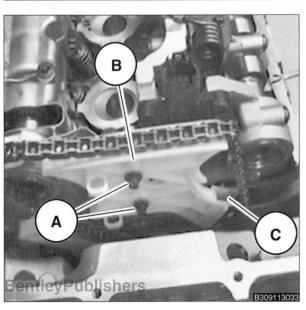

◄ Working at front of cylinder head:

- Remove timing chain module mounting bolts (**A**).
- Unclip chain module (**B**) at junction (**C**) and lift out.
- Place timing chain in cylinder head opening.

*CAUTION—*

- *Do not remove crankshaft locking tool. Rotating crankshaft may cause the timing chain to jam or jump teeth.*

*Cylinder head, removing (non-turbo)*

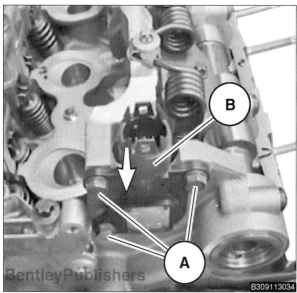

◄ Unbolt and remove valvetronic eccentric shaft sensor mounting bolts (**A**). Slide sensor (**B**) forward (**arrow**) to remove.

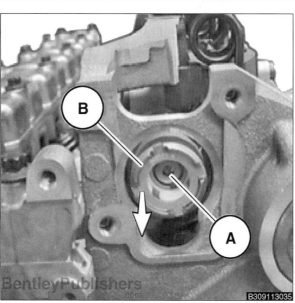

◄ Remove eccentric shaft magnet wheel mounting bolt (**A**). Slide magnet wheel (**B**) forward (**arrow**) to remove.

> **CAUTION—**
> - *Magnet wheel mounting bolt is non-magnetic. Do not allow it to fall into engine.*
> - *Magnet wheel is highly magnetic. Protect against metal filings by storing in sealed plastic bag.*

◄ Pretension eccentric shaft (**arrow**). Remove stop screw between cylinders 1 and 2 (**A**).

*Cylinder head, installing (non-turbo)*

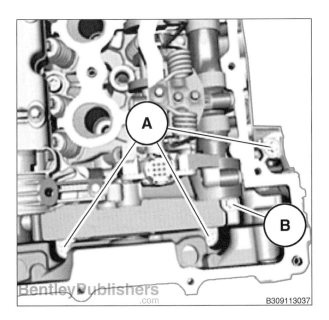

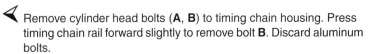

◀ Remove cylinder head bolts (**A**, **B**) to timing chain housing. Press timing chain rail forward slightly to remove bolt **B**. Discard aluminum bolts.

> **CAUTION—**
> - *Use mechanical gripper to prevent lower bolt(s) from falling down inside crankcase.*
> - *Measure and note down different bolt lengths for correct reinstallation.*

◀ Use BMW special tools 11 4 420 (Torx T50) and 11 8 580 (Torx T60) to loosen and remove M9 and M10 cylinder head bolts. (Intake and exhaust camshafts removed for purpose of illustration.)
- Loosen M9 bolts first.
- Loosen M10 bolts in crisscross pattern, starting with outside bolts.
- Note different bolt lengths.
- Discard aluminum bolts.

− Bolt lifting handles to cylinder head. Lift off head with help of assistant.

> **CAUTION—**
> - *Cylinder head weighs approx. 40 kg (88 lb).*
> - *Place cylinder head on work bench on its side. Putting it down on sealing surface risks damage to the valves.*
> - *Be sure to clean antifreeze out of cylinder head bolt holes in crankcase immediately.*

## Cylinder head, installing (non-turbo)

◀ Before cleaning engine block sealing surface, insert plugs (BMW special tools 11 4 430 or equivalent) into oil passages.
- Note cylinder head gasket ID at right front edge of gasket.

− Clean cylinder head and gasket surfaces of engine block and timing chain housing.

> **CAUTION—**
> - *Remove foreign matter and liquid from bolt holes. Trapped oil or coolant in bolt holes can cause damage to the engine block.*
> - *Do not use a metal scraper or wire brush to clean sealing surfaces. If necessary, use a hard wooden or plastic scraper. Also available are abrasive discs to be used in conjunction with an electric drill. Be sure to use the correct disc for the type of metal being cleaned.*

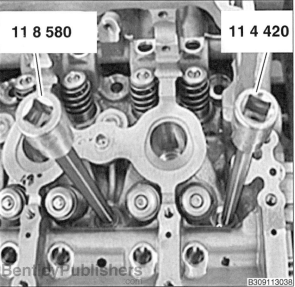

− Inspect cylinder head for visible cracks or other defects.

*Cylinder head, installing (non-turbo)*

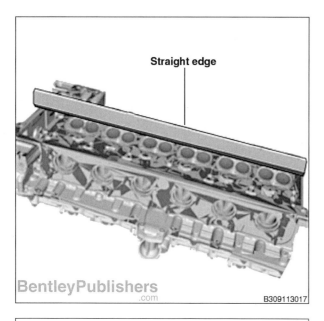

Straight edge

B309113017

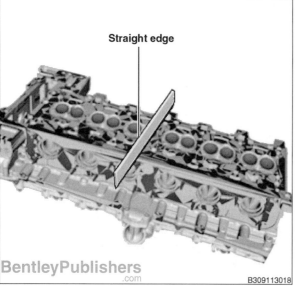

Straight edge

B309113018

— To check cylinder head for warpage:
  • Remove intake and exhaust camshafts and intermediate intake levers.

> **CAUTION—**
> • *Keep components in separate compartments and mark them for reassembly in their original positions.*

◄ Use straight edge to check evenness of cylinder head sealing surface in longitudinal direction.

◄ Use straight edge to check evenness of cylinder head sealing surface in transverse direction.

| Cylinder head warpage specifications | |
| --- | --- |
| Maximum warpage allowed<br>• Longitudinal<br>• Transverse | 0.10 mm (0.0039 in)<br>0.05 mm (0.0020 in) |

— Have cylinder head tested for coolant leaks and cracks.

— If cylinder head is warped but otherwise sound, machine a maximum of 0.3 mm (0.011 in) off sealing surface.

— Reassemble cylinder head, or use reconditioned BMW cylinder head. See **117 Camshaft Timing Chain**.

| Tightening torques | |
| --- | --- |
| Oil spray nozzle to valvetronic guide block (M6 x 30 mm bolt) | 10 Nm (7 ft-lb) |
| Valvetronic guide block to timing chain housing (M6 x 23 mm bolt) | 10 Nm (7 ft-lb) |
| Valvetronic torsion spring to cylinder head (M6 x 20 bolt) | 10 Nm (7 ft-lb) |
| Camshaft bearing strip to camshaft (M7 x 70 mm 10.9 steel bolt)<br>• Stage 1<br>• Stage 2 | <br><br>8 Nm (71 in-lb)<br>additional 60° |

> **CAUTION—**
> • *Once assembled with valves and camshafts, place cylinder head down on work bench on its side. Putting it down on sealing surface risks damage to the valves.*

◀ Check that two cylinder head aligning sleeves (**arrows**) are correctly positioned in engine block and are not damaged.

− Replace cylinder head gasket.

− If cylinder head is machined, use a special cylinder head gasket available from an authorized BMW dealer. The gasket is 0.3 mm (0.011 in) thicker than standard and is marked accordingly.

− Place cylinder head on engine block and fit to aligning sleeves.

B309113019

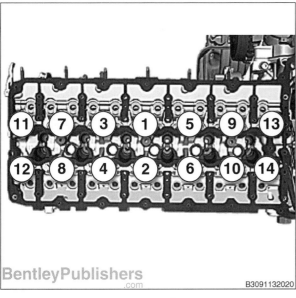

◀ Insert new aluminum cylinder head bolts:
  • Bolts 1 - 10: M10 x 125 mm
  • Bolts 11 - 14: M9 x 95 mm and M9 x 125 mm. Insert correct length bolts, as marked previously.

**NOTE**—
• Graphic shows intake and exhaust camshafts removed.

− Use BMW special tool 11 8 850 (Torx T60) to tighten bolts 1 - 10 in sequence shown below.

− Use BMW special tool 11 4 420 (Torx T50) to tighten bolts 11 - 14 in sequence shown below.

B3091132020

| Tightening torques and sequence | |
|---|---|
| Cylinder head to engine block: | |
| • Stage 1: All bolts, 1 - 14 | 30 Nm (22 ft-lb) |
| • Stage 2: All bolts, 1 - 14 | additional 90° |
| • Stage 3: Only bolts 1 - 10 | additional 90° |
| • Stage 4: All bolts, 1 - 14 | additional 45° |

**CAUTION**—
• Stage 3 applies to M10 bolts (1 - 10) only.

*Cylinder head, installing (non-turbo)*

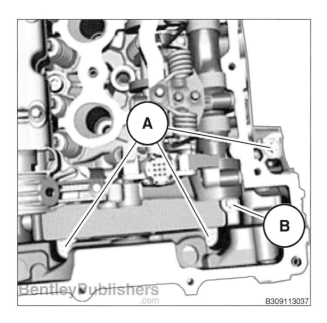

◄ Use new aluminum bolts (**A**, **B**) to attach cylinder head to timing chain housing. Press timing chain rail forward slightly to install lower bolt(s).

> **CAUTION—**
> - *Use mechanical gripper to prevent lower bolt(s) from falling down inside crankcase.*
> - *Place different bolt lengths in correct bores.*

| Tightening torques | |
|---|---|
| N52 engine cylinder head to timing chain housing (M9 x 30 mm or M9 x 70 mm): | |
| • Stage 1 | 15 Nm (11 ft-lb) |
| • Stage 2 | additional 90° |
| N52KP or N51 engine cylinder head to timing chain housing (M9 x 30 mm): | |
| • Stage 1 | 10 Nm (7 ft-lb) |
| • Stage 2 | additional 90° |
| N52KP or N51 engine cylinder head to timing chain housing (M9 x 70 mm): | |
| • Stage 1 | 10 Nm (7 ft-lb) |
| • Stage 2 | additional 135° |

– Reinstall eccentric shaft stop screw.

| Tightening torque | |
|---|---|
| Eccentric shaft stop screw to cylinder head (M6) | 10 Nm (7 ft-lb) |

– Replace eccentric shaft magnet wheel.

– Reinstall eccentric shaft sensor.

– Use wire hook to retrieve timing chain from inside timing chain housing. Place chain over chain module and clip module to lower chain rail. Reinstall chain module mounting bolts.

| Tightening torque | |
|---|---|
| Chain module to cylinder head (M6 x 35 mm Torx) | 8.5 Nm (6 ft-lb) |

◄ Use new bolts to reattach camshaft adjustment (VANOS) units. Note that exhaust and intake units are different and so marked. Camshaft sensor impulse wheel for intake and exhaust are the same.

> **CAUTION—**
> - *Use special tools shown in* **117 Camshaft Timing Chain** *to lock down camshafts.*

| Tightening torque | |
|---|---|
| Camshaft adjustment (VANOS) unit to camshaft (use new M10 x 94 mm bolt): | |
| • Stage 1 | 20 Nm (15 ft-lb) |
| • Stage 2 | additional 180° |

— Install chain tensioner and set camshaft timing. See **117 Camshaft Timing Chain**.

> **CAUTION—**
>
> • *If chain tensioner is reused, drain its oil chamber. Place tensioner on level working surface and compress slowly. Repeat twice.*
>
> • *No sealing ring is fitted to chain tensioner at the factory. When reassembling engine, be sure to use new sealing O-ring.*

| Tightening torque | |
|---|---|
| Timing chain tensioner to cylinder head (M22 x 1.5) (use new sealing O-ring) | 55 Nm (41 ft-lb) |

— Remainder of installation is reverse of removal. Remember to:

• Remove camshaft and crankshaft locking tools.

• Assemble cylinder head cover with new gasket.

• Reattach and tighten any ground cables removed.

• Reassemble fuel rail using new O-ring seals.

• Fill and bleed cooling system. See **170 Radiator and Cooling System**.

**113**

*Cylinder head cover components (turbo)*

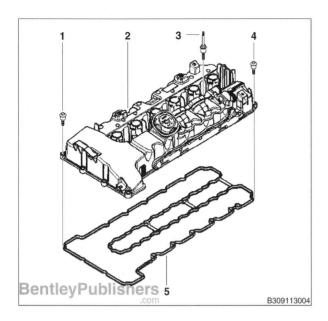

B309113004

## CYLINDER HEAD (TURBO ENGINE)

### Cylinder head cover components (turbo)

1. Cylinder head cover bolt (M6 x 38 mm)
   - Quantity: 2
   - Tighten to 8.5 Nm (75 in-lb)
2. Cylinder head cover
3. Threaded stud
   - Quantity: 3
   - Remove using BMW special tool 11 8 620 or equivalent deep 10 mm socket wrench.
4. Cylinder head cover bolt (M6 x 32.5 mm)
   - Quantity: 26
   - Tighten to 8.5 Nm (75 in-lb)
5. Cylinder head cover gasket

### Cylinder head cover, removing and installing (turbo)

− Disconnect negative (-) battery cable and cover battery terminal to keep cable from accidentally contacting terminal.

> **CAUTION—**
> - *Prior to disconnecting the battery, read the battery disconnection cautions given in* **001 Warnings and Cautions**.

− Use scan tool to read out and record ECM fault memory.

− Switch ignition OFF and remove key.

− Remove upper and lower cabin microfilter housings. See **640 Heating and Air-conditioning**.

− Remove right strut tower brace.

− Remove ignition coil cover (upper engine cover). See **020 Maintenance**.

− Remove ignition coils. See **120 Ignition System**.

− Unclip fuel injector and ignition coil wiring harness and set aside.

*Cylinder head cover, removing and installing (turbo)*

◀ Loosen high pressure fuel line junctions (**arrows**).

---

**WARNING—**

• *Fuel in the fuel line is under pressure (approx. 200 bar or 2900 psi) and may be expelled forcibly. Do not smoke or work near heaters or other fire hazards. Keep a fire extinguisher handy.*

• *Work only on fuel system when engine temperature is below 40°C (104°F).*

• *Unscrew the fuel tank cap to release pressure in the tank before working on the fuel line.*

• *Plug open fuel lines and fittings.*

• *Wrap a clean shop towel around fitting before disconnecting. Residual fuel pressure is present in the fuel line.*

• *To reduce fuel pressure, place towel over injector and carefully tap with a wrench.*

---

**CAUTION—**

• *Maintain a clean work area when servicing high pressure fuel system. Contaminants can cause a system malfunction.*

• *Fuel residue can break down the electrical resistance qualities of silicone used in ignition coil production, resulting in coil failure.*

• *Replace high pressure fuel lines if tightened 10 times.*

---

– Remove injector lines and mark them in order.

◀ Working at left front of cylinder head:

• Detach vacuum hoses (**A**) from vacuum lines.

• Unclip vacuum lines (**B**) from cylinder head cover.

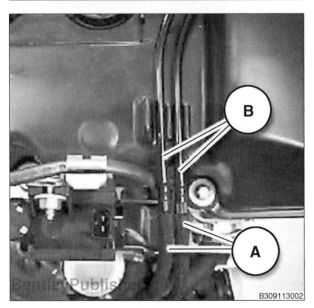

◀ Working at right front of cylinder head:

• Detach vacuum hoses (**A**) from vacuum lines.

• Unclip vacuum lines (**B**) and set aside.

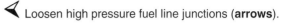

*Cylinder head cover, removing and installing (turbo)*

◄ Use BMW special tool 11 8 620 or equivalent deep 10 mm socket wrench to loosen and remove threaded studs (**arrow**) in center of cylinder head cover valley.

• Quantity: 3 studs

◄ Remove cylinder head cover bolts (**arrow**).

• M6 x 38 mm bolts, quantity: 2
• M6 x 32.5 mm bolts, quantity: 26

**NOTE—**
• *Make note of arrangement of fasteners during removal so that they can be reinstalled in their original locations.*

— Remove cylinder head cover and discard gasket.

— Inspect cylinder head cover fasteners. Replace as necessary.

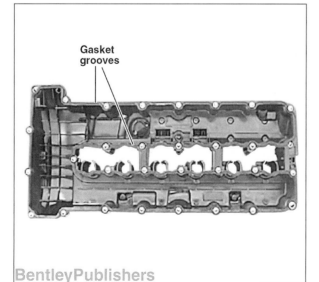

Gasket grooves

◄ Clean gasket residue from cylinder head sealing surface and from cylinder head cover grooves.

**CAUTION—**
• *To avoid gouging the cover, do not use metal scraping tool.*

— Coat cylinder head cover grooves with thin layer of anti-friction compound such as glycerine. Press gasket in place, making sure it is not stretched at any point.

*Cylinder head cover, removing and installing (turbo)*

− Reinstall cylinder head cover.

- Coat cylinder head and gasket contact surfaces with thin layer of anti-friction compound such as glycerine.
- Place small quantity of silicone sealant at metal-to-metal seams (such as timing cover to engine block).
- Install cylinder head cover fasteners in correct locations as noted previously.
- Tighten gradually in crisscross pattern, starting with inside fasteners.

| Tightening torque | |
|---|---|
| Cylinder head cover to cylinder head (M6) | 8.5 Nm (75 in-lb) |

◀ Reinstall high pressure fuel lines in correct locations, as marked previously.

- Coat nut threads with gear oil.
- Connect high pressure line (**A**) finger tight.
- High pressure line may only be retightened 10 times.

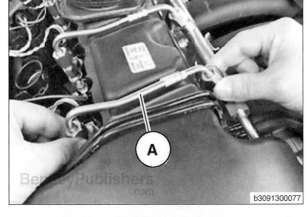

b3091300077

◀ If fuel lines cannot be easily installed, rock injector (**arrows**) to allow fuel line nipple threads to be started by hand.

- Tighten hold-down bracket fastener (**A**).

| Tightening torque | |
|---|---|
| Hold-down bracket to cylinder head | 13 Nm (9.5 ft-lb) |

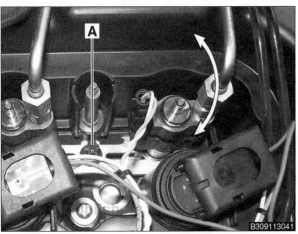

B309113041

◀ To tighten injector lines:

- Tighten nut (**A**) using special tool 37 1 151 while holding injector with wrench (**C**).
- Tighten nut (**B**) using special tool 37 1 151.

| Tightening torque | |
|---|---|
| High pressure line to injector | 23 Nm (17 ft-lb) |
| High pressure line to fuel rail | 23 Nm (17 ft-lb) |

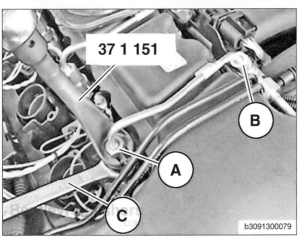

37 1 151

b3091300079

– Clean all fuel from ignition coil hole.

– Remainder of assembly is reverse of removal. Keep in mind the following:

• Make sure cabin microfilter housing seals correctly.

• Check fuel lines for leaks once engine starts.

| Tightening torque | |
|---|---|
| Ignition coil cover to cylinder head cover (M6) | 4 Nm (35 in-lb) |
| Strut tower brace to bulkhead (replace M12 bolt) • Stage 1 • Stage 2 | 100 Nm (74 ft-lb) additional 90° |
| Strut tower brace to strut tower (replace M10 bolt) • Stage 1 • Stage 2 | 40 Nm (30 ft-lb) additional 60° |

## Cylinder head and timing chain (turbo)

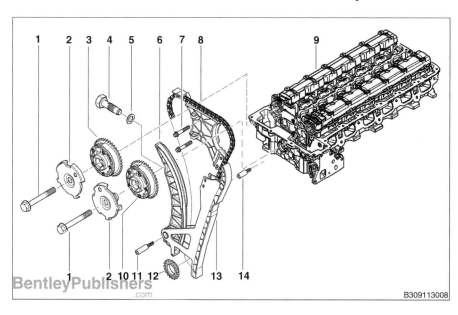

B309113008

1. Camshaft adjustment unit mounting bolt (M10 x 94 mm)

   • Replace with new

   • Tighten in 2 stages
     Stage 1: 20 Nm (15 ft-lb)
     Stage 2: Additional 180°

2. Camshaft impulse wheel

3. Exhaust camshaft adjustment unit

4. Chain tensioner (M22 x 1.5)

   • Tighten to 55 Nm (41 ft-lb)

5. Sealing O-ring

   • Install new

6. Chain tensioner rail

7. Chain module mounting bolts (M6 x 35 mm Torx)

   • Tighten to 8.5 Nm (6 ft-lb)

8. Timing chain

9. Cylinder head with camshafts

10. Intake camshaft adjustment unit

11. Chain guide mounting bolt (M8)

    • Tighten to 20 Nm (15 ft-lb)

12. Crankshaft sprocket

13. Chain guide

14. Chain guide mounting bolt (M7)

    • Tighten to 14 Nm (10 ft-lb)

## Cylinder head, removing and installing (turbo)

To remove the turbo engine cylinder head, first remove the engine. Special tools and procedures are required to remove and install camshaft adjustment units and to time camshafts. Read the entire procedure before beginning repairs.

> **CAUTION—**
> - *Disassembly, removal and assembly of camshafts, camshaft adjustment units or cylinder head without special tools poses the risk of damage or breakage:*
> -*Valves may be bent by contact with the piston crowns.*
> -*Camshaft may snap in two if bent by valve springs.*

> **NOTE —**
> - *Camshaft timing is covered in **117 Camshaft Timing Chain**.*

Cylinder head removal and installation procedures are described separately.

If you remove a cylinder head and determine that it requires significant reconditioning work, a remanufactured cylinder head is available from an authorized BMW dealer.

## Cylinder head, removing (turbo)

The cylinder head stretch bolts are aluminum. Replace them any time they are removed. Use angle protractor to torque.

> **WARNING —**
> - *To avoid personal injury, be sure the engine is cold before beginning the removal procedure.*

— Disconnect negative (–) cable from battery.

> **CAUTION—**
> - *Prior to disconnecting the battery, read the battery disconnection cautions in **001 Warnings and Cautions**.*

— Remove ignition coil cover (upper engine cover). See **020 Maintenance**.

— With engine fully cooled off, drain engine coolant. See **170 Radiator and Cooling System**.

— Remove engine. See **110 Engine Removal and Installation**.

— Remove cylinder head cover. See **Cylinder head cover, removing and installing (turbo)** in this repair group.

◀ Using vibration damper bolt to rotate crankshaft, place cylinder 1 in TDC firing position. In this position, lobes for cylinder 6 (rear of engine) intake and exhaust camshafts (**A**, **B**) point away from each other and down. Cylinder 6 camshaft lobes do not contact roller cam followers.

> **NOTE —**
> - *Use a mirror to check cylinder 6 cam lobe positions.*

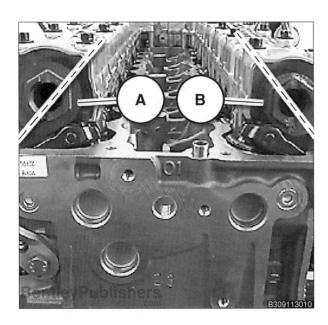

*Cylinder head, removing (turbo)*

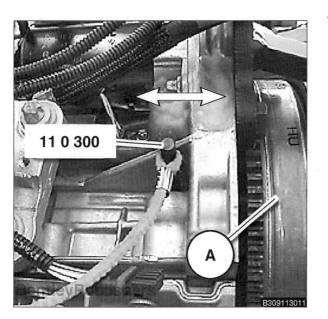

◀ Working underneath engine, slide out protective plug at lower left of engine bell housing flange. Install BMW special tool 11 0 300 (crankshaft locking tool) through bell housing flange port into flywheel (**A**) hole. If necessary, rock flywheel slightly back and forth to line up holes with tool. This locks crankshaft at TDC.

> **CAUTION—**
> • *Automatic transmission model: A short distance before the flywheel special tool bore for TDC position, there is a large bore which can be confused with the special tool bore. If the flywheel is locked using the correct bore, the engine can no longer be rotated at the vibration damper bolt.*

− Remove intake and exhaust camshaft adjustment units. See **117 Camshaft Timing Chain**.

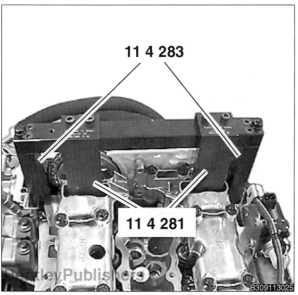

◀ Use BMW special tool set 11 4 280 to lock down camshafts.

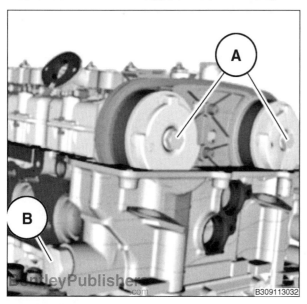

◀ Remove intake and exhaust camshaft adjustment units:
  • Loosen and remove adjustment unit mounting bolts (**1**). Discard bolts.
  • Remove timing chain tensioner (**2**). Be prepared to catch dripping oil with a shop towel. Do not allow oil to contaminate accessory belt.
  • Disengage timing chain from camshaft adjustment unit sprockets. Remove adjustment units and set aside.

**NOTE —**
• *Illustration does not show special tool set 11 4 280 in place.*

*Cylinder head, removing (turbo)*

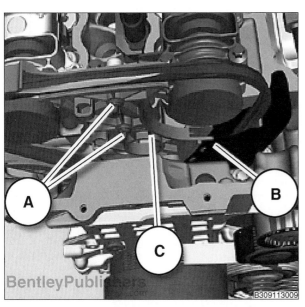

◀ Working at front of cylinder head:

- Remove timing chain module mounting bolts (**A**).
- Unclip chain module (**C**) at junction (**B**) and lift out.
- Place timing chain in cylinder head opening.

> **CAUTION—**
> - *Do not remove crankshaft locking tool. Rotating crankshaft may cause the timing chain to jam or jump teeth.*

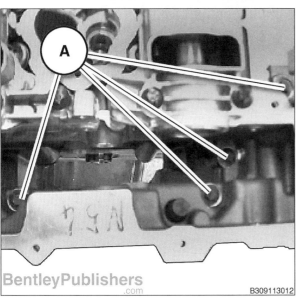

◀ Remove cylinder head bolts (**A**) to timing chain housing. Press timing chain rail forward slightly to remove lower bolt(s).

> **CAUTION—**
> - *Use mechanical gripper to prevent lower bolt(s) from falling down inside crankcase.*
> - *Measure and note down different bolt lengths for correct reinstallation.*

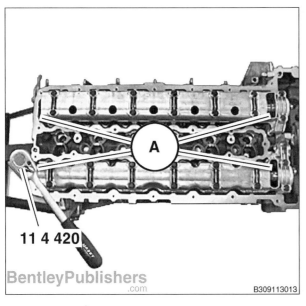

◀ Use BMW special tool 11 4 420 (Torx T50) to loosen and remove M9 cylinder head bolts.

- Note different bolt lengths.
- Discard all aluminum bolts.

*Cylinder head, installing (turbo)*

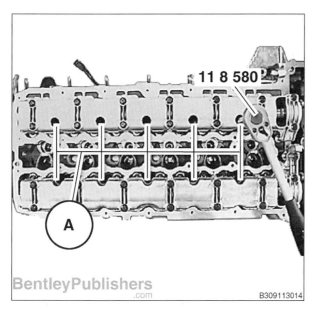

◄ Use BMW special tool 11 8 850 (Torx T60) to loosen and remove M11 cylinder head bolts (**A**).

- Start at outer corners and loosen bolts in crisscross pattern.

- Discard all aluminum bolts.

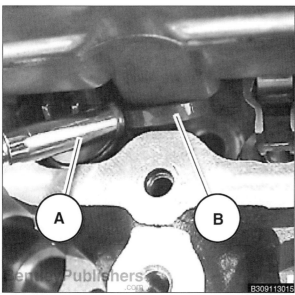

◄ Use magnet (**A**) to lift out cylinder head bolt washers (**B**) between surface of cylinder head and camshaft bearing strip.

– Bolt lifting handles to cylinder head. Lift off head with help of assistant.

> **CAUTION—**
> - *Cylinder head weighs approx. 40 kg (88 lb).*
> - *Place cylinder head down on work bench on its side. Putting it down on sealing surface risks damage to the valves.*
> - *Be sure to clean antifreeze out of cylinder head bolt holes in crankcase immediately.*

### Cylinder head, installing (turbo)

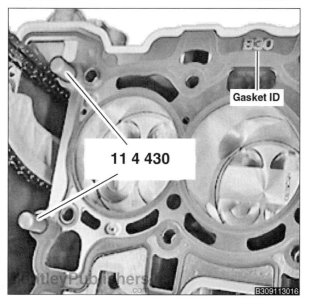

◄ Before cleaning engine block sealing surface, insert plugs (BMW special tools 11 4 430 or equivalent) into oil passages.

– Clean cylinder head and gasket surfaces of engine block and timing chain housing.

> **CAUTION—**
> - *Remove foreign matter and liquid from bolt holes. Trapped oil or coolant in bolt holes can cause damage to the engine block.*
> - *Do not use a metal scraper or wire brush to clean the aluminum cylinder head or pistons. If necessary, use a hard wooden or plastic scraper. Also available are abrasive discs to be used in conjunction with an electric drill. Be sure to use the correct disc for the type of metal being cleaned.*

– Inspect cylinder head for visible cracks or other defects.

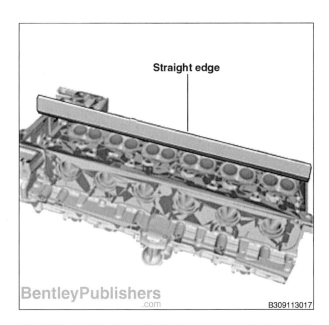

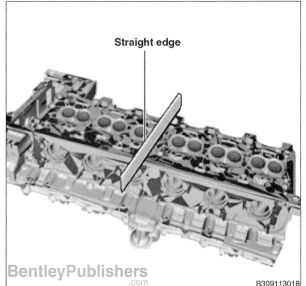

– To check cylinder head for warpage:

  • Remove intake and exhaust camshafts and roller cam followers.

  • Remove valve lifters and valves.

◀ Use straight edge to check evenness of cylinder head sealing surface in longitudinal direction.

◀ Use straight edge to check evenness of cylinder head sealing surface in transverse direction.

| Cylinder head warpage specifications | |
|---|---|
| Maximum warpage allowed <br> • Longitudinal <br> • Transverse | <br> 0.10 mm (0.0039 in) <br> 0.05 mm (0.0020 in) |

– Have cylinder head tested for coolant leaks and cracks.

– If cylinder head is warped but otherwise sound, machine a maximum of 0.3 mm (0.011 in) off sealing surface.

– Reassemble cylinder head, or use reconditioned BMW cylinder head.

| Tightening torque | |
|---|---|
| Camshaft bearing strip to camshaft <br> (M7 x 70 mm 10.9 steel bolt) <br> • Stage 1 <br> • Stage 2 | <br><br> 8 Nm (71 in-lb) <br> additional 60° |

**CAUTION—**

• *Once assembled with valves and camshafts, place cylinder head down on work bench on its side. Putting it down on sealing surface risks damage to the valves.*

◀ Check that two cylinder head aligning sleeves (**arrows**) are correctly positioned in engine block and are not damaged.

– Replace cylinder head gasket.

– If cylinder head is machined, use a special cylinder head gasket available from an authorized BMW dealer. The gasket is 0.3 mm (0.011 in) thicker than standard and is marked accordingly.

– Place cylinder head on engine block and fit to aligning sleeves.

*Cylinder head, installing (turbo)*

B3091132020

◀ Insert new aluminum cylinder head bolts:

• Bolts 1 - 10: M11 x 135 mm

• Bolts 11 - 14: M9 x 95 mm and M9 x 125 mm. Insert correct length bolts, as marked previously.

• Where necessary, use magnet to fit bolt washer.

***NOTE***—

• *Graphic shows intake and exhaust camshafts removed.*

— Use BMW special tool 11 8 850 (Torx T60) to tighten bolts 1 - 10 in sequence shown below.

— Use BMW special tool 11 4 420 (Torx T50) to tighten bolts 11 - 14 in sequence shown below.

| Tightening torques and sequence | |
|---|---|
| Cylinder head to engine block: | |
| • Stage 1: All bolts, 1 - 14 | 30 Nm (22 ft-lb) |
| • Stage 2: All bolts, 1 - 14 | additional 90° |
| • Stage 3: Only bolts 1 - 10 | additional 90° |
| • Stage 4: All bolts, 1 - 14 | additional 45° |

***CAUTION***—

• *Stage 3 applies to M11 bolts (1 - 10) only.*

◀ Install cylinder head bolts to timing chain housing (**A**). Press timing chain rail forward slightly to install lower bolt(s).

***CAUTION***—

• *Use mechanical gripper to prevent lower bolt(s) from falling down inside crankcase.*

• *Place different bolt lengths in correct bores.*

| Tightening torque | |
|---|---|
| Cylinder head to timing chain housing (M9 x 30 mm or M9 x 70 mm) | 22 Nm (16 ft-lb) |

— Use wire hook to retrieve timing chain from inside timing chain housing. Place chain over chain module and clip module to lower chain rail. Reinstall chain module mounting bolts.

| Tightening torque | |
|---|---|
| Chain module to cylinder head (M6 x 35 mm Torx) | 8.5 Nm (6 ft-lb) |

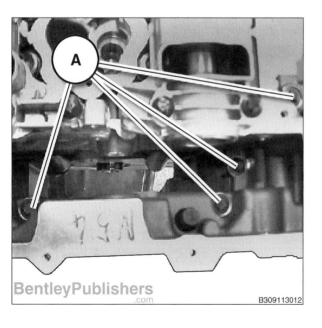

B3091113012

B309113023

◀ Use new bolts to reattach camshaft adjustment units. Note that exhaust and intake units are different and so marked. Camshaft sensor impulse wheel for intake and exhaust are the same.

> **CAUTION—**
> • *Use special tools shown in **117 Camshaft Timing Chain** to lock down camshafts.*

| Tightening torque | |
|---|---|
| Camshaft adjustment unit to camshaft (use new M10 x 94 mm bolt): | |
| • Stage 1 | 20 Nm (15 ft-lb) |
| • Stage 2 | additional 180° |

– Install chain tensioner and set camshaft timing. See **117 Camshaft Timing Chain**.

> **CAUTION—**
> • *If chain tensioner is reused, drain its oil chamber. Place tensioner on level working surface and compress slowly. Repeat twice.*
> • *No sealing ring is fitted to chain tensioner at the factory. When reassembling engine, be sure to use new sealing O-ring.*

| Tightening torque | |
|---|---|
| Timing chain tensioner to cylinder head (M22 x 1.5) (use new sealing O-ring) | 55 Nm (41 ft-lb) |

– Remainder of installation is reverse of removal. Remember to:

 • Remove camshaft and crankshaft locking tools.

 • Assemble cylinder head cover with new gasket.

 • Reattach and tighten any ground cables removed.

 • Reassemble fuel rail using new O-ring seals.

 • Reinstall engine, then fill and bleed cooling system. See **170 Radiator and Cooling System**.

# 117 Camshaft Timing Chain

## GENERAL

This repair group provides removal and repair information for crankshaft vibration damper, engine timing chain and camshaft adjustment (VANOS) units. Camshaft timing procedure is also included.

The 6-cylinder engine cylinder head is equipped with variable camshaft timing or VANOS (from the German words *VAriable NOckenwellen Steuerung*). Special tools and procedures are required to remove and install camshaft adjustment units and to time camshafts. Be sure to read each procedure through before starting work.

Camshaft removal and installation procedures are not included in this manual.

Repair procedures in this repair group assume that the engine is installed in the engine bay.

See also:

• **020 Maintenance**

• **100 Engine–General** for engine code and application information.

• **113 Cylinder Head Removal and Installation** for cylinder head cover removal

• **119 Lubrication System** for crankshaft seal replacement

• **130 Fuel Injection** for air filter housing and intake manifold removal

• **170 Radiator and Cooling System**

## Engine identification

Engine applications and specifications are detailed in **100 Engine–General**.

In the procedures that follow, non-turbo engine is used to refer to the 6-cylinder 3-liter normally-aspirated engine. There are 3 versions of this engine.

| Table a. Non-turbo engine identification | | |
| --- | --- | --- |
| **Engine designation** | **Year, model** | **Identifying feature** |
| N51 | 2007 and later 328i, 328ix with automatic transmission (sold in California, Connecticut, Maine, Massachusetts, New York, Oregon, Rhode Island, Vermont, Washington) | Secondary air injection pump Black plastic cylinder head cover Simple, not variable intake manifold |
| N52 | 2006 325i, 325ix, 330i, 330ix | Aluminum-magnesium cylinder head cover |
| N52KP | 2007 and later 328i, 328ix | Black plastic cylinder head cover |

The 6-cylinder turbo engine, N54, is referred to as turbo engine.

Fasteners and fastener torques differ among the versions. Read torque specifications carefully.

## Variable camshaft timing (VANOS)

Performance, torque, idle characteristics and exhaust emissions reduction are improved by variable camshaft timing or VANOS.

◄ VANOS units are mounted directly on the front of the camshafts and adjust the timing of the intake and exhaust camshafts from retarded to advanced. The engine control module (ECM) controls the operation of the VANOS solenoids which regulate oil pressure to rotate the VANOS units. Engine rpm, load and temperature inputs are used to regulate VANOS activation.

VANOS mechanical operation is dependent on engine oil pressure applied to the VANOS units. When oil pressure is applied to the units (via ports in the camshafts regulated by the solenoids), the camshaft hubs are rotated in the timing chain drive sprockets, thus advancing or retarding intake and exhaust camshaft timing.

The VANOS system is fully variable. When the ECM, using camshaft sensor signals, detects that the camshafts are in the optimum positions, the solenoids maintain oil pressure on the VANOS units to hold the camshaft timing.

VANOS solenoid operations are regulated according to OBD II requirements for emission control.

Exhaust camshaft adjustment (VANOS) unit — Intake camshaft adjustment (VANOS) unit

Intake camshaft sensor

Exhaust camshaft sensor
Exhaust VANOS solenoid

Intake VANOS solenoid

B309117036

VANOS solenoid

B309117037

## VANOS solenoids

◄ Separate VANOS solenoids, mounted through the front of the cylinder head, control oil flow to intake and exhaust camshaft ports. Each solenoid is equipped with a 4/3- way proportional valve activated by the ECM to direct oil flow. The solenoids are sealed to the cylinder head by a radial seal and secured by a retaining plate.

## Camshaft sensors and impulse wheels

◄ Intake and exhaust camshaft sensors are mounted at the front of the cylinder head and monitor the impulse wheels which are bolted to the front of the VANOS units.

The sensors are supplied power via engine electronics fuses. Ground is supplied via the ECM. The Hall effect sensors provide the ECM with a 5 volt square wave signal indicating camshaft position.

Camshaft sensor replacement is covered in **120 Ignition System**.

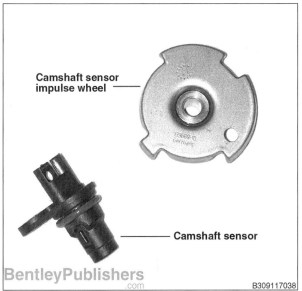

Camshaft sensor impulse wheel

Camshaft sensor

B309117038

## VANOS fault diagnosis

> **CAUTION—**
> • *A small amount of silicone introduced into VANOS actuator or solenoid can set faults.*

◄ A sticky VANOS solenoid may set a VANOS, camshaft or camshaft sensor fault code. To test for this problem:

• Swap VANOS solenoid positions.

• Clear and recheck for fault codes. If fault code swaps position, a solenoid is at fault.

— Remove faulty solenoid and use shop air to gently blow out particles and contaminants. Reinstall and retest.

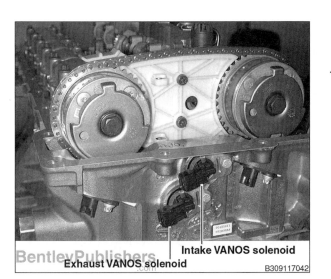

**Intake VANOS solenoid**

**Exhaust VANOS solenoid**

B309117042

| Tightening torque | |
|---|---|
| VANOS solenoid to cylinder head (replace sealing O-ring) | 9 Nm (7 ft-lb) |

## Warnings and Cautions

---

**WARNING** —

- To avoid personal injury, be sure the engine is cold before beginning work on engine components.

- The fuel system is designed to retain pressure even when the ignition is OFF. When working with the fuel system, loosen fuel lines slowly to allow residual fuel pressure to dissipate. Avoid spraying fuel. Use shop towels to capture leaking fuel.

- Before beginning work on the fuel system, place a fire extinguisher in the vicinity of the work area.

- Fuel is highly flammable. When working around fuel, do not disconnect wires that could cause electrical sparks. Do not smoke or work near heaters or other fire hazards.

- Wear eye protection and protective clothing to avoid injuries from contact with fuel.

- Unscrew the fuel tank cap to release pressure in the tank before working on fuel lines.

- Do not use a work light with an incandescent bulb near fuel. Fuel may spray on the hot bulb causing a fire.

- Make sure the work area is properly ventilated.

---

**CAUTION**—

- To avoid electrochemical corrosion to engine components made of aluminum-magnesium alloy, do not use steel fasteners. Use aluminum fasteners only.

- The end faces of aluminum fasteners are usually painted blue. For reliable identification, test fasteners for aluminum composition with magnet.

- To avoid camshaft damage, counter hold hexagon casting at rear of camshaft whenever loosening or tightening camshaft adjuster (VANOS) unit.

- Replace aluminum bolts each time they are loosened.

---

## CRANKSHAFT VIBRATION DAMPER

### Crankshaft vibration damper, removing and installing

The crankshaft vibration damper is also referred to as the front pulley.

> **WARNING** —
> • To avoid personal injury, be sure the engine is cold before beginning the procedure.

— Raise vehicle and support safely.

> **WARNING** —
> • Make sure the vehicle is stable and well supported at all times. Use a professional automotive lift or jack stands designed for the purpose. A floor jack is not adequate support.

— Remove engine compartment splash shield. See **020 Maintenance**.

— Remove engine accessory belt. See **020 Maintenance**.

◄ Remove vibration damper mounting Torx bolts (**A**). Lift off vibration damper.

> **CAUTION**—
> • Do not remove vibration damper hub bolt (**B**). If this bolt is removed, the timing chain drive sprocket becomes free to rotate, resulting in valve damage.

— Installation is reverse of removal.

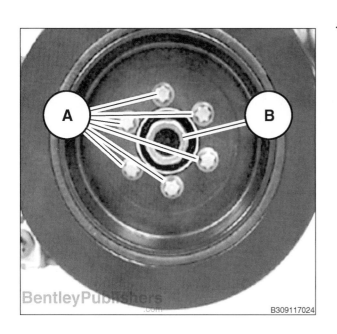

| Tightening torque | |
|---|---|
| Vibration damper to vibration damper hub (M8 x 16 mm Torx) | 35 Nm (26 ft-lb) |

B309117024

## CAMSHAFT TIMING CHAIN

### Camshaft timing chain components (non-turbo)

Camshaft timing chain, vibration damper (front pulley) and associated components of non-turbo and turbo engines are similar.

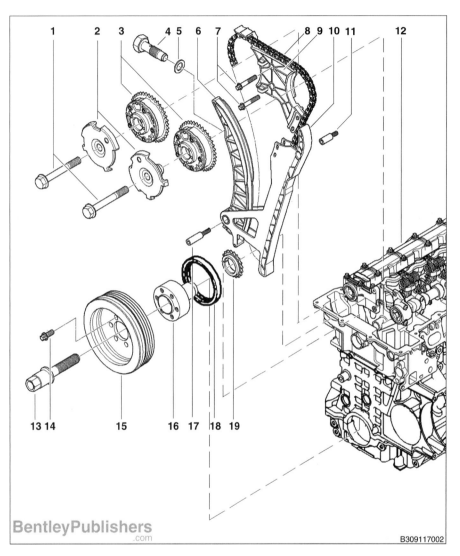

B309117002

1. **Camshaft adjustment (VANOS) unit mounting bolt (M10 x 94 mm)**
   - Replace with new
   - Tighten in 2 stages
     Stage 1: 20 Nm (15 ft-lb)
     Stage 2: Additional 180°

2. **Camshaft impulse wheel**

3. **Camshaft adjustment (VANOS) unit**
   - Different intake and exhaust adjustment units

4. **Chain tensioner (M22 x 1.5)**
   - Tighten to 55 Nm (41 ft-lb)

5. **Sealing O-ring**
   - Install new

6. **Chain tensioner rail**

7. **Chain assembly mounting bolts (M6 x 35 mm Torx)**
   - Tighten to 8.5 Nm (6 ft-lb)

8. **Timing chain**

9. **Chain assembly**

10. **Chain guide**

11. **Chain guide mounting bolt (M7)**
    - Tighten to 14 Nm (10 ft-lb)

12. **Cylinder head with camshafts**
    - Non-turbo cylinder head illustrated

13. **Vibration damper hub mounting bolt (M16 x 80 mm)**
    - Replace with new
    - Tighten in 2 stages
      Stage 1: 100 Nm (74 ft-lb)
      Stage 2: Additional 360°

14. **Vibration damper mounting bolt (M8 x 16 mm Torx)**
    - Tighten to 35 Nm (26 ft-lb)

15. **Vibration damper (front pulley)**

16. **Vibration damper hub**

17. **Chain tensioner rail mounting bolt (M8)**
    - Tighten to 20 Nm (15 ft-lb)

18. **Crankshaft front seal**

19. **Crankshaft sprocket**

## Camshaft timing chain, removing and installing

When removing and installing the camshaft timing chain, special tools and procedures are required to remove and install camshaft adjustment (VANOS) units and to time camshafts. Read the entire procedure before beginning repairs.

> **WARNING—**
> • To avoid personal injury, be sure the engine is cold before beginning the procedure.

> **CAUTION—**
> • Disassembly, removal and assembly of camshafts or camshaft adjustment units without special tools poses the risk of damage or breakage: Valves may be bent by contact with the piston crowns.
> • Throughout this procedure, unless otherwise specified, crankshaft and camshafts remain locked against rotation using BMW special tools.

— Use scan tool to read out and record ECM fault memory.

— Switch ignition OFF and remove key.

— Remove upper and lower cabin microfilter housings. See **640 Heating and Air-conditioning**.

— Remove right strut tower brace.

— Remove ignition coil cover (upper engine cover). See **020 Maintenance**.

— Detach ignition coil connectors. Lift ignition coil harness off cylinder head cover and set aside.

— Remove ignition coils. See **120 Ignition System**.

— Remove cylinder head cover. See **113 Cylinder Head Removal and Installation**.

— Remove spark plugs.

◁ Non-turbo engine: Using vibration damper bolt, rotate crankshaft to place cylinder 1 in TDC firing position. In this position, cylinder 1 intake camshaft lobe points upward at an angle (**dashed line**).

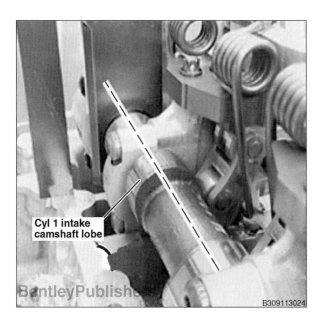

Cyl 1 intake camshaft lobe

B309113024

*Camshaft timing chain, removing and installing*

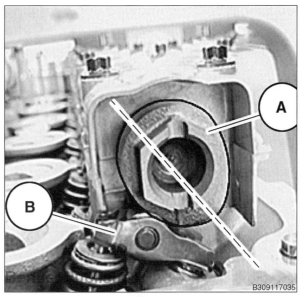

◀ Non-turbo engine: Cylinder 1 in TDC firing position: Cylinder 6 exhaust camshaft lobe (**A**) points downward at an angle (**dashed line**). Cam follower (**B**) is not actuated.

*NOTE—*

• *Use a mirror to check exhaust camshaft lobe position.*

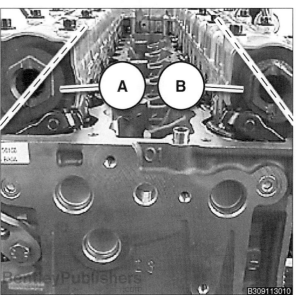

◀ Turbo engine: Using vibration damper bolt to rotate crankshaft, place cylinder 1 in TDC firing position. In this position, lobes for cylinder 6 (rear of engine) intake and exhaust camshafts (**A**, **B**) point away from each other and down. Cylinder 6 camshaft lobes do not contact roller cam followers.

*NOTE—*

• *Use a mirror to check cylinder 6 cam lobe positions.*

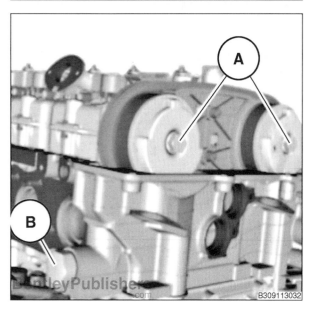

◀ Working at right front of cylinder head, remove timing chain tensioner (**B**). Be prepared to catch dripping oil with a shop towel. Do not allow oil to contaminate accessory belt.

— Raise vehicle and support safely.

*WARNING—*

• *Make sure the vehicle is stable and well supported at all times. Use a professional automotive lift or jack stands designed for the purpose. A floor jack is not adequate support.*

— Remove engine compartment splash shield. See **020 Maintenance**.

— Remove engine accessory belt. See **020 Maintenance**.

— Remove vibration damper (front pulley). See **Crankshaft vibration damper, removing and installing** in this repair group.

— Remove crankshaft front seal. See **119 Lubrication System**.

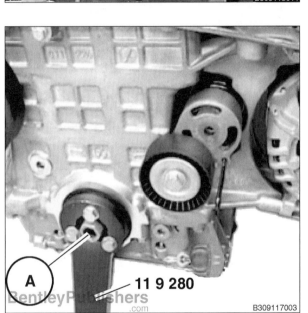

◁ Working underneath engine, slide out protective plug at lower left of engine bell housing flange. Install BMW special tool 11 0 300 (crankshaft locking tool) through bell housing flange port into flywheel (**A**) hole. If necessary, rock flywheel slightly back and forth to line up holes with tool. This locks crankshaft at TDC.

> **CAUTION—**
> * Models with automatic transmission: In the flywheel (torque plate), a short distance before the bore for TDC position, there is a large bore which can be confused with the special tool bore. If the flywheel is locked using the correct bore, the engine can no longer be rotated at the vibration damper bolt.
> * If special tool 11 0 300 does not slide easily into the bell housing flange bore, sand paint off the tool. Do not enlarge the bore.

◁ Remove vibration damper hub:
* Bolt BMW special tool 11 9 280 (counter hold tool) to hub.
* With help of assistant counter holding hub, loosen and remove hub bolt (**A**). Discard bolt.
* Pull hub off crankshaft, sliding it out of timing chain lower sprocket.

> **CAUTION—**
> * Counter hold hub securely. Do not rely on flywheel lock (special tool 11 0 300) to counter hold against crankshaft rotation.

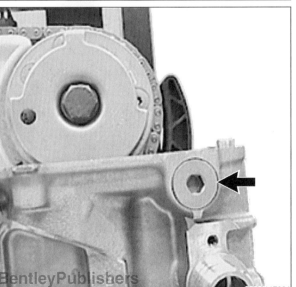

◁ Unscrew plug (**arrow**) at upper left of timing chain housing.

*Camshaft timing chain, removing and installing*

◄ Unscrew plug (**arrow**) at lower right of timing chain housing.

◄ Remove chain guide mounting bolt (**arrow**) at upper left of timing chain housing.

◄ Remove chain tensioning rail mounting bolt (**arrow**) at lower right of timing chain housing.

*Camshaft timing chain, removing and installing*

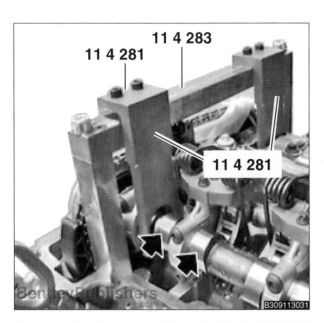

◁ Use BMW special tool set 11 4 280 to lock down camshafts.

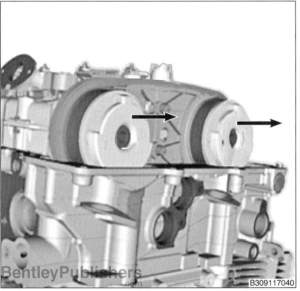

◁ Remove intake and exhaust camshaft adjustment units:

- Loosen and remove adjustment unit mounting bolts. Discard bolts.
- Disengage timing chain from camshaft adjustment unit sprockets.
- Remove adjustment units (**arrows**) and set aside. See **Camshaft adjustment (VANOS) units, removing and installing** in this repair group.

**NOTE** —

- *Illustration does not show special tool set 11 4 280 in place.*

◁ Working at front of cylinder head:

- Remove timing chain assembly mounting bolts (**A**).
- Lift timing chain, timing chain assembly and crankshaft sprocket straight up (**arrow**) out of timing chain housing.

*Camshaft timing chain, removing and installing*

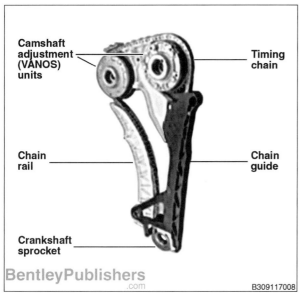

◄ Chain, chain assembly and crankshaft sprocket. Camshaft adjustment (VANOS) units shown installed on assembly for purposes of illustration.

– Disengage timing chain from guide and rail assembly and crankshaft sprocket and fit new chain.

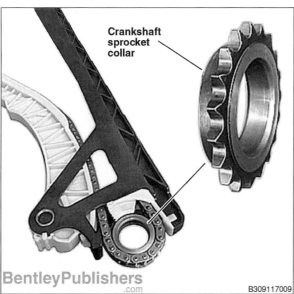

◄ Fit crankshaft sprocket to chain in orientation shown, with collar pointing to engine.

**CAUTION—**
• *Incorrect sprocket assembly results in engine damage.*

◄ Turbo engine: Note that friction plates (**arrows**) are fitted between timing chain sprocket and oil pump drive sprocket.

**CAUTION—**
• *If turbo engine is operated without friction plates, engine damage results.*

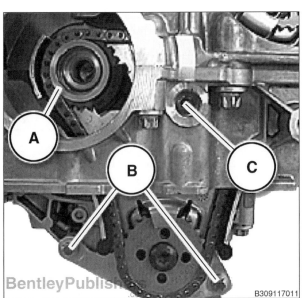

B309117011

B309117012

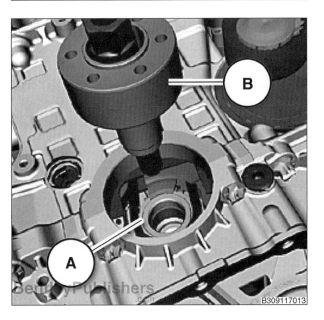

B309117013

◄ Turbo engine: Make sure oil pump drive sprocket friction plate (**A**) is in correct position.

**NOTE**—
• **B** and **C** are oil pump and oil pump chain guide mounting bolts.

– Pull timing chain taut until sprocket engages chain guide. Install timing chain and chain assembly in chain housing in this position, holding chain under tension at all times.

– Install and torque timing chain assembly, rail and guide bolts.

| Tightening torques | |
|---|---|
| Timing chain guide to cylinder head (M7) | 14 Nm (10 ft-lb) |
| Timing chain assembly to cylinder head (M6 x 35 mm Torx) | 8.5 Nm (6 ft-lb) |
| Timing chain rail to crankcase (M8) | 20 Nm (14 ft-lb) |

◄ Turbo engine: Slide friction plate on vibration damper hub shaft prior to inserting hub in crankcase bore.

◄ Line up timing chain and oil pump chain sprockets (**A**) inside crankcase bore, then insert vibration damper hub (**B**), sliding it through chain sprockets. Using new vibration damper bolt, attach hub finger tight to crankshaft.

– To achieve final torque on vibration damper hub, follow one of several alternative procedure steps for preventing crankshaft rotation recommended by BMW.

**CAUTION**—
• Do not rely on flywheel lock (special tool 11 0 300) to counter hold against crankshaft rotation.

*Camshaft timing chain, removing and installing*

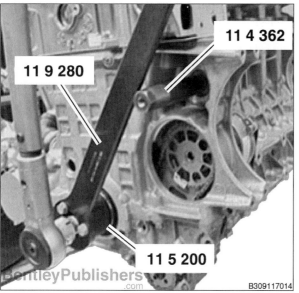

◄ Remove belt tensioner and screw in special tool 11 4 362.

- Bolt special tool 11 5 200 to vibration damper hub.
- Bolt special tool 11 9 280 to tool 11 5 200. Rest tool 11 9 280 against tool 11 4 362.
- Tighten to initial tightening torque.

| Tightening torque | |
|---|---|
| Vibration damper hub to crankshaft<br>• Stage 1 | 100 Nm (74 ft-lb) |

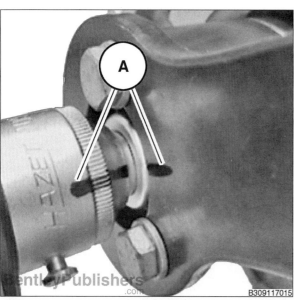

◄ Mark special tool 11 9 280 and socket wrench with paint (**A**).

- Tighten hub bolt to final torque with assistant helping to counter hold tool 11 9 280.

| Tightening torque | |
|---|---|
| Vibration damper hub to crankshaft<br>• Stage 2 | Additional 360° |

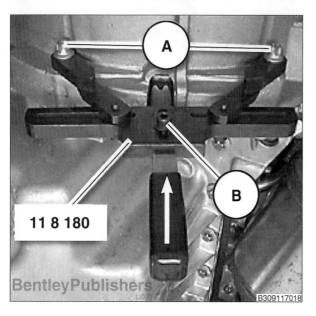

◄ Alternate method for manual transmission vehicle:

- Mount special tool 11 8 180 on transmission using bolts **A**.
- Slide lock handle up (**arrow**) and tighten bolt **B**.

*Camshaft timing chain, removing and installing*

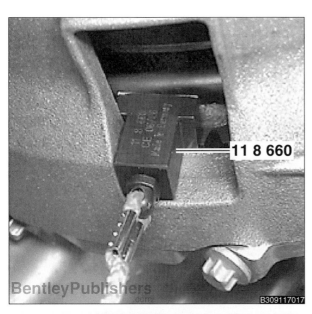

◄ Alternate method for automatic transmission vehicle:

- Secure flywheel with special tool 11 8 660 through transmission bell housing opening.

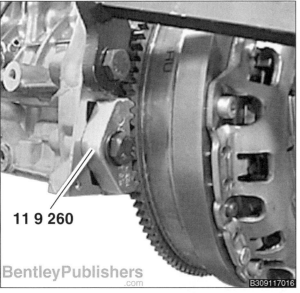

◄ Alternative method if transmission is removed:

- Secure flywheel with special tool 11 9 260.

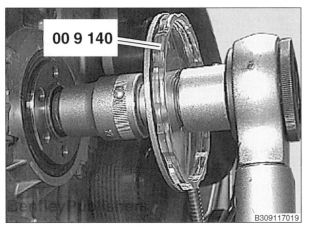

◄ Use angle protractor (BMW special tool 00 9 140 or equivalent) to torque hub bolt.

| Tightening torque | |
|---|---|
| Vibration damper hub to crankshaft<br>• Stage 1<br>• Stage 2 | 100 Nm (74 ft-lb)<br>Additional 360° |

– Install crankshaft front seal. See **119 Lubrication System**.

*Camshaft timing, adjusting*

B309113023

◄ Use new bolts to reattach camshaft adjustment (VANOS) units. Note that exhaust and intake units are different and so marked. Camshaft sensor impulse wheel for intake and exhaust are the same. See **Camshaft adjustment (VANOS) units, removing and installing** in this repair group.

| Tightening torque | |
| --- | --- |
| Camshaft adjustment (VANOS) unit to camshaft (use new M10 x 94 mm bolt): • Stage 1 • Stage 2 | 20 Nm (15 ft-lb) additional 180° |

– Install chain tensioner. See **Timing chain tensioner** in this repair group.

> **CAUTION—**
> • If chain tensioner is reused, drain its oil chamber. Place tensioner on level working surface and compress slowly. Repeat twice.
> • No sealing ring is fitted to chain tensioner at the factory. When reassembling engine, be sure to use new sealing O-ring.

| Tightening torque | |
| --- | --- |
| Timing chain tensioner to cylinder head (M22 x 1.5) (use new sealing O-ring) | 55 Nm (41 ft-lb) |

– Remove crankshaft and camshaft locking tools and rotate engine 2 full revolutions. Then check and, if necessary, reset camshaft timing. See **Camshaft timing, adjusting** in this repair group.

> **CAUTION—**
> • Remove crankshaft and camshaft locking tools before rotating or starting engine.

– Reassemble engine.

## Camshaft timing, adjusting

> **WARNING—**
> • To avoid personal injury, be sure the engine is cold before beginning the procedure.

– Use scan tool to read out and record ECM fault memory.

– Switch ignition OFF and remove key.

– Remove upper and lower cabin microfilter housings. See **640 Heating and Air-conditioning**.

– Remove right strut tower brace.

– Remove ignition coil cover (upper engine cover). See **020 Maintenance**.

– Detach ignition coil connectors. Lift ignition coil harness off cylinder head cover and set aside.

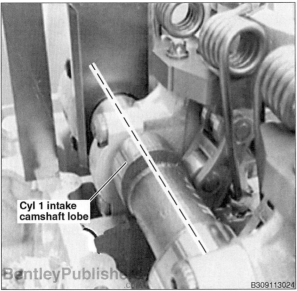

**Cyl 1 intake camshaft lobe**

B309113024

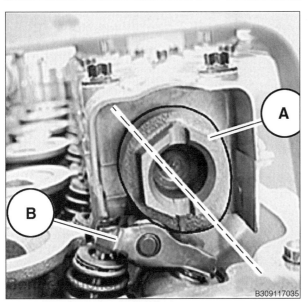

A

B

B309117035

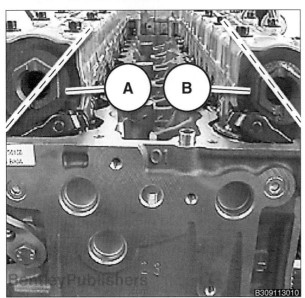

A  B

B309113010

- Remove ignition coils. See **120 Ignition System**.

- Remove cylinder head cover. See **113 Cylinder Head Removal and Installation**.

- Raise vehicle and support safely.

> **WARNING—**
> • *Make sure the vehicle is stable and well supported at all times. Use a professional automotive lift or jack stands designed for the purpose. A floor jack is not adequate support.*

- Remove engine compartment splash shield. See **020 Maintenance**.

◄ Non-turbo engine: Using vibration damper bolt, rotate crankshaft to place cylinder 1 in TDC firing position. In this position, cylinder 1 intake camshaft lobe points upward at an angle (**dashed line**).

◄ Non-turbo engine: Cylinder 1 in TDC firing position: Cylinder 6 exhaust camshaft lobe (**A**) points downward at an angle (**dashed line**). Cam follower (**B**) is not actuated.

> **NOTE—**
> • *Use a mirror to check exhaust camshaft lobe position.*

◄ Turbo engine: Using vibration damper bolt to rotate crankshaft, place cylinder 1 in TDC firing position. In this position, lobes for cylinder 6 (rear of engine) intake and exhaust camshafts (**A**, **B**) point away from each other and down. Cylinder 6 camshaft lobes do not contact roller cam followers.

> **NOTE—**
> • *Use a mirror to check cylinder 6 cam lobe positions.*

*Camshaft timing, adjusting*

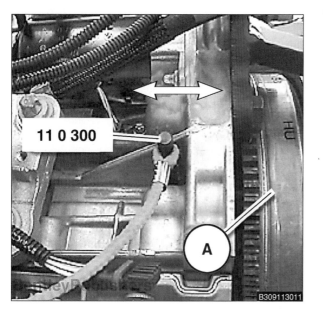

◄ Working underneath engine, slide out protective plug at lower left of engine bell housing flange. Install BMW special tool 11 0 300 (crankshaft locking tool) through bell housing flange port into flywheel (**A**) hole. If necessary, rock flywheel slightly back and forth to line up holes with tool. This locks crankshaft at TDC.

> **CAUTION—**
> - *Models with automatic transmission: In the flywheel (torque plate), a short distance before the bore for TDC position, there is a large bore which can be confused with the special tool bore. If the flywheel is locked using the correct bore, the engine can no longer be rotated at the vibration damper bolt.*
> - *If special tool 11 0 300 does not slide easily into the bell housing flange bore, sand paint off the tool. Do not enlarge the bore.*

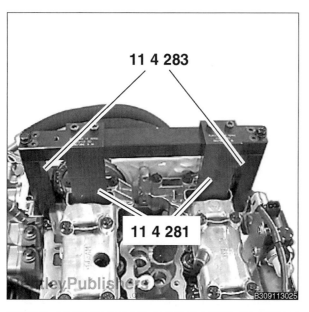

◄ Use BMW special tool set 11 4 280 to lock down camshafts.

− With crankshaft locked, if special tool 11 4 281 fits, camshaft timing is correct. Remove special tools and reassemble engine.

− If special tool 11 4 281 does not fit, use hexagon casting at rear of camshafts to rotate camshafts until tool fits. Proceed with camshaft timing procedure below.

◄ Working at front of camshafts:
- Loosen exhaust and intake camshaft adjustment (VANOS) unit mounting bolts (**A**, **B**).
- Discard bolts and replace with new.
- Tighten bolts finger tight.

 Install BMW special tool 11 8 520.

- Place tool up against camshaft adjustment unit sensor gears.
- Rotate sensor gears (**arrows**) until locating pins on tool line up with bores in sensor gears.
- Push tool firmly against sensor gears and lock down with M6 x 45 mm bolts (**A**).

◀ Working at front of cylinder head:

- Remove timing chain tensioner (**A**). Be prepared to catch dripping oil. Do not allow oil to contaminate accessory belt.
- Screw BMW special tool 11 9 340 (dummy chain tensioner) into cylinder head.
- Using BMW special tool 00 9 250 (low torque torque-wrench), rotate stud of special tool 11 9 340 to pretension timing chain to 0.6 Nm (5.3 in-lb).
- Tighten camshaft adjustment (VANOS) unit mounting bolts (**B**).

| Tightening torque | |
|---|---|
| Camshaft adjustment (VANOS) unit to camshaft: <br> • Stage 1 <br> • Stage 2 | 20 Nm (15 ft-lb) <br> additional 180° |

– Remove special tools and assemble engine. Reinstall chain tensioner using new sealing O-ring. See **Timing chain tensioner** in this repair group.

| Tightening torque | |
|---|---|
| Timing chain tensioner to cylinder head (M22 x 1.5) (use new sealing O-ring) | 55 Nm (41 ft-lb) |

## Timing chain tensioner

The timing chain tensioner is screwed into the right front of the cylinder head. When it is removed be sure to catch any dripping oil in a shop towel. Do not allow oil to contaminate accessory belt.

◀ If chain tensioner is reused, drain its oil chamber. Place tensioner vertically on level working surface and compress slowly (**arrow**). Repeat twice.

> **CAUTION—**
> • *No sealing ring is fitted to chain tensioner at the factory. When reassembling engine, be sure to use new sealing O-ring.*

| Tightening torque | |
|---|---|
| Timing chain tensioner to cylinder head (M22 x 1.5) (use new sealing O-ring) | 55 Nm (41 ft-lb) |

# CAMSHAFT ADJUSTMENT (VANOS) UNITS

## Camshaft adjustment (VANOS) units, removing and installing

Special tools and procedures are required to remove and install camshaft adjustment (VANOS) units and to time camshafts. Read the entire procedure before beginning repairs.

> **WARNING** —
> • To avoid personal injury, be sure the engine is cold before beginning the procedure.

> **CAUTION** —
> • Disassembly, removal and assembly of camshaft adjustment (VANOS) units without special tools poses the risk of damage or breakage: Valves may be bent by contact with the piston crowns.
> • Throughout this procedure, unless otherwise specified, crankshaft and camshafts remain locked against rotation using BMW special tools.
> • Keep VANOS components free of silicone sealant. A small amount of silicone introduced into VANOS actuator or solenoid can set faults.

— Use scan tool to read out and record ECM fault memory.

— Switch ignition OFF and remove key.

— Remove upper and lower cabin microfilter housings. See **640 Heating and Air-conditioning**.

— Remove right strut tower brace.

— Remove ignition coil cover (upper engine cover). See **020 Maintenance**.

— Detach ignition coil connectors. Lift ignition coil harness off cylinder head cover and set aside.

— Remove ignition coils. See **120 Ignition System**.

— Remove cylinder head cover. See **113 Cylinder Head Removal and Installation**.

— Raise vehicle and support safely.

> **WARNING** —
> • Make sure the vehicle is stable and well supported at all times. Use a professional automotive lift or jack stands designed for the purpose. A floor jack is not adequate support.

— Remove engine compartment splash shield. See **020 Maintenance**.

◄ Non-turbo engine: Using vibration damper bolt, rotate crankshaft to place cylinder 1 in TDC firing position. In this position, cylinder 1 intake camshaft lobe points upward at an angle.

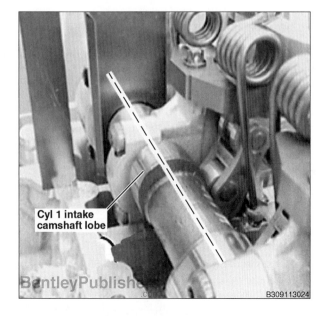

**Cyl 1 intake camshaft lobe**

*Camshaft adjustment (VANOS) units, removing and installing*

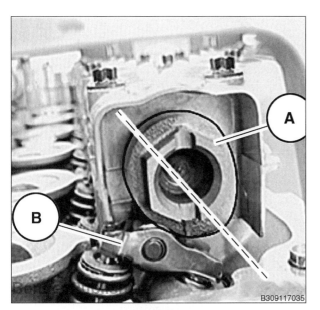

◀ Non-turbo engine: Cylinder 1 in TDC firing position: Cylinder 6 exhaust camshaft lobe (**A**) points downward at an angle (**dashed line**). Cam follower (**B**) is not actuated.

*NOTE* —

• *Use a mirror to check exhaust camshaft lobe position.*

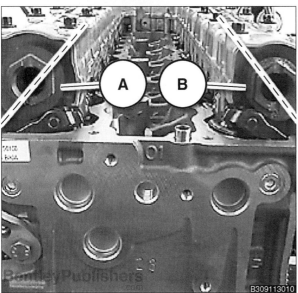

◀ Turbo engine: Using vibration damper bolt to rotate crankshaft, place cylinder 1 in TDC firing position. In this position, lobes for cylinder 6 (rear of engine) intake and exhaust camshafts (**A**, **B**) point away from each other and down. Cylinder 6 camshaft lobes do not contact roller cam followers.

*NOTE* —

• *Use a mirror to check cylinder 6 cam lobe positions.*

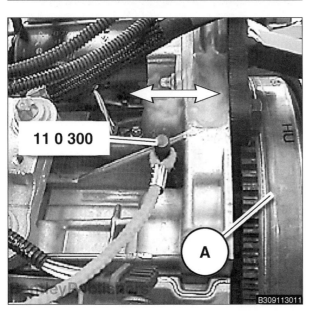

◀ Working underneath engine, slide out protective plug at lower left of engine bell housing flange. Install BMW special tool 11 0 300 (crankshaft locking tool) through bell housing flange port into flywheel (**A**) hole. If necessary, rock flywheel slightly back and forth to line up holes with tool. This locks crankshaft at TDC.

**CAUTION**—

• *Models with automatic transmission: In the flywheel (torque plate), a short distance before the bore for TDC position, there is a large bore which can be confused with the special tool bore. If the flywheel is locked using the correct bore, the engine can no longer be rotated at the vibration damper bolt.*

• *If special tool 11 0 300 does not slide easily into the bell housing flange bore, sand paint off the tool. Do not enlarge the bore.*

*Camshaft adjustment (VANOS) units, removing and installing*

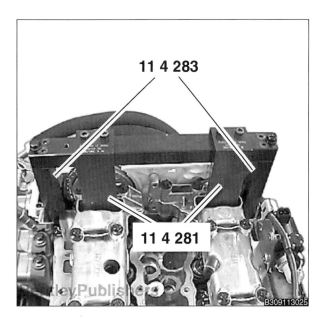

◄ Use BMW special tool set 11 4 280 to lock down camshafts.

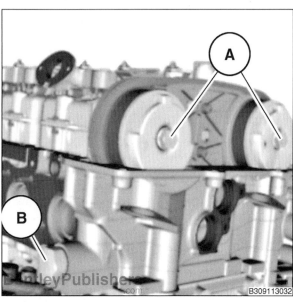

◄ Working at right front of cylinder head, remove timing chain tensioner (**B**). Be prepared to catch dripping oil with a shop towel. Do not allow oil to contaminate accessory belt.

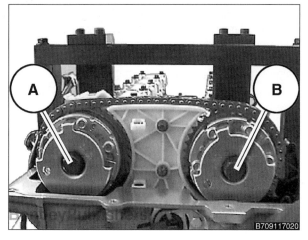

◄ Working at front of camshafts:

- Loosen and remove exhaust and intake camshaft adjustment (VANOS) unit mounting bolts (**A**, **B**). Discard bolts.
- Disengage timing chain from camshaft adjustment unit sprockets.
- Tilt adjustment units down to remove.

*Camshaft adjustment (VANOS) units, removing and installing*

◄ Use new bolts to reattach camshaft adjustment (VANOS) units.

- Note that exhaust and intake units are different and so marked.
- Camshaft sensor impulse wheel for intake and exhaust are the same.
- Adjustment units and sensor wheels may be installed in any position initially. Finger-tighten mounting bolts for now.

◄ Press chain into chain tensioner rail (**arrow**) by hand to make sure it is routed correctly. (Chain assembly and camshaft adjustment units shown removed from engine for purpose of illustration.)

− Adjust camshaft timing. See **Camshaft timing, adjusting** in this repair group. Then torque adjustment unit mounting bolts.

| Tightening torque | |
|---|---|
| Camshaft adjustment (VANOS) unit to camshaft (use new M10 x 94 mm bolt):<br>• Stage 1<br>• Stage 2 | <br><br>20 Nm (15 ft-lb)<br>additional 180° |

− Install chain tensioner. See **Timing chain tensioner** in this repair group.

> **CAUTION—**
> - *If chain tensioner is reused, drain its oil chamber. Place tensioner on level working surface and compress slowly. Repeat twice.*
> - *No sealing ring is fitted to chain tensioner at the factory. When reassembling engine, be sure to use new sealing O-ring.*

| Tightening torque | |
|---|---|
| Timing chain tensioner to cylinder head (M22 x 1.5) (use new sealing O-ring) | 55 Nm (41 ft-lb) |

− Reassemble engine.

> **CAUTION—**
> - *Remove crankshaft and camshaft locking tools before rotating or starting engine.*

# 119 Lubrication System

**119**

## GENERAL

This repair group covers lubrication system troubleshooting and crankshaft seal replacement. Oil pan removal and oil pump replacement are not covered in this manual.

See also:

• **020 Maintenance** for oil and oil filter change

• **100 Engine–General** for oil pump drive chain diagrams

### Engine lubricant

| Engine oil specification for N51, N52, N52KP or N54 engine | |
|---|---|
| BMW long-life rating (LL-01) synthetic oils for US market:<br>• Castrol Syntec European Formula SAE 0W - 30<br>• Mobil 1 SAE 0W - 40<br>• Pennzoil Platinum European Formula Ultra<br>  SAE 5W - 30<br>• Valvoline SynPower SAE 5W - 30 | API<br>rating<br>SM<br>or higher |

| Engine oil capacity | |
|---|---|
| 6-cylinder engines: N51, N52, N52KP, N54 | 6.5 liters (6.9 US qt) |

### Engine lubrication

◀ To meet the oiling requirements of 3 Series 6-cylinder engines, a chain-driven volumetric-flow controlled oil pump is utilized. The VANOS system requires a large volume of oil, particularly at low engine speeds.

The volumetric-flow controlled pump design allows:

• Increased power output

• Reduced weight

• Optimized fuel consumption

• Reduced exhaust emissions

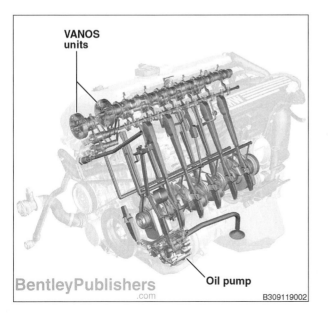

VANOS units

Oil pump

B309119002

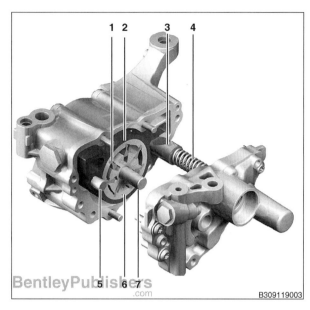

B309119003

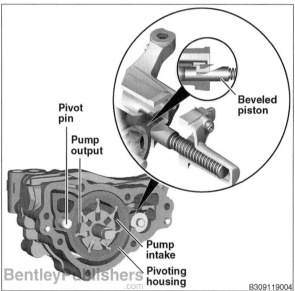

B309119004

## Engine oil pump

1. Sliding vane valve
2. Pivoting rotor housing
3. Beveled control piston
4. Compression spring
5. Pivot pin
6. Rotor
7. Pump shaft

The volumetric-flow controlled oil pump delivers only as much oil as is necessary. No surplus quantities of oil are delivered in low load operating ranges. This reduces the fuel consumption of the engine and slows down the oil wear rate.

The pump is designed with sliding vane valves. The pump shaft and rotor are positioned off-center in the pivoting rotor housing and the vanes are displaced radially during rotation. The vanes form chambers of differing volume depending on the position of the rotor housing.

◀ When the pump rotates, oil pressure acts on the control piston against the force of the compression spring. The beveled piston varies the position of the pivoting housing.

When the housing is centered on the rotor, changes in intake and output chamber volumes are small: Delivered oil volume is low. When the rotor housing is off-center in relation to the rotor, changes in input and output chamber volumes are greater: Delivered oil volume is high.

When the oil volume required by the engine increases, for example during VANOS operation, oil pressure in the lubricating system drops, reducing pressure on the beveled piston. In response, the compression spring presses the beveled piston against the pivoting housing control dog, forcing the housing further off-center and increasing oil volume. The opposite occurs as engine oil pressure increases and the need for delivered oil volume drops.

## Warnings and Cautions

**WARNING—**
- *Due to risk of personal injury, be sure the engine is cold before beginning work on engine components.*

**CAUTION—**
- *Prior to disconnecting the battery, read the battery disconnection cautions in **001 Warnings and Cautions**.*
- *To avoid electrochemical corrosion to engine components made of aluminum-magnesium alloy, do not use steel fasteners. Use aluminum fasteners only. For reliable identification, the end faces of aluminum fasteners are painted blue.*
- *Replace aluminum bolts each time they are loosened.*
- *Follow torque instructions, including angle of rotation specifications, when installing aluminum fasteners.*
- *Cover alternator with shop towel to protect from oil drips.*

## OIL PRESSURE WARNING SYSTEM

**CAUTION—**

• *If the red oil pressure warning light comes on or flashes on while driving, assume that the oil pressure is low. Stop the engine immediately and make arrangements to test oil pressure.*

## Oil pressure, checking

Test oil pressure by removing oil pressure switch and installing oil pressure gauge in its place.

— Loosen oil filter cover to allow engine oil to drain back down into oil pan. Tighten cover.

◀ Detach harness connector (**arrow**) from oil pressure switch. If necessary, remove ignition coil cover. See **020 Maintenance**.

— Remove switch. Be prepared to catch leaking oil with a shop towel.

**CAUTION—**

• *Thoroughly clean around the oil pressure switch before removing it.*

— Install pressure gauge in place of oil pressure switch. If necessary, use BMW special adapter 11 4 050 in place of oil pressure switch.

— With gauge installed, start engine and allow to reach operating temperature. Check oil pressure. See **Table a**.

**NOTE—**

• *For the most accurate test results, make sure the engine oil and filter are new and the oil of the correct grade.*

| Table a. Engine oil pressure | |
|---|---|
| At idle, engine at operating temperature | 1.5 bar (22 psi) |
| Maximum regulated pressure, engine at operating temperature | 4.0 - 6.0 bar (58 - 87 psi) |

— Remove pressure gauge and reinstall pressure switch with new sealing washer.

| Tightening torque | |
|---|---|
| Oil pressure switch to oil filter housing (M12 x 1.5) • Stage 1 • Stage 2 | 20 Nm (15 ft-lb) additional 16° |

If testing shows low oil pressure, one or more of the following conditions may be indicated:

- Worn or faulty oil pump or faulty pump pressure relief valve
- Worn or damaged engine bearings
- Severe engine wear

Any of these conditions indicate the need for major repairs.

## Oil pressure switch, replacing

— Loosen oil filter cover to allow engine oil to drain back down into oil pan. Tighten cover.

◀ Detach harness connector (**arrow**) from oil pressure switch. If necessary, remove ignition coil cover. See **020 Maintenance**.

— Remove switch. Be prepared to catch leaking oil with a shop towel.

> **CAUTION—**
> - *Thoroughly clean around the oil pressure switch before removing it.*

— Install new pressure switch with new sealing washer.

| Tightening torque | |
|---|---|
| Oil pressure switch to oil filter housing (M12 x 1.5) | |
| • Stage 1 | 20 Nm (15 ft-lb) |
| • Stage 2 | additional 16° |

## OIL CONDITION MONITORING

### Oil condition sensor (OZS)

◀ There is no oil dipstick. The engine oil level is measured by the oil condition sensor (OZS) and indicated in the instrument cluster or central information display. Engine oil temperature and condition are also monitored by the OZS.

Oil condition information is processed by the engine control module (ECM), then routed via PT-CAN and K-CAN buses to the instrument cluster and central information display. The ECM uses condition based service (CBS) software to determine optimal oil change interval.

Checking oil level is covered in **020 Maintenance**.

Oil filter cover

B309119012

Oil condition sensor (OZS)

B309119005

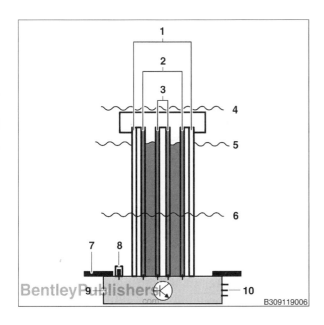

B309119006

## OZS operation

1. Housing
2. Outer metal tube
3. Inner metal tube
4. Engine oil (maximum)
5. Engine oil (average)
6. Engine oil (minimum)
7. Oil pan
8. Oil temperature sensor
9. Sensor electronics
10. Sensor connector

OZS consists of two cylindrical capacitors arranged one above the other. Oil condition is determined by the lower, smaller capacitor. Two metal tubes (**1**, **2**), arranged one inside the other, serve as capacitor electrodes. The dielectric is the engine oil between the electrodes. The electrical property of engine oil changes with age and break-down of oil additives, changing the OZS capacitance. This change is processed in the sensor electronics (**9**) and converted to a digital signal. The digital sensor signal is transferred to the ECM, which uses it to calculate the next oil change service due.

Engine oil level is determined in the upper part of the OZS. As oil level drops, sensor capacitance changes accordingly. This change is processed in the sensor electronics (**9**) and converted to a digital signal. The digital sensor signal is transferred to the ECM and displayed to the driver.

A platinum temperature sensor (**8**) is installed at the base of the oil condition sensor.

Engine oil level, temperature and condition are monitored continuously as long as voltage is applied at terminal 15 (ignition ON). OZS is powered via terminal 87.

## OZS fault evaluation

OZS electronic circuitry features a self-diagnosis function. In case of a fault in the sensor, an error message is sent to the ECM. The fault can be viewed using a BMW scan tool or equivalent.

## OZS, replacing

− Raise vehicle and support safely.

> **WARNING** —
> • *Make sure the vehicle is stable and well supported at all times. Use a professional automotive lift or jack stands designed for the purpose. A floor jack is not adequate support.*

− Remove splash shield underneath engine. See **020 Maintenance**.

− Drain engine oil. See **020 Maintenance**.

*Crankshaft front seal, removing and installing*

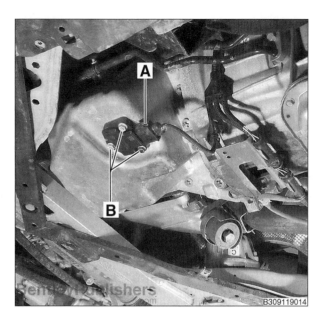

◄ With engine fully cooled off, disconnect OZS electrical connector (**A**) and remove mounting nuts (**B**). Lower level sensor. Be prepared to catch dripping oil.

– When reinstalling, replace sealing O-ring.

| Tightening torque | |
|---|---|
| OZS to oil pan | |
| • Stage 1 | 2 Nm (18 lb-in) |
| • Stage 2 | 8.5 Nm (75 lb-in) |

– Refill engine with oil and check for leaks after work is completed.

## CRANKSHAFT SEALS

### Crankshaft front seal, removing and installing

> **WARNING**—
> • To avoid personal injury, be sure the engine is cold before beginning the procedure.

> **CAUTION**—
> • When the crankshaft seal is replaced, its grooves and crankcase seams are filled with special Loctite® sealant to avoid oil leaks. Be sure to read the entire procedure before starting work.

– Raise vehicle and support safely.

> **WARNING**—
> • Make sure the vehicle is stable and well supported at all times. Use a professional automotive lift or jack stands designed for the purpose. A floor jack is not adequate support.

– Remove splash shield underneath engine. See **020 Maintenance**.

– Remove engine accessory belt. See **020 Maintenance**.

– Remove vibration damper (front pulley). See **117 Camshaft Timing Chain**.

> **CAUTION**—
> • Do not remove vibration damper hub bolt. If this bolt is removed, the timing chain drive sprocket becomes free to rotate, resulting in valve damage.

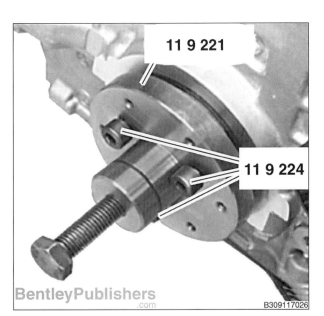

◄ Place BMW special tool 11 9 221 against vibration damper hub and tighten down using bolts (special tool 11 9 224). This pushes crankshaft seal inward approx. 1 mm, thus loosening it for subsequent removal.

| Tightening torque | |
|---|---|
| Special tool 11 9 221 to vibration damper hub | 20 Nm (15 ft-lb) |

– Remove special tools.

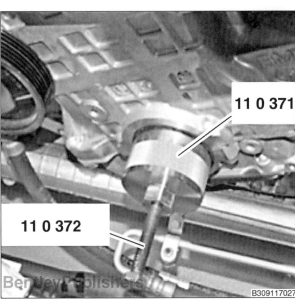

◄ Screw BMW special tool 11 0 371 into crankshaft seal with approx. 80 Nm (59 ft-lb) of torque. Then rotate special tool 11 0 371 clockwise to pull out seal. Repeat process if necessary.

◄ Carefully saw seal at **dashed line** and peel off tool.

*Crankshaft front seal, removing and installing*

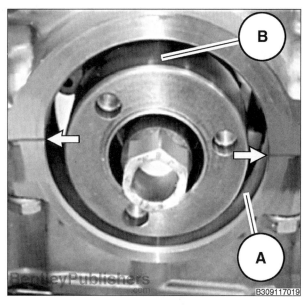

◄ Working at crankcase opening:

- Clean crankshaft seal seating surface (**A**).
- Degrease thoroughly area around crankcase seam (**arrows**).
- Lightly oil sealing surface (**B**) on vibration damper hub.

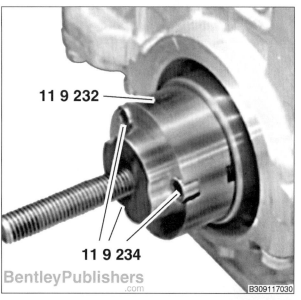

◄ Attach BMW special tool 11 9 232 to vibration damper hub using bolts (special tool 11 9 234).

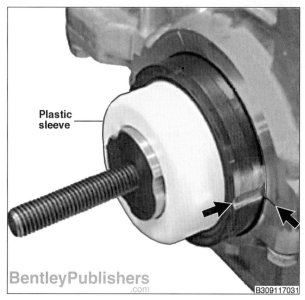

◄ Place crankshaft seal and installation sleeve over tool and against crankcase opening.

- Plastic sleeve is supplied with seal and is used as installation guide sleeve.
- Make sure seal grooves center on crankcase seam (**arrows**).
- Coat both grooves on seal with Loctite® 171000 (primer). Allow to dry for approx. 1 minute.

*Crankshaft front seal, removing and installing*

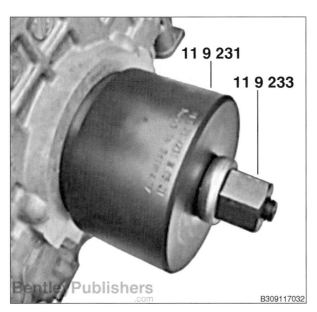

◀ Use BMW special tools 11 9 231 and 11 9 233 to press in seal.

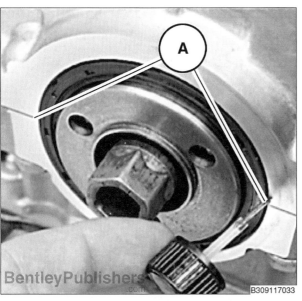

◀ Use brush to coat seal grooves and crankcase seams (**A**) with Loctite® 171000 (primer).

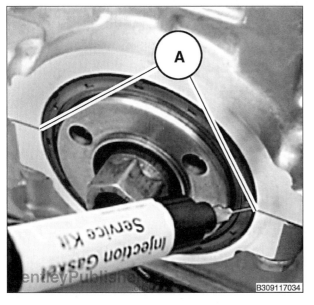

◀ Use injector kit to fill seal grooves and crankcase seams (**A**) with Loctite® 128357 (sealant).

– Coat sealed areas with Loctite® 171000 (primer) to bind sealant.

– Reinstall crankshaft vibration damper.

| Tightening torque | |
|---|---|
| Vibration damper to vibration damper hub (M8 x 16 mm Torx) | 35 Nm (26 ft-lb) |

– Remainder of assembly is reverse of disassembly.

## Crankshaft rear main seal, removing and installing

Crankshaft rear main seal (flywheel seal) replacement requires removal of the transmission and flywheel.

> **CAUTION—**
> - When the crankshaft seal is replaced, its grooves and crankcase seams are filled with special Loctite® sealant to avoid oil leaks. Be sure to read the entire procedure before starting work.

— Remove transmission. See **230 Manual Transmission** or **240 Automatic Transmission**.

— Manual transmission vehicles: Remove clutch pressure plate and disc. See **210 Clutch**.

— Remove flywheel. See **210 Clutch** or **240 Automatic Transmission**.

— Drain engine oil.

◄ Crankshaft rear main seal has six removal openings (**inset**). If necessary, scrape off rubber coating to expose openings.

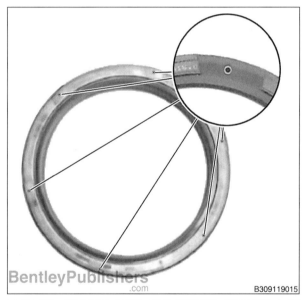

B309119015

◄ Fit BMW seal puller, special tool 11 9 200, to seal.
- Insert sheet metal screws (**arrows**) into seal removal openings. Tighten snugly but do not overtighten.
- Screw in seal remover spindle (**A**) slowly to pull out seal.

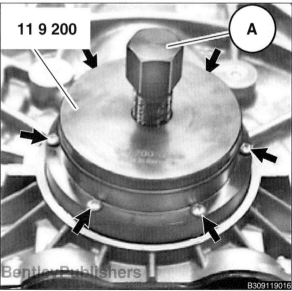

B309119016

*Crankshaft rear main seal, removing and installing*

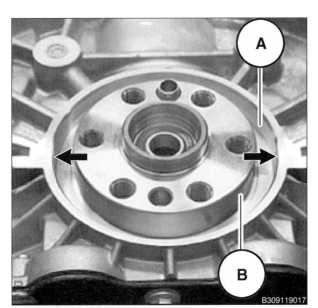

◄ Before installing new seal:

- Clean seal seating surface (**A**).
- Degrease crankcase seams (**arrows**) thoroughly.
- Apply light coal of engine oil to seal lip running surface (**B**) on crankshaft flange.

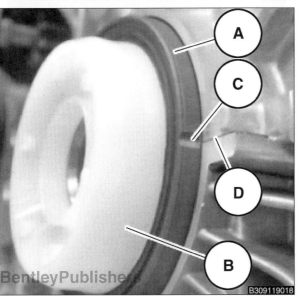

◄ Place crankshaft seal (**A**) and installation sleeve (**B**) against crankcase opening.

> **CAUTION—**
> - *Do not kink or damage the sealing lip. Do not touch with fingers.*

- Plastic installation sleeve is supplied with seal and is used as installation guide sleeve.
- Make sure seal grooves (**C**) center on crankcase seams (**D**).
- Coat both grooves on seal with Loctite® 171000 (primer). Allow to dry for approx. 1 minute.
- Press in seal as far as possible by hand, then remove installation sleeve.

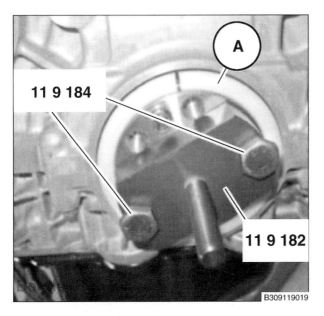

◄ Fit BMW special tools 11 9 182 and 11 9 184 to crankshaft flange.

- Fit spacer ring (**A**) over seal. Spacer ring is supplied with seal.

*Crankshaft rear main seal, removing and installing*

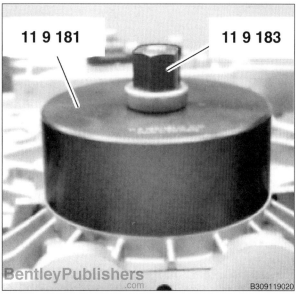

 Use BMW special tools 11 9 181 and 11 9 183 to press in seal.

− Remove special tools and spacer ring.

◄ Use brush to coat seal grooves and crankcase seams (**A**) with Loctite® 171000 (primer).

◄ Use injector kit to fill seal grooves and crankshaft seams (**A**) with Loctite® 128357 (sealant).

− Coat sealed areas with Loctite® 171000 (primer) to bind sealant.

− Remainder of assembly is reverse of disassembly.

• Install flywheel, clutch or torque converter and transmission.

• Fill engine with oil.

• Run engine and check for leaks.

# 120 Ignition System

120

## GENERAL

This repair group covers ignition component troubleshooting and replacement.

See also:

- **020 Maintenance** for spark plug replacement
- **100 Engine–General** for engine applications
- **130 Fuel Injection** for DME system applications, description and power supply fuses
- **ECL Electrical Component Locations**
- **ELE Electrical Wiring Diagrams**
- **OBD On-Board Diagnostics**

## Ignition firing order

| Table a. Firing order | |
|---|---|
| 6-cylinder engine | 1-5-3-6-2-4 |

◄ Cylinder 1 is at the front of the engine.

## Disabling ignition system

The ignition system operates in a lethal voltage range. Disable the ignition system any time engine service or repair work is being done that requires the ignition to be switched ON.

One way of disabling the ignition is by removing the DME main relay. The relay is located in the electronics box (E-box) in the right rear of the engine compartment. DME fuse, relay and power supply information is in **130 Fuel Injection**.

> *CAUTION—*
> * *Relay locations vary. Use care when identifying relays. See* **ECL Electrical Component Locations**.

## Warnings and Cautions

> *WARNING —*
> * *Do not touch or disconnect any cables from the ignition coils while the engine is running or being cranked by the starter.*
> * *The ignition system produces high voltages that can be fatal. Avoid contact with exposed terminals. Use extreme caution when working on a car with the ignition switched ON or the engine running.*
> * *Connect and disconnect the DME system wiring and test equipment leads when the ignition is OFF.*
> * *Before operating the starter without starting the engine (for example when testing compression), disable the ignition. See* **Disabling ignition system** *in this repair group.*

**CAUTION—**

- *Do not attempt to disable the ignition by removing the coils from the spark plugs.*

- *Do not connect any test equipment that delivers a 12-volt power supply to terminal 15 (+) of the ignition coil. The current flow may damage the engine control module (ECM). Connect test equipment only as specified by BMW or the equipment maker.*

- *Connect or disconnect ignition system wires, multiple wire connectors and ignition test equipment leads only while the ignition is OFF. Switch multimeter functions or measurement ranges with test probes disconnected.*

- *Do not disconnect the battery while the engine is running.*

- *Prior to disconnecting the battery cables, read the battery disconnection cautions in* **001 Warnings and Cautions**.

- *Wait at least 1 minute after switching the ignition OFF before removing the ECM connector. If the connector is removed before this time, residual power in the system relay may damage the control module.*

- *Use a digital multimeter for electrical tests. Use an LED test light for quick tests.*

- *To avoid electrochemical corrosion to engine components made of aluminum-magnesium alloy, do not use steel fasteners in place of aluminum. For reliable identification, the end faces of aluminum fasteners are painted blue.*

- *Replace aluminum bolts each time they are loosened.*

- *Follow torque instructions, including angle of rotation specifications, when installing aluminum fasteners.*

## DIGITAL MOTOR ELECTRONICS (DME) IGNITION SYSTEM

BMW E90 models are equipped with digital motor electronics (DME), also known as Motronic. In these systems, fuel injection and ignition are controlled by an integrated engine control module (ECM). Application information for DME systems is in **Table b**.

Most DME functions are described in **130 Fuel Injection**. In the topics that follow, functions that are traditionally associated with ignition are given fuller treatment.

| Table b. E90 engine management applications | | | |
|---|---|---|---|
| **Year, model** | **Engine code** | **Engine management** | **Features** |
| **2006** | | | |
| Sedan: 325i, 325xi Sport Wagon: 325xi Sedan: 330i, 330xi | N52 | Siemens MSV70 | Valvetronic, VANOS |
| **2007-2008** | | | |
| Sedan, Sport Wagon, Coupe, Convertible: 328i, 328xi (automatic transmission) | N51 | Siemens MSV80 SULEV II | Valvetronic, VANOS |
| Sedan, Sport Wagon: 328i, 328xi | N52KP | Siemens MSV70 | Valvetronic, VANOS |
| Coupe, Convertible: 328i, 328xi | N52KP | Siemens MSV80 | Valvetronic, VANOS |
| Sedan: 335i, 335xi Coupe: 335i Coupe: 335xi (2008 only) Convertible: 335i | N54 | Siemens MSD80/MSD81 | VANOS |
| **2009-2010** | | | |
| Sedan, Sport Wagon, Coupe, Convertible: 328i, 328xi (automatic transmission) | N51 | Siemens MSV80 SULEV II | Valvetronic, VANOS |
| Sedan, Coupe: 328i, 328xi Convertible: 328i Sport Wagon: 328i, 328xi | N52KP | Siemens MSV80 ULEV II | Valvetronic, VANOS |
| Sedan, Coupe: 335i, 335xi Convertible: 335i | N54 | Siemens MSD81 ULEV II | VANOS |

## Ignition coils

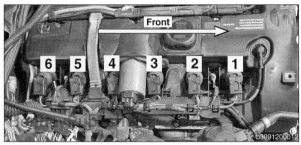

◀ E90 engines use a distributorless ignition system with individual ignition coils (**numbered**) for each cylinder. There is no distributor cap or ignition rotor. (N52 engine shown in photo.)

**120**

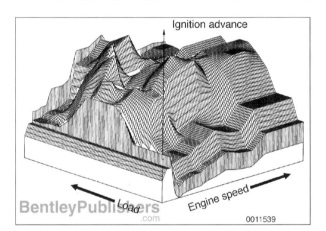

◀ Each coil is separately controlled and monitored by the ECM.

When the ignition is switched ON, the ECM receives wake-up (KL 15w) via the bus network and a hardwire KL15 wake-up signal directly from the car access system (CAS). It will then energize the ECM main relay to supply power to the engine electronics fuse carrier and to the ignition coils.

> **CAUTION—**
> • *Maintain a high level of cleanliness when servicing ignition coils. Fuel / oil residue can cause a breakdown the electrical resistance qualities of silicone used in production. This in turn can result in a failure of the ignition coil.*

◀ Ignition timing is electronically mapped and not adjustable. The ECM uses engine load, engine speed, coolant temperature, knock detection, and intake air temperature as the basic inputs for timing control.

A three-dimensional map similar to the one shown is digitally stored in the ECM. The initial ignition point is determined by the crankshaft sensor during cranking. Once the engine is running, the ECM refers to the stored map to continually adjust ignition timing based on operating conditions.

## Crankshaft sensor

The crankshaft sensor detects crankshaft position and rotation speed via a toothed pulse wheel mounted on flywheel. If the ECM does not receive an impulse signal from the crankshaft sensor during cranking, the engine does not start. If the OBD II system misfire detection protocol detects a catalyst damaging fault due to a malfunction in crankshaft sensor components, the malfunction indicator light (MIL) is illuminated.

The crankshaft position sensor is supplied 12 volts from the engine electronics fuses and ground from the ECM. It produces a 5 volt square wave signal to the ECM.

◄ Crankshaft sensor (**arrow**) is at left rear of cylinder block below starter.

The crankshaft sensor is also referred to as engine speed / reference sensor.

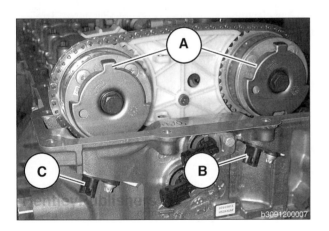

b3091200006

## Camshaft sensors

◄ Each camshaft sensor responds to an impulse wheel (**A**) mounted at the end of the camshaft. The signal from camshaft sensors are used by the ECM for cylinder recognition, spark timing, sequential fuel injection, VANOS (camshaft timing) and Valvetronic (variable valve lift) control. If a fault with the camshaft sensor is detected the malfunction indicator light (MIL) is illuminated

The camshaft position sensor is supplied 12 volts from the engine electronics fuses and ground from the ECM. It produces a 5 volt square wave signal to the ECM.

Intake camshaft sensor (**B**): Left front of cylinder head.

Exhaust camshaft sensor (**C**): Right front of cylinder head.

The camshaft sensor is also called the cylinder identification sensor.

*NOTE* —

• *A malfunctioning or sticking VANOS solenoid may set camshaft position sensor fault codes. If you suspect this, swap VANOS solenoid from bank with fault code to the other bank. If the camshaft position sensor fault code follows the location of the solenoid, the solenoid is at fault.*

b3091200007

## Knock sensors

Knock sensors monitor the combustion chamber for engine-damaging knock. A knock sensor is a piezoelectric microphone tuned to the frequencies of engine knock or detonation. If engine knock is detected, ignition spark is retarded by the ECM. If a fault with the knock sensor is detected the malfunction indicator light (MIL) is illuminated

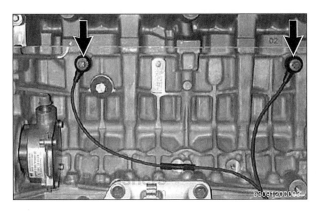

 Knock sensors are bolted to left side of cylinder block under intake manifold (**arrows**). They share an electrical connector and have to be replaced as a pair.

**120**

## TROUBLESHOOTING

### On-board diagnostics

◀ If faults arise, or if the malfunction indicator light (MIL) is illuminated, begin troubleshooting by connecting BMW scan tool or equivalent to the data link connector (DLC or OBD II plug). For information on how to access diagnostic trouble codes (DTCs), see **020 Maintenance**.

### Misfire detection

Engine misfire in one or more cylinders may be caused by malfunctions in various subsystems. The OBD II system incorporated into the engine management systems is designed to detect and warn of misfire faults during engine operation. See **OBD On-Board Diagnostics.**

> *WARNING—*
> * *Ignition misfires can cause high hydrocarbon exhaust emissions and catalytic converter damage. For this reason, if a severe misfire is detected, the fuel injector to the specific cylinder is switched OFF and the MIL is illuminated. A misfire may also overheat the catalytic converter(s), a fire hazard.*

### Oscilloscope diagnostic diagrams

One way to diagnose faulty engine management components or functions is to use an oscilloscope to analyze spark quality with the engine running.

See **Table c** for a list of common ignition coil voltage faults and related causes.

| Table c. Ignition secondary voltage diagnostics | | |
|---|---|---|
| | Secondary voltage low | Secondary voltage high |
| Spark plug electrode gap | Too small | Too big |
| Spark plug electrode condition | | Worn/burnt |
| Spark plug electrode temperature | Too high | Too low |
| Engine compression | Too low | Too high |
| Spark plug wires | | Faulty |
| Fuel air mixture | | Too lean |

◀ Normal scope trace of spark at idle

1. Start of ignition voltage peak
2. Level of ignition voltage
3. Level of combustion voltage
4. Period of combustion
5. Combustion curve characteristics
6. Start of spark decay
7. Termination oscillations

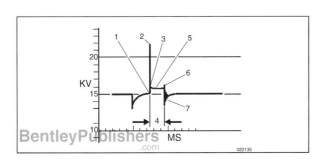

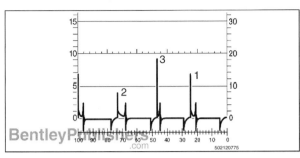

◄ Ignition spark at idle speed

1. Normal ignition voltage peak: Good spark plug
2. Low voltage peak: Closed plug gap
3. High voltage peak: Open plug gap

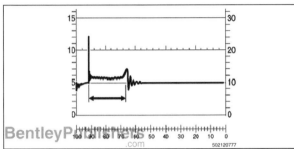

◄ Long combustion period: Small spark plug gap

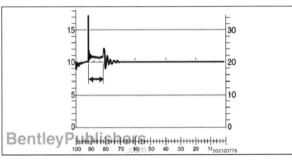

◄ Short combustion period: Large spark plug gap

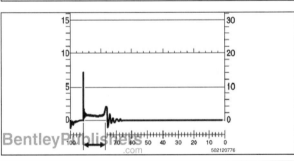

◄ Normal combustion period at idle

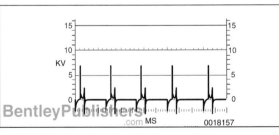

◄ Normal oscilloscope pattern for ignition system at idle

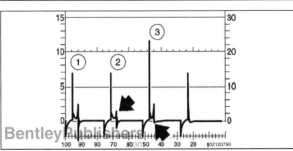

◄ Ignition voltage peaks at idle

1. Normal ignition peaks
2. Downward peak (**arrow**) shortened: Ignition coil defective
3. Downward peak (**arrow**) missing completely: Ignition coil defective

*Oscilloscope diagnostic diagrams*

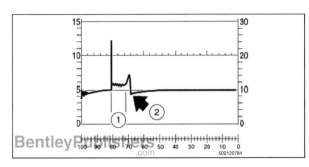

◁ Defective ignition coil
1. Short spark period
2. Spark voltage line (**arrow**) with very slight drop

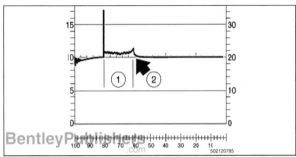

◁ Defective ignition coil
1. Normal combustion period
2. Spark voltage line (**arrow**) absent

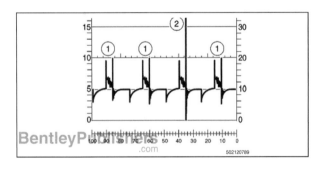

◁ Normal secondary voltage patterns (4–cylinder pattern shown)

◁ Ignition voltage peaks in response to sudden acceleration load:
1. Normal ignition pattern. Beginning of dying out pattern is not much higher than ignition voltage peak.
2. Beginning of dying out pattern considerably higher than ignition voltage peak. Fault in injection system:
   • Lean fuel mixture
   • Defective fuel injector
   • Low compression in cylinder

## IGNITION COIL SERVICE

There is a separate ignition coil above each spark plug. Spark plug replacement is covered in **020 Maintenance**.

### Ignition coil, replacing

– Make sure ignition is switched OFF.

– Remove ignition coil cover. See **020 Maintenance**.

◄ Unlock (**curved arrow**) ignition coil connector. Pull (**straight arrow**) connector off coil.

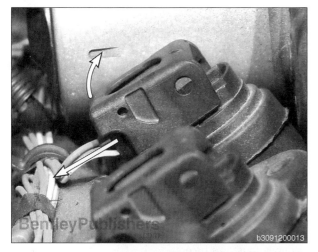

◄ Slide rod-shaped ignition coil straight out of spark plug hole.

> **CAUTION—**
> • Maintain a high level of cleanliness when servicing ignition coils. Fuel / oil residue can cause a breakdown in the electrical resistance qualities of silicone used in production. This in turn can result in a failure of the ignition coil.

– Installation is reverse of removal.

– Check for fault codes and reset ECM memory.

## CRANKSHAFT SENSOR SERVICE

### Crankshaft sensor, replacing

Crankshaft sensor is on left rear of engine block, underneath intake manifold and starter motor.

— Make sure ignition is OFF.

— Raise car and support in a safe manner.

> **WARNING—**
> • *Make sure the car is stable and well supported at all times. Use a professional automotive lift or jack stands designed for the purpose. A floor jack is not adequate support.*

◀ Working underneath starter:

- • Disconnect crankshaft sensor harness connector (**A**) from sensor (**B**).

— Remove sensor mounting fastener (**arrow**) and remove sensor from cylinder block. Be prepared to catch dripping oil.

— Installation is reverse of removal. Remember to:

- • Use new sealing O-ring when installing sensor.
- • Replace mounting bolt.
- • Be sure wiring is routed as before.
- • Check and clear fault codes from ECM memory.

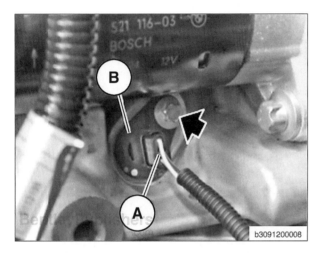

| Tightening torque | |
|---|---|
| Crankshaft sensor to engine block (M6, replace bolt) | 8 Nm (6 ft-lb) |

## CAMSHAFT SENSOR SERVICE

### Intake camshaft sensor, replacing

Intake camshaft sensor is mounted to left front of cylinder head.

– Make sure ignition is OFF.

– Remove upper engine covers. See **020 Maintenance**.

– Remove air filter housing and ducts. See **130 Fuel Injection**.

◄ Detach camshaft sensor electrical connector (**A**).

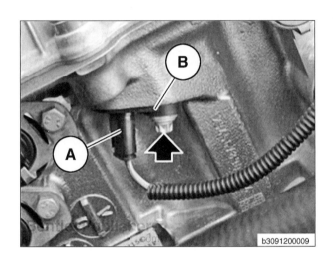

– Remove camshaft sensor mounting bolt (**arrow**). Remove sensor (**B**) from cylinder head. be prepared to catch dripping oil.

– Installation is reverse of removal. Remember to:
  • Replace camshaft sensor mounting bolt.
  • Use new sealing O-rings when installing sensor.
  • Be sure sensor harness is routed as before.
  • Check and clear fault codes from ECM memory.

| Tightening torques | |
|---|---|
| Intake camshaft sensor to cylinder head (M6, replace bolt) | 9 Nm (6.5 ft-lb) |

### Exhaust camshaft sensor, replacing

Exhaust camshaft sensor is mounted to right front of cylinder head.

– Make sure ignition is OFF.

– Remove upper engine covers. See **020 Maintenance**.

– Remove air filter housing and ducts. See **130 Fuel Injection**.

◄ Detach camshaft sensor electrical connector (**A**).

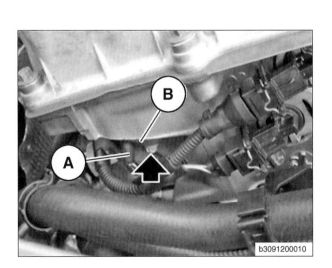

– Remove camshaft sensor mounting bolt (**arrow**). Remove sensor (**B**) from cylinder head. Be prepared to catch dripping oil.

– Installation is reverse of removal. Remember to:
  • Replace camshaft sensor mounting bolt.
  • Use new sealing O-rings when installing sensor.
  • Be sure sensor harness is routed as before.
  • Check and clear fault codes from ECM memory.

| Tightening torques | |
|---|---|
| Intake camshaft sensor to cylinder head (M6, replace bolt) | 9 Nm (6.5 ft-lb) |

## KNOCK SENSOR SERVICE

### Knock sensors, replacing (non-turbo)

Non-turbo engine knock sensors are under the intake manifold on the left side of the cylinder head.

— Disconnect negative (-) battery cable and cover battery terminal to keep cable from accidentally contacting terminal.

> **CAUTION—**
> • *Prior to disconnecting the battery, read the battery disconnection cautions given in* **001 Warnings and Cautions**.

— With engine fully cooled, remove intake manifold. See **130 Fuel Injection**.

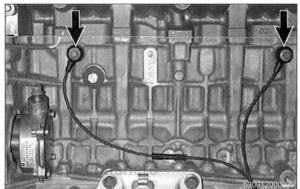

◄ Disconnect knock sensor electrical harness connector.

• Remove knock sensor mounting bolts (**arrows**) on side of cylinder block. Remove sensors.

> **CAUTION—**
> • *Note the installed angle of the knock sensor on the block before removing it. Reinstall the sensor in the same position. Be sure to use a torque wrench when tightening the sensor mounting bolt.*

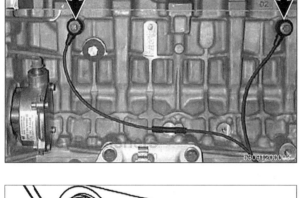

◄ Clean knock sensor contact surface on engine block and sensor (**arrow**) before installing knock sensor.

> **CAUTION—**
> • *Do not overtighten knock sensors.*

| Tightening torques | |
|---|---|
| Knock sensor to engine block (use new aluminum M8 fasteners) • Stage 1 • Stage 2 | 7 Nm (63 in-lb) additional 90° |

— Installation is reverse of removal. Remember to:

• Replace knock sensor mounting bolt.

• Be sure sensor harness is routed as before.

— Check and clear fault codes from ECM memory.

**120**

## Knock sensors, replacing (turbo)

Turbo engine knock sensors are under the intake manifold on the left side of the cylinder head.

— Disconnect negative (-) battery cable and cover battery terminal to keep cable from accidentally contacting terminal.

> **CAUTION—**
> • *Prior to disconnecting the battery, read the battery disconnection cautions given in* **001 Warnings and Cautions**.

— With engine fully cooled, remove intake manifold. See **130 Fuel Injection**.

◄ Disconnect electrical connectors (**A**), remove and seal fuel line connections (**B**). Be prepared to catch dripping fuel.

> **WARNING —**
> • *The fuel system is designed to retain pressure even when the ignition is OFF. When working with the fuel system, remove fuel lines slowly to allow residual fuel pressure to dissipate. Avoid spraying fuel, Use shop rags to capture leaking fuel*
> • *Electric fuel pump starts automatically when door is opened.*
> • *Carry out installation work on fuel system with coolant temperature below 40°C (104°F).*

> **CAUTION—**
> • *When working with high pressure fuel lines observe clean working habits. Any dirt or debris introduced into system will cause malfunctions.*

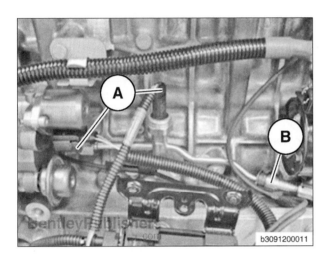

b3091200011

◄ Disconnect knock sensor electrical connector (**A**) on left side of engine block.

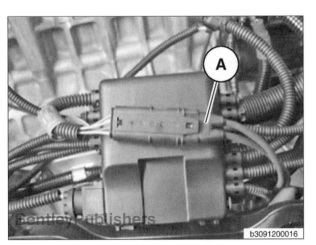

b3091200016

*Knock sensors, replacing (turbo)*

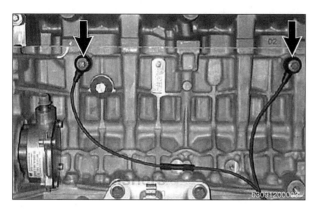

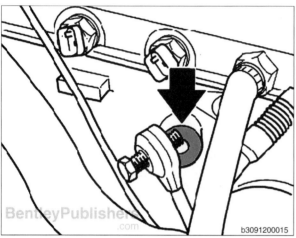

◄ Remove knock sensor mounting bolts (**arrows**) on side of cylinder block. Remove sensors.

> **CAUTION—**
> • *Note the installed angle of the knock sensor on the block before removing it. Reinstall the sensor in the same position. Be sure to use a torque wrench when tightening the sensor mounting bolt.*

◄ Clean knock sensor contact surface on engine block and sensor (**arrow**) before installing knock sensor.

> **CAUTION—**
> • *Do not overtighten knock sensors.*

| Tightening torques | |
|---|---|
| Knock sensor to engine block (use new aluminum M8 fasteners)<br>• Stage 1<br>• Stage 2 | 7 Nm (63 in-lb)<br>additional 90° |
| Fuel line nut to high pressure pump (coat thread with transmission fluid) | 30 Nm (22 ft-lb) |
| Fuel line mounting bracket to engine block | 8 Nm (87.5 in-lb) |

– Installation is reverse of removal. Remember to:

  • Replace knock sensor mounting bolt.

  • Be sure sensor harness is rerouted as before.

  • Check for fuel system leaks.

  • Check and clear fault codes from ECM memory.

# 121 Battery, Starter, Alternator

## GENERAL

This repair group covers the battery, alternator, starter and associated components of the electrical system.

See also:

- **020 Maintenance** for accessory belt replacement and battery routine service.
- **600 Electrical System–General** for bus system information, power reset procedure and general electrical troubleshooting
- **721 Airbag System (SRS)** for battery safety terminal (BST)
- **ECL Electrical Component Locations**
- **ELE Electrical Wiring Diagrams**

### Engine electrical system

The alternator and starter are wired directly to the battery. To prevent accidental shorts that might blow a fuse or damage wires and electrical components, disconnect the negative (–) battery cable before working on the electrical system.

Different versions of alternators, starters and batteries are used in E90 models. Replace components according to the original equipment specifications.

## Troubleshooting

Basic battery, starter and charging system troubleshooting information is in **Table a**.

**Table a. Battery, starter and charging system troubleshooting**

| Symptom | Probable cause | Corrective action |
|---|---|---|
| Engine does not crank | Fault in car access system (CAS). | Try another ignition key. If problem persists, contact your authorized BMW dealer. |
| Engine cranks slowly or not at all, solenoid clicks when starter is operated. | Battery cables loose, dirty or corroded. | Clean or replace cables. See **020 Maintenance**. |
| | Battery discharged. | Charge battery and test. Replace if necessary. |
| | Battery to body ground cable in trunk loose, dirty or corroded | Inspect ground cable. Clean, tighten or replace if necessary. |
| | Poor connection at starter motor terminal X6512. | Check connections at starter motor. |
| | Starter motor or solenoid faulty. | Test starter. |
| Battery does not stay charged more than a few days. | Short circuit draining battery. | Test for excessive current drain with everything electrical off. |
| | Short driving trips and high electrical drain on charging system does not allow battery to recharge. | Evaluate driving style. Where possible, reduce electrical consumption when making short trips. |
| | Engine accessory belt loose, worn or damaged. | Inspect or replace accessory belt. See **020 Maintenance**. |
| | Battery faulty. | Test battery and replace if necessary. |
| | Battery cables loose, dirty or corroded. | Clean or replace cables. See **020 Maintenance**. |
| | Alternator faulty. | Test alternator. |

## Warnings and Cautions

**WARNING** —

- *Wear goggles, rubber gloves, and a rubber apron when working around the battery or battery acid (electrolyte).*

- *Battery acid contains sulfuric acid and can cause skin irritation and burning. If acid is spilled on your skin or clothing, flush the area at once with large quantities of water. If electrolyte gets into your eyes, flush them with large quantities of clean water for several minutes and call a physician.*

- *A battery that is being charged or is fully charged gives off explosive hydrogen gas. Keep sparks and open flames away. Do not smoke.*

- *Battery lead and battery acid are both hazardous materials. When disposing of an old battery, follow federal, state and local regulations on hazardous waste disposal.*

***CAUTION—***

- *Use a digital multimeter when testing automotive electrical components.*

- *If a repair procedure specifies disconnecting the battery, follow the instruction for safety reasons.*

- *Prior to disconnecting the battery, read the battery disconnection cautions in* **001 Warnings and Cautions**.

- *Disconnecting the battery cables may erase fault codes stored in ECM memory.*

- *Using a conventional battery charger to jump start the vehicle may damage electronic control modules. Use an electronic vehicle power supply or another 12-volt battery for jump-starting. Jump starting is covered in* **020 Maintenance**.

- *Disconnect the negative (–) battery cable first and reconnect it last. Cover the battery post with an insulating material whenever the cable is removed.*

- *Do not disconnect battery, alternator or starter wires while the engine is running.*

- *Do not reverse the battery cables. Even a momentary wrong connection can damage the alternator or other electrical components.*

- *Do not depend on insulation color to tell battery positive and negative cables apart. Label cables before removing.*

- *Power windows and sunroof may fail to function properly after disconnecting and reconnecting the battery. Reinitialize windows and sunroof. See* **Battery reconnection notes** *in this repair group.*

- *Do not make any additional connections at the negative terminal of the battery.*

- *Do not modify the battery ground cable.*

- *Do not make any connections between the intelligent battery sensor (IBS) and the sensor screw.*

- *Do not use force when disconnecting the ground terminal from the battery.*

- *Do not pull at the ground cable.*

- *Do not use the IBS as a pivot point to lever off the ground terminal.*

- *Do not use the connections of the IBS as a lever.*

- *Use a torque wrench when reinstalling the battery ground cable.*

- *Do not release or tighten the IBS screw (screw with Torx head).*

- *To avoid electrochemical corrosion to engine components made of aluminum-magnesium alloy, do not use steel fasteners. Use aluminum fasteners only. For reliable identification, aluminum fastener heads are painted blue.*

- *Replace aluminum fasteners each time they are loosened.*

- *Follow torque instructions, including angle of rotation specifications, when installing aluminum fasteners.*

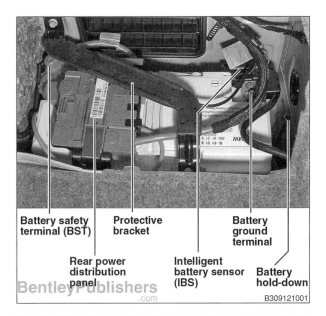

Battery safety terminal (BST) | Protective bracket | Battery ground terminal

Rear power distribution panel | Intelligent battery sensor (IBS) | Battery hold-down

B309121001

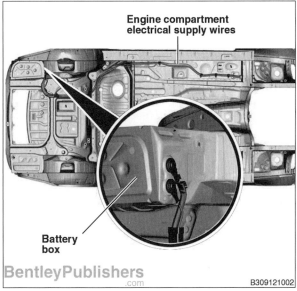

Engine compartment electrical supply wires

Battery box

B309121002

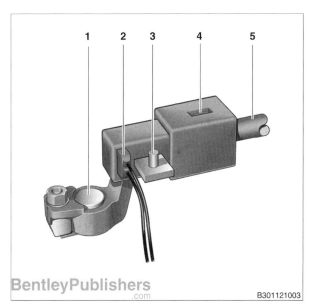

1  2  3  4  5

B301121003

# BATTERY

## Battery basics

The wet-cell lead-acid battery is rated by ampere / hours (Ah) and cold cranking amps (CCA) listed on the battery.

## Battery location and connections

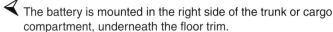 The battery is mounted in the right side of the trunk or cargo compartment, underneath the floor trim.

For rear power distribution panel details, see **ECL Electrical Component Locations**.

◀ Underneath the vehicle at the battery box are two power transfer points for the two cables that run to the engine compartment.

- One cable goes to the jump start terminal in the engine compartment and then connects to the starter and alternator.
- The second cable is used to supply power to engine electronics (DME and Valvetronic).

The power cables are routed in a protected area underneath the body of the vehicle.

## Battery safety terminal (BST)

1. Positive battery terminal (B+)
2. BST igniter connector
3. B+ to rear power distribution box (A46)
4. BST cover retaining clip
5. B+ to starter and alternator

The battery safety terminal (BST) is controlled by the multiple restraint system (MRS) control module. The system disconnects electrical power to the engine compartment in case of a significant crash. MRS fires an encapsulated pyrotechnic device in the positive (+) battery terminal that disconnects power to the engine compartment but maintains power to the exterior lights and interior of the vehicle.

See also **721 Airbag System (SRS)**.

B309121004

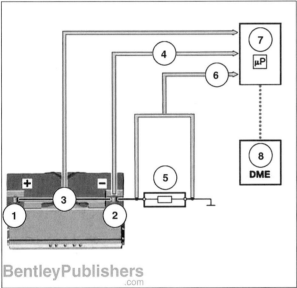

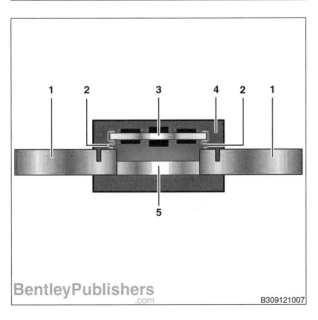

B309121007

## Intelligent battery sensor (IBS)

◀ Intelligent battery sensor (IBS) is connected to the negative battery terminal.

1. Battery ground cable
2. B+ connection to IBS
3. Bit-serial data (BSD) interface
4. Intelligent battery sensor (IBS)

The IBS is sensitive to mechanical stress and strain. See **Warnings and Cautions** in this repair group.

Replace IBS as a complete unit with the battery ground cable. The ground cable serves as a heat sink for the IBS.

If IBS is replaced, allow vehicle to rest unused at least 3 hours. Only then can the new IBS determine battery status.

◀ The IBS microprocessor monitors and measures battery conditions such as:

- Terminal voltage via measurement from B+ to ground
- Charge / discharge current via integrated shunt resistor
- Temperature of battery acid via integrated temperature sensor

1. B+ battery positive terminal
2. Battery ground terminal
3. Voltage measurement
4. Temperature measurement
5. Integrated shunt resistor
6. Current measurement
7. IBS microprocessor
8. Engine control module (ECM)

◀ IBS components:

1. Copper plate
2. Gull wing tabs
3. PC board with evaluation electronics
4. Housing
5. Manganin copper alloy resistor maintains constant temperature regardless of current flow, used to measure current flow.

## IBS evaluation function

IBS electronics continuously measure the following values under all vehicle operating conditions:

- Voltage (6 v to 16.5 v)
- Starting current (0 A to 1000 A)
- Charging current (20 A to 200 A)
- Temperature (-40°C to 105°C or -40°F to 221°F)
- Parasitic draw or closed circuit current (0 A to 10 A)

When the vehicle is stationary, the IBS is programmed to wake up every 40 seconds and makes battery condition measurements within approx. 50 ms in order to save power. The measured values, communicated to the engine control module (ECM) via binary serial data (BSD) interface, are used to calculate the following:

- State of charge (SoC) shows the current charge of the battery. SoC is used during key OFF periods to insure that the battery maintains a sufficient charge to start the engine at least one more time.

- State of health (SoH) tracks the history of the battery in the vehicle. Charge / discharge cycles and times are monitored. SoH helps the ECM determine correct battery charging rates and anticipated battery life. Internal resistance of the battery is calculated by IBS from current and voltage drop during engine start. These values are used by the ECM to calculate the SoH of the battery.

Software contained in the IBS microprocessor utilizes the measured values to calculate battery SoC during vehicle sleep mode and compares this information with that received from the ECM pertaining to the battery SoC / SoH during the period between engine OFF and deactivation of the DME main relay.

Battery data is stored every 2 hours over a 6 hour time frame, providing three snapshots of battery SoC information. The stored information / snapshot data is overwritten every 6 hours. Whenever the ignition is activated, IBS updates the ECM with the current closed circuit histogram / battery status information. The ECM evaluates the new data and, if a parasitic draw (closed-circuit current draw) is identified, a fault is stored in fault memory.

### IBS diagnosis

A fault code is stored in the ECM when the IBS is defective. The ECM boosts idle speed in order to sufficiently charge the battery.

The IBS can only be diagnosed through the ECM. The self-diagnosis function checks the voltage, current, temperature, terminal 15 wake up signal as well as system errors in the IBS.

### Voltage measurement

If IBS is shorted to ground, ECM fault code displays "Voltage Fault DME ON". The IBS is unable to wake up the ECM.

If IBS is shorted to B+, ECM fault code displays "Voltage Fault, DME not ON". The vehicle does NOT enter sleep mode.

### Current measurement

Current measurement is a dynamic process. If an implausible current flow value is detected, ECM fault code displays "Current Fault".

### IBS wake-up

The IBS constantly monitors battery SoC, even when the vehicle is asleep. A wake-up signal is sent to the ECM if the SoC falls below a predetermined threshold. Upon wake-up, the ECM switches OFF auxiliary electrical loads in order to preserve battery charge.

IBS wakes up the vehicle once during a key-off cycle. Once awakened, the vehicle returns to sleep mode.

### Wake-up signal faults

The IBS detects wake-up line faults under the following conditions:
- ECM switched ON.
- Ignition switched ON (voltage high at IBS).
- Terminal 15 running via alternator output at BSD.

If voltages at IBS terminal 15 and terminal 15 via the BSD are not equal, a fault is indicated either in the BSD line or the IBS.

## Battery, testing

BMW batteries are rated as follows:

- **Ah rating** is determined by the average amount of current the battery can deliver over time without dropping below a specified voltage.

- **CCA rating** is determined by the battery's ability to deliver starting current at 0°F (-18°C) without dropping below a specified voltage.

Battery testing determines battery condition and state of charge. Before testing the battery, check that the battery cables are tight and free of corrosion.

## Electronic battery testing

 Electronic battery testers such as Midtronics®MCR 717 are recommended for testing all battery types.

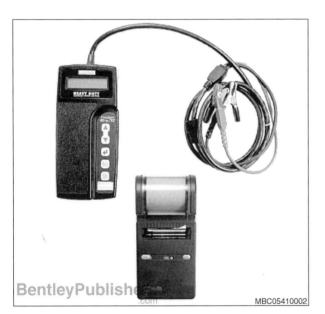

MBC05410002

## Hydrometer testing

On conventional or low-maintenance batteries, check the specific gravity of the electrolyte using a hydrometer. The more dense the concentration of sulfuric acid in the electrolyte, the higher the state of charge.

Before hydrometer testing, load the battery with 15 amperes for one minute. If the battery is installed in the vehicle, this can be done by switching the headlights ON for about one minute without the engine running. The state of battery charge based on specific gravity values are in **Table b**.

*Battery open-circuit voltage test*

Note that electrolyte temperature affects hydrometer reading. Check the electrolyte temperature with a thermometer. Add 0.004 to the hydrometer reading for every 6°C (10°F) that the electrolyte is above 27°C (80°F). Subtract 0.004 from the reading for every 6°C (10°F) that the electrolyte is below 27°C (80°F).

| Table b. Specific gravity of battery electrolyte at 27°C (80°F) | |
| --- | --- |
| **Specific gravity** | **State of charge** |
| 1.265 | Fully charged |
| 1.225 | 75% charged |
| 1.190 | 50% charged |
| 1.155 | 25% charged |
| 1.120 | Fully discharged |

If the specific gravity is at or above 1.225 but the battery lacks power for starting, determine the battery's service condition with a load voltage test. See **Battery load voltage test** in this repair group.

If the average specific gravity of the six cells is below 1.225, charge battery and retest. See **Battery charging notes** in this repair group.

## Battery open-circuit voltage test

— Before testing, load battery with 15 amperes for one minute with battery load-tester or switch headlights ON for about one minute without engine running. Connect digital voltmeter across battery terminals. Open-circuit voltage levels are given in **Table c.**

| Table c. Open-circuit voltage and battery charge | |
| --- | --- |
| **Open-circuit voltage** | **State of charge** |
| 12.6 or more | Fully charged |
| 12.4 | 75% charged |
| 12.2 | 50% charged |
| 12.0 | 25% charged |
| 11.7 or less | Fully discharged |

— If open-circuit voltage is OK but battery still lacks power for starting, perform a load voltage test. See **Battery load voltage test** in this repair group.

— If open-circuit voltage is below 12.4 volts, recharge battery and retest. See **Battery charging notes** in this repair group.

## Battery load voltage test

A battery load tester is required for a load voltage test. The test is made by applying a high resistive load to the battery terminals and simultaneously measuring battery voltage. For the most accurate results, make sure the battery is fully charged. Disconnect battery cables before making the test. Replace the battery if the voltage is below that listed in **Table d**.

> **WARNING** —
> • *Wear protective goggles and clothing when performing a load test.*

**Table d. Battery load test–minimum voltage**

| Ambient temperature | Voltage* |
|---|---|
| 27°C (80°F) | 9.6 |
| 16°C (60°F) | 9.5 |
| 4°C (40°F) | 9.3 |
| -7°C (20°F) | 8.9 |
| -18°C (0°F) | 8.5 |
| * Measure after applying a 200 amp load for 15 seconds. | |

## Battery parasitic draw, testing

If the vehicle battery is discharged for an unknown reason, perform the parasitic draw test designed to detect excessive current flow from the battery when everything in the vehicle is shut down. This is also known as a closed circuit current measurement.

— Check that battery voltage is 12 volts or higher. If lower, recharge battery.

◀ Remove negative cable and install battery isolation switch (OTC tool 7645 or equivalent).

— Close switch. Connect digital multimeter in series across switch. Set meter to milliamp (mA) scale.

— Turn trunk lock to locked position using screwdriver or similar (simulates trunk lid being closed). With exception of trunk, keep all other doors and lids closed.

— To simulate normal parasitic draw conditions: Switch ignition ON and activate all electrical consumers, including any accessories. Switch ignition OFF. Open and close driver's door (simulates somebody getting out). Lock car, arming alarm if installed.

— Open battery isolation switch and monitor current draw.
  • Vehicle without telematics (TCU): Wait 30 minutes.
  • Vehicle with telematics (TCU): Wait 60 - 70 minutes.

— Maximum allowable parasitic draw after waiting: Approx. 40 mA.

— If draw exceeds maximum allowable, find consumer(s) at fault by removing individual fuses and noting change in parasitic draw. Repair or replace component(s) found at fault.

Fuse locations and applications are in **ECL Electrical Component Locations**.

B309121029

*Battery charging notes*

**430-watt Deutronic power supply**

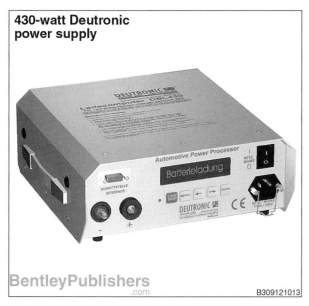

B309121013

**70-amp ACCTIVA Professional power supply**

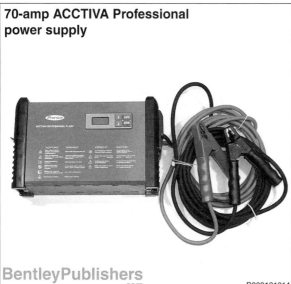

B309121014

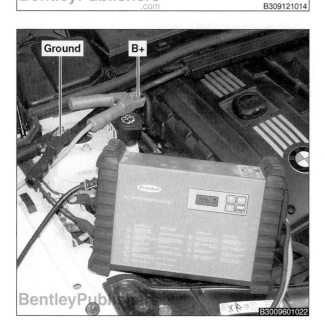

Ground    B+

B3009601022

## Battery charging notes

Consistent, clean voltage is essential when charging the battery or maintaining battery charge while coding or programming control modules. A transformer-based battery charger is inadequate for this task. BMW recommends the use of a vehicle power supply instead of a battery charger.

A power supply is a constant voltage, high-amperage power station with electronically controlled functions. It insures clean DC voltage and eliminates AC. It also provides fast, efficient and safe battery charging. Once proper battery voltage is obtained, the power supply floats the charge to maintain that voltage.

| Battery charging voltage | |
|---|---|
| BMW recommendation | 14.8 v |

Power supply units from different manufacturers are illustrated on this page.

If using a power supply, recharge battery without removing it. Otherwise, remove the battery from the trunk or cargo compartment during charging. See **Battery, removing and installing** in this repair group.

Prolonged charging with a conventional charger can cause battery electrolyte evaporation to a level that can damage. It is best to use a low-current charger (6 amperes or less) to prevent battery damage caused by overheating.

> **WARNING—**
> • Hydrogen gas given off by the battery during charging is explosive. Do not smoke. Keep open flames away from the top of the battery, and prevent electrical sparks by turning off the battery charger before connecting or disconnecting it.

> **CAUTION—**
> • Battery electrolyte (sulfuric acid) can damage the car. If electrolyte is spilled, clean the area with a solution of baking soda and water.
> • Allow a frozen battery to thaw before attempting to recharge it.
> • Do not exceed 16.5 charging voltage at the battery.

## Battery, charging

◄ Connect vehicle power supply charger to engine compartment B+ and ground. Follow manufacturer's instructions for setting charging voltage.

## Battery, removing and installing

**CAUTION—**
• *Prior to disconnecting the battery, read the battery disconnection cautions given in* **001 Warnings and Cautions**.

– Switch ignition OFF.

◄ Working in trunk or cargo compartment, open battery compartment. Twist plastic retainer counterclockwise (**arrow**) and remove right side trim.

◄ Working at top of battery, remove protective bracket mounting fasteners (**arrows**) and lift off bracket.

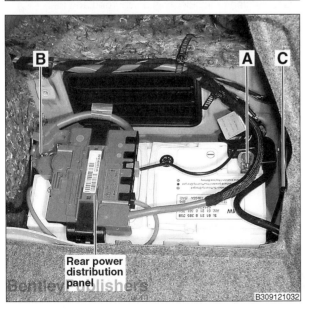

◄ Working at top of battery:

• Loosen fastener (**A**) and disconnect negative cable first.

• Unlock battery safety terminal plastic cover and loosen positive cable fastener (**B**).

• Carefully lift rear power distribution panel, positive cable, negative cable and intelligent battery sensor off battery and lay aside.

**CAUTION—**
• *Do not damage intelligent battery sensor (IBS), which is attached to ground cable. See* **Warnings and Cautions** *in this repair group.*

• Remove battery hold-down bolt (**C**).

• Disconnect battery vent hose at side of battery, if applicable.

– Lift battery out of trunk or cargo compartment.

— Clean away corrosion in and around battery tray and on cables ends.

— When reinstalling battery, reconnect negative cable last.

| Tightening torques | |
|---|---|
| Battery post pinch bolt | |
| • M6 | 5 Nm (44 in-lb) |
| • M8 | 15 Nm (11 ft-lb) |

Once the battery is reinstalled, the following steps are necessary:

• If higher rating battery is installed, recode CAS with correct battery specifications.

• Register battery. See **Replacement battery registration** in this repair group.

• Follow **Battery reconnection notes** in this repair group.

## Replacement battery registration

After fitting a new battery, connect BMW scan tool or equivalent and run service function "Register battery replacement" to notify vehicle power management (software in the engine electronics and intelligent battery sensor) that a new battery is fitted in the vehicle.

Without new battery registration, CAS and vehicle power management does not run properly and this can lead to function limitations; for example: reduction or deactivation of individual consumer functions.

During battery registration, the following operations are performed:

• Current mileage is stored.

• Stored values from old battery (charge status, current, voltage, temperature, etc.) are deleted.

• Power management is initialized.

## Battery reconnection notes

In addition to **Warnings and Cautions** in this repair group and in **001 Warnings and Cautions,** observe the following whenever the battery is disconnected or accidentally discharged and then reconnected.

### Clock

— Reset.

### Radio

— Enter presets.

### Steering angle sensor

— Adjust using BMW scan tool or equivalent.

### Power window regulator motors

Initialize as follows:

— Switch ignition ON and close window completely.

- Release window button, then hold switch in Close direction again for approx. 1 second.

- Open window completely.

- Release window button, then hold switch in Open direction again for approx. 1 second.

- Close window completely again.

- Release window button, then hold switch in Close direction again for approx. 1 second.

- Check to make sure one-touch control, anti-trapping and comfort functions are activated.

  See **512 Door Windows** for additional information.

### Sunroof

Initialize as follows (if applicable):

◀ Switch ignition ON and press and hold sunroof switch in Raised direction (**arrow**).

- After sunroof reaches Raised position, keep switch pressed for approx. 15 seconds longer.

- Initialization is complete when sunroof attempts briefly to lift again.

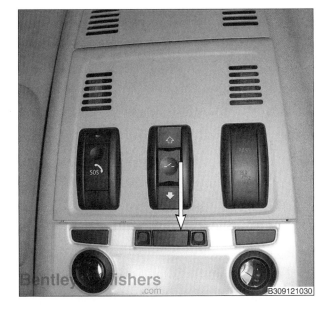

### Compass in interior mirror

Calibration (if applicable):

- Switch ignition ON

◀ Using thin bladed screwdriver or equivalent tool, press push button at base of mirror until C appears in compass display (**oval**).

- Drive vehicle 2 - 3 times in a circle at approx. 10 mph.

- Calibration is complete when direction display appears.

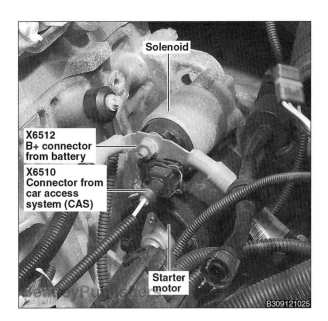

Solenoid

X6512
B+ connector
from battery

X6510
Connector from
car access
system (CAS)

Starter
motor

B309121025

# STARTER

## Starter troubleshooting

◄ The starter is bolted to the engine bell housing under the intake manifold. Starter wiring connects to the solenoid, above the starter, as follows:

• Large wire (X6512 or B+ connector) is direct battery voltage.

• Smaller wire (X6510) operates starter solenoid via ignition switch and car access system (CAS).

— If starter and solenoid click repeatedly without starting vehicle:

• Check battery state of charge.

• Inspect battery and starter cables, terminals, and ground connections for good contact. In particular, make sure ground connections between battery, body and engine are completely clean and tight.

• If no faults are found, starter may be faulty and should be replaced.

— If starter fails to operate, check the following:

• Car access system (CAS). Try another ignition key. If no faults can be found, have CAS checked using BMW scan tool equipment. CAS replacement is covered in **CAS module, removing and installing** in this repair group.

• Clutch switch module (manual transmission). Make sure clutch is pressed all the way to the floor. See **210 Clutch**.

**NOTE** —

• *Automatic transmission neutral safety switch function is built into transmission mechatronics electronics. Failure of this function causes a no-start condition.*

— Access to starter is difficult as it is under the intake manifold. If possible, check for battery voltage (12.6 volts) at B+ terminal (X6512).

— Check for battery voltage at terminal X6510 of starter motor with ignition in START position.

• If voltage is not present, check wiring between CAS and starter terminal.

• Check CAS and other inputs that disrupt power to solenoid. See **ELE Electrical Wiring Diagrams**.

• If voltage is present and no other visible wiring faults can be found, problem is most likely in starter motor.

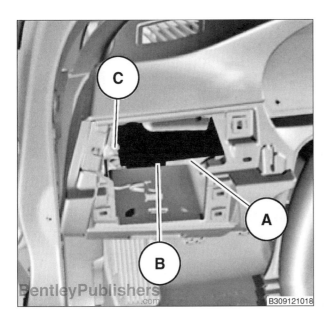

## CAS module, removing and installing

> **CAUTION—**
> • *CAS module is static sensitive. Static discharge may damage it permanently. Handle using static prevention equipment and techniques. See* **600 Electrical System–General**.

− Remove left side dashboard lower trim (pedal cluster trim). See **513 Interior Trim**.

◀ Working to left of steering column:

• Detach ribbon harness (**A**) from CAS module.

• Detach harness connector (**B**) from CAS module.

• Remove module mounting screw (**C**) and withdraw module to left and down to remove from dashboard.

− Inspect ribbon cable and replace if damaged. (Ribbon cable connects CAS to ignition key slot and Start / Stop button.)

− When installing, make sure CAS module guide fits correctly into mounting slot.

− After reassembly, carry out vehicle coding and programming. See **600 Electrical System–General**.

## Starter, removing and installing

− Switch ignition OFF. Disconnect negative (−) battery cable and cover battery terminal to keep cable from accidentally contacting terminal.

> **CAUTION—**
> • *Prior to disconnecting the battery, read the battery disconnection cautions in* **001 Warnings and Cautions**.

− Remove upper and lower cabin air microfilter housings. See **640 Heating and Air-conditioning**.

− Remove engine air filter housing and ducts. See **130 Fuel Injection**.

− Remove left front upper tension strut (crossbrace from rear engine compartment bulkhead to left strut tower).

− Remove ignition coil cover. See **020 Maintenance**.

− Remove intake manifold. See **130 Fuel Injection**.

> **CAUTION—**
> • *Do not detach fuel lines or injectors.*

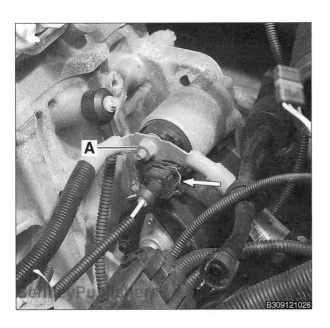

◀ Working at starter solenoid electrical connections:

• Remove fastener (**A**) and detach B+ cable from solenoid.

• Press in wire clip (**arrow**) to release solenoid wire connector.

B309121027

**Alternator**

**Idler pulley**

B309121017

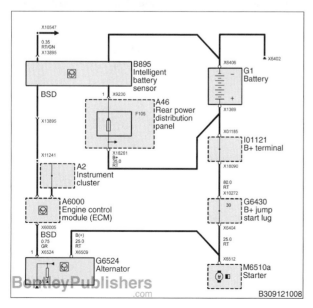

B309121008

 Remove starter mounting bolts (**arrows**). Discard aluminum bolts. (Aluminum bolt heads are not always marked with blue paint. Use a magnet to identify them.)

– Lift out starter motor.

– Before installing new starter, rotate engine and inspect flywheel or torque plate gear teeth through starter hole. Replace if damaged. See **210 Clutch** or **240 Automatic Transmission**.

– Reinstall starter and reattach electrical connectors.

| Tightening torques | |
| --- | --- |
| B+ cable to starter (M8) | 13 Nm (10 ft-lb) |
| Starter to bell housing (turbo) | 38 Nm (28 ft-lb) |
| Starter to bell housing (non-turbo) (replace M10 aluminum bolts) • Stage 1 • Stage 2 | 20 Nm (15 ft-lb) additional 180° |

## ALTERNATOR AND CHARGING SYSTEM

### Alternator basics

 The alternator is bolted to the left side of the engine block. It is driven by the engine accessory belt. A belt idler pulley is bolted to the bottom of the alternator housing. Accessory belt replacement is covered in **020 Maintenance**.

Several versions of alternators are used in E90 vehicles. Be sure that the replacement alternator is correct for the application.

### Alternator interface

The alternator communicates with the engine control module (ECM) via bit-serial data (BSD) interface. This single wire connection allows the ECM to adapt its calculations and control data to alternator output. The ECM controls the following functions:

• Alternator activation and deactivation.

• Informing the voltage regulator of the nominal voltage value to be set.

• Alternator load response control.

• BSD line diagnosis.

• Alternator fault code storage.

• Charge indicator light activation in instrument cluster.

## Charging system troubleshooting

Some charging system tests require special test equipment. If the test equipment is not available, charging system fault diagnosis can be performed by an authorized BMW dealer or other qualified repair shop. See **Table a** for general electrical component troubleshooting.

Before checking the alternator, make sure the battery is fully charged and capable of holding a charge. Check that the battery terminals are clean and tight and the engine accessory drive belt is properly tensioned and not severely worn.

### Charging system quick-check

— Use a digital multimeter to measure voltage across the battery terminals with ignition OFF and then again with engine running. Battery voltage should be about 12.6 volts with key OFF and between 13.5 and 14.5 volts with engine running.

— Run engine at about 2000 rpm and switch ON electrical loads (fans, lights, rear window defroster, and wipers). With all accessories on, battery voltage should be above 12.6 volts.

The regulated voltage (engine running, battery charged, accessories and lights OFF) is usually between 13.2 and 14.5, depending on temperature and operating conditions. If the voltage is higher than 14.8, the voltage regulator is most likely faulty.

### Charging system, checking

> **CAUTION—**
> • *Do not disconnect the battery while the engine is running. Damage to the alternator or engine electronic systems may result.*
> • *Only use a digital multimeter when testing charging system components.*

◄ Switch ignition ON. Check that battery warning light comes ON. If warning light does not come ON, check for fault codes.

◄ Check for battery voltage at alternator terminal 30 (B+):

- Pull off insulating cover at terminal 30 (**arrow**) at rear of alternator.
- Connect voltmeter between terminal 30 and ground and check for battery voltage. If voltage is not present, check wiring for faults.

— Connect oscilloscope to check alternator function:

- Positive test lead of oscilloscope to positive battery terminal.
- Negative test lead of oscilloscope to negative battery terminal.
- Set oscilloscope to A/C volts and a time base of 500ms.

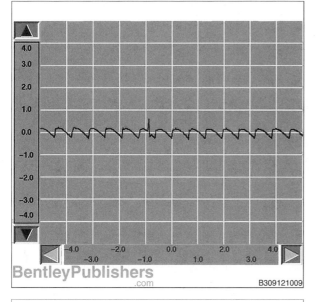

◄ Normal alternator pattern.

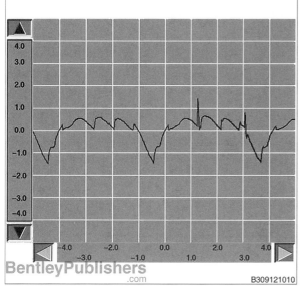

◄ Alternator with defective diode.

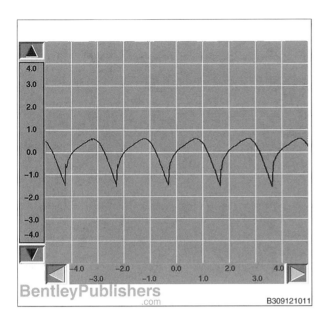

B309121011

◀ Alternator with broken winding.

– If test indicate a defective alternator, replace unit. Repair parts are not available for the alternator.

## Alternator, removing and installing (non-turbo)

– Switch ignition OFF. Disconnect negative (–) battery cable and cover battery terminal to keep cable from accidentally contacting terminal.

> **CAUTION—**
> • *Prior to disconnecting the battery, read the battery disconnection cautions in* **001 Warnings and Cautions**.

– Raise vehicle and support safely.

> **WARNING —**
> • *Make sure the vehicle is stable and well supported at all times. Use a professional automotive lift or jack stands designed for the purpose. A floor jack is not adequate support.*

– Remove splash shield underneath engine compartment. See **020 Maintenance**.

– Remove electric fan cowl and fan. See **170 Radiator and Cooling System**.

– Remove engine accessory belt. See **020 Maintenance**. Mark direction of rotation on belt before removing.

– Remove intake air filter housing. See **130 Fuel Injection**.

◀ Working at rear of alternator:
  • Detach harness connector (**A**)
  • Remove nut (**B**) and detach alternator cable.
  • Remove alternator mounting bolts (**arrows**) and discard (aluminum bolts).
  • Lift out alternator.

B301121020

*Alternator, removing and installing (turbo)*

B301121020a

 With alternator on work bench:

- Remove idler pulley (**C**) fastener plastic cover, if applicable.
- Remove idler pulley and transfer to new alternator.

| Tightening torques | |
|---|---|
| • Idler pulley to alternator housing | 80 Nm (59 ft-lb) |

– Reinstall alternator using new aluminium bolts. Reattach electrical harnesses.

| Tightening torques | |
|---|---|
| Alternator cable to alternator (M8) | 19 Nm (14 ft-lb) |
| Alternator to engine block (M8 x 82 mm aluminum bolts, replace with new) <br> • Stage 1 <br> • Stage 2 | <br><br> 10 Nm <br> additional 180° |

– Reassemble front of engine. Remember to:

- Reinstall accessory belt using previously made direction-of-rotation marks.
- Make sure accessory belt grooves engage pulleys correctly.
- After reconnecting battery, see **Battery reconnection notes** in this repair group.

## Alternator, removing and installing (turbo)

– Switch ignition OFF. Disconnect negative (–) battery cable and cover battery terminal to keep cable from accidentally contacting terminal.

> **CAUTION—**
> • *Prior to disconnecting the battery, read the battery disconnection cautions in* **001 Warnings and Cautions**.

– Raise vehicle and support safely.

> **WARNING—**
> • *Make sure the vehicle is stable and well supported at all times. Use a professional automotive lift or jack stands designed for the purpose. A floor jack is not adequate support.*

– Remove splash shield underneath engine compartment. See **020 Maintenance**.

– Remove electric fan cowl and fan. See **170 Radiator and Cooling System**.

– Remove engine accessory belt. See **020 Maintenance**. Mark direction of rotation on belt before removing.

– Remove intake air filter housing. See **130 Fuel Injection**.

– Remove left side charge air duct. See **130 Fuel Injection**.

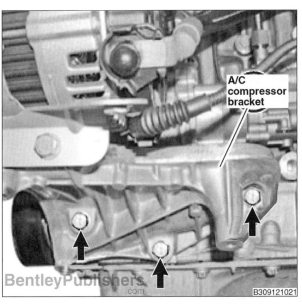

– Remove A/C compressor from mounting bracket and hang aside. See **640 Heating and Air-conditioning**. Do not detach A/C refrigerant lines.

◄ Loosen A/C compressor bracket bolts (**arrows**) a few turns. Do not remove bracket.

◄ Working at rear of alternator:
- Detach harness connector (**A**)
- Pull off plastic protective cover and remove nut (**B**) to detach alternator terminal 30 (B+) cable.

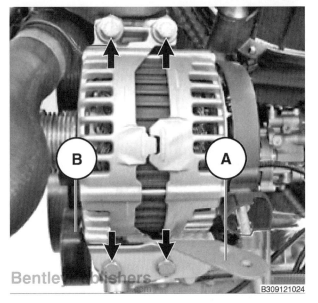

◄ Working at left side of engine:
- Remove alternator mounting bolts (**arrows**).
- Lift out alternator with bracket (**A**).

– With alternator on work bench:
- Remove idler pulley (**B**) fastener plastic cover, if applicable.
- Remove idler pulley and transfer to new alternator.

| Tightening torques | |
|---|---|
| Idler pulley to alternator housing | 80 Nm (59 ft-lb) |

– Reinstall alternator and reattach electrical harnesses.

| Tightening torques | |
|---|---|
| Alternator cable to alternator (M8) | 19 Nm (14 ft-lb) |
| Alternator to engine block (M8) | 19 Nm (14 ft-lb) |

– Tighten A/C compressor bracket bolts, then reinstall compressor.

| Tightening torque | |
|---|---|
| A/C compressor bracket to engine block | 19 Nm (14 ft-lb) |

– Reassemble front of engine. Remember to:

• Reinstall accessory belt using previously made direction-of-rotation marks.

• Make sure accessory belt grooves engage pulleys correctly.

• After reconnecting battery, see **Battery reconnection notes** in this repair group.

# 130 Fuel Injection

## GENERAL

This repair group covers service and repair of engine management systems. Information in this repair group is organized by engine (non-turbo, turbo).

See also:

- **020 Maintenance** for air filter, fuel filter and spark plug replacement
- **100 Engine–General** for engine identification
- **120 Ignition System** for ignition coil, camshaft sensor, crankshaft sensor and knock sensor service
- **160 Fuel Tank and Fuel Pump** for fuel pump and fuel pump relay service, fuel pressure tests and fuel pressure regulator replacement
- **180 Exhaust System** for oxygen sensor service
- **ECL Electrical Component Locations**
- **ELE Electrical Wiring Diagrams**
- **OBD On-Board Diagnostics**

## Warnings and Cautions

> *WARNING* —
> - *The fuel system is designed to retain pressure even when the ignition is OFF. When working with the fuel system, loosen the fuel lines slowly to allow residual fuel pressure to dissipate. Avoid spraying fuel. Use shop towels to capture leaking fuel.*
> - *Before beginning work on the fuel system, place a fire extinguisher in the vicinity of the work area.*
> - *Work only on fuel system when engine temperature is below 40°C (104°F).*
> - *When disconnecting a fuel line, clamp off the line and wrap a clean shop towel around the fitting before disconnecting. Residual fuel pressure is present in the line.*
> - *Fuel is highly flammable. When working around fuel, do not disconnect wires that could cause electrical sparks. Do not smoke or work near heaters or other fire hazards.*
> - *Wear eye protection and protective clothing to avoid injuries from contact with fuel.*
> - *When working on an open fuel system, wear suitable hand protection, as prolonged contact with fuel can cause illnesses and skin disorders.*
> - *Unscrew the fuel tank cap to release pressure in the tank before working on fuel lines.*
> - *Do not use a work light with an incandescent bulb near fuel. Fuel may spray on the hot bulb causing a fire.*
> - *Make sure the work area is properly ventilated.*
> - *Due to risk of personal injury, be sure the engine is cold before beginning work on engine components.*
> - *The ignition system produces high voltages that can be fatal. Avoid contact with exposed terminals. Use extreme caution when working on a car with the ignition switched ON or the engine running.*

**130**

**CAUTION—**

- *Renew fuel system hoses, clamps and O-rings any time they are removed.*

- *Prior to disconnecting the battery, read the battery disconnection cautions in* **001 Warnings and Cautions**.

- *Connect and disconnect the DME system wiring and test equipment leads only when the ignition is switched OFF.*

- *Wait at least 1 minute after switching the ignition OFF before removing the engine control module (ECM) connector. If the connector is removed before this time, residual power in the system relay may damage the control module.*

- *Tests or repair procedures in this section may set fault codes (DTCs) in the ECM and illuminate the MIL. After repairs are completed, access and clear DTC memory using a BMW scan tool or equivalent. See* **On-board diagnostics** *in this repair group.*

- *Fuel system cleaners and other chemical additives other than those specifically recommended by BMW may damage catalytic converters, oxygen sensors or other fuel supply components.*

- *Do not connect any test equipment that delivers a 12-volt power supply to terminal 15 (+) of the ignition coils. The current flow may damage the ECM. Connect test equipment only as specified by BMW or the equipment maker.*

- *Relay positions can vary. Be sure to confirm relay location and function by identifying the wiring in the socket using the wiring diagrams found in* **ELE Electrical Wiring Diagrams**.

- *Use a digital multimeter for electrical tests. Use an LED test light for quick tests.*

## DIGITAL MOTOR ELECTRONICS (DME)

BMW 3 Series models are equipped with digital motor electronics (DME), also known as Motronic. In these systems, fuel injection and ignition are controlled by an integrated engine control module (ECM). Application information for DME systems is in **Table a**.

| Table a. E90 engine management applications | | | |
|---|---|---|---|
| **Year, model** | **Engine code** | **Engine management** | **Features** |
| **2006** | | | |
| Sedan: 325i, 325xi Sport Wagon: 325xi Sedan: 330i, 330xi | N52 | Siemens MSV70 | Valvetronic, VANOS |
| **2007-2008** | | | |
| Sedan, Sport Wagon, Coupe, Convertible: 328i, 328xi (automatic transmission)* | N51 | Siemens MSV80 SULEV II | Valvetronic, VANOS |
| Sedan, Sport Wagon: 328i, 328xi | N52KP | Siemens MSV70 | Valvetronic, VANOS |
| Coupe, Convertible: 328i, 328xi | N52KP | Siemens MSV80 | Valvetronic, VANOS |
| Sedan: 335i, 335xi Coupe: 335i Coupe: 335xi (2008 only) Convertible: 335i | N54 | Siemens MSD80/MSD81 | VANOS |
| **2009-2010** | | | |
| Sedan, Sport Wagon, Coupe, Convertible: 328i, 328xi (automatic transmission)* | N51 | Siemens MSV80 SULEV II | Valvetronic, VANOS |
| Sedan, Coupe: 328i, 328xi Convertible: 328i Sport Wagon: 328i, 328xi | N52KP | Siemens MSV80 ULEV II | Valvetronic, VANOS |
| Sedan, Coupe: 335i, 335xi Convertible: 335i | N54 | Siemens MSD81 ULEV II | VANOS |

## DRIVEABILITY TROUBLESHOOTING

The self-diagnostic DME engine management systems monitor and store diagnostic trouble codes (DTCs). If the malfunction indicator light (MIL) illuminates, it indicates that an emissions-related fault has occurred and that one or more DTCs are stored in the engine control module (ECM).

◀ If faults arise, or if the MIL is illuminated, begin troubleshooting by connecting BMW scan tool or equivalent to the data link connector (DLC) in the engine compartment or OBD II plug under the dashboard.

The capabilities of OBD II software has the potential to save hours of diagnostic time and to help avoid incorrect component replacement and possible damage to system components. See **On-board diagnostics** in this repair group.

B309120017

## Basic engine settings

Idle speed, idle mixture (%CO), and ignition timing are not adjustable. The DME system is adaptive and automatically compensates for changes in the engine due to age, minor wear or small problems such as a disconnected vacuum hose. However, the adaptive range is limited. Once the limits are exceeded, driveability problems become noticeable.

Poor initial driveability may be encountered when the battery is disconnected and reconnected. When the battery is disconnected, ECM adaptive memory may be reset. The system readapts after about ten minutes of driving.

## System voltage

Digital motor electronics (DME) requires that the system (battery) voltage be maintained within a narrow range of DC voltage. DC voltage levels beyond or below the operating range, or any AC voltage in the electrical system can cause havoc.

— When troubleshooting an illuminated MIL, make sure the battery is fully charged and capable of delivering all its power to the electrical system. An undercharged battery can amplify AC alternator output ripple.

— To make a quick check of battery charge, measure voltage across battery terminals with all cables attached and ignition OFF. A fully charged battery measures 12.6 volts or slightly more, compared to 12.15 volts for a battery with a 25% charge.

The DME system operates at low voltage and current levels, making it sensitive to small increases in resistance. The electrical system is routinely subject to corrosion, vibration and wear, so faults or corrosion in the wiring harness and connectors are not uncommon.

— Check battery terminals for corrosion or loose cable connections. See **121 Battery, Starter, Alternator**.

*Main grounds*

– If a battery cable connection has no visible faults but is still suspect, measure voltage drop across the connection. A large drop indicates excessive resistance, meaning that the connection is corroded, dirty or damaged. Clean or repair and retest. See **600 Electrical System–General** for voltage drop test procedure.

– Visually inspect wiring, connectors, switches and fuses. Loose or damaged connectors can cause intermittent problems, especially small terminals in ECM connectors. Disconnect wiring harness connectors to check for corrosion, and use electrical cleaning spray to remove contaminants.

## Main grounds

Good grounds are critical to proper DME operation. If a ground connection has no visible faults but is still suspect, measure the voltage drop across the connection. A large voltage drop means high resistance. Clean or repair the connection and retest.

For voltage drop testing, see **600 Electrical System-General**.

For ground locations, see **ECL Electrical Component Locations**.

## On-board diagnostics

Second generation on-board diagnostics (OBD II) software and hardware is incorporated in the engine management systems. The OBD II system monitors components that influence exhaust and evaporative emissions. If a problem is detected, the OBD II system stores the associated diagnostic trouble code (DTC) and condition.

If vehicle emissions levels exceed 1.5 times Federally mandated criteria, the OBD II system illuminates a malfunction indicator light (MIL) in the instrument cluster.

◄ Scan tool connected to OBD II plug below left dashboard.

Professional diagnostic scan tools available at the time of this printing include the BMW GT1, ISTA and a small number of aftermarket BMW-specific tools.

In addition to professional scan tools, there are inexpensive generic OBD II scan tool software programs and handheld units available. Although these have limited capabilities as compared to the dedicated tools, they are powerful diagnostic tools.

For the DIY owner, a simple aftermarket DTC reader is available through http://www.peakeresearch.com. This tool is capable of checking for DTCs as well as switching the illuminated MIL OFF and resetting service indicator lights.

*NOTE —*

• *OBD II DTC memory (including an illuminated MIL) can only be reset using a BMW scan tool or equivalent. Removing the connector from the ECM or disconnecting the battery does not erase DTC memory.*

OBD 2 plug

B309020031

## ENGINE MANAGEMENT FUSES AND POWER SUPPLY COMPONENTS

### Power supply fuses

See **ECL Electrical Component Locations** for fuse panel access information.

◄ Rear distribution panel (A46) in trunk, installed directly on top of battery:

- **F108** 250A: Power supply to fuses (not replaceable separately): F54

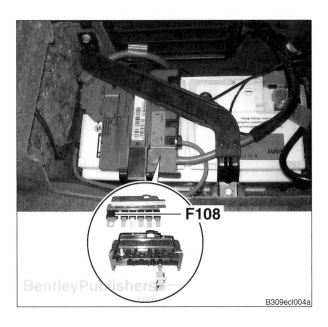

B309ecl004a

◄ 2006 fuse and relay panel behind glove compartment:

- **F54** 60A:
  Engine control module (ECM) (A6000)
  ECM main relay (K6300)
  Engine electronics fuse carrier (A8680)
  Engine electronics fuse carrier (A8681)

From 03/2007 fuse and relay panel may vary. See **ECL Electrical Component Locations** for specific vehicle fuse locations.

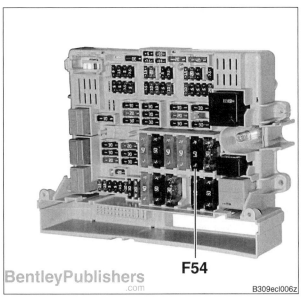

B309ecl006z

## SIEMENS DME (NON-TURBO)

### DME engine management system description

The DME manages and monitors the following functions:

**Air**

- Electronic throttle
- Mass air flow
- Resonance-turbulence intake control
- Valvetronic II

**Fuel**

- Fuel supply
- Fuel injection

**Ignition**

- Direct ignition
- Knock control
- Primary / secondary ignition monitoring

**Emissions**

- OBD II compliance
- Pre and post-catalyst oxygen sensors
- Electrically heated DME-mapped thermostat
- Misfire detection
- Evaporative emission control and leak detection
- Malfunction indicator light (MIL)

**Performance controls**

- Double VANOS control
- Output of injection signal (TI) for fuel economy gauge
- Output of engine rpm (TD) for tachometer
- A/C compressor control
- Electric radiator cooling fan
- CAN-bus communication
- Dynamic stability control (DSC) interface
- EWS (electronic immobilizer)
- Cruise control
- ECM programming

The accompanying IPO (input-processing-output) diagram illustrates DME features. In this type of stylized diagram, sensor inputs to the control module are on the left, control module processing is in the center and control module output commands are on the right of the diagram.

# DME IPO diagram (non-turbo)

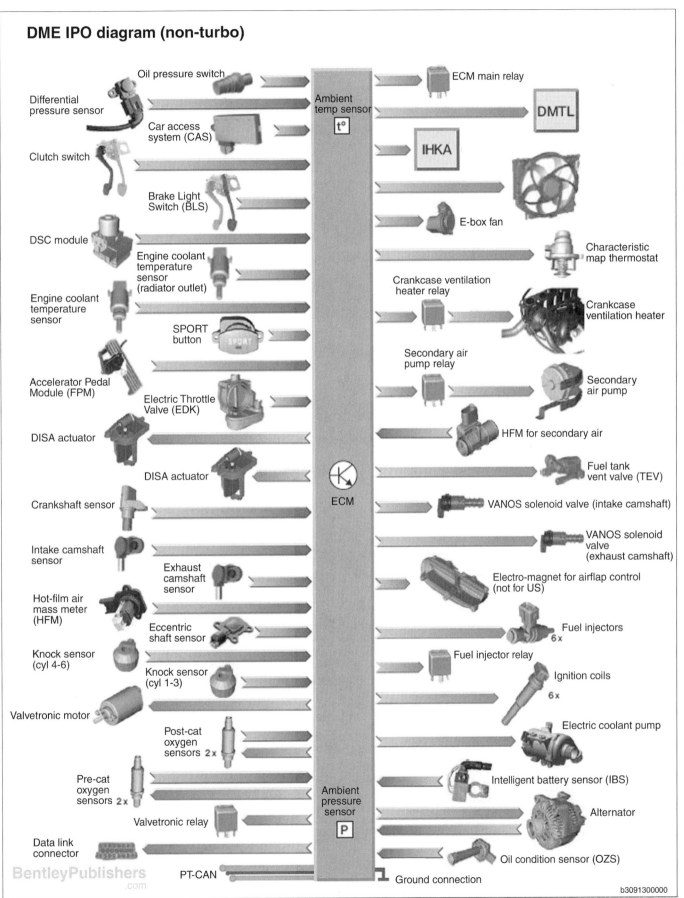

Oil pressure switch

Differential pressure sensor

Car access system (CAS)

Clutch switch

Brake Light Switch (BLS)

DSC module

Engine coolant temperature sensor (radiator outlet)

Engine coolant temperature sensor

SPORT button

Accelerator Pedal Module (FPM)

Electric Throttle Valve (EDK)

DISA actuator

DISA actuator

Crankshaft sensor

Intake camshaft sensor

Exhaust camshaft sensor

Hot-film air mass meter (HFM)

Eccentric shaft sensor

Knock sensor (cyl 4-6)

Knock sensor (cyl 1-3)

Valvetronic motor

Post-cat oxygen sensors 2 x

Pre-cat oxygen sensors 2 x

Valvetronic relay

Data link connector

PT-CAN

Ambient temp sensor t°

ECM

Ambient pressure sensor P

ECM main relay

DMTL

IHKA

E-box fan

Characteristic map thermostat

Crankcase ventilation heater relay

Crankcase ventilation heater

Secondary air pump relay

Secondary air pump

HFM for secondary air

Fuel tank vent valve (TEV)

VANOS solenoid valve (intake camshaft)

VANOS solenoid valve (exhaust camshaft)

Electro-magnet for airflap control (not for US)

Fuel injectors 6 x

Fuel injector relay

Ignition coils 6 x

Electric coolant pump

Intelligent battery sensor (IBS)

Alternator

Oil condition sensor (OZS)

Ground connection

b3091300000

*DME engine management system description*

b3091300001

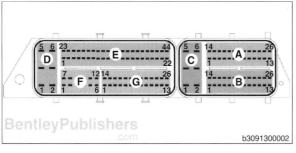

b3091300002

## Engine control module (ECM)

 The engine control module (ECM) (**arrow**) is mounted in the electronics box (E-box) at the right rear of the engine compartment.

 The ECM is flash-programmable and features 2 main electrical harness connectors, one with 4 modular connections and the other with 3 for a total of 7 subconnectors and 147 pins.

- **A:** X60001 (signals)
- **B:** X60002 (signals)
- **C:** X60003 (voltage, ground supply)
- **D:** X60004 (valvetronic)
- **E:** X60005 (signals)
- **F:** X60006 (ignition coils)
- **G:** X60007 (signals)

*NOTE —*

- *The EEPROM (chip) in the ECM is coded to the vehicle. ECMs cannot be swapped for testing purposes.*

## Fuel metering

The ECM meters pressurized fuel by changing the opening time (pulse width) of the fuel injectors. The exact amount of fuel injected is determined by the amount of time the injectors are open. To ensure that injector pulse width is the only factor that determines fuel metering, fuel pump pressure is maintained by a pressure regulator. The injectors are mounted to a common fuel rail.

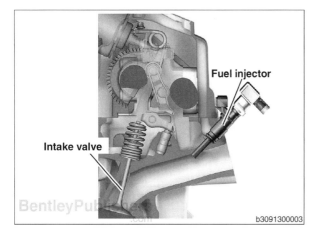

Fuel injector

Intake valve

b3091300003

The fuel injectors are mounted into a machined bore in the cylinder head. This design allows the fuel injectors to be closely mounted to the intake valves.

The injectors are a compact design manufactured by Deka with a resistance value of approximately 12 ohms each.

The ECM monitors engine operating conditions to determine injector opening duration. Each injector can be individually controlled for cylinder selective fuel trim.

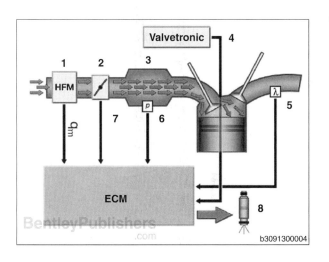

b3091300004

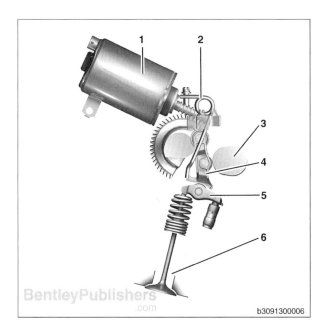

b3091300006

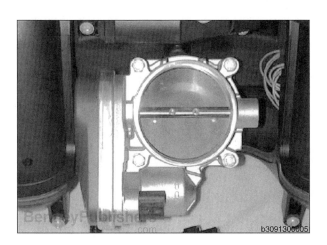

b3091300005

### Air intake

◄ Air entering the engine passes through a pleated paper element in the air filter housing. Intake air mass is then measured by a mass air flow sensor. A reference current is used to heat a thin film in the sensor when the engine is running. The current needed to hold the temperature of the film constant is used to calculate the mass of the intake air.

1.  Air mass measurement (HFM)
2.  Throttle valve
3.  Intake manifold
4.  Variable intake valve lift (valvetronic)
5.  Residual oxygen measurement in exhaust
6.  Inatke manifold vacuum
7.  Engine speed
8.  Injection timing

### Idle speed control

◄ The ECM controls Idle speed by varying intake valve lift via the valvetronic system.

1.  Valvetronic motor
2.  Return spring
3.  Intake camshaft
4.  Intermediate lever
5.  Intake rocker are
6.  Intake valve

Idle speed is not adjustable. The basic functions and parameters of idle speed control are as follows:

• Control of cold air intake volume.

• Smooth idle speeds regardless of load and inputs.

• Smooth transition from acceleration to deceleration.

Idle speed stabilization is active during the following conditions:

• Engine warm up

• Heating or A/C activation

• Drive gear selected (automatic transmission)

• Varying cooling fan speeds

### Throttle control

◄ The throttle module (EDK) is not needed for engine load control. Engine load control is carried out by the valvetronic function of the ECM. However, the throttle may be slightly closed to allow sufficient manifold vacuum for the crankcase ventilation and canister purge systems.

### Knock (detonation) control

Knock sensors monitor and control ignition knock through the ECM. The knock sensors function like microphones and are able to convert mechanical vibration (knock) into electrical signals. The ECM is programmed to react to frequencies that are characteristic of engine knock and adapt the ignition timing point accordingly.

Knock sensor replacement is covered in **120 Ignition System**.

## Secondary air injection (N51 engine)

The secondary air system pumps ambient air into the exhaust stream after a cold engine start to reduce the warm-up time of the catalytic converters and to reduce HC and CO emissions. The ECM controls and monitors the secondary air injection system.

The electric air pump draws in ambient air and supplies it to the secondary air valve. The air injection valve is opened by air pressure (from the pump) and is closed by an internal spring.

The secondary air valve is bolted to the right front of the cylinder head. Cast passageways within the cylinder head duct the secondary air directly into the cylinder head exhaust ports.

Secondary air injection power supply fuses and relay are shown in **ECL Electrical Component Locations**.

◄ Secondary air injection system components (6-cylinder engine)

1.  Air valve
2.  Air pump filter
3.  Secondary air mini-mass air flow sensor
4.  Air intake hose
5.  Air pump

b3091300007

◄ A miniature mass air flow sensor in the secondary air system detects the air mass supplied by the secondary-air pump. This function monitors the secondary air system for OBD compliance.

When the mini mass air flow sensor detects no air mass or insufficient air mass, a fault is stored in the ECM and the malfunction indicator light (MIL) is illuminated.

b3091300008

## Secondary air injection illustrations (N51 engine)

◀ Secondary air pump is in front of coolant expansion tank:

- **M63** Secondary air pump.
- **B2606** Mini mass air flow sensor (if equipped).
- **X166** Secondary air pump ground.

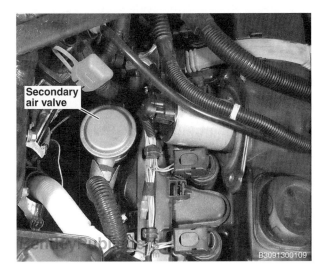

◀ Secondary air valve is bolted to right front of cylinder head.

## Air filter housing and ducts, removing and installing (non-turbo)

◀ Working at front of engine compartment above radiator, remove air intake hood screws (**A**). Detach air intake duct connection (**arrow**) and lift out of radiator support.

For air filter replacing, see **020 Maintenance**.

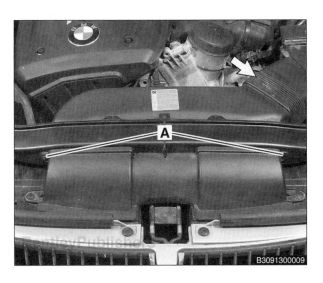

*Air filter housing and ducts, removing and installing (non-turbo)*

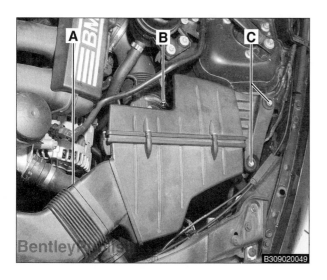

◄ Working at air filter housing:

- Detach air intake duct from filter housing (**A**).
- Loosen hose clamp (**B**) at mass air flow sensor.
- Remove filter housing mounting bolts (**C**) and lift housing out of engine compartment.

– Remove cabin microfilter housing. See **640 Heating and Air-conditioning**.

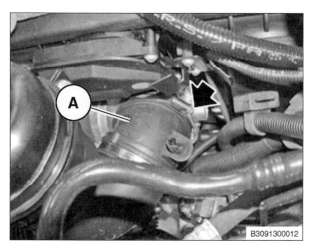

◄ Loosen duct clamp (**arrow**). Remove duct (**A**) from throttle body.

– Installation is reverse of removal.

– After reinstalling, check for fault codes and reset ECM memory.

## Mass air flow, measurement

◀ 3 Series non-turbo engines utilize two different air mass measurement systems.

b3091300013

**Analog mass air flow sensor** is used in models produced to 09 / 2006. The sensor, incorporating an electrically heated film in the air flow stream, sends to the ECM a varying voltage (approx. 0.5 - 4.5 volts) representing the mass of the intake air.

The ECM provides operating voltage and ground to the air flow sensor. As air flows through the sensor, the film is cooled. To maintain the film at a constant temperature, additional current is necessary. It is this additional current that is the basis for the input signal.

If there is no output signal from the air flow sensor, the ECM operates the engine using throttle position and engine rpm inputs. A faulty air flow sensor illuminates the MIL.

**Digital mass air flow sensor** is used in models from 09 / 2006. In this system, a duty cycle signal corresponds to changes in intake air mass. This eliminates the need for signal conversion in the ECM.

The intake air temperature sensor is integrated into the mass air flow sensor. The sensor is an NTC thermistor which receives a 5 volt reference current and ground from the ECM.

A faulty air flow sensor can produce the following problems:
• Difficult to restart when engine is hot.
• Engine starts then stalls.
• Engine starts and runs only with accelerator pedal depressed.

## Mass air flow sensor, replacing (non-turbo)

– Switch ignition OFF and remove key.

◀ Working at left front of engine compartment at air filter housing:
   • Detach mass air flow sensor electrical connector (**A**).
   • Remove fasteners (**arrows**).
   • Remove mass air flow sensor (**B**).

– Check intake ducts for cracks and vacuum leaks.

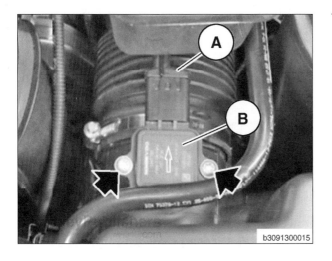

b3091300015

BentleyPublishers
.com

b3091300016

 Installation is reverse of removal.

• Inspect O-ring (**arrow**) and replace in necessary.

– After reinstalling, check for fault codes and reset ECM memory.

| Tightening torques | |
|---|---|
| Mass air flow sensor to housing | 3 Nm (26 in-lb) |

## Throttle housing, replacing (non-turbo)

The throttle housing (EDK) is not used for engine load control. Engine load control is carried out by the valvetronic function of the ECM. However, the throttle may be slightly closed to allow sufficient manifold vacuum for the crankcase ventilation and canister purge systems. There is no mechanical (cable) link between the accelerator pedal and the throttle plate.

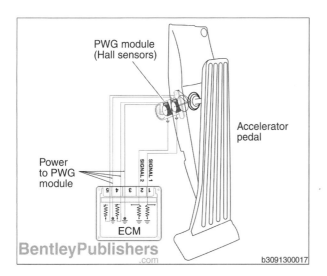 The accelerator pedal module (PWG) at the pedal assembly communicates pedal position directly to the ECM. The module provides two variable voltage signals (via two Hall sensors) to the ECM for pedal position and rate of movement.

The ECM provides an independent voltage and ground supply for each hall sensor. Each Hall sensor is provided with 5 volts and ground. As the accelerator pedal is moved from rest to full throttle, the sensors produce a variable voltage signal.

The output of the Hall sensors is checked for plausibility. The voltage range of Hall sensor 1 is approximately 0.5 to 4.5 volts. Hall sensor 2 ranges from approximately 0.5 to 2.5 volts.

The throttle housing unit is nonadjustable. If found to be faulty, replace as a complete unit.

After replacing the throttle housing, use BMW scan tool or equivalent to reset adaptation values.

> **CAUTION—**
> • *If the adaptation process is not completed correctly, the engine does not start.*

– Switch ignition OFF and remove key.

– Remove air filter housing and air intake ducts. See **Air filter housing and ducts, removing and installing (non-turbo)** in this repair group.

*Valvetronic motor, removing and installing (non-turbo)*

◀ Working at left side of intake manifold:

- Disconnect electrical connector (**A**).
- Remove fasteners (**arrows**) and remove throttle housing (**B**).

– Installation is reverse of removal.

– Replace profile gasket (sealing O-ring) between throttle assembly and intake manifold.

| Tightening torques | |
|---|---|
| Throttle housing to intake manifold | 9 Nm (80 in-lb) |

130

– Reattach throttle assembly connector with care. It is possible to twist the connector before plugging it in. This can cause damage to the harness and connector.

– After reinstalling, check for fault codes and reset ECM memory. Reset throttle plate adaptation values following on-screen directions.

## Valvetronic motor, removing and installing (non-turbo)

– Switch ignition OFF and remove key.

– Remove cabin microfilter housings. See **640 Heating and Air-conditioning**.

– Remove ignition coil cover. See **020 Maintenance**.

– Disconnect battery negative (-) cable.

> **CAUTION—**
> - *Prior to disconnecting the battery, read the battery disconnection cautions in* **001 Warnings and Cautions**.

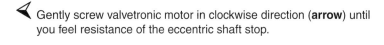

◀ Disconnect ignition coil electrical connectors and remove ignition coil overlay harness (**arrows**).

◀ Gently screw valvetronic motor in clockwise direction (**arrow**) until you feel resistance of the eccentric shaft stop.

*Fuel rail and injectors, removing and installing (non-turbo)*

◄ Remove valvetronic motor fasteners (**arrows**) and valvetronic motor support bracket fastener (**inset**).

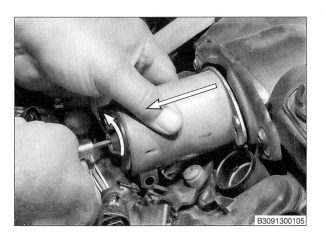

◄ Gently screw valvetronic motor in counterclockwise direction while sliding motor out of cylinder head cover (**arrow**).

– Installation is reverse of removal. Remember to:
  • Replace aluminum fasteners.
  • Route ignition harness correctly

| Tightening torque | |
|---|---|
| Valvetronic motor to cylinder head | 4 Nm (2.9 ft-lb) |

– After reinstalling, check for fault codes and reset ECM memory.

## Fuel rail and injectors, removing and installing (non-turbo)

Fuel injectors are electrically controlled solenoid valves that provide precisely metered and atomized fuel into the engine intake ports.

Injectors receive voltage from the DME main relay. The engine control module (ECM) controls injector opening by activating the ground circuit for the injector valve solenoids. The ECM varies the duration (in milliseconds) of injector opening to regulate air / fuel ratio.

– Switch ignition OFF and remove key.

– Remove cabin microfilter housing. See **640 Heating and Air-conditioning**.

– Remove ignition coil cover. See **020 Maintenance**.

– For a quick check of injectors, run engine and touch each injector with a screwdriver or stethoscope. You should feel a vibration or hear a buzzing. Switch engine OFF.

*Fuel rail and injectors, removing and installing (non-turbo)*

– Disconnect battery negative (-) cable.

> **CAUTION—**
> • *Prior to disconnecting the battery, read the battery disconnection cautions in* **001 Warnings and Cautions**.

◄ Working above engine, detach oxygen sensor connectors (**A**) and unclip wiring harness from holder.

> **CAUTION—**
> • *Be sure to mark oxygen sensor connectors so that they can be reassembled as before.*

◄ Unscrew schræder valve cap (**arrow**) from fuel rail. Connect air line adapter (**A**) to fitting.

• Unscrew fuel tank cap to release pressure.

• Using a brief burst of compressed air (maximum of 3 bar or 43.5 psi), blow fuel back into fuel tank.

> **WARNING—**
> • *Fuel in the fuel line is under pressure (approx. 3 - 5 bar or 45 - 75 psi) and may be expelled forcibly. Do not smoke or work near heaters or other fire hazards. Keep a fire extinguisher handy.*
> • *Unscrew the fuel tank cap to release pressure in the tank before working on the fuel line.*
> • *Plug open fuel lines and fittings.*

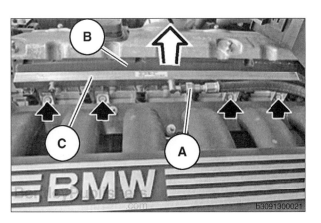

◄ Working above engine:

• Remove and detach fuel line (**A**).

• Disconnect connector strip (**B**) in direction of arrow.

• Remove fasteners (**arrows**).

• Remove fuel rail (**C**).

> **WARNING—**
> • *Wrap a clean shop towel around fitting before disconnecting. Residual fuel pressure is present in the fuel line.*

130

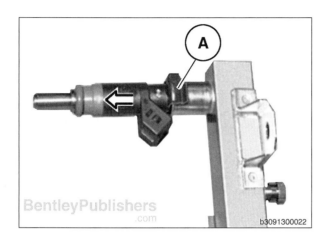

 Remove individual injectors:
- Pry retaining clip from injector (**A**).
- Pull injector from rail (**arrow**).

– Installation is reverse of removal. Remember to:
- Fit new sealing O-rings when installing injectors. For ease of installation, lightly lubricate O-rings with assembly lubricant.
- Check that injector electrical connections are correctly fitted and that injectors are fully seated prior to installing fuel rail mounting bolts.
- Replace wire ties.

| Tightening torque | |
|---|---|
| Fuel rail to cylinder head | 10 Nm (7 ft-lb) |

– After reinstalling, check for fault codes and reset ECM memory.

## Intake manifold, removing and installing (non-turbo)

– Disconnect battery negative (-) cable in cargo compartment.

> *CAUTION—*
> *• Prior to disconnecting the battery, read the battery disconnection cautions in* **001 Warnings and Cautions**.

– Remove cabin microfilter housing. See **640 Heating and Air-conditioning**.

– Remove ignition coil cover. See **020 Maintenance**.

– Remove air filter housing and air intake ducts. See **Air filter housing and ducts, removing and installing (non-turbo)** in this repair group.

 Remove tension strut (**arrow**).

*Intake manifold, removing and installing (non-turbo)*

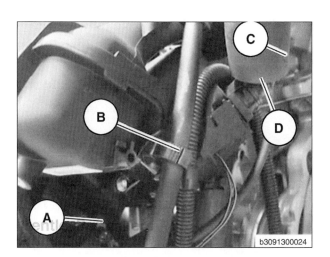

◀ Working at left side and underneath intake manifold:

- Open harness holder (**B**).
- Disconnect electrical connector (**A**).
- Release both crankcase breather connections (**C**,**D**).

**130**

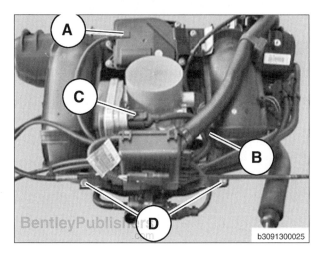

◀ Working at left side and underneath intake manifold:

- Disconnect electrical connectors (**A**,**C**).
- Remove fasteners (**D**).
- Detach engine wiring harness (**B**) from intake manifold and lay aside.

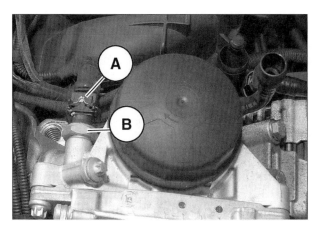

◀ Disconnect electrical connector (**A**) at oil pressure switch (**B**).

*Intake manifold, removing and installing (non-turbo)*

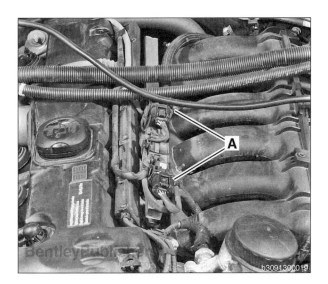

◀ Working above engine, detach oxygen sensor connectors (**A**) and unclip wiring harness from holder.

> **CAUTION—**
> • Be sure to mark oxygen sensor connectors so that they can be reassembled as before.

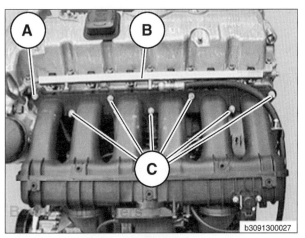

◀ Working above engine:

- Remove and lay fuel rail (**B**) aside. Do not disconnect fuel line.
- Remove fastener (**A**).
- Remove nuts (**C**).

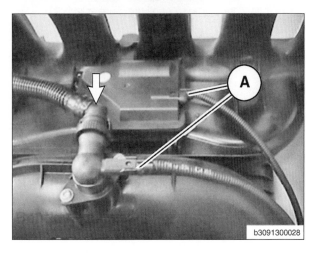

◀ Raise intake manifold approximately 10 cm (4 in). Working underneath:

- Disconnect electrical connector (**A**).
- Release fuel tank vent line (**arrow**) behind throttle valve assembly.
- Raise and remove intake manifold.

> **CAUTION—**
> • Plug open intake ports to prevent parts or debris from falling into the engine intake.

— Installation is reverse of removal. Remember to replace all seals.

| Tightening torque | |
|---|---|
| Manifold to cylinder head | 15 Nm (11 ft-lb) |

## Crankcase breather valve (non-turbo)

Non-turbo engine crankcase is ventilated by either a breather valve under the intake manifold or a breather valve integrated in the cylinder head cover. Engines with a metal cylinder head cover utilize an external breather valve, engines with a plastic valve cover utilize an internal breather valve.

◄ The crankcase ventilation system has an electrically heated crankcase breather valve. The pressure control valve and cyclonic oil separator are combined into one unit. The assembly is located under the intake manifold (**arrow**).

The pressure control valve varies the vacuum applied to the crankcase breather depending on engine load. The valve is balanced between spring pressure and the amount of manifold vacuum.

At idle when the intake manifold vacuum is high, vacuum reduces the valve opening, allowing a small amount of crankcase vapors to be drawn into the intake manifold.

At part to full load conditions when intake manifold vacuum is lower, the spring opens the valve and additional crankcase vapors are drawn into the intake manifold.

b3091300031

## Crankcase breather heating (non-turbo)

◄ Integrated into the design of the crankcase breather valve is an electric heating system (**arrow**) designed to prevent moisture buildup. Moisture buildup can eventually lead to ice at low ambient temperatures leading to malfunctions of the crankcase breather valve. The crankcase breather valve is insulated by a protective foam covering to provide additional shelter from low ambient temperatures.

The heating elements are integrated into the crankcase ventilation valve and hose assemblies. There is a junction point on the intake manifold which provides a connection point for the individual heating elements.

There is also a heating element located on the centrally located port on the intake manifold. This port is also provided with a separate heating circuit controlled by a PTC thermistor. For wiring schematic **ELE Electrical Wiring Diagrams**.

b3091300029

*Crankcase breather heating (non-turbo)*

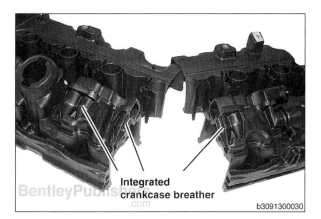

Integrated
crankcase breather

b3091300030

◀ The internal crankcase ventilation system is integrated into the plastic cylinder head cover. The crankcase breather valve is part of the cylinder head cover and is not serviceable as a separate component.

Oil separation is carried out via a labyrinth system and two cyclone separators incorporated into the cylinder head cover. By having the system components integrated into the cylinder head cover, the crankcase gases are heated by the engine rather than an electric heater as on the external system. However, there is still one electric heating element at the manifold inlet. Once the liquid oil is separated from the crankcase vapors, the oil is allowed to drain back through check valves back into the engine.

If the diaphragm valve in the breather housing leaks, full intake vacuum may be applied to the crankcase, resulting in excessive oil consumption, irregular idle, whistling or howling noises or oil smoke in the exhaust A faulty crankcase breather valve causes significant deviations from the values specified below:.

| Intake vacuum specifications (non-turbo engines) | |
| --- | --- |
| Operating pressure range<br>• N52<br>• N52KP | 24 to 28 mbar<br>28 to 32 mbar |
| Deviation to ambient pressure: | +20 mbar to -60 mbar |
| Fault condition:<br>• Clogged crankcase ventilation<br><br>• Internal leak in crankcase ventilation | +100 mbar over ambient pressure<br>-170 mbar under ambient pressure |

To access to breather valve, remove air filter housing and ducts. See **Air filter housing and ducts, removing and installing (non-turbo)** in this repair group.

## Engine coolant temperature (ECT) sensor, replacing (non-turbo)

The engine coolant temperature (ECT) sensor is an negative temperature coefficient (NTC) sensor. As coolant temperature rises, resistance through the sensor decreases.

The ECM varies ignition timing and air / fuel mixture based on engine coolant temperature. The ECT sensor is supplied a 5 volt reference voltage. The voltage drop across the sensor varies as the coolant temperature (sensor resistance) changes.

If the ECT sensor input is faulty or not plausible, the MIL is illuminated when OBD II fault criteria are exceeded. The ECM assumes a substitute value (80°C / 176°F) to maintain engine operation. The ignition timing is set to a safely conservative basic setting.

The ECT sensor is located in the left front of the engine near oil filter housing.

◄ With engine fully cooled off, disconnect ECT sensor connector (**A**).

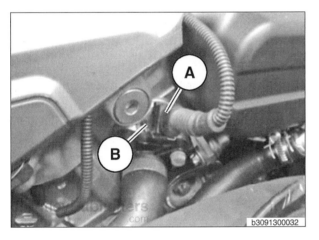

b3091300032

– Unscrew ECT sensor (**B**) from cylinder head. Be prepared to catch small amount of coolant.

– Installation is reverse of removal:
  • Use new copper sealing washer when installing sensor.
  • Replace lost coolant.

| Tightening torque | |
|---|---|
| Temperature sensor to cylinder head | 18 Nm (13 ft-lb) |

– After reinstalling, check for fault codes and reset ECM memory.

## DME main relay, testing (non-turbo)

The DME main relay is energized via the ECM and supplies battery positive (B+) power to the following:

- ECM
- Ignition coils
- Exhaust flap
- Mass air flow sensor
- Mini mass air flow sensor
- Fuel tank leak detection pump
- Crankshaft sensor
- Camshaft sensors
- Evaporative emissions valve
- EAC sensor
- Crankcase breather valve heater
- Oil condition sensor
- variable intake manifold (DISA) controllers
- Electric coolant pump
- Thermostat
- Oxygen sensor heaters

If the DME main relay is faulty, the engine does not start.

◄ With ignition off, remove DME main relay (**K6300**) in electronics box (E-box) at right rear of engine compartment.

### NOTE—

- *Relay locations can vary. Confirm relay identification by matching wiring colors and terminal numbers. See* **ELE Electrical Wiring Diagrams**.

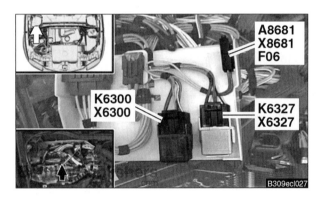

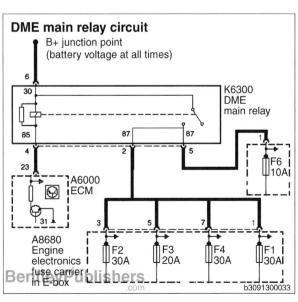

**DME main relay circuit**

◄ Check for voltage at terminal **6** of relay socket (corresponds to terminal **30** on relay).

– If battery voltage is present, continue testing.

– If battery voltage is not present, check the following:
- Large red wire in relay socket
- A2076 (battery positive junction) in E-box, right rear of engine compartment
- Fuse F54 in fuse and relay panel behind glove compartment. See **Power supply fuses** in this repair group.
- See **ELE Electrical Wiring Diagrams** for more details

– Check for ground at relay socket **4** (corresponds to terminal **85** on relay).

– If ground is present, continue testing.

— If ground is not present, signal from ECM is missing. Check wire between relay and ECM 44 pin connector X60005. See **ECM pin assignments (non-turbo)** in this repair group.

— If no faults are found:
  - Check ECM grounding.
  - ECM may be defective.

— With ignition ON and relay installed, check for battery voltage at relay sockets **2** and **5** (correspond to terminals **87** on relay).

### *NOTE*—
  - *In some models there is only one terminal 87.*

— If battery voltage is present, relay has energized and is functioning correctly.

— If battery voltage is not present and all earlier tests are OK, relay is faulty. Replace.

— If no faults are found during relay testing but power is not reaching ECM or other components, check fuses in engine electronics fuse carrier (A8680) in E-box. See **Power supply fuses** in this repair group.

— When finished testing, check for fault codes and reset ECM memory.

**130**

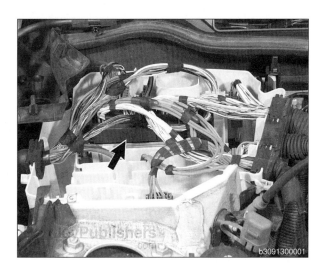

b3091300001

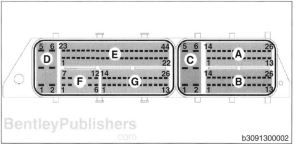

b3091300002

## ECM pin assignments (non-turbo)

◀ The engine control module (ECM) (**arrow**) is located in the right rear of the engine compartment in the E-box.

◀ The ECM has 2 main electrical harness connectors, one with 4 modular connections and the other with 3 for a total of 7 sub connectors and 147 pins.

- **A:** X60001 (signals)
- **B:** X60002 (signals)
- **C:** X60003 (voltage, ground supply)
- **D:** X60004 (valvetronic)
- **E:** X60005 (signals)
- **F:** X60006 (ignition coils)
- **G:** X60007 (signals)

ECM pin assignments for non-turbo engines are given in **Table b**. This information can be helpful when diagnosing faults to or from the ECM.

Generally, absence of voltage or continuity means there is a wiring or connector problem. Test results with incorrect values do not necessarily mean that a component is faulty. Check for loose, broken or corroded connections and wiring before replacing components. For engine management system electrical schematics, see **ELE Electrical Wiring Diagrams**.

When making checks at the ECM, use a break-out box to allow tests to be made with the connector attached to the ECM. This prevents damage to the small terminals in the connector. As an alternative, the connector housing can be separated so that electrical checks can be made from the back of the connector.

---

*CAUTION—*

- *Wait at least one minute after switching the ignition OFF before removing the connector from the ECM. If the connector is removed before this time, residual power in the system relay may damage the ECM.*

- *Connect or disconnect the control module connector and meter probes with the ignition OFF.*

---

**Table b. Non-turbo ECM pin assignments**

**Connector X60001 26-pin (signals)**

| Pin | Type | Component or function | Note |
|---|---|---|---|
| 1 | input/output | Signal PT-CAN low | Powertrain CAN-bus |
| 2 | input | Start signal | Car access system |
| 3 | input/output | BSD signal | Battery sensor |
| 4 | input | Brake light signal | Brake light switch |
| 5 | output | Exhaust flap signal | Exhaust flap |
| 6 | input | Radiator outlet temperature sensor signal | Temperature sensor at radiator outlet |
| 7 | input | Accelerator pedal module signal | Accelerator pedal module |
| 8 | output | Electric fan signal | Electric engine cooling fan |
| 9 | - | Not used | |
| 10 | ground | Accelerator pedal module | Accelerator pedal module |
| 11 | output | Accelerator pedal module supply voltage | Accelerator pedal module |
| 12 | - | Not used | |
| 13 | output | Secondary air pump relay signal | Secondary air pump relay |
| 14 | input/output | Signal PT-CAN high | Powertrain CAN-bus |
| 15 | input | EWS signal | Car access system |
| 16 | input | Brake light test signal | Brake light switch |
| 17 | input | Right rear wheel speed sensor signal | Connector X10186 (right rear wheel speed sensor) |
| 18 | input | Clutch switch signal | Clutch switch module |
| 19 | input | Radiator outlet temperature sensor signal | Temperature sensor at radiator outlet |
| 20 | input | Accelerator pedal module signal | Accelerator pedal module |
| 21 | input/output | TD signal | TD signal connector |
| 22 | - | Not used | |
| 23 | ground | Accelerator pedal module | Accelerator pedal module |
| 24 | output | Accelerator pedal module supply voltage | Accelerator pedal module |
| 25 | input | Mini mass air flow sensor signal | Mass air flow sensor secondary air |
| 26 | output | E-box fan signal | E-box fan |

**Connector X60002 26-pin (signals)**

| Pin | Type | Component or function | Note |
|---|---|---|---|
| 1 | input | Wake up signal, terminal 15 | Terminal 15 wake up connector |
| 2 | - | Not used | |
| 3 | - | Not used | |
| 4 | - | Not used | |
| 5 | input | Oxygen sensor signal | Bank 2 sensor 1 |
| 6 | input | Oxygen sensor signal | Bank 1 sensor 1 |
| 7 | input | Oxygen sensor signal | Bank 2 sensor 1 |

*ECM pin assignments (non-turbo)*

**Connector X60002 26-pin (signals) (continued)**

| Pin | Type | Component or function | Note |
|-----|------|----------------------|------|
| 8 | input | Oxygen sensor signal | Bank 1 sensor 1 |
| 9 | input | Oxygen sensor signal | Bank 2 sensor 1 |
| 10 | ground | Oxygen sensor | Bank 1 sensor 1 |
| 11 | ground | Oxygen sensor | Bank 2 sensor 1 |
| 12 | input | Oxygen sensor heating | Bank 1 sensor 1 |
| 13 | input | Oxygen sensor heating | Bank 2 sensor 1 |
| 14 | - | Not used | |
| 15 | input | DMTL valve signal | Diagnosis module for fuel tank leakage |
| 16 | input | DMTL pump signal | Diagnosis module for fuel tank leakage |
| 17 | input | DMTL heating signal | Diagnosis module for fuel tank leakage |
| 18 | input | Oxygen sensor signal | Bank 1 sensor 1 |
| 19 | input | Oxygen sensor signal | Bank 2 sensor 2 |
| 20 | input | Oxygen sensor signal | Bank 1 sensor 2 |
| 21 | - | Not used | |
| 22 | - | Not used | |
| 23 | ground | Oxygen sensor | Bank 1 sensor 2 |
| 24 | input | Oxygen sensor | Bank 2 sensor 2 |
| 25 | input | Oxygen sensor | Bank 2 sensor 2 |
| 26 | output | Oxygen sensor | Bank 1 sensor 2 |

**Connector X60003 6-pin (voltage, ground supply)**

| Pin | Type | Component or function | Note |
|-----|------|----------------------|------|
| 1 | input | Terminal 30 | B+ potential distributor |
| 2 | input | Terminal 87 | Fuse F03 |
| 3 | ground | Ground | Ground point |
| 4 | ground | Ground | Ground point |
| 5 | ground | Ground | Ground point |
| 6 | ground | Ground | Ground point |

**Connector X60004 6-pin (valvetronic)**

| Pin | Type | Component or function | Note |
|-----|------|----------------------|------|
| 1 | input | Terminal 87 | VVT relay |
| 2 | input | Terminal 87 | VVT relay |
| 3 | output | Valvetronic actuator signal | Valvetronic actuator timing actuator |
| 4 | output | Valvetronic actuator signal | Valvetronic actuator timing actuator |
| 5 | output | Valvetronic actuator signal | Valvetronic actuator timing actuator |
| 6 | output | Valvetronic actuator signal | Valvetronic actuator timing actuator |

**130**

**Connector X60005 44-pin (signals)**

| Pin | Type | Component or function | Note |
|-----|------|----------------------|------|
| 1 | - | Not used | |
| 2 | - | Not used | |
| 3 | - | Not used | |
| 4 | - | Not used | |
| 5 | - | Not used | |
| 6 | - | Not used | |
| 7 | - | Not used | |
| 8 | - | Not used | |
| 9 | - | Not used | |
| 10 | - | Not used | |
| 11 | - | Not used | |
| 12 | output | Crankcase breather valve heating activation | Crankcase breather valve heating relay |
| 13 | output | DME main relay activation | DME main relay |
| 14 | output | Throttle valve voltage supply | Throttle valve |
| 15 | input | Throttle valve signal | Throttle valve |
| 16 | input | Throttle valve signal | Throttle valve |
| 17 | - | Not used | |
| 18 | output | DISA changeover valve signal | DISA controller 2 |
| 19 | input | Knock sensor signal | Knock sensor |
| 20 | input | Knock sensor signal | Knock sensor |
| 21 | - | Not used | |
| 22 | - | Not used | |
| 23 | output | Fuel tank vent valve signal | Fuel tank vent valve |
| 24 | - | Not used | |
| 25 | output | Mass air flow sensor voltage supply | Mass air flow sensor |
| 26 | input | Mass air flow sensor signal | Mass air flow sensor |
| 27 | ground | Mass air flow sensor | Mass air flow sensor |
| 28 | input | Intake air temperature sensor signal | Intake air temperature sensor |
| 29 | input | Crankshaft position sensor signal | Crankshaft position sensor |
| 30 | ground | Crankshaft position sensor | Crankshaft position sensor |
| 31 | output | Intake manifold pressure sensor voltage supply | Intake manifold pressure sensor |
| 32 | ground | Intake manifold pressure sensor | Intake manifold pressure sensor |
| 33 | input | Intake manifold pressure sensor signal | Intake manifold pressure sensor |
| 34 | - | Not used | |
| 35 | input/output | BSD signal | BSD signal connector |
| 36 | input | Throttle valve signal | Throttle valve |
| 37 | input | Throttle valve signal | Throttle valve |

*ECM pin assignments (non-turbo)*

**Connector X60005 44-pin (signals) (continued)**

| Pin | Type | Component or function | Note |
|-----|------|----------------------|------|
| 38 | ground | Throttle valve | Throttle valve |
| 39 | - | Not used | |
| 40 | output | DISA changeover valve signal | DISA controller 1 |
| 41 | input | Knock sensor signal | Knock sensor |
| 42 | input | Knock sensor signal | Knock sensor |
| 43 | - | Not used | |
| 44 | - | Not used | |

**Connector X60006 12-pin (ignition coils)**

| Pin | Type | Component or function | Note |
|-----|------|----------------------|------|
| 1 | output | Ignition coil signal | Ignition coil signal 1 |
| 2 | output | Ignition coil signal | Ignition coil signal 2 |
| 3 | output | Ignition coil signal | Ignition coil signal 3 |
| 4 | output | Ignition coil signal | Ignition coil signal 4 |
| 5 | output | Ignition coil signal | Ignition coil signal 5 |
| 6 | output | Ignition coil signal | Ignition coil signal 6 |
| 7 | - | Not used | |
| 8 | - | Not used | |
| 9 | - | Not used | |
| 10 | - | Not used | |
| 11 | - | Not used | |
| 12 | - | Not used | |

**Connector X60007 26-pin (signals)**

| Pin | Type | Component or function | Note |
|-----|------|----------------------|------|
| 1 | output | Fuel injector signal | Fuel injector 1 |
| 2 | output | Fuel injector signal | Fuel injector 2 |
| 3 | output | Fuel injector signal | Fuel injector 3 |
| 4 | input | Engine coolant temperature signal | Engine coolant temperature sensor |
| 5 | output | Intake VANOS solenoid signal | Intake VANOS solenoid |
| 6 | input | Eccentric shaft sensor signal | Eccentric shaft sensor |
| 7 | input | Eccentric shaft sensor signal | Eccentric shaft sensor |
| 8 | input | Eccentric shaft sensor signal | Eccentric shaft sensor |
| 9 | input | Eccentric shaft sensor signal | Eccentric shaft sensor |
| 10 | ground | Wire shielding | Eccentric shaft sensor |
| 11 | input | Camshaft position sensor 1 signal | Camshaft position sensor 1 |
| 12 | input | Camshaft position sensor 2 signal | Camshaft position sensor 2 |
| 13 | input | Oil pressure switch signal | Oil pressure switch |

**Connector X60007 26-pin (signals) (continued)**

| Pin | Type | Component or function | Note |
|---|---|---|---|
| 14 | output | Fuel injector signal | Fuel injector signal 4 |
| 15 | output | Fuel injector signal | Fuel injector signal 5 |
| 16 | output | Fuel injector signal | Fuel injector signal 6 |
| 17 | ground | Engine coolant temperature sensor | Engine coolant temperature sensor |
| 18 | output | Exhaust VANOS solenoid signal | Exhaust VANOS solenoid |
| 19 | input | Thermostat signal | Thermostat |
| 20 | ground | Eccentric shaft sensor | Eccentric shaft sensor |
| 21 | output | Eccentric shaft sensor voltage supply | Eccentric shaft sensor |
| 22 | input | Eccentric shaft sensor signal | Eccentric shaft sensor |
| 23 | output | Valvetronic actuator relay signal | Valvetronic actuator relay |
| 24 | ground | Camshaft position sensor 1 | Camshaft position sensor 1 |
| 25 | ground | Camshaft position sensor 2 | Camshaft position sensor 2 |
| 26 | input/output | BSD signal | Electric coolant pump |

## SIEMENS DME (TURBO)

## DME engine management system description

The DME manages and monitors the following functions:

### Air

- Twin-turbo chargers
- Electronic throttle
- Charge air intercoolers

### Fuel

- Fuel supply
- Direct fuel injection

### Ignition

- Direct ignition
- Knock control
- Primary / secondary ignition monitoring

### Emissions

- OBD II compliance
- Pre- and post-catalyst oxygen sensors
- Electrically heated DME-mapped thermostat
- Misfire detection
- Evaporative emission control and leak detection
- Malfunction indicator light (MIL)

### Performance controls

- Double VANOS control
- Output of injection signal (TI) for fuel economy gauge
- Output of engine rpm (TD) for tachometer
- A/C compressor control
- Electric radiator cooling fan
- CAN-bus communication
- Dynamic stability control (DSC) interface
- EWS (electronic immobilizer)
- Cruise control
- ECM programming

### Engine control module (ECM)

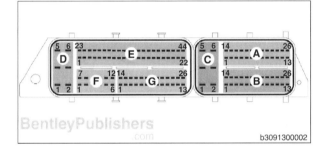

◄ The engine control module (ECM) (**arrow**) is mounted in the electronics box (E-box) at the right rear of the engine compartment.

b3091300001

◄ The ECM is flash-programmable and features 2 main electrical harness connectors, one with 4 modular connections and the other with 3 for a total of 7 sub connectors and 147 pins.

- **A:** X60001 (signals)
- **B:** X60002 (signals)
- **C:** X60003 (voltage, ground supply)
- **D:** X60004 (valvetronic)
- **E:** X60005 (signals)
- **F:** X60006 (ignition coils)
- **G:** X60007 (signals)

b3091300002

*NOTE*—

• *The EEPROM (chip) in the ECM is coded to the vehicle.*

### Fuel metering

The ECM meters pressurized fuel by changing the opening time (pulse width) of the fuel injectors. The exact amount of fuel injected is determined by the amount of time the injectors are open.

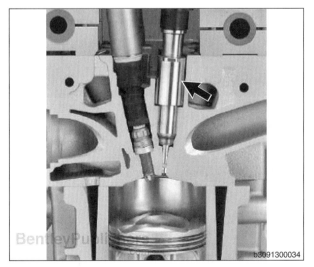

◄ 3 Series model turbo charged engines utilize direct fuel injection. The fuel injector (**arrow**) is mounted into a machined hole in the cylinder head near the spark plug.

A direct injection turbo charged engine achieves a higher compression ratio when compared to ones utilizing manifold injection. At the same time, the exhaust-gas temperature is reduced under full load. Another advantage of this injection process is the improved efficiency in part-load operation.

The ECM monitors engine operating conditions to determine injector opening duration. Each injector can be individually controlled for cylinder selective fuel trim.

b3091300034

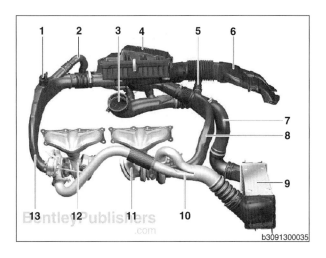

b3091300035

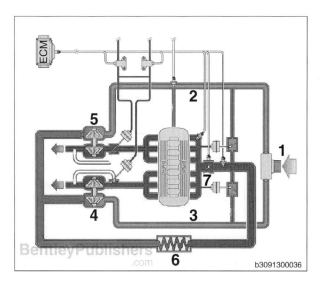

b3091300036

### Air intake

Air intake ducting plays a significant role due to the requirements of a turbocharged engine. In principle, the energy of escaping exhaust gases is utilized to precompress the inducted fresh air and thus introduce a greater air mass into the combustion chamber. This is only possible if the air intake ducting is leak free and installed properly.

1.  PTC heater for blow by gases
2.  Recirculated air line, bank 2
3.  Connection to throttle valve
4.  Air filter housing
5.  Recirculated air line, bank 1
6.  Air intake snorkel
7.  Charge air pressure line
8.  Charge air suction line, bank 1
9.  Charge air intercooler
10. Charge air manifold
11. Turbocharger, bank 1
12. Turbocharger, bank 2
13. Charge air suction line, bank 2

Fresh air is drawn in via the air cleaner (**1**) and charge-air suction lines (**2**, **3**) to the turbochargers compressors (**4**, **5**) and compressed. Because the turbochargers can get very hot during operation, they are connected to the engine coolant and engine oil circuits. The charge air is greatly heated when compressed in the turbocharger, making it necessary for the air to be cooled in an intercooler (**6**).

The compressed and cooled charge air is routed from the intercooler via the throttle valve (**7**) into the intake manifold. The system is equipped with several sensors and actuators in order to ensure that the volume of air is optimally adapted to engine operating conditions.

### Idle speed control

The ECM controls Idle speed by varying throttle valve actuation. Idle speed is not adjustable. The basic functions and parameters of idle speed control are as follows:

• Control of cold air intake volume.

• Smooth idle speeds regardless of load and inputs.

• Smooth transition from acceleration to deceleration.

Idle speed stabilization is active during the following conditions:

• Engine warm up

• Heating or A/C activation

• Drive gear selected (automatic transmission)

• Varying cooling fan speeds

*Air filter housing and ducts, removing and installing (turbo)*

### Throttle control

3 Series turbocharged engine features electronic throttle control (EDK). There is no throttle cable between the accelerator pedal and the throttle housing. EDK integrates the driver command with the requirements of the traction control system (DSC) and cruise control.

### Knock (detonation) control

Knock sensors monitor and control ignition knock through the ECM. The knock sensors function like microphones and are able to convert mechanical vibration (knock) into electrical signals. The ECM is programmed to react to frequencies that are characteristic of engine knock and adapt the ignition timing point accordingly.

Knock sensor replacement is covered in **120 Ignition System**.

## Air filter housing and ducts, removing and installing (turbo)

◄ Working at front of engine compartment above radiator, remove air intake hood screws (**A**). Detach air intake duct (**arrow**) and lift out of radiator support.

– Remove cabin microfilter housing. See **640 Heating and Air-conditioning**.

◄ Remove complete air cleaner housing, disconnecting and labeling connectors, ducting and hoses as necessary:

• Air duct hose clamp (**arrow**).

• Disconnect line (**A**) and detach from air intake housing (**B**).

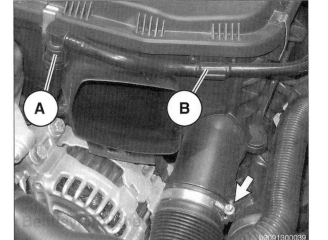

*Charge air ducts, left side, removing and installing (turbo)*

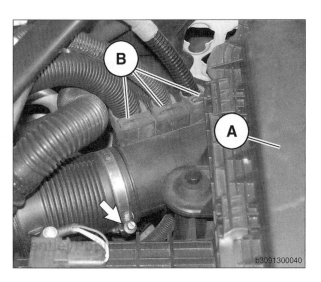

 Loosen clamp (**arrow**) and remove air intake hose.

- Pull off wiring harness holders (**B**) in upward direction.
- Detach intake filter housing (**A**) from rubber mounts then lift and remove.

– Installation is reverse of removal.

> **CAUTION—**
> • *Turbocharger failure may result if charge air ducts are not installed dry and free of grease. Install using antiseize compound only.*

– After reinstalling, check for fault codes and reset ECM memory.

## Charge air ducts, left side, removing and installing (turbo)

– Remove air filter housing and ducts. See **Air filter housing and ducts, removing and installing (turbo)** in this chapter.

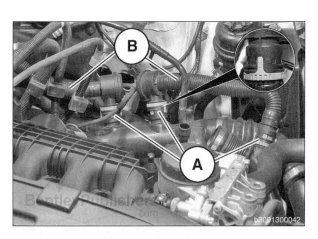

 Turn quick release coupling locks (**A**) 90° to disconnect. Detach recirculated air hoses (**B**) and lay aside. Note position of arrows on quick connector for reinstallation.

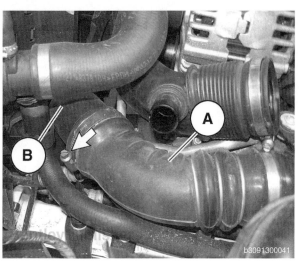

 Working at left charge air duct:

- Loosen clamp (**arrow**) and remove charge air hose (**A**) from duct (**B**).

*Charge air ducts, left side, removing and installing (turbo)*

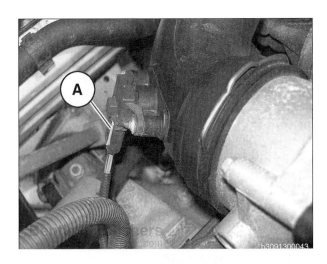

◄ Disconnect electrical connector (**A**) and place harness aside.

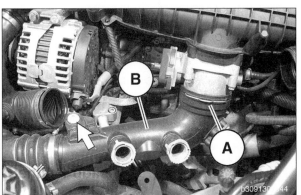

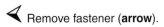

◄ Remove fastener (**arrow**).

　• Unlock quick connect (**A**) and remove charge air duct (**B**) from throttle valve.

— Raise vehicle and support safely.

> **WARNING** —
> • *Make sure the vehicle is stable and well supported at all times. Use a professional automotive lift or jack stands designed for the purpose. A floor jack is not adequate support.*

— Remove engine splash shield. See **020 Maintenance**.

◄ Working under vehicle at right front air charge duct:

　• Unlock quick connect (**arrow**) and disconnect charge air duct (**A**) from intercooler (**B**).

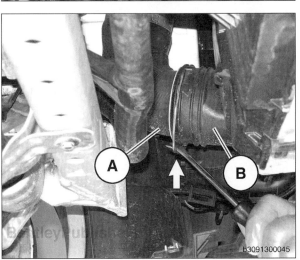

*Charge air ducts, right side, removing and installing (turbo)*

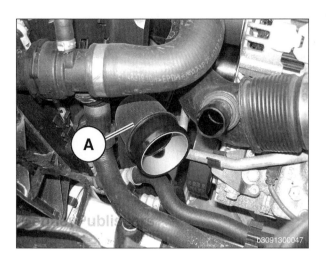

◀ Feed air charge duct (**A**) through top and remove.

– Installation is reverse of removal.

> **CAUTION—**
> • *Turbocharger failure may result if charge air ducts are not installed dry and free of grease. Install using antiseize compound only.*

– After reinstalling, check for fault codes and reset ECM memory.

## Charge air ducts, right side, removing and installing (turbo)

– Drain coolant and remove coolant expansion tank. See **170 Radiator and Cooling System**.

– Remove engine splash shield. See **020 Maintenance**.

◀ Working in right front engine compartment:
 • Label and remove vacuum lines (**A**).
 • Remove fasteners (**arrows**).

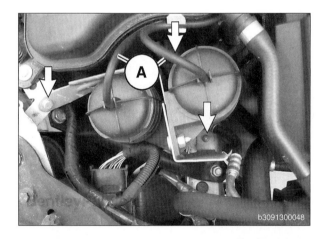

◀ Raise bracket (**A**) slightly, label and remove vacuum hoses (**B**) from bottom of canisters. Remove assembly.

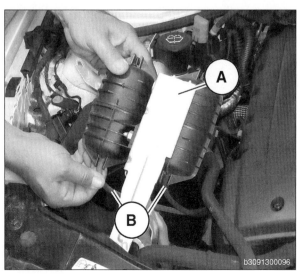

*Charge air ducts, right side, removing and installing (turbo)*

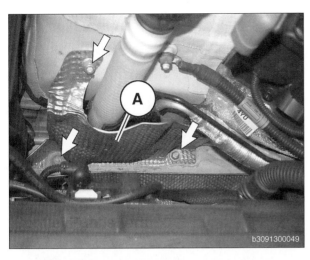

◄ Remove nuts (**arrows**) and remove heat shield (**A**).

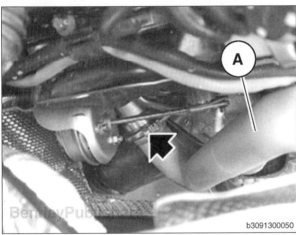

◄ Loosen clamp (**arrow**) and remove charge air duct (**A**).

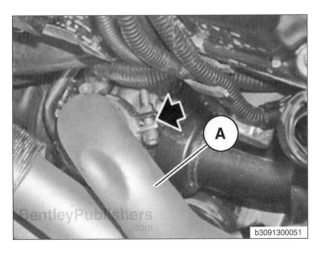

◄ Loosen clamp (**arrow**) and remove charge air duct (**A**).

*Charge air ducts, right side, removing and installing (turbo)*

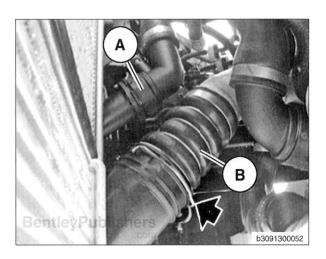

◄ Working beneath right front of vehicle:

- Unlock quick connect and remove radiator hose (**A**).
- Unlock quick connect (**arrow**) and remove charge air duct (**B**).

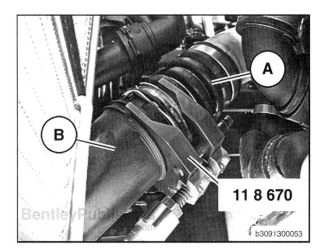

◄ When reinstalling charge air duct to intercooler use special tool 11 8 670.

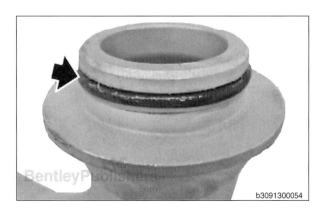

◄ Coat charge air duct O-ring (**arrow**) with antiseize before reinstalling.

— Remainder of installation is reverse of removal.

> **CAUTION—**
> • *Turbocharger failure may result if charge air ducts are not installed dry and free of grease. Install using antiseize compound only.*

— After reinstalling, check for fault codes and reset ECM memory.

**130**

## Mass air flow, measurement (turbo)

3 Series turbo engine utilizes a calculated air mass system. This calculation makes use of the following signals:

- VANOS setting (load acquisition)
- Throttle setting
- Intake air temperature (air density correction)
- Engine temperature (air density correction)
- Engine speed (cylinder charge)
- Intake manifold pressure (throttle correction)
- Ambient pressure (air density, altitude correction)

◄ The calculated air mass is adjusted with the oxygen sensor signal (mixture ratio) and injector timing and corrected if necessary.

1. Intake air temperature sensor
2. Throttle valve position
3. Intake manifold
4. Residual oxygen measurement in exhaust
5. Intake manifold vacuum
6. Engine speed
7. ECM with charge calculation model
8. Injection timing

In the event of an oxygen sensor failure, a fault code is stored in the ECM (air mass plausibility). The calculated air mass is not adjusted in this case.

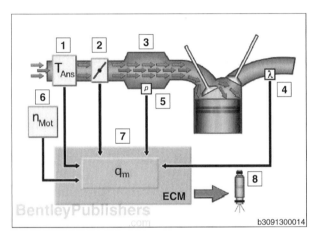

b3091300014

## Charge air duct pressure sensor, replacing (turbo)

− Switch ignition OFF and remove key.

Remove air filter housing and ducts. See **Air filter housing and ducts, removing and installing (turbo engine)** in this chapter.

◄ Working at throttle body charge air duct:
- Detach sensor electrical connector (**A**).
- Remove fasteners (**arrows**).
- Remove sensor (**B**).

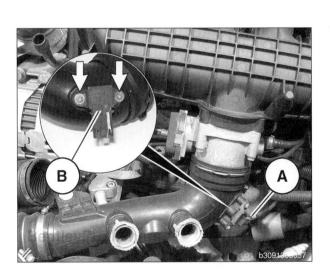

b3091300057

*Intake manifold charge air pressure sensor, replacing (turbo)*

b3091300056

◁ Installation is reverse of removal. Inspect O-ring (**arrow**) and replace in necessary.

– After reinstalling, check for fault codes and reset ECM memory.

| Tightening torques | |
|---|---|
| Sensor to charge air duct | 3.5 Nm (31 in-lb) |

## Intake manifold charge air pressure sensor, replacing (turbo)

– Switch ignition OFF and remove key.

– Remove cabin microfilter housing. See **640 Heating and Air-conditioning**.

◁ Working at rear of intake manifold:
  • Detach sensor electrical connector (**B**).
  • Remove fasteners (**arrows**).
  • Remove sensor (**A**).

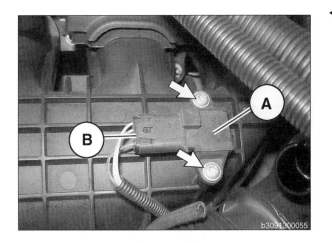

b3091300055

◁ Installation is reverse of removal.
  • Inspect O-ring (**arrow**) and replace if necessary.

– After reinstalling, check for fault codes and reset ECM memory.

| Tightening torques | |
|---|---|
| Sensor to intake manifold | 3.5 Nm (31 in-lb) |

b3091300056

## Throttle housing, replacing (turbo)

There is no mechanical (cable) link between the accelerator pedal and the throttle plate.

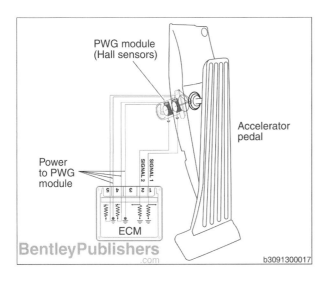

The accelerator pedal module (PWG) at the pedal assembly communicates pedal position directly to the ECM. The module provides two variable voltage signals (via two Hall sensors) to the ECM for pedal position and rate of movement.

The ECM provides an independent voltage and ground supply for each hall sensor. Each Hall sensor is provided with 5 volts and ground. As the accelerator pedal is moved from rest to full throttle, the sensors produce a variable voltage signal.

The output of the Hall sensors is checked for plausibility. The voltage range of Hall sensor 1 is approximately 0.5 to 4.5 volts. Hall sensor 2 ranges from approximately 0.5 to 2.5 volts.

The throttle housing unit is non-adjustable. If found to be faulty, replace as a complete unit.

After replacing the throttle housing, use BMW scan tool or equivalent to reset adaptation values.

> **CAUTION—**
> • *If the adaptation process is not completed correctly, the engine will not start.*

– Switch ignition OFF and remove key.

– Remove air filter housing and ducts. See **Air filter housing and ducts, removing and installing (turbo)** in this chapter.

– Remove charge air ducts. See **Charge air ducts, left side, removing and installing** in this chapter.

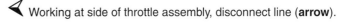
Working at side of throttle assembly, disconnect line (**arrow**).

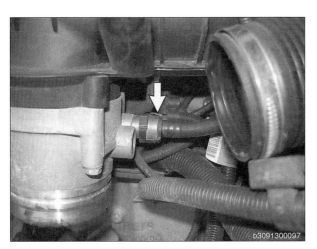

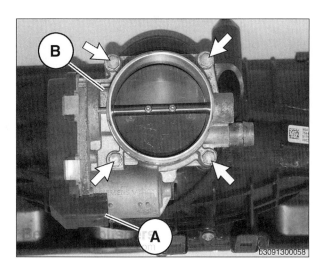

◄ Working under throttle assembly, disconnect electrical connector (**A**).

  • Remove fasteners (**arrows**) and remove throttle housing (**B**).

– Installation is reverse of removal.

– Reattach throttle assembly connector with care.

> **CAUTION—**
> • *It is possible to twist the connector before plugging it in. This can cause damage to the harness and connector.*

– Replace profile gasket (sealing O-ring) between throttle assembly and intake manifold.

| Tightening torques | |
|---|---|
| Throttle housing to intake manifold | 8 Nm (70 in-lb) |

– After reinstalling, check for fault codes and reset ECM memory. Reset throttle plate adaptation values following on-screen directions.

## Fuel injector service (turbo)

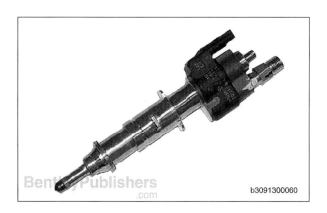

◄ Fuel injectors are electrically controlled solenoid valves that provide precisely metered and atomized fuel into the engine intake ports. E90 turbo engine utilizes a high precision injection (HPI) direct fuel injection system.

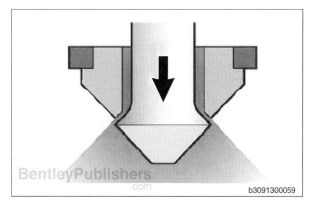

◄ The HPI system uses piezo-electric fuel injectors. These injectors open in an outward direction, which forms a precise tapered spray pattern. With the aid of high system pressure (200 bar), the HPI system is capable of providing a high level of efficiency.

Voltage from the ECM controls injector opening by activating the injector valve piezo element. The ECM varies the duration (in milliseconds) of injector opening to regulate air / fuel ratio.

During manufacture, the tolerance ranges for injector-quantity adjustment are determined and specified in a six-digit number combination. Make note of tolerance numbers. They are required for fuel injector adaptation. See **Fuel injector adaptation** in this repair group.

Information on the lift performance of the injector is also added for injector voltage adjustment. Injector adjustment is required because of the individual voltage demand of each piezo actuator. This data is programmed in the ECM. During engine operation, these values are used to compensate for deviations in the metering and switching performance.

When replacing an injector, it is essential to carry out an injector adjustment using BMW factory scan tool or equivalent.

If a fault is diagnosed in the system, such as failure of the high pressure sensor, the fuel-supply control valve is de-energized; fuel then flows bypasses into the rail. In the event of limp-home mode, turbocharging is deactivated by an opening of the wastegate valves.

Additional causes of limp-home mode can be:
- Implausible high-pressure sensor values
- Failure of the fuel-supply control valve
- Leakage in the high-pressure system
- Failure of the high-pressure pump
- Failure of the high-pressure sensor

## Fuel injectors, removing (turbo)

— Disconnect battery negative (-) cable in cargo compartment.

> **CAUTION—**
> • *Prior to disconnecting the battery, read the battery disconnection cautions in* **001 Warnings and Cautions**.

— Remove cabin microfilter housing. See **640 Heating and Air-conditioning**.

— Remove ignition coil cover. See **020 Maintenance**.

— Remove ignition coil at corresponding cylinder of fuel injector service. See **120 Ignition System**.

> **CAUTION—**
> • *Maintain a high level of cleanliness when servicing ignition coils. Fuel / oil residue can break down the electrical resistance qualities of silicone used in ignition coil production, resulting in coil failure.*

*Fuel injectors, removing (turbo)*

 Remove fuel line to corresponding fuel injector (**A**).

> **WARNING**—
> - *Fuel in the fuel line is under pressure (approx. 200 bar or 2900 psi) and may be expelled forcibly. Do not smoke or work near heaters or other fire hazards. Keep a fire extinguisher handy.*
> - *Work only on fuel system when engine temperature is below 40°C (104°F).*
> - *Unscrew the fuel tank cap to release pressure in the tank before working on the fuel line.*
> - *Plug open fuel lines and fittings.*
> - *Wrap a clean shop towel around fitting before disconnecting. Residual fuel pressure is present in the fuel line.*
> - *To reduce fuel pressure, place towel over injector and carefully tap with a wrench.*

> **CAUTION**—
> - *Maintain a clean work area when servicing high pressure fuel system. Contaminants can cause a system malfunction.*
> - *Seal all fuel system opening with protective caps.*
> - *Replace high pressure fuel lines if tightened 10 times.*

> **NOTE**—
> - *If several injectors are removed, ensure that each injector is reinstalled in its original location (cylinder).*

 Unlock and remove electrical connector (**A**). Remove fastener and remove hold-down bracket (**B**). Remove injector (**C**)

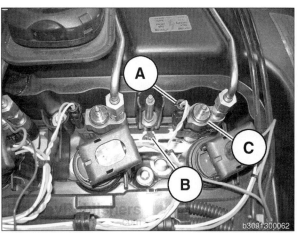

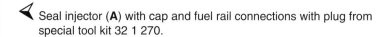 Seal injector (**A**) with cap and fuel rail connections with plug from special tool kit 32 1 270.

**32 1 270**

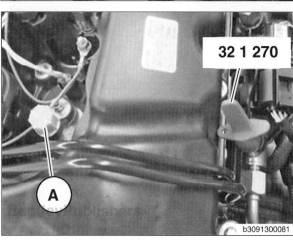

*Fuel injectors, removing (turbo)*

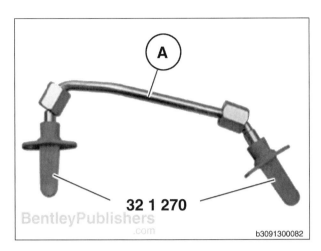

◁ Seal high pressure fuel lines (**A**) with caps from special tool kit 32 1 270.

The following procedure can be used if of an injector is stuck in the cylinder head.

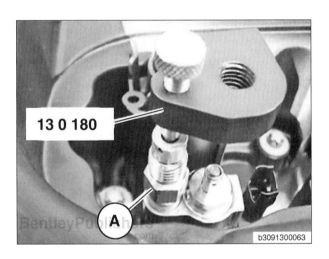

◁ Install special tool 13 0 180 on injector (**A**).

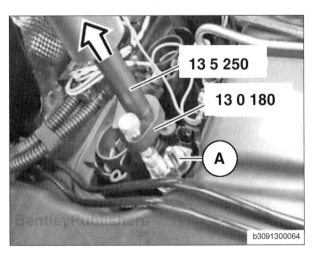

◁ Install special tool 13 5 250 and carefully knock fuel injector (**A**) out.

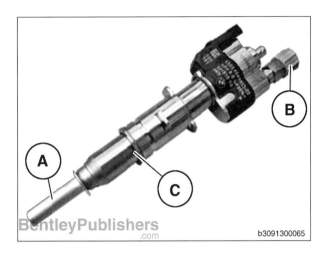

b3091300065

◄ Once injector (**C**) is removed. Install sealing caps to fuel line connection (**B**) and injector tip (**A**). Caps are available from BMW dealer parts department.

## Injector bore, cleaning (turbo)

Only use the following procedure if injector bores are dirty.

◄ To clean injector bore, slide injector, without uncoupling element (**A**) but with new PTFE sealing ring (**B**), in and out of injector bores several times. Replace PTFE sealing ring after cleaning.

– Clean contact surfaces of uncoupling element and cylinder head. Replace uncoupling element (**A**).

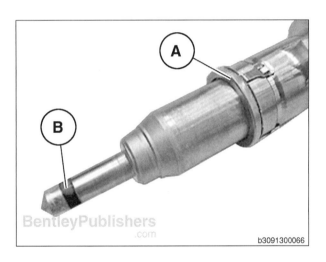

b3091300066

## Fuel injector PTFE seal, replacing (turbo)

◄ Before replacing PTFE sealing ring (**A**) make sure your hands and work surface are clean and free of oil. Avoid mechanical contact with injector tip (**B**).

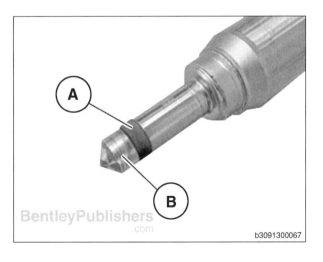

b3091300067

*Fuel injector PTFE seal, replacing (turbo)*

130

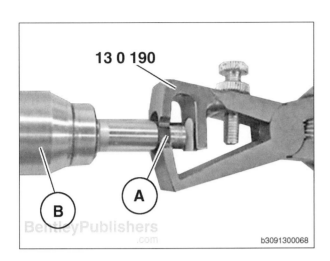

◀ Using special tool 13 0 190, remove PTFE sealing ring (**A**) from injector (**B**). Use a lint-free cloth to remove combustion residue from cylindrical part of injector tip. Do not clean injector tip.

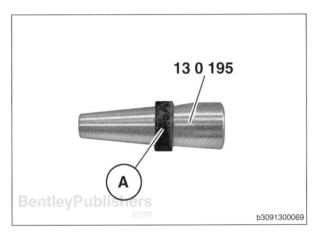

◀ Slide new PTFE sealing ring (**A**) onto mounting taper 13 0 195.

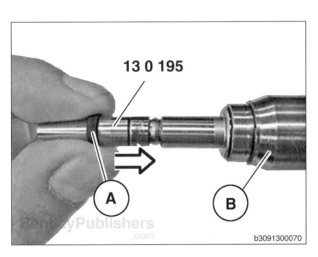

◀ Using fingers and mounting taper (13 0 195) install PTFE sealing ring (**A**) onto injector (**B**).

*Fuel injector PTFE seal, replacing (turbo)*

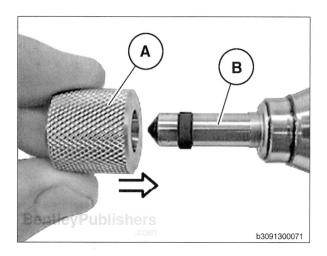

◄ To bring the PTFE sealing ring to its installation dimension, slide three mounting sleeves (**A**) with decreasing diameters on injector (**B**).

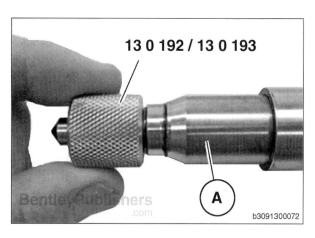

◄ First slide 13 0 192 (large diameter sleeve) onto injector (**A**). Then slide mounting sleeve 13 0 193 on injector (**A**).

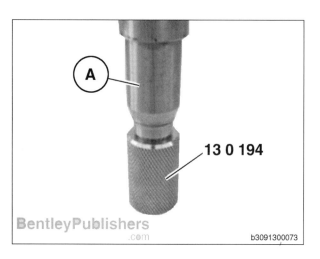

◄ Next press injector (**A**) into mounting sleeve 13 0 194 (small diameter). Install injector within 10 minutes of removing mounting sleeve.

## Fuel injectors, installing (turbo)

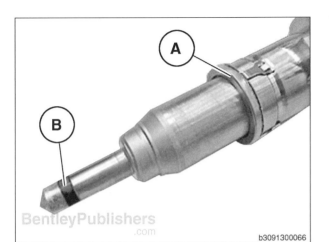

◀ Remember to:

- Replace uncoupling element (**A**).
- Replace PTFE sealing ring (**B**).
- Remove PTFE protective cap a maximum of 10 minutes before installing. Sealing ring swells up once cap is removed.
- If injector adaptation is needed note injector tolerance range numbers for each corresponding cylinder.

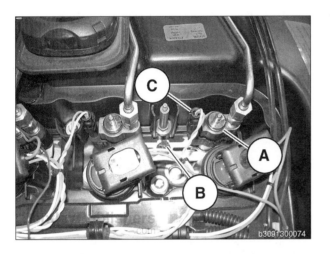
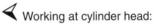

◀ Working at cylinder head:

- Install injector (**A**) into cylinder head.
- Install hold-down bracket (**B**). Fastener (**arrow**) should be finger tight allowing injector (**A**) to be adjusted.
- Install electrical connector (**C**).

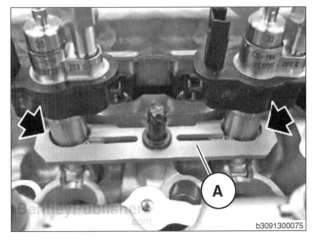

◀ Check that the hold-down bracket (**A**) is correctly installed (**arrows**).

*Fuel injectors, installing (turbo)*

◁ Copper seals on high pressure lines installed at factory are no longer needed. Remove and discard.

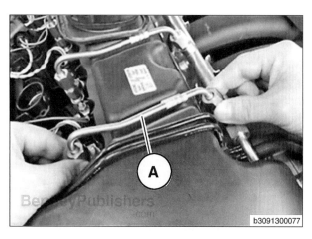

◁ Connect high pressure line (**A**) finger tight.

- If reusing high pressure line coat nut threads with gear oil.
- High pressure line may only be retightened 10 times.
- If both nuts on line cannot be installed easily by hand adjust position of injector using following step.

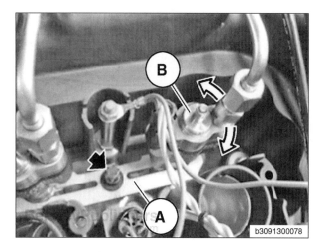

◁ If fuel lines cannot be easily installed by hand, rotate injector in direction of **arrows** until high pressure line nuts can be easily tightened by hand.

– Tighten fastener for hold-down bracket (**arrow**).

| Tightening torque | |
|---|---|
| Hold-down bracket to cylinder head | 13 Nm (9.5 ft-lb) |

◄ Use following tightening sequence:

- Tighten nut (**A**) using special tool 37 1 151 while holding injector with wrench (**C**).
- Tighten nut (**B**) using special tool 37 1 151.

− Clean all fuel from ignition coil hole.

− Check fuel system for leaks.

− Perform injector adaptation. See **Fuel injector adaptation** in this repair group.

− Check for fault codes and reset ECM memory.

| Tightening torque | |
|---|---|
| High pressure line to injector | 23 Nm (17 ft-lb) |
| High pressure line to fuel rail | 23 Nm (17 ft-lb) |

## Fuel injector adaptation (turbo)

− Connect BMW scan tool or equivalent and perform following tasks:

- Identify vehicle.
- Select **Function selection**.
- Select **Service functions**.
- Select **Adjustment programs**.
- Select **Adjust injectors**.
- Change **Test schedule**.

◄ For each replaced injector, enter fuel injector tolerance range (**inset**) to corresponding cylinder.

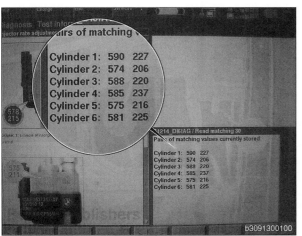

◄ Confirm the correct tolerance range (**inset**) has been entered for each injector.

## Fuel rail, removing (turbo)

– Disconnect battery negative (-) cable in cargo compartment.

> **CAUTION—**
> • *Prior to disconnecting the battery, read the battery disconnection cautions in* **001 Warnings and Cautions**.

– Remove cabin microfilter housing. See **640 Heating and Air-conditioning**.

– Remove ignition coil cover. See **020 Maintenance**.

– Remove ignition coils. See **120 Ignition System**.

> **CAUTION—**
> • *Maintain a high level of cleanliness when servicing ignition coils. Fuel / oil residue causes a breakdown of the electrical resistance qualities of silicone used in production. Resulting in failure of the ignition coil.*

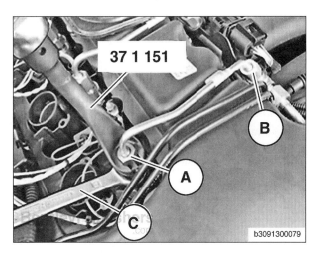

◀ Label position and remove high pressure fuel lines:
  • Using special tool 37 1 151 loosen nut (**A**) while holding injector with wrench.
  • Using special tool 37 1 151 loosen nut (**B**).

> **WARNING—**
> • *Fuel in the fuel line is under pressure (approx. 200 bar or 2900 psi) and may be expelled forcibly. Do not smoke or work near heaters or other fire hazards. Keep a fire extinguisher handy.*
> • *Work only on fuel system when engine temperature is below 40°C (104°F).*
> • *Unscrew the fuel tank cap to release pressure in the tank before working on the fuel line.*
> • *Plug open fuel lines and fittings.*
> • *Wrap a clean shop towel around fitting before disconnecting. Residual fuel pressure is present in the fuel line.*
> • *To reduce fuel pressure, place towel over injector and carefully tap with a wrench.*
> • *Protect alternator from dripping fuel and oil.*

> **CAUTION—**
> • *Maintain a clean work area when servicing high pressure fuel system. Contaminants can cause a system malfunction.*
> • *Seal all fuel system opening with protective caps.*
> • *Replace high pressure fuel lines if tightened 10 times.*

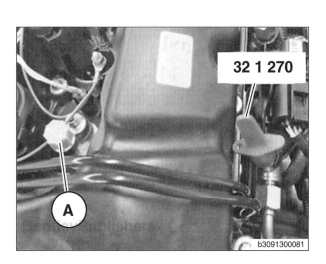

◀ Seal injector (**A**) with cap and fuel rail connections with plug from special tool kit 32 1 270.

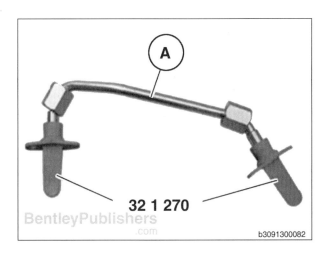

◄ Seal high pressure fuel lines (**A**) with caps from special tool kit 32 1 270.

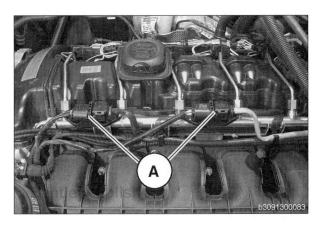

◄ Unlock and remove electrical connector (**A**) from fuel injector rail.

– Remove electrical connector holders from fuel injector rail.

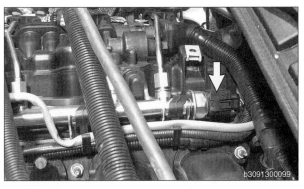

◄ Remove fuel rail pressure sensor electrical connector (**arrow**).

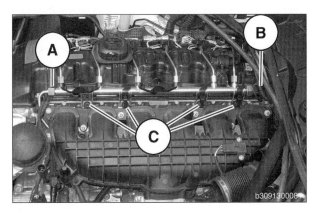

◄ Working at fuel injector rail:

- Loosen fuel line nut (**A**).

- Plug open fuel lines and fittings.

- Wrap a clean shop towel around fitting before disconnecting. Residual fuel pressure is present in fuel line.

- Remove fasteners (**B**) and remove fuel injector rail (**C**).

- Seal connections at high pressure line (**A**) and fuel rail (**C**).

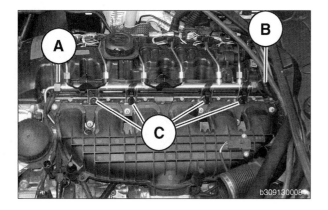

## Fuel rail, installing (turbo)

◀ Install high pressure rail:

- Connect nut (**A**) finger tight.
- Install fasteners (**C**) finger tight.
- Install electrical connector (**B**).

◀ Copper seals on high pressure lines installed at factory are no longer needed. Remove and discard.

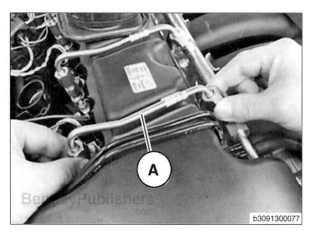

◀ Connect high pressure line finger tight.

- If reusing high pressure line coat nut threads with gear oil.
- High pressure line may only be retightened 10 times.
- If both nuts on line cannot be installed easily by hand adjust position of injector using following step.

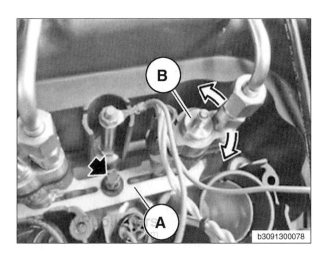

◀ If fuel lines cannot be easily installed by hand:

 • Loosen fastener (**arrow**)

 • Rotate injector in direction of **arrows** until high pressure line nuts can be easily tightened by hand.

— Tighten fastener for hold-down bracket (**arrow**).

| Tightening torque | |
|---|---|
| Hold-down bracket to cylinder head | 13 Nm (9.5 ft-lb) |

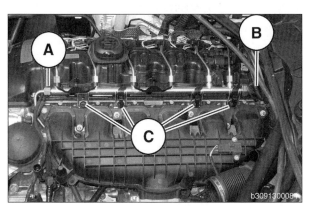

◀ Tighten fuel injector rail (**C**) fasteners (**B**).

— Tighten fuel line nut (**A**).

| Tightening torque | |
|---|---|
| Fuel injector rail to cylinder head | 13 Nm (9.5 ft-lb) |
| High pressure line to fuel rail | 30 Nm (22 ft-lb) |

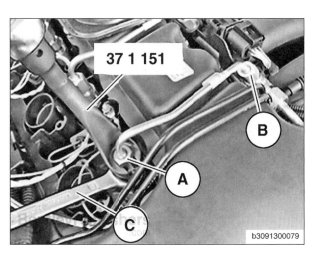

◀ Use following tightening sequence:

 • Tighten nut (**A**) using special tool 37 1 151 while holding injector with wrench (**C**).

 • Tighten nut (**B**) using special tool **37 1 151**.

— Clean all fuel from ignition coil hole.

— Check fuel system for leaks.

— Check for fault codes and reset ECM memory.

| Tightening torque | |
|---|---|
| High pressure line to injector | 23 Nm (17 ft-lb) |
| High pressure line to fuel rail | 23 Nm (17 ft-lb) |

## Intake manifold, removing and installing (turbo)

– Disconnect battery negative (-) cable in cargo compartment.

> *CAUTION—*
> • *Prior to disconnecting the battery, read the battery disconnection cautions in* **001 Warnings and Cautions**.

– Remove cabin microfilter housing. See **640 Heating and Air-conditioning**.

– Remove ignition coil cover. See **020 Maintenance**.

– Remove complete air filter housing and air intake ducts. See **Air filter housing and ducts, removing and installing (turbo)** in this repair group.

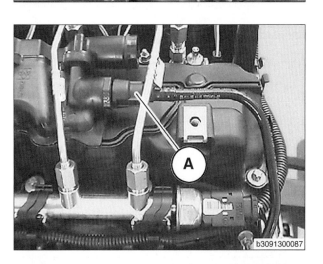

◀ Remove tension strut (**arrow**) if necessary.

◀ Disconnect crankcase breather line (**A**) at cylinder head cover if equipped.

> *NOTE—*
> • *Not all models have additional line.*

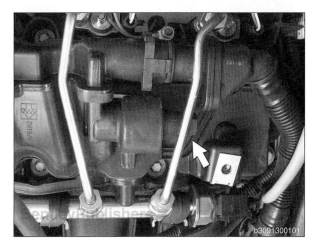

◀ Example of N54 engine without additional crankcase breather line. There will be a plug (**arrow**) in its place.

*Intake manifold, removing and installing (turbo)*

– Remove throttle housing. See **Throttle housing, replacing** in this repair group.

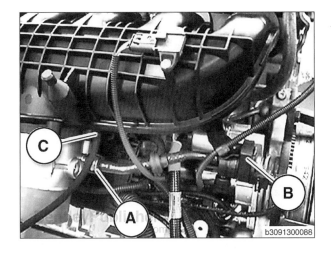

◄ Working at right side underneath intake manifold:

- Disconnect vacuum hose (**A**). If equipped.
- Remove fuel tank vent valve (**B**) from mounting bracket.
- Remove vacuum hose (**C**) and lay aside.

◄ Slide wiring harness junction box (**A**) off bracket under intake manifold.

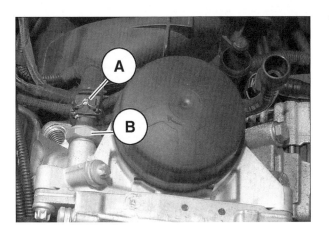

◄ Disconnect electrical connector (**A**) at oil pressure switch (**B**).

*Intake manifold, removing and installing (turbo)*

◄ Working at top of intake manifold, unhook electrical harness retainers (**A**) and place harness out of way.

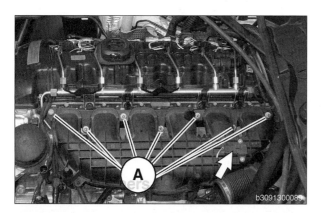

◄ Remove electrical connector (**arrow**) and remove fasteners (**A**).

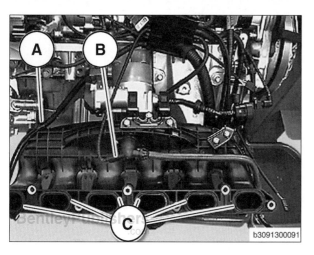

◄ Working at backside of intake manifold:

- Cut cable tie (**A**).
- Disconnect electrical connector (**B**). If equipped

> **CAUTION—**
> • *Plug open intake ports to prevent parts or debris from falling into the engine intake.*

− Installation is reverse of removal. Remember to replace intake manifold seals (**C**) if necessary.

| Tightening torque | |
|---|---|
| Manifold to cylinder head | 15 Nm (11 ft-lb) |

## Crankcase breather valve (turbo)

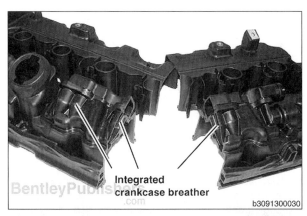

Integrated crankcase breather

b3091300030

◄ The crankcase breather valve is part of the cylinder head cover and is not serviceable as a separate component.

Oil separation is carried out via a labyrinth system and two cyclone separators incorporated into the cylinder head cover. By having the system components integrated into the cylinder head cover, the crankcase gases are heated by the engine.

b3091300104

◄ However, there is one electric heating element at the manifold inlet (**arrow**). Once the liquid oil is separated from the crankcase vapors, the oil is allowed to drain back through check valves back into the engine.

If the diaphragm valve in the breather housing leaks, full intake vacuum may be applied to the crankcase, resulting in excessive oil consumption, irregular idle, whistling or howling noises or oil smoke in the exhaust.

| Intake vacuum specifications (turbo engines) | |
|---|---|
| Operating pressure range | 7 to 11mbar |
| Deviation to ambient pressure: | +20 mbar to -60 mbar |
| Fault condition:<br>• Clogged crankcase ventilation<br><br>• Internal leak in crankcase ventilation | +100 mbar over ambient pressure<br>-170 mbar under ambient pressure |

## Engine coolant temperature (ECT) sensor, replacing (turbo)

The engine coolant temperature (ECT) sensor is an negative temperature coefficient (NTC) sensor. As coolant temperature rises, resistance through the sensor decreases.

The ECM varies ignition timing and air / fuel mixture based on engine coolant temperature. The ECT sensor is supplied a 5 volt reference voltage. The voltage drop across the sensor varies as the coolant temperature (sensor resistance) changes.

If the ECT sensor input is faulty or not plausible, the MIL is illuminated when OBD II fault criteria are exceeded. The ECM assumes a substitute value (80°C / 176°F) to maintain engine operation. The ignition timing is set to a safely conservative basic setting.

The ECT sensor is located in the front of cylinder head.

 With engine fully cooled off, remove fastener (**arrow**) and line (**A**).

> **CAUTION—**
> • *Be prepared to catch any dripping coolant*

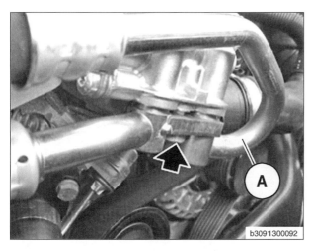

b3091300092

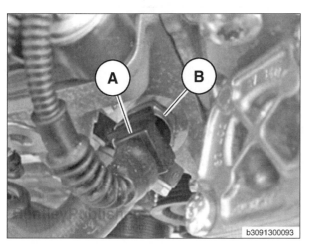

b3091300093

 Remove electrical connector (**A**). Unscrew ECT sensor (**B**) from cylinder head. Be prepared to catch small amount of coolant.

– Installation is reverse of removal:
  • Use new copper sealing washer when installing sensor.
  • Replace O-rings on coolant line.
  • Replace lost coolant.

| Tightening torque | |
|---|---|
| Temperature sensor to cylinder head | 19 Nm (14 ft-lb) |
| Coolant pipe to cylinder head | 19 Nm (14 ft-lb) |

– After reinstalling, check for fault codes and reset ECM memory.

## DME main relay, testing (turbo)

The DME main relay is energized via the ECM and supplies battery positive (B+) power to the following:

- ECM
- Ignition coils
- Exhaust flap
- E-box cooling fan
- Fuel tank leak detection pump
- Crankshaft sensor
- Camshaft sensors
- Evaporative emissions valve
- Crankcase breather valve heater
- Oil condition sensor
- Electric coolant pump
- Thermostat
- Oxygen sensor heaters

If the DME main relay is faulty, the engine does not start.

◀ With ignition off, remove DME main relay (**K6300**) in electronics box (E-box) at right rear of engine compartment.

*NOTE* —

- *Relay locations can vary. Confirm relay identification by matching wiring colors and terminal numbers. See* **ELE Electrical Wiring Diagrams**.

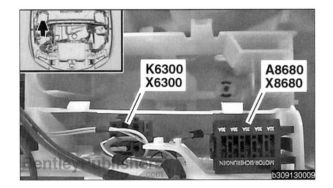

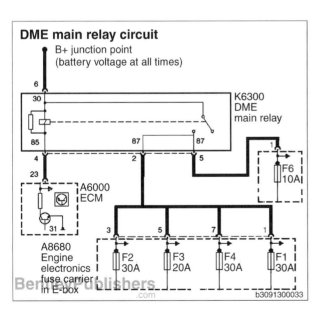

## DME main relay circuit

◀ Check for voltage at terminal **6** of relay socket (corresponds to terminal **30** on relay).

— If battery voltage is present, continue testing.

— If battery voltage is not present, check the following:

- Large red wire in relay socket
- A2076 (battery positive junction) in E-box, right rear of engine compartment
- Fuse F54 in fuse and relay panel behind glove compartment. See **Power supply fuses** in this repair group.
- Wiring can vary. See **ELE Electrical Wiring Diagrams** for more details.

— Check for ground at relay socket **4** (corresponds to terminal **85** on relay).

— If ground is present, continue testing.

— If ground is not present, signal from ECM is missing. Check wire between relay and ECM 44-pin connector X60005. See **ECM pin assignments (turbo)** in this repair group.

*DME main relay, testing (turbo)*

— If no faults are found:

  • Check ECM grounding.

  • ECM may be defective.

— With ignition ON and relay installed, check for battery voltage at relay sockets **2** and **5** (correspond to terminals **87** on relay).

***NOTE***—

• *In some models there is only one terminal 87.*

— If battery voltage is present, relay has energized and is functioning correctly.

— If battery voltage is not present and all earlier tests are OK, relay is faulty. Replace.

— If no faults are found during relay testing but power is not reaching ECM or other components, check fuses in engine electronics fuse carrier (A8680) in E-box. See **Power supply fuses** in this repair group.

— When finished testing, check for fault codes and reset ECM memory.

## ECM pin assignments (turbo)

◀ The engine control module (ECM) (**arrow**) is located in the right rear of the engine compartment in the E-box.

b3091300001

b3091300002

◀ The ECM has 2 main electrical harness connectors, one with 4 modular connections and the other with 3 for a total of 7 sub connectors and 147 pins.

- **A:** X60001 (signals)
- **B:** X60002 (signals)
- **C:** X60003 (voltage, ground supply)
- **D:** X60004 (ignition coils)
- **E:** X60005 (signals)
- **F:** X60006 (fuel injectors)
- **G:** X60007(signals)

ECM pin assignments for turbo engines are given in **Table b**. This information can be helpful when diagnosing faults to or from the ECM.

Generally, absence of voltage or continuity means there is a wiring or connector problem. Test results with incorrect values do not necessarily mean that a component is faulty. Check for loose, broken or corroded connections and wiring before replacing components. For engine management system electrical schematics, see **ELE Electrical Wiring Diagrams**.

When making checks at the ECM, use a break-out box to allow tests to be made with the connector attached to the ECM. This prevents damage to the small terminals in the connector. As an alternative, the connector housing can be separated so that electrical checks can be made from the back of the connector.

---

*CAUTION—*

- *Wait at least one minute after switching the ignition OFF before removing the connector from the ECM. If the connector is removed before this time, residual power in the system relay may damage the ECM.*

- *Connect or disconnect the control module connector and meter probes with the ignition OFF.*

---

*ECM pin assignments (turbo)*

**Table c. Turbo ECM pin assignments**

**Connector X60001 26-pin (signals)**

| Pin | Type | Component or function | Note |
|-----|------|----------------------|------|
| 1 | input/output | Signal PT-CAN low | Powertrain CAN-bus |
| 2 | input | Start signal | Car access system |
| 3 | input/output | BSD signal | Battery sensor |
| 4 | input | Brake light signal | Brake light switch |
| 5 | - | Not used | |
| 6 | input | Radiator outlet temperature sensor signal | Temperature sensor at radiator outlet |
| 7 | input | Accelerator pedal module signal | Accelerator pedal module |
| 8 | output | Electric fan signal | Electric engine cooling fan |
| 9 | - | Not used | |
| 10 | ground | Accelerator pedal module | Accelerator pedal module |
| 11 | output | Accelerator pedal module supply voltage | Accelerator pedal module |
| 12 | - | Not used | |
| 13 | - | Not used | |
| 14 | input/output | Signal PT-CAN high | Powertrain CAN-bus |
| 15 | input | EWS signal | Car access system |
| 16 | input | Brake light test signal | Brake light switch |
| 17 | input | Right rear wheel speed sensor signal | Connector X10186 (right rear wheel speed sensor) |
| 18 | input | Clutch switch signal | Clutch switch module |
| 19 | input | Radiator outlet temperature sensor signal | Temperature sensor at radiator outlet |
| 20 | input | Accelerator pedal module signal | Accelerator pedal module |
| 21 | input/output | TD signal | TD signal connector |
| 22 | - | Not used | |
| 23 | ground | Accelerator pedal module | Accelerator pedal module |
| 24 | output | Accelerator pedal module supply voltage | Accelerator pedal module |
| 25 | - | Not used | |
| 26 | - | Not used | |

**Connector X60002 26-pin (signals)**

| Pin | Type | Component or function | Note |
|-----|------|----------------------|------|
| 1 | input | Wake up signal, terminal 15 | Terminal 15 wake up connector |
| 2 | - | Not used | |
| 3 | - | Not used | |
| 4 | - | Not used | |
| 5 | input | Oxygen sensor signal | Bank 2 sensor 1 |
| 6 | input | Oxygen sensor signal | Bank 1 sensor 1 |
| 7 | input | Oxygen sensor signal | Bank 2 sensor 1 |

**Connector X60002 26-pin (signals) (continued)**

| Pin | Type | Component or function | Note |
|-----|------|----------------------|------|
| 8 | input | Oxygen sensor signal | Bank 1 sensor 1 |
| 9 | input | Oxygen sensor signal | Bank 2 sensor 1 |
| 10 | ground | Oxygen sensor | Bank 1 sensor 1 |
| 11 | ground | Oxygen sensor | Bank 2 sensor 1 |
| 12 | input | Oxygen sensor heating | Bank 1 sensor 1 |
| 13 | input | Oxygen sensor heating | Bank 2 sensor 1 |
| 14 | - | Not used | |
| 15 | - | Not used | |
| 16 | input | DMTL pump signal | Diagnosis module for fuel tank leakage |
| 17 | input | DMTL heating signal | Diagnosis module for fuel tank leakage |
| 18 | input | Oxygen sensor signal | Bank 1 sensor 1 |
| 19 | input | Oxygen sensor signal | Bank 2 sensor 2 |
| 20 | input | Oxygen sensor signal | Bank 1 sensor 2 |
| 21 | - | Not used | |
| 22 | - | Not used | |
| 23 | ground | Oxygen sensor | Bank 1 sensor 2 |
| 24 | input | Oxygen sensor | Bank 2 sensor 2 |
| 25 | input | Oxygen sensor | Bank 2 sensor 2 |
| 26 | output | Oxygen sensor | Bank 1 sensor 2 |

**Connector X60003 6-pin (voltage, ground supply)**

| Pin | Type | Component or function | Note |
|-----|------|----------------------|------|
| 1 | input | Terminal 30 | B+ potential distributor |
| 2 | input | Terminal 87 | Fuse F03 |
| 3 | ground | Ground | Ground point |
| 4 | ground | Ground | Ground point |
| 5 | ground | Ground | Ground point |
| 6 | ground | Ground | Ground point |

**Connector X60004 6-pin (ignition coils)**

| Pin | Type | Component or function | Note |
|-----|------|----------------------|------|
| 1 | output | Ignition coil signal | Ignition coil signal 1 |
| 2 | output | Ignition coil signal | Ignition coil signal 2 |
| 3 | output | Ignition coil signal | Ignition coil signal 3 |
| 4 | output | Ignition coil signal | Ignition coil signal 4 |
| 5 | output | Ignition coil signal | Ignition coil signal 5 |
| 6 | output | Ignition coil signal | Ignition coil signal 6 |

*ECM pin assignments (turbo)*

**Connector X60005 44-pin (signals)**

| Pin | Type | Component or function | Note |
|---|---|---|---|
| 1 | - | Not used | |
| 2 | - | Not used | |
| 3 | output | Volume control valve | Control signal |
| 4 | - | Not used | |
| 5 | - | Not used | |
| 6 | - | Not used | |
| 7 | output | Low pressure fuel sensor ground | Low pressure fuel sensor |
| 8 | output | Low pressure fuel sensor voltage supply | Low pressure fuel sensor |
| 9 | input | Boost pressure sensor signal | Boost pressure sensor |
| 10 | input | Boost pressure sensor signal | Boost pressure sensor |
| 11 | output | Boost pressure sensor voltage supply | Boost pressure sensor |
| 12 | - | Not used | |
| 13 | output | DME main relay activation | DME main relay |
| 14 | output | Throttle valve voltage supply | Throttle valve |
| 15 | input | Throttle valve signal | Throttle valve |
| 16 | input | Throttle valve signal | Throttle valve |
| 17 | input | Intake air temperature signal | Integral to boost pressure sensor |
| 18 | - | Not used | |
| 19 | input | Knock sensor signal | Knock sensor |
| 20 | input | Knock sensor signal | Knock sensor |
| 21 | - | Not used | |
| 22 | - | Not used | |
| 23 | output | Fuel tank vent valve signal | Fuel tank vent valve |
| 24 | - | Not used | |
| 25 | - | Not used | |
| 26 | - | Not used | |
| 27 | - | Not used | |
| 28 | - | Not used | |
| 29 | input | Crankshaft position sensor signal | Crankshaft position sensor |
| 30 | ground | Crankshaft position sensor | Crankshaft position sensor |
| 31 | output | Intake manifold pressure sensor voltage supply | Intake manifold pressure sensor |
| 32 | ground | Intake manifold pressure sensor | Intake manifold pressure sensor |
| 33 | input | Intake manifold pressure sensor signal | Intake manifold pressure sensor |
| 34 | input | Low pressure fuel sensor signal | Low pressure fuel sensor |
| 35 | input/output | BSD signal | BSD signal connector |
| 36 | input | Throttle valve signal | Throttle valve |
| 37 | input | Throttle valve signal | Throttle valve |

**Connector X60005 44-pin (signals) (continued)**

| Pin | Type | Component or function | Note |
|-----|------|----------------------|------|
| 38 | ground | Throttle valve | Throttle valve |
| 39 | - | Not used | |
| 40 | - | Not used | |
| 41 | input | Knock sensor signal | Knock sensor |
| 42 | input | Knock sensor signal | Knock sensor |
| 43 | - | Not used | |
| 44 | - | Not used | |

**Connector X60006 12-pin (ignition coils)**

| Pin | Type | Component or function | Note |
|-----|------|----------------------|------|
| 1 | output | Fuel injector voltage supply | Fuel injector 1 |
| 2 | output | Fuel injector voltage supply | Fuel injector 2 |
| 3 | output | Fuel injector voltage supply | Fuel injector 3 |
| 4 | output | Fuel injector voltage supply | Fuel injector 4 |
| 5 | output | Fuel injector voltage supply | Fuel injector 5 |
| 6 | output | Fuel injector voltage supply | Fuel injector 6 |
| 7 | output | Fuel injector trigger | Fuel injector 1 |
| 8 | output | Fuel injector trigger | Fuel injector 2 |
| 9 | output | Fuel injector trigger | Fuel injector 3 |
| 10 | output | Fuel injector trigger | Fuel injector 4 |
| 11 | output | Fuel injector trigger | Fuel injector 5 |
| 12 | output | Fuel injector trigger | Fuel injector 6 |

**Connector X60007 26-pin (signals)**

| Pin | Type | Component or function | Note |
|-----|------|----------------------|------|
| 1 | - | Not used | |
| 2 | - | Not used | |
| 3 | - | Not used | |
| 4 | input | Engine coolant temperature signal | Engine coolant temperature sensor |
| 5 | output | Intake VANOS solenoid signal | Intake VANOS solenoid |
| 6 | - | Not used | |
| 7 | output | Wastegate control valve signal | Wastegate control valve |
| 8 | input | Fuel rail pressure sensor signal | Fuel rail pressure sensor |
| 9 | output | Fuel rail pressure sensor signal | Fuel rail pressure sensor |
| 10 | output | Fuel rail pressure sensor voltage supply | Fuel rail pressure sensor |
| 11 | input | Camshaft position sensor 1 signal | Camshaft position sensor 1 |
| 12 | input | Camshaft position sensor 2 signal | Camshaft position sensor 2 |
| 13 | input | Oil pressure switch signal | Oil pressure switch |

*ECM pin assignments (turbo)*

**Connector X60007 26-pin (signals) (continued)**

| Pin | Type | Component or function | Note |
|-----|------|------------------------|------|
| 14 | output | Wastegate control valve signal | Wastegate control valve signal |
| 15 | - | Not used | |
| 16 | - | Not used | |
| 17 | ground | Engine coolant temperature sensor | Engine coolant temperature sensor |
| 18 | output | Exhaust VANOS solenoid signal | Exhaust VANOS solenoid |
| 19 | input | Thermostat signal | Thermostat |
| 20 | - | Not used | |
| 21 | - | Not used | |
| 22 | - | Not used | |
| 23 | - | Not used | |
| 24 | ground | Camshaft position sensor 1 | Camshaft position sensor 1 |
| 25 | ground | Camshaft position sensor 2 | Camshaft position sensor 2 |
| 26 | input/output | BSD signal | Electric coolant pump |

# 160   Fuel Tank and Fuel Pump

160

## GENERAL

This repair group covers service information for the fuel supply system.

See also:

- **100 Engine–General** for model year, engine code, and DME applications
- **130 Fuel Injection**
- **ECL Electrical Component Locations** for fuel pump fuse and relay access information

## Fuel tank

The saddle-shaped plastic fuel tank is mounted underneath the center of the car (underneath the rear seat). Mounted in the fuel tank are the electric fuel pump, fuel level sending units and suction jet pump. Connecting lines for the evaporative emission control system are also attached to the tank.

Fuel tank capacity for 3 Series models is listed in **Table a**.

| Table a. Fuel tank capacity for 3 Series models | |
| --- | --- |
| Tank capacity | 60 liters (15.8 gal) |
| Reserve capacity | 6 liters (1.5 gal) |

## Fuel delivery systems

3 Series models use two main fuel delivery systems:
- Non-turbo engines use a multi-port injection system
- Turbo models use a direct injection system.

Non-turbo engine fuel injectors are installed in machine-bored holes in the cylinder head. See **130 Fuel Injection**. An in-tank electric fuel pump delivers pressure-regulated fuel to the fuel rail. The fuel pump is a variable speed pump controlled by the EKP (electric fuel pump control) module delivers only the amount of fuel needed for engine operation. This eliminates excess fuel delivery and reduces pump wear. It can operate at up to 5 bar (72.5 psi) and 95 liters (25 gallons) per hour.

Direct fuel injection in the turbo engine allows for precise metering of mixture and higher compression. This is made possible by locating a fuel injector for each cylinder centrally between the valves. See **130 Fuel Injection**. The electric fuel pump delivers fuel to a high pressure fuel pump. The high pressure fuel pump is driven by a chain and can provide fuel pressure from 5 bar (72.5 psi) up to 200 bar (2900 psi).

## Electric fuel pump

An electric fuel pump is mounted in the fuel tank in tandem with the right side fuel level sender and suction jet pump. A suction jet pump is located in the left side of the tank to transfer fuel to the right side. The combined fuel filter / pressure regulator delivers pressurized fuel to the fuel injection system. The system is a non-return design; there is one fuel line to the fuel injectors and excess fuel flows directly from the fuel filter / pressure regulator back into the tank.

 Fuel pump self-diagnostics are built into the DME. A failure in the fuel pump circuit will set a fault code.

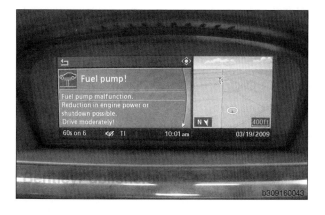

## Fuel system schematic (non-turbo)

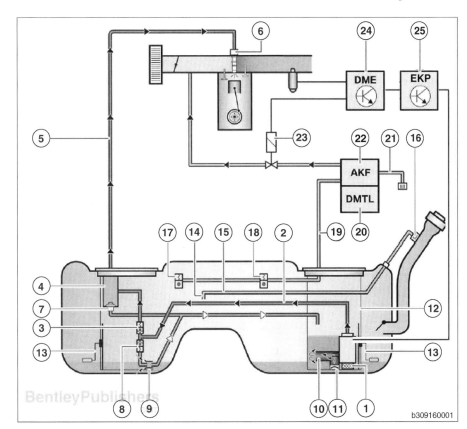

b309160001

1. Electric fuel pump
2. Supply line
3. Check valve
4. Fuel filter
5. Supply line to engine
6. Fuel injector
7. Pressure regulator
8. Check valve
9. Left suction jet pump
10. Suction jet pump
11. Initial filling valve
12. Fuel baffle
13. Fuel level sender
14. Refueling line connector
15. Refueling ventilation line
16. Refueling ventilation nipple
17. Left operation ventilation valve
18. Right operation ventilation valve
19. Operation ventilation line
20. Diagnosis pump for tank leakage (DMTL)
21. Fresh air vent line
22. Activated carbon canister
23. Fuel tank vent valve
24. Engine control module (ECM)
25. Fuel pump module (EKP)

160

## Fuel system schematic (turbo)

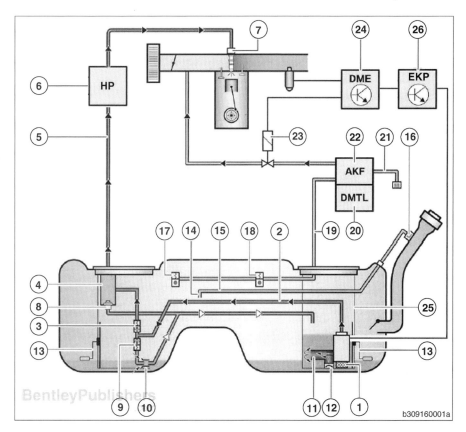

b309160001a

1. Electric fuel pump
2. Supply line
3. Check valve
4. Fuel filter
5. Supply line to engine
6. High pressure fuel pump
7. Fuel injector
8. Pressure regulator
9. Check valve
10. Left suction jet pump
11. Suction jet pump
12. Initial filling valve
13. Fuel level sender
14. Refueling line connector
15. Refueling ventilation line
16. Refueling ventilation nipple
17. Left operation ventilation valve
18. Right operation ventilation valve
19. Operation ventilation line
20. Diagnosis pump for tank leakage (DMTL)
21. Fresh air vent line
22. Activated carbon canister
23. Fuel tank vent valve
24. Engine control module (ECM)
25. Fuel baffle
26. Fuel pump module (EKP)

**160**

## Warnings and Cautions

*WARNING—*

- *The fuel system is designed to retain pressure even when the ignition is OFF. When working with the fuel system, loosen the fuel lines slowly to allow residual fuel pressure to dissipate. Avoid spraying fuel. Use shop towels to capture leaking fuel.*

- *Before beginning work on the fuel system, place a fire extinguisher in the vicinity of the work area.*

- *Work only on the fuel system when engine temperature is below 40°C (104°F).*

- *When disconnecting a fuel line, clamp off the line and wrap a clean shop towel around the fitting before disconnecting. Residual fuel pressure is present in the line.*

- *Electric fuel pump starts each time door is opened.*

- *Fuel is highly flammable. When working around fuel, do not disconnect wires that could cause electrical sparks. Do not smoke or work near heaters or other fire hazards.*

- *Wear eye protection, face shield and protective clothing to avoid injuries from contact with fuel.*

- *When working on an open fuel system, wear suitable hand protection, as prolonged contact with fuel can cause illnesses and skin disorders.*

- *Unscrew the fuel tank cap to release pressure in the tank before working on fuel lines.*

- *Do not use a work light with an incandescent bulb near fuel. Fuel may spray on the hot bulb causing a fire.*

- *Make sure the work area is properly ventilated.*

- *Due to risk of personal injury, be sure the engine is cold before beginning work on engine components.*

*CAUTION—*

- *Prior to disconnecting the battery, read the battery disconnection cautions given in* **001 Warnings and Cautions**.

- *Before making any electrical tests with ignition switched ON, disable the ignition system as described in* **120 Ignition System**. *Be sure the battery is disconnected when replacing components.*

- *To prevent damage to the ignition system or other DME components, including the engine control module (ECM), connect and disconnect wires and test equipment with ignition OFF.*

- *Cleanliness is essential when working with the fuel system. Thoroughly clean the fuel line unions before disconnecting any of the lines. Plug open fuel lines and ports.*

- *Use only clean tools. Keep removed parts clean and sealed or covered with a clean, lint-free cloth, especially if completion of the repair is delayed.*

- *Do not move the car while the fuel system is open.*

- *Avoid using high pressure compressed air to blow out lines and components. High pressure can rupture internal seals and gaskets.*

- *Use new seals, O-rings and hose clamps when replacing fuel system components*

## FUEL TANK EVAPORATIVE CONTROL SYSTEM

Evaporative control, also referred to as running losses control, is designed to prevent fuel system evaporative losses from venting into the atmosphere. The components of this system allow control and monitoring of evaporative losses by on-board diagnostic (OBD II) software incorporated into the engine control module (ECM).

Listed below are the main components of the evaporative control system and their functions:

• Carbon canister stores fuel vapors.

• Plumbing ducts vapors from fuel tank to canister and from canister to intake manifold.

• Carbon canister purge valve is controlled by engine control module (ECM).

• Pressure regulator shunts excess fuel volume directly back to fuel tank before it circulates through the fuel lines.

• Leak detection unit (DMTL) pressurizes fuel tank and evaporative system to monitor system leaks.

### Evaporative system troubleshooting

BX56020010

◄ Start by accessing diagnostic trouble codes (DTCs) using a BMW or compatible aftermarket scan tool.

• For purposes of OBD II emissions compliance, the DME system sets a diagnostic trouble code (DTC) when it detects a leak in the evaporative control system.

• Malfunction indicator light (MIL) is illuminated upon second recurrence of fault. See **OBD On-Board Diagnostics**.

− When leak testing, observe the following conditions to obtain plausible results:

• Fuel tank ¼ to ¾ full.

• Vehicle parked for at least 2 hours to allow fuel to reach ambient temperature. Ideal fuel temperature is 10°- 20°C (50° - 68°F).

• Do not refuel immediately before leak test.

− If a leak is detected, check the following areas:

• Fuel filler cap leaking or off.

• Fuel tank ventilation lines leaking at fuel tank or activated carbon canister.

• Tank ventilation valve leaking (in engine compartment).

• Fuel level sensor and fuel pump assembly cover leaking.

For evaporative system component replacement, see **Fuel Supply Components** in this repair group.

## Evaporative system leak test

Use the following leak test when diagnosing evaporative system leak fault codes.

— Working underneath left rear bumper: gain access to activated carbon canister. See **Activated carbon canister, removing and installing** in this repair group.

◄ Remove fresh air line (**inset**) from DMTL pump.

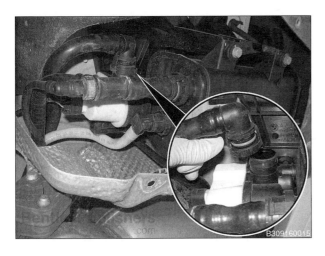

◄ Install BMW test adapter 83 30 0 433 207 (**B**) (or suitable substitute) at DMTL fresh air connection (**A**).

— Connect evaporative system smoke machine (**C**) to test adapter (**B**). BMW recommends VACUTEC 625-522B (nitrogen pressure swing absorption technology).

— Remove fuel filler cap.

— Activate smoke machine and fill fuel system with smoke until it escapes from fuel filler neck. Shut off smoke machine.

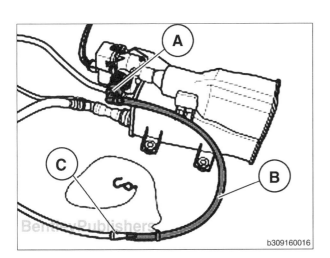

> **WARNING**—
> • *Use only smoke machine that utilizes nitrogen to pressurize fuel system.*
> • *The fuel system may release a substantial amount of fuel-rich gasoline vapors during testing. Work in a well ventilated area.*

— Reinstall fuel filler cap.

— Reactivate smoke machine and fill fuel system with smoke.

> **WARNING**—
> • *Do not exceed a maximum fuel system pressure of 0.3 bar (4 psi) when using smoke machine.*

— Examine fuel system components for signs of escaping smoke. Repair or replace faulty components.

— After completing tests:
  • Attach DMTL fresh air line.
  • Check for fault codes and reset ECM memory.

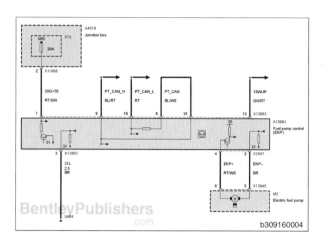

b309160004

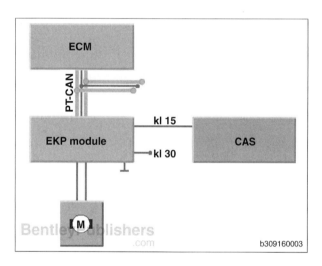

b309160003

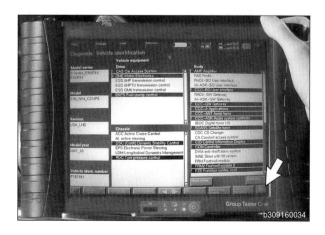

b309160034

# FUEL SYSTEM TROUBLESHOOTING

## Fuel pump fuse and module

Begin troubleshooting fuel system faults by checking fuel pump fuse. The fuel pump fuse is located in the junction box (JB) behind the glove compartment. See **ECL Electrical Component Locations** for access information.

◀ Fuel pump circuit is fuse-protected by:

- F70 up to 03/2007.
- F88 from 03/2007 to 09/2007.
- F70 0/20079 and up.

> **CAUTION—**
>
> - *Relay and fuse positions and wire colors vary. A good way to verify a relay position or wire colors is to compare the wiring colors at the relay socket to the colors indicated on the wiring diagrams in* **ELE Electrical Wiring Diagrams**.

◀ The ECM calculates the amount of fuel required at the given point in time and the electric fuel pump is activated as required. The total volume required is transmitted as a message to the EKP control module via PT-CAN.

The EKP module converts this message into an output voltage which controls the fuel pump. The fuel pump is capable of delivering up to 95 liters (25 gallons) per hour at a pressure of 5 bar (72.5 psi). On turbo engine models, if the ECM detects a fault in the low pressure fuel sensor, the fuel pump is activated to 100% or 5 bar (72.5 psi).

## Operating fuel pump for tests

This procedure explains how to operate the fuel pump for testing purposes without having to run the engine.

◀ Using BMW factory scan tool or equivalent:

- Identify vehicle
- Select **Next (arrow)**
- Select **Control Module Functions**
- Select **Complete Vehicle**
- Select **Drive**
- Select **DME**
- Select **Component Activation**
- Select **Fuel Pump**

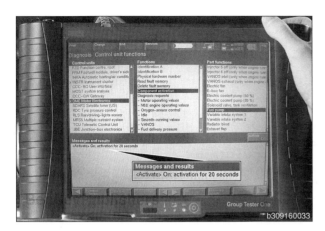

◄ Fuel pump will run at 100% (5 bar) for 20 seconds.

## Fuel pump electrical circuit, testing

If fuel pump does not operate or there is no fuel pressure, first test fuel pump electrical circuit.

– Remove rear seat to access fuel pump and fuel level sender. See **Accessing fuel pump and fuel level senders** in this repair group.

◄ Disconnect harness connector from fuel pump and fuel level sender.

◄ Connect voltmeter between fuel pump leads (**arrows**) on connector.

– Activate fuel pump. See **Operating fuel pump for tests** in this repair group.

– Use digital multimeter to test for battery voltage at fuel pump connector leads.

– If voltage and ground are present, fuel pump is probably faulty. If there is no voltage, check wiring between fuel pump and fuel pump module.

– After completing tests, reconnect fuel pump harness connector.

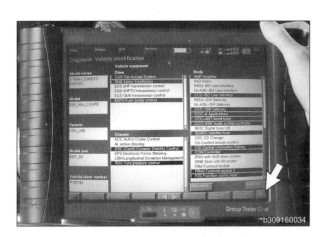

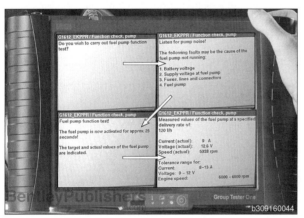

## Fuel pump power consumption, testing

If fuel delivery is erratic or poor, or if fuel pump makes abnormally loud noises, test pump power consumption.

 Using BMW factory scan tool or equivalent:

- Identify vehicle
- Select **Next (arrow)**
- Select **Function Selection**
- Select **DME**
- Select **Fuel Pump**
- Select **Control Current B1612_STR00**
- Select **Next (arrow)**

◁ Follow steps on screen to monitor fuel pump current.

| Fuel pump current | |
|---|---|
| Current consumption (activated with scan tool) | 8 - 13 amps |

An alternative method is to install a digital ammeter in fuel pump circuit using the following steps.

− Remove rear seat to access fuel pump and fuel level sender. See **Accessing fuel pump and fuel level senders** in this repair group.

◁ Disconnect harness connector from fuel pump.

− Make sure battery voltage at fuel pump connector is 12.6 volts. Charge battery if necessary.

*Fuel pressure gauge, installing (non-turbo)*

— Attach digital ammeter between pump lead and harness. Connect jumper wire between pump and harness.

> **CAUTION—**
> • *Do not allow the test leads to short to ground.*

◄ Activate fuel pump. See **Operating fuel pump for tests** in this repair group.

— Compare ammeter reading with specification listed in table.

| Fuel pump current | |
|---|---|
| Current consumption (activated with scan tool) | 8 - 13 amps |

— Higher than normal power consumption by fuel pump may indicate a worn pump, causing intermittent fuel starvation due to pump overheating and seizure. Replace pump.

— Lower than normal power consumption may indicate blockage in a fuel line. Before replacing fuel pump, be sure to check that return line and pump pickup (inside fuel tank) are not obstructed.

## Fuel pressure gauge, installing (non-turbo)

— Remove ignition coil cover. See **020 Maintenance**.

◄ Remove Schræder valve cap (**arrow**) at fuel rail and connect fuel pressure gauge.

— Use a fuel pressure gauge with a minimum range of 0 to 7 bar (0 to 100 psi).

> **WARNING—**
> • *The fuel system is designed to retain pressure even when the ignition is OFF. When working with the fuel system, loosen fuel lines slowly to allow residual fuel pressure to dissipate. Avoid spraying fuel. Use shop towels to capture leaking fuel.*
> • *Fuel pump starts each time door is opened.*
> • *Make sure the fuel pressure gauge is securely connected to the fuel rail to prevent it from coming loose under pressure.*

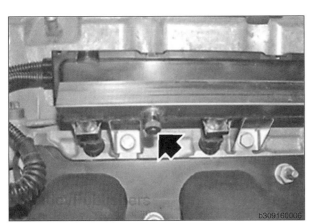

160

## Fuel pressure gauge, installing (turbo)

Use a fuel pressure gauge with a minimum range of 0 to 7 bar (0 to 100 psi).

> **WARNING —**
> * The fuel system is designed to retain pressure even when the ignition is OFF. When working with the fuel system, loosen fuel lines slowly to allow residual fuel pressure to dissipate. Avoid spraying fuel. Use shop towels to capture leaking fuel.
> * Fuel pump starts each time door is opened.
> * Make sure the fuel pressure gauge is securely connected to the fuel rail to prevent it from coming loose under pressure.

— Remove splash shield for transmission. See **020 Maintenance**.

◀ Working underneath vehicle on drivers side:

* Remove fasteners (**arrows**) for fuel line protective shield and remove protective shield.

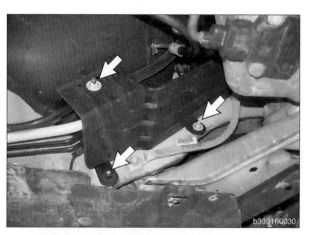

◀ Disconnect fuel line (**arrow**).

◀ Install compatible T-style test adapter and install fuel pressure gauge.

## Fuel pressure regulator

Fuel pressure is created by the fuel pump and maintained by the fuel pressure regulator.

Fuel pressure regulator is integrated into the fuel pump assembly. See **Fuel pump, removing and installing** in this repair group.

## Fuel delivery, testing

Checking fuel delivery is a fundamental part of troubleshooting and diagnosing the DME system. Fuel pressure directly influences fuel delivery. There are two significant fuel delivery values to be measured:

- **System pressure** is created by fuel pump and maintained by pressure regulator. System pressure is adjustable only by the ECM.

- **Residual pressure** is pressure maintained in closed system after engine and fuel pump are shut off.

### System pressure, engine not running

— Attach fuel pressure gauge. See **Fuel pressure gauge, installing (non-turbo) (turbo)** in this repair group.

— Activate fuel pump. See **Operating fuel pump for tests** in this repair group. Compare fuel pressure to specifications in accompanying table.

| Fuel pressure specification | |
|---|---|
| System pressure, engine not running | 5 ± 0.2 bar (72.5 ± 2.9 psi) |

> **CAUTION—**
> - *The fuel pump is capable of developing a higher pressure than that regulated by the pressure regulator. Do not allow pressure to rise above 6.5 bar (94 psi). Damage to the fuel lines or fuel system components could result.*

— After completing tests without running engine, check for fault codes and reset ECM memory.

### System pressure, engine running

If fuel pressure tests show normal pressure but engine lacks power under acceleration, test fuel pump pressure control regulation function.

— With fuel pressure gauge attached, start engine and check fuel pressure.

| Fuel pressure specification | |
|---|---|
| System pressure, engine running | 5 ± 0.2 bar (72.5 ± 2.9 psi) |

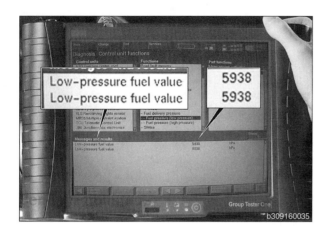

Low-pressure fuel value   5938
Low-pressure fuel value   5938

b309160035

> **CAUTION—**
>
> • *The fuel pump is capable of developing a higher pressure than that regulated by the pressure regulator. Do not allow pressure to rise above 6.5 bar (94 psi). Damage to the fuel lines or fuel system components could result.*

◄ On turbo engine models compare fuel pressure on gauge to data value on BMW factory scan tool or equivalent.

– If pressure does not match, replace fuel pressure regulator. See **Fuel pump, removing and installing** in this repair group.

– After completing tests, note the following:

• Non turbo: replace Schræder valve cap.

• Turbo reassemble fuel line.

• Check for fault codes and reset ECM memory.

### Residual pressure

For quick restarts and to avoid vapor lock when the engine is hot, the fuel injection system retains fuel pressure after the engine is shut off. This residual pressure is primarily maintained by the fuel pressure regulator and a check valve at the fuel pump outlet.

– Attach fuel pressure gauge. See **Fuel pressure gauge, installing** in this repair group.

– Start engine and allow it to run for approximately one minute. Note fuel pressure reading. Shut OFF engine.

– Note fuel pressure after approximately 20 minutes. Make sure pressure does not drop more than 0.5 bar from system pressure.

| Fuel pressure specification | |
|---|---|
| System pressure, engine not running | 5 ± 0.2 bar (72.5 ± 2.9 psi) |

– When finished, disconnect pressure gauge and fitting, and replace Schræder valve cap.

– If fuel system does not maintain pressure:

• Visually check for leaks in fuel lines and unions.

• Check for leaking injector(s).

• Check for faulty fuel pump check valve.

## FUEL PUMP AND FUEL LEVEL SENDERS

### Accessing fuel pump and fuel level senders

*NOTE—*

* *Right side fuel pump / fuel level sender shown. Accessing left side fuel level sender is similar.*

— Remove rear seat cushion. See **520 Seats**.

◄ Working at ride side fuel tank:

* Remove fasteners (**A**).
* Remove fuel pump access cover (**B**).

— Installation is reverse of removal.

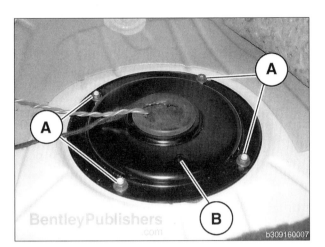

### Fuel pump and fuel level sender (right side), removing

— Drain fuel tank. See **Fuel tank, draining** in this repair group.

— Disconnect negative cable from battery.

> *CAUTION—*
> * *Prior to disconnecting the battery, read the battery disconnection cautions given in **001 Warnings and Cautions**.*

— Remove fuel pump access cover. See **Accessing fuel pump and fuel level senders** in this repair group.

◄ Remove electrical connectors (**A**) and fuel lines (**B**).

> *WARNING—*
> * *When disconnecting fuel hose, wrap shop towel around end of hose to prevent spray of fuel under pressure.*

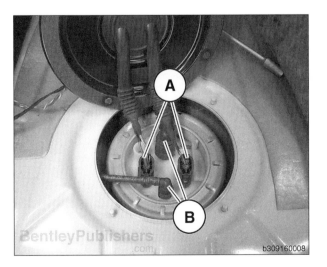

*Fuel pump and fuel level sender (right side), removing*

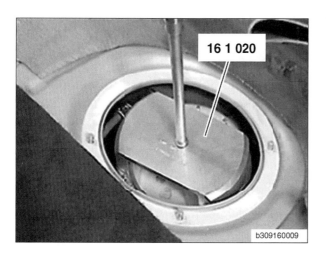

◀ Using special tool 16 1 020, remove fuel pump service cap.

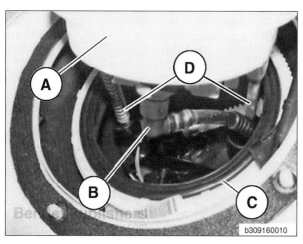

◀ Carefully raise service cap (**A**) and disconnect fuel line (**B**). Remove and discard O-ring (**C**).

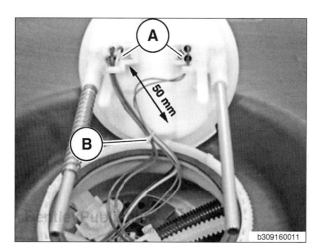

◀ Disconnect electrical connectors (**A**), cut and dispose of wire tire (**B**).

*Fuel pump and fuel level sender (right side), installing*

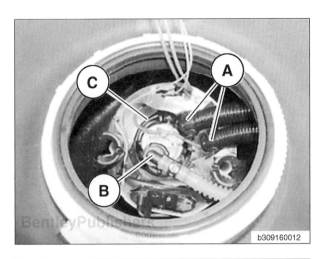

b309160012

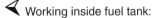

◄ Working inside fuel tank:

- Disconnect black fuel return lines (**A**).
- Unlock and disconnect fuel line (**B**) using only your fingers.
- Carefully lift fuel pump and fuel level sender (**C**) out of tank. If necessary rotate 90° counterclockwise and tilt towards fuel level sender.

> **CAUTION—**
> • *Do not bend fuel sender arm.*

**160**

> **NOTE—**
> • *Be prepared to catch any dripping fuel.*

To replace fuel level sender use following step.

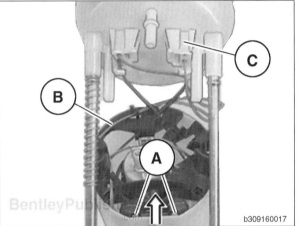

b309160017

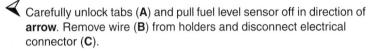

◄ Carefully unlock tabs (**A**) and pull fuel level sensor off in direction of **arrow**. Remove wire (**B**) from holders and disconnect electrical connector (**C**).

— Installation of fuel level sender is reverse of removal. **See Fuel pump and fuel level sender (right side), installing** in this repair group for fuel pump installing.

## Fuel pump and fuel level sender (right side), installing

◄ Working inside fuel tank:

- Carefully install fuel pump and fuel level sender (**C**). If necessary rotate 90° clockwise and tilt toward fuel level sender.
- Connect black fuel return lines (**A**).
- Connect and lock fuel line (**B**) using only your fingers.

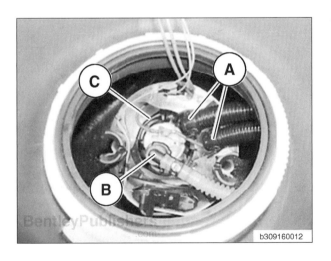

b309160012

*Fuel pump and fuel level sender (right side), installing*

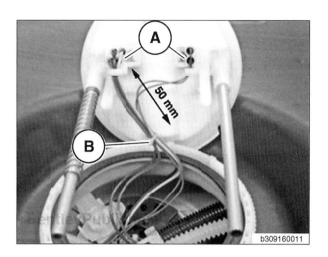

◄ Connect electrical connectors (**A**), and attach wires with wire tie (**B**).

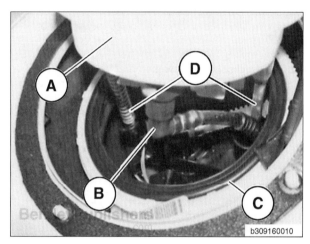

◄ Clean sealing area for O-ring (**C**). Remember to replace O-ring (**C**) with new.

– Carefully install service cap (**A**) while aligning locating rods (**D**). Check to see service cap freely, do not force.

– Connect vent line (**B**).

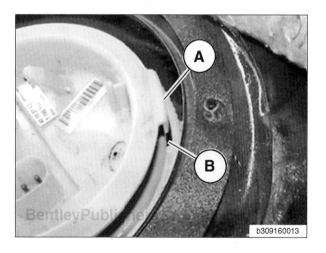

◄ When installing, check to see that service cap lug (**A**) engages with corresponding slot of fuel tank (**B**).

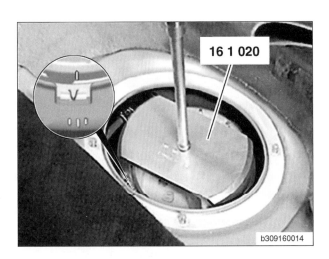

◄ Install service cap hand tight.

− Using special tool 16 1 020 tighten service cap until marking on service cap point to notch on fuel tank (**inset**).

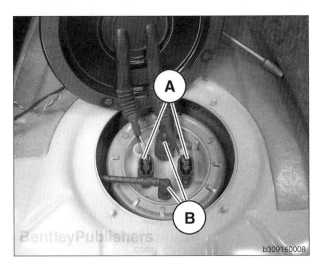

◄ Connect electrical connectors (**A**) and fuel lines (**B**).

− Install fuel tank access cover.

> **CAUTION—**
> • After finishing repairs but before starting engine, be sure there is at least 5 liters (1.5 gallons) of fuel in the tank. The fuel pump is damaged if run without fuel.

## Fuel level sender (left side), removing

− Drain fuel tank. See **Fuel tank, draining** in this repair group.

− Disconnect negative cable from battery.

> **CAUTION—**
> • Prior to disconnecting the battery, read the battery disconnection cautions given in **001 Warnings and Cautions**.

− Remove fuel sender access cover. See **Accessing fuel pump and fuel level senders** in this repair group.

− Remove left side fuel level sender. See **Fuel pump and fuel level sender (right side), removing**, in this repair group

◄ Disconnect electrical connector (**C**). Using only your fingers press gray ring (**A**) toward sensor and pull fuel supply (**B**) line straight out.

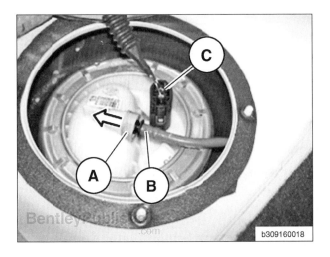

*Fuel level sender (left side), removing*

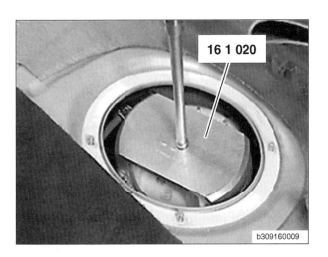

◅ Using special tool 16 1 020, remove fuel pump service cap.

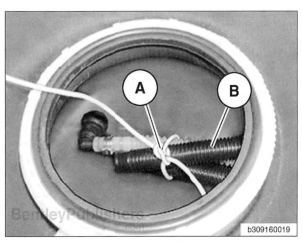

◅ Attach stiff wire (**A**) to hose pack (**B**) through right side fuel tank opening. The wire is pulled through to the left side to aid installation.

◅ To remove assembly, press tab (**B**) against spring force and carefully lift sender (**A**) out of tank with hose pack. Remember to replace fuel tank seals (O-rings).

## Fuel level sender (left side), installing

– Carefully feed hose pack through tank with mechanics wire and guide fuel level sender into position.

◄ When installing check to see that service cap lug (**A**) engages with corresponding slot of fuel tank (**B**).

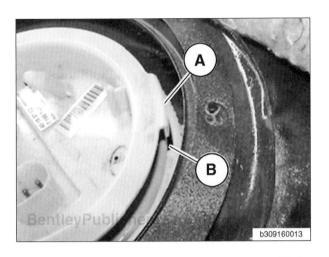

◄ Install service cap hand tight.

– Using BMW special tool 16 1 020 tighten service cap until marking on service cap point to notch on fuel tank.

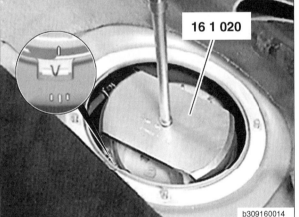

◄ Connect electrical connector (**C**) and fuel line (**B**).

– Install fuel tank access cover.

> **CAUTION—**
> • *After finishing repairs but before starting engine, be sure there is at least 5 liters (1.5 gallons) of fuel in the tank. The fuel pump is damaged if run without fuel.*

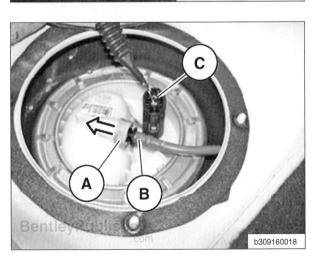

## High-pressure fuel pump, removing (turbo)

– Remove intake manifold. See **130 Fuel Injection**.

◄ Remove electrical connectors (**A**) and lay harness aside.

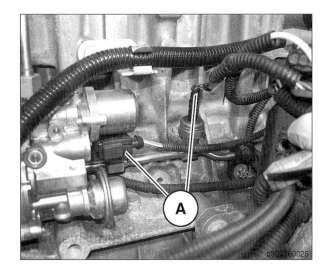

◄ Remove aluminum fastener (**arrow**) and discard. Detach fuel line (**A**). Seal fuel lines with BMW special tools 13 5 281 and 13 5 282. Remember to replace aluminum fastener (**arrow**) with new.

> **WARNING**—
> • *Wear gloves and face shield when loosening fuel lines.*

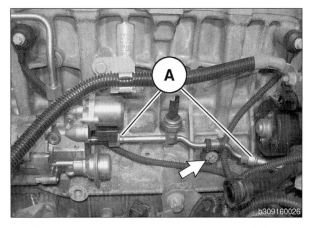

◄ Loosen fuel line nut (**A**) and fuel line nut (**B**) in this order. Remove fuel line bracket fastener (**C**) and remove fuel line (**D**). Seal fuel line connections with matching plugs from BMW special tool kit 32 1 270.

> **WARNING**—
> • *Wear gloves and face shield when loosening fuel lines.*

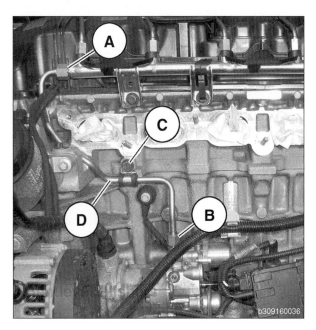

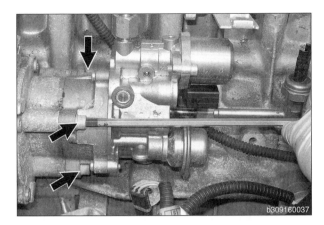

◄ Remove high-pressure fuel pump mounting fasteners (**arrows**) and remove high-pressure fuel pump. Be prepared to catch any dripping oil with shop cloth.

**160**

## High-pressure fuel pump, installing (turbo)

◄ Replace high-pressure fuel pump O-ring (**A**) and clean mounting surfaces.

◄ When installing, rotate pump (**A**) in direction of **arrow** until flush with mounting surface.

*High-pressure fuel pump, installing (turbo)*

◀ Install high-pressure fuel pump fasteners (**arrows**) finger tight.

◀ Prior to installing high-pressure fuel lines, dispose of any copper sealing rings installed at the factory. They are no longer needed.

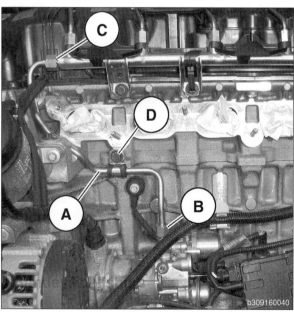

◀ Use the following sequence when installing the fuel line.

- Coat fuel line connections with transmission fluid.
- Preinstall fuel line (**A**).
- Tighten nuts (**B**) (**C**) finger tight.
- Tighten nut (**B**) to proper torque.
- Tighten nut (**C**) to proper torque.
- Tighten fuel line bracket fastener (**D**).

| Tightening torques | |
|---|---|
| Fuel line to high-pressure fuel pump | 30 Nm (22 ft-lb) |
| Fuel line to fuel rail | 30 Nm (22 ft-lb) |
| Fuel line mount to cylinder head | 13 Nm (9.5 ft-lb) |

*High-pressure fuel pump, installing (turbo)*

◄ Before installing high-pressure fuel pump supply line, confirm it has the updated elastomer mounting clamp (**arrow**). If it has a soldered hold down clamp replace fuel supply line with updated part.

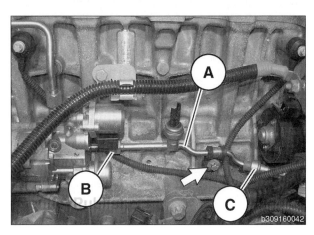

◄ Use the following sequence when installing the fuel supply line.

- Coat fuel line connections with transmission fluid.
- Pre-install fuel line (**A**).
- Tighten nut (**B**) and mount fastener (**arrow**) finger tight. Remember to replace fuel line bracket aluminum fastener with new.
- Connect fuel line (**C**) to fuel supply line (**A**). Listen for audible click.
- Tighten nut (**B**) to proper torque.
- Tighten fuel line bracket fastener (**arrow**).

| Tightening torques | |
|---|---|
| Fuel line to high-pressure fuel pump | 30 Nm (22 ft-lb) |
| Fuel line bracket to engine<br>• Stage 1<br>• Stage 2 | 10 Nm (7.3 ft-lb)<br>Additional 90° ± 15° |

− Reassemble engine.

− Check fuel system for leaks.

− Check for fault codes and reset ECM memory.

## FUEL SUPPLY COMPONENTS

### Fuel tank, draining

When draining fuel tank, use a safe storage unit and an approved fuel pumping device.

> **WARNING—**
> • *Before starting to work on tank removal, make sure hot components, such as the exhaust system, are completely cooled down.*
> • *Fuel may be spilled. Do not smoke or work near heaters or other fire hazards.*

— Start engine and allow to run 10 - 15 seconds to fill fuel compensating siphon assembly. This allows both lobes of fuel tank to be drawn off through fuel filler pipe.

— Disconnect negative cable from battery.

> **CAUTION—**
> • *Prior to disconnecting the battery, read the battery disconnection cautions given in* **001 Warnings and Cautions**.

— Remove fuel tank filler cap.

— Slide suction hose into filler neck about 130 cm (51 in), twisting as necessary. Withdraw fuel into storage unit.

— Monitor fuel level reduction in both lobes:

• Remove rear seat cushion and access both fuel tank sender harness connectors. See **Accessing fuel pump and fuel level senders** in this repair group.

• Use multimeter to measure resistance at both senders. Resistance should drop as fuel level drops.

— If siphoning mechanism is faulty, drain left tank lobe separately by removing sender cover and pumping fuel directly out of left lobe.

— Remove suction hose from tank filler neck carefully to avoid damaging filler neck baffle plate.

> **CAUTION—**
> • *After finishing repairs but before starting engine, be sure there is at least 5 liters (1.5 gallons) of fuel in tank. The fuel pump is damaged if run without fuel.*

## Fuel filter

The fuel filter is a lifetime filter. It is integrated into the left side fuel level sender. See **Fuel level sender (left side), removing** in this repair group.

## Fuel pressure regulator

The fuel pressure regulator is integrated into the left side fuel level sender. See **Fuel level sender (left side), removing** in this repair group.

## Fuel pump module (EKP), removing and installing

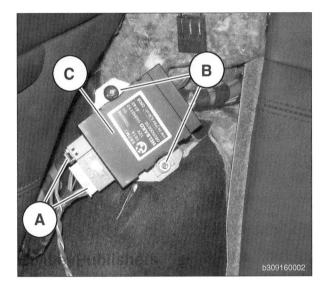

‒ E90: Remove rear seat backrest. See **520 Seats**.

‒ E91, E92: Remove rear right backrest side bolster. See **520 Seats**.

◀ Working at EKF module:

 • Remove electrical connectors (**A**).

 • Remove fasteners (**B**) and remove EKP module (**C**).

‒ Installation is reverse of removal.

 • Remember to perform coding / programming on EKP module if replaced. See **600 Electrical System-General**.

‒ Check for fault codes and reset ECM memory.

## Activated carbon canister, removing and installing

The carbon canister is on the left side underneath the rear bumper.

‒ Raise rear end of car and support safely.

> **CAUTION—**
> • *Make sure the car is stable and well supported at all times. Use a professional automotive lift or jack stands designed for the purpose. A floor jack is not adequate support.*

◀ Remove left side rear bumper splash shield fasteners (**arrows**).

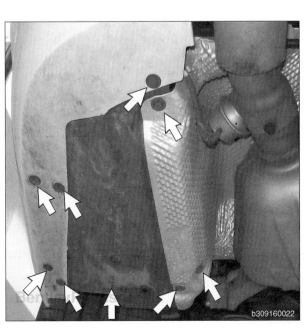

*Fuel tank leak detection unit (DMTL), removing and installing*

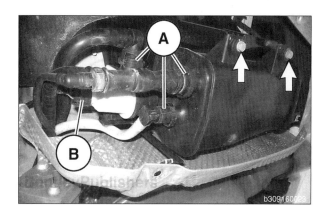

◀ Remove activated carbon canister:

- Remove line connections at leak detection pump (**A**).
- Disconnect electrical harness connector (**B**).
- Remove fasteners (**arrows**) and remove carbon canister from vehicle.

– Installation is reverse of removal.

### Fuel tank leak detection unit (DMTL), removing and installing

The DMTL is mounted to the activated carbon canister.

– Raise car and support safely.

> **WARNING**—
> • *Make sure the car is stable and well supported at all times. Use a professional automotive lift or jack stands designed for the purpose. A floor jack is not adequate support.*

– Remove activated carbon canister. See **Activated carbon canister, removing and installing** in this repair group.

◀ Remove fasteners (**A**) and pull DMTL unit out of carbon canister in direction of **arrow**.

– Installation is reverse of removal.

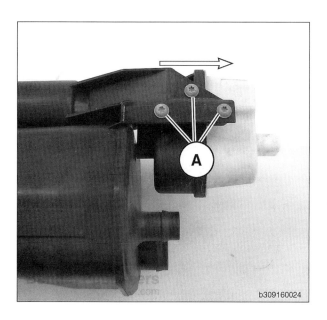

# 170 Radiator and Cooling System

## GENERAL

This repair group covers component repair information for the engine cooling system.

See also:

• **020 Maintenance** for coolant hose inspection

• **100 Engine–General** for engine code and application information

• **130 Fuel Injection** for engine coolant temperature (ECT) sensor service

### Electric coolant pump

 An externally mounted electric coolant pump is bolted to the right front of the engine block. The electric pump allows for more efficient heating and cooling of the engine. It can operate regardless of whether the engine is ON or OFF.

A low coolant flow rate is used during cold start situations to speed engine warm-up. A high flow rate (including flow with engine OFF) is used for rapid cool-down. In this way the electric coolant pump helps ensure engine efficiency and longevity.

The pump is DME controlled. The DME use engine load, the operating range and various temperature sensors to determine coolant pump operation and speed.

The electric coolant pump is self-diagnosable and can identify and store the following faults:

• Impeller speed deviation

• Stiff operation or blocked by foreign objects

• Incorrect mixture ratio coolant/water

• Air in cooling system

## Electrically heated thermostat

An electrically heated, DME controlled thermostat is externally mounted above the coolant pump. The engine control module (ECM) activates the thermostat to maintain engine coolant temperature within a narrow range.

If the electronics fail, the mechanical function of the thermostat acts as a fail-safe.

## Radiator and expansion tank

◀ The radiator is a crossflow design. An expansion tank provides for coolant expansion at higher temperatures and easy monitoring of the coolant level.

Automatic transmission fluid (ATF) is circulated through an additional heat exchanger (ATF cooler).

N51 engines use a manganese oxide coated radiator that works to reduce ambient air ozone. This radiator uses an EAC (Environmental Air Catalyst) sensor to check that the special coated radiator if fitted to the vehicle.

*NOTE—*

• *The EAC sensor is hard wired to the radiator so that it cannot be disconnected. In the event of failure of the EAC sensor, it can be replaced once. If the EAC sensor fails again, it must always be replaced together with the radiator.*

• *The EAC sensor continuously transmits a signal to the engine control module. If an uncoated radiator without an EAC sensor is installed, the engine control module will illuminate the check engine lamp.*

## Electric cooling fan

◀ Models covered by this manual use an electric cooling fan mounted on the engine side of the radiator.

The electric cooling fan is controlled by the engine control module (ECM) via the output final stage.

The output final stage is mounted on the fan housing, next to the fan motor. The fan is operated using a pulse width modulated signal.

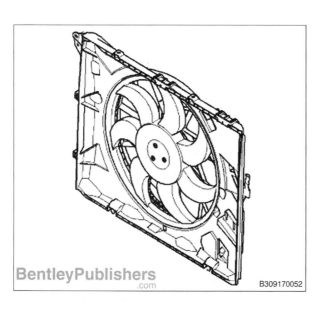

BentleyPublishers.com    B309170053

BentleyPublishers.com    B309170052

Fan circuit wiring is protected by a high-amp fuse. Electric fan activation is based on the following inputs to the ECM:

• Radiator outlet temperature

• Calculated catalytic converter temperature

• Vehicle speed

• Battery voltage

• Calculated refrigerant pressure

When the vehicle is first started, the ECM activates the electric fan briefly at 20% of its maximum speed, then switches OFF. This is for diagnostic monitoring. The voltage generated by the fan when it slows down (acting as a generator) must match the stored rpm values in the fan output stage to confirm that the fan is operating correctly.

**NOTE —**

• *If the ECM fault memory indicates a cooling fan fault, check that the fan is not seized and that it spins freely.*

• *When A/C is switched ON, the electric fan is not immediately turned on.*

• *After the engine is switched OFF, the fan may continue to run at varying speeds for up to 10 minutes, based on calculated catalyst temperature.*

## Automatic transmission fluid (ATF) cooler

ATF lines connect the transmission to the ATF cooler (heat exchanger) at back of radiator.

On cold engine start-up, the engine coolant is heated more quickly than the transmission fluid. Heat from engine coolant is used to warm up the ATF faster, reducing drag in the transmission and improving fuel mileage.

Once ATF reaches normal operating temperature it is hotter than the engine coolant. The ATF heat exchanger then acts as a cooling device.

## Warnings and Cautions

Observe the following warnings and cautions when working on the cooling system.

**WARNING —**

• *At normal operating temperature the cooling system is pressurized. Allow the system to cool as long as possible before opening (a minimum of one hour), then release the cap slowly to allow safe release of pressure.*

• *Releasing cooling system pressure lowers the coolant boiling point. The coolant may boil suddenly. Use heavy gloves and wear eye and face protection to guard against scalding.*

• *Use extreme care when draining and disposing of engine coolant. Coolant is poisonous and lethal to humans and pets. Pets are attracted to coolant because of its sweet smell and taste. Seek medical attention immediately if coolant is ingested.*

> **CAUTION—**
> - *Avoid adding cold water to the coolant while the engine is hot or overheated. If it is necessary to add coolant to a hot system, do so only with the engine running and coolant pump operating.*
> - *To avoid excess silicate gel precipitation in the cooling system and loss of cooling capacity, use BMW coolant or equivalent low silicate antifreeze.*
> - *If oil enters the cooling system, the radiator, expansion tank and heating circuit must be flushed with cleaning agent. BMW recommends removal of the radiator and expansion tank to flush.*
> - *When working on the cooling system, cover the alternator to protect it against coolant drips.*
> - *Prior to disconnecting the battery, read the battery disconnection cautions given in* **001 Warnings and Cautions**.

## TROUBLESHOOTING

Begin the diagnosis of cooling system problems with a thorough visual inspection. If no visual faults are found, check the engine control module (ECM) fault memory for stored diagnostic trouble codes (DTCs) using BMW scan tool or equivalent.

Common cooling system faults can be grouped into one of 4 categories:
- Cooling system leaks
- Poor coolant circulation
- Radiator cooling fan faults
- Electrical / electronic faults

### Cooling system inspection

— Check operation of electric radiator fan:
  - Start engine, turn A/C on, MAX setting. Electric fan should run.

— Check coolant hoses for cracks or softness. Check clamps for looseness. Check coolant level and check for evidence of coolant leaks from engine.

— Check that radiator fins are not blocked with dirt or debris. Clean radiator using low-pressure water or compressed air. Blow outward from engine side out.

— Check operation of electric coolant pump:
  - Turn ignition key on.
  - Adjust heat to max. setting.
  - Press accelerator pedal to floor.
  - Pump should audibly run after about 10 seconds.

— At normal operating temperature, cooling system is pressurized. This raises boiling point of coolant. Leaks may prevent system from becoming pressurized. Pressure test cooling system to help pinpoint hard-to-find leaks. See **Cooling system pressure test**.

— If cooling system is full of coolant and holds pressure:

- Use an appropriate scan tool to interrogate engine control module (ECM) for radiator fan or DME control circuit faults.
- Check for failed thermostat or coolant pump impeller.
- Check for clogged / plugged radiator or coolant passages.

## Cooling system pressure test

A cooling system pressure tester is used to test for coolant leaks, including internal ones. Common sources of internal coolant leaks are a faulty cylinder head gasket, a cracked cylinder head, or a cracked engine block.

> **WARNING—**
>
> - *At normal operating temperature the cooling system is pressurized. Allow the system to cool before opening. Remove the cap slowly to allow safe release of pressure.*

— With engine cold, install pressure tester (BMW special tools 17 0 101 / 17 0 113 or equivalent) to expansion tank. Pressurize system to specification listed in **Table a**.

- Pressure should not drop more than 0.1 bar (1.45 psi) for at least two minutes.
- If pressure drops rapidly and there is no sign of external leakage, cylinder head gasket may be faulty. Perform compression and leak-down tests.
- Test expansion tank cap using pressure tester with correct adapter (BMW special tool 17 0 114 or equivalent). Replace faulty cap or cap gasket.

> **CAUTION—**
>
> - *Exceeding the specified test pressure could damage the radiator or other system components.*

**Table a. Cooling system test pressures**

| Component | Test Pressure |
|---|---|
| Radiator | 1.5 bar (21.75 psi) |
| Radiator cap | 2 bar (29 psi) |

## Combustion chamber leak test

— If you suspect that combustion chamber pressure is leaking into the cooling system past the cylinder head gasket, use an exhaust gas analyzer to test the vapors rising from the coolant at the expansion tank.

> **CAUTION—**
>
> - *Use an extension tube above the reservoir neck to maintain distance between the tip of the coolant and the gas analyzer nozzle. The gas analyzer is easily damaged if it is allowed to inhale liquid coolant.*
> - *While running engine to check for causes of overheating, observe coolant temperature carefully in order to avoid engine damage.*

## Thermostat

If the engine overheats or runs too cool and no other cooling system tests indicate trouble, the thermostat may be faulty.

The electrically heated thermostat is monitored by the OBD II diagnostic software. The fault may lie in the DME software or hardware, or it may lie in the wiring to the thermostat. See **OBD On-Board Diagnostics**.

## COOLING SYSTEM SERVICE

### Coolant, draining and filling

> **WARNING—**
> • Allow cooling system to cool before opening or draining the cooling system.

– Raise car and support safely.

> **WARNING—**
> • Make sure the car is stable and well supported at all times. Use a professional automotive lift or jack stands designed for the purpose. A floor jack is not adequate support.

– Remove splash shield from under engine.

◄ Remove cap from radiator expansion tank.

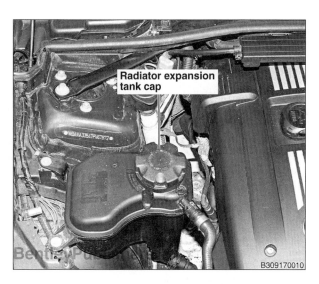

Radiator expansion tank cap

B309170010

> **CAUTION—**
> • Cover alternator when working on oil, coolant or fuel circuits to protect from damage.

◄ Release fasteners (**1**) on radiator cover (**2**) and remove cover in direction of **arrow**.

– Turbo models: Remove intercooler. See **Intercooler removing and installing** in this repair group.

– Place a 5-gallon pail underneath radiator.

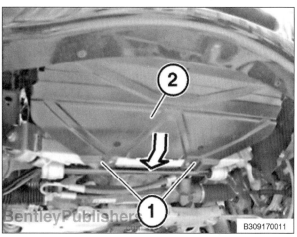

B309170011

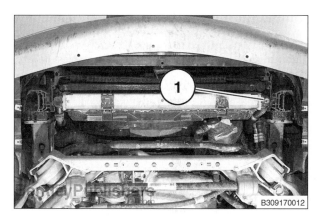

B309170012

◀ Release drain plug (**1**) on bottom of radiator and allow coolant to drain.

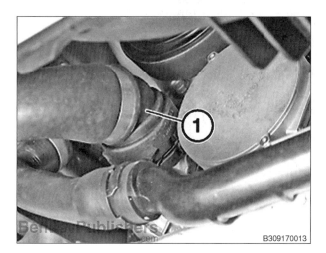

B309170013

◀ Disconnect radiator hose from thermostat housing and allow coolant to drain.

— Catch and dispose of coolant properly.

> **WARNING—**
> • *Coolant is poisonous. It is especially lethal to pets. Clean up spills immediately and rinse the area with water. If coolant is ingested, immediately seek medical attention.*

— To fill cooling system, reattach removed hoses and close drain plugs.

— Using a coolant mixture of 50% antifreeze and 50% distilled water, fill expansion tank slowly to top.

> **CAUTION—**
> • *Open radiator bleed screw when filling cooling system.* See **Cooling system, bleeding**
> • *Tap water may cause corrosion of radiator and engine components.*
> • *Do not reuse coolant.*

— Bleed cooling system. See **Cooling system, bleeding** in this repair group.

> **CAUTION—**
> • *Strict adherence to the factory bleeding procedure is necessary to avoid incomplete filling of cooling system, overheating and engine damage.* See **Cooling system, bleeding** in this repair group.

| Tightening torque | |
|---|---|
| Radiator drain plug to radiator (replace O-ring with new) | 2.5 Nm (22 in-lb) |

## Cooling system, filling and bleeding

Trapped air in the cooling system can prevent proper coolant circulation and cause overheating. Whenever the coolant is drained and filled, bleed the cooling system.

Models covered by this manual feature an electric coolant pump. The bleeding procedure operates the coolant pump for approximately 12 minutes to remove trapped air and ensure that the cooling system is filled to capacity.

> **CAUTION—**
>
> • *This procedure should be carried out when replacing cooling system components or refilling the cooling system. Failure to follow this procedure may result in incomplete filling of cooling system, overheating and engine damage.*

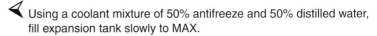

◀ Using a coolant mixture of 50% antifreeze and 50% distilled water, fill expansion tank slowly to MAX.

> **CAUTION—**
>
> • *Cover alternator when working on oil, coolant or fuel circuits to protect from damage.*

B309170014

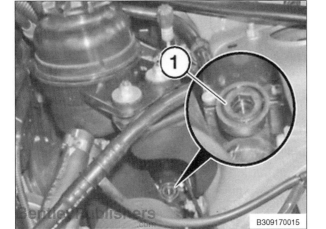

B309170015

◀ Open bleed screw on radiator hose (**1**) (if equipped). Continue to fill expansion tank slowly until coolant starts to emerge. Close bleed screw.

◀ Open bleed screw on coolant expansion tank (**arrow**). Fill coolant expansion tank until coolant starts to emerge from bleed screw.

– Close bleed screw.

– Fill coolant expansion tank to lower edge of filler neck.

◀ Close cap on coolant expansion tank and perform the following steps:

1. Connect battery charger.

2. Switch on ignition.

3. Set heater to MAX temperature and turn fan to lowest speed.

4. Press accelerator pedal for 10 seconds to floor.

5. Bleeding procedure begins when accelerator pedal is pressed and takes approximately 12 minutes. (Electric coolant pump turns ON and OFF automatically after approx. 12 minutes).

**CAUTION—**

• *Do not open expansion tank cap while electric coolant pump is ON.*

6. Fill coolant expansion tank 100 ml above MAX (dimension **A**).

7. Check cooling system for leaks

8. If leaks are found, remove ignition key and wait approximately 3 minutes before repeating cooling system bleeding procedure.

◀ When bleeding procedure is complete, close coolant expansion tank cap until marks on cap and tank (**arrows**) line up.

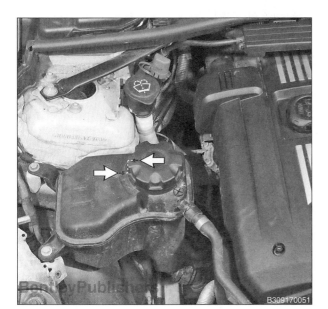

| Table b. Cooling system capacities | |
|---|---|
| **Engine** | **Capacity** |
| N51, N52, N54<br>• Manual transmission<br>• Automatic transmission | <br>8.2L (2.17 gal)<br>8.4L (2.23 gal) |

170

## Radiator, removing and installing

— Raise car and support safely

> **WARNING —**
> • Make sure the car is stable and well supported at all times. Use a professional automotive lift or jack stands designed for the purpose. A floor jack is not adequate support.

— Remove splash shield from under engine.

— Drain radiator. See **Coolant draining and filling** in this repair group.

> **WARNING —**
> • Allow cooling system to cool before opening or draining system.

— Remove fan cowl. See **Electric cooling fan and cowl, removing and installing** in this repair group.

— Unlock coolant hose and detach from radiator.

— Turbo models: Release clamp at charge-air duct and remove duct.

◄ Automatic transmission: Release bolts (**arrow**) and disconnect hose (**1**) for ATF heat exchanger.

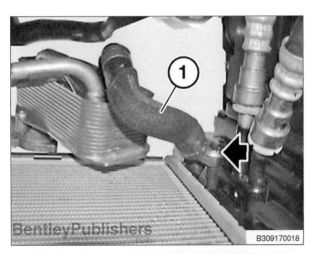

◄ Remove fasteners (**arrows**) and carefully lift radiator (**1**) up and out of engine compartment.

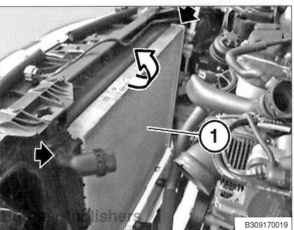

— Installation is reverse of removal. Make sure:
  • Radiator seats firmly in lower mounts.
  • Electric cooling fan cowl clips securely at bottom.
  • Refill and bleed cooling system. See **Cooling system, bleeding** in this repair group.
  • Check cooling system for leaks.

| Tightening torques | |
|---|---|
| Radiator to body | 10 Nm (ft-lb) |

## Electric cooling fan and cowl, removing and installing

— Use a BMW factory scan tool, or equivalent, to read and clear fault codes.

— Switch ignition OFF.

— Remove intake air duct.

— Remove splash shield from under engine.

◀ Automatic transmission: Remove fastener (**arrow**) and remove ATF cooler (**1**) from fan shroud (**2**).

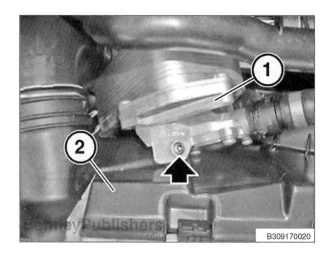

B309170020

◀ Detach electrical connector (**1**) and unclip line (**2**) from fan cowl.

— Detach cable strap (**3**) and remove fastener (**arrow**).

— Turbo models: Release charge air duct from rubber mount on fan cowl.

— Unlock clip (**inset**) on lower edge of fan cowl and lift electric fan and cowl up and out of engine compartment.

— Installation is reverse of removal. Make sure:
- Fan cowl snaps securely into clips on lower edge.
- Fan electrical connector snaps firmly into place and wires and hose are routed as before.

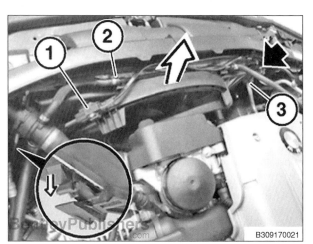

B309170021

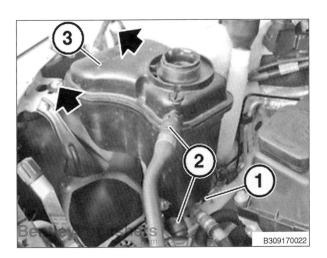

B309170022

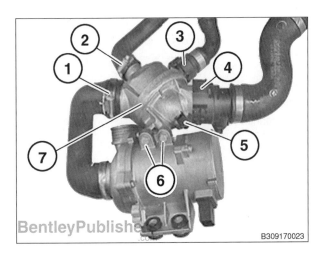

B309170023

## Coolant expansion tank, removing and installing

— Drain cooling system. See **Coolant, draining and filling** in this repair group.

— Turbo models: Unclip vacuum hoses from perimeter of expansion tank.

◄ Remove expansion tank fasteners (**arrows**).

— Raise tank slightly (if necessary) and release electrical connector for coolant level switch (**1**).

— Release clamps on coolant hoses (**2**) and remove expansion tank.

— Installation is reverse of removal. Remember to:
  • Make sure locating pin at bottom of tank fits securely into rubber grommet.
  • Refill and bleed cooling system. See **Cooling system, bleeding** in this repair group.
  • Check cooling system for leaks.

| Tightening torque | |
|---|---|
| Expansion tank to body | 8 Nm (71 in-lb) |

## Thermostat, removing and installing

— Remove splash shield from under engine.

— Drain cooling system. See **Coolant, draining and filling** in this repair group.

◄ Working above engine coolant pump, release hose clamps (**1** and **2**) and disconnect hoses.

— Unlock fasteners (**3** and **4**) and remove hoses.

— Disconnect electrical connector (**5**).

— Remove bolts (**6**) and remove thermostat (**7**).

— Installation is reverse of removal. Remember to:
  • Refill and bleed cooling system. See **Cooling system, bleeding** in this repair group.
  • Check cooling system for leaks.

| Tightening torque | |
|---|---|
| Thermostat to coolant pump: | |
| • non-turbo engine | 9 Nm (80 in-lb) |
| • turbo engine | 8 Nm (71 in-lb) |

## Coolant pump, removing and installing

– Remove splash shield from under engine.

– Drain cooling system. See **Coolant, draining and filling** in this repair group.

– Remove coolant thermostat. See **Thermostat, removing and installing** in this repair group.

◀ Release hose clamps (**1**) and disconnect coolant hoses from back of pump.

– Disconnect electrical connector (**4**) at front of pump.

– Remove bolts (**5**) and remove pump from side of engine.

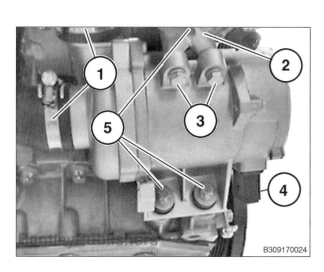

B309170024

> **CAUTION—**
>
> • *If coolant pump is to be reused, fill with mixture of 50% antifreeze and 50% distilled water immediately after removing, and plug openings to avoid contamination.*

– Installation is reverse of removal. Remember to:

• Mechanically rotate coolant pump impeller one full revolution before installing.

• Replace aluminum fasteners (fasteners with heads painted blue) with new.

> **CAUTION—**
>
> • *Do not use steel fasteners in place of aluminum. Electrochemical corrosion will result.*

• Reinstall thermostat.

• Refill and bleed cooling system. See **Cooling system, bleeding** in this repair group.

• Check cooling system for leaks.

| Tightening torque | |
|---|---|
| Thermostat to coolant pump<br>• non-turbo engine<br>• turbo engine | 9 Nm (80 in-lb)<br>8 Nm (71 in-lb) |
| Coolant pump to engine block<br>(replace aluminum fasteners with new<br>and observe torque angle) | 10 Nm (89 in-lb)<br>+ 90° turn |

170

## Automatic transmission fluid (ATF) cooler, removing and installing

− Remove splash shield from under engine.

− Drain cooling system. See **Coolant, draining and filling** in this repair group.

> **CAUTION—**
> • *Cover alternator when working on oil, coolant or fuel circuits to protect from damage.*

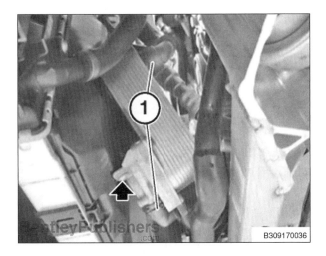

◄ Remove coolant hoses (**1**) and remove screw (**arrow**) from underside of ATF cooler.

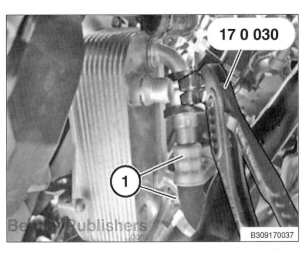

◄ Use BMW special tool 17 0 030 to unlock transmission fluid from hydraulic lines and remove ATF cooler.

− Installation is reverse of removal. Remember to:

• Check automatic transmission fluid level. See **020 Maintenance**.

• Refill and bleed cooling system. See **Cooling system, bleeding** in this repair group.

• Check cooling system for leaks.

## Power steering cooling loop, removing and installing

— Remove splash shield from under engine.

— Drain cooling system. See **Coolant, draining and filling** in this repair group.

> **CAUTION—**
> • *Cover alternator when working on oil, coolant or fuel circuits to protect from damage.*

— Remove radiator. See **Radiator, removing and installing** in this repair group.

— Place a suitable container beneath power steering cooling loop connections to catch dripping fluid. Dispose of properly.

◄ Press hydraulic line (**1**) towards cooling loop (**2**). Pull back on locking ring and remove line.

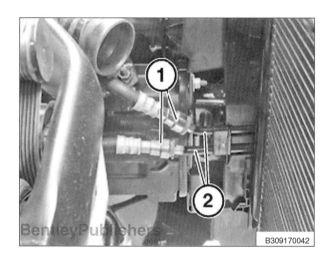

B309170042

◄ Working at A/C condenser, release clip (**1**) and remove fastener (**arrow**).

> **WARNING—**
> • *Do not disconnect A/C refrigerant lines.*

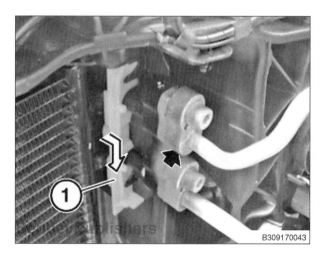

B309170043

*Power steering cooling loop, removing and installing*

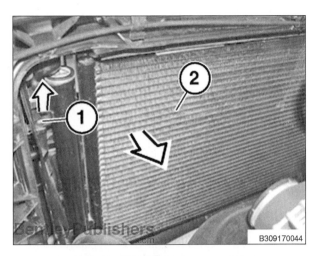

◀ Release condenser lock (**1**) in direction of **arrow**. Gently tilt condenser towards engine to gain access to power steering cooling loop. Make sure condenser and refrigerant lines are not stressed or damaged.

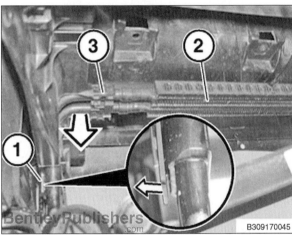

◀ Working in front of condenser, release clip (**1**). Release cooling loop (**2**) from clip (**3**) and remove cooling loop.

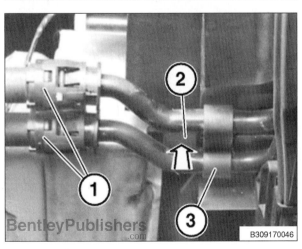

◀ Installation is reverse of removal. Remember to:

- Make sure cooling loop hydraulic lines (**1**) connect securely.
- Check that cooling loop lines (**3**) snap securely into holder (**2**).
- Refill and bleed cooling system. See **Cooling system, bleeding** in this repair group.
- Check cooling system for leaks.
- Replace lost power steering fluid.

## Intercooler, removing and installing (turbo engine)

— Raise car and support safely

> **WARNING—**
> • *Make sure the car is stable and well supported at all times. Use a professional automotive lift or jack stands designed for the purpose. A floor jack is not adequate support.*

— Remove splash shield from under engine.

— Disconnect intake air duct from left and right side of intercooler.

◀ Working at front of radiator, release lock on intercooler cover in direction of **arrow**.

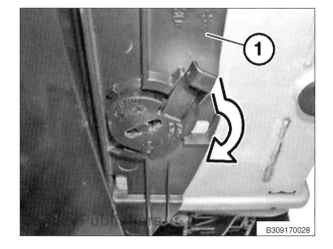

◀ Release cover (**1**) in direction of **arrows** and remove.

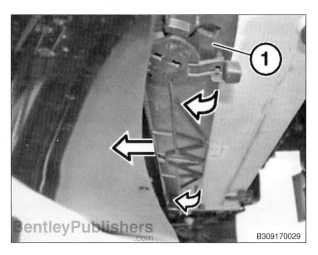

*Intercooler, removing and installing (turbo engine)*

◁ Remove fasteners (**arrows**) at sides of intercooler and remove from below.

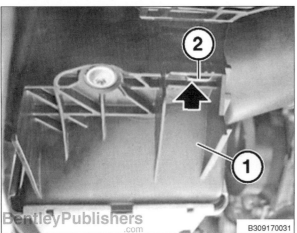

◁ When installing, make sure sides of intercooler (**1**) fits securely into notch of intercooler bracket (**2**).

– Coat sealing rings of intake air ducts with antiseize paste.

> **NOTE**—
> • *Fitting air ducts to intercooler without antiseize paste is nearly impossible.*

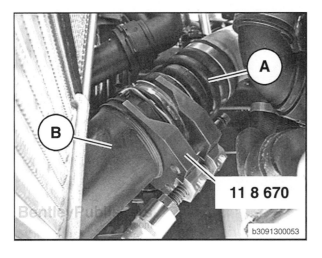

◁ Reattach intake air ducts using BMW special tool 11 8 670. Ducts must snap audibly into place.

> **CAUTION**—
> • *Special clamping jaws (special tool 11 8 670) are strongly recommended for proper installation and to prevent damage to air ducts.*
> • *Right side shown, left side is similar.*

# 180 Exhaust System

180

## GENERAL

This repair group covers removal and replacement of the exhaust system including exhaust manifolds, turbochargers and oxygen sensors.

### Warnings and Cautions

> **WARNING—**
> • *The exhaust system and catalytic converter operate at very high temperatures. Allow components to cool before servicing. Wear protective clothing to prevent burns. Do not use flammable chemicals near a hot catalytic converter.*
> • *Corroded exhaust system components crumble easily and often have exposed sharp edges. To avoid injury, wear eye protection and heavy gloves when working with old exhaust parts.*

## EXHAUST SYSTEM

The exhaust system is designed to be maintenance free, although regular inspection is warranted due to the harsh operating conditions. Under normal conditions, catalytic converters do not require replacement unless damaged

Use new fasteners, clamps, rubber mounts and gaskets when replacing exhaust components. A liberal application of penetrating oil to the exhaust system nuts and bolts in advance may make removal easier.

## Exhaust system, removing and installing

The removal and installation procedures given here are general procedures for all models. Where model-specific differences exist, they are noted in the text. The removal of the exhaust system as a complete unit is recommended. Once the complete system is removed from the car, individual pipes and mufflers can be more easily replaced.

> **WARNING—**
> • Exhaust gases are colorless, odorless, and very toxic. Run the engine only in a well-ventilated area. Immediately repair any leaks in the exhaust system or structural damage to the car body that might allow exhaust gases to enter the passenger compartment.

> **CAUTION—**
> • Use care not to drag or bang oxygen sensors. Oxygen sensors are easily damaged.
> • When detaching and reattaching oxygen sensor connectors, make sure front and rear connectors are not mixed up.
> • The exhaust system is heavy. Work with an assistant

– Raise vehicle and support safely.

> **WARNING—**
> • Make sure the vehicle is stable and well supported at all times. Use a professional automotive lift or jack stands designed for the purpose. A floor jack is not adequate support.

– Sport Wagon and Coupe models: Remove tension strut on rear axle. See **330 Rear Suspension**.

– Support exhaust using BMW special tool 31 2 220 or equivalent and suitable jack.

◄ Remove fasteners for front exhaust at exhaust manifold flange (**arrows**).

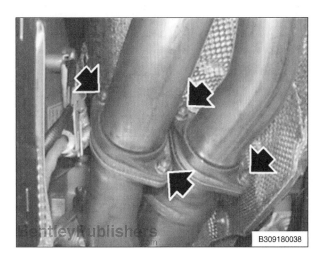

B309180038

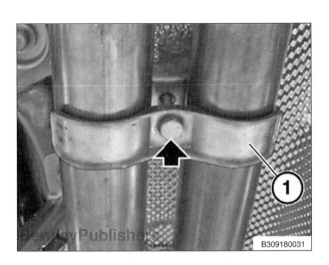

◀ Remove fastener (**arrow**) and front support bracket (**1**).

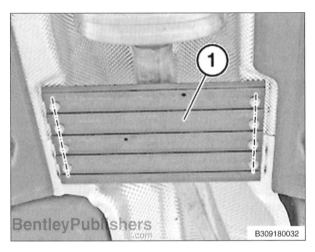

◀ Remove reinforcement plate bolts and remove plate (**1**).

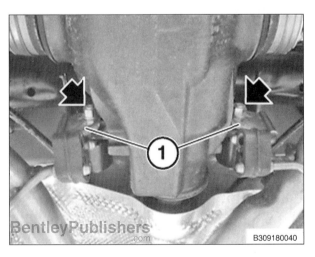

◀ Working at rear differential, release fasteners (**arrows**) and remove exhaust hanger brackets (**1**).

*Exhaust system components, removing and installing*

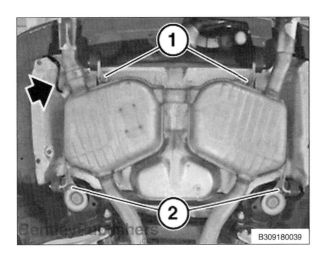

B309180039

 Working at rear mufflers, remove vacuum hose (**arrow**). Remove exhaust hanger fasteners at rear chassis (**1**) and wheel carrier (**2**).

> **CAUTION—**
> • *Exhaust system is heavy. Lower with the help of an assistant.*

– Carefully lower complete exhaust system and remove.

– Installation is reverse of removal. Remember to:

  • Use new gaskets and hardware. Coat hardware threads with anti-seize paste.

  • Make sure there is sufficient clearance between exhaust system and vehicle underbody at every point.

  • Loosely install exhaust system mounting hardware and hangers before tightening fasteners to their final torque.

  • Check exhaust system for leaks.

| Tightening torques | |
| --- | --- |
| Exhaust to manifold flange:<br>• non-turbo<br>• turbo | <br>45 Nm (33 ft-lb)<br>21 Nm (15 ft-lb) |
| Front exhaust clamp to transmission | 20 Nm (15 ft-lb) |
| Exhaust hanger to rear differential:<br>• non-turbo<br>• turbo | <br>30 Nm (22 ft-lb)<br>35 Nm (26 ft-lb) |
| Exhaust hanger to wheel carrier | 21 Nm (15 ft-lb) |
| Exhaust hanger to rear chassis | 20 Nm (15 ft-lb) |

## Exhaust system components, removing and installing

BMW offers individual exhaust components as replacement parts. Originally installed exhaust components are welded together at the factory and must be cut off to be replaced.

Component replacement is best accomplished by first removing the complete exhaust system. See **Exhaust system, removing and installing** in this repair group.

> **NOTE—**
> • *Rear muffler can be replaced without removing exhaust system.*

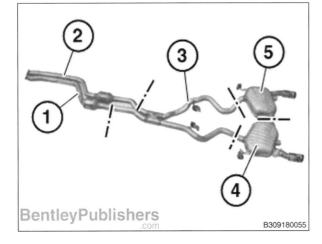

BentleyPublishers
.com

B309180055

◀ Cut lines for exhaust components are designated by notches in the exhaust system.

1.  Rear catalytic converter, left
2.  Rear catalytic converter, right
3.  Center muffler
4.  Rear muffler, left
5.  Rear muffler, right

> **NOTE—**
> • *335i exhaust shown.*

*Exhaust manifold (cylinders 1- 3), removing and installing (non-turbo)*

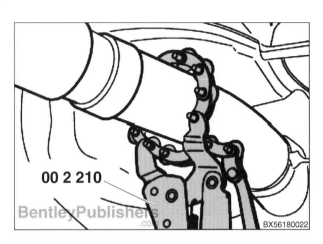

◀ Use exhaust pipe cutter (BMW special tool 00 2 210 or equivalent) to cut pipe(s). Deburr cut pipe end(s).

00 2 210

BX56180022

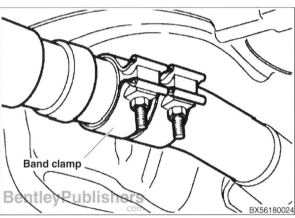

Band clamp

BX56180024

◀ Assemble pipes using band clamps.

— Installation is reverse of removal. Remember to:
  • Make sure there is sufficient clearance between exhaust system and vehicle underbody at every point.
  • Check exhaust system for leaks.

| Tightening torque | |
|---|---|
| Band clamp to exhaust pipes | 45 Nm (33 ft-lb) |

## EXHAUST MANIFOLDS (NON-TURBO)

The N51 and N52 engines uses two exhaust manifolds. Each manifold includes an integral pre-catalytic converter. Should the pre-catalyst need replacing, replace the appropriate exhaust manifold / pre-catalyst unit. See **Exhaust Components** in this repair group.

### Exhaust manifold (cylinders 1- 3), removing and installing (non-turbo)

— Remove rear exhaust manifold. See **Exhaust manifold (cylinders 4 - 6), removing and installing** in this repair group.

— Remove oxygen sensors. See **Oxygen sensors, removing and installing** in this repair group.

◀ Remove fasteners (**arrows**) from front exhaust manifold (**1**) and remove manifold.

— Installation is reverse of removal. Remember to:
  • Clean sealing surfaces of manifold and cylinder head.
  • Use new gaskets and hardware.
  • Check exhaust system for leaks.

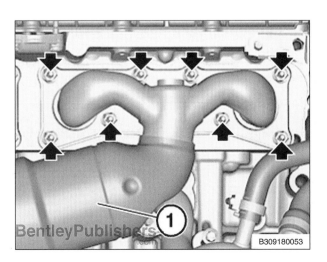

1

B309180053

| Tightening torque | |
|---|---|
| Exhaust manifold to cylinder head | 20 Nm (15 ft-lb) |

180

## Exhaust manifold (cylinders 4 - 6), removing and installing (non-turbo)

– Remove ignition coil cover. See **020 Maintenance**.

– Remove coolant expansion tank. See **170 Radiator and Cooling System**.

– Remove lower engine cover. See **020 Maintenance**.

– Remove complete exhaust system. See **Exhaust system, removing and installing** in this repair group.

– Remove oxygen sensors. See **Oxygen sensors, removing and installing** in this repair group.

◄ Remove fasteners (**arrows**) from rear exhaust manifold (**1**) and remove manifold.

– Installation is reverse of removal. Remember to:
  • Clean sealing surfaces of manifold and cylinder head.
  • Use new gaskets and hardware.
  • Check exhaust system for leaks.

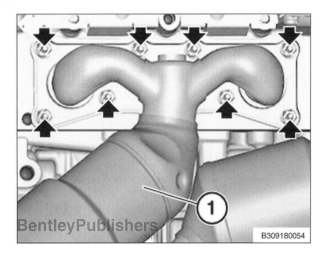

| Tightening torque | |
|---|---|
| Exhaust manifold to cylinder head | 20 Nm (15 ft-lb) |

## EXHAUST MANIFOLDS AND TURBOCHARGERS

The N54 engine is equipped with two exhaust manifolds each with an integral turbocharger. A pre-catalytic converter is attached downstream of each turbocharger. Should the pre-catalyst need replacing, it is removable and available separately. See **Exhaust Components** in this repair group.

## Exhaust manifold and turbocharger (cylinders 1- 3), removing and installing

– Remove both pre-catalytic converters. See **Pre-catalytic converters (turbo)** in this repair group.

– Release right side tie rod from steering rack. See **320 Steering and Wheel Alignment**.

– Remove intercooler. See **170 Radiator and Cooling System**.

– Drain engine coolant and remove coolant expansion tank. See **170 Radiator and cooling system**.

– Remove coolant pump. See **170 Radiator and Cooling System**.

– Remove turbocharger vacuum reservoirs. See **130 Fuel Injection**.

– Remove air box and air intake duct. See **130 Fuel Injection**.

*Exhaust manifold and turbocharger (cylinders 1- 3), removing and installing*

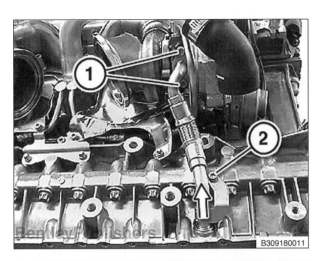

◄ Remove fasteners on oil return line (**1**) and oil return line bracket (**2**). Gently pull oil return line out of engine block in direction of **arrow**.

◄ Working between turbochargers, remove fasteners (**1** and **2**) and remove coolant supply lines (**3** and **4**).

**NOTE**—

• *If necessary grasp coolant supply line flange with pliers to remove. Do not use pliers on pipes.*

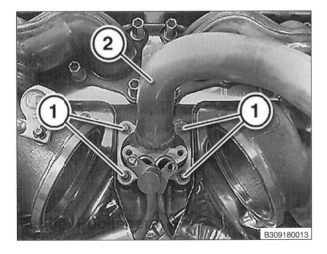

◄ Remove fasteners (**1**) at coolant inlet pipe (**2**) and remove pipe.

*Exhaust manifold and turbocharger (cylinders 1- 3), removing and installing*

◄ Remove coolant return pipe fasteners (**1** and **3**) and remove return pipe (**4**).

**NOTE—**

• *If necessary grasp coolant return line flange (**2**) with pliers to remove. Do not use pliers on pipes.*

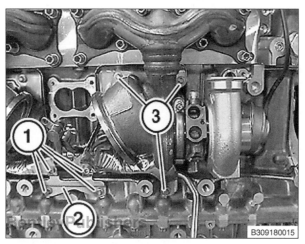

◄ Remove fasteners (**1**) at retaining plate (**2**). Remove heat shield fasteners (**3**).

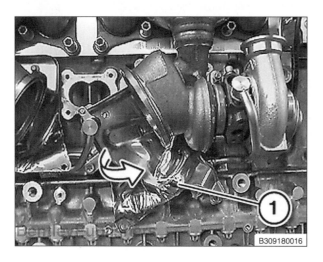

◄ Remove heat shield (**1**) in direction of **arrow**. Make sure shield and coolant pipes are not damaged.

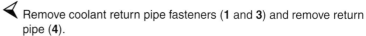

*Exhaust manifold and turbocharger (cylinders 1- 3), removing and installing*

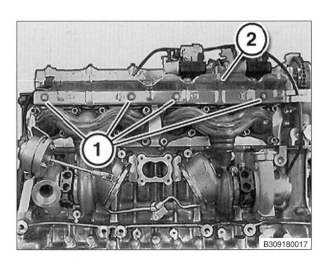

◄ Remove fasteners (**1**) from bracket (**2**). Lay bracket on top of cylinder head.

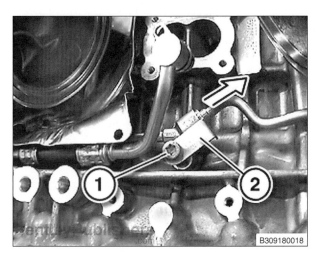

◄ Remove oil supply line bracket fastener (**1**). Remove oil supply line in direction of **arrow**.

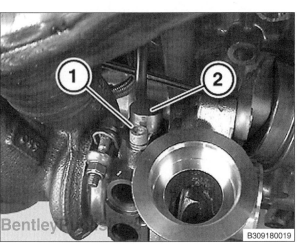

◄ Remove fastener (**1**) and remove oil supply line.

**NOTE**—

• *If necessary grasp oil supply line flange (**2**) with pliers to remove. Do not use pliers on pipes.*

*Exhaust manifold and turbocharger (cylinders 1- 3), removing and installing*

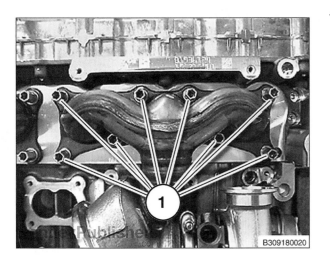

◀ Remove exhaust manifold fasteners (**1**). Detach vacuum hose from wastegate valve and remove exhaust manifold / turbocharger towards the top.

**NOTE —**

• *Take care not to damage wastegate valve linkage.*

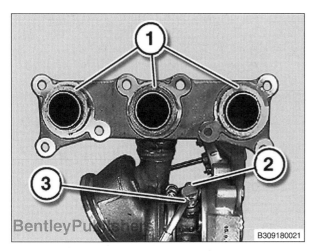

◀ If replacing turbocharger, remove fastener (**2**) for oil supply line (**3**) and install supply line on new unit. Always replace graphite gaskets (**1**).

– Remainder of installation is reverse of removal. Remember to:

   • Use new O-rings, gaskets and hardware. Coat hardware threads with anti-seize paste.
   • Check and clear fault memory using BMW scan tool.
   • Check air intake system for leaks.
   • Check exhaust system for leaks.

| Tightening torques | |
|---|---|
| Bracket to cylinder head | 9 Nm (7 ft-lb) |
| Coolant supply line to crankcase | 9 Nm (7 ft-lb) |
| Coolant return line to crankcase | 8 Nm (6 ft-lb) |
| Coolant return line to turbocharger | 8 Nm (6 ft-lb) |
| Coolant supply line to supply line | 8 Nm (6 ft-lb) |
| Exhaust manifold heat shield to crankcase | 8 Nm (6 ft-lb) |
| Oil supply line to crankcase | 20 Nm (15 ft-lb) |
| Oil pressure line to turbocharger | 8 Nm (6 ft-lb) |
| Oil return line to crankcase | 8 Nm (6 ft-lb) |
| Oil return line to turbocharger | 8 Nm (6 ft-lb) |
| Turbocharger to exhaust manifold | 20 Nm (15 ft-lb) |

*Turbocharger and exhaust manifold (cylinders 4-6), removing and installing*

## Turbocharger and exhaust manifold (cylinders 4-6), removing and installing

— Remove both pre-catalytic converters. See **Pre-catalytic converters (turbo)** in this repair group.

— Release right side tie rod from steering rack. See **320 Steering and Wheel Alignment**.

— Remove intercooler. See **170 Radiator and Cooling System**.

— Drain engine coolant and remove coolant expansion tank. See **170 Radiator and Cooling system**.

— Remove coolant pump. See **170 Radiator and cooling system**.

— Remove turbocharger vacuum reservoirs. See **130 Fuel Injection**.

— Remove air box and air intake duct. See **130 Fuel Injection**.

◀ Remove fasteners on oil return line (**1**) and oil return line bracket (**2**). Gently pull oil return line out of engine block in direction of **arrow**.

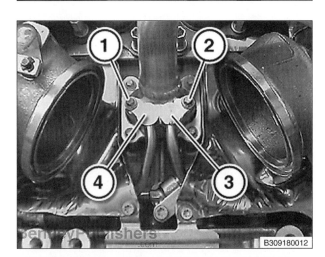

◀ Working between turbochargers, remove fasteners (**1** and **2**) and remove coolant supply lines (**3** and **4**).

*NOTE —*
* *If necessary grasp coolant supply line flange with pliers to remove. Do not use pliers on pipes.*

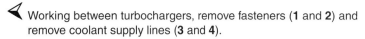

◀ Remove fasteners (**1**) at coolant inlet pipe (**2**) and remove pipe.

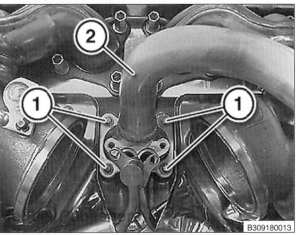

*Turbocharger and exhaust manifold (cylinders 4-6), removing and installing*

◁ Remove fastener (**1**) at coolant return line clamp and remove line.

**NOTE** —

- *If necessary grasp coolant return line flange with pliers to remove. Do not use pliers on pipes.*

◁ Remove fastener (**1**) and remove coolant return line (**2**) and coolant supply line (**3**).

**NOTE** —

- *If necessary grasp flange with pliers to remove. Do not use pliers on pipes.*
- *Take care not to damage wastegate valve linkage.*

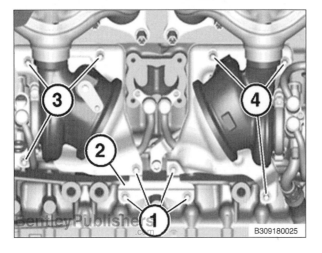

◁ Remove fasteners (**1**) at retaining plate (**2**). Remove heat shield fasteners (**3** and **4**).

*Turbocharger and exhaust manifold (cylinders 4-6), removing and installing*

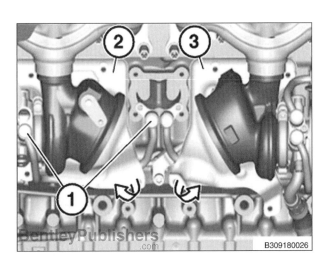

◄ Carefully swing out heat shields (**2** and **3**) in direction of **arrow**. Coolant supply pipe (**1**) can be removed along with heat shield.

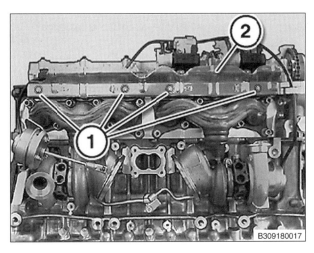

◄ Remove fasteners (**1**) from bracket (**2**). Lay bracket on top of cylinder head.

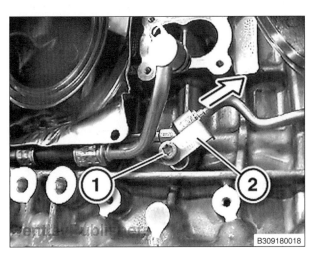

◄ Remove oil supply line bracket fastener (**1**). Remove oil supply line in direction of **arrow**.

*Turbocharger and exhaust manifold (cylinders 4-6), removing and installing*

 Remove exhaust manifold fasteners (**1**). Detach vacuum hose from wastegate valve and remove exhaust manifold / turbocharger towards the top.

**NOTE** —

• *Take care not to damage wastegate valve linkage.*

◄ f replacing turbocharger, remove fastener (**2**) for oil supply line (**3**) and install supply line on new unit. Always replace graphite gaskets (**1**).

— Remainder of installation is reverse of removal. Remember to:

• Use new O-rings, gaskets and hardware. Coat hardware threads with anti-seize paste.
• Check and clear fault memory using BMW scan tool.
• Check air intake system for leaks.
• Check exhaust system for leaks.

| Tightening torques | |
|---|---|
| Bracket to cylinder head | 9 Nm (7 ft-lb) |
| Coolant supply line to crankcase | 9 Nm (7 ft-lb) |
| Coolant return line to crankcase | 8 Nm (6 ft-lb) |
| Coolant return line to turbocharger | 8 Nm (6 ft-lb) |
| Coolant supply line to supply line | 8 Nm (6 ft-lb) |
| Exhaust manifold heat shield to crankcase | 8 Nm (6 ft-lb) |
| Oil supply line to crankcase | 20 Nm (15 ft-lb) |
| Oil pressure line to turbocharger | 8 Nm (6 ft-lb) |
| Oil return line to crankcase | 8 Nm (6 ft-lb) |
| Oil return line to turbocharger | 8 Nm (6 ft-lb) |
| Turbocharger to exhaust manifold | 20 Nm (15 ft-lb) |

**180**

## OXYGEN SENSORS

### Oxygen sensors, removing and installing

Oxygen sensors are installed at the front and rear of the catalytic converters. Prior to sensor removal, use BMW scan tool or equivalent to read out and clear ECM fault codes.

> **CAUTION—**
> • *Use care not to drag or bang oxygen sensors. Oxygen sensors are easily damaged.*
> • *To avoid possible engine damage, do not mix up oxygen sensor connectors. Mark connectors before disassembling.*

– Remove upper engine cover. See **020 Maintenance**.

– Raise vehicle and support safely.

> **WARNING—**
> • *Make sure the vehicle is stable and well supported at all times. Use a professional automotive lift or jack stands designed for the purpose. A floor jack is not adequate support.*

– Disconnect oxygen sensor harness connectors.

**Pre-catalyst oxygen sensors**

– Release right side tie rod from steering rack. See **320 Steering and Wheel Alignment**.

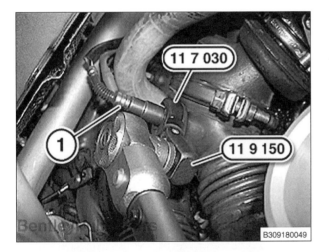

◄ Pre-catalyst oxygen sensor for cylinders 1 - 3 shown with BMW special tools 11 7 030 and 11 9 150.

> **NOTE—**
> • *Cylinders 1 - 3 harness connector colored black.*

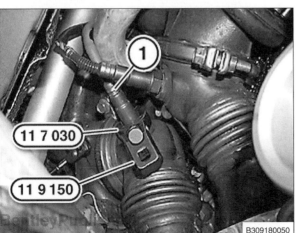

◄ Pre-catalyst oxygen sensor for cylinders 4 - 6 shown with BMW special tools 11 7 030 and 11 9 150.

> **NOTE—**
> • *Cylinders 4 - 6 harness connector colored grey*

*Oxygen sensors, removing and installing*

– Installation is reverse of removal. Remember to:

   • Apply a small amount of anti-seize compound to sensor threads.

   • Make sure sensor electrical harness connectors are routed as before and connected correctly.

---

**CAUTION—**

   • *Do not overuse anti-seize paste. Do not contaminate tip of sensor with paste or lubricants.*

---

| Tightening torques | |
| --- | --- |
| Oxygen sensor to exhaust pipe:<br>• Using BMW special tool 11 7 030<br>  together with 11 9 150<br>• Using BMW special tool 11 7 020 | 47 Nm (35 ft-lb)<br>50 Nm (37 ft-lb) |

*NOTE —*

   • *When tool 11 7 030 is used together with swivel tool 11 9 150, reduce tightening torque by 3 Nm to 47 Nm (35 ft-lb).*

### Post-catalyst oxygen sensors

◄ Post-catalyst oxygen sensor for cylinders 1 - 3 shown with BMW special tools 11 7 030 and 11 9 150.

*NOTE —*

   • *Cylinders 1 - 3 harness connector colored black.*

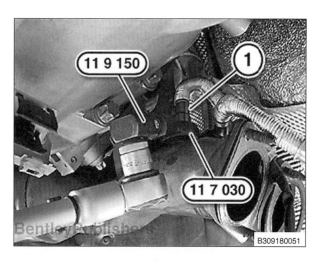

B309180051

◄ Post-catalyst oxygen sensor for cylinders 4 - 6 shown with BMW special tool 11 7 020.

*NOTE —*

   • *Cylinders 4 - 6 harness connector colored grey.*

– Installation is reverse of removal. Remember to:

   • Apply a small amount of anti-seize compound to sensor threads.

   • Make sure sensor electrical harness connectors are routed as before and connected correctly.

---

**CAUTION—**

   • *Do not overuse anti-seize paste. Do not contaminate tip of sensor with paste or lubricants.*

---

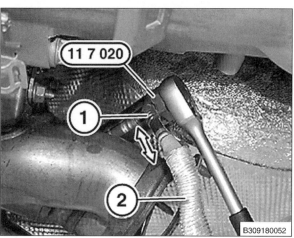

B309180052

| Tightening torques | |
|---|---|
| Oxygen sensor to exhaust pipe: | |
| • Using BMW special tool 11 7 030 together with 11 9 150 | 47 Nm (35 ft-lb) |
| • Using BMW special tool 11 7 020 | 50 Nm (37 ft-lb) |

**180**

**NOTE**—

• When tool 11 7 030 is used together with swivel tool 11 9 150, reduce tightening torque by 3 Nm to 47 Nm (35 ft-lb).

## CATALYTIC CONVERTERS

Catalytic converters are used in the exhaust pipes to force oxidation or conversion of unburned hydrocarbons and nitrogen oxides. E90 models use two pre-catalytic converters and two post-catalytic converters in the exhaust pipes.

### Pre-catalytic converters (non-turbo)

N51 and N52 engines include an integral pre-catalytic converter in each exhaust manifold. To replace pre-catalyst, see **Exhaust manifold (non-turbo)** in this repair group.

### Pre-catalytic converters (turbo)

N54 engines include a separate pre-catalytic converter clamped to each turbocharger. To replace N54 pre-catalyst, follow the procedures below.

— Remove lower engine cover. See **020 Maintenance**.

— Remove exhaust system. See **Exhaust system, removing and installing** in this repair group.

— Working at side of transmission: Remove holder for oxygen sensor wiring harness.

— Remove oxygen sensors. See **Oxygen sensors, removing and installing** in this repair group.

**Pre-catalytic converter, cylinders 1 - 3 (turbo)**

◀ Remove nuts (**arrows**) from catalytic converter bracket.

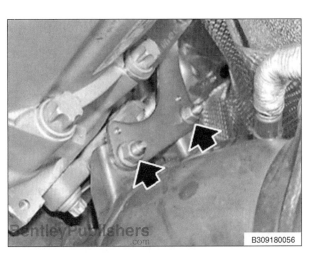

B309180056

*Pre-catalytic converters (turbo)*

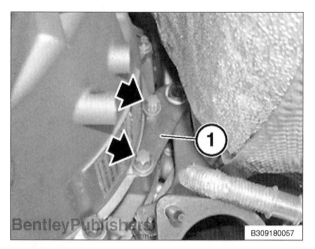

◁ Remove bolts (**arrows**) from catalytic converter bracket.

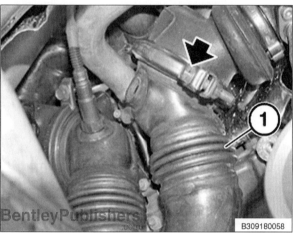

◁ While supporting catalytic converter: Remove clamp (**arrow**) and lower converter (**1**) downwards to remove.

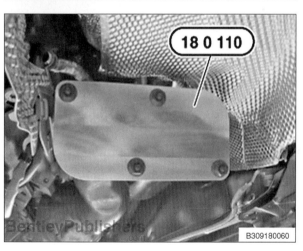

◁ Installation is reverse of removal. Remember to:

- Clean sealing surfaces and replace seal between converter and turbocharger.
- Hold catalytic converter in position using BMW special tool 18 0 110 or equivalent and install clamp.
- Check exhaust system for leaks.

| Tightening torque | |
|---|---|
| Catalytic converter to turbocharger | 13 Nm (10 ft-lb) |

### Pre-catalytic converter, cylinders 4 - 6 (turbo)

— Remove pre-catalytic converter for cylinders 1 - 3.

— Remove oxygen sensors. See **Oxygen sensors, removing and installing** in this repair group.

◄ While supporting catalytic converter: Remove clamp (**arrow**) and lower converter (**1**) downwards to remove.

B309180059

◄ Installation is reverse of removal. Remember to:

- Clean sealing surfaces and replace seal between converter and turbocharger.

- Hold catalytic converter in position using BMW special tool 18 0 110 or equivalent and install clamp.

- Check exhaust system for leaks.

| Tightening torque | |
|---|---|
| Catalytic converter to turbocharger | 13 Nm (10 ft-lb) |

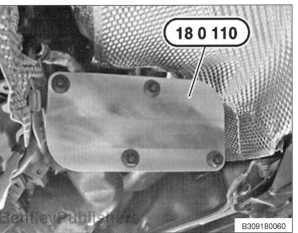

B309180060

## Post-catalytic converters

N51, N52 and N54 engines include post-catalytic converters that are welded into the originally installed exhaust system and must be cut off to be replaced.

To replace N51, N52 or N54 engine post-catalyst, See **Exhaust system components, removing and installing** in this repair group.

## EXHAUST COMPONENTS

### Exhaust components (non-turbo)

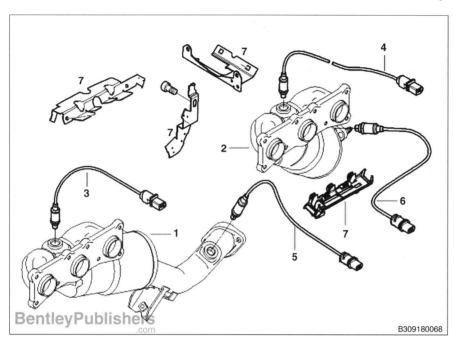

B309180068

1. Exhaust manifold, front
2. Exhaust manifold, rear
3. Pre-catalyst oxygen sensor, front
4. Pre-catalyst oxygen sensor, rear
5. Post-catalyst oxygen sensor, front
6. Post-catalyst oxygen sensor, rear
7. Bracket

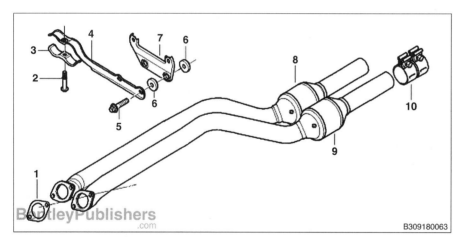

B309180063

1. Gasket
2. Bolt
3. Exhaust hanger, lower
4. Exhaust hanger, upper
5. Bolt
6. Washer
7. Bracket
8. Post-catalytic converter, front
9. Post-catalytic converter, rear
10. Dual clamp

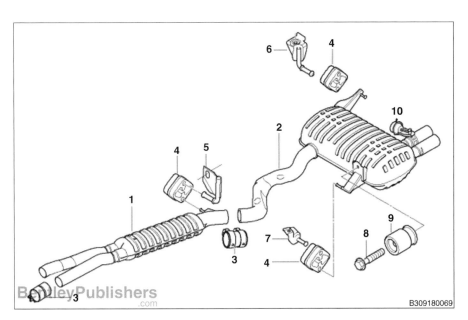

1. Resonator
2. Muffler
3. Dual clamp
4. Hanger
5. Bracket, front
6. Bracket, rear
7. Bracket, center
8. Bolt
9. Vibration dampener
10. Vacuum valve

B309180069

## Exhaust components (turbo)

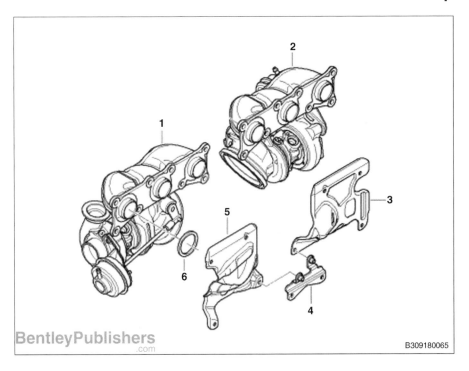

1. Exhaust manifold / turbocharger, front
2. Exhaust manifold / turbocharger, rear
3. Heat shield
4. Bracket
5. Heat shield
6. Gasket

B309180065

*Exhaust components (turbo)*

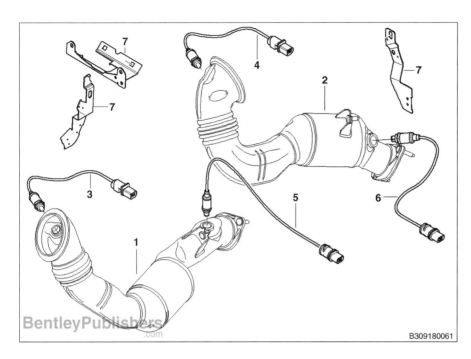

1. Pre-catalytic converter, front
2. Pre-catalytic converter, rear
3. Pre-catalyst oxygen sensor, front
4. Pre-catalyst oxygen sensor, rear
5. Post-catalyst oxygen sensor, front
6. Post-catalyst oxygen sensor, rear
7. Bracket

B309180061

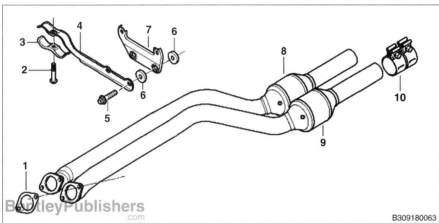

1. Gasket
2. Bolt
3. Exhaust hanger, lower
4. Exhaust hanger, upper
5. Bolt
6. Washer
7. Bracket
8. Post-catalytic converter, front
9. Post-catalytic converter, rear
10. Dual clamp

B309180063

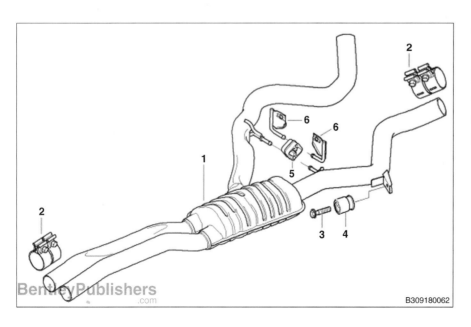

1. Resonator
2. Dual clamp
3. Bolt
4. Vibration dampener
5. Hanger
6. Bracket

B309180062

*Exhaust components (turbo)*

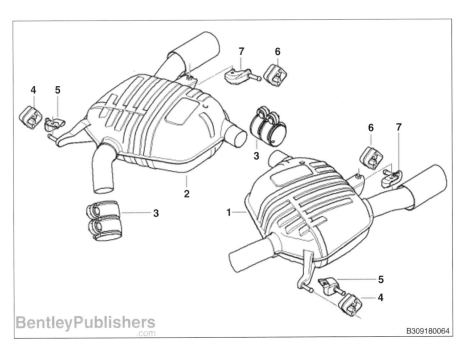

B309180064

1. Muffler, left

2. Muffler, right

3. Dual clamp

4. Hanger

5. Bracket, front

6. Hanger

7. Bracket, rear

**180**

# 200 Transmission–General

**200**

## GENERAL

This section provides general information for drivetrain components such as clutch, transmission, driveshafts and xDrive transfer case.

See also:

- **119 Lubrication System** for rear main seal replacement
- **210 Clutch** for clutch mechanical and hydraulic repairs and flywheel replacement
- **230 Manual Transmission** for manual transmission fluid service, seal replacement and transmission replacement
- **240 Automatic Transmission** for ATF change and transmission replacement
- **260 Driveshafts** for front and rear driveshaft repairs
- **270 Transfer Case** for xDrive transfer case replacement
- **311 Front Axle Differential** for front differential, front drive axles and front CV joints
- **331 Rear Axle Differential** for rear differential, rear drive axles and rear CV joints

## Drivetrain

3 Series models are equipped with a longitudinal drivetrain. The transmission is bolted directly to the rear of the engine. In rear wheel drive models, a driveshaft connects the output shaft of the transmission to the rear differential. On xDrive models, a transfer case is mounted to the rear of the transmission, with drive shafts leading to front and rear differentials. Individual drive axles with integrated constant velocity joints transfer rotational power from the differentials to the drive wheels.

## Manual Transmission

◀ A 6-speed manual transmission is standard on all models. 325i and 328i models use a Getrag type I unit while 325xi, 328xi, 330i, and 330xi a models use a Getrag type H unit. 335i and 335xi models use a more robust ZF type G unit. See **Table a**. Transmission gear ratio information is in **230 Manual Transmission**.

BentleyPublishers.com
B309020001

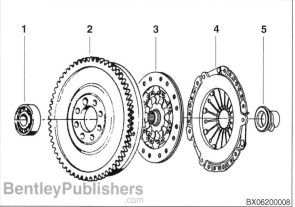

BentleyPublishers.com
BX06200008

◀ Manual transmission vehicles are equipped with a single-disc clutch and dual-mass flywheel.

1. Pilot bearing
2. Dual-mass flywheel
3. Clutch disc
4. Clutch pressure plate
5. Clutch release bearing

For further information, see **210 Clutch**.

Manual transmission has metal ID plate mounted on side of transmission. Do not rely on numbers cast on transmission case for identification.

| Table a. Manual transmission applications | | |
|---|---|---|
| **Model** | **Transmission** | **Manufacturer id** |
| 325i, 328i | GS6-17BG | Getrag type I |
| 325xi, 328xi, 330xi 330i | GS6X-37BZ GS6-37BZ | ZF type H |
| 335i 335xi | GS6-53DZ GS6X-53DZ | ZF type G |

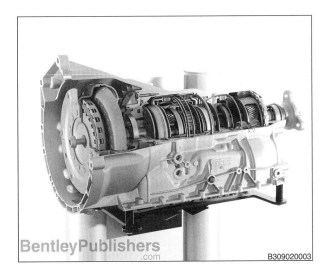

B309020003

## AUTOMATIC TRANSMISSION

◀ The automatic transmission is a 6-speed Steptronic that offers a choice of Normal, Sport, and Manual mode. Sport mode is engaged by moving the shift lever out of Drive and into the Sport / Manual shift gate. In Sport mode, shifts occur at a higher rpm than normal. Additionally, the driver can tip the lever forward (downshifts) or backward (upshifts) to manually select a gear. Automatic transmission applications are in **Table b**.

**200**

| Table b. Automatic transmission applications | | |
|---|---|---|
| **Model** | **Transmission** | **Manufacturer id** |
| 328i, 328xi | GA6L45R (6-speed) | GM GM6 |
| 325i, 325xi, 330i, 330xi, 335i, 335xi | GA6HP19Z (6-speed) | ZF 6HP19 |

◀ GM transmission identification tag (**arrow**) is on left side of transmission, just above transmission pan, behind transmission selector cable.

BX56200014

◀ ZF transmission identification tag (**arrow**) is on left rear of transmission, just above transmission pan.

BX06200002

## xDrive

BMW's advanced all-wheel drive system is known as xDrive. It includes a transfer case with electronically controlled clutch that regulates the front to rear torque split for best traction.

### Transfer case

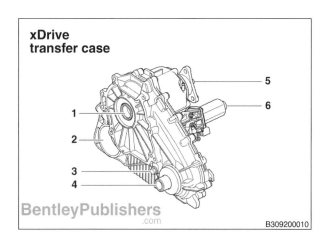

xDrive
transfer case

B309200010

 The xDrive transfer case, bolted to the rear of the transmission, directs power from the transmission to both the front and rear differentials via driveshafts. The transfer case is permanently engaged to drive all four wheels all of the time.

1.  Transfer case input shaft
2.  Transmission and transfer case mount
3.  Fill plug
4.  Front driveshaft output
5.  Rear driveshaft output
6.  xDrive clutch actuator

### Clutch

In the xDrive system, an electronically controlled clutch allows for infinitely variable distribution of front to rear torque for best traction.

 xDrive components consist of:

1.  Transmission output shaft
2.  Electronically controlled clutch
3.  Rear driveshaft
4.  Front driveshaft
5.  Power transfer chain
6.  xDrive clutch actuator

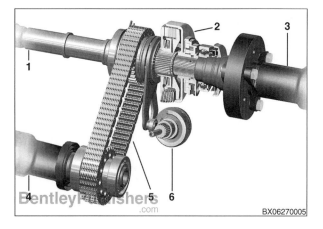

BX06270005

xDrive functions are integrated with ABS / DSC. Under normal driving conditions, 60% of engine power goes to the rear axle, 40% to the front. If a wheel begins to slip or if the DCS steering angle sensor and acceleration sensors signal excessive "yaw" in the vehicle, xDrive reacts by transferring power to the wheel or wheels with best traction, usually before a wheel is able to spin. This significantly reduces the risk of under- or oversteer, improving agility and safety on the road.

Torque and engine power are redistributed by xDrive within a few milliseconds. As a result, the driver normally does not notice a change in power distribution.

In addition to controlling power distribution, xDrive and DSC may intervene via braking. If a wheel starts to spin without transmitting power, the brakes are applied at that wheel. In this case, the differential automatically supplies more power to the opposite wheel.

For additional information on xDrive and DSC functions, see **340 Brakes**.

## DRIVETRAIN LUBRICANTS

### Transmission fluids

Manual and automatic transmissions are filled with lifetime lubrication. No oil change is required for the entire service life of the transmission. If repairs have to be made to the transmission or transmission oil cooler, use only the recommended lifetime fluid to refill. See **Table c** or **Table d**.

| Table c. Manual transmission fluids | | |
|---|---|---|
| **Transmission** | **Year range** | **Fluid type** |
| Getrag GS6-17BG | All | MTF-LT-3 |
| ZF GS6-37BZ | To 03/2007<br>From 03/2007 | MTF-LT-2<br>MTF-LT-3 |
| ZF GS6-53BZ | To 03/2007<br>From 03/2007 | MTF-LT-2<br>MTF-LT-3 |
| *MTF-LT-2 (Lifetime fluid) BMW part no. 83 22 0 309 031* | | |
| *MTF-LT-3 (Lifetime fluid) BMW part no. 83 22 7 533 818* | | |

| Table d. Automatic transmission fluids | | |
|---|---|---|
| **Type** | **BMW part no.** | **Manufacturer part no.** |
| GA6L45R | 83 22 0 397 114 | Dexron VI |
| GA6HP19Z | 83 22 0 142 516 | Shell M-1375.4 |

◄ A label on manual transmission specifies original lubricant used at the factory.

For manual transmission fluid service, see **230 Manual Transmission**.

◄ ATF is specified on colored label on automatic transmission sump.

For automatic transmission fluid service, including checking fluid level and ATF filter replacement, see **240 Automatic Transmission**.

## Transfer case fluid

**xDrive models**: Transfer case fluid specifications are in **Table e**.

| Table e. Transfer case fluid specifications | |
|---|---|
| **Type** | **BMW part no.** |
| xDrive (all) | 83 22 0 397 244 |

For transfer case fluid service, see **270 Transfer Case**.

## Differential oil

Differentials are filled with lifetime lubrication. No oil change is required for the entire service life of the differential. If repairs have to be made to the differential, use only the recommended lifetime oil to refill. See **Table f**.

| Table f. Differential oil (lifetime) | |
|---|---|
| BMW specification | SAF-XO Synthetic |

**xDrive models**: Front differential is bolted to left side of engine oil pan.

For front differential oil service, see **311 Front Axle Differential**.

 Rear differential is bolted to rear suspension subframe.

For rear differential oil service, see **331 Rear Axle Differential**.

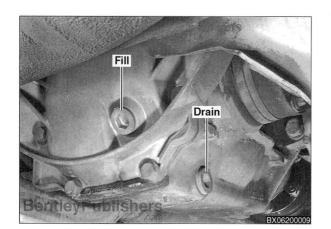

# 210 Clutch

**210**

## GENERAL

This repair group covers replacement of clutch mechanical and hydraulic components.

See also:

- **200 Transmission–General** for transmission application information
- **230 Manual Transmission** for transmission removal
- **270 Transfer Case** for xDrive transfer case removal

### Warnings and Cautions

*CAUTION—*

- *When performing any repair which involves separating the engine and transmission, check that the bellhousing dowels are undamaged and properly in place before reassembly. If the alignment of the engine flywheel to the transmission input shaft or torque converter is incorrect any of the following complaints may result: Clutch slipping, shudder, or poor disengagement; noise from transmission input shaft; transmission popping out of gear; difficulty changing gears; or internal damage to the transmission.*

- *For engines with a magnesium crankcase only aluminum fasteners and dowels may be used. Consult with an authorized BMW dealer parts department for the correct fasteners and dowels for the engine and model concerned.*

# CLUTCH HYDRAULICS

The clutch is hydraulically actuated by the master and slave cylinders. Clutch disc wear is automatically taken up through the self-adjusting clutch (SAC) pressure plate springs, making periodic adjustments unnecessary.

A soft or spongy feel to the clutch pedal, long pedal free-play, or grinding noises from the gears while shifting can all indicate problems with the clutch hydraulics. In these circumstances it is best to start with a clutch fluid flush, followed, if necessary, by replacement of the hydraulic parts.

The clutch hydraulic system shares the fluid reservoir and fluid with the brake hydraulic system.

Models prior to 08/2006 are equipped with metal slave cylinder. Later models are equipped with a plastic slave cylinder. Differences are noted in the text where they occur.

## Clutch hydraulic system, bleeding and flushing

If the clutch and brake fluid is murky or muddy, or has not been changed within the last two years, flush the system using a brake system pressure bleeder.

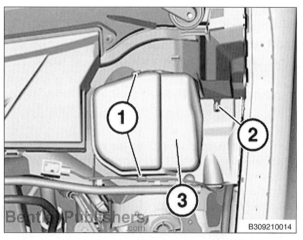

B309210014

— Raise vehicle and support safely.

> **WARNING**—
> • *Make sure the vehicle is stable and well supported at all times. Use a professional automotive lift or jack stands designed for the purpose. A floor jack is not adequate support.*

— Remove splash shield under transmission. See **020 Maintenance**.

◄ Working on left side of engine compartment, release locking tabs (**1**) and remove brake fluid reservoir cover (**3**).

— Remove brake fluid reservoir cap. Using a clean syringe, remove brake fluid from reservoir. Refill reservoir with clean DOT4 low viscosity brake fluid.

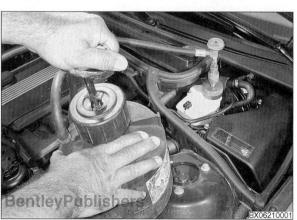

BX06210001

◄ Attach pressure brake bleeder to fluid reservoir and pump bleeder a few times to pressurize hydraulic fluid system.

> **CAUTION**—
> • *Do not exceed 2 bar (29 psi) pressure at the fluid reservoir when bleeding or flushing the hydraulic system.*
> • *Brake fluid is poisonous, highly corrosive and dangerous to the environment. Wear safety glasses and rubber gloves when working with brake fluid. Do not siphon brake fluid with your mouth. Immediately clean away any fluid spilled on painted surfaces and wash with water, as brake fluid will remove paint.*
> • *Use new brake fluid from a fresh, unopened container. Brake fluid absorbs moisture from the air. This can lead to corrosion problems in the hydraulic systems, and also lowers the brake fluid boiling point. Dispose of brake fluid properly.*

## Clutch hydraulics, bleeding

◄ Connect a length of hose from clutch slave cylinder bleeder valve (**arrow**) to a container.

– Open bleeder valve and allow brake fluid to expel until clean fluid comes out free of air bubbles.

– Close bleeder valve and disconnect pressure bleeding equipment from fluid reservoir. Hose on bleeder valve remains connected.

– Slowly operate clutch pedal about 10 times. Fill reservoir with clean fluid as necessary.

## Clutch hydraulics, bleeding using BMW special tool 21 5 030

Slave cylinder   **21 5 030**

◄ Working underneath vehicle, unbolt slave cylinder from transmission. Fit BMW special tool 21 5 030 to slave cylinder. Rotate threaded tool spindle to press slave cylinder pushrod completely into slave cylinder.

– Attach pressure brake bleeder to fluid reservoir.

– Hold slave cylinder so that bleeder valve is at highest point.
  • Open bleeder valve.
  • If bubble-free brake fluid emerges, use tool spindle to retract slave cylinder push rod slightly, then press in again.
  • If bubbles appear, repeat procedure until fluid runs clear and without bubbles. Once brake fluid appears without air bubbles, close bleeder valve.
  • Release pressure bleeder and detach special tool. Disconnect bleeder hose.

> **CAUTION—**
> • Do not detach special tool from slave cylinder if fluid is pressurized. The slave cylinder push rod can blow out of cylinder.

– Reinstall slave cylinder to transmission. Add clean brake fluid to reservoir as necessary. Check clutch operation.

| Tightening torque | |
|---|---|
| Clutch slave cylinder to transmission | 22 Nm (16 ft-lb) |

## Clutch master cylinder, replacing

The clutch master cylinder is mounted to the pedal assembly directly above the clutch pedal.

◄ Working on left side of engine compartment, release locking tabs (**1**) and remove brake fluid reservoir cover (**3**).

– Remove brake fluid reservoir cap. Using a clean syringe, remove brake fluid from reservoir.

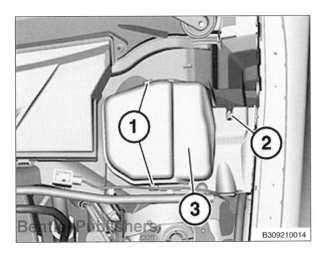

*Clutch master cylinder, replacing*

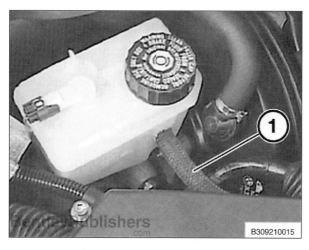

◅ Disconnect clutch fluid supply line (**1**) from brake fluid reservoir. Place a pan under hose to catch dripping fluid.

– Working at pedal cluster, remove lower left trim panel under dashboard (pedal cluster trim). See **513 Interior Trim**.

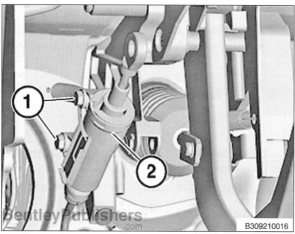

◅ Remove fasteners (**1**) on master cylinder (**2**).

**NOTE** —

• *Clutch pedal shown removed to aid illustration.*

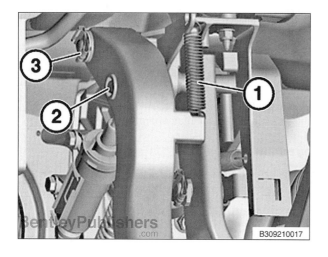

◅ Remove clutch pedal return spring (**1**).

– Remove locking clip (**3**) to release clutch pedal and master cylinder from bearing block.

– Press pin ends (**2**) together and remove pin so that master cylinder is free from clutch pedal.

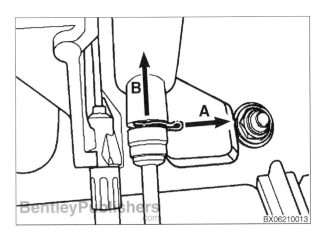

◀ Remove pressure line locking clip (**A**) and pull master cylinder (**B**) off line.

> **CAUTION—**
> • *To prevent brake fluid spill, wrap clutch master cylinder with shop towels when removing hydraulic fluid lines from master cylinder.*
> • *Brake fluid damages paint and stains carpets. Clean off any brake fluid on or in the vehicle immediately.*

– Remove supply hose from master cylinder. Do not pull supply hose into vehicle interior.

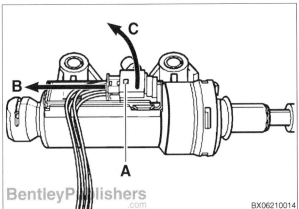

◀ Remove switch module from master cylinder.
  • Press locking button (**A**) to release harness connector.
  • Pull harness connector (**B**) off switch module.
  • Use screwdriver to lever off switch module (**C**).

– Installation is reverse of removal. Make sure switch module snaps audibly into place on master cylinder housing.

| Tightening torques | |
| --- | --- |
| Clutch master cylinder to pedal cluster | 9 Nm (80 in-lb) |

– Fill brake fluid reservoir with clean fluid and bleed clutch hydraulics. See **Clutch hydraulic system, bleeding and flushing** in this repair group.

## Clutch switch, replacing

The clutch switch is a single module, attached to the clutch master cylinder. It performs both cruise control and starter immobilization functions.

– Remove driver side footwell trim. See **513 Interior Trim**.

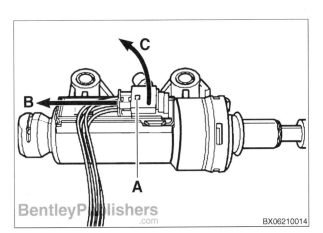

◀ Remove switch module from master cylinder.
  • Press locking button (**A**) to release harness connector.
  • Pull harness connector (**B**) off switch module.
  • Use screwdriver to lever off switch module (**C**).

– Installation is reverse of removal. Make sure switch module snaps firmly into place.

## Clutch slave cylinder, replacing

— Working on left side of engine compartment, remove brake fluid reservoir cover.

◄ Use BMW special tool 13 3 010 or equivalent hose clamping tool to pinch off brake reservoir to clutch master cylinder supply hose.

— Raise vehicle and support safely.

> **WARNING** —
> • *Make sure the vehicle is stable and well supported at all times. Use a professional automotive lift or jack stands designed for the purpose. A floor jack is not adequate support.*

— Remove lower engine and transmission splash shields as necessary. See **020 Maintenance**.

— **Models with metal slave cylinder:** Working underneath transmission, disconnect fluid line from slave cylinder on side of transmission. Place pan under hose to catch dripping fluid.

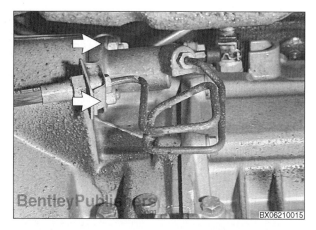

◄ Remove slave cylinder mounting nuts (**arrow**) from clutch bellhousing and remove cylinder.

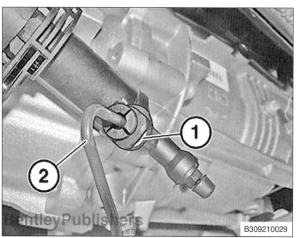

◄ **Models with plastic slave cylinder:** Remove slave cylinder mounting nuts from clutch bellhousing and remove cylinder.

— Working underneath transmission, release retaining clip (**1**) and remove hydraulic line (**2**). Place pan under hose to catch dripping fluid.

B309210030

B309210031

◄ To reinstall, press cylinder piston in by hand. Reconnect hydraulic line with cylinder fully depressed.

– Working at brake fluid reservoir, remove hose clamp tool (BMW special tool 13 3 010 or equivalent) from hydraulic line

◄ Hold cylinder with piston facing down. Press piston into cylinder 5 times.

– **All models:** Remainder of installation is reverse of removal. Note the following:

  • Check for wear on slave cylinder. Any wear except on tip is caused by misalignment of clutch components.

  • Lightly coat pushrod tip with molybdenum disulfide grease (Molykote® Longterm or equivalent).

  • During installation be sure pushrod tip engages recess in clutch release lever.

  • Make sure spacer (if equipped) between fuel line and hydraulic line remains in installed position.

  • Fill brake fluid reservoir with clean fluid and bleed clutch hydraulics. See **Clutch hydraulic system, bleeding and flushing** in this repair group.

| Tightening torques | |
|---|---|
| Clutch slave cylinder to transmission | 22 Nm (16 ft-lb) |
| Fluid line to slave cylinder | 14.5 Nm (11 ft-lb) |

**210**

## Clutch assembly and hydraulics

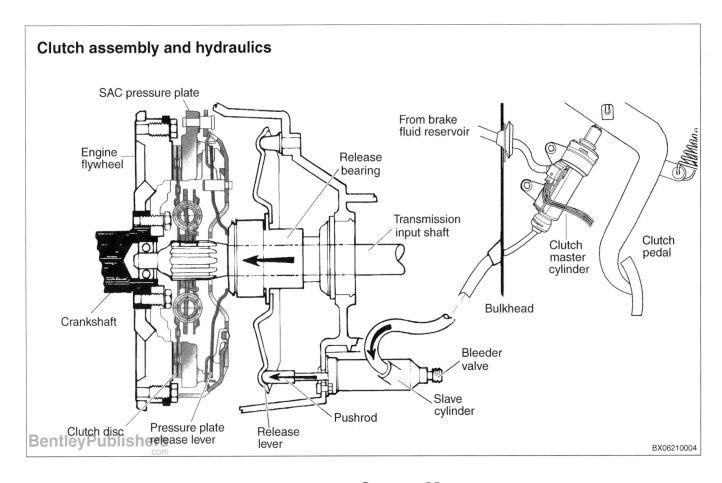

BX06210004

## CLUTCH MECHANICAL

Clutch replacement requires removal of the transfer case (xDrive models) and transmission.

Clutch disc, pressure plate and release bearing are usually replaced during a clutch overhaul. Check flywheel for wear and scoring. Replace if necessary.

Be sure to check the bottom of the bellhousing for oil. If engine oil is found, check for faulty rear crankshaft (rear main) oil seal. Rear main seal replacement is covered in **119 Lubrication System**.

 Use special tools for removing and installing self-adjusting clutch (SAC). The SAC pressure plate uses a wedge ring which rotates against the diaphragm springs to accommodate for clutch disc wear. The wedge ring adjusts by means of spring tension, so special tools are needed to apply and relieve spring tension as the clutch pressure plate is removed and installed.

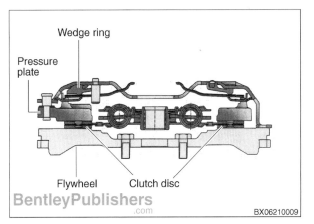

BX06210009

## Clutch, removing

– Raise vehicle and support safely.

> **WARNING** —
> • *Make sure the vehicle is stable and well supported at all times. Use a professional automotive lift or jack stands designed for the purpose. A floor jack is not adequate support.*

– Remove splash shield under transmission.

– Remove intermediate muffler and heat shield. See **180 Exhaust System**.

> **WARNING** —
> • *Make sure exhaust system is fully cooled off before starting removal.*

– Detach front (xDrive models) and rear driveshaft. Tie to side. See **260 Driveshafts**.

– Remove transfer case (xDrive models). See **270 Transfer Case**.

– Remove transmission from engine. See **230 Manual Transmission**.

◄ Lock flywheel in position using BMW special tool 11 9 260 or equivalent.

◄ Loosen 6 clutch mounting bolts (**arrows**) evenly.

– Remove pressure plate and clutch disc.

> **WARNING** —
> • *Friction material in the clutch disc produces dangerous dust. Do not breathe in dust. Use water to wet down components and collect dripping mixture in a shop towel.*

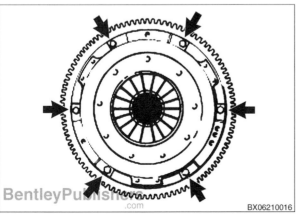

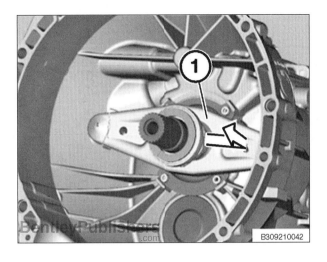

◀ Remove clutch release bearing / lever module from transmission input shaft as a complete unit.

— Remove release module (**1**) from spring clip in direction of **arrow**.

> **CAUTION—**
> • *To avoid installing incorrectly, do not disassemble bearing from combined release bearing / lever module.*

## Clutch components, inspecting

— Inspect clutch disc for wear, cracks, loose rivets, contamination or excessive runout (warping). Replace if necessary.

— Measure depth of clutch lining at lining rivets. If shallowest rivet depth is less than 1 mm (0.04 in), replace clutch disk.

— Inspect flywheel for scoring, hot spots, cracks or loose or worn guide pins. Replace flywheel if any faults are found. See **Flywheel, removing and installing** in this repair group.

> **CAUTION—**
> • *If flywheel is removed from engine, install using new bolts.*

— Check to make sure transmission pilot bearing rotates smoothly without play. Replace if faulty. See **Transmission pilot bearing, replacing** in this repair group.

— Inspect and clean release bearing module.

◀ Check release bearing ball stud and spring retainer. Replace if damaged or worn.

— Clean release bearing guide sleeve.

> **CAUTION—**
> • *Do not grease release bearing module or guide sleeve. If guide sleeve is greased, release bearing may stick to it.*

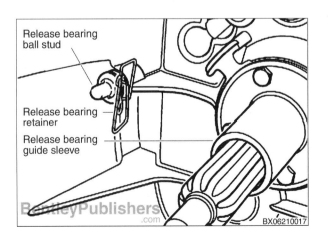

Release bearing ball stud

Release bearing retainer

Release bearing guide sleeve

## Clutch, installing (new SAC components)

The SAC pressure plate, when new, comes from the factory with a lock plate at the center which maintains spring tension on the self-adjusting springs. Do not remove this lock plate until the pressure plate is securely installed on the flywheel with clutch disk in place.

> **CAUTION—**
> • *Avoid contaminating clutch friction surfaces with oil or grease. Do not touch these surfaces.*

◄ Center clutch disc on flywheel using the appropriate BMW (or equivalent) centering tool.

> **CAUTION—**
> • *Be sure clutch disc is facing the correct way. The disc is marked "engine side" or "transmission side".*

**NOTE—**
• *The large bolt in the clutch disc centering tool is used to install and remove the tool only. Once the disc is in place on the flywheel, remove the bolt to make room for the SAC pressure plate.*

— Lock flywheel in position using BMW special tool 11 9 260 or equivalent.

— Install SAC pressure plate on dowel pins at flywheel. Install clutch mounting bolts and tighten each one turn at a time until pressure plate is fully seated. Torque to specification in 2 stages.

| **Tightening torque** | |
|---|---|
| Clutch to flywheel (use new M8 ZNS bolts) | |
| • Stage 1 | 15 Nm (11 ft-lb) |
| • Stage 2 (torque angle) | additional 90° ± 5° |

◄ Use 14 mm Allen wrench to unscrew (clockwise or counterclockwise) lock plate in center of pressure plate.

**NOTE—**
• *The spring lock plate may make snapping noises while being unscrewed.*

— Using large bolt, pull out clutch disc centering tool.

— Remove flywheel locking tool.

— Inspect and clean clutch release bearing / lever module.

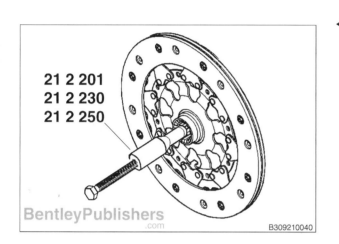

21 2 201
21 2 230
21 2 250

BentleyPublishers
.com

B309210040

BX06210025

*Clutch, installing (used SAC components)*

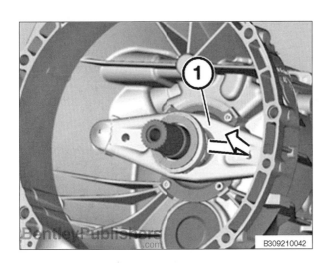

◄ Install clutch release bearing / lever module (**1**).

– Install transmission. See **230 Manual Transmission**.

---
**CAUTION—**
- *Replace aluminum bolts each time they are loosened.*
- *Follow torque instructions, including angle of rotation specifications, when installing aluminum fasteners.*
---

| **Tightening torques** | |
|---|---|
| Front end reinforcement to front end (use new fasteners): • Stage 1 • Stage 2 | 56 Nm (41 ft-lb) additional 90° |
| Slave cylinder to transmission | 22 Nm (16 ft-lb) |
| Transmission rear support to body (M8) | 19 Nm (14 ft-lb) |
| Transmission mount to rear support (M8) | 19 Nm (14 ft-lb) |
| Transmission to engine (use new alum. bolts) • M10 x 30 mm   Stage 1   Stage 2 • M10 x 85 mm   Stage 1   Stage 2 • M12   Stage 1   Stage 2 | 20 Nm additional 90° - 110° 20 Nm additional 180° - 200° 25 Nm additional 130° + 20° |
| Vibration mount to trans. rear support (M10) | 38 Nm (28 ft-lb) |

## Clutch, installing (used SAC components)

When reinstalling a previously used self-adjusting clutch (SAC), special tools are needed to reset the self-adjusting ring to its original position.

– Place SAC pressure plate on clean work surface.

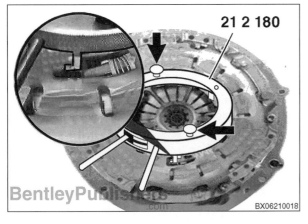

21 2 180

◄ Place BMW special tool 21 2 180 on pressure plate.
- Note that locating hooks of special tool engage pressure plate adjusting ring openings (**inset**).
- Grip tool firmly and squeeze special tool handles together.
- Tighten down special tool knurled screws (**arrows**).
- SAC adjustment ring is now in its original position.

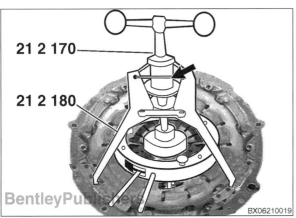

21 2 170

21 2 180

◄ Install BMW special tool 21 2 170 on SAC pressure plate.
- Fit fingers of special tool in slots above dowel pin bores.
- Tighten down knurled nut (**arrow**) finger-tight.
- Screw in T-handle until pressure plate diaphragm spring is pretensioned to stop.

---
**CAUTION—**
- *Avoid contaminating clutch friction surfaces with oil or grease. Do not touch these surfaces.*
---

*Clutch, installing (used SAC components)*

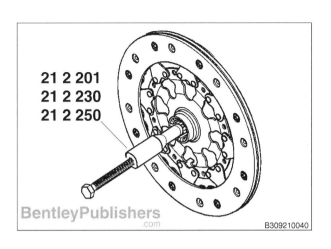

21 2 201
21 2 230
21 2 250

BentleyPublishers
.com

B309210040

◀ Center clutch disc on flywheel using the appropriate BMW (or equivalent) centering tool.

> **CAUTION—**
> • Be sure clutch disc is facing the correct way. The disc is marked "engine side" or "transmission side".

> **NOTE—**
> • The large bolt in the clutch disc centering tool is used to install and remove the tool only. Once the disc is in place on the flywheel, remove the bolt to make room for the SAC pressure plate.

— Lock flywheel in position using BMW special tool 11 9 260 or equivalent.

— Install SAC pressure plate on dowel pins at flywheel. Install clutch mounting bolts and tighten each one turn at a time until pressure plate is fully seated. Torque to specification in 2 stages.

| Tightening torque | |
|---|---|
| Clutch to flywheel (use new M8 ZNS bolts) <br> • Stage 1 <br> • Stage 2 (torque angle) | 15 Nm (11 ft-lb) <br> additional 90° ± 5° |

— Using large bolt, pull out clutch disc centering tool.

— Remove flywheel locking tool.

— Inspect and clean release bearing lever.

◀ Install clutch release bearing / lever module (**1**).

— Install transmission. See **230 Manual Transmission**.

> **CAUTION—**
> • Replace aluminum bolts each time they are loosened.
> • Follow torque instructions, including angle of rotation specifications, when installing aluminum fasteners.

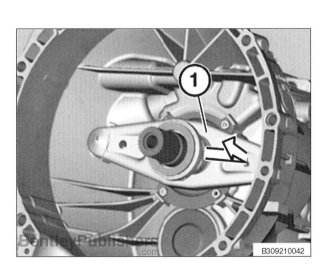

B309210042

| Tightening torques | |
|---|---|
| Front end reinforcement to front end (use new fasteners): <br> • Stage 1 <br> • Stage 2 | 56 Nm (41 ft-lb) <br> additional 90° |
| Slave cylinder to transmission | 22 Nm (16 ft-lb) |
| Transmission rear support to body (M8) | 19 Nm (14 ft-lb) |
| Transmission mount to rear support (M8) | 19 Nm (14 ft-lb) |
| Transmission to engine (use new fasteners) <br> • M10 x 30 mm <br>   Stage 1 <br>   Stage 2 <br> • M10 x 85 mm <br>   Stage 1 <br>   Stage 2 <br> • M12 <br>   Stage 1 <br>   Stage 2 | <br> <br> 20 Nm <br> additional 90° - 110° <br> <br> 20 Nm <br> additional 180° - 200° <br> <br> 25 Nm <br> additional 130° + 20° |
| Vibration mount to trans. rear support (M10) | 38 Nm (28 ft-lb) |

210

## Self-adjusting clutch (SAC), breaking in

In normal driving, approx. 800 to 1000 gearshifts are needed for a new SAC clutch lining to be fully broken in. To ensure correct operation and long life, break in the SAC gradually, with light to medium loads. Fast sports-style driving and abrupt clutch engagement may destroy a new clutch. The following procedure helps to break in the clutch.

— Drive at 20 mph (30 kph) on level grade. Start, upshift and downshift through the gears at approx. 2000 rpm.

— Increase speed. Upshift and downshift through the gears at approx. 3500 - 4000 rpm.

— On medium grade (approx. 12% and up): Start off at approx. 2500 rpm 3 - 5 times.

## Flywheel, removing and installing

This procedure is for vehicles with manual transmission. Flywheel and torque plate removal for automatic transmission vehicle is covered in **240 Automatic Transmission**.

— Remove splash shield under transmission.

— Remove intermediate muffler and heat shield. See **180 Exhaust System**.

> **WARNING** —
> • *Make sure exhaust system is fully cooled off before starting removal.*

— Detach front (xDrive models) and rear driveshaft. Tie to side. See **260 Driveshafts**.

— Remove transfer case (xDrive models). See **270 Transfer Case**.

— Remove transmission. See **230 Manual Transmission**.

— Remove clutch. See **Clutch, removing** in this repair group.

— Inspect flywheel for scoring, hot spots, cracks or loose or worn guide pins. Replace flywheel if any faults are found.

◄ Lock flywheel in position using BMW special tool 11 9 260 or equivalent.

— Loosen and remove flywheel mounting bolts. Remove flywheel.

— Clean flywheel bolt threads in crankshaft.

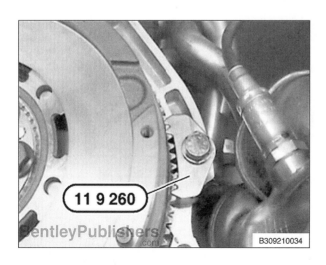

B309210034

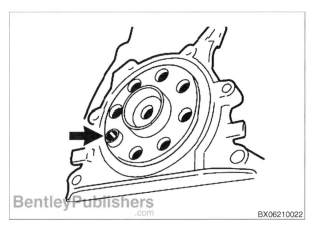

◀ Check flywheel location dowel sleeve (**arrow**) for damage and correct installation.

BX06210022

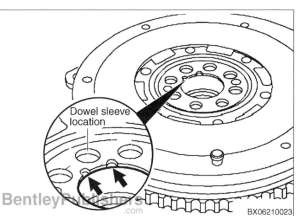

Dowel sleeve location

BX06210023

◀ When reinstalling flywheel, position dowel sleeve next to two locating notches (**arrows**).

– Install flywheel using new self-locking bolts.

| Tightening torque | |
| --- | --- |
| Flywheel to crankshaft (use new self-locking bolts) | 120 Nm (89 ft-lb) |

> **CAUTION—**
> • *Use new self-locking bolts to install flywheel. Do not reuse the old stretch-type bolts. Do not install bolts with Loctite® or similar thread-locking compound.*

## Transmission pilot bearing, replacing

– Remove splash shield under transmission.

– Remove intermediate muffler and heat shield. See **180 Exhaust System**.

> **WARNING—**
> • *Make sure exhaust system is fully cooled off before starting removal.*

– Detach front (xDrive models) and rear driveshaft. Tie to side. See **260 Driveshafts**.

– Remove transfer case (xDrive models). See **270 Transfer Case**.

– Remove transmission. See **230 Manual Transmission**.

– Remove clutch. See **Clutch, removing** in this repair group.

– Remove flywheel. See **Flywheel, removing and installing** in this repair group.

210

*Transmission pilot bearing, replacing*

BX06210024

◄ Use hydraulic press and BMW special tool 21 2 051 to press transmission pilot bearing out of dual-mass flywheel. Press from engine side of flywheel.

> **CAUTION—**
> • *Do not drive bearing in or out using a chisel or punch.*

– Place new pilot bearing on BMW special tool 21 2 052. Use hydraulic press to press bearing into flywheel as far as it will go. Press from clutch side of flywheel.

# 230  Manual Transmission

## GENERAL

This repair group covers external service of manual transmission, including transmission removal and installation. Internal transmission repair is not covered. Special tools and procedures are required to disassemble and service the internal geartrain.

See also:

- **210 Clutch**
- **250 Gearshift Linkage**
- **260 Driveshafts**
- **270 Transfer Case**

---

*CAUTION—*

- *When performing any repair which involves separating the engine and transmission, check that the bellhousing dowels are undamaged and properly in place before reassembly. If the alignment of the engine flywheel to the transmission input shaft or torque converter is incorrect any of the following complaints may result: Clutch slipping, shudder, or poor disengagement; noise from transmission input shaft; transmission popping out of gear; difficulty changing gears; or internal damage to the transmission.*

- *For engines with a magnesium crankcase only aluminum fasteners and dowels may be used. Consult with an authorized BMW dealer parts department for the correct fasteners and dowels for the engine and model concerned.*

---

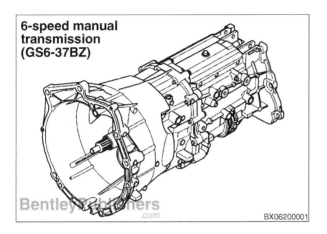

6-speed manual transmission (GS6-37BZ)

BX06200001

## Manual transmission applications and ratios

◀ Several manual transmission are used in the various 3 Series models. See **Table a**. For gear ratio specifications, see **Table b**.

**Table a. Manual transmission applications**

| Model | Transmission | Manufacturer id |
|-------|-------------|-----------------|
| 325i, 328i | GS6-17BG | Getrag type I |
| 325xi, 328xi, 330xi 330i | GS6X-37BZ GS6-37BZ | ZF type H |
| 335i 335xi | GS6-53DZ GS6X-53DZ | ZF type G |

**Table b. Manual transmission gear ratios**

| Gear | GS6-17BG | ZF GS6-37BZ | ZF GS6-53DZ |
|------|----------|-------------|-------------|
| 1st | 4.32 | 4.35 | 4.06 |
| 2nd | 2.46 | 2.50 | 2.40 |
| 3rd | 1.66 | 1.66 | 1.58 |
| 4th | 1.23 | 1.23 | 1.19 |
| 5th | 1.00 | 1.00 | 1.00 |
| 6th | 0.85 | 0.85 | 0.87 |
| Reverse | 3.94 | 3.93 | 3.68 |
| Final drive | 3.23 | 3.38 | 3.08 |

## TRANSMISSION FLUID SERVICE

Manual transmissions in 3 Series models are provided with lifetime lubrication. No oil change is required for the entire service life of these transmissions. If repairs have to be made to the transmission, use only the recommended lifetime fluid to refill.

◀ ZF GS6-53BZ transmission filled with MTF-LT-3 lifetime oil is identified with a blue label near the transmission fill plug.

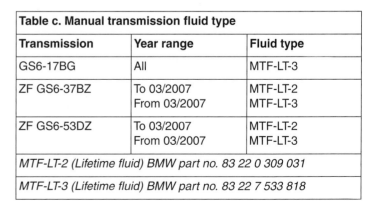

B309230038

**Table c. Manual transmission fluid type**

| Transmission | Year range | Fluid type |
|--------------|-----------|------------|
| GS6-17BG | All | MTF-LT-3 |
| ZF GS6-37BZ | To 03/2007 From 03/2007 | MTF-LT-2 MTF-LT-3 |
| ZF GS6-53DZ | To 03/2007 From 03/2007 | MTF-LT-2 MTF-LT-3 |
| *MTF-LT-2 (Lifetime fluid) BMW part no. 83 22 0 309 031* | | |
| *MTF-LT-3 (Lifetime fluid) BMW part no. 83 22 7 533 818* | | |

## Transmission fluid level, checking

– Drive vehicle for a few miles to warm transmission.

– Raise and safely support vehicle to access transmission filler plug. Make sure vehicle is level.

> **WARNING—**
> • *Make sure the vehicle is stable and well supported at all times. Use a professional automotive lift or jack stands designed for the purpose. A floor jack is not adequate support.*

◄ Remove fill plug (**2**). Be prepared to catch dripping fluid.

– Insert finger in fill hole to check fluid level.

• If fluid level is up to bottom of fill hole (finger is wetted by transmission fluid), level is correct.

• If level is low, slowly fill transmission with fluid until fluid overflows fill hole.

– Install and torque fill plug.

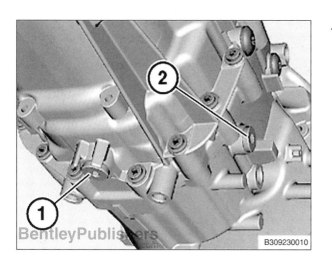

B309230010

| Tightening torque | |
|---|---|
| Drain or fill plug to transmission case: | |
| • M12 x 1.5 | 25 Nm (18 ft-lb) |
| • M18 x 1.5 | 35 Nm (26 ft-lb) |

## Transmission fluid, replacing

– Drive vehicle for a few miles to warm transmission.

– Raise and safely support vehicle to access drain plug.

> **WARNING—**
> • *Make sure the vehicle is stable and well supported at all times. Use a professional automotive lift or jack stands designed for the purpose. A floor jack is not adequate support.*

◄ Place drain pan under transmission and remove drain plug (**1**) at bottom of transmission.

• Drain fluid.

• Install and torque drain plug.

• Remove fill plug (**2**) from side of transmission.

• Slowly fill transmission with fluid until fluid overflows fill hole.

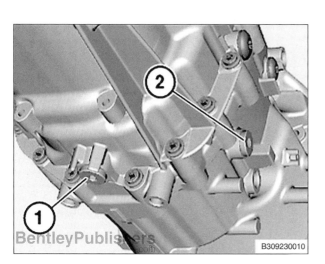

B309230010

| Table d. Manual transmission fluid capacities | | |
|---|---|---|
| Transmission | Initial fill, new or rebuilt unit | Fluid change |
| GS6-17BG | 1.4 liter (1.5 US qt) | 1.3 liter (1.4 US qt) |
| ZF GS6-37BZ | 1.6 liter (1.7 US qt) | 1.5 liter (1.6 US qt) |
| ZF GS6-53DZ | 1.6 liter (1.7 US qt) | 1.5 liter (1.6 US qt) |

230

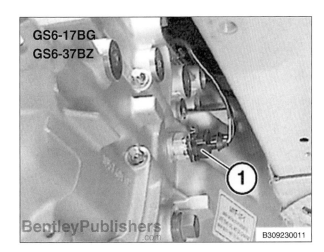

GS6-17BG
GS6-37BZ

B309230011

– Install and torque fluid fill plug.

| Tightening torque | |
|---|---|
| Drain or fill plug to transmission case:<br>• M12 x 1.5<br>• M18 x 1.5 | 25 Nm (18 ft-lb)<br>35 Nm (26 ft-lb) |

## TRANSMISSION EXTERNAL SERVICE

### Back-up light switch, replacing

– Raise and safely support vehicle to access back-up light switch.

> **WARNING** —
> • *Make sure the vehicle is stable and well supported at all times. Use a professional automotive lift or jack stands designed for the purpose. A floor jack is not adequate support.*

◄ Unscrew switch (**1**) from transmission.

> **NOTE** —
> • *Back-up light switch location on transmission varies.*

– Install new switch.

| Tightening torque | |
|---|---|
| Back-up light switch to transmission | 18 Nm (13 ft-lb) |

– Check transmission fluid level before lowering vehicle. Top off as necessary. See **Transmission Fluid Service** in this repair group.

### Selector shaft seal, replacing

This repair can be performed with transmission installed in vehicle.

– Place transmission into second gear.

– Raise vehicle and support safely.

> **WARNING** —
> • *Make sure the vehicle is stable and well supported at all times. Use a professional automotive lift or jack stands designed for the purpose. A floor jack is not adequate support.*

– Remove underbody splash shields.

– Remove exhaust system. See **180 Exhaust System**.

> **WARNING** —
> • *Make sure exhaust system is fully cooled off before removing.*

– Remove exhaust heat shields.

– xDrive models: Remove front drive shaft. See **260 Driveshafts**.

- All models: Remove rear driveshaft from output flange:

  • Remove driveshaft center bearing support fasteners. Support center of driveshaft.

  • Detach rear driveshaft flex-disc from transfer case.

  • Lower center of driveshaft sufficiently to disengage flex-disc from transfer case flange. Tie driveshaft to side.

> **CAUTION—**
> • *To prevent damage to rear driveshaft CV joint, do not allow driveshaft to hang down unsupported.*

- Free harnesses for oxygen sensors and back-up light switch from rear transmission support.

◀ Support end of transmission with suitable jack. Remove mounting fasteners (**arrows**) for rear transmission support.

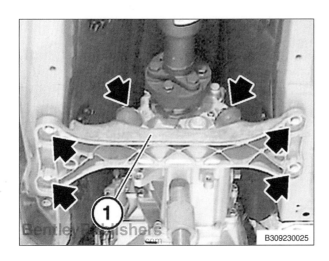

B309230025

◀ Working at top rear of transmission at shifter console, pry locking spring (**A**) out of groove and press pin (**B**) out of shift coupling.

  • Detach shift coupling and shift linkage from selector shaft and tie aside.

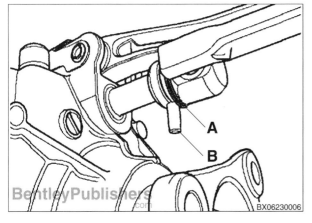

BX06230006

◀ Carefully pry out selector shaft oil seal with BMW special tool 23 0 210, or with a narrow seal remover or small screwdriver.

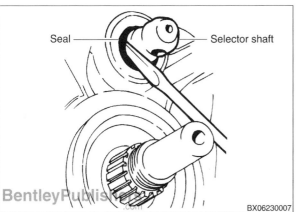

Seal ——— ——— Selector shaft

BX06230007

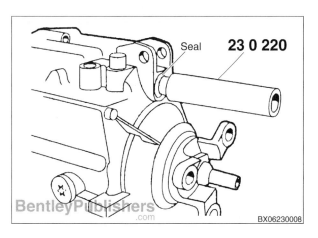

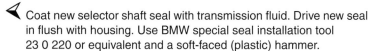

BX06230008

◄ Coat new selector shaft seal with transmission fluid. Drive new seal in flush with housing. Use BMW special seal installation tool 23 0 220 or equivalent and a soft-faced (plastic) hammer.

– Remainder of installation is reverse of removal. Check transmission and transfer case oil level, topping up as necessary.

| Tightening torques | |
|---|---|
| Transfer case to transmission | 43 Nm (31 ft-lb) |

## Transmission input shaft seal, replacing

– Remove transmission from vehicle. See **Transmission, removing and installing** in this repair group.

– Remove clutch release bearing / release lever module from inside bellhousing. See **210 Clutch**.

◄ Remove bolts (**arrows**) for clutch release-bearing guide sleeve. Remove guide sleeve.

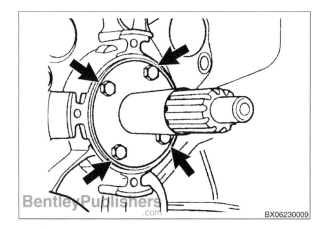

BX06230009

◄ Two covered removal holes (**1**) are present in seal. Thread BMW special tool 23 0 490 or equivalent slide hammer seal puller into one hole and remove seal.

B309230017

B309230019

◀ To install new seal:

- Push radial seal onto BMW special tool 23 0 320.
- Coat sealing lip of new seal with transmission oil.
- Slide tool onto input shaft.
- Use plastic hammer to drive in seal until fully seated.

— Thoroughly clean clutch release bearing guide sleeve mounting bolts, sealing surfaces, and threads. Apply Loctite®243 or equivalent thread locking compound to guide sleeve bolts. Reinstall guide sleeve and spacer (if equipped).

| Tightening torque | |
|---|---|
| Guide sleeve to transmission housing | |
| • M8 X 30 | 25 Nm (18 ft-lb) |
| • M8 X 22 | 18 Nm (13 ft-lb) |
| • M6 | 10 Nm (7 ft-lb) |

— Replace clutch release bearing / release lever module. See **210 Clutch**.

— Reinstall transmission.

## Transmission output shaft seal, replacing

— Disconnect negative (-) cable from battery.

> *CAUTION—*
> • *Prior to disconnecting the battery, read the battery disconnection cautions given in* **001 Warnings and Cautions**.

— Raise and safely support vehicle.

> *WARNING—*
> • *Make sure the vehicle is stable and well supported at all times. Use a professional automotive lift or jack stands designed for the purpose. A floor jack is not adequate support.*

— Remove underbody splash shields.

— Remove complete exhaust system. See **180 Exhaust System**.

> *WARNING—*
> • *Make sure exhaust system is fully cooled off before removing.*

— Remove exhaust system heat shields.

**230**

– Remove rear driveshaft from output shaft:

- Remove driveshaft center bearing support fasteners. Support center of driveshaft.

- Detach rear driveshaft flex-disc from transfer case.

- Lower center of driveshaft sufficiently to disengage flex-disc from transfer case flange. Tie driveshaft to side.

> **CAUTION—**
> - *To prevent damage to rear driveshaft CV joint, do not allow driveshaft to hang down unsupported.*

– xDrive models: Remove transfer case. See **270 Transfer Case**.

◄ Counterhold output flange with BMW special tool 23 0 020 and release flange collar nut using BMW special tool 23 1 210.

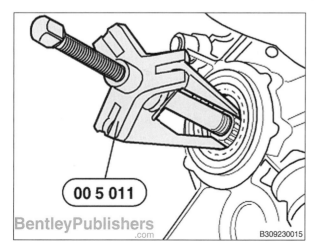

◄ Remove output flange using BMW special tool 33 1 150 or suitable puller.

◄ Remove output shaft seal using BMW special tool 00 5 011 or suitable seal puller.

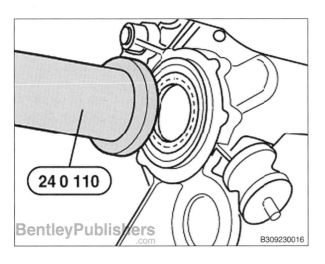

◀ When installing new seal, coat seal lips with transmission fluid. Use BMW special tool 24 0 110 and plastic hammer to drive seal in flush.

— Remainder of installation is reverse of removal. Remember to:

  • Replace collar nut with new.

  • Use Loctite® 431 on output shaft threads when installing collar nut.

  • Follow 3 step tightening procedure (tighten, release, tighten down).

  • Check transmission fluid level and check system for leaks.

| Tightening torque | |
|---|---|
| Transmission output flange to transmission (GS6-17BG and GS6-37BZ transmission) | |
| • Pretension | 170 Nm (125 ft-lb) |
| • Release | Release tension |
| • Tighten down | 120 Nm (89 ft-lb) |
| Transmission output flange to transmission (GS6-53DZ transmission) | |
| • Pretension | 200 Nm (148 ft-lb) |
| • Release | Release tension |
| • Tighten down | 140 Nm (103 ft-lb) |

## TRANSMISSION REMOVAL AND INSTALLATION

Removal and installation of the transmission is best accomplished with the vehicle on a lift and using a transmission jack. Support engine using equipment which allows the engine to pivot on its mounts to access the upper bolts at the transmission bellhousing.

> **WARNING —**
> • The removal of the transmission may upset the balance of the vehicle on a lift.

## Transmission, removing and installing

— Disconnect negative (-) cable from battery.

> **CAUTION—**
> • Prior to disconnecting the battery, read the battery disconnection cautions given in **001 Warnings and Cautions**.

— Raise and safely support vehicle.

> **WARNING —**
> • Make sure the vehicle is stable and well supported at all times. Use a professional automotive lift or jack stands designed for the purpose. A floor jack is not adequate support.

— Remove underbody splash shields.

— Remove compete exhaust system. See **180 Exhaust System**.

> **WARNING —**
> • Make sure exhaust system is fully cooled off before removing.

— Remove exhaust system heat shields.

*Transmission, removing and installing*

– xDrive models: Remove front drive shaft. See **260 Driveshafts**.

– All models: Remove rear driveshaft from output flange:

  • Remove driveshaft center bearing support fasteners. Support center of driveshaft.

  • Detach rear driveshaft flex-disc from transfer case.

  • Lower center of driveshaft sufficiently to disengage flex-disc from transfer case flange. Tie driveshaft to side.

> **CAUTION—**
> • *To prevent damage to rear driveshaft CV joint, do not allow driveshaft to hang down unsupported.*

– Disconnect harness connector from back-up light switch on transmission. See **Back up light switch, replacing** in this repair group.

◄ Remove fasteners (**1**) and remove exhaust bracket (**2**).

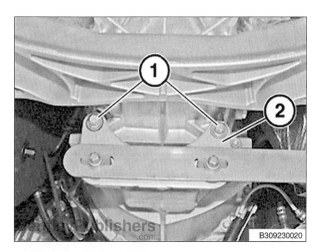

◄ Remove brackets for underbody splash shields (**1**).

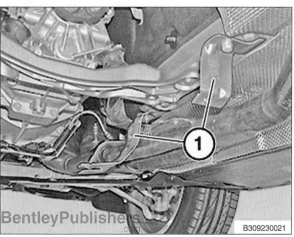

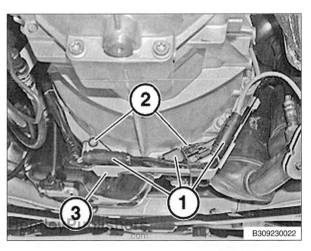

◁ Disconnect oxygen sensor harness connectors (**1**) and remove fasteners (**2**) from connector bracket (**3**).

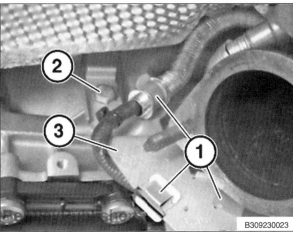

◁ Unclip oxygen sensor harness (**1**) from bracket (**2**). Remove fastener and remove bracket (**3**) from transmission.

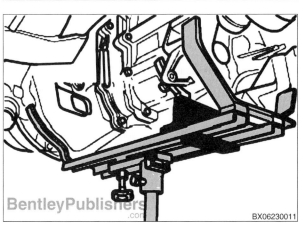

◁ Support transmission on transmission jack. Secure transmission to jack.

*Transmission, removing and installing*

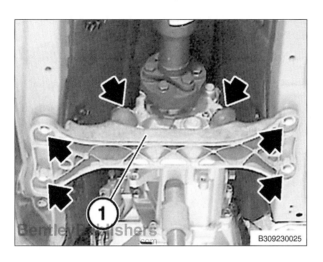

◅ Remove mounting fasteners (**arrows**) for rear transmission support.

– xDrive models: Remove transfer case. See **270 Transfer Case**.

  • Be sure to detach xDrive servomotor harness connectors at transfer case.

– Lower transmission jack slowly, allowing engine and transmission assembly to tilt back and down slightly.

> *CAUTION—*
>
> • *Tilting the engine to lower the transmission can lead to damage to engine compartment components due to lack of clearance at rear of engine. Lower transmission carefully while checking engine rear clearance.*

– Unbolt clutch slave cylinder from side of transmission. Do not disconnect fluid hose. Suspend slave cylinder from chassis using stiff wire.

> *CAUTION—*
>
> • *Unbolt clutch slave cylinder slowly to prevent air being drawn into hydraulic system.*
>
> • *Do not operate clutch pedal with slave cylinder removed from transmission.*

◅ Remove shift rod clip and disconnect shift linkage from selector shaft coupling.

> *NOTE —*
>
> • *A new, more secure, shift rod clip is fitted as of 04/2008. Use new specification shift rod clip when reassembling.*

– Disconnect shift console from top of transmission. See **250 Gearshift Linkage**.

– Support front of engine with tall jack stand or hydraulic jack.

◅ Release locking clips (**1**) and lift out shift arms.

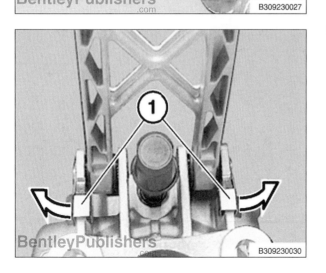

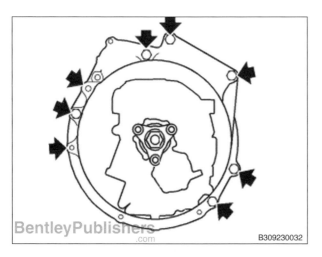

◄ Remove transmission mounting Torx-head bolts (**arrows**). Note length and location of bolts.

> **CAUTION—**
> • *Number, size and location of fasteners varies with transmission installed.*

— Remove transmission by pulling backward until transmission input shaft clears clutch disc splines, then pull downwards. Lower transmission jack to remove transmission.

> **CAUTION—**
> • *Do not allow transmission to hang from input shaft.*

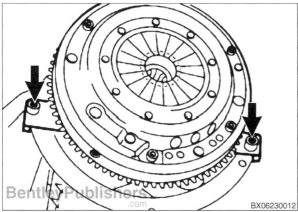

◄ Be sure bellhousing alignment dowel sleeves (**arrows**) are located correctly. Replace damaged sleeves.

— Inspect clutch, clutch release bearing and flywheel. See **210 Clutch**. Repair as necessary.

— Check and repair transmission seals. See **Transmission External Service** in this repair group.

— Reinstall transmission and xDrive transfer case (if equipped), keeping in mind the following:

   • If installing a new transmission, be sure to transfer parts from old transmission.

   • Thoroughly clean input shaft and clutch disc splines. Lightly lubricate transmission input shaft splines before installing.

| Tightening torques | |
|---|---|
| Slave cylinder to transmission | 22 Nm (16 ft-lb) |
| Transmission to engine<br>• M6 Allen bolt<br>• M8 Torx bolt<br>• M10 Torx bolt<br>• M12 Torx bolt | <br>9 Nm (t ft-lb)<br>22 Nm (16 ft-lb)<br>43 Nm (32 ft-lb)<br>72 Nm (53 ft-lb) |

◄ Reinstall transmission support. Center rear of transmission in driveshaft tunnel before tightening support bracket bolts (**arrows**).

| Tightening torques | |
|---|---|
| Transfer case to transmission | 43 Nm (31 ft-lb) |
| Transfer case support<br>• To chassis (M10)<br>• To transfer case rubber mount (M12) | <br>42 Nm (30 ft-lb)<br>74 Nm (55 ft-lb) |

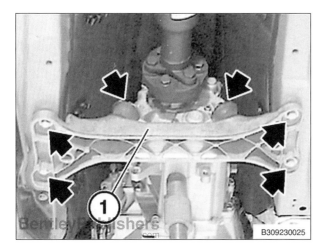

— Reinstall driveshafts using new self-locking nuts. See **260 Driveshafts**.

> **CAUTION—**
> • *To avoid damaging flex-disc rubber, be sure to hold bolts stationary while tightening nuts.*

| Tightening torques | |
|---|---|
| Front driveshaft flex-disc to front differential flange (replace fasteners) (M10 10.9) | 60 Nm (44 ft-lb) |
| Rear driveshaft flex-disc to transfer case output flange | 100 Nm (74 ft-lb) |

– xDrive models: Refill transfer case. See **270 Transfer Case**.

| Tightening torque | |
|---|---|
| Fill plug to transfer case | 33 Nm (24 ft-lb) |

– Refill transmission before starting or towing vehicle. See **Transmission Fluid Service** in this repair group.

| Tightening torque | |
|---|---|
| Drain or fill plug to transmission case:<br>• M12 x 1.5<br>• M18 x 1.5 | <br>25 Nm (18 ft-lb)<br>35 Nm (26 ft-lb) |

# 240 Automatic Transmission

## GENERAL

This repair group covers maintenance and replacement of the automatic transmission.

Automatic transmission internal repairs are not covered. Transmission repairs require special service equipment and knowledge. If transmission internal service is required, consult an authorized BMW dealer about a factory reconditioned unit or a transmission rebuild.

See also:

- **119 Lubrication System** for crankshaft rear main (flywheel) seal.
- **170 Radiator and Cooling System** for ATF cooler and heat exchanger.
- **200 Transmission–General** for drivetrain information.
- **260 Driveshafts** for front (xDrive) and rear driveshaft.
- **270 Transfer Case** for xDrive equipped models.

## Automatic transmission applications

Automatic transmissions are configured with adaptive transmission control and Steptronic. Automatic transmission applications are in **Table a**.

| Table a. Automatic transmission applications | | |
|---|---|---|
| **Model** | **Transmission** | **Manufacturer id** |
| 328i, 328xi | GA6L45R (6-speed) | GM GM6 |
| 325i, 325xi, 330i, 330xi, 335i, 335xi | GA6HP19Z (6-speed) | ZF 6HP19 |

## Steptronic

The Steptronic function makes it possible to shift the automatic transmission manually. Manual mode is engaged when the selector lever is moved left from automatic gate into manual gate. In manual mode, pressing the selector lever forward or backward closes electrical contacts, resulting in upshift or downshift.

BX06240006

## Bus systems

To handle electrical complexity, E90 vehicles are equipped extensively with bus systems. Signals are shared digitally among electrical components on a bus, eliminating the need for separate connections for each pair of components. The use of bus communication for controls and accessories reduces wiring complexity and improves system response time.

Data transfer over a bus is similar to a telephone conference. A component on the bus transmits a stream of data which other components receive at the same time. Each component is then free to use or ignore this data.

The benefits of the bus method of data transfer are as follows:

- As data and programs are modified and extended, only software modifications are necessary.
- Continuous verification of transmitted data leads to low error rate.
- Sensors and signal wires can be simplified or eliminated due to the transmittal of multiplexed digital data.
- Control modules transfer data at a high rate.
- Control module sizes and connector sizes are smaller.
- Bus architecture conforms to international standards. This facilitates data interchange between components of different manufacture.

See **600 Electrical System–General** for additional details.

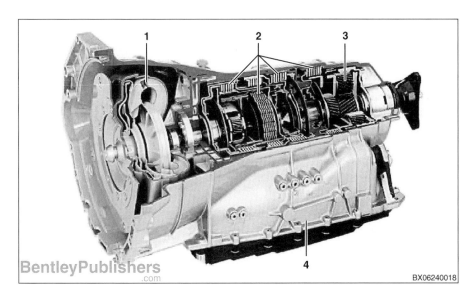

BX06240018

## 6-speed automatic transmission assembly

1. Torque converter
   - Capable of torque multiplication
2. Multi-plate clutch packs
3. Planetary gear assembly
4. Mechatronics module
   - Valve body (hydraulic unit)
   - Transmission control module (A7000a)

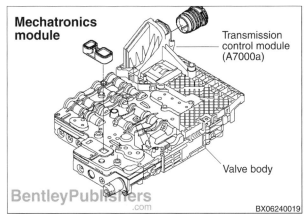

**Mechatronics module**

Transmission control module (A7000a)

Valve body

BX06240019

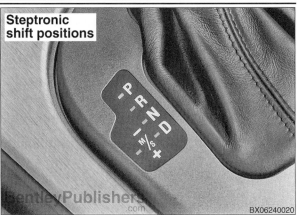

**Steptronic shift positions**

BX06240020

## 6-speed automatic transmission overview

The 6-speed automatic transmission system utilizes the following components:

- 6-speed automatic gearbox.
- Mechatronics module inside the transmission housing, combining hydraulic unit (valve body) and transmission control module (TCM)(A7000a).
- Selector lever with positions P(ARK), R(EVERSE) and N(EUTRAL) as well as D(RIVE) for automatic mode and M/S for manual and Steptronic mode.
- Instrument cluster displaying shift selector range and drive program.
- Brake light switch signal affects function of selector lever shiftlock.
- Engine control module (ECM) signals engine speed, torque and other parameters. TCM signals current transmission operating status back to ECM.
- DSC control module signals cornering, acceleration and traction data.
- Accelerator pedal module signals driver power demand data.

240

OBD 2
plug

B309020031

## Troubleshooting

Minor automatic transmission problems may be corrected by changing the automatic transmission fluid (ATF) and filter. Begin by checking ATF level and condition. Check to see if the fluid is dirty or has a burned odor indicating overheated fluid. The burned odor may be the results of burned discs in the clutch packs. The friction material from the burned disc can clog valve body passages.

Software in the transmission control module (TCM) monitors transmission operation for faults and alerts the driver by illuminating the transmission fault indicator on the instrument panel. The self-diagnostic software stores diagnostic trouble codes (DTCs) which may be accessed as follows:

◀ Connect BMW diagnostic scan tool to OBD 2 plug on left door post. (Plug is behind plastic trim.)

− Place transmission selector lever in PARK or NEUTRAL. Engage parking brake.

− Switch ignition ON.

− Follow scan tool instructions as they appear on scan tool screen.

− For a listing of scan tool suppliers, see **020 Maintenance**.

## Cautions

*CAUTION—*

• *When performing any repair which involves separating the engine and transmission, check that the bellhousing dowels are undamaged and properly in place before reassembly. If the alignment of the engine flywheel to the transmission input shaft or torque converter is incorrect, shudder, noise and internal damage to the transmission may result.*

• *For engines with a magnesium crankcase only aluminum fasteners and dowels may be used. Consult with an authorized BMW dealer parts department for the correct fasteners and dowels for the engine and model concerned.*

• *Do not mix BMW transmission oils, and do not replace with another oil.*

• *ATF does not circulate unless the engine is running. When transporting the vehicle, use a flat bed truck or raise the wheels off the ground.*

## AUTOMATIC TRANSMISSION FLUID (ATF) SERVICE

3 Series automatic transmission fluid has a condition based service interval of approximately 100,000 miles (160,935 km). If service or repairs have to be made to the transmission or ATF cooler, use only the approved transmission fluid.

Check ATF level if there is evidence of a leak, a complaint related to fluid level or after transmission repairs.

The automatic transmission is not equipped with a dipstick. Check ATF level while monitoring ATF temperature with special equipment. Make sure transmission is at operating temperature and vehicle is level throughout tests.

Be sure necessary equipment, catch bin, transmission fluid and fluid pump are available before starting the fluid level checking procedure.

**Table b. ATF service interval**

| Condition based - check instrument cluster to monitor service interval | approximately 100,000 miles |
|---|---|

## ATF level, checking

Transmission fluid expands with temperature. BMW requires that the ATF of all 3 Series transmissions be checked when fluid temperature is between 30 - 50°C (86 - 122°F).

— Drive vehicle to warm up ATF to operating temperature.

◀ Connect BMW diagnostic scan tool to OBD 2 plug on left door post. (Plug is behind plastic trim.) Set scan tool to measure ATF temperature.

— With engine running, switch on air-conditioning to increase engine idle speed.

— Apply parking brake.

— While applying foot brake firmly move gear shift selector lever through all gear positions, pausing in each gear briefly.

— Raise and safely support vehicle. Place oil drip pan underneath.

> **CAUTION—**
> • *Make sure the vehicle is stable and well supported at all times. Use a professional automotive lift or jack stands designed for the purpose. A floor jack is not adequate support.*

OBD 2 plug

B309020031

*ATF level, checking*

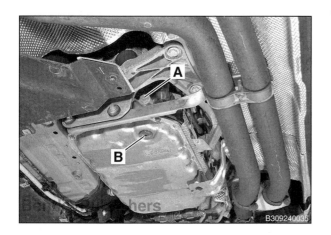

B309240035

◄ With engine running, selector lever in PARK and temperature as specified, remove fill plug (**A**).

*NOTE* —

- *GM transmission fill plug shown. ZF fill plug is on right side of transmission.*

> **WARNING** —
> - *Hot ATF can scald. Wear eye protection and protective clothing and gloves during the check. If the transmission is overfilled, hot ATF spills from the fill hole when the fill plug is removed.*

| ATF level checking | |
|---|---|
| Fluid temperature | 30° - 50°C (86° - 120°F) |

*NOTE* —

- *For best results, check fluid level at 30°C (85°F).*
- *An accurate level check is not possible if fluid temperature rises above 50ºC (120°F).*

— Level is correct if small stream of fluid runs out of fill hole.

— If no fluid runs out, add fluid until it starts to overflow.

> **CAUTION** —
> - *Do not mix BMW transmission oils, and do not replace with another oil.*

| Automatic transmission fluid (6-speed transmission) | | |
|---|---|---|
| **Type** | **BMW part no.** | **Manufacturer part no.** |
| GA6L45R | 83 22 0 397 114 | Dexron VI |
| GA6HP19Z | 83 22 0 142 516 | Shell M-1375.4 |

— Install fill plug using new sealing ring.

| Tightening torques | |
|---|---|
| Drain plug to transmission sump:<br>• GA6L45R (M12 x 1.75)<br>• GA6HP19Z (M10 x 1 metal sump)<br>• GA6HP19Z (M16 x 1.5 plastic) | 14 Nm (10 ft-lb)<br>12 Nm (9 ft-lb)<br>8 Nm (6 ft-lb) |
| Fill plug to transmission sump:<br>• GA6L45RM (M18 x 1.5)<br>• GA6HP19Z (M18 x 1.5) | 19 Nm (14 ft-lb)<br>35 Nm (26 ft-lb) |

— Connect BMW diagnostic tool and call up "Service functions (drive)." Follow the on-screen instructions to complete fluid level check.

## ATF, draining and filling

*NOTE* —

• *Draining and filling of the GM transmission is shown throughout this procedure. Draining and filling the ZF transmission is similar.*

– Raise vehicle and support safely.

> *WARNING* —
>
> • *Make sure the vehicle is stable and well supported at all times. Use a professional automotive lift or jack stands designed for the purpose. A floor jack is not adequate support.*

– Remove splash shield under transmission. If necessary to improve access, remove splash shield and exhaust brackets.

◄ Remove ATF drain plug (**B**) and drain fluid into container.

> *WARNING* —
>
> • *Make sure ATF is warm when draining. Hot ATF can scald. Wear eye protection, protective clothing and gloves.*

– Remove transmission sump mounting bolts and remove sump.

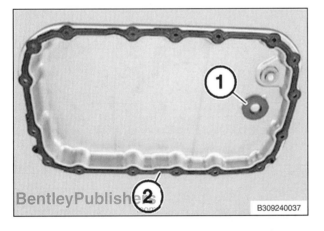

◄ Clean sump and sump magnet (**1**) using a lint-free cloth. Remove sump gasket (**2**) and clean gasket sealing surface.

*NOTE* —

• *Models with plastic sump lack magnet.*

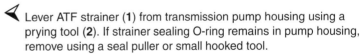

◄ Lever ATF strainer (**1**) from transmission pump housing using a prying tool (**2**). If strainer sealing O-ring remains in pump housing, remove using a seal puller or small hooked tool.

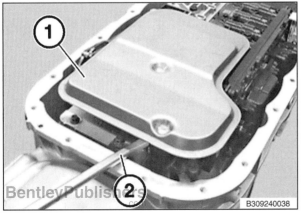

*ATF, draining and filling*

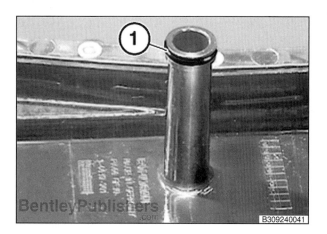

◄ Using new sealing O-ring (**1**), replace ATF strainer.

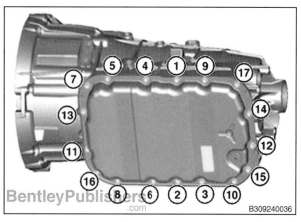

◄ Install transmission sump using new gasket. Make sure locating tabs of gasket engage in openings of sump. Use new ATF sump bolts purchased from BMW. Alternatively, clean old bolts and coat with Loctite® thread locking compound or equivalent. Tighten transmission pan bolts in order shown, gradually and in several stages.

| Tightening torques | |
|---|---|
| ATF sump to transmission (M6) | 10 Nm (7 ft-lb) |

— Replace drain plug using new sealing ring.

| Tightening torques | |
|---|---|
| Drain plug to transmission sump:<br>• GA6L45R (M12 x 1.75)<br>• GA6HP19Z (M10 x 1 metal sump)<br>• GA6HP19Z (M16 x 1.5 plastic) | 14 Nm (10 ft-lb)<br>12 Nm (9 ft-lb)<br>8 Nm (6 ft-lb) |
| Fill plug to transmission sump:<br>• GA6L45R (M18 x 1.5)<br>• GA6HP19Z (M18 x 1.5) | 19 Nm (14 ft-lb)<br>35 Nm (26 ft-lb) |

— Top off transmission and check fluid level. See **ATF level, checking** in this repair group.

| Automatic transmission fluid (6-speed transmission) | | |
|---|---|---|
| **Type** | **BMW part no.** | **Manufacturer part no.** |
| GA6L45R | 83 22 0 397 114 | Dexron VI |
| GA6HP19Z | 83 22 0 142 516 | Shell M-1375.4 |

| Table c. ATF capacities | |
|---|---|
| GA6L45R<br>(with torque converter drained) | approx. 9.5 liters (10 US qt) |
| GA6HP19Z<br>(with torque converter drained) | approx. 9.5 liters (10 US qt) |

*NOTE —*

• *If not draining torque converter, measure fluid removed and replace with same amount.*

## TRANSMISSION REMOVAL AND INSTALLATION

Removal and installation of the transmission is best accomplished on an automotive lift using a transmission jack. Use caution and safe workshop practices when working underneath vehicle and lowering transmission. Be sure to have appropriate tools on hand before starting the job.

> **CAUTION—**
> - *Replace aluminium fasteners each time they are released. Do not use steel fasteners in place of aluminium. Electrochemical corrosion will result.*
> - *Magnesium crankcase requires aluminum fasteners exclusively.*
> - *When replacing aluminium fasteners, follow tightening torque and angle of rotation specification strictly.*

## Transmission, removing and installing

Automatic transition removal varies slightly depending on installed transmission. Although the following procedure is specific to the GM (GA6L45R) 6-speed transmission, it can be used as a guide for all models.

> **WARNING—**
> - *Allow engine and transmission to cool down before starting work on the transmission.*

### Transmission, removing

— Disconnect negative (-) cable from battery.

> **CAUTION—**
> - *Prior to disconnecting the battery, read the battery disconnection cautions given in* **001 Warnings and Cautions**.

— Remove electric radiator fan. See **170 Radiator and Cooling System**.

◀ Support engine from above with suitable hoist.

— Raise and safely support vehicle.

> **WARNING—**
> - *Make sure the vehicle is stable and well supported at all times. Use a professional automotive lift or jack stands designed for the purpose. A floor jack is not adequate support.*

— Remove splash shields and supporting brackets under engine and transmission.

— Remove chassis reinforcement plate (if equipped).

— Remove exhaust system. See **180 Exhaust System**.

— Remove exhaust heat shields.

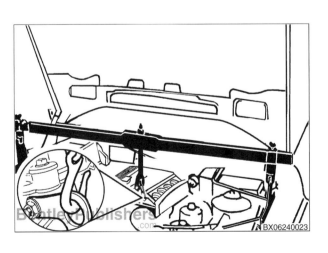

BX06240023

*Transmission, removing and installing*

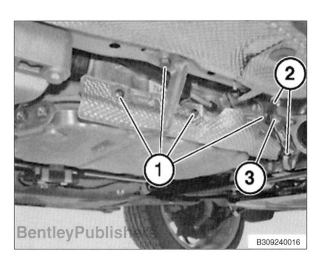

◄ Remove fasteners (**1**) and remove heat shield. Unclip lines (**2**) and remove support bracket (**3**).

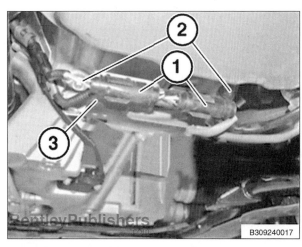

◄ Release electrical connector (**1**) Remove fasteners (**2**) and remove retaining plate (**3**).

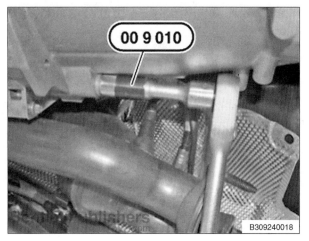

◄ Using BMW special tool 00 9 010 (or equivalent), remove aluminium fastener next to electrical connector brackets.

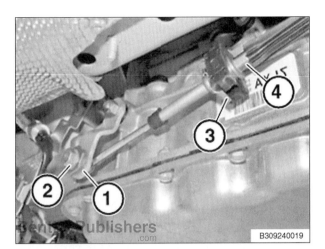

◄ Counterhold clamping sleeve (**1**) and loosen nut (**2**). Use a screwdriver to remove retainer (**3**) downwards and pull cable (**4**) out of holder.

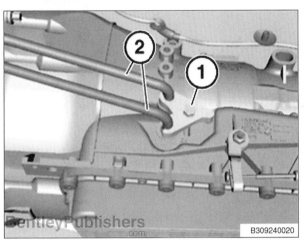

◄ Remove hold-down bolt (**1**) and disconnect hydraulic lines to transmission fluid cooler.

> **CAUTION—**
> • *Be prepared to catch dripping fluid.*
> • *Make sure hydraulic line O-rings are removed with line and discarded. Always replace O-rings with new.*

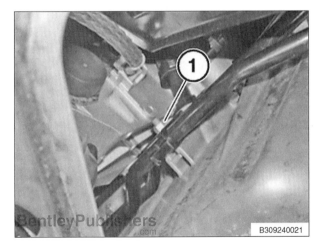

◄ Remove nut (**1**) and bracket holding hydraulic lines to sump.

*Transmission, removing and installing*

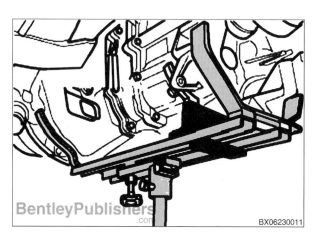

◁ Support transmission with suitable hoist.

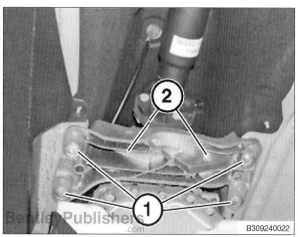

◁ Remove fasteners (**1** and **2**) and remove transmission cross-member.

— xDrive models: Remove front drive shaft. Be prepared to catch dripping fluid. See **260 Driveshafts**.

— Rear driveshaft:

  • Remove driveshaft center bearing support fasteners. Support center of driveshaft.

  • Detach rear driveshaft flex-disc from transfer case.

  • Lower center of driveshaft sufficiently to disengage flex-disc from transfer case flange. Tie driveshaft to side. See **260 Driveshafts**.

> **CAUTION—**
> • *To prevent damage to rear driveshaft CV joint, do not allow driveshaft to hang down unsupported.*

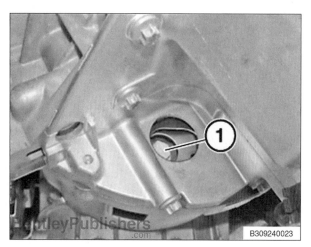

◁ Crank engine by hand in direction of rotation using bolt on crankshaft dampener until fastener (**1**) is visible through access hole in transmission bell housing.

— Remove fastener (**1**). Continue to rotate engine and remove remaining torque converter fasteners.

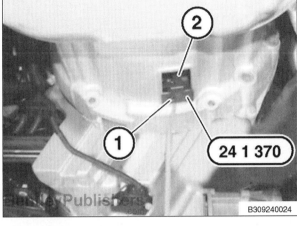

◄ Insert torque converter locking tool (BMW special tool 24 1 370 or equivalent) and secure with fastener (**1**). Make sure lug (**2**) points in opposite direction of vehicle travel.

**240**

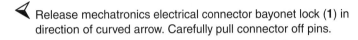

◄ Release mechatronics electrical connector bayonet lock (**1**) in direction of curved arrow. Carefully pull connector off pins.

– Insert BMW special tool 24 2 390 in place of mechatronics connector to protect delicate pins.

> **CAUTION—**
> • *Do not touch pins.*

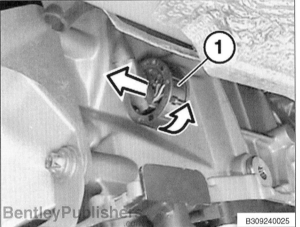

◄ Remove remainder of aluminium fasteners from transmission bell housing.

– Remove transmission by pulling back and down. Lower jack slowly while watching carefully to make sure no lines, hoses or wires become snagged.

> **WARNING —**
> • *Be sure the vehicle is properly supported. The removal of the transmission may upset the balance of the vehicle on the lift.*

> **CAUTION—**
> • *Tilting the engine to remove the transmission can lead to damage to various components due to lack of clearance.*
> • *Do not allow the torque converter to fall off the transmission input shaft. Use BMW special tool 24 1 370 or equivalent to hold torque converter in place during transmission removal.*

– Blow out oil cooler lines with low-pressure compressed air and flush cooler with clean ATF twice.

> **CAUTION—**
> • *Wear safety glasses when working with compressed air.*
> • *Do not reuse ATF used for flushing.*

— Inspect engine drive plate and flywheel for cracks or elongated holes. Replace if necessary.

— If torque converter seal is leaky, or torque converter position on transmission input shaft was disturbed during removal, replace torque converter seal. See **Torque converter oil seal, removing and installing** in this repair group.

**Transmission, installing**

◀ Rotate flywheel until bore (**1**) is accessible through opening in engine oil pan.

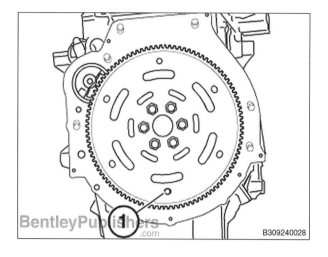

B309240028

◀ Check that dowel sleeves are in good shape and correctly seated. Replace if needed.

— Check that torque converter is seated correctly in transmission.

— Rotate torque converter until bore in converter is flush with bore in driving disk.

— Join transmission to engine.

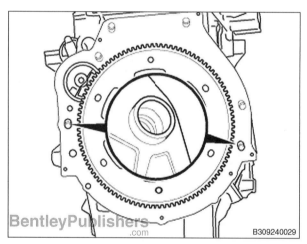

B309240029

◀ When attaching transmission, replace all aluminium fasteners and follow tightening sequence.

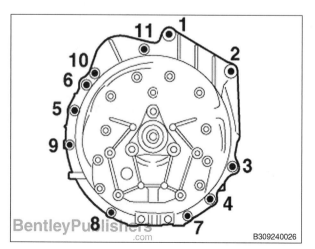

B309240026

◄ Tighten new aluminium bolts at bell housing to initial torque.

— Secure torque angle tool (BMW special tools 00 9 120 / 00 9 130 or equivalent) and tighten fasteners to final torque angle.

| Tightening torques | |
|---|---|
| Transmission to engine (M10x30 aluminium): | |
| • Initial torque | 20 Nm (15 ft-lb) |
| • Torque angle | + 90 - 110° |
| Transmission to engine (M10x85 aluminium): | |
| • Initial torque | 20 Nm (15 ft-lb) |
| • Torque angle | + 180 - 200° |
| Transmission to engine (M12 aluminium): | |
| • Initial torque | 25 Nm (18 ft-lb) |
| • Torque angle | + 130° |
| Transmission cross member to body (M8) | 19 Nm (14 ft-lb) |
| Transmission cross member to transmission | 19 Nm (14 ft-lb) |
| Torque converter to flywheel: | |
| • M8 | 26 Nm (19 ft-lb) |
| • M10x8.8 | 45 Nm (33 ft-lb) |
| • M10x10.9 | 56 Nm (41 ft-lb) |

> **CAUTION—**
>
> • *To avoid damaging driveshaft flex-disc rubber, hold bolts stationary while tightening nuts.*

— Remainder of installation is reverse of removal. Remember to:

• Install new sealing washers or O-rings on ATF cooling line fittings.

• Adjust gearshift mechanism. See **250 Gearshift Linkage**.

• Fill transmission with clean ATF. See **ATF, draining and filling** in this repair group.

| Tightening torques | |
|---|---|
| Drain plug to transmission sump: | |
| • GA6L45R (M12 x 1.75) | 14 Nm (10 ft-lb) |
| • GA6HP19Z (M10 x 1 metal sump) | 12 Nm (9 ft-lb) |
| • GA6HP19Z (M16 x 1.5 plastic) | 8 Nm (6 ft-lb) |
| Fill plug to transmission sump: | |
| • GA6L45R (M18 x 1.5) | 19 Nm (14 ft-lb) |
| • GA6HP19Z (M18 x 1.5) | 35 Nm (26 ft-lb) |

| Automatic transmission fluid (6-speed transmission) | | |
|---|---|---|
| Type | BMW part no. | Manufacturer part no. |
| GA6L45R | 83 22 0 397 114 | Dexron VI |
| GA6HP19Z | 83 22 0 142 516 | Shell M-1375.4 |

**240**

## Torque converter, removing and installing

– Remove transmission. See **Automatic transmission, removing and installing** in this repair group.

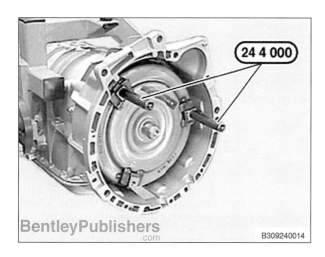

◀ Screw BMW special tools 24 4 000 into torque converter. Pull converter straight off transmission input shaft.

> **CAUTION—**
> • *When torque converter is removed, transmission fluid will drain out. Be prepared to catch dripping fluid.*

◀ Remove torque converter slowly and set down vertically to avoid spilling additional transmission fluid.

– Reinstall torque converter, taking care to not damage new seal. Lightly oil converter seal surface and rotate converter during installation, applying slight pressure until recesses in converter locate audibly in ATF pump. Then press converter in firmly.

> **CAUTION—**
> • *If torque converter is not installed correctly, impeller driver in converter is destroyed when transmission is mated to engine.*

## Torque converter oil seal, removing and installing

ATF leaking from the torque converter seal usually collects at the bottom of the bellhousing and drips out.

Torque converter oil seal leakage is often caused by a worn or scored bushing in the torque converter hub. Check bushing when replacing seal. A damaged bushing rapidly wears the new seal.

— Remove transmission. See **Transmission, removing and installing** in this repair group.

— Carefully slide torque converter off transmission input shaft. Be prepared to catch ATF as it flows out of torque converter.

◄ Check converter bushing surface (**arrow**) for scoring or wear.

• Remove sharp edges and burrs with fine emery cloth.

• If hub is deeply scored, replace torque converter.

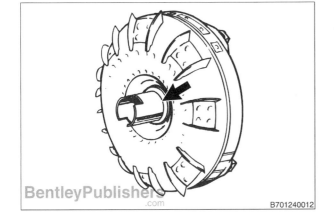

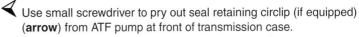

◄ Use small screwdriver to pry out seal retaining circlip (if equipped) (**arrow**) from ATF pump at front of transmission case.

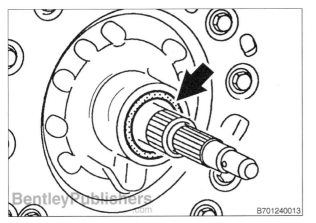

◄ Attach BMW special tool (24 2 353 / 24 2 354, depending on transmission) to transmission input shaft.

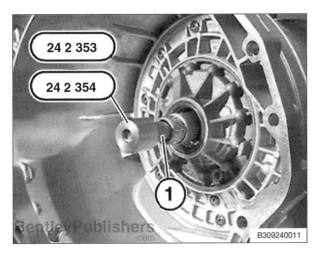

240

*Torque converter oil seal, removing and installing*

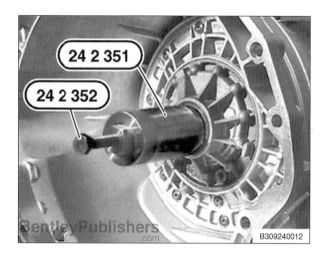

◄ Screw BMW special tool 24 2 351 into seal. Use BMW special tool 24 2 352 to gradually draw out seal.

◄ Coat sealing lips of new seal with transmission fluid. Use BMW special tool (24 2 360 / 24 2 400, depending on transmission) and soft-faced hammer to drive seal into transmission as far as it will go.

− Reinstall retaining circlip (if equipped).

− Reinstall torque converter, taking care to not damage new seal. Lightly oil converter seal surface and rotate converter during installation, applying slight pressure until recesses in converter locate audibly in ATF pump. Then press converter in firmly.

> **CAUTION—**
> • If torque converter is not installed correctly, impeller driver in converter is destroyed when transmission is mated to engine.

## Torque plate and flywheel, removing and installing

Crankshaft rear main (flywheel) seal replacement is covered in **119 Lubrication System**.

– Remove transmission. See **Transmission, removing and installing** in this repair group.

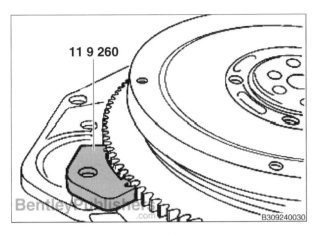

◄ Use BMW special tool 11 9 260 or equivalent to lock flywheel.

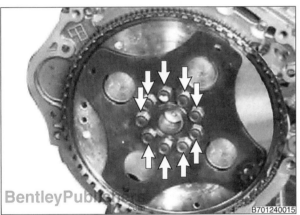

◄ Loosen and remove flywheel bolts (**arrows**) and discard.

– Remove torque plate and flywheel.

– Clean bolt threads in crankshaft.

◄ When installing:

• Note that flywheel is located with dowel sleeve (**arrow**).

• Make sure torque converter mounting holes in torque plate and flywheel line up.

• Use new flywheel bolts.

| Tightening torque | |
|---|---|
| Flywheel and torque plate to crankshaft (M12 x 1.5) (use new bolts) | 130 Nm (96 ft-lb) |

– Reinstall transmission.

## Mechatronic notes

The mechatronic connection is delicate. Use care when removing and replacing the multi-pin connector. If pins are damaged, the complete mechatronic module must be replaced.

Leaks around the mechatronic sleeve can be misdiagnosed as coming from the transmission pan gasket. If a leak at the mechatronic sleeve is confirmed, replace the sleeve.

An incorrectly installed mechatronic sleeve can cause damaged connector pins and intermittent transmission communication faults. Example faults include:

• Serial wire message missing (FC 5079)
• Serial line signal plausibility (FC 507A)
• Transmission Emergency Program light illuminated
• Transmission entering failsafe mode

◄ Push the sealing sleeve (**1**) into the mechatronic housing. Use new O-rings and lubricate sleeve with transmission fluid.

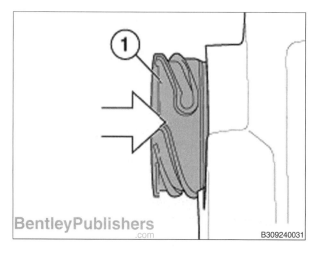

B309240031

– Reattach mechatronic connector making sure connector pins are not damaged. Close white locking tab on connector. Do not use excessive force. Excessive force indicates an incorrectly installed sleeve.

◄ With the harness connector installed and locked, the distance between the connector and the housing surface (**B**) should not exceed 3 mm.

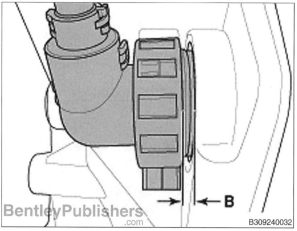

B309240032

◄ If the distance between the connector and housing surface (**A**) measures approximately 7 - 8 mm, the sealing sleeve was installed incorrectly. An incorrectly installed mechatronic sleeve may permanently damage the connector pins.

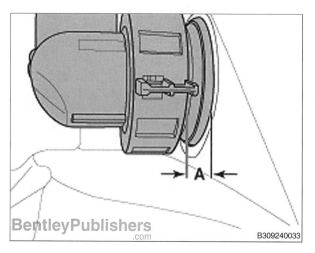

B309240033

# 250 Gearshift Linkage

**250**

## GENERAL

This repair group covers transmission gearshift service for manual and automatic transmission models.

To gain access to the complete gearshift mechanism, remove the transfer case, intermediate muffler and rear driveshaft. See:

- **180 Exhaust System**
- **260 Driveshafts**
- **270 Transfer Case**
- **310 Front Suspension** for front end reinforcement

### Neutral safety switch function

In models with automatic transmission, the electronic immobilizer function (EWS) prevents starter operation unless the gear position is (P)ARK or (N)EUTRAL. This serves as the neutral safety switch.

### Gearshift knob, removing

Gearshift knob removal is the same on manual and automatic models. Make sure the engine is OFF when removing gearshift knob.

◄ Starting from left side of shift boot (**A**), press in on shift boot frame to release boot from center console.

– Pull gearshift knob straight up (**arrow**) to remove. It may require up to 90 lbs. of force to do this.

> **CAUTION—**
> - *Some versions of shift boot and knob are one piece. Always release boot from console before removing knob.*
> - *To prevent damage to locating tabs, do not twist knob.*

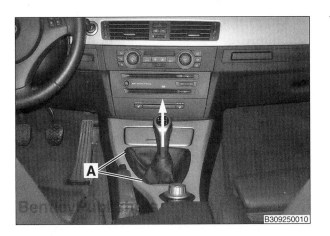

B309250010

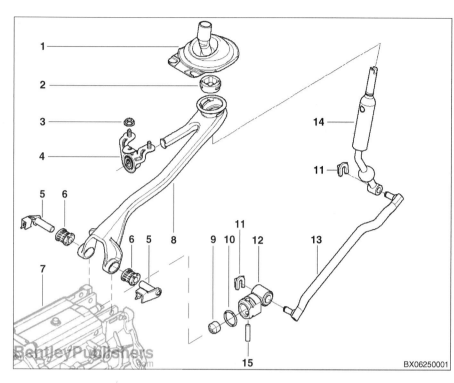

BX06250001

## MANUAL TRANSMISSION GEARSHIFT

### Manual gearshift linkage

1. Rubber boot
2. Shift lever bearing
3. M8 nut
4. Shift arm support bearing
5. Lock pin
6. Bushing
7. Transmission housing
8. Shift arm
9. Bushing
10. Lock ring
11. Circlip
12. Shifter coupling
13. Selector rod
14. Shift lever
15. Dowel

### Gearshift lever, removing and installing (manual transmission)

— Remove shift boot and shift knob. See **Gearshift knob, removing** in this repair group.

> **CAUTION—**
> • *Some versions of shift boot and knob are one piece. Always release boot from console before removing knob.*
> • *To prevent damage to locating tabs, do not twist knob.*

— Remove sound insulation at base of shift lever.

— Raise vehicle to gain access to underside of vehicle.

> **WARNING—**
> • *Make sure the vehicle is stable and well supported at all times. Use a professional automotive lift or jack stands designed for the purpose. A floor jack is not adequate support.*

— Remove exhaust system and heat shields. See **180 Exhaust System**.

◄ Support transmission with a suitable jack. Remove transmission support bracket (**arrows**) and lower transmission slightly to gain access to gearshift lever.

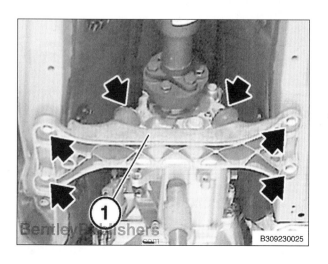

B309230025

◀ Working above transmission, disconnect selector rod:

• Pull off selector rod retaining circlip (**arrow**).

• Disengage selector rod from gearshift lever.

**NOTE—**

• *A new, more secure, shift rod clip is fitted as of 04/2008. Use new shift rod clip when reassembling.*

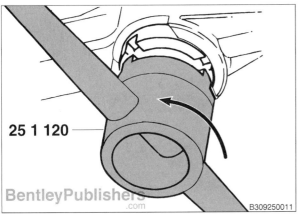

◀ Release shift lever bearing from below using BMW special spanner 25 1 120. Turn tool 90° (¼ turn) counterclockwise.

• Push shift lever and bearing up to remove from shift arm.

— Lower vehicle. Working from inside passenger compartment, pull up on shift lever to remove it together with inner rubber boot and shift lever bearing.

— Clean old grease from shift lever ball and mounting ring. Also clean shift arm bowl. Lubricate with molybdenum disulfide grease.

— Insert shift lever together with inner boot and bearing into shift arm.

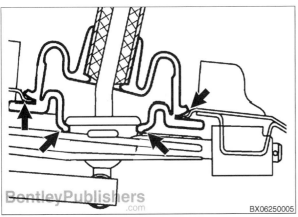

◀ Pull inner rubber boot over shift arm bowl (**arrows**) to seal base of shift lever. Install rubber boot with arrow pointing toward front of vehicle.

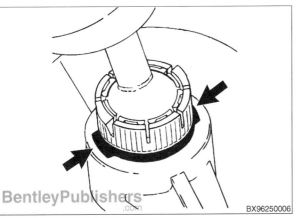

◀ When installing shift lever bearing:

• Align locking tabs with slots (**arrows**) in shift arm bowl.

• Make sure arrow on shift lever bearing points to front of vehicle.

• Press down until bearing snaps into place.

— Remainder of installation is reverse of removal.

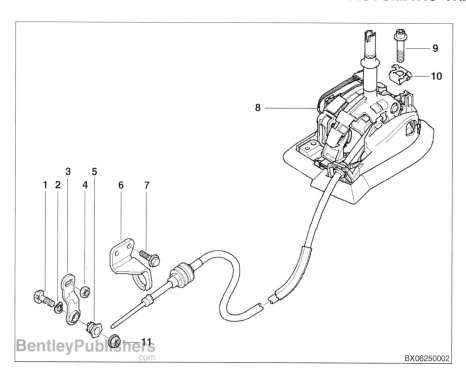

BX06250002

## AUTOMATIC TRANSMISSION GEARSHIFT

### Steptronic gearshift assembly

1. Clamping bolt
2. Washer
3. Transmission shift arm on side of transmission
4. M8 self-locking nut
5. Bushing
6. Support bracket
7. M6 bolt
8. Steptronic shift mechanism
9. M6 Torx screw
10. Cage nut
11. M8 self-locking nut

### Gearshift mechanism, adjusting

*NOTE* —

• *Gearshift mechanism varies with model. Adjustment is similar.*

– Position gearshift lever in P(ARK).

– Raise vehicle to gain access to shift linkage.

> **WARNING** —
> • *Make sure the vehicle is stable and well supported at all times. Use a professional automotive lift or jack stands designed for the purpose.*

 Working at transmission selector lever at side of transmission:

• Counterhold cable clamping bushing (**A**).
• Loosen cable clamping nut (**B**).
• Push transmission shift arm forward toward engine (**arrow 1**) (PARK position).
• Push shifter cable end backward away from engine (**arrow 2**). Release pressure on cable.
• Tighten clamping nut.

> **CAUTION**—
> • *Do not overtighten the nut so that it twists the cable.*

| Tightening torque | |
|---|---|
| Shift cable clamping nut | 10 Nm (7 ft-lb) |

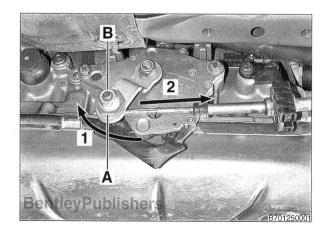

B701250001

## Automatic shiftlock, checking function

The automatic shiftlock uses an electric solenoid to lock the selector lever in P(ARK) or N(EUTRAL). Depressing the foot brake with the ignition ON energizes the solenoid, allowing the lever to be moved into R(EVERSE) or D(RIVE). The solenoid is energized only when engine speed is below 2,500 rpm and vehicle speed is below 3 mph (5 kph). The solenoid is mounted in the right side of the selector lever housing.

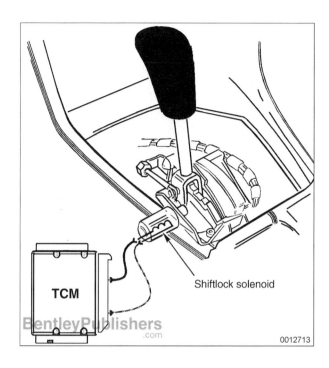

TCM

Shiftlock solenoid

0012713

◀ Automatic shiftlock prevents drive gear selection until brake pedal is depressed.

- With engine running and vehicle stopped, place selector lever in P.
- Without depressing brake pedal, check that selector lever is locked in P.
- Depress brake pedal firmly and listen to solenoid clicking audibly.
- Check that selector lever can now be moved out of P.

*NOTE —*

- *Perform the next test in an open area with the parking brake ON and with extreme caution.*

– With selector lever in P and brake pedal depressed, raise engine above 2,500 rpm. Check that selector lever cannot be moved out of P.

– If any faults are found:

- Check electrical operation of shiftlock solenoid
- Check for wiring faults to or from transmission control module (TCM). See **ECL Electrical Component Locations** and **ELE Electrical Wiring Diagrams**.

*NOTE —*

- *The solenoid is controlled via the transmission control module (TCM), using brake pedal position, engine speed, and road speed as controlling inputs.*

**250**

# 260 Driveshafts

260

## GENERAL

This repair group covers repair and replacement of front and rear driveshafts and driveshaft components.

xDrive models include a transfer case bolted to the rear of the transmission with front and rear driveshafts. Rear-drive models include a single driveshaft attached directly to the rear of the transmission.

Front driveshaft repairs are limited to replacement of the complete driveshaft. Rear driveshaft repairs consist of replacement of the flex-discs, center mount and bearing. If rear driveshaft universal joints are defective, replace the complete driveshaft.

3 Series vehicles are equipped with aluminium driveshafts and ZNS (shiny zinc-coated) fasteners. Always replace ZNS fasteners with same.

See also:

• **270 Transfer case**

• **310 Front Suspension** for front end components

• **311 Front Axle Differential** for front drive axle repairs

• **331 Rear Axle Differential** for rear drive axle repairs

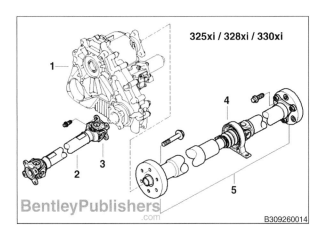

B309260014

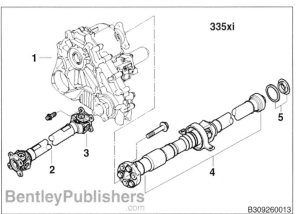

B309260013

## Driveshaft assemblies

### 325xi, 328xi and 330xi components

1. Transfer case
2. Front driveshaft
3. Front driveshaft universal joint
4. Rear driveshaft center bearing
   • Rubber mounted
5. Rear driveshaft flex-discs

### 335xi components

1. Transfer case
2. Front driveshaft
3. Front driveshaft universal joint
4. Rear driveshaft center bearing
   • Rubber mounted
5. Rear driveshaft
   • Flange nut
   • Collar

## Cautions

> **CAUTION—**
>
> • *Be sure the wheels are off the ground before removing the driveshaft. Set the parking brake before removing the driveshaft.*
>
> • *Use only ZNS (zinc-coated) fasteners with aluminium driveshaft components.*
>
> • *ZNS fasteners are designed to be used only once. Replace during reassembly.*
>
> • *Do not move vehicle using engine power once a driveshaft is removed.*
>
> • *Driveshaft are balanced to close tolerances. Whenever driveshafts are removed or disassembled, mark mounting flanges and driveshaft sections with paint before proceeding with work. This ensures that the driveshaft can be reassembled and installed in exactly the original orientation.*

Driveshafts 260-3

Front driveshaft, removing and installing

## FRONT DRIVESHAFT SERVICE

If detecting vibration or noise from the front driveshaft, check front universal joints for play. Pull and twist driveshaft while watching universal joint. Specified tolerance for play is very small, so almost any noticeable play indicates a problem.

| Universal joint play | |
|---|---|
| Maximum allowable | 0.15 mm (0.006 in) |

## Front driveshaft, removing and installing

— Raise car and support safely.

> **WARNING —**
> • Make sure the car is stable and well supported at all times. Use a professional automotive lift or jack stands designed for the purpose. A floor jack is not adequate support.

— Remove splash guard under engine. Remove front end reinforcement (if equipped). See **310 Front Suspension**.

— If driveshaft is to be reinstalled, mark mounting flanges and driveshaft sections with paint to preserve original orientation.

◄ Front driveshaft components:

1. Transfer case
2. ZNS bolt (replace with new)
3. Driveshaft
4. Universal joint

— Working at front differential input flange, remove universal joint bolts.

— Working at transfer case flange, remove universal joint bolts and remove driveshaft.

— Installation is reverse of removal. Remember to:
  • Observe marks made previously (if applicable).
  • Replace ZNS fasteners with new.

| Tightening torque | |
|---|---|
| Front driveshaft to transfer case / differential (use new ZNS bolts) | 20 Nm (15 ft-lb) + additional 45° |

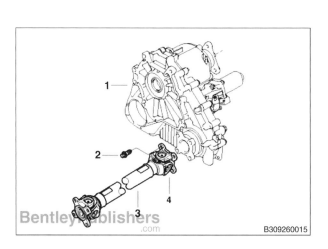

B309260015

BentleyPublishers.com
BentleyPublishers.com—All Rights Reserved

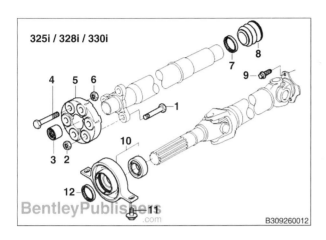

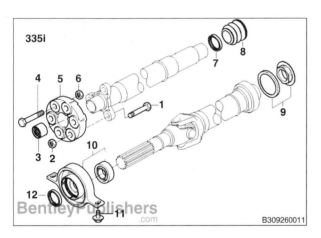

## REAR DRIVESHAFT SERVICE

### Rear driveshaft components

 325i, 328i and 330i rear driveshaft components:

1. ZNS bolt (replace)
2. Self-locking nut (replace)
3. Centering sleeve
4. ZNS bolt (replace)
5. Flex-disc
6. Self-locking nut (replace)
7. Dust cover
8. Boot
9. ZNS bolt (replace)
10. Center bearing and housing
11. Bolt
12. Spacer

 335i rear driveshaft components

1. ZNS bolt (replace)
2. Self-locking nut (replace)
3. Centering sleeve
4. ZNS bolt (replace)
5. Flex-disc
6. Self-locking nut (replace)
7. Dust cover
8. Boot
9. Flange nut and collar
10. Center bearing and housing
11. Bolt
12. Spacer

### Troubleshooting

Sources of driveline vibrations and noise may be difficult to pinpoint. Engine, transmission, front or rear axle or wheel vibrations may be transmitted through the driveshafts to the car body.

Noises in the interior of vehicle may be caused by:

• Differential problems
• Faulty wheel bearings
• Damaged drive axle(s)
• Worn or improperly inflated tires

Driveshaft noise or vibrations are usually caused by worn or damaged components.

− To inspect or remove rear driveshaft, remove exhaust system and exhaust heat shield. See **180 Exhaust System**.

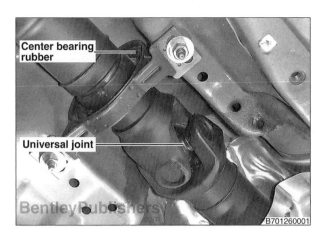

Center bearing rubber

Universal joint

B701260001

◀ Check driveshaft universal joint for play. Pull and twist driveshaft while watching universal joint. Specified tolerance for play is very small, so almost any noticeable play indicates a problem.

| Universal joint play | |
|---|---|
| Maximum allowable | 0.15 mm (0.006 in) |

– Check fastener torque at flange connections.

– Check flex-disc and center bearing rubber for deterioration or tearing.

– Check driveshaft for broken or missing balance weights. Weights are welded tabs on driveshaft tubes.

– Use paint to matchmark front and rear flanges. Remove driveshaft. See **Rear driveshaft, removing (universal joint at rear differential)** or **Rear driveshaft, removing (flange nut at rear differential)** in this repair group.

– Check universal joints for wear or binding. If it is difficult to move or binds, replace driveshaft.

– Check centering guide at output flange for damage or misalignment.

– Check runout at transmission / transfer case output flange and output shaft, and at rear differential input flange.

| Driveshaft flange wear limits | |
|---|---|
| Runout at transfer case output flange (max. allowable): • Axial play • Radial play | 0.10 mm (0.004 in) 0.07 mm (0.003 in) |
| Rear differential input flange radial play (measured at driveshaft center lip) | 0.07 mm (0.003 in) |

– Check bolt bores at transmission / transfer case output flange and rear differential input flange for wear and elongation.

– Spin driveshaft center bearing and check for smooth operation without play.

If inspection reveals nothing wrong with driveshaft, it may need to be rebalanced. This can be done by a speciality driveshaft repair shop.

Sometimes a minor driveshaft vibration can be corrected by disconnecting at transfer case and repositioning it 90°, 180° or 270° in relation to differential input flange.

**Table a** lists symptoms of rear driveshaft problems and their probable causes. Most of the repair information is contained within this repair group. There are references to other repair groups, where applicable.

260

**Table a. Rear driveshaft problems and causes**

| Symptom | Probable cause | Corrective action |
|---|---|---|
| Vibration when starting off (forward or reverse). | Center bearing rubber deteriorated. | Inspect center bearing and rubber. Replace if necessary. See **Center bearing assembly, replacing** in this repair group. |
| | Flex-disc damaged or worn. | Inspect flex-disc. Replace if necessary. See **Flex-disc, replacing** in this repair group. |
| | Engine or transmission mounts faulty. | Inspect engine and transmission mounts. Align or replace, if necessary. |
| | Front centering guide worn, or driveshaft mounting flanges out of round. | Check front centering sleeve and replace if necessary. See **Front centering sleeve, replacing** in this repair group. Also check runout of driveshaft flanges. |
| | Universal joint worn or seized. | Check universal joint play and movement. Replace driveshaft if necessary. |
| Noise during on / off throttle or when engaging clutch. | Differential components worn or damaged (excessive pinion-to-ring-gear clearance). | Remove differential and repair. See **311 Front Axle Differential** or **331 Rear Axle Differential**. |
| | Drive axle or CV joint faulty. | Inspect drive axles and CV joints. Repair or replace as necessary. See **311 Front Axle Differential** or **331 Rear Axle Differential**. |
| Vibration at 25 to 30 mph (40 to 50 kph). | Front centering sleeve worn, or driveshaft mounting flanges out of round or damaged. | Check front centering sleeve and replace if necessary. See **Front centering sleeve, replacing** in this repair group. Also check runout of driveshaft flanges. |
| | Universal joint worn or seized. | Check universal joint play and movement. Replace driveshaft if necessary. |
| | Flex-disc damaged or worn. | Inspect flex-disc. Replace if necessary. See **Flex-disc, replacing** in this repair group. |
| | Center bearing rubber deteriorated. | Inspect center bearing. Replace if necessary. See **Center bearing assembly, replacing** in this repair group. |
| Vibration, audible rumble over 35 mph (60 kph). | Front centering sleeve worn, or driveshaft mounting flanges out of round or damaged. | Check front centering sleeve and replace if necessary. See **Front centering sleeve, replacing** in this repair group. Also check runout of driveshaft flanges. |
| | Mounting flange bolts loose or holes worn. | Remove rear driveshaft and check transfer case output flange and differential input flange. Replace if necessary. |
| | Rear driveshaft unbalanced. | Check driveshaft for loose or missing balance weights. Have driveshaft rebalanced or replace if necessary. |
| | Universal joint worn or seized. | Check universal joint play and movement. Replace rear driveshaft if necessary. |
| | Rear driveshaft center bearing faulty. | Replace center bearing. See **Center bearing assembly, replacing** in this repair group. |
| | Rear differential rubber bushing(s) faulty. | Inspect differential rubber bushing. Replace as necessary. See **331 Rear Axle Differential**. |

## Rear driveshaft, removing (universal joint at rear differential)

− Raise vehicle and support safely.

> **WARNING**—
> • Make sure the vehicle is stable and well supported at all times. Use a professional automotive lift or jack stands designed for the purpose. A floor jack is not adequate support.

− Remove exhaust system and exhaust heat shields. See **180 Exhaust System**.

> **WARNING**—
> • Make sure exhaust system is fully cooled off before removing.

− Mark mounting flanges and driveshaft sections with paint to preserve original orientation.

◄ Working at driveshaft front flex-disc, counterhold bolt heads (**arrows**) and remove nuts at transmission / transfer case output flange. Discard old fasteners.

> **CAUTION**—
> • To avoid damaging flex-disc rubber, be sure to hold bolts stationary while loosening nuts.

− Hang driveshaft front section from body using stiff wire.

− Working at driveshaft rear universal joint, remove mounting nuts at differential input flange. Discard nuts. If necessary, use pry bar at groove to pry universal joint free.

− Hang driveshaft rear section from body using stiff wire.

◄ Remove driveshaft center support bearing mounting nuts (**arrows**).

− Remove driveshaft. Pull down on center of driveshaft to facilitate removal.

| Tightening torque | |
|---|---|
| Driveshaft center bearing support to body | 21 Nm (15 ft-lb) |

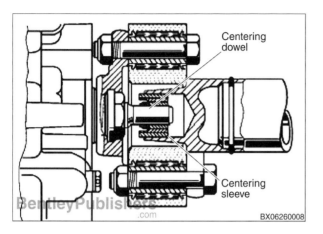

Centering dowel

Centering sleeve

BX06260008

## Rear driveshaft, installing (universal joint at rear differential)

 Prior to installation:

- Inspect centering dowel on transmission / transfer case output flange.
- Inspect centering sleeve inside driveshaft flex-disc.
- Replace damaged components. See **Front centering sleeve, replacing** in this repair group.
- When installing centering sleeve over centering dowel, apply thin coat of molybdenum disulfide grease (Molykote Longterm 2 Plus® or equivalent).

– Bend driveshaft slightly at center universal joint to install.

– Align matchmarks on driveshaft to matchmarks on differential and transfer case flanges.

– Fit driveshaft to differential input flange. Using new ZNS fasteners, alternately tighten two opposite nuts to draw joint evenly into flange. Once seated, tighten down remaining nuts.

> **CAUTION—**
> - *Do not reuse fasteners. They are designed to be used only once.*
> - *Do not allow driveshaft to hang unsupported.*

– Attach front flex-disc to transmission / transfer case output flange using new fasteners.

> **CAUTION—**
> - *To avoid damaging flex-disc rubber, be sure to hold bolts stationary while tightening nuts.*

| Tightening torque | |
|---|---|
| Front driveshaft to transmission / transfer case (flex-disc) | |
| • M10x10.9 (replace ZNS fasteners) | 20 Nm (15 ft-lb) + 90° |
| • M12x10.9 (replace ZNS fasteners) | 55 Nm (41 ft-lb) + 90° |
| Rear driveshaft to differential (flex-disc) | |
| • M10x10.9 (replace ZNS fasteners) | 20 Nm (15 ft-lb) + 90° |
| • M12x10.9 (replace ZNS fasteners) | 55 Nm (41 ft-lb) + 90° |
| Rear driveshaft to differential (universal joint) | |
| • M10x10.9 (bolt with ribbed teeth) (replace ZNS fasteners) | 40 Nm (30 ft-lb) + 45° |
| • M10x10.9 (and M3 models) (replace ZNS fasteners) | 20 Nm (15 ft-lb) + 90° |
| Rear driveshaft to differential (flange nut) | 75 Nm (55 ft-lb) |

*Rear driveshaft, removing (flange nut at rear differential)*

— Reinstall center bearing support.

| Tightening torque | |
|---|---|
| Driveshaft center bearing support to body | 21 Nm (15 ft-lb) |

— Install heat shields. Install exhaust system. See **180 Exhaust System**.

— Road test vehicle to check for noise or vibration.

## Rear driveshaft, removing (flange nut at rear differential)

— Raise vehicle and support safely.

> **WARNING**—
> • Make sure the vehicle is stable and well supported at all times. Use a professional automotive lift or jack stands designed for the purpose. A floor jack is not adequate support.

— Remove exhaust system and exhaust heat shields. See **180 Exhaust System**.

> **WARNING**—
> • Make sure exhaust system is fully cooled off before removing.

— Mark mounting flanges and driveshaft sections with paint to preserve original orientation.

◄ Working at driveshaft front flex-disc, counterhold bolt heads (**arrows**) and remove nuts at transfer case output flange. Discard old fasteners.

> **CAUTION**—
> • To avoid damaging flex-disc rubber, be sure to hold bolts stationary while loosening nuts.

— Hang driveshaft front section from body using stiff wire.

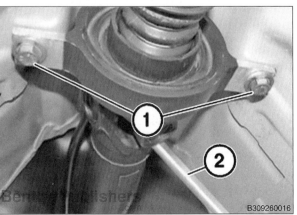

◄ Working at center support bearing, loosen fasteners (**1**) but do not remove. Use a pry bar or equivalent tool (**2**) to brace driveshaft at center universal joint.

*Rear driveshaft, installing (flange nut at rear differential)*

◄ Working at rear differential, release insert nut clockwise using BMW special tools 33 5 040 and 33 5 070.

> **CAUTION—**
> • *Do not use flange nut to counter hold driveshaft. Rear differential may be damaged.*

– Hang driveshaft rear section from body using stiff wire.

– Remove driveshaft center support bearing mounting nuts.

– Remove driveshaft. Pull down on center of driveshaft to facilitate removal.

| Tightening torque | |
|---|---|
| Driveshaft center bearing support to body | 21 Nm (15 ft-lb) |

## Rear driveshaft, installing (flange nut at rear differential)

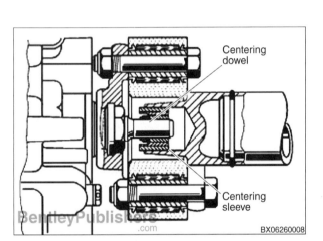

Centering dowel

Centering sleeve

◄ Prior to installation:

• Inspect centering dowel on transmission / transfer case output flange.

• Inspect centering sleeve inside driveshaft flex-disc.

• Replace damaged components. See **Front centering sleeve, replacing** in this repair group.

• When installing centering sleeve over centering dowel, apply thin coat of molybdenum disulfide grease (Molykote Longterm 2 Plus® or equivalent).

◄ Remove retaining clip (**1**) and seal (**2**)

*Rear driveshaft, installing (flange nut at rear differential)*

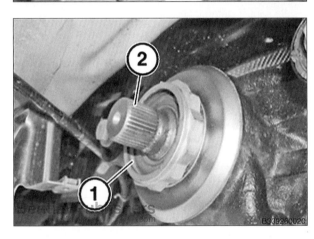

◀ Remove insert nut (**1**).

> **CAUTION—**
> • *Always replace retaining clip, seal and insert nut at rear differential with new.*

◀ Clean insert collar (**1**), flange nut and spline teeth on bevel pinion (**2**). Fill insert collar (**1**) with thin coat of molybdenum disulfide grease (Molykote Longterm 2 Plus® or equivalent).

◀ Clean threads of joint hub (**1**) to remove all trace of residue. Clean hub teeth (**2**) and coat with thin coat of molybdenum disulfide grease (Molykote Longterm 2 Plus® or equivalent).

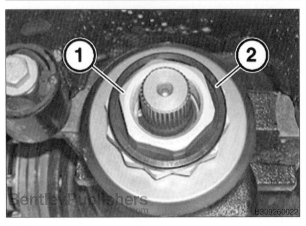

◀ Using new parts, place insert nut (**1**) with seal in insert collar of flange nut. Install retaining clip (**2**).

– Align matchmarks on driveshaft to matchmarks on differential and transfer case flanges.

– Attach front flex-disc to transmission / transfer case output flange using new fasteners.

> **CAUTION—**
> • *To avoid damaging flex-disc rubber, be sure to hold bolts stationary while tightening nuts.*

**260**

*Rear driveshaft, installing (flange nut at rear differential)*

– Bend driveshaft slightly at center universal joint to aid installation.

> **CAUTION—**
> - *Observe the following installation sequence:*
>   - *Attach driveshaft to transmission.*
>   - *Attach driveshaft to rear differential.*
>   - *Attach center mount.*
> - *Observe the following tightening sequence:*
>   - *Insert nut to driveshaft.*
>   - *Flex-disc to transmission / transfer case.*
>   - *Center mount to chassis.*

◀ Slide driveshaft (**1**) as far as it will go onto insert nut and secure finger tight. Use a pry bar or equivalent tool to brace driveshaft at center universal joint. Tighten insert nut to final torque.

> **CAUTION—**
> - *Final tightening of insert nut must occur within 5 minutes.*
> - *Do not use flange nut to counter hold driveshaft. Rear differential may be damaged.*
> - *Do not reuse fasteners. They are designed to be used only once.*
> - *Do not allow driveshaft to hang unsupported.*

| Tightening torque | |
| --- | --- |
| Front driveshaft to transmission / transfer case (flex-disc) | |
| • M10x10.9 (replace ZNS fasteners) | 20 Nm (15 ft-lb) + 90° |
| • M12x10.9 (replace ZNS fasteners) | 55 Nm (41 ft-lb) + 90° |
| Rear driveshaft to differential (flex-disc) | |
| • M10x10.9 (replace ZNS fasteners) | 20 Nm (15 ft-lb) + 90° |
| • M12x10.9 (replace ZNS fasteners) | 55 Nm (41 ft-lb) + 90° |
| Rear driveshaft to differential (universal joint) | |
| • M10x10.9 (bolt with ribbed teeth) (replace ZNS fasteners) | 40 Nm (30 ft-lb) + 45° |
| • M10x10.9 (and M3 models) (replace ZNS fasteners) | 20 Nm (15 ft-lb) + 90° |
| Rear driveshaft to differential (flange nut) | 75 Nm (55 ft-lb) |

– Reinstall center bearing support.

| Tightening torque | |
| --- | --- |
| Driveshaft center bearing support to body | 21 Nm (15 ft-lb) |

– Install heat shields. Install exhaust system. See **180 Exhaust System**.

– Road test vehicle to check for noise or vibration.

## Flex-disc, replacing

— Check flex-disc for cracks, tears, missing pieces or distortion. Check for worn bolt hole bores in flange.

— Remove driveshaft center bearing support fasteners. Support center of driveshaft.

— Detach driveshaft flex-disc from transmission / transfer case.

— Lower center of driveshaft sufficiently to disengage flex-disc from transfer case flange. Tie driveshaft to side.

— Remove fasteners and detach flex-disc from driveshaft.

> *CAUTION—*
> • *To avoid damaging rear driveshaft CV joint, do not allow driveshaft to hang down unsupported.*
> • *To avoid damaging flex-disc rubber, be sure to hold bolts stationary while loosening nuts.*

◀ Install new flex-disc using new ZNS fasteners.

• Molded arrows (**arrows**) on coupling point toward flange arms.

• Counterhold bolts while tightening nuts.

> *CAUTION—*
> • *To avoid damaging flex-disc rubber, be sure to hold bolts stationary while tightening nuts.*

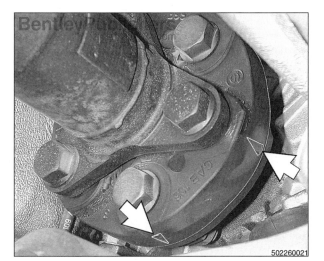

| Tightening torques | |
|---|---|
| Front driveshaft to transmission / transfer case (flex-disc) | |
| • M10x10.9 (replace ZNS fasteners) | 20 Nm (15 ft-lb) + 90° |
| • M12x10.9 (replace ZNS fasteners) | 55 Nm (41 ft-lb) + 90° |

## Center bearing assembly, replacing

The rear driveshaft center bearing assembly consists of a grooved ball bearing in a rubber mount. The bearing assembly is pressed on the driveshaft.

— Remove driveshaft. See **Rear driveshaft, removing (universal joint at rear differential)** or **Rear driveshaft, removing (flange nut at rear differential)** in this repair group.

— Use paint to matchmark front and rear driveshaft sections before separating. Do not scratch or punch marks in driveshaft metal.

◀ Remove bolt (**arrow**) securing front and rear halves of driveshaft and pull driveshaft apart.

— Remove shim and dust shield, where fitted.

— Use puller to remove center bearing assembly from driveshaft.

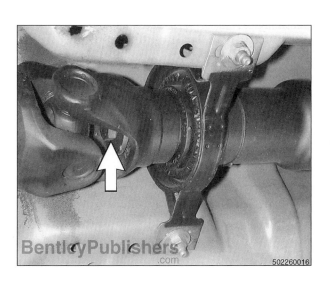

— On installation, drive new center bearing firmly to stop. Reassemble driveshaft using matchmarks made prior to disassembly.

— Clean threads and install bolt securing driveshaft halves. Use thread locking compound Loctite® or equivalent.

| Tightening torque | |
|---|---|
| Driveshaft front half to rear half (use thread locking compound) | 97 Nm (72 ft-lb) |

— Install driveshaft. See **Rear driveshaft, installing (universal joint at rear differential)** or **Rear driveshaft, installing (flange nut at rear differential)** in this repair group.

## Front centering sleeve, replacing

◄ The front centering sleeve centers the rear driveshaft in relation to the transfer case flange. The guide is press-fit into a cavity in the flex-disc and slides on a dowel on the transfer case output flange.

No specifications are given for wear of the guide. Check to make sure that the sleeve fits snugly over the dowel.

— Remove rear driveshaft. See **Rear driveshaft, removing (universal joint at rear differential)** or **Rear driveshaft, removing (flange nut at rear differential)** in this repair group.

— Pack cavity behind centering guide with heavy grease until grease is flush with bottom edge of guide.

— Insert 14 mm (approximately $^9/_{16}$ in) diameter mandrel or metal rod into guide. Strike guide with hammer to force centering guide out. Make sure mandrel fits snugly in the centering guide so that grease cannot escape around the sides of the mandrel.

— Remove old grease from driveshaft, lubricate new centering guide with molybdenum disulfide grease (Molykote Longterm 2 Plus® or equivalent) and drive into driveshaft.

◄ When installing new driveshaft centering guide, be sure sealing lip of guide faces outward. Drive guide into driveshaft to a protrusion depth of 4 - 6 mm (0.16 - 0.24 in).

— Install driveshaft. See **Rear driveshaft, installing (universal joint at rear differential)** or **Rear driveshaft, installing (flange nut at rear differential)** in this repair group.

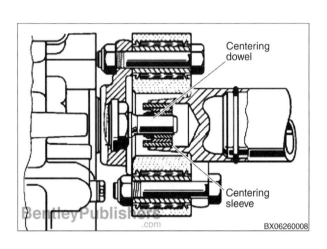

Centering dowel

Centering sleeve

BX06260008

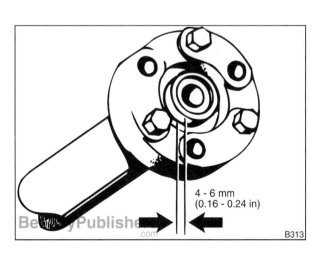

4 - 6 mm
(0.16 - 0.24 in)

B313

# 270 Transfer Case

## GENERAL

This repair group covers the all-wheel drive transfer case. Internal transfer case repair is not covered. Special press tools and procedures are required to disassemble and service the internal geartrain.

See also:

- **180 Exhaust System**
- **260 Driveshafts**

### Transfer case

 The xDrive transfer case, bolted to the rear of the transmission, directs power from the transmission to both the front and rear differentials via driveshafts. The transfer case is permanently engaged to drive all four wheels all of the time.

xDrive includes active torque control (ATC). ATC uses electronics to control torque split and traction.

For additional information, see

- **200 Transmission–General**
- **260 Driveshafts**

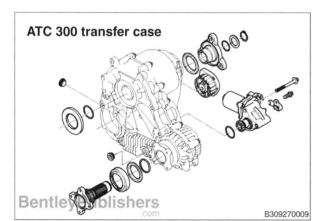

**ATC 300 transfer case**

B309270009

## TRANSFER CASE SERVICE

### Transfer case fluid service

xDrive transfer case oil monitoring is performed by the transfer case control module to determine when oil change is due.

— After performing work on transfer case, check fluid level. Be sure to use correct specification fluid.

◄ Remove drain plug (**1**) to drain transfer case.

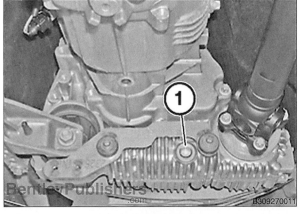

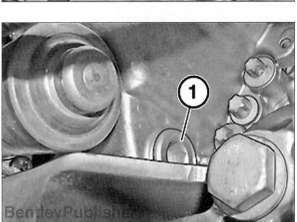

◄ Fill case to lower edge of filler plug (**arrow**).

| Transfer case fluids | |
|---|---|
| Capacity | 0.52 ltr (0.55 qt) |
| Specification | BMW part no. 83 22 0 397 244 |

> *CAUTION—*
> * *In order to prevent serious damage to transfer case, use only the recommended fluid.*

| Tightening torque | |
|---|---|
| Drain / fill plug to transfer case (M22) | 60 Nm (44 ft-lb) |

**270**

## Transfer case, removing and installing

– Raise vehicle and support safely.

> **WARNING**—
> • *Make sure the vehicle is stable and well supported at all times. Use a professional automotive lift or jack stands designed for the purpose. A floor jack is not adequate support.*

– Remove splash guard under engine. Remove front end reinforcement (if applicable). See **310 Front Suspension**.

– Remove exhaust system and exhaust heat shield. See **180 Exhaust System**.

> **WARNING**—
> • *Make sure exhaust system is fully cooled off before removing.*

– Remove support brackets for heat and splash shields as needed.

◀ Remove front driveshaft at transfer case output flange. Tie driveshaft to side.

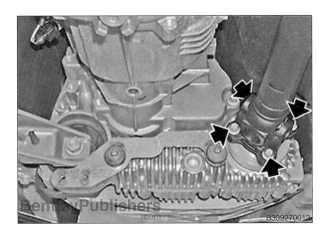

| Tightening torque | |
|---|---|
| Front driveshaft to transfer case (use new ZNS bolts) | 20 Nm (15 ft-lb) + 45° |
| Front driveshaft to front differential (use new ZNS bolts) | 20 Nm (15 ft-lb) + 45° |

– Rear driveshaft:

• Working at transfer case output flange, use paint to matchmark rear driveshaft flex-disc flanges.

• Remove driveshaft center bearing support fasteners. Support center of driveshaft.

• Detach rear driveshaft flex-disc from transfer case.

> **CAUTION**—
> • *To avoid damaging flex-disc rubber, be sure to hold bolts stationary while loosening nuts.*

– Lower center of driveshaft sufficiently to disengage flex-disc from transfer case flange. Tie driveshaft to side. See **260 Driveshafts**.

> **CAUTION**—
> • *To prevent damage to rear driveshaft CV joint, do not allow driveshaft to hang down unsupported.*

*Transfer case, removing and installing*

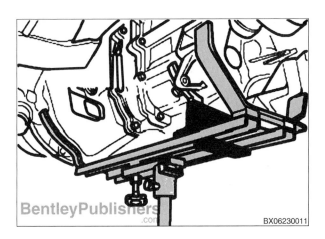

◀ Support transmission on transmission jack.

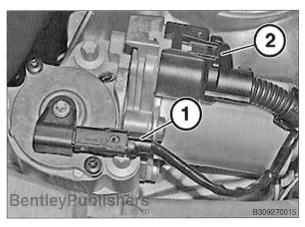

◀ Detach xDrive clutch actuator electrical harnesses (**1** and **2**).

− Detach vent line from transfer case.

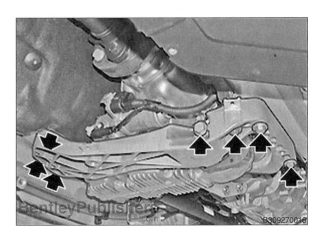

◀ Remove mounting fasteners (**arrows**) for transmission cross member and remove cross member.

| Tightening torque | |
| --- | --- |
| Transmission cross member to rubber mounts (M12) | 68 Nm (50 ft-lb) |
| Transmission cross member to chassis (M8) | 19 Nm (14 ft-lb) |

− While supporting transfer case, remove transfer case mounting bolts. Lower transfer case. Check carefully to make sure no lines, hoses or wires become snagged.

*Transfer case, removing and installing*

◀ When installing:

- Inspect dowel sleeves (**1**) and replace if damaged.

- Transfer vents hose, covers and protective caps to new transfer case

- Replace transfer case input shaft sealing O-ring, if applicable.

- Apply thin coat of Weicon® antiseize grease to dowel pin and input shaft splines.

| Tightening torques | |
|---|---|
| Front driveshaft to transfer case (use new ZNS bolts) | 20 Nm (15 ft-lb) + 45° |
| Front driveshaft to front differential (use new ZNS bolts) | 20 Nm (15 ft-lb) + 45° |
| Front driveshaft to transmission / transfer case (flex disc) • M10x10.9 (use new ZNS fasteners) • M12x10.9 (use new ZNS fasteners) | 20 Nm (15 ft-lb) + 90° 55 Nm (41 ft-lb) + 90° |
| Transfer case to transmission (M10) | 43 Nm (32 ft-lb) |
| Transmission cross member to rubber mounts (M12) | 68 Nm (50 ft-lb) |
| Transmission cross member to chassis (M8) | 19 Nm (14 ft-lb) |

— After completion of work, check and top off fluid level. See **Transfer case fluid service** in this repair group.

— After filling transfer case, drive vehicle approximately 200 meters (600 ft) and recheck fluid level.

— Use BMW diagnostic tool to carry out "Repair" service function and complete transfer case programing / coding.

# 300 Suspension, Steering and Brakes– General

## GENERAL

This repair group includes overview information for the front and rear suspension, braking and steering systems. Also covered is tire pressure monitoring (TPM) system initialization. For additional information, see:

• **200 Transmission–General** for xDrive transfer case information

• **600 Electrical System–General** for bus information

• **ECL Electrical Component Locations**

### Suspension, steering, brakes and drivetrain, overview (rear-wheel drive Coupe)

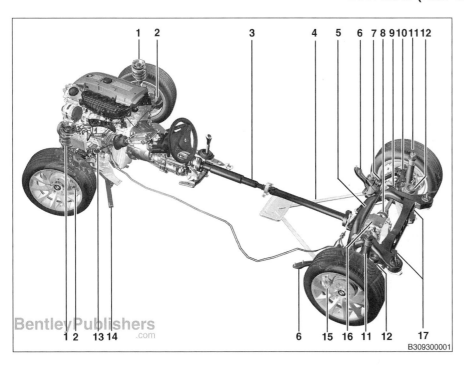

B309300001

1. Front strut and spring assembly
2. Front brake caliper
3. Rear driveshaft
4. Rear body reinforcement
5. Rear axle carrier (rear subframe)
6. Thrust link
7. Guide arm
8. Rear drive axle
9. Stabilizer bar
10. Upper control arm
11. Rear shock absorber
12. Rear coil spring
13. Steering shaft universal joint
14. Front body reinforcement
15. Rear brake caliper
16. Rear differential
17. Rear toe link

## Aluminum suspension components

In order to reduce vehicle weight, some aluminum suspension components are used. A test with a magnet easily reveals the metal used. If working with aluminum components, follow the cautions below.

> *CAUTION—*
> * *Due to the chemical and corrosion characteristics of aluminum, do not bring into contact with battery acid.*
> * *Do not use wire brushes with brass or iron bristles. Only use brushes with stainless steel bristles.*
> * *Do not expose to flying sparks from grinding or cutting operations.*
> * *Do not subject to steel welding splashes.*
> * *Do not expose to temperatures over 80°C (176°F), even for short periods. Temperatures in painting facilities are not a problem.*

## FRONT SUSPENSION

The 3 Series front suspension is a double-pivot, strut-type design with dual lower control arms. An axle carrier (front subframe) is used as a rigid mounting platform for the front suspension arms, stabilizer bar and steering rack.

The tension struts (thrust arms) are connected to the axle carrier using hydraulic mounts. The lower control arms are connected to the steering knuckles in a double pivot configuration.

Each front strut assembly includes a tubular strut and a coil spring. The upper strut mount includes a bearing.

 The lower end of each strut housing is pinch-fitted to the steering knuckle.

The wheel bearing and hub assemblies are either bolted to the steering knuckles (rear drive models) or pressed on the steering knuckles (xDrive models) and require several special tools to remove.

Front suspension repairs are covered in **310 Front Suspension**.

The front differential is bolted to the left side of the engine oil pan. Drive axles with constant velocity (CV) joints at each end drive the front wheels.

Front differential and drive axle repairs are covered in **311 Front Axle Differential**.

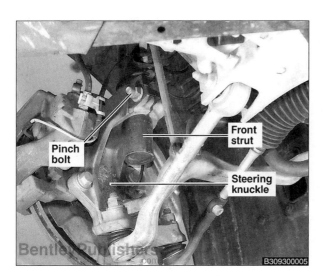

Pinch bolt

Front strut

Steering knuckle

B309300005

*Front suspension components (rear-wheel drive Coupe)*

## Front suspension components (rear-wheel drive Coupe)

B309200002

1. Front axle carrier (front subframe)
2. Hydraulic mount
3. Tension strut (thrust arm)
4. Front stabilizer bar
5. Steering rack
6. Front strut and coil spring assembly
7. Steering knuckle (wheel bearing carrier)
8. Steering tie rod
9. Stabilizer bar link
10. Control arm
11. Front body reinforcement

300

*Front suspension components (rear-wheel drive Coupe)*

## REAR SUSPENSION

The rear suspension is a 5-link design. The rear axle carrier (subframe) and links are made from high strength steel.

On xDrive (AWD) version of the car, the wheel bearing carrier is slightly bigger to allow for bigger wheel bearings.

Rear suspension repairs are covered in **330 Rear Suspension**.

The rear differential mounts to the subframe using two rubber bushings in front and one hydraulic mount at rear. Drive axles with constant-velocity (CV) joints at both ends transfer power from the differential to the road wheels.

Rear differential and drive axle repairs are covered in **331 Rear Axle Differential**.

 Rear control arms and links:

1. Rear drive axle
2. Lower control arm (swing arm)
3. Upper control arm
4. Toe link
5. Wheel bearing carrier
6. Guide arm (traction strut)
7. Trailing arm

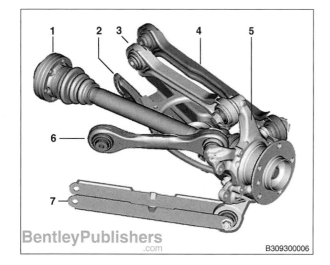

## Rear suspension components

1. Thrust link
2. Guide arm (traction strut)
3. Wheel hub
4. Upper control arm
5. Stabilizer link
6. Shock absorber
7. Coil spring
8. Toe link
9. Lower control arm (swing arm)
10. Stabilizer bar
11. Rear axle carrier (rear subframe)
12. Trailing arm

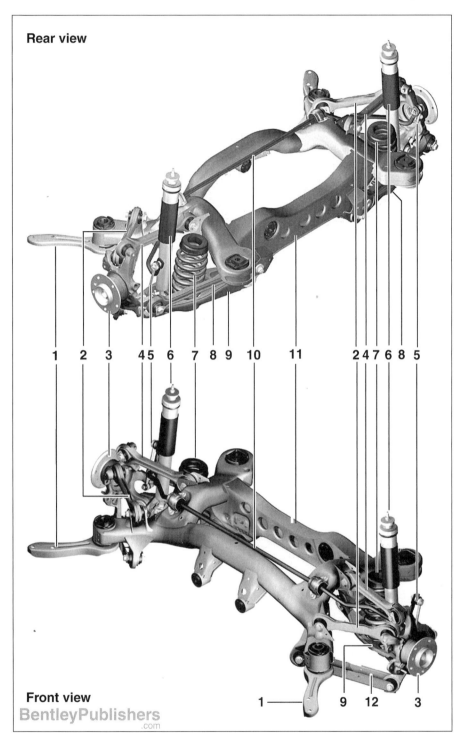

**Rear view**

**Front view**

**300**

*Steering column components*

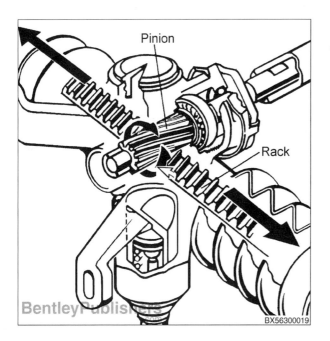

## STEERING

◀ The rack-and-pinion steering system features speed-sensitive variable power assist provided by an engine-driven hydraulic pump.

## Steering column components

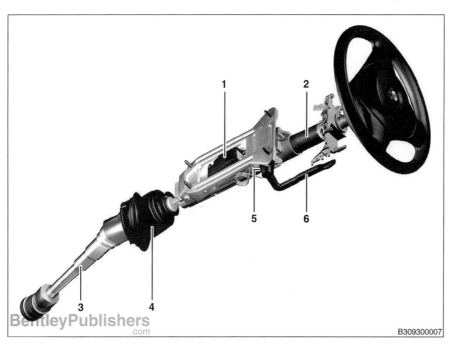

1. Electric steering lock or ELV (2006 only)
2. Crash absorbing element
3. Lower steering shaft spindle
4. Rubber boot
5. Steering column adjustment lock
6. Steering column adjustment lever

## BRAKE SYSTEM

3 Series vehicles covered by this manual are equipped with power disc brakes with integral antilock brakes (ABS) and dynamic stability control (DSC). See **340 Brakes** for details.

The parking brake is a dual-drum system integrated with the rear brake rotors.

Each disc brake uses a caliper with a single hydraulic cylinder. Brake pads in the left front and right rear contain wear sensors. When brake pads need replacement, the sensors illuminate a light on the dashboard.

Power assist is provided by a vacuum booster when the engine is running. The brake pedal pushrod is connected directly to the master cylinder, so failure of the vacuum booster does not normally result in total brake failure.

In order to provide adequate vacuum for the brake booster, an additional vacuum pump is fitted. The pump is driven off the oil pump chain.

◄ Non-turbo (N52) engine: Vacuum pump is attached to rear of timing chain housing.

Vacuum pump

B309300008

◄ Turbo (N54) engine: Vacuum pump in tandem with high pressure fuel pump is attached to rear of timing chain housing, below and to right of alternator.

See **100 Engine–General** for additional information.

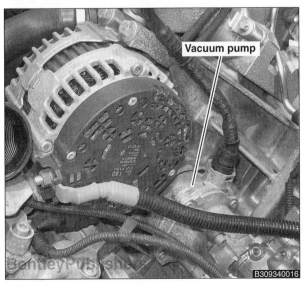

Vacuum pump

B309340016

300

## WHEEL ALIGNMENT

Use electronic alignment equipment to check and set camber and toe for all 4 wheels. Be sure to check and adjust ride height prior to attempting wheel alignment.

For ride height and alignment specifications and procedures, see **320 Steering and Wheel Alignment**.

## WHEELS AND TIRES

Run-flat tires are standard on 3 Series cars covered by this manual. Several different styles of wheels in 16, 17, 18 and 19 inch diameters are available from an authorized BMW dealer.

### Tire pressure monitoring (TPM)

◁ To conform to US legal requirements, tire pressures are automatically monitored by the tire pressure monitoring system (TPM). A TPM antenna in each wheel communicates tire pressure data to a pick-up antenna in each wheel housing.

Tire pressure monitor antenna

B309300009

◁ Tire pressure data from the run-flat tires is monitored by the tire pressure monitoring (TPM) system. If a substantial loss of tire pressure is detected, warning lights in yellow and red illuminate in the instrument cluster and a tire failure message appears in Check Control display. In addition, an acoustic signal sounds.

> **WARNING—**
> - *In case of run-flat tire failure, drive cautiously and do not exceed a speed of 50 mph or 80 km/h. With tire pressure loss, vehicle handling changes. This includes reduced tracking stability in braking, extended braking distance and altered steering characteristics.*
> - *If unusual vibration or loud noises occur while driving on a damaged tire, this may be an indication that the tire has failed completely. Reduce speed and pull over as soon as possible at a suitable location. Otherwise parts of the tire could come loose, resulting in an accident. Do not continue driving.*
> - *TPM does not work correctly if it is not initialized.*
> - *TPM cannot indicate a flat tire if a wheel without TPM electronics is mounted.*

Tire failure!

B309119001

Avoid sudden braking and steering maneuvers. At the next opportunity, check air pressure in all four tires. Tire pressure specifications are given on a sticker on the driver door jamb.

Immediately after correcting tire pressures or mounting a new wheel, reinitialize TPM.

### TPM, reinitializing in instrument cluster

– Start engine, but do not drive off.

◄ Working at turn signal lever:

- Toggle button **1** up or down to scroll through instrument cluster menu items.
- When **INIT** appears, press button **2** (BC button) to select it.
- Press and hold button **2** (BC button) for approx. 5 seconds until **INIT** is displayed with check box. TPM is now ready for initialization. If no check box appears, TPM cannot be initialized due to a fault. Diagnose system using BMW scan tool or equivalent.

– Start to drive. Initialization completes automatically while vehicle is on the move.

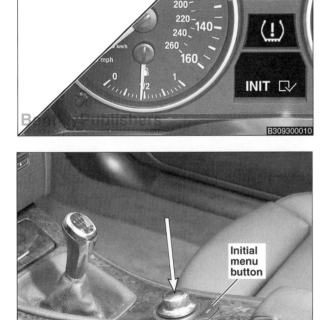

### TPM, reinitializing using iDrive

– Switch ignition ON.

◄ Press down iDrive controller (**arrow**) to select **Info sources | Settings** menu.

*NOTE —*
- *Early style iDrive shown. Later version iDrive operates similarly.*

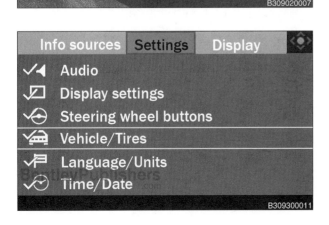

◄ Rotate controller to **Settings**.

– Press down controller to select **Settings**, then rotate to **Vehicle/Tires**.

*Tire pressure monitoring (TPM)*

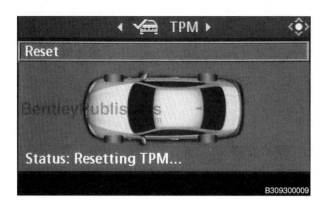

◄ Press down controller to select **Vehicle/Tires**. In similar manner, navigate to **TPM** screen.

– Start engine, but do not drive off.

– Select **Reset** and press controller.

– Select **Yes** and press controller.

– Start to drive. Initialization completes automatically while vehicle is on the move.

# 310 Front Suspension

**310**

## GENERAL

This repair group covers the repair and replacement of front suspension components.

All models are equipped with a rack and pinion type steering system mounted to a steel subframe. The subframe is strengthened by a reinforcing struts and, on xDrive models, a front end reinforcement plate.

See **300 Suspension, Steering and Brakes–General** for a description of the front suspension and components.

See **320 Steering and Wheel Alignment** for specifications on setting ride height.

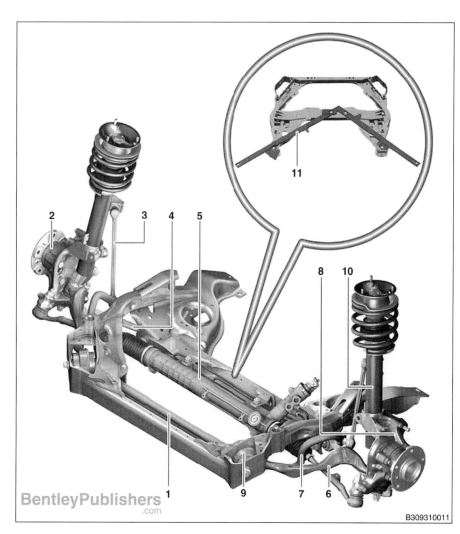

B309310011

## Front suspension components

1.  Front axle carrier
2.  Wheel hub
3.  Stabilizer bar link
4.  Control arm
5.  Steering rack
6.  Tension strut
7.  Stabilizer bar
8.  Steering knuckle (swivel bearing)
9.  Hydro-mount
10. Spring strut
11. Reinforcing strut

## Front end reinforcement plate, removing and installing

◄  xDrive models include a reinforcement plate (**1**) to provide additional rigidity to the subframe (front axle carrier).

> **CAUTION—**
> • *Do not drive vehicle with front end reinforcement plate removed.*

—  Raise vehicle support safely.

> **WARNING—**
> • *Make sure the vehicle is stable and well supported at all times. Use a professional automotive lift or jack stands designed for the purpose. A floor jack is not adequate support.*

—  Remove fasteners (**2**) and remove reinforcement plate.

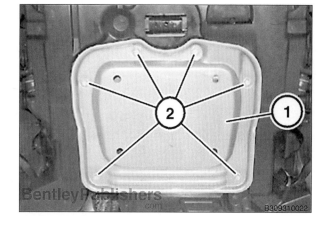

B309310022

— Installation is reverse of removal. Remember to replace fasteners with new.

| Tightening torque | |
|---|---|
| Front end reinforcement plate to subframe (use new fasteners): | |
| • Stage 1 | 56 Nm (41 ft-lb) |
| • Stage 2 | + additional 90° |

## Strut brace, removing and installing

3 Series models include 2 strut tower braces to provide additional rigidity to the front suspension.

| CAUTION— |
|---|
| • *Do not drive vehicle with strut tower brace removed.* |

◄ Working at cowl cover, use a large flat blade screwdriver to release center cover (**1**) for left and right strut brace fastener.

— Make sure tab (**2**) and seal (**3**) are not damaged. A damaged cover can allow water to infiltrate the cabin.

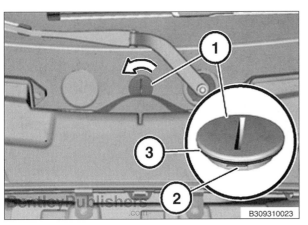

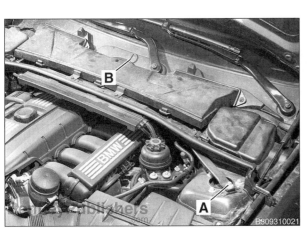

◄ Release fastener (**A**) at strut top. Loosen fastener (**B**) under center cover at cowl cover.

— Slide strut brace out of engine compartment.

> *NOTE—*
> • *A grommet in cowl cover properly locates strut brace when reinstalling. If grommet becomes dislodged, remove microfilter housing to access. See* **640 Heating and Air-conditioning**.

— Installation is reverse of removal.

| Tightening torque | |
|---|---|
| Strut brace to chassis (M12 use new fasteners): | |
| • Stage 1 | 100 Nm (74 ft-lb) |
| • Stage 2 | + additional 100° |
| Strut brace to strut tower (M10 use new fasteners): | |
| • Stage 1 | 40 Nm (30 ft-lb) |
| • Stage 2 | + additional 60° |

## Warning

**WARNING**—
- *Do not reuse self-locking fasteners. They are designed to be used only once and may fail if reused. Replace with new.*

## FRONT STRUT ASSEMBLY

◀ The front suspension shock absorbers on 3-Series models are MacPherson struts. The strut is a major component of the front suspension and supports the spring. Most strut assembly components are available as replacement parts. Replace struts and springs in pairs.

Front strut, upper strut mount or spring replacement is a two-step procedure:

- Removal of strut assembly from vehicle
- Disassembly and replacement of components on work bench

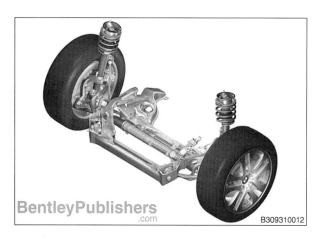
BentleyPublishers.com
B309310012

## Front strut assembly, removing and installing

– Raise car and remove front wheel.

**WARNING**—
- *Make sure the vehicle is stable and well supported at all times. Use a professional automotive lift or jack stands designed for the purpose. A floor jack is not adequate support.*

◀ Remove clips (**A**) securing brake fluid hydraulic line to front strut.

– Detach wheel speed sensor wire harness and brake pad wear sensor wire harness (**B** and **C**) from strut housing.

– Remove upper stabilizer bar connecting link mounting nut. Use a thin wrench to counterhold shaft of stabilizer bar link ball joint while removing nut.

– Support steering knuckle with suitable jack.

BentleyPublishers.com
B309310018

◀ Remove front strut pinch bolt (**arrow**).

– Loosen control arm and tension strut bolts at subframe to avoid damaging bonded rubber bushings.

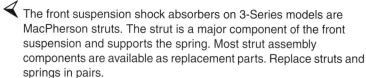

*Front strut assembly, removing and installing*

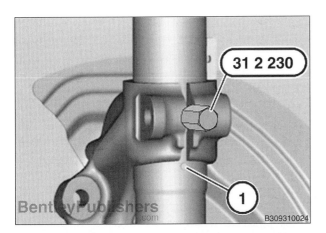

◄ If necessary, use BMW special too 31 2 230 to spread steering knuckle pinch collar.

◄ Working in engine compartment, remove strut brace (**A**). See **Strut brace, removing and installing** in this repair group.

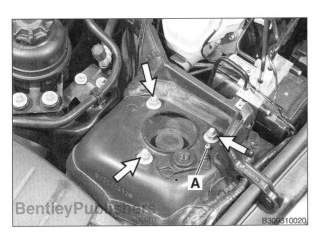

◄ Note position of strut centering pin (**A**). If centering pin is missing, mark position of strut top bearing studs on strut tower.

> **CAUTION—**
> • If strut centering pin is missing from strut top bearing, mark the position of the studs to the strut tower to maintain original camber.

– Secure spring strut against falling out.

– Remove upper strut top bearing fasteners (**arrows**).

> **WARNING—**
> • Do not remove center strut retaining nut.

– Remove strut downwards out of wheel arch.

– If replacing strut, disassemble and reassemble strut assembly on bench. See **Front strut assembly, disassembling and assembling** in this repair group.

> **NOTE—**
> • Letter on strut tube designates mounting location. Struts are marked R for right and L for left.

*Front strut assembly, removing and installing*

— Remainder of installation is reverse of removal. Remember to:

• Face bolt head of strut to steering knuckle bolt in direction of travel.

• Make sure steering knuckle contacts stop on strut.

• When attaching stabilizer link to strut, use a thin wrench to counterhold link ball joint while tightening nut.

• Tighten bonded rubber fasteners with car on ground and loaded. Bounce suspension a few times before final tightening.

• Check alignment when job is complete.

| Tightening torques | |
|---|---|
| Control arm to subframe<br>• M12 8.8 bolt (replace with new)<br>• M12 10.9 bolt (replace with new) | 68 Nm (50 ft-lb) +90°<br>100 Nm (74 ft-lb) +90° |
| Tension strut to subframe<br>• M12 8.8 bolt (replace with new)<br>• M12 10.9 bolt (replace with new) | 68 Nm (50 ft-lb) +90°<br>100 Nm (74 ft-lb) +90° |
| Road wheel to hub | 120 Nm (89 ft-lb) |
| Stabilizer bar link to strut<br>• M10 bolt (replace with new) | 58 Nm (43 ft-lb) |
| Strut assembly to steering knuckle<br>• M10 pinch bolt (replace with new)<br>• M12 pinch bolt (replace with new) | 45 Nm (34 ft-lb)<br>81 Nm (60 ft-lb) |
| Strut top bearing to chassis<br>• M8 bolt (replace with new) | 34 Nm (25 ft-lb) |

## Front strut assembly components

1. Cap
2. Upper strut self-locking nut
3. Washer
4. Strut top bearing reinforcement
5. Strut mount self-locking nut
6. Upper strut mount
7. Dust protector collar
8. Spacer
9. Upper spring seat
10. Upper spring pad
11. Coil spring
12. Rubber stop
13. Dust boot
14. Lower spring pad
15. Strut with lower spring seat

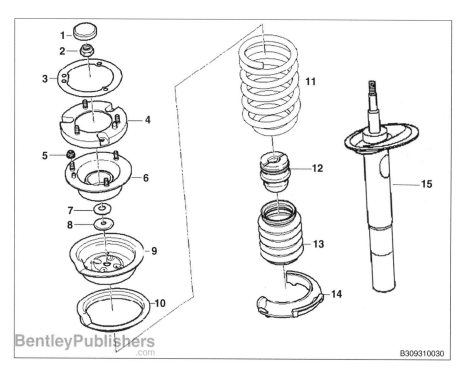

BentleyPublishers.com

B309310030

*NOTE*—

• *Illustration shows a typical E90 strut assembly. Other models are similar but not identical.*

## Front strut assembly, disassembling and assembling

Replacing the strut, upper strut mount or spring requires that the strut assembly first be removed from the car and disassembled. See **Front strut assembly, removing and installing** in this repair group.

◄ Clamp spring compressor (BMW special tool 31 3 340 or equivalent) in shop vise.

> **WARNING** —
> * Do not attempt to disassemble the strut assembly without a spring compressor designed specifically for this job.
> * Prior to each use, check special tool for functionality.
> * Do not use a damaged tool.
> * Do not make any modifications to tool.
> * Use correct size spring retainers when compressing coil spring.
> * When assembling BMW spring compressor (special tool 31 3 340), make sure spring retainer plates are felt and heard snapping into place. Check seating of spring retainers carefully.

◄ Position coil spring between spring holders so that 3 coils lie between spring holders (**arrows**). Compress spring.

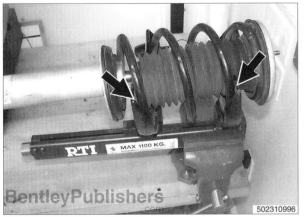

> **WARNING** —
> * When tensioned, the spring coils must rest completely in the spring holder recess.
> * Do not tighten or loosen spring compressor with an impact tool.
> * Only tighten down the coil springs until stress on the thrust bearing is relieved.
> * Only loosen strut nut if spring coils are completely inserted in the spring holder grooves. If necessary, loosen compressor, reposition and recompress.

◄ Use BMW special tool 31 2 210 or equivalent to remove strut nut. Counterhold strut shaft using 6 mm Allen wrench.

> **CAUTION** —
> * Do not remove strut nut with impact tool.

— Remove upper strut bearing and related components.

— If a new coil spring is being installed, relieve tension on spring compressor and remove coil spring.

— Check strut dust boot, rubber stop and spring pads. Replace as necessary.

— Replace strut, upper strut mount or spring, as needed.

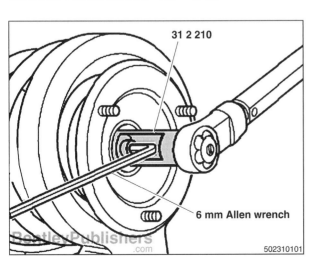

31 2 210

6 mm Allen wrench

310

*Front strut assembly, disassembling and assembling*

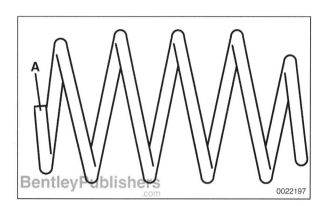

◄ Replace springs in matched pairs only. BMW ID number is stamped near end (**A**).

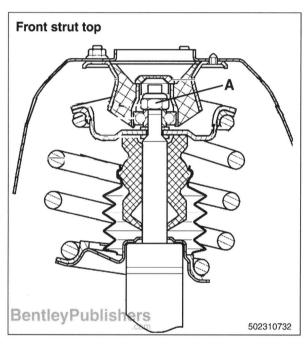

**Front strut top**

◄ Assembly is reverse of disassembly, noting the following:

• Use a new upper strut self-locking nut (**A**). Tighten nut fully before releasing spring compressor.

> **CAUTION—**
> • *Do not tighten strut nut with impact tool.*

> **NOTE—**
> • *Illustration shows a typical BMW strut assembly. 3 Series models are similar but not identical.*

◄ Be sure upper and lower spring pads (**arrows**) are correctly installed to spring seats before releasing spring compressor.

• Release spring compressor carefully and evenly, allowing spring to expand slowly.

• Have car professionally aligned when job is complete.

| Tightening torques | |
| --- | --- |
| Strut shaft to strut top bearing (replace with new) | 64 Nm (47 ft-lb) |

## FRONT SUSPENSION ARMS

Control arms and tension struts are attached to the front subframe through rubber bushings and to the steering knuckles by ball joints.

*NOTE* —

- *Tension struts are sometimes called thrust arms or thrust rods.*

- *Control arms or tension struts are sometimes called lower front arms or lower rear arms.*

Inspect ball joints for wear and looseness. Inspect bushings for wear or fluid leaks. The ball joint can only be replaced as part of an entire suspension arm assembly. Some suspension arm bushings are available as replacement parts. Always replace in pairs.

*NOTE* —

- *Steering wheel vibration during braking (usually at road speeds of 50 to 60 mph) are often caused by faulty suspension arm bushings, not out-of-true brake rotors.*

Some special tools may be required to remove suspension arms and to replace bushings. Read procedures through before beginning the job.

## Control arm, removing and installing

— Raise car and remove front wheel.

> *WARNING* —
> - *Make sure that the car is firmly supported on jack stands designed for the purpose. Place jack stands underneath structural chassis points. Do not place jack stands under suspension parts.*

— If equipped, remove ride height sensor link rod clamp from control arm.

◄ Remove control arm fasteners (**A** and **B**). Lightly tap inner control arm mounting bolt out of front subframe.

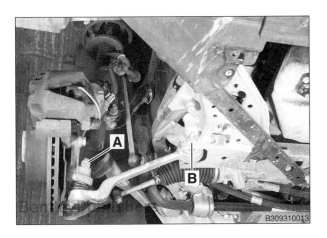

B309310013

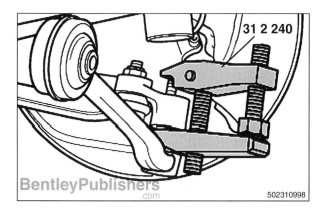

BentleyPublishers.com
31 2 240
502310998

◀ Use BMW special tool 31 2 240 or equivalent to separate ball joint from steering knuckle.

− Installation is reverse of removal. Remember to:

• Make sure thread bores, bolts, nuts and mating surfaces are clean.

• Install bushing end of control arm to subframe using new fasteners. Do not tighten nut at this time.

• Install control arm ball joint to steering knuckle using new self-locking nut. Tighten fully.

• Install ride height sensor link rod to control arm (if applicable).

• Install wheel and lower car.

• Tighten bushing end of control arm to subframe with car on ground and loaded. Bounce suspension a few times before final tightening.

• Use BMW scan tool to carry out steering angle sensor alignment.

• Check vehicle alignment.

| Tightening torques | |
|---|---|
| Control arm to steering knuckle<br>• M14 8.8 bolt (replace with new)<br>• M14 10.9 bolt (replace with new) | 80 Nm (59 ft-lb)<br>165 Nm (122 ft-lb) |
| Control arm to subframe<br>• M12 8.8 bolt (replace with new)<br>• M12 10.9 bolt (replace with new) | 68 Nm (50 ft-lb) + 90°<br>100 Nm (74 ft-lb) + 90° |
| Road wheel to hub | 120 Nm (89 ft-lb) |

## Control arm bushing, replacing

− Raise car and remove wheel.

> **WARNING** —
> • Make sure that the car is firmly supported on jack stands designed for the purpose. Place jack stands underneath structural chassis points. Do not place jack stands under suspension parts.

− Remove control arm. See **Control arm, removing and installing** in this repair group.

− Using a service press and appropriate press tools, press bushing out of control arm.

− Clean bushing bore and press in new bushing.

> **CAUTION**—
> • Draw in rubber mount from chamfered side of control arm bore.

− Press bushing in so it protrudes equally from both sides of arm.

− Install control arm.

## Tension strut, removing and installing

– Raise car and remove wheel.

> **WARNING**—
> • Make sure that the car is firmly supported on jack stands designed for the purpose. Place jack stands underneath structural chassis points. Do not place jack stands under suspension parts.

– Remove lower engine cover.

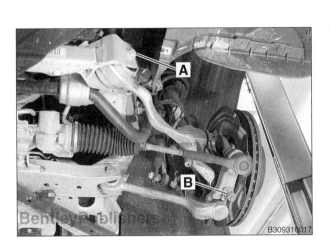

B309310017

◄ Remove tension strut fasteners (**A**). Lightly tap tension strut mounting bolt out of front subframe.

– Remove tension strut nut (**B**). If necessary, use a Torx socket (T40) to prevent joint from turning.

– Separate ball joint from steering knuckle and remove tension strut.

> **CAUTION**—
> • Take care not to damage the ball joint threads if the tension strut is to be reused.

– Installation is reverse of removal

• Make sure thread bores, bolts, nuts and mating surfaces are clean.

• Install bushing end of tension strut to subframe using new fasteners. Do not tighten nut at this time.

• Install tension strut ball joint to steering knuckle using new self-locking nut. Tighten fully.

• Install wheel and lower car.

• Tighten bushing end of tension strut to subframe with car on ground and loaded. Bounce suspension a few times before final tightening.

• Use BMW scan tool to carry out steering angle sensor alignment.

• Check vehicle alignment.

| Tightening torques | |
|---|---|
| Road wheel to hub | 120 Nm (89 ft-lb) |
| Tension strut to steering knuckle (replace with new) | 165 Nm (122 ft-lb) |
| Tension strut to subframe • M12 8.8 (replace with new) • M12 10.9 (replace with new) | 68 Nm (50 ft-lb) + 90° 100 Nm (74 ft-lb) + 90° |

**310**

## Tension strut bushing, replacing

Replace tension strut bushings in pairs. Bushings may only be replaced once.

– Raise car and remove wheel.

> **WARNING** —
> • Make sure that the car is firmly supported on jack stands designed for the purpose. Place jack stands underneath structural chassis points. Do not place jack stands under suspension parts.

– Remove tension strut. See **Tension strut, removing and installing** in this repair group.

– Using a service press and appropriate press tools, press bushing out of tension strut.

◄ Clean bushing bore and press in new bushing while aligning mark on bushing with mark on tension strut (**arrows**).

> **CAUTION** —
> • To avoid damaging the new bushing, press only on the outer steel sleeve during installation.

– Press bushing in so it protrudes equally from both sides of tension strut.

– Install tension strut.

> **CAUTION** —
> • Tighten the tension strut bushing through-bolt to its final torque only with car on the ground and the suspension normally loaded as described earlier.

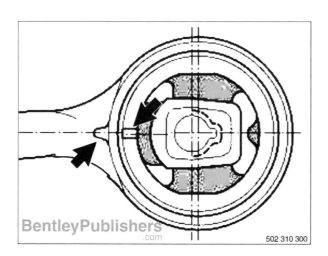

502 310 300

*Front wheel bearing, removing and installing (rear drive models)*

## STEERING KNUCKLE AND FRONT WHEEL BEARINGS

The steering knuckle (also called swivel bearing) serves as the outboard attachment point for the suspension arms and as the wheel hub / wheel bearing carrier.

The wheel bearings are permanently sealed and require no maintenance. The wheel bearing and hub assembly is either bolted to the steering knuckle (rear drive models), or pressed onto the steering knuckle and requires several special tools to remove (xDrive models).

On xDrive models, the bearing is destroyed when the wheel hub is removed. Consult the procedure appropriate for your model.

## Front wheel bearing, removing and installing (rear drive models)

— Raise car and remove front wheel.

> **WARNING—**
> • *Make sure that the car is firmly supported on jack stands designed for the purpose. Place jack stands underneath structural chassis points. Do not place jack stands under suspension parts.*

— Unbolt brake caliper and hang to side with stiff wire. Do not disconnect brake hose. Remove brake disc. See **340 Brakes**.

◄ Remove wheel hub fasteners (**A**).

— Remove wheel bearing / hub unit off steering knuckle.

— Installation is reverse of removal. Remember to:
  • Make sure wheel hub and steering knuckle mating surfaces are clean.
  • If reusing wheel bearing / hub unit, recut bolt hole threads.
  • Replace fasteners with new.

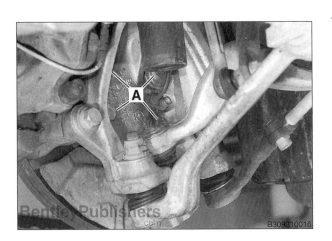

| Tightening torques | |
|---|---|
| Road wheel to hub | 120 Nm (89 ft-lb) |
| Wheel bearing / hub unit to steering knuckle (replace bolts with new) | 110 Nm (81 ft-lb) |

**310**

## Front wheel bearing, removing and installing (xDrive models)

– Raise car and remove front wheel.

> **WARNING** —
> • *Make sure that the car is firmly supported on jack stands designed for the purpose. Place jack stands underneath structural chassis points. Do not place jack stands under suspension parts.*

– Using a suitable drift, release staked side of collar nut.

◄ With an assistant holding down brake, remove collar nut using BMW special tool 31 2 080. Do not reuse collar nut.

– Unbolt brake caliper and hang to side with stiff wire. Do not disconnect brake hose. Remove brake disc. See **340 Brakes**.

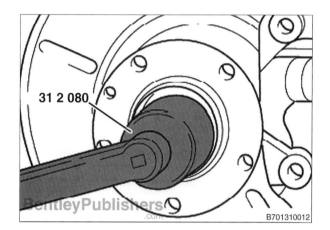

◄ Remove wheel hub using BMW special tools 33 2 160 / 33 2 116 / 33 4 200 and 5 wheel lugs.

> **NOTE** —
> • *Point rounded inside edge of special tool 33 2 160 towards wheel hub.*

> **WARNING** —
> • *Bearing is destroyed when wheel hub is removed. Replace wheel bearing and wheel hub together.*

– Remove steering knuckle and clamp in bench vice with aluminum clamping jaws. See **Steering knuckle, removing and installing** in this repair group.

◄ Use snap ring pliers to remove wheel bearing circlip.

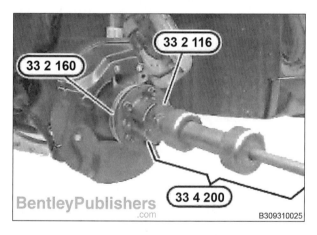

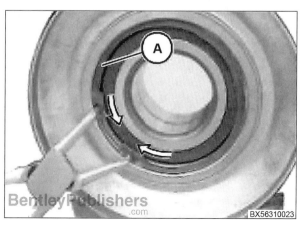

*Front wheel bearing, removing and installing (xDrive models)*

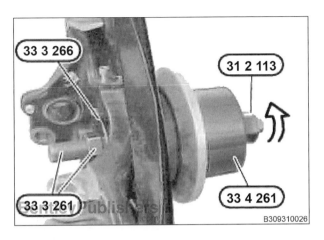

◄ Remove wheel bearing using BMW special tools 31 2 113 / 33 4 261 / 33 3 266 / 33 3 261.

— Check dust sleeve. Replace if necessary.

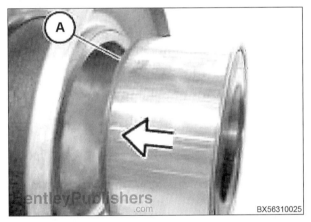

◄ Make sure steering knuckle bearing surface is clean and coat 50% of its length with Loctite 638®. Note that wide chamfer of bearing (**A**) points towards steering knuckle.

◄ With wide chamfer of bearing pointing towards steering knuckle, draw new bearing into hub using BMW special tools 31 2 113 / 22 1 018 / 33 4 262 / 33 3 261.

— Install new wheel bearing circlip. Make sure circlip is correctly seated.

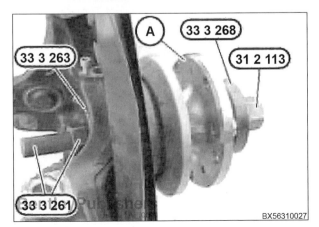

◄ Replace wheel hub (**A**) and draw into steering knuckle using BMW special tools 32 2 113 / 33 3 268 / 33 3 263 / 33 3 261.

– Install steering knuckle. See **Steering knuckle, removing and installing** in this repair group.

– Draw front axle into steering knuckle.

– Install front brake disc and caliper. See **340 Brakes**.

– Apply light coating of oil to contact surfaces. With an assistant holding down brake, tighten axle nut to specified torque.

| Tightening torque | |
|---|---|
| Road wheel to hub | 120 Nm (89 ft-lb) |
| Wheel hub to axle shaft (replace axle nut with new) | 420 Nm (310 ft-lb) |

– Using a suitable drift, stake side of axle nut to axle.

## Steering knuckle, removing and replacing

Rear drive and xDrive procedures vary. Differences are noted in the text.

– Raise car and remove front wheel.

> **WARNING—**
> • *Make sure that the car is firmly supported on jack stands designed for the purpose. Place jack stands underneath structural chassis points. Do not place jack stands under suspension parts.*

– **xDrive**: Using a suitable drift, release staked side of collar nut.

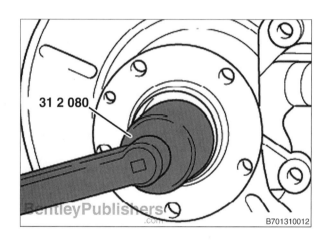

◄ **xDrive**: With an assistant holding down brake, remove collar nut using BMW special tool 31 2 080. Do not reuse collar nut.

– Unbolt brake caliper and hang to side with stiff wire. Do not disconnect brake hose.

– Remove front brake disc. See **340 Brakes**.

– Remove wheel speed sensor. See **340 Brakes**.

– Remove tie rod end from steering knuckle. See **320 Steering and Wheel Alignment**.

– Remove tension strut from steering knuckle. See **Tension strut, removing and installing** in this repair group.

– Remove control arm from steering knuckle. See **Control arm, removing and installing** in this repair group.

– **xDrive**: Press drive axle out of steering knuckle.

◁ Using a suitable jack, support steering knuckle. Remove pinch bolt (**arrow**) securing front strut to steering knuckle.

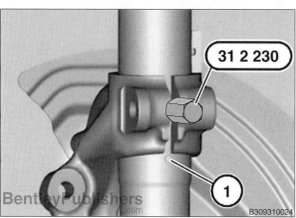

◁ If necessary, use BMW special too 31 2 230 to spread steering knuckle pinch clamp. Remove steering knuckle.

– Remainder of installation is reverse of removal. Remember to:

• Face bolt head of steering knuckle pinch bolt in direction of travel.

• Replace self locking fasteners with new.

• Make sure steering knuckle contacts stop on strut.

• Tighten bonded rubber fasteners to final torque specification with car on ground and loaded. Bounce suspension a few times before final tightening.

| **Tightening torques** | |
|---|---|
| Control arm to steering knuckle<br>• M14 8.8 bolts (replace with new)<br>• M14 10.9 bolts (replace with new) | 80 Nm (59 ft-lb)<br>165 Nm (122 ft-lb) |
| Control arm to subframe<br>• M12 8.8 bolts (replace with new)<br>• M12 10.9 bolts (replace with new) | 68 Nm (50 ft-lb)+90°<br>100 Nm (74 ft-lb)+90° |
| Road wheel to hub | 120 Nm (89 ft-lb) |
| Stabilizer bar link to strut<br>• M10 bolts (replace with new) | 58 Nm (43 ft-lb) |
| Strut assembly to steering knuckle<br>• M10 bolts (replace with new)<br>• M12 bolts (replace with new) | 45 Nm (34 ft-lb)<br>81 Nm (60 ft-lb) |
| Strut top bearing to chassis<br>• M8 bolts (replace with new) | 34 Nm (25 ft-lb) |
| Tension strut to steering knuckle | 165 Nm (122 ft-lb) |
| Tension strut to subframe<br>• M12 8.8 bolts (replace with new)<br>• M12 10.9 bolts (replace with new) | 68 Nm (50 ft-lb)+90°<br>100 Nm (74 ft-lb)+90° |
| Tie rod end to steering knuckle<br>(replace nut with new) | 80 Nm (59 ft-lb) |
| Wheel bearing / hub unit to steering knuckle<br>(replace bolts with new) | 110 Nm (81 ft-lb) |
| Wheel hub to axle shaft (replace with new) | 420 Nm (310 ft-lb) |

**310**

## FRONT STABILIZER BAR

The stabilizer bar mounts to the front subframe. The front stabilizer bar links attach to the strut assemblies.

### Stabilizer bar, removing and installing

– Raise vehicle support safely.

> **WARNING** —
> • Make sure the vehicle is stable and well supported at all times. Use a professional automotive lift or jack stands designed for the purpose. A floor jack is not adequate support.

– Remove engine splash shield and reinforcement plate (if equipped).

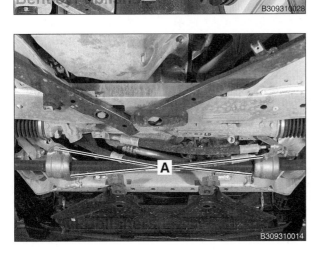

◄ Remove stabilizer bar connecting link mounting nut (**A**). Use a thin wrench to counterhold shaft of stabilizer bar link ball joint (**B**) while removing nut.

> **NOTE** —
> • If replacing stabilizer bar links, remove upper stabilizer bar link ball joint from strut.

◄ Remove stabilizer bar anchor bushing nuts (**A**) on right and left sides.

– Installation is reverse of removal. Remember to:
  • Replace fasteners with new.
  • Check rubber mounts for damage. Replace as needed.
  • Tighten stabilizer bar mount fasteners with car on ground and loaded. Bounce suspension a few times before final tightening.

| Tightening torques | |
|---|---|
| Stabilizer bar link to stabilizer bar<br>• M8 bolts (replace with new)<br>• M10 bolts (replace with new) | 21 Nm (16 ft-lb)<br>60 Nm (44 ft-lb) |
| Stabilizer bar link to strut<br>• M10 bolts (replace with new) | 58 Nm (43 ft-lb) |

# 311 Front Axle Differential

## GENERAL

This repair group covers service and replacement of front drive axles and front differential. Front differential internal repair is not covered.

See **300 Suspension, Steering and Brakes–General** for a general description of the front suspension.

For additional information, see also the following repair groups:

• **260 Driveshafts** for front driveshaft removal

• **310 Front Suspension**

### Front differential and drive axles

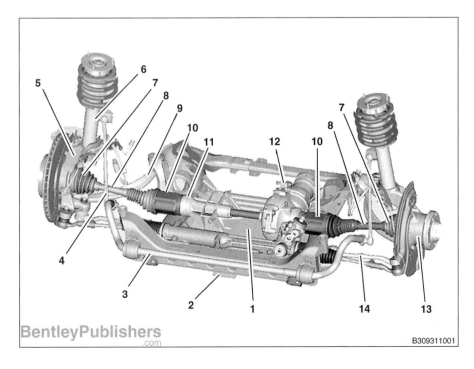

1. Reinforcement plate
2. Axle carrier
3. Stabilizer bar
4. Stabilizer link
5. Steering knuckle
6. Spring strut
7. Outer CV joint
8. Front drive axle
9. Tension strut
10. Inner CV joint
11. Right side bearing pedestal
12. Differential
13. Wheel bearing hub
14. Control arm

B309311001

311

## System description

The front axle differential and the right side bearing pedestal bolt to each side of a modified oil pan. Power is transmitted to the front differential from the transfer case via a driveshaft, and out to front drive hubs through two drive axles. The right drive axle inner constant velocity (CV) joint shaft extends through the oil pan into the front differential.

## Warning

> **WARNING —**
> • Do not reuse self-locking fasteners. They are designed to be used only once and may fail if reused. Replace with new.

## DRIVE AXLES

Front drive axles use two different types of CV joint.

- **Outer CV joint**: Traditional design allows power to be delivered from axle to wheel hub continuously while allowing suspension and steering motion.
- **Inner joint**: Triple roller bearing joint minimizes the amount of vibration and noise transmitted back through vehicle drivetrain while allowing axle to move in and out to compensate for suspension travel.

To replace a CV joint or boot, remove the drive axle from the vehicle.

## Drive axle, removing and installing

◄ Pry center cap off road wheel. Use a suitable drift to unstake drive axle collar nut at wheel hub.

– With an assistant applying brakes, break free drive axle collar nut (**arrow**). Do not remove completely.

> **WARNING —**
> • The drive axle collar nut is tightened to a high torque. Make sure car is firmly on ground.

– Raise front of vehicle and support safely.

> **WARNING —**
> • Make sure the vehicle is stable and well supported at all times. Use a professional automotive lift or jack stands designed for the purpose. A floor jack is not adequate support.

– Remove front wheel.

– Remove splash shield and front end reinforcement (if applicable). See **310 Front Suspension**.

– Remove ABS wheel speed sensor. See **340 Brakes**.

– Remove front brake caliper and tie up. Do not detach brake fluid line. See **340 Brakes**.

*Drive axle, removing and installing*

— Detach tie rod end from steering knuckle. See **320 Steering and Wheel Alignment**.

— Detach tension strut and bushing from steering knuckle. See **310 Front Suspension**.

— Detach control arm from steering knuckle. See **310 Front Suspension**.

— Detach stabilizer bar link at suspension strut. See **310 Front Suspension**.

— Remove drive axle collared nut.

◄ Use BMW special tool kit 33 2 100 / 33 2 200 to press drive axle shaft inward and disengage axle from steering knuckle:

• Use all five lug nuts to attach special tool 33 2 203, 33 2 207 and 33 2 201 to drive flange.

• Counterhold flange using special tools 33 2 202 and 33 5 070.

• Press out drive axle and tie to chassis using strong wire.

> **CAUTION—**
> • *BMW specifies 2 special tool kits (33 2 200 and 33 2 100). This procedure shows special tool kit 33 2 200.*
> • *Do not pound on end of drive axle shaft.*

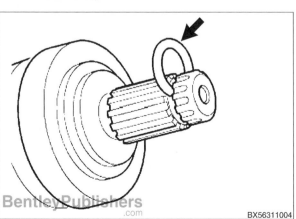

◄ Use BMW special tool 31 5 110 or equivalent prying tool to force drive axle inner CV joint shaft out of front differential or right bearing pedestal output flange. Be prepared to catch dripping oil.

— Replace differential or bearing pedestal flange seal while axle is removed from vehicle. See **Front differential flange seal, replacing** in this repair group.

— Replace CV joint boots as necessary. See **Outer CV joint boot, replacing** or **Inner CV joint boot, replacing** in this repair group.

◄ Replace inner CV joint locking circlip (**arrow**).

— When installing:

• Coat sealing lip of flange seal with transmission fluid.

• Push inner CV joint shaft into differential or bearing pedestal flange until locking circlip snaps in place.

*Drive axle, removing and installing*

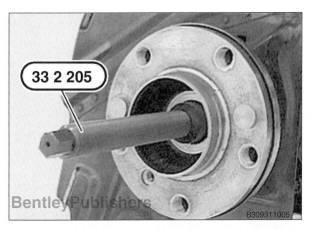

◄ Lightly oil drive axle spline teeth and insert drive axle into wheel hub.

– Screw BMW special tool 33 2 2 05 into drive axle.

> **CAUTION—**
> • *Do not oil axle or collar nut threads.*

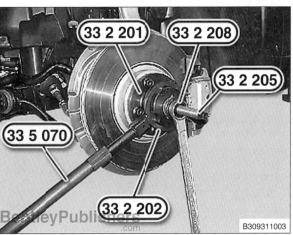

◄ Use three lug nuts to attach BMW special tool 33 2 201 to wheel hub.

– Draw axle into wheel hub using special tool 33 2 208. Counterhold hub with special tools 33 2 202 and 33 5 070.

– Remainder of installation is reverse of removal. Remember to:
  • Use new collar nut at outboard end of drive axle. Restake nut after tightening. Caulk axle threads.
  • Install front end reinforcement plate using new fasteners. See **310 Front Suspension**.
  • Check front differential oil level and top off if necessary. See **Front differential oil, checking** in this repair group.

| Tightening torques | |
|---|---|
| Brake pad carrier to steering knuckle | 110 Nm (81 ft-lb) |
| Control arm to subframe:<br>• M12 8.8 (replace with new)<br><br>• M12 10.9 (replace with new) | 68 Nm (50 ft-lb)<br>+ additional 90°<br>100 Nm (74 ft-lb)<br>+ additional 90° |
| Drive axle collar nut to front hub (replace nut) | 420 Nm (310 ft-lb) |
| Oil drain / filler plug to differential | 60 Nm (44 ft-lb) |
| Reinforcement plate to front subframe (replace fasteners) | 56 Nm (41 ft-lb)<br>+ additional 90° |
| Road wheel to hub | 120 Nm (89 ft-lb) |
| Stabilizer bar link to strut<br>• M10 (replace with new) | 58 Nm (43 ft-lb) |
| Tension strut to subframe:<br>• M12 8.8 (replace with new)<br><br>• M12 10.9 (replace with new) | 68 Nm (50 ft-lb)<br>+ additional 90°<br>100 Nm (74 ft-lb)<br>+ additional 90° |
| Tie rod to steering knuckle | 80 Nm (59 ft-lb) |

*Front differential flange seal, replacing*

## Front differential flange seal, replacing

– Raise front of vehicle and support safely.

> **WARNING** —
> • *Make sure the vehicle is stable and well supported at all times. Use a professional automotive lift or jack stands designed for the purpose. A floor jack is not adequate support.*

– Remove front wheel.

– Remove splash shield and front end reinforcement (if applicable) from below engine compartment. See **310 Front Suspension**.

– Remove front ABS wheel speed sensor. See **340 Brakes**.

– Remove front brake caliper and tie up. Do not detach brake fluid line. See **340 Brakes**.

– Detach tie rod end from steering knuckle. See **320 Steering and Wheel Alignment**.

– Detach tension strut and bushing from steering knuckle. See **310 Front Suspension**.

– Detach control arm from steering knuckle. See **310 Front Suspension**.

◄ Remove pinch-bolt (**arrow**) securing front strut to steering knuckle. See **310 Front Suspension**.

> **NOTE** —
> • *Rear drive shown. xDrive is similar.*

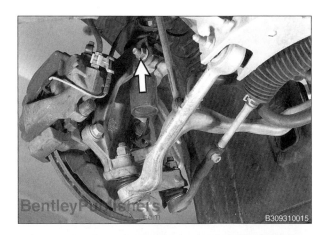

B309310015

◄ Use BMW special tool 31 5 110 or equivalent prying tool to force drive axle inner CV joint shaft out of front differential or right bearing pedestal output flange. Be prepared to catch dripping oil.

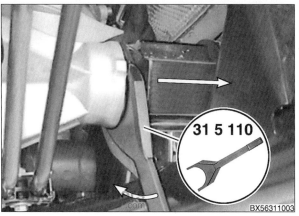

31 5 110

BX56311003

*Front differential flange seal, replacing*

◀ Note that drive axle is removed along with steering knuckle as a single unit.

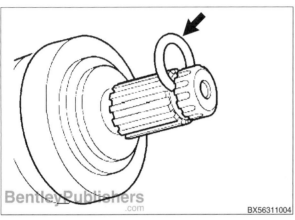

◀ Replace inner CV joint locking circlip (**arrow**).

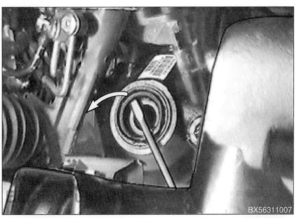

◀ Use seal removal tool or screw driver to pry flange seal out of differential or bearing pedestal.

− Remove protective sleeve from new flange seal and save for use during drive axle installation. Seal is equipped with protective covering to prevent sealing lip from damage during installation.

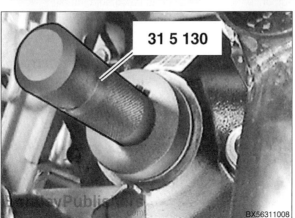

◀ Use BMW special tool 31 3 130 or equivalent seal driver to drive flange seal into differential or bearing pedestal as far as it will go.

− Coat sealing lip of flange seal with transmission fluid.

− Insert protective sleeve into seal.

– Install drive axle:

  • Insert inboard end of drive axle partially into differential housing or bearing pedestal.

  • Withdraw protective sleeve from sealing lip, cut protective sleeve and remove sleeve.

  • Continue pressing drive axle in until spring clip snaps audibly into place.

– Remainder of installation is reverse of removal. Check front differential oil level and top off if necessary. See **Front differential oil, checking** in this repair group.

| Tightening torques | |
|---|---|
| Brake pad carrier to steering knuckle | 110 Nm (81 ft-lb) |
| Control arm to subframe:<br>• M12 8.8 (replace with new)<br><br>• M12 10.9 (replace with new) | 68 Nm (50 ft-lb)<br>+ additional 90°<br>100 Nm (74 ft-lb)<br>+ additional 90° |
| Reinforcement plate to front subframe (replace fasteners) | 56 Nm (41 ft-lb)<br>+ additional 90° |
| Road wheel to hub | 120 Nm (89 ft-lb) |
| Stabilizer bar link to strut:<br>• M10 (replace with new) | 58 Nm (43 ft-lb) |
| Strut to steering knuckle pinch bolt:<br>• M10 (replace with new)<br>• M12 (replace with new) | 45 Nm (34 ft-lb)<br>81 Nm (60 ft-lb) |
| Tension strut to subframe:<br>• M12 8.8 (replace with new)<br><br>• M12 10.9 (replace with new) | 68 Nm (50 ft-lb)<br>+ additional 90°<br>100 Nm (74 ft-lb)<br>+ additional 90° |
| Tie rod to steering knuckle | 80 Nm (59 ft-lb) |

**311**

## Outer CV joint boot, replacing

When replacing CV boot, use a complete boot repair kit available from an authorized BMW dealer parts department. The kit includes new boot, clamping bands, special lubricant and a new CV joint shaft circlip.

– Remove drive axle. See **Drive axle, removing and installing** in this repair group. Place axle in shop vice with aluminum jaws.

– Release retaining clamps from both ends of outer CV boot. Cut off boot and discard.

– Using a soft-faced hammer, pound outer CV joint off drive axle.

– Using a flat blade screw driver, pry spring clip off drive axle splines.

– Clean old lubricant off axle splines.

*Outer CV joint boot, replacing*

– Inspect CV joint carefully.

- Look for galling, pitting and other signs of wear or physical damage.
- Polished surfaces or visible ball tracks alone are not necessarily cause for replacement.
- Discoloration (overheating) indicates lack of lubrication.

– Place new clamping bands and CV boot over drive axle.

– Replace spring clip on splined end of drive axle.

– Apply Loctite® 270 or an equivalent heavy-duty locking compound to drive axle splines.

> **CAUTION—**
> - *Do not let locking compound contact balls in joint. Apply only a thin coat to cover splines.*

– Pack joint with fresh CV joint grease.

| CV joint lubricant capacity | |
|---|---|
| Outer CV joint | 80 grams (2.8 oz) |

– Tap CV joint onto splined end of drive axle until spring clip snaps audibly into place.

– Using clamp pliers, secure retaining clamp into position tightly sealing large end of boot against CV joint.

◄ Before installing small boot clamp:

- Flex CV joint as far over as it will go.
- Insert small screw-driver between boot and axle-shaft to "burp" boot.

– With outer boot full of grease, and any air eliminated from boot, secure small end of boot on CV joint by pinching clamp with pliers.

– Remainder of installation is reverse of removal. See **Drive axle, removing and installing** in this repair group.

– Check front differential oil level and top off if necessary. See **Front differential oil, checking** in this repair group.

BX56311009

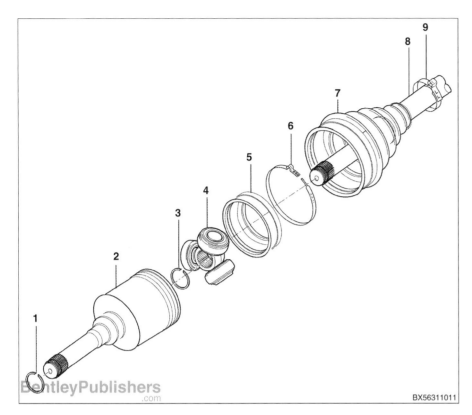

BX56311011

## Inner CV joint (triple-roller)

1. Locking circlip
2. Inner CV joint housing
3. Circlip
4. Triple roller bearing
5. Inner CV joint boot adapter
6. Clamp
7. Inner CV joint boot
8. Drive axle shaft
9. Clamp

## Inner CV joint boot, replacing

When replacing CV boot, use a complete boot repair kit available from an authorized BMW dealer parts department. The kit includes new boot, clamping bands, special lubricant and a new outer CV joint axle circlip.

– Remove drive axle. See **Drive axle, removing and installing** in this repair group.

– Release retaining clamp on both ends of inner CV boot. Pull back inner boot and detach inner CV joint housing.

– Remove circlip retaining triple roller bearing to drive axle and remove triple roller bearing.

– Slide boot off drive axle. Separate inner CV joint boot adapter from boot.

– Clean old lubricant off axle splines and triple roller bearing splines.

– Install new inner CV joint boot:
  • Attach boot to boot adapter.
  • Slide retaining clamps and boot over drive axle.
  • Secure retaining clamp using clamp pliers, tightly sealing small end of boot against drive axle.

311

*Front differential oil level, checking*

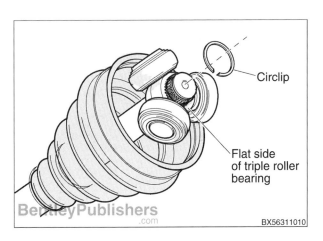

Circlip

Flat side
of triple roller
bearing

BX56311010

◀ Install triple roller bearing with flat edge of joint facing retaining
circlip.

– Replace inner CV joint housing shaft circlip.

– Pack triple roller bearing and boot with fresh CV joint grease.

| CV joint lubricant capacity | |
| --- | --- |
| Inner CV joint | 80 grams (2.8 oz) |

– Insert triple roller bearing into inner CV joint housing.

– Secure boot connection to boot adapter using clamp supplied with
boot kit.

– Remainder of installation is reverse of removal. See **Drive axle,
removing and installing** in this repair group.

– Check front differential oil level and top off if necessary. See **Front
differential oil, checking** in this repair group.

## FRONT DIFFERENTIAL

The front differential on xDrive models is filled with lifetime oil that
ordinarily does not need to be changed. If service is required, BMW
recommends using only a specially formulated synthetic gear oil
(SAF-XO). For additional information on this lubricant and any other
lubricants that may be compatible, contact an authorized BMW
dealer parts department.

Replacement of O-ring seal between engine oil pan and front
differential is covered in **Front differential, removing and
installing** in this repair group.

Replacement of O-ring seal between engine oil pan and right side
bearing pedestal is covered in **Right axle bearing pedestal,
removing and installing** in this repair group.

| Table a. Differential fluid | |
| --- | --- |
| Capacity | 0.6 ltr (0.63 qt) |
| BMW specification | SAF-XO Synthetic |

### Front differential oil level, checking

– Drive vehicle a short distance to warm differential oil.

– Raise vehicle and support safely.

> **WARNING —**
> • *Make sure the vehicle is stable and well supported at all times.
> Use a professional automotive lift or jack stands designed for
> the purpose. A floor jack is not adequate support.*

– Remove splash shield and front end reinforcement (if applicable).
See **310 Front Suspension**.

*Front differential oil, draining and filling*

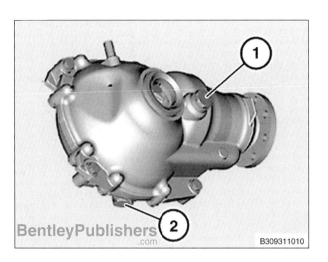

B309311010

◄ With vehicle level, check oil at filler plug (**1**):
- Place a drain pan under oil filler plug.
- Oil level is correct when it just reaches edge of filler hole.

— If necessary, top up fluid with synthetic gear oil (SAF-XO).

— Replace filler plug sealing ring.

— Install and tighten oil filler plug when oil level is correct.

| Tightening torque | |
|---|---|
| Oil drain / fill plug to differential | 60 Nm (44 ft-lb) |

## Front differential oil, draining and filling

— Drive vehicle a short distance to warm differential oil.

— Raise vehicle and safely support.

> **WARNING—**
> • Make sure the vehicle is stable and well supported at all times. Use a professional automotive lift or jack stands designed for the purpose. A floor jack is not adequate support.

— Remove splash shield and front end reinforcement (if applicable). See **310 Front Suspension**.

◄ With vehicle level, Change oil at drain plug (**2**):
- Place a drain pan under oil drain plug.
- Remove drain plug and allow oil to drain into pan.

> **WARNING—**
> • Pull the loose plug away quickly to avoid being scalded by hot oil. Use gloves to protect your hands.

— When oil flow has diminished to an occasional drip, reinstall drain plug with new sealing ring.

— Remove filler plug (**1**).

— Add synthetic gear oil (SAF-XO) and check level. See **Front differential oil level, checking** in this repair group.

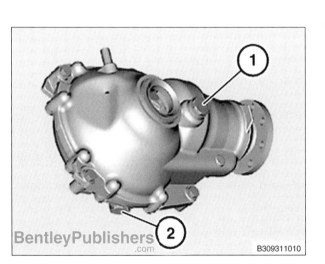

B309311010

| Tightening torque | |
|---|---|
| Oil drain / fill plug to differential | 60 Nm (44 ft-lb) |

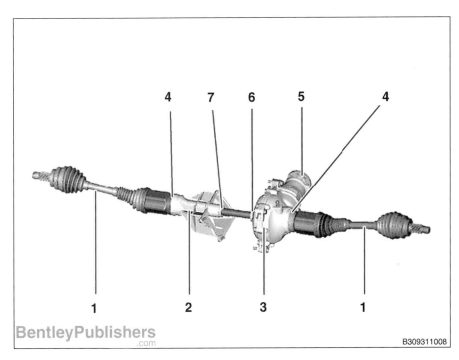

B309311008

## Front differential and right bearing pedestal components

1. Drive axles and boots

2. Right bearing pedestal

3. Front differential

4. Output shaft seal

5. Drive flange seal

6. O-ring, differential

7. O-ring, right bearing pedestal

## Front differential, removing and installing

— Disconnect negative (-) battery cable.

> **CAUTION—**
> • *Prior to disconnecting the battery, read the battery disconnection cautions in* **001 Warnings and Cautions**.

— Remove cabin microfilter housing. See **640 Heating and Air-conditioning**.

— Remove air intake hood above radiator.

— Remove upper engine cover (ignition coil cover). See **020 Maintenance**.

— Non-turbo engine: Remove air filter housing. See **020 Maintenance**.

— Raise engine hood into assembly position. See **410 Fender, Engine Hood**.

— Raise vehicle and support safely.

> **WARNING—**
> • *Make sure the vehicle is stable and well supported at all times. Use a professional automotive lift or jack stands designed for the purpose. A floor jack is not adequate support.*

— Remove splash shield and front end reinforcement (if applicable) from under engine. See **310 Front Suspension**.

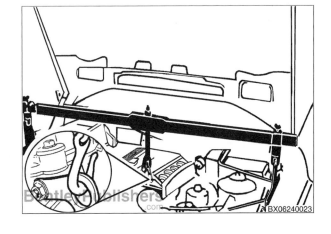

BX06240023

◀ Install engine support brace across engine bay. Raise engine slightly (¼ - ½ in) to release load on engine mounts.

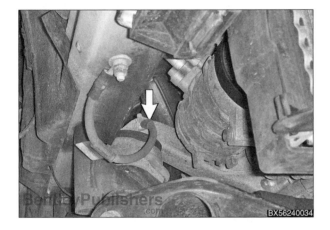

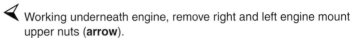

◁ Working underneath engine, remove right and left engine mount upper nuts (**arrow**).

– Remove left front wheel.

– Remove left front ABS wheel speed sensor. See **340 Brakes**.

– Remove front brake caliper and tie up. Do not detach brake fluid line. See **340 Brakes**.

– Detach left tie rod end from steering knuckle. See **320 Steering and Wheel Alignment**.

– Detach left tension strut and bushing from steering knuckle. See **310 Front Suspension**.

– Detach left control arm from steering knuckle. See **310 Front Suspension**.

◁ Remove pinch-bolt (**arrow**) securing front strut to steering knuckle. See **310 Front Suspension**.

*NOTE* —
• *Rear drive shown. xDrive is similar*

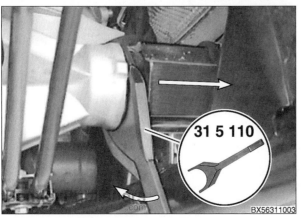

◁ Use BMW special tool 31 5 110 or equivalent prying tool to force left front drive axle inner CV joint shaft out of front differential output flange. Be prepared to catch dripping oil.

◀ Note that drive axle is removed along with steering knuckle as a single unit.

– Unbolt steering spindle universal joint from steering rack.

◀ Support front subframe with block of wood placed on transmission jack.

**NOTE—**
- *Steering rack remains bolted to front subframe.*

– Unbolt front subframe from vehicle frame. Carefully lower by approx. 46 mm (2 in) and insert longer bolts to support it.

> **CAUTION—**
> - *Lower subframe without damaging power steering lines. Make sure it is adequately supported throughout the remainder of this procedure.*

– Remove left engine mount.

– Pull off front differential vent hose.

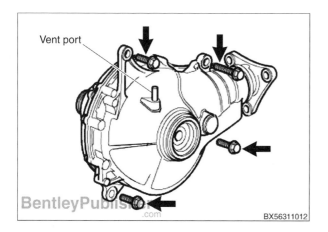

Vent port

◀ Remove bolts (**arrows**) and lower differential carefully, making sure that no lines, hoses or harnesses become snagged.

*Right axle bearing pedestal, removing and installing*

— Replace O-ring between oil pan and differential before reinstalling differential. Coat O-ring with differential oil.

— Install differential to oil pan.

| Tightening torques | |
|---|---|
| Front differential to oil pan | 65 Nm (48 ft-lb) |

— Remainder of assembly is reverse of removal. Keep in mind:

  • Replace drive axle flange seal before installing drive axle.

  • Check front differential oil level and top off if necessary. See **Front differential oil, checking** in this repair group.

  • Use BMW scan tool to carry out steering angle sensor adjustment.

| Tightening torques | |
|---|---|
| Brake pad carrier to steering knuckle | 110 Nm (81 ft-lb) |
| Control arm to steering knuckle:<br>• M14 8.8 (replace with new)<br>• M14 10.9 (replace with new) | 80 Nm (59 ft-lb)<br>165 Nm (122 ft-lb) |
| Tension strut to steering knuckle | 165 Nm (122 ft-lb) |
| Oil filler plug to differential | 60 Nm (44 ft-lb) |
| Reinforcement plate to front subframe (replace fasteners) | 56 Nm (41 ft-lb)<br>+ 90° |
| Road wheel to hub | 120 Nm (89 ft-lb) |
| Tie rod end to steering knuckle (replace with new) | 80 Nm (59 ft-lb) |
| Engine mount to engine bracket<br>• M10 10.9 grade<br>• E92 M10 | 56 Nm (41 ft-lb)<br>38 Nm (28 ft-lb) |
| Front subframe to chassis:<br>• M12<br>• M10 | 108 Nm (80 ft-lb)<br>56 Nm (41 ft-lb)<br>+ additional 90° |
| Steering spindle universal joint to steering rack (pinch bolt) | 21 Nm (16 ft-lb) |
| Strut assembly to steering knuckle:<br>• M10 (replace with new)<br>• M12 (replace with new) | 45 Nm (34 ft-lb)<br>81 Nm (60 ft-lb) |

**311**

**Right axle bearing pedestal, removing and installing**

*Differential input flange seal, replacing*

— Raise vehicle and support safely.

> **WARNING—**
> • Make sure the vehicle is stable and well supported at all times. Use a professional automotive lift or jack stands designed for the purpose. A floor jack is not adequate support.

— Remove splash shield and front end reinforcement (if applicable) from under engine. See **310 Front Suspension**.

— Remove right front wheel.

— Remove right front ABS wheel speed sensor. See **340 Brakes**.

— Remove right front brake caliper and tie up. Do not detach brake fluid line. See **340 Brakes**.

— Detach right tie rod end from steering knuckle. See **320 Steering and Wheel Alignment**.

— Detach right tension strut and control arm from steering knuckle. See **310 Front Suspension**.

— Remove pinch-bolt securing right front strut to steering knuckle.

— Use BMW special tool 31 5 110 or equivalent prying tool to force right front drive axle inner CV joint shaft out of right axle bearing pedestal flange. Be prepared to catch dripping oil.

◄ Note that drive axle is removed along with steering knuckle as a single unit.

BX56311006a

◄ Remove bearing pedestal mounting bolts (**arrows**) at side of oil pan. Lift off pedestal.

— When reinstalling:
  • Replace sealing O-ring (**arrow**). Coat O-ring with assembly fluid.
  • Replace drive axle flange seal before installing drive axle.

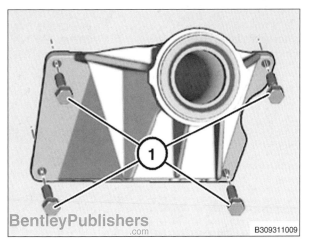

B309311009

## Differential input flange seal, replacing

**Tightening torques**

| | |
|---|---|
| Bearing pedestal to oil pan | 27 Nm (20 ft-lb) |
| Brake pad carrier to steering knuckle | 110 Nm (81 ft-lb) |
| Control arm to steering knuckle:<br>• M14 8.8 (replace with new)<br>• M14 10.9 (replace with new) | <br>80 Nm (59 ft-lb)<br>165 Nm (122 ft-lb) |
| Tension strut to steering knuckle | 165 Nm (122 ft-lb) |
| Reinforcement plate to front subframe<br>(replace fasteners) | 56 Nm (41 ft-lb)<br>+ additional 90° |
| Road wheel to hub | 120 Nm (89 ft-lb) |
| Strut assembly to steering knuckle:<br>• M10 (replace with new)<br>• M12 (replace with new) | <br>45 Nm (34 ft-lb)<br>81 Nm (60 ft-lb) |
| Tie rod end to steering knuckle<br>(replace with new) | 80 Nm (59 ft-lb) |

— Raise vehicle and support safely.

> **WARNING —**
> • Make sure the vehicle is stable and well supported at all times. Use a professional automotive lift or jack stands designed for the purpose. A floor jack is not adequate support.

— Remove front driveshaft. See **260 Driveshafts**.

— Pry out input flange retaining nut lock plate.

◀ Using a center punch, mark relation of input flange retaining nut to shaft.

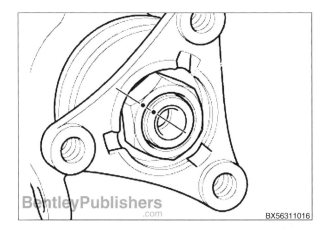

◀ Counterhold input flange using BMW special tool 23 0 020 and remove nut.

— Remove input flange out of differential using hub puller. Be prepared to catch dripping oil.

— Remove input seal dust shields.

— Using a seal puller or flat screwdriver, pry seal out of differential housing.

— Coat sealing edges of seal with transmission fluid and drive into differential housing using BMW special tool 31 5 130 or equivalent drift.

— Replace dust shields.

**23 0 020**

*Differential input flange seal, replacing*

— Clean input flange and install into differential housing.

  • Tighten down nut until punch marks align.

  • Install new input flange retaining nut locking plate.

> **CAUTION—**
> • *Do not torque input flange retaining nut beyond match marks. Over-torquing can damage differential internals.*
> • *Do not replace input flange or input flange locking nut.*

— Remainder of installation is reverse of removal. Check front differential oil level and top off if necessary. See **Front differential oil, checking** in this repair group.

| Tightening torque | |
|---|---|
| Oil drain / fill plug to differential | 60 Nm (44 ft-lb) |

# 320  Steering and Wheel Alignment

**320**

## GENERAL

This repair group covers steering wheel and column removal and steering system service, including wheel alignment information. For additional information, see:

- **513 Interior Trim** for steering column trim
- **612 Switches** for steering column switch cluster (SZL) and START / STOP switch
- **721 Airbag System (SRS)** for driver airbag

### Steering system

3 Series models are equipped with a power-assisted steering rack mounted to a steel subframe. Power boost for the steering is provided by an engine-driven hydraulic pump.

The steering wheel connects to the steering rack via an adjustable steering column which incorporates a sliding spindle to dampen vibration and noise.

Power steering fluid is supplied from the fluid reservoir to the pump and to the steering rack via rubber and metal lines.

The return line from the steering rack to the reservoir loops into the airstream in front of the radiator and acts as the steering fluid cooler.

The steering system requires no maintenance other than alignment and periodic inspection for worn components. Inspect tie rod end boots periodically for tears or damage. Replace tie rod end if necessary.

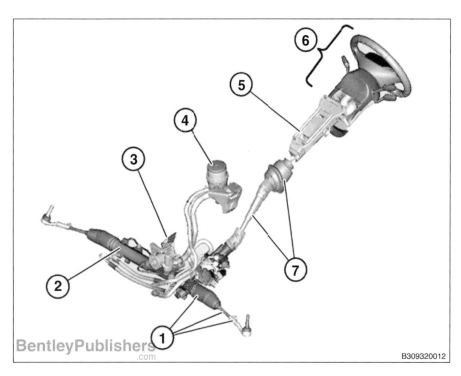

BentleyPublishers.com

B309320012

## Steering components

1. Tie rod end, tie rod, steering rack boot

2. Steering rack

3. Power steering pump

4. Power steering reservoir

5. Steering column (upper) and adjustment mechanism

6. Steering wheel and switch housing

7. Lower steering spindle and sleeve

## Warnings and Cautions

**WARNING —**

- *The airbag mounted in the steering wheel is an explosive device. Treat it with extreme caution. Follow the airbag removal procedure in 721 Airbag System (SRS).*

- *Serious injury may result if airbag system service is attempted by persons unfamiliar with the BMW SRS and its approved service procedures.*

- *Before performing any work involving airbags, disconnect the negative (-) battery cable.*

- *Prior to disconnecting the battery, read the battery disconnections cautions given in 001 Warnings and Cautions.*

- *BMW airbags are equipped with a back-up power supply inside the airbag control module. Observe a 5 second waiting period after disconnecting the battery cable to allow the reserve power supply to discharge.*

- *Do not reuse self-locking nuts. They are designed to be used only once and may fail if reused. Replace with new.*

- *Do not install bolts and nuts coated with undercoating wax, as correct tightening torque cannot be assured. Clean the threads with solvent before installation, or install new parts.*

- *Do not attempt to weld or straighten steering components. Replace damaged parts.*

**CAUTION—**

- *When working with power steering components, maintain absolute cleanliness to ensure proper operation of the hydraulic system.*

- *Follow local, state and federal regulations for safe disposal of power steering fluid.*

- *To avoid electrochemical corrosion to engine components made of aluminum-magnesium alloy, do not use steel fasteners. Use aluminum fasteners only.*

- *The end faces of aluminum fasteners are usually painted blue. For reliable identification, test fasteners for aluminum composition with magnet.*

- *Replace aluminum bolts each time they are loosened.*

- *Follow torque instructions, including angle of rotation specifications, when installing aluminum fasteners.*

- *To prevent marring interior trim, work with plastic prying tools or wrap the tips of screwdrivers and pliers with tape before prying out switches or trim.*

**320**

## STEERING WHEEL

3 Series vehicles are equipped with one of two different styles of steering wheel:

### Multifunction steering wheel switches

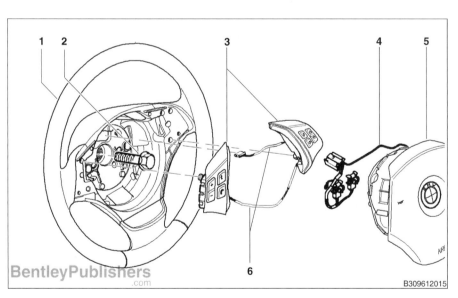

1. Multifunction steering wheel

2. Mounting bolt (M16)
   - Tighten to 63 Nm (46 ft-lb)

3. Multifunction switches

4. Airbag and horn electrical harness

5. Airbag unit and horn button

6. Multifunction switch electrical harness

BentleyPublishers.com

B309612015

## Sport steering wheel switches

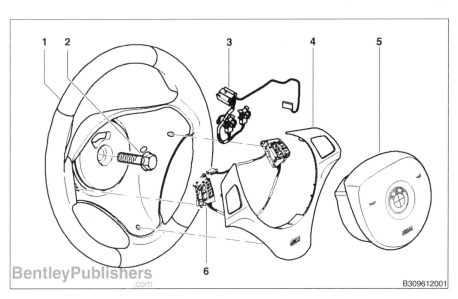

1. Sport steering wheel
2. Mounting bolt (M16)
   • Tighten to 63 Nm (46 ft-lb)
3. Airbag and horn electrical harness
4. Plastic trim
5. Airbag unit and horn button
6. Radio and telephone control switches

## Steering angle sensor

The steering angle sensor is integral with the steering column switch cluster (SZL). For more information, including removal and installation of the SZL, see **612 Switches**.

To reset steering angle sensor, connect vehicle to BMW diagnostic tool and carry out steering angle sensor adjustment system function.

## Steering wheel, removing and installing

− Center steering wheel. Make sure front wheels are pointed straight ahead.

− Disconnect negative (-) cable from battery.

> **CAUTION—**
> • *Prior to disconnecting the battery, read the battery disconnection cautions given in **001 Warnings and Cautions***.

− Extend steering wheel as far back and as low as possible.

− Remove driver airbag in steering wheel. See **721 Airbag System (SRS)**.

> **WARNING —**
> • *The steering wheel mounted airbag is an explosive device. Treat with extreme caution. Follow the airbag removal procedure in **721 Airbag System (SRS)***.
> • *Airbag removal may set SRS fault codes. The SRS indicator light remains ON until problems are corrected and fault memory cleared.*

◄ Remove steering wheel center bolt (**arrow**).

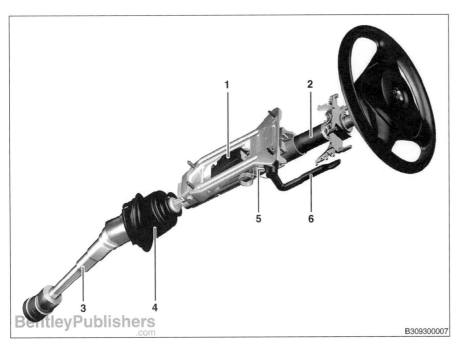

> **CAUTION—**
> • *The SRS contact reel (also known as airbag contact ring / slip ring) is integral with the steering column switch block. The contact reel is a wound coil of wire that ensures continuous electrical contact for the airbag and steering wheel electrical components. When the steering wheel is removed the contact reel is locked and its position must not be altered.*

◀ Check for proper alignment of steering column marks (**arrow**) before removing steering wheel.

> **NOTE—**
> • *The steering column and steering wheel are match marked at the factory.*

– Remove steering wheel.

– When installing steering wheel:
  • Align steering wheel and column match marks.
  • Align steering wheel to alignment pins located on steering column switch block.
  • Install steering column center bolt. Do not over-torque.

| Tightening torques | |
|---|---|
| Steering wheel to steering shaft (M14) | 63 Nm (47 ft-lb) |

– Carefully install airbag. See **721 Airbag System (SRS)**.

## STEERING COLUMN

### Steering column components

1. Electric steering lock or ELV (2006 only)
2. Crash absorbing element
3. Lower steering shaft spindle
4. Rubber boot
5. Steering column adjustment lock
6. Steering column adjustment lever

**320**

## Steering column, removing and installing

— Disconnect negative (-) battery cable and cover battery terminal to keep cable from accidentally contacting terminal.

> **CAUTION—**
> • Prior to disconnecting the battery, read the battery disconnection cautions given in **001 Warnings and Cautions**.

— Extend steering wheel as far back and as low as possible.

— Remove driver airbag. See **721 Airbag System (SRS)**.

> **WARNING —**
> • The steering wheel mounted airbag is an explosive device. Treat with extreme caution. Follow the airbag removal procedure in **721 Airbag System (SRS)**.
> • Airbag removal may set SRS fault codes. The SRS indicator light remains ON until problems are corrected and fault memory cleared.

— Remove steering wheel. See **Steering wheel, removing and installing** in this repair group.

> **CAUTION—**
> • Do not move front wheels from straight-ahead position while steering wheel is off.
> • Do not turn or twist the airbag and horn contact spring.

— Remove steering column trim, left lower dashboard trim and left dashboard panel. See **513 Interior Trim**.

— Remove left footwell duct.

— Disconnect harness connectors for steering column switch cluster.

— Remove wiring harness from steering column.

◀ Working in footwell, slide sleeve (**1**) for steering spindle upwards on steering column.

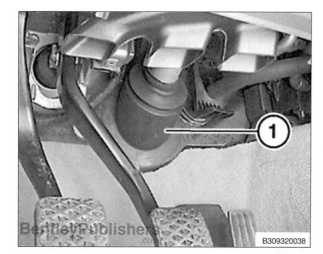

◀ Remove pinch bolt (**1**) joining upper section of steering spindle (**2**) to lower section.

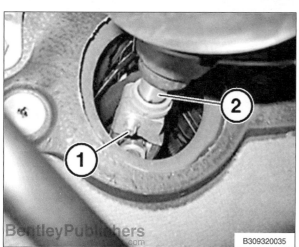

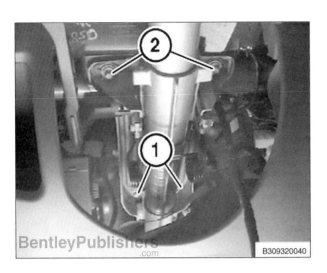

B309320040

◀ Working underneath steering column:

  • Loosen and remove steering column fasteners (**1**).

  • Have an assistant support column and remove fasteners (**2**). Guide column off of steering spindle swivel joint and remove.

— Remainder of installation is reverse of removal. Remember to:

  • Make sure spindle sleeve is slid on column.

  • Clean all threads of residual adhesive.

  • Align upper steering column with lower spindle clamp. Pinch bolt must rest in groove of steering column. Use new pinch bolt.

  • Fit spindle sleeve back into opening in floorboard. Align marks on sleeve and floorboard.

  • Use new bolts to mount column to dashboard brace.

| Tightening torque | |
| --- | --- |
| Steering column to dashboard (M8) | 21 Nm (15.5 ft-lb) |
| Steering column to lower spindle (M8) | 21 Nm (15.5 ft-lb) |

— Check steering system for freedom of movement through entire steering column adjustment range.

— Carry out steering angle sensor adjustment using BMW scan tool. If replacing steering angle sensor, code using BMW scan tool before performing steering angle offset check.

## Lower steering spindle, removing and installing

— Extend steering wheel as far back and as high as possible.

— Move steering wheel to straight ahead position and remove ignition key.

— Remove left lower dashboard trim. See **513 Interior Trim**.

— Working in footwell, push upper spindle towards column and secure.

— Non turbo models: Working in engine compartment, remove intake air filter housing and ductwork. See **130 Fuel Injection**.

◀ Release pinch bolt (**1**) at steering spindle swivel joint (**2**).

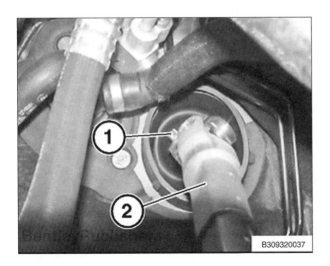

B309320037

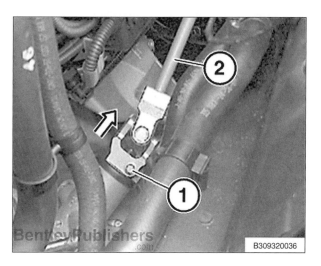

B309320036

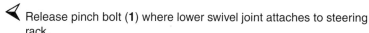Release pinch bolt (**1**) where lower swivel joint attaches to steering rack.

– Detach lower steering spindle (**2**) from rack in direction of **arrow**.

– Detach lower steering spindle from upper spindle and remove.

– Installation is reverse of removal. Remember to:

  • Clean all threads of residual adhesive.

  • Pinch bolts must rest in groove of steering column and steering rack. Use new pinch bolts.

| Tightening torque | |
|---|---|
| Steering lower spindle to steering rack (M8) | 21 Nm (15.5 ft-lb) |
| Steering upper spindle to lower spindle (M8) | 21 Nm (15.5 ft-lb) |

– Check steering system for freedom of movement through entire steering column adjustment range.

– Carry out steering angle sensor adjustment using BMW scan tool. If replacing steering angle sensor, code using BMW scan tool before performing steering angle offset check.

## POWER STEERING PUMP

Power assist is provided by a belt-driven pump at the lower left front of the engine. The power steering fluid reservoir is located at the left side of the engine compartment.

### Power steering system, bleeding and filling

The power steering system is permanently filled with either CHF or ATF hydraulic fluid. Routinely adding fluid is not required unless the system is leaking.

> **CAUTION—**
> • *Power steering reservoir cap is marked with the type of fluid being used— ATF or CHF. Do not mix.*

B309020078

◄ To check power steering fluid level in fluid reservoir:
  • Park vehicle on level ground with engine off.
  • Level is correct if it is between **MIN** and **MAX** marks on dipstick.
  • If level is below **MIN** mark, add fluid to reservoir to bring level up.

> *CAUTION—*
> • *Correct power steering fluid level can show as much as 10 mm (0.4 in) high when engine is at normal operating temperature. Do not draw off fluid to* **MAX** *mark when checking fluid with engine warmed up.*

– To bleed power steering system, start engine. Turn steering wheel twice to left lock and right lock.

– Recheck fluid level with engine off. Fill to MAX.

– Hand-tighten reservoir cap.

| Power steering fluid application | |
| --- | --- |
| 3 Series (E90, E91, E92, E93):<br>• Green label (check cap)<br>• Black label (check cap) | Pentosin CHF 11 S<br>ATF Dexron III |

## Power steering pump, removing and installing

– Remove intake air filter housing. See **130 Fuel Injection**.

– Drain power steering fluid reservoir using clean syringe. Do not reuse fluid.

– Raise front of car.

> *WARNING—*
> • *Make sure the car is firmly supported on jack stands designed for the purpose. Place jack stands underneath structural chassis points, not underneath suspension parts.*

– Remove splash shield from under engine.

– Remove accessory belt from power steering pump. See **020 Maintenance**. Mark direction of rotation if reusing belt.

◄ Working under vehicle, release hose clamp (**1**) and detach low pressure fluid hose (**2**) from pump. Be prepared to catch dripping fluid.

– Plug openings in pump and hose ends to prevent contamination.

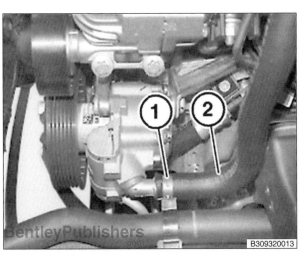

*Power steering pump, removing and installing*

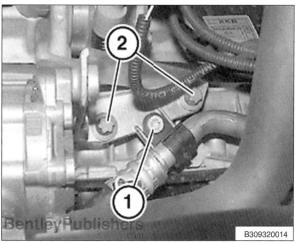

◀ Remove fastener (**1**) for A/C refrigerant line clamp.

– Remove fasteners (**2**) for power steering pump bracket.

◀ Remove banjo bolt (**1**) and detach high pressure fluid hose from pump. Be prepared to catch dripping fluid.

– Plug openings in pump and hoses to prevent contamination.

– Remove fasteners (**2**) and remove power steering pump out from below.

– When installing pump, replace aluminium fasteners with new, tighten pump fasteners finger tight and observe the following tightening sequence:

1. Tighten side bracket fasteners to 2 Nm (18 in-lb).

2. Tighten front bracket fasteners to 2 Nm (18 in-lb)

3. Tighten front bracket fasteners to final specification.

4. Release side bracket fasteners and make sure bracket is flush with engine block.

5. Tighten side bracket fasteners to final specification.

| Tightening torques | |
|---|---|
| Power steering pump to block (except N54 engine) | 20 Nm (15 ft-lb) + 90° |
| Power steering pump to block (N54 engine) | 38 Nm (28 ft-lb) |

– Remainder of installation is reverse of removal. Remember to:

• Replace sealing rings on high pressure fluid hose.

• Fill and bleed hydraulic system.

• Check for leaks.

| Tightening torque | |
|---|---|
| Hydraulic line to power steering pump (replace sealing rings) | 35 Nm (26 ft-lb) |

## MECHANICAL STEERING COMPONENTS

### Steering rack, removing and installing

— Drain power steering fluid reservoir using clean syringe. Do not reuse fluid.

— Raise front of car and remove front wheels.

> **WARNING—**
> • *Make sure the car is firmly supported on jack stands designed for the purpose. Place jack stands underneath structural chassis points, not underneath suspension parts.*

— Remove splash shield from underneath engine. See **020 Maintenance**.

— Detach tie rod ends from steering knuckles. See **Tie rod (outer), replacing** in this repair group.

— If necessary, remove heat shield from power steering rack.

— Remove steering spindle universal joint pinch bolt and disengage spindle from steering rack.

◀ Release banjo bolt fasteners (**1** and **4**). Remove pressure line (**2**) and return line (**3**) from steering rack. Be prepared to catch dripping fluid.

— Tie hydraulic lines off to side. If necessary, remove hydraulic line bracket from power steering pump. See **Power steering pump, removing and installing** in this repair group.

— Plug openings in rack and hoses to prevent contamination.

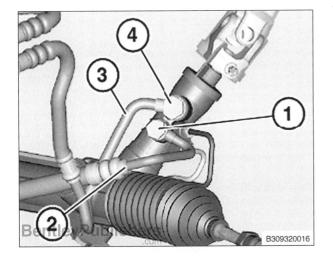

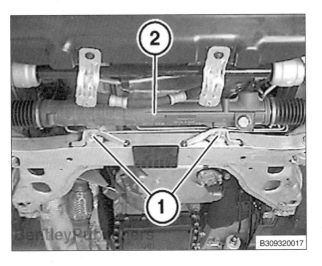

◀ Release fasteners (**1**) and remove steering rack (**2**) forward and down.

— Installation is reverse of removal, keeping in mind the following:
  • Make sure all threaded bores, bolts, nuts, splines and mating surfaces are clean.
  • Replace banjo bolt sealing O-rings. Do not overtorque banjo bolts.
  • Make sure power steering fluid lines are routed without tension and with sufficient spacing to nearby components.
  • Use new steering rack mounting bolts. Tighten in two stages.
  • Replace steering spindle double universal joint pinch bolt(s).
  • Use new self-locking fasteners wherever applicable.

| Tightening torques | |
|---|---|
| Hydraulic lines to steering rack:<br>• M14<br>• M16 | 30 Nm (22 ft-lb)<br>35 Nm (26 ft-lb) |
| Steering rack to subframe M10<br>(replace fasteners with new) | 56 Nm (41 ft-lb)<br>+ 90° |
| Tie rod end to steering knuckle<br>(replace fastener with new) | 80 Nm (59 ft-lb) |

— Rotate steering wheel and check that steering spindle and steering double universal joint do not contact vehicle chassis or front subframe. If necessary, loosen steering rack and rotate in slotted holes for better steering spindle clearance.

— After reassembling steering and front suspension:

• Fill and bleed power steering system. Check system for leaks. See **Power steering system, bleeding and filling** in this repair group.

• Have car professionally aligned.

• Carry out steering angle sensor adjustment using BMW scan tool.

## Steering rack boot, replacing

— Raise front of car. Remove road wheel.

> **WARNING—**
> • *Make sure the car is firmly supported on jack stands designed for the purpose. Place jack stands underneath structural chassis points, not underneath suspension parts.*

— Remove splash shield underneath engine.

◀ Make length reference mark on tie rod, then remove outer tie rod end. See **Tie rod (outer), replacing**.

— Cut rack boot band clamps and slide off boot. Inspect boot for any sign of damage. Replace if necessary.

> **NOTE—**
> • *New rack boot kit comes with new band clamps.*

— Grease tie rod taper so that small end of rack boot slides on tie rod when tie rod is tightened, preventing rack boot from twisting.

— Slide new boot into position and replace band clamps. Reinstall tie rod end using previously made reference marks.

B309320043

| Tightening torques | |
|---|---|
| Tie rod end to tie rod (pinch bolt) | 40 Nm (30 ft-lb) |
| Tie rod to steering knuckle (use new nut) | 80 Nm (59 ft-lb) |

— After reassembling steering:

• Have car professionally aligned.

• Carry out steering angle sensor adjustment using BMW scan tool.

## Tie rod (outer), replacing

— Raise front of car. Remove road wheel.

> **WARNING**—
> • Make sure the car is firmly supported on jack stands designed for the purpose. Place jack stands underneath structural chassis points, not underneath suspension parts.

— Remove splash shield underneath engine.

◄ Make reference measurement (**A**) of outer tie rod end to tie rod. Record measurement.

> **NOTE**—
> • Accurate measurement of tie rod end with reference to tie rod helps approximate correct wheel alignment when new parts are installed.
> • Note correct placement of inner taper on locking ring.

◄ Working at outer end of tie rod:
   • Remove tie rod lock nut (**A**) at steering knuckle.
   • Loosen tie rod adjustment lock nut (**B**).

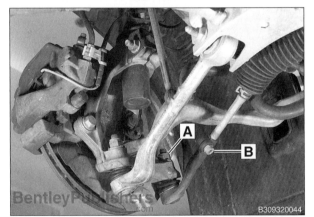

◄ Use BMW special tool 32 3 090 or equivalent to press tie rod end out of steering knuckle.

— Unscrew tie rod end from tie rod shaft.

— Installation is reverse of removal.
   • Make sure threaded parts are clean.
   • Use anti-seize paste on inner tie rod threads.
   • Use new self-locking nuts where applicable.
   • Use previously made reference marks to set toe temporarily.

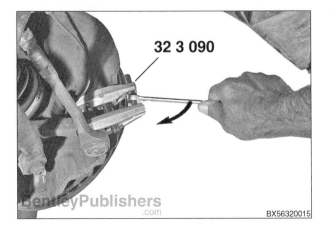

| Tightening torques | |
| --- | --- |
| Tie rod end to tie rod (pinch bolt) | 40 Nm (30 ft-lb) |
| Tie rod to steering knuckle (use new nut) | 80 Nm (59 ft-lb) |

— After reassembling steering:
   • Have car professionally aligned.
   • Carry out steering angle sensor adjustment using BMW scan tool.

## Tie rod (inner), replacing

– Raise front of car. Remove road wheel.

> **WARNING—**
> • *Make sure the car is firmly supported on jack stands designed for the purpose. Place jack stands underneath structural chassis points, not underneath suspension parts.*

– Make length reference mark on tie rod, then remove outer tie rod end. See **Tie rod (outer), replacing**.

– Cut rack boot clamps and slide boot off.

◄ Loosen and remove inner tie rod shaft (**1**) from steering rack.

> **CAUTION—**
> • *To avoid damage to steering rack while removing tie rod, turn steering until end of rack is as far as possible inside rack housing.*

B309320018

– When reassembling, grease tie rod taper so that rack boot support buffer or small end of rack boot slides on tie rod when tie rod is tightened, preventing rack boot from twisting.

– Inspect boot for any signs of damage. Replace boot if necessary, using new band clamps.

> **NOTE—**
> • *New rack boot comes with new band clamps.*

– Installation is reverse of removal, noting the following:
  • Make sure threaded parts are clean.
  • Use anti-seize paste on inner tie rod threads.
  • Tighten inner tie rod to rack in 2 stages.
  • Use new self-locking nuts where applicable.
  • Use previously made reference marks to set toe temporarily.

| Tightening torques | |
|---|---|
| Tie rod end to tie rod (pinch bolt) | 40 Nm (30 ft-lb) |
| Tie rod to steering knuckle | 80 Nm (59 ft-lb) |
| Tie rod to steering rack:<br>• ZF rack (fluid = Pentosin CHF 11S)<br>• TRW rack (fluid = ATF Dexron III) | 110 +10 Nm (81 +7 ft-lb)<br>100 +10 Nm (74 +7 ft-lb) |

– After reassembling steering:
  • Have car professionally aligned.
  • Carry out steering angle sensor adjustment using BMW scan tool.

## WHEEL ALIGNMENT

Proper handling, stability and driving ease depend upon the correct alignment of all four wheels. The front axle is aligned in relation to the rear axle, then the front wheels are aligned in relation to one another. This is known as a four-wheel or thrust-axis alignment.

BMW vehicles use a sophisticated multi-link suspension at the front and rear of the car. Proper alignment requires computerized alignment equipment.

For front and rear alignment specifications, see **Alignment specifications** in this repair group.

## Front toe, setting

Set front toe before adjusting camber. Camber and toe influence each other. Toe is the difference in the distance between the front of the wheels and the rear of the wheels. It is adjusted by altering the length of the tie rods.

Make toe adjustments with vehicle in normal loaded position. See **Normal loaded position** in this repair group.

– Clean threads on tie rod.

◀ Loosen tie rod adjuster pinch bolt (**A**).

• To adjust toe, grip tie rod end (**B**) and turn inner tie rod (**C**) to change length.

*NOTE—*

• *Center steering rack by aligning centering mark on steering shaft with lug on steering rack.*

• *To keep steering wheel centered, adjust both tie rods equal amounts.*

• *Make sure the rack boot moves freely on the tie rod and does not become twisted.*

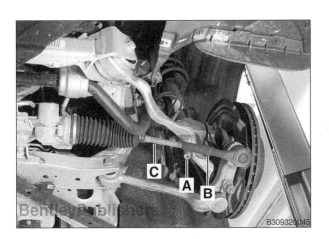

| Tightening torques | |
|---|---|
| Tie rod end to tie rod (pinch bolt) | 40 Nm (30 ft-lb) |

**320**

## Front camber, adjusting

Set front toe before adjusting camber. Camber and toe influence each other. Camber is the deviation of each wheel from vertical. If necessary, adjust camber by removing front strut top centering pin.

> **CAUTION—**
> • Do not attempt to straighten out accident-caused changes in axle geometry by adjusting the camber.

— Working in engine compartment, remove upper strut brace. See **310 Front Suspension**.

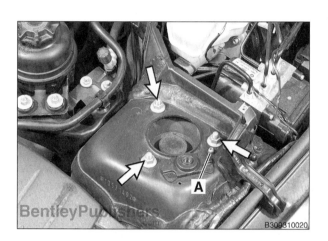

◄ Working at strut top bearing:

• Pry off protective cap.

• Remove centering pin (**A**).

• Loosen strut top bearing mounting nuts (**arrows**) 1 - 1½ turns.

— Raise vehicle until wheels are off ground. Support vehicle safely.

> **WARNING—**
> • Make sure the vehicle is stable and well supported at all times. Use a professional automotive lift or jack stands designed for the purpose. A floor jack is not adequate support.

— Working below vehicle, use compressed air to clean off debris in wheel housing near strut top bearing.

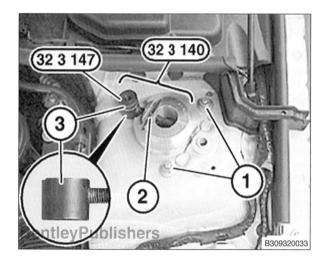

◄ Fit BMW special tool 33 3 140 and 32 3 147 over inboard strut top nut.

• Face short end of guide sleeve (**3**) up.

• Lower vehicle on alignment rack and bounce vehicle to make sure suspension is in loaded position and free from tension.

• Remove outboard strut top bearing nuts (**1**). Reinstall finger tight.

• Turn nut (**2**) in special tool to adjust camber to specified value.

• Tighten down outboard strut top mounting nuts (**1**).

— Remove special tool and replace inboard strut top mounting nut.

— Check directional stability of vehicle. If necessary, reset toe. See **Front toe, setting**.

| Tightening torque | |
|---|---|
| Strut top bearing to chassis (replace M8 shoulder nuts) | 34 Nm (25 ft-lb) |

## Rear camber, adjusting

Adjust rear camber before setting toe. A camber change means a toe change as well. Camber is the deviation of each wheel from vertical.

— Raise vehicle and support safely.

> **WARNING—**
> • *Make sure the vehicle is stable and well supported at all times. Use a professional automotive lift or jack stands designed for the purpose. A floor jack is not adequate support.*

◄ Working at swing arm (**A**) underneath rear suspension:

- Replace nut on swing arm eccentric bolt (**arrow**). Tighten to 5 Nm (finger tight).
- Lower vehicle on alignment rack and use eccentric bolt to adjust camber (**curved arrow**).
- Tighten swing arm eccentric bolt to specification with vehicle in normal loaded position.

| Tightening torque | |
|---|---|
| Swing arm eccentric fastener to rear subframe (replace nut, tighten with suspension loaded) | 165 Nm (122 ft-lb) |

## Rear toe, setting

Adjust rear camber before setting toe. A camber change means a toe change as well. Toe is the difference in the distance between the front of the wheels and the rear of the wheels.

◄ Working at toe link in rear (**B**):

- Replace nut (**arrow**) on eccentric bolt. Tighten to 5 Nm (finger tight).
- Lower vehicle on alignment rack and use eccentric bolt to set toe (**curved arrow**).
- Tighten toe link eccentric bolt to specification with vehicle in normal loaded position.

| Tightening torque | |
|---|---|
| Traction strut eccentric fastener to rear subframe (replace nut, tighten with suspension loaded) | 100 Nm (74 ft-lb) |

## Caster

Front and rear caster are fixed and deviations are usually the result of worn or damaged suspension or body parts.

— Check front suspension arms and bushings for wear, damage and deformation if front caster problems are present.

— Check rear axle subframe and traction struts if rear caster problems are present.

## Preparing for alignment

The following conditions are necessary prior to wheel alignment:

• Correct wheels and tires in good condition and inflated correctly.

• Steering and suspension parts and bushings undamaged and showing no signs of abnormal wear.

• Wheel bearings in good condition.

• Ride height in accordance with specifications. See **Ride height** in this repair group.

• Vehicle in normal loaded position. See **Normal loaded position** in this repair group.

## Normal loaded position

BMW defines vehicle normal loaded position as follows.

| Normal loaded position | |
|---|---|
| Each front seat | 68 Kg (150 lb) |
| Center of rear seat | 68 Kg (150 lb) |
| Cargo compartment | 21 Kg (46 lb) |
| Fuel tank | Full |

## Ride height

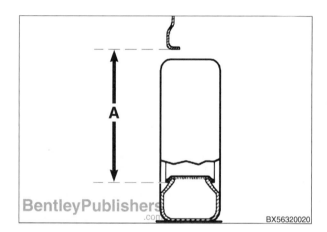

◀ Measure ride height (**A**) from center of fender arch to bottom of wheel rim.

• Car in normal loaded position on the ground. See **Normal loaded position** in this repair group.

• Specified tires and wheels, correct tire pressure, even tire wear

• Correct wheel bearing play

— If ride height is outside specification listed, install new springs. Suspension spring removal and installation is covered in **310 Front Suspension** and **330 Rear Suspension**.

BentleyPublishers.com

BX56320020

| Table a. Front ride height (measurement A) | |
|---|---|
| **Wheel size** | **Ride height in mm (in)** |
| 16 inch | 584 (22.99) |
| 17 inch | 599 (23.58) |
| 18 inch | 612 (24.09) |
| 19 inch | 625 (24.60) |
| Maximum combined deviation from specification: 10 mm (0.4 in) | |

| Table b. Rear ride height (measurement A) | |
|---|---|
| **Wheel size** | **Ride height in mm (in)** |
| 16 inch | 565 (22.24) |
| 17 inch | 580 (22.83) |
| 18 inch | 593 (23.35) |
| 19 inch | 605 (23.82) |
| Maximum combined deviation from specification: 10 mm (0.4 in) | |

**NOTE**—

• *Due to fender shape or model variation, ride height may vary by 1 mm (0.04 in) from specifications.*

## Alignment specifications

| Table c. Alignment specifications | |
|---|---|
| **Parameter** | **Specification** |
| **Front axle** | |
| Total toe | 0° 14' ± 10' |
| Camber (difference between left / right, maximum 30') | - 18' ± 25' |
| Toe angle difference with 20° lock on inside wheel (difference between left / right, maximum 30') | -1° 40' ± 30' |
| **Front caster (difference between left / right maximum 30'):** | |
| Front wheel displacement | 0° ± 15' |
| **Maximum wheel lock** | |
| Inside wheel (approx.) | 41° 05' |
| Outside wheel (approx.) | 33° 18' |
| **Rear axle** | |
| Total toe | 0° 18' ± 6' |
| Camber (difference between left / right maximum 30'): | -1° 30' ± 15' |
| Geometrical axis deviation | 0° ± 4' |

**NOTE**—

• *These specifications are for vehicles with standard suspension.*

# 330 Rear Suspension

## GENERAL

This repair group covers removal and replacement of 3 Series rear suspension components. For related information see:

- **300 Suspension, Steering and Brakes–General** for a general description of the 3 Series suspension.
- **310 Front Suspension** for front suspension component replacement.
- **320 Steering and Wheel Alignment** for ride height and alignment specifications.

Special service tools are required for some of the work described in this repair group. Most of these tools are specialized press jigs and pullers that may be replaced by standard pullers of various sizes. Read the procedures through before beginning any job.

## Rear suspension description

The 3 Series rear suspension uses a subframe as a rigid mounting platform for the differential (also called final drive) and rear suspension components. The differential is mounted to the subframe and the subframe is bolted to the body through rubber bushings which help isolate drivetrain noise and vibration.

The 3 Series rear suspension is known as a multi-link system. Five control arms on each side locate the rear wheels. The lower control arm, called the swing arm, is attached to the wheel bearing carrier.

The rear suspension uses conventional shock absorbers and coil springs. The bottom of each shock absorber bolts to the swing arm (lower control arm). The top shock absorber mount bolts to the body.

## Warnings and Cautions

> **WARNING—**
> • *Do not reuse self-locking nuts, bolts or fasteners. They are designed to be used only once and may fail if reused. Replace them with new self-locking fasteners.*

> **CAUTION—**
> • *3 Series models are equipped with hardened steel suspension components. Do not heat, weld on or bend.*

## REAR SHOCK ABSORBERS AND COIL SPRINGS

### Rear shock absorber, removing and installing

— Working in luggage compartment, remove wheel arch trim.

— Raise car and remove rear wheel.

> **WARNING—**
> • *Make sure the car is firmly supported on jack stands designed for the purpose. Place jack stands underneath structural chassis points, not underneath suspension parts.*

— Support swing arm from below with a suitable jack.

> **CAUTION—**
> • *The shock absorber prevents the drive axle and wheel bearing carrier from dropping too far. Supporting the wheel bearing carrier before disconnecting the shock absorber mounting fasteners prevents damage to the brake hose, parking brake cable and drive axle CV joints.*

Remove upper shock absorber mount fastener (**A**) along with washer (**B**).

*Rear shock absorber thrust bearing removing and installing*

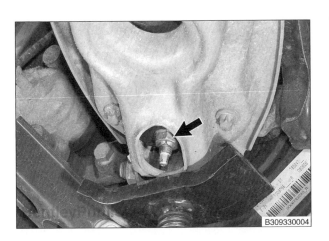

◅ Remove shock absorber lower mounting bolt (**arrow**).

– Compress and remove shock absorber from vehicle.

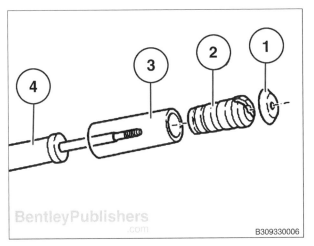

◅ If replacing shock absorber, transfer top mount, dust cover (if applicable) and related components to new shock absorber. Counterhold piston rod with suitable wrench:

1.  Washer plate
2.  Bump stop
3.  Damper protective tube
4.  Rear shock absorber

– Installation is reverse of removal, noting the following:
- Make sure all threaded bolts, nuts and mating surfaces are clean.
- Install shock absorber upper mount to subframe using new self-locking nuts.
- Do not mix up shock brands on a single axle. Use BMW part number to match manufacturers.
- Tighten fasteners to final torque only after vehicle has been lowered and suspension has settled.

| Tightening torques | |
| --- | --- |
| Shock absorber to body (replace fastener) | |
| • M10 | 27 Nm (19.9 ft-lb) |
| • M14 | 37 Nm (27.2 ft-lb) |
| Shock absorber to swing arm (replace fastener) | 38 Nm (28 ft-lb) |
| Road wheel to hub | 120 Nm (88.5 ft-lb) |

## Rear shock absorber thrust bearing removing and installing

– Remove shock absorber. See **Shock absorber, removing and installing** in this repair group.

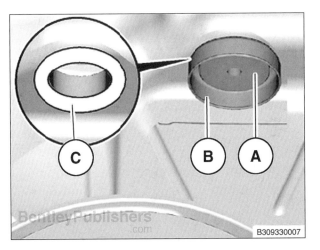

◅ Pull shock absorber support bearing (**A**) with sealing grommet (**B**) out of shock absorber mounting (**C**).

– Installation is reverse of removal. Remember to clean contact area (**C**) on mounting surface.

## Coil spring, removing and installing

**NOTE** —

• *Replace coil springs in pairs per axle.*

— Raise car and remove rear wheel.

> **WARNING** —
> • *Make sure the car is firmly supported on jack stands designed for the purpose. Place jack stands underneath structural chassis points, not underneath suspension parts.*

◄ Insert BMW special tool 33 5 012 centrally into coil spring and rotate to lowest coil. Guide BMW special tools 33 5 013, 33 5 014, 33 5 015 from below through swing arm and BMW special tool 33 5 012.

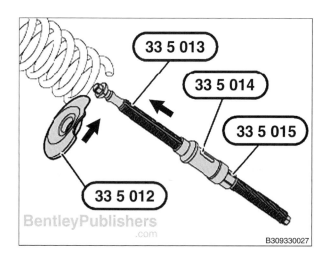

B309330027

◄ Insert BMW special tool 33 5 011 sideways into coil spring and turn to uppermost coil. Pull BMW special tool (spindle) 33 5 013 downwards.

**NOTE** —

• *Make sure BMW special tool 33 5 013 hexagon (inset) is correctly seated in BMW special tool 33 5 011.*

— Install BMW special tools (spring tensioner) centrally in order to gain the most contact area on spring.

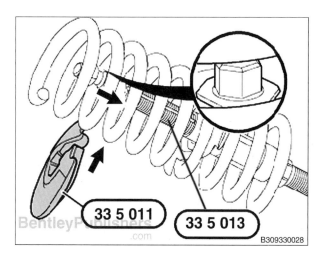

B309330028

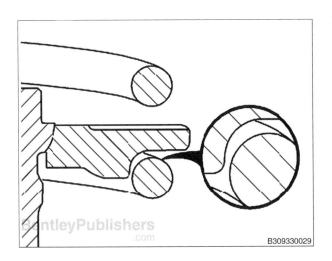

◄ Check that coil spring is correctly positioned in spring plates.

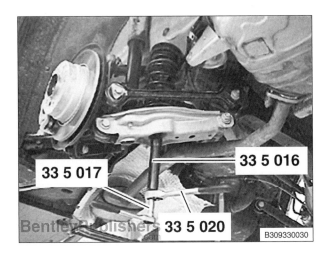

◄ Using BMW using special tools 33 5 016 and 33 5 020, gripping spindle of spring tensioner with special tool 33 5 017 in the process, compress and remove coil spring upwards.

– Slowly decompress spring tensioner tool and remove tool from coil spring.

**330**

◄ Installation is reverse of removal. Remember to:
- Inspect coil spring mounts for wear and replace if necessary.
- Inspect coil spring for any surface damage or corrosion.
- Properly align upper and lower coil spring mounts (**arrow**).
- Check and adjust headlight aim if necessary. See **630 Lights**.

## REAR SUSPENSION ARMS, SUBFRAME AND BUSHINGS

### Rear suspension arm components

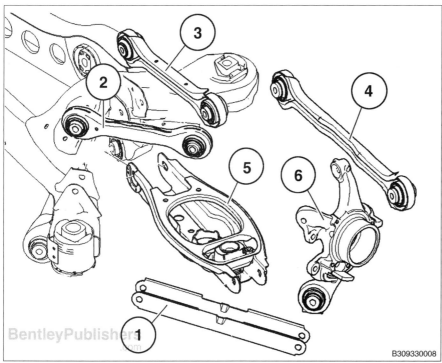

B309330008

1. Trailing arm
2. Guide arm (traction strut)
3. Upper control arm
4. Toe link
5. Lower control arm (swing arm)
6. Wheel bearing carrier

### Trailing arm, removing and installing

**NOTE** —
• *Check wheel alignment if trailing arm is removed.*

– Raise car and remove rear wheel.

> **WARNING** —
> • *Make sure the car is firmly supported on jack stands designed for the purpose. Place jack stands underneath structural chassis points, not underneath suspension parts.*

– Support rear wheel bearing carrier with suitable jack.

◄ Remove fasteners (**A**) and remove trailing arm (**B**) in a downward direction.

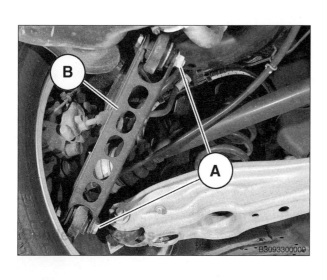

B309330009

— Installation is reverse of removal, noting the following:

- Use new self-locking nuts.

- Tighten fasteners to final torque only after vehicle has been lowered and suspension has settled.

- Have car professionally aligned when job is complete.

| Tightening torques | |
|---|---|
| Trailing arm to rear subframe (use new self-locking nut) | 100 Nm (73.7 ft-lb) |
| Trailing arm to wheel bearing carrier (use new self-locking nut) | 100 Nm (73.7 ft-lb) |
| Road wheel to hub | 120 Nm (88.5 ft-lb) |

## Trailing arm bushings, removing and installing

*NOTE —*

- *Replace trailing arm bushings in sets.*

- *Check wheel alignment if trailing arm is removed.*

— Raise car and remove rear wheel.

> *WARNING —*
> - *Make sure the car is firmly supported on jack stands designed for the purpose. Place jack stands underneath structural chassis points, not underneath suspension parts.*

— Support rear wheel bearing carrier with suitable jack.

— Remove trailing arm. See **Trailing arm, removing and installing** in this repair group.

◄ Working at wheel bearing carrier: Using BMW special tools 33 4 465, 33 4 466, 33 4 475, 33 4 474 and 33 4 472, remove bushing from wheel bearing carrier

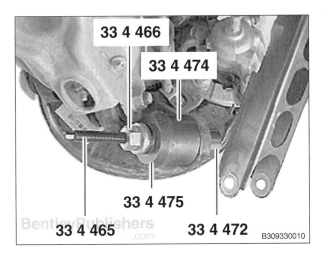

330

*Trailing arm bushings, removing and installing*

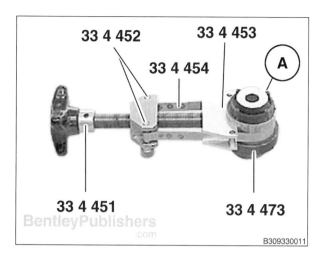

B309330011

◣ Using BMW special tools 33 4 451, 33 4 452, 33 4 454, 33 4 453, compress new bushing (**A**) and insert bushing into BMW special tool 33 4 473 with spray on point facing upwards.

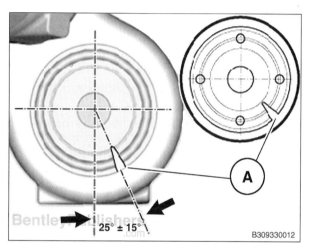

B309330012

◣ When installing bushing into wheel bearing carrier, align slot (**A**) at specified angle with spray on points facing rear of vehicle.

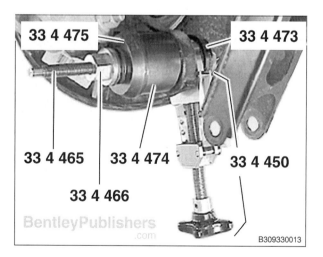

B309330013

◣ Using BMW special tools 33 4 465, 33 4 466, 33 4 475, 33 4 474 and 33 4 473, slightly draw rubber bushing into wheel bearing carrier. Remove BMW special tool 33 4 450 and press rubber bushing in as far as it will go.

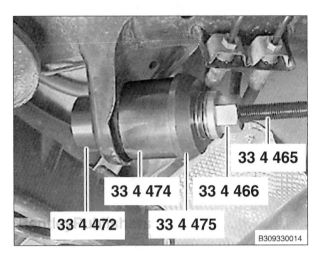

— Working at rear subframe: Mark bushing slot alignment on subframe.

◄ Using BMW special tools 33 4 472, 33 4 474, 33 4 475, 33 4 466 and 33 4 465, remove bushing from subframe.

— Clean rubber bushing mounting hole.

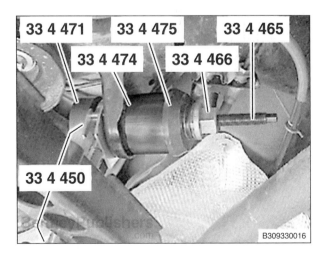

◄ When installing bushing into subframe, align slot (**A**) at specified angle with spray on points facing rear of vehicle.

— Align rubber mount slot with your mark on subframe.

**330**

◄ Using BMW special tools 33 4 471, 33 4 474, 33 4 475, 33 4 466 and 33 4 465, slightly draw rubber bushing into subframe. Remove special tool 33 4 450. Apply a thin coating of Loctite 638 to rubber bushing. Press rubber bushing in as far as it will go.

— Remainder of installation is reverse of removal, noting the following:

• Use new self-locking nuts.

• Tighten fasteners to final torque only after vehicle has been lowered and suspension has settled.

• Have car professionally aligned when job is complete.

| Tightening torques | |
|---|---|
| Trailing arm to rear subframe | 100 Nm (73.7 ft-lb) |
| Trailing arm to wheel bearing carrier | 100 Nm (73.7 ft-lb) |
| Road wheel to hub | 120 Nm (88.5 ft-lb) |

## Upper control arm, removing and installing

***NOTE***—
* *Check wheel alignment if control arm is removed.*

— Raise car and remove rear wheel.

> ***WARNING***—
> * *Make sure the car is firmly supported on jack stands designed for the purpose. Place jack stands underneath structural chassis points, not underneath suspension parts.*

— Support rear wheel bearing carrier with suitable jack.

◄ Working at wheel bearing carrier: Remove fastener (**arrow**) and discard.

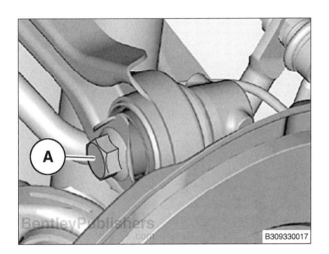

B309330017

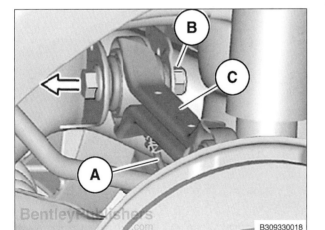

B309330018

◄ Unclip wiring harness from control arm (**A**). Remove control arm fastener (**B**) and remove control arm (**C**).

— installation is reverse of removal, noting the following:
* Use new self-locking nuts.
* Tighten fasteners to final torque only after vehicle has been lowered and suspension has settled.
* Have car professionally aligned when job is complete.

| Tightening torques | |
|---|---|
| Control arm to rear subframe (use new self-locking nuts) | 100 Nm (73.7 ft-lb) |
| Control arm to wheel bearing carrier (replace fastener) | 100 Nm (73.7 ft-lb) +90° |
| Road wheel to hub | 120 Nm (88.5 ft-lb) |

## Guide arm (traction strut), removing and installing

*NOTE—*

• *Check wheel alignment if guide arm is removed.*

— Raise car and remove rear wheel.

> *WARNING—*
>
> • *Make sure the car is firmly supported on jack stands designed for the purpose. Place jack stands underneath structural chassis points, not underneath suspension parts.*

— Support rear wheel bearing carrier with suitable jack.

— Remove stabilizer links and rotate stabilizer bar upwards. See **Stabilizer link, removing and installing** in this repair group.

◄ Working at wheel bearing carrier, remove fastener (**arrow**) and discard.

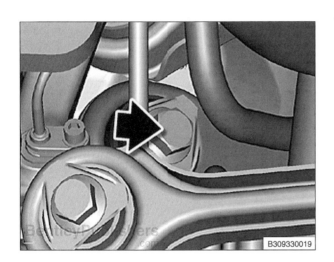

B309330019

◄ Remove guide arm fastener (**A**) and remove guide arm (**B**).

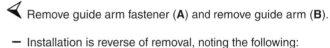

— Installation is reverse of removal, noting the following:

• Make sure subframe guide arm fastener head faces rear of vehicle.

• Use new self-locking nuts.

• Tighten fasteners to final torque only after vehicle has been lowered and suspension has settled.

• Have car professionally aligned when job is complete.

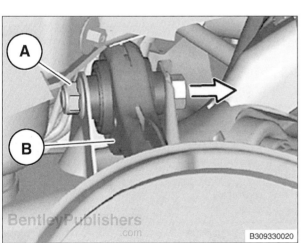

B309330020

| Tightening torques | |
| --- | --- |
| Guide arm to rear subframe (use new self-locking nuts) | 100 Nm (73.7 ft-lb) |
| Guide arm to wheel bearing carrier (replace fastener) | 100 Nm (73.7 ft-lb) +90° |
| Road wheel to hub | 120 Nm (88.5 ft-lb) |

330

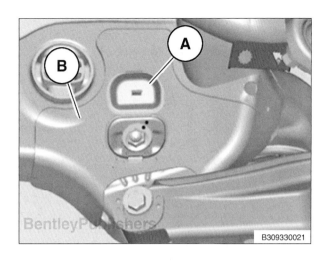

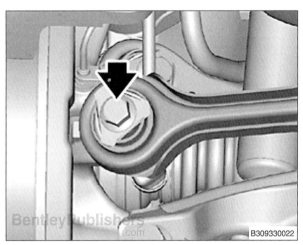

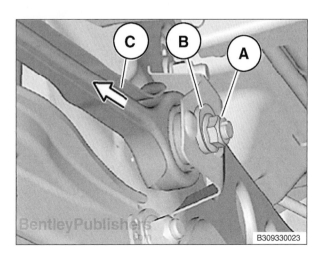

## Toe link, removing and installing

**NOTE—**
* *Check wheel alignment if guide arm is removed.*

— Raise car and remove rear wheel.

> **WARNING—**
> * *Make sure the car is firmly supported on jack stands designed for the purpose. Place jack stands underneath structural chassis points, not underneath suspension parts.*

— Support rear wheel bearing carrier with suitable jack.

◀ Open cover (**A**) and mark eccentric washer location on subframe (**arrow**).

◀ Working at wheel bearing carrier: Remove fastener (**arrow**) and discard.

◀ Remove nut (**A**) and discard. Remove eccentric washer (**B**), bolt and remove toe link (**C**).

— Installation is reverse of removal, noting the following:
* Use new self-locking nuts.
* Tighten fasteners to final torque only after vehicle has been lowered and suspension has settled.
* Have car professionally aligned when job is complete.

| Tightening torques | |
| --- | --- |
| Toe link to rear subframe (use new self-locking nuts) | 100 Nm (73.7 ft-lb) |
| Toe link to wheel bearing carrier | 100 Nm (73.7 ft-lb) |
| Road wheel to hub | 120 Nm (88.5 ft-lb) |

### Lower control arm (swing arm), removing and installing

**NOTE** —

• *Check wheel alignment if swing arm is removed.*

— Raise car and remove rear wheel.

> **WARNING** —
>
> • *Make sure the car is firmly supported on jack stands designed for the purpose. Place jack stands underneath structural chassis points, not underneath suspension parts.*

— Support rear wheel bearing carrier with suitable jack.

— Remove coil spring. See **Coil spring, removing and installing** in this repair group.

— Remove ride height sensor if equipped.

◄ Remove lower shock absorber fastener (**arrow**).

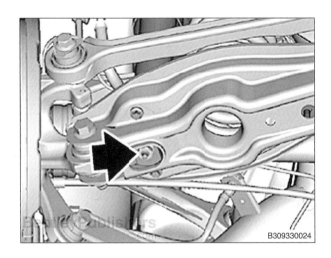

B309330024

◄ Remove lower shock absorber mount fasteners (**A**) and remove mount (**B**).

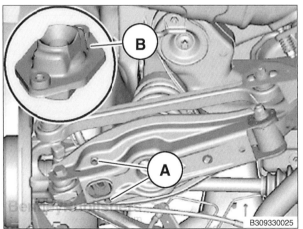

B309330025

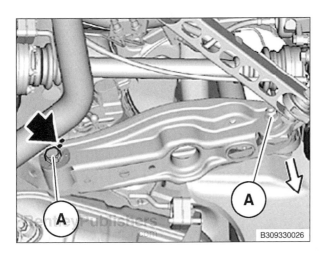

B309330026

◀ Mark eccentric washer location on subframe (**arrow**). Remove fasteners (**A**) and eccentric washer and remove swing arm from vehicle.

– Installation is reverse of removal, noting the following:

  • Make sure subframe swing arm fastener head faces rear of vehicle.

  • Use new self-locking nuts.

  • Tighten fasteners to final torque only after vehicle has been lowered and suspension has settled.

– Have car professionally aligned when job is complete.

| Tightening torques | |
|---|---|
| Swing arm to rear subframe (use new self-locking nut) | 165 Nm (121.6 ft-lb) |
| Swing arm to wheel bearing carrier (use new self-locking nut) | 165 Nm (121.6 ft-lb) |
| Shock absorber to swing arm (use new self-locking nut) | 38 Nm (28 ft-lb) |
| Shock absorber mount to swing arm (replace fasteners) | 60 Nm (44.2 ft-lb) |
| Road wheel to hub | 120 Nm (88.5 ft-lb) |

## Lower control arm (swing arm) ball joint, removing and installing

*NOTE —*

• *Replace ball joints in pairs.*

– Raise car and remove rear wheel.

> *WARNING —*
> • *Make sure the car is firmly supported on jack stands designed for the purpose. Place jack stands underneath structural chassis points, not underneath suspension parts.*

– Support rear wheel bearing carrier with suitable jack.

– Remove coil spring. See **Coil spring, removing and installing** in this repair group.

– Remove ride height sensor if equipped.

– Remove rear shock absorber. See **Rear shock absorber, removing and installing** in this repair group.

– Remove swing arm. See **Swing arm, removing and installing** in this repair group.

– Remove trailing arm. See **Trailing arm, removing and installing** in this repair group.

*Lower control arm (swing arm) ball joint, removing and installing*

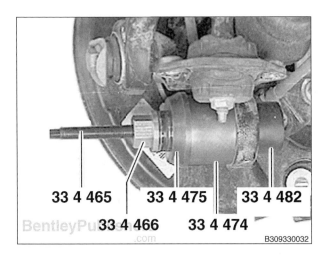

◄ Using BMW special tools special tools 33 4 465, 33 4 466, 33 4 475, 33 4 474 and 33 4 482, press out ball joint from wheel bearing carrier.

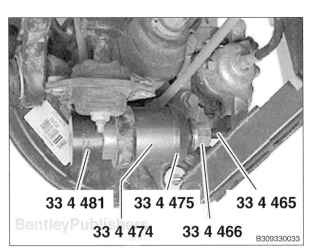

◄ Draw in new ball joint using BMW special tools 33 4 481, 33 4 474, 33 4 475, 33 4 466 and 33 4 465 as far as it will go.

– Remainder of installation is reverse of removal, noting the following:

 • Use new self-locking nuts.

 • Tighten fasteners to final torque only after vehicle has been lowered and suspension has settled.

– Have car professionally aligned when job is complete.

| Tightening torques | |
|---|---|
| Swing arm to rear subframe (use new self-locking nut) | 165 Nm (121.6 ft-lb) |
| Swing arm to wheel bearing carrier (use new self-locking nut) | 165 Nm (121.6 ft-lb) |
| Shock absorber to swing arm (use new self-locking nut) | 38 Nm (28 ft-lb) |
| Shock absorber mount to swing arm (replace fasteners) | 60 Nm (44.2 ft-lb) |
| Trailing arm to rear subframe (use new self-locking nut) | 100 Nm (73.7 ft-lb) |
| Trailing arm to wheel bearing carrier (use new self-locking nut) | 100 Nm (73.7 ft-lb) |
| Road wheel to hub | 120 Nm (88.5 ft-lb) |

*Lower control arm (swing arm) bushing, removing and installing*

B309330034

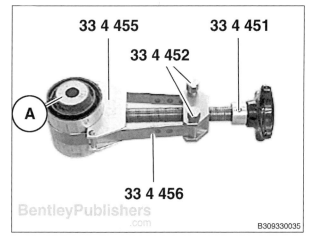

B309330035

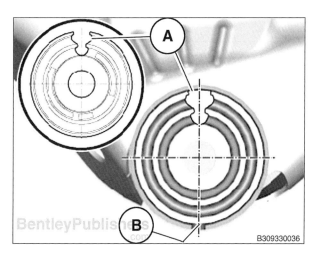

B309330036

## Lower control arm (swing arm) bushing, removing and installing

*NOTE* —

• *Replace bushings in pairs.*

– Raise car and remove rear wheel.

> *WARNING* —
> • *Make sure the car is firmly supported on jack stands designed for the purpose. Place jack stands underneath structural chassis points, not underneath suspension parts.*

– Support rear wheel bearing carrier with suitable jack.

– Remove coil spring. See **Coil spring, removing and installing** in this repair group.

– Remove ride height sensor if equipped.

– Remove swing arm. See **Swing arm, removing and installing** in this repair group.

◄ Using BMW special tools 33 4 462, 33 4 464, 33 4 463, 33 4 466 and 33 4 465, remove bushing from subframe.

◄ Using BMW special tools 33 4 455, 33 4 456, 33 4 452 and 33 4 451, compress new bushing (**A**).

◄ During installation align rubber bushing slot (**A**) with center line mark (**B**).

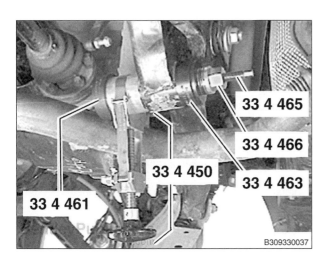

◀ Using BMW special tools 33 4 461, 33 4 463, 33 4 466 and 33 4 465 press mount in as far as possible, then remove special tool 33 4 450 and draw in rubber mount as far as it will go.

– Remainder of installation is reverse of removal, noting the following:
  • Use new self-locking nuts.
  • Tighten fasteners to final torque only after vehicle has been lowered and suspension has settled.

– Have car professionally aligned when job is complete.

| Tightening torques | |
| --- | --- |
| Swing arm to rear subframe (use new self-locking nut) | 165 Nm (121.6 ft-lb) |
| Swing arm to wheel bearing carrier (use new self-locking nut) | 165 Nm (121.6 ft-lb) |
| Shock absorber to swing arm (use new self-locking nut) | 38 Nm (28 ft-lb) |
| Shock absorber mount to swing arm (replace fasteners) | 60 Nm (44.2 ft-lb) |
| Road wheel to hub | 120 Nm (88.5 ft-lb) |

## Rear subframe components

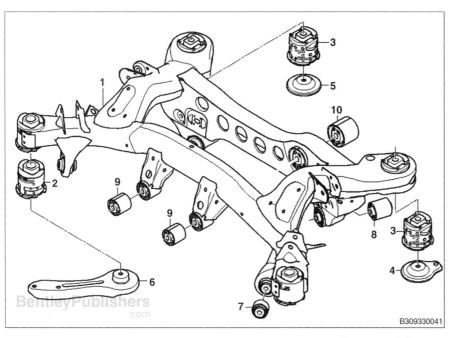

1. Rear subframe
2. Subframe mount
3. Subframe mount
4. Stop plate
5. Stop plate
6. Thrust rod
7. Trailing arm bushing
8. Swing arm bushing
9. Differential mount
10. Differential mount (round)

## Rear subframe and axle assembly, removing and installing

– In order to maintain even weight distribution in vehicle, load the luggage compartment with a minimum of 100 kg (220 lbs) before lowering / removing the rear axle carrier.

– Remove both rear wheels.

– Remove rear driveshaft. See **260 Driveshafts**.

*Rear subframe and axle assembly, removing and installing*

**CAUTION—**
- *When supporting rear subframe, make sure that the vehicle can no longer be raised or lowered and the vehicle does not lift off the locating plates on the lifting platform.*

— Remove both rear coil springs. See **Coil spring, removing and installing** in this repair group.

— Remove both rear wheel speed sensors, unclip wiring harness from control arm and subframe. See **340 Brakes**.

— Disconnect electrical connector for brake pad wear sensor. See **340 Brakes**.

— Disconnect electrical connector for ride-height sensor and unclip line from subframe if equipped.

— Disengage both parking brake cables from parking brake. See **340 Brakes**.

— Remove both rear shock absorbers. See **Rear shock absorbers, removing and installing** in this repair group.

◄ Insert pedal prop and depress brake pedal slightly. This prevents brake fluid from escaping when brake lines are detached.

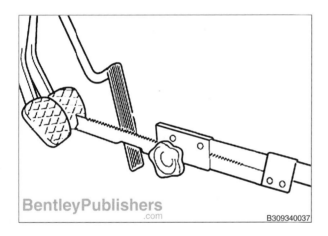

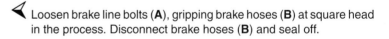

◄ Loosen brake line bolts (**A**), gripping brake hoses (**B**) at square head in the process. Disconnect brake hoses (**B**) and seal off.

**NOTE—**
- *Be prepared to catch any dripping brake fluid.*

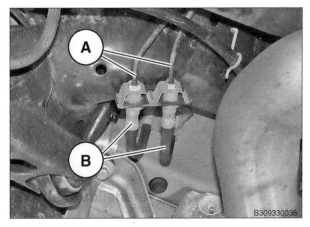

*Rear subframe and axle assembly, removing and installing*

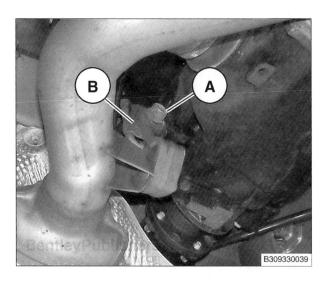

◁ Remove exhaust mount fastener (**A**) and rotate bracket (**B**) towards rear of vehicle.

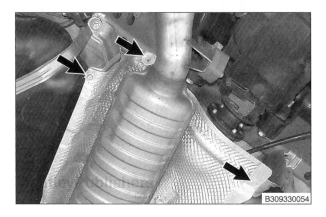

◁ Remove fasteners (**arrows**) and rest heat shield on exhaust.

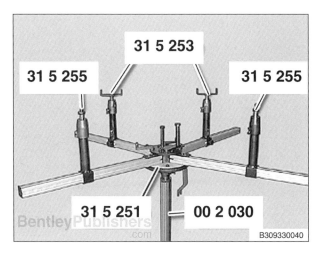

◁ Assemble BMW special tools 31 5 251, 31 5 253, 31 5 255 and 00 2 030 (subframe jack assembly).

**330**

*Rear subframe and axle assembly, removing and installing*

◀ Align subframe jack assembly and raise jack until subframe is supported.

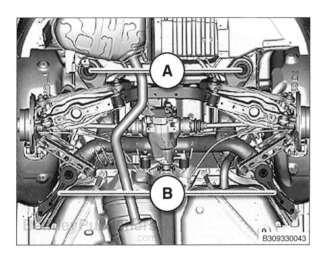

◀ Remove rear subframe fasteners (**A**) and front subframe / tension strut fasteners (**B**).

> **WARNING—**
> • *Removing the rear subframe alters the vehicle's center of gravity. Make sure vehicle remains securely in place on lift or jacks.*

– Slowly lower and remove rear subframe assembly from vehicle.

– To install, jack subframe into position. Install tension struts in their original position and tighten subframe mounting bolts.

| Tightening torque | |
|---|---|
| Rear subframe to body (M12) | 100 Nm (73.7 ft-lb) |

– Remainder of installation is reverse of removal, noting the following.

- Tighten suspension arms and shock absorber fasteners to final torque only after vehicle is lowered and suspension has settled.
- Bleed entire brake system before driving car. See **340 Brakes**.
- Adjust emergency brake.
- Have car professionally aligned when job is complete.

| Tightening torques | |
|---|---|
| Subframe mounts to body (replace fasteners) | 100 Nm (73.7 ft-lb) |
| Tension strut to body (replace fasteners) | 47 Nm (34.6 ft-lb) +90° |
| Vibration dampener to subframe (Convertible) M8 M10 | 27 Nm (19.9 ft-lb) 56 Nm (41.3 ft-lb) |
| Shock absorber to swing arm (use new self-locking nut) | 38 Nm (28 ft-lb) |
| Shock absorber mount to swing arm (replace fasteners) | 60 Nm (44.2 ft-lb) |
| Brake line nut to hose | 12 Nm (9 ft-lb) |
| Road wheel to hub | 120 Nm (88.5 ft-lb) |

## Rear subframe mounting bushings, removing and installing

– Lower subframe approximately 40 - 45 mm (1½ - 2 in). See **Rear subframe and axle assembly, removing and installing** in this repair group.

◄ To remove subframe mounting bushing:

- Coat top edge of mount with Circolight® anti-friction agent.
- Install BMW special tool **33 4 431** on top edge of subframe mounting bushing.
- Install BMW special tool **33 4 140** through opening in subframe mounting bushing.
- Using BMW special tools **33 4 436**, **33 4 437**, **33 4 140** and **33 4 431**, remove subframe mounting bushing from subframe.

◄ To install subframe mounting bushing:

- Coat new mount with Circolight® anti-friction agent.
- Align rubber mount by way of **arrow** to front of vehicle.
- Using BMW special tools **33 4 432**, **33 4 433**, **33 4 435** and **33 4 434**, install subframe mounting bushing as far as it will go.

– Remainder of installation is reverse of removal. Bleed entire brake system before driving car. See **340 Brakes**.

| Tightening torques | |
|---|---|
| Road wheel to hub | 120 Nm (88.5 ft-lb) |

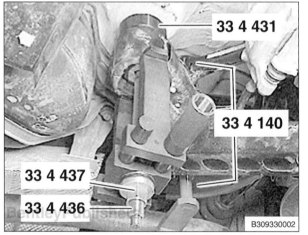

33 4 431
33 4 140
33 4 437
33 4 436

B309330002

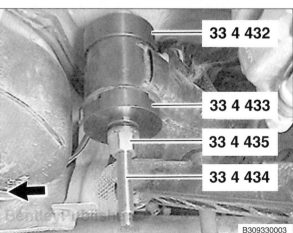

33 4 432
33 4 433
33 4 435
33 4 434

B309330003

## REAR WHEEL BEARINGS

The rear wheel bearing is pressed into the rear wheel bearing carrier. The wheel bearing can be replaced without removing the rear wheel bearing carrier. The rear wheel hub is pressed into the rear wheel bearing. Removing the hub destroys the wheel bearing. To service the wheel bearing, remove the wheel hub and replace the wheel bearing.

### Rear wheel bearing carrier, removing and installing

– Raise vehicle and remove rear wheel.

> **WARNING** —
> • *Make sure the car is firmly supported on jack stands designed for the purpose. Place jack stands underneath structural chassis points, not underneath suspension parts.*

– Remove coil spring. See **Coil spring, removing and installing** in this repair group.

– Remove brake calipers and brake discs. Hang brake calipers aside with stiff wire. Do not disconnect brake fluid hoses. See **340 Brakes**.

– Remove ABS wheel speed sensor from wheel bearing carrier. See **340 Brakes**.

– Disconnect parking brake cable from brake shoe expander. See **340 Brakes**.

– Remove rear drive axle. See **331 Rear Axle Differential**.

– Remove shock absorber. See **Shock absorber, removing and installing** in this repair group.

– Remove control arm. See **Control arm, removing and installing** in this repair group.

– Remove trailing arm. See **Trailing arm, removing and installing** in this repair group.

– Remove guide arm. See **Guide arm, removing and installing** in this repair group.

– Remove swing arm. See **Swing arm, removing and installing** in this repair group.

– Remove toe link. See **Toe link, removing and installing** in this repair group.

– Installation is reverse of removal. Remember to:
  • Adjust parking brake.
  • Have car professionally aligned when job is complete.

## Rear wheel hub, removing and installing

– Raise vehicle and remove wheel.

> **WARNING** —
> • Make sure the car is firmly supported on jack stands designed for the purpose. Place jack stands underneath structural chassis points, not underneath suspension parts.

◀ With an assistant applying brakes, break free and remove staked collar nut (**arrow**).

– Disconnect brake pad sensor connector at brake caliper.

– Remove brake caliper assembly and rotor. See **340 Brakes**. Leave brake hose connected to caliper. Suspend caliper assembly from chassis using stiff wire.

– Disconnect parking brake cables from brake shoe expanders. See **340 Brakes**.

– Remove ABS wheel speed sensor at wheel bearing carrier.

– Remove rear drive axle. See **331 Rear Axle Differential**.

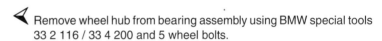

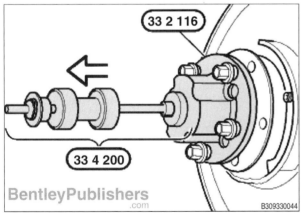

◀ Remove wheel hub from bearing assembly using BMW special tools 33 2 116 / 33 4 200 and 5 wheel bolts.

> **CAUTION** —
> • The wheel bearing is destroyed when the hub is removed.

– Replace wheel bearing. See **Rear wheel bearing, replacing** in this repair group.

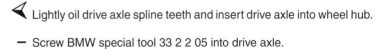

◀ Lightly oil drive axle spline teeth and insert drive axle into wheel hub.

– Screw BMW special tool 33 2 2 05 into drive axle.

> **CAUTION** —
> • Do not oil axle or collar nut threads.

> **NOTE** —
> • Depending on axle bearing outside diameter BMW special tools 33 2 118 or 33 2 119 may be substituted.

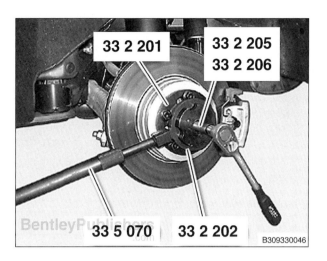

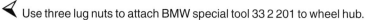
◄ Use three lug nuts to attach BMW special tool 33 2 201 to wheel hub.

– Draw axle into wheel hub using special tool 33 2 208. Counterhold hub with special tools 33 2 202 and 33 5 070.

**NOTE—**

• *Depending on axle bearing outside diameter BMW special tools 33 2 116, 33 2 111, 33 2 117, 33 5 070 and 33 2 202 may be substituted.*

– The remainder of installation is reverse of removal. Remember to:

• Use new collar nut at outboard end of drive axle.

• Restake nut after tightening.

• Remember to adjust parking brake when job is complete.

| Tightening torques | |
|---|---|
| Drive axle collar nut to wheel hub<br>• M24<br>• M27 | <br>250 Nm (184.3 ft-lb)<br>420 Nm (310 ft-lb) |
| Road wheel to hub | 120 Nm (88.5 ft-lb) |

## Rear wheel bearing, replacing

– Remove drive flange. See **Rear wheel hub, removing and installing** in this repair group.

**CAUTION—**

• *The wheel bearing is destroyed when the drive flange is removed. Replace wheel bearing.*

– Press wheel bearing inner race off wheel hub shaft.

◄ Using a pair of needle nose pliers, remove snap ring (**A**) from wheel bearing carrier.

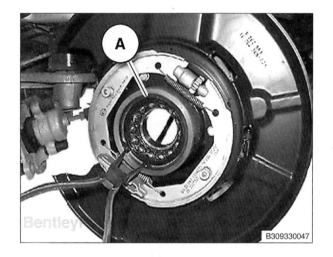

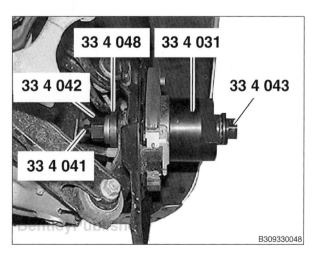

◄ Using BMW special tools 33 4 041, 33 4 042, 33 4 031, 33 4 048 and 33 4 043, pull wheel bearing out of wheel bearing carrier.

**NOTE—**

• *Wheel bearing cannot be reused.*

• *85 mm outside diameter bearing will use BMW special tools 33 3 2 61, 33 3 263, 33 3 262 and 33 2 261.*

B309330050

◄ 85 mm outside diameter wheel bearings:

- Black seal (**A**) points towards center of vehicle.

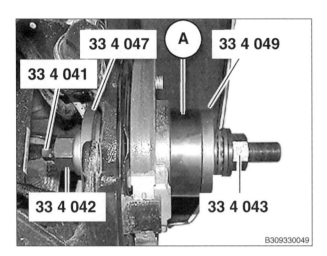

B309330049

◄ Using BMW special tools 33 4 041, 33 4 042, 33 4 049, 33 4 047 and 33 4 043, draw wheel bearing (**A**) into wheel bearing carrier.

**NOTE—**

- *85 mm outside diameter bearing will use BMW special tools 33 3 2 61, 33 3 264 and 33 2 265.*

— The remainder of installation is reverse of removal. Remember to:

- Use new collar nut at outboard end of drive axle.
- Restake nut after tightening.
- Remember to adjust parking brake when job is complete.

| Tightening torques | |
|---|---|
| Drive axle collar nut to wheel hub<br>• M24<br>• M27 | <br>250 Nm (184.3 ft-lb)<br>420 Nm (310 ft-lb) |
| Road wheel to hub | 120 Nm (88.5 ft-lb) |

**330**

## REAR STABILIZER BAR

The rear stabilizer bar is mounted to the rear subframe and attached to the swing arms with stabilizer bar links.

### Rear stabilizer bar components

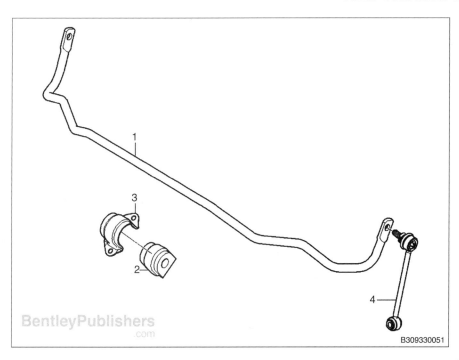

1. Stabilizer bar
2. Stabilizer mount
3. Stabilizer bushing
4. Stabilizer link

### Stabilizer bar, removing and installing

– Raise vehicle and safely support.

> **WARNING** —
> • *Make sure the car is firmly supported on jack stands designed for the purpose. Place jack stands underneath structural chassis points, not underneath suspension parts.*

– Mark stabilizer bar on left side for ease of assembly.

– Remove both coil springs. See **Coil spring, removing and installing** in this repair group.

– Remove left side control arm. See **Control arm, removing and installing** in this repair group.

– Remove stabilizer links. See **Stabilizer links, removing and installing** in this repair group.

– Lower rear subframe. See **Rear subframe and axle assembly, removing and installing** in this repair group.

◀ Remove stabilizer support bracket fasteners (**A**) on each side and remove stabilizer bar (**B**).

– Check rubber mounts. Replace if necessary.

– Installation is reverse of removal. Use previously made mark for reassembly.

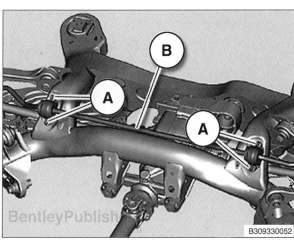

| Tightening torques | |
|---|---|
| Stabilizer bar bracket to subframe (M8) | 21 Nm (15.4 ft-lb) |
| Stabilizer link to stabilizer bar (M10) | 58 Nm (42.7 ft-lb) |

## Stabilizer link, removing and installing

– Raise vehicle and safely support.

> **WARNING**—
> • *Make sure the car is firmly supported on jack stands designed for the purpose. Place jack stands underneath structural chassis points, not underneath suspension parts.*

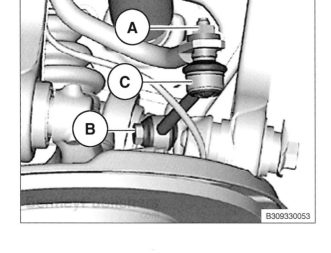

B309330053

◄ Remove stabilizer link mounting nut (**A**) at stabilizer bar.

– Remove stabilizer link mounting fastener (**B**) at swing arm.

– Press out stabilizer link ball joints and remove stabilizer link (**C**).

– Installation is reverse of removal.

| Tightening torques | |
|---|---|
| Stabilizer bar bracket to subframe (M8) | 21 Nm (15.4 ft-lb) |
| Stabilizer link to stabilizer bar (M10) | 58 Nm (42.7 ft-lb) |

**330**

# 331 Rear Axle Differential

## GENERAL

This repair group covers removal and repair information for the rear differential (final drive), axle shafts, CV joints, CV joint boots, and differential seal replacement.

Internal repairs of the differential assembly are not covered in this manual.

## REAR DIFFERENTIAL

### Rear differential applications

Several rear differentials are used in the various 3 Series models. See **Table a**.

| Table a. Rear differential applications | | |
| --- | --- | --- |
| **Engine** | **Rear differential** | **Capacity** |
| Non-turbo | 188L / 188LW | 1.0 ltr (1.05 qt) |
| Turbo | 215L / 215LW | 1.2 ltr (1.3 qt) |

### Differential oil, draining and filling

The 3 Series rear differential is filled with lifetime oil that ordinarily does not need to be changed. BMW recommends using only a specially formulated synthetic gear oil (SAF-XO) that is available through an authorized BMW dealer parts department. For additional information on this lubricant and any other lubricants that may be compatible, contact an authorized BMW dealer service department.

— Operate vehicle to warm differential oil.

*Differential oil level, checking*

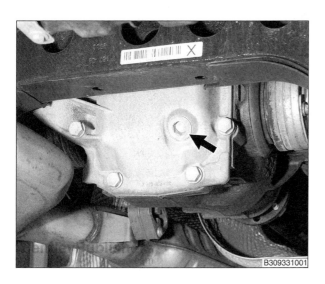

B309331001

◄ Remove differential plug (**arrow**). Using a suction gun, remove fluid from differential.

− Drain oil into a suitable container.

− Replace plug and seal.

− Add rear differential oil and check level. See **Differential oil level, checking** in this repair group.

| Tightening torque | |
|---|---|
| Fill / drain plug to rear differential housing:<br>• Plug with sealing O-ring | 60 Nm (44 ft-lb) |

## Differential oil level, checking

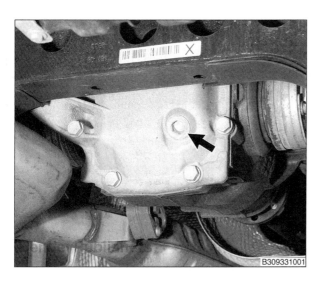

B309331001

◄ Check lubricant level with vehicle on a level surface:
- Remove differential plug (**arrow**).
- Level is correct when fluid just reaches edge of plug hole.
- If necessary, top up fluid.
- Replace plug sealing O-ring.
- Install and tighten oil filler plug when oil level is correct.

| Tightening torque | |
|---|---|
| Fill / drain plug to rear differential housing:<br>• Plug with sealing O-ring | 60 Nm (44 ft-lb) |

## Differential, removing and installing

− Raise car and support safely.

> **WARNING**—
> • Make sure the car is firmly supported on jack stands designed for the purpose. Place jack stands underneath structural chassis points, not underneath suspension parts.

− Disconnect rear drive shaft from differential. See **260 Driveshaft**.

◄ Remove drive axle CV joint bolts (**arrows**) at left and right sides. Suspend drive axles from body using stiff wire.

B309331002

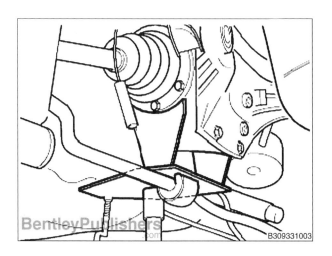

◀ Support differential with BMW special tool 33 4 420. Make sure special tool does not damage output flange dust covers:

- Remove front differential mounting bolts.
- Remove rear differential mounting bolt.
- Remove vent line from differential.
- Carefully lower differential unit.

— To install, use BMW special tool 33 4 420 to lift differential into place:

- Install mounting bolts finger tight (replace nuts and bolts).
- Remove differential support.
- Tighten both front mounting bolts.
- Tighten rear mounting bolt.

— Remainder of installation is reverse of removal. Remember to check differential oil. See **Differential oil level, checking** in this repair group.

| Tightening torques | |
|---|---|
| Differential to subframe<br>• Front mounting bolts (M12)<br>• Rear mounting bolts (M14) | <br>100 Nm (74 ft-lb)<br>165 Nm (122 ft-lb) |
| Rear driveshaft to differential (flex-disc)<br>• M10x10.9<br>  (replace ZNS fasteners)<br>• M12x10.9<br>  (replace ZNS fasteners) | <br><br>20 Nm (15 ft-lb)<br>+ 90°<br>55 Nm (41 ft-lb)<br>+ 90° |
| Rear driveshaft to differential (universal joint)<br>• M10x10.9 (bolt with ribbed teeth)<br>  (replace ZNS fasteners)<br>• M10x10.9 (and M3 models)<br>  (replace ZNS fasteners) | <br>40 Nm (30 ft-lb)<br>+ 45°<br>20 Nm (15 ft-lb)<br>+ 90° |
| Rear driveshaft to differential (flange nut) | 75 Nm (55 ft-lb) |
| Drive axle to differential flange:<br>• Torx M8 (replace bolts and washers)<br>• Torx M10 (replace bolts and washers)<br>• Torx M12 (replace bolts and washers) | <br>52 Nm (38.3 ft-lb)<br>70 Nm (51.6 ft-lb)<br>120 Nm (88.5 ft-lb) |

**331**

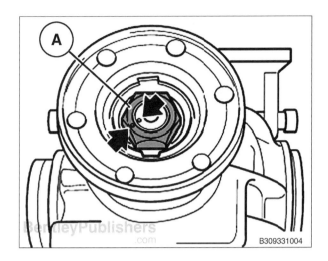

B309331004

## Differential input shaft seal, replacing

– Remove exhaust system. See **180 Exhaust System**.

– Remove drive shaft. See **260 Driveshaft**.

– Lift out collar nut locking plate.

◀ Mark position of collar nut (**A**) on driveshaft flange with a center punch.

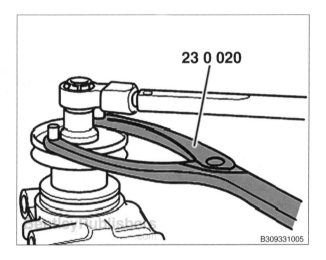

23 0 020

B309331005

◀ Using BMW special tool **23 0 020** or equivalent, brace driveshaft flange and remove collar nut.

**NOTE** —

• *For clarity, illustration shows differential removed.*

33 1 150

B309331006

◀ 188L / 188LW rear differential: Using BMW special tool 33 1 150 or equivalent, remove differential input flange.

*Differential input shaft seal, replacing*

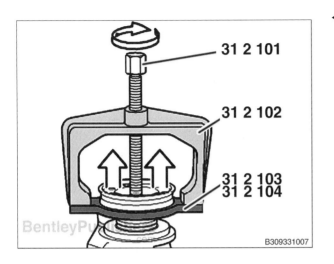

◄ 215L / 215LW rear differential: Using BMW special tools 31 2 101, 31 2 102, 31 2 103 and 31 2 104 or equivalent, remove differential input flange.

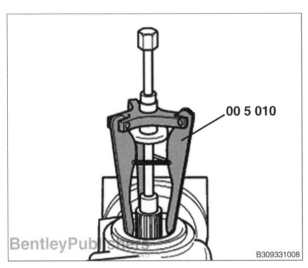

◄ Using BMW special tool 00 5 010 or equivalent remove seal from differential housing.

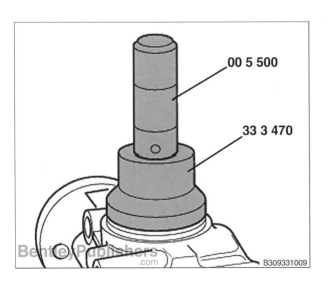

◄ Using BMW special tools 00 5 500 and 33 3 470 or equivalent, drive new seal into place until fully seated.

*Differential input shaft seal, replacing*

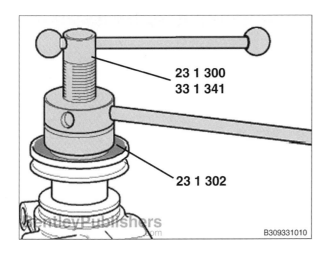

23 1 300
33 1 341

23 1 302

B309331010

◀ Coat drive flange sealing area and seal lip with differential oil:

• Install drive flange on pinion shaft.

• Using BMW special tools 23 1 300, 33 1 341 and 23 1 302, press drive flange on pinion shaft just far enough to allow collar nut to be installed.

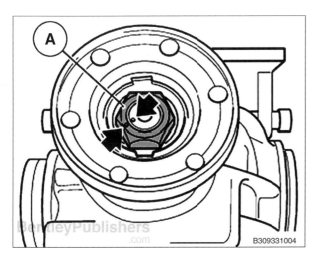

A

B309331004

◀ Tighten collar nut only until previously marked points are aligned (**arrow**).

> **CAUTION—**
> • *Do not under any circumstances tighten collar nut beyond the marked points, otherwise clamping sleeve inside differential housing will have to be replaced.*

– Using a suitable drift pin punch, install new collar nut locking plate. Stake plate in place.

– Remainder of installation is reverse of removal.

– Check differential oil level. See **Differential oil level, checking** in this repair group.

| Tightening torques | |
|---|---|
| Rear driveshaft to differential (flex-disc)<br>• M10x10.9<br>  (replace ZNS fasteners)<br>• M12x10.9<br>  (replace ZNS fasteners) | 20 Nm (15 ft-lb)<br>+ 90°<br>55 Nm (41 ft-lb)<br>+ 90° |
| Rear driveshaft to differential (universal joint)<br>• M10x10.9 (bolt with ribbed teeth)<br>  (replace ZNS fasteners)<br>• M10x10.9 (and M3 models)<br>  (replace ZNS fasteners) | 40 Nm (30 ft-lb)<br>+ 45°<br>20 Nm (15 ft-lb)<br>+ 90° |
| Rear driveshaft to differential (flange nut) | 75 Nm (55 ft-lb) |

## Differential output shaft seals, replacing

– Remove exhaust system (if necessary). See **180 Exhaust System**.

◄ Remove drive axle CV joint bolts (**arrows**). Suspend drive axle from body using stiff wire.

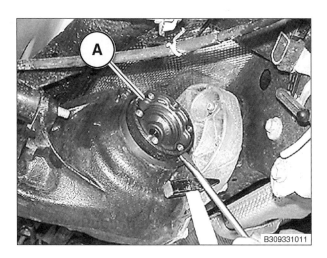

◄ Using a suitable prybar and a hammer (acting as a rest), lever axle flange (**A**) out of differential.

**NOTE**—

• *Be careful not to damage output flange dust covers (if applicable).*

– Pry off output flange dust cover (if applicable).

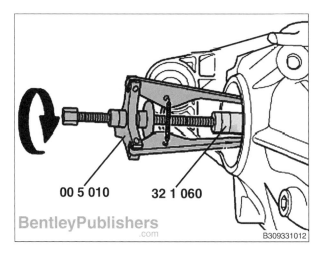

◄ Remove seal using BMW special tools 00 5 010 and 32 1 060 / 33 1 308 or equivalent.

00 5 010    32 1 060

331

*Differential output shaft seals, replacing*

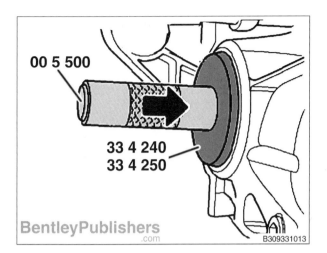

◀ Coat seal with differential oil and drive into place using BMW special tools 00 5 500 and 33 4 240 / 33 4 250 or equivalent.

Tool dimensions:

- 188L / 188LW rear differential: 33 4 240 (90x44x10mm)
- 215L / 215LW rear differential: 33 4 250 (100x50x10mm)

– Replace output flange dust cover (if applicable).

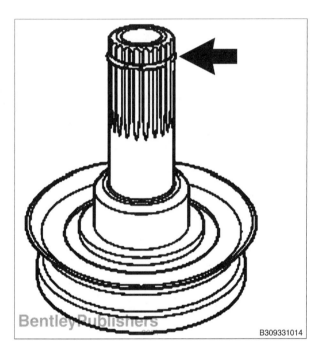

◀ Replace snap ring (**arrow**) on differential output flange shaft:

- Coat output flange shaft with differential oil where it contacts shaft seal.
- Push output flange into differential until flange splines engage splines of differential gear and snap ring can be heard to snap into place.

– Remainder of installation is reverse of removal. Remember to:

- Check differential oil level. See **Differential oil level, checking** in this repair group.

| Tightening torques | |
| --- | --- |
| Drive axle to differential flange: | |
| • Torx M8 (replace bolts and washers) | 52 Nm (38.3 ft-lb) |
| • Torx M10 (replace bolts and washers) | 70 Nm (51.6 ft-lb) |
| • Torx M12 (replace bolts and washers) | 120 Nm (88.5 ft-lb) |

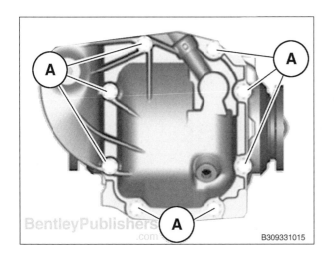

B309331015

## Differential cover, removing and installing

– Drain rear differential oil to a suitable container.

– Remove differential. See **Differential, removing and installing**.

◄ 188L / 188LW rear differential:
- Remove fasteners (**A**).
- Clean cover and differential housing sealing surfaces.
- Install new gasket with cover.
- Remainder of installation is reverse of removal.

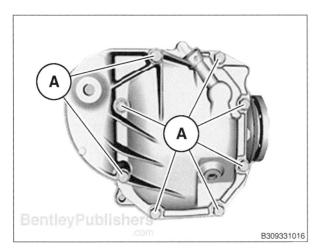

B309331016

◄ 215L / 215LW rear differential:
- Remove fasteners (**A**).
- Clean cover and differential housing sealing surfaces.
- Install new gasket with cover.
- Remainder of installation is reverse of removal.

– Refill differential with oil. See **Differential oil, draining and filling** in this repair group.

| Tightening torque | |
|---|---|
| Differential cover to differential housing: | |
| • 188L / 188LW | 55 Nm (40.5 ft-lb) |
| • 215L / 215LW | 90 Nm (66.3 ft-lb) |

## Differential mounts, replacing

– Remove differential. See **Differential, removing and installing** in this repair group.

### Rear differential mounts

– Remove rear differential rubber mounts using suitable puller.

◄ Coat new mount with Circolight® anti-friction agent and install, noting the following:
- Do not mix up rubber (**A**) and hydraulic mounts (**B**).
- Draw mount in firmly using suitable press.

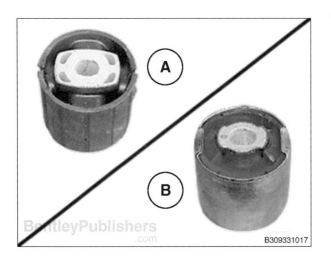

B309331017

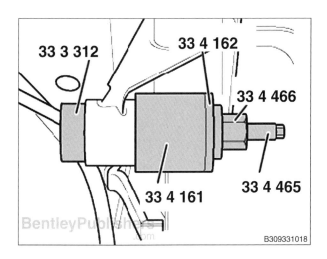

### Front differential mounts

◄ Using BMW special tools 33 3 312, 33 4 161, 33 4 162, 33 4 465 and 33 4 466, remove front differential mount.

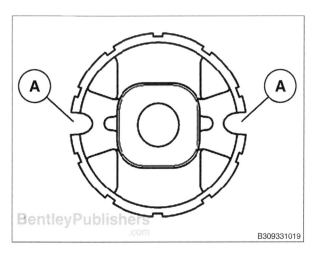

◄ Position slots (**A**) horizontally in rear axle support (A = 90° ± 7°).

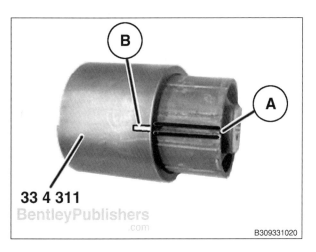

◄ Coat bearing sleeve in rear subframe and rubber mount with Circolight® anti-friction agent:

- Slide rubber mount from side with large diameter into BMW special tool 33 4 311.

- Slot **A** must line up with mark **B**.

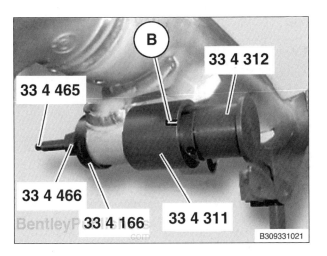

B309331021

◀ Using BMW special tools 33 4 166, 33 4 311, 33 4 312, 33 4 465 and 33 4 466, install front differential mount as far as it will go.

– Remainder of installation is reverse of removal.

## DRIVE AXLES

Drive axles use constant-velocity (CV) joints on both ends. For replacement parts, only CV joint boots or complete axles are offered by BMW.

### Drive axle assembly

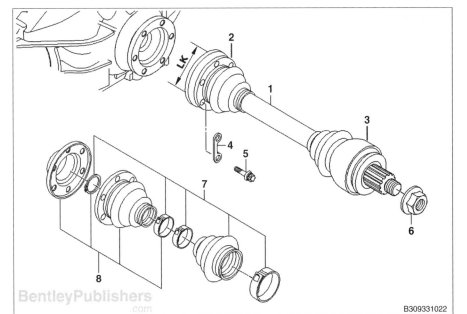

B309331022

1. **Drive axle**
2. **Inner CV joint**
3. **Outer CV joint**
4. **Reinforcement**
5. **Torx bolt**
6. **Collar nut**
7. **Outer CV boot kit**
8. **Inner CV boot kit**

**331**

## Drive axle, removing and installing

◄ With an assistant applying brakes, break free staked collar nut (**arrow**) at center of rear wheel hub. Do not remove completely.

**NOTE** —

• *The wheel hub collar nut is tightened to a high torque. Make sure the car is firmly on the ground.*

– Raise rear of car. Remove rear wheel.

> **WARNING** —
>
> • *Make sure that the car is firmly supported on jack stands designed for the purpose. Place the jack stands beneath structural chassis points. Do not place jack stands under suspension parts.*

– Remove exhaust components as needed. See **180 Exhaust System**.

◄ Remove drive axle mounting bolts (**arrows**) from differential flange.

– Support rear wheel bearing carrier with a suitable jack.

– Using jack, lift wheel bearing carrier so that inboard side of drive axle clears the differential.

◄ Remove staked collar nut and press output shaft out of wheel hub.

– Remove drive axle towards center of vehicle.

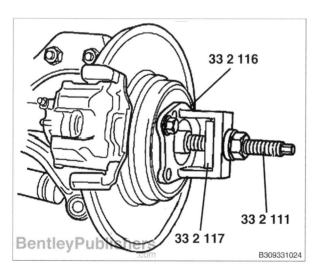

— Installation is reverse of removal, noting the following:

• Use a new collar nut.

• Apply a light coating of oil to contact face of collar nut and tighten firmly, but not to final torque.

• Install road wheel and lower car to ground.

• With an assistant applying brakes, tighten drive axle collar nut to its final torque. Stake collar nut.

| Tightening torques | |
| --- | --- |
| Drive axle collar nut to wheel hub<br>• M24<br>• M27 | <br>250 Nm (184.3 ft-lb)<br>420 Nm (310 ft-lb) |
| Drive axle to differential flange:<br>• Torx M8 (replace bolts and washers)<br>• Torx M10 (replace bolts and washers)<br>• Torx M12 (replace bolts and washers) | <br>52 Nm (38.3 ft-lb)<br>70 Nm (51.6 ft-lb)<br>120 Nm (88.5 ft-lb) |
| Road wheel to hub | 120 Nm (88.5 ft-lb) |

## CV joint boots

*NOTE —*

• *When replacing a CV joint boot, use a complete CV joint boot repair kit. The kit will include a new boot, clamping bands, special lubricant, and a new inner CV joint circlip. The kit is available from an authorized BMW dealer parts department.*

• *The outer CV joint cannot be removed from the axle shaft. In order to replace the outer CV boot, it is necessary to remove the inner joint and boot first.*

• *If the CV joints are worn or defective, a complete rebuilt axle shaft is available from an authorized BMW dealer parts department.*

— Remove axle shaft. See **Drive axle, removing and installing** in this repair group.

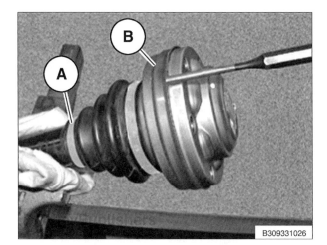

◄ Working with axle shaft at bench, cut off old boot clamps and remove boot (**A**) from inner joint (**B**) with suitable tool. Clean old grease off joint and shaft.

— Remove dust cover from inner CV joint.

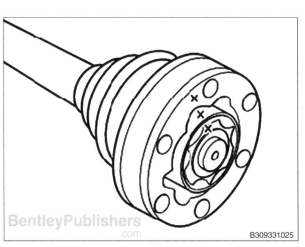

◄ Mark CV joint component positions in relation to each other.

• Ball hub

• Ball cage

• CV joint

*NOTE —*

• *This will aid in reassembly if CV joint comes apart.*

B309331026

B309331025

331

*CV joint boots*

◄ Remove circlip (**A**).

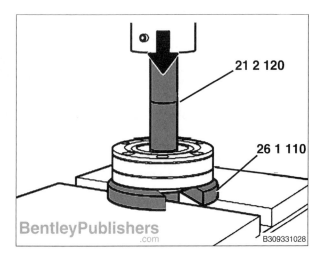

◄ Support inner hub with BMW special tool 26 1 110 and press axle shaft out of joint using BMW special tool 21 2 120.

— Clean all old lubricant off shaft splines and inner joint splines.

> **CAUTION—**
> • If the CV joint must be disassembled for cleaning and inspection, be sure to matchmark inner and outer race and intermediate ball cage. This allows reassembly of parts in their original positions.

**NOTE—**

• To inspect a CV joint, clean away the grease and look for galling, pitting, and other signs of wear or physical damage. Polished surfaces or visible ball tracks alone are not necessarily cause for replacement. Discoloration due to overheating indicates lack of lubrication and need for a new CV joint.

• Do not let the ball hub pivot too far in the outer ring of the joint. The balls will fall out.

◄ If replacing outer CV joint boot, cut off old boot clamps (**A**) and remove boot (**B**) from outer CV joint. Clean old grease off CV joint and shaft and carefully separate joint from axle.

— Clean all old lubricant off shaft splines and inner joint splines.

**NOTE—**

• To inspect a CV joint, clean away the grease and look for galling, pitting, and other signs of wear or physical damage. Polished surfaces or visible ball tracks alone are not necessarily cause for replacement. Discoloration due to overheating indicates lack of lubrication and need for a new CV joint.

— Slide outer CV joint boot on axle shaft.

**NOTE—**

• Do not let the ball hub pivot too far in the outer ring of the joint. The balls will fall out.

• Before installing each small boot clamp be sure to "burp" the boot by flexing the CV joint. A small screwdriver inserted between the boot and the axle shaft will help the process.

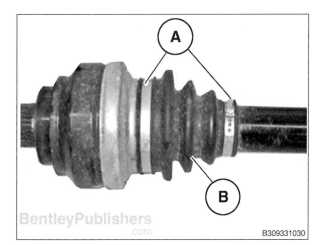

— Install new boot clamps.

**NOTE—**

• *Apply Loctite® 270 or an equivalent heavy-duty locking compound to inner drive axle splines.*

---

**CAUTION—**

• *Do not let the locking compound contact the balls in the joint. Apply only a thin coat to cover the splines.*

---

— Slide inner CV joint boot on axle shaft.

◀ While supporting axle shaft with BMW special tool 33 2 100, press inner hub of CV joint onto shaft. Install a new circlip.

— Install new boot clamps.

**NOTE—**

• *Before installing each small boot clamp be sure to "burp" the boot by flexing the CV joint. A small screwdriver inserted between the boot and the axle shaft will help the process.*

— Use sealing gel to seal dust cover to CV joint prior to reinstallation.

— Remainder of installation is reverse of removal.

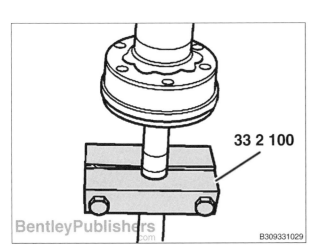

33 2 100

B309331029

| Tightening torques | |
|---|---|
| Drive axle collar nut to wheel hub<br>• M24<br>• M27 | 250 Nm (184.3 ft-lb)<br>420 Nm (310 ft-lb) |
| Drive axle to differential flange:<br>• Torx M8 (replace bolts and washers)<br>• Torx M10 (replace bolts and washers)<br>• Torx M12 (replace bolts and washers) | 52 Nm (38.3 ft-lb)<br>70 Nm (51.6 ft-lb)<br>120 Nm (88.5 ft-lb) |
| Road wheel to hub | 120 Nm (88.5 ft-lb) |

331

# 340 Brakes

**340**

## GENERAL

This repair group covers service for the brake system and for electronic braking and stability control (traction control) systems.

See also:

- **020 Maintenance** for basic brake system checks
- **300 Suspension, Steering and Brakes–General**
- **612 Switches** for brake light switch
- **ECL Electrical Component Locations** for fuse and component access
- **ELE Electrical Wiring Diagrams**

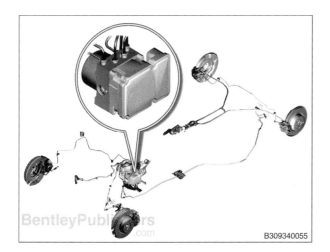

B309340055

## Brake system

3 Series models are equipped with vacuum power-assisted four-wheel disc brakes with integral antilock braking system (ABS). Single-piston calipers act on vented front and rear rotors. Two-stage brake pad wear sensors work along with condition based service (CBS) system to indicate when brake pads need replacement. The first stage is activated when brake pad linings reach a thickness of 6 mm, the second is activated at a thickness of 4 mm. The dual drum-type parking brake system is integrated with the rear brake rotors.

## Electronic braking and stability control

3 Series models are equipped with dynamic stability control (DSC). DSC is a computer controlled traction control system that uses the ABS system in conjunction with engine management controls to control wheel spin during acceleration and maintain vehicle stability while braking.

## Troubleshooting

Brake performance is mainly affected by three factors:

• Level and condition of brake fluid

• Ability of brake system to create and maintain pressure

• Condition of friction components

Air in brake fluid makes the brake pedal feel spongy during braking or increases the brake pedal force required to stop. Fluid contaminated by moisture or dirt corrodes the system. Inspect the brake fluid inside the reservoir. If it is dirty or murky, or is more then two years old, replace fluid. See **Brake system, bleeding** in this repair group.

To check the function of the master cylinder, hold the brake pedal down hard with the engine running. If the pedal slowly falls to the floor, either the master cylinder is leaking internally or fluid is leaking externally.

Inspect the brake rotors for glazing, discoloration and scoring. Steering wheel vibration while braking at speed is often caused by warped rotors, but can also be caused by worn suspension components.

When troubleshooting, keep in mind that tire inflation, wear and temperature can all have an affect on braking. See **300 Suspension, Steering and Brakes–General** for additional suspension and brake system troubleshooting.

**Table a** lists symptoms of brake problems, probable causes, and suggested corrective actions. Unless noted otherwise, relevant repairs are described later in this repair group.

**Table a. Brake system troubleshooting**

| Symptom | Probable cause | Repairs |
|---|---|---|
| Brake squeal | Brake pad carriers dirty or corroded or pads loose (poor fit) in pad carrier | Remove brake pads and clean calipers. Use original equipment pads for proper fit and use BMW anti-squeal compound during installation. |
| | Brake pads heat-glazed or oil-soaked | Replace brake pads. Clean rotors. Replace leaking calipers as required. |
| | Wheel bearings worn (noise most pronounced when turning) | Replace worn bearings. See **310 Front Suspension** or **330 Rear Suspension**. |
| | Incorrectly installed brake pads, parking brake shoes, or brake parts | Check component installation. Check/replace anti-rattle springs. |
| Pedal goes to floor when braking | Brake fluid loss due to system leaks | Check fluid level and inspect for signs of leakage. |
| | Master cylinder or traction control system faulty | Replace master cylinder. Diagnose traction control system using factory or compatible diagnostic tool. |
| Low pedal after system bleeding | Master cylinder faulty | Replace master cylinder. |
| Pedal spongy or brakes work only when pedal is pumped | Air in brake fluid | Bleed system using factory or compatible diagnostic tool. |
| | Master cylinder or traction control system faulty | Replace master cylinder. Diagnose traction control system using factory or compatible diagnostic tool. |
| Excessive braking effort | Brake pads wet | Use light pedal pressure to dry pads while driving. |
| | Brake pads heat-glazed or fluid-soaked | Replace brake pads and rotors. Replace leaking calipers. |
| | Vacuum booster or vacuum hose connections to booster faulty | Inspect vacuum lines. Test vacuum booster and replace as required. Test brake booster check valve for one-way flow. |
| Brakes pulsate, chatter or grab | Warped brake rotors | Resurface or replace rotors. |
| | Brake pads worn | Replace brake pads. |
| | Brake pads heat-glazed or oil-soaked | Clean rotors. Replace leaking calipers. |
| Uneven braking, car pulls to one side, rear brakes lock | Incorrect tire pressures or worn tires | Inspect tire condition. Check and correct tire pressures. |
| | Brake pads on one side of car heat-glazed or fluid-soaked | Replace brake pads. Clean rotors. Replace leaking calipers. |
| | Caliper or brake pads binding | Clean and recondition brakes. |
| | Worn suspension components | Inspect for worn or damaged suspension components. See **310 Front Suspension** or **330 Rear Suspension**. |
| Brakes drag, bind or overheat | Brake caliper or brake pads binding | Clean or replace caliper. |
| | Master cylinder or traction control system faulty | Replace master cylinder. Diagnose traction control system using factory or compatible diagnostic tool. |

**340**

## Warnings and Cautions

---

*WARNING*—

• Make sure that the brake system is bled using a BMW scan tool or equivalent. See **Bleeding Brakes** in this repair group.

• Semi-metallic and metallic brake friction materials in brake pads or shoes produce dangerous dust. Treat all brake dust as a hazardous material. Do not create dust by grinding, sanding, or cleaning brake friction surfaces with compressed air.

• Brake fluid is poisonous, corrosive and dangerous to the environment. Wear safety glasses and rubber gloves when working with brake fluid. Do not siphon brake fluid with your mouth. Dispose of brake fluid properly.

• Do not reuse self-locking nuts, bolts or fasteners. They are designed to be used only once and may fail if reused. Replace them with new self-locking fasteners.

• A car with electronic stability control is still subject to normal physical laws. Avoid excessive speeds for the road conditions encountered.

---

*CAUTION*—

• Brake fluid damages paint. Immediately clean brake fluid spilled on painted surfaces and wash with water.

• Use new brake fluid from a fresh, unopened container. Brake fluid absorbs moisture from the air. This can lead to corrosion problems in the braking system and also lowers the fluid boiling point.

• When working on brake fluid lines:
-Do not mix up fluid lines at the master cylinder or hydraulic unit. Label unions before disconnecting.
-Do not kink brake lines.
-Plug open lines and brake fluid ports to prevent contamination.

• Tighten brake hoses on front wheels with wheels in straight ahead position.

• If carrying out electric welding work, be sure to disconnect electrical harness connector from electronic control module.

• Do not expose electronic control modules to high sustained heat. Maximum heat exposure:
-95°C (203°F) for short periods of time
-85°C (185°F) for long periods of time (approx. 2 hours)

---

## BLEEDING BRAKES

> **WARNING—**
>
> • The BMW traction control system uses electronic controls and a sophisticated hydraulic unit in the brake system. Once air enters the hydraulic unit, it is very difficult to remove using traditional methods. For this reason, use BMW scan tool or equivalent to pressure bleed brakes.
>
> • When flushing brake fluid from the system, use extreme care to not let the brake fluid reservoir run dry. If air enters the hydraulic unit, be sure to use the BMW scan tool to bleed the brake system before the vehicle is driven.

Brake bleeding is usually done for one of two reasons:

• To replace old brake fluid as part of routine maintenance

• To expel trapped air in the system that resulted from opening the brake hydraulic system during repairs.

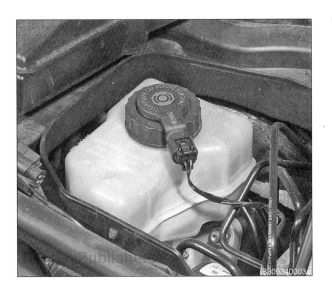

 BMW recommends completely replacing the brake fluid at least once every two years. When replacing brake fluid or bleeding brakes, use the correct specification brake fluid according to **Table b**.

| Table b. Brake fluid application | |
|---|---|
| BMW preferred fluid | Low viscosity DOT 4 brake fluid |
| *Low viscosity DOT 4 brake fluid may be used in all 3 Series vehicles. DOT 4 and low viscosity DOT 4 brake fluid can be mixed.* | |

When adding or replacing brake fluid, add new brake fluid from an unopened container. It is important to bleed the entire system when any part of the hydraulic system is opened.

If you are certain no air was introduced into the master cylinder or DSC hydraulic unit, bleed the brakes at the calipers using a pressure bleeder. See **Brake calipers, bleeding** in this repair group.

However, if air enters the DSC hydraulic unit, bubbles may adhere to the edges and internal valves of the unit and these cannot be removed via conventional flushing. In that case it is necessary to bleed brakes using a BMW scan tool or equivalent. The special tool creates pulsations or vibrations which loosen and flush the bubbles.

Therefore, if you are in any doubt about introduced air into the brake system, use the service tools to bleed the system or have the brakes bled by an authorized BMW dealer. See **Brake system, bleeding** in this repair group.

When bleeding the brakes, start at the wheel farthest from the master cylinder and progress in the following order:

• right rear brake

• left rear brake

• right front brake

• left front brake

340

## Brake calipers, bleeding

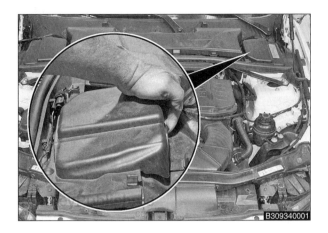

◄ Remove cover (**inset**) to access brake fluid reservoir.

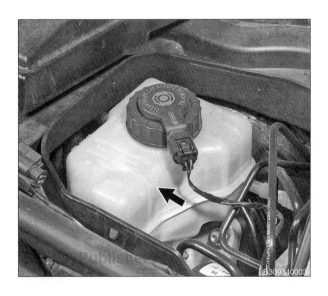

◄ Top off brake fluid reservoir (**arrow**).

– Connect pressure bleeder to reservoir. Pressurize system to approximately 2 bar (29 psi).

> **CAUTION—**
> • *Do not exceed a pressure of 2 bar (29 psi) when pressure bleeding the brake system. Excessive pressure damages the brake fluid reservoir.*

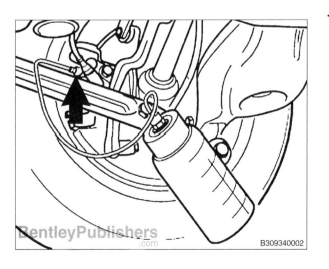

◄ Connect bleeder hose and bottle to **right rear** caliper bleeder screw (**arrow**). Have a helper hold brake pedal down.

◄  Open bleeder screw (**arrow**). Have helper slowly pump brakes about 10 times with bleeder screw open, holding pedal down on last pump. When escaping fluid is free of air bubbles, close bleeder screw.

> **CAUTION—**
> • *Make sure bleeder hose remains submersed in clean brake fluid whenever the bleeder valve is open.*

—  Close bleeder screw and release brake pedal. Refill brake fluid reservoir and proceed to left rear wheel.

—  Continue bleeding remaining wheels in the following order:
- **left rear**
- **right front**
- **left front**

| Tightening torques | |
|---|---|
| Bleeder to caliper: | |
| • 9 mm screw | 7 - 11 Nm (5 - 8 ft-lb) |
| • 11 mm screw | 12 - 18 Nm (9 - 13 ft-lb) |

## Brake system, bleeding

The procedure below requires the use of BMW scan tool or equivalent.

◄  Remove cover (**inset**) to access brake fluid reservoir.

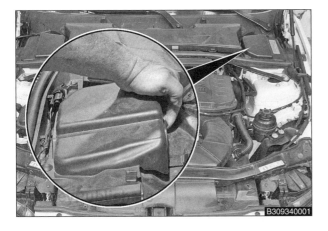

◄  Top off brake fluid reservoir (**arrow**).

—  Connect pressure bleeder to reservoir. Pressurize system to approximately 2 bar (29 psi).

> **CAUTION—**
> • *Do not exceed a pressure of 2 bar (29 psi) when pressure bleeding the brake system. Excessive pressure damages the brake fluid reservoir.*

—  Connect BMW scan tool or equivalent to OBD II plug on underside of dash in left footwell.

340

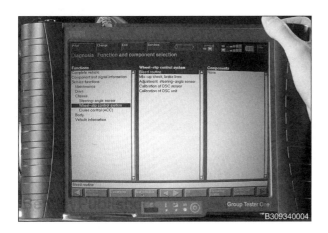

◁ Set tool to service function Bleeding ABS / DSC.

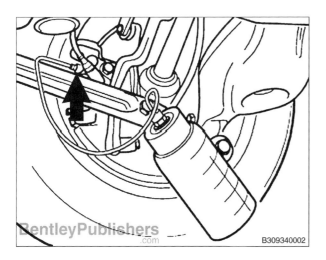

◁ Connect bleeder hose and bottle to **right rear** caliper bleeder screw (**arrow**). Have a helper hold brake pedal down.

◁ Open bleeder screw (**arrow**). Carry out bleeding procedure using BMW scan tool on-screen instructions until clear, bubble-free fluid flows.

– After BMW scan tool bleeding routine has finished, press brake pedal to floor 5 times until clear, bubble-free fluid flows. Close bleeder.

> **CAUTION—**
> • *Make sure bleeder hose remains submersed in clean brake fluid whenever the bleeder valve is open.*

– Repeat procedure at **left rear** brake.

– Repeat procedure at **right front** brake.

– Repeat procedure at **left front** brake.

— Remove brake bleeding apparatus and disconnect BMW scan tool. Top off brake fluid. Check to make sure brake fluid reservoir cap seal is intact.

| Tightening torques | |
|---|---|
| Bleeder to caliper: | |
| • 9 mm screw | 7 - 11 Nm (5 - 8 ft-lb) |
| • 11 mm screw | 12 - 18 Nm (9 - 13 ft-lb) |

## BRAKE PADS, CALIPERS AND ROTORS

### Braking system components

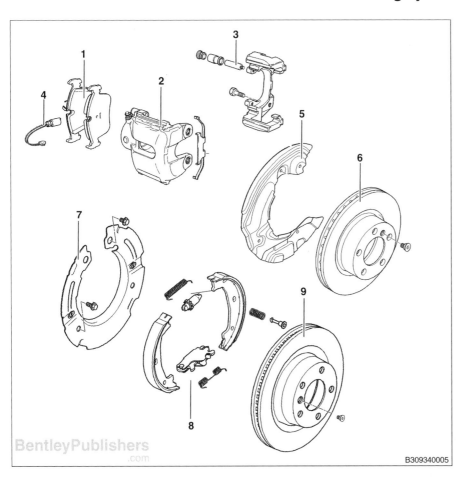

B309340005

1. Brake pads
   • Wear limit: 3 mm (0.12 in).
   • Follow directional marking when installing.

2. Brake caliper

3. Brake caliper guide bolt
   • Tighten to 30 ± 2 Nm (22 ± 1 ft-lb).

4. Brake pad wear sensor
   • On left front, right rear inner pad.
   • Replace with new pads.
   • Replace if brake pad wear warning light illuminated.

5. Front brake backing plate

6. Front brake rotor
   • See **Table d** or **Table e** for brake rotor specifications.
   • Clean off preservative before installing new rotor.

7. Rear brake backing plate

8. Parking brake shoes with hardware

9. Rear brake rotor

340

## Brake pads, checking and replacing

Brake pads can be replaced without disconnecting the brake fluid hose from the caliper or having to bleed the brakes. The rotors can be replaced without disassembling wheel hub and bearing. Front and rear brake pad replacement procedures are similar.

Replace pads in sets.

— Raise car and support safely. Remove wheels.

> **WARNING—**
> • *Make sure the car is stable and well supported at all times. Use a professional automotive lift or jack stands designed for the purpose. A floor jack is not adequate support.*

 To measure brake pad lining thickness, insert BMW special tool 34 1 260 at either right front or left rear wheel.

- Move wheel until notch for brake wear indicator can be seen through wheel opening.
- Insert tip of tool into notch so that body of tool rests on brake pad backing plate (**A**), and tip touches brake rotor (**B**).
- Replace pads if at minimum thickness. See **Table c**.

| Table c. Brake pad lining minimum thickness | |
|---|---|
| Minimum pad thickness, front or rear | 2.4 mm (0.9 in) |

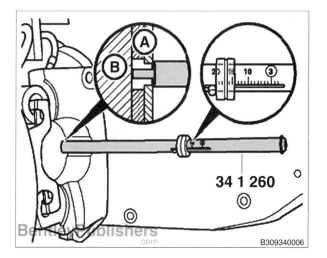

B309340006

 Pry off brake caliper anti-rattle spring in direction of **arrows**.

B309340011

*Brake pads, checking and replacing*

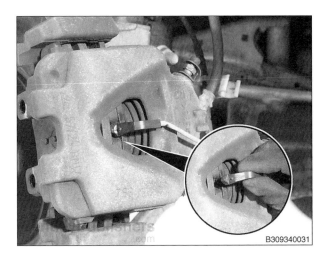

◄ Using your fingers, carefully remove brake pad wear sensor from brake pad.

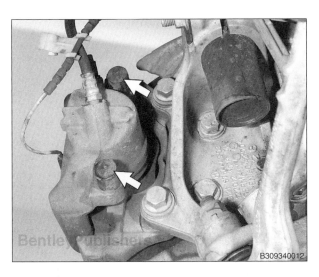

◄ Remove plastic caps from caliper guide bolts (**arrows**).

**340**

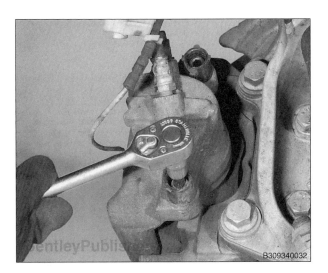

◄ Use BMW special tool 34 1 080 (7 mm Allen wrench) to remove caliper guide bolts. Remove caliper from pad carrier.

> ***CAUTION—***
> • *Do not let the brake caliper assembly hang from the brake hose. Support caliper from chassis with strong wire.*

**NOTE—**
• *If there is a ridge on brake rotor edge, press caliper pistons back into caliper before removing caliper.*

— Check brake rotor thickness. Inspect for rust or damage. If necessary replace or machine brake rotors. See **Brake rotor, removing and installing** in this repair group. Brake rotor specifications are in **Table d** and **Table e**.

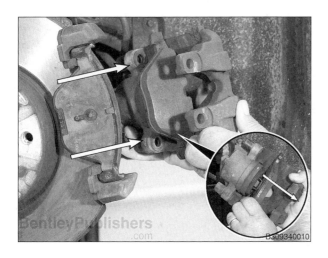

◀ Remove brake pads in direction of **arrows**.

**NOTE** —
• *Inner brake pad (**inset**) has a spring to locate it in the caliper piston.*

◀ Compress caliper piston using BMW special tool 34 1 050 or equivalent.

**CAUTION**—
• *Pressing caliper pistons in may cause brake fluid reservoir to overflow. To prevent this, use a clean syringe to first remove some fluid from reservoir.*

– Check caliper dust boots for damage and replace if necessary.

– Clean contact surfaces between caliper and caliper carrier.

◀ Apply thin coating of BMW anti-squeal compound to caliper contact face (**arrows**).

• Do not apply grease to brake pad backing plate.

**CAUTION**—
• *Do not let caliper rubber dust sleeve come in contact with anti-squeal compound. The compound causes rubber to swell and deteriorate.*

*Brake pads, checking and replacing*

B309340007

◄ Apply thin coating of BMW anti-squeal compound to brake pad rests (**arrows**) on pad carrier.

*NOTE—*

• *In order to preserve brake caliper surface coating use brake cleaner only to clean.*

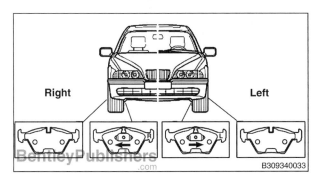

**Right**     **Left**

B309340033

◄ When installing directional brake pads, install marked pads as shown.

*NOTE—*

• *BMW-supplied (OEM) front brake pads may be marked as directional pads. Aftermarket brands are generally not labeled as directional. When installing directional pads, be sure to install them as indicated in the illustration.*

– Where applicable, insert brake pad wear sensor into cutout in new pad. Push sensor into pad cutout until it locks into place. Brake pad wear sensor is fragile, be careful not to damage during installation.

*NOTE—*

• *If brake pad wear sensor light illuminated prior to brake pad replacement, replace wear sensor or reset CBS data. Brake pad sensor can only be installed once, then needs replacing. See **020 Maintenance**.*

– Route pad wear sensor wiring through caliper opening and under bleeder dust cap.

– Remainder of installation is reverse of removal.

• Clean brake caliper guide bolts (7 mm Allen). Replace ones which are not in perfect condition. Do not grease.

• Top off brake fluid to MAX marking.

• Before driving car, pump brake pedal several times so that brake pads contact brake rotors.

• Check that brake fluid level is correct. Top off if necessary.

• Hold ignition key for at least 30 seconds in accessory position without starting engine. This clears fault codes in memory and turns brake pad warning light OFF. If light remains on reset condition based service (CBS) system. See **020 Maintenance**.

| Tightening torques | |
|---|---|
| Brake caliper to pad carrier (7 mm Allen) | 30 ± 2 Nm (22 ± 1 ft-lb) |
| Road wheel to hub | 120 Nm (88.5 ft-lb) |

## Brake caliper and pad carrier, removing and installing

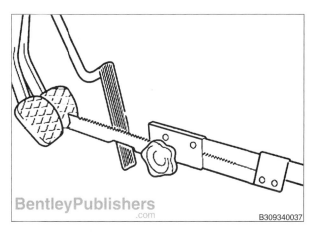

◀ Insert pedal prop and depress brake pedal slightly. This prevents brake fluid from escaping when brake lines are detached.

− Raise car and support safely. Remove wheels.

> **WARNING** —
> • *Make sure the car is stable and well supported at all times. Use a professional automotive lift or jack stands designed for the purpose. A floor jack is not adequate support.*

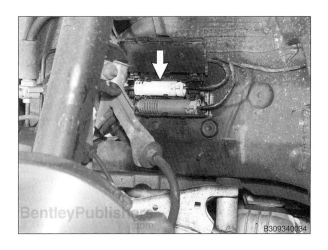

◀ Left front wheel: Working in junction box in wheel housing, separate brake pad warning sensor electrical harness (**arrow**).

− Right rear wheel: Remove right rear wheel well housing liner. See **410 Fenders, Engine Hood**.

◀ Working in junction box in wheel housing, separate brake pad warning sensor electrical harness (**arrow**).

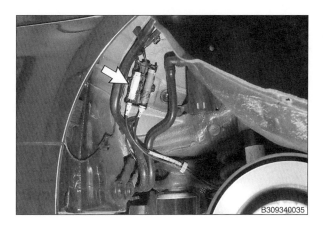

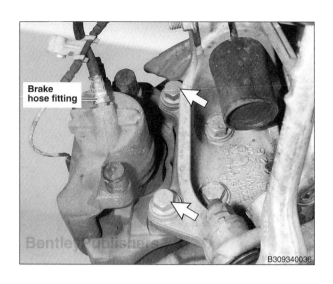

Brake
hose fitting

B309340036

◀ Working at brake caliper:

- Loosen brake hose fitting at caliper. Use shop towels to catch dripping brake fluid.
- Remove pad carrier and caliper mounting bolts (**arrows**) from steering knuckle (front caliper) or from wheel bearing carrier (rear caliper).

— Lift off caliper and spin assembly off hose. Plug open fluid lines and ports.

— Inspect brake caliper for signs of leakage. Check that caliper piston slides smoothly into caliper. Replace caliper if any faults are found.

— Installation is reverse of removal. Bleed entire brake system before driving car. See **Brake calipers, bleeding** in this repair group.

| Tightening torques | |
|---|---|
| Brake caliper to pad carrier | 30 ± 2 Nm (22 ± 1 ft-lb) |
| Brake fluid hose to caliper | 24 ± 2 Nm (17.7 ± 1 ft-lb) |
| Brake hose to steel line | 12 Nm (8.8 ft-lb) |
| Front pad carrier to steering knuckle | 110 Nm (81 ft-lb) |
| Rear pad carrier to wheel bearing carrier | 65 Nm (50 ft-lb) |
| Road wheel to hub | 120 Nm (88.5 ft-lb) |

## Brake rotor, removing and installing

Measure brake rotor diameter on vehicle and check against corresponding brake rotor specifications in **Table d** (front brakes) or **Table e** (rear brakes). Additional application information is available through parts data and authorized BMW dealer parts department.

| Table d. Front brake rotor specifications in mm (inches) | | |
|---|---|---|
| Diameter | Thickness (new) | Thickness (min.) |
| 360 (14.2) | 30 (1.18) | 28.4 (1.12) |
| 348 (13.7) | 30 (1.18) | 28.4 (1.12) |
| 338(13.3) | 26 (1.02) | 24.4 (0.96) |
| 330 (13.0) | 24 (0.94) | 22.4 (0.88) |
| 312 (12.3) | 24 (0.94) | 22.4 (0.88) |
| 300 (11.8) | 24 (0.94) | 22.4 (0.88) |
| 292 | 22 (0.87) | 20.4 (0.80) |
| Max. machine limit per friction ring side: 0.8 mm (0.03 in). Do not machine M3 brake rotors. | | |
| Wear warning from residual lining thickness: 3.7 mm (0.15 in). | | |

**340**

| Table e. Rear brake rotor specifications in mm (inches) | | |
|---|---|---|
| Diameter | Thickness (new) | Thickness (min.) |
| 350 (13.8) | 24 (0.94) | 22.4 (0.88) |
| 336 (13.2) | 22 (0.87) | 20.4 (0.80) |
| 300 (11.8) | 20 (0.79) | 18.4 (0.72) |
| 296 (11.7) | 10 (0.39) | 8.4 (0.33) |
| Max. machine limit per friction ring side: 0.8 mm (0.03 in). Do not machine M3 brake rotors. | | |
| Wear warning from residual lining thickness: 3.7 mm (0.15 in) | | |

Machine or replace brake rotors in pairs per axle.

− Raise car and support safely. Remove wheels.

> **WARNING**—
> • *Make sure the car is stable and well supported at all times. Use a professional automotive lift or jack stands designed for the purpose. A floor jack is not adequate support.*

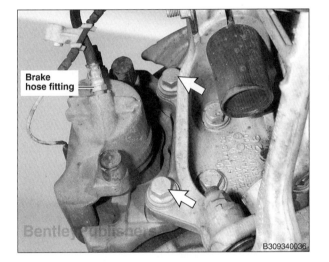

◄ Remove brake caliper carrier bolts (**arrows**). Suspend brake caliper from chassis using stiff wire.

> **NOTE**—
> • *Hydraulic brake line remains connected.*

◄ Remove brake rotor mounting screw (**arrow**) and remove rotor.

− Inspect rotor for cracks, signs of overheating and scoring.

− Minimum allowable thickness (MIN TH) is stamped on rotor hub. Measure rotor braking surface with a micrometer at eight to ten different points and use the smallest measurement. Compare to specifications in **Table d** or **Table e**.

− If rotor does not pass minimum thickness requirements or is damaged, replace rotor.
  • Clean rotor with brake cleaner before installing.
  • When installing new rear brake rotors, adjust parking brake. See **Parking brake, adjusting** in this repair group.

| Tightening torques | |
|---|---|
| Brake rotor to hub | 16 Nm (12 ft-lb) |
| Front brake pad carrier to steering knuckle | 110 Nm (81 ft-lb) |
| Rear brake pad carrier to wheel bearing carrier | 65 Nm (48 ft-lb) |
| Road wheel to hub | 120 Nm (88.5 ft-lb) |

## MASTER CYLINDER

The brake master cylinder is mounted to the front of the vacuum booster on the driver side bulkhead.

> **WARNING**—
> • *Make sure that the brake system is bled using the BMW scan tool or equivalent. See* **Bleeding Brakes** *in this repair group.*

## Master cylinder, removing and installing

> **CAUTION**—
> • *Brake fluid is highly corrosive and dangerous to the environment. Dispose of it properly.*

– Remove cabin microfilter housings. See **640 Heating and Air-conditioning**.

– Remove left lower dashboard trim. See **513 Interior Trim**.

◄ Working at brake fluid reservoir at left rear of engine compartment:
  • Detach brake fluid level sensor connector (**arrow**).
  • Remove reservoir cap.
  • Using a clean syringe, empty brake fluid reservoir.
  • Plug open brake fluid lines and ducts to prevent fluid leakage and contamination.

– Remove brake fluid reservoir by tilting sideways out of grommets.

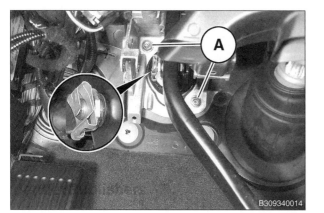

◄ Slacken brake booster:
  • Remove fasteners (**A**).
  • Disconnect brake pedal from push rod (**inset**).

**340**

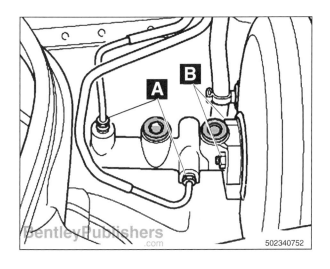

◀ Disconnect master cylinder brake lines (**A**).

- Plug open brake lines to prevent contamination.
- Remove master cylinder mounting nuts (**B**) and remove master cylinder.

– During reinstallation, make sure all nuts, fluid couplings, thread bores, and mating surfaces are clean.

– Mount master cylinder to brake booster using new sealing O-ring and new self-locking nuts.

> **CAUTION—**
> - *Be sure to align master cylinder pushrod and booster pushrod.*
> - *Do not over-torque master cylinder mounting nuts. This could damage the brake booster and prevent proper vacuum build-up.*

| Tightening torque | |
|---|---|
| Brake master cylinder to brake booster | 21 ± 3 Nm (15.4 ± 2 ft-lb) |

– Connect brake fluid lines to master cylinder.

| Tightening torque | |
|---|---|
| Brake fluid line to master cylinder | 12 Nm (8.8 ft-lb) |

– Reinstall fluid reservoir using new sealing grommets.

– Fasten brake booster.

| Tightening torque | |
|---|---|
| Brake booster to body panel<br>• M8 | 21 Nm (15.4 ft-lb) |

– Remainder of installation is reverse of removal. Remember to:

- Top up with fresh brake fluid.
- Bleed entire brake system. See **Brake system, bleeding** in this repair group.

## Brake booster check valve

The check valve in the brake booster vacuum line prevents contamination from engine backfires and other sources from entering the brake booster. The check valve is attached to brake booster.

– Remove DSC hydraulic control unit. See **DSC hydraulic control unit, removing and installing** In this repair group.

– Pump brake pedal a few times to reduce vacuum in brake booster. This makes removal of check valve easier.

◀ Disconnect quick connect coupler (**arrow**).

◄ Remove valve to test or replace. Valve is pressed into grommet in vacuum booster (**inset**), pry it out carefully.

— Reinstall valve using new hose clamps. Install valve so that molded arrow is pointing toward intake manifold.

## Auxiliary brake booster vacuum pump

◄ 3 Series models use an auxiliary pump to supply vacuum to the brake booster, rather than using traditional manifold vacuum.

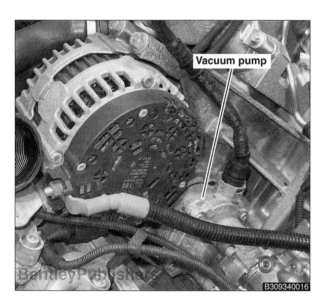

Vacuum pump

# PARKING BRAKE

## Parking brake components

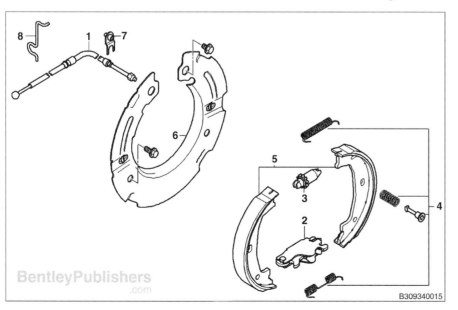

1. Parking brake bowden cable
2. Expanding lock
3. Adjuster
4. Brake shoe hardware
5. Brake shoes
6. Backing plate
7. Spring clip
8. Bowden cable bracket

## Parking brake, adjusting

The parking brake is a brake drum system integrated into the rear brake rotors. Adjust with rear of car raised off the ground and the wheels installed.

Adjusting parking brake under the following circumstances:

- After replacing parking brake shoes
- After replacing rear brake rotors
- Excessive stroke of parking brake handle required for actuation (more then 10 clicks)
  - After replacement of brake shoe adjuster or parking brake cable(s)

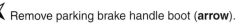 Remove parking brake handle boot (**arrow**).

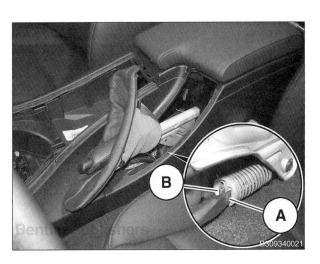

◄ relieve parking brake cable tension: Using a screwdriver, lock parking brake handle adjuster by pressing stop (**A**) spring back to engage hook (**B**). **Inset** shows hook engaged.

— Raise rear of car.

> **WARNING—**
> • *Make sure that the car is firmly supported on jack stands designed for the purpose. Place jack stands beneath structural chassis points. Do not place jack stands under suspension parts.*

◄ Remove one rear wheel stud and rotate wheel until parking brake adjuster is visible through wheel stud hole (**arrow**).

◁ Using a screwdriver turn parking brake adjuster (**inset**) until wheel can no longer be rotated. Back adjuster off corresponding amount of notches. See table below.

| Parking brake adjusting (initial) | |
| --- | --- |
| 185 diameter brake rotor | 8 notches |
| 160 diameter brake rotor | 9 notches |

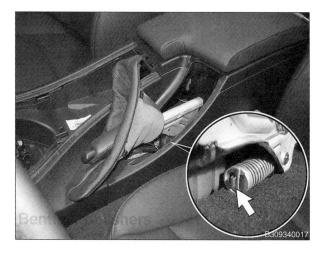

◁ Unlock parking brake handle adjuster by levering out restraining hook (**arrow**) with a screwdriver.

– Working inside car, set parking brake several times to seat brakes.

– Release lever and make sure rear wheels turn freely.

– Switch ignition ON. Pull up parking brake lever 1 notch and make sure that parking brake warning light comes on. If not, adjust parking brake warning light contact switch.

– Install parking brake lever boot. Install road wheel lug bolts.

| Tightening torque | |
| --- | --- |
| Road wheel to hub | 120 Nm (88.5 ft-lb) |

## Parking brake shoes, removing and installing

◁ Remove parking brake handle boot (**arrow**).

*Parking brake shoes, removing and installing*

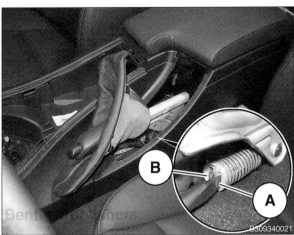

◄ relieve parking brake cable tension: Using a screwdriver, lock parking brake handle adjuster by pressing stop (**A**) spring back to engage hook (**B**). **Inset** shows hook engaged.

– Raise rear of car and remove wheels.

> **WARNING—**
> • *Make sure the car is firmly supported on jack stands designed for the purpose. Place jack stands beneath structural chassis points. Do not place jack stands under suspension parts.*

– Without disconnecting brake fluid hose, remove rear brake calipers from trailing arms. Remove rear brake rotors. See **Brake rotor, removing and installing** in this repair group.

> **CAUTION—**
> • *Do not let the brake caliper assembly hang from the brake hose. Support caliper from chassis with strong wire.*

◄ Unhook upper return spring (**A**) from brake shoes. Note position of parking brake shoe adjuster (**B**).

◄ Unhook lower return spring (**arrow**) from brake shoes.

◁ Rotate hub flange to align lug hole with return spring. Remove brake shoe retaining pins using 6 mm allen wrench.

- Rotate retainer ¼ turn to release.
- Spread shoes apart and lift out.

– Apply thin coat of grease to sliding parts and pins before reassembly.

– Installation is reverse of removal. Be sure to adjust parking brake. See **Parking brake, adjusting** in this repair group.

| Tightening torque | |
|---|---|
| Road wheel to hub | 120 Nm (88.5 ft-lb) |

## Parking brake cable, replacing

The parking brake is actuated by two separate Bowden cables. Each cable can be replaced separately.

– Working inside car, gain access to base of parking brake handle by removing center console. See **513 Interior Trim**.

– Remove airbag control module. See **721 Airbag System (SRS)**.

◁ relieve parking brake cable tension: Using a screwdriver, lock parking brake handle adjuster by pressing stop (**A**) spring back to engage hook (**B**). **Inset** shows hook engaged.

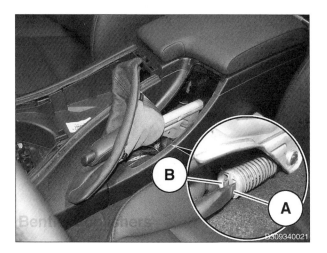

◁ Press cable retainer (**A**) forward in direction of **arrows**.

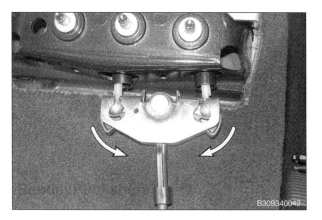

**340**

*Parking brake cable, replacing*

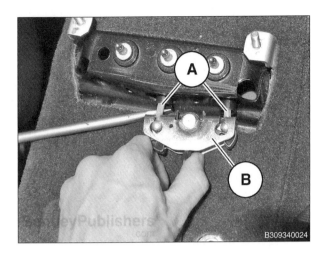

◄ Remove parking brake cables (**A**) from balance arm (**B**).

– Raise rear of car and remove wheels.

> **WARNING** —
> • *Make sure the car is firmly supported on jack stands designed for the purpose. Place jack stands beneath structural chassis points. Do not place jack stands under suspension parts.*

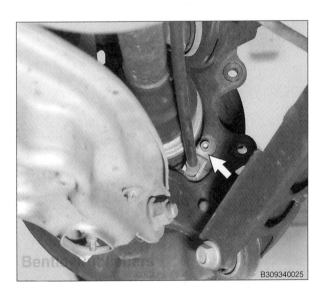

◄ Remove fastener and cable hold down (**arrow**).

◄ Rotate brake rotor to align stud hole until cable end and expander are visible through hole (**arrow**).

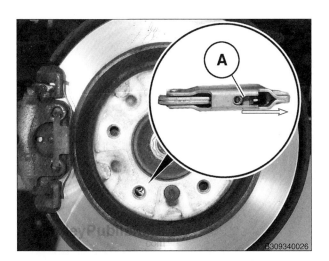

◄ Press and release spring (**A**) in direction of **arrow** while pulling parking brake cable out of expander and backing plate.

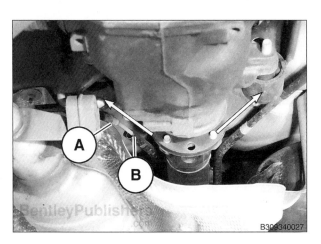

◄ Pull parking brake cable (**A**) out of guide tube (**B**) in direction of **arrow** and detach from routing brackets, noting correct routing for reinstallation.

– Installation is reverse of removal. Adjust parking brake. See **Parking brake, adjusting** in this repair group.

340

## ANTILOCK BRAKE AND STABILITY CONTROL

3 Series vehicles are equipped with antilock brakes (ABS) with dynamic stability control (DSC). This manual refers to these systems as ABS. DSC is specified when necessary.

### Antilock brake system (ABS)

The electronically controlled antilock brake system (ABS) maintains vehicle stability and control during emergency braking by preventing wheel lock-up. ABS provides optimum deceleration and stability during adverse conditions. It automatically adjusts brake system hydraulic pressure at each wheel to prevent wheel lock-up.

### Dynamic stability control (DSC)

DSC works in conjunction with ABS and the engine management system to enhance vehicle control. The main DSC function is to maintain contact between the tires and the road surface under all driving conditions. This is achieved through exact application and management of braking and drivetrain forces.

DSC is active throughout the driving range, helping to stabilize the vehicle in cornering and avoidance maneuvers by adjusting engine controls such as throttle, ignition, fuel injection and the application of brake pressure individually to the wheels.

The DSC control module uses various inputs to determine vehicle instability during braking, cornering, or reduced traction situations. Based upon these inputs the ABS / DSC control module sends outputs to the engine control module and the ABS / DSC hydraulic unit to activate torque reduction protocols and braking intervention.

The ABS / DSC control module, operating through the ABS hydraulic control unit, modulates braking force at the wheels. In addition, DSC overrides throttle opening to reduce engine torque and maintain vehicle traction. Because throttle is controlled electronically, the driver cannot increase engine power output during DSC intervention regardless of how far the accelerator pedal is pushed.

Traction control also comes into operation during deceleration. Decelerating on snowy or icy road surfaces can lead to rear wheel slip. If a rear wheel starts to drag or lock up, DSC can limit the problem by adjusting throttle, fuel injection and ignition timing.

◄ DSC can be toggled ON and OFF by a switch labeled DTC, **(inset)** mounted on the center console switching center. Turning DSC OFF does not disable ABS functions.

B309340028

### CAN-bus and traction control

◄ The CAN-bus (controller area network) is a serial bus system in which the ECM, transmission control module (TCM), longitudinal management system (LDM), active cruise control (ACC) and ABS / DSC control module send and receive signals. The connection consists of two data links (CAN-low and CAN-high). See **600 Electrical System–General** for additional details.

B309340029

### DSC acceleration sensor

The DSC acceleration sensor utilizes two yaw rate sensor elements to detect yaw (rotation about the vertical axis) rate and lateral acceleration (G-force) rate.

◄ For rotational acceleration (yaw), the sensor produces a reference signal and a linear voltage signal. The sensor also produces a linear voltage signal for lateral acceleration. The DSC control module uses this input to determine rotational and side forces acting on the vehicle.

B309340047

### Steering angle sensor

◄ The steering angle sensor is located in the steering column switch cluster (SZL). It optically measures the angle of rotation of the steering wheel to determine steering angle and rate of steering.

After repairs to the steering or suspension system, use a BMW scan tool or equivalent to calibrate the sensor. Once calibration is complete, the sensor sends an identification number over the CAN-bus to the DSC control module. The ID confirms that the sensor is calibrated correctly.

DSC control module logic checks the plausibility of the steering angle sensor signal against other inputs such as wheel speeds and acceleration inputs.

If battery voltage is interrupted, steering wheel angle of rotation is recalculated by the DSC control module evaluating the wheel speeds. If replacing, steering angle sensor, remember to recalibrate sensor.

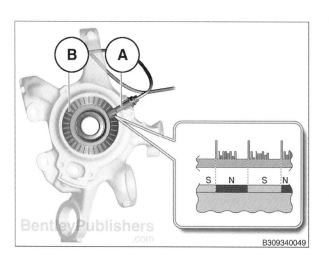

Encoded disc

Steering column switch cluster

Optical sensor

B309340048

### Wheel speed sensors

◄ A wheel speed sensor (**A**) is mounted at each wheel along with a ring of magnets (**B**) used to measure direction of wheel rotation and speed. The electrical resistance of the wheel speed sensor changes under the influence of the magnetic field. Each increment generates 2 pulses in the wheel speed sensor (96 pulses / revolution of wheel). When vehicle is stationary the sensor sends one pulse every 0.75 second.

B309340049

### DSC and xDrive

xDrive uses information from the DSC system to control a multi-plate clutch in the transfer case. The multi plate clutch varies torque split between front and rear wheels.

xDrive calculates the necessary torque split from information supplied by DSC:

- Accelerator pedal position
- Engine torque
- Dynamic state of vehicle (drive dynamic state)

## DSC COMPONENTS AND REPAIRS

> *CAUTION—*
> - *If the tires on the car are of different makes, the DSC system may overreact. Only fit tires of the same make and tread pattern.*
> - *In adverse conditions, such as trying to rock the car out of deep snow or other soft surface, or when snow chains are fitted, switch traction control OFF and allow the car driveline to operate conventionally.*

3 Series models are equipped with Dynamic Stability Control (DSC). DSC is a computer controlled traction control system that uses the ABS system in conjunction with engine management controls to control wheel spin during acceleration and maintain vehicle stability while braking.

### On-board diagnostics, coding

DSC systems are self-diagnosing and store fault codes (diagnostic trouble codes or DTCs) in the DSC control module. For information on how to access DTCs, see **020 Maintenance**.

ABS / DSC components are coded to each other and to the vehicle using BMW scan tool or equivalent. If you do not have access to a scan tool, be sure to have newly installed ABS / DSC components coded at a BMW dealer service department or other qualified shop with the correct equipment.

### DSC power supply

See **ECL Electrical Component Locations** for fuse panel access information.

Rear power distribution panel A46 (**arrow**) is located directly on top of battery. A46 supplies power to junction box A4010 which houses DSC fuses. See **ECL Electrical Component Locations** for specific fuse assignment according to model / year.

B309340043

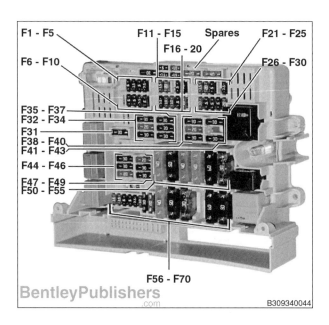

F1 - F5
F6 - F10
F11 - F15
F16 - 20
Spares
F21 - F25
F26 - F30
F35 - F37
F32 - F34
F31
F38 - F40
F41 - F43
F44 - F46
F47 - F49
F50 - F55

F56 - F70

B309340044

◄ Fuse panel, above glove box (A4010):

• **F20** 5A: DSC control module
• **F35** 30A: DSC control module
• **F65** 40A: DSC control module

***NOTE*—**

• *2006 model fuse panel shown, see* **ECL Electrical Component Locations** *for specific fuse locations for your model.*

## DSC controls

B309340028

◄ Lower dashboard above center console:

• **DTC** (dynamic traction control) switch

B309340045

◄ Left side engine compartment (**arrow**):

• Combined DSC control module / hydraulic unit / brake pressure sensors

340

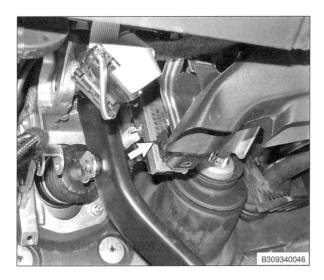

 Above brake pedal, underneath left side dashboard (**arrow**):

- **S29** Brake light switch

## DSC hydraulic control unit, removing and installing

> **CAUTION—**
> - *Brake fluid is highly corrosive and dangerous to the environment. Dispose of it properly.*

- Remove cabin microfilter upper and lower housings. See **640 Heating and Air-conditioning**.

- Using a syringe, remove brake fluid from master cylinder reservoir.

 Working at DSC hydraulic control unit:

- Disconnect electrical connector (**arrow**).
- Remove brake lines (**A**).

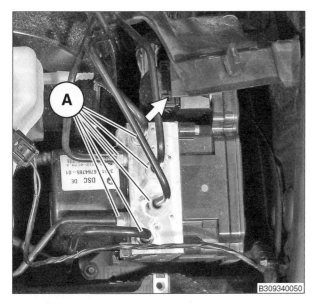

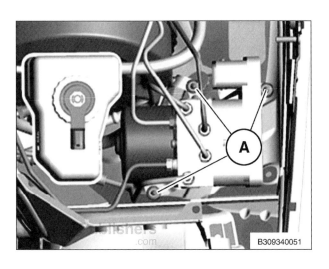

◄ Remove fasteners (**A**).

– Tilt unit in direction of fender and remove.

– Installation is reverse of removal.

| Tightening torque | |
|---|---|
| Brake line to DSC control unit | 12 Nm (8.8 ft-lb) |
| DSC control unit mounting fasteners | 8 Nm (5.9 ft-lb) |

– Bleed entire brake system. See **Brake system, bleeding** in this repair group.

– Program using BMW scan tool or equivalent.

## Wheel speed sensor, replacing

– Raise car and support safely.

> **WARNING** —
> • *Make sure the car is stable and well supported at all times. Use a professional automotive lift or jack stands designed for the purpose. A floor jack is not adequate support.*

### Front wheel speed sensor

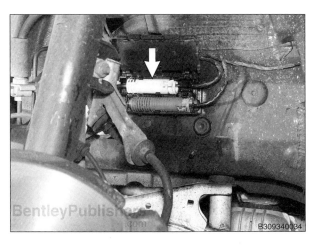

◄ Working in junction box in wheel housing, separate wheel speed sensor electrical harness (**arrow**). (Left front junction box illustrated. Right front contains single harness connector.)

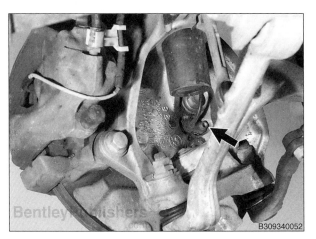

◄ Unscrew sensor mounting bolt (**arrow**) at steering knuckle and remove sensor.

– Installation is reverse of removal. Apply thin coat of Staburags®NBU 12/K or equivalent grease to speed sensor and housing.

| Tightening torque | |
|---|---|
| ABS wheel speed sensor to steering knuckle | 8 Nm (6 ft-lb) |

**340**

### Rear wheel speed sensor

– Remove right wheel well housing liner. See **410 Fenders, Engine Hood**.

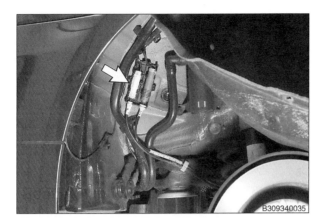

◄ Working in junction box in wheel housing, separate wheel speed sensor electrical harness (**arrow**).

◄ Unscrew mounting bolt (**arrow**) in rear wheel bearing carrier.

– Installation is reverse of removal. Apply thin coat of Staburags®NBU 12/K or equivalent grease to speed sensor and housing.

| Tightening torque | |
|---|---|
| ABS wheel speed sensor to rear wheel bearing carrier | 8 Nm (6 ft-lb) |

## ABS impulse wheel

The front and rear ABS impulse wheels are integral with the inner wheel bearing seal and not available as separate parts. See **310 Front Suspension** or **330 Rear Suspension** for wheel bearing replacement procedures.

## DSC acceleration sensor, removing and installing

– Remove left front seat. See **520 Seats**.

– Remove left door sill trim. See **513 Interior Trim**.

◄ Remove fasteners (**arrows**) and subwoofer speaker grill if equipped.

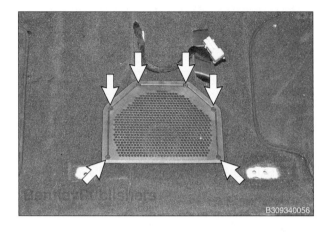

◄ Lift carpet (**A**), lay aside and remove carpet underlay (**B**).

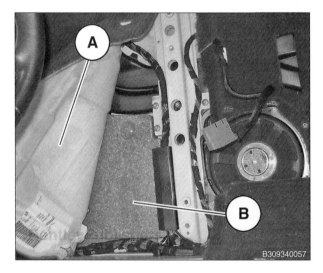

◄ Remove DSC acceleration sensor mounting fastener (**A**). Loosen fasteners (**B**) enough to slide sensor out from under seat rail. Disconnect electrical connector and remove sensor.

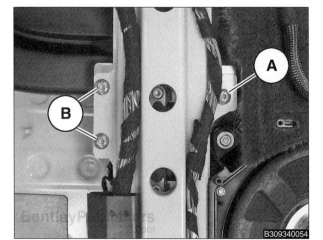

340

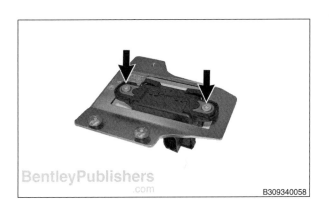

B309340058

◀ Remove fasteners (**arrows**) and remove sensor from bracket.

– Installation is reverse of removal.

> **CAUTION—**
> • Be sure to tighten the DSC acceleration sensor and mounting bracket, if applicable, to specified torques. The sensor is vibration sensitive and causes DSC malfunctions if installed improperly.

| Tightening torques | |
| --- | --- |
| DSC acceleration sensor to bracket | 8 Nm (6 ft-lb) |
| DSC acceleration sensor bracket to body | 8 Nm (6 ft-lb) |

– Program using BMW scan tool or equivalent.

## DSC steering angle sensor, replacing

– Remove steering column switch assembly. See **612 Switches**.

◀ Separate steering angle sensor (**A**) from steering column switch assembly (**B**).

– Installation is reverse of removal.

– Program using BMW scan tool or equivalent.

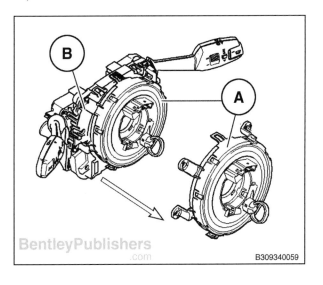

B309340059

# 400  Body–General

## GENERAL

This chapter covers system descriptions and general information for the repair groups in partitions **4 Body** and **5 Body Equipment**.

The 2006 3 Series chassis was introduced in the North America market as a Sedan (E90) and Sport Wagon (E91) in fall 2005. Both rear-wheel drive and all-wheel drive (xDrive) versions were offered.

In subsequent years, a Coupe (E92) and a Convertible (E93) became available.

B309400001

## BODY ASSEMBLY

### Dimensions

In the accompanying illustrations, dimensions for 2006 - 2008 vehicles are given in inches / mm.

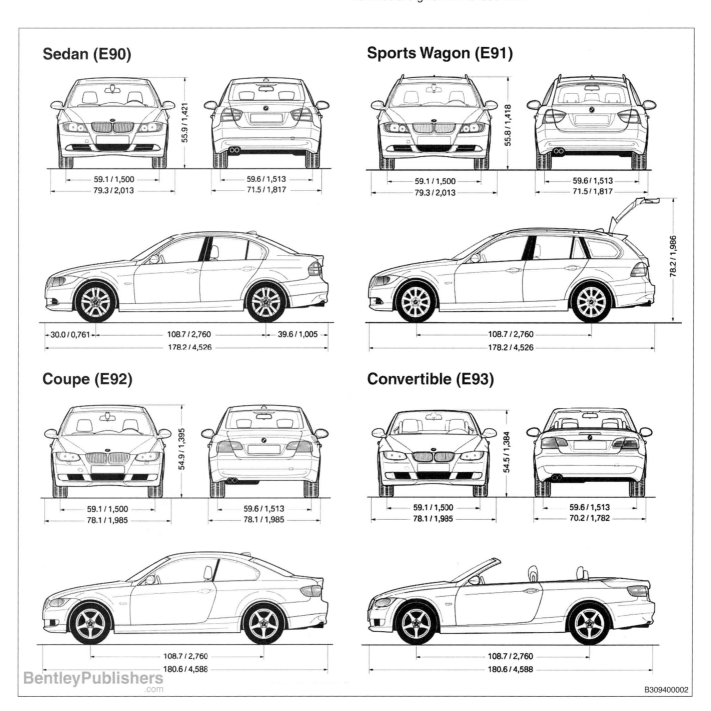

### Sedan (E90)

59.9 / 1,421

59.1 / 1,500
79.3 / 2,013

59.6 / 1,513
71.5 / 1,817

30.0 / 0,761   108.7 / 2,760   39.6 / 1,005
178.2 / 4,526

### Sports Wagon (E91)

55.8 / 1,418

59.1 / 1,500
79.3 / 2,013

59.6 / 1,513
71.5 / 1,817

78.2 / 1,986

108.7 / 2,760
178.2 / 4,526

### Coupe (E92)

54.9 / 1,395

59.1 / 1,500
78.1 / 1,985

59.6 / 1,513
78.1 / 1,985

108.7 / 2,760
180.6 / 4,588

### Convertible (E93)

54.5 / 1,384

59.1 / 1,500
78.1 / 1,985

59.6 / 1,513
70.2 / 1,782

108.7 / 2,760
180.6 / 4,588

B309400002

## Body

◁ Sedan (E90) and Sport Wagon (E91) bodies are conventionally manufactured from steel, fully galvanized and equipped with a safety passenger cell. Vehicle performance, weight optimization, body stiffness and safety are inherent in the body design.

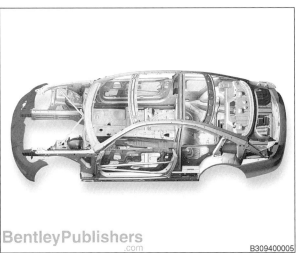

◁ The bodies of the Sedan and Sports Wagon were developed in parallel. This made it possible from the start not only to identify the identical components required but also to take into account parts and components specific to each.

◁ The Sports Wagon floor assembly does not require any reinforcement because the lightweight design of the E91 was combined with increased load-carrying capacity. Without additional reinforcements vehicle weight is reduced and interior space and load capacity expanded.

◄ The inclusion of strong but light weight side-frames accommodates the special demands made by the large roof opening for the panorama sunroof. The static stiffness of the Sport Wagon is approx. 19000 Nm/degree, while the dynamic stiffness is approximately 29 Hz.

◄ The cargo compartment volume of the Sports Wagon offers 16.24 cu. ft. (460 liters) of space and expands to 49 cu. ft. (1385 liters) with the rear seat backrests folded down. The indentation in the rear bumper reduces the height of the loading sill and makes loading easier.

◄ The E92 Coupe, introduced in 2007, features a strong, light body constructed of a combination of different types of materials including thermo plastic. Structural rigidity and support were enhanced without increasing overall vehicle weight.

◀ The E93 Convertible features a retractable hardtop which operates electrohydraulically and stows in the trunk.

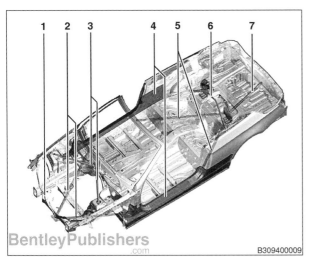

◀ Significant torsional (twisting) forces are introduced into the Convertible body structure while driving due to the run-flat tires and sporty suspension. Consequently, high body rigidity targets were set when the body was designed. The main means for increasing body rigidity include strengthened sills and bolt-on struts.

1. Engine compartment strut
2. Front subframe struts
3. Front strut tower struts
4. Sills
5. Rear underbody struts
6. Strut in rollover protection system
7. Tension strut

Vehicle side sills are the main load-bearing components. A horizontal flange is used between the inner and outer sill shell in order to optimize bending and torsional rigidity. In addition, the sills are reinforced with transverse bulkheads.

## SAFETY AND SECURITY

### Passenger safety

◀ BMW passive safety is based on the principle of protecting the passenger compartment with dynamic deformation zones. Body structures with a high load bearing capacity isolate the extremely rigid passenger cell. In case of accident, the passenger cage is designed to absorb the impact and route the deformation around the passengers.

**400**

B309400011

## Restraint system

◁ The passive restraint system consists of seat belts with pyrotechnic (explosive) tensioners and a minimum of 6 airbags.

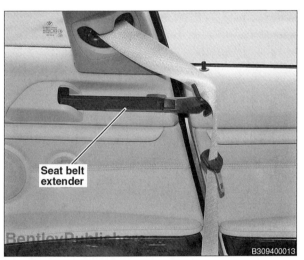

**Seat belt extender**

B309400013

◁ The E92 Coupe features large doors. As a result, the B-pillar is located further toward the rear relative to front seat position, making it difficult for the driver or front passenger to reach the seat belt. For this reason, an electrically operated seat belt extender is installed on the E92. The extender pushes the seat belt approximately 25 cm (10 inches) forward.

For additional restraint system information, see:

• **720 Seat belts**

• **721 Airbag System (SRS)**

## Door handles

◁ In vehicle equipped with comfort access, the front door handle contains the components of the electronic outer door handle module (TAGE).

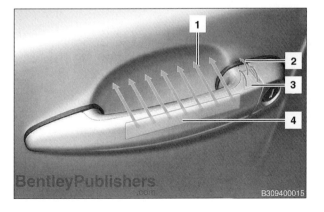

B309400015

1.  Electric field, capacitor 1
2.  Electric field, capacitor 2
3.  Capacitor plate, capacitive sensor 2
4.  Capacitor plate, capacitive sensor 1

If a vehicle remote key is in the vicinity of the vehicle, a hand inserted between the door handle and the door automatically unlocks the car.

See **515 Central Locking and Anti-theft**.

Remote key

B309400016

## Central locking

◄ All doors locks as well as trunk lid lock, tailgate lock and fuel filler flap lock are integrated into central locking and can be operated via the following:

- Remote key
- Driver's door lock barrel (door lock)
- Central locking button
- Electronic outer door handle module (TAGE) (comfort access vehicle)

1. Car access system (CAS) module
2. Footwell module (FRM)
3. Junction box electronic module (JBE)

### Antitheft alarm (DWA)

When armed, the antitheft system monitors door lock contacts and trunk and engine hood locks and sounds an alarm if it detects tampering. Included in the enhanced system is a tilt sensor to protect against the vehicle being towed away, and an interior motion sensor.

For more information, see **515 Central Locking and Anti-theft**.

## INTERIOR FEATURES

### Instruments, iDrive

◄ The instrument cluster and dashboard layout is similar to other BMW models with all of the controls in easy reach of the driver.

The dashboard is equipped with the optional iDrive central information display (CID) or car information computer (CIC). The display screen is used for a variety of vehicle control and diagnostic tasks and is also capable of displaying navigation information.

**400**

Central information display (CID)

B309400014

◄ Navigation, climate control, sound system and other functions are controlled via iDrive controller, if equipped.

B309400017

B309400019

Functions and controls essential to the driver are logically grouped and easy to reach. Instruments and controls are fully integrated into the overall design of the vehicle.

- Tilt-telescopic steering wheel has 30 mm (1.2 in) of vertical and longitudinal adjustment.
- Multifunction steering wheel contains two key pads containing controls for the sound system, telephone and cruise control.

## Seats

Ergonomically engineered seats are constructed from polyurethane foam containing areas or zones of different firmness. They offer superior lateral support without constricting the occupant.

In cars equipped with seat position memory, two different seat configurations can be memorized by the seat control module. Seat memory coordinates with outside mirror memory. These functions are controlled by the seat memory module.

For additional information, see **520 Seats**.

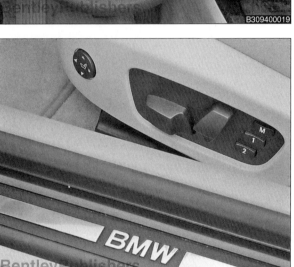

B309400018

## BODY ELECTRONICS

3 Series vehicles are equipped with an integrated complex of electronic modules connected via the bus system. An overview of the bus system is in **600 Electrical System–General**. For details of electrical functions, see:

- **512 Door Windows**
- **515 Central Locking and Anti-theft**
- **520 Seats**
- **611 Wipers and Washers**
- **620 Instruments**
- **630 Lights**

# 410 Fenders, Engine Hood

## GENERAL

This repair group covers replacement of the front fenders and removal and installation of the engine hood.

> **CAUTION—**
> • The body is painted at the factory after assembly. Realignment of body panels may expose unpainted metal. Paint all exposed metal once the work is complete.

### Special tools

Most body repairs can be performed using regular automotive service tools. Special BMW tools are required to set engine hood into service position.

## FRONT FENDERS

### Front wheel housing liner, removing and installing

— Raise front of vehicle and remove wheel.

> **WARNING—**
> • Make sure that the car is firmly supported on jack stands designed for the purpose. Place jack stands beneath structural chassis points. Do not place jack stands under suspension parts.

◄ Remove clips (**arrows**) from fender edge by driving center out with a suitable sized punch, then prying out clip with suitable plastic prying tool.

> **NOTE—**
> • The clips are not reusable, replace with new.

**410**

B309410022

◄ Remove fasteners (**arrows**) from rear section of wheel housing liner.

– Remove rear section of liner (**A**).

◄ Remove front wheel housing liner screws and nut (**arrows**) and disconnect plug at tire pressure control antenna.

– Remove front section of liner.

– Installation is reverse of removal.

## Front fender, removing and installing

– Raise hood to service position. See **Engine hood, raising to service position** in this repair group.

– Remove front wheel housing liner. See **Front wheel housing liner, removing and installing** in this repair group.

◄ Fastener locations shown for Sedan and Sport Wagon models.

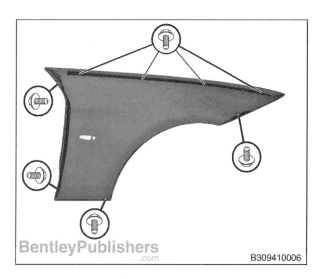

*Front fender, removing and installing*

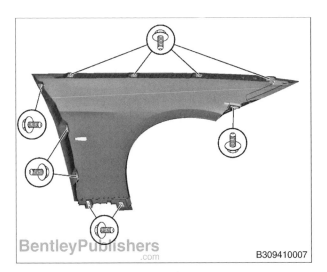

◀ Fastener locations shown for Coupe and Convertible models.

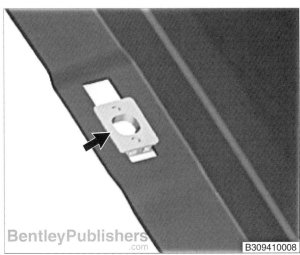

◀ On Coupe and Convertible models make sure sliding element (**1**) is securely seated in fender.

| Tightening torque | |
|---|---|
| Fender to body (M6) | 7.6 Nm (67 in-lb) |

410

## ENGINE HOOD

### Engine hood latch components

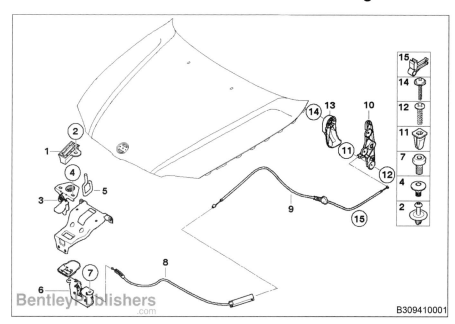

1. Twist protection

2. Expanding rivet

3. Hood latch

4. Torx bolt with washer, M6 x 12 mm

5. Safety bracket

6. Hood lock

7. Torx bolt with washer, M6 x 9 mm

8. Bowden cable, hood mechanism

9. Rear Bowden cable

10. Combination bracket

11. Expanding nut

12. Sheet metal screw

13. Hood release lever

14. Phillips screw, 5 x 25 mm

15. Cable holder

B309410001

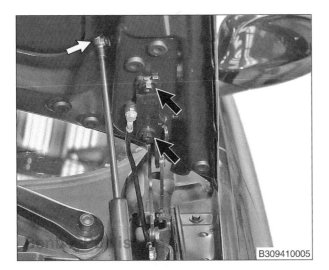

B309410005

## Engine hood, aligning

When installing hood, align hinges as close to original painted surface as possible. Movement of hood on its attaching hardware may require touch up paint.

◀ With help of assistant, support hood and remove retaining clips (**white arrow**) on upper end of pressurized lifting struts. Pull struts off hood.

– Loosen left upper and lower hinge mounting bolts (**black arrows**). Hood must be able to be moved.

– Repeat on right.

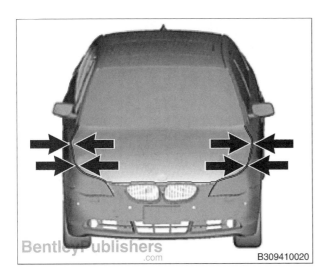

B309410020

◀ Align hood so gap (**arrows**) to fender is as even as possible.

| Tightening torque | |
|---|---|
| Hood to hood hinge (M8) | 15 Nm (11 ft-lb) |

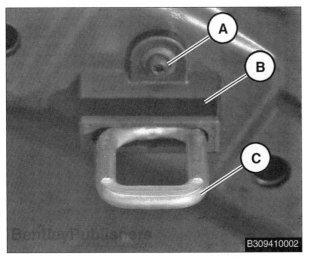

B309410002

◀ If front height adjustment is off, adjust safety brackets:
- Release screw (**A**).
- Remove cover (**B**).
- Adjust height by turning latch (**C**).

*Engine hood, raising to service position*

B309410021

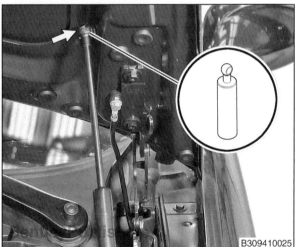

B309410025

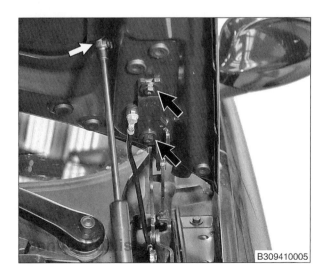

B309410005

◄ If height adjustment of engine hood lid to front fenders is off, turn front buffer stops (**arrow**) on left and right.

> **CAUTION—**
> • To avoid excessive wind noise, make sure hood does not protrude beyond front fenders.

## Engine hood, raising to service position

◄ With hood open and help of an assistant, support hood and remove retaining clips (**arrow**) on upper end of left pressurized lifting strut.

– Slide BMW special tool 51 2 170 (**inset**) over housing of gas spring strut then clip ball socket of special tool on ball stud on hood.

– Repeat on right.

## Engine hood, removing and installing

> **WARNING —**
> • The hood is heavy. Before removing the hood supports, be sure to have an assistant help support the hood.

– Mark position of hood hinge mounting plates.

◄ With help of assistant, support hood and remove retaining clips (**white arrow**) on upper end of pressurized lifting struts. Pull struts off hood.

– Loosen upper hinge mounting bolts and remove lower bolts (**black arrows**). Lift hood off carefully.

– Installation is reverse of removal noting the following:
  • Repair any paint damage and paint any exposed metal.
  • Check hood alignment. See **Engine hood, aligning** in this repair group.

| Tightening torque | |
|---|---|
| Hood to hood hinge (M8) | 15 Nm (11 ft-lb) |

# 411 Doors

## GENERAL

This repair group covers front and rear door repair information and includes door trim panel service.

> **CAUTION—**
> * The body is painted at the factory after assembly. Realignment of body panels may expose unpainted metal. Paint exposed metal once work is complete.

For additional information, see:

* **512 Door Windows** for power door windows and door glass replacement
* **515 Central Locking and Anti-theft** for power door locks

## Cautions

> **CAUTION—**
> * Prior to disconnecting the battery, read the battery disconnection cautions given in **001 Warnings and Cautions**.
> * To avoid damaging plastic interior trim, use a plastic prying tool or a screwdriver with the tip wrapped with masking tape.

**411**

# DOORS

## Door check, replacing

– Close door window completely.

– Disconnect negative (-) battery cable.

> **CAUTION—**
> • Prior to disconnecting the battery, read the battery disconnection cautions given in **001 Warnings and Cautions.**

– Remove interior door panel. See **Door trim panel, removing and installing** in this repair group.

◄ Remove door check seal (**C**).

– Release screws (**A** and **B**) on door check.

– Working inside door, remove door check assembly (**A**).

– Installation is reverse of removal.

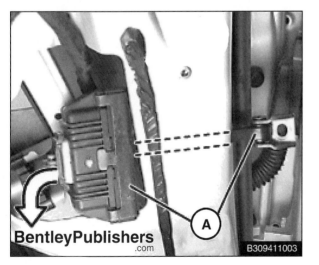

| Tightening torques | |
|---|---|
| Door check to body | 22 Nm (16 ft-lb) |
| Door check to door | 12 Nm (9 ft-lb) |

## Door hinge assembly, front

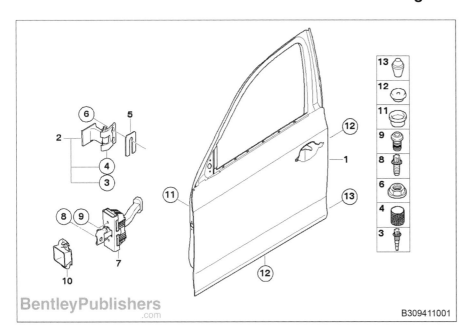

B309411001

1. Front left door
2. Door hinge
3. Hinge pin bolt
4. Hinge bushing
5. Shim
6. Nut with plate, M8
7. Door check
8. Torx bolt with washer, M8 x 20 mm
9. Torx bolt with washer, M6 x 12 mm
10. Door check gasket
11. Protection cap
12. Blind plug
13. Bump stop

## Door, adjusting

Front and rear door adjustment procedure are similar.

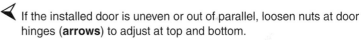

◀ If the installed door is uneven or out of parallel, loosen nuts at door hinges (**arrows**) to adjust at top and bottom.

– If more adjustment is necessary, spacers (or shims) can be used to correct its position. Spacers are placed behind hinge.

B309411009

**411**

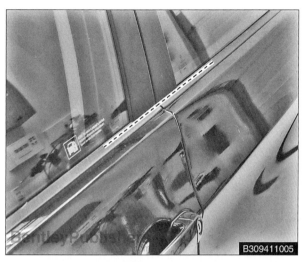

◁ Check that adjoining body parts are flush in terms of height (**dotted line**) and correct if necessary. After adjustment, tighten hinge nuts and screws.

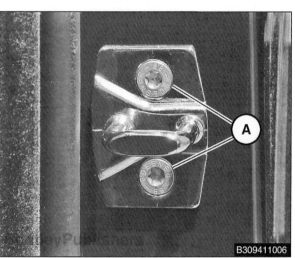

◁ Loosen screws (**A**) to adjust lock striker.

**NOTE**—

• *When door is closed, lock striker must not touch or brush against door lock. Avoid scratching door.*

| Tightening torques | |
|---|---|
| Door to door hinge (M8 nut) | 20 Nm (15 ft-lb) |
| Door striker to body | 18.5 Nm (13.5 ft-lb) |

## Door, removing and installing

Front and rear door removal and installation are similar.

Disconnect negative (-) battery cable.

**CAUTION**—

• *Prior to disconnecting the battery, read the battery disconnection cautions given in **001 Warnings and Cautions**.*

◁ Remove harness connector mounting bolt (**arrow**) at door pillar.

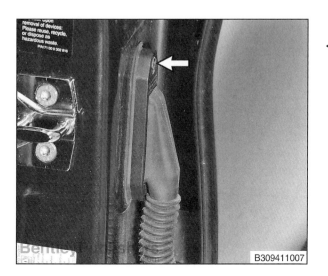

*Door, removing and installing*

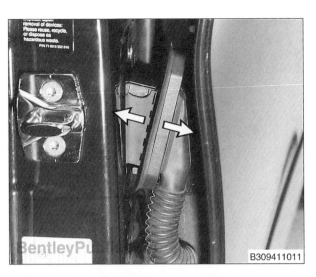

◄ Pull plug connection from door pillar by lifting it up and out.

– Detach plug connection (**arrows**).

◄ Pull back door check gasket (**A**).

– Remove door check mounting bolt (**B**).

411

◄ With door fully open, unscrew door hinge pin bolts (**arrows**) from top and bottom hinges.

*Door trim panel, removing and installing*

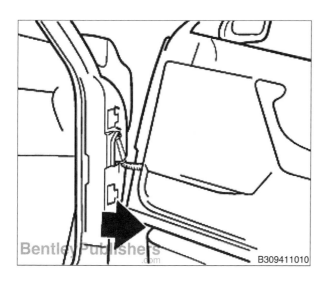

B309411010

◄ Remove door by pulling out sideways.

– Installation is reverse of removal. Keep in mind the following:

- Mount and align rear doors first (if applicable), followed by the front doors.
- Align door so that panel gaps are equal on either side. If necessary, adjust door hinges. See **Door, adjusting** in this repair group.
- Adjust door striker so that trailing edge of front door is slightly higher than leading edge of rear door.
- Repair paint damage and paint exposed metal.

| Tightening torques | |
|---|---|
| Door check to body | 22 Nm (16 ft-lb) |
| Door electrical harness to body (M5 x 16 mm) | 3 Nm (27 in-lb) |
| Door hinge pin bolts | 25 Nm (18 ft-lb) |

## DOOR PANELS

Left front door panel of sedan is illustrated. Door panels used on other models are similar.

### Door trim panel, removing and installing

– Disconnect negative (-) battery cable.

> **CAUTION—**
> • *Prior to disconnecting the battery, read the battery disconnection cautions given in* **001 Warnings and Cautions**.

◄ Pry out decorative panel (**A**) on driver's side using plastic prying tool.

– Remove screws (**arrows**).

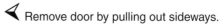

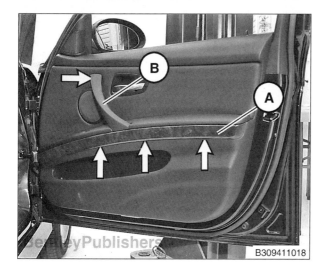

B309411022

◄ On passenger side, pry out decorative panel (**A**) and door handle cover (**B**) using plastic prying tool.

– Remove screws (**arrows**).

B309411018

*Door trim panel, removing and installing*

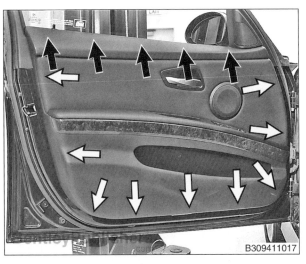

B309411017

◁ Detach clips (**white arrows**) on door trim panel with plastic prying tool.

— Unclip door trim panel at top (**black arrows**) using a plastic prying tool. Feed door trim panel out of unlocking button.

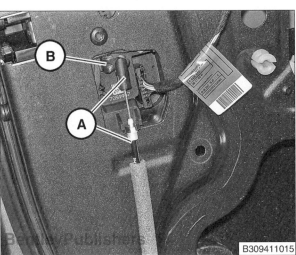

B309411015

◁ Unhook Bowden cable (**A**) from inner door opener by unlatching tab (**B**).

— Disconnect wiring harness for window switch panel and remove door trim panel.

— Installation is reverse of removal. To reattach bowden cable snap into position.

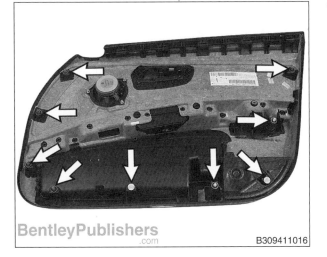

B309411016

◁ If necessary, replace any broken clips including sealing ring (**arrows**). Check door-lock mechanism and window for ease of movement and proper function.

| Tightening torque | |
|---|---|
| Door trim panel to door | 4 Nm (35 in-lb) |

**411**

# 412 Trunk lid, Tailgate

## GENERAL

This repair group covers trunk lid and tailgate removal and installation. Also included here are replacement procedures for gas-charged support struts that hold trunk lid or tailgate in open position.

> *CAUTION—*
> • *Body is painted at factory after assembly. Realignment of body panels may expose unpainted metal. Paint exposed metal once work is complete.*

## TRUNK LID (SEDAN AND COUPE)

### Trunk lid, removing and installing (Sedan and Coupe)

— Raise trunk lid.

 Detach emergency release handle (**A**) from clip (**B**) and disconnect Bowden cable from handle (**A**).

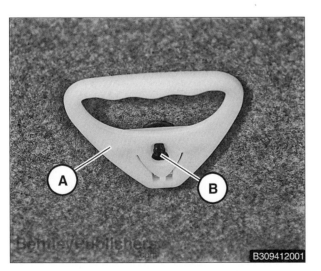

B309412001

*Trunk lid, aligning (Sedan and Coupe)*

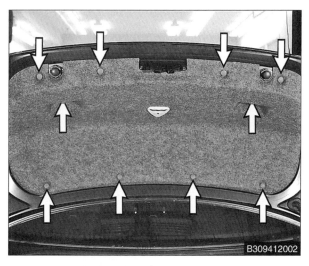

◁ Release clips (**arrows**) and remove trunk lid trim panel.

− Disconnect all electrical connectors.

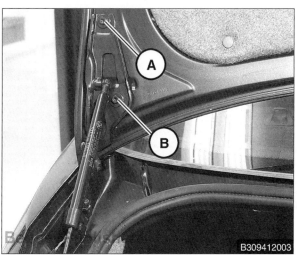

◁ While supporting trunk lid, loosen top hinge bolts (**A**) and remove lower bolts (**B**) from left and right sides.

> *NOTE* —
> • *Before loosening hinge bolts, mark hinge and hinge bolt locations for reinstallation.*

− Installation is reverse of removal. If necessary, align trunk lid to body. See **Trunk lid, aligning (Sedan and Coupe)** in this repair group.

| Tightening torque | |
|---|---|
| Trunk lid to hinge (M8) | 15 Nm (11 ft-lb) |

## Trunk lid, aligning (Sedan and Coupe)

◁ Loosen top hinge bolts (**A** and **B**) so that trunk lid can be moved.

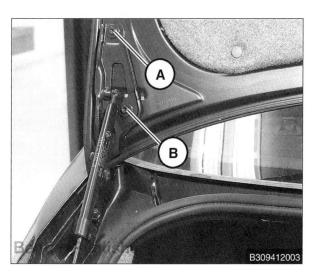

*Trunk lid, aligning (Sedan and Coupe)*

◁ To adjust trunk lid height in relation to side panel, loosen bolts (**A**) so that trunk lid can be moved.

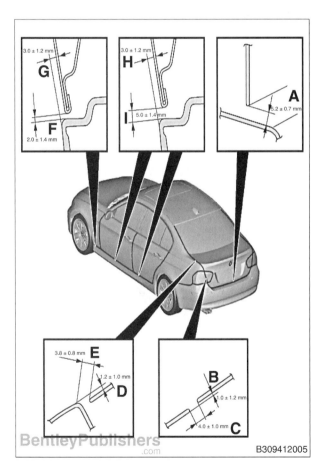

◁ Sedan: Set gap measurements as listed below.

**Trunk lid gap specifications (Sedan)**

- Dimension **A** . . . . . . . . . . . . .5.2 ± 0.7 mm (0.20 ± 0.03 in)
- Dimension **B** . . . . . . . . . . . . .1.0 ± 1.2 mm (0.04 ± 0.05 in)
- Dimension **C** . . . . . . . . . . . . .4.0 ± 1.0 mm (0.16 ± 0.04 in)
- Dimension **D** . . . . . . . . . . . . .1.2 ± 1.0 mm (0.05 ± 0.04 in)
- Dimension **E**. . . . . . . . . . . . .3.8 ± 0.8 mm (0.15 ± 0.03 in)

**CAUTION—**
- *Before closing trunk lid, be sure that trunk lid and body do not scrape.*

412

*Trunk lid, aligning (Sedan and Coupe)*

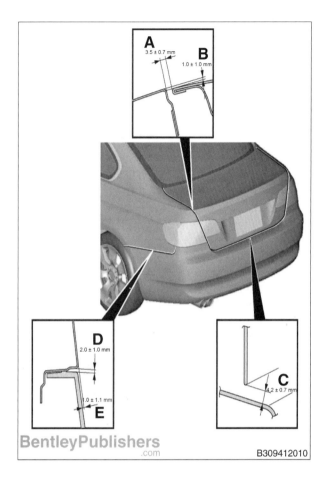

◄ Coupe: Set gap measurements as listed below.

**Trunk lid gap specifications (Coupe)**

- Dimension **A** . . . . . . . . . . . . 3.5 ± 0.7 mm (0.14 ± 0.03 in)
- Dimension **B** . . . . . . . . . . . . 1.0 ± 1.0 mm (0.04 ± 0.04 in)
- Dimension **C** . . . . . . . . . . . . 4.2 ± 0.7 mm (0.17 ± 0.03 in)
- Dimension **D** . . . . . . . . . . . . 2.0 ± 1.0 mm (0.08 ± 0.04 in)
- Dimension **E** . . . . . . . . . . . . 1.0 ± 1.1 mm (0.04 ± 0.04 in)

**CAUTION—**
- *Before closing trunk lid, be sure that trunk lid and body do not scrape.*

| Tightening torques | |
| --- | --- |
| Trunk lid to hinge (M8) | 15 Nm (11 ft-lb) |
| Trunk lid hinge to body (M8) | 20 Nm (15 ft-lb) |

**Adjusting trunk lock**

◄ Screw in left and right trunk lid detent buffers (**arrows**) completely.

*Trunk lid support strut, removing and installing (Sedan and Coupe)*

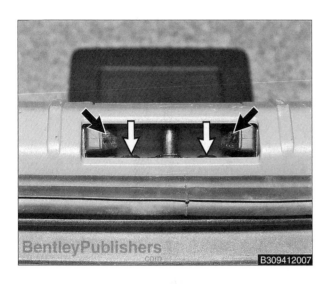

◀ Inspect pads (**black arrows**) on each side of striker assembly for damage or wear. Replace if necessary.

– Loosen trunk striker screws (**white arrows**) so that striker is just able to move. Close trunk lid to center striker.

– Open trunk lid and tighten striker screws.

– Check adjustment of trunk lock and striker. Repeat adjustment process if necessary.

– Unscrew trunk lid detent buffers until left and right sides of lid rest on buffers with trunk lid closed.

> **CAUTION—**
> • *Be sure top surface of trunk lid is even with top surfaces of fenders.*

| Tightening torque | |
| --- | --- |
| Trunk striker to body | 10 Nm (7 ft-lb) |

## Trunk lid support strut, removing and installing (Sedan and Coupe)

> **WARNING—**
> • *Be sure to support trunk lid before removing strut.*

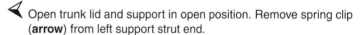

◀ Open trunk lid and support in open position. Remove spring clip (**arrow**) from left support strut end.

– Remove strut from trunk lid.

– Repeat on right.

– Installation is reverse of removal. Replace spring clips damaged during removal.

**412**

*Trunk lid, removing and installing (Convertible)*

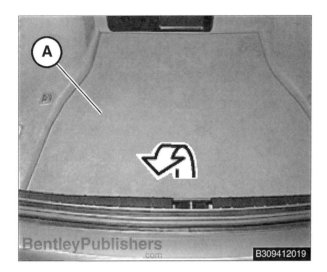

## TRUNK LID (CONVERTIBLE)

### Trunk lid, removing and installing (Convertible)

– Raise trunk lid.

◄ Remove trunk floor trim panel (**A**).

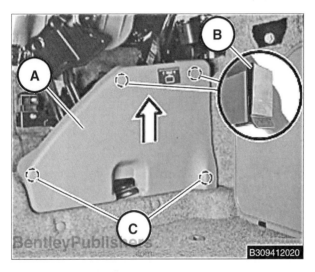

◄ Move luggage compartment cover so that panel (**A**) is accessible.

– Slide panel (**A**) up to release from retainers (**B**) and catches (**C**) and remove panel.

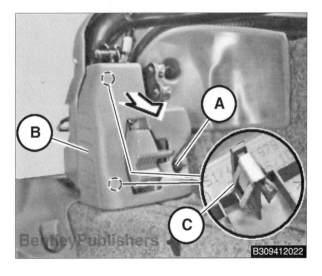

◄ Turn clip (**A**) 90º (¼ turn) and remove left rear trunk trim panel (**B**) in direction of **arrow**.

– Repeat on right.

*Trunk lid, removing and installing (Convertible)*

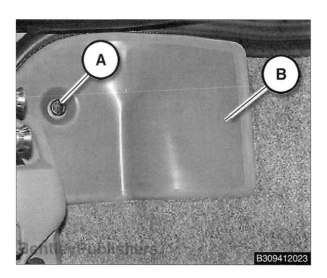

◁ Release clip (**A**) and remove left side trunk trim panel (**B**).

– Open convertible top lid.

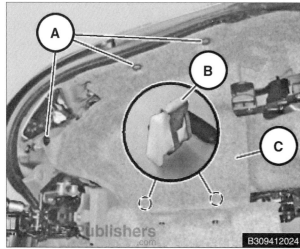

◁ Release clips (**A** and **B**) and remove panel (**C**).

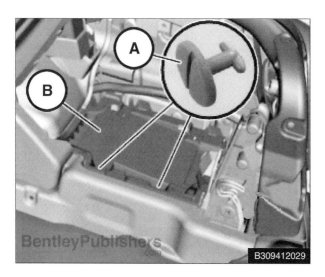

◁ On right side, release clips (**A**) and remove battery cover (**B**).

412

*Trunk lid, removing and installing (Convertible)*

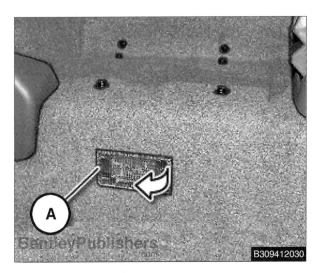

◀ Pry out trunk light (**A**) in direction of **arrow** and disconnect electrical connection.

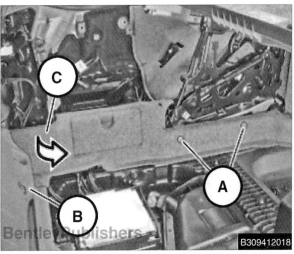

◀ Release clips (**A**).

– Pry left and right side member trim panels (**B**) away from trim (**C**) and remove in direction of **arrow**.

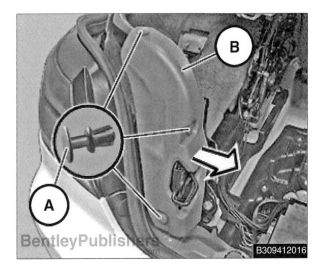

◀ Release clips (**A**) and remove tail panel trim (**B**) in direction of **arrow**.

– Remove trunk lid support struts. See **Trunk lid support strut, removing and installing (Convertible)** in this repair group.

*Trunk lid, removing and installing (Convertible)*

◁ Disconnect electrical connections (**arrow**).

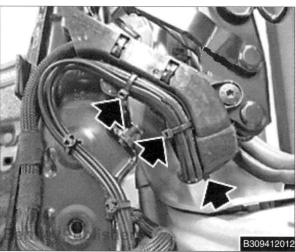

◁ Cut cable ties (**arrows**).

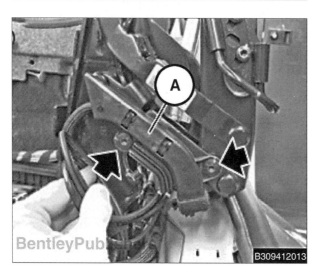

◁ Remove screws (**arrows**) and cable duct (**A**).

**412**

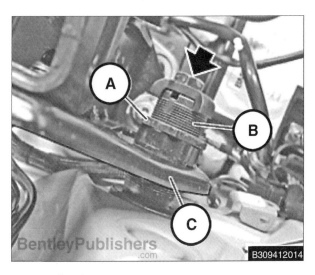

◀ Remove convertible top main bearing bolt (**arrow**).

– Loosen nut (**A**).

– Loosen barrel screw (**B**) so that wiring harness can be removed between body and frame (**C**).

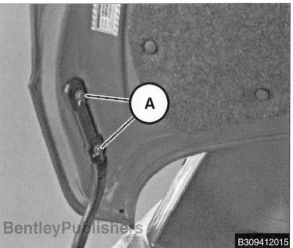

◀ Remove bolts (**arrow**) and lift off trunk lid.

***NOTE***—

• *Before loosening hinge bolts, mark hinge and hinge bolt locations for reinstallation.*

– Installation is reverse of removal. If necessary, align trunk lid to body. See **Trunk lid, aligning (Convertible)** in this repair group.

| Tightening torques | |
|---|---|
| Trunk lid to hinge (M8 x 25 mm) | 20 Nm (15 ft-lb) |
| Main bearing to body and bracket (M8) | 19 Nm (14 ft-lb) |
| Barrel screw to frame, rear module | 0.2 Nm (1.6 in-lb) |

## Trunk lid, aligning (Convertible)

### Aligning trunk lid

◀ Loosen upper hinge bolts (**A**) so that trunk lid can be moved.

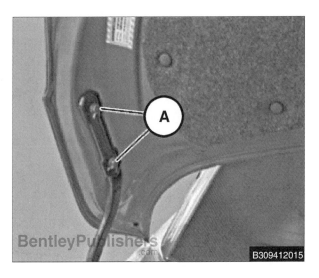

*Trunk lid, aligning (Convertible)*

◀ Set gap measurements as listed below.

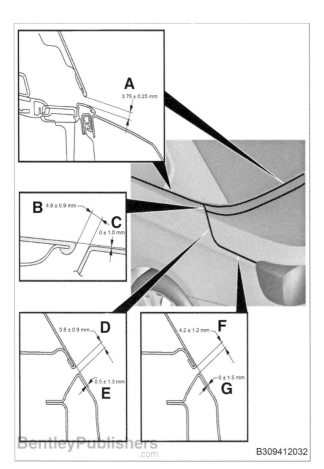

**Trunk lid gap specifications (Convertible)**

- Dimension **A** . . . . . . . . . . 3.75 ± 0.25 mm (0.15 ± 0.01 in)
- Dimension **B** . . . . . . . . . . . . 4.8 ± 0.9 mm (0.18 ± 0.04 in)
- Dimension **C** . . . . . . . . . . . . . . 0 ± 1.0 mm (0.0 ± 0.04 in)
- Dimension **D** . . . . . . . . . . . . . 3.8 ± 0.9 mm (0.15 ± 0.04 in)
- Dimension **E**. . . . . . . . . . . . . 0.5 ± 1.3 mm (0.02 ± 0.05 in)
- Dimension **F**. . . . . . . . . . . . 4.2 ± 1.2 mm (0.17 ± 0.05 in)
- Dimension **G** . . . . . . . . . . . . . . . 0 ± 1.5 mm (0.0 ± 0.06 in)

*CAUTION—*
- *Before closing trunk lid, be sure that trunk lid and body do not scrape.*

◀ Set gap measurements as listed below.

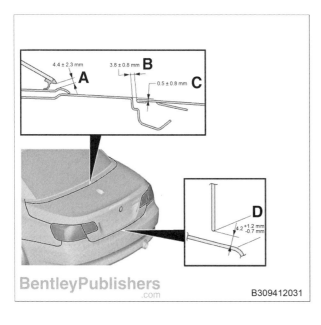

**Trunk lid gap specifications (Convertible)**

- Dimension **A** . . . . . . . . . . . . . 4.4 ± 2.3 mm (0.17 ± 0.09 in)
- Dimension **B** . . . . . . . . . . . . 3.8 ± 0.8 mm (0.15 ± 0.03 in)
- Dimension **C** . . . . . . . . . . . . 0.5 ± 0.8 mm (0.02 ± 0.03 in)
- Dimension **D** 4.2 + 1.2 mm / - 0.7 mm (0.17 + 0.05in / - 0.03 in)

*CAUTION—*
- *Before closing trunk lid, be sure that trunk lid and body do not scrape.*

| Tightening torque | |
|---|---|
| Trunk lid to hinge (M8 x 25 mm) | 20 Nm (15 ft-lb) |

B309412032

B309412031

412

*Trunk lid, aligning (Convertible)*

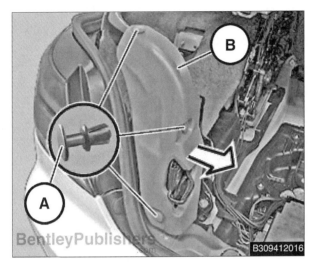

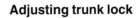

### Adjusting trunk lock

◄ Release clips (**A**) and remove tail panel trim (**B**) in direction of **arrow**.

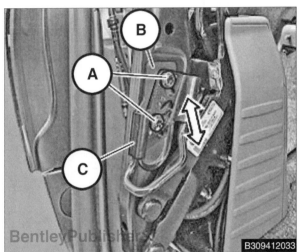

◄ Loosen screws (**A**) so that lock striker (**C**) can be moved.

– Slide lock striker in direction of **arrow**.

– Tighten screws (**A**) and check alignment of rear lid and lock striker.

– Add or remove shims (**B**) as necessary.

| Tightening torque | |
|---|---|
| Lock striker to convertible top module | 10 Nm (7 ft-lb) |

### Adjusting buffer stops

◄ Version 1: Turn buffer stop (**arrow**) left or right to adjust height.

*Trunk lid support strut, removing and installing (Convertible)*

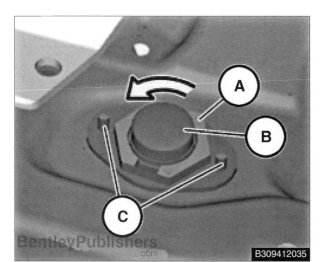

◀ Version 2: Turn lock (**A**) counterclockwise 90º (¼ turn). Pull buffer stop (**B**) up. Close trunk lid slowly until it is at the same height as the side panel. Open trunk lid and turn lock (A) 90º (¼ turn) clockwise.

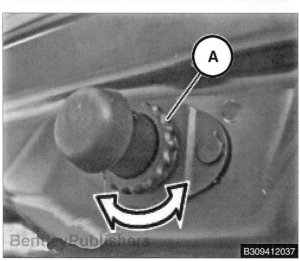

◀ Version 3: Turn buffer stop (**A**) left or right to adjust height.

## Trunk lid support strut, removing and installing (Convertible)

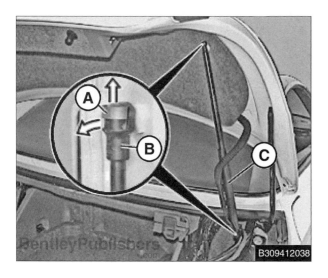

> **WARNING—**
> • Be sure to support trunk lid before removing strut.

◀ Open trunk lid and support in open position. Remove spring clips (**A**) from support strut ends (**B**).

– Remove strut (**C**) from trunk lid.

– Installation is reverse of removal. Replace spring clips damaged during removal.

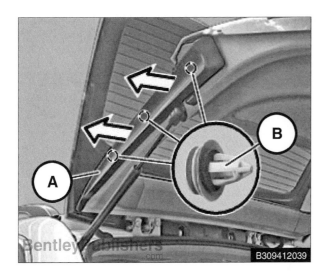

B309412039

## TAILGATE (SPORTS WAGON)

### Tailgate, removing and installing

– Raise tailgate.

◄ Remove tailgate left and right inside trim (**A**) by releasing trim clips (**B**).

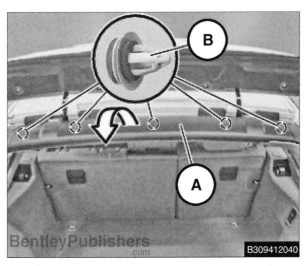

B309412040

◄ Remove tailgate upper inside trim (**A**) by releasing trim clips (**B**).

– Disconnect electrical connectors from tailgate lock, rear wiper, rear window defogger, center brake light and license plate light assembly. Remove wiring harness from tailgate.

– Disconnect left and right support struts. See **Tailgate support strut, removing and installing** in this repair group.

B309412041

◄ While supporting tailgate, remove left tailgate hinge bolt (**arrow**).

– Repeat on right.

> **CAUTION—**
> • *The tailgate is very heavy. Use assistance to support both sides prior to removal of hinge bolts.*

– Installation is reverse of removal. To align, see **Tailgate, aligning** in this repair group.

| Tightening torque | |
|---|---|
| Tailgate to tailgate hinge (M8) | 30 Nm (22 ft-lb) |

### Tailgate support strut, removing and installing

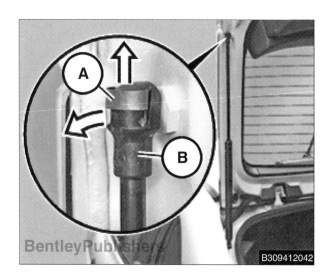

B309412042

◁ Fully open tailgate and support with suitable jack. Remove retaining clip (**A**) on upper end of pressurized support strut (**B**).

> **CAUTION—**
> • *The tailgate is very heavy and will close without both pressurized struts installed. Properly support tailgate prior to removal of a strut.*

– Pull support strut (**B**) off tailgate.

– Remove retaining clip from lower end of support strut. Remove support strut.

– Installation is reverse of removal. Replace retaining clips if damaged during removal.

## Tailgate, aligning

◁ Loosen tailgate hinge screws (**A**) so tailgate can be moved left or right.

– Loosen tailgate hinge screws (**B**) so tailgate can be moved up or down.

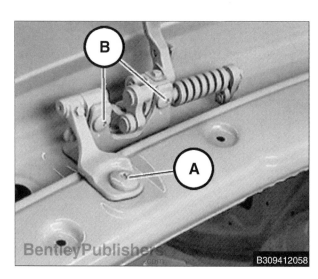

B309412058

412

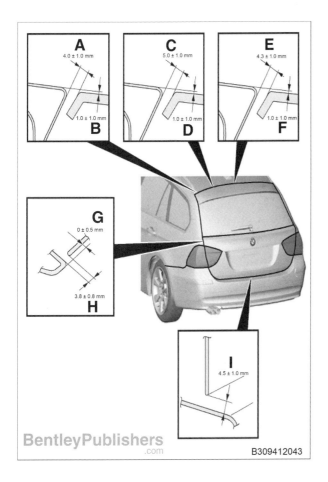

Set gap measurements as listed below for Sport Wagon.

**Trunk lid gap specifications (Sport Wagon)**

- Dimension **A** . . . . . . . . . . . . 4.0 ± 1.0 mm (0.16 ± 0.04 in)
- Dimension **B** . . . . . . . . . . . . 1.0 ± 1.0 mm (0.04 ± 0.04 in)
- Dimension **C** . . . . . . . . . . . . 5.0 ± 1.0 mm (0.20 ± 0.04 in)
- Dimension **D** . . . . . . . . . . . . 1.0 ± 1.0 mm (0.04 ± 0.04 in)
- Dimension **E** . . . . . . . . . . . . 4.3 ± 1.0 mm (0.17 ± 0.04 in)
- Dimension **F** . . . . . . . . . . . . 1.0 ± 1.0 mm (0.04 ± 0.04 in)
- Dimension **G** . . . . . . . . . . . . 0.0 ± 0.5 mm (0.00 ± 0.02 in)
- Dimension **H** . . . . . . . . . . . . 3.8 ± 0.8 mm (0.15 ± 0.03 in)
- Dimension **I** . . . . . . . . . . . . 4.5 ± 1.0 mm (0.18 ± 0.04 in)

**CAUTION—**
- *Before closing truck lid, be sure that trunk lid and body do not scrape.*

### Adjusting tailgate lock

Remove protective cap (**A**) and fully screw in buffer stop (**B**).

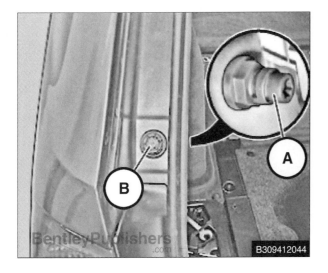

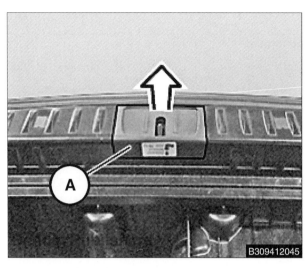

◀ Unclip and remove tailgate lock striker cover (**A**).

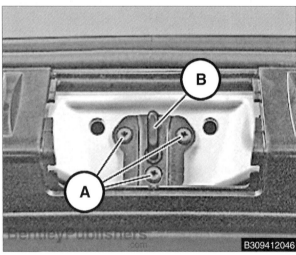

◀ Loosen screws (**A**) so that tailgate lock striker (**B**) can be moved.

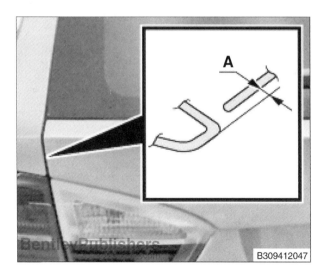

◀ Adjust tailgate at striker so that tailgate rests below side panel on left and right sides (**A**).

| Trunk lid gap specification |
| --- |
| • Dimension **A** . . . . . . . . . . . . 1.0 to 1.5 mm (0.04 ± 0.06 in) |

**412**

*Rear spoiler, removing and installing*

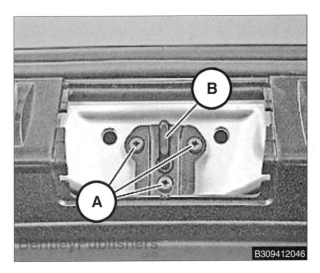

B309412046

◀ Tighten screws (**A**).

| Tightening torque | |
|---|---|
| Striker to body (M8) | 10 Nm (7 ft-lb) |

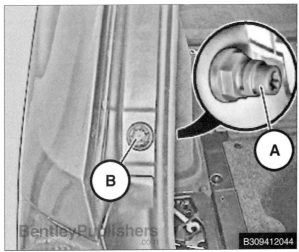

B309412044

◀ Unscrew buffer stops (**B**) until tailgate is flush with side panel. Replace protective cap (**A**).

## REAR SPOILER (SPORTS WAGON)

### Rear spoiler, removing and installing

**Removing**

◀ Pry out plugs (**A**, **B** and **C**) and remove fasteners underneath.

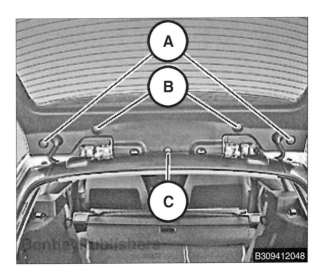

B309412048

*Rear spoiler, removing and installing*

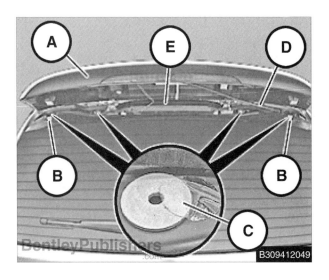

◄ Pull rear spoiler (**A**) toward rear and feed out of guides (**B**). If shims (**C**) are in installed, note location and reinstall using original fasteners.

− Tilt rear spoiler (**A**) upward, remove cover (**E**) and disconnect electrical connections underneath.

− Disconnect rear window washer hose (**D**) and remove rear spoiler (**A**).

**Installing**

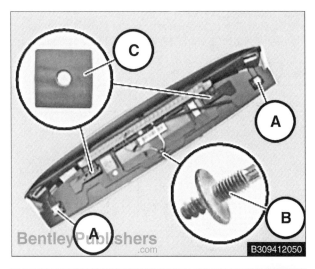

◄ Replace adjusting screw (**B**) if missing or damaged.

− Replace slide nuts (**A** and **C**) and retaining clips. Slide nuts (**C**) vary by vehicle build date. Consult authorized BMW parts dealer for correct part information.

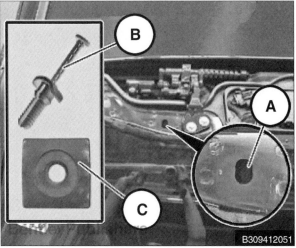

◄ Replace expanding rivet (**B**) and slide nut (**C**) (early vehicle shown, late vehicle similar).

412

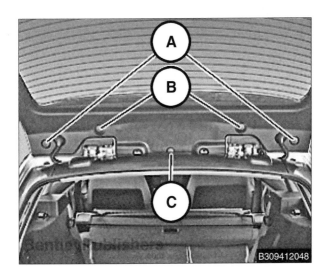

◁ Observe correct installation sequence:

- Tighten screws (**A**).
- Adjust rear spoiler. See **Adjusting rear spoiler** in this repair group.
- Tighten nut (**C**).
- Secure expanding rivets (**B**).

## Rear spoiler, adjusting

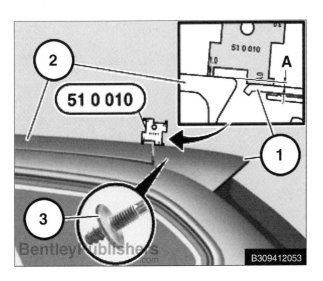

◁ Press on rear spoiler (**1**) and measure negative protrusion of rear spoiler (**1**) to rear window (**2**) with BMW tool 51 0 010 or equivalent.

| Rear spoiler gap specification |
|---|
| • Dimension **A** . . . . . . . . . . . . . 1.0 to 1.0 mm (0.04 ± 0.04 in) |

— If necessary, adjust rear spoiler (**1**) by turning adjusting screw (**3**).

# 510 Exterior Trim, Bumpers

## GENERAL

This repair group includes repair information for the outside rear view mirrors, front and rear bumpers, and the easily removable exterior trim parts.

### NOTE—

• *The procedures outlined in this group apply specifically to a 2007 330i. Other models may vary slightly from the illustrations shown.*

See also:

• **411 Doors** for door panels
• **513 Interior Trim**

**510**

## OUTSIDE REAR VIEW MIRROR

### Outside mirror glass, removing and installing

Move mirror glass carefully and slowly. For added protection, cover glass completely with masking tape or wear hand protection when removing.

> **CAUTION—**
> • *Make sure mirror glass is at or above room temperature before removing. Otherwise, small plastic parts or glass may break.*

– Tilt mirror housing out.

– With mirror glass squarely positioned in housing frame, push bottom of glass fully into housing.

◄ Insert plastic wedge under center of glass and gently pry glass up until glass disengages from retaining clips.

– Lift glass out and store mirror glass safely.

– When installing:
  • Position mirror glass in housing while aligning plastic retainers.
  • Carefully lever top center of glass down to engage retaining clips.
  • Check that mirror moves freely in all directions.

### Outside mirror housing, removing and installing

– Remove interior door trim panel. See **411 Doors**.

– Remove door window frame cover.

◄ Disconnect electrical connector (**A**).

– Support mirror from outside and remove fasteners (**arrows**).

– Installation is reverse of removal.

> **NOTE—**
> • *Check mirror function before reinstalling door panel trim.*

| Tightening torques | |
|---|---|
| Outside mirror to door | |
| • Previously installed mirror | 6 Nm (4.5 ft-lb) |
| • New mirror | 8 Nm (6 ft-lb) |

## BUMPERS

### Front bumper assembly

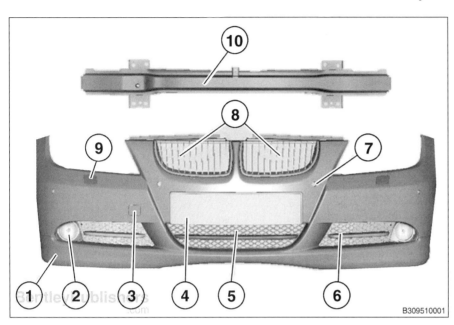

1. Front bumper trim
2. Fog light
3. Towing eye cover
4. License plate holder
5. Center trim grill
6. Side trim grill
7. Parktronic sensor
8. Radiator grill
9. Headlight washer nozzle cover
10. Front bumper support

B309510001

### Front bumper, removing and installing

◄ Remove headlight washer nozzle cover if equipped.

– Pull headlight washer nozzle (**A**) out by cover (**B**).

– Firmly grasp headlight washer nozzle (**A**) and remove cover (**B**) in direction of **arrows**. Allow headlight washer nozzle to retract slowly once cover is removed.

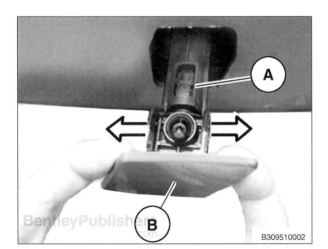

B309510002

◄ Remove front bumper fasteners (**arrows**).

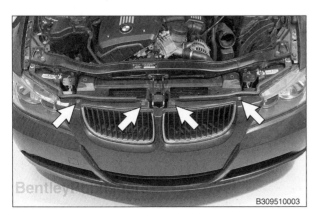

B309510003

510

*Front bumper, removing and installing*

◁ Working in left front wheel well, remove wheel housing trim fasteners (**arrows**).

**NOTE** —

• *Repeat procedure for right side of vehicle.*

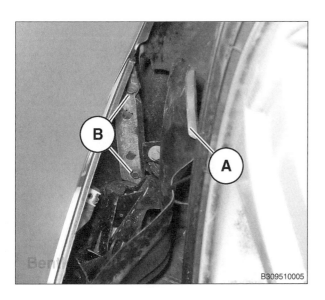

◁ Push wheel housing trim (**A**) aside and remove bumper fasteners (**B**).

**NOTE** —

• *Repeat procedure for right side of vehicle.*

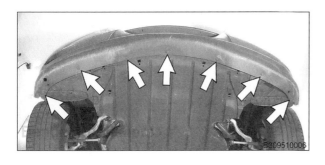

◁ Remove bumper fasteners (**arrows**).

◀ Detach bumper at sides in direction of **arrows**.

– Slide bumper (**A**) forward just enough to disconnect electrical connectors for fog lights and parktronic sensors if equipped.

– Remove bumper forward with help from an assistant.

– Installation is reverse of removal.

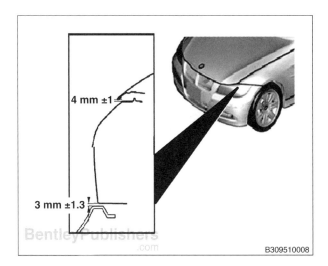

◀ Adjust bumper body gap if necessary.

## Rear bumper assembly

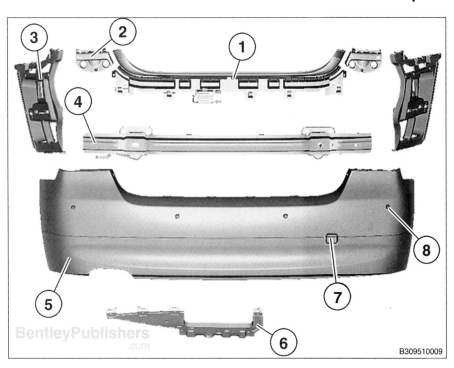

1. Middle guide
2. Side guide
3. Side holder
4. Rear carrier
5. Bumper
6. Bottom guide
7. Towing eye cover
8. Parktronic sensor

510

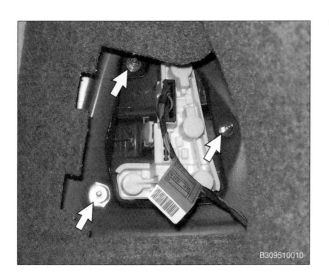

## Rear bumper, removing and installing

◀ Working at left tail light assembly:

- Disconnect electrical connector.
- Remove fasteners (**arrows**).
- Remove tail light assembly from body panel.

***NOTE***—

- *Repeat procedure for right side of vehicle.*

◀ Using a screwdriver, pry out covers (**arrows**) and remove fasteners underneath.

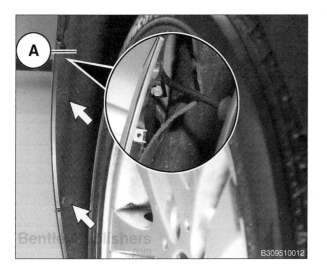

◀ Working in left rear wheel well:

- Remove fasteners (**arrows**).
- Pull wheel housing trim (**A**) aside and remove fastener (**inset**).

***NOTE***—

- *Repeat procedure for right side of vehicle.*

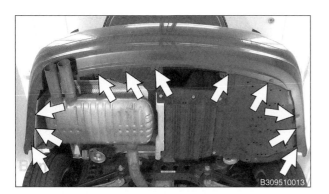

◄ Remove fasteners (**arrows**).

◄ Unclip bumper by pushing front edges in area (**A**) and pulling upper edge out of retaining clips.

– Remove by pulling bumper back and up (**arrow**).

**NOTE** —
   • *Repeat procedure for right side of vehicle.*

– Disconnect electrical connectors for parktronic sensors.

– Remove bumper with help from an assistant. Be careful not to damage bumper catches.

– Installation is reverse of removal.

## Rear bumper impact absorber, replacing

– Remove rear bumper. See **Rear bumper, removing and installing** in this repair group.

◄ If necessary, release rubber mount (**A**) on impact absorber (**B**).

– Remove fasteners (**arrows**) and remove impact absorber (**B**).

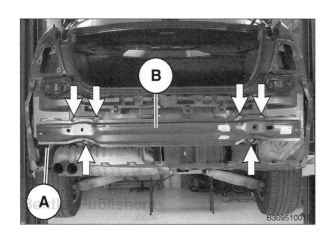

**510**

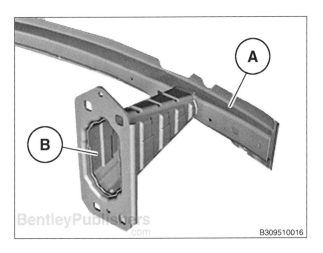

B309510016

◁ Installation is reverse of removal. Remember to:
- replace defective panel nuts (**D**).
- Seal all cavities (**B**) of impact absorber (**A**) with cavity sealant.

| Tightening torques | |
|---|---|
| Impact absorber to body | 66 Nm (48.6 ft-lb) |

## EXTERIOR TRIM

Exterior trim is attached to the body with plastic clips and fasteners that may be damaged during removal. Be sure to have necessary fasteners on hand when reinstalling exterior trim pieces.

### BMW emblem, removing and installing

The procedure given below applies to both front and rear emblems.

– Wrap end of a screwdriver with tape.

> **CAUTION—**
> • *Protect hood paint by covering area around emblem with tape.*

◁ Pry up emblem carefully on either side (**arrows**).

> **NOTE —**
> • *Notice tape on screwdriver tips.*

– Installation is reverse of removal.
- Replace plastic inserts in body if damaged.
- If emblem fits loosely, use a small amount of body molding tape or adhesive on rear of emblem before installing.

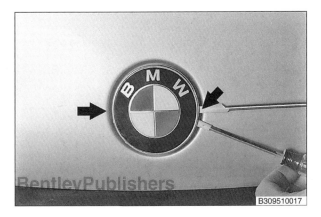

B309510017

## Radiator grill, removing and installing

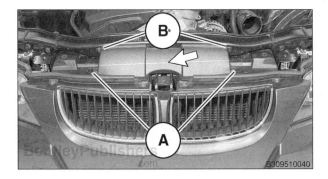

◄ Remove fasteners (**B**) and trim clips (**A**) and remove air duct (**arrow**).

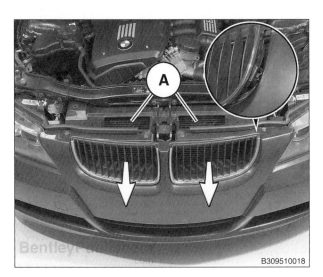

◄ Reach behind grill through air duct openings (**A**), release catches (**inset**) and remove radiator grill in direction of **arrows**.

– Once grill is removed, pry remaining tabs to separate inner grill from chrome trim ring.

– Before installation, assemble chrome trim ring and grill insert securely. Replace components if tabs or catches are broken or missing.

– Install grill and trim ring in appropriate location in hood. Press on trim ring until grill snaps into place.

**510**

# 512  Door Windows

## GENERAL

This repair group covers door glass and window regulator repair information. The windshield, rear window, and fixed rear door glass are bonded using special adhesives and tools. For bonded glass replacement, see an authorized BMW service facility or an automotive glass installer.

See also:

- **411 Doors** for door trim panel
- **515 Central Locking and Anti-theft**
- **612 Switches** for electric window switch replacement
- **721 Airbag System (SRS)** for side-impact airbag information

### Power window features

- Door window motors controlled by the car access system (CAS) footwell module (FRM) and / or junction box electronics (JBE).
- One-touch operation in both directions on all four windows.
- Cable-type window regulator used for all door windows.
- Anti-trap protection provided by monitoring window motor torque.
- Convenience opening / closing of the windows from driver's lock cylinder and from remote unlocking feature of remote key.
- Window operation can be owner customized with Car Memory function. See **515 Central Locking and Anti-theft.**
- After ignition is switched OFF, electric windows can be operated until a door is opened, or until 16 minutes has elapsed.
- Window drop down feature (Coupe, Convertible). Window glass drops out of window seal when the door is opened

*Power window control modules*

## Power window control modules

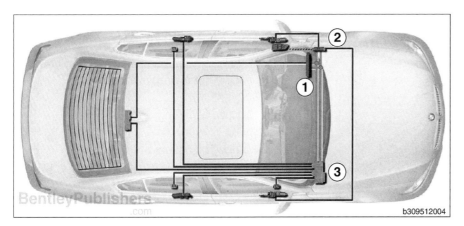

b309512004

1. Car access system (CAS)

2. Footwell module (FRM)

3. Junction box electronics module (JBE)

**Car access system (CAS)** is the master control module for lowering and raising the windows.

**Footwell module (FRM)** contains relays for the driver and passenger front windows.

**Junction box electronics module (JBE)** contains relays for the driver and passenger rear windows.

CAS is the central control module for electric opening and closing of the power windows. CAS issues the signal to enable the open and close function for the power windows. FRM and the JBE activate the power window motors.

By monitoring motor speed of the power window motors FRM and JBE can respond to overheating or the event of an object being trapped in the windows.

## Window switches

### Drivers window switch cluster

◄ When the power window switch for the window in the driver's door or front passenger's door is operated the drivers window switch cluster sends a signal via the LIN-bus to the FRM. The FRM then actuates the corresponding power window motor.

When the power window switch for the window in a rear door is operated the drivers window switch cluster sends a signal via the LIN-bus to the FRM. FRM sends the signal via the K-CAN to JBE, JBE then actuates the window motors.

### Passenger window switches

When the power window switch in the front passenger's door is operated the JBE sends a signal via the K-CAN to the footwell module, the FRM then actuates the power window motor.

◄ When the power window switches in the rear doors are operated the switch sends a signal to JBE, JBE then actuates the power window motor.

◄ Window switch positions:
1. Off
2. Open
3. One touch open
4. Close
5. One touch close

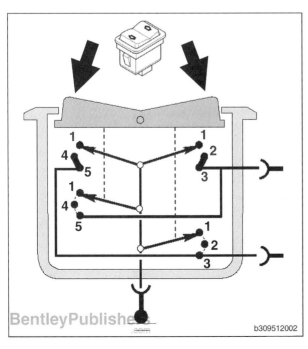

The window toggle switch provides the corresponding control module with a coded ground signal. Holding a switch at the first detent provides a single ground signal on one wire requesting the general module to open the window. When released, the ground signal is removed and the window motor stops.

Momentarily pushing the switch to the second detent and releasing provides an additional ground signal on the second wire requesting one touch mode. The corresponding module lowers the window automatically until it reaches the end position.

### Rear window child lockout switch

 The rear window child lockout switch (**arrow**) is incorporated in the driver's window switch block. When activated, it provides a signal VIA the LIN bus to the footwell module (FRM), preventing the windows from being operated from the rear door switches.

The lockout switch signal is overridden if a multiple restraint system (MRS) crash signal is received.

### Power window motors

The window motors are mounted on cable regulators. The window motor control circuit consists of two wires for operating the motor in both directions.

The motors are activated by relays in the FRM and JBE. The relays provide either power or ground depending on the direction of window travel. FRM and JBE controls the polarity based on a request to run the window from a window switch or a convenience opening / closing signal.

### Convenience opening / closing

The CAS module provides the convenience open / close feature, providing control of the power windows (and sunroof) from outside the vehicle using the key in the driver's door lock, or with the remote key and the drivers door handle.

Anti-trap protection is active during convenience closing from the driver's door lock.

If the CAS module receives a request to operate convenience closing or opening for more than 110 seconds, the function is deactivated and a fault code is stored.

### Window anti-trap protection

Anti-trapping function does not prevent an object being trapped but rather limits the trapping force to maximum 80 Nm. The power window motor is reversed when this force is exceeded.

Anti-trapping function is based on the evaluation of power window motor Hall sensor pulses. During initialization speed of the Hall sensor pulses are learned. Speed fluctuations within a certain range triggers the anti-trapping function.

*NOTE—*

- *If window is not initialized or a faulty hall sensor is detected the window will only move in small increments.*

## Panic mode

Panic mode can be used to close a window in the event of an emergency. It is triggered by overpulling - releasing - overpulling (overpulling = pulling beyond limit stop) the power window switches. It is necessary to release and overpull the switch again in order to deactivate the anti-trapping protection function, which is still active the first time the switch is overpulled.

Overpulling the power window switch the second time within 4 s closes the window with maximum force.

*NOTE* —

• *Anti-trapping function is not active during panic mode. The window closes at the maximum closing force and does not reverse.*

## Window motor thermal protection

FRM and JBE monitor power window motor temperature. Motor temperature is determined based on outside ambient temperature, motor running time and the time the motor is stationary.

Each motor can be switched off individually to prevent the window motor overheating during operation of the window regulator. The motor is deactivated for a period of time.

Thermal protection function does not prevent windows from being opened in case of trapping. Once started, a power window function is not interrupted by the thermal protection facility.

*NOTE* —

• *In panic mode the window can still be closed even when the thermal protection function is active.*

## Warnings and Cautions

*WARNING* —

• *E90 models are fitted with side-impact airbags in the front seats. When servicing the door windows on cars with side-impact airbags, always disconnect the negative (–) battery cable. See **721 Airbag System (SRS)** for cautions and procedures relating to the airbag system.*

• *Always wear hand and eye protection when working with broken glass.*

• *If a window is broken, all of the glass bits should be vacuumed out of the door cavity. Use a blunt screwdriver to clean out any remaining glass pieces from the window guide rails.*

• *When servicing the door windows, the harness connector to the window regulator should always be disconnected to prevent pinching fingers in the moving window mechanism.*

*CAUTION* —

• *Prior to disconnecting the battery, read the battery disconnection cautions given in **001 Warnings and Cautions**.*

**512**

*Front door window, removing and installing (Sedan, Sports Wagon)*

## WINDOW SERVICE

### Front door window, removing and installing (Sedan, Sports Wagon)

– Remove door panel. See **411 Doors**.

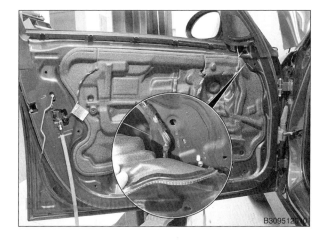

◀ Remove vapor barrier from inside of door (**inset**).

> **CAUTION—**
> • *Use care when peeling back vapor barrier. A damaged vapor barrier should be replaced to prevent possible water leaks.*

◀ Reconnect window switch and lower window down to 105 mm (4.1 in.) (**A**). Turn ignition OFF and disconnect window switch.

– Disconnect electrical connector from power window motor.

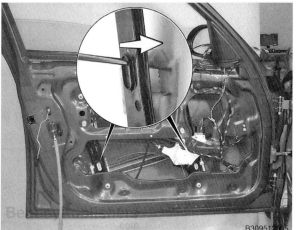

◀ Release door window catches with screwdriver in direction of **arrow** while an assistant lifts window out of window regulator guides.

*Front door window, removing and installing (Coupe, Convertible)*

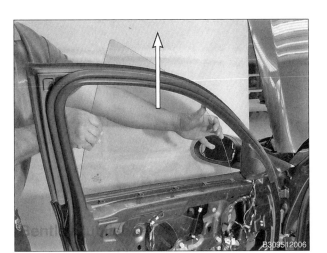

◅ Tilt and lift glass out of door in direction of **arrow**.

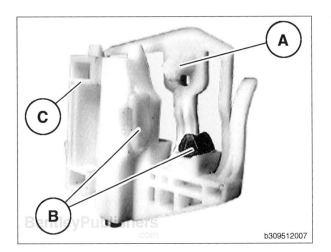

◅ Installation is reverse of removal, noting the following:

- Be careful not to break catch (**A**) or buffer stop (**B**) on window guide (**C**).
- Adjust door window if necessary. See **Front door window, adjusting, (Sedan, Sports Wagon)** in this repair group.
- Initialize power window. See **Initializing windows** in this repair group.

## Front door window, removing and installing (Coupe, Convertible)

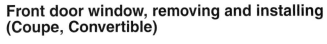

– Remove door panel. See **411 Doors**.

◅ Remove vapor barrier from inside of door (**inset**).

> **CAUTION—**
> - *Use care when peeling back vapor barrier. A damaged vapor barrier should be replaced to prevent possible water leaks.*

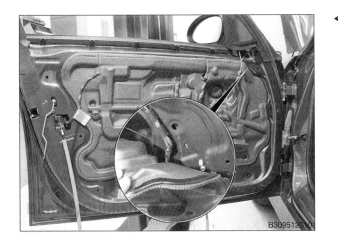

*Front door window, removing and installing (Coupe, Convertible)*

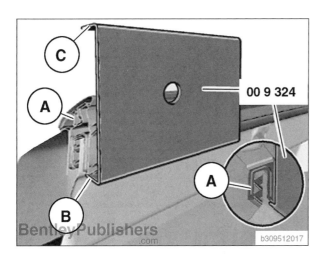

◁ Lower door window and install BMW special tool 00 9 324 on external window cavity trim strip as shown:

- Window cavity trim strip (**A**).
- BMW special tool 00 9 324 narrow edge (bottom) (**B**).
- BMW special tool 00 9 324 top (**C**).

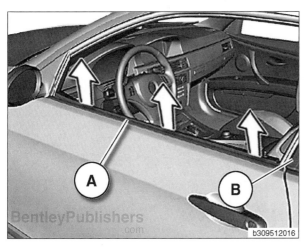

◁ Using special tool 00 9 324, remove external window cavity trim strip (**A**) starting at B-pillar (**B**).

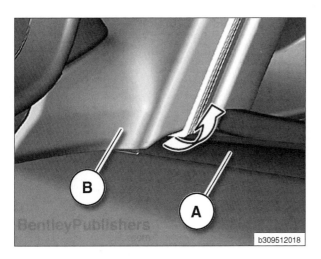

◁ Remove external window cavity trim strip (**A**) out from under mirror (**B**) in direction or **arrow**.

*Front door window, removing and installing (Coupe, Convertible)*

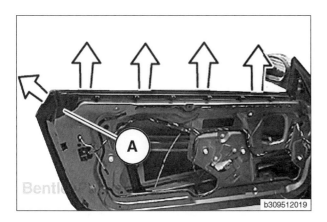

◀ Remove interior window cavity strip (**A**) in directions of **arrows**.

− Remove outside door handle. See **515 Central Locking and Anti-Theft**.

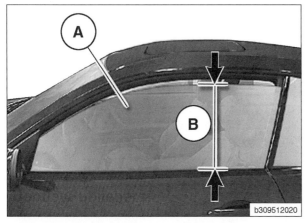

◀ Raise door window (**A**) to 335 mm (14 in) (**B**).

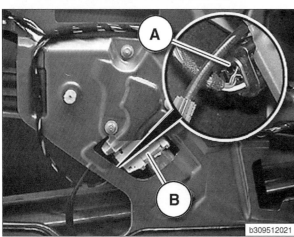

◀ Disconnect electrical connector (**A**) from power window motor (**B**).

512

*Front door window, removing and installing (Coupe, Convertible)*

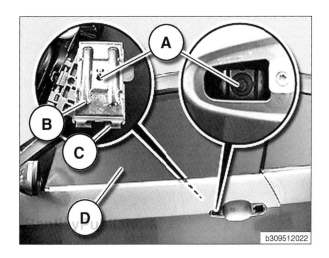

◄ Remove door window mounting clamp (**B**) fastener (**A**) through outside door handle opening.

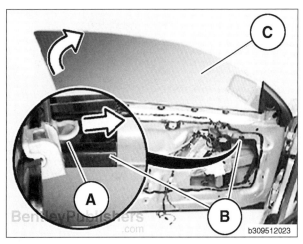

◄ Slide locking clip (**A**) in direction of **arrow**.

- Remove door window (**C**) from power window regulator.
- Rotate door window (**C**) in direction if **arrow** and feed towards top rear out of guide rail (**B**).

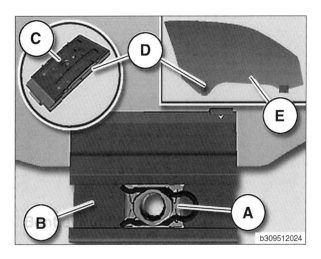

◄ Installation is reverse of removal, noting the following:

- Check that slide (**B**) and clip (**A**) are correctly installed in window regulator.
- Check that clamp (**C**) is correctly attached to clamping plate (**D**) on door window (**E**).
- Adjust front door window. See **Front door window adjusting, Coupe Convertible** in this repair group.
- Initialize power window in necessary. See **Initializing windows** in this repair group.

| Tightening torques | |
|---|---|
| Door window regulator | 10 Nm (7.3 ft-lb) |

## Front door window adjusting (Sedan, Sports Wagon)

◄ At time of publication no BMW factory procedure for adjusting door windows was available for Sedan or Sports Wagon models. However the window regulator mounting holes are slotted (**arrow**) and do have room for adjustment. The following procedure can be used if adjustment is needed.

– Remove front door panel. See **411 Doors**.

◄ Remove vapor barrier from inside of door (**inset**).

> **CAUTION—**
> • *Use care when peeling back vapor barrier. A damaged vapor barrier should be replaced to prevent possible water leaks.*

– Reconnect window switch and slightly lower door window.

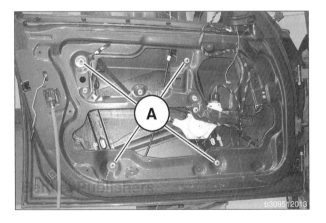

◄ Loosen fasteners for window regulator (**A**) then snug fasteners but do not tighten.

– Fully close window and tighten window regulator fasteners (**A**).

| Tightening torques | |
|---|---|
| Window regulator to door | 10 Nm (7.3 ft-lb) |

– Initialize power window. See **Initializing windows** in this repair group.

**512**

## Front door window adjusting (Coupe, Convertible)

Window regulator service varies dependent on model. Read through entire procedure before beginning work as window adjustment on some models require BMW special tools.

- Park vehicle on level ground.

- Confirm front door is properly adjusted. See **411 Doors**.

- Delete power window initialization. See **Initializing windows** in this repair group.

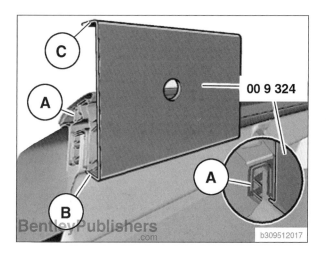

◀ Install special tool 00 9 324 on external window cavity trim strip as shown:

- Window cavity trim strip (**A**).
- Special tool 00 9 324 narrow edge (bottom) (**B**).
- Special tool 00 9 324 top (**C**).

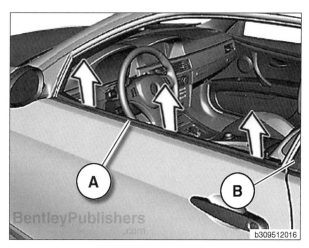

◀ Using special tool 00 9 324, remove external window cavity trim strip (**A**) starting at B-pillar (**B**).

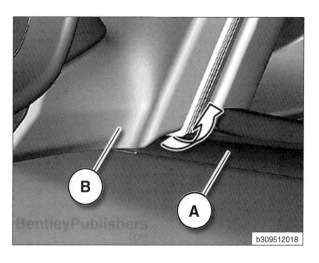

◀ Remove external window cavity trim strip (**A**) out from under mirror (**B**) in direction or **arrow**.

*Front door window adjusting (Coupe, Convertible)*

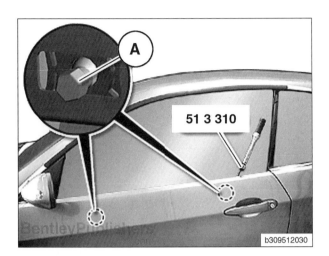

b309512030

### Longitudinal / retraction depth adjustment

◄ Using ratchet extension tool (BMW special tool 51 3 310), loosen fasteners (**A**) until door window can be moved.

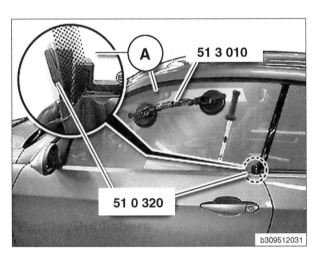

b309512031

◄ Attach suction cup handle (BMW special tool 51 3 010), to door window (**A**).

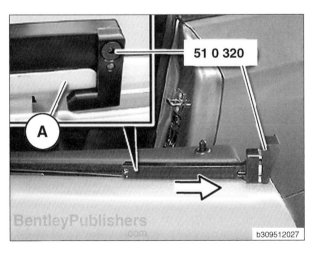

b309512027

◄ Install BMW special tool 51 0 320 on front door and press back as far as it will go in direction of **arrow**. Tool should rest against door and reach the stop on guide (**A**).

**512**

*Front door window adjusting (Coupe, Convertible)*

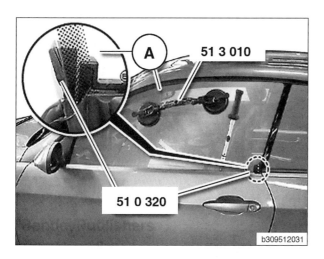

◄ Slide door window (**A**) up against BMW special tool no. 51 0 320 and hold in place.

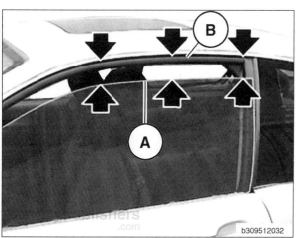

◄ Adjust top edge of door window (**A**) so it is parallel to contour of water drain (**B**).

• Be careful not to damage seals on A-pillar and retractable hardtop.

• When door window is retracted into seals, the seals should not be distorted.

— Temporarily tighten adjustment fasteners.

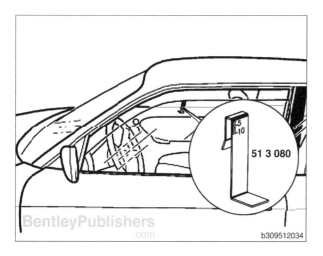

◄ Using BMW special tool 51 3 080 measure window retraction depth.

*Front door window adjusting (Coupe, Convertible)*

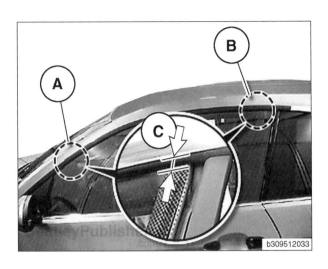

◀ Adjust retraction depth (**C**) if necessary.

| Retraction depth | |
| --- | --- |
| Area **A** | 2.5 mm ± 0.5 mm |
| Area **B** | 3.5 mm ± 0.5 mm |

- Area **A** located 30mm from mirror triangular point.
- Area **B** in located next to DOT screen.

— Tighten fasteners once adjustments are complete.

| Tightening torques | |
| --- | --- |
| Window adjustment fasteners<br>• Using ratchet extension (BMW special tool 51 3 310) | 7 Nm (5.1 ft-lb) |

— Initialize power windows. See **Initializing windows** in this repair group.

## Pretension adjustment

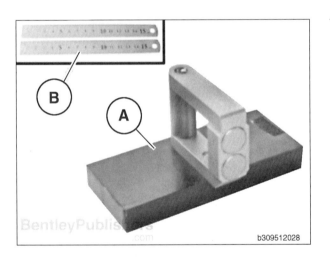

◀ Pretension can be checked with or without door window cavity strip installed. Pretension is 1.0 mm less with window cavity strip installed. The magnet built into BMW special tool 51 0 341 (**A**) creates the correct tension on door window seal for measurement. No force should be placed on door or door window during pretension measurement.

- **A** BMW special tool 51 0 341
- **B** BMW special tool 51 0 342

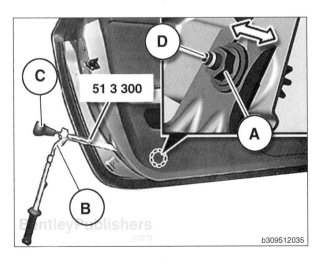

◀ Loosen nut (**A**) with ratcheting wrench and BMW special tool 51 3 300.

— Turn knob (**C**) to rotate pretension adjustment stud.

512

*Front door window adjusting (Coupe, Convertible)*

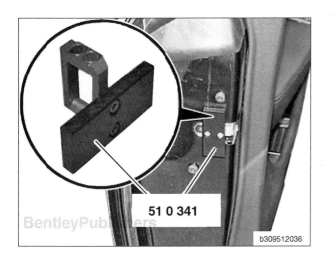

◀ Install BMW special tool 51 0 341 in vehicle door latch and carefully close door.

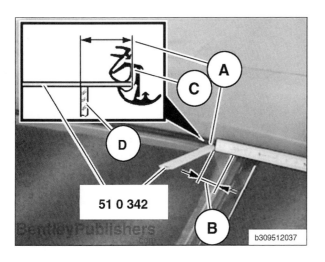

◀ Slide BMW special tool 51 0 342 at distance (**B**) to door window side edge into seal (**C**) and measure dimension (**A**) to outside edge of door window (**D**).

| Pretension measurement | |
|---|---|
| Dimension **A**<br>• With window cavity strip installed<br>• Without window cavity strip installed | <br>42 mm ± 1.0 mm<br>43 mm ± 1.0 mm |
| Dimension **B** | 10 mm |

– Tighten fasteners once adjustment has been made.

| Tightening torques | |
|---|---|
| Window adjustment fasteners | 10 Nm (7.3 ft-lb) |

– Initialize power windows. See **Initializing windows** in this repair group.

## WINDOW REGULATOR SERVICE

Window regulator service varies dependent on model. Read through entire procedure before beginning work as window adjustment on some models require BMW special tools.

*NOTE—*

- *The electronically-controlled window motor does not have mechanical end positions. For this reason the motor can be removed and installed with the window in any position.*

### Front window regulator, removing and installing (Sedan, Sports Wagon)

There are two window rails in each front window regulator, only one in the rear window regulator. Otherwise the front and rear regulators are similar.

*NOTE—*

- *Remove window regulator and motor as one unit. If necessary, separate the two on the bench.*

– Remove front door panel. See **411 Doors.**

– Remove window glass. See **Front door window removing and installing** in this repair group.

◀ Disconnect window motor electrical connector (**arrow**).

◀ Remove window regulator fasteners (**A**).

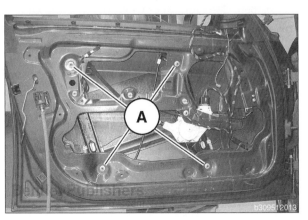

*Front window regulator, removing and installing (Coupe, Convertible)*

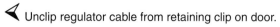 Unclip regulator cable from retaining clip on door.

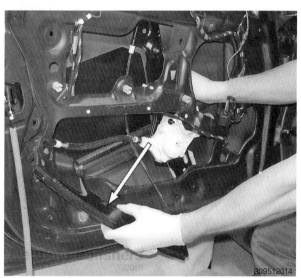

◁ Feed window regulator (**A**) out of door cavity.

– Installation is reverse of removal, noting the following:

  • Route wiring harnesses to keep them away from moving window mechanism. Use new wire ties as necessary.

  • Initialize power window. See **Initializing windows** in this repair group.

| Tightening torques | |
|---|---|
| Window regulator to door | 10 Nm (7.3 ft-lb) |
| Motor to window regulator | 6 Nm (4.4 ft-lb) |

## Front window regulator, removing and installing (Coupe, Convertible)

*NOTE —*

• *Remove window regulator and motor as one unit. If necessary, separate the two on the bench.*

– Remove door window. See **Front door window, removing and installing Coupe, Convertible** in this repair group.

◁ Remove plastic plug (**A**) and remove fastener (**B**).

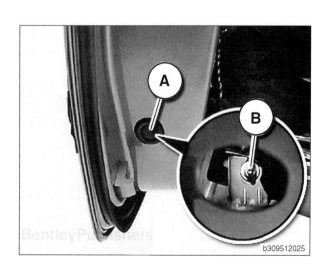

*Front window regulator, removing and installing (Coupe, Convertible)*

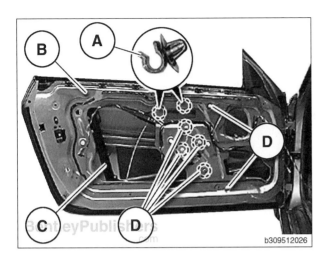

b309512026

◄ Remove window regulator cables from clips (**A**).

  • Remove fastener (**B**) and feed out front window regulator rail (**C**).

  • Remove fasteners (**D**) and feed rear window regulator rail out of door.

— Installation is reverse of removal, noting the following:

  • Route wiring harnesses to keep them away from moving window mechanism. Use new wire ties as necessary.

  • Replace fasteners for window regulator motor if removed.

  • Adjust front door window. See **Front door window adjusting, Coupe Convertible** in this repair group.

  • Initialize power window. See **Initializing windows** in this repair group.

| Tightening torques | |
|---|---|
| Window regulator to door | 10 Nm (7.3 ft-lb) |
| Motor to window regulator | 6 Nm (4.4 ft-lb) |

## INITIALIZING WINDOWS

Two parameters are learned during initialization:

• Upper end stop (normalization of the power windows).

• Power characteristic curve for opening and closing (learning the characteristic curve).

The initialization can be carried out using the control switch in each door or the power-window switch block in the driver's door.

The following requirements are necessary for initialization to be carried:

• Vehicle stationary.

• Adequate battery voltage present (12.4 volts), connect vehicle power supply if necessary.

• Terminal R (radio readiness) or terminal 15 switched ON (ignition ON) See **020 Maintenance** for vehicle key states.

• All doors closed.

### Deleting a previous initialization

Deleting an initialization and subsequent re-initialization can remedy sporadic, incorrect shutdowns in one touch operation mode.

Open the window of each door completely. Press and hold the control switch completely (switch position: one touch operation mode) for longer than 15 seconds and less than 20 seconds.

Deletion of the initialization was successful when one touch operation mode is no longer possible for window close function.

512

*Front window regulator, removing and installing (Coupe, Convertible)*

### Performing initialization

— Fully close window by pulling the switch so that the top end stop is reached (normalization).

— Open the window completely so that the lower end stop is reached.

— Pull the control switch into one touch operation mode, close (one touch operation, close) position and hold it there until the window has reached the top end stop (learning the characteristic curve).

The initialization was successful if the window can be opened and closed without faults in one touch operation mode.

*NOTE* —

• *Windows will move in small increments if not initialized.*

# 513  Interior Trim

## GENERAL

This repair group covers interior trim removal and installation.

Photos in this repair group illustrate a 2008 3 Series Sedan. Other models are similar.

See also:

- **411 Doors** for interior door trim panel removal
- **520 Seats** for rear side bolster removal
- **612 Switches**
- **620 Instruments**
- **640 Heating and Air-conditioning**
- **650 Radio**
- **721 Airbag System (SRS)** for passenger airbag

**513**

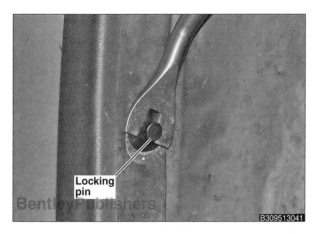

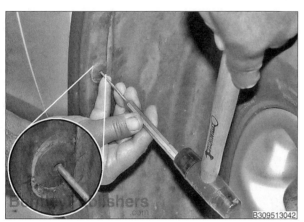

## Trim clips

Interior trim and finish panels are clipped or screwed into place. When removing trim that is held in place with clips, be sure to have spare clips (also known as plastic rivets) on hand before beginning the job.

 Many trim clips may be reused if removed correctly:
- Carefully pry out center locking pin.
- Lever out clip using removal tool.

 Other trim retaining clips are designed to be used only once:
- Use thin pin punch to drive in headless pin (**inset**) in center of clip.
- Lever out clip using removal tool.

## Warnings and Cautions

---

**WARNING**—
- *Serious injury may result if airbag system service is attempted by persons unfamiliar with the BMW SRS and its approved service procedures.*
- *Before performing any work involving airbags, disconnect the negative (-) battery cable. See **721 Airbag System (SRS)**.*
- *BMW airbags are equipped with a back-up power supply inside the airbag control module. Observe a 5 second waiting period after disconnecting the battery cable to allow the reserve power supply to discharge.*

---

**CAUTION**—
- *When working on electrical switches or lights, disconnect the negative (-) battery cable and insulate the cable end to prevent accidental reconnection.*
- *Prior to disconnecting the battery, read the battery disconnection cautions given in **001 Warnings and Cautions**.*
- *To prevent marring the trim, work with a plastic prying tool or wrap a screwdriver tip with masking tape before prying out trim panels, switches or electrical accessories.*

---

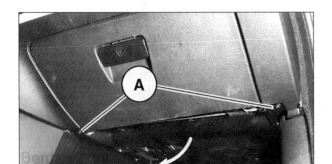

## DASHBOARD

### Right lower dashboard trim, removing and installing

– Move passenger seat all the way back.

◄ Remove trim panel fasteners (**A**) and feed trim panel in direction of **arrow**.

– Disconnect footwell light electrical connector if equipped.

– Remove trim panel.

– Installation is reverse of removal.

### Left lower dashboard trim, removing and installing

– Move driver seat all the way back.

◄ Remove trim panel fasteners (**A**).

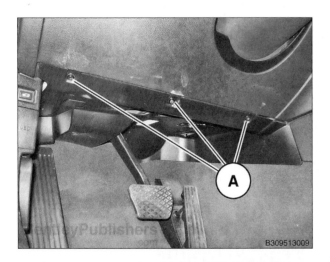

◄ Lower trim panel and disconnect fiber optic programming connector and footwell light electrical connector (**arrows**).

– Remove trim panel.

– Installation is reverse of removal.

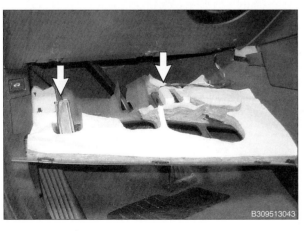

**513**

## CENTER CONSOLE

### Center console, removing and installing

– Coupe, Convertible: Remove rear center console. See **Rear center console (Coupe, Convertible) removing and installing** in this repair group.

– Remove shift knob. See **250 Gearshift Linkage**.

◁ Manual transmission: Remove shift boot by grasping boot material and pulling up to release tabs (**arrows**). Be careful not to break retaining tabs (**arrows**).

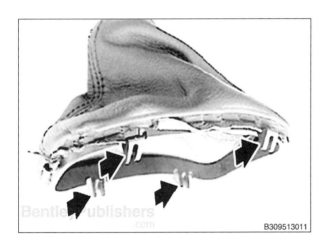

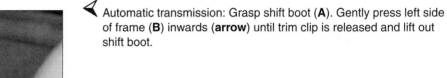

◁ Automatic transmission: Grasp shift boot (**A**). Gently press left side of frame (**B**) inwards (**arrow**) until trim clip is released and lift out shift boot.

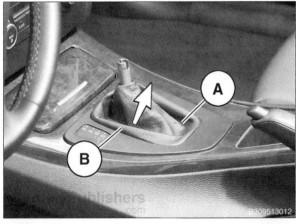

◁ Automatic transmission: Using a plastic prying tool, lever out trim piece (**A**). Disconnect electrical connectors and remove in direction of **arrows**.

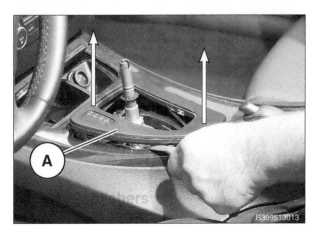

*Center console, removing and installing*

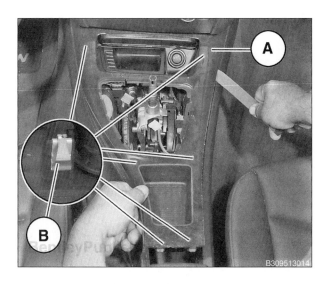

◀ All models: Pry off trim piece (**A**) in area of trim clips (**B**).

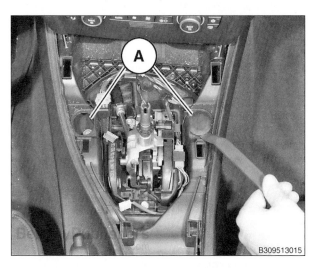

◀ Pry out covers (**A**) and remove fasteners underneath.

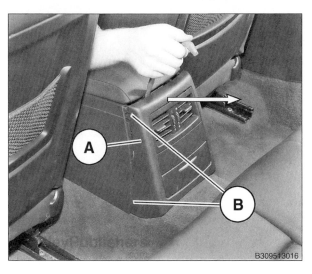

◀ Pry trim panel (**A**) off in direction of arrow while carefully unclipping trim clips (**B**).

**513**

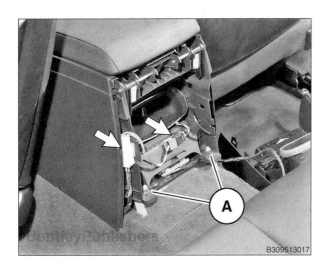

◄ Remove fasteners (**A**) and disconnect electrical connectors (**arrows**).

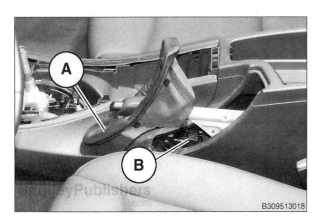

◄ Pull parking brake handle boot (**A**) over handle. Disconnect phone system electrical connector (**B**) if equipped.

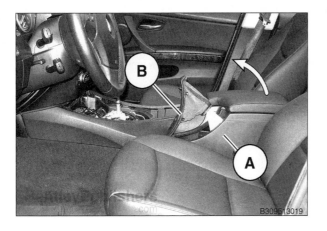

◄ Raise center console (**A**) at rear in direction of **arrow** while feeding parking brake lever boot (**B**) through opening. Disconnect electrical connectors and remove center console (**A**).

– Installation is reverse of removal. Remember to:

• Connect electrical connectors.

• Connect air ducts.

• Replace any damaged panel clips.

## Rear center console (Coupe, Convertible) removing and installing

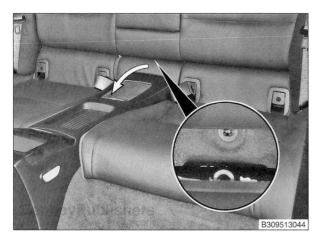

◀ Remove rear seat filler element in direction of **arrow** detaching guide loop (**inset**).

◀ Remove left and right rear seat cushions in direction of **arrows** while feeding seat belt buckles through opening in seat cushion.

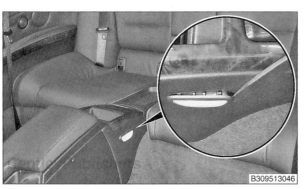

◀ Using a plastic prying tool, remove left and right rear footwell lights (**inset**).

**513**

*Rear center console (Coupe, Convertible) removing and installing*

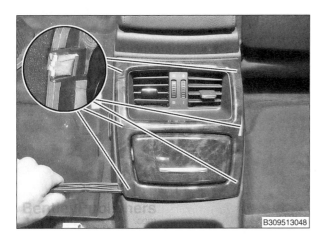

◄ using a plastic prying tool, release clips (**inset**) and remove rear trim piece from center console.

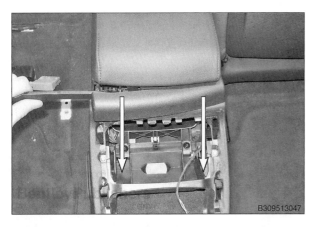

◄ Using a plastic prying tool, remove center trim piece in direction of **arrows**.

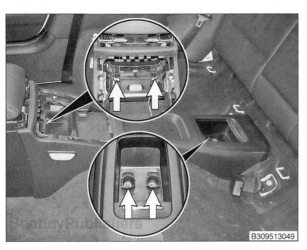

◄ Remove center console fasteners (**arrows**).

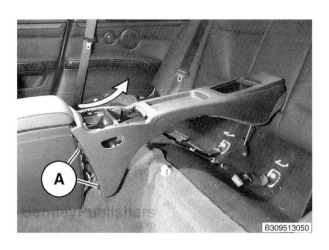

◁ Using a plastic prying tool, release catches on both sides and lift center console out in direction of **arrow**.

– Installation is reverse of removal. Remember to:
  • Connect electrical connectors.
  • Connect air ducts.
  • Replace any damaged panel clips.

## GLOVE COMPARTMENT

### Glove compartment, removing and installing

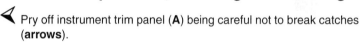

◁ Pry off instrument trim panel (**A**) being careful not to break catches (**arrows**).

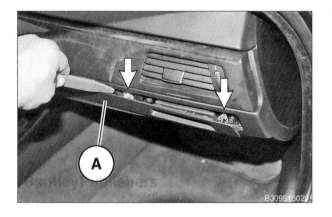

◁ Remove fasteners (**arrows**) and cupholders (**A**).

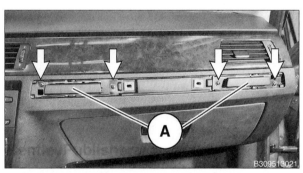

◁ Remove fasteners (**A**) and pull glove compartment out slightly in direction of **arrows**.

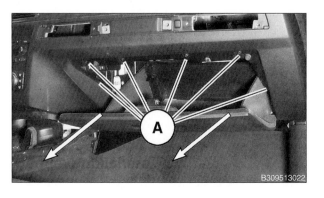

**513**

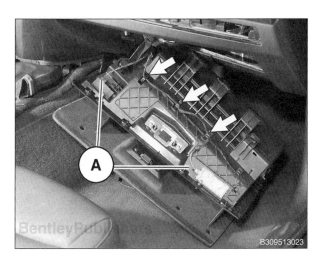

◀ Disconnect electrical connectors (**A**), remove wires from clips (**arrows**) and remove glove compartment.

– Installation is reverse of removal. Remember to:
   • Connect electrical connectors.
   • Replace any damaged panel clips.

## COVERS AND TRIM PANELS

### Steering column upper trim, removing and installing

– Adjust steering column to fully extended and lowered position.

◀ Unclip steering column upper trim piece (**arrow**) from side with plastic prying tool.

◀ Tilt steering column upper trim panel (**A**) forward and unclip (**arrows**) from cover (**B**).

– Installation is reverse of removal.

### Steering column lower trim, removing and installing

— Remove steering column upper trim panel. See **Steering column upper trim, removing and installing** in this repair group.

◄ Press detent lug (**arrow**) on each side of trim panel outwards and unclip trim panel.

— Installation is reverse of removal.

### Door sill trim, removing and installing

◄ Using a plastic prying tool unclip door sill trim (**A**) clips (**B**) starting at rear.

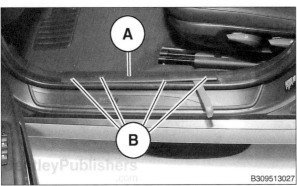

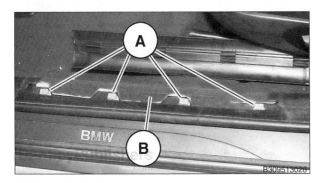

◄ Remove panel clips (**A**) left in floor panel (**B**) after trim panel removal if necessary.

— Installation is reverse of removal. Replace any damaged panel clips.

**513**

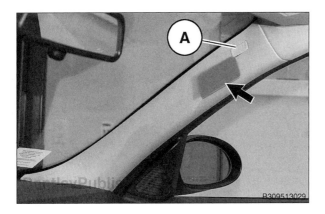

## A-pillar trim, removing and installing

◀ Using plastic trim tool (**arrow**) remove cover (**A**).

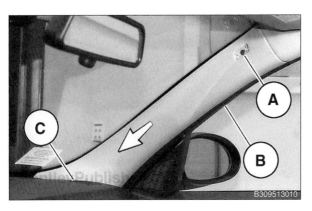

◀ Remove fastener (**A**) then release door seal (**B**) from A-pillar trim.

– Unclip trim from A-pillar and out of instrument panel (**C**) in direction of **arrow**.

– Installation is reverse of removal. Replace any damaged panel clips

## B-pillar trim, removing and installing

– Remove driver door sill trim. See **Door sill trim, removing and installing** in this repair group.

### Lower B-pillar trim

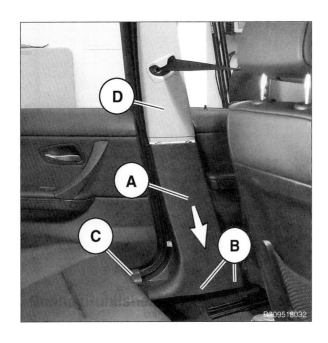

◀ Snap trim (**A**) out of trim clips at bottom (**B**) and feed trim panel out of rear door sill trim (**C**) and door seal.

– Carefully guide trim panel (**A**) out of upper trim panel (**D**).

**Upper B-pillar trim**

◄ Using a plastic prying tool unclip release tab for seat belt trim cover (**arrow**).

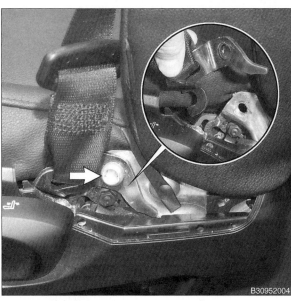

◄ Remove fastener for seat belt (**arrow**) and discard. Disconnect seat belt from tab (**inset**) and lay aside.

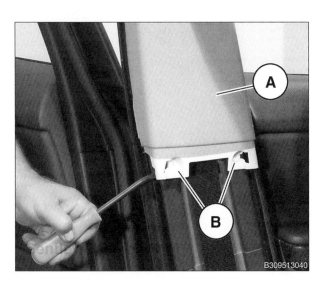

◄ Disconnect trim panel (**A**) trim clips (**B**).

513

◀ Remove trim panel in direction of **arrow**.

− Installation is reverse of removal. Remember to:
  • Replace any damaged panel clips.
  • Replace fastener for seat belt.

| Tightening torque | |
|---|---|
| Seatbelt to front seat (Replace bolt) | 44 Nm (32.4 ft-lb) |

## C-pillar trim, removing and installing

◀ Remove cap (**A**) and fastener underneath. Remove door seal (**B**) from trim panel (**D**).

− Pull trim panel (**D**) in direction of **arrow** to disconnect clips (**C**) and remove.

− Installation is reverse of removal. Replace any damaged panel clips

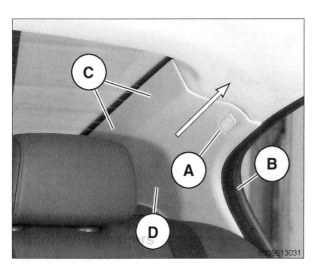

## Trunk lid trim panel, removing and installing

◀ Remove emergency trunk release handle by pushing lever and releasing cable (**inset**).

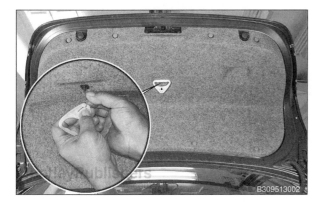

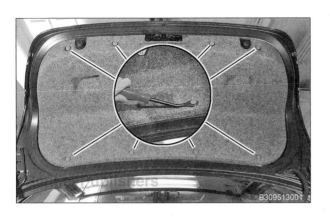

◀ Remove trim panel clips (**inset**) and remove trunk lid trim panel.

– Installation is reverse of removal. Remember to replace damaged trim panel clips.

## Trunk lower trim panel, removing and installing

◀ Remove luggage compartment floor trim panel in direction of **arrow**.

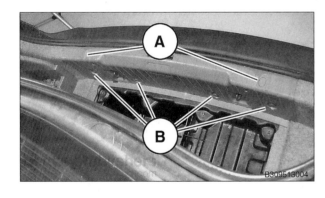

◀ Remove plastic cover and fasteners (**A**). Remove trim panel clips (**B**) then lift out and remove trunk trim panel.

– Installation is reverse of removal. Remember to replace damaged trim panel clips.

## Tailgate lid trim panel, removing and installing

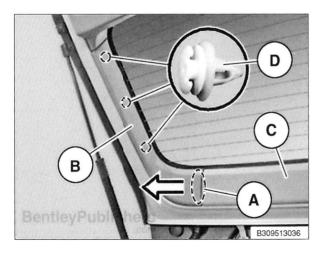

◀ Remove left and right side window trim panels:
  • Release trim clips (**D**) with trim tool.
  • Feed window trim panel (**B**) in area (**A**) out of trim panel (**C**) in direction of arrow.

**513**

*Tailgate lid trim panel, removing and installing*

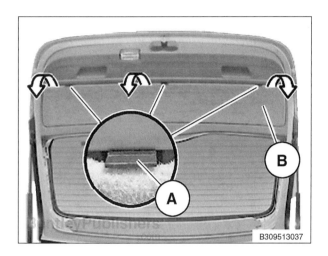

B309513037

◁ Release catches (**A**) and rotate panel (**B**) downwards.

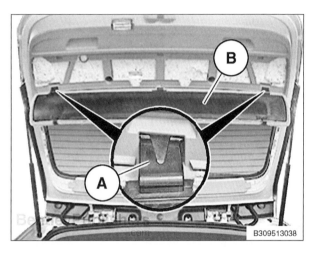

B309513038

◁ Carefully compress tabs (**A**) and remove insert (**B**).

– Remove tailgate light housing.

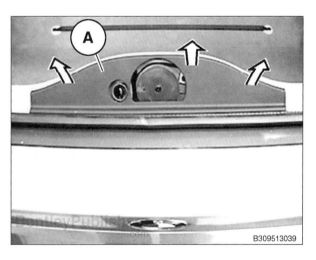

B309513039

◁ Pull up on trim panel (**A**) to unclip (**arrows**).

*Tailgate lid trim panel, removing and installing*

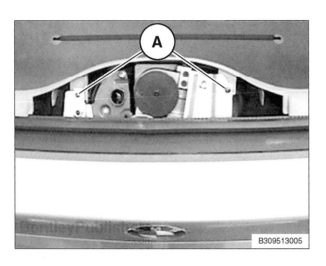

◄ Remove fasteners (**A**).

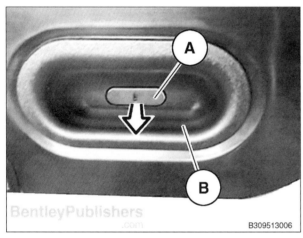

◄ Remove plastic cover (A) and screw behind it. Remove recessed handle (**B**). Right side shown; left is similar.

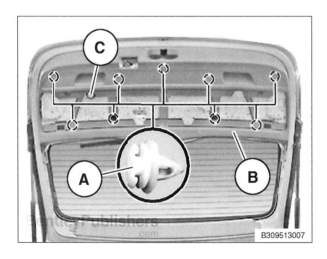

◄ Release panel clips (**A**) on trim panel **B**. Feed out eyelet (**C**) and lower trim panel **B**.

– Installation is reverse of removal. Remember to replace damaged trim panel clips.

**513**

# 515 Central Locking and Anti-theft

## GENERAL

This section covers repair information for door and tailgate locks, central locking, electronic immobilization (EWS) and anti-theft alarm (DWA).

3 Series vehicles are equipped with sophisticated self-diagnostic electrical systems. When experiencing malfunctions relating to central locking or anti-theft systems, start the diagnosis process using the BMW factory scan tool or equivalent. An advanced diagnostic scan tool can usually pinpoint electrical faults quickly and safely.

See also:

• **411 Doors** for inner door trim removal

• **513 Interior Trim** for tailgate trim removal

• **600 Electrical System–General**

• **ECL Electrical Component Locations**

• **ELE Electrical Wiring Diagrams**

**515**

B309515051

## Fuel filler flap emergency opening

The fuel filler flap can be unlocked manually in the event of an electrical defect. The emergency release is located in the luggage compartment on the right behind the luggage compartment cover.

◄ Remove cover (**arrow**).

B309515052

◄ Pull green knob (**inset**) with fuel pump symbol to release fuel filler flap.

*Fuel filler flap emergency opening*

## CENTRAL LOCKING

Central locking in 3 Series vehicles controls the door locks, trunk lid lock and fuel filler flap lock.

Central locking is distributed over several control modules. This offers the advantage that sensors and actuators are connected directly to a control module in the vicinity of their installed location, which result is shorter cable connections. By interlinking the control modules, it is possible to exchange sensor data between them.

The primary control modules for central locking in the 3 Series are:

1. Car access system (CAS)

2. Footwell module (FRM)

3. Junction box electronics (JBE)

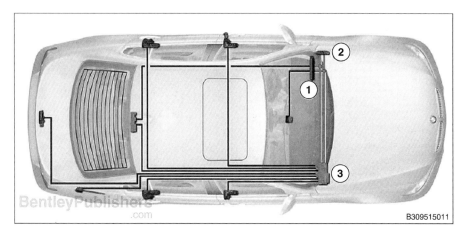

B309515011

Central locking can be operated via the following components:

- Remote control / remote key.
- Driver's door lock barrel (door lock).
- Center-lock button.
- Electronic outer door handle module (TAGE) in connection with comfort access.

### Car access system (CAS)

 Car access system (CAS) is the master control module for the central locking system, it issues the enable signal to activate a lock / unlock function. When CAS receives a lock / unlock signal from the remote control receiver, it checks whether the remote key is valid and belongs to the vehicle. If the check / authentication is successful CAS will forward the request to activate central locking via the body bus system (K-CAN) to JBE.

*NOTE—*

- *For summary of CAS functions see **600 Electrical System– General**.*

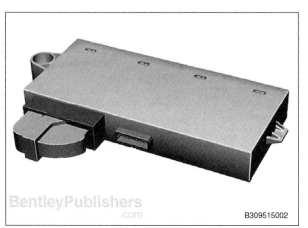

B309515002

515

*Fuel filler flap emergency opening*

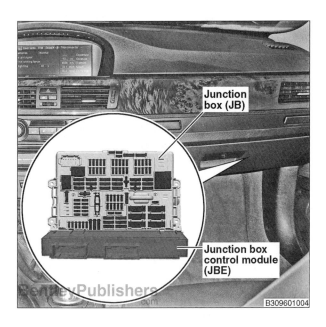

### Junction box control module (JBE)

 JBE is responsible for the locking and unlocking the entire vehicle. It contains relays which drive the respective lock / unlock motors.

The following central locking relays are activated by JBE:
- Driver door
- Front passenger door
- Rear doors
- Fuel filler flap

The central locking function for the trunk lid is activated by the JBE.

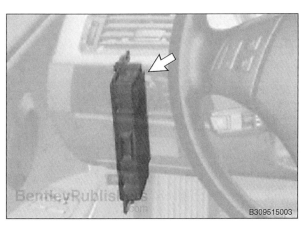

### Footwell module (FRM)

 FRM (**arrow**) monitors Hall sensors in the door contacts to determine if a door is open or closed. CAS indirectly obtains the door status and uses the information to determine if a lock / unlock authorization signal is to be provided to JBE.

## Central locking inputs, outputs

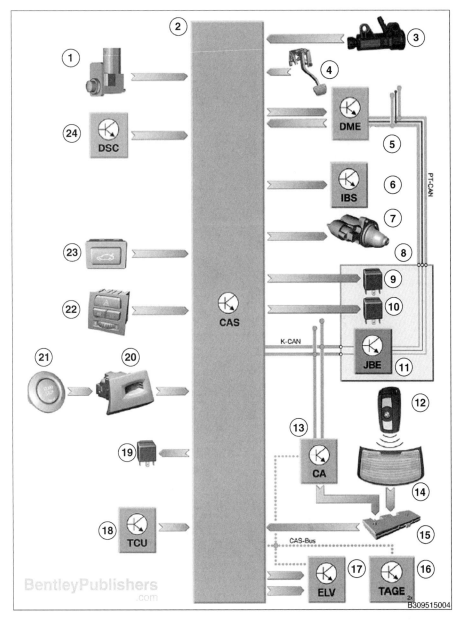

1. Hood contact switch
2. Car access system (CAS)
3. Clutch switch
4. Brake light switch
5. Digital motor electronics (DME)
6. Intelligent battery sensor (IBS)
7. Starter motor
8. Junction box (JB)
9. Terminal 30g relay
10. Terminal 15, load shielding relay
11. Junction box electronics module (JBE)
12. Identification transmitter
13. Comfort access (CA)
14. Remote control receiver
15. Rear window antenna
16. Electronic door handle module (TAGE)
17. Electric steering lock (ELV)
18. Telematics control unit (TCU)
19. Fuel injector relay
20. Remote key slot
21. Start stop switch
22. Central lock button
23. Trunk lid button
24. Dynamic stability control (DC)

B309515004

## Central locking features

Central locking can be activated when the driver door is closed.

Vehicle locking / unlocking is initiated by the following components:
• Remote key / identification transmitter.
• Central locking button on center dashboard.
• Mechanical key / spare key.

Driver identification is incorporated within the remote key and is also used for the optional comfort access (CA) system. CA module activates the identification transmitter in the remote key by way of a radio signal. This makes it possible to unlock the vehicle without actively using the remote key.

The central locking system activates the following system components:

- Driver and front passenger door locks.
- Rear door locks.
- Fuel filler flap lock.
- Trunk lid or tailgate.

### Unlocking / locking

When the remote key unlock button is pressed, the signal is received by the rear window antenna and forwarded to the remote control receiver in the diversity module. The remote control receiver forwards the signal to CAS.

The signal from the remote key is verified in CAS. If the signal is valid, JBE is authorized to unlock the vehicle. JBE now activates the relay to trigger vehicle unlocking.

Remote key signal path:

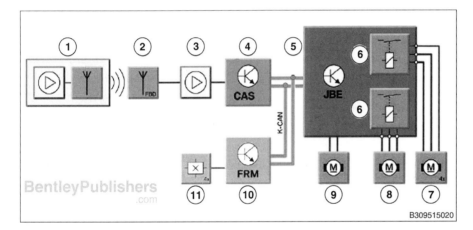

1. Remote key
2. Rear window antenna
3. Remote key receiver
4. Car access system (CAS)
5. Junction box electronics (JBE)
6. Central locking relays
7. Lock actuators, passenger door, rear doors and fuel filler flap
8. Lock actuator, driver door
9. Lock actuator, trunk / tailgate
10. Footwell module (FRM)
11. Door contacts

The vehicle can be locked after the CAS signals to the FRM that the doors are closed.

### Mechanical key locking / unlocking

The vehicle can be locked / unlocked with the mechanical key in the driver door lock. The footwell module (FRM) monitors the Hall sensor signal for the lock barrel in the driver door. When the lock is turned a change in the Hall sensor state initiates locking / unlocking.

 Door key positions for electrical / manual locking and unlocking are:

1. Turn once: Unlocks driver door
   Turn twice: Unlocks remaining doors, trunk, tailgate, fuel filler
   Turn and hold (door closed): Opens windows, sunroof
2. Turn once: Locks all doors, tailgate, fuel filler
   Turn and hold (door closed): Closes windows, sunroof

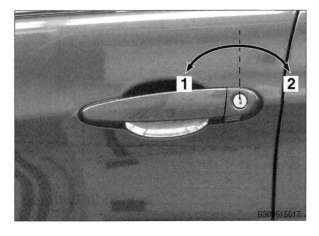

### Selective unlocking

When unlocking with the key or the identification transmitter, the first unlock request only unlocks the driver's door. A second unlock request unlocks the remaining doors, tailgate and fuel flap.

### Central locking button

◀ The central locking button (**arrow**) is in the center of dashboard.

- The central locking button only locks the doors and tailgate. The filler flap remains unlocked for refueling purposes.

- If a door is opened from inside while centrally locked, the remaining doors remain locked.

The open door can be relocked, when closed, by manually locking or pressing the central locking button twice. This synchronizes the door locks.

### Single lock and double lock function

Each door lock actuator incorporates two lock positions.

Single lock controls the mechanical lock mechanism when the central lock switch is pressed. The lock mechanism is fully locked at this point but can still be opened from the interior by pulling the interior door handle twice or by pressing the central lock switch again. When single lock function is activated, the fuel filler flap is not locked.

Double lock, also known as central arrest, is activated only when the vehicle is locked from the outside at the driver's door lock with a key or when CAS receives a lock request from the remote key. In this case the double lock motor is activated, mechanically offsetting an internal rod in the lock actuator. This disables the actuator from unlocking the vehicle from the interior and prevents the doors from being unlocked by any means other than an unlock request at the driver's door or via the remote key.

### Vehicle accident unlocking

During a vehicle accident the multiple restraint system (MRS) module sends a signal to CAS to unlock the vehicle. The remote key and central locking button are disabled until ignition status (terminal R) is changed from ON to OFF back to ON.

### Center console emergency opening (convertible)

Convertible 3 Series models have a locking center console cover that is activated by the central locking system.

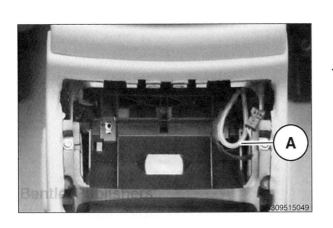

◀ In case of battery discharge or center console locking actuator failure, use the emergency release cable (**A**) to unlock and open center console.

– Unclip and remove rear air vents and air ducts.

– Pull cable (**A**) to release center console cover.

**515**

## Car memory / key memory (personalization)

A number of features and functions can be customized to the driver(s) preference. The identity of the vehicle user is provided by a signal from the remote key.

Car memory and key memory are two separate functions, although they are marketed as a combined feature.

### Car memory

Prior to new vehicle delivery, the BMW factory scan tool is used to code driver preferences into the appropriate control modules. Thereafter these choices cannot be changed without recoding using a BMW factory scan tool or equivalent. Only one car memory setting setting per vehicle is possible.

The functions that can be set using car memory include:

- Audible confirmation (siren chirp) and visual confirmation (via turn signal lights) when alarm is armed. Siren chirp can be de-activated with BMW factory scan tool or equivalent.
- Daytime running lamps ON or OFF.
- Pathway lighting allows use of the dimmer switch to turn on the headlights and interior lights for 40 seconds.
- Automatic locking of central locking system once vehicle reaches 10 mph.
- Selective unlocking. Unlocks only drivers door on first actuation of unlock button on remote key. Unlocks all doors, trunk and fuel filler door after second actuation of button on remote key.

### Key memory

 Whenever a remote keys (identification transmitter) is used to lock or unlock the car, the user is identified by CAS. Multiple keys can be programmed with the personalization feature. The use of the personalized key then triggers car memory functions such as heating and air-conditioning settings or memory seat position adjustment.

Most key memory options can be programed using the iDrive menu. Some programming requires the use of BMW factory scan tool or equivalent.

Available Key memory functions vary based on vehicle equipment. The functions that can be set include:

- Audio tone settings and radio presets.
- Language of displays and voice functions.
- Climate control temperature.
- Seat / mirror memory settings.
- Lighting preferences.

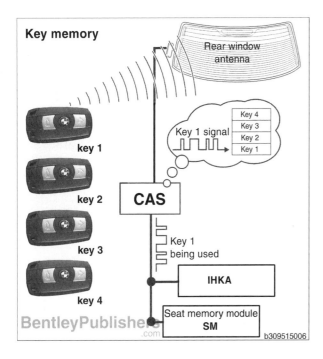

Key memory

Rear window antenna

Key 1 signal

Key 4
Key 3
Key 2
Key 1

key 1

key 2

CAS

key 3

Key 1 being used

key 4

IHKA

Seat memory module
SM

b309515006

## Comfort access (CA)

Comfort access (CA), optional in 3 Series models, is a passive access system which allows the vehicle to be unlocked by grasping the outer door handle, provided the remote key is located within a radius of no more than approx. 0.5 - 1.5 m (1½ - 4½ ft) from the vehicle. With CA it is sufficient for the driver to carry the remote key on his or her person in order to open or start the vehicle.

Modules and other components which control and operate CA:

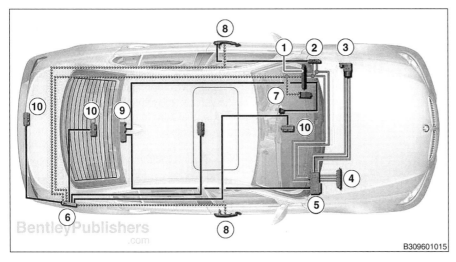

1. Car access system (CAS)
2. Footwell module (FRM)
3. Dynamic stability control (DSC) module
4. Engine control module (ECM)
5. Junction box module (JBE)
6. Comfort access (CA) module
7. Electric steering lock (ELV)
8. Door handle module (TAGE)
9. Remote control receiver
10. Antennas

When a remote key comes into range of the CA antennas, the signal is sent to CAS to be verified. If seen as valid the lock / unlock function is granted.

### Comfort access antennas

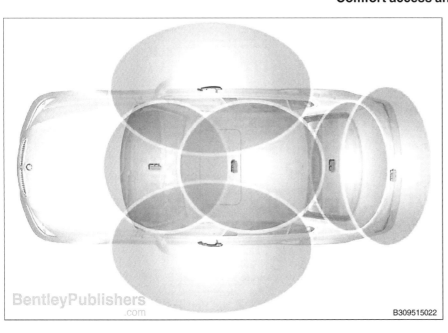

- Driver door handle
- Passenger door handle
- Rear bumper
- Luggage compartment
- Interior front
- Interior center

**515**

## Comfort access features

### Passive entry

Passive entry enables access to the vehicle without operating the remote key. The vehicle recognizes the presence of a valid remote key and access is granted by grasping the outer door handle.

### Unlocking

A capacitive sensor in the door handle module (TAGE) recognizes that the handle has been grasped and activates the transmit antenna. The transmit antenna sends a signal to the remote key. In turn, the identification transmitter sends a 315 MHz high frequency signal to the remote control receiver, which contains the authentication request. CAS checks the authentication code of the remote key. Following successful authentication, CAS issues an enable signal to unlock the vehicle and initiates the vehicle unlocking procedure. JBE executes the unlocking procedure. The electronic steering lock (ELV) is not yet unlocked (if equipped).

1.  Door handle module (TAGE)
2.  Remote key
3.  Rear window antenna
4.  Remote key receiver
5.  Car access system (CAS)
6.  Electronic steering lock (ELV)

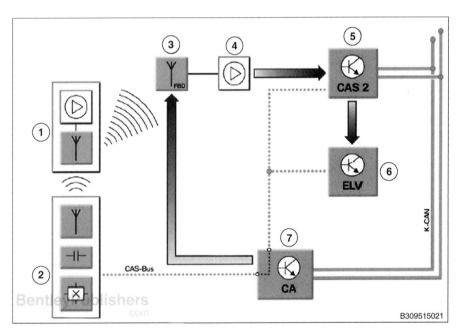

B309515021

### Trunk lid / tailgate unlocking

An authentication check takes place when a remote key is located within the rear area of the vehicle. After successful authentication, the trunk lid or tailgate can be unlocked and opened with the outer trunk lid / tailgate button.

### Passive go

When a valid remote key is located within the vehicle interior, the passive go function makes it possible to start the vehicle without the remote key inserted in the slot in instrument panel.

After a door has been opened, CAS starts a check after 3 seconds to establish whether a valid remote key is in the vehicle. The remote replies with data for the electronic vehicle immobilizer. CAS enables engine start by sending a signal to the ECM. If equipped, the electric steering lock (ELV) is unlocked.

### Passive exit

Passive exit makes it possible to lock the vehicle without using the remote control. After the vehicle door is closed, the locking procedure is started by touching the recognition area on the outer door handle. The door handle module (TAGE) sends the request to CAS to lock the vehicle.

If a valid remote key is detected in the interior of the vehicle during locking with another valid remote key from the exterior, the key left in the vehicle is deactivated until the vehicle in unlocked again.

## DOOR HANDLES AND LOCKS

In the procedures that follow, door handle removal, door lock cylinder removal and door latch removal are covered for the left front door. Other doors are similar although simpler, due to the lack of lock cylinder.

Inner door panel removal is covered in **411 Doors**.

### Door lock cylinder, removing and installing

◁ Open door. Working at door rear edge, pry out plastic cover from access hole.

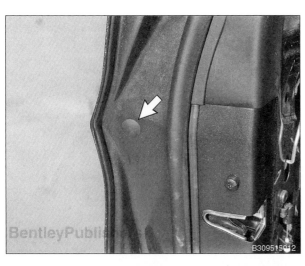

◁ Use 4 mm Allen wrench to remove lock cylinder mounting screw (**arrow**).

*Door handle, removing and installing*

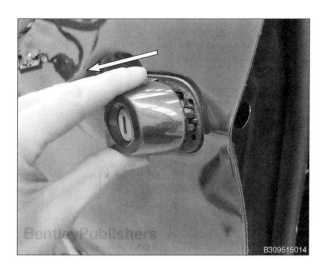

◁ Slide lock cylinder slightly toward rear of car and out of door.

– Installation is reverse of removal.

• Replace door handle gaskets if damaged.

• Reset comfort access (CA) by disconnecting and reconnecting battery. See **121 Battery, Starter, Alternator**.

## Door handle, removing and installing

– Remove door lock cylinder. See **Door lock cylinder, removing and installing** in this repair group.

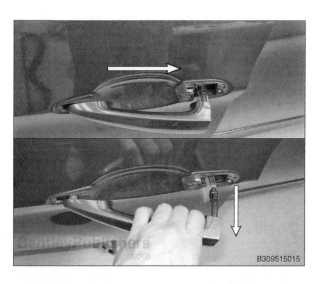

◁ Pull door handle out and in direction of **arrow**. Carefully feed wire out with handle and disconnect electrical connector if equipped with comfort access.

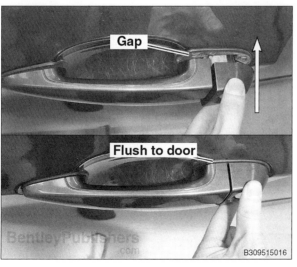

◁ Installation is reverse of removal.

• Replace door handle gaskets if damaged.

• Handle will not sit flush until lock cylinder is installed.

• Reset comfort access (CA) by disconnecting and reconnecting battery. See **121 Battery, Starter, Alternator**.

## Door latch, removing and installing

***NOTE***—
• *Do not use silicone lubricant on door latch. Latch faults have been traced to silicone contamination.*

— Remove door trim panel. See **411 Doors**.

◀ Carefully peel (**inset**) off vapor barrier covering inner door cavity.

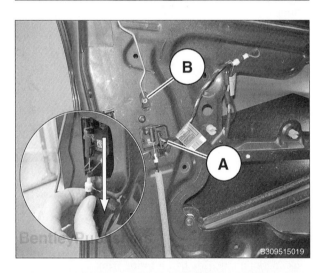

> **CAUTION**—
> • *Use care when peeling back vapor barrier. A damaged vapor barrier should be replaced to prevent possible water leaks.*

— Partially remove window regulator to gain access to door latch. See **512 Door Windows**.

◀ Working at corner of door at door latch assembly:
• Detach electrical connector (**A**) from latch assembly.
• Detach door lock rod (**B**) from latch assembly.
• Pull down in direction of **arrow** to detach Bowden cable from latch assembly.

— Remove door lock cylinder. See **Door lock cylinder, removing and installing** in this repair group.

◀ Working inside door:
• Disconnect Bowden cable (**A**) from latch (**B**).
• Detach electrical harness from latch (**arrows**).

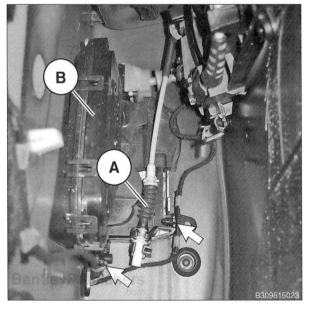

515

◁ Remove latch fasteners (**arrows**).

– Remove latch assembly from inside door.

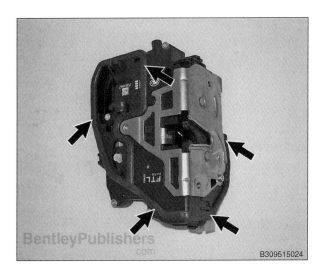

◁ Installation is reverse of removal, keeping in mind the following:

- Do not bend door lock button metal rod when inserting through door skin opening.
- Hand tighten fasteners to properly seat door latch seal (**arrows**) before tightening.
- Replace latch mounting screws and use threadlock compound.
- Make sure seal on latch is not damaged.
- Make sure inner door cavity vapor barrier is installed intact and leak-proof.

| Tightening torque | |
|---|---|
| Latch assembly to door (replace screws) | 9.5 Nm (7 ft-lb) |

## TRUNK AND TAILGATE LOCKS

### Trunk lock cylinder

– Remove trunk lid trim panel. See **513 Interior Trim**.

◁ Unclip and remove trunk lock cylinder trim cover (**arrow**).

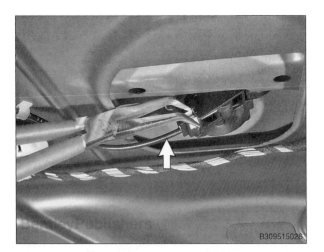

◄ Working inside trunk at rear of lock cylinder, disconnect bowden cable from lock cylinder (**arrow**).

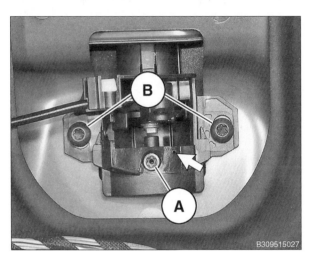

◄ Working inside trunk at rear of lock cylinder:

- Insert a 2 mm diameter punch into hole (**arrow**) and press down catch.
- Rotate lock release (**A**) 90° counterclockwise and remove punch.
- Remove fasteners (**B**) and remove lock cylinder.

– Installation is reverse of removal. Remember to:

- Inspect and replace lock cylinder seal if necessary.
- Properly seat seal.
- Rotate lock release (**A**) 90° clockwise once lock is in place.

| Tightening torque | |
|---|---|
| Lock cylinder to trunk lid | 10 Nm (7.3 ft-lb) |

## Trunk lock assembly

– Remove trunk lid trim panel. See **513 Interior Trim**.

◄ Disconnect electrical connector (**arrow**) from trunk lock assembly.

– Remove fasteners (**A**) and pull latch assembly out of trunk lid.

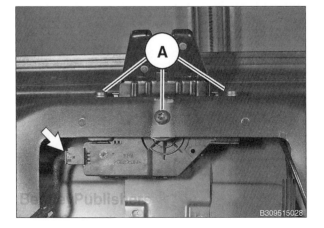

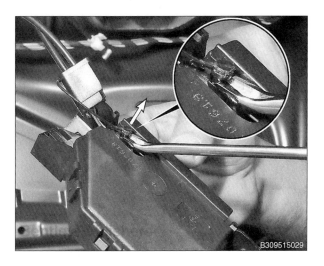

◁ Lever out locking pin (**inset**) in direction of **arrow** and remove bowden cable from lock assembly.

– Installation is reverse of removal.

| Tightening torque | |
|---|---|
| Lock assembly to trunk lid | 10 Nm (7.3 ft-lb) |

## Trunk lock striker, removing and installing

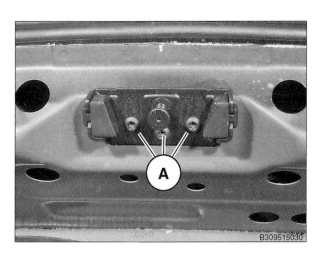

– Remove lower trunk trim panel. See **513 Interior**.

◁ Remove trunk lock striker fasteners (**A**) then remove striker.

– Installation is reverse of removal. Adjust striker if necessary. See **Trunk lock striker, adjusting** in this repair group.

| Tightening torque | |
|---|---|
| Trunk lock striker to body | 10 Nm (7.3 ft-lb) |

## Trunk lock striker, adjusting

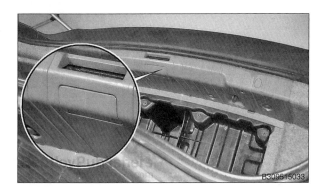

◁ Remove trunk lock striker access cover (**inset**).

*Trunk lock striker, adjusting*

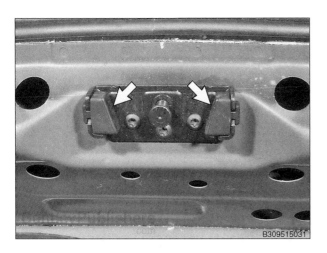

◄ Inspect fulcrum pads (**arrows**) for wear of damage, replace if necessary. Interior trim panel removed for clarity.

◄ Screw in trunk lid detent buffers (**arrows**) completely.

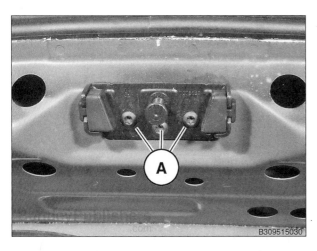

◄ Loosen trunk lock striker fasteners (**A**) slightly, just enough so it is able to move and center itself.

– Close trunk lid. This allows for the trunk lock striker to adjust itself.

– Open trunk and tighten fasteners. Check adjustment and repeat procedure if necessary.

| Tightening torque | |
|---|---|
| Trunk lock striker to body | 10 Nm (7.3 ft-lb) |

– Reassemble trunk interior trim.

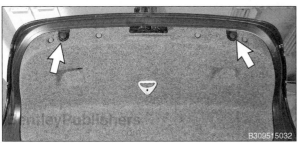

◄ Unscrew trunk lid detent buffers (**arrows**) until closed rear trunk lid left / right detent buffers make contact with body panels. Trunk lid should be even with rear body panels.

515

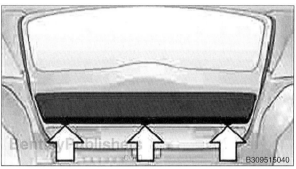

## Tailgate, emergency opening

In case of battery failure or other electrical problems, open tailgate as follows.

◄ Working inside the vehicle, swing tailgate trim up (**arrows**).

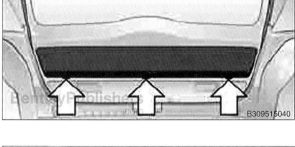

◄ Pull ring upwards (**inset**) to unlock tailgate.

## Tailgate lock

To gain access to tailgate locking mechanisms, remove tailgate trim. See **513 Interior Trim**.

### Tailgate lock assembly, removing and installing

— Open upper tailgate and remove trim. See **513 Interior Trim**.

◄ Remove tailgate lock fasteners (**A**).

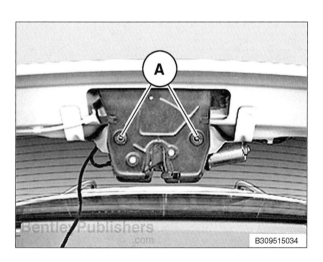

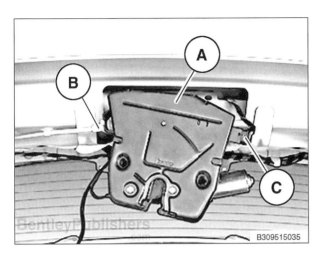

◀ Pull tailgate lock (**A**) slightly out of lid. Remove bowden cable (**B**) and disconnect electrical connector (**C**).

– Installation is reverse of removal.

| Tightening torque | |
|---|---|
| Lock to tailgate lid | 10 Nm (7.3 ft-lb) |

### Tailgate striker assembly, removing and installing

◀ Snap out cover (**A**) in direction of **arrow** and remove.

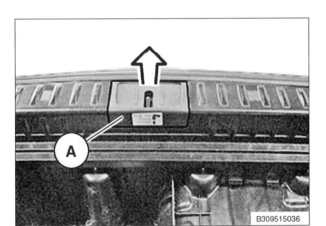

◀ Remove fasteners (**A**) and remove striker (**B**).

– Installation is reverse of removal.

| Tightening torque | |
|---|---|
| Lock to tailgate lid | 10 Nm (7.3 ft-lb) |

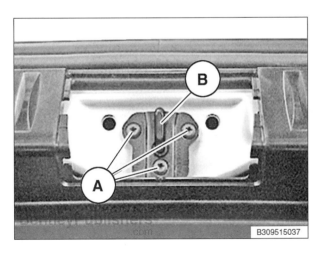

**515**

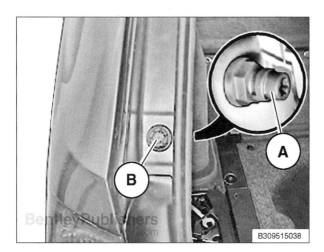

B309515038

### Tailgate striker assembly, adjusting

◁ Remove protective caps (**A**) on left and right side bump stops (**B**) and fully screw in.

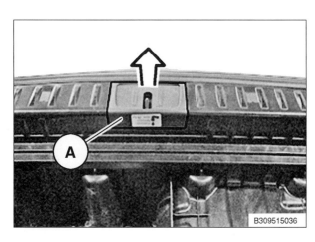

B309515036

◁ Snap out cover (**A**) in direction of **arrow** and remove.

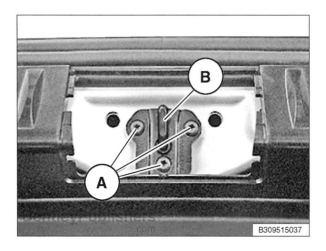

B309515037

◁ Loosen tailgate striker fasteners (**A**) slightly, just enough so it is able to move and center itself.

> **CAUTION—**
> • *Check that tailgate fasteners do not strike tailgate during adjustment.*

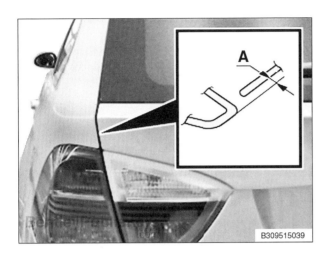

◀ Adjust tailgate striker until tailgate in recessed 1.0 to 1.5 mm (**A**).

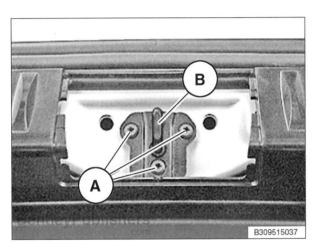

◀ Tighten tailgate striker fasteners (**A**).

| Tightening torque | |
|---|---|
| Lock to tailgate lid | 10 Nm (7.3 ft-lb) |

– Install striker trim panel.

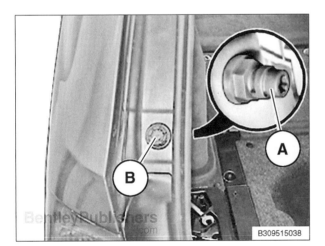

◀ Unscrew bump stops (**B**) until tailgate flush with side body panel. Install bump stop cover (**A**).

– Check for proper adjustment and tailgate operation. Repeat adjustment if necessary.

**515**

### Rear window lock assembly

The rear window (tailgate glass) lock assembly is part of the rear wiper motor. For removing and installing see **611 Wipers and Washers**.

### Rear window lock, adjusting

– Check that tailgate is adjusted properly.

◄ Remove plastic covers (**A**). Be careful not to break catches (**B**).

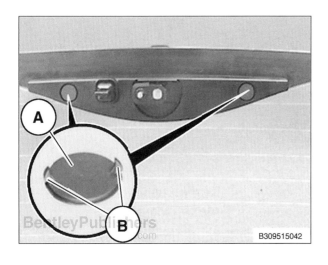

◄ Remove fasteners (**A**) then trim panel (**B**).

◄ Loosen nut (**A**). Adjust striker by turning in or out (**B**).

– Tighten nut and recheck adjustment.

– Install tailgate trim panels.

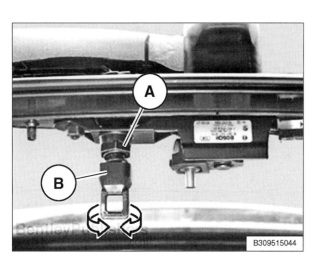

## ELECTRONIC IMMOBILIZER (EWS)

EWS is a shared system between car access system (CAS) and digital motor electronics (DME). If an authorized key is recognized by CAS a start signal is authorized and sent to the DME. Troubleshooting is performed with a BMW factory scan tool or equivalent.

## ANTI-THEFT SYSTEM (DWA)

### DWA components

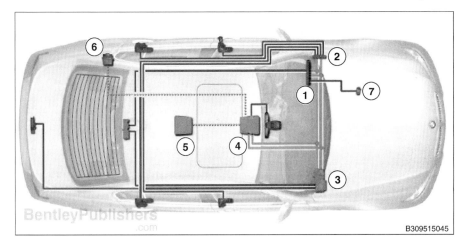

B309515045

1. **Car access system (CAS)**
2. **Footwell module (FRM)**
3. **Junction box electronics (JBE)**
4. **Roof function center (FZD)**
5. **Ultra sonic sensor (USIS)**
6. **Tilt sensor / alarm siren (SINE)**
7. **Hood switch**

### DWA operation

When the anti-theft system (DWA) is armed:

- The doors, hood, windows, and trunk lid are monitored against forcible entry
- A tilt sensor protects the vehicle from being jacked up or towed away.
- Movement inside the vehicle is monitored.
- Battery voltage is monitored.

The system responds to unauthorized vehicle entry or attempted theft by activating the following:

- Alarm siren sounds for 30 seconds.
- Hazard warning lights and high beams flash for approx. 5 minutes.

The system is armed or disarmed from the driver's door lock or the remote transmitter when the vehicle is locked or unlocked. The interior compartment monitor is activated approx. 30 seconds after the vehicle is locked.

The system indicates that it is armed by flashing the hazard warning lights once and emitting a brief chirp from the siren.

If the alarm is activated, the tailgate may still be opened using button **3** on the remote key. The alarm resets when the tailgate is closed.

Following the triggering of an alarm, the system resets and can trigger again if further tampering to the vehicle is detected.

**515**

*DWA LED display*

The interior protection ultrasonic sensor (USIS) is in the DWA main control module. It monitors the passenger compartment and receives inputs from corresponding modules for alarm activation, deactivation and triggering.

• FRM monitors door contacts.

• JBE monitors trunk lid and tailgate status.

• CAS monitors engine hood contact switch.

## DWA LED display

◄ The DWA status LED (**arrow**) is below the interior rear view mirror. LED displays are listed in **Table a**.

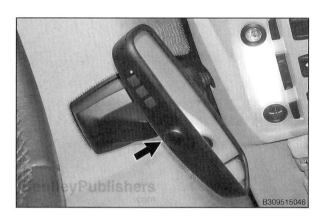

| Table a. DWA LED status | |
|---|---|
| **DWA status** | **LED signal** |
| Disarmed | OFF |
| Armed | Continual slow flash |
| Armed with tailgate or door not fully closed | Rapid flash for 10 second, then continual slow flash. Interior motion sensor not activated. |
| Alarm activated | Rapid flash for 5 minutes, then continual slow flash |
| Disarmed after activated alarm | Blinks for 5 minutes then goes OFF, or goes off when remote key in inserted. |

## DWA alarm siren

◄ The DWA alarm siren (**arrow**) is at the left side rear inner fenderwell, behind the plastic inner fenderwell.

The siren is powered by a separate rechargeable battery. This battery is recharged by the vehicle electrical system when DWA is not armed.

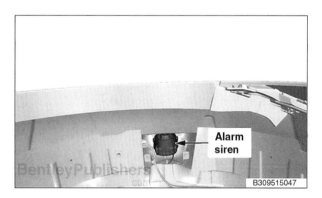

Alarm siren

## Tilt sensor

The tilt sensor is integrated into the alarm siren. It registers the vehicles rest position when armed and detects changes in position, for example jacking of the vehicle.

When flat-bed transporting the vehicle, lock the vehicle twice within 10 seconds to switch tilt sensor OFF.

## Interior protection

◄ The interior motion ultrasonic sensor (USIS) is in the center of the headliner. Due to the design of the vehicle interior, install sensor in the correct direction to ensure proper operation of the system. Arrow (**inset**) points toward front of vehicle

As with the tilt sensor, when flat-bed transporting the vehicle, lock the vehicle twice within 10 seconds to switch interior motion sensor OFF.

The USIS system uses ultrasound to sense motion inside its detection cone. Every time DWA is armed, the USIS sensor adapts to whatever objects are stationary in the interior. USIS also checks for background hiss (wind noise through a partially open window) and adapts for this.

- If detected echoes and sounds are consistent, no movement is detected.

- If the echoes are altered (inconsistent), USIS determines motion in the interior compartment.

- If motion is detected, the USIS changes from a pulsed signal to a constant signal and the echo is compared again.

- If the inconsistency is still present USIS triggers the alarm.

## Panic mode

B309515048

◁ If the tailgate button (**3**) is pressed and held for more than 2 seconds, USIS activates the siren in panic mode. This function is available with either an armed or disarmed DWA.

## Emergency disarming

Emergency disarming occurs automatically when a recognized remote key is inserted into the key holder. If the key is accepted by CAS, the doors are unlocked and the alarm deactivated.

515

# 520 Seats

## GENERAL

This repair group covers removal and installation of the front and rear seats.

See also:

- **ECL Electrical Component Locations**
- **ELE Electrical Wiring Diagrams**

### Seat memory

 Seat and outside rear-view mirror positions can be memorized and stored in the seat control module for two different users. The seat control module is mounted to the bottom of the seat (**inset**).

**520**

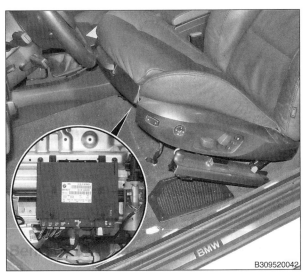

B309520042

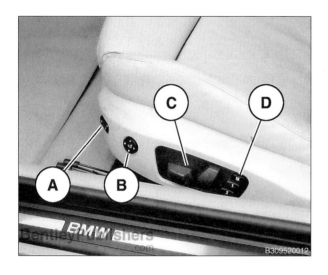

## Seat memory position, setting

— With transmission range selector in P, switch ignition ON and adjust seat and mirrors to desired position.

◄ Press M on memory switch and press one of the two memory switches (**D**).

- The current position of the mirrors, seat and steering column is now stored in memory.

Power seat controls.

- **A** — Backrest width adjustment
- **B** — Lumbar support
- **C** — Seat adjustment
- **D** — Memory buttons

## FRONT SEATS

Seat repair and component replacement is possible once the seat has been removed from the vehicle. Before servicing front seats read safety regulations on handling airbags and pyrotechnic seat belt tensioners. See **720 Seat Belts** and **721 Airbag System (SRS)**.

> **WARNING—**
> - *The front seats are equipped with side impact airbags and pyrotechnic seat belt tensioners. These tensioners are powerful devices. Handle with extreme care. Incorrect handling can trigger off the airbag or tensioner and cause injury.*
> - *BMW recommends that repair or replacement work on airbag and pyrotechnic devices be carried out by a qualified BMW technician.*
> - *Be sure to disconnect the battery and wait 5 seconds before attempting to work on pyrotechnic devices.*
> - *During body straightening and welding with an electric arc welder, disconnect the battery and the connection to the pyrotechnic gas generators.*

## Front seat, removing and installing

— Switch ignition OFF.

— Move seat as far back as possible.

◄ Remove front seat mounting bolts (**arrows**) and discard.

— Move seat as far forward as possible.

◁ Using plastic prying tool, unclip seat belt trim cover in direction of **arrow**.

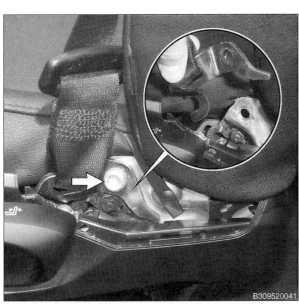

◁ Remove fastener for seat belt (**arrow**) and discard. Disconnect seat belt hook (**inset**) from seat and lay aside.

◁ Remove rear seat mounting bolts (**arrows**) and discard.

520

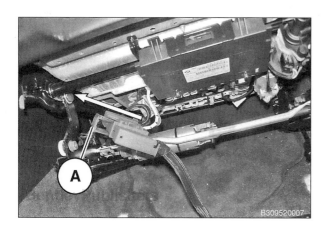

◀ Tilt seat back and use a screwdriver to unlock harness connector lock (**A**) in direction of **arrow**. Disconnect connector.

– Cover door sill with protective covers and remove front seat from car.

**NOTE** —

• *Use a blanket to protect the seat upholstery from damage if placing the seat upside down for repairs.*

– Installation is reverse of removal. Use wire ties or equivalent means to keep seat harness wiring from fraying.

| Tightening torques | |
| --- | --- |
| Front seat to floor (replace bolts) | 44 Nm (32.4 ft-lb) |
| Seatbelt to front seat (replace bolt) | 44 Nm (32.4 ft-lb) |

## Front seat control switches, removing and installing

– Remove front seat. See **Front seat, removing and installing** in this repair group.

– Place seat backrest down on a soft surface.

◀ Remove mounting screw or release catch (**C**). Using your finger, unclip lugs (**A**) out of catches (**B**).

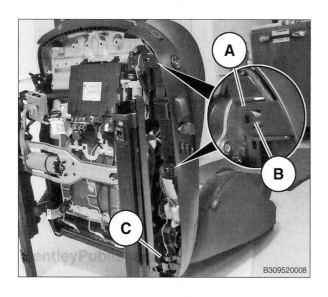

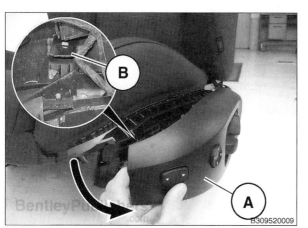

◀ Working at front of seat carefully pull cover (**A**) with switches away from seat. Release unlocking lug (**B**) above seat switches with screwdriver and detach cover (**A**) from seat.

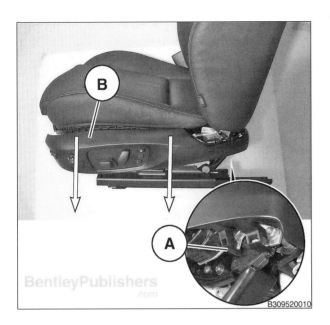

◁ Unlock lug (**A**). Reach between seat cushion and cover (**B**) and disconnect trim piece.

– Disconnect seat switch electrical connectors.

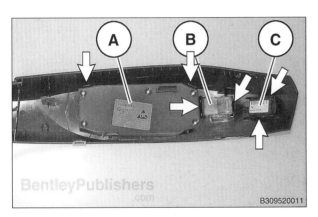

◁ Unlock catches of switch housing (**arrows**) and remove switches.
- **A** Combination switch
- **B** Lumbar support
- **C** Backrest adjustment

– Installation is reverse of removal.

## Passenger seat occupancy sensor

Vehicles covered by this manual are equipped with a passenger seat occupancy sensor in the passenger seat bottom. This device is part of the two-stage deployment airbag system. Access to the seat occupancy sensor is described below. 3 Series models use an OC3 mat which is integrated in the seat cushion. The seat cushion and occupancy mat are replaced as a unit.

– Using BMW factory scan tool or equivalent, disable occupancy detection mat from restraint control module.

– Remove passenger seat. See **Front seat, removing and installing** in this repair group.

– Remove seat control switches. See **Front seat control switches, removing and installing** in this repair group.

◁ Remove fastener (**A**) and seat cover clip panel (**B**). Remove trim panel (**C**) in direction of **arrow**.

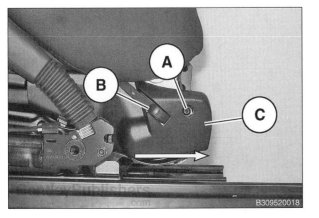

**520**

*Passenger seat occupancy sensor*

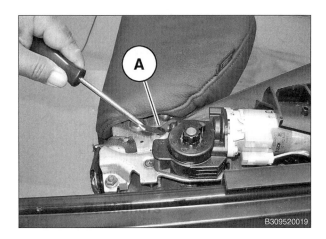

◁ Using a panel clip tool, pry clip (**A**) out of seat cover on right side of seat.

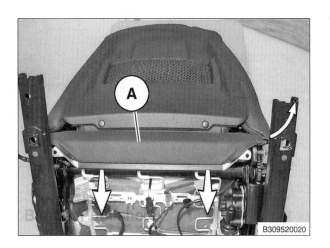

◁ Unhook seat bottom upholstery (**A**) at rear of seat and pull it away from seat frame (**arrows**).

**NOTE** —

• *Having an assistant push down on seat bottom cushion helps to unhook it from the seat frame.*

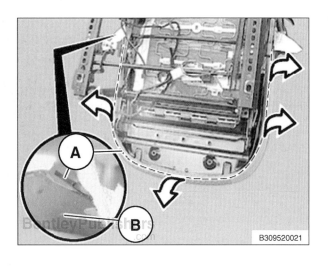

◁ Pull out cover welt (**A**) completely from seat frame (**B**).

*Front seat backrest rear panel, removing and installing*

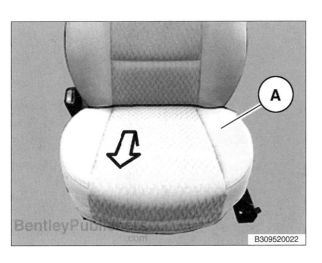

◄ Move seat cover with cushion (**A**) from seat frame in direction of **arrow**. Carefully feed bracing cloth through gap in backrest.

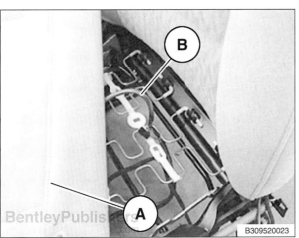

◄ Disconnect harness connector (**B**) for seat occupancy sensor and seat heating if equipped.

– Remove seat cushion (**A**) while carefully detaching wire retainers.

– Installation is reverse of removal. Remember to enable occupancy mat with BMW factory scan tool or equivalent.

## Front seat backrest rear panel, removing and installing

The back of the front seat is accessible by removing the rigid backrest panel.

◄ Cut panel clips (**A**) with diagonal cutters and remove backrest panel (**B**) downward with a turning action to remove (**arrows**).

– Installation is reverse of removal.
  • Remove remnants of panel clips (**A**).
  • Replace panel clips (**A**).

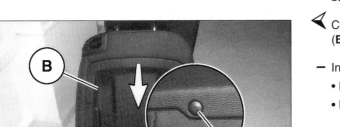

**520**

## REAR SEATS

### Rear seat, removing and installing

◄ Pull seat bottom up and away (**arrows**) from pedestal and feed seat belt buckles (**A**) through opening in seat. Lift out rear seat.

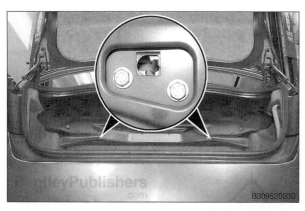

◄ Working in trunk, locate backrest locks (**inset**).

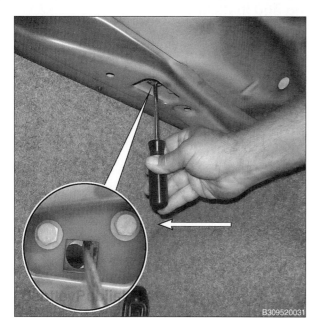

◄ Using a screwdriver release backrest lock (**inset**) in direction of **arrow**.

*Rear seat headrest, removing and installing*

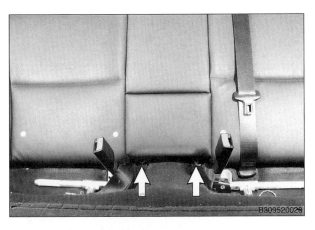

◅ Remove backrest fasteners (**arrows**).

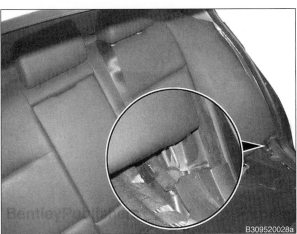

◅ Tilt backrest forward while lifting guides (**inset**) out of body panel.

– Lift backrest while feeding out seat belts and remove backrest.

– Installation is reverse of removal.

| Tightening torque | |
|---|---|
| Rear seat belt to body | 31 Nm (22.8 ft-lb) |

## Rear seat headrest, removing and installing

– Remove rear seat. See **Rear seat, removing and installing** in this repair group.

– Slide headrest as far up as possible.

◅ Press lock (**B**) and pull headrest (**A**) upward to remove.

– Installation is reverse of removal.

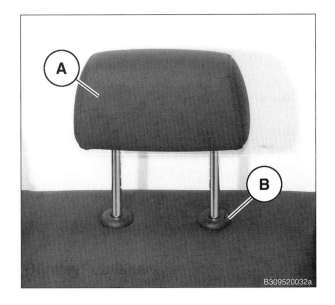

**520**

## SEAT CONTROL COMPONENT LOCATIONS

| Component | ID | Location | Page |
|---|---|---|---|
| Backrest angle adjustment motor | M58a | Side of passenger seat | 520-12 |
| Backrest width adjustment switch | S289 S0298 | Side of driver or passenger seat | 520-12 |
| Lumbar support vacuum pump | M55b M56b | Driver or passenger seat backrest | 520-11 |
| Lumbar support valve block, left or right | Y193 Y194 | Driver or passenger seat backrest | 520-11 |
| Seat angle adjustment motor | M61a | Underneath passenger seat | 520-12 |
| Seat backrest heater, driver, passenger | E56a E59a | Behind seat backrest | 520-11 |
| Seat belt buckle contact switch, driver seat, passenger seat | S58a S59a | Seat belt buckle, driver seat belt, passenger seat belt | 520-12 |
| Seat forward-backward adjustment motor | M60a | Underneath driver seat | 520-12 |
| Seat heater, driver, passenger | E57a E58a | Underneath seat cushion | 520-11 |
| Seat heating module | A186a | Underneath center of right front seat | 520-11 |
| Seat heating module | A187a | Underneath center of left front seat | 520-10 |
| Seat height adjustment motor | M59a | Underneath driver seat | 520-12 |
| Seat lumbar support switch, driver | S52 | Left side of driver seat | 520-12 |
| Seat lumbar support switch, passenger | S55 | Right side of passenger seat | 520-12 |
| Seat occupancy sensor module | A113 | Center rear of right front seat, underneath cushion | 520-10 |

## Seat control components

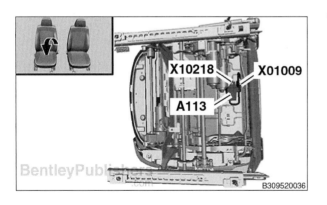

◀ Right front seat cushion (**arrow**):

- **A113** Seat occupancy sensor
- **X01009** Connector
- **X10218** Connector

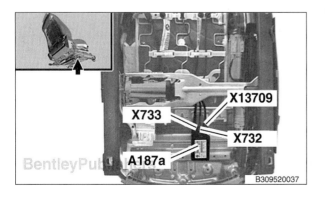

◀ Underneath left front seat (**arrow**):

- **A187a** Driver seat heating module
- **X187a** Connector
- **X733** Connector
- **X13709** Connector

*Seat control components*

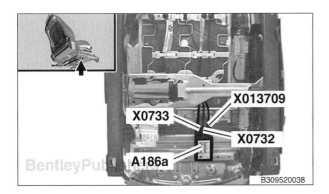

◀ Underneath right front seat (**arrow**):

- **A186a** Passenger seat heating module
- **X0187a** Connector
- **X0733** Connector
- **X013709** Connector

◀ Behind seat backrest (**arrow**):

- **E56a** Backrest heater
- **E57a** Seat heater
- **E58a** Seat heater
- **E59a** Backrest heater

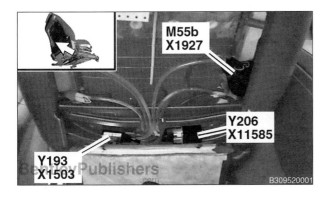

◀ In driver seat backrest (**arrow**):

- **M55b** Lumbar support vacuum pump
- **Y193** Lumbar control valve block
- **Y206** Backrest width adjustment valve
- **X1503** Connector
- **X1927** Connector
- **X11585** Connector

**520**

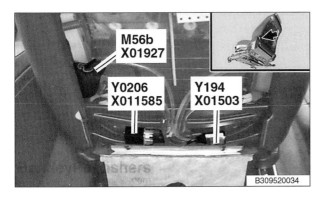

◀ Passenger seat backrest lumbar controls (**arrow**):

- **M56b** Lumbar support vacuum pump
- **Y194** Lumbar control valve block
- **Y0206** Backrest width adjustment valve

*Seat control components*

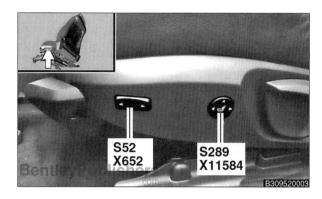

◄ Side of driver seat (**arrow**):
- **S52** Lumbar control switch
- **S289** Backrest width adjustment control switch
- **X652** Connector
- **X11584** Connector

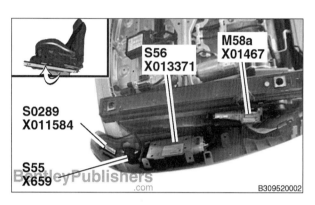

◄ Side of passenger seat (**arrow**):
- **M58a** Backrest angle adjustment motor
- **S55** Lumbar control switch
- **S0289** Backrest width adjustment control switch
- **X659** Connector
- **X01467** Connector
- **X011584** Connector
- **X013371** Connector

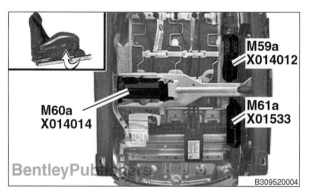

◄ Underneath driver / passenger seat (**arrow**):
- **M59a** Seat height adjustment motor
- **M60a** Seat forward-backward adjustment motor
- **M61a** Seat angle adjustment motor
- **X01533** Connector
- **X014012** Connector
- **X014014** Connector

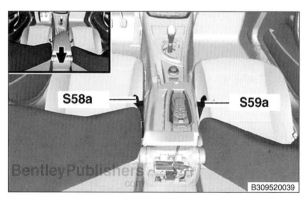

◄ Seat belt buckle, driver and passenger (**arrow**):
- **S58a** Driver seat belt buckle switch
- **S59a** Passenger seat belt buckle switch

# 541  Convertible Top

## GENERAL

This repair group covers the automatic electrohydraulic convertible hard top. Information on the rollover protection system is also included here.

### Convertible top basics

The E93 convertible top system opens and closes the top using hydraulic cylinders and an electrohydraulic pump.

The convertible top system features:

- Convertible top module (CTM) with fault memory storage.
- Electrohydraulic operation.
- Convenience opening / closing using the remote key or driver door lock cylinder.
- Convenience trunk loading / unloading using remote key.
- Top monitoring using hall sensors and microswitches.

### Emergency operation

An emergency closing procedure for the consumer is not provided by the factory due to multiple BMW special tools needed to perform the procedure. Contact a BMW service facility in the event of convertible top failure.

### Hydraulic fluid level, checking or filling

The convertible top electrohydraulic pump is filled with lifetime fluid. In the event there is a leak or service is performed and the fluid level has to be topped off, fill to the mark on oil reservoir. Use Aral Vitamol fluid available through BMW parts.

**541**

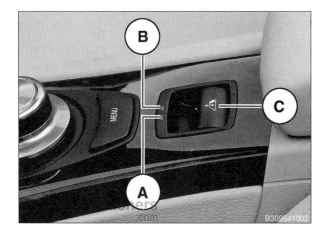

## Convertible top switch

 The convertible top switch is located in the center console (**C**). When the switch is pressed or pulled the top opens or closes. Operation of the switch is similar to that of the power windows.

— Pushing the switch opens the hardtop; pulling the switch closes it.

— The green LED (**A**) in the switch lights up while the hardtop is moving.

— If the switch is released while the hardtop is moving, movement of the hardtop, the rear module or the side windows stops. The red LED (**B**) flashes. Hardtop movement can be resumed by pressing the switch again. Movement of the side windows can be resumed within 10 seconds.

— If the red LED (**B**) is lit continuously. One of the convertible top operating condition have not been met. See **Convertible top operating conditions** in this repair group.

## Convertible top operating conditions

The convertible top can be opened and closed using the button in the center console when the following conditions are met:

• Terminal R activated.

• Outside temperature above -12°C (10°F).

• Trunk lid closed.

• Vehicle stationary (driving speed 0 mph).

• Luggage compartment divider in lowest position.

• Lateral inclination of the vehicle less than 8°.

• Power windows initialized.

• Battery voltage greater than 9.5 V.

• Fewer than five consecutive successive opening / closing operations.

• Temperature of the hydraulic fluid.
  Opening: maximum 90°C (194°F)
  Closing: maximum 105°C (221°F)

## Convenience operation

Convenience opening or closing is possible using the remote key or drivers door lock. A convenience loading / unloading feature can be used to access luggage compartment when the convertible top is open.

 To open convertible top using remote key press and hold unlock button (**arrow**). Windows will open first, followed by convertible top.

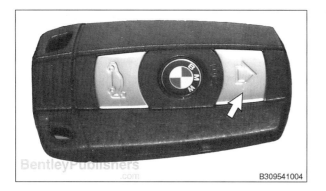

*Convenience operation*

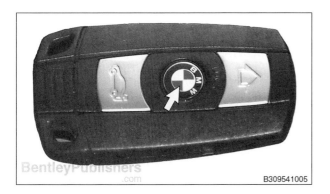

◄ To close convertible top using remote key press and hold center button (**arrow**).

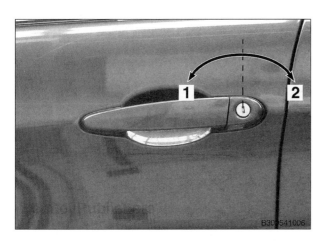

◄ To open or close top using lock cylinder turn and hold lock cylinder in unlock position (**1**) to open or locked position (**2**) to close. Windows will open first, followed by convertible top.

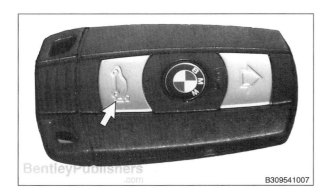

◄ Press and hold trunk button (**arrow**) on remote key to activate convenience trunk loading.

541

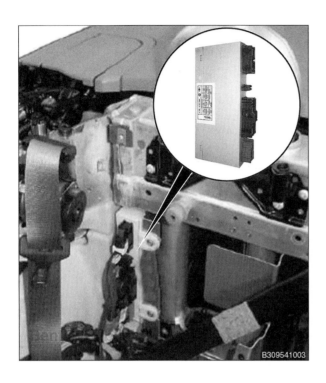

B309541003

## CONVERTIBLE TOP OPERATION

### Convertible top module (CTM)

◀ The convertible top module (CTM) is located behind the passenger rear seat on the right (**inset**). It contains the processing, controlling and monitoring electronics for top operation.

The CTM communicates with the car access system (CAS), footwell module (FRM) and door modules for operation of the convertible top.

The CTM is fully self-diagnostics and is capable of monitoring and storing faults. Fault code access and diagnosis requires a BMW factory scan tool or equivalent.

### Convertible top locking

The roof sections of the convertible top are interlocked when opened or closed. The convertible top locks into the windshield in two places. Each roof section locks together.

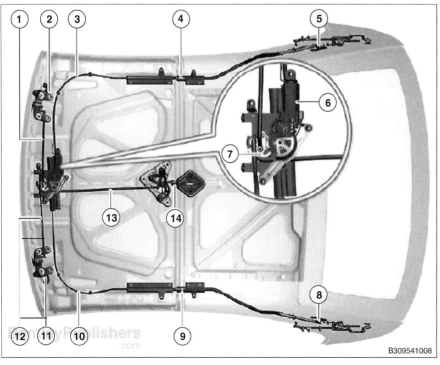

B309541008

1.  Connecting rod for right catch hook.

2.  Right catch hook.

3.  Right drive cable.

4.  Locking pin for center roof panel to center right roof panel.

5.  Locking pin for center roof panel to right rear roof panel.

6.  Electric motor

7.  Control disk

8.  Locking pin for center roof panel to left rear roof panel.

9.  Locking pin for front center roof panel to left center roof panel.

10. Left drive cable.

11. Left catch hook.

12. Connecting rod for left catch hook.

13. Connecting rod for locking catch hook.

14. Locking hook

## Convertible top position sensors

The various positions of the convertible top and the rear module are monitored with 9 Hall sensors and 5 microswitches. The CTM monitors these sensors for opening, closing and fault detection.

◀ Cowl panel microswitch (**A**) is built into the left cowl panel on the vehicle. When the front roof panel guide pin has reached the cowl panel, the microswitch is closed. Beginning at this position, the electric motor is activated and the roof sections are locked.

Catch hook locking microswitch (**B**) is installed on the left below the hardtop locking mechanism electric motor. The contacts of the microswitch are opened if the catch hooks are locked. The catch hooks lock both at the cowl panel and at the base plate in the luggage compartment.

Catch hook unlocking microswitch (**C**) is installed on the right below the hardtop locking mechanism electric motor. The contacts of the microswitch are opened if the catch hooks on the cowl panel are unlocked.

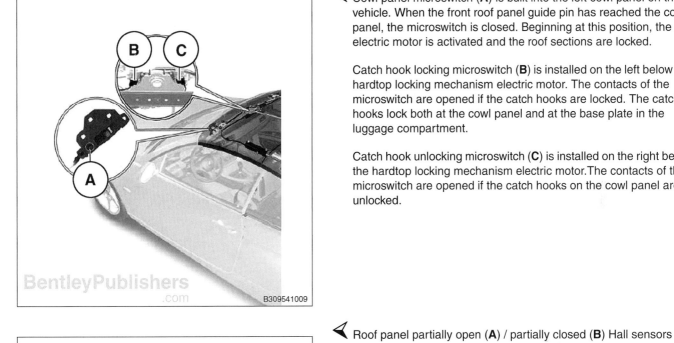

B309541009

◀ Roof panel partially open (**A**) / partially closed (**B**) Hall sensors detect movement of the piston in the roof panel. When the piston is extended or completely retracted, a signal is sent from the roof panel partially open Hall sensor to the CTM.

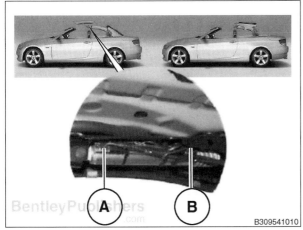
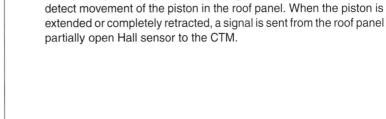

B309541010

541

*Convertible top position sensors*

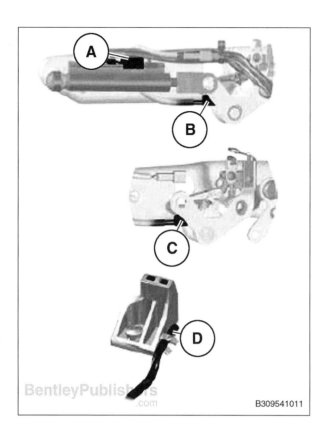

B309541011

◄ Right closure open Hall Sensor (**A**) is located on the right closure cylinder. It transmits a signal to the CTM when the closure cylinder piston is fully extended.

Left / right closure closed microswitches (**B**) (**C**) are on both the left and right closure cylinders. When the closure is locked these microswitches transmit a signal to the CTM.

Trunk lid closed Hall sensor (**D**) is installed on the right of the trunk lid divider. When the trunk lid bow reaches the bottom position it transmits a signal to the CTM.

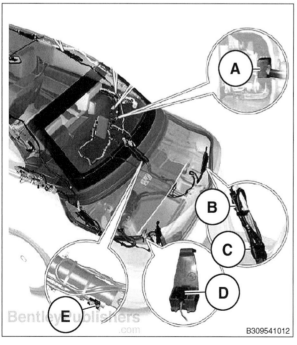

B309541012

◄ Roof package Hall sensor (**A**) is installed on the right base plate in the luggage compartment. When the guide pin of the front roof panel has reached the guide in the base plate it transmits a signal to the CTM.

Rear module open (**B**) / almost closed (**C**) Hall sensors detect rear module piston movement. If the piston is extended, a signal is sent from the top rear module open Hall sensor to the CTM. The lower rear module almost closed Hall sensor sends a signal to the CTM when the piston in the rear module cylinder is almost completely extended.

Luggage compartment Hall sensor (**D**) signals that the luggage compartment divider is in the bottom position. If this signal is missing, the convertible top cannot be operated.

Roof package Hall sensor (**E**) is installed on the right rear pillar cylinder. when the piston in the rear pillar cylinder is extended it sends a signal to the CTM.

## Convertible top hydraulics

Movement of the convertible top and rear module are determined by corresponding valve positions and by reversing rotation direction of the hydraulic pump. The hydraulic pump is driven by an electric motor that operates in two directions. Both rotation directions are actuated with a relay.

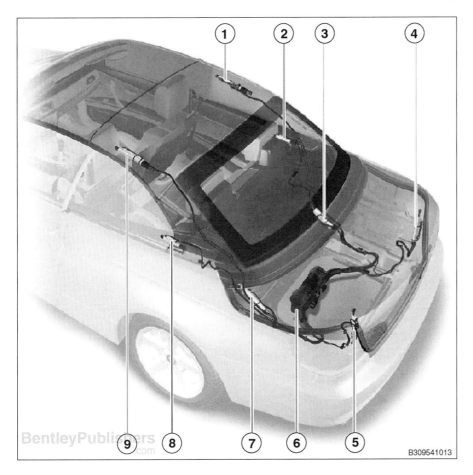

1. Roof panel cylinder
2. Right closure cylinder
3. Right main pillar cylinder
4. Right rear module cylinder
5. Left rear module cylinder
6. Hydraulic assembly
7. Left main pillar assembly
8. Left closure cylinder
9. Left roof panel cylinder

B309541013

### Electrohydraulic pump assembly

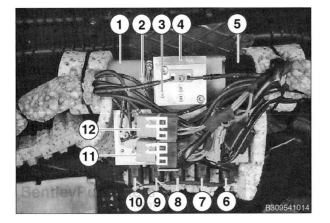

1. Fluid reservoir
2. Fill level mark
3. Bleed screw for emergency actuation
4. Hydraulic pump
5. Electric pump motor
6. Valve 1
7. Valve 3
8. Valve 5
9. Valve 4
10. Valve 2
11. Relay for counterclockwise pump operation
12. Relay for clockwise pump operation

B309541014

541

*Convertible top hydraulics*

## CONVERTIBLE TOP COMPONENT LOCATIONS

| Component | ID | Location | Page |
|---|---|---|---|
| Navigation module | A112a | Trunk floor under floor covering | 520-11 |
| Convertible top coupling fastener microswitch | I01197 | Left C-pillar | 520-9 |
| Convertible top rear module Hall sensors | I01198 I01199 | Right rear of trunk behind trim | 520-10 |
| Convertible top front lock microswitches | I01200 I01201 | Front of convertible top, under trim | 520-10 |
| Convertible top coupling fastener | I01202 I01208 | Right C-pillar | 520-9 |
| Convertible top Hall sensor | I01203 | Right C-pillar | 520-9 |
| Convertible top Hall sensor | I01205 I01206 | Convertible top railside, behind trim panel | 520-10 |
| Convertible top Hall sensors | I01204 I01207 | Right C-pillar | 520-10 |
| Convertible top front lock | I01209 | Front of convertible top, under trim | 520-10 |
| Convertible top drive motor relays | K18363a K18364a | Underneath trunk floor covering | 520-9 |
| Trunk lid soft-close motor, left, right | M79a M85 | Convertible: Trunk lid lock assembly | 520-11 |
| Convertible top drive motor | M101 | Underneath trunk floor covering | 520-9 |
| Cowl microswitch | S41 | Behind left side trim panel | 520-11 |
| Rear lid lock microswitch | S149 | Left side lid, behind trim panel | 520-11 |
| Rear lid lock microswitch | S167b | Right side lid, behind trim panel | 520-11 |
| Convertible top switch | S700 | Between front seats on center console | 520-2 |
| Convertible top drive valves | Y802 Y804 Y805 | Underneath trunk floor covering | 520-9 |

## Convertible top components

### Trunk

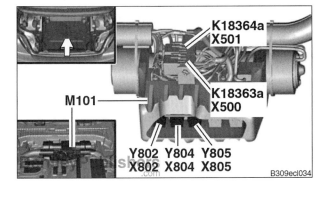

◄ Trunk floor covering removed (**arrow**):

- **K18363a**, **K18364a** Convertible top drive motor relays
- **M101** Convertible top drive motor
- **X500** Connector
- **X501** Connector
- **X802** Connector
- **X804** Connector
- **X805** Connector
- **Y802** Valve
- **Y804** Valve
- **Y805** Valve

### Left C-pillar

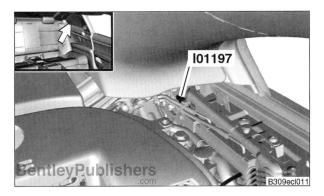

◄ Behind trim panel (**arrow**):

- **I01197** Convertible top coupling fastener microswitch

### Right C-pillar

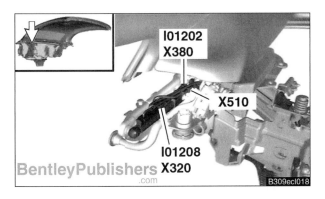

◄ Behind trim panel (**arrow**):

- **I01202** Convertible top coupling fastener microswitch
- **I01208** Convertible top coupling fastener microswitch
- **X320** Connector
- **X380** Connector
- **X510** Connector

### Right C-pillar

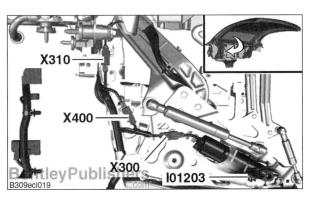

◄ Behind trim panel (**arrow**):

- **I01203** Convertible top Hall sensor (roof up)
- **X300** Connector
- **X310** Connector
- **X400** Connector

541

*Convertible top components*

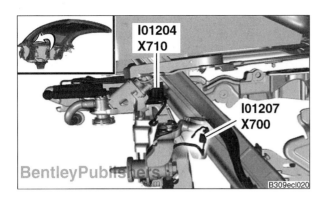

### Right C-pillar

◁ Behind trim panel (**arrow**):

- **I01204** Convertible top Hall sensor (roof down)
- **I01207** Convertible top rear module Hall sensor (closed)
- **X700** Connector
- **X710** Connector

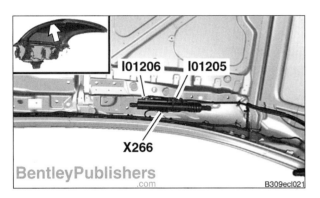

### Convertible top right side rail

◁ Behind trim panel (**arrow**):

- **I01205** Convertible top Hall sensor (roof partially closed)
- **I01206** Convertible top rear module Hall sensor (roof partially open)
- **X266** Connector

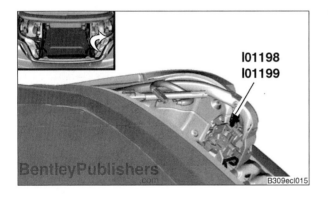

### Right rear trunk

◁ Behind trim panel (**arrow**):

- **I01198** Convertible top rear module Hall sensor (almost closed)
- **I01199** Convertible top rear module Hall sensor (open)

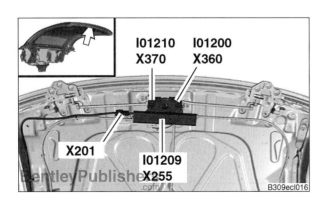

### Front of convertible top

◁ Behind trim panel (**arrow**):

- **I01200** Convertible top front locks Hall switch (locked)
- **I01201** Convertible top front locks Hall switch (unlocked)
- **I01209** Convertible top lock
- **X201** Connector
- **X255** Connector
- **X360** Connector
- **X370** Connector

*Convertible top components*

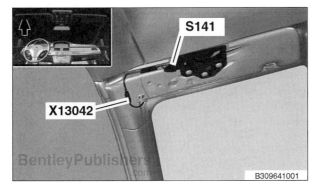

 ### Top of windshield frame

Behind trim panel
- **S41** Cowl microswitch
- **X13042** Connector

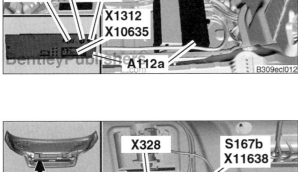

 ### Trunk

Trunk floor covering removed (**arrow**):
- **A112a** Navigation module
- **X1312** Connector, OPPS adapter
- **X4293** Connector
- **X10635** Connector, OPPS adapter
- **X14243** Connector
- **X14321** Connector

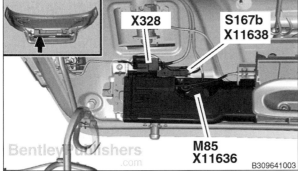

 ### Trunk lid

Right side, behind trim panel
- **M85** Trunk lid lock assembly
- **S167b** Rear lid lock microswitch
- **X328** Connector
- **X11636** Connector
- **X11638** Connector

Left side, behind trim panel
- **M79a** Trunk lid lock assembly
- **S149** Rear lid lock microswitch
- **X329** Connector
- **X11635** Connector
- **X11640** Connector

541

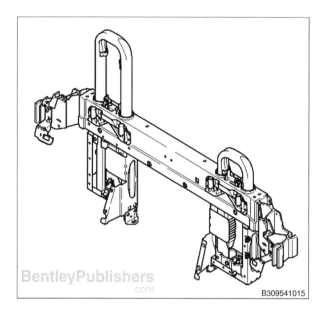

B309541015

## ROLLOVER PROTECTION SYSTEM

 Two spring-loaded rollbar cassettes are mounted behind the rear seat. The cassettes are bolted into the reinforced carrier behind the seat backs.

A rollover control unit (ROC), mounted in the rear behind the left rear seat back on the rollbar cassette, contains the electronics for rollover detection and deployment final stage for triggering the rollover bar solenoids.

The ROC performs a self-check every time the ignition is switched on. The ROC is connected to the restraint control module for troubleshooting purposes.

If faults are detected, the warning lamp in the instrument cluster lights up. In case of a crash, the system attempts to trigger the rollover cassettes to deploy even if a fault code is stored in fault memory.

*NOTE —*

• *Diagnosis of convertible top and Rollover Protection System are beyond the scope of this book. Your authorized BMW dealer has proper diagnostic equipment and tools to carry out these tasks.*

After deployment, the detent pawl in a rollover protection cassette can be retracted by press the toothed strap back so that rollbar can be pushed down and locked into the solenoids.

> *WARNING —*
> • *Ensure that area above and adjacent to rollover bars remains clear and unobstructed at all times.*

> *CAUTION—*
> • *It is not possible to close convertible top with rollover bars extended.*

# 600 Electrical System–General

## GENERAL

This section presents a brief description of the principal parts of the electrical system. Also covered here are basic electrical system troubleshooting tips.

See also:

- **121 Battery, Starter, Alternator**
- **ECL Electrical Component Locations** for common BMW acronyms as well as component location information
- **ELE Electrical Wiring Diagrams**
- **OBD On-Board Diagnostics**

### Electrical test equipment

Many electrical tests described in this manual call for measuring voltage, current or resistance using a digital multimeter. A digital meter is preferred for precise measurements and for electronics work because it is generally more accurate than an analog meter

**600**

(swing-needle). An analog meter may draw enough current to damage sensitive electronic components.

An LED test light is a safe, inexpensive tool that can be used to perform many simple electrical tests that would otherwise require a digital multimeter. The LED indicates when voltage is present between any two test-points in a circuit.

The integrated safety, comfort, security and handling systems on 3 Series vehicles are designed with self-diagnostic capabilities. The quickest way to diagnose many problems is to start with a scan tool read-out of diagnostic trouble codes (DTCs). See **Scan tool basics** in this repair group.

## Static damage prevention

Electronic circuits can be easily damaged by static electricity held by the human body and vehicle electrical components. To avoid static electricity damage, take precautions to ground the static electricity before touching any internal components of a circuit.

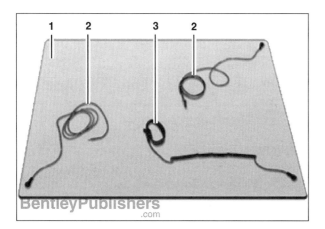

◄ Wearing an electrostatic discharge (ESD) wrist strap or working on an anti-static mat prevents static electricity damage.

1. ESD mat
2. Grounding lead
3. ESD wrist strap

## Warnings and Cautions

> **WARNING—**
> • Airbags and pyrotechnic seat belt tensioners utilize explosive devices. Handle with extreme care. See warnings and cautions in **721 Airbag System (SRS)**.
>
> • The ignition system operates at lethal voltages. If you have a weak heart or wear a pacemaker, do not expose yourself to ignition system electric currents. Take extra precautions when working on the ignition system or when servicing the engine while it is running or the key is ON. See **120 Ignition System** for additional ignition system warnings and cautions.
>
> • Keep hands, clothing and other objects clear of the electric engine cooling fan when working on a warm engine. The fan may start at any time, even when the ignition is switched OFF.

**CAUTION—**

- *Do not disconnect the battery with the engine running.*

- *Prior to disconnecting the battery, read the battery disconnection cautions given in* **001 Warnings and Cautions**.

- *Switch the ignition OFF and remove the negative battery cable before removing any electrical components. Connect and disconnect electrical connectors and ignition test equipment leads only while the ignition is switched OFF.*

- *Relay and fuse positions are subject to change and may vary from vehicle to vehicle. If questions arise, an authorized BMW dealer is the best source for the most accurate and up-to-date information.*

- *Use a digital multimeter for electrical tests. Switch the multimeter to the appropriate function and range before making test connections.*

- *Many control modules are static sensitive. Static discharge damages them permanently. Handle the modules using static prevention equipment and techniques. See* **Static damage prevention** *in this repair group.*

- *To avoid damaging harness connectors or relay panel sockets, use jumper wires with flat-blade connectors that are the same size as the connector or relay terminals.*

- *Do not try to start the engine of a vehicle which has been heated above 176°F (80°C) (for example, in a paint drying booth). Allow it to cool to normal temperature.*

- *Disconnect the battery before doing any electric welding on the vehicle.*

- *Do not wash the engine while it is running, or any time the ignition is ON.*

- *Choose test equipment carefully. Use a digital multimeter with at least 10 MΩ input impedance or an LED test light. An analog meter (swing-needle) or a test light with a normal incandescent bulb may draw enough current to damage sensitive electronic components.*

- *Do not use an ohmmeter to measure resistance on solid state components such as control modules.*

- *Disconnect the battery before making resistance (ohm) measurements on a circuit.*

**600**

## VEHICLE ELECTRICAL SYSTEM

### Voltage and polarity

 The vehicle operates on a 12-volt direct current (DC) negative-ground system. Power is supplied by a lead-acid battery in the trunk or cargo compartment.

A voltage regulator controls system voltage at approximately 12 volts. All circuits are grounded by direct or indirect connection to the negative (–) terminal of the battery. A number of ground connections throughout the vehicle connect the wiring harness to chassis ground. These circuits are completed by the battery cable or ground strap between the body and the battery negative (–) terminal.

Fuses are color coded to indicate current capacities.

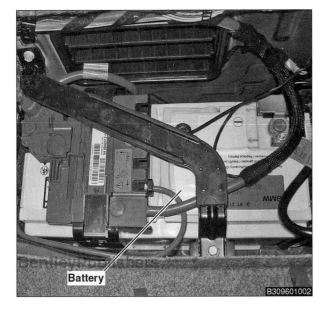

**Battery**

B309601002

Electrical components connect using one of the following:

- Heavy cables with lug-type connectors (battery, starter, alternator).
- Electrical harnesses with keyed, push-on connectors that lock into place.
- Buses with modular connectors.

Relays and control modules are mounted in various places throughout the vehicle.
See **ECL Electrical Component Locations**.

## Battery connections

◀ From the battery, power is supplied to consumers in the vehicle via three main supply cables.

1. Rear power distribution panel (high amperage fuses)
2. Starter
3. Alternator (generator)
4. Battery
5. Line to junction box
   Copper 40 mm$^2$ (1 gauge)
6. Line to engine electronics (ECM, Valvetronic control module)
   Copper 10 mm$^2$ (7 gauge)
7. Line to B junction, starter and alternator
   Aluminum 80 mm$^2$ (000 gauge)
8. Junction box (JB)
9. E-box containing engine electronics fuse carriers and control modules
10. B+ junction (jump start connector) in engine compartment

## Power distribution

1. Alternator (generator)
2. Starter
3. Junction box (JB)
4. Junction box control module (JBE)
5. Car access system (CAS)
6. Engine control module (ECM)
7. Rear power distribution panel
8. Battery safety terminal
9. Battery
10. Intelligent battery sensor (IBS)

The high amperage fuses (fusible links) in the rear power distribution panel are not replaceable separately.
See **ECL Electrical Component Locations**.

The junction box (JB) underneath right side dashboard serves as the primary power distribution point. See **Junction box (JB)** in this repair group.

The junction box control module (JBE) is the primary bus system gateway. See **Bus Systems** in this repair group.

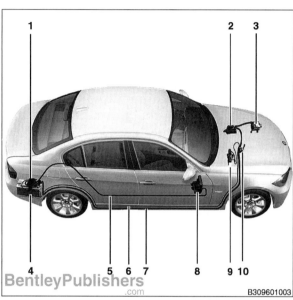

B309601003

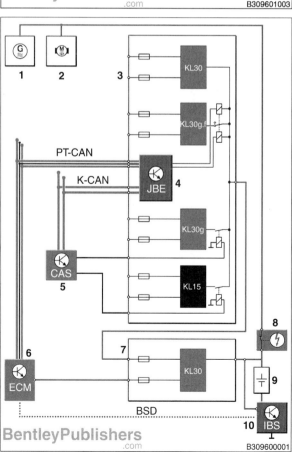

B309600001

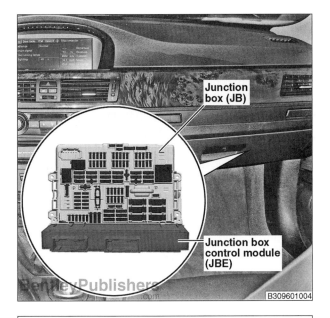

B309601004

To ensure efficient energy management in the vehicle, an energy management function is incorporated into the ECM operating software. See **Power Management** in this repair group

## Junction box (JB)

◄ The junction box (JB), underneath right side of the dashboard behind the glove compartment, carries fuses, relays and the junction box control module (JBE).

For fuse ratings and locations, see **ECL Electrical Component Locations**.

Some JB relays are plugged into the box while others are soldered to the PC board. JB relay locations are shown in **ECL Electrical Component Locations**. The following relays are soldered:

• Horn relay

• Terminal 30g_f relay

• Terminal 15 relay

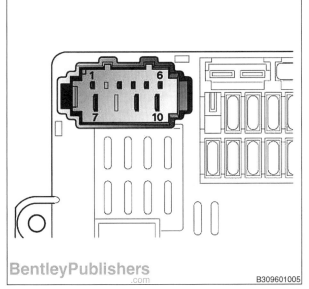

BentleyPublishers
.com

B309601005

◄ Upper left corner of JB interfaces directly to vehicle wiring harness. Its function is relay actuation and supplying power to various loads.

1. Secondary air pump actuation ground
2. not used
3. ECM terminal 87, secondary air pump
4. Fuel pump actuation, ground
5. Terminal 15 actuation
6. Terminal 30g actuation
7. Ground
8. not used
9. Wiper stage 1
10. Wiper stage 2

## Junction box control module (JBE)

◄ JBE module uses 4 connectors:

1. **X14270** Connector to wiring harness (47 pin)
2. **X4010** Connector to junction box (JB) (23 pin)
3. **X14271** Connector to wiring harness (54 pin)
4. **X14272** Connector to instrument cluster (54 pin)

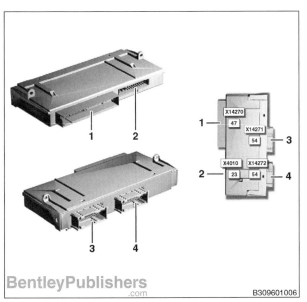

BentleyPublishers
.com

B309601006

**600**

*JBE module failure*

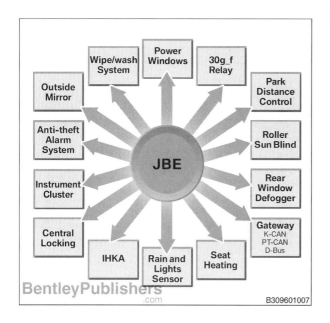

BentleyPublishers.com

B309601007

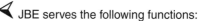

JBE serves the following functions:

- Gateway module, vehicle bus systems (pass-through function for F-CAN)
- Data from engine coolant level sensor, washer fluid level sensor, fuel level sensor and parking brake switch evaluated and transmitted to instrument cluster
- Data from automatic recirculation air control and refrigerant pressure evaluated and transmitted to IHKA module
- Actuation of A/C compressor valve and rear window defogger from IHKA module
- Wiper and washer functions, heated washer jets, seat heating, mirror heating, coolant valve, terminal 30g_f, rear power windows, rear window sun blind actuation
- Vehicle locking, unlocking
- Outside temperature sensor data pass-through

Soldered relays controlled by JBE:

- Rear power windows
- Central locking (except trunk)

Plug-in relays controlled by JBE:

- Rear window defroster
- Headlight washer
- Terminal 30g_f (deactivation of off-load power consumers)
- Wiper stages 1 and 2

## JBE module failure

In vehicles with N51 (non-turbo) engine, the following sporadic and seemingly unrelated electrical problems while driving may indicate JBE module failure:

- A/C stops working.
- Fuel gauge display is implausible (shows empty).
- Rear windows one-touch function is inoperative.
- Windshield wipers work without being switched ON.
- Various instrument cluster warning lights illuminate.

During the course of diagnosis, several fault codes are detected in the JBE module:

- A6E5 or A6E4 (fuel sensor signal plausibility)
- 9C5E (A/C refrigerant sensor signal)
- A72A, A72B, A72C or A72D (rear window Hall sensor signal)
- 9C69 (rear stratification potentiometer)

Also, fuel sensor plausibility faults may be stored:

- 2DE4 or 2DE5 in the ECM
- 9319 or 931A in the instrument cluster.

Additionally, the JBE module may show signs of local overheating. First check harness and ground connections at JBE module.

The problem may be that the right side fuel sending unit ground wire is intermittently shorted to the B+ terminal of the electric fuel pump inside the fuel tank. Battery voltage, traveling via the fuel sender ground path, overloads the ground circuits of the JBE module, causing its failure.

To inspect fuel sender wiring for chafing, see **160 Fuel Tank and Fuel Pump**. For JBE module replacement, see **JBE module, removing and installing** in this repair group.

## JBE module, removing and installing

— Disconnect negative (-) battery cable and cover battery terminal to keep cable from accidentally contacting terminal.

> **CAUTION—**
> • *Prior to disconnecting the battery, read the battery disconnection cautions given in* **001 Warnings and Cautions**.

— Remove glove compartment and right side dashboard lower trim (trim above right footwell). See **513 Interior Trim**.

◄ Working at JBE module, detach electrical connectors (**arrows**).

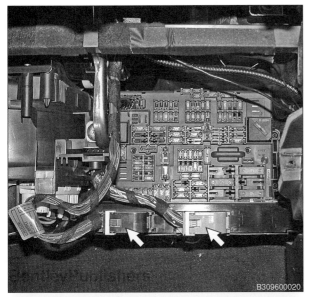

◄ Remove JBE mounting screws (**arrows**).

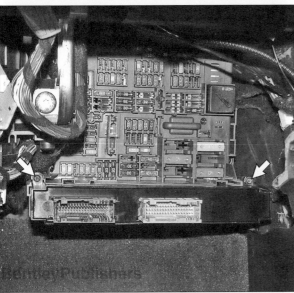

600

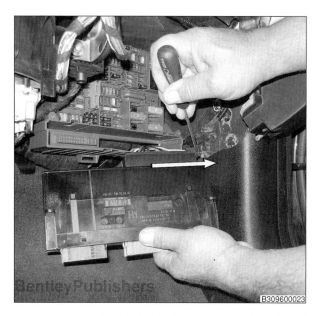

B309600023

◁ Pull JBE out of junction box. Slide connector lock to right (**arrow**) to detach connector.

– When installing, make sure JBE module is seated correctly on plug connections.

– After reassembly, carry out vehicle coding and programming. See **Coding, Programming, Adaptation** in this repair group.

### Car access system (CAS)

◁ Car access system (CAS) module underneath steering column uses 2 connectors:

• Connector to vehicle wiring harness (42 pin)
• Ribbon cable connector (14 pin)

CAS removal and installation is covered in **121 Battery, Starter, Alternator**.

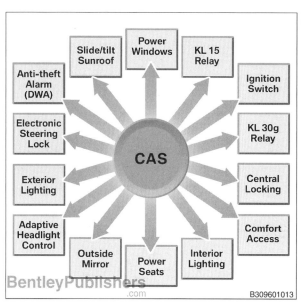

B309601013

◁ CAS serves the following functions:

• Ignition switch control
• Central locking, comfort access, power windows, sunroof master controller (issues enable command)
• Electronic steering lock actuation and control
• Key validation, electronic immobilization
• Vehicle data storage, also known as vehicle order or VO (redundant with FRM)
• Condition based service (CBS) data storage
• Terminal 15, terminal 30g relays control

Note that electronic immobilization (EWS) is a function of CAS.

The accompanying IPO (input-processing-output) diagram illustrates CAS inputs and outputs. In this type of stylized diagram, sensor inputs to the control module are on the left, control module processing is in the center and control module output commands are on the right of the diagram.

**Car access
system (CAS)
inputs / outputs**

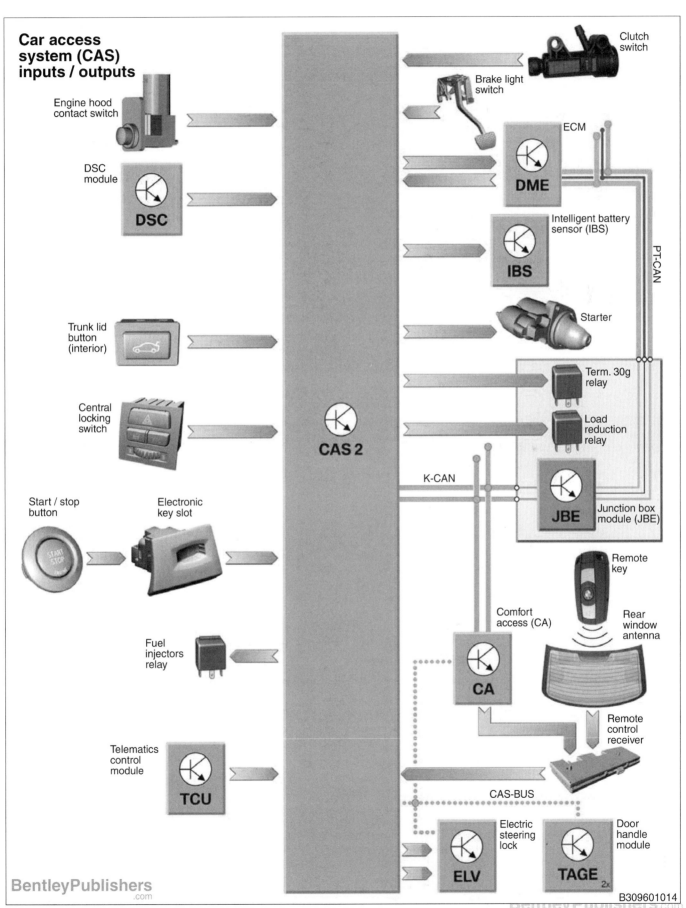

Engine hood
contact switch

DSC
module

**DSC**

Trunk lid
button
(interior)

Central
locking
switch

Start / stop
button

Electronic
key slot

Fuel
injectors
relay

Telematics
control
module

**TCU**

**CAS 2**

Clutch
switch

Brake light
switch

ECM

**DME**

Intelligent battery
sensor (IBS)

**IBS**

Starter

Term. 30g
relay

Load
reduction
relay

**JBE**

Junction box
module (JBE)

K-CAN

PT-CAN

Remote
key

Comfort
access (CA)

Rear
window
antenna

**CA**

Remote
control
receiver

CAS-BUS

Electric
steering
lock

Door
handle
module

**ELV**

**TAGE** 2x

600

B309601008

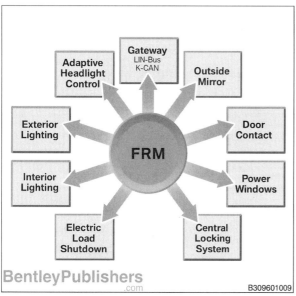

B309601009

## Footwell module (FRM)

◄ Footwell module (FRM), behind left footwell trim, uses 3 connectors:

1. Connector to instrument cluster (46 pin)
2. Connector to vehicle wiring harness (51 pin)
3. Connector to vehicle wiring harness (51 pin)

◄ FRM serves the following functions:

- Gateway module, LIN-bus and K-CAN (outside mirrors, driver door switch cluster)
- Door contact switches and door lock cylinders data evaluation
- Exterior lights, adaptive headlights evaluation, actuation
- Front power windows, electric load shut-down control
- Window anti-trap actuator
- Vehicle data storage, also known as vehicle order or VO (redundant with CAS module)

## Footwell module (FRM), removing and installing

– Disconnect negative (-) battery cable and cover battery terminal to keep cable from accidentally contacting terminal.

> **CAUTION—**
> - *Prior to disconnecting the battery, read the battery disconnection cautions given in* **001 Warnings and Cautions**.

– Remove driver door sill trim, left side dashboard lower trim (pedal cluster trim) and left kick panel trim. See **513 Interior Trim**.

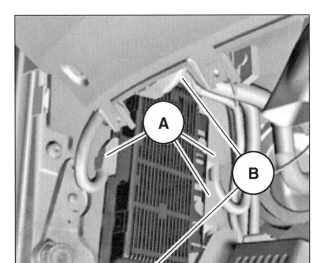

◄ Working at FRM:
- Detach electrical connectors (**A**).
- Remove mounting fasteners (**B**).
- Lift FRM out of vehicle.

– After reassembly, carry out vehicle coding and programming. See **Coding, Programming, Adaptation** in this repair group.

## Roof function center (FZD)

◄ Roof function center (FZD) in front center of headliner uses 4 connectors:

1. Connector to vehicle wiring harness (20 pin)
2. Connector to interior rear view mirror (20 pin)
3. Connector to vehicle wiring harness (4 pin)
4. Connector to rear interior lighting (20 pin)

For roof function center (FZD) removal and installation, see **Interior light bulb replacement** in **630 Lights**.

Sunroof, interior lights, rain sensor and other functions controlled by the FZD (roof function center) may fail owing to incorrect FZD software. To check, remove and reinstall FZD fuses in the junction box (JB) behind the glove compartment. If functionality is restored, use BMW scan tool to update FZD software.

◄ FZD serves the following functions:
- Sunroof control
- Rain-light sensor data transmitted via LIN-bus, then via K-CAN to other modules
- Condensation sensor data evaluated to calculate relative humidity, transmitted via K-CAN to IHKA module
- Electrochromatic inside rear view mirror data converted and transmitted to FRM via K-CAN. (FRM dims outside rear view mirrors.)
- Garage door opener power
- Vanity mirror lights, map lights, reading lights and interior lights actuation
- Passenger airbag light, microphone, and emergency call button integration

**600**

## Bus Systems

### Bus basics

To handle electrical complexity, 3 Series vehicles are equipped extensively with bus systems. Signals are shared digitally among electrical components on a bus, eliminating the need for separate connections for each pair of components. The use of bus communication for controls and accessories reduces wiring complexity and improves system response time.

Data transfer over a bus is similar to a telephone conference. A component on the bus transmits a stream of data which other components receive at the same time. Each component is then free to use or ignore this data.

The benefits of the bus method of data transfer are as follows:

• As data and programs are modified and extended, only software modifications are necessary.

• Continuous verification of transmitted data leads to low error rate.

• Sensors and signal wires can be simplified or eliminated due to the transmittal of multiplexed digital data.

• Control modules transfer data at a high rate.

• Control module sizes and connector sizes are smaller.

• Bus architecture conforms to international standards. This facilitates data interchange between components of different manufacture.

### Distributed functions

 The 3 Series bus system allows system functions to be distributed over multiple control modules. For example, central locking, power window control and interior lighting functions are distributed among the following control modules:

1.  Junction box module (JBE)

2.  Roof function center (FZD)

3.  Car access system (CAS)

4.  Footwell module (FRM)

5.  Comfort access (CA) module

In addition, due to the increase in interconnectivity allowed by bus systems, some sensors are not connected to the main control module for that system but rather to the control module closest to the sensor or actuator. The information is then transferred to the main controller via the bus system. By utilizing the closest module as a data transfer point, cable length and the number of connectors is reduced.

BentleyPublishers
.com

B309ecl001

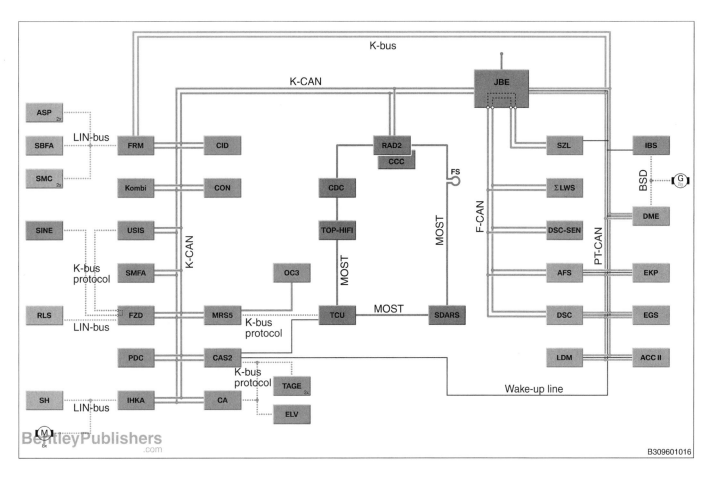

B309601016

## Bus system connections

**ACCII** Active cruise control

**ASP** Outside mirror(s)

**CA** Comfort access

**CAS2** Car access system

**CCC** Car communications computer

**CDC** CD changer

**CID** Central information display

**CON** iDrive controller

**DME** Engine control module (ECM)

**DSC** Dynamic stability control module

**DSC-SEN** DSC sensor

**EGS** Automatic transmission control module

**EKP** Fuel pump control module

**ELV** Electric steering lock

**FRM** Footwell module

**FS** MOST direct access

**FZD** Roof function center

**G** Battery

**IBS** Intelligent battery sensor

**IHKA** Automatic climate control

**JBE** Junction box module

**KOMBI** Instrument cluster

**LDM** Longitudinal dynamics management

**LWS** Steering angle sensor

**MRS5** Multiple restraint system

**OC3** Seat occupancy sensor

**PDC** Park distance control

**RAD2** Radio

**RLS** Rain-lights sensor

**SBFA** Driver door switch block

**SDARS** Satellite radio

**SH** Seat heater

**SINE** Emergency siren with tilt sensor

**SMC** Seat motor controller(s)

**SMFA** Driver seat module

**SZL** Steering column switch cluster

**TAGE** Door handle module

**TCU** Telematics control module

**TOP-HIFI** Amplifier

**USIS** Ultrasonic passenger compartment sensor

600

## Bus types

3 Series vehicles are equipped with two groups of bus systems:

- Main bus systems are
  D-bus (diagnostic bus)
  K-CAN (body bus)
  PT-CAN (powertrain bus)
  F-CAN (chassis bus)
  MOST (communications)

- Sub-bus system are
  K-bus (body bus)
  K-bus protocol (protocol body bus)
  LIN-bus (local interconnect network bus)
  BSD (bit-serial data interface)

Main bus systems exchange data between control modules throughout the vehicle. *Example:* Door contacts status is relayed to footwell module (FRM) when doors are locked. This information is transmitted via K-CAN to junction box module (JBE) which activates central locking drive units.

Sub-bus systems exchange relatively small quantities of data within one system. *Example:* Rain-lights sensor (RLS) data is relayed to the roof function center (FZD) via LIN-bus, then forwarded via K-CAN to JBE and FRM.

**Table a** shows characteristics of main bus and sub-bus systems.

| Table a. Bus system properties | | | |
|---|---|---|---|
| **Bus** | **Name** | **Data rate** | **Properties** |
| **Main bus** | | | |
| D-bus | Diagnostic bus | 10.5 / 115 Kbit/s | Linear, 1-wire |
| K-CAN | Body CAN-bus | 100 Kbit/s | Linear, 2-wire |
| PT-CAN | Powertrain CAN-bus | 500 Kbit/s | Linear, 2-wire |
| F-CAN | Chassis CAN-bus | 500 Kbit/s | Linear, 2-wire |
| MOST | Multimedia oriented system transport | 22.5 Mbit/s | Ring, fiber optic |
| **Sub-bus** | | | |
| K-bus | Body bus | 9.6 Kbit/s | Linear, 1-wire |
| K-bus protocol | Protocol body bus | 9.6 Kbit/s | Linear, 1-wire |
| LIN-bus | Local interconnect network bus | 9.6 / 19.2 Kbit/s | Linear, 1-wire |
| BSD | Bit-serial data interface | 9.6 Kbit/s | Linear, 1-wire |

## Terminating resistors

Terminating resistors, located in control modules, are used to ensure exact data transmission in bus systems.

- K-CAN terminating resistors are in each control module connected to the bus.

- F-CAN terminating resistors are in two module on the bus (SZL and DSC).

- PT-CAN terminating resistors are in two modules on the bus (EKP and DSC).

## POWER MANAGEMENT

### Power management basics

During vehicle operation, engine mechanical energy is converted by the alternator into electrical energy and made available to electric loads in the vehicle. Most electric loads receive power primarily via switched terminal 30g and terminal 30g_f relays in the junction box (JB). Certain electric loads are supplied unswitched battery power directly by terminal 30 or terminal R. *Example:* Anti-theft alarm system is active when the vehicle is parked and engine is shut OFF. Therefore anti-theft power is from an unswitched terminal.

The power management portion of the engine control module (ECM) operating program is able to:

• Regulate idle speed and charging voltage while the engine is running.

• Regulate power consumption of electric loads with relatively high power demands, or switch OFF those loads if needed.

• Switch OFF electric loads when the engine is stationary either as a timed function (via CAS and terminal 30g relay) or in response to electrical faults (via the ECM, JB and terminal 30g_f relay).

• Generate and store fault codes to help with vehicle or battery diagnosis.

### Idle speed boost

Although the alternator may be operating at maximum speed, the idle speed can be increased by up to 200 rpm as soon as current is drawn from the battery.

### Electric load reduction (engine running)

In addition to increasing idle speed and charging voltage, power management may reduce or switch OFF electric loads to reduce power consumption in critical situations. Electric loads are shut down only under the following two conditions:

• Battery charge status in critical range

• Alternator at maximum output

**Table b** shows measures implemented if these two conditions are detected.

**600**

| Table b. Electric load reduction | | |
|---|---|---|
| **Load (function)** | **Operation** | **Control module** |
| Heater blower | Reduced to 75% | IHKA |
| Heater blower | Reduced to 50% | IHKA |
| Heater blower | Reduced to 25% | IHKA |
| Mirror heating | Off | FRM |
| Rear window defogger | Timed | IHKA |
| Rear window defogger | Off | IHKA |
| Seat heating | Reduced to stage 2 | Seat control module, JBE |
| Seat heating | Reduced to 50% | Seat control module, JBE |
| Seat heating | Off | Seat control module, JBE |

## Electric load cut-off (engine OFF)

Even if the engine is OFF and the closed-circuit current monitoring feature of power management is in operation, some electric loads may be active:

• Required electric loads such as side lights and hazard warning system.

• Convenience load such as radio or telephone.

Under normal conditions, power management recognizes these activities and accepts the higher power consumption until the systems are deactivated. Then power management logs off the relevant control modules.

If power management detects a problem in the battery state of charge, it sends a request to switch OFF active convenience loads (radio, telephone, etc.) with the vehicle stationary. As a result of the request, these electric loads deactivate and reach their preprogrammed closed-circuit current within 5 minutes. Required electric loads (lights, hazard warning, etc.) are excluded from this function.

◀ Most control modules in the 3 Series electrical system are powered by the following relays in the junction box (JB):

**Terminal 30g relay** Controlled by CAS
CAS switches connected control modules OFF after 30 minutes. Switch OFF time extended to 60 minutes if equipped with telephone.

**Terminal 30g_f relay** Controlled by JBE
(bistable (latching) relay switches power OFF if a fault is detected:

• Invalid wake-up procedure within bus systems.

• Control units keep bus systems constantly active.

• Limit of battery power for starting reached.

Bistable (latching) relay switches power ON if:

• Vehicle is unlocked.

• Terminal change from R OFF to R ON or terminal 15

• Change in trunk lid, engine hood or door status.

**Terminal 30 relay** Unswitched, controlled by CAS

**Terminal 15 relay** Controlled by CAS, switched ON with ignition. Switches PDC control module.

JB
KL30
KL30g.f
PT-CAN
K-CAN
JBE
KL30g
CAS
KL15
ECM
KL30
BSD
IBS

B309600017

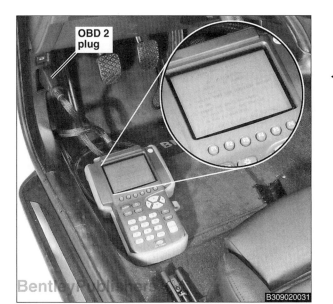

B309020031

## CODING, PROGRAMMING, ADAPTATION

### Scan tool basics

◄ The scan tool, shown here connected to the OBD 2 plug, is an electronic device used for the following:

- Displaying vehicle data such as engine, engine management and transmission versions
- Viewing and clearing fault codes (diagnostic trouble codes or DTCs)
- Coding and programming new control modules and other electronic equipment
- Clearing and resetting adaptations

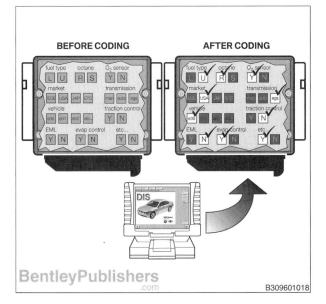

B309601018

### Coding

◄ The procedure of assigning one labeled group of data to the operating program of a control module or component is referred to as coding. A codable control module has a basic operating program already installed along with several variations of operating data. The coding process allows a specific set of operating data to be assigned to the basic operating program of that module or component to match a specific application.

Here are some types of operating requirements:

- Nominal values of device input signals (0.25 - 2.5 volts, 5 - 25 watts, etc.)
- Type of device input signal (PWM, square wave, analog)
- Operational parameters (device activation or deactivation time)
- Market specific operations (oxygen sensors, fuel type, emission standards)
- Country specific regulations (USA, Canada, Japan, UK, EU)
- Powertrain configurations (manual transmission, automatic transmission, TLEV, ULEV, SULEV, Diesel)

### Programming

◄ Programming loads application and system-specific operating instructions (program) into a coded module. Programming is also a means of updating data and operating instructions previously installed in a control module.

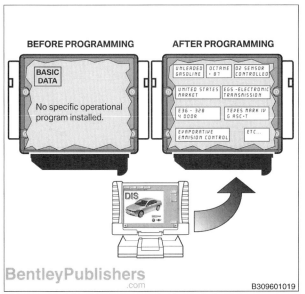

B309601019

600

## Adaptation

The engine control model (ECM), automatic transmission control module (EGS), dynamic stability control (DSC) module and other modules and components in the vehicle are adaptive. The software in each module learns from use and becomes adapted to other accompanying modules.

When installing a new module or component, be sure to use the scan tool to clear old adaptations in order to allow the components to readapt.

## Vehicle data storage

In the 3 Series vehicle, data such as engine type, engine management, transmission type and other control module information as well as odometer mileage reading and service information is called vehicle order (VO). This is equivalent to the central coding key (ZCS) in other BMW models and is stored redundantly in two locations: the footwell module (FRM) and car access system (CAS).

The VO is retrieved by coding software whenever a new module is coded. However, if possible, before removing the old module, use the scan tool to retrieve application information such as hardware and software level. Record this information for later reference.

## Coding and programming procedure

Ground    B+

B3009601022

◀ Before starting the coding and programming procedure, use a vehicle power supply to maintain correct voltage throughout the electrical system. See **121 Battery, Starter, Alternator**.

For the most up-to-date data and program information, make sure the scan tool has the current version of CIP (coding, individualization & programming) installed.

Connect BMW scan tool or equivalent to OBD II plug under dashboard. See **Scan tool basics** in this repair group. In addition to BMW scan tools, there are a number of aftermarket tools available. See **Tools** in **020 Maintenance**.

## ELECTRICAL TROUBLESHOOTING

Four things are required for current to flow in any electrical circuit:
• Voltage source.
• Wires or connections to transport voltage.
• Load or device that uses electricity.
• Connection to ground.

Most problems can be found using a digital multimeter (volt / ohm / ammeter) to check the following:
• Voltage supply.
• Breaks in the wiring (infinite resistance / no continuity).
• A path to ground that completes the circuit.

Electric current is logical in its flow, always moving from the voltage source toward ground. Electrical faults can usually be located through a process of elimination. When troubleshooting a complex circuit, separate the circuit into smaller parts. General tests outlined below may be helpful in finding electrical problems. The information is most helpful when used with wiring diagrams.

Be sure to analyze the problem. Use wiring diagrams to determine the most likely cause. Get an understanding of how the circuit works by following the circuit from ground back to the power source.

When making test connections at connectors and components, use care to avoid spreading or damaging the connectors or terminals. Some tests may require jumper wires to bypass components or connections in the wiring harness. When connecting jumper wires, use blade connectors at the wire ends that match the size of the terminal being tested. The small internal contacts are easily spread apart, and this can cause intermittent or faulty connections that can lead to more problems.

## Voltage and voltage drop

Wires, connectors, and switches that carry current are designed with very low resistance so that current flows with a minimum loss of voltage. A voltage drop is caused by higher than normal resistance in a circuit. This additional resistance actually decreases or stops the flow of current. Excessive voltage drop can be noticed by problems ranging from dim headlights to sluggish wipers. Some common sources of voltage drops are corroded or dirty switches, dirty or corroded connections or contacts, and loose or corroded ground wires and ground connections.

A voltage drop test is a good test to perform if current is flowing through the circuit but the circuit is not operating correctly. A voltage drop test helps pinpoint a corroded ground strap or a faulty switch. Normally, there should be less than 1 volt drop across most wires or closed switches. A voltage drop across a connector or short cable should not exceed 0.5 volt.

A voltage drop test is generally more accurate than a simple resistance check because the resistances involved are often too small to measure with most ohmmeters. For example, a resistance as small as $0.02 \ \Omega$ results in a 3 volt drop in a typical 150 amp starter circuit. (150 amps x $0.02 \ \Omega$ = 3 volts).

**600**

Keep in mind that voltage with ignition key ON and voltage with engine running are not the same. With ignition ON and engine OFF, fully charged battery voltage is approximately 12.6 volts. With engine running (charging voltage), normal voltage is approximately 14.0 volts. Measure voltage at battery with ignition ON and then with engine running to get exact measurements.

## Voltage, measuring

◄ Connect digital multimeter negative lead to a reliable ground point on vehicle.

**NOTE** —

• The negative (-) battery terminal is always a good ground point.

— Connect digital multimeter positive lead to point in circuit you wish to measure.

— Check that voltage reading does not deviate more than 1 volt from voltage at battery. If voltage drop is more than this, check for a corroded connector or loose ground wire.

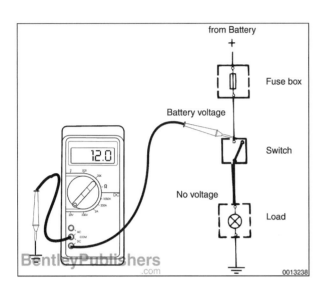

## Voltage drop, testing

Check voltage drop only when there is a load on the circuit, such as when operating the starter motor or turning on the headlights. Use a digital multimeter to ensure accurate readings.

◄ Connect digital multimeter positive lead to positive (+) battery terminal or a positive power supply close to battery source.

— Connect digital multimeter negative lead to other end of cable or switch being tested.

— With power switched ON and circuit working, meter shows voltage drop (difference between two points). This value should not exceed 1 volt.

— Maximum voltage drop in an automotive circuit, as recommended by the Society of Automotive Engineers (SAE), is as follows:

• 0 volt for small wire connections

• 0.1 volt for high current connections

• 0.2 volt for high current cables

• 0.3 volt for switch or solenoid contacts

— On longer wires or cables, the drop may be slightly higher. In any case, a voltage drop of more than 1.0 volt usually indicates a problem.

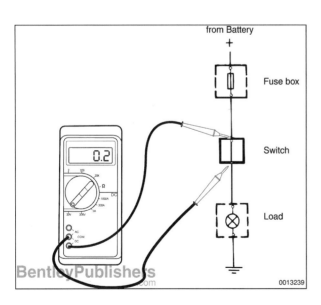

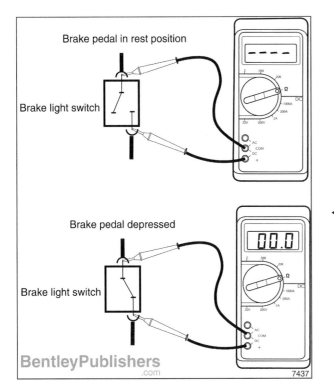

## Continuity, checking

Use continuity test to check a circuit or switch. Because most automotive circuits are designed to have little or no resistance, a circuit or part of a circuit can be easily checked for faults using an ohmmeter. An open circuit or a circuit with high resistance does not allow current to flow. A circuit with little or no resistance allows current to flow easily.

When checking continuity, switch ignition OFF. On circuits that are powered at all times, disconnect battery. Using the appropriate wiring diagram, test circuit for faulty connections, wires, switches, relays and engine sensors by checking for continuity.

◀ Example: Test brake light switch for continuity:

- With brake pedal in rest position (switch open) there is no continuity (infinite $\Omega$).

- With pedal depressed (switch closed) there is continuity (0 $\Omega$).

## Short circuits, testing

Short circuits are exactly what the name implies. Current in the circuit takes a shorter path than it was designed to take. The most common short that causes problems is a short to ground where the insulation on a positive (+) wire wears away and the metal wire is exposed. When the wire rubs against a metal part of the vehicle or other ground source, the circuit is shorted to ground. If the exposed wire is live (positive battery voltage), a fuse blows or the circuit may be damaged.

Short circuits vary in nature and are often difficult to locate. They can be found using a logical approach based on knowledge of the current path.

Use a digital multimeter to locate short circuits.

**CAUTION—**
- *In circuits protected with high rating fuses (25 amp and greater), wires or circuit components may be damaged before the fuse blows. Check for wiring damage before replacing fuses of this rating. Also, check for correct fuse rating.*

### Testing with ohmmeter

— Remove blown fuse from circuit and disconnect cables from battery. Disconnect harness connector from circuit load or consumer.

◀ Using an ohmmeter, connect one test lead to load side of fuse terminal (terminal leading to circuit) and other test lead to ground.

— If there is continuity to ground, there is a short to ground.

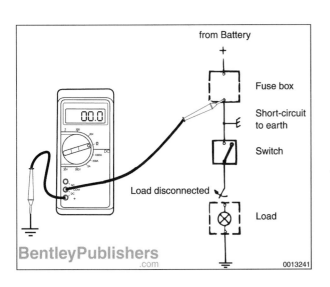

600

*Short circuits, testing*

− If there is no continuity, work from wire harness nearest to fuse and relay panel and move or wiggle wires while observing meter. Continue to move down harness until meter displays a reading. This is the location of the short to ground.

− Visually inspect wire harness at this point for any faults. If no faults are visible, carefully slice open harness cover or wire insulation for further inspection. Repair any faults found.

### Testing with voltmeter

− Remove blown fuse from circuit. Disconnect harness connector from circuit load or consumer.

*NOTE —*

• *Most fuses power more than one consumer. Be sure all consumers are disconnected when checking for a short circuit.*

◄ Using a digital multimeter, connect test leads across fuse terminals. Make sure power is present in circuit. If necessary switch ignition ON.

− If voltage is present at voltmeter, there is a short to ground.

− If voltage is not present, work from wire harness nearest to fuse and relay panel and move or wiggle wires while observing meter. Continue to move down harness until meter displays a reading. This is the location of the short to ground.

Visually inspect wire harness at this point for any faults. If no faults are visible, carefully slice open harness cover or wire insulation for further inspection. Repair any faults found.

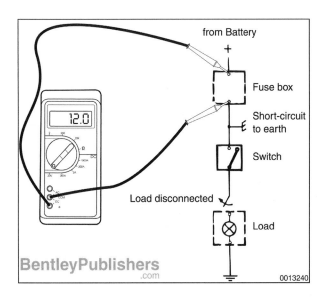

from Battery

Fuse box

Short-circuit to earth

Switch

Load disconnected

Load

BentleyPublishers.com

0013240

# 611 Wipers and Washers

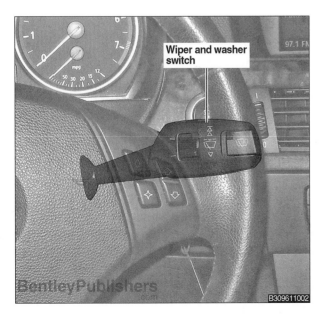

Wiper and washer switch

B309611002

**611**

## GENERAL

This repair group covers repair information for windshield, headlight and rear window wiper and washer systems.

See also:

- **612 Switches** for steering column switch cluster replacement
- **640 Heating and Air-conditioning** for cabin microfilter housing removal
- **ECL Electrical Component Locations** for wiper and washer system fuse and relay locations and applications
- **ELE Electrical Wiring Diagrams**

### Wiper and washer system operation

Wiper and washer functions in 3 Series vehicles are controlled by the junction box control module (JBE), located behind the glove compartment.

 Driver input to wiper and washer system is via multi-function stalk switch to right of steering column.

*Wiper and washer system components (Sedan)*

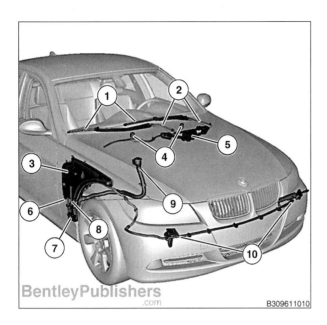

B309611010

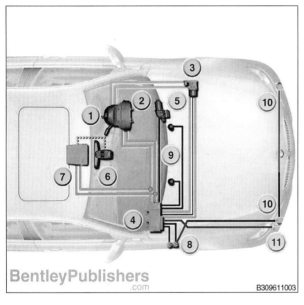

B309611003

## Wiper and washer system components (Sedan)

1. Wiper blades
2. Wiper arms
3. Washer fluid reservoir
4. Heated windshield washer jets
5. Wiper motor assembly
6. Washer fluid level switch
7. Windshield washer pump
8. Headlight washer pump
9. Washer reservoir filler neck
10. Headlight washer jets

## Wiper and washer system schematic (Sedan)

1. Wiper and washer switch, steering column switch cluster
2. Instrument cluster
3. DSC control module
4. Junction box module (JBE)
5. Windshield wiper motor
6. Rain and lights sensor (RLS)
7. Roof function center (FZD)
8. Washer fluid pumps
9. Heated windshield washer jets
10. Headlight washer jets
11. Outside temperature sensor

## Wiper and washer system inputs-outputs (Sedan)

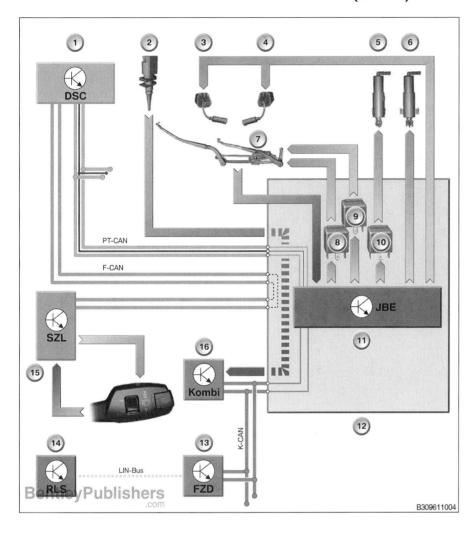

B309611004

1. DSC control module
   - Provides vehicle speed signal
   - Steering column switch center (SZL) interface

2. Outside temperature sensor

3. Heated windshield washer jet, driver's
   - PTC resistor limits current

4. Heated windshield washer jet, passenger
   - PTC resistor limits current

5. Headlight washer pump
   - In washer fluid reservoir behind right front wheel housing
   - Activated by relay in junction box (JB)

6. Windshield washer pump
   - In washer fluid reservoir behind right front wheel housing
   - Activated directly by junction box module (JBE)

7. Windshield wiper motor
   - 2-speed
   - Equipped with reset contact

8. Wiper relay 1
   - Plugged in JB

9. Wiper relay 2
   - Soldered in JB

10. Headlight washer relay
    - Plugged in JB

11. Junction box module (JBE)
    - Master control for wiper and washer functions
    - Plugged in JB

12. Junction box (JB)
    - Behind glove compartment

13. Roof function center (FZD)
    - Connected to rain and lights sensor via LIN-bus

14. Rain and lights sensor (RLS)

15. Wiper switch
    - Component of steering cluster switch center (SZL)
    - 4-stage optical switch

16. Instrument cluster

611

*Wiper and washer system components (Sports Wagon)*

## Wiper and washer system components (Sports Wagon)

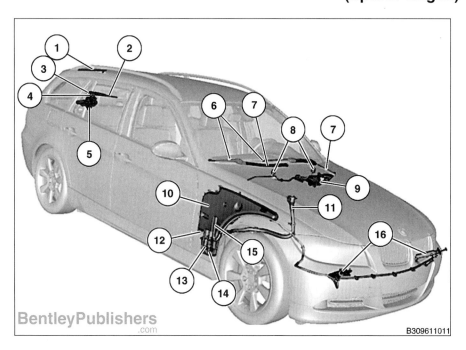

B309611011

1. Rear window washer jet
2. Rear wiper blade
3. Rear wiper arm
4. Rear wiper pivot
5. Rear wiper motor assembly
6. Windshield wiper blades
7. Windshield wiper arms
8. Heated windshield washer jets
9. Windshield wiper motor assembly
10. Washer fluid reservoir
11. Washer reservoir filler neck
12. Washer fluid level switch
13. Rear window washer pump
14. Windshield washer pump
15. Headlight washer pump
16. Headlight washer jets

## Wiper and washer system inputs-outputs (Sports Wagon)

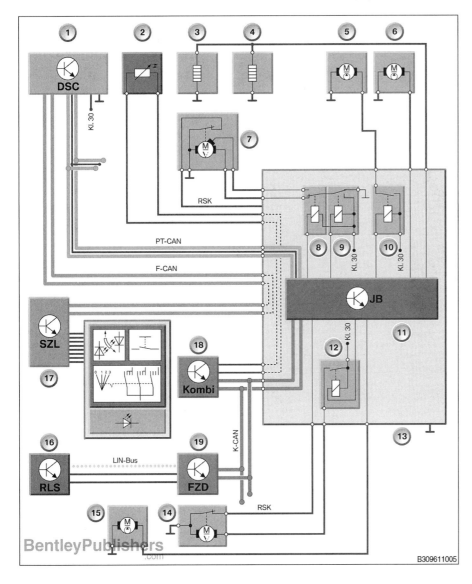

B309611005

1.  DSC control module
    - Provides vehicle speed signal
    - Steering column switch center (SZL) interface

2.  Outside temperature sensor

3.  Heated windshield washer jet, driver's
    - PTC resistor limits current

4.  Heated windshield washer jet, passenger
    - PTC resistor limits current

5.  Headlight washer pump
    - In washer fluid reservoir behind right front wheel housing
    - Activated by relay in junction box (JB)

6.  Windshield washer pump
    - In washer fluid reservoir behind right front wheel housing
    - Activated directly by junction box module (JBE)

7.  Windshield wiper motor
    - 2-speed
    - Equipped with reset contact

8.  Wiper relay 1
    - Plugged in JB

9.  Wiper relay 2
    - Soldered in JB

10. Headlight washer relay
    - Plugged in JB

11. Junction box module (JBE)
    - Master control for wiper and washer functions
    - Plugged in JB

12. Rear wiper relay
    - Plugged in JB

13. Junction box (JB)
    - Behind glove compartment

14. Rear window wiper motor
    - Intermittent when vehicle moving forward
    - Continuous wipe when vehicle in reverse

15. Rear window washer pump
    - In washer fluid reservoir behind right front wheel-housing
    - Activated directly by junction box module (JBE)

**611**

## Wiper and washer system inputs-outputs (Sports Wagon) *(continued)*

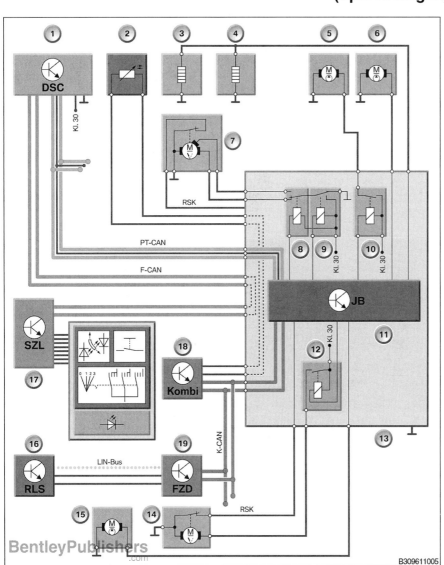

**16.** Rain and lights sensor (RLS)

**17.** Wiper switch
- Component of steering cluster switch center (SZL)
- 4-stage optical switch

**18.** Instrument cluster

**19.** Roof function center (FZD)
- Connected to rain and lights sensor via LIN-bus

B309611005

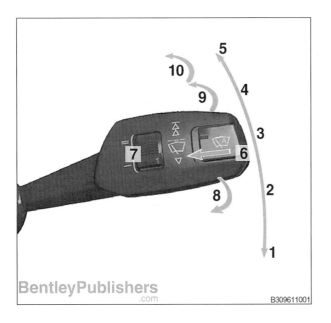

BentleyPublishers
.com

B309611001

## Wiper and washer switch operation

1. Single wipe
   • Hold stalk switch down
2. Off
3. Interval windshield wipe
4. Slow windshield wipe
   • Automatically switches to interval when car is stopped
5. Fast windshield wipe
   • Automatically switches to slow speed when car is stopped
6. Automatic interval switch with LED
   • Push inward to activate
7. Sensitivity adjustment thumb wheel for interval control
8. Windshield wash
   • Pull stalk toward driver
9. Rear window wipe (Sports Wagon)
   • Push stalk away from driver
10. Rear window wash (Sports Wagon)
    • Push stalk away from driver

## WIPER BLADES AND ARMS

### Wiper blade cleaning problems

Common problems with the wipers include streaking or sheeting, water drops after wiping, and blade chatter.

**Streaking** is usually caused when wiper blades are coated with road film or car wash wax.

— Clean blades using soapy water. If cleaning does not cure problem, replace blades.

   *NOTE* —

   • *BMW recommends replacing the wiper blades twice a year, before and after the cold season.*

**Drops** that remain behind after wiping are usually caused by oil, road film, or diesel exhaust residue on the glass.

— Use an alcohol or ammonia solution or other non-abrasive cleaner to clean glass.

**Chatter** may be caused by dirty or worn blades, or by twisted wiper arms, causing incorrect wiper blade contact angle.

— Clean blades and glass as described above.

— Check and adjust wiper arm twist. See **Wiper arm twist, adjusting** in this repair group.

— If problems persist, replace wiper blades and arms. See **Windshield wiper blade, replacing**, in this repair group.

**611**

## Windshield wiper blade, replacing

– Pivot wiper arm off windshield.

◄ Working at wiper blade pivot:
  • Press on locking clip (**arrow**) to release plastic cap.
  • Lift off cap (**curved arrow**).

◄ Position wiper blade approximately perpendicular to wiper arm and slide off wiper arm pin (**arrow**).

> **CAUTION—**
> • *Do not allow wiper arm to snap back against windshield when wiper blade is off.*

– Installation is reverse of removal. Make sure plastic cap is intact and snaps into place.

## Windshield wiper arm, removing and installing

– Open engine hood.

◄ Pry off (**arrow**) wiper pivot nut plastic cap.

◀ Remove wiper arm mounting nut (**arrow**).

◀ Use BMW special tool 61 6 210 or equivalent puller to remove wiper arm from pivot.

> **CAUTION—**
> • *Do not bend wiper arm while removing.*

– Before installing wiper arms, make sure wipers are in PARK position:

  • Switch ignition ON.

  • Switch wipers ON and allow two cycles to complete.

  • Switch wipers OFF. Wait for wiper motor to come to rest, then switch ignition OFF.

– Attach wiper arms and tighten down mounting nuts temporarily, then check and adjust wiper blade positions. See **Windshield wiper blades, adjusting position** in this repair group.

– Tighten arms to final torque.

| Tightening torque | |
| --- | --- |
| Front wiper arm to wiper pivot (M10) | 30 Nm (22 ft-lb) |

– If necessary, adjust wiper arm twist (wiper blade contact angle). See **Windshield wiper arm twist, adjusting** in this repair group.

**611**

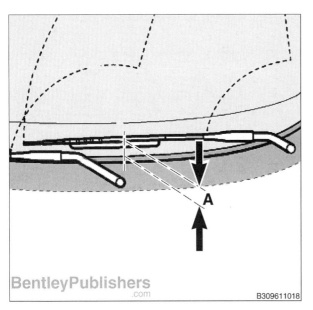

B309611018

## Windshield wiper blades, adjusting position

◄ Wiper blade position is set in relation to top of cowl cover at base of windshield:

- Make sure wipers are in PARK position.
- Loosen wiper arm nut. See **Windshield wiper arm, removing and installing** in this repair group.
- Measure from center of wiper blade to base of windshield. See **Table a**. Reset wiper arm position as necessary.

| Table a. Wiper blade position above top of cowl cover (wipers in PARK position) | | |
|---|---|---|
| **Distance A** | **Sedan, Sports Wagon (E90, E91)** | **Coupe, Convertible (E92, E93)** |
| Right side | 88 ± 3 mm (3.5 ± 0.1 in) | 75 ± 3 mm (3.0 ± 0.1 in) |
| Left side | 95 ± 3 mm (3.7 ± 0.1 in) | 84 ± 3 mm (3.3 ± 0.1 in) |

– When finished, tighten arms to final torque.

| Tightening torque | |
|---|---|
| Front wiper arm to wiper pivot (M10) | 30 Nm (22 ft-lb) |

## Windshield wiper arm twist, adjusting

◄ Wiping action is improved if contact angle (**A**) of wiper blade to plane of windshield is set correctly by adjusting wiper arm twist.

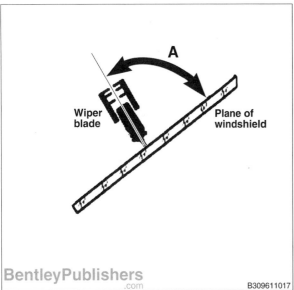

A

Wiper blade

Plane of windshield

B309611017

◄ Slide wiper blade off wiper arm pin (**arrow**). See **Windshield wiper blade, replacing** in this repair group.

> **CAUTION—**
> - *Do not allow wiper arm to snap back against windshield when wiper blade is off.*

B309611006

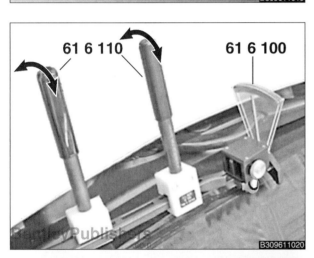

◄ Slide BMW special tool 61 6 100 on wiper arm pin. Place tool on windshield and read off degrees on scale.

| Table b. Windshield wiper blade contact angle | |
|---|---|
| Angle of wiper blade to windshield: | |
| • Right wiper | 86.7° ± 1° |
| • Left wiper | 86° ± 1° |

◄ If angle is incorrect, use BMW special tool set 61 6 110 to twist wiper arm for correct wiper blade contact angle.

### Rear wiper blade, replacing

– Pivot wiper arm off rear window.

◄ Slide blade (**arrow**) off wiper arm.

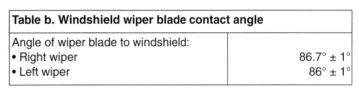

**611**

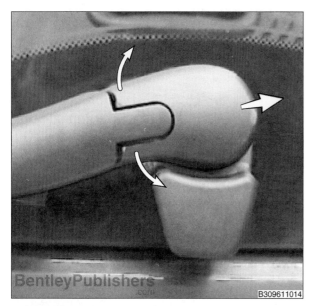

## Rear wiper arm, removing and installing

◀ Spread wiper pivot plastic cap catches (**curved arrows**) and remove cap (**flared arrow**).

◀ Pivot wiper arm off rear window, then remove mounting nut (**arrow**).

− Use BMW special tool 61 6 060 or equivalent puller to remove wiper arm from pivot.

− Before installing wiper arm, make sure wiper assembly is in PARK position:

• Switch ignition ON.

• Switch rear wiper ON and allow two cycles to complete.

• Switch wiper OFF. Wait for wiper motor to come to rest, then switch ignition OFF.

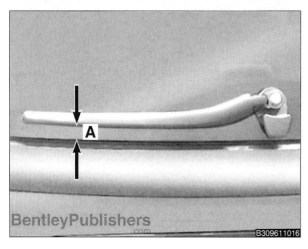

◀ Attach wiper arm and tighten down mounting nut temporarily, then check and adjust wiper blade position.

| Rear wiper blade position | |
|---|---|
| Measurement **A** (distance between bottom of wiper arm and rear window lower edge | 35 ± 3 mm (1.4 ± 0.1 in) |

− Tighten arm to final torque.

| Tightening torque | |
|---|---|
| Rear wiper arm to wiper pivot (M8) | 10 Nm (7 ft-lb) |

## WIPER ASSEMBLIES

## Windshield wiper assembly, removing and installing

> **CAUTION—**
> • *Make sure wipers are parked (stalk switch in OFF position) and the ignition is also OFF.*
> • *Use fender cover to protect windshield.*
> • *To avoid damaging the wiper arms and pivots, do not manually slide or force the wiper arms across the windshield.*

– Remove wiper arms. See **Windshield wiper arm, removing and installing** in this repair group.

– Remove upper and lower cabin microfilter housings. See **640 Heating and Air-conditioning**.

◄ Working at right side of cowl cover:
  • Detach windshield washer hose (**A**).
  • Separate washer jet electrical connectors (**B**).
  • Remove rubber seal (**C**).

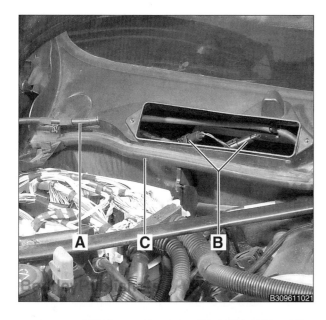

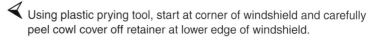

◄ Using plastic prying tool, start at corner of windshield and carefully peel cowl cover off retainer at lower edge of windshield.

**611**

*Windshield wiper assembly, removing and installing*

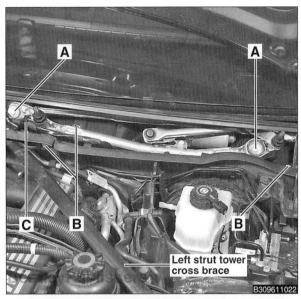

◄ Working at left side of plenum chamber:

- Remove wiper motor assembly mounting screws (**A**).

- Remove left side plenum chamber bulkhead fasteners (**B**). If necessary, unbolt one end of left strut tower cross brace for access to rightmost bolt.

- Detach wiper motor wiring harness (**C**) from bracket.

Left strut tower cross brace

B309611022

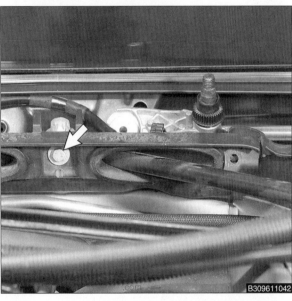

◄ Remove center plenum chamber bulkhead bolt (**arrow**). This allows removal of left plenum chamber bulkhead.

B309611042

◄ Pull wiper assembly out of plenum chamber and detach electrical connector.

B309611043

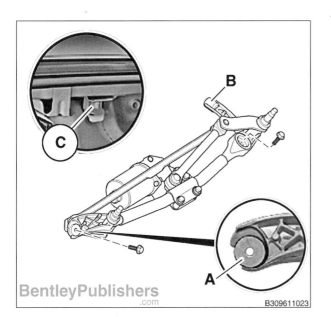

BentleyPublishers.com

B309611023

◄ When installing wiper assembly:

• Check that rubber buffers **A** and **B** are intact and in place.

• Place wiper assembly in plenum chamber. Note that buffer **B** fits in bracket **C**.

| Tightening torque | |
|---|---|
| Wiper motor assembly to bulkhead (M6) | 10 Nm (7 ft-lb) |

— When reinstalling cowl cover, to avoid water leaks into cabin, check that seals and grommets are intact and seat correctly.

— Before reinstalling wiper arms, make sure wiper motor is in PARK position. Reset wiper blade positions and contact angle. See **Windshield wiper blades, adjusting position** and **Windshield wiper arm twist, adjusting** in this repair group.

## Rear wiper assembly

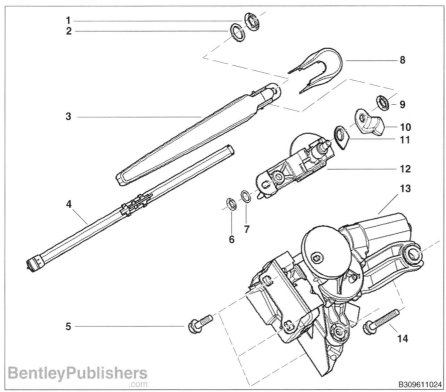

BentleyPublishers.com

B309611024

1. Wiper arm nut (M8)
   • Tighten to 10 Nm (7 ft-lb)

2. Wave washer

3. Wiper arm

4. Wiper blade

5. Torx bolt (M6 x 9 mm)
   • Tighten to 10 Nm (7 ft-lb)

6. Wiper pivot nut (M6)
   • Tighten to 8 Nm (6 ft-lb)

7. Gasket

8. Cover

9. Lock nut

10. Rear window lock release button

11. Gasket

12. Wiper pivot assembly

13. Wiper motor assembly

14. Torx bolt (M6 x 22 mm)
    • Tighten to 10 Nm (7 ft-lb)

## Rear wiper motor, removing and installing

The rear wiper motor is bolted to the Sports Wagon tailgate. The wiper arm and blade are mounted to the rear window which is hinged at the top. The motor drives the rear wiper arm via a pivot assembly mounted on the rear window. For the window to close correctly and rear wiper to operate, align the pivot assembly on the glass with the drive on the wiper motor using BMW special tool 61 1 370.

The rear window lock is bolted to the rear wiper motor assembly.

611

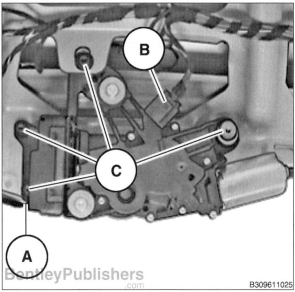

B309611025

- Remove tailgate inner trim panel. See **513 Interior Trim**.

◀ Working at rear wiper motor:
  - Detach electrical connectors (**A**, **B**).
  - Remove mounting bolts (**C**).
  - Lift off wiper motor.

- If replacing motor: Separate rear window lock from rear wiper motor assembly and bolt to new unit.

- Reinstall wiper motor but tighten mounting bolts finger tight at first.

- Attach wiper motor electrical harness. Switch ignition ON. Cycle rear wiper twice to make sure wiper motor is in PARK position. Switch ignition OFF.

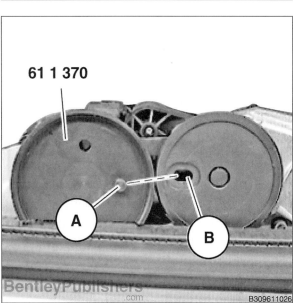

61 1 370

B309611026

◀ Align assembly using BMW special tool 61 1 370: Position special tool so that pin (**A**) on tool inserts into slot (**B**) in wiper motor drive.

B309611027

◀ With rear wiper arm vertical to glass, close rear window and allow journal of wiper pivot assembly to snap into bore (**arrow**). Close window completely.

- Tighten rear wiper motor mounting bolts.

| Tightening torque | |
|---|---|
| Rear wiper motor to tailgate | 10 Nm (7 ft-lb) |

- Open window and remove special tool.

- Replace tailgate trim.

## Rear window wiper pivot, removing and installing

— Remove rear wiper arm. See **Rear wiper arm, removing and installing** in this repair group.

— Use duct tape to hold window lock release button in place.

◄ Remove nut (**arrow**) securing pivot to window lock release button.

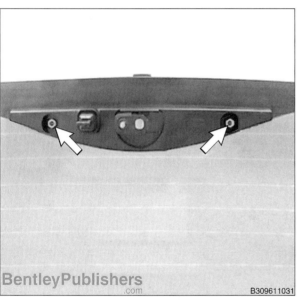

◄ With window open:

- Carefully pry out wiper pivot assembly trim covers.
- Remove trim cover mounting nuts (**arrows**) and pull off cover.

◄ With window open:

- Detach window lock release button electrical connector.
- Remove pivot assembly mounting nut (**arrow**) and remove pivot (**flared arrow**).

— Installation is reverse of removal.

| Tightening torques | |
|---|---|
| Window lock release button to glass | 10 Nm (7 ft-lb) |
| Wiper pivot to glass (M6) | 8 Nm (6 ft-lb) |

— Synchronize wiper pivot and wiper motor drive. See **Rear wiper motor, removing and installing** in this repair group.

611

## WASHER SYSTEMS

The windshield washer system includes electrically heated spray jets under the engine hood, the washer fluid pump, and washer fluid reservoir behind the right front wheel housing.

The headlight washer system (optional) consists of front washer fluid reservoir (shared with windshield washer system), a separate washer pump, and washer jets in the front bumper.

The rear window washer consists of the fluid reservoir (shared with windshield washer system), a separate washer pump, and a washer jet at the top of the rear window.

### Windshield washer jet, removing and installing

– Remove cabin microfilter housing. See **640 Heating and Air-conditioning**.

◀ Working inside fresh air intake opening in cowl cover:

- Press on lock clip and separate washer jet electrical connector (**arrow**).
- Detach washer fluid hose (**B**) from jet.

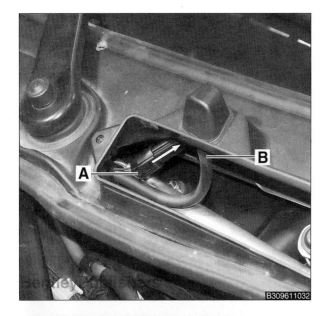

◀ Tilt (**arrow**) washer jet to detach and remove from cowl cover.

– When installing, check that the retaining clips and hose connection are intact.

– Check windshield washer function. Washer jet nozzle aim is set at the factory and cannot be adjusted.

## Headlight washer jet, removing and installing

– Remove right front wheel housing trim. See **410 Fender, Engine Hood**.

◄ To avoid washer fluid spillage, pinch off washer hose with hose pinch tool 13 3 010 or equivalent.

◄ Pull headlight washer jet out of bumper using trim cover, then detach cover by prying carefully at side clips (**arrows**).

> **CAUTION—**
> • *In order to avoid damage to washer jet, do not let it snap back. Slide it back slowly into bumper opening*

◄ Working through bumper cover opening (bumper cover removed for purpose of illustration):

• Press on catches (**arrows**) to release jet housing.

• Push housing backward and detach high pressure washer fluid line. Remove housing.

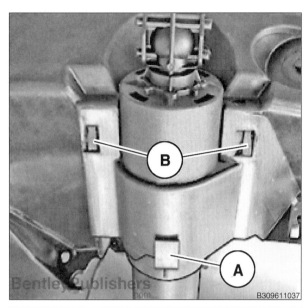

B309611037

◄ When reinstalling:

- Keep high pressure washer fluid line and connections clean and grease-free.
- Make sure guide (**A**) seats correctly.
- Make sure catches (**B**) snap audibly into place.

– Check headlight washer function. If necessary, adjust jet nozzles using needle-nosed pliers.

## Rear window washer jet, removing and installing

– Remove rear spoiler. See **412 Trunk Lid, Tailgate**.

– Remove center brake light from spoiler. See **630 Lights**.

◄ Unlock clip (**arrow**) and pull washer jet off brake light housing.

– Separate washer fluid hose from washer jet.

– Installation is reverse of removal.

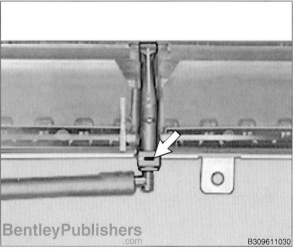

B309611030

## Washer fluid reservoir, removing and installing

– Open engine hood. Working at right side of engine compartment, siphon out washer fluid from reservoir.

– Raise front of vehicle and support safely.

> **WARNING—**
> • *Make sure the vehicle is stable and well supported at all times. Use a professional automotive lift or jack stands designed for the purpose. A floor jack is not adequate support.*

– Remove right front wheel.

– Remove right front wheel housing trim. See **410 Fenders, Engine Hood**.

– Remove right side indicator light. See **630 Lights**.

*Washer fluid reservoir, removing and installing*

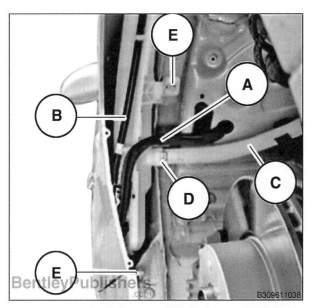

B309611038

◄ Working underneath right front wheel housing at washer fluid reservoir:

- Unhook electrical harness (**A**) out of bracket(s).
- Unhook washer fluid hose (**B**).
- Unlock filler hose (**C**) and detach from fluid reservoir (**D**). Be prepared to catch dripping washer fluid.
- Remove fluid reservoir mounting screws (**E**).
- Pull fluid reservoir forward to remove from under fender.

– For individual component replacement, see **Washer fluid reservoir components service** in this repair group.

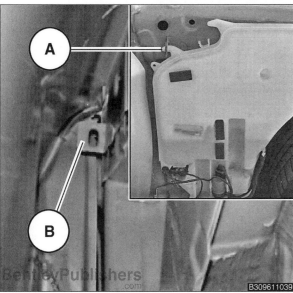

B309611039

◄ When installing:

- Make sure fluid reservoir lug (**A**) hooks into bracket (**B**) under fender.
- Check to see that fluid hoses are not kinked.
- Fill reservoir and check for leaks.

**611**

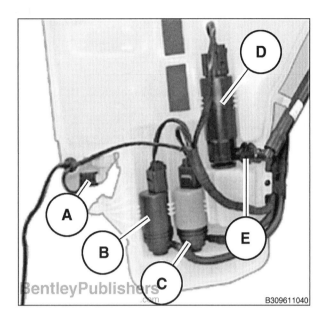

B309611040

## Washer fluid reservoir components service

— Remove washer fluid reservoir. See **Washer fluid reservoir, removing and installing** in this repair group.

◄ Washer fluid level switch (**A**):

- Detach electrical connector.
- Rotate switch clockwise and pry out of reservoir. Be prepared to catch dripping fluid.

— Rear window washer pump (**B**):

- Detach electrical connector.
- Cut or loosen hose clamp and detach hose from pump.
- Rotate pump clockwise and pry out of reservoir. Be prepared to catch dripping fluid.

— Windshield washer pump (**C**):

- Detach electrical connector.
- Cut or loosen hose clamp and detach hose from pump.
- Rotate pump clockwise and pry out of reservoir. Be prepared to catch dripping fluid.

— Headlight washer pump (**D**):

- Detach electrical connector.
- Separate high pressure fluid hose at split connector (**E**).
- Rotate pump clockwise and pry out of reservoir. Be prepared to catch dripping fluid.

— Installation is reverse of removal, noting the following:

- Replace strainers on washer pumps.
- Coat grommet at base of pump or sensor with anti-friction agent.
- Use new hose clamps, if applicable.
- After installation, check that fluid hoses are not kinked.

— Fill reservoir and check for leaks.

# 612 Switches

## GENERAL

This repair group covers replacement of electrical switches at the steering wheel, steering column, dashboard, pedal cluster, center console and door panels.

See also the following sections:

- **210 Clutch** for clutch switch
- **230 Manual Transmission** for manual transmission back-up light switch
- **240 Automatic Transmission** for automatic transmission back-up light switch function
- **250 Gearshift Linkage** for automatic shiftlock
- **320 Steering and Wheel Alignment** for steering wheel and steering column components
- **520 Seats** for seat position control switches
- **541 Convertible Top** for convertible top microswitches
- **ECL Electrical Component Locations**
- **ELE Electrical Wiring Diagrams**

**612**

## Cautions

> **CAUTION—**
> • When working on electrical switches or lights, disconnect the negative (–) cable from the battery and insulate the cable end to prevent accidental reconnection.
>
> • Prior to disconnecting the battery, read the battery disconnection cautions given in **001 Warning and Cautions**.
>
> • To prevent marring interior trim, work with plastic prying tools or wrap the tips of screwdrivers and pliers with tape before prying out switches or trim.

## STEERING WHEEL SWITCHES

The steering wheel of vehicles covered by this manual are equipped with the following:

• SRS airbag and horn button

• Horn contact

• Cellular telephone controls

• Radio controls

To replace the steering wheel switches and buttons, remove the airbag first. The horn button is integrated with the airbag and is not replaceable separately.

### Multifunction steering wheel switches

1. Multifunction steering wheel

2. Mounting bolt (M16)
   • Tighten to 63 Nm (46 ft-lb)

3. Multifunction switches

4. Airbag and horn electrical harness

5. Airbag unit and horn button

6. Multifunction switch electrical harness

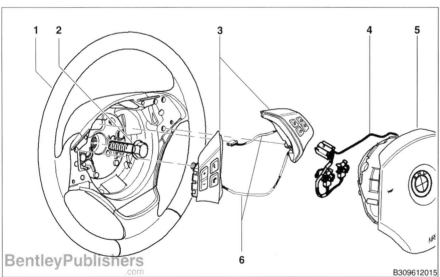

B309612015

## Sport steering wheel switches

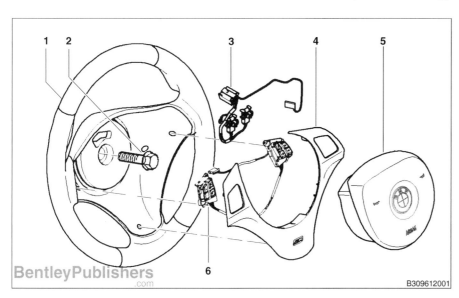

1. Sport steering wheel

2. Mounting bolt (M16)
   • Tighten to 63 Nm (46 ft-lb)

3. Airbag and horn electrical harness

4. Plastic trim

5. Airbag unit and horn button

6. Radio and telephone control switches

## Steering wheel switches, removing and installing

− Disconnect negative (-) battery cable and cover battery terminal to keep cable from accidentally contacting terminal.

> **CAUTION—**
> • *Prior to disconnecting the battery, read the battery disconnection cautions given in* **001 Warnings and Cautions**.

− Remove driver airbag in steering wheel. See **721 Airbag System (SRS).**

> **WARNING—**
> • *The steering wheel mounted airbag is an explosive device. Treat with extreme caution. Follow the airbag removal procedure in* **721 Airbag System (SRS)**.
> • *Airbag removal may set SRS fault codes. The SRS indicator light remains ON until problems are corrected and fault memory cleared.*

 Multifunction steering wheel:
   • Use plastic prying tool to pry switches off steering wheel.
   • Detach switch electrical harness. Detach harness loom from steering wheel and remove switches.

− Sport steering wheel:
   • Use plastic prying tool to pry plastic trim and multifunction switches off steering wheel. Separate switches from trim.
   • Detach switch electrical harness. Detach harness loom from steering wheel and remove switches.

− Installation is reverse of removal.

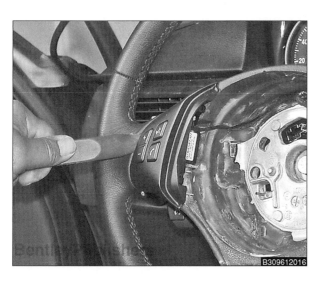

612

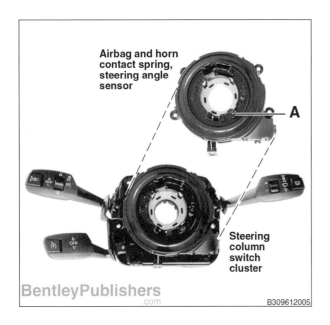

Airbag and horn
contact spring,
steering angle
sensor

A

Steering
column
switch
cluster

B309612005

# STEERING COLUMN SWITCH CLUSTER (SZL)

## Steering column switch cluster (SZL) basics

◄ The steering column switch cluster (SZL) integrates the following functions:

- Wiper and washer switch
- Headlight beam switch
- Turn signal switch
- Cruise control
- Airbag and horn contact spring, steering angle sensor with stop pin (**A**)
- On-board computer (BC) switch

SZL switches are optical devices.

## SZL system overview

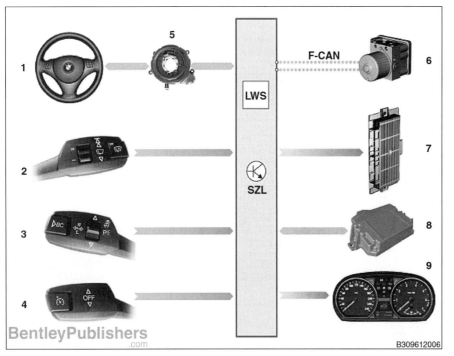

F-CAN

LWS

SZL

B309612006

1. Steering wheel and driver airbag

2. Wiper and washer switch

3. Turn signal switch
   Headlight beam switch
   On-board computer switch

4. Cruise control switch

5. Airbag and horn contact spring, steering angle sensor

6. DSC control module

7. Footwell module (FRM)

8. Multiple restraint system (MRS) control module

9. Instrument cluster

- **F-CAN** Chassis CAN-bus
- **LWS** Steering angle sensor
- **SZL** Steering column switch cluster

## SZL system schematic

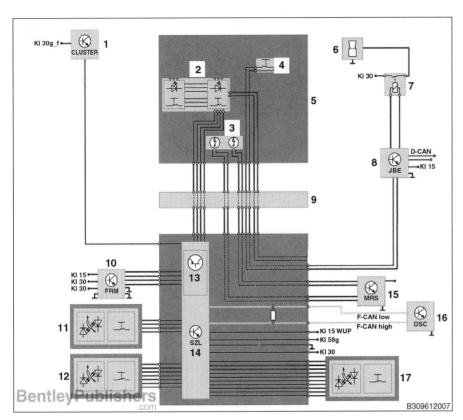

1. Instrument cluster
2. Multifunction steering wheel switches
3. Driver airbag
4. Horn switch
5. Multifunction steering wheel
6. Horn
7. Horn relay in junction box (JB)
8. Junction box control module (JBE)
9. Airbag and horn contact spring
10. Footwell module (FRM)
11. Cruise control switch
12. Turn signal switch
    Headlight beam switch
13. Steering angle sensor (LWS)
14. Steering column switch cluster (SZL)
15. Multiple restraint system (MRS) control module under center console
16. DSC control module
17. Wiper and washer switch

## SZL connector pin assignments

◄ 6-pin connector:

1. Horn button ground
2. Horn button signal wire
3. Driver airbag data line, stage 2
4. Driver airbag data line, stage 2
5. Driver airbag data line, stage 1
6. Driver airbag data line, stage 1

12-pin connector:

1. Right turn signal
2. Not used
3. Terminal 58g light
4. Not used
5. Left turn signal
6. F-CAN low
7. Terminal 31 (ground)
8. Headlight flasher and headlight beam switch
9. SZL control module voltage supply (terminal 30)
10. Terminal 15 wake-up wire
11. On-board computer signal
12. F-CAN high

**612**

## Steering column switch cluster (SZL), removing and installing

– Disconnect negative (-) battery cable and cover battery terminal to keep cable from accidentally contacting terminal.

> **CAUTION—**
> • *Prior to disconnecting the battery, read the battery disconnection cautions given in* **001 Warnings and Cautions**.

– Remove driver airbag in steering wheel. See **721 Airbag System (SRS).**

> **WARNING—**
> • *The steering wheel mounted airbag is an explosive device. Treat with extreme caution. Follow the airbag removal procedure in* **721 Airbag System (SRS)**.
> • *Airbag removal may set SRS fault codes. The SRS indicator light remains ON until problems are corrected and fault memory cleared.*

– Extend steering column as far back and as low as possible.

– Remove steering wheel. See **320 Steering and Wheel Alignment**.

> **CAUTION—**
> • *Do not move front wheels from straight-ahead position while steering wheel is off.*
> • *While steering wheel is off, do not turn or twist the airbag and horn contact spring.*

◄ Use plastic prying tool to unclip upper steering column cover at sides.

◄ Tilt trim up and unclip gap cover pins (**arrows**). Remove trim.

– Convertible: Detach hands-free microphone from trim.

– Place steering column in extended position and as high as possible. Do not lock manual adjustment lever.

*Airbag and horn contact spring, steering angle sensor, removing and installing*

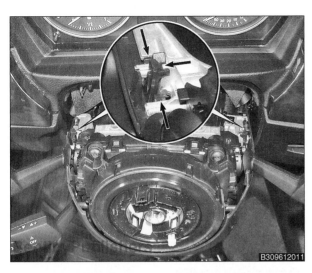

◀ Release steering column lower trim cover detent lugs (**arrows**) and detach lower trim.

◀ Remove SZL mounting screws (**arrows**) and pull cluster back.

– Detach electrical connectors and remove SZL.

– Installation is reverse of removal. Be sure to connect BMW scan tool or equivalent and carry out steering angle sensor adjustment.

## Airbag and horn contact spring, steering angle sensor, removing and installing

– Remove SZL. See **Steering column switch cluster (SZL), removing and installing** in this repair group.

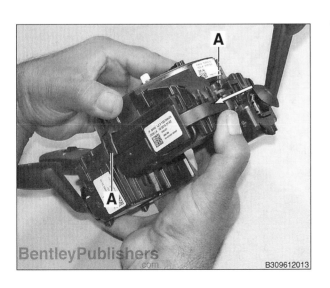

◀ Working at contact spring module:
• Unlock catches **A**.
• Press lock (**arrow**) and pull contact spring off SZL (**arrow**).

**CAUTION—**
• *Do not rotate inner ring of contact spring. If necessary, secure ring using adhesive tape.*

612

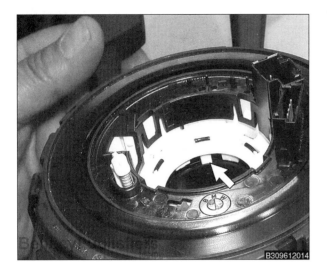

◁ When installing contact spring, make sure guide (**arrow**) slides into notch in switch cluster.

## DASHBOARD SWITCHES

### Light switch, removing and installing

◁ Use plastic prying tool to pry out left side dashboard trim strip and vent (**arrow**).

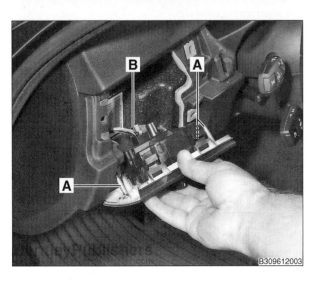

◁ Use plastic prying tool to lever out light switch bezel with switch.

- Note that switch bezel snaps into dashboard using lugs **A**.
- Unclip switch electrical connector (**B**).

– Detach switch from bezel and replace.

## START STOP switch, removing and installing

— Remove hazard warning and central locking switch. See **Hazard warning, central locking and DTC switch assembly, removing and installing** in this repair group.

◁ Use plastic prying tool to pry off right side dashboard decorative strip.

◁ Pull back decorative strip and press on lock tabs (**arrow**) to separate ignition ribbon harness from START STOP switch.

— Press together catches on START STOP switch to remove from decorative strip.

— Installation is reverse of removal.

## Hazard warning, central locking and DTC switch assembly, removing and installing

◁ Use plastic prying tools to lever out hazard warning, central locking and DTC switches on center dashboard. Detach electrical harness from back of switch assembly after pulling it out slightly.

— Installation is reverse of removal.

**612**

## OTHER SWITCHES

### Back-up light switch

For manual transmission back-up light switch replacement, see **230 Manual Transmission**.

Automatic transmission electronics combines the following functions:

• Neutral safety switch.

• Back-up light switch.

### Brake light switch, removing and installing

– Remove left lower dashboard trim (above pedals). See **513 Interior Trim**.

◀ Working at pedal cluster, disconnect electrical harness connector (**arrow**) from brake light switch.

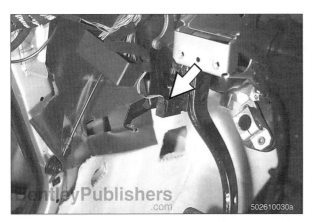

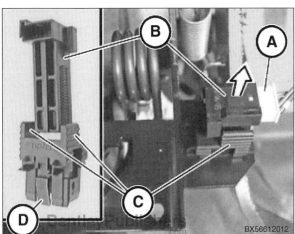

◀ Pull brake light switch (**B**) from bracket mounting in direction of **arrow**.

– To install, depress brake pedal and hold down with brake pedal prop tool.

– Slide brake light switch (**B**) as far as it will go into brake light switch holder (**C**).

– Attach harness connector (**A**).

– Grip brake light switch holder (**C**), slowly return brake pedal to rest position and pull switch back to stop.

– Check function of brake light switch with helper.

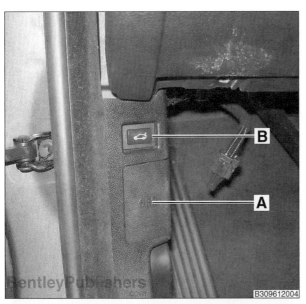

## Trunk lid or tailgate release button, replacing

◄ Working at left door jamb:

- Remove OBD II plug cover (**A**).
- Reach through opening and push out trunk lid or tailgate switch (**B**).
- Detach electrical connector.

– Installation is reverse of removal.

## iDrive controller, removing and installing

– Remove shifter knob. See **250 Gearshift Linkage**.

◄ Use plastic prying tool to pry up center console cover. Note locations of locking clips on underside of cover (**arrows**).

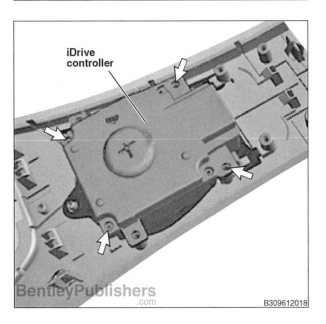

◄ Working at underside of center console cover:

- Remove iDrive controller mounting screws (**arrows**).
- Slide controller forward to remove.

– If installing new controller:

- Use plastic prying tool to pry controller knob off old unit and press on new unit.
- Use BMW scan tool or equivalent to program and code new unit.

**612**

### Driver door switch module, removing and installing

The master front and rear window switches are ganged with child safety switch and outside mirror control switch on the driver door arm rest.

◄ Using plastic prying tool, pry complete assembly out of arm rest.

− Disconnect electrical harnesses and remove module.

− Installation is reverse of removal.

### Passenger door power window switch, removing and installing

− Using plastic prying tool, pry door switch unit from door arm rest.

− Disconnect harness connector from switch unit.

− Installation is reverse of removal.

# 620 Instruments

## GENERAL

This repair group covers removal and installation of the instrument cluster. The cluster does not contain any replaceable components. If necessary, replace the entire unit.

See **020 Maintenance** for an explanation of condition based service (CBS) and Check Control, both of which use instrument cluster displays.

## INSTRUMENT CLUSTER

### Instrument cluster layout

1. Speedometer

2. Indicator and warning lights

3. Tachometer

4. Trip odometer reset button

5. Fuel gauge

6. Clock
   Outside temperature
   Check Control
   Indicator and warning lights

7. Automatic transmission gear selected
   On-board computer (BC)
   Next scheduled service
   Odometer
   Trip odometer
   Flat tire monitor (FTM) initialization
   Engine oil level
   Settings and information

8. Fuel mileage gauge

**620**

*Instrument cluster replacement*

## INSTRUMENT CLUSTER SERVICE

### Instrument cluster replacement

If replacing the instrument cluster, keep in mind that vehicle odometer reading and other data is redundantly stored in the instrument cluster, footwell module (FRM) and car access system (CAS) module.

If FRM, CAS and the instrument cluster are replaced simultaneously, the odometer reading may be lost as a result.

### Instrument cluster, removing and installing

– Extend steering column as far back and down as it will go.

◄ Remove instrument cluster fasteners (**arrows**). Tilt cluster backward (**curved arrow**) out of dashboard.

– Unlock and disconnect harness connectors from back of cluster. Slide cluster sideways to clear steering wheel.

– Installation is reverse of removal, noting the following:

• Make sure instrument cluster harness connector locking levers are in fully unlocked position before installing connector.

• Recode new or replacement cluster using BMW scan tool or equivalent.

| Tightening torque | |
|---|---|
| Instrument cluster to dashboard | 1.5 Nm (8.5 in-lb) |

# 630 Lights

## GENERAL

This repair group covers interior and exterior lights.

See also:

- **600 Electrical System–General** for bus system basics and footwell module (FRM) replacement
- **611 Wipers and Washers** for headlight washer system
- **612 Switches** for light switch replacement
- **620 Instruments** for instrument cluster removal
- **ECL Electrical Component Locations**
- **ELE Electrical Wiring Diagrams**

**630**

## Bulb applications

Bulb applications for Sedan and Sports Wagon models are in **Table a**; for Coupe and Convertible models in **Table b**.

| Table a. Bulb applications: Sedan, Sports Wagon | |
|---|---|
| **Location** | **Type and wattage** |
| **Headlights**<br>• Low beam (halogen)<br>• Low beam (xenon)<br>• High beam | <br>H7 55 w<br>D1S<br>H7 55 w |
| **Back-up lights** | P21 w |
| **Brake light**<br>• Sides<br>• Center | <br>21 w<br>LEDs |
| **Licence plate lights**<br>• to 09 / 2007<br>• from 09 / 2007 | <br>Festoon 5 w<br>LEDs |
| **Adaptive brake light** | H21 w |
| **Taillights** | 21 w |
| **Turn signals**<br>• Front<br> to 09 / 2008<br> from 09 / 2008<br>• Rear<br>• Side | <br><br>21 w<br>LEDs<br>21w<br>WY5 w ST |
| **Interior lights** | |
| • Cargo area light (D-pillar) | W5 w |
| • Dome and map lights, front or rear | Xenon W6 w |
| • Door courtesy lights | W3 w |
| • Footwell lights | W5 w |
| • Glove compartment | Festoon C5 w |
| • Trunk light | Festoon C10 w |
| • Vanity mirror | Festoon C10 w |

| Table b. Bulb applications: Coupe, Convertible | |
|---|---|
| **Location** | **Type and wattage** |
| **Headlights**<br>• Driving light (xenon)<br>• Parking light<br>• Turning light | <br>D1S<br>H8 35 w<br>H3 55 w |
| **Back-up lights** | W16 w |
| **Brake light**<br>• Sides<br>• Center | <br>W16 w<br>LEDs |
| **Licence plate lights**<br>• to 09 / 2007<br>• from 09 / 2007 | <br>Festoon 5 w<br>LEDs |
| **Adaptive brake light** | H21 w |
| **Taillights** | LEDs |
| **Turn signals**<br>• Front<br>  to 09 / 2008<br>  from 09 / 2008<br>• Rear<br>• Side | <br><br>24 w<br>LEDs<br>21 w<br>WY5 w ST |
| **Interior lights** | |
| • Dome and map lights, front or rear | Xenon W6 w |
| • Door courtesy lights | W3 w |
| • Footwell lights | W5 w |
| • Glove compartment | Festoon C5 w |
| • Trunk light | Festoon C10 w |
| • Vanity mirror | Festoon C10 w |

## Exterior lights overview

The exterior lighting system consists of:

• Headlights with low beams, high beams and parking (side) lights

• Turn signal lights

• Brake lights including center brake light

• Side turn signals

• Taillights

• Back-up lights

• Front foglights

• Rain and light sensor with automatic driving light control

The optional bi-xenon headlights are available in conjunction with adaptive headlights.

**630**

## Exterior lighting control modules

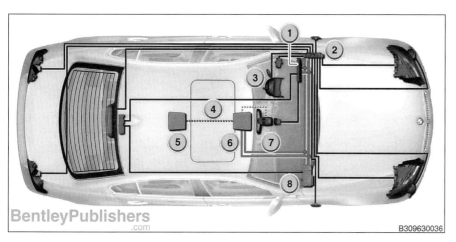

1. Car access system (CAS)
2. Footwell module (FRM)
3. Steering column switch cluster (SZL)
4. Multiple restraint system (MRS)
5. Ultrasonic passenger compartment sensor (USIS)
6. Roof function center (FZD)
7. Rain and light sensor (RLS)
8. Junction box electronic module (JBE)

**Footwell module (FRM)** is the master control module for all exterior lighting functions. Exterior light systems (headlights and side and parking lights) are switched ON and OFF by the light switch via the FRM. The hazard light switch is connected directly to the FRM.

**Steering column switch cluster (SZL)** directly provides information to flash headlights, activate high beams or activate turn signal indicators to the FRM via a hard wired connection.

**Rain and light sensor (RLS)** provides the FRM with light switching information in the "automatic" driving lights setting.

**Junction box electronics module (JBE)** provides a pass-through function for the signals from the SZL, which are transmitted on the F-CAN to the DSC module.

**Junction box (JB)** fuses supply power to the FRM.

**Car access system (CAS)** provides ignition switch information to the FRM.

**Roof function center (FZD)** routes information from RLS to FRM via K-CAN. RLS provides information to switch headlights ON or OFF based on ambient light levels.

**Ultrasonic passenger compartment protection sensor (USIS)** is part of the optional alarm system. If the alarm is triggered, a request is sent to the FRM to trigger a visual alarm by flashing the lights. Flashing of the lights in association with arming and disarming the alarm system can be set using car / key memory (personal profile). See **515 Central Locking and Anti-theft**.

**Multiple restraint system (MRS)** sends a crash signal to the FRM to activate the hazard lights and illuminate the interior lights.

## Exterior lighting functions

◀ **Automatic headlight control** is activated by turning the light switch to the AUTO headlight position. Driving lights are switched ON together with the side lights by the automatic driving lights control system. Lights activation is based on input from the rain and light sensor (RLS), depending on ambient lighting conditions (tunnel, twilight, rain or snow).

In case of RLS malfunction, FRM illuminates the headlights.

> **WARNING—**
> • The automatic headlight control cannot serve as a substitute for personal judgement in determining when to switch the lights ON. For example: The system cannot detect fog.

**Foglights** are activated by pressing the foglight button; switch parking lights or low beam headlights ON first.

**Turn signals** are activated via the turn signal stalk on the SZL, an optical switch. A defective bulb in the front or rear turn signals results in the remaining lights flashing at double the normal rate.

The one- touch function flashes the turn signals three times. The function can be modified using car / key memory (personal profile). See **515 Central Locking and Anti-theft**.

◀ **Hazard lights** are activated by depressing the hazard light switch (ganged with the central locking and DTC switches and stratification thumbwheel) located in the center of the dashboard.

Turn signals have priority if the hazard flashers are activated first. Hazard flashers have priority if the turn signal is activated first.

Vehicle with alarm system: Hazard lights flash for up to 6 minutes if alarm is triggered and not switched off. FRM receives the flasher request via K-CAN from USIS module.

When central locking is activated, CAS supplies a signal to FRM via K-CAN to flash the hazard lights indicating that the vehicle is locked. This visual feedback can be deactivated using car / key memory (personal profile). See **515 Central Locking and Anti-theft**.

**Taillights**. In case of a taillight bulb failure or other malfunction, the brake light bulbs are used as a substitute. The bulbs are dimmed by a pulsed signal to provide substitute taillights.

**630**

*Exterior lighting functions*

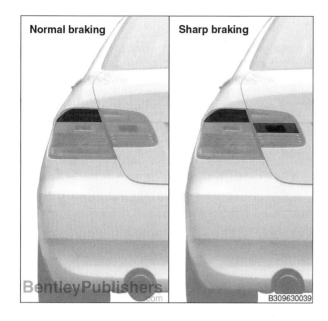

Normal braking | Sharp braking

B309630039

**Brake lights, brake force display**. Brake lights illuminate in two stages, depending on how sharply the brakes are applied:

• Normal braking: Outboard and center brake lights illuminate

• Sharp braking: brake light bulb in trunk lid or tailgate also illuminates.

Brake force display, standard on 3 Series vehicles, is activated at speeds above 5 kph (3 mph). The threshold for triggering brake force display is deceleration above $5 \text{ m} / \text{s}^2$ (0.003 mach).

The brake light switch is powered by a 5 v signal from CAS with terminal R ON.

**Back-up lights**. Automatic transmission signal for activating back-up lights is communicated from EGS module via PT-CAN to FRM.

Manual transmission back-up light signal is communicated by reverse gear switch to FRM.

**Bulb monitoring**. FRM monitors the exterior lighting system with the lights switched ON or OFF if terminal 15 is active (ignition ON).

Cold monitoring with lights OFF: Brief current pulses, so short that bulbs are not illuminated, are used for measurement purposes. FRM evaluates individual bulb outputs to establish whether there is a line break or a bulb is defective.

The number of current pulses is large during the first 4 seconds after terminal 15 ON to check whether bulbs are in working order before setting off. This function is referred to as the predrive check. The number of pulses is then reduced after the predrive check. Pulsed power is then applied to the bulbs every 1.5 minutes.

The center brake light is not included in the cold monitoring system because LEDs react too fast to the current pulse and would consequently light up. The bi-xenon headlight is also not included in the cold monitoring because of legal restrictions.

Hot monitoring with lights ON is based on measuring the current of individual bulbs, used to detect an overload or interruption (break).

**Pathway / follow me home light** is activated by the headlight flasher position on the SZL stalk.

## Exterior lighting circuit diagram

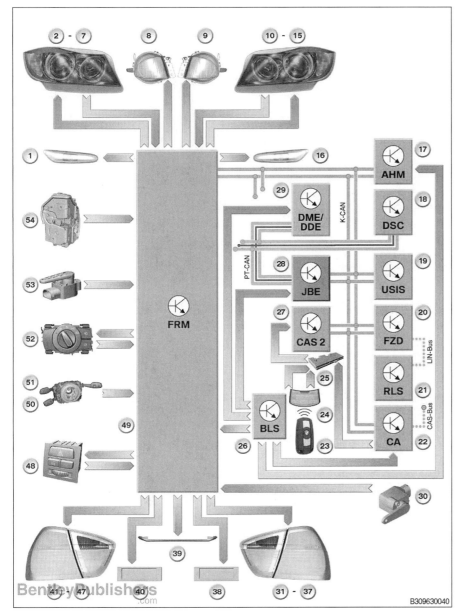

1. Left side turn signal
2. Left headlight vertical aim control stepper motor
3. Left front turn signal
4. Left high beam shutter
5. Left side light
6. Left low beam
7. Left high beam
8. Left front foglight
9. Right front foglight
10. Right high beam
11. Right low beam
12. Right side light
13. Right high beam shutter
14. Right front turn signal
15. Right headlight vertical aim control stepper motor
16. Right side turn signal
17. Not used
18. Dynamic stability control (DSC)
19. Ultrasonic passenger compartment protection sensor (USIS)
20. Roof function center (FZD)
21. Rain and light sensor (RLS)
22. Comfort access (CA) module
23. Remote key (identification transmitter)
24. Rear window antenna
25. Remote control receiver
26. Brake light switch
27. Car access system (CAS)
28. Junction box electronic module (JBE)
29. Engine control module (ECM)
30. Rear ride height sensor
31. Right rear turn signal
32. Right taillight, outboard
33. Right brake light
34. Right brake force display light
35. Right rear foglight
36. Right taillight, inboard
37. Right back-up light
38. Right license plate light

**630**

## Exterior lighting circuit diagram (continued)

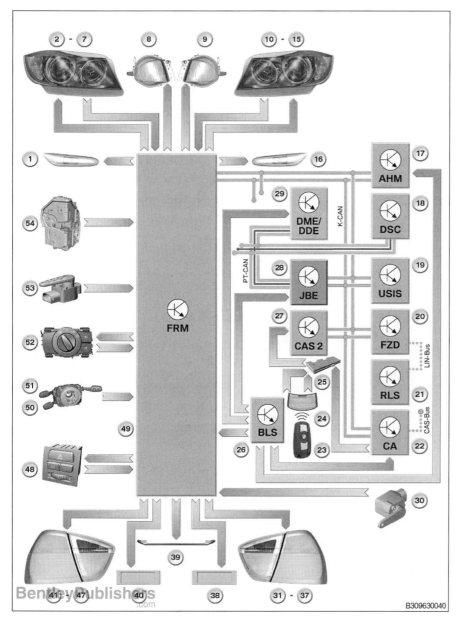

**39.** Center brake light

**40.** Left license plate light

**41.** Left back-up light

**42.** Left taillight, inboard

**43.** Left rear foglight

**44.** Left brake force display light

**45.** Left brake light

**46.** Left taillight, outboard

**47.** Left rear turn signal

**48.** Hazard warning switch

**49.** Footwell module (FRM)

**50.** Steering column high beam and turn signal switch

**51.** Steering column switch cluster (SZL)

**52.** Light switch

**53.** Front ride height sensor

**54.** Door contact switch

• **CAS-bus** K-bus protocol

• **K-CAN** Body bus

• **LIN-bus** Local interconnected network bus

• **PT-CAN** Powertrain bus

B309630040

## Bi-xenon headlights

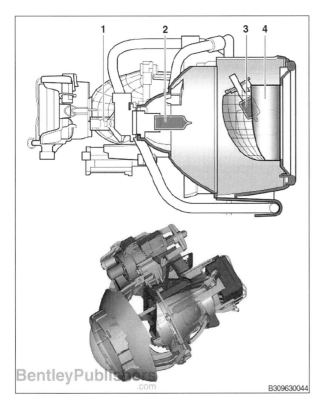

The optional bi-xenon headlight is equipped with an electrically activated shutter which directs the low beam cone of light in the same direction as the high beam.

1.   Xenon bulb
2.   H8 bulb for side light and daytime running light
3.   H3 bulb for cornering light
4.   Mirror for cornering light

## Adaptive headlight control

The bi-xenon headlights are equipped with an adaptive headlight control system.

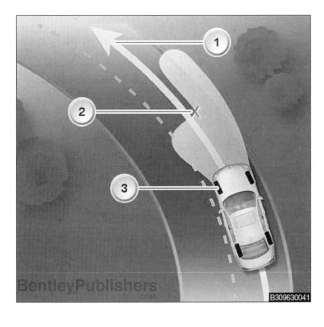

Adaptive headlights rotate slightly as the front wheels (**3**) turn, providing an enhanced lighting path as the vehicle travels through a turn. The light / dark transition point (**2**) is designed to be to the right of the anticipated curve of the vehicle (**1**) in order to reduce the risk of glare to oncoming traffic.

Headlights are rotated via a stepper motor in each headlight assembly. Footwell module (FRM) controls the amount of headlight rotation based on the following information:

• Steering angle (from steering angle sensor)
• Road speed (from vehicle speed sensors)
• Yaw rate (from DSC acceleration sensor)

**630**

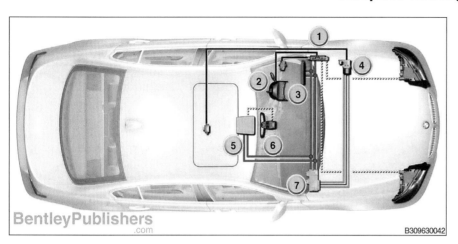

BentleyPublishers.com

B309630042

## Adaptive headlight control modules

1. Footwell module (FRM)
2. Steering column switch cluster (SZL)
3. Car access system (CAS)
4. Dynamic stability control (DSC) module
5. Roof function center (FZD)
6. Rain and light sensor (RLS)
7. Junction box electronic module (JBE)

## Adaptive headlight functions

**Car access system (CAS)** provides ignition switch information to footwell module (FRM).

**Footwell module (FRM)** controls adaptive headlight system. FRM is connected to:

- K-CAN
- PT-CAN
- LIN-bus.

FRM is gateway between K-CAN and LIN-bus. FRM receives data via PT-CAN, K-CAN and LIN-bus, but it only transmits data via K-CAN and LIN-bus. If FRM is replaced, use BMW scan tool to enter VIN and to code FRM to vehicle. This adaptation activates adaptive headlights. FRM replacement is covered in **600 Electrical System–General**.

**Dynamic stability control (DSC) module** sends yaw rate and vehicle speed signals to FRM.

**Junction box electronics module (JBE)** transmits steering angle data from steering column switch cluster (SZL) to FRM.

**Rain and light sensor (RLS)** is at base of inside rear view mirror. RLS signals switch automatic driving lights ON and activate adaptive headlight control in FRM.

**Roof function center (FZD)** is gateway for RLS. FZD transfers LIN-bus signal of RLS via K-CAN to FRM.

**Ultrasonic passenger compartment protection sensor (USIS)** transmits anti-theft alarm system signal via K-CAN to FRM.

**Multiple restraint system (MRS)** supplies crash signal to FRM.

**Bi-xenon headlight control module** is mounted on the headlight assembly and supplies power and ignition voltage for the bi-xenon light bulb, integrated in the swivel section of the adaptive headlight.

**Zero position Hall sensor** registers zero position of swivel module.

**Stepper motor** rotates the swivel module. A separate stepper motor controls headlight vertical aim control.

If the headlight is replaced, headlight-specific coding is necessary for the stepper motor controller. If this adaptation is not performed, adaptive function appear to operate, but not correctly. The swivel range and zero point can vary from vehicle model to vehicle model.

**Stepper motor controller** is mounted on side of bi-xenon headlight and controls and monitors movement of both stepper motors. If controller is replaced, use BMW scan tool to store VIN and enter headlight related coding in controller. Adaptive headlights do not function without this adaptation.

Take care when replacing stepper motor controller to ensure that controller housing gasket is fitted and seals correctly.

**Turn signal and high beam switch** is integrated in steering column switch cluster (SZL). Signal from this switch goes directly to FRM via hard-wired connection.

**DSC sensor** provides vehicle yaw (rotation of vehicle about the vertical axis) data via DSC module to FRM.

**Wheel speed sensors** supply vehicle speed data via DSC module to FRM.

**Steering angle sensor**, integrated in the SZL, is optical sensor providing steering wheel angle data via DSC module to FRM.

**Front and rear ride-height sensors** on front and rear axles provide signals for headlight vertical aim control and are evaluated by FRM.

**Brake light switch** signal is used by FRM to adjust headlight vertical aim.

## Adaptive headlight system diagnosis

Use BMW scan tool or equivalent to set adaptive headlights to diagnosis mode for following:

• Read-out of relevant bus signals with vehicle stationary:
  Road speed
  Yaw rate
  Steering angle
• Checking signal plausibility
• Checking that conditions for activation are fulfilled:
  Rain and light sensor status
  Light switch status.

Missing or non-plausible bus signals are stored as fault codes in FRM. Fault types are stored in the stepper motor controller, accessed via FRM.

Note that if headlight rotation function is being checked while vehicle is standing still, headlights only rotate right.

**630**

## Adaptive headlight control inputs-outputs

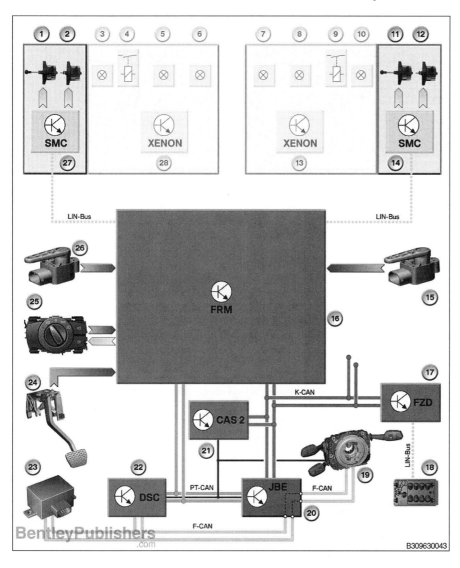

B309630043

1. Left headlight vertical aim control stepper motor

2. Left headlight adaptive stepper motor

3. Left side light

4. Left high beam shutter

5. Left bi-xenon bulb

6. Left high beam bulb

7. Right high beam bulb

8. Right bi-xenon bulb

9. Right high beam shutter

10. Right side light

11. Right headlight adaptive stepper motor

12. Right headlight vertical aim control stepper motor

13. Right bi-xenon control module

14. Right stepper motor controller

15. Rear ride-height sensor

16. Footwell module (FRM)

17. Roof function center (FZD)

18. Rain and light sensor (RLS)

19. Steering column switch cluster (SZL)

20. Junction box electronics module (JBE)

21. Car access system (CAS)

22. Dynamic stability control (DSC) module

23. DSC sensor

24. Brake light switch

25. Light switch

26. Front ride height sensor

27. Left stepper motor controller

28. Left bi-xenon control module

• **F-CAN** Chassis bus

• **K-CAN** Body bus

• **LIN-bus** Local interconnected network bus

• **PT-CAN** Powertrain bus

## Adaptive headlight control circuit diagram

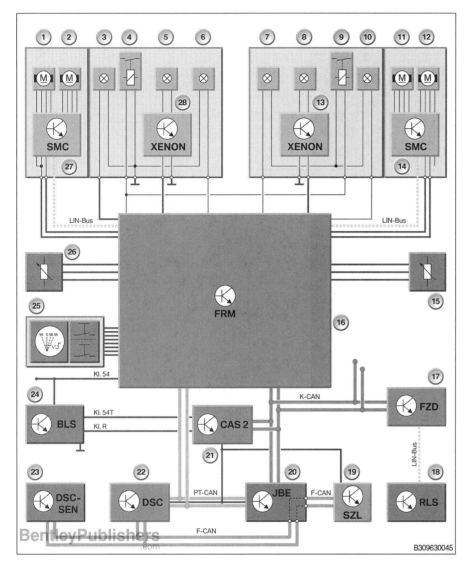

B309630045

1. Left headlight vertical aim control stepper motor
2. Left headlight adaptive stepper motor
3. Left side light
4. Left high beam shutter
5. Left bi-xenon bulb
6. Left high beam bulb
7. Right high beam bulb
8. Right bi-xenon bulb
9. Right high beam shutter
10. Right side light
11. Right headlight adaptive stepper motor
12. Right headlight vertical aim control stepper motor
13. Right bi-xenon control module
14. Right stepper motor controller
15. Rear ride-height sensor
16. Footwell module (FRM)
17. Roof function center (FZD)
18. Rain and light sensor (RLS)
19. Steering column switch cluster (SZL)
20. Junction box electronics module (JBE)
21. Car access system (CAS)
22. Dynamic stability control (DSC) module
23. DSC sensor
24. Brake light switch
25. Light switch
26. Front ride height sensor
27. Left stepper motor controller
28. Left bi-xenon control module
- **F-CAN** Chassis bus
- **K-CAN** Body bus
- **LIN-bus** Local interconnected network bus
- **PT-CAN** Powertrain bus

**630**

## Interior lights–overview

Interior lights consist of:
- Front dome lights with switches
- Rear dome lights with switches
- Reading lights with switches
- Trunk light (Sedan, Coupe, Convertible)
- Cargo compartment light (Sports Wagon)
- D-pillar lights (Sports Wagon)
- Vanity mirror light, driver and passenger
- Footwell lights, driver and passenger
- Door courtesy lights
- Door handle courtesy lights

## Interior lighting modules

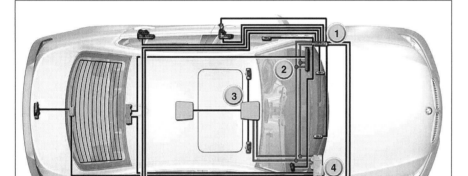

1. Footwell module (FRM)
2. Car access module (CAS)
3. Roof function center (FZD)
4. Junction box electronics module (JBE)

B309630046

## Interior lighting modules and functions

Interior lighting function is distributed over several control module that communicate with each other via K-CAN.

### Footwell module (FRM)

FRM is responsible for switching interior lighting ON and OFF.

FRM interior lighting outputs are pulse-width modulated to ensure that interior lighting functions are at a constant brightness level despite voltage fluctuations. Pulse-width modulation is also used for the soft ON / OFF function.

FRM controls the following:
- Switching interior lighting ON / OFF
- Electric load shut-down after 16 minutes
- Instrument lighting (terminal 58g)

FRM signals to switch interior lighting ON are either internal to FRM or received via K-CAN (body bus):

- Central locking signals from remote key via CAS
- Crash signal from MRS
- Door contact signal from FRM
- Driver door lock cylinder unlocked
- Interior light switch via FRM and FZD
- Trunk lid or tailgate opening via JB

FRM signals to switch interior lighting OFF are via K-CAN or are obtained indirectly by the FRM:

- Central locking in central arrest, all doors and the trunk lid closed.
- Terminal R OFF after 16 minutes.
- Interior lighting button pressed for longer than 3 seconds.
- Terminal R ON with doors closed.
- Terminal 58 ON and terminal R OFF.

Interior lighting is switched OFF:

- If no door is opened within 20 seconds after remote unlocking.
- Terminal R is OFF and a vehicle door is opened for longer than 1 minute.
- Power down via diagnosis of low battery power by intelligent battery sensor (IBS).

### Electric load shutdown

Interior lighting is switched off by the FRM after 16 minutes by way of terminal R OFF. For this purpose, FRM sends the electric load shutdown information via K-CAN. FZD receives this information and switches dome lights OFF. The interior lights that are switched ON directly by FRM are also switched OFF.

### Instrument lights

 Instrument lighting via terminal 58g and K-CAN is pulse-width modulated and features two brightness levels:

- Brightness level for instrument lighting is toggled via switch on turn signal lever (lights ON).
- Brightness level for function lighting is not dimmed and is switched on at full brightness.

See **Instrument lights dimming** in this repair group.

On-board computer button

Instrument lights dimmer

B309630047

**630**

## Warnings and Cautions

> **WARNING—**
> - There is high pressure inside a halogen bulb. Bulb temperature may exceed 700° Celsius. Wear safety glasses and gloves when removing and installing a halogen bulb.
> - Do not look directly at an operating xenon bulb. The UV emissions are approximately 2.5 times that of a comparable halogen bulb.
> - When working on electrical systems, remove the fuse protecting the circuit under repair. See **ECL Electrical Component Locations** for fuse locations.

> **CAUTION—**
> - Xenon bulbs and igniter modules are electrically sensitive. Use an antistatic mat and work with caution. See **600 Electrical System–General**.
> - Do not operate the xenon control module unless a bulb is connected.
> - Before servicing the headlight system, switch electrical consumers OFF. Switch ignition OFF and remove ignition key.
> - Do not handle bulb glass with bare fingers. Dirt and skin oils cause a bulb to fail prematurely. If necessary, wipe bulb using a clean cloth dampened with rubbing alcohol.
> - Use only original equipment replacement bulbs. Non-original bulbs may cause false failure readings on the Check Control display.
> - To avoid marring car paint or trim, work with plastic prying tools or wrap the tips of tools with tape.

## HEADLIGHTS

### Halogen headlight components

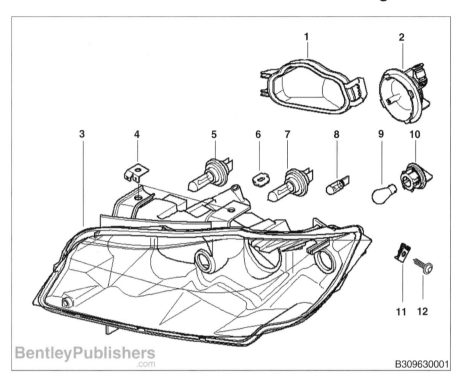

1. High beam bulb cover
2. Low beam bulb cover
3. Headlight assembly
4. Sheet metal nut
5. High beam bulb
   • H7 55 w
6. Adjusting element
7. Low beam bulb
   • H7 55 w
8. Front driving light
   • 5 w
9. Turn signal bulb
   • 21 w (amber)
10. Turn signal socket
11. Sheet metal nut
12. Sheet metal screw

### Xenon headlight components (to 09 / 2008)

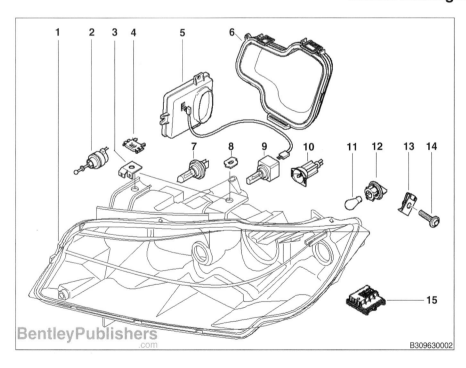

1. Headlight assembly
2. Headlight vertical aim stepper motor
3. Sheet metal nut
4. Adjusting element
5. Xenon bulb ignition unit
6. Bulb cover
7. Halogen high beam bulb
   • H7 55 w
8. Adjusting element
9. Xenon low beam bulb
   • D1S
10. Light rings
11. Turn signal bulb
   • 21 w (amber)
12. Turn signal socket
13. Sheet metal nut
14. Sheet metal screw
15. Adaptive headlight control module

**630**

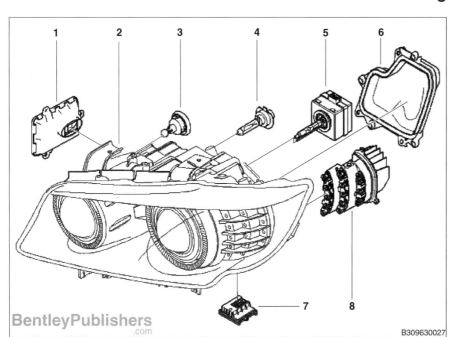

## Xenon headlight components (from 09 / 2008)

1. Xenon control module
2. Headlight assembly
3. Headlight vertical aim stepper motor
4. High beam bulb
5. Xenon low beam bulb with ignition unit
6. Bulb cover
7. Adaptive headlight control module
8. LED turn signal unit

## Headlight aim, adjusting

Adjust headlight aim with correct tire pressures, fuel tank full, and weight of one person (approximately 75 kg or 165 lb) in driver seat.

When adjusting xenon headlights, switch lights ON, then wait 80 seconds before proceeding with adjustment. Do not move or vibrate vehicle during that time.

◄ Working above and in rear of headlight housing, use screws to adjust headlight aim:

• **A**: Primarily vertical aim adjustment
• **B**: Primarily lateral aim adjustment

Adjuster **B** is hidden under plastic plug in fender edge.

Note that turning each adjuster affects both planes of adjustment.

*Headlight bulb, replacing (halogen headlight assembly)*

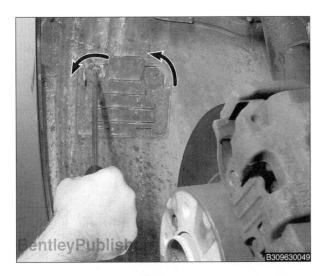

# Headlight bulb, replacing (halogen headlight assembly)

– Switch lights OFF.

– Left headlight: Remove air filter housing. See **020 Maintenance**.

### Low beam bulb access

◀ Working at front wheel housing liner, twist plastic retainers (**arrows**) and remove trapdoor behind headlight assembly.

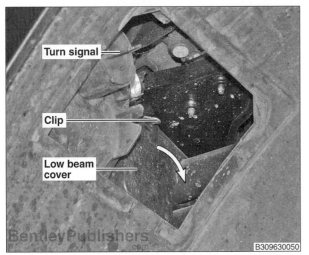

◀ Release clip and remove (**arrow**) plastic low beam bulb cover.

### High beam bulb access

◀ Working in engine compartment behind headlight, release clip and remove (**arrow**) plastic high beam bulb cover.

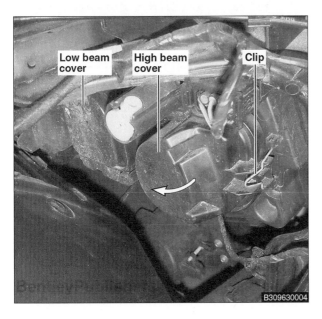

### Bulb replacement

◄ Working at back of headlight bulb (high beam bulb shown; low beam similar):

- Detach electrical connector (**A**).
- Unlock bulb retainer (**B**).
- Pull bulb out of reflector hole.

– Replace bulb. Do not touch bulb surface with bare finger. Grease from skin can cause bulb to fail prematurely.

– Installation is reverse of removal. Make sure cover is firmly seated on headlight.

## Headlight bulb, replacing (xenon headlight assembly)

Vehicles equipped with the optional xenon headlights (also known as high intensity discharge or HID headlights) utilize a special high voltage bulb and control unit for the low beam headlights. High beam bulbs are conventional halogens.

– Remove headlight fuse(s). See **ECL Electrical Component Locations**.

> **WARNING** —
>
> - *High voltage in xenon headlights is hazardous. Disconnect xenon headlight components from power supply before removing.*
>
> - *The physical and mechanical properties of xenon bulb and igniter module are very sensitive. Use an antistatic mat and work with caution.*

– Remove wheel housing trim. See **410 Fenders, Engine Hood**.

◄ Unlock headlight bulb cover retaining clips (**black arrows**) and remove cover (**curved arrow**).

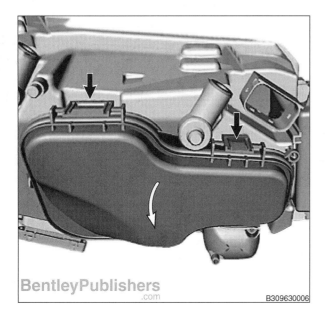

*Headlight assembly, removing and installing*

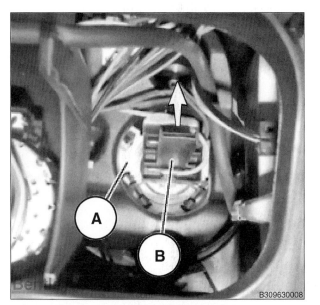

B309630008

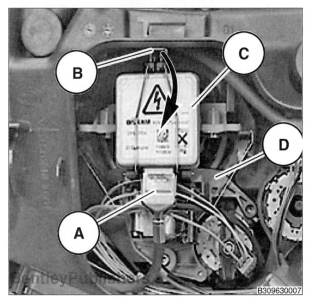

B309630007

### Halogen high beam bulb, replacing

◀ Working at back of high beam bulb:

- Grip bulb socket (**B**) and pull out of headlight (**arrow**).
- Detach bulb (**A**) from socket and remove bulb.

– Replace bulb. Do not touch bulb surface with bare finger. Grease from skin can cause bulb to fail prematurely.

– Installation is reverse of removal. Make sure cover is firmly seated on headlight.

### Xenon low beam bulb, replacing

◀ Working at back of low beam bulb:

- Detach harness connector (**A**) from xenon bulb ignition unit.
- Unlock ignition unit retainer (**B**) and fold down (**arrow**).
- Remove ignition unit (**C**) and xenon bulb together from headlight.
- When installing, make sure ignition unit seats correctly on headlight (**D**).

– Installation is reverse of removal. Make sure cover is firmly seated on headlight.

## Headlight assembly, removing and installing

– Xenon headlight: Remove headlight fuse(s). See **ECL Electrical Component Locations**.

> **WARNING—**
> • *High voltage in xenon headlights is hazardous. Disconnect xenon headlight components from power supply before removing.*
> • *The physical and mechanical properties of xenon bulb and igniter module are very sensitive. Use an antistatic mat and work with caution.*

– Remove wheel housing trim. See **410 Fenders, Engine Hood**.

– Remove front bumper cover. See **510 Exterior Trim, Bumpers**.

– Remove headlight washer system high-pressure nozzle, if equipped. See **611 Wipers and Washers**.

**630**

*Headlight assembly, removing and installing*

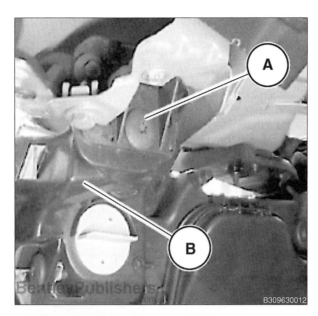

◄ Working from underneath wheel housing arch, remove screw (**A**) on headlight arm (**B**).

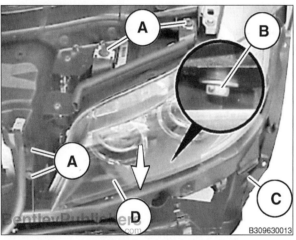

◄ Working in front of headlight:

- Remove headlight assembly mounting screws (**A**).
- Detach wiring harness fastener (**C**) on headlight arm. Remove high-pressure line and wiring harness from headlight arm.
- Pull out headlight (**D**) slightly and disconnect harness connector in back. Remove headlight in direction of arrow.

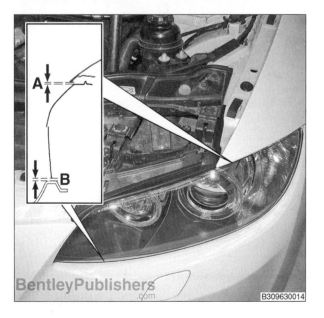

◄ When installing, set gaps from top (below fender) and bottom (above bumper cover) according to specifications.

**Headlight installation gaps**

| | |
|---|---|
| Dimension **A** (below fender edge) | 4.0 ± 1.0 mm (0.16 ± 0.04 in) |
| Dimension **B** (above bumper cover) | 3.0 ± 1.3 mm (0.12 ± 0.05 in) |

**Tightening torques**

| | |
|---|---|
| Headlight arm to headlight assembly | 6.0 Nm (53 in-lb) |
| Headlight assembly to body member | 6.0 Nm (53 in-lb) |

– Adjust headlight aim when done. See **Headlight aim, adjusting** in this repair group.

## EXTERIOR LIGHTS

### Taillight failure

In E92 (Coupe) model produced up to January 21, 2008, a "rear bulb failure" fault message or code may indicate poor contact between taillight bulb socket and bulb.

— In case of taillight failure, inspect taillight bulbs and sockets, noting the following:

- Updated bulb sockets produced up to mid-April 2008 have an additional bulb retention collar.
- Updated bulb sockets produced mid-April 2008 and later have extended bulb retention clips but no retention collar.
- The production date code is shown on the label in the format dd.mm.yy.

— Check with an authorized BMW parts department for the updated taillight socket by part number. Replace as necessary. Note that a new socket comes equipped with a new bulb.

### Brake force display light failure

In E92 (Coupe) or E93 (Convertible) model produced from August 31, 2006 to July 2, 2007, REAR LIGHT FAILURE displayed in Check Control or an inoperative brake force display lights may indicate light bulb failure or loose contact between light bulb and socket.

Depending on the version of the FRM (footwell module) the following fault codes may be set:

- A8C0 / 9320 Brake force display right defective
- A8BF / 931F Brake force display left defective

◄ Brake force display bulb and socket are in trunk lid taillight housing (**arrow**).

B309630009

630

*Front turn signal bulb, replacing*

◁ Open trunk lid, remove trunk lid trim and remove brake force display bulb and socket (**arrow**).

◁ Check bulb for failure. Use a 12 volt power supply if necessary.

– If bulb is faulty, replace.

– If bulb is not faulty, replace both sockets.

– Vehicle produced before July 3, 2007: Replace both sockets regardless of bulb condition.

| Brake force display replacement bulb and socket | |
|---|---|
| Bulb | Part no. 63 21 7 160 788 |
| Socket | Part no. 63 21 7 207 528 |

– When finished, clear fault codes using BMW scan tool or equivalent.

## Front turn signal bulb, replacing

◁ Working at front wheel housing liner, twist plastic retainers (**arrows**) and remove trapdoor behind headlight assembly.

◄ Twist turn signal bulb socket base to remove.

– Replace bulb. Do not touch bulb surface with bare finger. Grease from skin can cause bulb to fail prematurely.

– Installation is reverse of removal.

## LED front turn signal unit, replacing

– Remove headlight assembly. See **Headlight assembly, removing and installing** in this repair group.

◄ With headlight on workbench, remove turn signal unit mounting bolts (**A**).

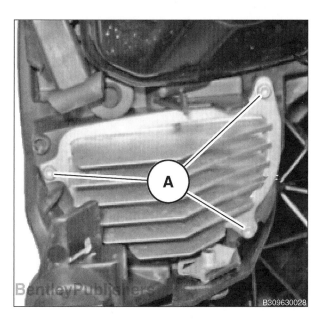

◄ Detach electrical connector (**A**) and remove turn signal unit.

– Installation is reverse of removal.

| Tightening torque | |
|---|---|
| LED turn signal unit to headlight | 1.5 Nm (13 in-lb) |

**630**

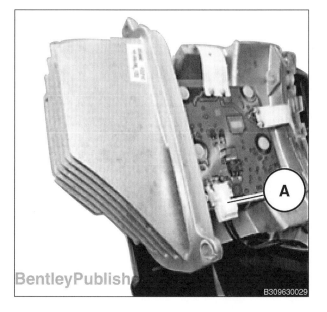

## Side turn signal bulb, replacing

◀ Use plastic prying tool or finger to push side turn signal housing forward (**white arrow**). Pivot housing away from fender (**curved arrow**) and remove.

– Rotate bulb socket and remove. Replace bulb. Do not touch bulb surface with bare finger. Grease from skin can cause bulb to fail prematurely.

– Installation is reverse of removal.

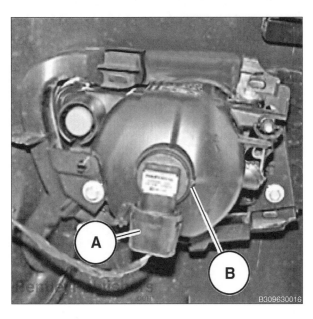

## Front foglight bulb, replacing

– Remove wheel housing trim. See **410 Fenders, Engine Hood**.

◀ Working behind end of front bumper cover:
   • Detach foglight harness connector (**A**).
   • Twist foglight socket (**B**) to remove.

– Replace bulb. Do not touch bulb surface with bare finger. Grease from skin can cause bulb to fail prematurely.

– Installation is reverse of removal.

– Adjust foglight aim through slot in front bumper cover.

## Taillight assembly (Sedan, Sports Wagon)

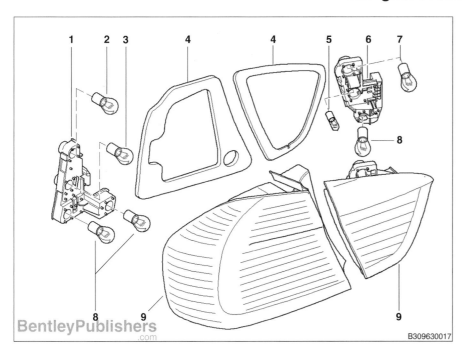

BentleyPublishers.com

B309630017

1. Taillight socket, outboard
2. Turn signal bulb
   - 21 w
3. Taillight and parking light bulb
   - 21 w
4. Sealing gasket
5. Brake force display light
   - H21 w
6. Taillight socket, inboard
7. Back-up light bulb
   - 21 w
8. Brake light bulb
   - 21 w
9. Taillight lens

## Taillight assembly (Coupe, Convertible)

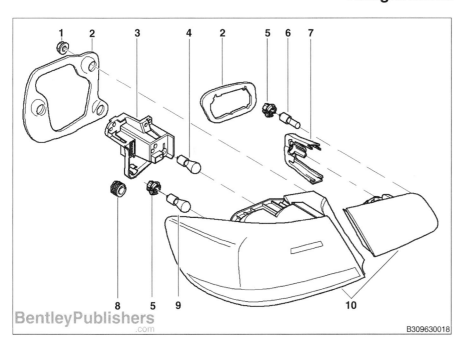

BentleyPublishers.com

B309630018

1. Nut with washer, M5
2. Sealing gasket
3. Taillight socket, outboard
4. Bulb (back-up, brake lights)
   - 16 w
5. Bulb socket
6. Brake force display light
   - H21 w
7. Mounting bow
8. Spacer
9. Amber bulb
   - 21 w
10. Taillight lens

**630**

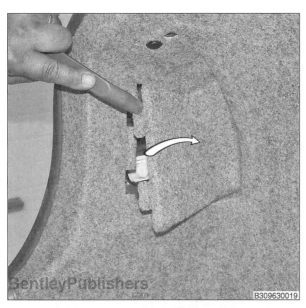

B309630019

## Taillights service

### Outboard taillight bulbs

◄ At side rear of trunk or cargo compartment, open taillight access hatch (**arrow**).

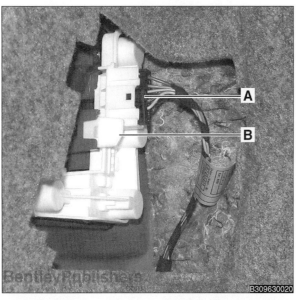

B309630020

◄ Working at taillight socket:

- Detach electrical connector (**A**).
- Press locking clip (**B**) to unlock socket.
- Remove socket to replace bulb(s). Do not touch bulb surface with bare finger. Grease from skin can cause bulb to fail prematurely.

– Installation is reverse of removal.

### Inboard taillight bulbs

– Open trunk lid or tailgate. Partially remove trunk lid or tailgate trim. See **412 Trunk Lid, Tailgate**.

– Sports Wagon: Cut out and remove sound-insulation in tailgate cavity behind taillight.

◄ Working at taillight socket:

- Detach electrical connector (**A**).
- Press (**arrow**) locking clip (**B**) to unlock socket.
- Remove socket to replace bulb(s). Do not touch bulb surface with bare finger. Grease from skin can cause bulb to fail prematurely.
- Installation is reverse of removal.

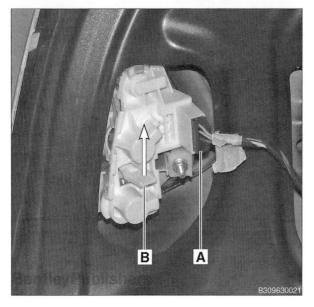

B309630021

## Center brake light service

Center brake light bulbs consist of varying numbers of LEDs. In case of bulb failure, replace the entire LED strip.

### Sedan, Coupe center brake light

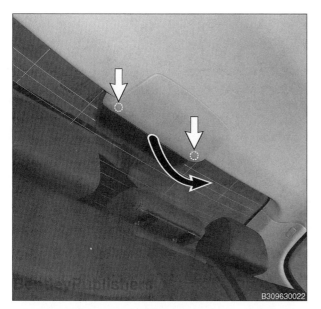

◀ Working at top of rear window, pull off center brake light cover. Cover is held by plastic clips (**white arrows**).

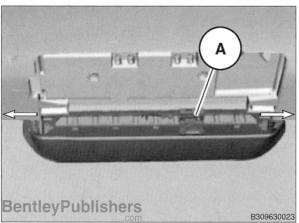

◀ Working at center brake light assembly:
  • Detach electrical connector (**A**).
  • Press (**arrows**) locking clips to unlock assembly.
  • Remove assembly to replace LED strip.

− Installation is reverse of removal.

### Sports Wagon center brake light

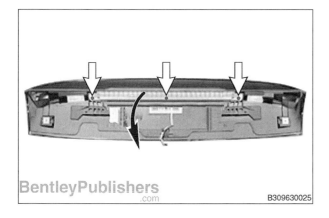

− Remove rear spoiler. See **412 Trunk Lid, Tailgate**.

◀ Remove screws (**white arrows**) and remove brake light assembly from spoiler.

− Replace LED strip.

− Installation is reverse of removal.

**630**

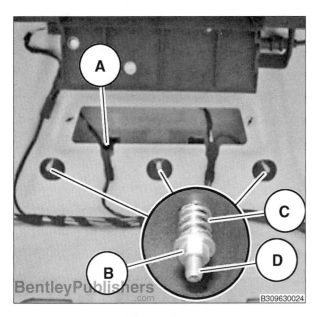

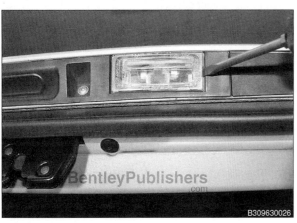

## Convertible center brake light

– Open trunk lid. Partially remove trunk lid trim. See **412 Trunk Lid, Tailgate**.

◄ Working underneath trunk lid:

- Detach electrical connector (**A**).
- Working inside trunk lid cavity, remove nuts (**B**) and pull off springs (**C**).
- Push on brake light assembly threaded studs (**D**) to remove assembly and replace LED strip.

– Installation is reverse of removal.

| Tightening torque | |
|---|---|
| Center brake light assembly to trunk lid (M5) | 2.5 ± 0.5 Nm (22 ± 4 in-lb) |

## License plate light bulb, replacing

◄ Use small screwdriver to carefully pry out license plate light. Detach electrical connector.

– Replace bulb. Do not touch bulb surface with bare finger. Grease from skin can cause bulb to fail prematurely.

– Installation is reverse of removal.

## INTERIOR LIGHTS

Sunroof, interior lights, rain sensor and other functions controlled by the FZD (roof function center) may fail owing to incorrect FZD software. To check, remove and reinstall FZD fuses in the junction box (JB) behind the glove compartment. If functionality is restored, use BMW scan tool to update FZD software.

### Sedan interior lights

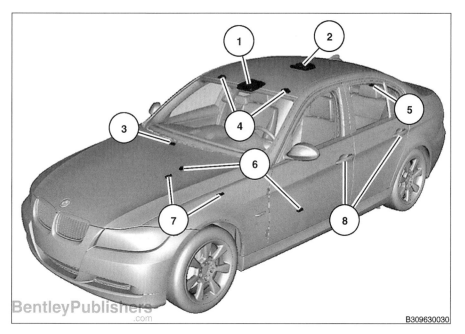

B309630030

1. Roof function center (FZD)
2. Rear dome lights
3. Glove compartment light
4. Vanity mirror lights
5. Trunk light
6. Door courtesy lights
7. Footwell lights
8. Door handle courtesy lights

### Instrument lights dimming

Instrument cluster removal and installation is covered in **620 Instruments**. Instrument lighting is via LED bulbs which are not replaceable separately.

◀ Use turn signal lever buttons to activate service information:
- Toggle button **1** up or down to scroll through instrument cluster menu items.
- When icon for instrument lights appears, press button **2** to select it.
- Toggle button **1** to increase or decrease lights brightness.
- Press button **2** to confirm selection and exit menu.

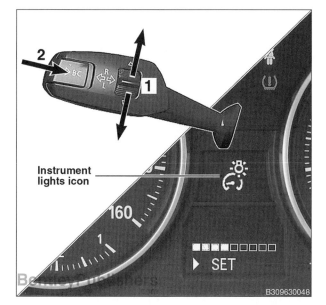

Instrument lights icon

160

SET

B309630048

**630**

B309020085

## Interior light bulb replacement

### Dome light bulbs

This procedure applies to roof function center (front dome lights) and rear dome light assembly.

◀ Use plastic prying tool to lever off dome light front plastic cover.

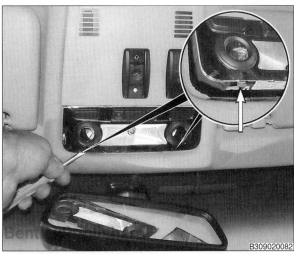

B309020082

◀ Remove roof control module (FZD).

• Retaining clips (**inset**) are aligned with center line of reading lights. Pry carefully (**arrow**) with thin bladed screwdriver

B309630052

◀ Light bulb sockets (**arrows**) are accessible from back of unit. Outer bulbs are reading lights; Inner bulb is dome light. Replace as necessary

– Installation is reverse of removal.

### Glove compartment light bulb

◄ Open glove compartment and use plastic prying tool to lever off light fixture.

– Replace light bulb.

– Installation is reverse of removal.

### Door courtesy light bulb

◄ Working at bottom of door trim panel, use plastic prying tool to remove courtesy light.

– Replace bulb.

– Installation is reverse of removal.

### Trunk light bulb

◄ Open trunk and use plastic prying tool to lever off light fixture (**arrow**).

– Replace light bulb.

– Installation is reverse of removal.

**630**

### Cargo compartment light bulb

◄ Open tailgate and use plastic prying tool to lever off light fixture.

– Replace light bulb.

– Installation is reverse of removal.

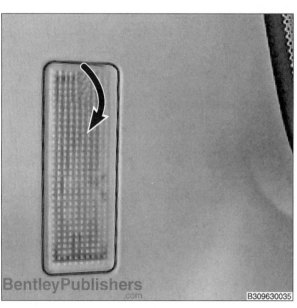

### D-pillar light bulb

◄ Open tailgate and use plastic prying tool to lever off light fixture.

– Replace light bulb.

– Installation is reverse of removal.

# 640   Heating and Air-conditioning

## GENERAL

This repair group covers heating and air-conditioning operation and component replacement.

If the air-conditioning system requires evacuation and recharging of refrigerant, use equipment specially designed for A/C system service and follow the equipment manufacturer's instructions.

See also:

• **020 Maintenance** for cabin microfilter service

• **170 Radiator and Cooling System** for cooling system service and electric cooling fan removal and installation

• **600 Electrical System–General**

### A/C system fluids

The air-conditioning refrigerant used in modern automobiles is R134a, known chemically as *tetrafluoroethane*. Strict regulations govern the handling and disposal of automotive refrigerant. Be sure to read **Warnings and Cautions** in this repair group if working with A/C and heating components.

A sticker in the engine compartment gives the manufacturer's recommendation for refrigerant capacity.

| Table a. A/C system refrigerant capacity | |
|---|---|
| R134a | 590 ± 10 grams (20.8 ± 0.4 oz) |

A synthetic oil, *polyalkylene glycol* (PAG), is used to lubricate the A/C compressor. This type of oil is highly hygroscopic (absorbs water). Be sure to immediately reseal an opened container after use.

**640**

**IHKA control panel**

**Seat heater controls**

B309640002

## IHKA basics

 The 3 Series is equipped with an integrated automatic climate control system (IHKA). The dashboard mounted control panel shares functions with iDrive (if equipped).

IHKA includes the following features:

• Dual zone control system allows driver and passenger to control temperature settings separately.

• Residual heat (REST) function allows brief periods of cabin-heating with the engine OFF.

• Condensation sensor at base of interior rear view mirror.

• Eight air control flap stepper motors (seven are identical).

• Stepper motors control via LIN-bus.

• Seat heater control.

• Rear window defogger control.

• Clutchless A/C compressor.

## IHKA system circuit diagram

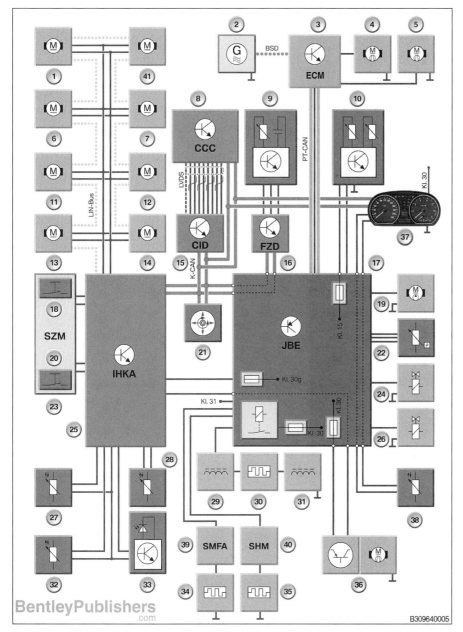

B309640005

1. Rear air distribution stepper motor
2. Alternator
3. Engine control module (ECM)
4. Electric coolant pump
5. Engine cooling fan
6. Ventilation stepper motor
7. Front air distribution stepper motor
8. Car communication computer (CCC)
9. Condensation sensor
10. Air quality (AUC) sensor
11. Fresh air - recirculation stepper motor
12. Blend flap stepper motor, left
13. Defroster flap stepper motor
14. Footwell flap stepper motor
15. Central information display (CID)
16. Roof function center (FZD)
17. Junction box electronics module (JBE)
18. Seat heater button, left
19. A/C compressor valve
20. Seat heater button, right
21. iDrive controller
22. Refrigerant pressure sensor
23. Center console switch cluster (SZM)
24. Heater valve
25. IHKA control panel
26. Auxiliary coolant pump (not for US)
27. Evaporator temperature sensor
28. Footwell temperature sensor
29. Rear window defogger lockout circuit
30. Rear window defogger
31. Rear window defogger lockout circuit
32. Ventilation temperature sensor
33. Solar sensor
34. Seat heating element, left
35. Seat heating element, right
36. Blower motor and final stage
37. Instrument cluster
38. Outside temperature sensor
39. Driver seat module
40. Seat heating module, right
41. Blend flap stepper motor, right

**640**

## IHKA control panel

1. Windshield air distribution
2. Maximum A/C setting
3. Driver temperature setting display
4. Blower speed display
5. Passenger temperature setting display
6. Residual heat (REST) button
7. Windshield defrost program
8. Face vent air distribution
9. Footwell air distribution
10. Driver temperature control knob
11. Automatic program button
12. Blower speed control (toggle switch)
13. Interior air temperature sensor intake vent
14. Recirculation control button
15. Passenger temperature control knob
16. Rear window defogger button
17. A/C button

## IHKA control panel functions

Climate control sensor data is processed in the IHKA control panel. Driver and passenger climate control settings and requests are also entered in the panel. However, the panel does not directly control all functions and components but rather makes use of other control modules for this purpose. The IHKA control panel directly monitors the following:

• Center console switch cluster (SZM) input (if equipped).
• Solar sensor input.
• Receives rear air distribution knob (rheostat) signal.
• Receives ventilation, footwell, and evaporator temperature sensor signals.

The IHKA control panel indirectly receives the following:
• Condensation sensor signal via K-CAN.

The IHKA control panel illuminates function and backlighting LEDs.

## IHKA additional controls

**Engine control module (ECM)** climate control functions are:
• Actuates engine cooling fan for cooling of A/C condenser.
• Interfaces with IHKA control panel via bus network for compressor ON signal.
• Interfaces with IHKA control panel for operation of electric coolant pump for residual heat feature.

**Junction box electronic module (JBE)** climate control functions are:

- Output signal for seat heating.
- Rear window defogger.
- Blower motor operating voltage.
- Refrigerant control valve (in A/C compressor).
- PT-CAN gateway for bidirectional communication between IHKA and ECM.
- Receives rear air distribution knob (rheostat) signal.
- Receives refrigerant pressure sensor signal.
- Receives air quality (AUC) sensor signal.
- Splice point for outside air temperature sensor.

**Roof control panel (FZD)** relays condensation sensor signal to IHKA via K-CAN.

**Car access system (CAS)** assigns a personal identification code to each remote control key. Personal identification codes are transmitted to IHKA control panel via K-CAN. When vehicle enters sleep mode, current climate control settings are stored in IHKA control panel for remote control key in use at that time.

When vehicle is unlocked via remote control key, settings for this key are called up and executed.

**Car communication computer (CCC)** processes IHKA menu and submenu signals and displays them in the dashboard mounted central information display (CID), if equipped with iDrive.

**Central information display (CID)**. Use iDrive controller to activate the following functions and display selections in CID:

- Air distribution setting. positions for defrost flaps, ventilation flaps and footwell flaps may be individually set in air distribution submenu.
- Automatic IHKA mode. Climate control intensity (low, medium or high) may be set in automatic mode submenu.

◀ **Center console switch cluster (SZM)**. Seat heater switches in SZM (if equipped) are connected via 14-wire ribbon cable directly to IHKA control panel.

**640**

Seat heater switches

B309640006

## IHKA sensors

**Interior temperature sensor**, mounted on IHKA control panel, samples cabin air by using a small electrical fan (non-replaceable) to suck air through the grill on the front face of the control panel. Sensor output is used by the IHKA panel to modulate interior temperature.

**Evaporator temperature sensor**, mounted close to the evaporator, transfers data directly via cable to IHKA control panel.

**Outside temperature sensor** is hard wired to the instrument cluster.

**Vent flap temperature sensors** are 3 NTC type sensors wired directly to the IHKA control panel:

- Stratified temperature sensor
- Ventilation temperature sensor
- Footwell temperature sensor

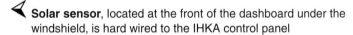

**Solar sensor**, located at the front of the dashboard under the windshield, is hard wired to the IHKA control panel

**Refrigerant pressure sensor** is in the pressure line between the A/C condenser and the evaporator. In case of excessively high or low refrigerant pressure, A/C compressor output is reduced via signal from IHKA control panel to JBE. Sensor power is provided by JB.

Solar sensor

B309640008

**Air quality (AUC) sensor**, mounted on the cabin microfilter housing, is controlled and powered by JB. AUC sensor detects the following:

- Carbon monoxide (CO)
- Hydrocarbons (HC)
- Oxides of nitrogen ($NO_X$).

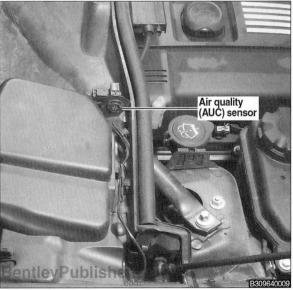

Air quality (AUC) sensor

B309640009

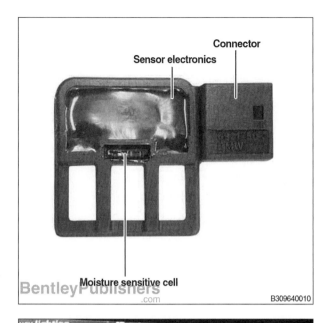

Connector

Sensor electronics

Moisture sensitive cell

BentleyPublishers.com

B309640010

◄ **Condensation sensor**, mounted under the rain and light sensor (RLS) on interior mirror base at top of windshield, is controlled and powered by the roof control module (FZD).

When moisture is detected on the windshield by the condensation sensor, the following occurs if IHKA system is set on automatic operation:

- Defroster flaps open further.
- Fresh air flaps open 100%.
- Blower speed is increased.
- Footwell flaps are closed.
- Temperature setting increases.
- Evaporator temperature threshold goes to minimum.

Front air distribution thumbwheel

B309640011

◄ **Front air distribution thumbwheel** is ganged with hazard, central locking and DTC switches located in the center of the dashboard.

Thumbwheel analog voltage signal is hard wired to IHKA control panel. The panel sends position signals to the front mixing flap stepper motor via LIN-bus.

**Rear air distribution thumbwheel** is located to the right of the rear center vent, between the front seat backs. Thumbwheel analog voltage signal is hard wired to JBE. JBE converts this signal into a digital signal, transmitted via K-CAN to IHKA control panel, which then sends the position signals to rear mixing flap stepper motor via LIN-bus.

**640**

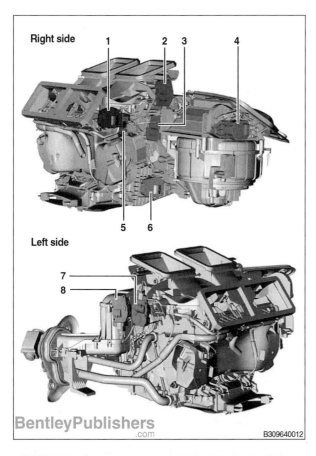

B309640012

## IHKA outputs

◄ **Stepper motors** in climate control housing under the dashboard:

1. Dashboard ventilation flaps stepper motor
2. Defroster flaps stepper motor
3. Right side blend flap stepper motor
4. Fresh air – recirculation flap stepper motor
5. Rear air distribution flap stepper motor
6. Footwell flaps stepper motor
7. Left side blend flap stepper motor
8. Front air distribution flap stepper motor

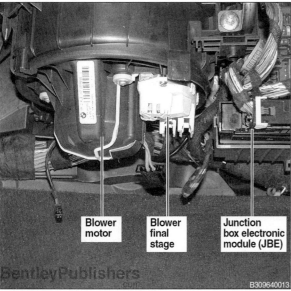

| Blower motor | Blower final stage | Junction box electronic module (JBE) |

B309640013

◄ **Blower** and **blower output stage** are mounted in the climate control housing behind the glove compartment.

Blower output stage is activated via pulse-width modulation by IHKA control panel. This connection is spliced through junction box (JB). Operating power for the blower motor is supplied by JB.

**Heater valve** controls amount of heated engine coolant sent to the heater core. Blend flaps are used to control the temperature settings on the two sides of the dual zone climate control system.

Heater valve is opened via a spring. It is operated via band pulse width modulated signal from JBE.

**A/C compressor** is clutchless. A swash plate in the compressor housing varies the amount of compression on the refrigerant. The compressor valve is controlled and powered by JBE.

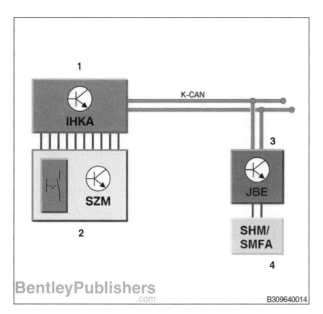

BentleyPublishers.com

B309640014

◀ **Seat heating** is controlled and powered by JBE. Request for seat heating activation is initiated from center console switch cluster (SZM) directly to IHKA control panel, then via K-CAN to JBE.

1.  IHKA control panel
2.  Center console switch cluster (SZM)
3.  Junction block electronic module (JBE)
4.  Seat heating module
    Driver seat module

**Rear window defogger** is controlled and powered by JBE. Defogging request is sent to JB from IHKA control panel via K-CAN.

BentleyPublishers.com

B309640015

◀ **Electric coolant pump** is electronically controlled by the engine control module (ECM). When residual heat (REST) function is activated, IHKA control panel interfaces with ECM to activate the coolant pump, circulating hot or warm coolant through the heater core to warm up the passenger cabin.

## IHKA non-electrical components

**Refrigerant circuit** consists of A/C compressor, expansion valve, evaporator and condenser. The system features:

* Aluminum refrigerant lines.
* Receiver-drier (with replaceable desiccant) integrated in the condenser.
* Clutchless compressor controlled by IHKA logic via JBE.
* Expansion valve accessible from engine compartment.

**Heating circuit.** Heated engine coolant is pumped by electric coolant pump through heater valve to heater core (heat exchanger). From here, coolant is routed back to engine and coolant thermostat.

**640**

B309640016

◀ **Cabin microfilter**. The microfilter with activated carbon is accessible from the engine compartment. For microfilter replacement, see **020 Maintenance**. Microfilter housing removal is covered in this repair group.

Filter service is indicated by condition based service (CBS) system. Microfilter condition is monitored by the IHKA control panel using a calculation model (algorithm) based on the following factors:

• Outside temperature.

• Signal from rain and light sensor.

• Signal from solar sensor.

• Blower voltage.

• Air quality, recognized from frequency of recirculation mode usage.

• Average vehicle road speed.

• Service interval display (SIA) timer.

IHKA panel communicates with instrument cluster via K-CAN to detect and report the following:

• Odometer reading.

• Microfilter availability in percent.

• Time remaining until next microfilter service.

## IHKA functions

◀ **Manual air distribution**. For the best possible air distribution, manually adjust air vents using IHKA panel buttons. However, automatic fine adjustment for each side is possible if vehicle is equipped with iDrive.

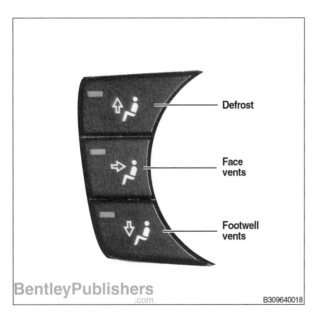

Defrost

Face vents

Footwell vents

B309640018

Driver temperature control knob

BentleyPublishers.com

B309640017

◀ **Temperature** is adjusted using separate driver and passenger temperature control knobs on IHKA control panel. Interior temperature is calculated from values measured by interior temperature sensor on IHKA panel and footwell temperature sensors. System also responds to outside temperature sensor signals.

Temperature control is via 2 air blend flaps in climate control housing.

**MAX** button selects maximum cooling with just one press of button. With MAX button pressed:

• Defrost deactivates.

• Temperature control deactivates

• Air-conditioning activates.

• Ventilation flaps open fully.

• Recirculation mode activates.

BentleyPublishers.com

B309640019

◀ **AUTO** button activates automatic airflow control using programmed blower and flap settings. If one or more automatically controlled functions are set manually, automatic control for those functions is cancelled, but other functions remain automatically controlled.

In this mode, the following applies

• Dynamic pressure compensation: Air volume at air inlet grills increases disproportionately with increasing road speed. This effect is compensated for by programmed reduction of opening angle of fresh-air flaps as vehicle speed increases.

• Blower control: If necessary, vehicle power management reduces blower output via K-CAN. See **600 Electrical System–General**.

• Starting: When engine is cranked (terminal 50 ON), electric coolant pump and blower are switched OFF to reduce load on battery.

◀ **Blower speed control** is via toggle switch at center of IHKA panel. Current blower speed setting is shown by display icon.

**OFF.** IHKA control panel is switched OFF when blower speed is set to 0.

**640**

BentleyPublishers.com

B309640022

*IHKA functions*

B309640023

Passenger
temperature
control knob

B309640020

◀ **Recirculation mode** blocks flow of outside air to prevent pollution from entering vehicle. Air inside vehicle is continually recirculated.

To make sure that there is a sufficient supply of fresh air, recirculation mode is only available for 30 minutes. The system then switches to partial fresh air circulation for 30 minutes, then switches back to full recirculation

**Automatic air quality control**. If air quality (AUC) sensor detects an increased level of automotive pollutants, IHKA automatically switches to recirculation mode.

To make sure there is a sufficient supply of fresh air, automatic recirculation is only available for a limited time:

- Outside temperature under 0°C (32°F):
  2 minute recirculated air mode
  20 seconds fresh air mode
  2 minute recirculated air mode, etc.

- Outside temperature 0° - 6°C (32° - 43°F):
  3 minute recirculated air mode
  20 seconds fresh air mode
  3 minute recirculated air mode, etc.

- Outside temperature above 6°C (43°F), no A/C:
  4 minute recirculated air mode
  20 seconds fresh air mode
  4 minute recirculated air mode, etc.

- Outside temperature above 6°C (43°F), with A/C:
  12 minute recirculated air mode
  20 seconds fresh air mode
  12 minute recirculated air mode, etc.

When the engine is started and AUC function activated, fresh-air mode is selected for approx. 40 seconds due to warming phase of AUC sensor.

◀ **Residual heat (REST)** function allows hot or warm engine coolant to heat up vehicle interior when engine is not running. This function is available for a run-down period of approx. 15 minutes from the time ignition is switched OFF (terminal 15 OFF).

Pressing REST button signals ECM via bus system to activate electric coolant pump and circulate coolant.

REST switch-on conditions:

- Terminal 15 OFF.
- Run-down period (up to 15 minutes after terminal 15 OFF).
- REST button in IHKA controls ON.
- Outside temperature below 25°C (77°F).
- Engine temperature above 60°C (140°F).
- Battery voltage over 11.4 volts.

REST switch-off conditions:

- Terminal 15 ON.
- Residual heat ON past 15 minutes.
- REST button in IHKA control panel OFF.
- Power management switches auxiliary consumers OFF.
- Battery voltage below 11 volts.

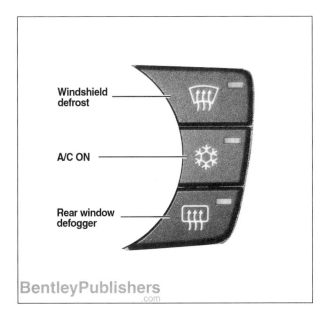

Windshield defrost

A/C ON

Rear window defogger

◀ **Defrost button** opens windshield defroster flaps fully. Fresh air - recirculation flaps move to fresh air position. Other flaps are closed. Blower is run at maximum speed.

**A/C button** switches cooling function ON in order to cool and dehumidify incoming air before it is heated. This function helps prevent or reduce condensation on windows.

**Rear window defogger**, toggled ON or OFF by pressing button. Defogging switches OFF automatically after programmed rear window heating time expires.

There are two rear window defogging programs. First program:

• After vehicle starts, the first time defogger is switched ON, defogging time is as follows:
  Outside temperature down to 15°C (59°F): 10 minutes
  Outside temperature below 15°C (59°F): 17 minutes.

• After initial defogging phase, rear window is heated for 25 minutes with pulsed heat output:
  40 seconds ON
  80 seconds OFF.

Second program:

• Each subsequent time defogger button is pressed:
  Defogging is switched ON for 30 minutes.
  After second heating period, output is again pulsed.

**Evaporator** temperature is regulated by evaporator temperature sensor and expansion valve. The minimum evaporator temperature is set to 2°C (36°F) to avoid risk of icing. Actual evaporator temperature ranges 2° - 7°C (36° - 45°F), depending on outside temperature, vent temperature and refrigerant pressure. Variable evaporator temperature control reduces excessive dehumidification of vehicle interior.

**Solar sensor** (active in IHKA automatic mode) modifies the following functions, depending on sunlight intensity:

• Blower output increased or reduced.

• Temperature settings using temperature control knobs increased or reduced.

Driver and passenger side (dual-zone) functions are not modified separately.

**Condensation sensor** operates with engine running and IHKA in automatic mode. IHKA control panel evaluates condensation sensor signal (humidity). If condensation on windshield is imminent, the following measures are initiated in sequence:

• Open defrost flaps further.

• If in recirculation mode, switch to partial fresh-air mode.

• If in partial recirculation mode, switch to fresh air.

• Increase blower speed.

• Reduce footwell air volume.

• Increase set temperature value.

If one measure proves to be ineffective, the next measure is initiated. Once successful, the measures previously performed are performed in reverse order.

**640**

## Warnings and Cautions

---

**WARNING —**

- Do not discharge or charge the A/C system without proper equipment and training. Damage to the vehicle and personal injury may result.

- Wear hand and eye protection (gloves and goggles) when working around the A/C system.

- If refrigerant come in contact with your skin or eyes:
  -Do not rub skin or eyes.
  -Immediately flush skin or eyes with cool water for 15 minutes.
  -Rush to a doctor or hospital.
  -Do not attempt to treat yourself.

- Work in a well ventilated area. Switch on exhaust / ventilation systems when working on the refrigerant system.

- Do not expose any component of the A/C system to high temperatures (above 80°C or 176°F) or open flames. Excessive heat causes a pressure increase which could burst the system.

- Keep refrigerant away from open flames. Poisonous gas is produced if it burns. Do not smoke near refrigerant gases for the same reason.

- The A/C system is filled with refrigerant gas which is under pressure. Pressurized refrigerant in the presence of oxygen may form a combustible mixture. Do not introduce compressed air into any refrigerant container (full or empty).

- Electric welding near refrigerant hoses causes R-134a to decompose. Discharge system before welding.

- At normal operating temperature the cooling system is pressurized. Allow the system to cool as long as possible before opening (a minimum of one hour), then release the cap slowly to allow safe release of pressure.

---

**CAUTION—**

- In the United States, any person who services a motor vehicle air-conditioner must, by law, be properly trained and certified, and use approved refrigerant recycling equipment. Technicians must complete an EPA-approved recycling course to be certified.

- Comply with state and local governments which may have additional requirements regarding air-conditioning servicing.

- It is recommended that all A/C service be left to an authorized BMW dealer or other qualified A/C service facility.

- Do not top off a partially charged refrigerant system. Discharge system, evacuate and then recharge system.

- The mixture of refrigerant oil (PAG oil) and refrigerant R-134a attacks some metals and alloys (for example, copper) and breaks down certain hose materials. Use only hoses and lines that are identified with a green mark (stripe) or marked with R-134a.

- Immediately plug open connections on A/C components and lines to prevent dirt and moisture contamination.

- Do not steam clean the A/C condenser or evaporator. Use only cold water or compressed air.

- To avoid damaging plastic interior trim, use a plastic prying tool or a screwdriver with the tip wrapped with masking tape.

## IHKA Component Replacement

### IHKA control panel, removing and installing

#### Version 1: Model without iDrive

◄ Use plastic prying tool to carefully pry out IHKA control panel.

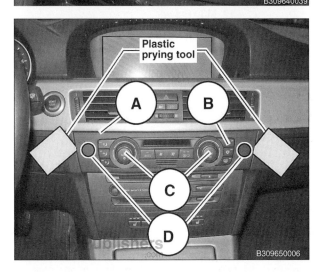

#### Version 2: Model with iDrive

◄ Use plastic prying tool to pry off IHKA control panel (**B**). Unclip front face (**A**) using knobs (**C**). Plastic pins are located at **D**.

◄ Pull panel back and unlock connector locks to detach.

– Installation is reverse of removal. Use BMW scan tool to program and code new panel. See **600 Electrical System–General**.

**640**

## IHKA housing and components

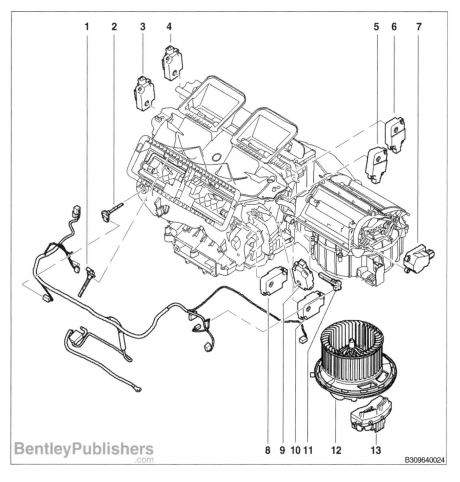

BentleyPublishers.com

B309640024

1. **B62** Center vent temperature sensor

2. **B109a** Footwell vent temperature sensor

3. **M153** Blend flap stepper motor, left

4. **M4729** Air distribution flap motor, front

5. **M154** Blend flap stepper motor, right

6. **M35a** Defroster flap stepper motor

7. **M111** Fresh air - recirculation flap stepper motor

8. **M38** Center vent flap stepper motor

9. **M31** Footwell flap stepper motor

10. **M4723** Air distribution flap motor, rear

11. **B14b** Evaporator temperature sensor

12. **M30** Blower

13. **N2** Blower final stage

### Stepper motors

The IHKA system utilizes eight stepper motors that are wired in series for climate control operation. IHKA control panel operates stepper motors via LIN-bus.

Stepper motors can be replaced without removing the dashboard or climate control housing.

Seven of the eight stepper motors used are identical and have the same part number. A different stepper motor is used only for the fresh air – recirculation motor.

After replacement, use BMW scan tool or equivalent to program stepper motor locations.

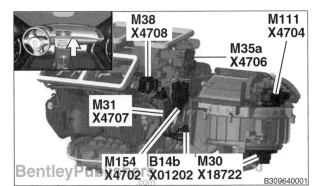

B309640001

## Right side stepper motors

- **B14b** Evaporator temperature sensor
- **M30** Blower motor
- **M31** Footwell flap stepper motor
- **M35a** Defroster flap stepper motor
- **M38** Center vent flap stepper motor
- **M111** Fresh air - recirculation flap stepper motor
- **M154** Blend flap stepper motor, right
- **X4702** Connector
- **X4704** Connector
- **X4706** Connector
- **X4707** Connector
- **X4708** Connector
- **X01202** Connector
- **X18722** Connector

- **A4010** Junction box (JB)
- **A4010a** Junction box electronics module (JBE)
- **M30** Blower
- **M111** Fresh air - recirculation flap stepper motor

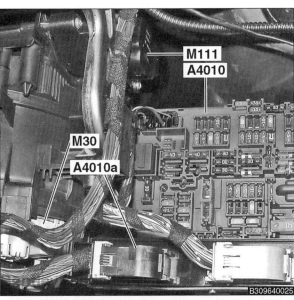

B309640025

- **A4010a** Junction box electronics module (JBE)
- **M30** Blower
- **N2** Blower final stage
- **M4723** Air distribution flap motor, rear

– To gain access to right side stepper motors:
- Remove right lower dashboard trim. See **513 Interior Trim**.
- Remove glove compartment. See **513 Interior Trim**.

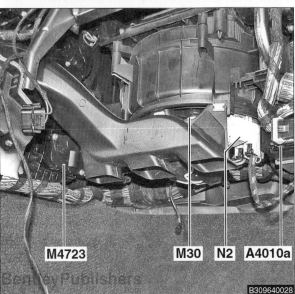

B309640028

640

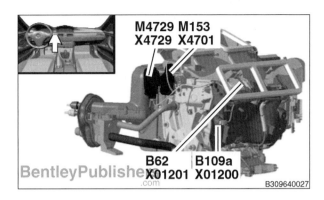

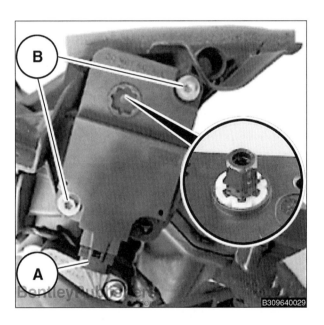

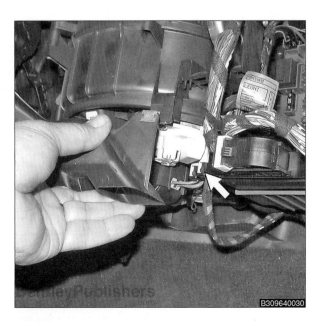

## Left side stepper motors

- **B62** Center vent temperature sensor
- **B109a** footwell vent temperature sensor
- **M153** Blend flap stepper motor, left
- **M4729** Air distribution flap motor, front
- **X4701** Connector
- **X4729** Connector
- **X01200** Connector
- **X01201** Connector

– To gain access to left side stepper motors, remove left lower dashboard trim (pedal cluster trim). See **513 Interior Trim**.

## Stepper motor, removing and installing

◀ To remove stepper motor:
- Detach electrical connector (**A**).
- Remove mounting bolts (**B**) and tilt motor out of housing.

– During installation, do not twist teeth of motor drive (**inset**).

– After replacement, use BMW scan tool or equivalent to program stepper motor locations.

## Blower, removing and installing

– Remove right lower dashboard trim. See **513 Interior Trim**.

◀ Working at blower:
- Pull off right footwell duct
- Detach electrical connector (**arrow**) at blower final stage.

*NOTE—*
- *Glove compartment removed for purpose of illustration.*

*Cabin microfilter housings, upper and lower, removing*

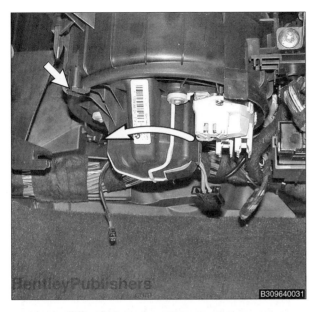

◀ Press carefully on lock lug (**arrow**) and rotate blower in direction of **curved arrow** to remove.

◀ If necessary, separate blower final stage by removing screws (**arrows**).

— When installing blower, make sure lock lug snaps audibly into place.

## Cabin microfilter housings, upper and lower, removing

— Open engine hood and place in service position. See **020 Maintenance**.

◀ Remove upper microfilter housing screws (**arrows**). Lift off microfilter upper housing and microfilter.

Microfilter replacement is covered in **020 Maintenance**.

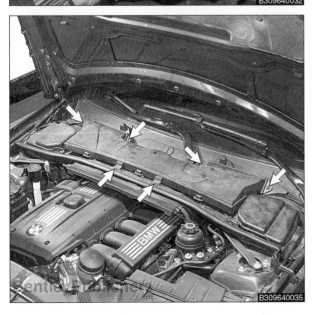

**640**

*Cabin microfilter housings, upper and lower, removing*

◀ Right side: Unclip E-box cover and detach rubber lock tab ((**arrow**) to lift off cover. Detach AUC sensor and wire from lower microfilter housing and lay aside.

− Left side: Brake fluid reservoir cover removal is similar.

◀ Unclip locking tabs (**arrows**) for engine wiring loom cover and take off cover.

◀ Lift wiring harnesses over edge of plastic loom (**arrows**).

*Cabin microfilter housings, upper and lower, removing*

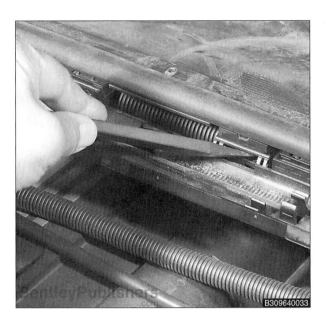

◀ Reach through wire loom opening with plastic prying too and unclip engine wiring loom cover underneath microfilter housing.

◀ Working at left side of housing, remove housing hold-down screw (**A**) and detach rubber lock tab (**B**). Repeat operation on right side of housing.

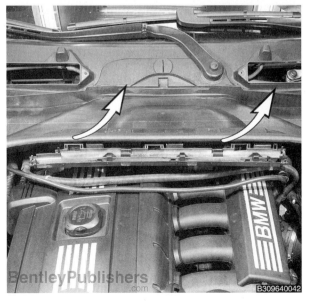

◀ Slide housing forward and up (**arrows**) to remove.

– Installation is reverse of removal.

> **CAUTION—**
> • *Make sure upper microfilter housing seals securely to lower housing. A bad seal may allow water leaks into the cabin, IHKA housing or blower.*

**640**

*Air-conditioning components in engine compartment*

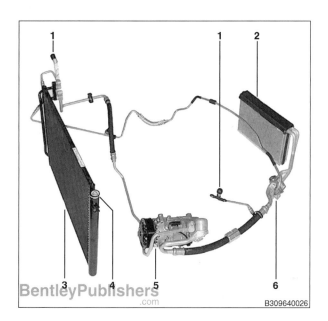

B309640026

## Air-conditioning components in engine compartment

1. Refrigerant service port
2. Evaporator
3. Condenser
4. Receiver-dryer port
5. A/C compressor
6. Expansion valve

# 650 Radio

## GENERAL

This section covers BMW factory-installed sound and navigation systems.

### Radio

The two radio versions supplied with E90 models are both on the MOST (optical cable) bus and have CD playing capabilities.

The base radio, with a single cd drive and a two-line LCD display, is referred to as RAD2. The basic 180 watt radio may be upgraded to Top-HiFi Logic7 with 420 watts of power.

The high-end radio is the car communication computer (CCC) which also serves as the navigation system. The CCC is controlled by the iDrive controller and utilizes the navigation video screen or central information display (CID) as a visual monitor. This system comes with the Top-HiFi Logic7 system with 420 watts of power as standard.

### MOST-bus (media oriented systems transport)

 Sound system and navigation components are connected using MOST-bus, a fiber optic network.

**650**

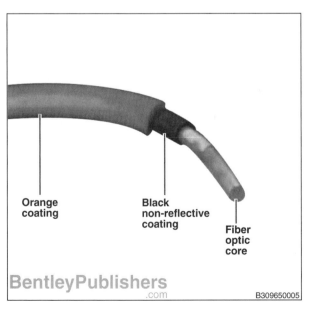

Orange coating

Black non-reflective coating

Fiber optic core

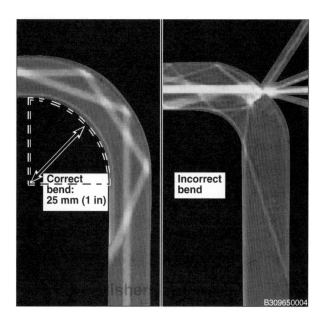

Correct bend: 25 mm (1 in)

Incorrect bend

B309650004

◁ Make sure any bend in MOST-bus fiber optic harness has a radius of 25 mm (1 in) or greater.

> **CAUTION—**
> • *Signal transmission through a fiber optic harness that is bent excessively is impaired.*

## Cautions

> **CAUTION—**
> • *Before beginning work on the radio or sound system, verify that the radio is an original equipment BMW radio and that the wiring harness is not modified.*
> • *Refer servicing of aftermarket sound equipment to an authorized agent of the equipment manufacturer.*
> • *When handling electronic equipment (monitors, control modules, relays), use anti-static tools and techniques to prevent static discharge damage. See* **600 Electrical System– General***.*
> • *To avoid damaging plastic interior trim, use a plastic prying tool or a screwdriver with the tip wrapped with masking tape.*

## COMPONENT LOCATIONS

### Sedan audio equipment

#### RAD2 audio system (basic radio)

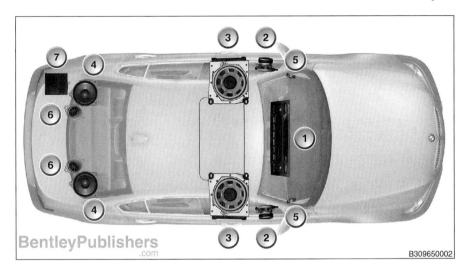

1. Radio (RAD2)
2. Front midrange speakers
3. Floor-mounted woofers
4. Rear midrange speakers
5. Front tweeters
6. Rear tweeters
7. Amplifier

B309650002

#### CCC audio system (high-end radio)

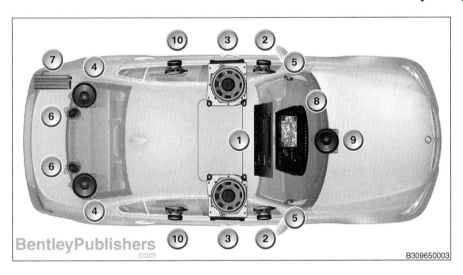

1. Car communication computer (CCC)
2. Front midrange speakers
3. Floor-mounted woofers
4. Rear midrange speakers
5. Front tweeters
6. Rear tweeters
7. Amplifier
8. Central information display (CID)
9. Front center midrange speaker
10. Rear door midrange speakers

B309650003

**650**

### Antennas

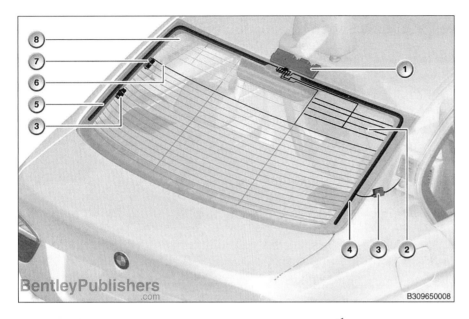

1. Antenna amplifier, diversity module
2. Remote key antenna (FBD)
3. Rear window defogger suppressor filter
4. FM3, TV1 antenna
5. FM2, TV2 antenna
6. FM1 antenna
7. Center brake light filter
8. AM antenna

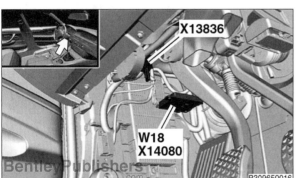

◀ Underneath left side dashboard (**arrow**):
- **W18** Bluetooth antenna
- **X13836** Connector
- **X14080** Connector

### Audio equipment

◀ In trunk, front section, underneath trunk floor carpet:
- **N47** Satellite radio
- **U400** Telematics control unit (TCU)
- **W13** Comfort access antenna

## Sports Wagon audio and communication equipment

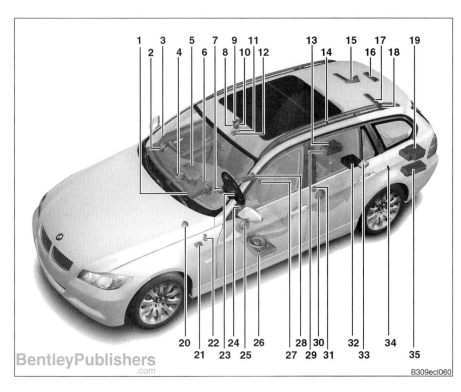

B309ecl060

1. Radio
2. Door-mounted midrange speaker
3. Door-mounted tweeter
4. Dashboard midrange speaker
5. Central information display (CID)
6. Floor-mounted woofer
7. Controller
8. Microphone
9. Roof-mounted tweeter
10. Roof-mounted midrange speaker
11. Microphone
12. Emergency call button
13. Satellite radio (SDARS)
14. Wheel speed sensor, right rear
15. Sharkfin (satellite radio, navigation, telephone antenna)
16. Antenna amplifier, diversity module
17. Electrodynamic planar speaker
18. Rear window defogger and center brake light suppressor filter
19. CD changer
20. Emergency speaker
21. Bluetooth antenna
22. MOST direct access port
23. Multifunction (MFL) steering wheel
24. Door-mounted tweeter
25. Door-mounted midrange speaker
26. Floor-mounted woofer
27. Auxiliary audio input
28. Telephone
29. Subwoofer
30. Door-mounted midrange speaker
31. Door-mounted tweeter
32. IBOC tuner
33. Emergency response antenna
34. Wheel speed sensor, left rear
35. Amplifier

650

**Antennas**

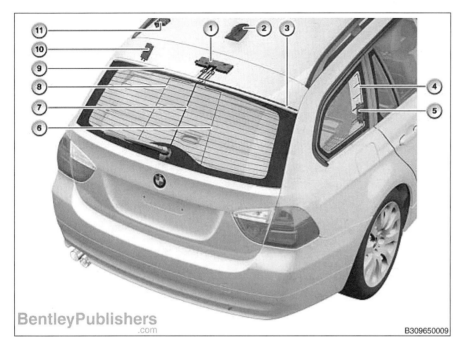

1. Antenna amplifier, diversity module

2. Sharkfin (satellite radio, navigation, telephone antenna)

3. FM1 antenna

4. TV antenna

5. TV antenna

6. FM3 antenna

7. Remote key antenna (FBD)

8. FM2 antenna

9. AM antenna

10. Rear window defogger and center brake light suppressor filter

## Convertible communication equipment

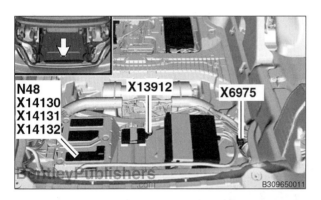

◄ Trunk, rear section, underneath floor carpet (**arrow**):

- **N48** Digital tuner
- **X6975** Connector
- **X13912** Connector
- **X14130** Connector
- **X14131** Connector
- **X14132** Connector

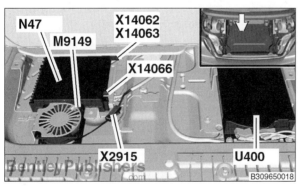

◄ Trunk, front section, underneath floor carpet (**arrow**):

- **M9149** Trunk ventilation fan
- **N47** Amplifier
- **U400** Telematics control module (TCU)
- **X2915** Connector
- **X14062** Connector
- **X14063** Connector
- **X14066** Connector

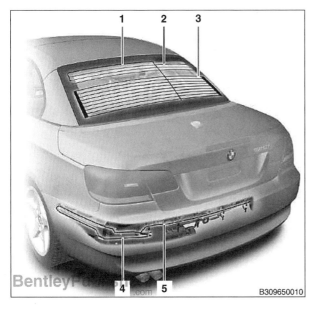

B309650010

### Antennas

◀ Behind rear bumper:

1. FM1 antenna
2. AM antenna
3. FM3 antenna
4. FM2 antenna
5. FM4 antenna

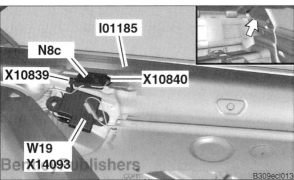

B309ecl013

◀ Underneath left quarter window, behind trim panel (**arrow**):

- **I01185** FM1 antenna
- **N8c** Antenna amplifier
- **W19** Emergency call antenna
- **X10839** Connector
- **X10840** Connector
- **X14093** Connector

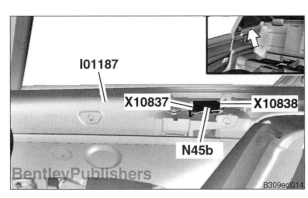

B309ecl014

◀ Underneath right quarter window, behind trim panel (**arrow**):

- **I01187** FM3 antenna
- **N45b** Antenna amplifier
- **X10837** Connector
- **X10838** Connector

**650**

## Sound System

### Radio service mode

Use service mode to check radio functions directly at the radio. This procedure differs for the RAD2 (basic radio) and CCC (high end radio with iDrive and navigation).

#### RAD2 service mode

— Switch radio ON.

— Within 8 seconds, press and hold M button for at least 8 seconds. Service mode is enabled.

— Select menus while in service mode.

— Switch radio OFF to exit service mode.

#### RAD2 reset

— Switch radio ON, then OFF.

— Disconnect radio from vehicle electrical system.

— Reconnect radio and use BMW scan tool or equivalent to reset.

#### CCC service mode

The only information available through the CCC service mode are software, hardware, and system status numbers. This information is primarily intended for equipment developers.

— Using iDrive controller, open Start menu.

— Press and hold iDrive controller for at least 10 seconds.

— Move controller 3 stops to right. Read and follow menus.

— Move controller 3 stops to left. Read and follow menus.

— Move controller 1 stop to right. Read and follow menus.

— Move controller 1 stop to left. Read and follow menus.

— Move controller 1 stop to right. Read and follow menus.

— Press controller once.

— Press Menu button to exit service mode.

#### CCC reset

— Simultaneously press and hold eject buttons on DVD or CD player and iDrive controller for approximately 10 seconds.
  • Central information display (CID) becomes blank.
  • CCC then restarts.

## Radio, removing and installing

– Disconnect negative (-) battery cable and cover battery terminal to keep cable from accidentally contacting terminal.

> **CAUTION—**
> • *Prior to disconnecting the battery, read the battery disconnection cautions given in* **001 Warnings and Cautions**.

◄ Use plastic prying tool to pry off right side dashboard decorative strip.

– Version without iDrive: Use plastic prying tool to pry off IHKA control panel and lower panel underneath radio. See **640 Heating and Air-conditioning**.

– Version with iDrive:

 • Use plastic prying tool to pry off IHKA control panel

 • Pry off center console switch cluster (SZM) panel below radio.

◄ Working below radio face plate, remove mounting screws (**arrows**) and pull radio out of center dashboard.

◄ Use pointed tool such as screwdriver to detach harness connector at rear of radio.

– Installation is reverse of removal. Check to make sure MOST bus is not kinked. See **MOST-bus (media oriented systems transport)** in this repair group.

– Use BMW scan tool to code and program new radio. See **600 Electrical System–General**.

**650**

## TELEMATICS

Telematics combines information and communications technology such as GPS and cell telephone to send and receive data via telecommunications devices. As implemented in BMW vehicles, Telematics can assist the driver in a wide range of situations and deliver useful information directly to the vehicle. The system consists of several different services which are provided via subscription.

**BMW Assist** features include the following:

• Vehicle position data (can be transmitted if an emergency request is sent)

• Automatic collision notification.

• Enhanced roadside assistance.

• Customer relations.

• Vehicle service status or required inspections.

• Remote door unlock (in case of lost remote key).

• Stolen vehicle recovery.

• Critical calling (allows a limited number of telephone calls when the driver's mobile phone is not available).

**BMW Online** features include the following:

• Location information for restaurants, hotels, theaters, etc.

• Traffic news, enabling the navigation system to calculate a route that avoids traffic jams.

**BMW TeleServices** monitors the condition of key vehicle parts and, if required, contacts a BMW service center automatically to arrange for service.

## NAVIGATION SYSTEM

### Navigation basics

 Vehicle navigation systems utilize signals from global positioning system (GPS) satellites.

The 3 Series navigation system operates via the car communication computer (CCC) and features the following range of functions:

• Navigation with map and arrow mode.

• Display on 8.8" color central information display (CID).

• Split-screen view.

• Perspective map presentation.

• Input via iDrive controller with electrically controlled feedback.

• Input optionally controlled by voice commands (SVS).

GPS receiver

B309650019

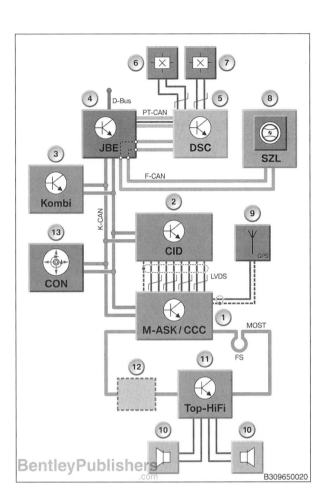

◁ Navigation system schematic

1. Car communication computer (CCC)
2. Central information display (CID)
3. Instrument cluster
4. Junction box electronic module (JBE)
5. DSC control module
6. Left rear wheel speed sensor
7. Right rear wheel speed sensor
8. Steering column switch cluster (SZL)
9. GPS antenna
10. Audio speakers
11. Amplifier
12. MOST components (optional)

## Central information display (CID), removing and installing

− Make sure ignition is OFF.

◁ Working at CID screen:

• Remove mounting screws (**arrows**) at top.
• Tilt screen backward (**curved arrow**) and remove.

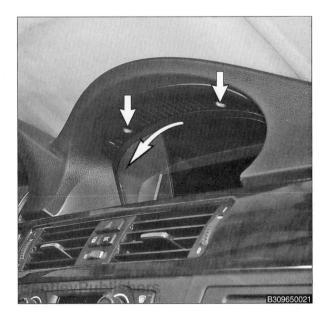

650

*Central information display (CID), removing and installing*

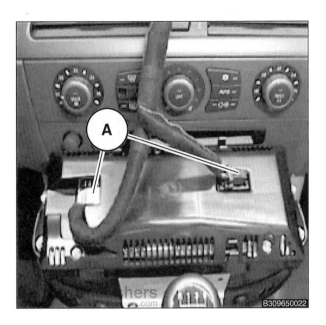

◄ Detach CID screen electrical connectors.

– When installing, make sure cables are routed without kinking.

– Use BMW scan tool to code and program new CID. See **600 Electrical System–General**.

# 720 Seat Belts

## GENERAL

This section covers mechanical repairs to seat belts and seat belt tensioner components. Airbag system electronics integrate seat belt operations and airbag deployment. Airbag system information is covered in **721 Airbag System (SRS)**.

See also:

• **513 Interior Trim**
• **520 Seats**

### Troubleshooting

Check that seat belt reel locks when driving quickly through curves and during severe braking. The automatic reel does not require any servicing. Replace if it is found faulty.

In case of an accident, follow the seat belt troubleshooting procedures presented in **Table a**.

| Table a. Seat belt troubleshooting | | |
|---|---|---|
| **Problem** | **Probable cause** | **Repairs** |
| Damage to seat belt. | Accident in which bumper impact absorbers were permanently deformed. | Replace complete automatic seat belt. Also check and replace, if necessary, seat belt mounting on car body and seat belt mounting on seat runner. |
| Belt creased, unraveled, pinched, cut or melted. Belt buckle or belt lock plastic casing worn, damaged or missing. | Seat belts aged or worn. | Replace complete automatic seat belt. |
| Seat belt buckle not ejected with spring pressure when red button on seat belt lock pressed. | Seat belt lock mechanism worn or damaged. | Replace seat belt buckle. |

**720**

| Table a. Seat belt troubleshooting | | |
| --- | --- | --- |
| **Problem** | **Probable cause** | **Repairs** |
| Seat belt automatic reel does not lock when pulled out suddenly. | Automatic reel defective. | Replace reel assembly. |
| Seat belt automatic reel jams when pulled out. | Automatic reel loose.<br>Return spring broken inside reel. | Tighten reel mounting bolt.<br>Replace reel assembly. |
| Seat belt does not retract automatically (see note below). | Automatic reel loose.<br>Return spring broken inside reel. | Tighten reel mounting bolt.<br>Replace reel assembly. |
| Automatic belt squeaks when fastened or unfastened. | Excessive friction in belt guides<br>Automatic reel loose.<br>Return spring broken inside reel. | Replace reel assembly.<br>Tighten reel mounting bolt.<br>Replace reel assembly. |
| Seat belt pyrotechnic tensioner triggered. | Accident triggered pyrotechnic deployment. | Replace complete automatic seat belt. Also check retaining bracket of belt tensioner for twist. |

*NOTE—*

• *The rear bench seat belt strap may not retract fully due to increased friction between strap and seat cover. A small remaining loop in belt strap when fully retracted is acceptable.*

## Warnings

*WARNING—*

• *For maximum protection from injury, replace seat belts and hardware if subjected to occupant loading in a collision.*

• *Do not modify or repair seat belts or seat belt mounting points.*

• *Do not bleach or dye seat belt webbing. Webbing that is severely faded or redyed does not meet the strength requirements of a collision. Replace it.*

• *Clean belts with a luke-warm soap solution only.*

• *Periodically inspect seat belts for webbing defects such as cuts or pulled threads.*

• *Immediately after replacing a damaged or worn seat belt, destroy the old belt to prevent it from being used again.*

• *Pyrotechnic seat belt tensioners are powerful devices. Handle with extreme care. Incorrect handling can trigger the tensioner.*

• *BMW recommends that repair or replacement work on pyrotechnic devices be carried out by a qualified BMW technician.*

• *Be sure to disconnect the battery and wait 1 minute before attempting to work on pyrotechnic devices.*

• *Pyrotechnic devices cannot be repaired. Always replace them.*

• *Do not treat pyrotechnic components with cleaning agents or grease.*

• *Do not expose pyrotechnic components to temperatures above 75°C (167°F).*

• *Do not fire a pyrotechnic gas generator prior to disposal. It must be fired by a special disposal company or shipped back to BMW in the packaging of the new component.*

• *During body straightening and welding with an electric arc welder, disconnect the battery and the connection to the pyrotechnic gas generators.*

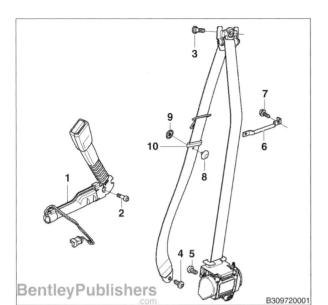

B309720001

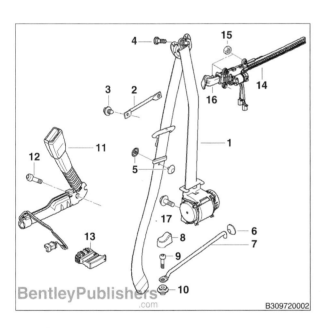

B309720002

## FRONT SEAT BELTS

### Front seat belt components

**Sedan, Sports Wagon**

1. Seat belt buckle assembly with pyrotechnic (explosive) tensioner

2. M10 x 22 mm self-locking bolt, replace with new
   Tighten to 38 Nm (28 ft-lb)

3. B-pillar bolt
   Tighten to 36 Nm (27 ft-lb)

4. M10 x 15 mm seat belt anchor self-locking bolt, replace with new
   Tighten to 44 Nm (32 ft-lb)

5. M10 x 22 mm seat belt reel self-locking bolt, replace with new
   Tighten to 36 Nm (27 ft-lb)

6. Belt guide

7. ST5.5 x 13 mm sheet metal screw
   Tighten to 3.5 Nm (31 in-lb)

8. Plastic button

9. Plastic button

10. Plastic stop

### Coupe

1. Driver seat belt

2. Belt guide

3. ST5.5 x 13 mm sheet metal screw
   Tighten to 3.5 Nm (31 in-lb)

4. B-pillar bolt
   Tighten to 36 Nm (27 ft-lb)

5. Plastic button

6. Plastic trim

7. Slide bar

8. Plastic trim

9. M10 x 55 mm bolt
   Tighten to 36 Nm (27 ft-lb)

10. Spacer bushing

11. Seat belt buckle assembly with pyrotechnic (explosive) tensioner

12. M10 x 22 mm self-locking bolt, replace with new
    Tighten to 38 Nm (28 ft-lb)

13. Plastic trim

14. Seat belt extender

15. M5 nut
    Tighten to 2.5 Nm (22 in-lb)

16. Belt extender tip

17. M10 x 22 mm seat belt reel self-locking bolt, replace with new
    Tighten to 36 Nm (27 ft-lb)

**720**

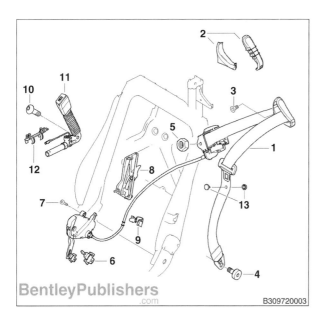

BentleyPublishers.com

B309720003

### Convertible

1. Driver seat belt

2. Belt guide

3. Belt guide M6 bolt
   To 09 / 2008: Tighten to 9 Nm (90 in-lb)
   From 09 / 2008: Tighten to 8 Nm (71 in-lb)

4. M10 x 22 mm seat belt anchor self-locking bolt, replace with new
   Tighten to 36 Nm (27 ft-lb)

5. M10 seat belt reel self-locking nut, replace with new
   Tighten to 36 Nm (27 ft-lb)

6. Coupling gear stud
   Tighten to 3 Nm (27 in-lb)

7. Coupling gear screw
   Tighten to 2.5 Nm (22 in-lb)

8. Support plate

9. Clip

10. M10 x 22 mm self-locking bolt, replace with new
    Tighten to 38 Nm (28 ft-lb)

11. Seat belt buckle assembly with pyrotechnic (explosive) tensioner

12. Plastic bracket

13. Plastic button

## Front seat belt buckle and tensioner, removing and installing

The front seat belt buckle is equipped with pyrotechnic (explosive charge) automatic tensioner designed to automatically retract and tension the seat belt by 55 mm (approximately 2 inches) in case of an accident.

> **WARNING—**
> • *The side impact airbag and pyrotechnic seat belt tensioner attached to the front seat are powerful and potentially dangerous devices. Handle with extreme care. Incorrect handling can trigger off the airbag or tensioner and cause injury.*

— Disconnect battery negative (–) cable in trunk.

> **CAUTION—**
> • *Prior to disconnecting the battery, read the battery disconnection cautions given in* **001 Warnings and Cautions**.

— Remove front seat. See **520 Seats**.

◄ Working underneath seat:

- Pull electrical connectors out of plug housing (**arrow**).

- Cut wire ties and detach wire harnesses from seat base.

B309720004

*Front seat belt reel, removing and installing (Sedan, Sports Wagon)*

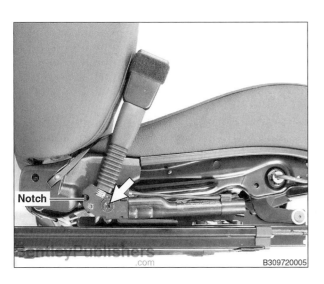

◀ Working at lower side of seat, remove belt buckle mounting bolt (**arrow**) and discard.

— When installing:

• Secure base of belt buckle to seat using aligning notch.

• Use new self-locking belt buckle bolt.

| Tightening torque | |
|---|---|
| Belt buckle to base of seat (M10 x 22 mm self-locking bolt, replace with new) | 38 Nm (28 ft-lb) |

— Replace wire ties and reconnect harness connectors before reinstalling seat.

| Tightening torque | |
|---|---|
| Front seat to floor (replace bolts) | 44 Nm (32 ft-lb) |

## Front seat belt reel, removing and installing (Sedan, Sports Wagon)

— Remove B-pillar plastic trim. See **513 Interior Trim**.

◀ Using plastic prying tool, unclip seat belt anchor bolt cover and remove (**arrow**).

◀ Remove seat belt anchor bolt (**arrow**) and discard. Disconnect seat belt anchor hook (**inset**) from seat.

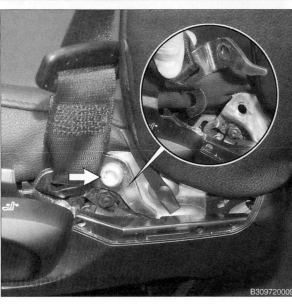

*Front seat belt reel, removing and installing (Coupe)*

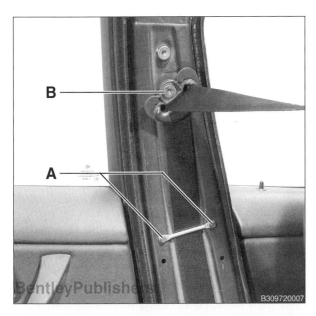

◀ Working at upper B-pillar:

• Remove belt guide mounting screws (**A**). Remove guide.

• Remove upper seat belt bolt (**B**).

– Set upper part of seat belt aside temporarily.

◀ Working at lower B-pillar, remove automatic seat belt reel mounting bolt (**arrow**) and lift out reel with seat belt.

– When installing:

• Make sure reel locating tab fits B-pillar slot.

• Replace self-locking hardware with new.

• Position trim retaining clips back into trim panels before installing.

• Replace damaged trim retaining clips or trim panels.

| Tightening torques | |
| --- | --- |
| Seat belt to upper B-pillar | 36 Nm (27 ft-lb) |
| Seat belt guide to B-pillar (ST5.5 x 13 mm sheet metal screw) | 3.5 Nm (31 in-lb) |
| Seat belt reel to lower B-pillar (M10 x 22 mm self-locking bolt, replace with new) | 36 Nm (27 ft-lb) |
| Seat belt anchor to seat (M10 x 15 mm self-locking bolt, replace with new) | 44 Nm (32 ft-lb) |

## Front seat belt reel, removing and installing (Coupe)

– Remove B-pillar plastic trim. See **513 Interior Trim**.

– Slide seat forward.

◀ Working at door sill next to seat:

• Remove slide bar plastic cap.

• Remove slide bar mounting bolt (**arrow**). Note position of spacer and washer for reinstallation.

• Twist bar to remove from floor. Disengage seat belt from bar.

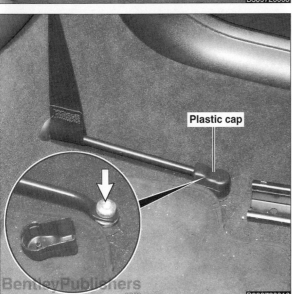

*Front seat belt reel, removing and installing (Coupe)*

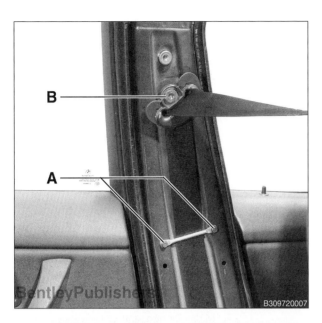

◄ Working at upper B-pillar:

- • Remove belt guide mounting screws (**A**). Remove guide.
- • Remove upper seat belt bolt (**B**).

– Set upper part of seat belt aside temporarily.

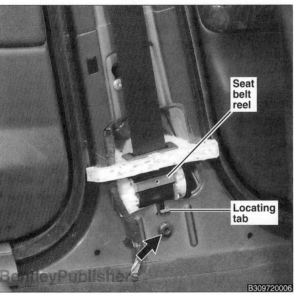

Seat belt reel

Locating tab

◄ Working at lower B-pillar, remove automatic seat belt reel mounting bolt (**arrow**) and lift out reel with seat belt.

– When installing:

- • Make sure reel locating tab fits B-pillar slot.
- • Replace self-locking hardware with new.
- • Position trim retaining clips back into trim panels before installing.

– Replace damaged trim retaining clips or trim panels.

| Tightening torques | |
|---|---|
| Seat belt to upper B-pillar | 36 Nm (27 ft-lb) |
| Seat belt guide to B-pillar (ST5.5 x 13 mm sheet metal screw) | 3.5 Nm (31 in-lb) |
| Seat belt reel to lower B-pillar (M10 x 22 mm self-locking bolt, replace with new) | 36 Nm (27 ft-lb) |
| Slide bar to floor (M10 x 55 mm) | 36 Nm (27 ft-lb) |

720

## REAR SEAT BELTS

### Rear seat belt assembly (Sedan, Sports Wagon)

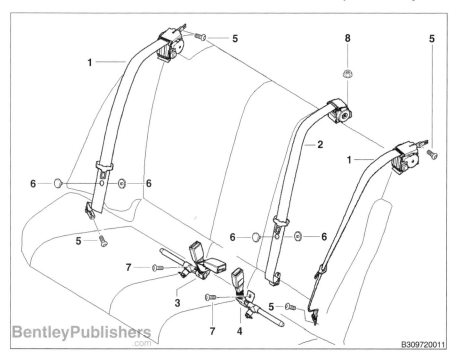

1. Rear seat belt, outboard

2. Rear seat belt, center
   Sports Wagon: Seat belt integrated with left backrest

3. Right rear and center rear seat belt buckles with pyrotechnic tensioner

4. Left seat belt buckle with pyrotechnic tensioner

5. M10 x 26 mm seat belt reel or anchor self-locking bolt, replace with new
   Tighten to 36 Nm (27 ft-lb)

6. Plastic buttons

7. M12 x 27 mm seat belt buckle self-locking bolt, replace with new
   Tighten to 38 Nm (28 ft-lb)

8. M10 nut, replace with new
   Sedan: Tighten to 36 Nm (27 ft-lb)
   Sports Wagon: Does not apply

### Rear seat belt, removing and installing (Sedan, Sports Wagon)

In Sports Wagon model with split rear seat backrest, the center seat belt is integrated with the left backrest.

– Sedan: Remove rear parcel shelf

– Sports Wagon:
  • Remove C-pillar and D-pillar trim. See **513 Interior Trim**.
  • Remove inner rear wheel housing trim.
  • Remove rear seat backrest upper trim.

– Remove rear seat. See **520 Seats**.

◄ Remove seat belt reel mounting bolt (**arrow**).

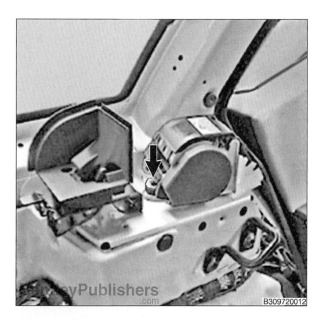

*Rear seat belt buckles and tensioners, removing and installing*

◀ Remove seat belt anchor bolt (**arrow**) at base of backrest and lift out seat belt.

– Installation is reverse of removal.

• Place seat belt anchor correctly on locating pin.

• Make sure tab on seat belt reel engages body slot.

• Use new self-locking bolts.

| Tightening torques | |
|---|---|
| Seat belt anchor to body (M10 x 26 mm self-locking bolt, replace with new) | 36 Nm (27 ft-lb) |
| Seat belt reel to body (M10 x 26 mm self-locking bolt, replace with new) | 36 Nm (27 ft-lb) |

## Rear seat belt buckles and tensioners, removing and installing

Rear seat belt buckles are equipped with pyrotechnic (explosive charge) automatic tensioners designed to automatically retract and tension the seat belts by 55 mm (approximately 2 inches) in case of an accident.

> **WARNING—**
> • *Pyrotechnic seat belt tensioners are powerful and potentially dangerous devices. Handle with extreme care. Incorrect handling can trigger off the tensioner and cause injury.*

– Disconnect battery negative (–) cable in trunk.

> **CAUTION—**
> • *Prior to disconnecting the battery, read the battery disconnection cautions given in* **001 Warnings and Cautions**.

– Remove rear seat. See **520 Seats**.

◀ Working at seat belt tensioners:

• Detach electrical connectors.

• Loosen and remove mounting fasteners (**arrows**). Lift out tensioners and store in a safe place.

– When installing:

• Make sure tab on seat belt buckle engages body slot.

• Use new self-locking bolts.

| Tightening torques | |
|---|---|
| Seat belt tensioner to body (M12 x 27 mm self-locking bolt, replace with new) | 38 Nm (28 ft-lb) |

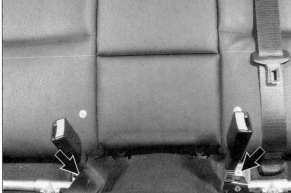

**720**

# 721 Airbag System (SRS)

## GENERAL

This repair group covers the airbag system and component replacement. Airbag system problems can only be diagnosed using BMW scan tool or equivalent.

See also:

• **121 Battery, Starter, Alternator** for battery safety terminal

• **411 Doors** for door panel removal

• **513 Interior Trim** for center console and glove compartment removal

• **520 Seats** for seat removal

• **612 Switches** for steering column switch cluster

• **720 Seat Belts**

• **ECL Electrical Component Locations**

### Airbag system overview

The BMW airbag system, including pyrotechnic seat belt tensioners and battery safety terminal, is called multiple restraint system (MRS). (The industry name is supplemental restraint system or SRS.)

| Airbag system application | |
|---|---|
| Year | Restraint system |
| From 2006 | MRS 5 |

1. Side rear airbag

2. Driver airbag

3. Passenger airbag

4. Curtain side airbag

5. Side front airbag (seat backrest)

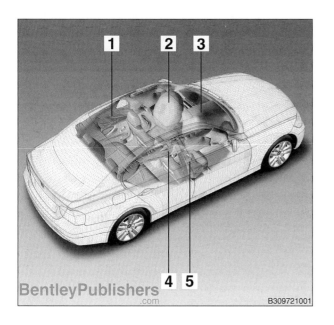

B309721001

**721**

B309721002

## MRS components

◄ The MRS system consists of the following components:

- MRS control module (**1**) under center console
- Crash sensors in B-pillars
- Crash sensors in engine compartment
- Door pressure sensors
- Warning light in instrument cluster
- Driver airbag and horn contact spring
- Passenger seat occupancy sensor (OC-3 mat)
- Driver and passenger airbags (**2**, **3**)
- Driver and passenger thorax (side) airbags (**4**)
- Right and left curtain airbags (**5**)
- Front and rear seat belt pyrotechnic tensioners (**6**)
- Seat belt buckle microswitches
- Battery safety terminal (BST) (**7**)

## MRS control module

◄ The MRS control module, located under the center console between the parking brake handle and the gear selector lever, connects to other MRS system components and vehicle electronics via two connectors:

- 26-pin connector to instruments
- 54-pin connector to vehicle harness.

The module houses two crash sensors.

Communication with other control modules in the vehicle network takes place via K-CAN. In case of a crash, a K-bus protocol is transmitted via a separate data line to the telematics control module (TCU) and an emergency call is triggered.

For a description of vehicle bus systems, see **600 Electrical System–General**.

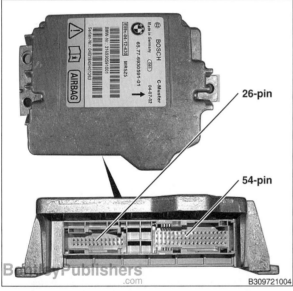

26-pin

54-pin

B309721004

◄ The red MRS warning LED in the instrument cluster is illuminated for a short period after switching the ignition ON.

If a fault is stored in the MRS control module, the LED illuminates and remains ON until the ignition is switched OFF. A check control icon also appears in either yellow or red depending on the system fault along with a brief text message.

With the warning LED illuminated, MRS may not operate in case of a collision.

MRS warning

B309721005

## Crash sensors

In addition to two acceleration sensors in the MRS control module, satellite sensors are installed in the B-pillars, frame rails and doors. Together with the acceleration sensors in the control module, the longitudinal and transverse acceleration sensors and door pressure sensors serve the purpose of detecting side crashes.

The longitudinal acceleration sensors detect front end and rear end crashes.

◄ **B-pillar satellite**, a combined longitudinal and transverse acceleration sensor, detects frontal, side and rear end crashes. The left and right sensors are identical and are mechanically coded to side during installation.

◄ Acceleration sensor data is converted to digital signals and transmitted to the MRS control module as data telegrams every 228 microseconds ($\mu$s). The main sensors in the control module provide a directional signal so that the control module recognizes the direction of impact.

**B-pillar sensor**

B309721006

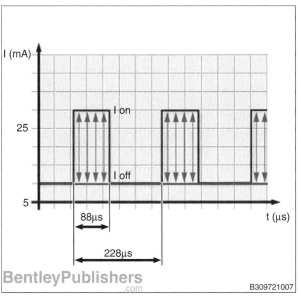

B309721007

◄ **Front sensors** on the front frame rails detect frontal impacts and provide the MRS control module with initial information on the progression and severity of the impact. The front sensor consists of an acceleration sensor for detecting deceleration, a signal converter and a microprocessor for data transmission.

Front sensors transmit a digital data message cyclically every 228 $\mu$s. Power supply of 5 - 10 mA is via a current-signal interface.

**Front sensor**

B309721008

721

*Driver airbag and horn contact spring*

**Door pressure sensor** in the front door cavity measures the pressure inside the door, providing supplementary side impact detection. In case of a side crash, the outer door panel is pushed inward, thus compressing the space inside the door and increasing the pressure, detected by the door pressure sensor.

The door pressure sensor contains a pressure sensor and an electronic module which digitizes and transmits data cyclically to the MRS control module. At the same time, side impact is detected by the B-pillar satellite sensor. The MRS module processes the two signals and triggers the restraint system on the basis of the information provided.

### Driver airbag and horn contact spring

The contact spring on the steering column switch cluster (SZL) behind the steering wheel provides the electrical interface between the fixed wiring harness and the moveable driver airbag. SZL service is covered in **612 Switches**.

The contact spring cassette consists of outer and inner housings with integral connectors and contains a ribbon type flexible cable.

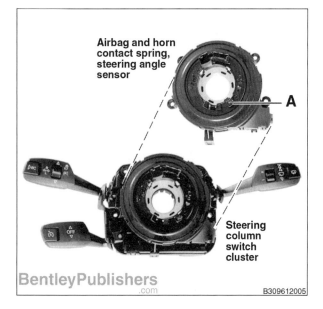

## Passenger seat occupancy sensor (OC-3 mat)

◄ The passenger seat occupancy sensor (occupant classifier or OC-3 mat) is integrated into the seat area of the passenger seat. The sensor consists of conductors with pressure-dependent resistor (force sensitive resistance or FSR) elements connected to an electronic analyzer.

The FSR elements are wired in such a way that they can be sampled individually. When the mechanical load on a sensor element increases, its electrical resistance decreases and the current changes accordingly. By analyzing the signals from different sections of the mat, the analyzer maps the occupancy of the seat surface and can identify local concentrations of weight.

The purpose of the OC-3 mat is to monitor the presence of a person or object placed on the front passenger seat and determine whether to deactivate passenger side airbags. The mat is capable of detecting a child seat that conforms to the NHTSA FMVSS 208 standard by the weight pattern on the seat. If detected, passenger airbags are deactivated.

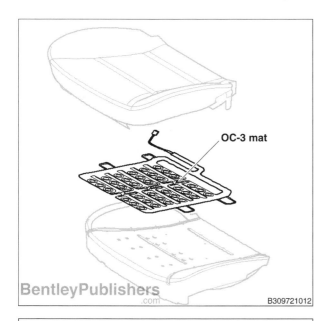

◄ The OC-3 mat is capable of distinguishing between a one-year-old child in a child's seat (**A**) and a light person (**B**). The distances between the areas where pressure is applied and the concentrations of pressure reveal who occupies the seat.

The OC-3 mat analyzer transmits a message to the MRS control module via the K-CAN. If the system detects that the seat is unoccupied or that a child seat for a child up to one year old is fitted, the airbags on the passenger side are deactivated. If a child seat is detected, the passenger airbag status light illuminates, indicating that passenger side airbags are deactivated.

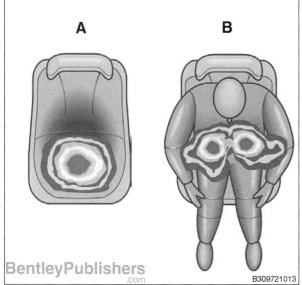

## Airbag status light

◄ The airbag status light in the roof function center (FZD) glows yellow when the front passenger airbag and the side passenger airbag are deactivated.

721

B309721016

## Pyrotechnic devices

◄ **Driver airbag**, of two-stage design, is attached to the steering wheel by spring clips. Electrical connection to the MRS control module is provided via the driver airbag and horn contact spring in the steering column.

Once the airbag is fully inflated, vents in the airbag prevent further pressure build-up, so that progressive deceleration is provided as the driver contacts the cushion and injury due to sudden impact forces is prevented.

Passenger airbag

B309721017

◄ **Passenger airbag,** of two-stage design, is above the glove compartment, directly in front of the passenger seat, mounted to the body crossbeam.

Upon deployment, the airbag tears the dashboard cover through several predetermined shear points. Once free of the housing and fascia, the airbag inflates to its full extent to provide a protective cushion between the front seat passenger and the windshield.

Vents in the airbag prevent excess pressure bursting the bag and, as soon as the material in the gas generator is exhausted, the airbag deflates.

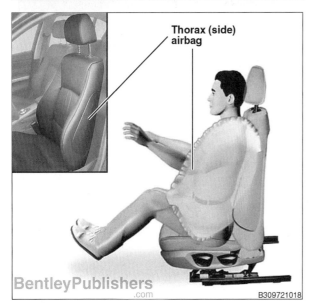

Thorax (side) airbag

B309721018

◄ **Thorax (side) airbag**, mounted to the front seat backrest frame, is designed to protect the front seat occupant during a side impact. Side airbags are activated by a signal from the MRS control module in case of a side impact or a front angled impact of sufficient severity to cause both front and side airbag deployment.

The side airbag module consists of a molded plastic case housing a folded nylon fabric bag, gas generating capsules and an igniter squib. Two studs at the rear of the side airbag module are used for mounting the module to the seat frame and are secured in position by two nylon locknuts.

The side airbag module has a 2-pin connector under the seat where it connects to the vehicle main harness.

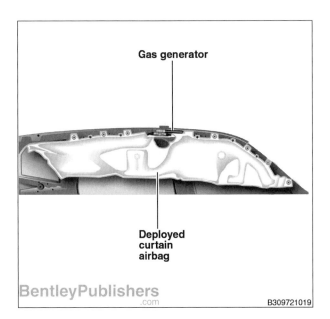

Gas generator

Deployed curtain airbag

B309721019

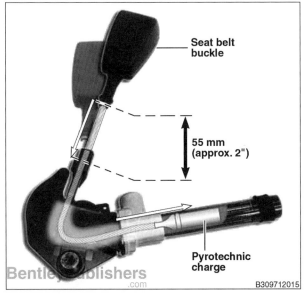

Seat belt buckle

55 mm (approx. 2")

Pyrotechnic charge

B309712015

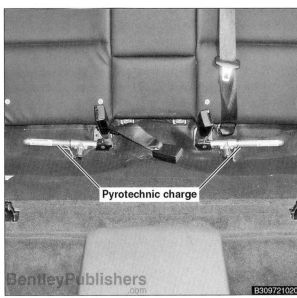

Pyrotechnic charge

B309721020

◄ **Curtain airbag**, extending all the way from the A-pillar to the C-pillar, covering the entire side-window area, inflates between the vehicle occupants and the side windows and pillar trims.

The curtain airbag reduces the risk of occupant's head or other extremities protruding through the windows in a sideways collision. Advantages of the system are:

• Extended covered area for side windows, front and rear.

• Protection against glass splinters and penetrating objects.

• Optimized protective area offering protection for occupants of differing sizes.

The curtain airbag is positioned along the line of the roof side member, folded up. It consists of a gas generator, two gas nozzles and curtain. In the event of a severe enough side collision, the generator is detonated and the gas flows through the two gas nozzles into the curtain. Simultaneous inflation of the curtain at the front and back achieves more even deployment.

Because the curtain generators and curtain are a sealed system, the curtain airbag retains its shape and strength for several seconds.

◄ **Seat belt tensioner.** Each seat belt buckle is equipped with a pyrotechnic (explosive charge) tensioner capable of cinching the belt an additional 55 mm (approx. 2 inches) in case of an accident. The belt buckle is attached via steel cable to a tube containing explosive propellant and a piston. An igniter (squib) in the base of the tube provides an ignition source when triggered by a signal from the MRS control module. A 2-pin connector located on a bracket underneath the seat frame links the igniter to MRS wiring.

The MRS control module deploys the pyrotechnic seat belt tensioners at a slightly lower impact threshold level than the front airbags.

**Belt buckle Hall microswitch** in the front seat belt buckle is used to detect whether the seat belt is fastened or not. The detection signal is used by the MRS control module as a criterion for selective triggering of airbags and seat belt tensioners in case of a crash.

The switch is supplied current by the MRS control module via a current-signal interface. The current draw of the switch is the signal for switch position. The belt buckle switch is monitored while the ignition is ON.

◄ **Rear belt tensioners** are also equipped with pyrotechnic devices.

Seat belt tensioner replacement is covered in **720 Seat Belts**.

**721**

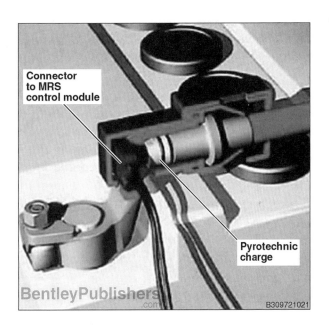

Connector to MRS control module

Pyrotechnic charge

◀ **Battery safety terminal (BST)** is used to minimize the possibility of a short circuit at the heavy gauge B+ wire that runs the length of the vehicle in case of an accident.

The BST consists of a conventional clamp that is screwed to the positive terminal from above and connected with a hollow cylinder. A propellant charge is stored in this hollow cylinder. As with airbags and seat belt tensioners, this pyrotechnic device is controlled and ignited by the MRS control module. The unit is enclosed in a plastic shell that captures the cable if it is forced out via BST deployment and locks it so that a renewed contact is no longer possible.

See also **121 Battery, Starter, Alternator**.

## MRS system inputs, outputs

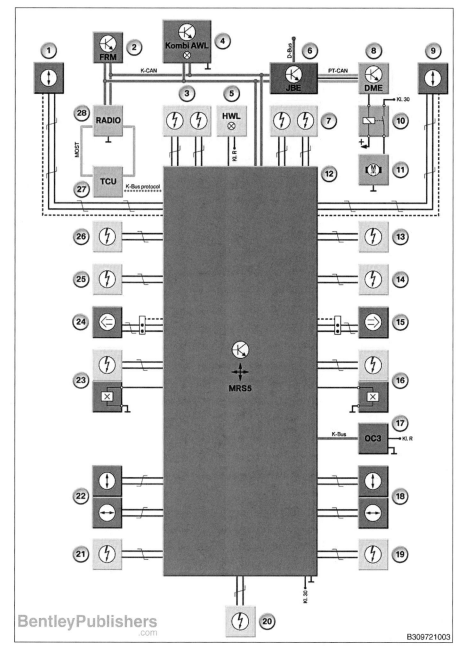

1. Left front crash sensor
2. Footwell module (FRM)
3. Driver airbag
4. Instrument cluster
5. Airbag warning light
6. Junction box electronic module (JBE)
7. Passenger airbag
8. Engine control module (ECM)
9. Right front crash sensor
10. Fuel pump relay
11. Fuel pump
12. MRS control module
13. Right side curtain airbag
14. Passenger thorax (side) airbag
15. Passenger door pressure sensor
16. Right front belt buckle status and seat belt tensioner
17. Passenger seat occupancy sensor (OC-3)
18. Right B-pillar sensor crash sensor
19. Right rear seat belt tensioner
20. Battery safety terminal (BST)
21. Left rear seat belt tensioner
22. Left B-pillar crash sensor
23. Left front belt buckle status and seat belt tensioner
24. Left front door pressure sensor
25. Driver thorax (side) airbag
26. Left curtain airbag
27. Telematics control module (TCU)
28. Radio (RAD2 or CCC)

B309721003

721

## Principles of operation

MRS control module performs the following functions:

• Crash detection and determining triggering point.

• Triggering ignition output stages.

• Documentation of crash data.

• System self-test.

• Cyclic monitoring.

• Display of system standby status.

• Fault indication and fault code storage.

• Fault output (diagnosis).

• Output of a crash telegram for other users in communication system network.

• Activation of airbag indicator light when passenger airbag is deactivated.

### Crash detection

The MRS control module determines whether a crash has occurred based on the values detected by crash sensors and calculated by a triggering algorithm. Deceleration signals from two independent sensors are needed to indicate a crash. In the case of a frontal crash for example, the acceleration values from the B-pillar satellite and from the longitudinal acceleration sensor (in the control module) are needed.

Signals from different sensors help determine crash severity and direction. Based on this information, the stored algorithm determines the triggering (ignition) points of the restraint systems to be activated.

### Triggering output stages

Signals from two different sensors, B-pillar satellite and MRS control module sensor, triggers airbag ignition output stages.

With ignition ON, voltage is supplied to the MRS control module, which becomes operational once it completes a system self-test. In case of a crash, a capacitor provides the energy reserve for airbag ignition even if electrical power is interrupted.

### Documentation of actuator triggering

The triggering (ignition) commands are recorded in case of a crash where one or several actuators are triggered. The most important crash event data are stored in the form of a crash telegram in the non-volatile memory of the MRS control module. This data is only available to the manufacturer.

A maximum of 3 crash telegrams can be stored, after which the control module needs to be replaced.

### System self-test

The control module performs a system self-test when the ignition is switched ON. The airbag warning light is illuminated for 3 - 5 seconds during system self-test.

If system self-test finds no faults, the airbag warning light switches OFF and the system is ready for operation.

## Cyclic monitoring

Once system self-test is successfully concluded and the system is ready for operation, cyclic fault monitoring is performed as long as ignition is ON.

## Indication of system operability

System operability is indicated by the airbag warning light switching OFF in the instrument cluster.

## Fault code storage

A fault in the system is indicated by the airbag warning light and stored in nonvolatile control module memory. A distinction is made between internal and external faults.

## Fault output (diagnosis)

Using BMW scan tool or equivalent, fault codes can be read out via the diagnosis interface. After rectifying faults, the fault codes can be cleared by means of "clear fault code memory" diagnosis command.

## Crash telegram output

In case of a crash which triggers restraint system components, the MRS control module sends a crash telegram via bus system. The following control modules then perform the following functions depending on crash severity:

| Crash telegram responses | |
|---|---|
| Fuel pump control module (EKP) | Switches fuel pump OFF |
| Engine control module (ECM) | Switches alternator OFF |
| Junction box module (JBE) | Releases central locking |
| Footwell module (FRM) | Activates hazard warning lights |
| Footwell module (FRM) | Activates interior lights |
| Telematic control module (TCU) | Places emergency call |

## Deactivation of passenger airbags

MRS control module utilizes the OC-3 mat signal to deactivate the front and side passenger airbags when a child seat is mounted on the passenger side. Airbag deactivation is indicated by a yellow airbag indicator light.

## Seat belt reminder

The seat belt reminder (SBR) function monitors whether the driver or passenger has fastened his or her seat belt. If the seat belt is not worn or is unbuckled while driving at a speed in excess of approx. 1 kph (0.6 mph), a reminder is illuminated and a chime is sounded.

Left and right front seat belt buckle microswitches are monitored separately.

**721**

## Warnings and Cautions

> **WARNING —**
>
> - The airbag is inflated by an explosive device. Handled improperly or without adequate safeguards, it can be very dangerous. Observe special precautions prior to any work at or near airbags.
>
> - Serious injury may result if system service is attempted by persons unfamiliar with the BMW airbag system and its approved service procedures. BMW advises that airbag system inspection and service be performed by an authorized BMW dealer.
>
> - Special test equipment is required to retrieve airbag fault codes, diagnose system faults and switch the airbag warning light OFF. The warning light remains ON until problems are corrected and fault memory cleared.
>
> - If the airbag warning light is ON, there is a risk that airbags are not triggered in case of an accident. Be sure to have the system inspected and repaired immediately.
>
> - Disconnect the battery and cover the negative (–) battery terminal with an insulator before starting diagnostic, troubleshooting or service work associated with the airbags, and before doing any welding on the car.
>
> - After disconnecting the battery, wait 1 minute before beginning work on airbag components.
>
> - If an airbag deploys due to an accident, BMW specifies that airbag components be replaced. For more information on post-collision airbag service, see an authorized BMW dealer.
>
> - If the driver airbag deploys in an accident, BMW specifies that the steering column be replaced during repairs.
>
> - Do not fire an airbag unit prior to disposal. It must be fired by a special disposal company or shipped back to BMW in the packaging of the new components.
>
> - Wear gloves and avoid skin contact when removing a deployed airbag unit. In case of skin contact, wash with water.
>
> - Do not allow airbag system components to come in contact with cleaning solutions or grease. Do not subject airbag components to temperatures above 75°C (167°F). When reconnecting the battery, make sure no person is inside the vehicle.
>
> - Place a removed airbag unit with the padded side facing upward. Do not leave an airbag unit unattended.
>
> - If the airbag unit or airbag control module is dropped from a height of ½ meter (1½ feet) or more, do not use it.

> **CAUTION —**
>
> - To avoid damaging plastic interior trim, use a plastic prying tool or a screwdriver with the tip wrapped with masking tape.

## MRS COMPONENT REPLACEMENT

### MRS control module, replacing

— Disconnect negative (–) cable from battery and cover negative terminal with insulating material.

> **CAUTION—**
> • *Prior to disconnecting the battery, read the battery disconnection cautions given in* **001 Warnings and Cautions**.

— Remove center console between front seats. See **513 Interior Trim**.

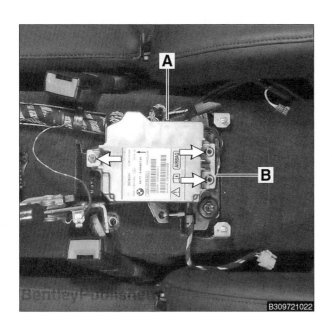

◀ Remove MRS control module mounting fasteners (**arrows**) and lift up module. Disconnect electrical harness connectors (**A**).

— Installation is reverse of removal. Make sure ground (**B**) is on threaded stud before reinstalling module.

| Tightening torque | |
|---|---|
| MRS control module to center tunnel | 8 Nm (6 ft-lb) |

— Use BMW scan tool or equivalent to code new module.

### Driver airbag, removing and installing

Vehicles covered by this manual are equipped with either a multifunction steering wheel or a sport steering wheel. Follow applicable procedure below to remove airbag.

— Disconnect negative (–) cable from battery and cover negative terminal with insulating material.

> **WARNING—**
> • *After disconnecting the battery, wait 1 minute before beginning work on airbag components.*

> **CAUTION—**
> • *Prior to disconnecting the battery, read the battery disconnection cautions given in* **001 Warnings and Cautions**.

#### Multifunction steering wheel

◀ Insert Torx screwdriver (T20) or equivalent vertically from below into opening on back side of steering wheel up to stop (approx. 5.5 cm or 2 in). Swing screwdriver sideways against spring retainer until one side of airbag unit is unlocked.

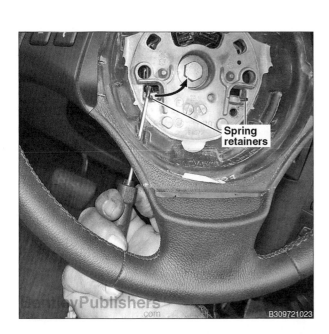

Spring retainers

— Repeat procedure on other side and tilt back airbag.

**721**

◀ Press on electrical connector lock (**arrow**) to detach, then remove airbag unit.

> **WARNING—**
> • *Place a removed airbag unit with the padded side facing upward. Do not leave an airbag unit unattended.*
> • *Do not pinch airbag harness in center of steering wheel when removing or installing airbag.*

– Installation is reverse of removal:
  • Make sure electrical lead is positioned correctly.
  • Press airbag directly down on steering wheel until it snaps in place.

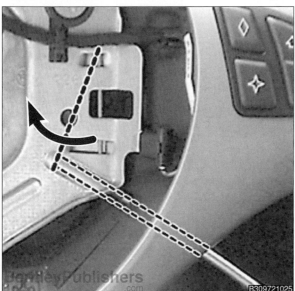

### Sport steering wheel

◀ Insert Torx screwdriver (T25) at an angle into concealed opening on back side of steering wheel until spring resistance is felt (approx. 1.5 cm or 0.6 in). Increase pressure on spring until airbag unit is unlocked.

– Repeat procedure on other side and tilt back airbag.

◀ Disconnect electrical connectors (**arrows**) and remove airbag unit.

> **WARNING—**
> • *Place a removed airbag unit with the padded side facing upward. Do not leave an airbag unit unattended.*
> • *Do not pinch airbag harness in center of steering wheel when removing or installing airbag.*

– Installation is reverse of removal:
  • Make sure electrical leads are positioned correctly. Connect same color connectors to each other.
  • Press airbag directly down on steering wheel until it snaps in place.

## Passenger airbag, removing and installing

If the passenger airbag deploys, it tears a hole through the dashboard surface. Be prepared to replace the dashboard.

— Disconnect negative (–) cable from battery and cover negative terminal with insulating material.

> **WARNING**—
> • After disconnecting the battery, wait 1 minute before beginning work on airbag components.

> **CAUTION**—
> • Prior to disconnecting the battery, read the battery disconnection cautions given in **001 Warnings and Cautions**.

— Remove glove compartment. See **513 Interior Trim**.

◄ Working from below right side of dashboard:

• Detach electrical connectors (**A**).

• While supporting airbag unit, remove mounting fasteners (**arrows**), then lower airbag.

> **WARNING**—
> • Place a removed airbag unit with the padded side facing upward. Do not leave an airbag unit unattended.

> **NOTE**—
> • Airbag unit shown is in 2007 vehicle. Models built before 03 / 2006 are equipped with one electrical connector.

— Models from 03 / 2006: Installation is reverse of removal.

| Tightening torque | |
|---|---|
| Passenger airbag to body crossbeam | 7 Nm (5 ft-lb) |

◄ Models to 03 / 2006:

• Attach updated (2-connector) harness to new airbag module. Connect same color connectors to each other.

• Tape harness to airbag, making sure that approx 190 ± 10 mm (7.5 ± 0.5 in) of cable is free.

• Attach foam pads to airbag as indicated.

• Install airbag and plug in single harness connector.

| Tightening torque | |
|---|---|
| Passenger airbag to body crossbeam | 7 Nm (5 ft-lb) |

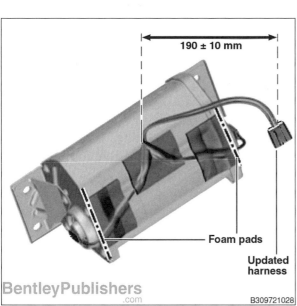

**190 ± 10 mm**

**Foam pads**

**Updated harness**

721

# ECL Electrical Component Locations

## GENERAL

This repair group covers electrical component location information. Fuse locations and ground points are also covered.

Electrical equipment and accessories included vary with model and model year. Confirm component identification whenever you begin work on the electrical system.

See also:

- **130 Fuel Injection** for engine management components
- **520 Seats** for seat control and seat heating components
- **541 Convertible Top** for retractable hard top components
- **600 Electrical System–General** for bus systems
- **640 Air-conditioning and Heating** for climate control system components
- **650 Radio** for communication equipment components
- **ELE Electrical Wiring Diagrams** for electrical schematics

**ECL**

## BMW acronyms

BMW uses many abbreviations and acronyms in the technical literature, service bulletins, wiring diagrams and parts bulletins it distributes. See **Table a** for common BMW and industry acronyms.

| Table a. Common BMW acronyms | |
|---|---|
| **Acronym** | **Component or system** |
| A/C | air-conditioning |
| ABS | antilock brakes |
| ACC | active cruise control |
| AGS | adaptive gearbox system |
| AUC | automatic air recirculation control |
| BST | battery safety terminal |
| CA | comfort access |
| CAN | controller area network (bus) |
| CAS | car access system (module) |
| CBS | condition-based service |
| CCC/M-ASK | car communications computer / audio system controller |
| CID | central information display |
| CIC | car information computer |
| DISA | variable intake manifold system |
| DME | digital motor electronics |
| DM-TL | diagnosis module—tank leakage |
| DSC | dynamic stability control |
| DWA | antitheft alarm |
| ECM | engine control module |
| ECT | engine coolant temperature (sensor) |
| EDK | electronic throttle |
| EEPROM | flash programmable read-only memory |
| EGS | electronic transmission control |
| ELV | electronic steering lock |
| EPROM | erasable / programmable read-only memory |
| EVAP | fuel tank evaporative control system |
| EWS | electronic immobilizer |
| FH | power windows |
| FRM | footwell module |
| FZD | roof function center |
| GPS | global positioning system |
| HPS | head protection airbag |
| IAT | intake air temperature (sensor) |
| IB | interior lighting |
| IHKA | automatic heating and air-conditioning system |
| IKE | integrated instrument cluster module |

| Table a. Common BMW acronyms | |
|---|---|
| **Acronym** | **Component or system** |
| ITS | inflatable tubular structure (head protection airbag) |
| JB | junction box |
| JBE | junction box electronic module |
| KL R | battery positive, ignition on accessories |
| KL 15 | battery positive, ignition switch on RUN |
| KL 30 | battery positive (B+), power |
| KL 31 | battery / chassis ground |
| KL 50 | ignition start position, power |
| LDP | fuel tank leak diagnosis pump |
| LED | light emitting diode |
| LEV | low emissions vehicle |
| LIN | local interconnected network (bus) |
| MIL | malfunction indicator light |
| MRS | multiple restraint system (airbags) |
| NAV | navigation system |
| NLEV | national low emissions vehicle |
| NTC | negative temperature coefficient (resistor) |
| OBD II | second generation on-board diagnostics |
| PDC | park distance control |
| PWG | accelerator pedal module |
| RAM | random access memory |
| RDC | tire pressure control |
| RXD | receive data line |
| SHD | sunroof module |
| SRS | supplemental restraint system (airbags) |
| SZL | steering column switch cluster |
| TAGE | electronic outer door handle module |
| TCM | automatic transmission control module |
| TCU | telematics control module |
| TDC | top dead center |
| TI | injection signal |
| TLEV | transitional low emissions vehicle |
| TPM | tire pressure monitoring |
| TXD | transmit data line |
| ULEV | ultra low emissions vehicle |
| VANOS | variable camshaft timing |
| VVT | Valvetronic |

## Warnings and Cautions

> **WARNING—**
> • The battery safety terminal, pyrotechnic seat belt tensioners and airbags utilize explosive devices. Handle with extreme care. See warnings and cautions in **121 Battery, Alternator, Starter**, **720 Seat Belts**, and **721 Airbag System (SRS)**.

> **CAUTION—**
> • Prior to disconnecting the battery, read the battery disconnection precautions in **001 Warnings and Cautions**.
> • Relay and fuse positions vary from car to car. If questions arise, an authorized BMW dealer is the best source for the most accurate and up-to-date information.
> • A good way to verify a relay position is to compare the wiring colors at the relay socket to the colors indicated on the wiring diagrams in **ELE Electrical Wiring Diagrams**.
> • Switch the ignition OFF and remove the negative (-) battery cable before removing any electrical components. Connect and disconnect ignition system wires, multiple connectors, and ignition test equipment leads while the ignition is switched OFF.
> • Use a digital multimeter for electrical tests.

## ELECTRICAL COMPONENTS

### Electrical components table

**Table b** is a cross-referenced listing of electrical components in E90 vehicles.

• **Column 1**: Components alphabetized by names in current usage
• **Column 2**: BMW alphanumeric code
• **Column 3**: Location in vehicle
• **Column 4**: Figure number in this repair group, if illustrated
• **Column 5**: Page number for illustration

Photos in this repair group illustrate a 2007 328i unless indicated otherwise.

**Table b. E90 component locations**

| Component | Code | Location | Fig # | Page # |
|---|---|---|---|---|
| 12v socket, center console | E840 | Center console behind parking brake handle | | |
| 12v socket, rear | A14112 | Right side trunk or cargo compartment | | |
| 12v socket, rear | X18846 | Left side trunk or cargo compartment | **Fig 44** | **Pg 43** |
| 30g_f relay | | *see* Bistable relay (30g_f) | | |
| A/C and heating control panel (module) | A11a | Center dashboard | | |
| A/C and heating electrical components | | *see* **640 Heating and Air-conditioning** *see also* Heater | | |
| A/C compressor | Y2 | Right side of engine | | |
| ABS | | *see also* DSC entries | | |
| ABS / DSC control module | A65a | Left rear engine compartment in air intake plenum | **Fig 11** **Fig 12** | **Pg 33** **Pg 34** |

**ECL**

*Electrical components table*

| Table b. E90 component locations | | | | |
|---|---|---|---|---|
| **Component** | **Code** | **Location** | **Fig #** | **Page #** |
| ABS wheel speed sensor | B1, B2 B3, B4 | Wheel hub, left front, right front, left rear, or right rear wheel *see also* **340 Brakes** | | |
| Accelerator pedal module | A234a B10 | Underneath accelerator pedal | | |
| Active cruise control module | A144a | Center of front bumper, underneath right kidney grille | **Fig 48** | **Pg 45** |
| Active steering control module | A467 | Left footwell behind kick panel trim | **Fig 48** | **Pg 45** |
| AGS | | *see* Automatic transmission control module | | |
| Airbag | | *see also* MRS | | |
| Airbag contact spring, driver side | | Underneath steering wheel, at steering column switch cluster | | |
| Airbag control module | A12 | Between front seats, under center console | **Fig 35** | **Pg 41** |
| Airbag deactivation switch, passenger airbag | S559 | Right end of dashboard | | |
| Airbag sensor, driver, passenger | B10508a, B10509a | Engine compartment inner fender, left, right | | |
| Airbag sensor, front side airbag | B78 B79 | Front of front door, left, right | | |
| Airbag sensor, rear side airbag | A173 A174 | Coupe, Convertible: Behind B-pillar behind trim | | |
| Airbag sensor, rear side airbag | A173 A174 | Sedan, Sports Wagon: Lower left or right B-pillar behind trim | | |
| Airbag, driver | G5 | In steering wheel under horn button | | |
| Airbag, head protection, left, right | G17, G18 | Top of B-pillar, left, right | | |
| Airbag, passenger | G6 | Under right end of dashboard | | |
| Airbag, side, driver | G14b | Left edge of driver seat backrest | | |
| Airbag, side, passenger | G15b | Right edge of passenger seat backrest | | |
| Alarm | | *see* Anti-theft | | |
| Alternator (generator) | G6524 | Left front of engine | **Fig 20** | **Pg 36** |
| Amplifier | A18 | Left side trunk or cargo compartment behind trim | **Fig 48** | **Pg 45** |
| Antenna | | *see* **650 Radio** *see also* Tire pressure control | | |
| Anti-theft siren (DWA) | H1 | Left rear inner fender well | | |
| AUC sensor | | *see* Automatic air recirculation (AUC) sensor | | |
| Audio system components | | *see* **650 Radio** | | |
| Audio system controller / car communications computer (CCC/M-ASK) | N38a | Center dashboard | | |
| Audio-visual socket | A18807 | Center console behind parking brake handle | | |
| Automatic air recirculation (AUC) sensor | B414 | Right rear engine compartment in fresh air plenum | | |
| Automatic transmission control module (TCM) | A7000a | In transmission housing, rear | | |
| Automatic transmission range indicator light | E82 | Under selector lever bezel | | |
| B+ jump start terminal | G6430 | Right rear engine compartment | **Fig 11** **Fig 12** | **Pg 33** **Pg 34** |
| B+ power | A2076 | Right rear engine compartment in electronics box (E-box) | **Fig 7** | **Pg 26** |
| Back-up light switch | S8511 | Manual transmission: Right rear transmission housing | **Fig 23** | **Pg 37** |

**Table b. E90 component locations**

| Component | Code | Location | Fig # | Page # |
|---|---|---|---|---|
| Battery | G1 | Right side trunk or cargo compartment, behind trim | Fig 1<br>Fig 47 | Pg 16<br>Pg 44 |
| Battery safety terminal (BST) | G19a | Positive battery terminal, in trunk or cargo compartment | Fig 1 | Pg 16 |
| Battery sensor | B895 | Top of battery, in trunk or cargo compartment | Fig 1<br>Fig 48 | Pg 16<br>Pg 45 |
| Bistable relay (30g_f) | I01139 | Junction box (JB), behind glove compartment | | |
| Blower | M30 | Under right side dashboard | | |
| Blower output stage | N2 | On blower under right side dashboard | | |
| Brake fluid level switch | B18a | Brake fluid reservoir, left rear engine compartment | Fig 11<br>Fig 12 | Pg 33<br>Pg 34 |
| Brake light switch | S29 | Above brake pedal | | |
| Brake pad wear sensor | B16a<br>B17a | Brake caliper, left front, right rear | | |
| BST | | *see* Battery safety terminal (BST) | | |
| Camshaft sensor, intake, exhaust | B6214,<br>B6224 | Front of cylinder head, left, right | Fig 13 | Pg 35 |
| Car access system | | *see* CAS module | | |
| Cargo compartment roller cover motor release, left, right | M300<br>M301 | D-pillar behind quarter glass, left, right | | |
| CAS module | A149a | Underneath left side dashboard, left of steering column | | |
| CCC/M-ASK | | *see* Audio system controller / car communications computer (CCC/M-ASK) | | |
| CD changer | | Left side trunk or cargo compartment behind trim | Fig 48 | Pg 45 |
| Center brake light | H34 | Convertible: Top of trunk lid | | |
| Center brake light | H34a | Non-convertible: Above rear window | Fig 43 | Pg 43 |
| Center console switch center | A169 | Above center console in lower center dashboard | | |
| Central information display | A165a | Center dashboard | Fig 10<br>Fig 48 | Pg 32<br>Pg 45 |
| Central locking switch | | Ganged with hazard warning and DSC switches, upper center dashboard | | |
| Classification resistor | | *see* xDrive classification resistor | | |
| Closed circuit latching relay | | *see* Bistable relay (30g_f) | | |
| Clutch switch | S805a | Above clutch pedal | | |
| Comfort access control module | A215 | Right side trunk or cargo compartment behind trim | Fig 47<br>Fig 48 | Pg 44<br>Pg 45 |
| Compressor | | *see* A/C compressor | | |
| Condensation sensor | B100 | Top center of windshield | | |
| Convertible top components | | *see* **541 Convertible Top** | | |
| Coolant | | *see* Engine coolant | | |
| Crankcase breather heater | E65390 | Non-turbo: Intake manifold | Fig 17 | Pg 36 |
| Crankcase breather heater | E65390 | Turbo: Behind left rear of cylinder head | Fig 19 | Pg 36 |
| Crankcase breather heater relay | K6539 | Right rear engine compartment in electronics box (E-box) | Fig 5 | Pg 25 |
| Crankshaft sensor | B6203a | Left rear of engine block near bell housing | | |
| DISA controllers | | *see* Variable intake manifold (DISA) controllers | | |
| DLC | | *see* OBD II socket | | |

ECL

*Electrical components table*

**Table b. E90 component locations**

| Component | Code | Location | Fig # | Page # |
|---|---|---|---|---|
| DME main relay | K6300 | Right rear engine compartment in electronics box (E-box) | **Fig 5**<br>**Fig 6** | **Pg 25**<br>**Pg 26** |
| Door handle control module, driver door, passenger door | S263<br>S264 | Outer door handle, driver door, passenger door | | |
| Door locks, driver door, passenger door | S47<br>S49 | Rear of door in door cavity, left, right | | |
| Door locks, right rear, left rear | M14a<br>M15a | Rear lower edge of door inside door cavity, right, left, | | |
| Door switch cluster, driver door | A23b | Driver door arm rest | | |
| Driver seat control module | A187 | Underneath center of driver seat | | |
| DSC | | *see also* ABS | | |
| DSC acceleration sensor | B9801 | Under driver seat front rail, bolted to floor | **Fig 48** | **Pg 45** |
| DSC control module | | *see* ABS / DSC control module | | |
| DSC hydraulic unit | | On DSC control module | | |
| DSC steering angle sensor | | Steering column switch center (SZL)<br>*see* **612 Switches** | | |
| DSC switch | | Ganged with hazard warning and central locking switches, upper center dashboard | | |
| Dynamic stability control | | *see* ABS / DSC<br>*see also* DSC | | |
| EAC sensor | | *see* Environmental air catalyst (EAC) sensor | | |
| E-box | | Right rear engine compartment under cover | **Fig 11**<br>**Fig 12** | **Pg 33**<br>**Pg 34** |
| E-box fan | M6506 | Base of E-box | | |
| Eccentric shaft sensor | B60213 | Non-turbo: Top front of cylinder head cover | | |
| ECM | | *see* Engine control module (ECM) | | |
| Electric cooling fan cutoff relay | K9137 | Right rear engine compartment in electronics box (E-box) | **Fig 8**<br>**Fig 9** | **Pg 28**<br>**Pg 28** |
| Electronic power steering | | *see* Steering | | |
| Electronics box | | *see* E-box | | |
| Engine control module (ECM) | A6000 | Right rear engine compartment in electronics box (E-box) | **Fig 5**<br>**Fig 8**<br>**Fig 9**<br>**Fig 10**<br>**Fig 48** | **Pg 25**<br>**Pg 28**<br>**Pg 28**<br>**Pg 32**<br>**Pg 45** |
| Engine control module relay | | *see* DME main relay | | |
| Engine coolant level switch | S63b | Bottom of coolant reservoir, right front engine compartment | | |
| Engine coolant pressure sensor | B8 | Right side engine compartment underneath coolant reservoir | | |
| Engine coolant pump, electric | M6035 | Right front lower engine compartment | **Fig 14**<br>**Fig 15** | **Pg 35**<br>**Pg 35** |
| Engine coolant temperature (ECT) sensor | B6236 | Turbo: Left front of cylinder head, on thermostat housing cover | **Fig 13** | **Pg 35** |
| Engine coolant temperature (ECT) sensor | B6236a | Non-turbo: Right front engine compartment on thermostat housing | | |
| Engine coolant temperature sensor, radiator outlet | B604b | Lower radiator hose, right front engine compartment | | |

### Table b. E90 component locations

| Component | Code | Location | Fig # | Page # |
|---|---|---|---|---|
| Engine cooling fan | M9 | Between radiator and engine | | |
| Engine electronics fuse carriers | A8680 A8681 A8682 A8684 A8685 | *see* **Fuse Locations and Ratings** in this repair group *see also* **E-box engine electronics fuse carriers** in this repair group | | |
| Engine hood contact switch | S19a | Left rear engine compartment behind plenum bulkhead | | |
| Engine mount changeover valve | B2231 | Right rear of engine | | |
| Environmental air catalyst (EAC) sensor | B111 | N51 engine: Behind right side of radiator | | |
| Evaporative emissions valve | Y6120 | Non-turbo: Underneath intake manifold | **Fig 18** | **Pg 36** |
| Evaporative emissions valve | Y6120 | Turbo: Behind cylinder head | **Fig 19** | **Pg 36** |
| Exhaust camshaft sensor | | *see* Camshaft sensor | | |
| Exhaust flap | Y198 | Tailpipe | | |
| Final stage unit | | *see* Blower final stage | | |
| Foglight switch | | On dashboard, left of steering column | | |
| Footwell module | A4011 | Left lower A-pillar behind kick panel | **Fig 48** | **Pg 45** |
| Fuel filler flap lock motor | M16 | Right side trunk or cargo compartment behind trim | **Fig 47** **Fig 49** | **Pg 44** **Pg 46** |
| Fuel injector relay | K6327 | Right rear engine compartment in electronics box (E-box) | **Fig 5** | **Pg 25** |
| Fuel injectors | Y6101 - Y6106 | Non-turbo: Intake manifold Turbo: Top of cylinder head | | |
| Fuel level sensor | B25a | Top of fuel tank, underneath right rear seat | | |
| Fuel pressure sensor, low pressure | B6125a | Turbo: Left lower engine, underneath throttle housing | **Fig 20** | **Pg 36** |
| Fuel pump | M2 | Underneath right rear seat cushion, top of fuel tank | | |
| Fuel pump control module | A13663 | Sedan, Sports Wagon: Right C-pillar behind rear seat side bolster | **Fig 41** **Fig 48** | **Pg 42** **Pg 45** |
| Fuel pump control module | A13663 | Convertible: Behind rear seat backrest, lower right | **Fig 42** **Fig 48** | **Pg 42** **Pg 45** |
| Fuel pump relay | K96 | Junction box, underneath right side dashboard, behind glove compartment | **Fig 27** | **Pg 38** |
| Fuel rail pressure sensor | B2261 | Turbo: Fuel rail, top of engine | **Fig 20** | **Pg 36** |
| Fuel tank flap emergency release cable | | Trunk or cargo compartment, behind right trim | | |
| Fuel tank leakage diagnostic module | M119a | Underneath vehicle, behind left rear wheel housing | | |
| Fuel volume control valve | Y2381 | Turbo: high pressure pump, left side engine | **Fig 20** | **Pg 36** |
| Fuse carrier, engine electronics | | *see* **E-box engine electronics fuse carriers** in this repair group | | |
| Fuses | | *see* **Fuse Locations and Ratings** in this repair group | | |
| Gearshift paddles | I01091 I01092 | On steering wheel spokes | | |
| Generator | | *see* Alternator (generator) | | |
| GPS | | *see* Audio system controller / car communications computer (CCC/M-ASK) *see also* Navigation | | |
| Grounds | | *see* **Grounds** in this repair group | | |
| Hall effect camshaft position sensor | | *see* Camshaft sensor | | |

ECL

*Electrical components table*

**Table b. E90 component locations**

| Component | Code | Location | Fig # | Page # |
|---|---|---|---|---|
| Hand-free microphone | B402 B403 | Dome light unit, left, right | Fig 48 | Pg 45 |
| Hazard warning switch | S18a | Ganged with central locking and DSC switches, upper center dashboard | | |
| Headlight aim control motor, right, left | E126 E127 | Rear of headlight assembly, right, left | | |
| Headlight washer pump | M7 | Washer fluid reservoir, behind right wheel housing | Fig 21 | Pg 37 |
| Headlight washer relay | K6 | Junction box (JB), underneath right side dashboard, behind glove compartment | Fig 27 | Pg 38 |
| Heated oxygen sensor | | *see* Oxygen sensor | | |
| Heater valve | Y4 | Left rear engine compartment | | |
| Heating | | *see* Air-conditioning and heating | | |
| High amperage fuses | A46 | Top of battery, in trunk or cargo compartment | Fig 1 | Pg 16 |
| Horn relay | K2 | Junction box (JB), underneath right side dashboard, behind glove compartment | Fig 27 | Pg 38 |
| Horn switch | S4a | Steering wheel | | |
| Horns | H2a H3a | Behind front bumper, left, right | | |
| Hot-film mass air flow sensor | | *see* Mass air flow sensor | | |
| iDrive controller | A167a | Center console between front seats | | |
| Ignition coil suppression capacitor | I01046 | Top of cylinder head cover in ignition coil harness | Fig 11 | Pg 33 |
| Ignition coils | T6151 - T6156 | Top of cylinder head cover above spark plugs | Fig 11 Fig 12 | Pg 33 Pg 34 |
| Ignition key slot | | *see* Slide-in compartment | | |
| Ignition switch | S2 | Right of steering column | | |
| IHKA | | *see* **640 Air-conditioning and Heating** | | |
| IKE | | *see* Instrument cluster module | | |
| Information display module | | *see* Central information display | | |
| Instrument cluster module | A2a | Dashboard | Fig 48 | Pg 45 |
| Intake camshaft sensor | | *see* Camshaft sensor | | |
| Intake pressure sensor | B6239 | Non-turbo: Left rear cylinder head, on cylinder head cover | Fig 11 Fig 17 | Pg 33 Pg 36 |
| Intake resonance valve | | *see* Variable intake manifold (DISA) controllers | | |
| Interference suppressor filter, radio | U410 | Left C-pillar | Fig 40 | Pg 42 |
| Interior movement sensor (ultrasonic detector) | A121a | Sedan: Dome light unit | Fig 10 | Pg 32 |
| Interior movement sensor (ultrasonic detector) | A121a | Sports Wagon: Roof function module | Fig 48 | Pg 45 |
| JB | | *see* Junction box (JB) | | |
| JBE | | *see* Junction box electronic control module (JBE) | | |
| Junction box (JB) | A4010 | Underneath right side dashboard, behind glove compartment | Fig 2 Fig 10 Fig 27 Fig 28 Fig 48 | Pg 18 Pg 32 Pg 38 Pg 39 Pg 45 |

**Table b. E90 component locations**

| Component | Code | Location | Fig # | Page # |
|---|---|---|---|---|
| Junction box electronic control module (JBE) | A4010a | Junction box (JB), underneath right side dashboard, behind glove compartment | **Fig 27** **Fig 28** | **Pg 38** **Pg 39** |
| Knock sensors | B62400 | Left side engine block | **Fig 20** | **Pg 36** |
| Level sensor | | *see* Ride height sensor, front, rear | | |
| Light sensor | | *see* Rain / light sensor | | |
| Light switch | S8 | Left of steering column | | |
| Lockout circuit | | *see* Rear window defroster suppressor filter, right, left | | |
| Longitudinal dynamics management module | A14282 | Sedan: Underneath left side dashboard behind light switch | | |
| Longitudinal dynamics management module | A14282 | Sports Wagon: Junction box behind glove compartment | | |
| Low fuel pressure sensor | | *see* Fuel pressure sensor, low pressure | | |
| Mass air flow sensor | B6207b | Non-turbo: Air intake duct between air filter housing and throttle housing *see also* Secondary air injection intake mass air flow sensor | | |
| Memory switch | S50 | Seat control switch | | |
| Mirror module, electrochromic (inside) | A22 | Top center of windshield | | |
| Mirror, outside, left, right | Y5 Y6 | Driver door, passenger door | | |
| MOST-bus connector | I14255 | Left C-pillar, behind rear seat side bolster | **Fig 38** | **Pg 41** |
| MRS | | *see* Airbag entries | | |
| Multifunction switch assemblies | I01032 I01033 | On steering wheel spokes | | |
| Multiple restraint system | | *see* Airbag entries | | |
| Navigation module | A112a | Convertible: Rear center trunk floor under cover | | |
| Navigation module | A112a | Non-convertible: Left side trunk or cargo compartment behind trim | | |
| Neutral safety switch | Y19 | Under selector lever bezel, center console | **Fig 34** | **Pg 40** |
| O₂ sensor | | *see* Oxygen sensor | | |
| OBD II socket | X19527 | Edge of driver door post | | |
| Oil condition sensor | B62540 | Non-turbo: Rear of oil pan | **Fig 22** | **Pg 37** |
| Oil pressure switch | B6231 | Left front of cylinder head | **Fig 11** **Fig 12** **Fig 20** | **Pg 33** **Pg 34** **Pg 36** |
| Outside temperature sensor | B21a | Behind front bumper, right of center | | |
| Overhead function control module | A14286 | Front dome light unit | | |
| Oxygen sensor | B62101a B62102a B62201a B62202a | In exhaust pipes before and after catalytic converters | **Fig 22** **Fig 23** | **Pg 37** **Pg 37** |
| Oxygen sensor connectors (post-catalyst) | X62102 X62202 | Non-turbo engine: Underneath transmission bell housing | **Fig 22** | **Pg 37** |
| Oxygen sensor connectors (precatalyst) | X62101 X62201 | Non-turbo engine: Above intake manifold | **Fig 11** **Fig 12** | **Pg 33** **Pg 34** |
| Park / neutral position switch | | *see* Neutral safety switch | | |
| Park distance control (PDC) module | A81a | Right side trunk behind trim | **Fig 47** | **Pg 44** |

**ECL**

*Electrical components table*

| Table b. E90 component locations | | | | |
|---|---|---|---|---|
| Component | Code | Location | Fig # | Page # |
| Park distance control sensor, rear | B34a - B37a | Rear bumper | | |
| Park distance control sensors, front | B30a - B33a | Front bumper | | |
| Park distance control signal | H45 | Coupe, Convertible: Right quarter panel, behind trim | **Fig 36** **Fig 37** | **Pg 41** **Pg 41** |
| Parking brake warning switch | S31a | Base of parking brake handle, under center console | **Fig 35** | **Pg 41** |
| PDC | | *see* Park distance control (PDC) entries | | |
| Power steering | | *see* Steering | | |
| Pressure sensor | | *see* Engine coolant pressure sensor | | |
| Radiator outlet coolant temperature sensor | | *see* Engine coolant temperature sensor, radiator outlet | | |
| Radio | N9 | Center dashboard *see also* **650 Radio** | | |
| Rain / light sensor | B57b | Top center of windshield | | |
| RDC | | *see* Tire pressure control (RDC) entries | | |
| Rear window defroster | E9 | Rear window | | |
| Rear window defroster relay | K13 | Junction box (JB), underneath right side dashboard, behind glove compartment | **Fig 27** | **Pg 38** |
| Rear window defroster suppressor filter, right, left | Z1 Z2 | Sedan, Coupe: Right C-pillar, left C-pillar | **Fig 40** | **Pg 42** |
| Rear window lock motor | M96a | Sports Wagon: Center tailgate behind trim | | |
| Rear window release button | S147a | Sports Wagon: Base of rear window | | |
| Rear window washer pump | M95 | Washer fluid reservoir, behind right wheel housing | **Fig 21** | **Pg 37** |
| Relay, terminal 15 | I01069 | Junction box (JB), underneath right side dashboard, behind glove compartment (on PC board) | **Fig 27** | **Pg 38** |
| Relay, terminal 30g | I01068 | Junction box (JB), underneath right side dashboard, behind glove compartment | **Fig 27** **Fig 28** | **Pg 38** **Pg 39** |
| Resonance valve | | *see* Variable intake manifold (DISA) controllers | | |
| Ride height sensor, front, rear | B42b B64a | Left front, right rear suspension | | |
| Seat belt positioner motor, left, right | M49 M62 | Coupe, Convertible: Behind B-pillar behind trim | **Fig 37** | **Pg 41** |
| Seat belt positioner, left, right | I01157 - I01158 | Coupe, Convertible: Behind B-pillar behind trim | **Fig 37** | **Pg 41** |
| Seat belt pyrotechnic tensioner, driver seat belt, passenger seat belt | G12 G13 | Seat belt buckle, driver seat belt, passenger seat belt | | |
| Seat belt pyrotechnic tensioner, left rear, right rear | G27 G28 | Seat belt buckle, left rear, right rear | | |
| Seat control, seat heater components | | *see* **520 Seats** | | |
| Secondary air injection intake mass air flow sensor | B6206 | N51 engine: Right front engine compartment in secondary air intake hose | | |
| Secondary air injection pump | M63 | N51 engine: Right front, mounted to coolant reservoir | | |
| Secondary air injection pump relay | K6304 | N51 engine: Junction box (JB), underneath right side dashboard, behind glove compartment | **Fig 27** | **Pg 38** |
| Secondary air injection pump relay | K6304a | 2009-2010 non-turbo: Right rear engine compartment in electronics box (E-box) | **Fig 16** | **Pg 35** |

**Table b. E90 component locations**

| Component | Code | Location | Fig # | Page # |
|---|---|---|---|---|
| Selector lever position switch | S227 | Under selector lever bezel, center console | **Fig 34** | **Pg 40** |
| Slide-in compartment | S14028 | Right of steering column | | |
| Solar sensor | B66 | Front center of dashboard | | |
| Speakers | | *see* **650 Radio** | | |
| Speed (rpm) sensor | | *see* Crankshaft sensor | | |
| SRS | | *see* Airbag entries | | |
| Starter | M6510 | Left side of engine under intake manifold | **Fig 20** | **Pg 36** |
| Steering angle sensor | | *see* Steering column switch center | | |
| Steering column switch cluster | A72 | Behind steering wheel on steering column | **Fig 10** **Pg 32** | **Pg 32** **Pg 45** |
| Steering control module | A60233 | On steering rack | | |
| Steering lock | M137a | Underneath steering column | | |
| Steering lock | Y14035 | On electric steering rack | | |
| Steering module | | *see* Active steering control module | | |
| Steering rack, electric | M179 | Underneath vehicle, center front | **Fig 24** | **Pg 37** |
| Steering torque sensor | I01096 | Top of steering rack | | |
| Stepper motor | | *see* **640 Heating and Air-conditioning** | | |
| Steptronic switch | S224a | Under selector lever bezel, center console | **Fig 34** | **Pg 40** |
| Suction jet pump valve | Y6165a | Left side engine compartment | | |
| Sunroof control module | A14102 | Sports Wagon: Above center of windshield, behind dome light unit | | |
| Sunroof drive unit | A33c | Above center of windshield, behind dome light unit | | |
| Sunroof motors | M14104 M14105 | Sports Wagon: Above center of windshield, behind headliner | | |
| Sunshade motor, rear window | M74 | Underneath rear parcel shelf | | |
| Supplemental restraint system | | *see* Airbag entries | | |
| Suspension level sensor | | *see* Ride height sensor, front, rear | | |
| Tailgate lock motor | M17a | Tailgate lock | | |
| Tailgate release button | S172a | Sports Wagon: Base of tailgate, outside | | |
| TCM | | *see* Automatic transmission control module (TCM) | | |
| Telephone | | *see* **650 Radio** | | |
| Telematics control module (TCU) | U400a | Right side trunk *see also* **650 Radio** | **Fig 10** **Fig 48** | **Pg 32** **Pg 45** |
| Temperature sensor, outside | B21a | Behind front bumper, right | | |
| Thermostat, coolant | Y6279 | Right front lower engine compartment on coolant pump housing | **Fig 14** **Fig 15** | **Pg 35** **Pg 35** |
| Throttle valve | Y6390 Y63900 | Underneath intake manifold | **Fig 18** | **Pg 36** |
| Tire pressure control (RDC) control module | A85a | Convertible: Left front trunk behind rear seat | | |
| Tire pressure control (RDC) control module | A85a | Non-convertible: Right side trunk or cargo compartment behind trim | | |
| Tire pressure control (RDC) transmitter | B43a - B47a | Left front, right front, left rear, right rear fender housing | **Fig 25** | **Pg 38** |

**ECL**

*Electrical components table*

**Table b. E90 component locations**

| Component | Code | Location | Fig # | Page # |
|---|---|---|---|---|
| Tire pressure control (RDC) wheel electronics | B43b - B47b | Inside each wheel | | |
| Towing hitch release | S492 | Sports Wagon: Left side cargo compartment | | |
| Towing hitch release | A195 | Right side trunk or cargo compartment behind trim | | |
| Trailer module | A6 | Right side trunk behind trim | | |
| Transfer case control module | A70006 | Underneath floor mat in front of passenger seat | | |
| Transmission | | *see* Automatic transmission | | |
| Trunk fan | M9149 | Convertible: Left side trunk underneath floor covering | | |
| Trunk lid lock motor | M17a | Trunk lid lock | | |
| Trunk lid lock switch, left, right | S419 S167b | Convertible: Trunk lid lock assembly | | |
| Trunk lid lock switch, right, left | S167b S419 | Convertible: Trunk lid lock assembly | | |
| Trunk lid release | S172a | Center trunk lid above license plate lights | | |
| Trunk lid soft-close motor, left, right | M79a M85 | Convertible: Trunk lid lock assembly | | |
| Trunk partition microswitch | B6229 | Convertible: Behind rear seat backrest | | |
| Turbo bypass valve | B2409 | Right side of engine at exhaust manifold | | |
| Turbo control valve | B2408 | Right side of engine at exhaust manifold | | |
| Turbo intake temperature-boost pressure sensor | B6583 | Turbo: Rear of intake manifold | | |
| Turbo wastegate valve | B2407 | Right side of engine at exhaust manifold | | |
| Turn signal / high beam switch | S7 | Steering column stalk switch | | |
| Tweeter | | *see* **650 Radio** | | |
| Ultrasonic detector | | *see* Interior movement sensor (ultrasonic detector) | | |
| Valvetronic drive motor | M6352 | Non-turbo: Top center of cylinder head cover | **Fig 11** | **Pg 33** |
| Valvetronic relay | K6319 | Right rear engine compartment in electronics box (E-box) | **Fig 5** **Fig 8** | **Pg 25** **Pg 28** |
| Vanity mirror switch, left, right | S77 S78 | Sun visor, left, right | | |
| VANOS solenoid, intake, exhaust | Y6275, Y6276 | Front of cylinder head | **Fig 13** | **Pg 35** |
| Variable intake manifold (DISA) controllers | Y6540 Y6541 | Non-turbo: Intake manifold | **Fig 17** | **Pg 36** |
| Ventilation temperature sensor | B62 | Top of center vent on dashboard | | |
| Video module | A197 | Left side trunk or cargo compartment behind trim | | |
| Volume control valve | | *see* Fuel volume control valve | | |
| VTG actuator | | *see* xDrive clutch (VTG) actuator | | |
| Washer fluid level switch | S136a | Washer fluid reservoir behind right front wheel, behind wheel housing liner | **Fig 21** | **Pg 37** |
| Washer pumps | M4 M7 M95 | Washer fluid reservoir behind right front wheel, behind wheel housing liner | **Fig 21** | **Pg 37** |
| Wastegate valve | Y6039 Y6723 | Turbo: side cylinder head | | |

| Table b. E90 component locations | | | | |
|---|---|---|---|---|
| **Component** | **Code** | **Location** | **Fig #** | **Page #** |
| Wheel speed sensor | | *see* ABS wheel speed sensor<br>*see also* **340 Brakes** | | |
| Window regulator motors, left front, right front | M21<br>M23 | Center of front door inside door cavity, left, right | | |
| Window regulator motors, left rear, right rear | M20b<br>M22b | Center of rear door inside door cavity, left, right | | |
| Window switch, driver | | *see* Door switch cluster, driver door | | |
| Window switch, passenger | S127 | Passenger door armrest | | |
| Window switches, left rear, right rear | S41a<br>S42a | Rear door armrests, left, right | | |
| Windshield washer nozzle heater, left, right | E51a<br>E52a | Base of windshield | | |
| Windshield washer pump | M4 | Washer fluid reservoir, behind right wheel housing | **Fig 21** | **Pg 37** |
| Wiper and washer control module, rear | A36 | Below center of tailgate window, behind trim | | |
| Wiper motor, windshield | M3a | Underneath plenum chamber cover, left rear engine compartment | | |
| Wiper relay, rear | K91 | Junction box (JB), underneath right side dashboard, behind glove compartment | **Fig 27** | **Pg 38** |
| Wiper relays | K36, K37 | Junction box (JB), underneath right side dashboard, behind glove compartment | **Fig 27**<br>**Fig 28** | **Pg 38**<br>**Pg 39** |
| X connector | | *see* **Harness connectors, wire splices (X connectors)** in this repair group. | | |
| X ground | | *see* **Grounds** in this repair group | | |
| xDrive classification resistor | R8554 | Rear of transfer case | | |
| xDrive clutch (VTG) actuator | M8533 | Rear of transmission housing | | |
| xDrive control module | | *see* Transfer case control module | | |

**ECL**

## Harness connectors, wire splices (X connectors)

BMW electrical components connect to the electrical harness via X connectors. Most connectors bear the same numerical designation as the component they attach to. For example, the connector for Y6279 (coolant thermostat) is designated X6279.

**Table c** lists harness connectors and wire splices not attached directly to components and gives brief location information for each.

| Table c. E90 X connectors | | | | |
|---|---|---|---|---|
| **Code** | **Description and application** | **Location** | **Fig #** | **Page #** |
| X01091 | Seat control, passenger | Base of seat | | |
| X018812 | Seat control, passenger | Base of seat | | |
| X10183 | DSC control module to navigation system | Behind instrument cluster | **Fig 32** | **Pg 40** |
| X10237 | Passenger seat occupancy sensor, front seat belt buckle sensors, rollover sensor controller to ground | Behind center right dashboard | | |
| X10545 X10546 | ECM, fuel pump control module, longitudinal dynamics management to PT CAN-bus | Behind glove compartment | **Fig 33** | **Pg 40** |
| X10547 | CAS, battery sensor, longitudinal dynamics management, DSC control module, active steering, transfer box control module, automatic transmission control module, fuel pump control module to junction box | 2006: Behind center dashboard from 2006: Behind glove compartment | **Fig 30** | **Pg 39** |
| X10548 X10549 | Powertrain CAN-bus to footwell module | Behind instrument cluster | **Fig 31** | **Pg 39** |
| X10550 | Battery sensor, longitudinal dynamics management, DSC control module, active steering to junction box | Behind instrument cluster | | |
| X1108 | Amplifier, sound system to junction box | Left footwell underneath carpet | **Fig 29** | **Pg 39** |
| X11366 | Convertible top module, towing hitch release to CAS | Convertible: Right of battery in trunk | | |
| X11619 | Park distance control signal | Coupe, Convertible: Right quarter panel, behind trim | **Fig 36** **Fig 37** | **Pg 41** **Pg 41** |
| X1256 | License plate lights, right taillights, trunk lock connector | Trunk | | |
| X13007 | Center brake light, right inner taillight, right license plate light to ground | Convertible: Trunk lid under trim | | |
| X13172 | Tailpipe flap connector | Left side trunk behind trim | **Fig 46** | **Pg 43** |
| X13337 | Compensator connector | | **Fig 46** | **Pg 43** |
| X13722 X13722 | DSC control module, DSC sensor, junction box to F CAN-bus | Left footwell underneath dashboard | **Fig 33** | **Pg 40** |
| X13727 | Headlights to footwell module | Behind center dashboard | **Fig 32** | **Pg 40** |
| X13916 X13917 | Antenna diversity module connectors | Convertible: Left side trunk behind trim | **Fig 46** | **Pg 43** |
| X15001 X15002 | Junction box, roof function control center to K CAN-bus | Behind glove compartment | **Fig 33** | **Pg 40** |
| X15003 X15004 | Footwell module, radio, iDrive to K CAN-bus | Behind instrument cluster | **Fig 32** | **Pg 40** |
| X15005 X15006 | Park distance control module, comfort access module, trailer module to K CAN-bus | Right side trunk, to right of battery | | |

| Code | Description and application | Location | Fig # | Page # |
|------|---------------------------|----------|-------|--------|
| X1771 | Taillights connector to footwell module | Convertible: Right of battery in trunk | | |
| X181 | Brake light switch | Behind instrument cluster | **Fig 31** | **Pg 39** |
| X217 | Components under dash board | Behind instrument cluster | **Fig 31** | **Pg 39** |
| X219 | Washer nozzle heaters to ground | Behind glove compartment | **Fig 32** | **Pg 40** |
| X256 X257 | Door components, passenger door, driver door | Door hinge, passenger, driver | | |
| X275 X279 | Seat control, driver, passenger | Under seat, driver, passenger | | |
| X3255 X3257 | Footwell module to taillights | Convertible: Footwell module, left footwell | | |
| X329 | Taillight connector | Convertible: Center trunk lid, near trunk lid lock assembly, under trim | | |
| X3313 | Telephone, antenna splitter | Behind left rear seat bolster | **Fig 39** | **Pg 42** |
| X60552 | Engine harness connector | Right rear engine compartment in electronics box (E-box) | **Fig 5** | **Pg 25** |
| X62400 | Knock sensor connector | Underneath intake manifold | **Fig 18** | **Pg 36** |
| X6460 X6462 X6463 | Engine components to ground | Engine wiring harness, top of E-box, right rear engine compartment | | |
| X82 | Engine cooling fan connector | Upper left fan shroud | | |
| X834 X835 | Door harness connector, left rear, right rear | Under door panel, near lower hinge, left rear, right rear | | |
| X849 X891 | Door harness connector, driver door, passenger door | Under door panel, near lower hinge, driver door, passenger door | | |
| X908 | Front cigar lighter, gear indicator, front dome light, passenger door power switch, passenger door window control, radio, courtesy lights right, driver door switch cluster to footwell module | 2006: Behind center dashboard from 2006: Behind glove compartment | **Fig 30** | **Pg 39** |
| X9331 | iDrive, CAS control module, MRS control module, telephone transceiver to junction box | Left footwell underneath carpet | **Fig 29** | **Pg 39** |
| X9985 | License plate lights to footwell module | Convertible: Right side trunk | | |

**Table c. E90 X connectors**

ECL

B309ecl005

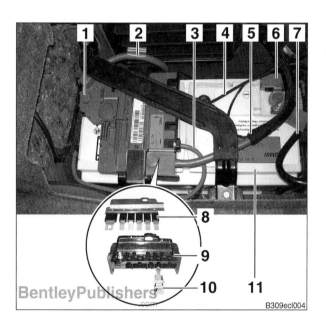

B309ecl004

## Fuse Locations and Ratings

### Fuse panels

For a description of the power supply system, see **600 Electrical System–General**.

◄ Fuses and fusible links in E90 vehicle are located as follows:

1. **A46** Rear power distribution panel in trunk or cargo compartment, attached to top of battery. High amperage fuses (fusible links) are not replaceable separately.
   See **Rear power distribution panel (high amperage fuses) (A46)** in this repair group.

2. **A4010** Junction box under right side dashboard, behind glove compartment.
   See **Junction box (A4010) fuse panel** in this repair group.

3. **A8680**, **A8681**, **A8682**, **A8684**, **A8685** Engine electronics fuse carriers in E-box, right rear engine compartment.
   See **E-box engine electronics fuse carriers** in this repair group.

### Rear power distribution panel (high amperage fuses) (A46)

**Fig 1   Inside trunk or cargo compartment, top of battery**

◄ Rear power distribution panel (A46) is installed directly on top of battery.

1. **G19a** Battery safety terminal (BST)
2. Line to B+ junction, starter and alternator
3. Line to engine electronics
4. Line to IBS electronics
5. Line to junction box (A4010)
6. **B895** Battery sensor (IBS)
7. Battery ground cable
8. **A46** High amperage fuses (fusible links)
9. Housing
10. High current connector
11. **G1** Battery

Fuse ratings for high amperage fuses are in **Table d** and **Table e**.

| Table d. High amperage fuses in rear power distribution panel (A46) (to 03 / 2007) | | |
|---|---|---|
| **Fuse** | **Rating in amps** | **Protected circuits** |
| F104 | | Intelligent battery sensor (IBS) (B895) |
| F105 | 100 | Electronic power steering (A60233) |
| F106 | 100 | Auxiliary heater (R6138) |
| F106 | 100 | Electric auxiliary heater |
| F108 | 250 | Junction box (A4010) |

**Table d. High amperage fuses in rear power distribution panel (A46) (to 03 / 2007)**

| Fuse | Rating in amps | Protected circuits |
|------|------|------|
| F203 | 100 | B+ terminal (engine compartment) (G6430), starter, battery |

**Table e. High amperage fuses in rear power distribution panel (A46) (from 03 / 2007)**

| Fuse | Rating in amps | Protected circuits |
|------|------|------|
| F101 | 250 | Junction box (A4010) |
| F102 | 100 | B+ terminal (engine compartment) (G6430), starter, battery |
| F103 | 100 | Electronic power steering (A60233) |
| F104 | 100 | Auxiliary heater (R6138) |
| F105 | | Intelligent battery sensor (IBS) (B895) |
| F106 | 100 | Electric auxiliary heater |

Rear power distribution panel fuses are not replaceable separately.

## Junction box (A4010) fuse panel

The junction box or JB (A4010) is underneath right side of the dashboard, behind the glove compartment.

 Open glove compartment. Twist plastic retainers (**arrows**) 90° to remove fuse cover. Cover lists fuse applications and ratings.

Fuse applications and ratings vary by year. Fuse applications for each model year are shown in **Table f** (2006 models), **Table g** (2007 models) and **Table h** (2008 models).

*NOTE—*

- *No vehicle is equipped with every one of the components or fuses in the fuse tables.*
- *Model year changes usually take effect in September of the previous year. 2008 model changes are usually incorporated in 09 / 2007 production.*

For junction box relays and modules, see **Fig 27, Pg 38** in this repair group.

B309ecl008

ECL

*Junction box (A4010) fuse panel*

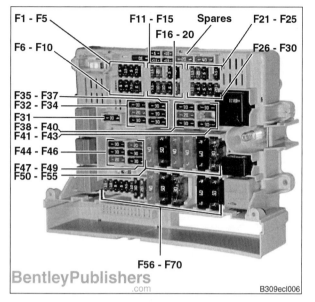

B309ecl006

**Fig 2    Behind glove compartment (to 03 / 2007)**

◀ **A4010** Junction box (JB) fuse panel.

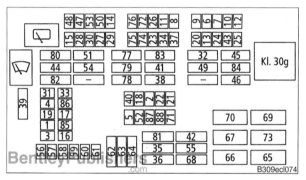

B309ecl074

**Fig 3    Behind glove compartment (03 / 2007 - 09 / 2007)**

◀ **A4010** Junction box (JB) fuse panel.

*NOTE —*

• *Fuses in this version of JB are not numbered in order.*

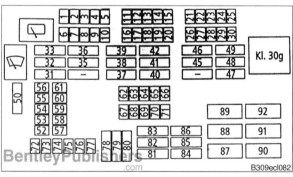

B309ecl082

**Fig 4    Behind glove compartment (09 / 2007 and later)**

◀ **A4010** Junction box (JB) fuse panel.

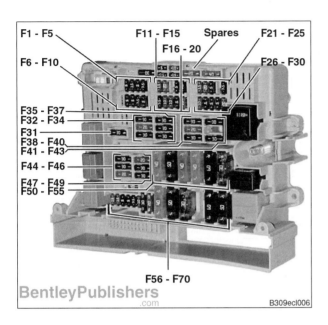

F1 - F5
F11 - F15   Spares   F21 - F25
F16 - 20
F6 - F10   F26 - F30
F35 - F37
F32 - F34
F31
F38 - F40
F41 - F43
F44 - F46
F47 - F49
F50 - F55

F56 - F70

BentleyPublishers.com

B309ecl006

## 2006 fuses (to 03 / 2007)

| | Rating | |
|---|---|---|
| **Fuse** | **in amps** | **Protected circuits** |
| F1 | | not used |
| F2 | 5 | Diversity antenna |
| F3 | 20 | Passenger seat heating |
| F4 | 5 | Car access system |
| F5 | 7.5 | Roof function control center |
| F6 | 15 | Transmission control module |
| F7 | 20 | Auxiliary heater control module |
| F8 | 5 | CD changer<br>Diversity antenna |
| F9 | 10 | Active cruise control |
| F10 | | not used |
| F11 | 10 | Radio |
| F12 | 20 | Convertible top or sunroof control<br>Roof function center (FZD) |
| F13 | 5 | iDrive controller |
| F14 | | not used |
| F15 | 5 | AUC sensor |
| F16 | 15 | Horns |
| F17 | 5 | Telephone eject box<br>Telephone transceiver |
| F18 | 5 | CD changer |

**Table f. 2006 fuses F1 - F88 in junction box (A4010)**

| | Rating | |
|---|---|---|
| **Fuse** | **in amps** | **Protected circuits** |
| F19 | 7.5 | Comfort access control module<br>Front door outer handles control modules<br>Siren and tilt alarm sensor |
| F20 | 5 | DSC<br>Transfer case control module |
| F21 | 7.5 | Driver door switch cluster<br>Outside rear view mirrors |
| F22 | 10 | Longitudinal dynamics management<br>Towing hitch release speaker |
| F23 | 10 | Digital tuner<br>Satellite radio |
| F24 | 5 | Tire pressure control (RDC) |
| F25 | 10 | Front seat belts positioner control modules |
| F26 | 10 | Shift selector lighting<br>Telephone eject box<br>Telephone transceiver |
| F27 | 5 | Driver door switch cluster<br>Telephone transceiver |
| F28 | 5 | Roof function control center<br>Park distance control (PDC) |
| F29 | 5 | AUC sensor<br>Front seat heating modules |
| F30 | 20 | 12-volt utility sockets<br>Front cigar lighter |
| F31 | 20 | CCC/M-ASK<br>Radio |
| F32 | 30 | Driver seat heating module<br>Driver seat module |
| F33 | 30 | Front seat control |
| F34 | 30 | Sound system amplifier |
| F35 | 30 | DSC |
| F36 | 30 | Footwell module |
| F37 | 30 | Driver seat control |
| F38 | 30 | Transfer case control module |
| F39 | 30 | Wipers |
| F40 | 20 | Fuel pump (EKPS) |
| F41 | 30 | Footwell module |
| F42 | 30 | Trailer module |
| F43 | 30 | Headlight washer pump |
| F44 | 30 | Trailer module |
| F45 | 40 | Active steering |

ECL

*2006 fuses (to 03 / 2007)*

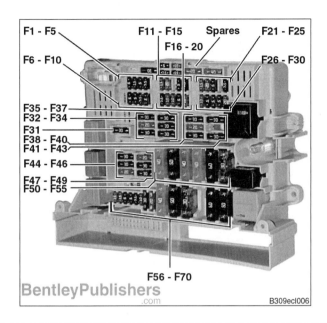

F1 - F5
F11 - F15    Spares    F21 - F25
F16 - 20
F6 - F10    F26 - F30
F35 - F37
F32 - F34
F31
F38 - F40
F41 - F43
F44 - F46
F47 - F49
F50 - F55
F56 - F70

B309ecl006

| Table f. 2006 fuses F1 - F88 in junction box (A4010) | | |
|------|------|------|
| **Fuse** | **Rating in amps** | **Protected circuits** |
| F46 | 30 | Rear window defroster |
| F47 | 20 | Trailer socket |
| F48 | 20 | Rear wiper and washer control |
| F49 | 30 | Passenger seat heating |
| F50 | 40 | Active steering |
| F51 | 50 | Car access system |
| F52 | 50 | Footwell module |
| F53 | 50 | Footwell module |
| F54 | 60 | B+ potential distributor |
| F55 | | not used |
| F56 | 15 | Central locking |
| F57 | 15 | Central locking |
| F58 | 5 | Instrument cluster OBD II socket |
| F59 | 5 | Steering column switch cluster |
| F60 | 7.5 | A/C and heating system |
| F61 | 10 | Cargo compartment lights Central information display Glove compartment light Trunk light |
| F62 | 30 | Window control |
| F63 | 30 | Window control |
| F64 | 30 | Window control |
| F65 | 40s | DSC |

| Table f. 2006 fuses F1 - F88 in junction box (A4010) | | |
|------|------|------|
| **Fuse** | **Rating in amps** | **Protected circuits** |
| F66 | 50 | Fuel heater (Diesel) |
| F67 | 50 | Blower output stage |
| F68 | 50 | Vacuum pump relay |
| F69 | 50 | Engine cooling fan |
| F70 | 50 | Secondary air injection pump |
| F71 | 20 | Trailer socket |
| F72 | | not used |
| F73 | | not used |
| F74 | | not used |
| F75 | | not used |
| F76 | | not used |
| F77 | 30 | Fuel injectors Ignition coils Interference suppression capacitor |
| F78 | | not used |
| F79 | | not used |
| F80 | | not used |
| F81 | | not used |
| F82 | | not used |
| F83 | | not used |
| F84 | | not used |
| F85 | | not used |
| F86 | | not used |
| F87 | | not used |
| F88 | | not used |

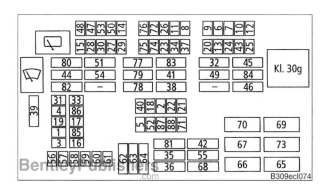

## 2007 fuses (03 / 2007 - 09 / 2007)

| Fuse | Rating in amps | Protected circuits |
|---|---|---|
| | | **Table g. 2007 fuses F1 - F88 in junction box (A4010)** |
| F1 | 10 | Rollover protection control module |
| F2 | 5 | Instrument cluster<br>OBD II plug |
| F3 | 20 | Passenger seat heating |
| F4 | 5 | Car access system |
| F5 | | not used |
| F6 | 15 | Transmission control module |
| F7 | 20 | Auxiliary heater control module |
| F8 | 20 | Sound system amplifier |
| F9 | 10 | Active cruise control |
| F10 | 15 | Trailer module |
| F11 | 10 | Radio |
| F12 | 20 | Convertible top or sunroof control<br>Roof function center (FZD) |
| F13 | 5 | iDrive controller<br>Tire pressure control (RDC) |
| F14 | | not used |
| F15 | 5 | AUC sensor |
| F16 | 15 | Horns |
| F17 | 5 | Telephone eject box<br>Telephone transceiver |
| F18 | 5 | *Convertible:*<br>Diversity antenna<br>Gearshift bezel lighting<br>*Non-convertible:*<br>Electrochromic rear view mirror<br>Gearshift bezel lighting |
| F19 | 7.5 | Siren and tilt alarm sensor |
| F20 | 5 | DSC<br>Transfer case control module |

| Fuse | Rating in amps | Protected circuits |
|---|---|---|
| | | **Table g. 2007 fuses F1 - F88 in junction box (A4010)** |
| F21 | 7.5 | Driver door switch cluster<br>Outside rear view mirrors |
| F22 | 10 | Longitudinal dynamics management |
| F23 | 10 | Digital tuner<br>Satellite radio |
| F24 | 5 | DC converter<br>Fan cutout relay |
| F25 | 10 | Front seat belts positioner control modules |
| F26 | 10 | Telephone eject box<br>Telephone transceiver |
| F27 | 5 | Driver door switch cluster<br>Telephone transceiver |
| F28 | 5 | Roof function control center<br>Park distance control (PDC) |
| F29 | 5 | Front seat heating modules |
| F30 | 20 | 12-volt utility sockets<br>Front cigar lighter |
| F31 | 20 | CCC/M-ASK |
| F32 | 30 | Driver seat module |
| F33 | 5 | Comfort access control module<br>Front door outer handles control modules |
| F34 | 5 | CD changer<br>Diversity antenna |
| F35 | 30 | DSC |
| F36 | 30 | Footwell module |
| F37 | 10 | Front seat control |
| F38 | 30 | Transfer case control module |
| F39 | 30 | Wipers |
| F40 | 7.5 | Roof function control center |
| F41 | 30 | Footwell module |
| F42 | 40 | Footwell module |
| F43 | | not used |
| F44 | 30 | Trailer module |
| F45 | 40 | Active steering |
| F46 | 30 | Rear window defroster |
| F47 | 20 | Trailer socket |
| F48 | 20 | Rear wiper and washer control |
| F49 | 30 | Passenger seat module |
| F50 | 10 | Engine control module (ECM) |
| F51 | 40 | Car access system |

*2007 fuses (03 / 2007 - 09 / 2007)*

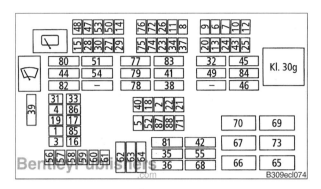

B309ecl074

| Table g. 2007 fuses F1 - F88 in junction box (A4010) | | |
|---|---|---|
| **Fuse** | **Rating in amps** | **Protected circuits** |
| F52 | 20 | Driver seat heating |
| F53 | 20 | Passenger seat heating |
| F54 | 30 | Trailer module |
| F55 | | not used |
| F56 | 15 | Central locking |
| F57 | 15 | Central locking |
| F58 | 5 | Instrument cluster<br>OBD II socket |
| F59 | 5 | Steering column switch cluster |
| F60 | 5 | Central information display |
| F61 | 10 | Cargo compartment lights<br>Central information display<br>Glove compartment light<br>Trunk light |
| F62 | 30 | Window control |
| F63 | 30 | Window control |
| F64 | 30 | Window control |
| F65 | 10 | Selector lever illumination<br>Longitudinal dynamics management |
| F66 | 50 | Fuel heater (Diesel) |
| F67 | 40 | Blower output stage |
| F68 | 40 | Footwell module |
| F69 | 50 | 400 watt engine cooling fan |
| | 60 | 600 watt engine cooling fan |
| F70 | 40 | Secondary air injection pump |
| F71 | 20 | Trailer socket |
| F72 | | not used |
| F73 | | not used |

| Table g. 2007 fuses F1 - F88 in junction box (A4010) | | |
|---|---|---|
| **Fuse** | **Rating in amps** | **Protected circuits** |
| F74 | 10 | Engine control module (ECM)<br>Exhaust flap<br>Fuel tank leakage diagnostic module<br>Nitrogen oxide sensor |
| F75 | 10 | EAC sensor<br>E-box fan<br>ECM<br>Secondary air pump relay |
| F76 | 30 | Crankshaft sensor<br>Fuel tank vent valve<br>Mass air flow sensor<br>Oil condition sensor<br>Variable intake manifold controllers<br>Volume control valve |
| F77 | 30 | Fuel injectors<br>Ignition coils<br>Ignition coil interference suppression capacitor |
| F78 | 30 | Camshaft sensors<br>Coolant thermostat<br>Electric coolant pump<br>Engine control module (ECM)<br>VANOS valves<br>Waste gate valves |
| F79 | 30 | Crankcase breather heating<br>Oxygen sensor heating |
| F80 | 40 | *Non-turbo:*<br>Electric coolant pump |
| F81 | 30 | Trailer module |
| F82 | | not used |
| F83 | 40 | Footwell module |
| F84 | 30 | Headlight washer pump |
| F85 | | not used |
| F86 | | not used |
| F87 | | not used |
| F88 | 20 | Fuel pump (EKPS) |

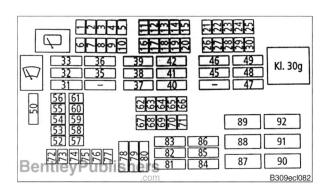

B309ecl082

## 2008 fuses (from 09 / 2007)

| Fuse | Rating in amps | Protected circuits |
|---|---|---|
| | | **Table h. 2008 fuses F1 - F92 in junction box (A4010)** |
| F1 | 10 | Rear wiper and washer |
| F2 | 5 | Instrument cluster<br>OBD II plug |
| F3 | 20 | Passenger seat heating |
| F4 | 10 | Engine control module (ECM)' |
| F5 | | not used |
| F6 | 5 | AUC sensor<br>DC converter |
| F7 | 20 | Roof function center (FZD)<br>Park distance control (PDC) |
| F8 | 20 | Cigar lighters<br>Utility 12 volt outlets |
| F9 | 5 | Driver door switch cluster<br>Telephone |
| F10 | 5 | Front seat heating |
| F11 | 20 | Crankshaft sensor<br>Engine control module (ECM)<br>Fuel tank vent valve<br>Fuel volume control valve<br>Mass air flow sensor<br>Oil condition sensor<br>Variable intake manifold controllers |
| F12 | 15 | Vacuum pump relay |
| F13 | 5 | Telephone<br>USB hub |
| F14 | 10 | Radio |
| F15 | 20 | Amplifier |
| F16 | 10 | EAC sensor<br>E-box fan<br>Engine control module (ECM)<br>Radiator shutter control<br>Secondary air pump relay |

| Fuse | Rating in amps | Protected circuits |
|---|---|---|
| | | **Table h. 2008 fuses F1 - F92 in junction box (A4010)** |
| F17 | 10 | Engine control module (ECM)<br>Exhaust flap<br>Fuel tank leakage diagnostic module |
| F18 | 10 | Digital tuner<br>Satellite radio |
| F19 | 5 | CD changer<br>*Convertible:*<br>Diversity antenna |
| F20 | 10 | Seat control |
| F21 | 10 | Active cruise control |
| F22 | 15 | Automatic transmission control module |
| F23 | 20 | Auxiliary heater control |
| F24 | 15 | Towing module |
| F25 | 20 | Convertible top module<br>Roof control center (FZD) |
| F26 | 5 | Dynamic stability control (DSC)<br>Transfer case control module |
| F27 | 5 | iDrive controller<br>Tire pressure control (RDC) |
| F28 | 5 | Cooling fan cut-out relay<br>DC converter |
| F29 | 5 | Sunroof |
| F30 | 10 | Seat belt positioner controllers |
| F31 | 30 | Trailer module |
| F32 | 30 | Trailer module |
| F33 | 40 | Electric coolant pump |
| F34 | 5 | CD changer<br>Diversity antenna |
| F35 | 30 | DSC |
| F36 | 40 | Car access system (CAS) |
| F37 | 30 | Camshaft sensors<br>Coolant thermostat<br>ECM<br>Electric coolant pump<br>VANOS valves<br>Waste gate valves |
| F38 | 30 | Crankcase breather heating<br>Engine control module (ECM)<br>Oxygen sensor heating |
| F39 | 30 | Fuel injectors<br>Ignition coils<br>Ignition coil interference suppression capacitor |
| F40 | 30 | Transfer case control |

**ECL**

*2008 fuses (from 09 / 2007)*

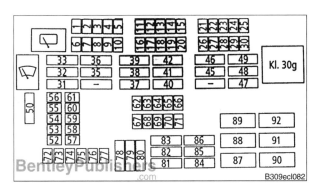

Kl. 30g

B309ecl082

| Table h. 2008 fuses F1 - F92 in junction box (A4010) | | |
|---|---|---|
| **Fuse** | **Rating in amps** | **Protected circuits** |
| F41 | 30 | Footwell module (FRM) |
| F42 | 40 | Footwell module |
| F43 | 30 | Headlight washer pump |
| F44 | 30 | Trailer module |
| F45 | 30 | Passenger seat module |
| F46 | 30 | Driver seat module |
| F47 | 30 | Rear window defogger |
| F48 | 30 | Headlight washer<br>Rear wiper and washer control |
| F49 | 40 | Passenger seat module |
| F50 | 30 | Wiper control |
| F51 | 40 | Car access system |
| F52 | | not used |
| F53 | 10 | Rollover protection |
| F54 | 7.5 | Anti-theft alarm siren, tilt sensor<br>*Convertible:*<br>Door microwave sensors |
| F55 | 5 | Car access system (CAS) |
| F56 | 20 | CCC/M-ASK |
| F57 | 15 | Horns |
| F58 | 5 | Instrument cluster<br>OBD II socket |
| F59 | 5 | Telephone |
| F60 | 5 | Central information display |
| F61 | 5 | Comfort access control module<br>Dual remote control receiver<br>Front door handle control module |
| F62 | 7.5 | Roof function control center (FZD) |
| F63 | 5 | Diversity antenna<br>Electrochromic rear-view mirror<br>Selector lever illumination |

| Table h. 2008 fuses F1 - F92 in junction box (A4010) | | |
|---|---|---|
| **Fuse** | **Rating in amps** | **Protected circuits** |
| F64 | 5 | OBD II plug |
| F65 | 10 | Selector lever illumination<br>Longitudinal dynamics management |
| F66 | 7.5 | Driver door switch cluster<br>Passenger outside mirror |
| F67 | 20 | DSC |
| F68 | 20 | Driver seat heating module |
| F69 | | not used |
| F70 | 20 | Fuel pump (EKPS) |
| F71 | 20 | Trailer module |
| F72 | 15 | Central locking |
| F73 | 15 | Central locking |
| F74 | 5 | Instrument cluster |
| F75 | 5 | Passenger seat module |
| F76 | 5 | Radio |
| F77 | 10 | Glove compartment light<br>Heating and air-conditioning<br>Trunk or cargo compartment light |
| F78 | 30 | Window control |
| F79 | 30 | Wiper control |
| F80 | 30 | Window control |
| F81 | 30 | Footwell module |
| F82 | 30 | DSC control module |
| F83 | 40 | Footwell module |
| F84 | 40 | Footwell module |
| F85 | 30 | Car access system (CAS) |
| F86 | 40 | Footwell module |
| F87 | | not used |
| F88 | 40 | Blower |
| F89 | 40 | Secondary air pump relay |
| F90 | 40 | DSC control module |
| F91 | | not used |
| F92 | 50 | 400 watt engine cooling fan |
| | 60 | 600 watt engine cooling fan |

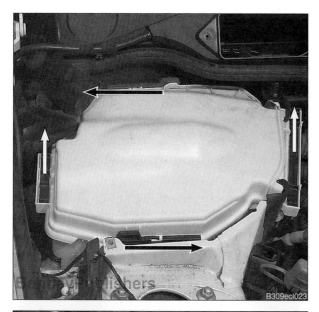

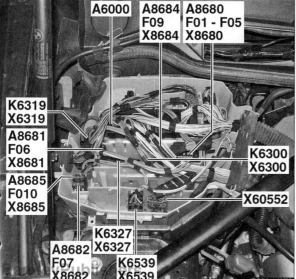

## E-box engine electronics fuse carriers

**To 03 / 2007:** Fuses F01 through F010 are in several fuse holders in engine compartment electronics box (E-box).

**From 03 / 2007:** Fuse 07 is in fuse holder in engine compartment electronics box (E-box).

- Open engine hood and prop in service position. See **410 Fenders, Engine Hood**.

- Remove upper and lower microfilter housings at rear of engine compartment. See **640 Heating and Air-conditioning**.

◄ Working at right rear of compartment:

- Slide E-box cover locks in direction of **black arrows**.

- Pull up on left and right side clips (**white arrows**) and remove E-box cover.

**Fig 5    Engine electronics fuses F01 - F07, F09 - F010 (non-turbo to 03 / 2007)**

◄ E-box cover off:

- **A6000** engine control module (ECM)

- **A8680** Fuse carrier
  Fuse applications and ratings in **Table i**

- **A8681** Fuse carrier
  Fuse applications and ratings in **Table i**

- **A8682** Fuse carrier
  Fuse applications and ratings in **Table i**

- **A8684** Fuse carrier
  Fuse applications and ratings in **Table i**

- **A8685** Fuse carrier
  Fuse applications and ratings in **Table i**

- **K6300** DME main relay

- **K6319** Valvetronic (VVT) relay

- **K6327** Fuel injector relay

- **K6539** Crankcase breather heating relay

- **X6300** Connector

- **X6319** Connector

- **X6327** Connector

- **X6539** Connector

- **X8680** Connector

- **X8681** Connector

- **X8682** Connector

- **X8684** Connector

- **X8685** Connector

- **X60552** Connector

*E-box engine electronics fuse carriers*

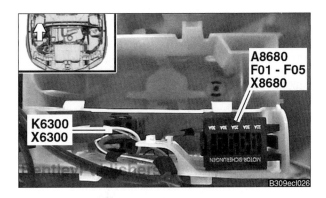

**Fig 6 Engine electronics fuses F01 - F05 (turbo to 03 / 2007)**

◄ Engine compartment electronics box (E-box) cover off (**arrow**).

- **A8680** fuse carrier
  Fuse applications and ratings in **Table j**

- **K6300** DME main relay

- **X6300** Connector

- **X8680** Connector

**Fig 7 Engine electronics fuses F06 - F07 (turbo to 03 / 2007)**

◄ Engine compartment electronics box (E-box) cover off (**arrow**).

- **A2076** B+ power

- **A8681** Fuse carrier
  Fuse application and rating in **Table j**

- **A8682** Fuse carrier
  Fuse application and rating in **Table j**

- **X8681** Connector

- **X8682** Connector

- **X18326** Connector

- **X64101** Connector

- **X64102** Connector

◄ If replacing fuses F01 - F05, unplug fuse carrier A8680.

*E-box engine electronics fuse carriers*

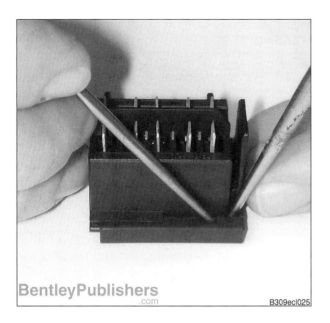

BentleyPublishers
.com

B309ecl025

◀ Pry open cover A 8680 using sharp tools. Fuse ratings are in **Table i** and **Table j**.

**Table i. Engine electronics fuses in A8680, A8681, A8682, A8684, A8685 (non-turbo to 03 / 2007)**

| Fuse | Rating in amps | Protected circuits |
|------|------|------|
| F01 | 30 | Ignition coils (T6151 - T6156)<br>Interference suppression capacitor (I01046) |
| F02 | 30 | Coolant thermostat (B6279)<br>Electric coolant pump (M6035)<br>Exhaust camshaft sensor (B6224a)<br>Exhaust VANOS solenoid (Y6276)<br>Intake camshaft sensor (B6214a)<br>Intake VANOS solenoid (Y6275) |
| F03 | 20 | Crankshaft sensor (B6203a)<br>Engine control module (ECM)(A6000)<br>Fuel tank vent valve (Y6120)<br>Mass air flow sensor (B6207b)<br>Oil condition sensor (B62540a)<br>Variable intake manifold controllers (Y6540, Y6541) |
| F04 | 30 | Crankcase breather heater (E65390)<br>Oxygen sensor heaters |
| F05 | 30 | Fuel injector relay (K6327) |
| F06 | 10 | EAC sensor (B111)<br>E-box fan (M6506)<br>Exhaust flap (Y198)<br>Fuel tank leakage diagnostic module (M119a)<br>Junction box (A4010)<br>Secondary air injection mass airflow sensor (B6206) |
| F07 | 40 | Valvetronic (VVT) relay |
| F09 | 30 | Electric coolant pump (M6035) |
| F010 | 5 | Crankcase breather heating relay (K6539) |

**Table j. Engine electronics fuses in A8680, A8681 (turbo to 03 / 2007)**

| Fuse | Rating in amps | Protected circuits |
|------|------|------|
| F01 | 30 | Ignition coils (T6151 - T6156)<br>Interference suppression capacitor (I01046) |
| F02 | 30 | Coolant thermostat (B6279)<br>Electric coolant pump (M6035)<br>Engine control module (ECM)(A6000)<br>Exhaust camshaft sensor (B6224a)<br>Exhaust VANOS solenoid (Y6276)<br>Intake camshaft sensor (B6214a)<br>Intake VANOS sensor (Y6275)<br>Wastegate valves (Y6039, Y6723) |

**ECL**

*E-box engine electronics fuse carriers*

**Table j. Engine electronics fuses in A8680, A8681 (turbo to 03 / 2007)**

| Fuse | Rating in amps | Protected circuits |
|------|------|------|
| F03 | 20 | Crankshaft sensor (B6203a)<br>Fuel tank vent valve (Y6120)<br>Oil condition sensor (B62540a)<br>Volume control valve (Y2381) |
| F04 | 30 | Crankcase breather heaters (E6539, E65390)<br>Oxygen sensor heaters |
| F05 | | not used |
| F06 | 10 | E-box fan (M6506)<br>Exhaust flap (Y198)<br>Fuel tank leakage diagnostic module (M119a) |
| F07 | 40 | Electric coolant pump |

**Fig 8    Engine electronics fuse F07 (non-turbo from 03 / 2007)**

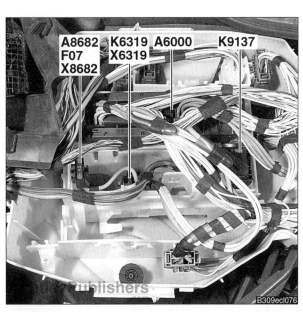

◁ Engine compartment electronics box (E-box) cover off (**arrow**).

- **A6000** Engine control module (ECM)
- **A8682** Fuse carrier
  Fuse applications and ratings in **Table k**
- **K6319** Valvetronic relay
- **K9137** Electric cooling fan cutoff relay
- **X6319** Connector
- **X8682** Connector

**Table k. Engine electronics fuse in A8682 (non-turbo)**

| Fuse | Rating in amps | Protected circuits |
|------|------|------|
| F07 | 40 | Valvetronic (VVT) relay |

**Fig 9    Engine electronics fuse F07 (turbo from 03 / 2007)**

◁ Engine compartment electronics box (E-box) cover off (**arrow**).

- **A6000** Engine control module (ECM)
- **A8682** Fuse carrier
  Fuse application and rating in **Table l**
- **K9137** Electric cooling fan cutoff relay
- **X8682** Connector

**Table l. Engine electronics fuse in A8684 (turbo)**

| Fuse | Rating in amps | Protected circuits |
|------|------|------|
| F07 | 50 | Electric coolant pump (M6035) |

## GROUNDS

### Ground distribution

Grounds are distributed throughout the vehicle body. Many are found under the interior carpets or behind trim panels. Several components grounds are often ganged. Ground positions vary among models. Lugs and connectors attached to ground are susceptible to damage and corrosion. Clean or renew as necessary.

Most ground positions are illustrated in photos in this repair group. See figure and page references in **Table m**. Ground applications are detailed in **Table n**.

**Table m. Ground locations**

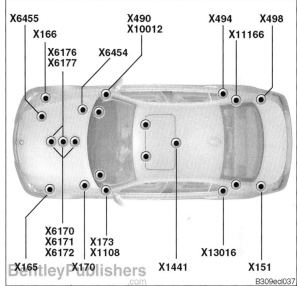

| Code | Location, application | Fig # | Page # |
|------|----------------------|-------|--------|
| X10012 | Right footwell underneath carpet, see **Table n** | Fig 30 | Pg 39 |
| X1108 | Left footwell underneath carpet, see **Table n** | Fig 29 | Pg 39 |
| X11166 | Convertible: Behind rear seat backrest, lower right | Fig 42 | Pg 42 |
| X13016 | C-pillar, behind seat side bolster, see **Table n** | Fig 38 | Pg 41 |
| X1441 | Underneath center console, see **Table n** | Fig 35 | Pg 41 |
| X151 | Left side trunk behind trim, see **Table n** | | |
| X165 | Left front engine compartment on inner fender, see **Table n** | Fig 11 | Pg 33 |
| X166 | Right front engine compartment on inner fender, see **Table n** | Fig 11 | Pg 33 |
| X170 | Left rear engine compartment, DSC control module | | |
| X173 | Left footwell underneath carpet, see **Table n** | Fig 29 | Pg 39 |
| X490 | Right footwell underneath carpet, see **Table n** | Fig 30 | Pg 39 |
| X494 | Right rear, behind seat side bolster, see **Table n** | Fig 41 | Pg 42 |
| X498 | Right side trunk or cargo compartment behind trim, see **Table n** | | |
| X6170 X6171 X6172 | Turbo: Top of cylinder head underneath ignition coil cover; ignition coil grounds | | |
| X6454 | Right strut tower, see **Table n** | | |
| X6455 | Right lower engine block, electric coolant pump | Fig 14 Fig 15 | Pg 35 Pg 35 |

**ECL**

*Ground applications*

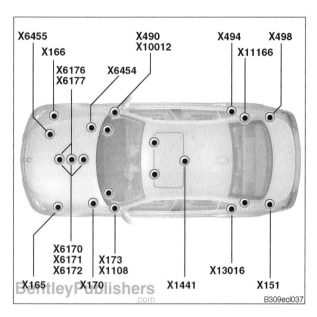

X6455  X166
X490  X10012  X494  X498  X11166
X6176  X6454
X6177

X6170  X173
X6171  X1108
X6172
X165  X170  X1441  X13016  X151

B309ecl037

## Ground applications

| Table n. Ground applications | | | |
|---|---|---|---|
| Circuit | Ground | Fig # | Pg # |
| 12v utility socket, center console | X173 | **Fig 29** | Pg 39 |
| 12v utility socket, trunk | X151 | | |
| A/C compressor valve | X6454 | | |
| Amplifier | X13016 | **Fig 38** | Pg 41 |
| AUC sensor | X10012 | **Fig 30** | Pg 39 |
| Auxiliary heating control | X165 | **Fig 11** | Pg 33 |
| Back-up light switch | X6454 | | |
| Blower output stage | X490 | **Fig 30** | Pg 39 |
| Brake fluid level switch | X1108 | **Fig 29** | Pg 39 |
| Brake light switch | X1108 | **Fig 29** | Pg 39 |
| Brake light, center | X494 | **Fig 41** | Pg 42 |
| Cargo compartment roller cover | X498 | | |
| CAS | X173 | **Fig 29** | Pg 39 |
| CAS | X1108 | **Fig 29** | Pg 39 |
| CD changer | X13016 | **Fig 38** | Pg 41 |
| Clutch pedal switch | X1108 | **Fig 29** | Pg 39 |
| Comfort access control module | X494 | **Fig 41** | Pg 42 |
| Coolant level switch | X1108 | **Fig 29** | Pg 39 |
| Coolant pump, auxiliary | X165 | **Fig 11** | Pg 33 |
| Coolant pump, electric | X6455 | **Fig 14** **Fig 15** | Pg 35 Pg 35 |
| Courtesy light, left door | X151 | | |
| Courtesy light, left rear door | X151 | | |
| Courtesy light, right door | X494 | **Fig 41** | Pg 42 |
| Courtesy light, right rear door | X494 | **Fig 41** | Pg 42 |
| Crankcase breather heater | X6454 | | |

| Table n. Ground applications | | | |
|---|---|---|---|
| Circuit | Ground | Fig # | Pg # |
| Cruise control | X166 | **Fig 11** | Pg 33 |
| Digital tuner | X13016 | **Fig 38** | Pg 41 |
| Dome light, front | X173 | **Fig 29** | Pg 39 |
| Dome light, front | X490 | **Fig 30** | Pg 39 |
| DSC control module | X170 | | |
| ECM | X6454 | | |
| Engine cooling fan | X166 | **Fig 11** | Pg 33 |
| Footwell light, front | X173 | **Fig 29** | Pg 39 |
| Footwell light, passenger | X490 | **Fig 30** | Pg 39 |
| Footwell module | X10012 | **Fig 30** | Pg 39 |
| Footwell module | X1108 | **Fig 29** | Pg 39 |
| Footwell module | X173 | **Fig 29** | Pg 39 |
| Footwell module | X494 | **Fig 41** | Pg 42 |
| Footwell module | X498 | | |
| Front cigar lighter | X173 | **Fig 29** | Pg 39 |
| Front seat belt buckle contacts, left, right | X1441 | **Fig 35** | Pg 41 |
| Fuel heater | X165 | **Fig 11** | Pg 33 |
| Fuel injector relay | X6454 | | |
| Fuel pump | X494 | **Fig 41** | Pg 42 |
| Gear indicator light | X10012 | **Fig 30** | Pg 39 |
| Headlight, left | X1108 | **Fig 29** | Pg 39 |
| Headlight, right | X10012 | **Fig 30** | Pg 39 |
| Heater valve | X165 | **Fig 11** | Pg 33 |
| Hood contact switch | X1108 | **Fig 29** | Pg 39 |
| Horn, left | X165 | **Fig 11** | Pg 33 |
| Horn, right | X166 | **Fig 11** | Pg 33 |
| Ignition coil suppression capacitor | X6176 | | |
| Ignition coils (N52) | X6176 X6177 | | |
| Ignition coils (N54) | X6170 X6171 X6172 | | |
| Interference suppressor | X151 | | |
| Junction box | X10012 | **Fig 30** | Pg 39 |
| Junction box | X490 | **Fig 30** | Pg 39 |
| Keyless entry receiver | X498 | | |
| License plate lights | X498 | | |
| Lights, left front | X165 | **Fig 11** | Pg 33 |
| Lights, right front | X166 | **Fig 11** | Pg 33 |
| Lock motor, left rear door | X151 | | |
| Lock motor, right rear door | X494 | **Fig 41** | Pg 42 |
| Lock-out circuit, rear window defroster | X151 | | |

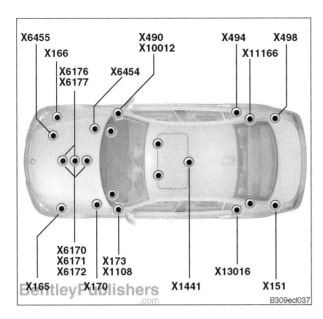

X6455 X490 X494 X498
X166 X10012 X11166
X6176 X6454
X6177
X6170
X6171 X173
X6172 X1108 X13016
X165 X170 X1441 X151

B309ecl037

**Table n. Ground applications**

| Circuit | Ground | Fig # | Pg # |
| --- | --- | --- | --- |
| Longitudinal dynamics management | X1108 | **Fig 29** | **Pg 39** |
| Lumbar control, driver seat | X173 | **Fig 29** | **Pg 39** |
| Lumbar control, passenger seat | X490 | **Fig 30** | **Pg 39** |
| Metering pump | X151 | | |
| Microwave sensor, left rear | X151 | | |
| Mirror, interior | X10012 | **Fig 30** | **Pg 39** |
| MRS control module | X1441 | **Fig 35** | **Pg 41** |
| Navigation system | X13016 | **Fig 38** | **Pg 41** |
| OBD II socket | X1108 | **Fig 29** | **Pg 39** |
| OBD II socket | X173 | **Fig 29** | **Pg 39** |
| Oil condition sensor | X6454 | | |
| Park distance control | X10012 | **Fig 30** | **Pg 39** |
| Passenger seat occupancy sensor | X1441 | **Fig 35** | **Pg 41** |
| Radio | X13016 | **Fig 38** | **Pg 41** |
| Rear window defroster | X498 | | |
| Rear window lock button | X498 | | |
| Rear wiper and washer | X498 | | |
| Roller cover release, left | X151 | | |
| Rollover protection control module | X1441 | **Fig 35** | **Pg 41** |
| Roof function control center | X173 | **Fig 29** | **Pg 39** |
| Roof function control center | X490 | **Fig 30** | **Pg 39** |
| Satellite radio | X13016 | **Fig 38** | **Pg 41** |
| Seat belt positioner, left | X151 | | |
| Seat belt positioner, right | X494 | **Fig 41** | **Pg 42** |
| Seat heating, driver seat | X173 | **Fig 29** | **Pg 39** |
| Seat heating, passenger seat | X490 | **Fig 30** | **Pg 39** |

**Table n. Ground applications**

| Circuit | Ground | Fig # | Pg # |
| --- | --- | --- | --- |
| Secondary air injection mass air flow sensor | X165 | **Fig 11** | **Pg 33** |
| Secondary air pump | X166 | **Fig 11** | **Pg 33** |
| Steptronic switch | X10012 | **Fig 30** | **Pg 39** |
| Sunroof | X498 | | |
| Taillights, inner | X494 | **Fig 41** | **Pg 42** |
| Taillights, left | X151 | | |
| Taillights. inner | X498 | | |
| Tilt sensor | X151 | | |
| Tire pressure control (RDC) | X498 | | |
| Towing hitch release | X498 | | |
| Trailer module | X498 | | |
| Transfer case control module | X490 | **Fig 30** | **Pg 39** |
| Transmission control module | X6454 | | |
| Trunk lid lock | X498 | | |
| Trunk lid release, interior | X1108 | **Fig 29** | **Pg 39** |
| Variable intake manifold control | X6454 | | |
| Video module | X13016 | **Fig 38** | **Pg 41** |
| Washer fluid level switch | X10012 | **Fig 30** | **Pg 39** |
| Washer nozzle heaters | X490 | **Fig 30** | **Pg 39** |
| Washer pumps | X166 | **Fig 11** | **Pg 33** |
| Wave trap, rear window defroster | X151 | | |
| Window motor, left rear door | X151 | | |
| Window motor, right rear door | X494 | **Fig 41** | **Pg 42** |
| Wiper motor | X490 | **Fig 30** | **Pg 39** |

## COMPONENT LOCATION PHOTOS

### Sedan components

**Fig 10   Control modules**

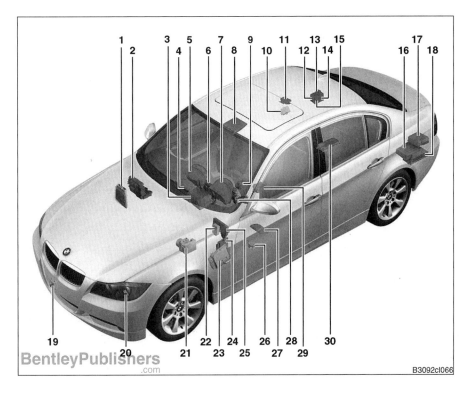

B3092cl066

1. **A6000** Engine control module (ECM)
2. **A4010** Junction box (JB)
3. **N38a** Car communications computer (CCC)
4. **A186** Passenger seat module
5. **A165a** Central information display
6. **A11a** IHKA control module
7. **A2a** Instrument cluster
8. **A121b** Interior movement sensor
9. **A167a** iDrive controller
10. **M2** Fuel pump
11. **A121a** Interior movement sensor (ultrasonic detector)
12. **A215** Comfort access control module
13. **A195** Towing hitch release
14. **A6** Trailer module
15. **A81a** Park distance control (PDC) module
16. **A18** Amplifier
17. **A197** Video module
18. **N22** CD changer
19. **U400b** Telematics control module (TCU)
20. **A12** Airbag (MRS) control module
21. **A72** Steering column switch cluster
22. **A187** Driver seat module
23. **B9801** DSC acceleration sensor
24. **A149a** Car access system (CAS) module
25. **A4011** Footwell module (FRM)
26. **A467** Active steering control module
27. **A14282** Longitudinal dynamics management control module
28. **A65a** DSC control module
29. Xenon headlight control
30. **A144a** Active cruise control module

## Engine compartment components

Fig 11   **Engine compartment, covers removed (328i non-turbo)**

1. Electronics box (E-box)
2. **G5430** B+ jump start terminal
3. **M6352** Valvetronic driver motor
4. **T6151 -T6156** Ignition coils
5. **X62101, X62201** Oxygen sensor connectors, precatalyst
6. **B6239** Intake pressure sensor
7. Power steering reservoir
8. Refrigerant port
9. **B18a** Brake fluid level switch
10. **A65a** ABS / DSC control module, hydraulic unit
11. **X166** Ground
    See **Ground applications** in this repair group
12. **I01046** Ignition coil suppression capacitor
13. **B6231** Oil pressure switch
14. Vacuum motor line connection
15. **X165** Ground
    See **Ground applications** in this repair group

**ECL**

**Fig 12 Engine compartment, covers removed (335i turbo)**

1. Electronics box (E-box)
2. **G5430** B+ jump start terminal
3. **T6151 -T6156** Ignition coils
4. **X62101, X62201** Oxygen sensor connectors, precatalyst
5. Refrigerant port
6. **B18a** Brake fluid level switch
7. **A65a** ABS / DSC control module, hydraulic unit
8. Vacuum reservoirs
9. **B6231** Oil pressure switch
10. Power steering reservoir

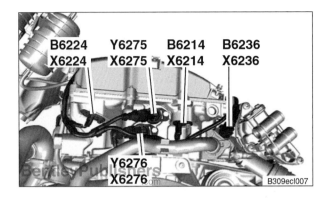

**Fig 13   Front of cylinder head (turbo)**

◄ Top of timing chain housing:
- **B6214** Intake camshaft sensor
- **B6224** Exhaust camshaft sensor
- **B6236** Engine coolant temperature (ECT) sensor
- **X6214** Connector
- **X6224** Connector
- **X6236** Connector
- **X6275** Connector
- **X6276** Connector
- **Y6275** Intake VANOS solenoid
- **Y6276** Exhaust VANOS solenoid

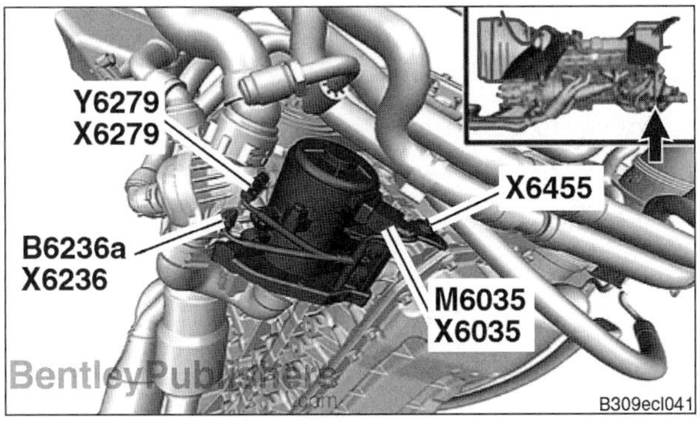

**Fig 14   Right front engine compartment (non-turbo)**

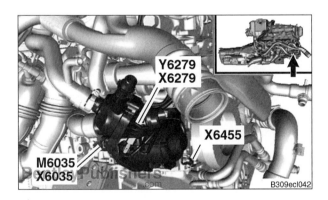

◄ Bolted to lower front right of engine (**arrow**):
- **B6236a** Engine coolant temperature (ECT) sensor
- **M6035** Electric coolant pump
- **X6035** Connector
- **X6236** Connector
- **X6279** Connector
- **X6455** Ground
  Electric coolant pump
- **Y6279** Coolant thermostat

**Fig 15   Right front engine compartment (turbo)**

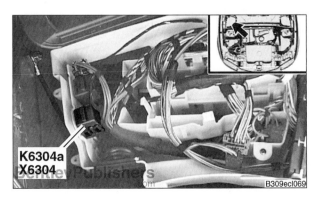

◄ Bolted to lower front right of engine (**arrow**):
- **M6035** Electric coolant pump
- **X6035** Connector
- **X6455** Ground
  Electric coolant pump
- **X6279** Connector
- **Y6279** Coolant thermostat

**Fig 16   Right rear engine compartment (2009-2010 non-turbo)**

◄ In E-box:
- **K6304a** Secondary air injection pump relay
- **X6304** Connector

ECL

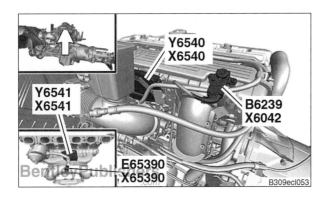

## Fig 17   Left side cylinder head (non-turbo)

◀ Top of intake manifold (**arrow**):
- **B6239** Intake pressure sensor
- **E65390** Crankcase breather heater
- **X6042** Connector
- **X6540** Connector
- **X6541** Connector
- **X65390** Connector
- **Y6540** Variable intake manifold (DISA) controller 1
- **Y6541** Variable intake manifold (DISA) controller 2

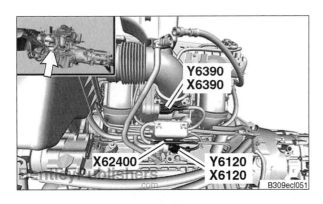

## Fig 18   Left side cylinder head (non-turbo)

◀ Underneath intake manifold (**arrow**):
- **X6120** Connector
- **X6390** Connector
- **X62400** Knock sensor connector
- **Y6120** Evaporative emissions valve
- **Y6390** Throttle valve

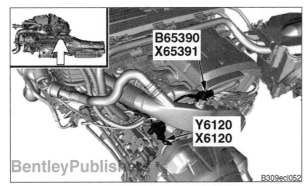

## Fig 19   Engine rear (turbo)

◀ Behind cylinder head (**arrow**):
- **B65390** Crankcase breather heater
- **X6120** Connector
- **X65391** Connector
- **Y6120** Evaporative emissions valve

## Fig 20   Left side engine (turbo)

◀ Intake manifold removed:
- **B2261** Fuel rail pressure sensor
- **B6125a** Low fuel pressure sensor
- **B6231** Oil pressure switch
- **B62400** Knock sensor
- **G6524** Alternator
- **M6510** Starter
- **Y2381** Fuel volume control valve

## Components underneath vehicle

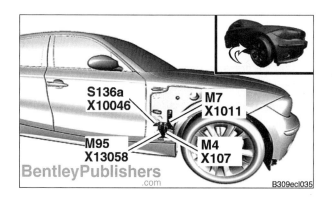

### Fig 21   Behind right front wheel

◄ Behind wheel housing liner:
- **M4** Windshield washer pump
- **M7** Headlight washer pump
- **M95** Rear window washer pump (Sports Wagon)
- **S136a** Washer fluid level switch
- **X107** Connector
- **X1011** Connector
- **X10046** Connector
- **X13058** Connector

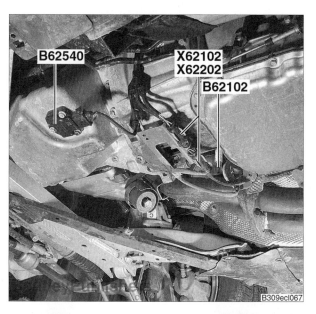

### Fig 22   Underneath vehicle (non-turbo)

◄ Engine rear, transmission bell housing:
- **B62102** Oxygen sensor (post-catalyst)
- **B62540** Oil condition sensor
- **X62102**, X62202 Connectors, oxygen sensors (post-catalyst)

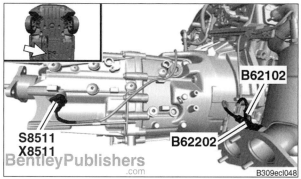

### Fig 23   Underneath vehicle

◄ Right rear manual transmission housing (**arrow**):
- **S8511** Back-up light switch
- **B62102** Oxygen sensor
- **B62202** Oxygen sensor
- **X8511** Connector

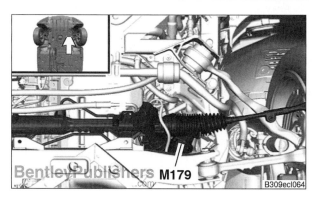

### Fig 24   Underneath vehicle

◄ Steering rack (**arrow**):
- **M179** Electric steering rack

**ECL**

*Components in passenger compartment*

B309ecl080

### Fig 25   Behind right rear wheel

◄ Wheel housing liner removed:
- B44a Right rear tire pressure control (RDC) transmitter
- X377 Right rear wheel speed sensor connector
- X18146 Right rear brake pad warning sensor connector

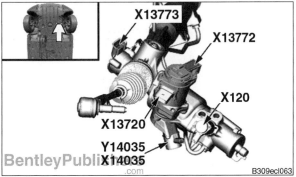

B309ecl063

### Fig 26   Underneath vehicle at steering rack

◄ Steering rack (**arrow**):
- **X120** Connector
- **X13720** Connector
- **X13772** Connector
- **X13773** Connector
- **X14035** Connector
- **Y14035** Steering lock

## Components in passenger compartment

### Fig 27   Junction box (A4010) relays and modules (to 03 / 2007)

◄ Behind glove compartment:
- **A4010a** Junction box electronic control module
- **I01068** Relay, terminal 30g
- **I01069** Relay, terminal 15 (on PC board)
- **K2** Horn relay (on PC board)
- **K6** Headlight washer relay
- **K13** Rear window defroster relay
- **K36** Wiper relay 1
- **K37** Wiper relay 2
- **K91** Rear wiper relay (Sports Wagon)
- **K6304** Secondary air injection pump relay

For junction box fuses, see **Fig 2**, **Pg 18** in this repair group.

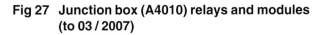

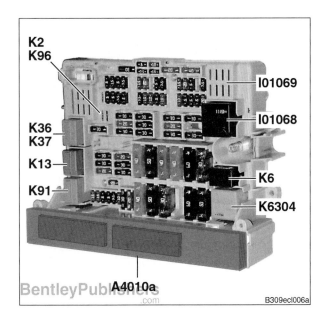

B309ecl006a

*Components in passenger compartment*

### Fig 28   Junction box (A4010) relays and modules (03 / 2007 and later)

◄ Behind glove compartment:
- **A4010a** Junction box electronic control module (JBE)
- **I01068** Relay, terminal 30g
- **K36** Wiper relay 1
- **K37** Wiper relay 2

For junction box fuses, see **Fig 3** and **Fig 4**, **Pg 18** in this repair group.

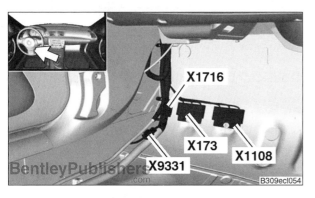

### Fig 29   Left footwell

◄ Underneath carpet (**arrow**):
- **X173** Ground
  See **Ground applications** in this repair group.
- **X1108** Ground
  See **Ground applications** in this repair group.
- **X1716** Connector
- **X9331** Connector

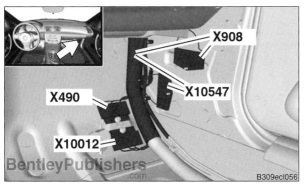

### Fig 30   Right footwell

◄ Underneath carpet (**arrow**):
- **X490** Ground
  See **Ground applications** in this repair group.
- **X908** Connector (2006)
  **X908** Splice in harness (from 2006)
- **X10012** Ground
  See **Ground applications** in this repair group.
- **X10547** Connector (2006)
  **X10547** Splice in harness (from 2006)

### Fig 31   Underneath dashboard

◄ Wiring harness (**arrow**):
- **X181** Splice
- **X217** Splice
- **X436** Splice
- **X1065** Splice
- **X10548** Splice
- **X13660** Splice
- **X14051** Splice

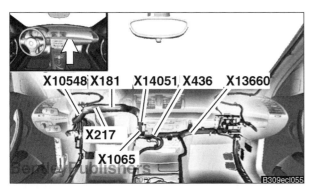

ECL

*Components in passenger compartment*

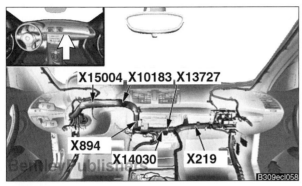

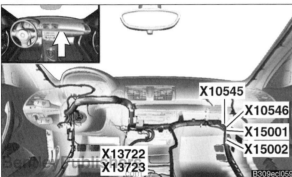

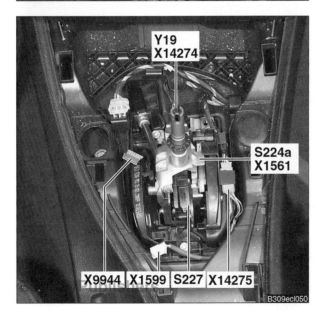

### Fig 32   Underneath dashboard

◄ Wiring harness (**arrow**):
- **X219** Splice
- **X894** Splice
- **X10183** Splice
- **X13727** Splice
- **X14030** Splice
- **X15004** Splice

### Fig 33   Underneath dashboard

◄ Wiring harness (**arrow**):
- **X10545** Splice
- **X10546** Splice
- **X13722** Splice
- **X13723** Splice
- **X15001** Splice
- **X15002** Splice

### Fig 34   At selector lever (automatic transmission)

◄ Selector lever bezel removed:
- **S224a** Steptronic switch
- **S227** Selector lever position switch
- **X1561** Connector
- **X1599** Connector (to selector lever position switch)
- **X9944** Connector (to selector lever illumination)
- **X14274** Connector
- **X14275** Connector (to A70000 transmission control module)
- **Y19** Neutral safety switch

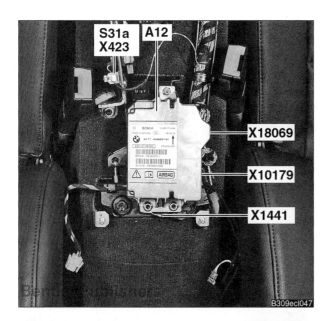

### Fig 35   On center tunnel

◄ Underneath center console:
- **A12** MRS control module
- **S31a** Parking brake warning switch
- **X423** Connector
- **X1441** Ground
  See **Ground applications** in this repair group.
- **X10179** Connector
- **X18069** Connector

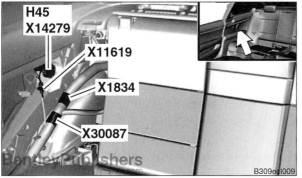

### Fig 36   Behind right B-pillar (Convertible)

◄ Behind trim panel (**arrow**):
- **H45** Park distance control signal
- **X1834** Splice
- **X11619** Splice
- **X14279** Park distance control signal connector
- **X30087** Splice, footwell module to trailer module

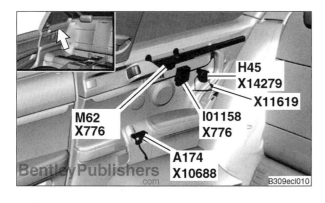

### Fig 37   Behind right B-pillar (Coupe)

◄ Behind trim panel (**arrow**):
- **A174** Airbag sensor, rear side airbag
- **H45** Park distance control signal
- **I01158** Seat belt positioner
- **M62** Seat belt positioner motor
- **X776** Seat belt positioner connector
- **X10688** Airbag sensor connector
- **X11619** Connector
- **X14279** Park distance control signal connector

### Fig 38   Left C-pillar (Sedan, Sports Wagon)

◄ Behind rear seat side bolster (**arrow**):
- **I14255** MOST-bus connector
- **W19** Emergency call antenna
- **X13016** Ground
  See **Ground applications** in this repair group
- **X14093** Connector

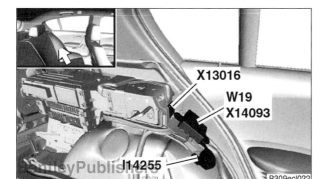

ECL

*Components in passenger compartment*

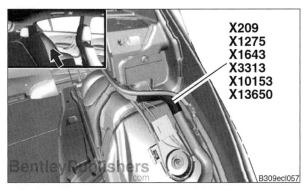

### Fig 39   Left C-pillar

◄ Behind rear seat side bolster (**arrow**):
- **X209** Splice
- **X1275** Splice
- **X1643** Splice
- **X3313** Splice
- **X10153** Splice
- **X13650** Splice

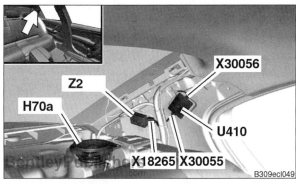

### Fig 40   Left upper C-pillar (Sedan)

◄ Behind trim panel (**arrow**):
- **H70a** Mid-range speaker
- **U410** Interference suppressor filter
- **X18265** Connector
- **X30055** Connector
- **X30056** Connector
- **Z2** Rear window defroster suppressor filter

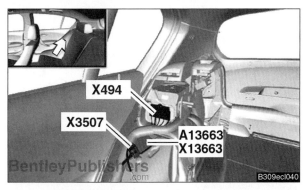

### Fig 41   Right C-pillar (Sedan, Sports Wagon)

◄ Behind rear seat side bolster (**arrow**):
- **A13663** Fuel pump control module
- **X494** Ground
  See **Ground applications** in this repair group.
- **X3507** Connector to fuel pump
- **X13663** Connector

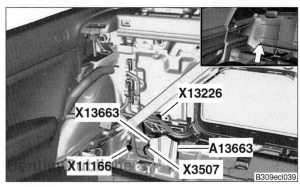

### Fig 42   Behind rear seat (Convertible)

◄ Behind backrest, lower right (**arrow**):
- **A13663** Fuel pump control module
- **X3505** Connector to fuel pump
- **X11166** Ground
- **X13226** Connector
- **X13663** Connector

### Fig 43 Above rear window (non-Convertible)

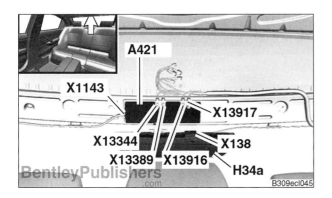

◀ Behind headliner (**arrow**):
- **A421** Antenna diversity module
- **H34a** Center brake light assembly
- **X138** Connector, center brake light
- **X1143** Connector, antenna diversity
- **X13344** Connector, antenna diversity
- **X13389** Connector, antenna diversity
- **X13916** Connector, antenna diversity
- **X13917** Connector, antenna diversity

## Components in trunk

### Fig 44 Left side trunk (non-Convertible)

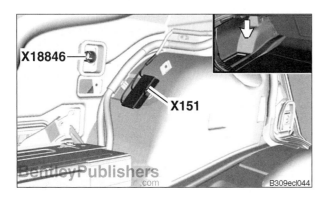

◀ Behind trim (**arrow**):
- **X151** Ground
  See **Ground applications** in this repair group.
- **X18846** Rear 12v utility socket

### Fig 45 Left front trunk (Convertible)

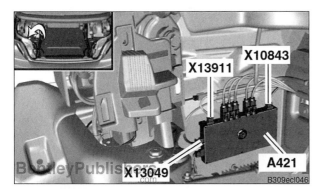

◀ Behind trim (**arrow**):
- **A421** Antenna diversity module
- **X10843** Connector
- **X13049** Connector
- **X13911** Connector

### Fig 46 Left side trunk (Convertible)

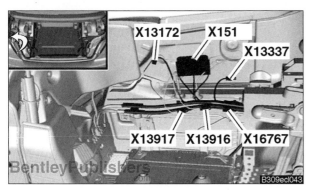

◀ Behind trim (**arrow**):
- **X151** Ground
  See **Ground applications** in this repair group.
- **X13172** Connector
- **X13337** Connector
- **X13916** Splice
- **X13917** Splice
- **X16767** Splice

**ECL**

*Components in trunk*

**Fig 47  Right side trunk**

Behind trim:

- **A215** Comfort access control module
- **G1** Battery
- **M16** Fuel filler flap lock motor
- **X312** Connector
- **X13354** Connector

## Sports Wagon components

### Fig 48   Control modules

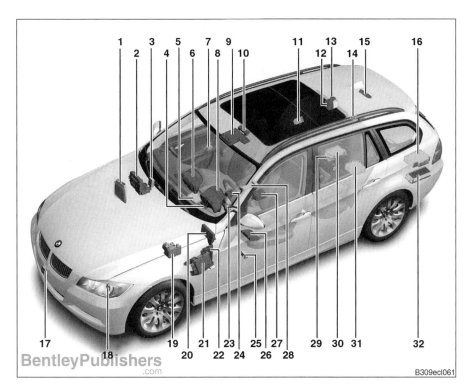

B309ecl061

1. **A6000** Engine control module (ECM)

2. **A4010** Junction box (JB)

3. **A14282** Longitudinal dynamics management control module

4. **A11a** IHKA control module

5. **A9** Radio

6. **A165a** Central information display

7. **B57b** Rain / light sensor

8. **A2a** Instrument cluster

9. **A14286** Roof function center (FZD)

10. **A121a** Interior movement sensor (ultrasonic detector)

11. **A13663** Fuel pump control module (N54 engine)

12. **A81a** Park distance control (PDC) module

13. **A215** Comfort access control module

14. **B895** Intelligent battery sensor

15. **A14102** Sunroof control module

16. **N22** CD changer

17. **A144a** Active cruise control module

18. Xenon headlight control

19. **A65a** DSC control module

20. **A149a** Car access system (CAS) module

21. **A467** Active steering control module

22. **A4011** Footwell module (FRM)

23. **A72** Steering column switch cluster

24. **I01032, I01033** Multifunction (MFL) steering wheel switch assemblies

25. **B9801** DSC acceleration sensor

26. **A187** Driver seat module

27. **A12** Airbag (MRS) control module

28. Universal charging and hands-free kit

29. **U400b** Telematics control module (TCU)

30. **N47** Satellite radio SDARS

31. **A197** Video module (not USA)

32. **A18** Amplifier

**ECL**

*Sports Wagon components*

## Fig 49    Tailgate

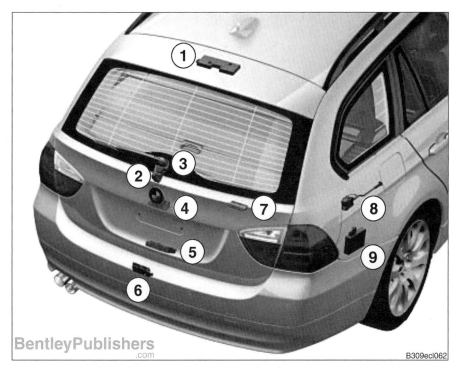

1. **A421** Antenna diversity module
2. **M96a** Rear window lock motor
3. **S147a** Rear window release button
4. **S172a** Tailgate release button
5. **M17a** Tailgate lock motor
6. Comfort access antenna
7. Comfort access antenna
8. **M16** Fuel filler flap motor
9. **A215** Comfort access control module

B309ecl062

# ELE Electrical Wiring Diagrams

## ELECTRICAL COMPONENT LOCATIONS (relay and fuse positions, ground locations)see **Repair Group ECL**

### GENERAL

This section contains selected electrical wiring diagrams for E90 3 Series models. A detailed index of the diagrams and electrical component is listed in the opening pages.

## Schematic conventions

▽ The schematics (wiring diagrams) divide the vehicle electrical system into individual circuits. Interacting electrical components are shown on one schematic.

Electrical components are represented in such a way that their general layout and function are self-explanatory. They are usually arranged in the diagrams so that the current path can be followed from positive at the top to negative at the bottom.

• If a schematic spans several pages, this fact is clearly indicated at the top of each page.

• A component (or connector) which is completely represented in the schematic is shown as a solid box.

• A component (or connector) which has other connectors in addition to the ones shown in the schematic is shown with a dashed line.

• Switches and relays are always shown in rest position (generally OFF).

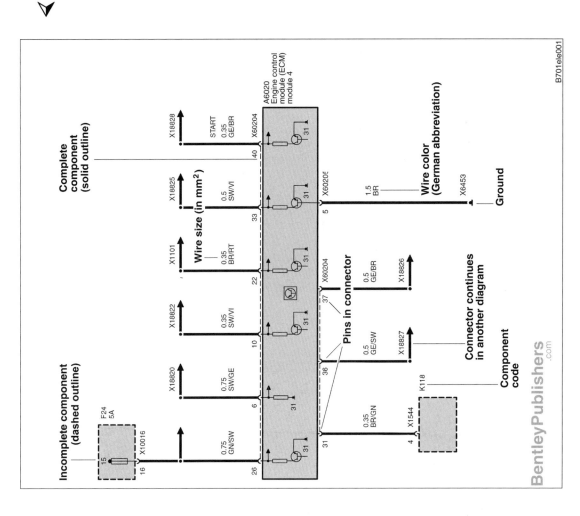

BentleyPublishers
.com

B701ele001

## Symbols

▽ The schematics utilize simplified electrical symbols.

| Fuse | Resistor | LED |
| Ignition coil | Bulb | Ground |
| Heater element | Connector (removable) | Switch |
| Variable resistor | Wire connection | |
| Control module | Shielded wire | Light sensitive diode |
| Motor | Relay | |

B701ele002

▽ Wire insulation colors in this section are given with German color abbreviations.

Wire sizes follow the DIN (European) convention.

**Example:** 0.5 wire is ½ mm$^2$ in cross-section area. This corresponds to approx. SAE 16 gauge wire.

BMW identifies many electrical circuits with unique designations which follow the DIN standard. Also, BMW designates electrical components, junctions and grounds with a unique alphanumeric designation, most of which also follow the DIN standard.

**Wiring color code**

| BL | = blue |
| BR | = brown |
| GE | = yellow |
| GN | = green |
| GR | = grey |
| RT | = red |
| SW | = black |
| WS | = white |
| VI | = violet |

B701ele003

**Fuse F01**
**N52 and N54 engines**
**(to 03 / 2007)**

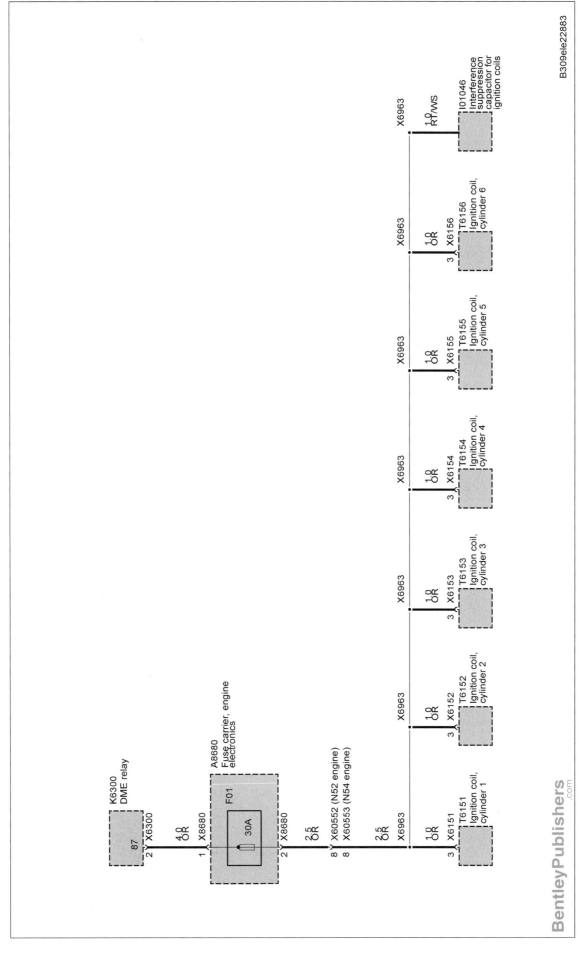

B309ele22883

**Fuse F02**
**N52 engine**
**(to 03 / 2007)**

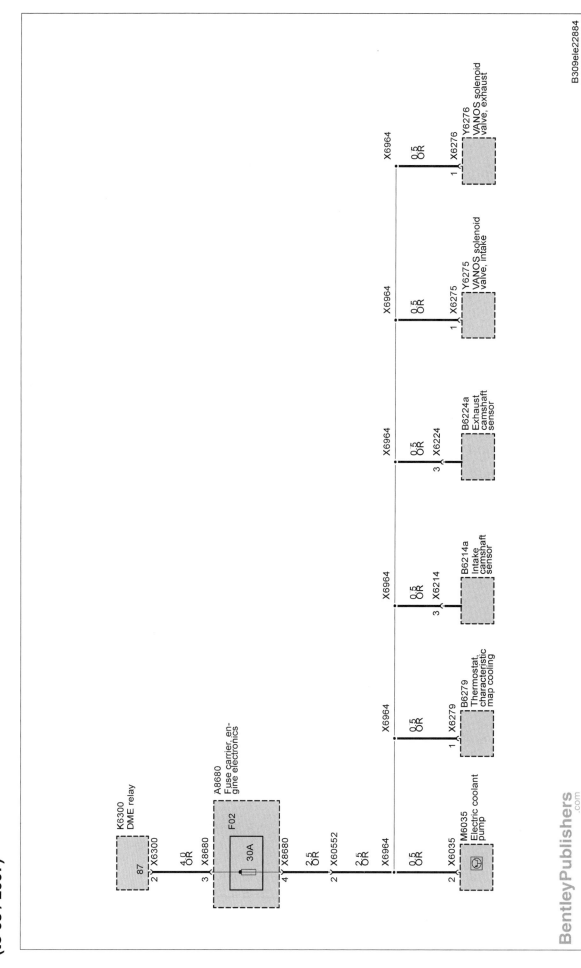

B309ele22884

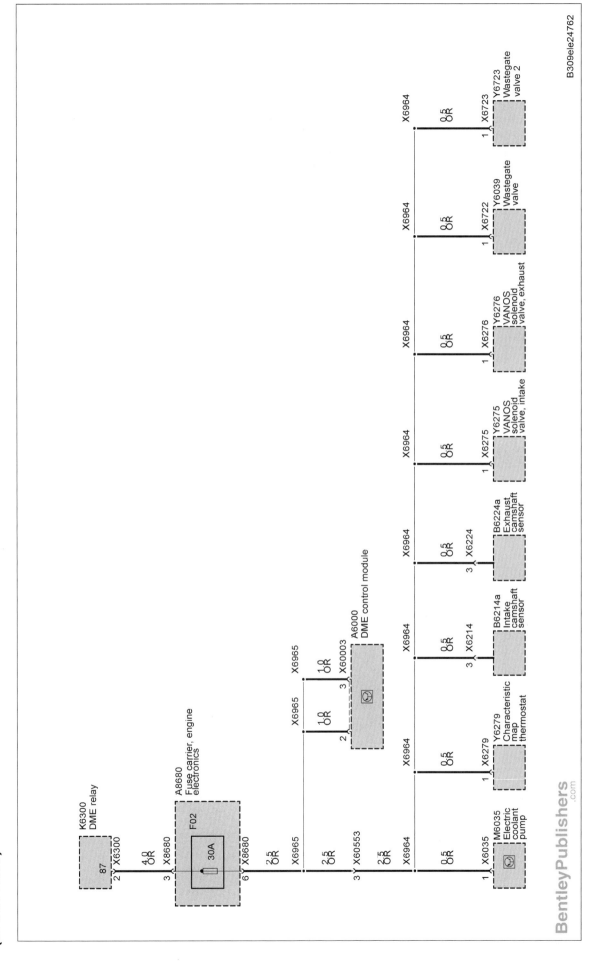

**K6300**
DME relay

**A8680**
Fuse carrier, engine
electronics

**A6000**
DME control module

**M6035**
Electric
coolant
pump

**Y6279**
Characteristic
map
thermostat

**B6214a**
Intake
camshaft
sensor

**B6224a**
Exhaust
camshaft
sensor

**Y6275**
VANOS
solenoid
valve, intake

**Y6276**
VANOS
solenoid
valve, exhaust

**Y6039**
Wastegate
valve

**Y6723**
Wastegate
valve 2

**Fuse F03**
**N52 engine**
**(to 03 / 2007)**

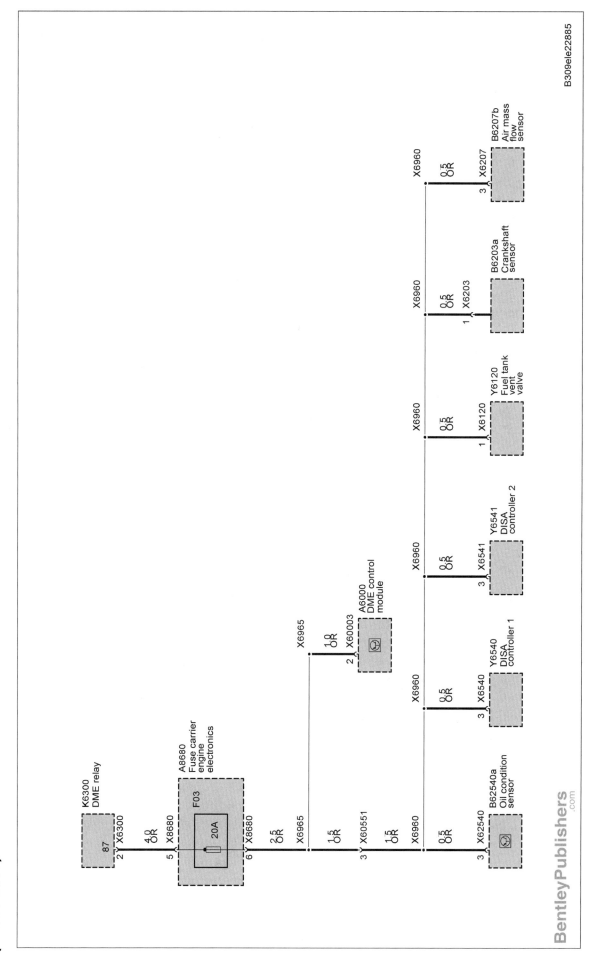

B309ele22885

**Fuse F03**
**N54 engine**
**(to 03 / 2007)**

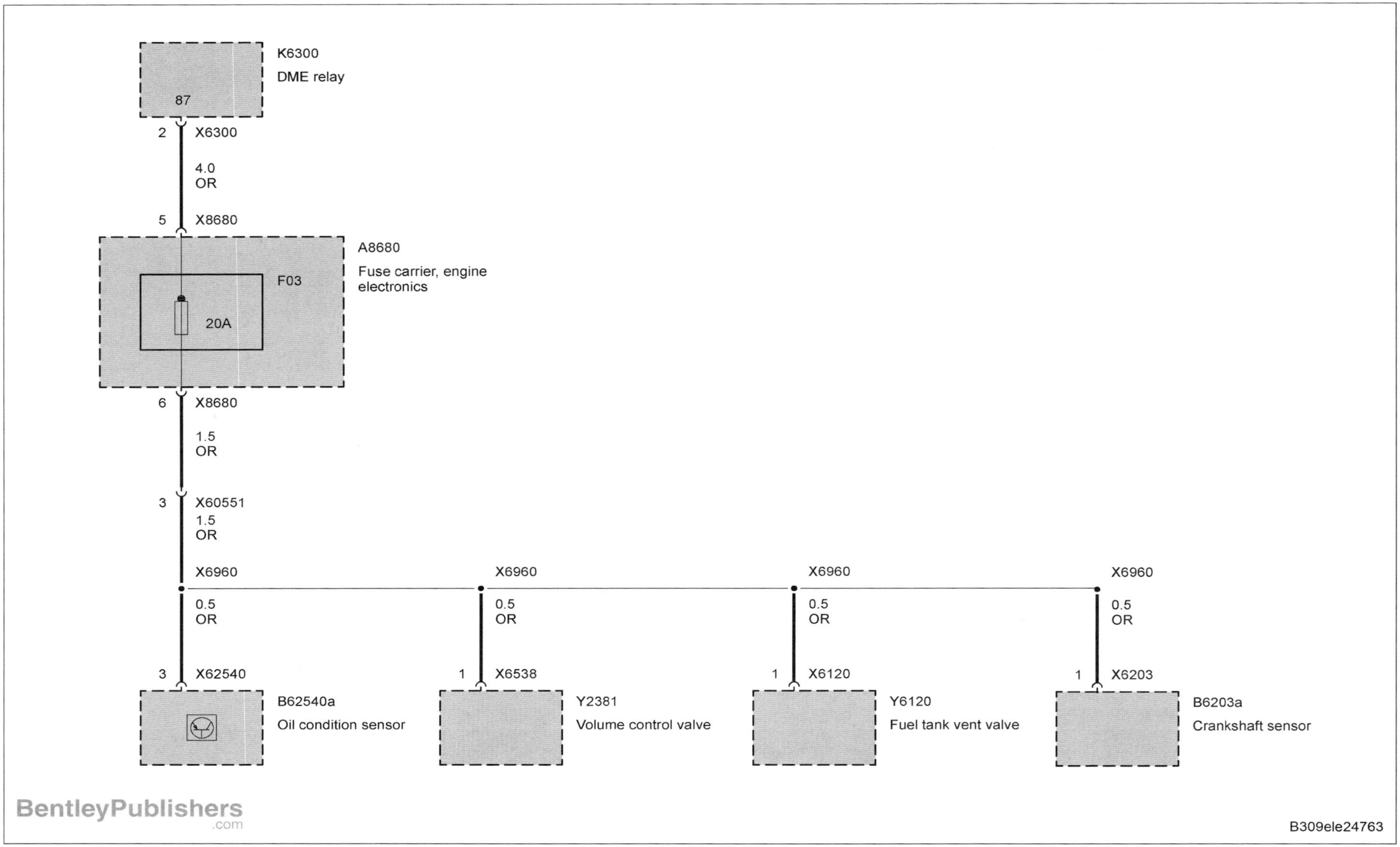

K6300
DME relay

87 X6300
4.0
OR
X8680

A8680
Fuse carrier, engine
electronics

F03

20A

2  5  6 X8680
1.5
OR
X60551
1.5
OR
X6960
0.5
OR
X62540

3

B62540a
Oil condition sensor

X6960

X6960
0.5
OR
X6538
1

Y2381
Volume control valve

X6960

X6960
0.5
OR
X6120
1

Y6120
Fuel tank vent valve

X6960

X6960
0.5
OR
X6203
1

B6203a
Crankshaft sensor

Electrical Wiring Diagrams  **ELE-11**

**Fuse F04**
**N52 and N54 engines**
**(to 03 / 2007)**

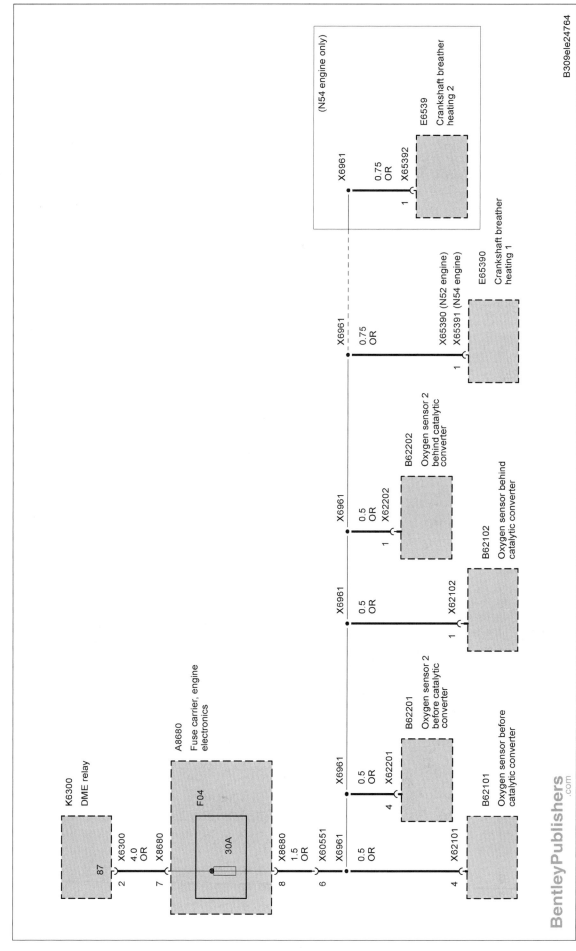

B309ele24764

**Fuse F06**
**N54 engine**
**(to 03 / 2007)**

**Fuse F05**
**N52 engine**
**(to 03 / 2007)**

B309ele24765

B309ele22887

K6300 DME relay
87 — X6300 — 1.0 OR — X8681
A8681 Fuse carrier, engine electronics
F06 10A
5 / 1
X8681 — 0.75 OR — X6011 — 0.5 RT/WS — X11212
7
2
0.5 RT/WS — X13172 — Y198 Exhaust flap
2
X11212 — 0.5 RT/WS — X6506 — M6506 E-box fan
2
X11212 — 0.75 RT/WS — X1714 — M119a Diagnostic module for fuel tank leakage
4

A2076 B+ potential distributor
X64102 — X6411
1
2.5 RT — X8680
A8680 Fuse carrier, engine electronics
F05 30A
9
X8680 — 2.5 RT — X6327
10
6
K6327 Relay, fuel injectors

BentleyPublishers.com

BentleyPublishers.com

**Fuse F06**
**N52 and N51 engines**
**(to 03 / 2007)**

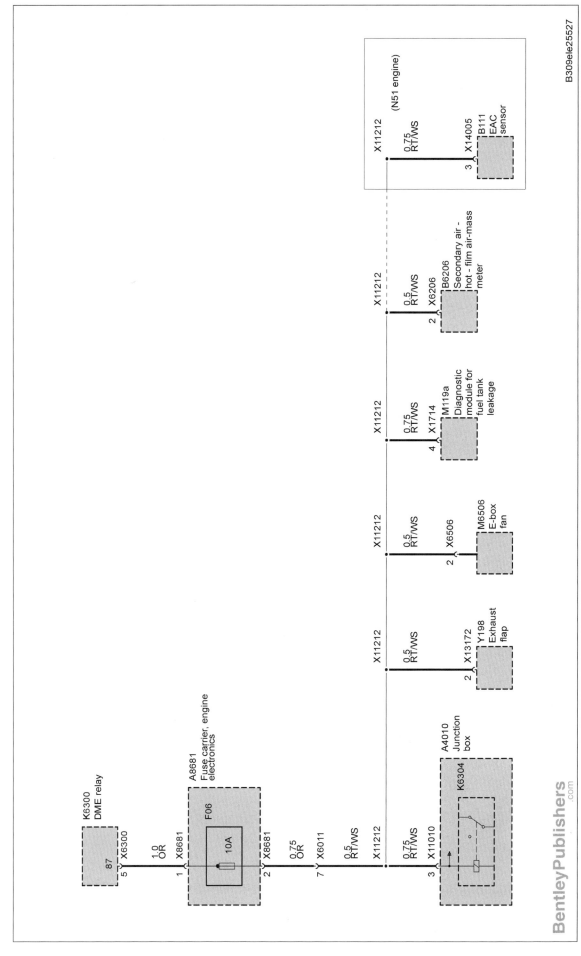

B309ele25527

**Fuse F09**
**N52 engine**

**Fuse F07**
**N52 and N54 engines**

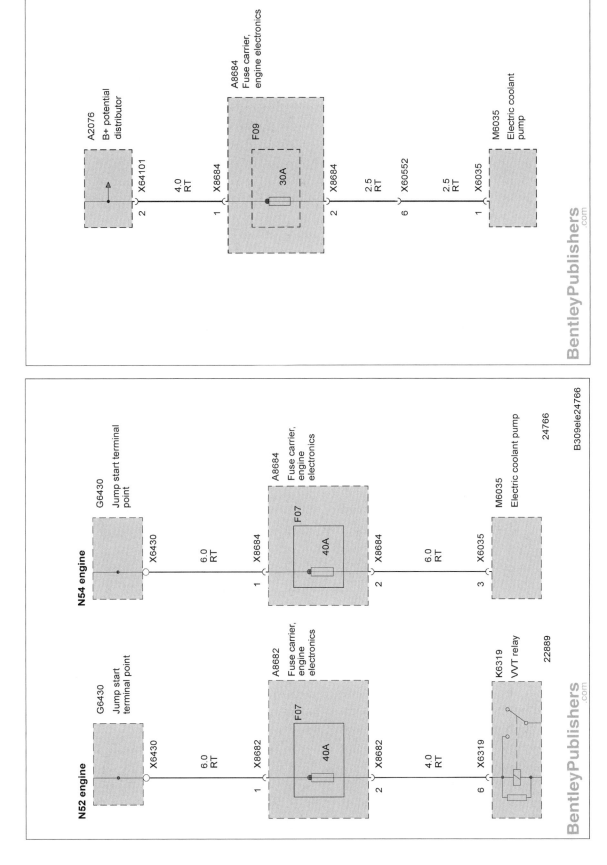

B309ele22890

B309ele24766

BentleyPublishers.com

BentleyPublishers.com

**Fuse F09 N52 engine diagram:**

A2076 B+ potential distributor

2  X64101

4.0 RT

1  X8684

A8684 Fuse carrier, engine electronics

F09

30A

2  X8684

2.5 RT

6  X60552

2.5 RT

1  X6035

M6035 Electric coolant pump

**N54 engine diagram:**

G6430 Jump start terminal point

X6430

6.0 RT

1  X8684

A8684 Fuse carrier, engine electronics

F07

40A

2  X8684

6.0 RT

3  X6035

M6035 Electric coolant pump

24766

**N52 engine diagram:**

G6430 Jump start terminal point

X6430

6.0 RT

1  X8682

A8682 Fuse carrier, engine electronics

F07

40A

2  X8682

4.0 RT

6  X6319

K6319 VVT relay

22889

Fuse F1

Fuse F010
N52 engine
(to 03 / 2007)

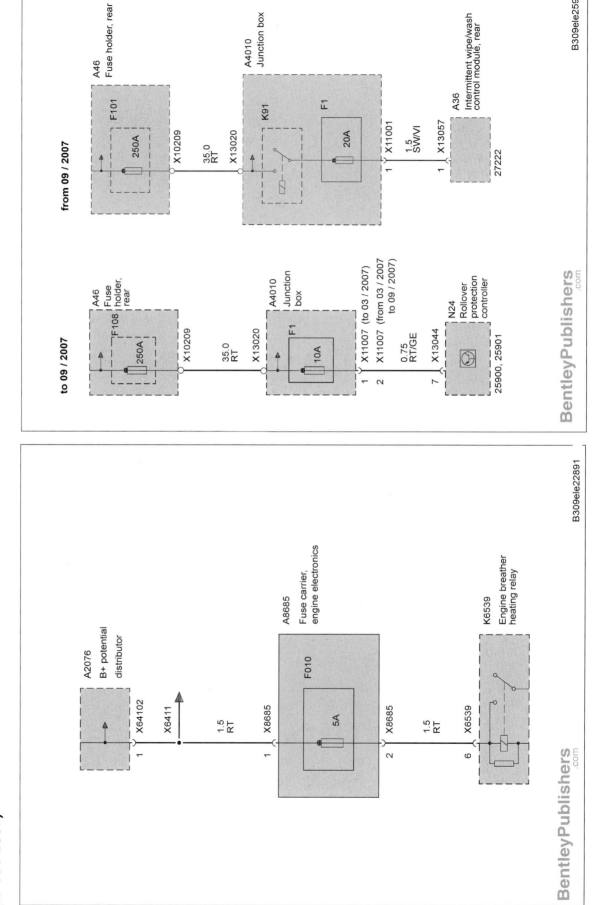

**to 09 / 2007**

A46
Fuse holder, rear

F108

250A

X10209

35.0
RT

X13020

A4010
Junction box

F1

10A

1    X11007 (to 03 / 2007)
2    X11007 (from 03 / 2007 to 09 / 2007)

0.75
RT/GE

7    X13044

N24
Rollover protection controller

25900, 25901

**from 09 / 2007**

A46
Fuse holder, rear

F101

250A

X10209

35.0
RT

X13020

A4010
Junction box

K91

F1

20A

1    X11001

1.5
SW/VI

1    X13057

A36
Intermittent wipe/wash control module, rear

27222

A2076
B+ potential distributor

X64102

X6411

1.5
RT

1    X8685

A8685
Fuse carrier, engine electronics

F010

5A

X8685

1.5
RT

2    X6539

6    K6539
Engine breather heating relay

# Fuse F3

# Fuse F2

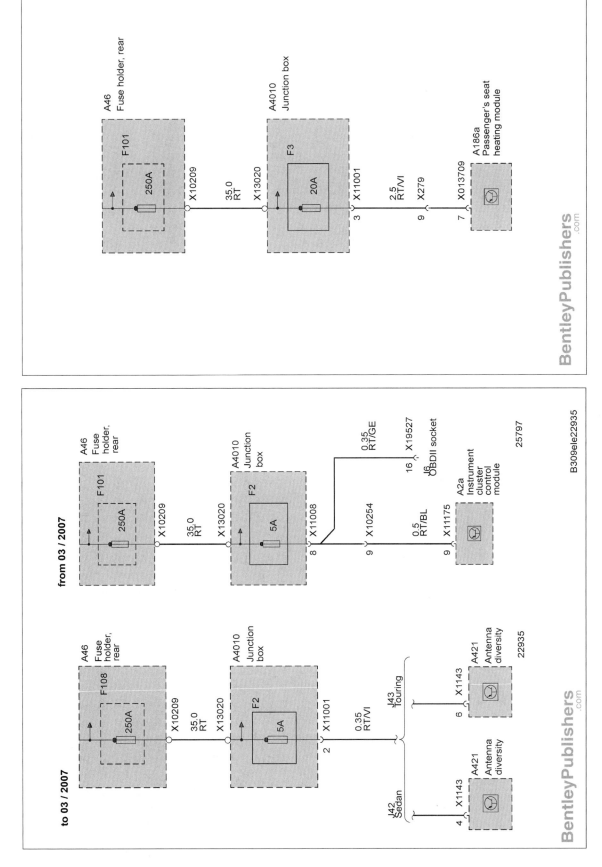

B309ele27223

B309ele22935

**Fuse F3 panel (top):**

A46 Fuse holder, rear

F101

250A

X10209

35.0 RT

X13020

A4010 Junction box

F3

20A

X11001

3

2.5 RT/VI

X279

9

X013709

7

A186a Passenger's seat heating module

**Fuse F2 panel — from 03 / 2007:**

A46 Fuse holder, rear

F101

250A

X10209

35.0 RT

X13020

A4010 Junction box

F2

5A

X11008

8

0.35 RT/GE

X19527

16

OBDII socket

X10254

9

0.5 RT/BL

X11175

9

A2a Instrument cluster control module

25797

**Fuse F2 panel — to 03 / 2007:**

A46 Fuse holder, rear

F108

250A

X10209

35.0 RT

X13020

A4010 Junction box

F2

5A

X11001

2

0.35 RT/VI

J43 Touring

X1143

6

A421 Antenna diversity

J42 Sedan

X1143

4

A421 Antenna diversity

22935

## Fuse F5

## Fuse F4

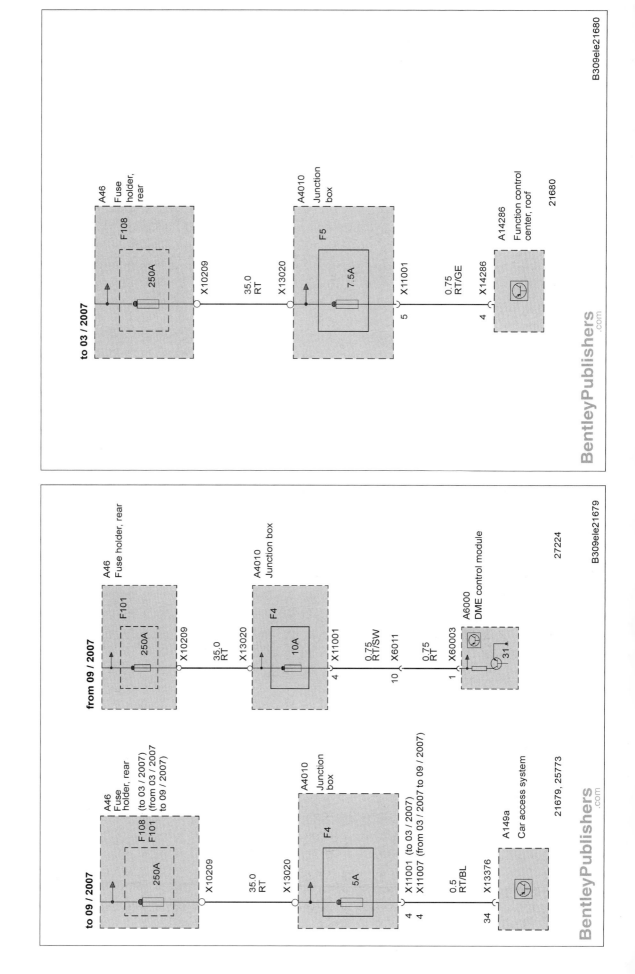

B309ele21680

B309ele21679

**Fuse F6**

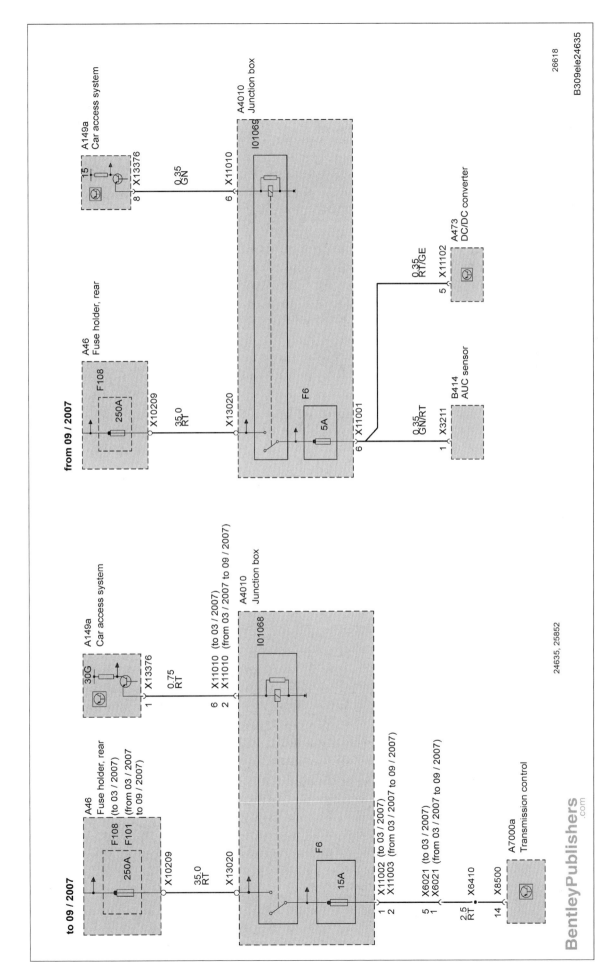

B309ele24635

26618

**from 09 / 2007**

A149a
Car access system

15   X13376

0.35
GN

X11010   6

A4010
Junction box

I01069

A46
Fuse holder, rear

F108

250A

X10209

35.0
RT

X13020

F6

5A

X11001   6

0.35
RT/GE   X11102   5

A473
DC/DC converter

0.35
GN/RT   X3211   1

B414
AUC sensor

**to 09 / 2007**

A149a
Car access system

30G   X13376   1

0.75
RT

X11010 (to 03 / 2007)
X11010 (from 03 / 2007 to 09 / 2007)   6
2

A4010
Junction box

I01068

A46
Fuse holder, rear (to 03 / 2007)
F108   (from 03 / 2007
F101   to 09 / 2007)

250A

X10209

35.0
RT

X13020

F6

15A

X11002 (to 03 / 2007)   1
X11003 (from 03 / 2007 to 09 / 2007)   2

X6021 (to 03 / 2007)   5
X6021 (from 03 / 2007 to 09 / 2007)   1

2.5
RT

X6410

X8500   14

A7000a
Transmission control

24635, 25852

**Fuse F7**

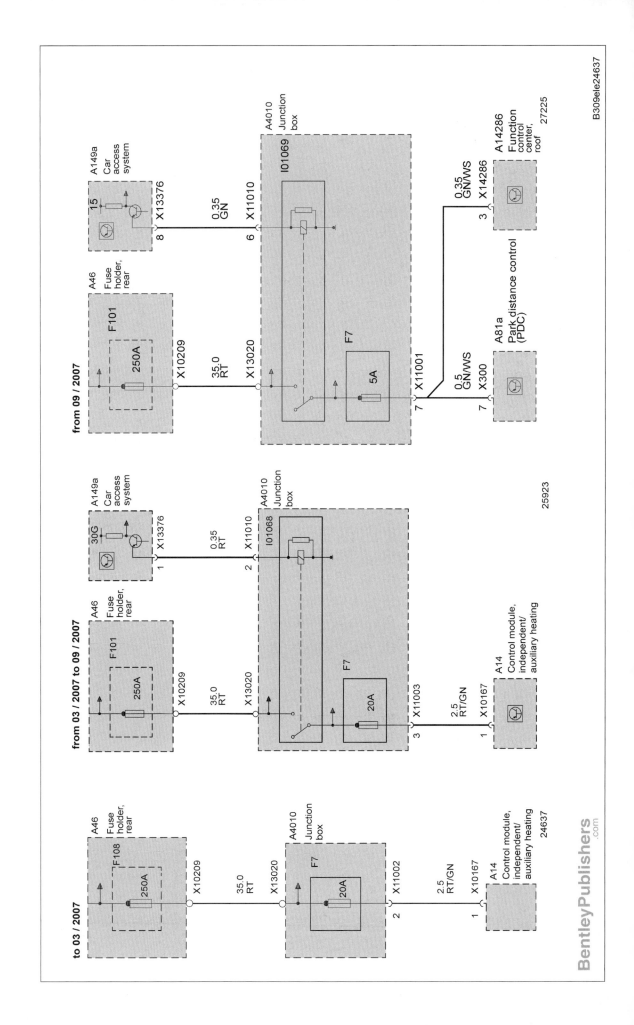

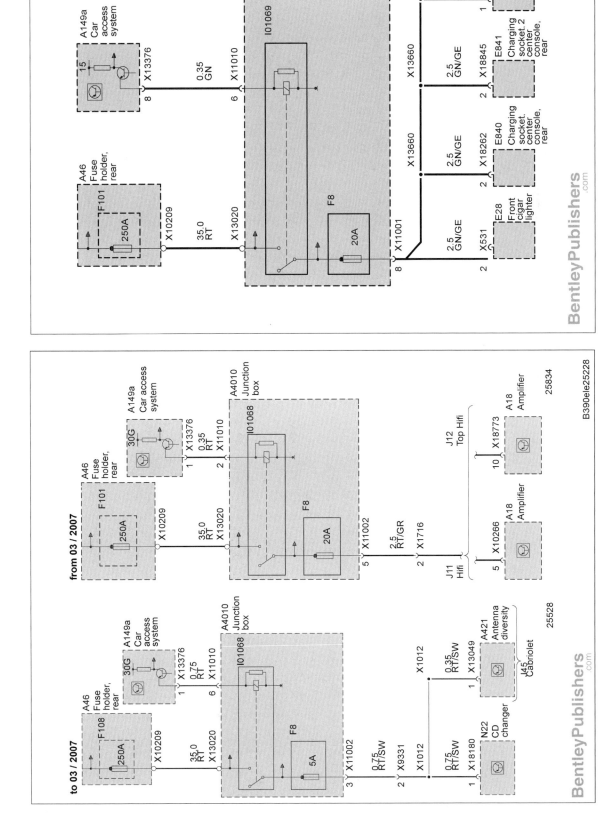

**Fuse F8**
**(from 09 / 2007)**

B309ele27317

A149a
Car
access
system

15

X13376

8

0.35
GN

X11010

6

A4010
Junction
box

I01069

A46
Fuse
holder,
rear

F101

250A

X10209

35.0
RT

X13020

F8

20A

X11001

8

X13660

2.5
GN/GE

X18846

A14112
Luggage
compartment
socket
outlet

1

X13660

2.5
GN/GE

X18845

E841
Charging
socket 2
center
console,
rear

2

X13660

2.5
GN/GE

X18262

E840
Charging
socket,
center
console,
rear

2

X531

2.5
GN/GE

E28
Front
cigar
lighter

2

---

**Fuse F8**
**(to 09 / 2007)**

B390ele25228

**from 03 / 2007**

A149a
Car access
system

30G

X13376

1

0.35
RT

X11010

2

A4010
Junction
box

I01068

A46
Fuse
holder,
rear

F101

250A

X10209

35.0
RT

X13020

F8

20A

X11002

5

2.5
RT/GR

X1716

2

J11
Hifi

5

X10266

A18
Amplifier

J12
Top Hifi

10

X18773

A18
Amplifier

25834

---

**to 03 / 2007**

A149a
Car
access
system

30G

X13376

1

0.75
RT

X11010

6

A4010
Junction
box

I01068

A46
Fuse
holder,
rear

F108

250A

X10209

35.0
RT

X13020

F8

5A

X11002

3

0.75
RT/SW

X9331

2

X1012

X1012

0.35
RT/SW

X13049

1

A421
Antenna
diversity

J45
Cabriolet

25528

0.75
RT/SW

X18180

1

N22
CD
changer

**Fuse F9**
**(from 09 / 2007)**

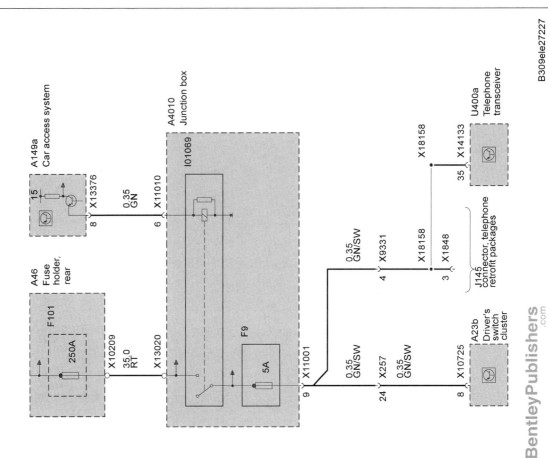

B309ele27227

**Fuse F9**
**(to 09 / 2007)**

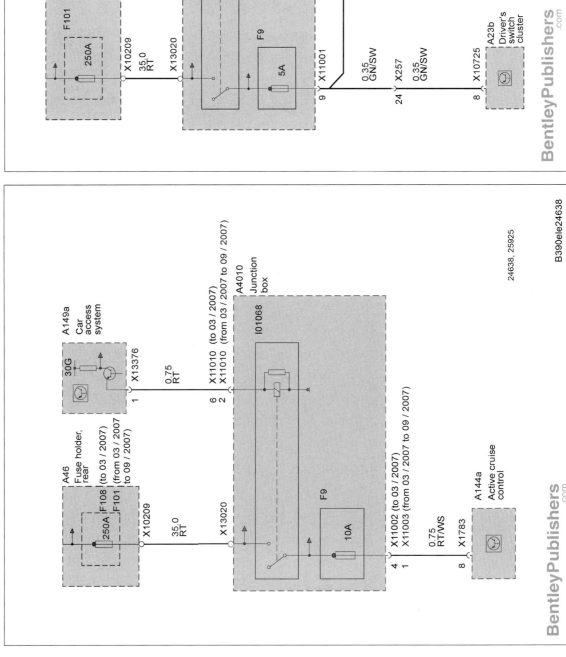

24638, 25925

B390ele24638

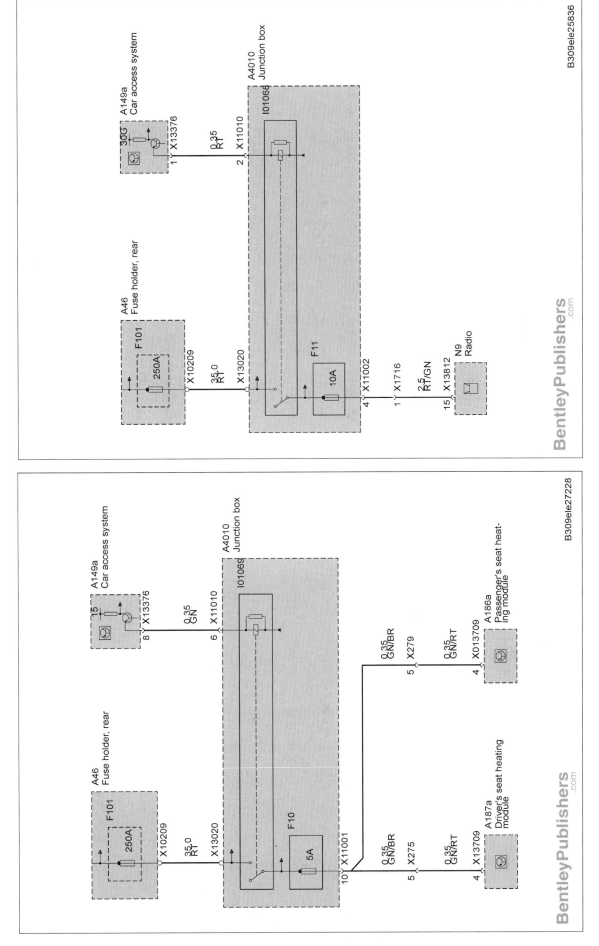

**Fuse F11**
**(to 09 / 2007)**

**Fuse F10**
**(from 09 / 2007)**

B309ele25836

B309ele27228

BentleyPublishers
.com

BentleyPublishers
.com

**Fuse F11 (to 09 / 2007)**

A149a
Car access system

30G
X13376

0.35
RT
X11010

A4010
Junction box
I01068

A46
Fuse holder, rear

F101
250A
X10209

35.0
RT
X13020

F11
10A
X11002

X1716

2.5
RT/GN
X13812

N9
Radio

**Fuse F10 (from 09 / 2007)**

A149a
Car access system

15
X13376

0.35
GN
X11010

A4010
Junction box
I01069

A46
Fuse holder, rear

F101
250A
X10209

35.0
RT
X13020

F10
5A
X11001

0.35
GN/BR
X279

0.35
GN/RT
X013709

A186a
Passenger's seat heat-
ing module

0.35
GN/BR
X275

0.35
GN/RT
X13709

A187a
Driver's seat heating
module

**Fuse F11**
**N52 or N51 engine**
**(from 09 / 2007)**

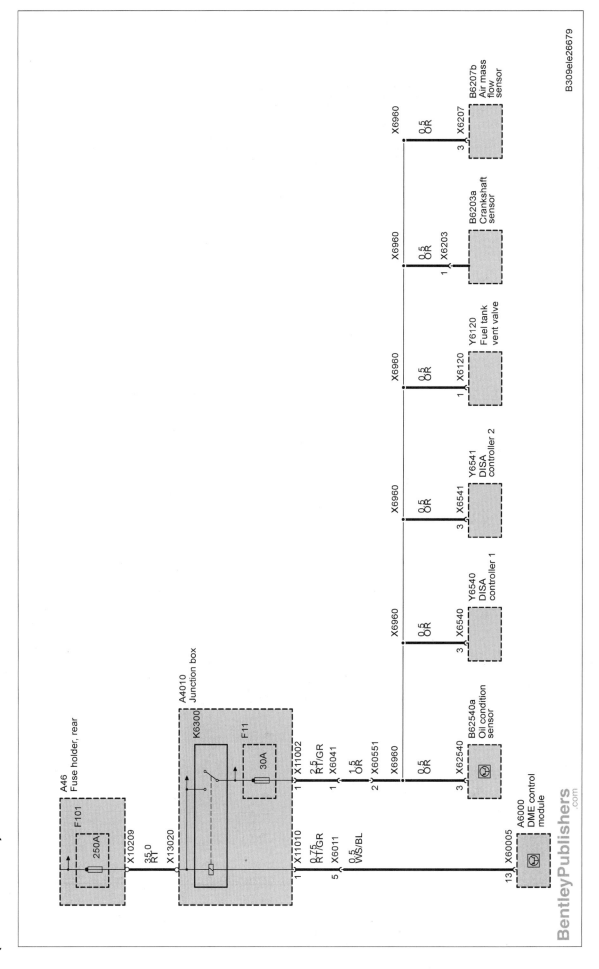

B309ele26679

**A46** Fuse holder, rear

F101

250A

X10209

35.0
RT

X13020

**A4010** Junction box

K6300

F11

20A

X11002

1

2.5
RT/GR

X6041

1

1.5
OR

X60551

2

X6960

0.5
OR

X62540

3

**B62540a** Oil condition sensor

X11010

1

0.75
RT/GR

X6011

5

0.5
WS/BL

X60005

13

**A6000** DME control module

X6960

0.5
OR

X6538

1

**Y2381** Volume control valve

X6960

0.5
OR

X6120

1

**Y6120** Fuel tank vent valve

X6960

0.5
OR

X6203

1

X6960

**B6203a** Crankshaft sensor

Electrical Wiring Diagrams  **ELE-25**

B309ele27287

**Fuse F12**
**(from 03 / 2007 to 09 / 2007)**

A149a
Car access system

30G

X13376

A4010
Junction
box

I01068

X11010   convertible
X11010   ex. convertible

0.75
RT

6
2

1

A46
Fuse holder, rear

convertible
ex. convertible

F108
F101

250A

X10209

35.0
RT

X13020

F12

20A

X11003

A96a
Convertible
top module
(CTM)

2.5
RT/GR

X13039

22

convertible

25899

A14102
Multi-drive
sunroof

2.5
RT/GR

X14102

1

Sports Wagon

25911

A14286
Function control
center, roof

2.5
RT/GR

X14287

5

2

sedan or
coupe

25813

B309ele25813

**Fuse F12**
**(to 03 / 2007)**

A149a
Car access system

30G

X13376

A4010
Junction
box

I01068

0.75
RT

X11010

6

1

A46
Fuse
holder,
rear

F108

250A

X10209

35.0
RT

X13020

F12

20A

X11003

A96a
Convertible
top module
(CTM)

2.5
RT/GR

X13039

22

convertible

25503

A14102
Multi-drive
sunroof

2.5
RT/GR

X14102

1

Sports Wagon

23503

A14286
Function control
center, roof

2.5
RT/GR

X14287

2

2

sedan or
coupe

21714

B390ele21714

**Fuse F12**
**(from 09 / 2007)**

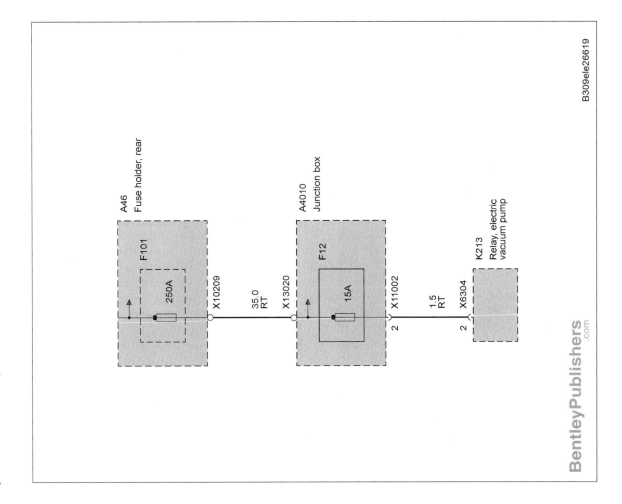

A46
Fuse holder, rear

F101

250A

X10209

35.0
RT

X13020

A4010
Junction box

F12

15A

X11002

2

1.5
RT

X6304

2

K213
Relay, electric
vacuum pump

B309ele26619

**Fuse F13**

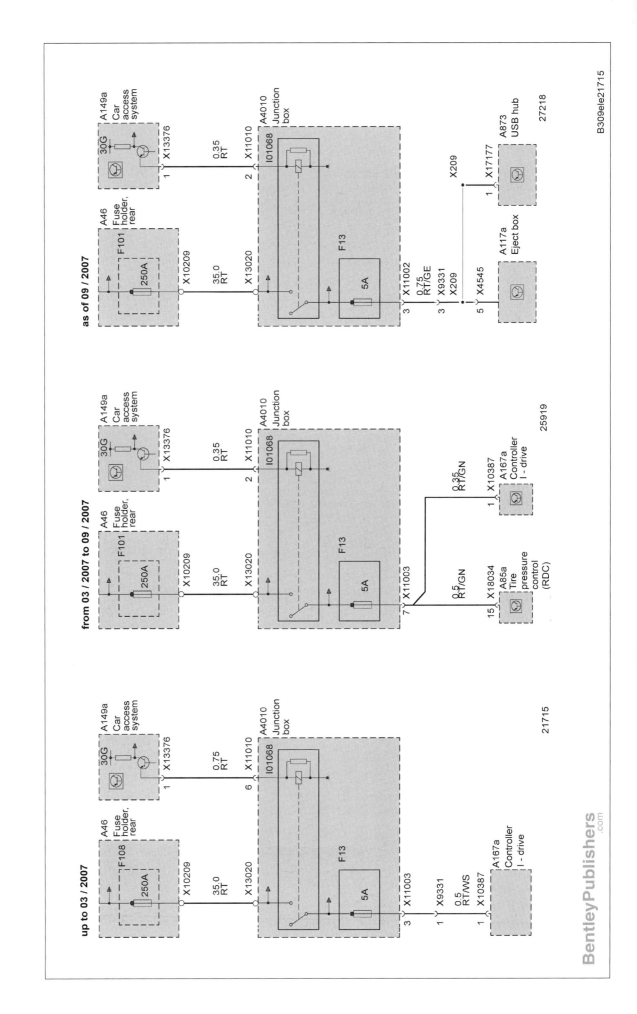

B309ele21715

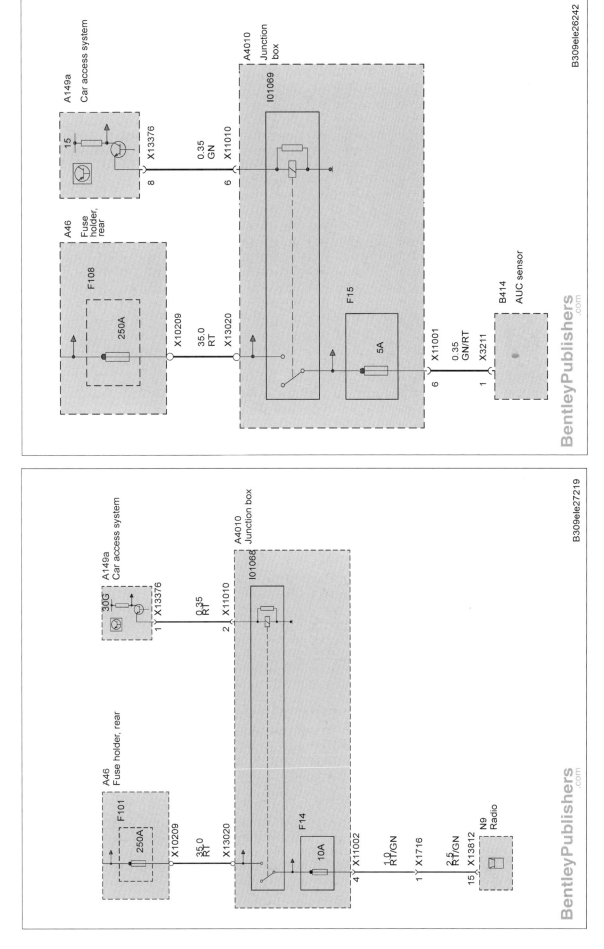

**Fuse F15**
**(to 09 / 2007)**

A149a
Car access system

A46
Fuse holder, rear

A4010
Junction box

I01069

15
X13376
8

0.35
GN
X11010
6

F108

250A
X10209

35.0
RT
X13020

F15
5A

X11001
6

0.35
GN/RT
X3211
1

B414
AUC sensor

B309ele26242

---

**Fuse F14**
**(from 09 / 2007)**

A149a
Car access system

A46
Fuse holder, rear

A4010
Junction box

I01068

30G
X13376
1

0.35
RT
X11010
2

F101

250A
X10209

35.0
RT
X13020

F14
10A

X11002
4

1.0
RT/GN
X1716
1

2.5
RT/GN
X13812
15

N9
Radio

B309ele27219

**Fuse F16
(to 09 / 2007)**

**Fuse F15
(from 09 / 2007)**

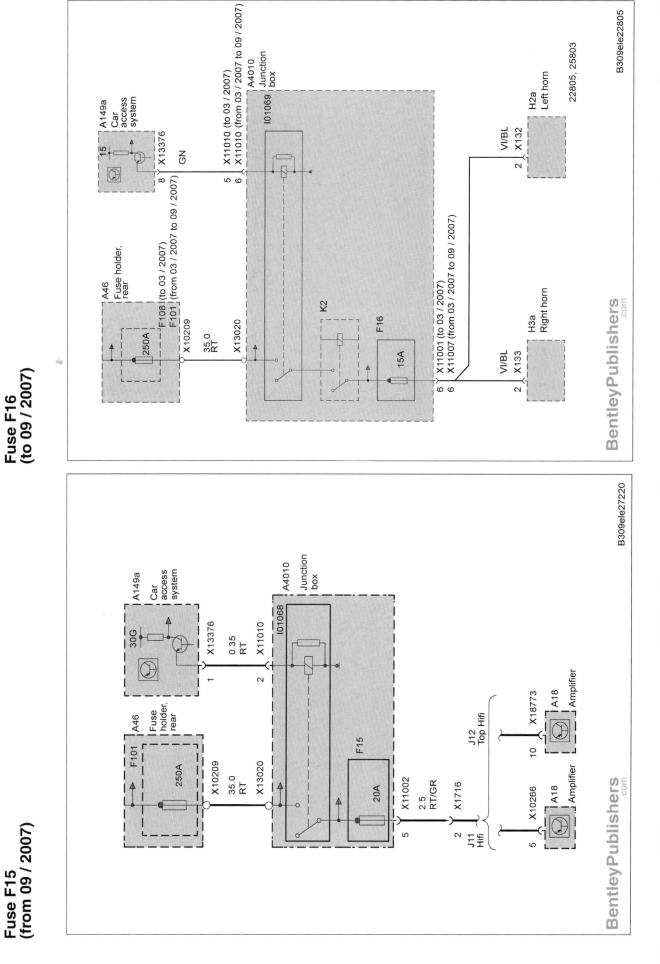

B309ele22805

B309ele27220

**Fuse F16**
**N52 and N54 engines**
**(from 09 / 2007)**

**Fuse F16**
**N51 engine**
**(from 09 / 2007)**

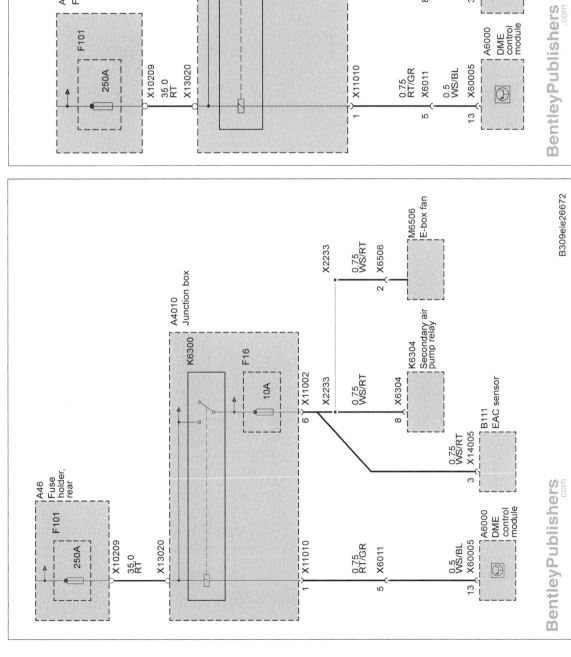

B309ele27297

B309ele26672

BentleyPublishers
.com

BentleyPublishers
.com

**Fuse F17**
**N52 and N51 engines**
**(from 09 / 2007)**

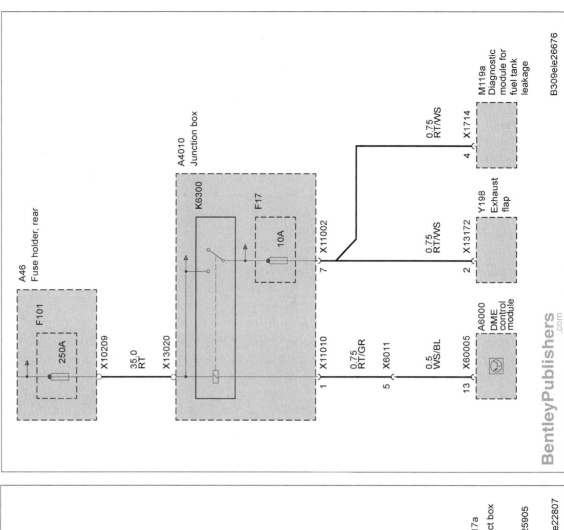

**Fuse F17**
**(to 09 / 2007)**

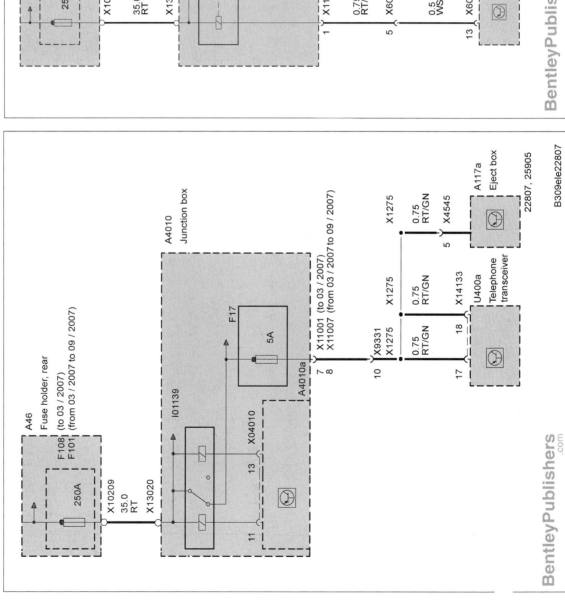

**Fuse F18**
**(to 03/ 2007)**

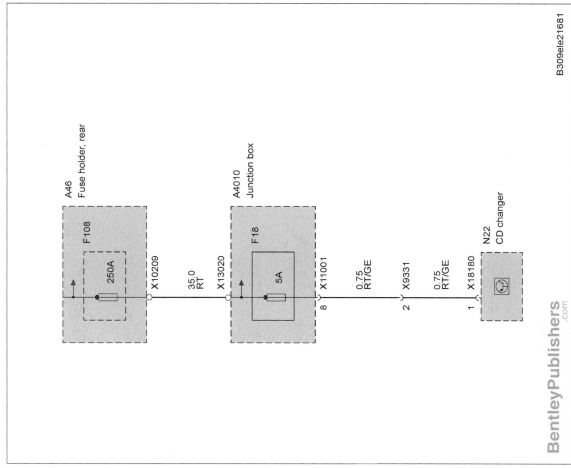

B309ele21681

A46
Fuse holder, rear

F108

250A

X10209

35.0
RT

X13020

A4010
Junction box

F18

5A

X11001

8

0.75
RT/GE

X9331

2

0.75
RT/GE

X18180

1

N22
CD changer

**Fuse F17**
**N54 engine**
**(from 09 / 2007)**

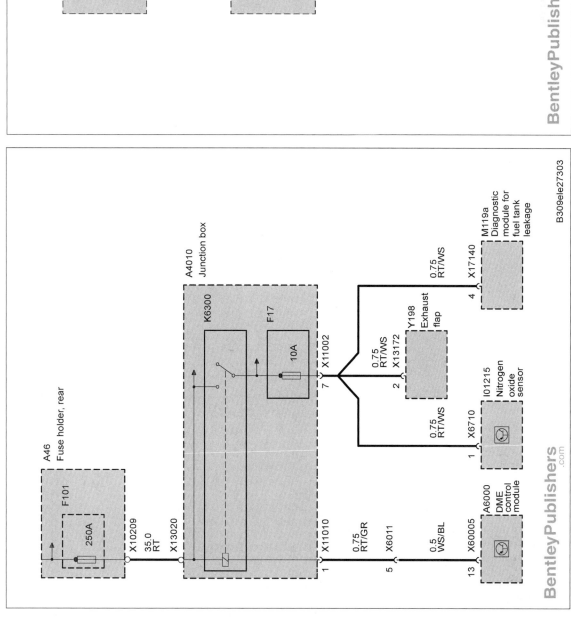

B309ele27303

A46
Fuse holder, rear

F101

250A

X10209

35.0
RT

X13020

A4010
Junction box

K6300

F17

10A

X11002

7

X11010

1

0.75
RT/WS

X13172

2

0.75
RT/WS

X6710

1

0.75
RT/WS

X17140

4

Y198
Exhaust
flap

I01215
Nitrogen
oxide
sensor

M119a
Diagnostic
module for
fuel tank
leakage

0.75
RT/GR

X6011

5

0.5
WS/BL

X60005

13

A6000
DME
control
module

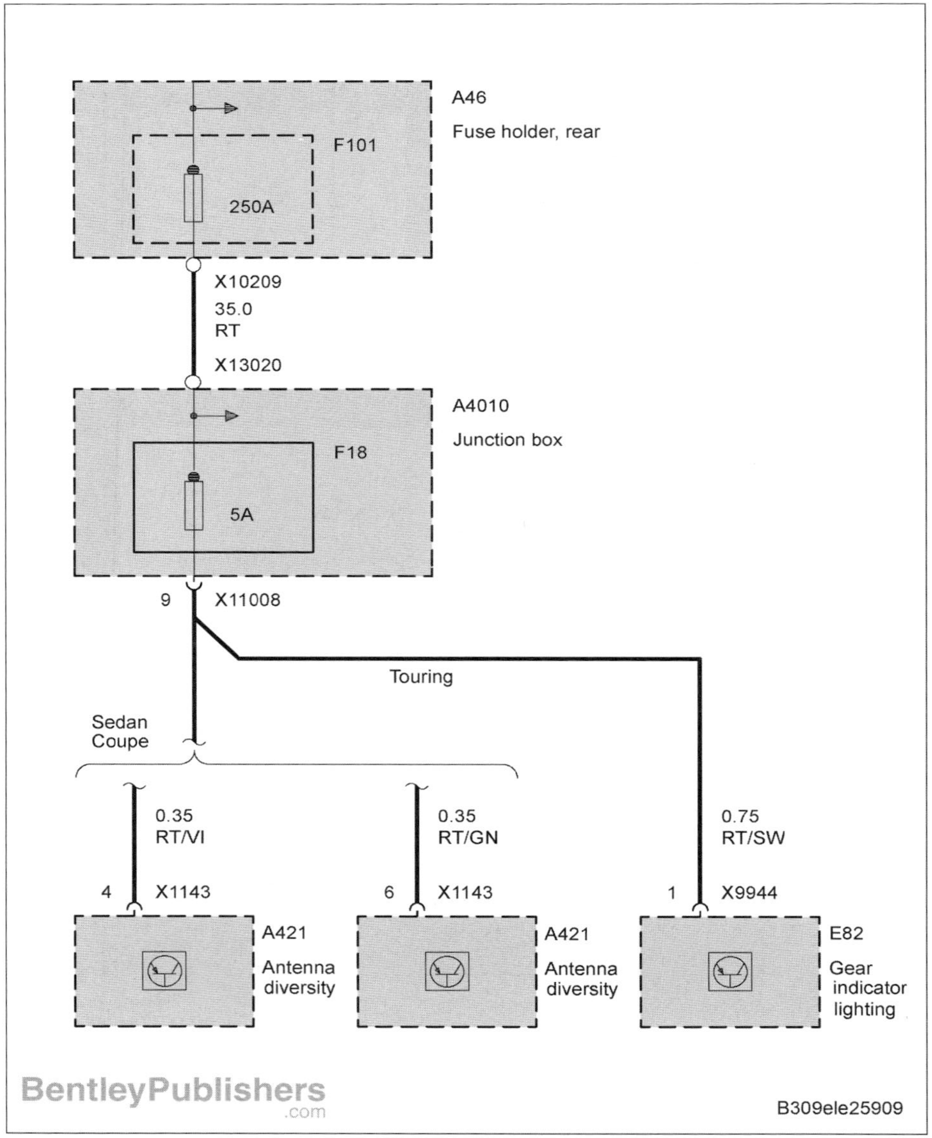

## Fuse F18
## non-Convertible
### (from 03 / 2007 to 09 / 2007)

B309ele27009

## Fuse F18
## Convertible
### (from 03 / 2007 to 09 / 2007)

B309ele25909

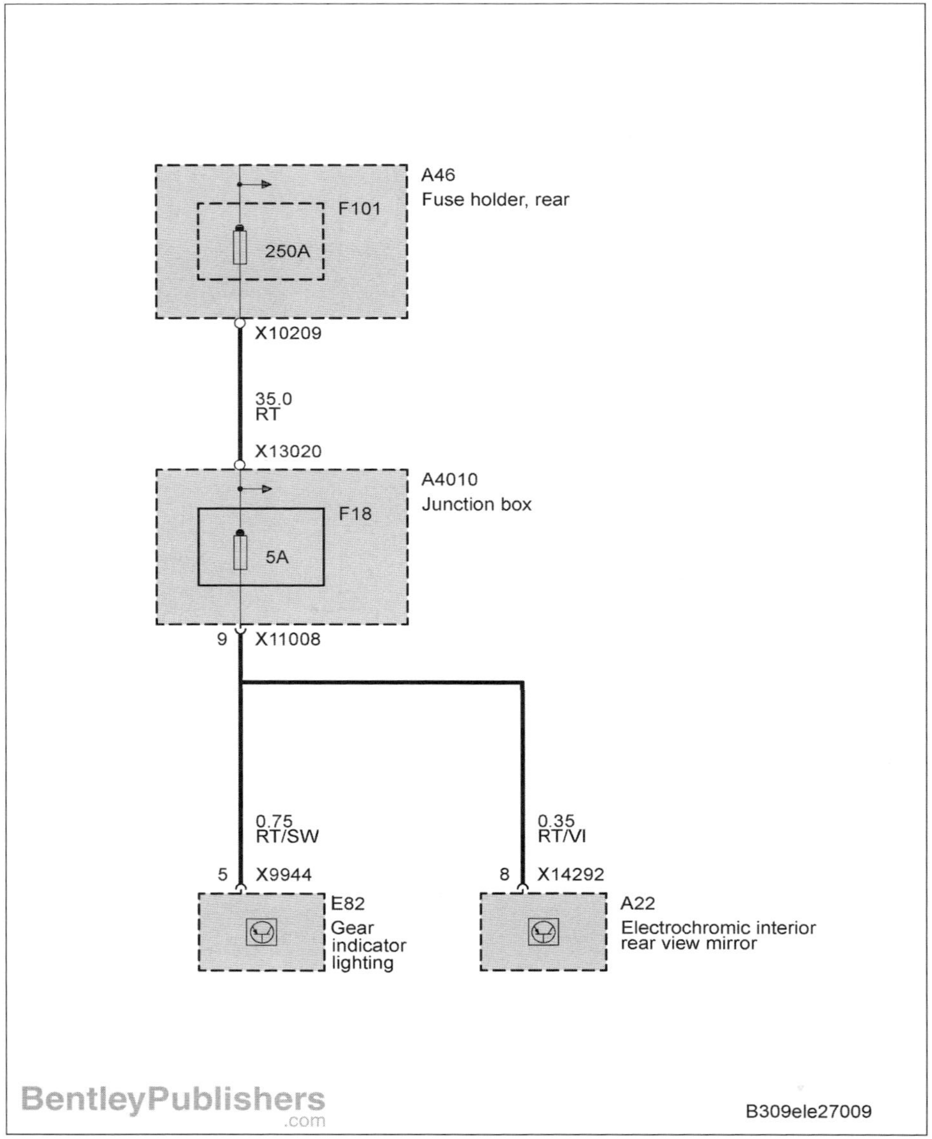

**Fuse F19
(to 03 / 2007)**

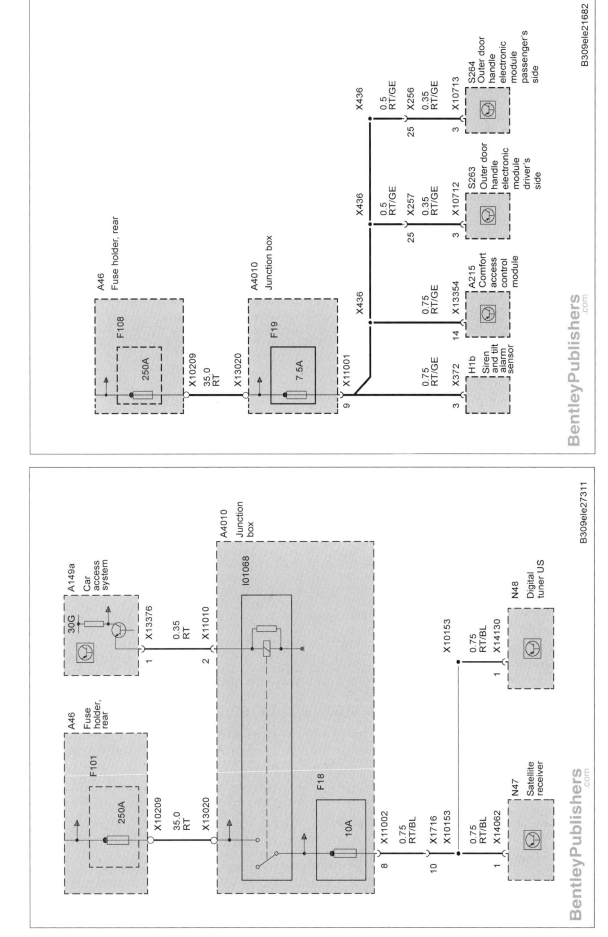

B309ele21682

**Fuse F18
(from 09 / 2007)**

B309ele27311

**Fuse F20**
**(to 09 / 2007)**

A149a
Car access system

30G

X13376

RT

X11010  (to 03 / 2007)
X11010  (from 03 / 2007 to 09 / 2007)

A4010 Junction box

I01068

A46 Fuse holder, rear
(to 03 / 2007)
(from 03 / 2007 to 09 / 2007)

F108
F101

250A

X10209

35.0 RT

X13020

F20

5A

X11001 (to 03 / 2007)
X11003 (from 03 / 2007 to 09 / 2007)

10
6

0.35 RT/GR X10594

A70006 Control module, transfer box

8

all-wheel drive

0.35 RT/GR X1746

A65a Dynamic stability control (DSC)

7

0.35 RT/GR X18303

A65a Dynamic stability control (DSC)

17

not all-wheel drive

23504, 25913

B309ele23504

BentleyPublishers.com

---

**Fuse F19**
**(from 03 / 2007)**

A149a
Car access system

30G

X13376

0.35 RT

X11010

A4010 Junction box

I01068

A46 Fuse holder, rear

from 09 / 2007

F101

250A

X10209

35.0 RT

X13020

F19

5A

X11002

9

X1716

9

X1069

0.35 RT/SW X13049

A421 Antenna diversity

1

Cabriolet

27008

0.35 RT/SW X18180

N22 CD changer

1

B309ele25775

from 03 / 2007
to 09 / 2007

A46 Fuse holder, rear

F101

250A

X10209

35.0 RT

X13020

A4010 Junction box

F19

7.5A

X11007

3

0.5 RT/BR X372

H1b Siren and tilt alarm sensor

3

25775

BentleyPublishers.com

**Fuse F20
(from 09 / 2007)**

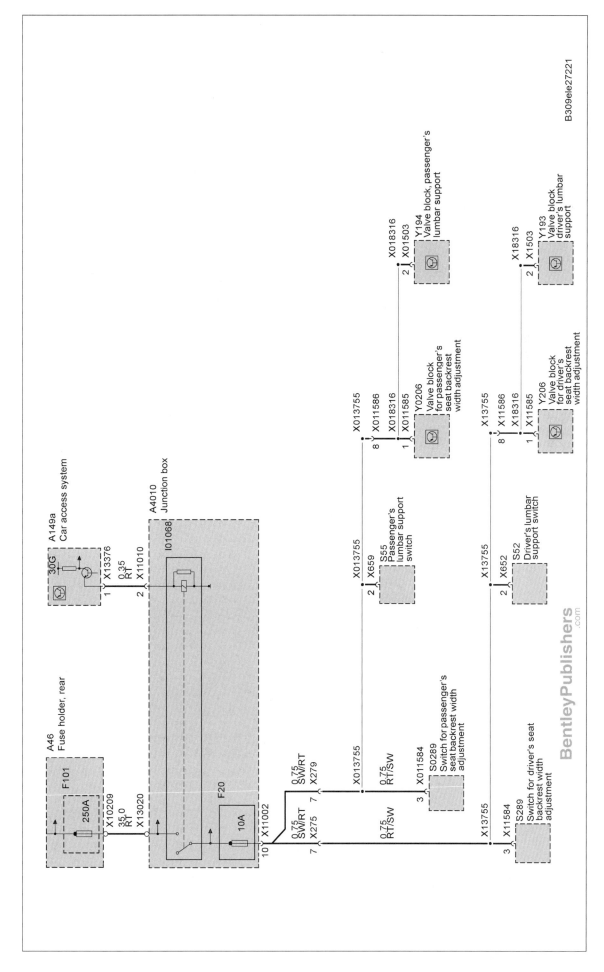

B309ele27221

BentleyPublishers
.com

**Fuse F21
(from 09 / 2007)**

A149a
Car access system

30G

X13376

0.35
RT

X11010

A4010
Junction box

I01068

1

2

A46
Fuse holder, rear

F101

250A

X10209

35.0
RT

X13020

F21

10A

X11003

0.75
RT/WS

X1783

1

8

A144a
Active cruise control

B309ele27273

**Fuse F21
(to 09 / 2007)**

A149a
Car access system

30G

X13376

0.75
RT

X11010 (to 03 / 2007)
X11010 (from 03 / 2007 to 09 / 2007)

A4010
Junction box

I01068

1

6
2

A46
Fuse holder, rear

(to 03 / 2007)
(from 03 / 2007
to 09 / 2007)

F108  F101

250A

X10209

35.0
RT

X13020

F21

7.5A

X11002 (to 03 / 2007)
X11008 (from 03 / 2007 to 09 / 2007)

6
6

X256

8

0.75
RT/GR

X624

6

Y6
Outside mirror,
passenger's side

21718, 25819

X257

8

0.75
RT/GR

X10275

13

A23b
Driver's switch
cluster

B309ele21718

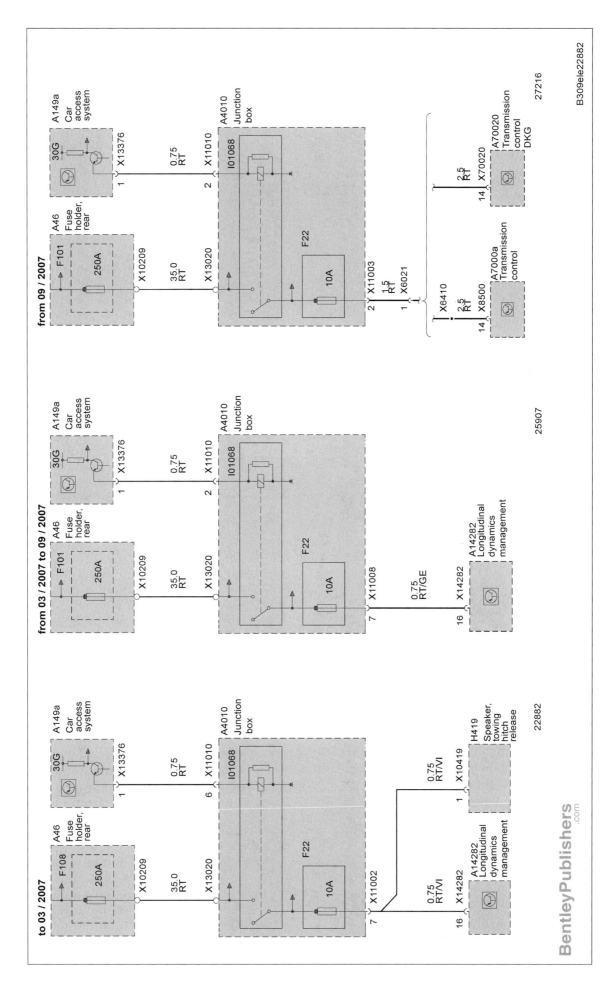

B309ele22882

**Fuse F23**

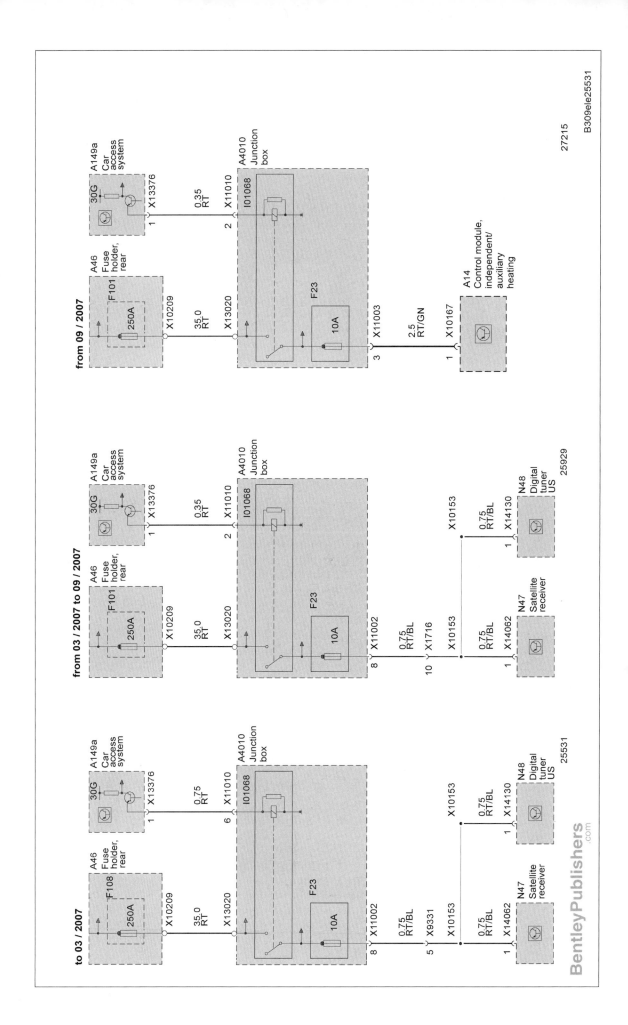

27215

B309ele25531

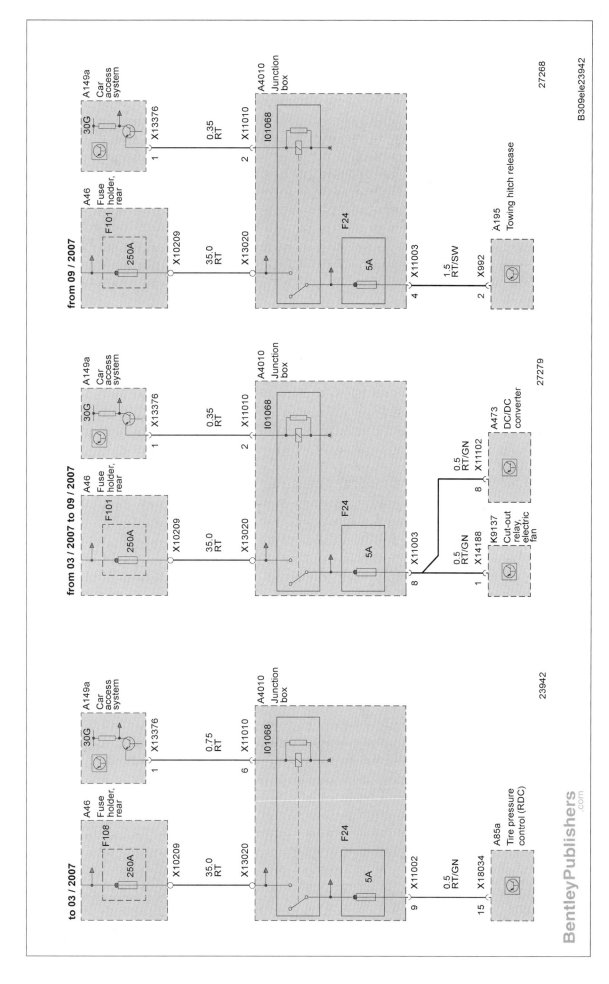

B309ele23942

## Fuse F25

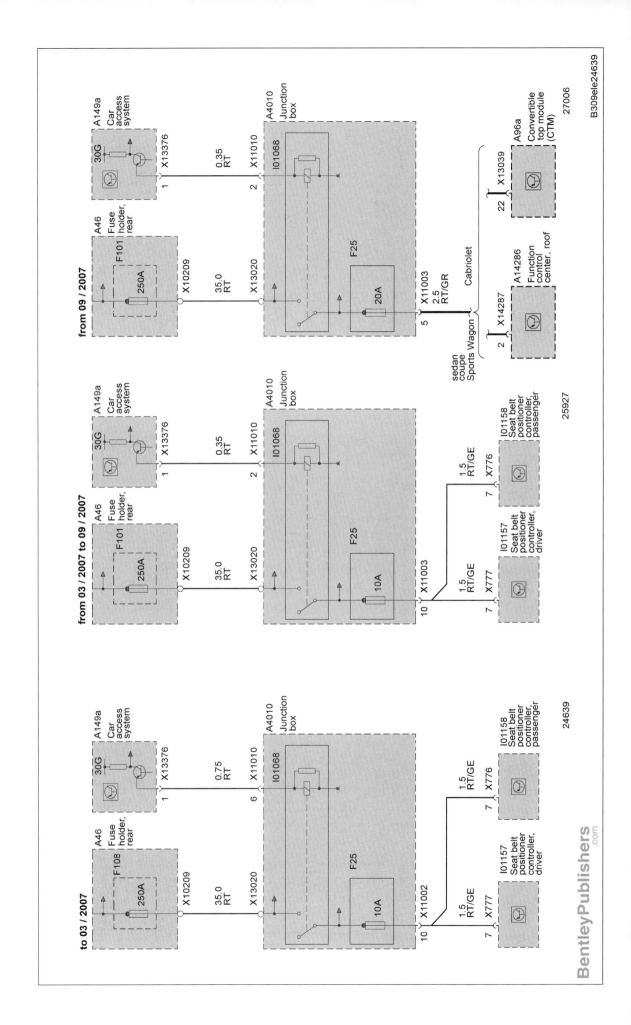

B309ele24639

27006

25927

24639

**Fuse F26
without TCU or ULF
(to 03 / 2007)**

B309ele22333

A149a
Car
access
system

30G

X13376

1

0.75
RT

X11010

A4010
Junction
box

I01068

6

A46
Fuse
holder,
rear

F108

250A

X10209

35.0
RT

X13020

F26

10A

X11003

6

X9331

3

X209

0.75
RT/GE

X695

17

U400a
Telephone
transceiver

X209

0.5
RT/GE

X1765

1

N27a
Compensator

X209

0.75
RT/GE

X4545

5

A117a
Eject
box

X209

0.75
RT/GE

X1848

1

connector, telephone
retrofit packages

E82
Gear
indicator
lighting

5

X9944

0.35
RT/GE

BentleyPublishers
.com

---

**Fuse F26
with TCU or ULF
(to 03 / 2007)**

B309ele26264

A149a
Car
access
system

30G

X13376

1

0.75
RT

X11010

A4010
Junction
box

I01068

6

A46
Fuse
holder,
rear

F108

250A

X10209

35.0
RT

X13020

F26

10A

X11003

6

X9331

3

X209

0.75
RT/GE

18

U400a
Telephone
transceiver

17

X14133

X209

0.75
RT/GE

A117a
Eject
box

5

X4545

X209

0.75
RT/GE

BentleyPublishers
.com

**Fuse F26**
**with TCU or ULF from**
**(03 / 2007 to 09 / 2007)**

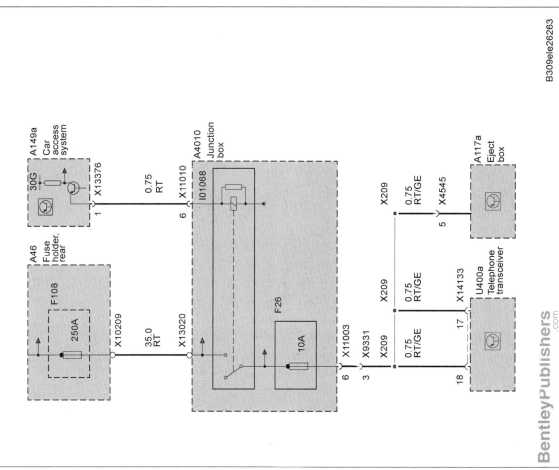

**Fuse F26**
**without TCU or ULF**
**(from 03 / 2007 to 09 / 2007)**

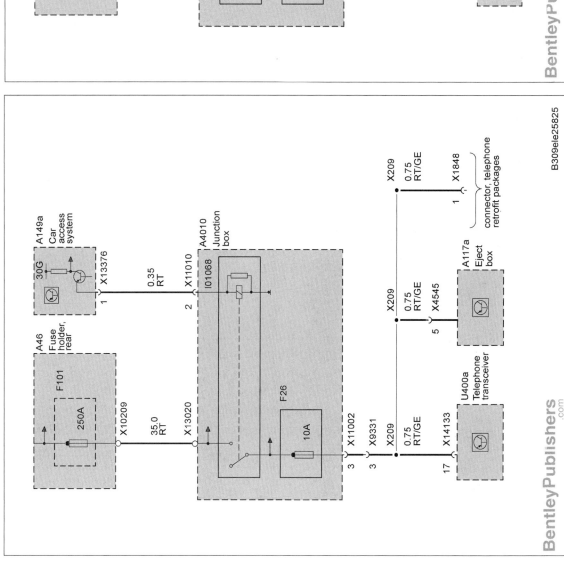

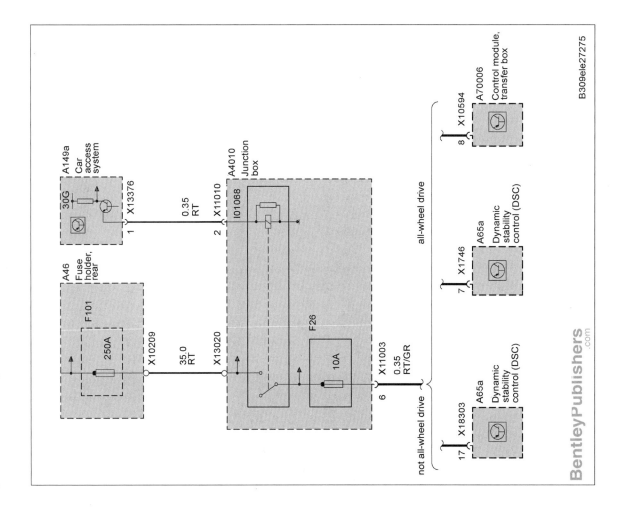

B309ele27275

**Fuse F27**
**(from 09 / 2007)**

A149a Car access system

30G

X13376

0.35 RT

X11010

A4010 Junction box

IO1068

1

2

A46 Fuse holder, rear

F101

250A

X10209

35.0 RT

X13020

F27

5A

X11003

7

0.35 RT/VI

X10387

A167a Controller

1

A85a Tire pressure control (RDC)

0.5 RT/VI

X18034

15

B309ele27007

**Fuse F27**
**(to 09 / 2007)**

A149a Car access system

15

X13376

GN

X11010 (to 03 / 2007)
X11010 (from 03 / 2007 to 09 / 2007)

8

5
6

A4010 Junction box

IO1069

A46 Fuse holder, rear

(to 03 / 2007)
(from 03 / 2007
to 09 / 2007)

250A F108 F101

X10209

35.0 RT

X13020

F27

5A

X11003 (to 03 / 2007)
X11001 (from 03 / 2007 to 09 / 2007)

7
9

0.5 GN/SW

X257

24

0.5 GN/SW

X10725

A23b Driver's switch cluster

8

0.75 GN/SW

X9331

3

0.75 GN/SW

X1643

0.75 GN/SW

X1848

3

connector, telephone retrofit packages

X1643

0.75 GN/SW

X695

35

U400a Telephone transceiver

21710, 25805

B309ele21710

# Fuse F28

## to 03 / 2007

**A46** Fuse holder, rear
F108
250A
X10209

35.0 RT
X13020

**A149a** Car access system
15
X13376
8

0.75 GN
X11010
5

**A4010** Junction box
I01069

F28
5A
X11003
8

0.35 GN/WS
X14286
3
**A14286** Function control center, roof

0.35 GN/WS
X300
7
**A81a** Park distance control (PDC)

21711

## from 03 / 2007 to 09 / 2007

**A46** Fuse holder, rear
F101
250A
X10209

35.0 RT
X13020

**A149a** Car access system
15
X13376
8

0.35 GN
X11010
6

**A4010** Junction box
I01069

F28
5A
X11001
7

0.35 GN/WS
X14286
3
**A14286** Function control center, roof

0.35 GN/WS
X300
7
**A81a** Park distance control (PDC)

25807

## from 09 / 2007

**A149a** Car access system
30G
X13376
8

0.35 RT
X11010
2

**A46** Fuse holder, rear
F101
250A
X10209

35.0 RT
X13020

**A4010** Junction box
I01068

F28
5A
X11003
8

0.5 RT/GN
X11102
8
**A473** DC/DC converter

0.5 RT/GN
X14188
1
**K9137** Cut-out relay, electric fan

27277

BentleyPublishers
.com

**Fuse F29
(from 03 / 2007)**

B309ele25809

A149a
Car access system

15
X13376
8

0.35
GN

X11010
6

A4010
Junction box

I01069

A46
Fuse holder, rear

F101

250A
X10209

35.0
RT

X13020

F29

5A

X11001
10

X013709
0.35
GN/BR
X279
5
0.35
GN/RT
X013709
4

A186a
Passenger's seat heating module

0.35
GN/BR
X275
5
0.35
GN/RT
X13709
4

A187a
Driver's seat heating module

BentleyPublishers.com

---

**Fuse F29
(to 03 / 2007)**

B309ele21712

A149a
Car access system

15
X13376
8

0.75
GN

X11010
5

A4010
Junction box

I01069

A46
Fuse holder, rear

F108

250A
X10209

35.0
RT

X13020

F29

5A

X11003
9

X9454
0.35
GN/RT
X279
5
X013709
4

A186a
Passenger's seat heating module

0.35
GN/RT
X9454
0.35
GN/RT
X275
5
X13709
4

A187a
Driver's seat heating module

0.5
GN/RT

X3211
1

B414
AUC sensor

BentleyPublishers.com

# Fuse F30

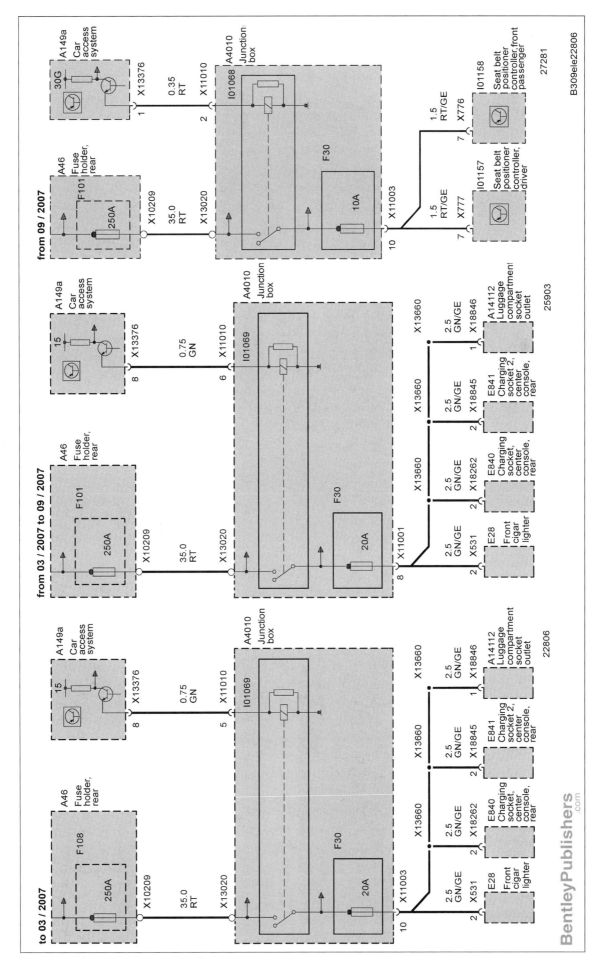

BentleyPublishers.com

B309ele22806

**Fuse F31**
**(to 03 / 2007)**

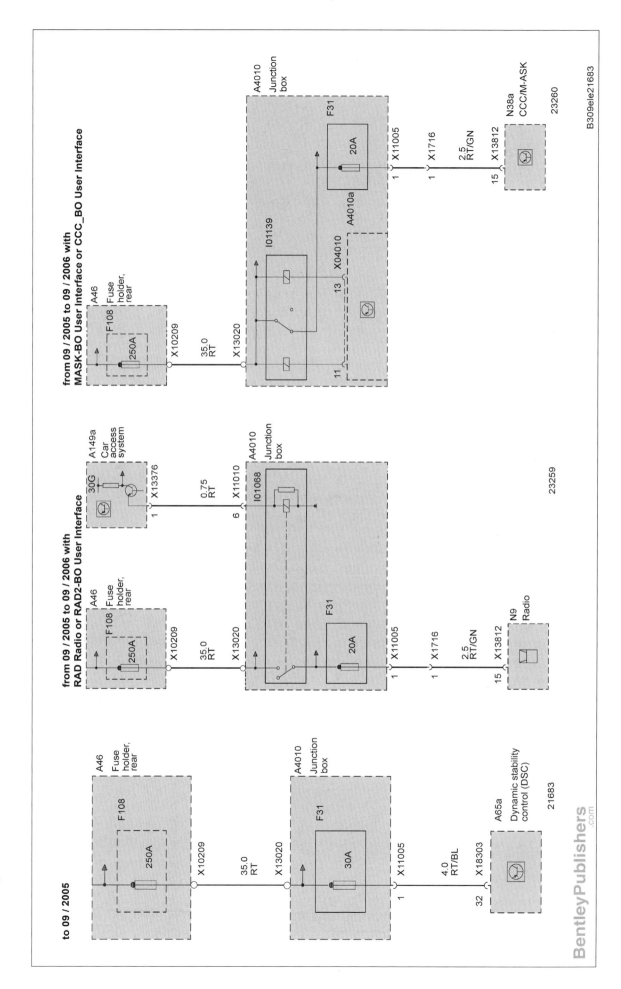

B309ele21683

BentleyPublishers
.com

**Fuse F31**
**(from 09 / 2007)**

**Fuse F31**
**(from 03 / 2007 to 09 / 2007)**

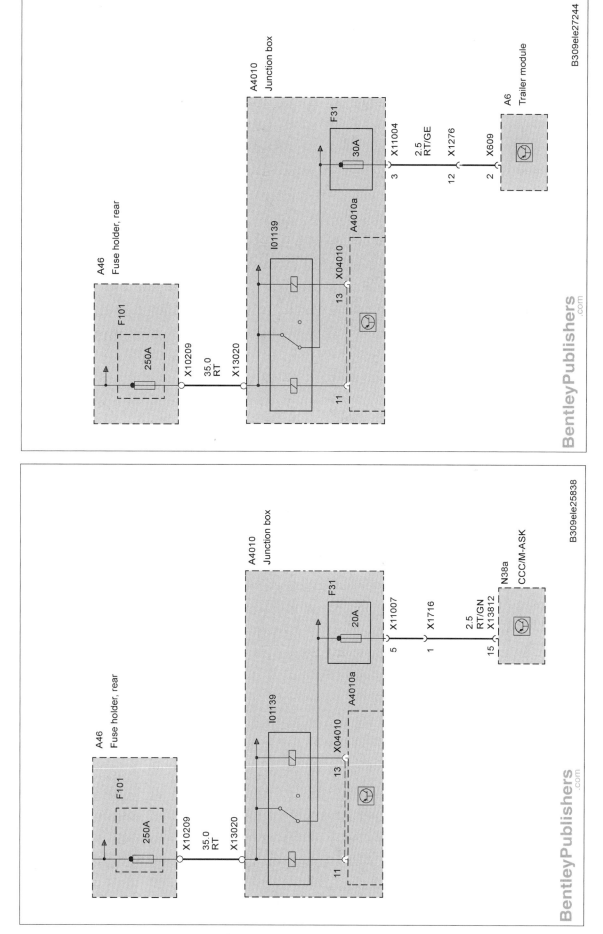

B309ele27244

B309ele25838

**Fuse F32**

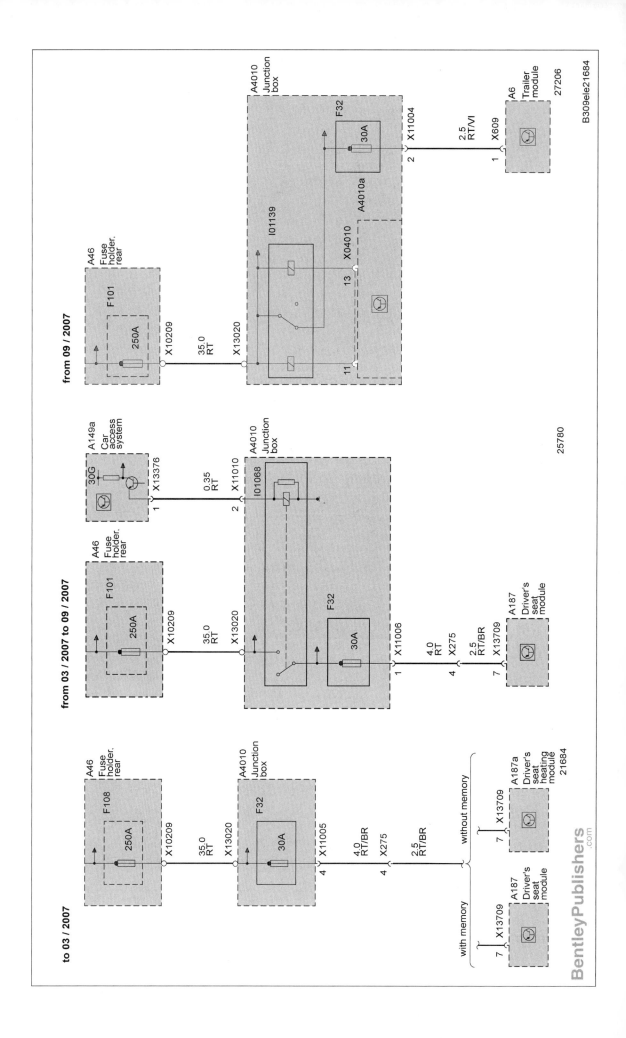

**Fuse F33**
**(from 03 / 2007 to 09 / 2007)**

**Fuse F33**
**(to 03 / 2007)**

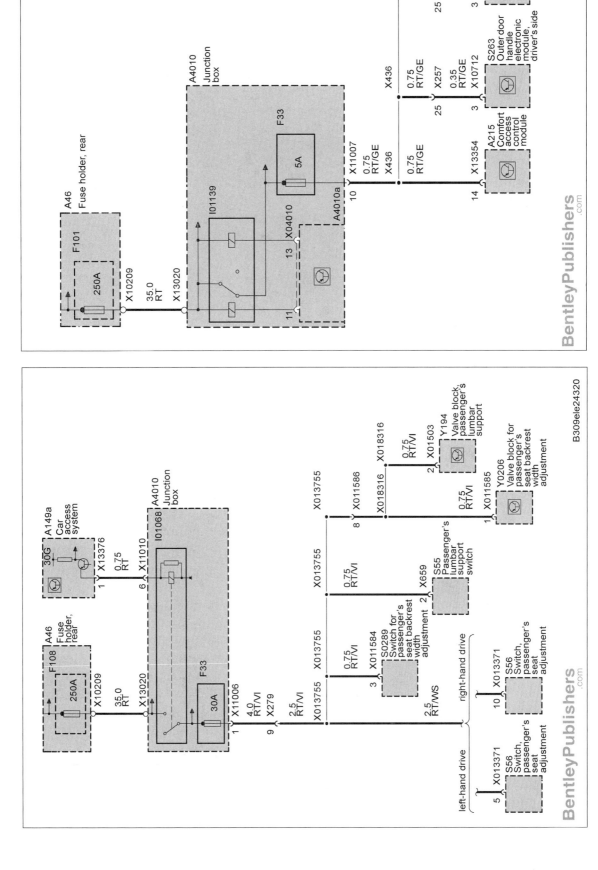

B309ele25778

B309ele24320

**Fuse F34
(to 03 / 2007)**

A149a
Car access system

30G

X13376
1

0.75
RT
X11010
6

A4010
Junction box

I01068

A46
Fuse
holder,
rear

F108

250A

X10209

35.0
RT
X13020

F34

30A

X11006
4

X1716
5

2.5
RT/GR

Top Hifi

A18
Amplifier

X18773
10

Hifi

A18
Amplifier

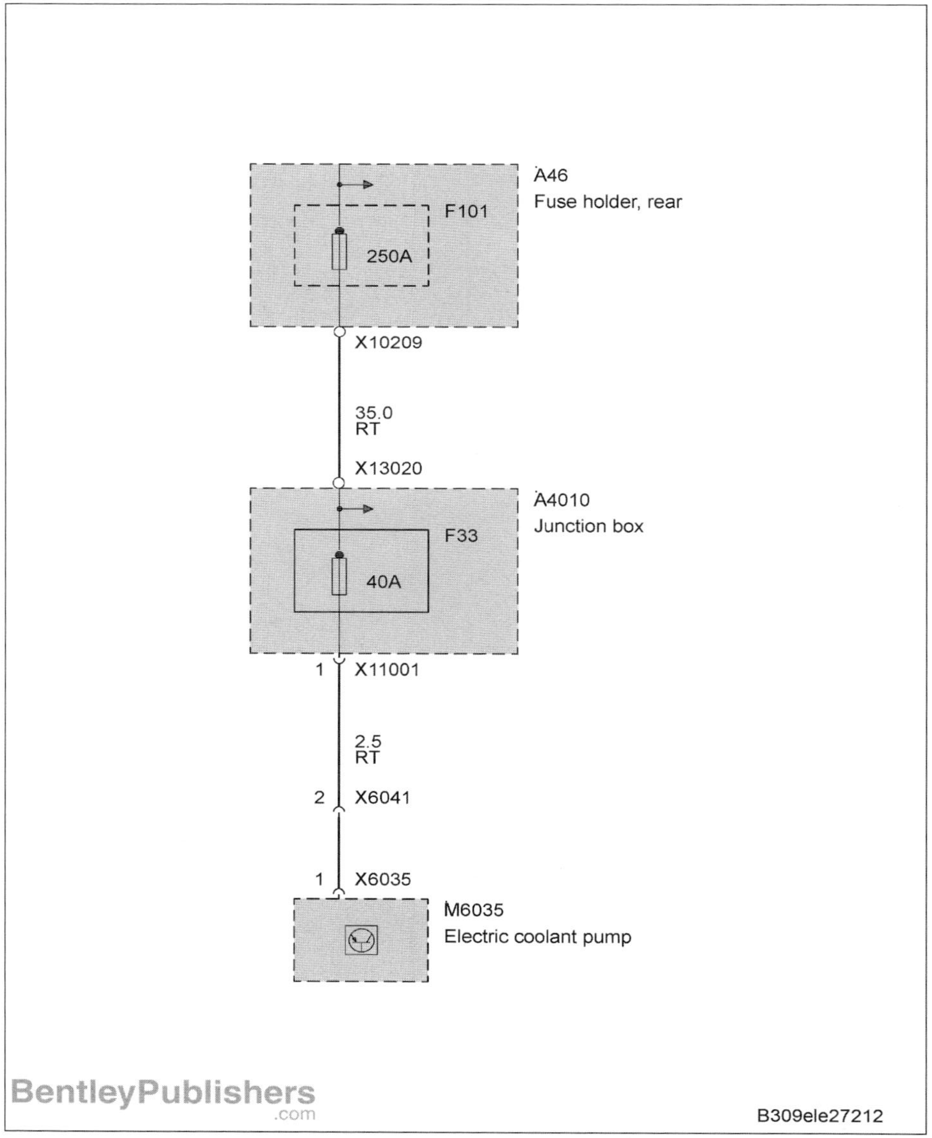

X10266
5

B309ele21721

**Fuse F33
(from 09 / 2007)**

A46
Fuse holder, rear

F101

250A

X10209

35.0
RT
X13020

A4010
Junction box

F33

40A

X11001
1

2.5
RT
X6041
2

M6035
Electric coolant pump

X6035
1

B309ele27212

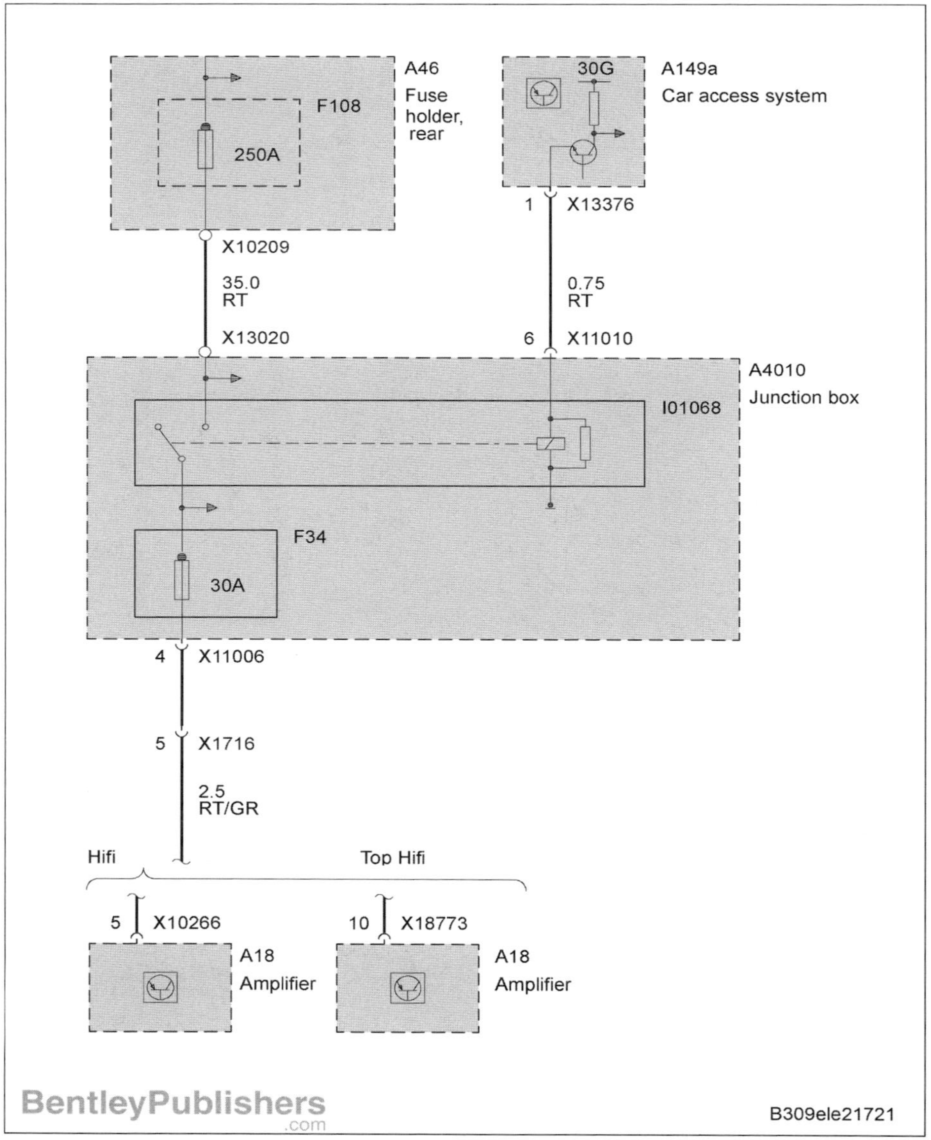

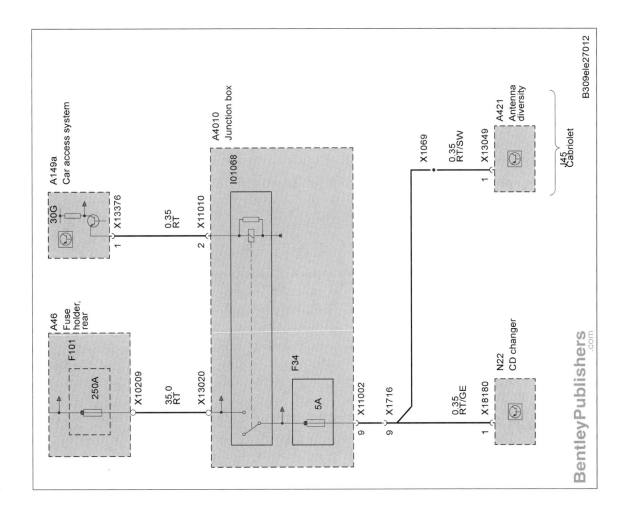

**Fuse F34
(from 03 / 2007)**

A149a
Car access system

A4010
Junction box

A421
Antenna diversity

J45
Cabriolet

A46
Fuse holder, rear

N22
CD changer

30G

F101

250A

I01068

F34

5A

X13376

X11010

X13049

X1069

X18180

X10209

X13020

X11002

X1716

0.35
RT

0.35
RT/SW

35.0
RT

0.35
RT/GE

BentleyPublishers.com

B309ele27012

## Fuse F35

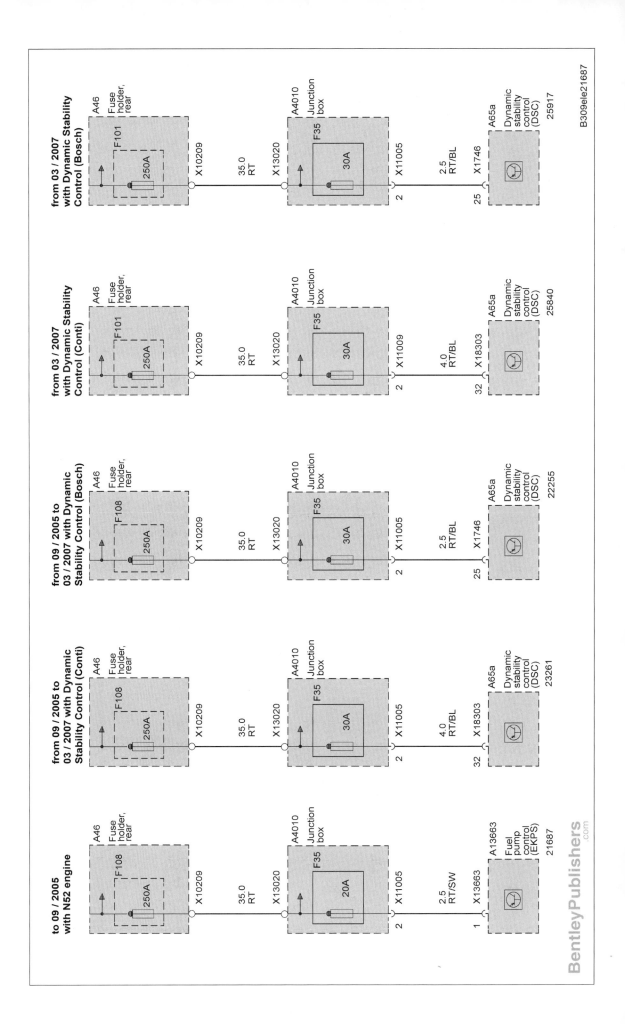

B309ele21687

**Fuse F36**

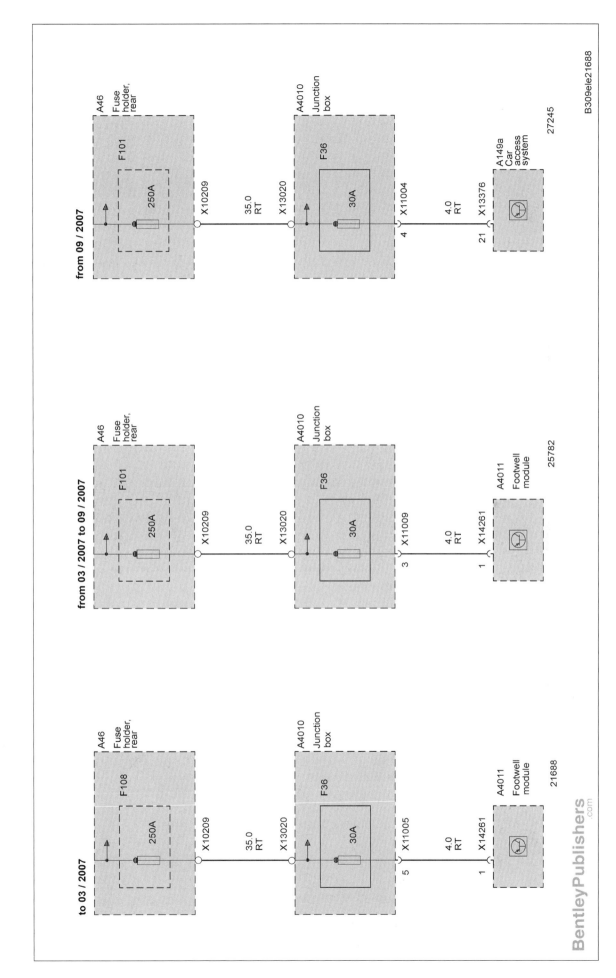

**to 03 / 2007**

A46
Fuse holder, rear

F108

250A

X10209

35.0
RT

X13020

A4010
Junction box

F36

30A

X11005

5

4.0
RT

X14261

1

A4011
Footwell module

21688

**from 03 / 2007 to 09 / 2007**

A46
Fuse holder, rear

F101

250A

X10209

35.0
RT

X13020

A4010
Junction box

F36

30A

X11009

3

4.0
RT

X14261

1

A4011
Footwell module

25782

**from 09 / 2007**

A46
Fuse holder, rear

F101

250A

X10209

35.0
RT

X13020

A4010
Junction box

F36

30A

X11004

4

4.0
RT

X13376

21

A149a
Car access system

27245

Electrical Wiring Diagrams  **ELE-57**

B309ele21688

**Fuse F37**
**(from 03 / 2007 to 09 / 2007)**

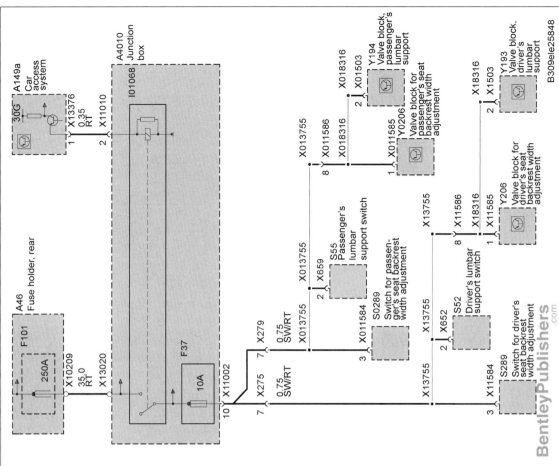

**Fuse F37**
**(to 03 / 2007)**

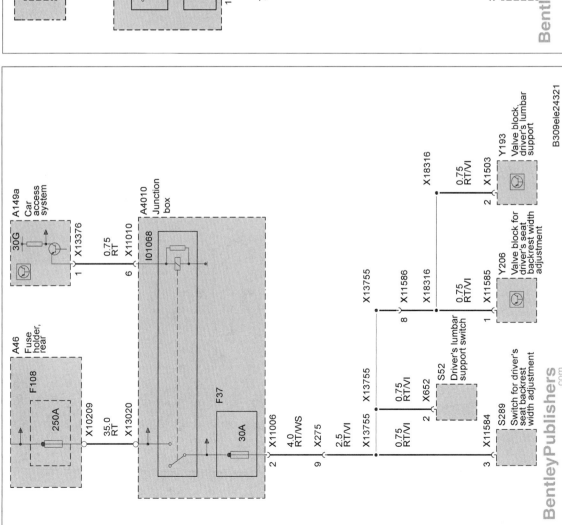

**Fuse F37**
**N52 or N51 engine**
**(from 09 / 2007)**

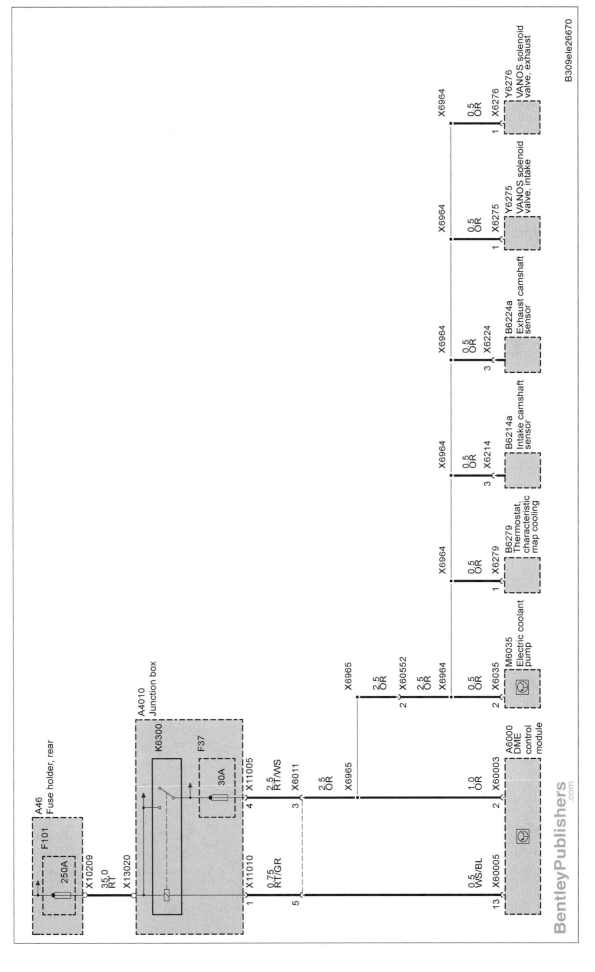

B309ele26670

**Fuse F37**
**N54 engine**
**(from 09 / 2007)**

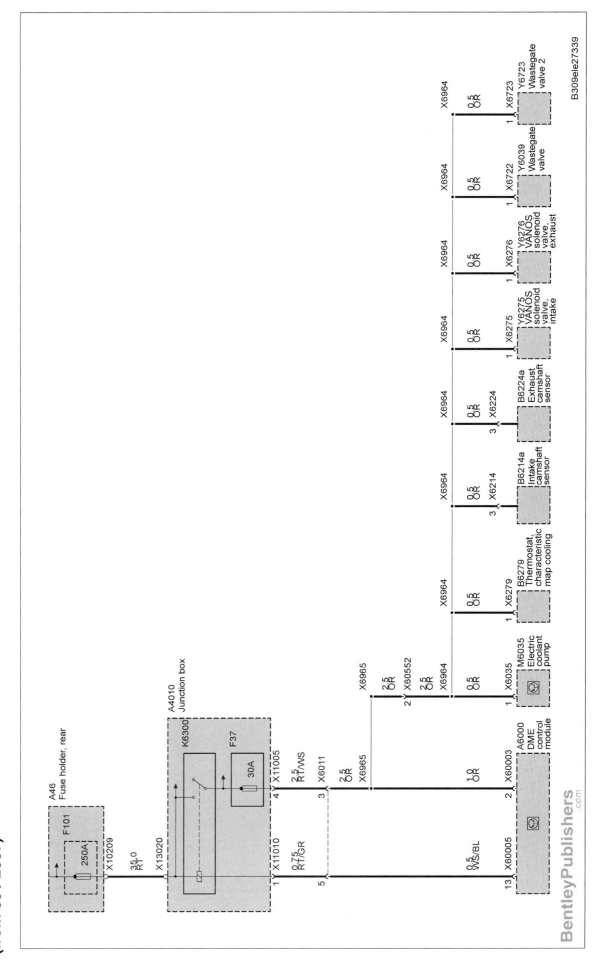

B309ele27339

BentleyPublishers
.com

# Electrical Wiring Diagrams  ELE-61

**Fuse F38
(from 09 / 2007)**

**Fuse F38
(to 09 / 2007)**

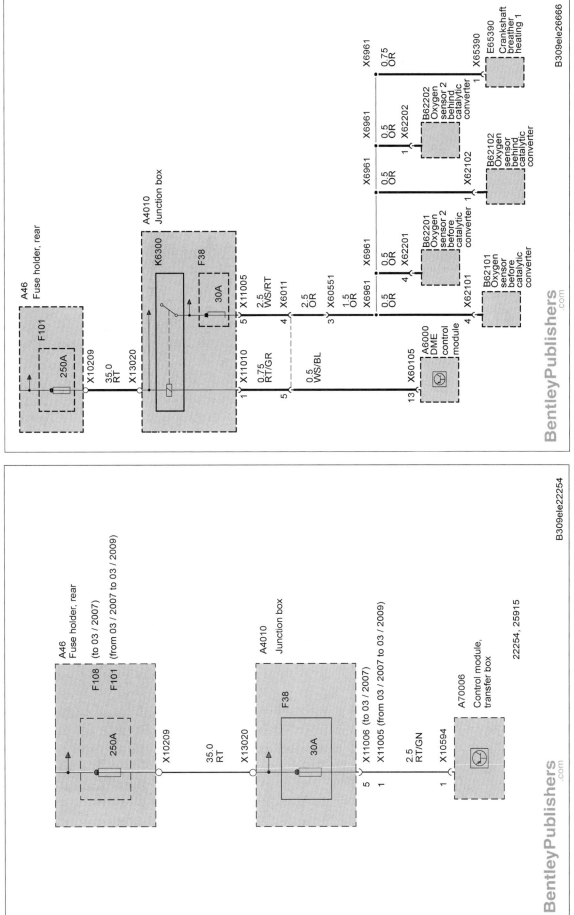

B309ele26666

B309ele22254

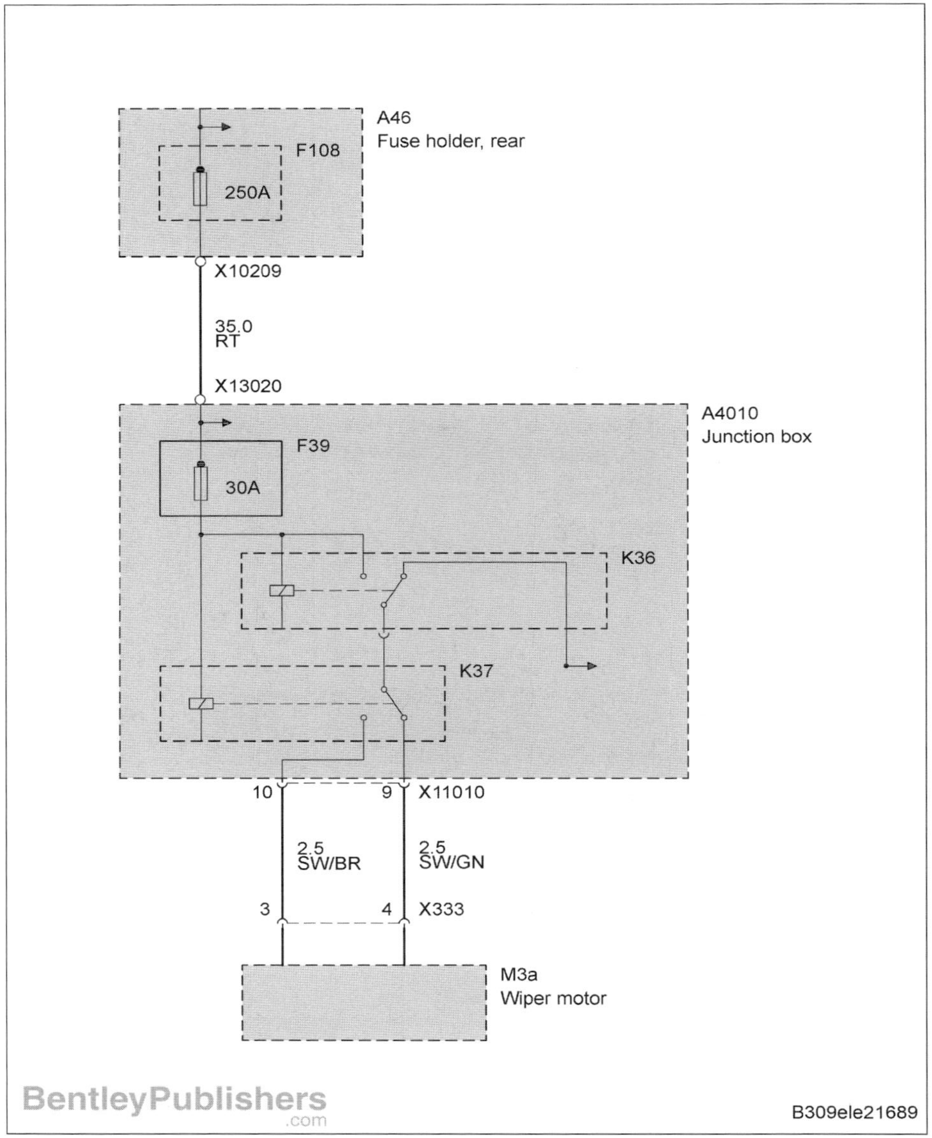

## Fuse F39
### (from 03 / 2007 to 09 / 2007)

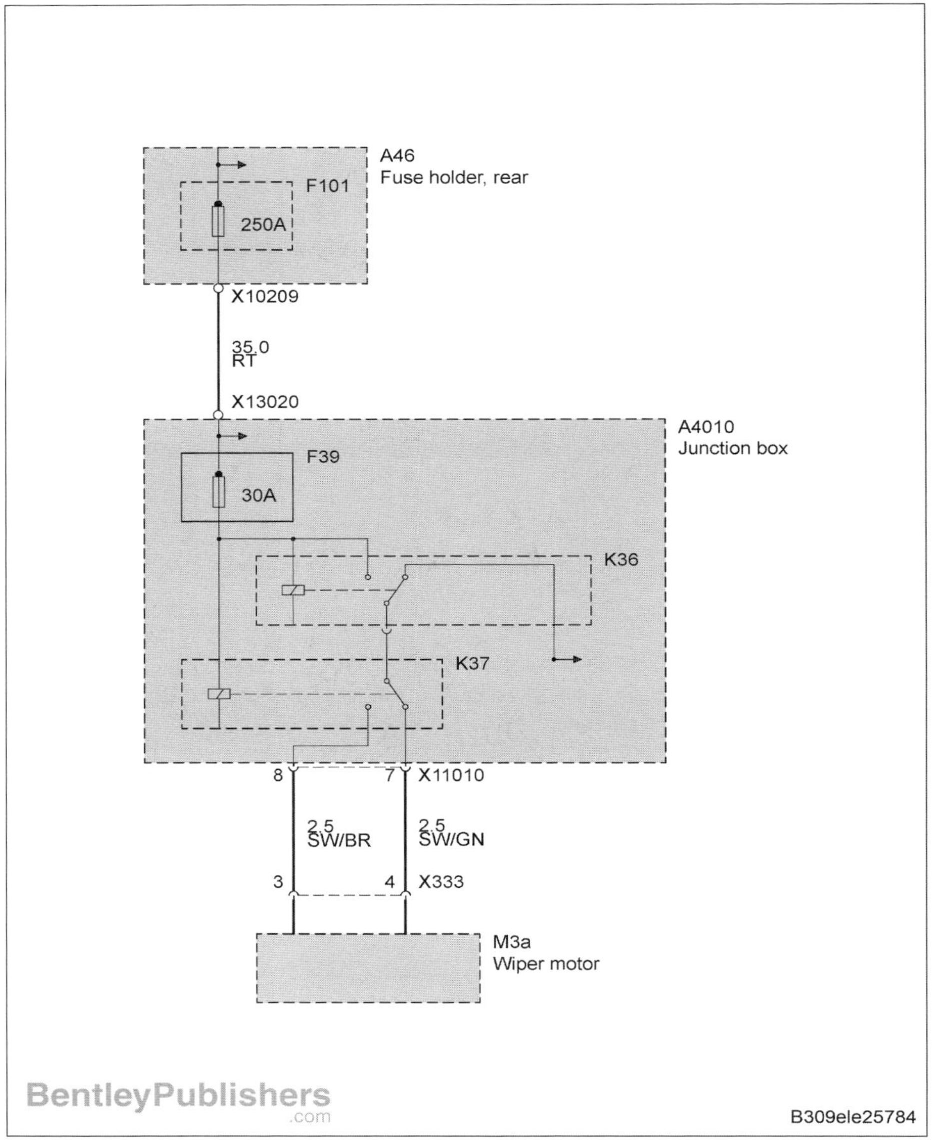

B309ele25784

## Fuse F39
### (to 03 / 2007)

B309ele21689

**A46** Fuse holder, rear

F101
250A
X10209
35.0
RT
X13020

**A4010** Junction box

K6300

F39
30A

X11005
2.5
RT/VI
6
X6011
5

X11010
0.75
RT/GR
1
5

**A6000** DME control module
0.5
WS/BL
X60005
13

X6966
X6966
8
2.5
OR

X60552
X6970
1.5
OR
1
X6970

Y6101 Fuel injector, cylinder 1
X6101
0.5
OR
1

Y6102 Fuel injector, cylinder 2
X6970
X6102
0.5
OR
1

Y6103 Fuel injector, cylinder 3
X6970
X6103
0.5
OR
1

Y6104 Fuel injector, cylinder 4
X6970
X6104
0.5
OR
1

Y6105 Fuel injector, cylinder 5
X6970
X6105
0.5
OR
1

Y6106 Fuel injector, cylinder 6
X6970
X6106
0.5
OR
1

X6963
1.0
OR
X6151
3
T6151 Ignition coil, cylinder 1

X6963
X6152
1.0
OR
3
T6152 Ignition coil, cylinder 2

X6963
X6153
1.0
OR
3
T6153 Ignition coil, cylinder 3

X6963
X6154
1.0
OR
3
T6154 Ignition coil, cylinder 4

X6963
X6155
1.0
OR
3
T6155 Ignition coil, cylinder 5

X6963
X6156
1.0
OR
3
T6156 Ignition coil, cylinder 6

X6963
0.75
OR
I01046 Interference suppression capacitor for ignition coils

B309ele26664

**Fuse F40
(from 03 / 2007)**

**(from 09 / 2007)**

A46
Fuse
holder,
rear

F101

250A

X10209

35.0
RT

X13020

A4010
Junction
box

F40

30A

X11005

2.5
RT/GN

X10594

1

A70006
Control
module,
transfer
box

27335

1

B309ele25774

**(from 03 / 2007 to 09 / 2007)**

A46
Fuse
holder,
rear

F101

250A

X10209

35.0
RT

X13020

A4010
Junction
box

F40

7.5A

X11008

0.5
RT/WS

X14286

10

A14286
Function
control
centre,
roof

25774

4

BentleyPublishers.com

**Fuse F40
(to 03 / 2007)**

A149a
Car
access
system

30G

X13376

0.75
RT

X11010

1

6

A4010
Junction
box

I01068

F40

20A

X11005

2.5
RT/SW

X13663

3

1

A13663
Fuel pump control
(EKPS)

A46
Fuse
holder,
rear

F108

250A

X10209

35.0
RT

X13020

B309ele23263

BentleyPublishers.com

**Fuse F42
(to 03 / 2007)**

**Fuse F41**

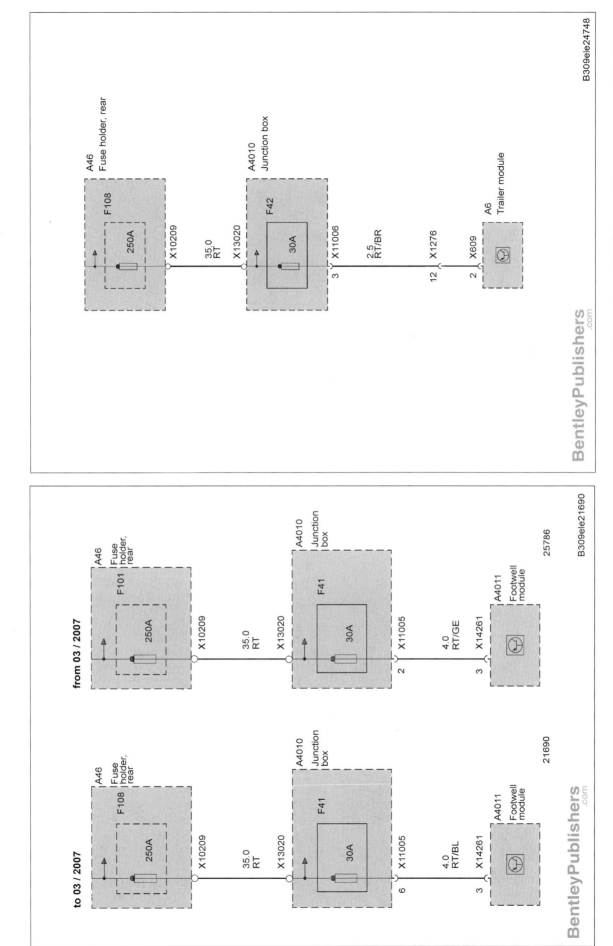

A46
Fuse holder, rear

F108

250A

X10209

35,0
RT

X13020

A4010
Junction box

F42

30A

3  X11006

2,5
RT/BR

12  X1276

2  X609

A6
Trailer module

B309ele24748

**from 03 / 2007**

A46
Fuse
holder,
rear

F101

250A

X10209

35,0
RT

X13020

A4010
Junction
box

F41

30A

2  X11005

4,0
RT/GE

3  X14261

A4011
Footwell
module

25786

B309ele21690

**to 03 / 2007**

A46
Fuse
holder,
rear

F108

250A

X10209

35,0
RT

X13020

A4010
Junction
box

F41

30A

6  X11005

4,0
RT/BL

3  X14261

A4011
Footwell
module

21690

**Fuse F43**

**Fuse F42
(from 03 / 2007)**

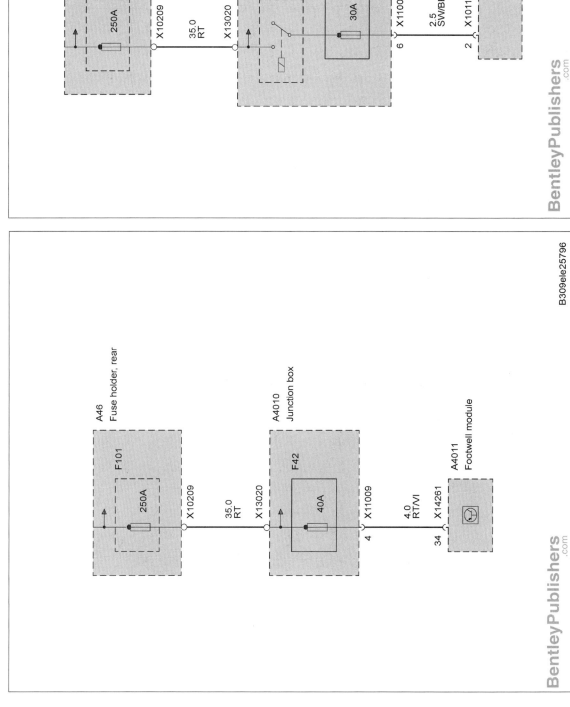

B309ele21692

B309ele25796

## Fuse F44

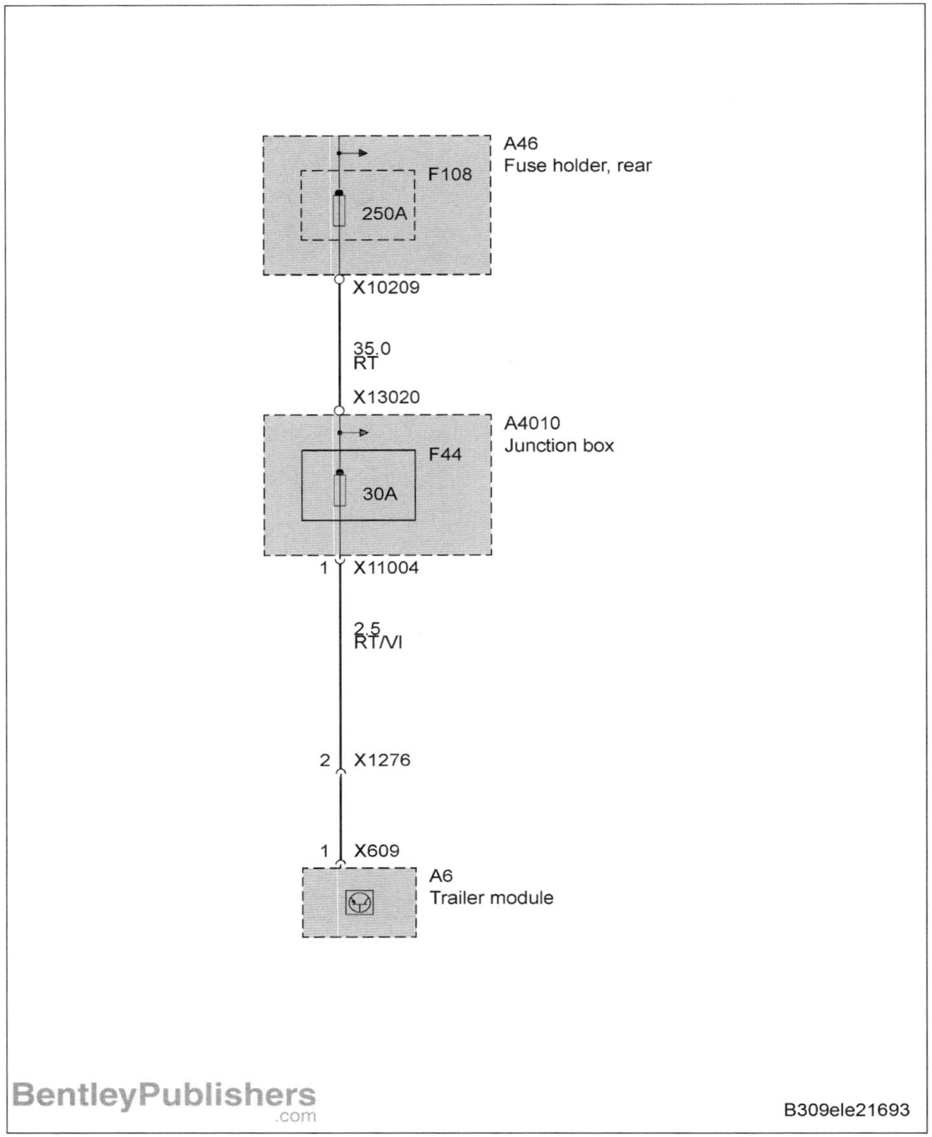

A46
Fuse holder, rear
F108
250A
X10209
35.0
RT
X13020
A4010
Junction box
F44
30A
1
X11004
2.5
RT/VI
2
X1276
1
X609
A6
Trailer module
BentleyPublishers
.com
B309ele21693

**Fuse F45**

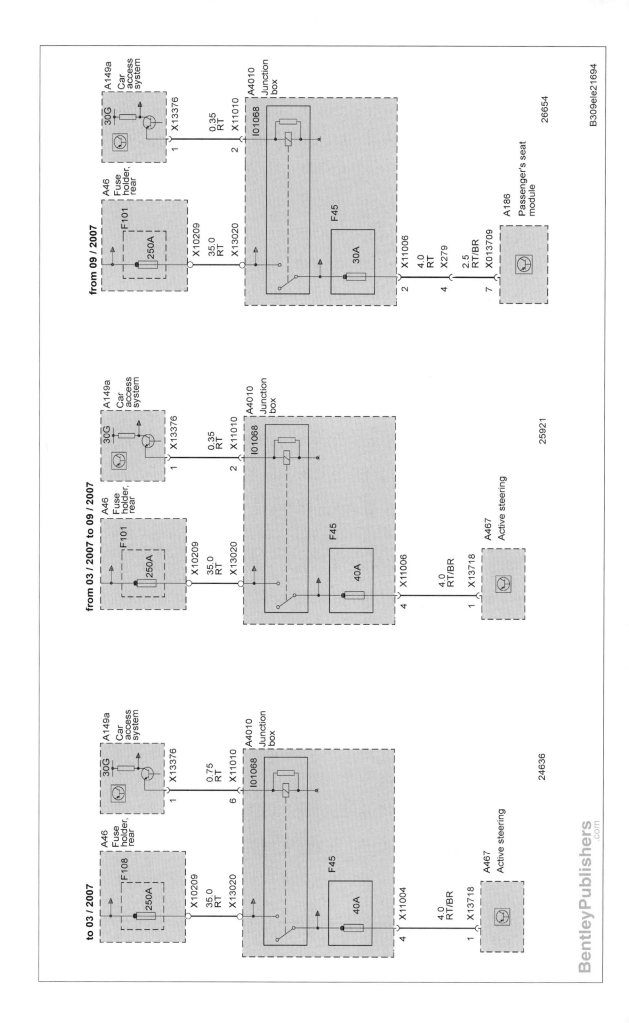

**Fuse F46**
**(from 03 / 2007 to 09 / 2007)**

**Fuse F46**
**(to 03 / 2007)**

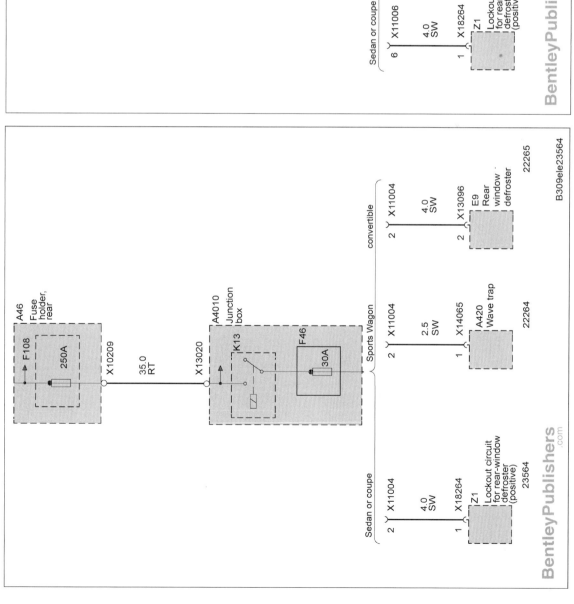

A46
Fuse holder, rear

F108
250A

X10209

35.0
RT

X13020

A4010
Junction box

K13

F46
30A

Sports Wagon

X11006
6

2.5
SW

X14065
1

A420
Wave trap

27343

convertible

X11006
6

4.0
SW

X13096
2

E9
Rear window defroster

27344

Sedan or coupe

X11006
6

4.0
SW

X18264
1

Z1
Lockout circuit for rear-window defroster (positive)

27342

B309ele27342

BentleyPublishers.com

A46
Fuse holder, rear

F108
250A

X10209

35.0
RT

X13020

A4010
Junction box

K13

F46
30A

Sports Wagon

X11004
2

2.5
SW

X14065
1

A420
Wave trap

22264

convertible

X11004
2

4.0
SW

X13096
2

E9
Rear window defroster

22265

Sedan or coupe

X11004
2

4.0
SW

X18264
1

Z1
Lockout circuit for rear-window defroster (positive)

23564

B309ele23564

BentleyPublishers.com

**Fuse F47**
**(to 09 / 2007)**

A46
Fuse holder, rear

F108

250A

X10209

35.0
RT

X13020

A4010
Junction box

F47

20A

X11004

5

2.5
RT/BL

X1276

1

X630

9

Trailer socket

B309ele23264

**Fuse F46**
**(from 09 / 2007)**

A149a
Car
access
system

30G

X13376

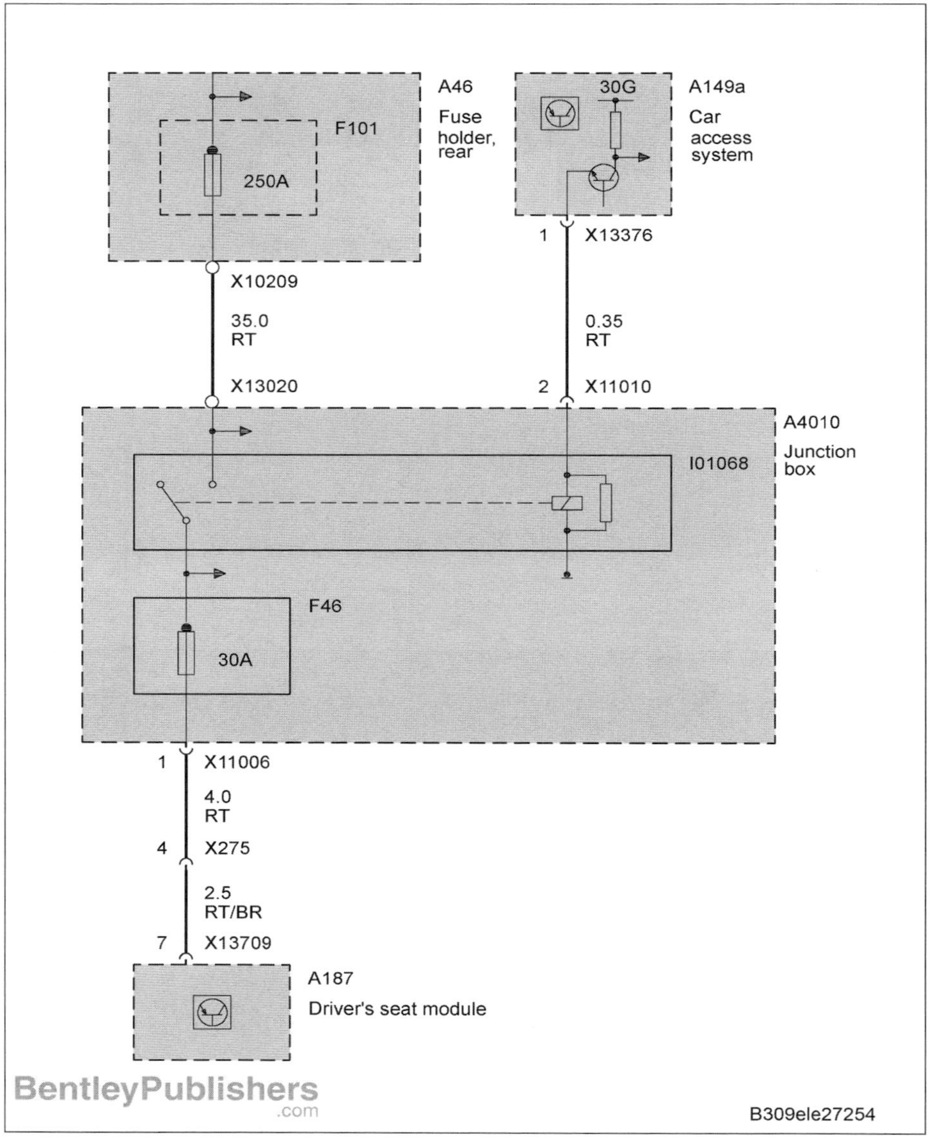

1

0.35
RT

X11010

2

A4010
Junction
box

I01068

A46
Fuse
holder,
rear

F101

250A

X10209

35.0
RT

X13020

F46

30A

X11006

1

4.0
RT

X275

4

2.5
RT/BR

X13709

7

A187
Driver's seat module

B309ele27254

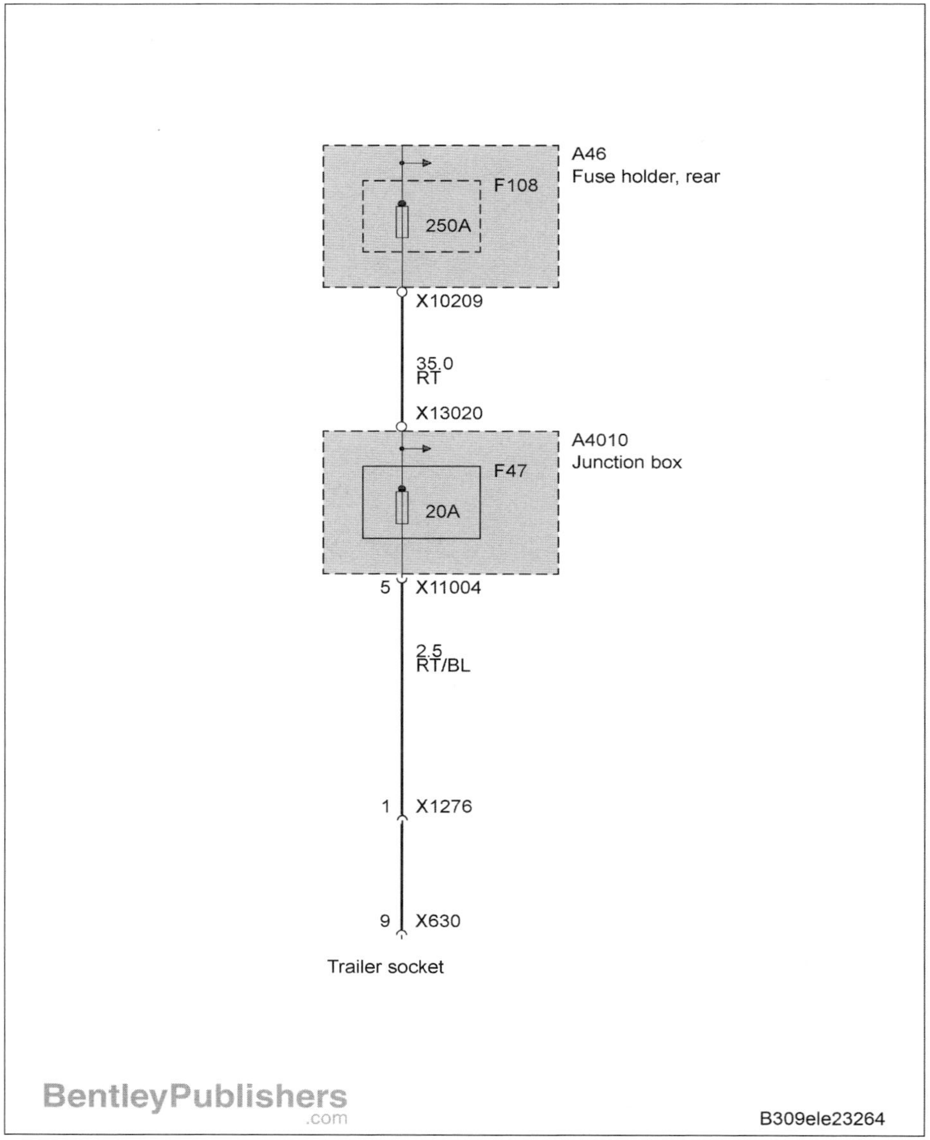

**Fuse F48**

**Fuse F47
(from 09 / 2007)**

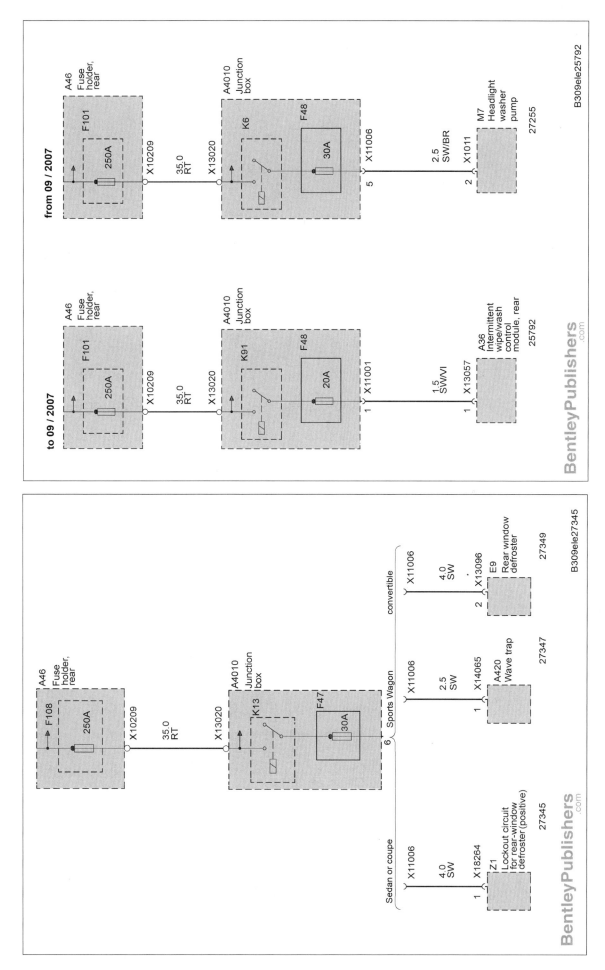

from 09 / 2007

A46 Fuse holder, rear
F101
250A
X10209
35.0 RT
X13020
A4010 Junction box
K6
F48
30A
X11006
5
2.5 SW/BR
X1011
M7 Headlight washer pump
2
27255

B309ele25792

to 09 / 2007

A46 Fuse holder, rear
F101
250A
X10209
35.0 RT
X13020
A4010 Junction box
K91
F48
20A
X11001
1
1.5 SW/VI
X13057
A36 Intermittent wipe/wash control module, rear
1
25792

A46 Fuse holder, rear
F108
250A
X10209
35.0 RT
X13020
A4010 Junction box
K13
F47
30A
6

convertible
X11006
4.0 SW
X13096
E9 Rear window defroster
2
27349

Sports Wagon
X11006
2.5 SW
X14065
A420 Wave trap
1
27347

Sedan or coupe
X11006
4.0 SW
X18264
Z1 Lockout circuit for rear-window defroster (positive)
1
27345

B309ele27345

27345

**Fuse F49**

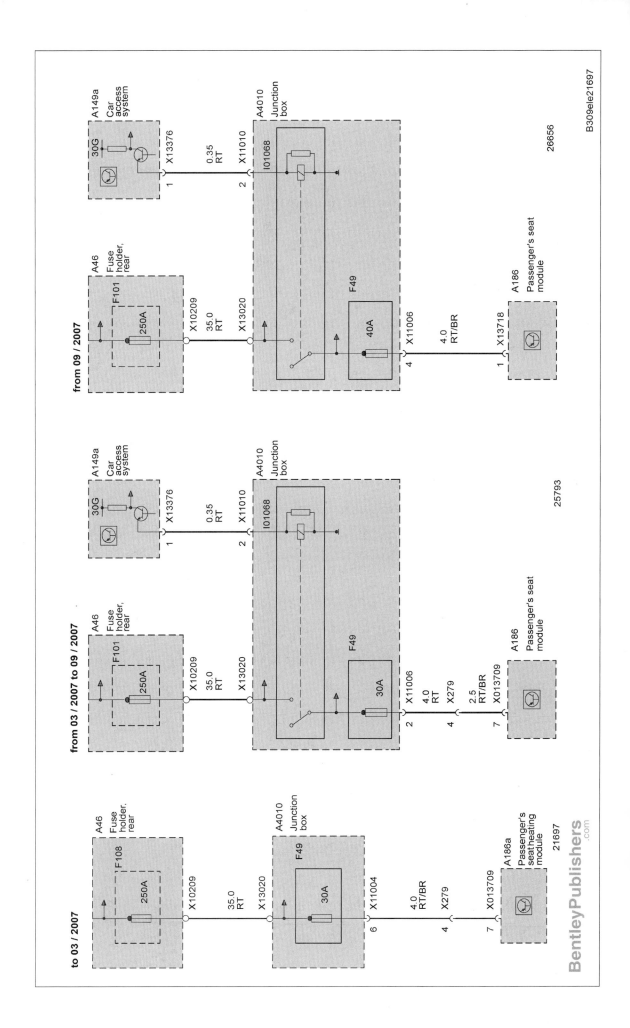

**Fuse F51**

**Fuse F50**

B309ele21698

25794

21698

B309ele22257

26234

22257

**Fuse F53**

**Fuse F52**

B309ele21699

**Fuse 54
Convertible**

**Fuse F54
ex. Convertible**

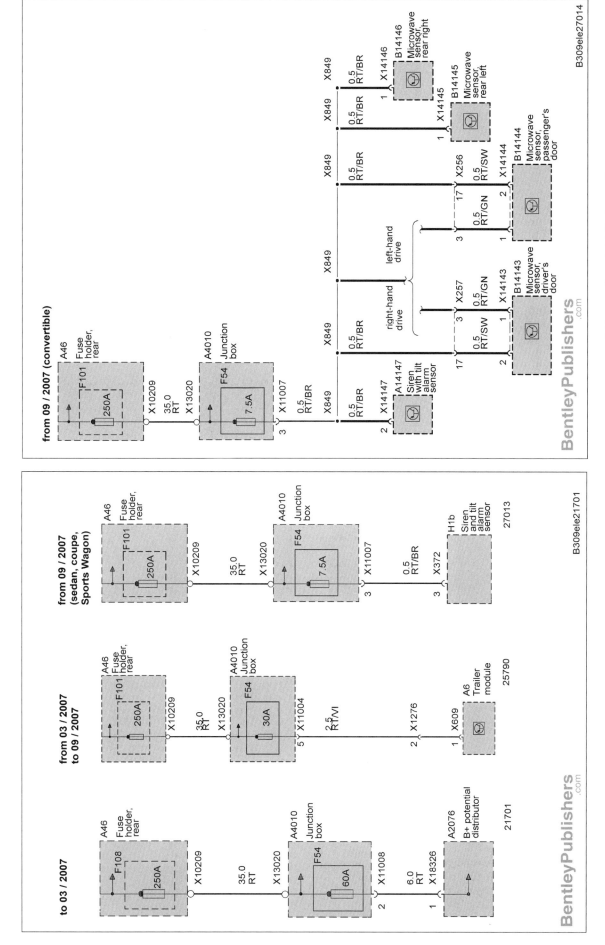

B309ele27014

B309ele21701

BentleyPublishers
.com

BentleyPublishers
.com

**Fuse F55**
**(from 09 / 2007)**

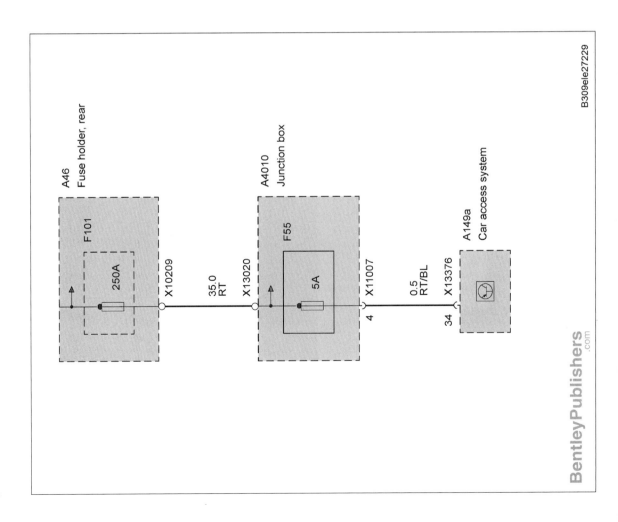

A46
Fuse holder, rear

F101

250A

X10209

35.0
RT

X13020

A4010
Junction box

F55

5A

X11007

4

0.5
RT/BL

X13376

34

A149a
Car access system

B309ele27229

**Fuses F56 and F57 and junction box
(to 09 / 2007)
page 1 of 2**

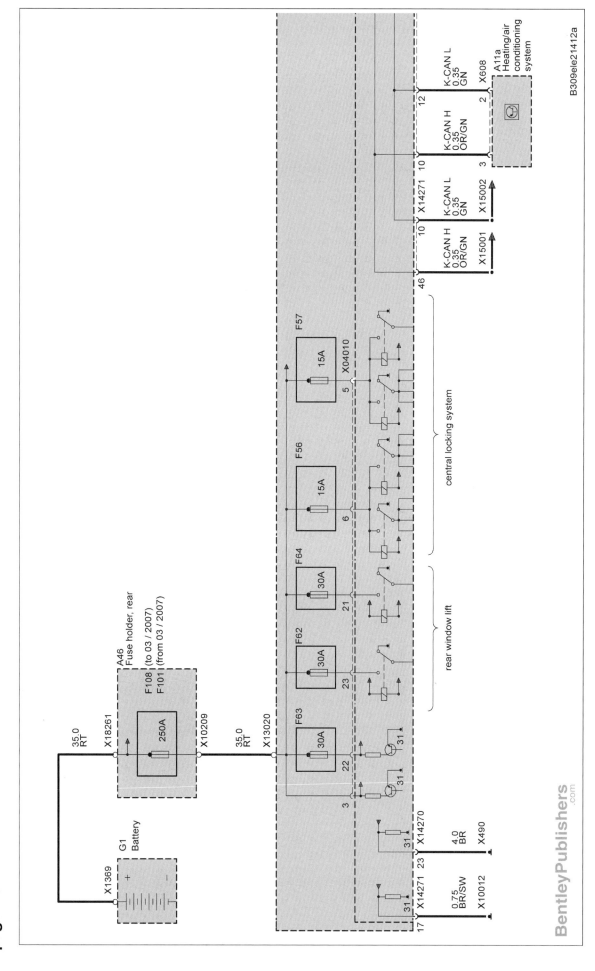

B309ele21412a

BentleyPublishers
.com

**Fuses F56 and F57 and junction box
(to 09 / 2007)
page 2 of 2**

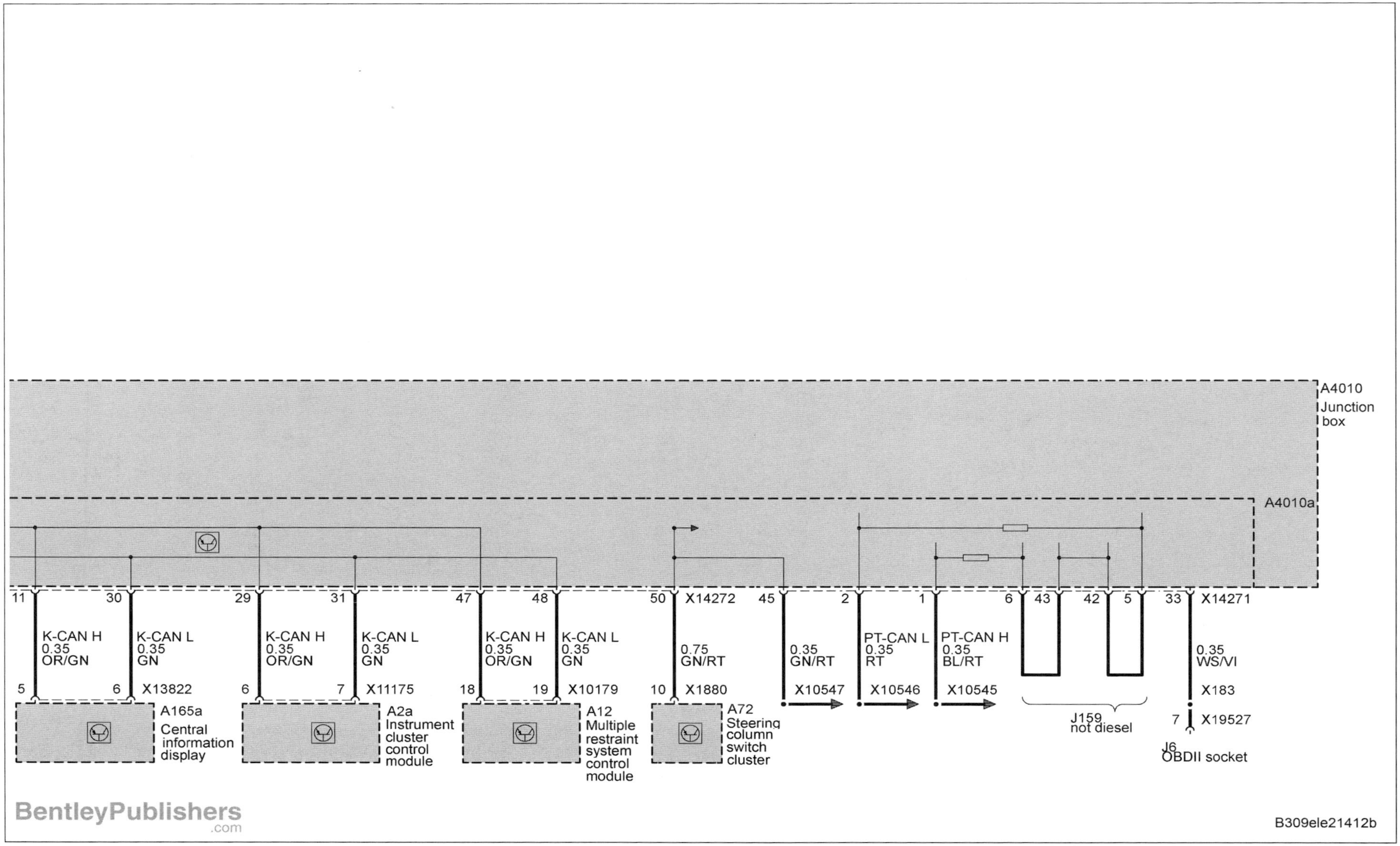

A4010
Junction box

A4010a

X14271

33 | 0.35 WS/VI | X183 | X19527
7 | J6 OBDII socket

5

42

43

6

J159
not diesel

1 | PT-CAN H | 0.35 BL/RT | X10545

2 | PT-CAN L | 0.35 RT | X10546

45 | 0.35 GN/RT | X10547

X14272

50 | 0.75 GN/RT | X1880

A72
Steering column switch cluster
10

48 | K-CAN H | 0.35 OR/GN | 19 | K-CAN L | 0.35 GN | X10179

A12
Multiple restraint system control module
18

47

31 | K-CAN H | 0.35 OR/GN | 7 | K-CAN L | 0.35 GN | X11175

A2a
Instrument cluster control module
6

29

30 | K-CAN H | 0.35 OR/GN | 6 | K-CAN L | 0.35 GN | X13822

A165a
Central information display
6

11

5

B309ele21412b

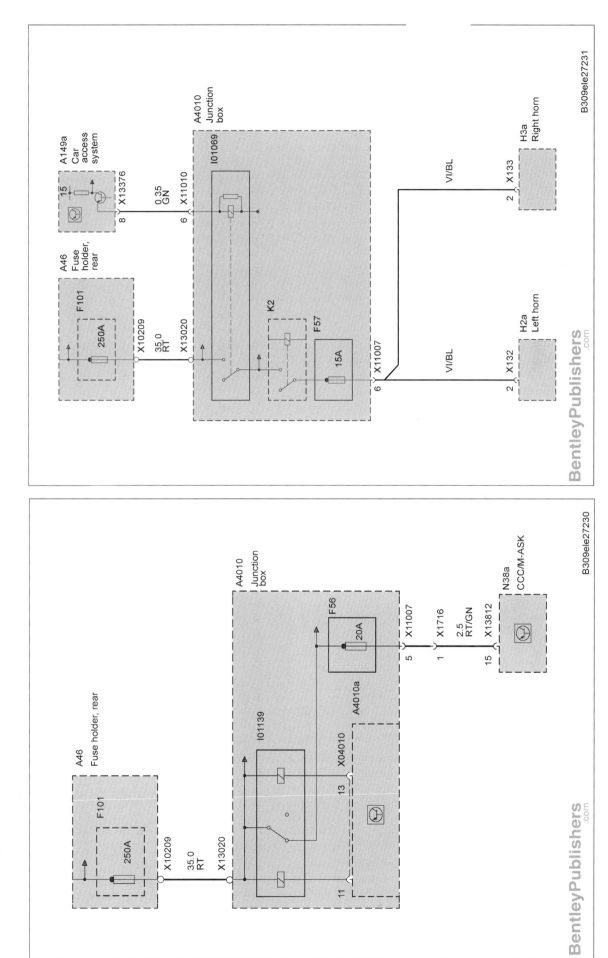

**Fuse F57**
**(from 09 / 2007)**

**Fuse F56**
**(from 09 / 2007)**

B309ele27231

B309ele27230

BentleyPublishers .com

BentleyPublishers .com

**Fuse F58**

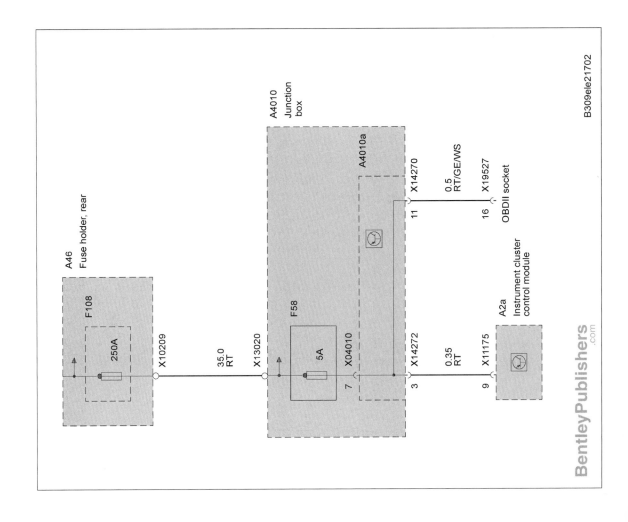

B309ele21702

**Fuse F59**

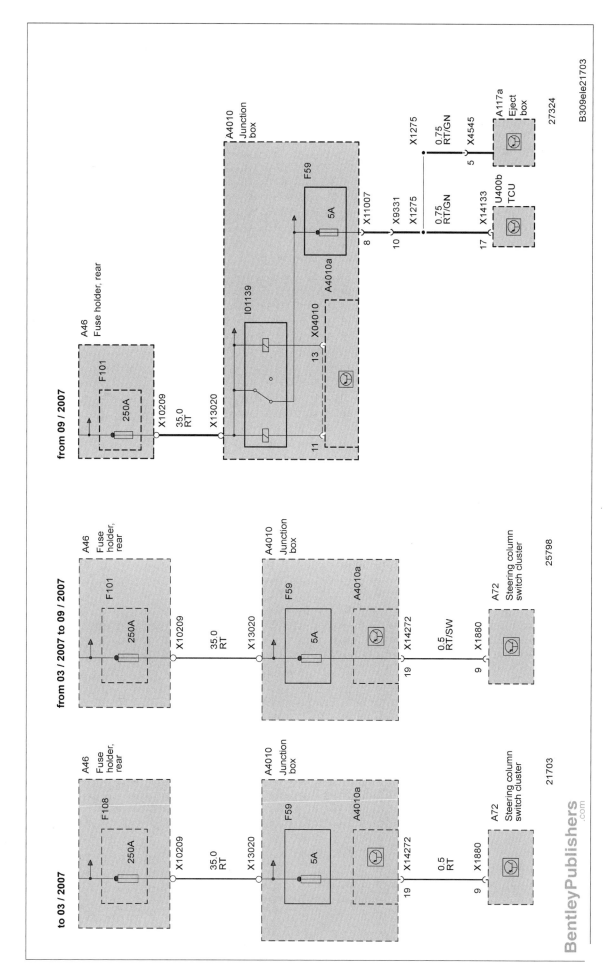

B309ele21703

BentleyPublishers.com

**Fuse F60
(from 03 / 2007)**

**Fuse F60
(to 03 / 2007)**

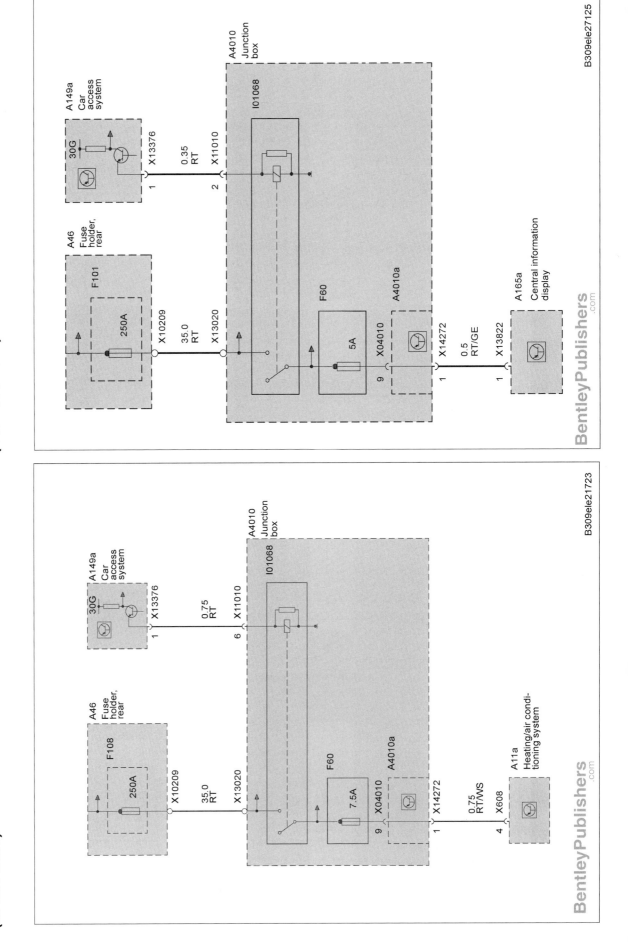

B309ele27125

B309ele21723

**Fuse F61
Sports Wagon
(to 03 / 2007)**

**Fuse F61
Sedan and Coupe
(to 03 / 2007)**

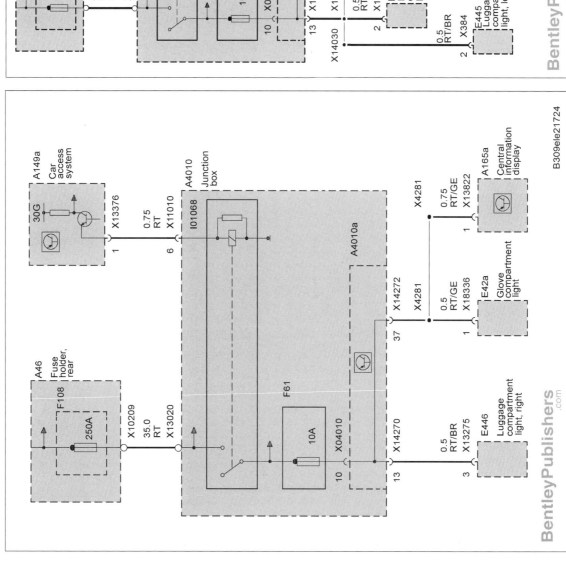

BentleyPublishers.com

B309ele23941

B309ele21724

## Fuse F61
### (from 03 / 2007 to 09 / 2007)

## Fuse F61
### (Convertible to 03 / 2007)

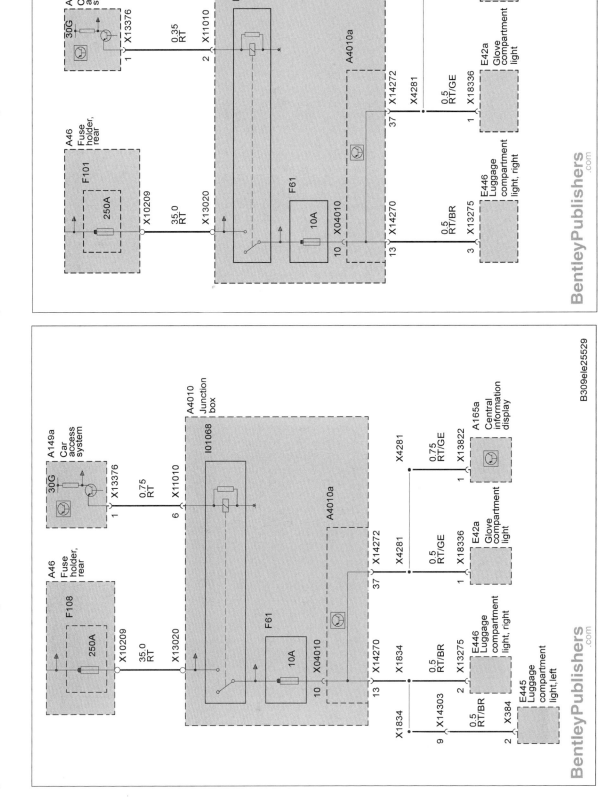

B309ele25831

B309ele25529

**Fuse F61
(from 09 / 2007)**

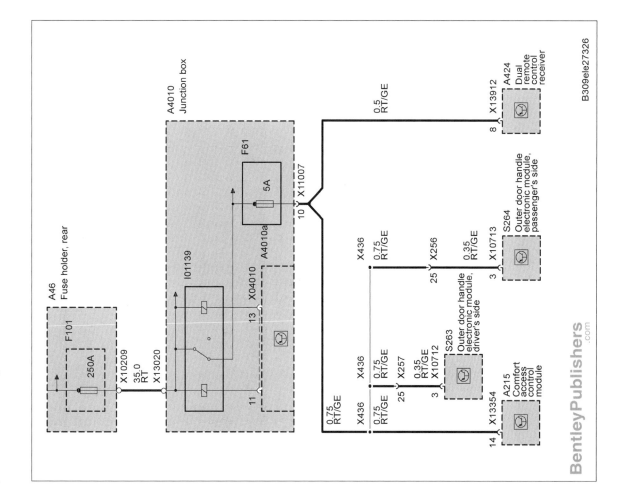

B309ele27326

**Fuses F62, F63, and F64
(to 09 / 2007)
page 1 of 2**

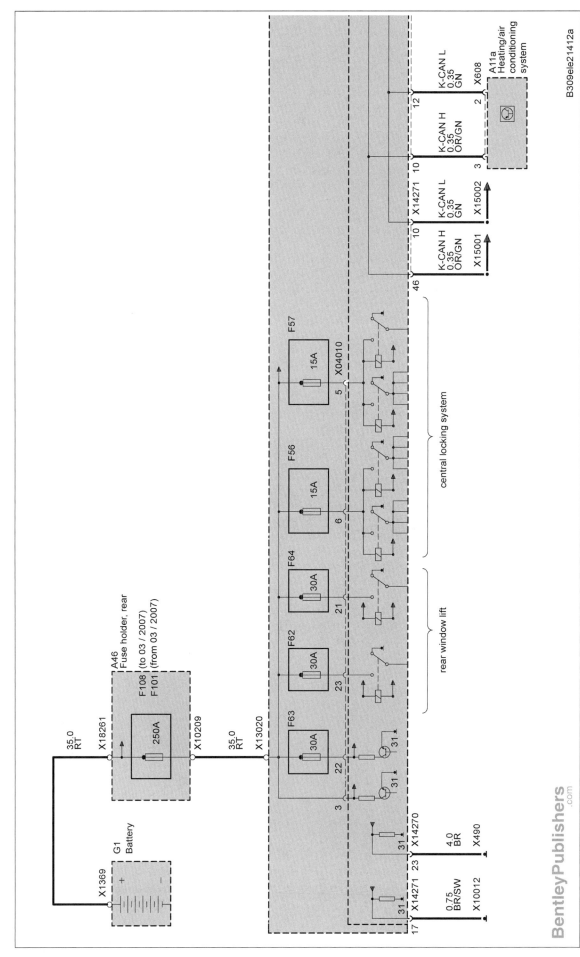

B309ele21412a

Electrical Wiring Diagrams  ELE-87

A4010
Junction
box

A4010a

X14271

0.35
WS/VI

X183

X19527

33

OBDII socket
7

J159
not diesel

5

42

43

6

PT-CAN H
0.35
BL/RT

X10545

1

PT-CAN L
0.35
RT

X10546

2

0.35
GN/RT

X10547

45

X14272

0.75
GN/RT

X1880

A72
Steering
column
switch
cluster

50

10

K-CAN L
0.35
GN

X10179

A12
Multiple
restraint
system
control
module

48

K-CAN H
0.35
OR/GN

19

47

18

K-CAN L
0.35
GN

X11175

A2a
Instrument
cluster
control
module

31

K-CAN H
0.35
OR/GN

7

29

6

K-CAN L
0.35
GN

X13822

A165a
Central
information
display

30

K-CAN H
0.35
OR/GN

6

11

5

B309ele21412b

**Fuse F63**
**Sedan, Sports Wagon and Coupe**
**(from 09 / 2007)**

**Fuse F62**
**(from 09 / 2007)**

**Fuse F64
(from 09 / 2007)**

**Fuse F63
Convertible
(from 09 / 2007)**

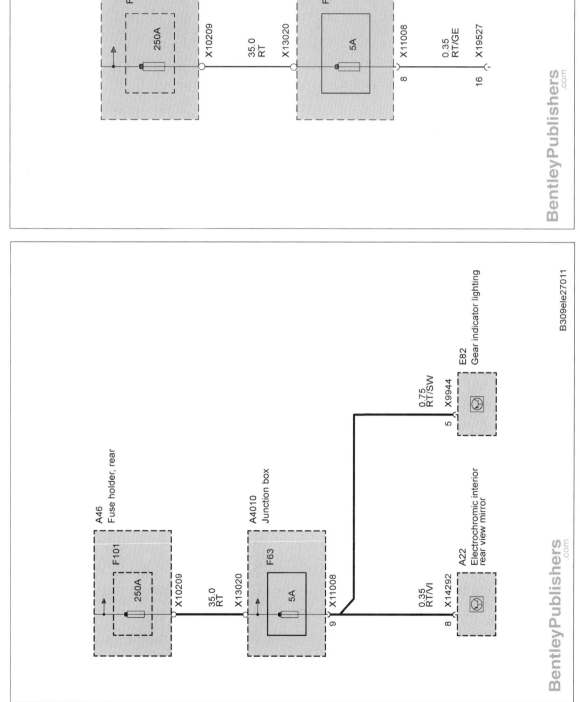

**Fuse F66**

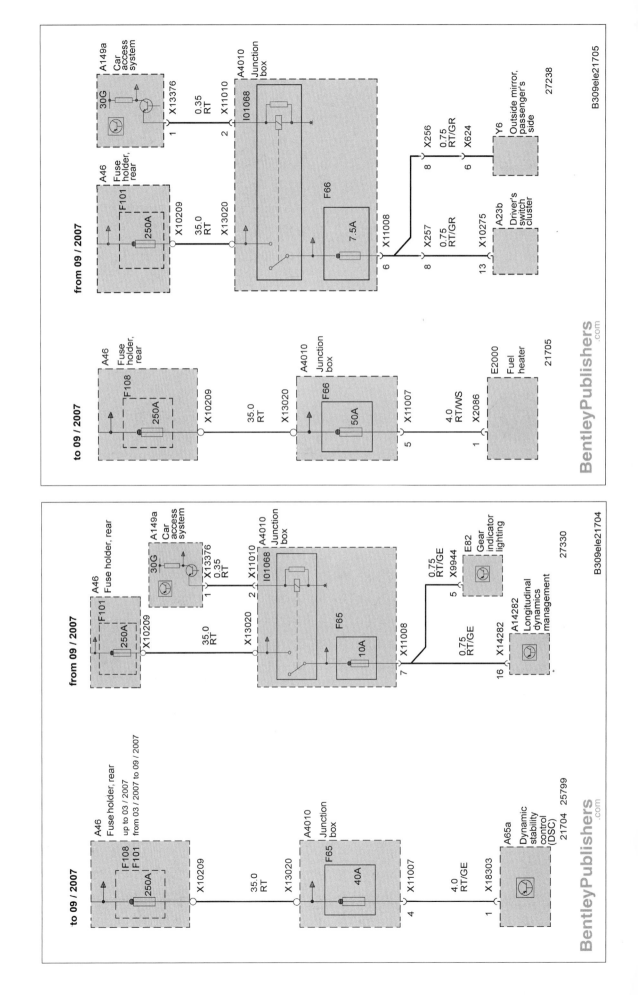

**Fuse F65**

**Fuse F68**

**Fuse F67**

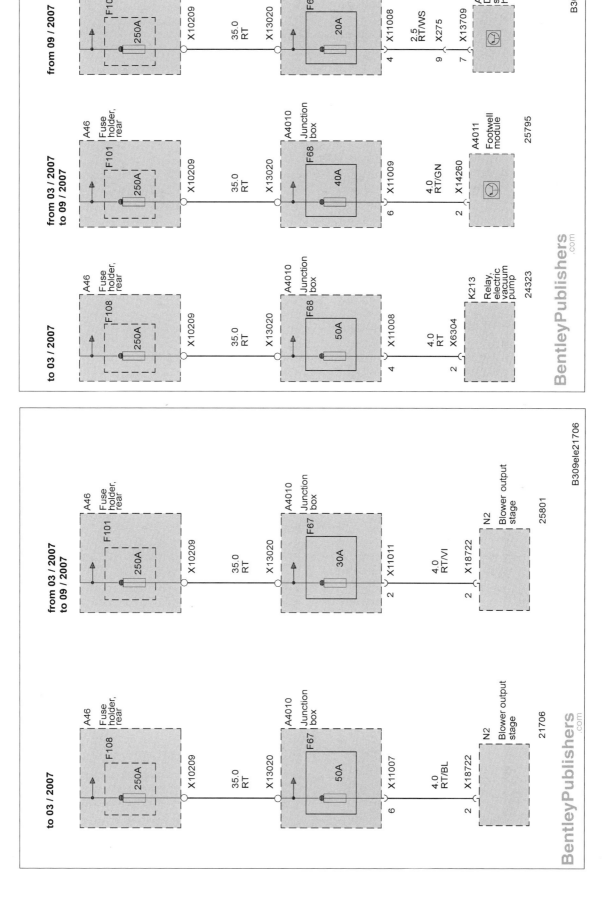

**Fuse F70**
**N51 engine**
**(to 09 / 2007)**

**Fuse F69**

(from 03 / 2007 to 09 / 2007)

A4010 Junction box

F70
30 | 40A
X11011
3
4.0 RT
X6304
2
K6304 Secondary air pump relay
1
X6304
4.0 SW/RT/GE
X1124
2
M63 Secondary air pump
M
1
X1124
4.0 BR
X166
26276

F75
87 | 10A
X11002
6
0.75 WS/RT
8
4
0.35 BR/BL
X60001
13
A6000 DME control module
31

B309ele26276

(to 03 / 2007)

A4010 Junction box

K6304
F70
50A
X11008
X11010 6
4.0 SW/RT/GE
X1124
2
M63 Secondary air pump
M
1
X1124
4.0 BR
X166

1
0.75 BR/BL
X60001
13
A6000 DME control module
31

22379

BentleyPublishers
.com

---

from 03 / 2007

A46 Fuse holder, rear
F101 | 250A
X10209
35.0 RT
X13020
A4010 Junction box
F69 | 60A
X11011
6
electric fan 600 Watt

A46 Fuse holder, rear
F101 | 250A
X10209
35.0 RT
X13020
A4010 Junction box
F69 | 50A
X11011
6
electric fan 400 Watt

6.0 RT/BL
X14188
3
K9137 Cut-out relay, electric fan

27234

B309ele21707

to 03 / 2007

A46 Fuse holder, rear
F108 | 250A
X10209
35.0 RT
X13020
A4010 Junction box
F69 | 50A
X11008
5
6.0 RT/BL
electric fan 600 Watt
X1797
2
M9 Electric fan

electric fan 400 Watt
X82
4
M9 Electric fan

21707

BentleyPublishers
.com

**Fuse F71**

**Fuse F70
(from 09 / 2007)**

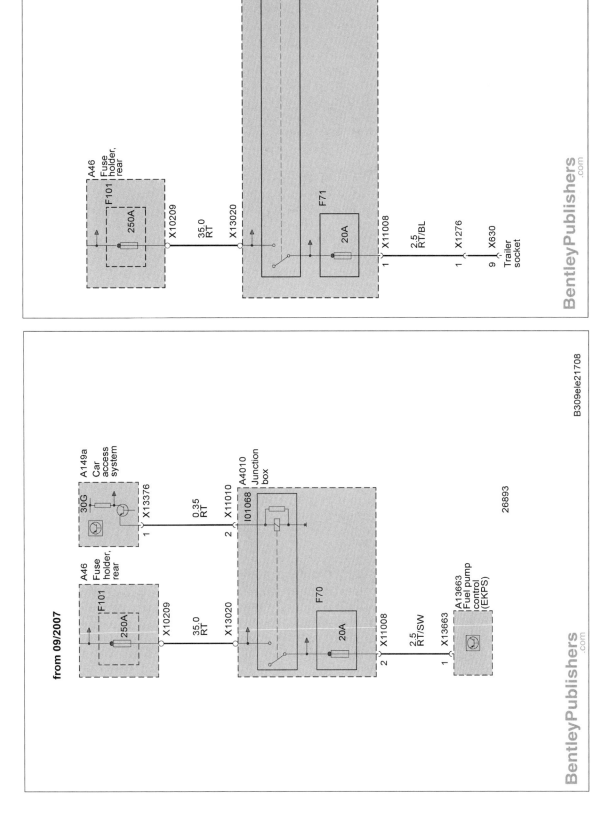

A149a
Car access system

30G

X13376

0.35
RT

X11010

A4010
Junction box

I01068

A46
Fuse holder, rear

F101

250A

X10209

35.0
RT

X13020

F71

20A

X11008

2.5
RT/BL

X1276

X630
Trailer socket

9

B309ele25846

from 09/2007

A149a
Car access system

30G

X13376

0.35
RT

X11010

A4010
Junction box

I01068

A46
Fuse holder, rear

F101

250A

X10209

35.0
RT

X13020

F70

20A

X11008

2.5
RT/SW

X13663

A13663
Fuel pump control (EKPS)

26893

B309ele21708

**Fuses F72 and F73
(from 09 / 2007)
page 1 of 2**

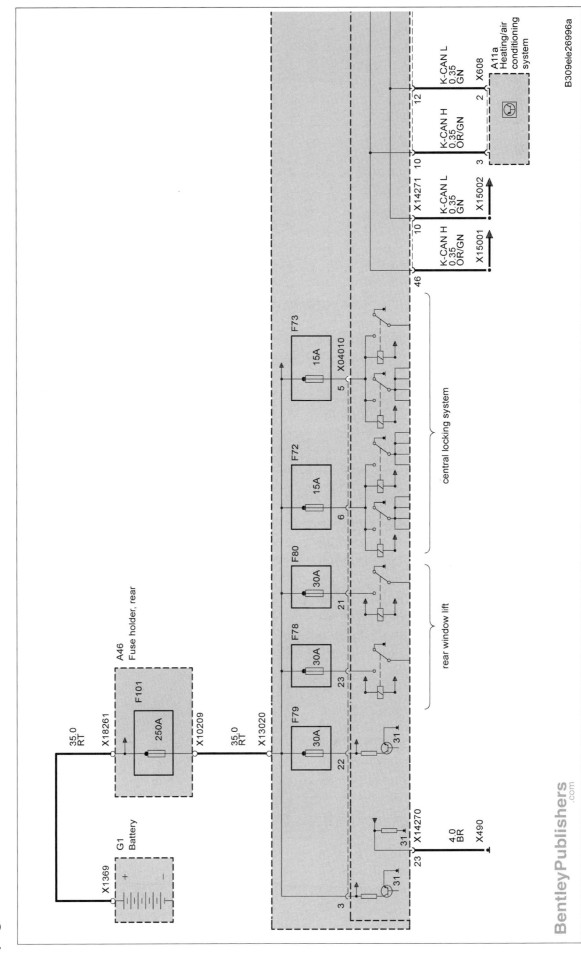

B309ele26996a

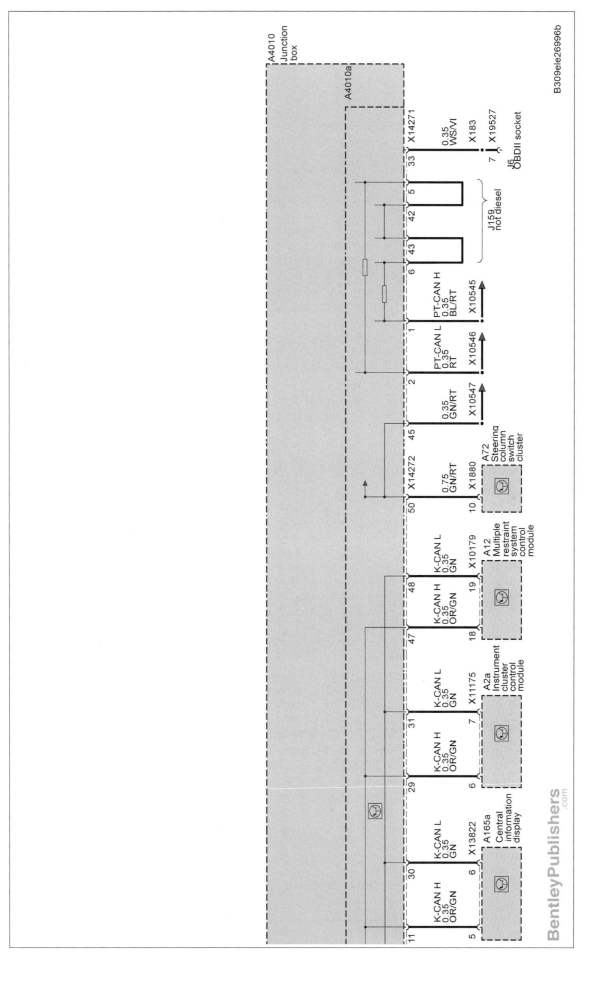

**Fuse F74**

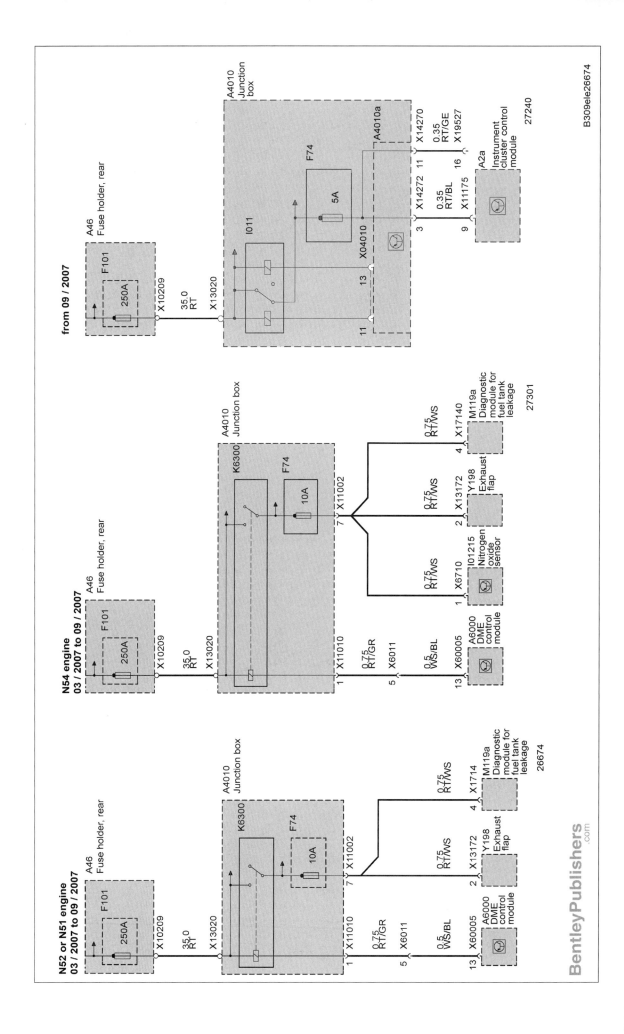

**Fuse F75**
**N51 engine**
**(from 03 / 2007 to 09 / 2007)**

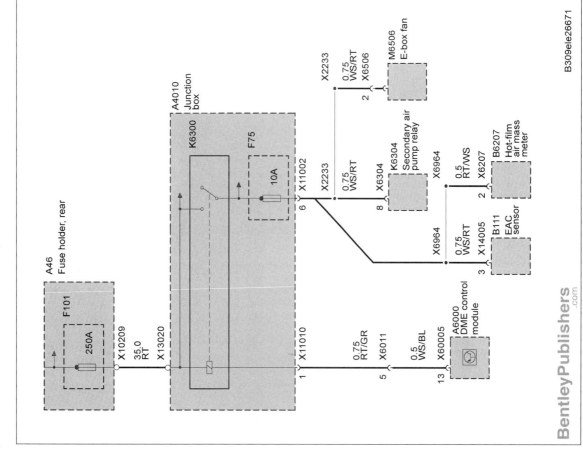

B309ele26671

Fuse F76
N54 engine
(from 03 / 2007 to 09 / 2007)

Fuse F76
N52 and N51 engine
(from 03 / 2007 to 09 / 2007)

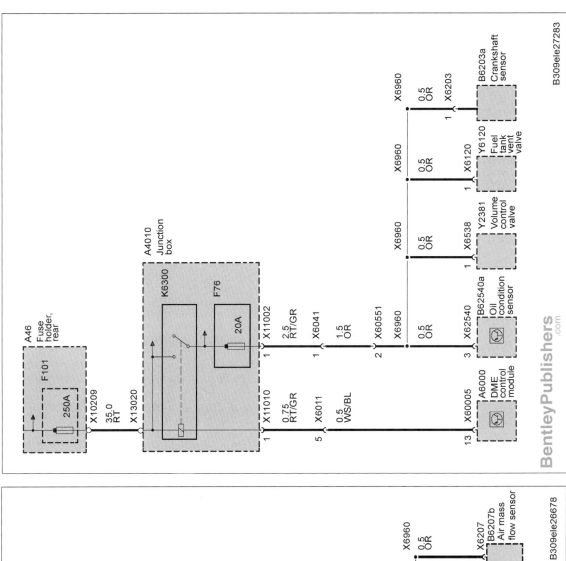

B309ele27283

B309ele26678

**Fuse F77**
**N52 or N51 engine**
**(to 03 / 2007)**

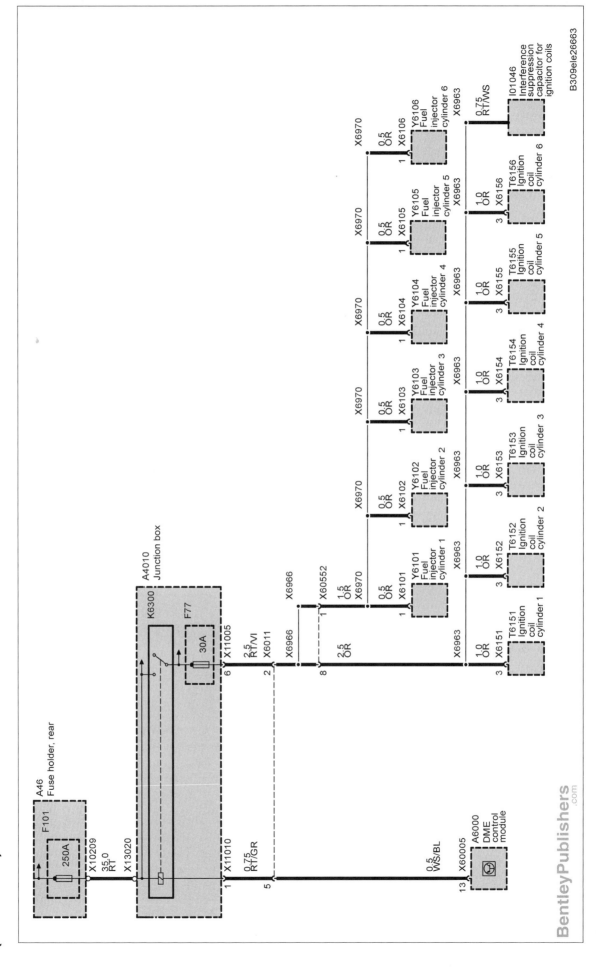

B309ele26663

**Fuse F78**
**N52 or N51 engine**
**(from 03 / 2007 to 09 /2007)**

**Fuse F77**
**(from 09 / 2007)**

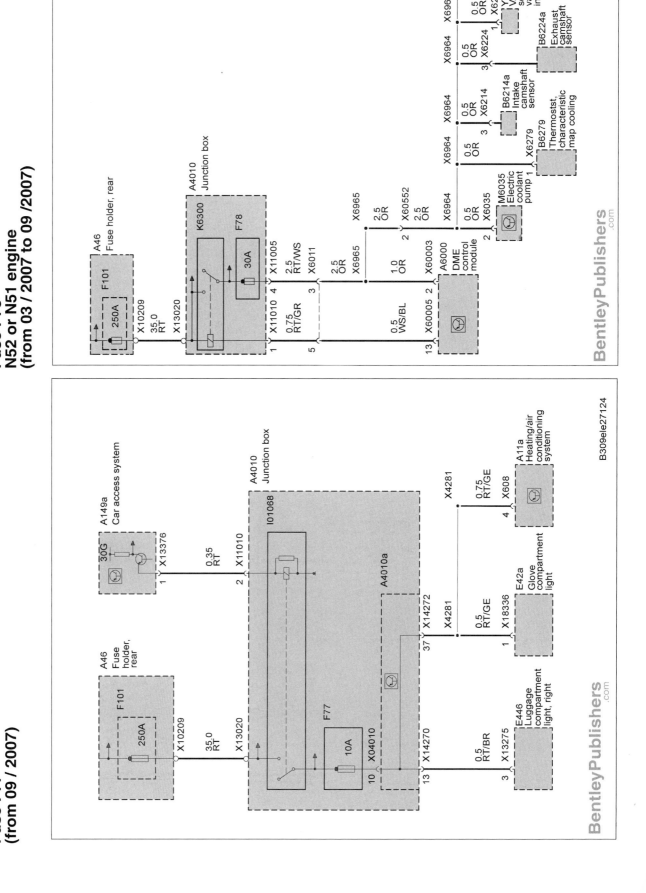

B309ele26668

B309ele27124

**Fuse F80**
(from 03 / 2007 to 09 / 2007)

**Fuse F79**
**N52 or N51 engine**
(from 03 / 2007 to 09 / 2007)

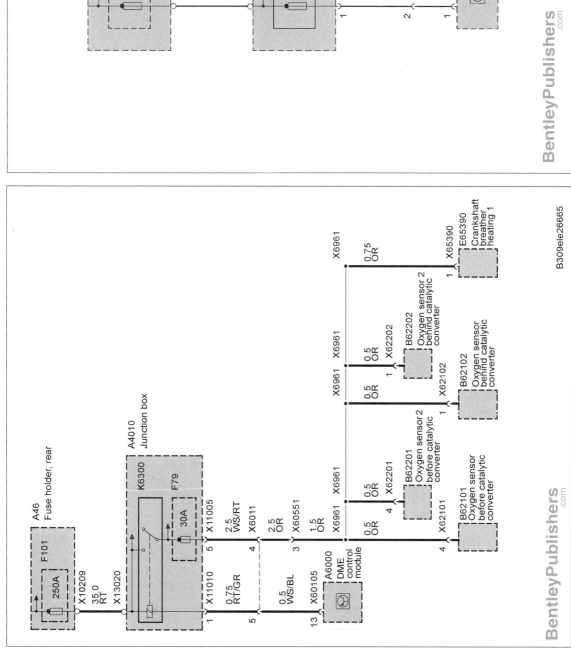

B309ele27208

B309ele26665

BentleyPublishers
.com

## Fuses F78, F79 and F80
**(from 09 / 2007)**
**page 1 of 2**

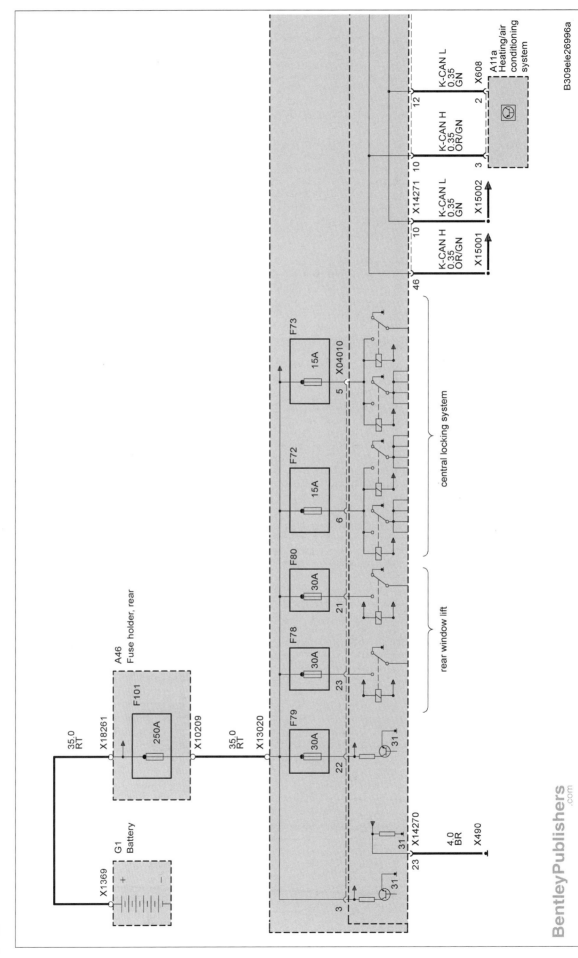

B309ele26996a

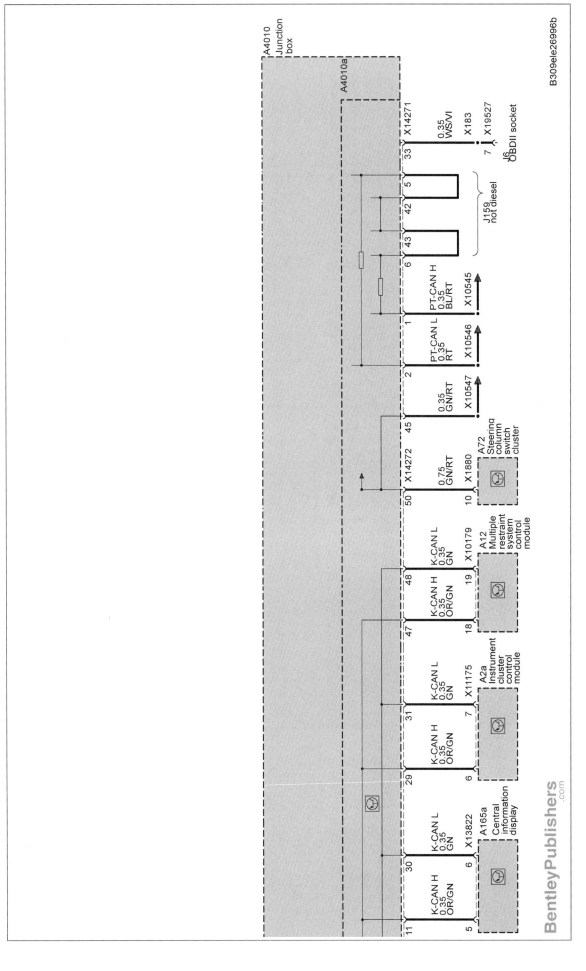

**Fuse F82
from 09 / 2007**

**Fuse F81**

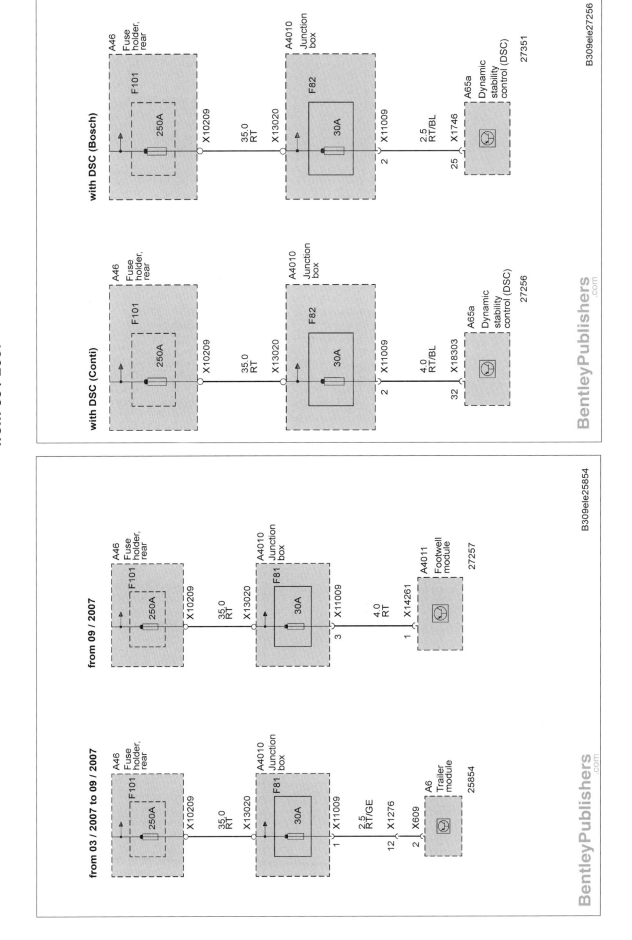

with DSC (Bosch)

A46 Fuse holder, rear
F101 250A
X10209
35.0 RT
X13020
A4010 Junction box
F82 30A
X11009
2
2.5 RT/BL
X1746
25
A65a Dynamic stability control (DSC)
27351

B309ele27256

with DSC (Conti)

A46 Fuse holder, rear
F101 250A
X10209
35.0 RT
X13020
A4010 Junction box
F82 30A
X11009
2
4.0 RT/BL
X18303
32
A65a Dynamic stability control (DSC)
27256

BentleyPublishers.com

from 09 / 2007

A46 Fuse holder, rear
F101 250A
X10209
35.0 RT
X13020
A4010 Junction box
F81 30A
X11009
3
4.0 RT
X14261
1
A4011 Footwell module
27257

B309ele25854

from 03 / 2007 to 09 / 2007

A46 Fuse holder, rear
F101 250A
X10209
35.0 RT
X13020
A4010 Junction box
F81 30A
X11009
1
2.5 RT/GE
X1276
12
X609
2
A6 Trailer module
25854

BentleyPublishers.com

**Fuse F85**
**from 09 / 2007**

A46
Fuse holder, rear

F101

250A

X10209

35.0
RT

X13020

A4010
Junction box

F85

30A

X11009

4.0
RT/WS/GE

X11102

5

2

A473
DC/DC converter

B309ele27260

**Electrical Wiring Diagrams   ELE-105**

---

**Fuse F84**

**from 09 / 2007**

A46
Fuse holder, rear

F101

250A

X10209

35.0
RT

X13020

A4010
Junction box

F84

40A

X11009

4.0
RT/GN

X14260

6

2

A4011
Footwell module

27259

B309ele25788

**from 03 / 2007 to 09 / 2007**

A46
Fuse holder, rear

F101

250A

X10209

35.0
RT

X13020

A4010
Junction box

K6

F84

30A

X11006

2.5
SW/BR

X1011

5

2

M7
Headlight washer pump

25788

**Fuse F88**

from 09 / 2007

A46 Fuse holder, rear
F101
250A
X10209
35.0 RT
X13020
A4010 Junction box
F88
40A
X11011
4.0 RT/VI
X18722
N2 Blower output stage
2
2
26617
B309ele25844

from 03 / 2007 to 09 / 2007

A149a Car access system
30G
X13376
0.35 RT
X11010
A4010 Junction box
I01068
F88
1
2
A46 Fuse holder, rear
F101
250A
X10209
35.0 RT
X13020
20A
X11008
2.5 RT/SW
X13663
A13663 Fuel pump control (EKPS)
2
1
25844

**Fuse F86**

A46 Fuse holder, rear
F101
250A
X10209
35.0 RT
X13020
A4010 Junction box
F86
40A
X11009
4.0 RT/VI
X14261
A4011 Footwell module
4
34

B309ele27258

**Fuse F90**
**from 09 / 2007**

**Fuse F89**
**N51 engine (from 09 / 2007)**

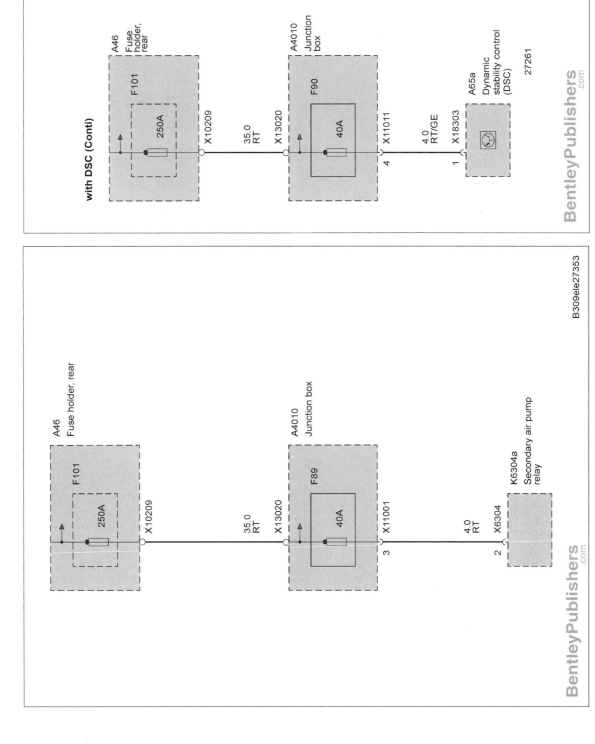

with DSC (Bosch)

A46
Fuse
holder,
rear

F101

250A

X10209

35.0
RT

X13020

A4010
Junction
box

F90

40A

X11011

4

4.0
RT/GE

X1746

A65a
Dynamic
stability control
(DSC)

27354

with DSC (Conti)

A46
Fuse
holder,
rear

F101

250A

X10209

35.0
RT

X13020

A4010
Junction
box

F90

40A

X11011

4

4.0
RT/GE

X18303

A65a
Dynamic
stability control
(DSC)

27261

A46
Fuse holder, rear

F101

250A

X10209

35.0
RT

X13020

A4010
Junction box

F89

40A

X11001

3

4.0
RT

X6304

K6304a
Secondary air pump
relay

2

B309ele27261

B309ele27353

Electrical Wiring Diagrams ELE-107

**Fuse F92**
**from 09 /2007**

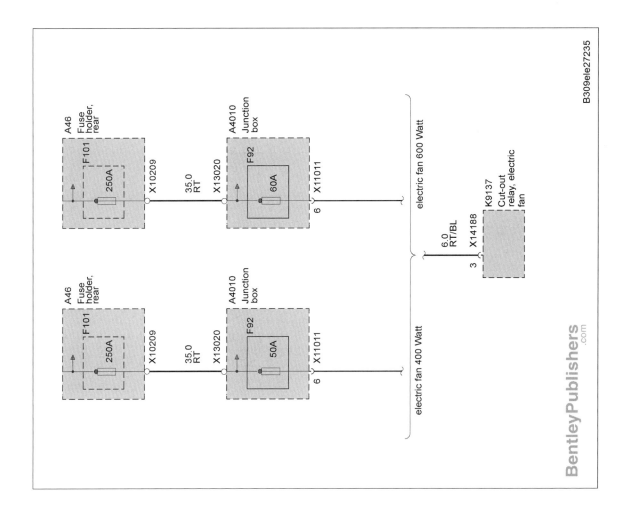

A46
Fuse
holder,
rear

F101

250A

X10209

35.0
RT

X13020

A4010
Junction
box

F92

60A

X11011

6

electric fan 600 Watt

A46
Fuse
holder,
rear

F101

250A

X10209

35.0
RT

X13020

A4010
Junction
box

F92

50A

X11011

6

electric fan 400 Watt

6.0
RT/BL

X14188

3

K9137
Cut-out
relay, electric
fan

B309ele27235

**Fuses F101, F102, F103, F104, F105 and F106
(from 03 / 2007)**

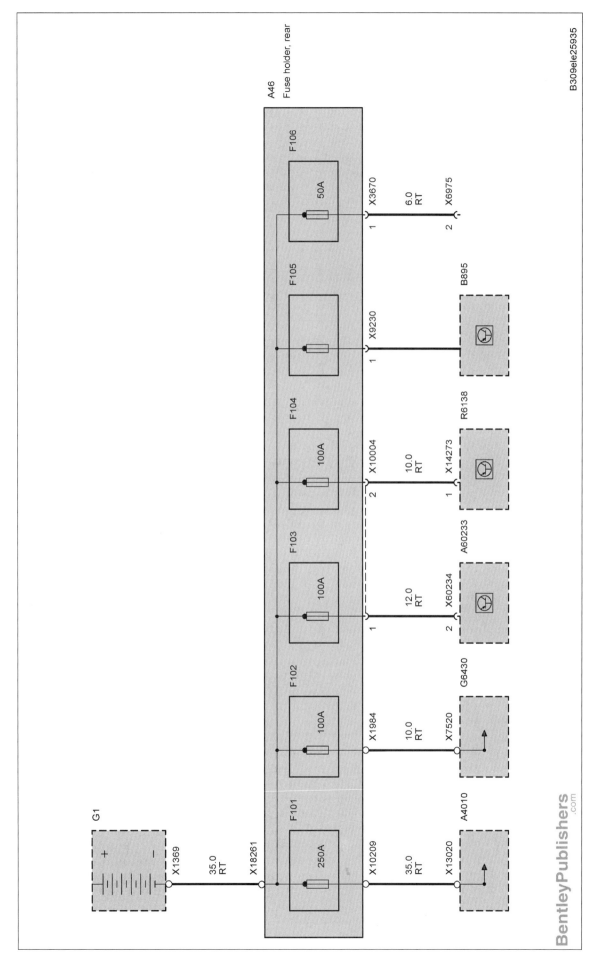

B309ele25935

BentleyPublishers
.com

## Fuse F104
## (to 03 / 2007)

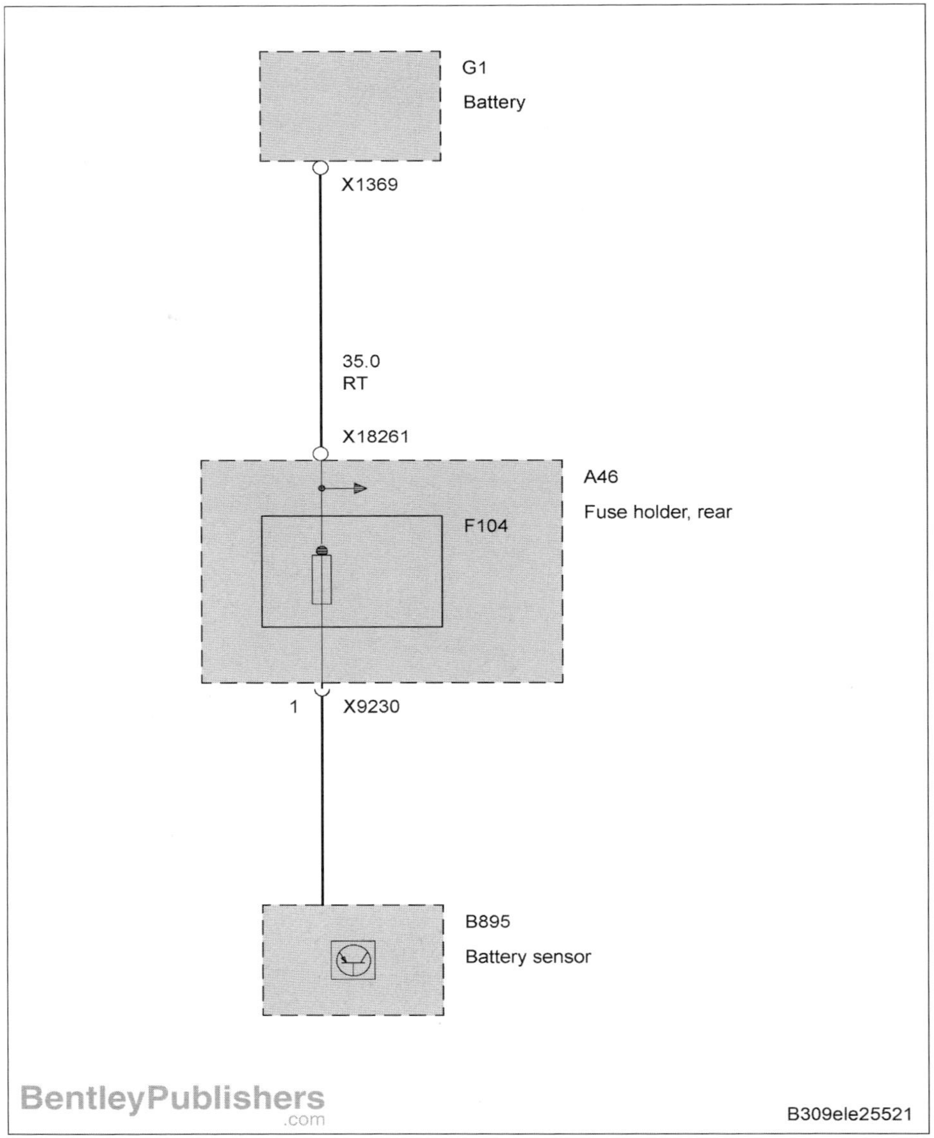
G1
Battery
X1369
35.0
RT
X18261
A46
Fuse holder, rear
F104
1
X9230
B895
Battery sensor
BentleyPublishers.com
B309ele25521

## Fuse F105
## (to 03 / 2007)

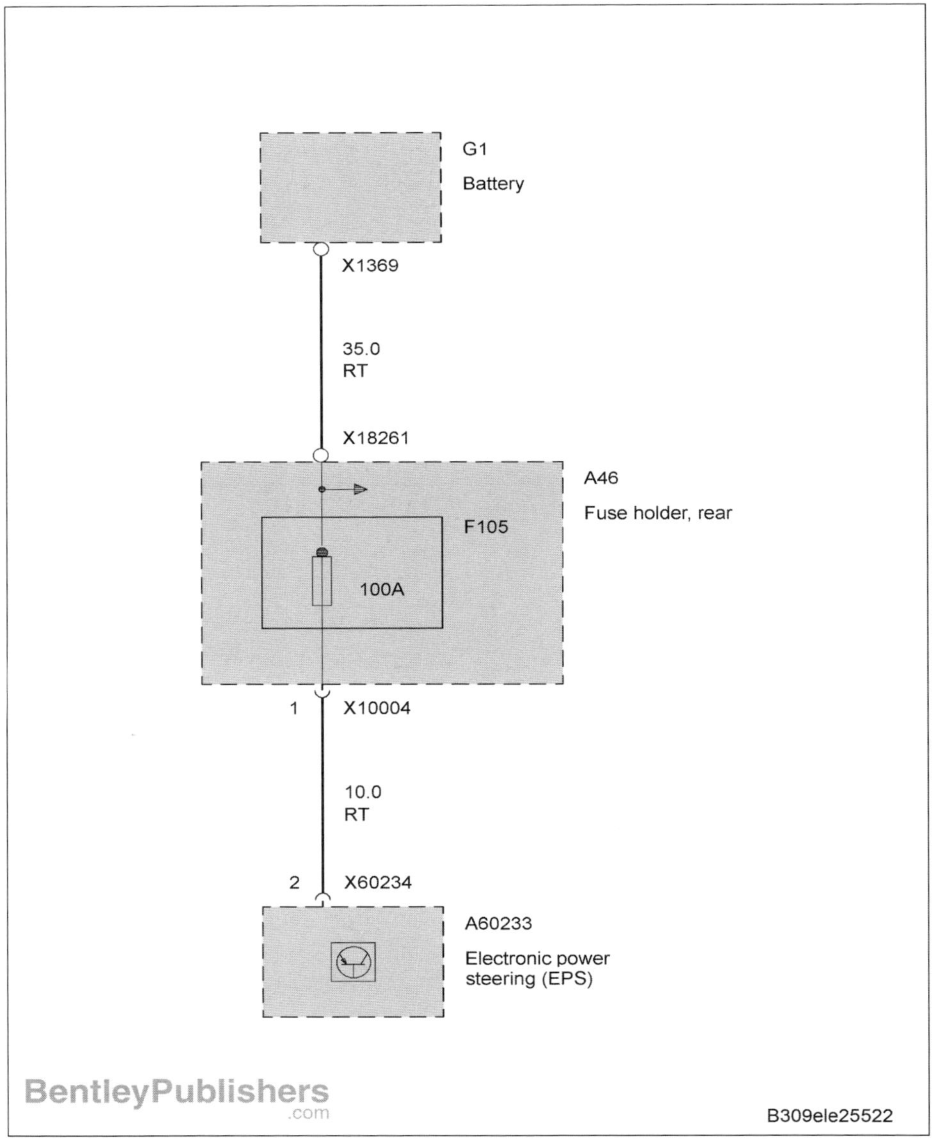
G1
Battery
X1369
35.0
RT
X18261
A46
Fuse holder, rear
F105
100A
1
X10004
10.0
RT
2
X60234
A60233
Electronic power
steering (EPS)
BentleyPublishers.com
B309ele25522

**Fuse F108**

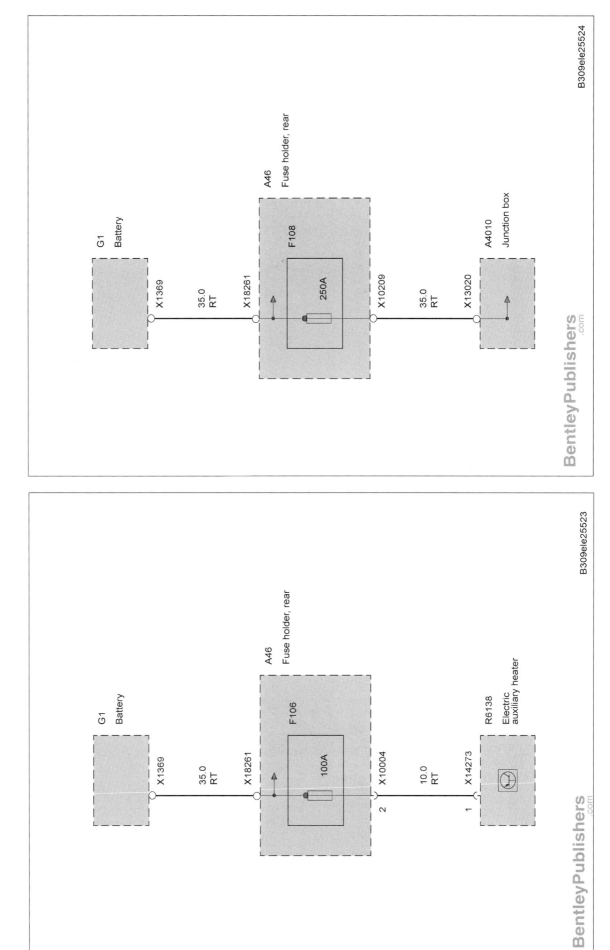

**Fuse F106**

B309ele25524

B309ele25523

G1
Battery

A46
Fuse holder, rear

F108

250A

A4010
Junction box

X1369

35.0
RT

X18261

X10209

35.0
RT

X13020

G1
Battery

A46
Fuse holder, rear

F106

100A

R6138
Electric
auxiliary heater

X1369

35.0
RT

X18261

X10004

10.0
RT

X14273

2

1

BentleyPublishers
.com

BentleyPublishers
.com

**Engine control module, overview
N52 and N51 engines
page 1 of 7**

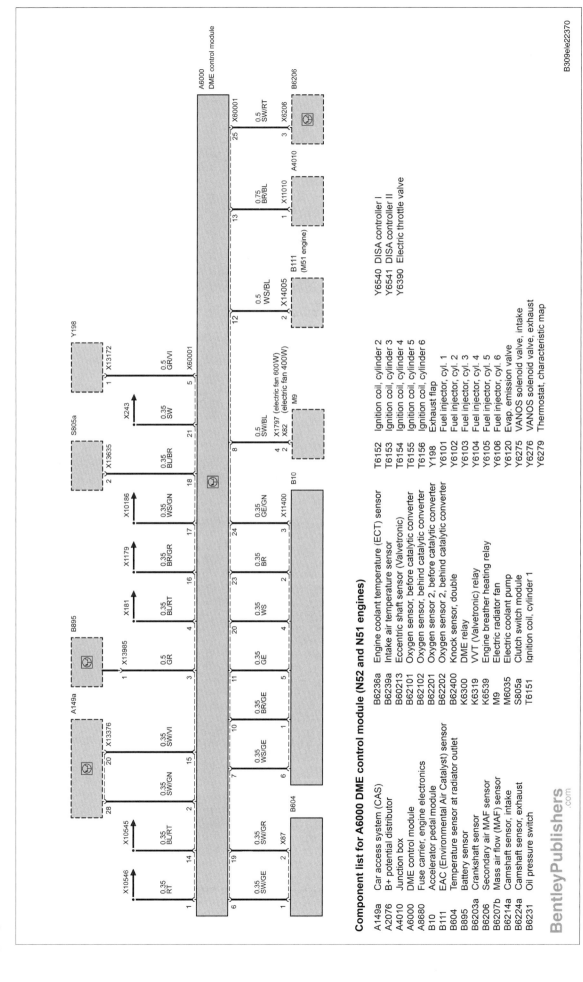

## Component list for A6000 DME control module (N52 and N51 engines)

| | | | | |
|---|---|---|---|---|
| A149a | Car access system (CAS) | B6236a | Engine coolant temperature (ECT) sensor | T6152 Ignition coil, cylinder 2 |
| A2076 | B+ potential distributor | B6239a | Intake air temperature sensor | T6153 Ignition coil, cylinder 3 |
| A4010 | Junction box | B60213 | Eccentric shaft sensor (Valvetronic) | T6154 Ignition coil, cylinder 4 |
| A6000 | DME control module | B62101 | Oxygen sensor, before catalytic converter | T6155 Ignition coil, cylinder 5 |
| A8680 | Fuse carrier, engine electronics | B62102 | Oxygen sensor, behind catalytic converter | T6156 Ignition coil, cylinder 6 |
| B10 | Accelerator pedal module | B62201 | Oxygen sensor 2, before catalytic converter | Y198 Exhaust flap |
| B111 | EAC (Environmental Air Catalyst) sensor | B62202 | Oxygen sensor 2, behind catalytic converter | Y6101 Fuel injector, cyl. 1 |
| B604 | Temperature sensor at radiator outlet | B62400 | Knock sensor, double | Y6102 Fuel injector, cyl. 2 |
| B895 | Battery sensor | K6300 | DME relay | Y6103 Fuel injector, cyl. 3 |
| B6203a | Crankshaft sensor | K6319 | VVT (Valvetronic) relay | Y6104 Fuel injector, cyl. 4 |
| B6206 | Secondary air MAF sensor | K6539 | Engine breather heating relay | Y6105 Fuel injector, cyl. 5 |
| B6207b | Mass air flow (MAF) sensor | M9 | Electric radiator fan | Y6106 Fuel injector, cyl. 6 |
| B6214a | Camshaft sensor, intake | M6035 | Electric coolant pump | Y6120 Evap. emission valve |
| B6224a | Camshaft sensor, exhaust | S805a | Clutch switch module | Y6275 VANOS solenoid valve, intake |
| B6231 | Oil pressure switch | T6151 | Ignition coil, cylinder 1 | Y6276 VANOS solenoid valve, exhaust |
| | | | | Y6279 Thermostat, characteristic map |
| | | | | Y6540 DISA controller I |
| | | | | Y6541 DISA controller II |
| | | | | Y6390 Electric throttle valve |

BentleyPublishers.com

**Engine control module, overview
N52 and N51 engines
page 2 of 7**

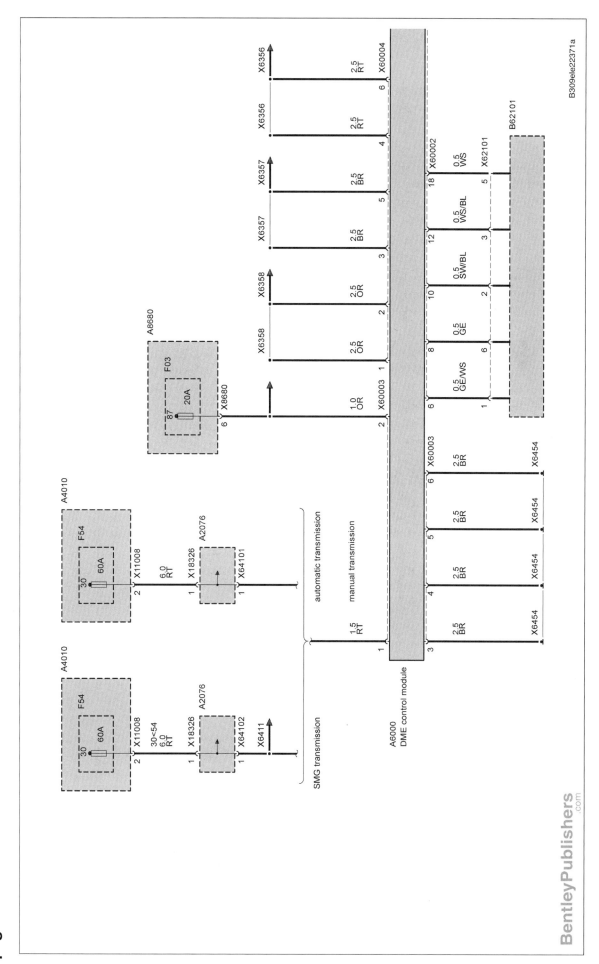

B309ele22371a

**Engine control module, overview
N52 and N51 engines
page 3 of 7**

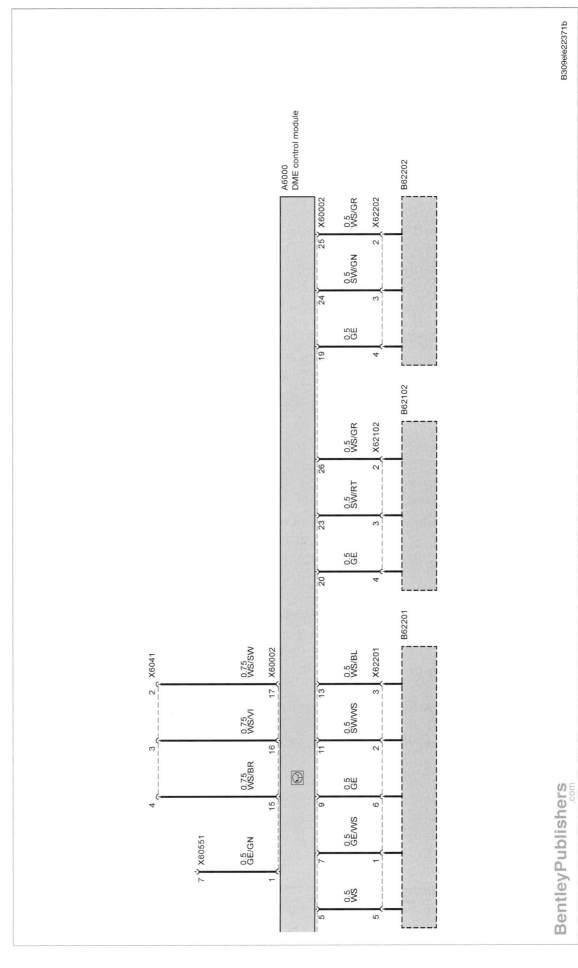

B309ele22371b

**Engine control module, overview
N52 and N51 engines
page 4 of 7**

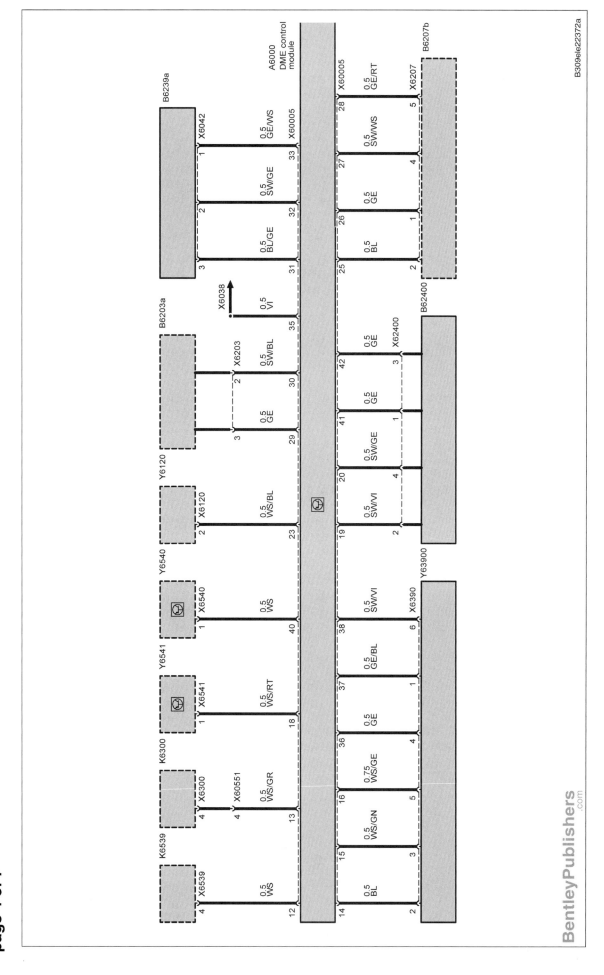

**Engine control module, overview
N52 and N51 engines
page 5 of 7**

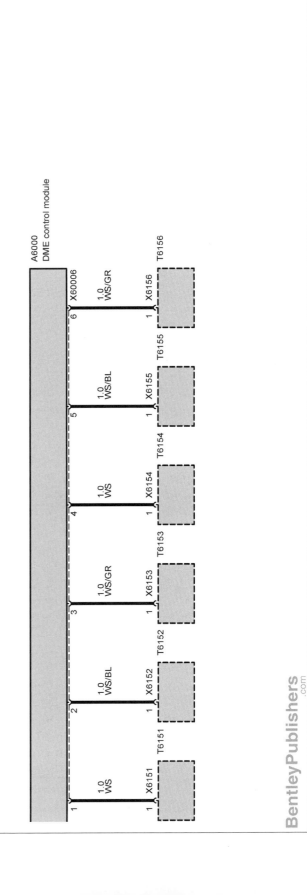

B309ele22372b

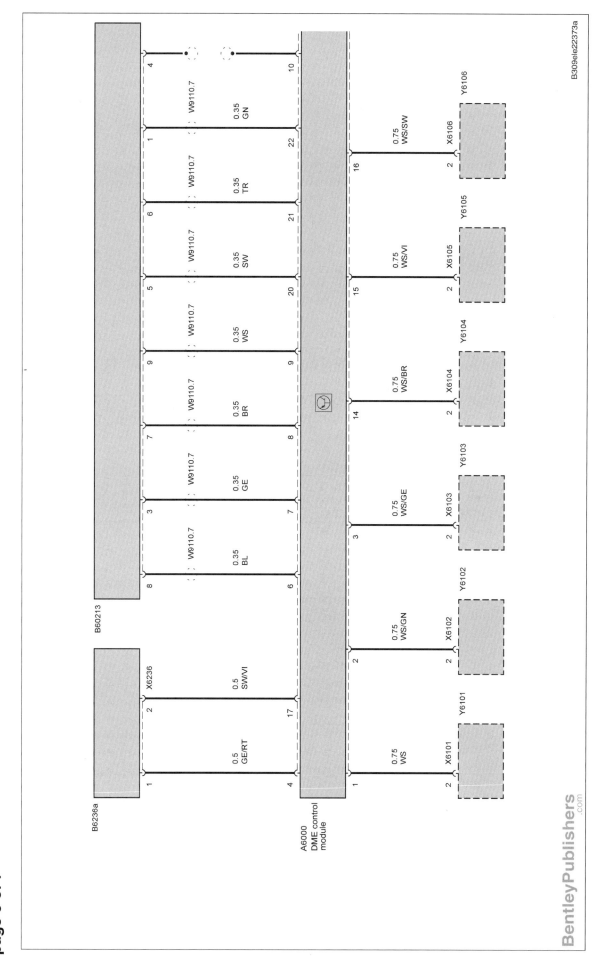

**Engine control module, overview**
**N52 and N51 engines**
**page 6 of 7**

B309ele22373a

**Engine control module, overview
N52 and N51 engines
page 7 of 7**

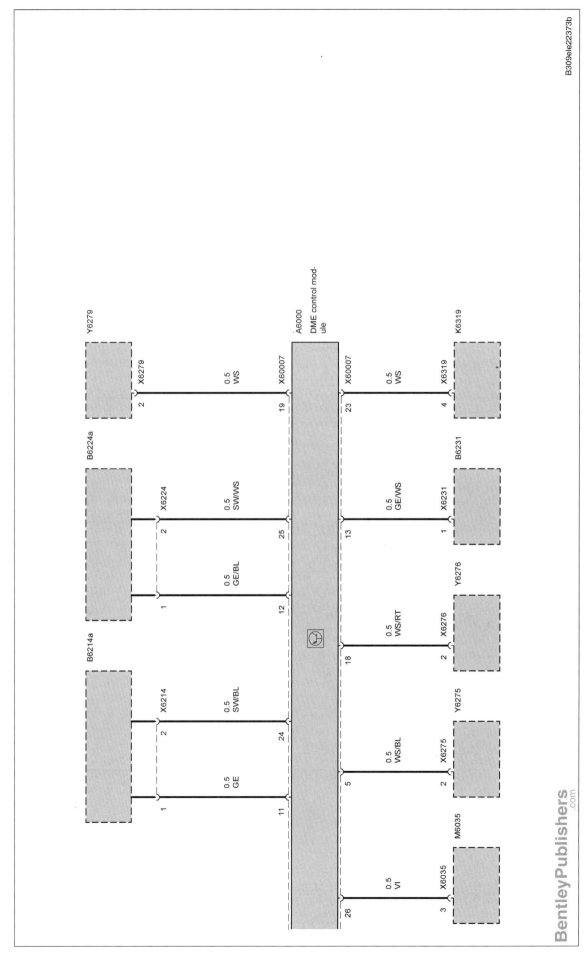

B309ele22373b

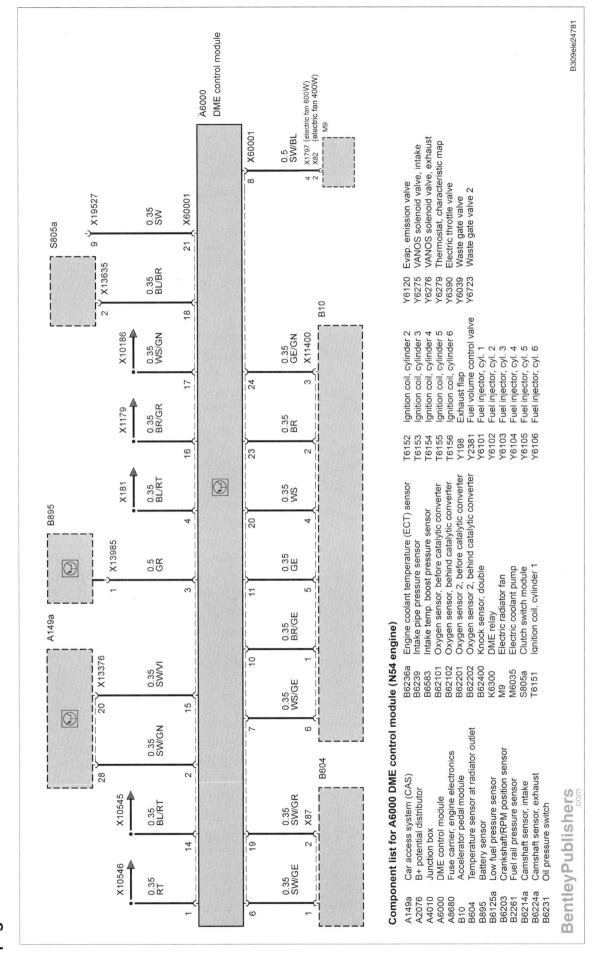

**Component list for A6000 DME control module (N54 engine)**

| | | | | |
|---|---|---|---|---|
| A149a | Car access system (CAS) | B6236a | Engine coolant temperature (ECT) sensor | Y6120 | Evap. emission valve |
| A2076 | B+ potential distributor | B6239 | Intake pipe pressure sensor | Y6275 | VANOS solenoid valve, intake |
| A4010 | Junction box | B6583 | Intake temp. boost pressure sensor | Y6276 | VANOS solenoid valve, exhaust |
| A6000 | DME control module | B62101 | Oxygen sensor, before catalytic converter | Y6279 | Thermostat, characteristic map |
| A8680 | Fuse carrier, engine electronics | B62102 | Oxygen sensor, behind catalytic converter | Y6390 | Electric throttle valve |
| B10 | Accelerator pedal module | B62201 | Oxygen sensor 2, before catalytic converter | Y6039 | Waste gate valve |
| B604 | Temperature sensor at radiator outlet | B62202 | Oxygen sensor 2, behind catalytic converter | Y6723 | Waste gate valve 2 |
| B895 | Battery sensor | B62400 | Knock sensor, double | | |
| B6125a | Low fuel pressure sensor | K6300 | DME relay | | |
| B6203 | Crankshaft/RPM position sensor | M9 | Electric radiator fan | | |
| B2261 | Fuel rail pressure sensor | M6035 | Electric coolant pump | | |
| B6214a | Camshaft sensor, intake | S805a | Clutch switch module | | |
| B6224a | Camshaft sensor, exhaust | T6151 | Ignition coil, cylinder 1 | | |
| B6231 | Oil pressure switch | | | | |

| | |
|---|---|
| T6152 | Ignition coil, cylinder 2 |
| T6153 | Ignition coil, cylinder 3 |
| T6154 | Ignition coil, cylinder 4 |
| T6155 | Ignition coil, cylinder 5 |
| T6156 | Ignition coil, cylinder 6 |
| Y198 | Exhaust flap |
| Y2381 | Fuel volume control valve |
| Y6101 | Fuel injector, cyl. 1 |
| Y6102 | Fuel injector, cyl. 2 |
| Y6103 | Fuel injector, cyl. 3 |
| Y6104 | Fuel injector, cyl. 4 |
| Y6105 | Fuel injector, cyl. 5 |
| Y6106 | Fuel injector, cyl. 6 |

B309ele24781

**Engine control module, overview**
**N54 engine**
**page 2 of 7**

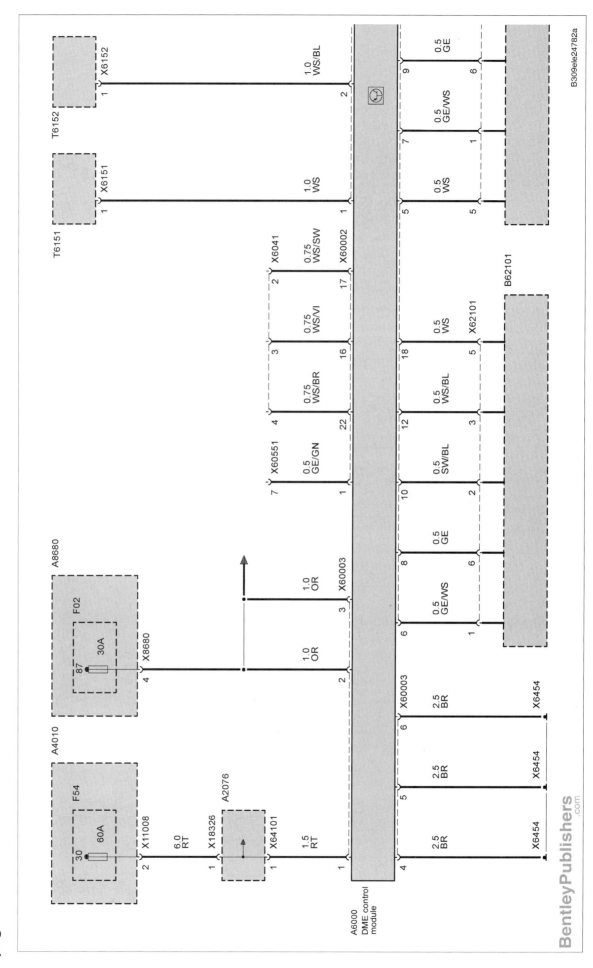

B309ele24782a

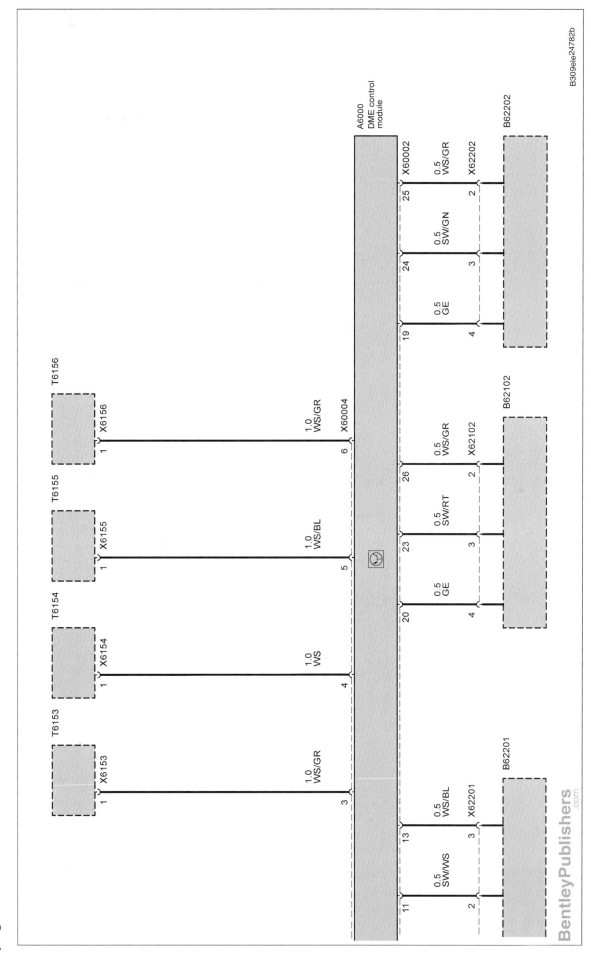

B309ele24782b

**Electrical Wiring Diagrams   ELE-121**

**Engine control module, overview**
**N54 engine**
**page 4 of 7**

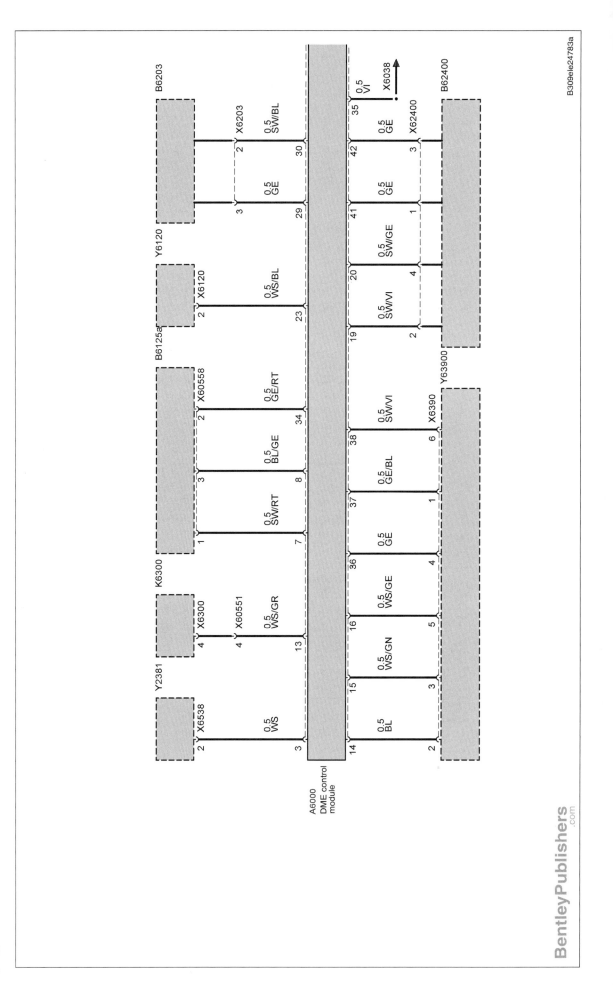

B309ele24783a

**Engine control module, overview**
**N54 engine**
**page 5 of 7**

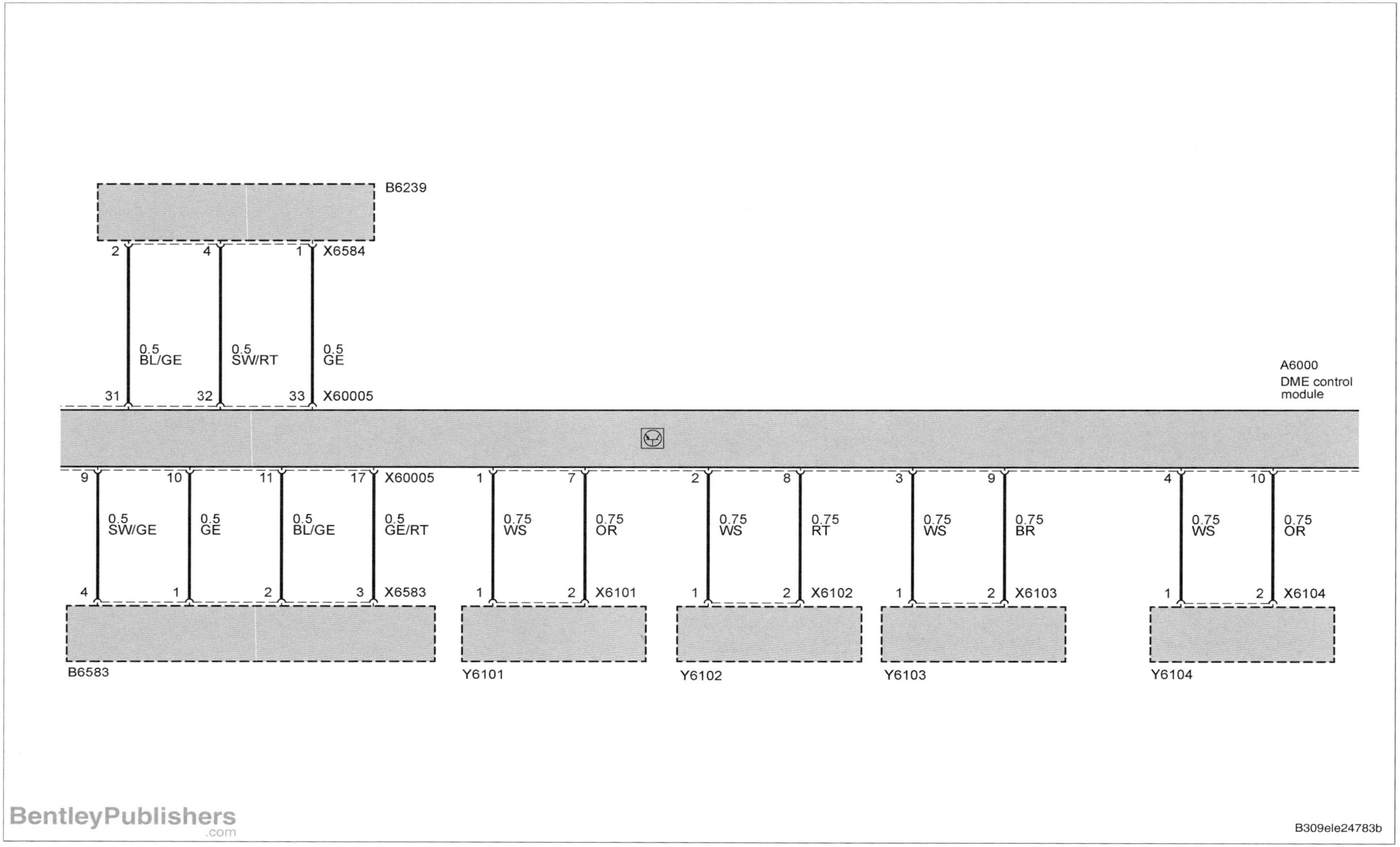

A6000
DME control module

B6239

X6584

| | | |
|---|---|---|
| 1 | 4 | 2 |
| 0.5 GE | 0.5 SW/RT | 0.5 BL/GE |
| 33 | 32 | 31 |

X60005

X60005
0.5 GE/RT
X6583

| | | | |
|---|---|---|---|
| 17 | 11 | 10 | 9 |
| 0.5 GE/RT | 0.5 BL/GE | 0.5 GE | 0.5 SW/GE |
| 3 | 2 | 1 | 4 |

B6583

Y6101
| | |
|---|---|
| 7 | 1 |
| 0.75 OR | 0.75 WS |
| X6101 | |
| 2 | 1 |

Y6102
| | |
|---|---|
| 8 | 2 |
| 0.75 RT | 0.75 WS |
| X6102 | |
| 2 | 1 |

Y6103
| | |
|---|---|
| 9 | 3 |
| 0.75 BR | 0.75 WS |
| X6103 | |
| 2 | 1 |

Y6104
| | |
|---|---|
| 10 | 4 |
| 0.75 OR | 0.75 WS |
| X6104 | |
| 2 | 1 |

Electrical Wiring Diagrams   ELE-123

B309ele24783b

**Engine control module, overview**
**N54 engine**
**page 6 of 7**

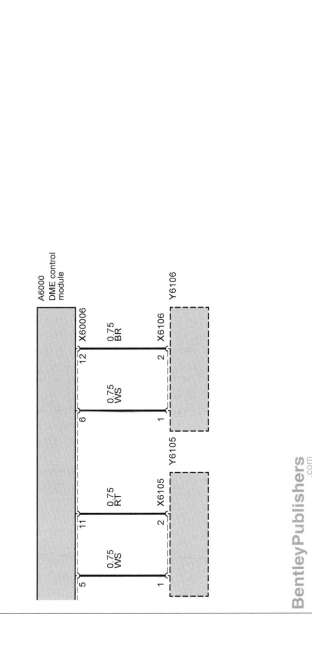

B309ele24783c

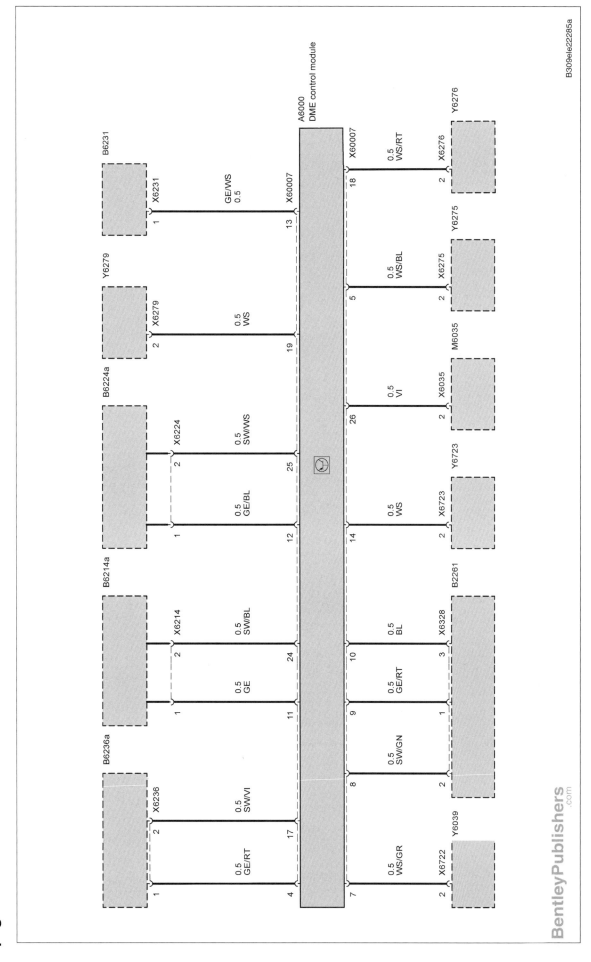

## OBD II socket

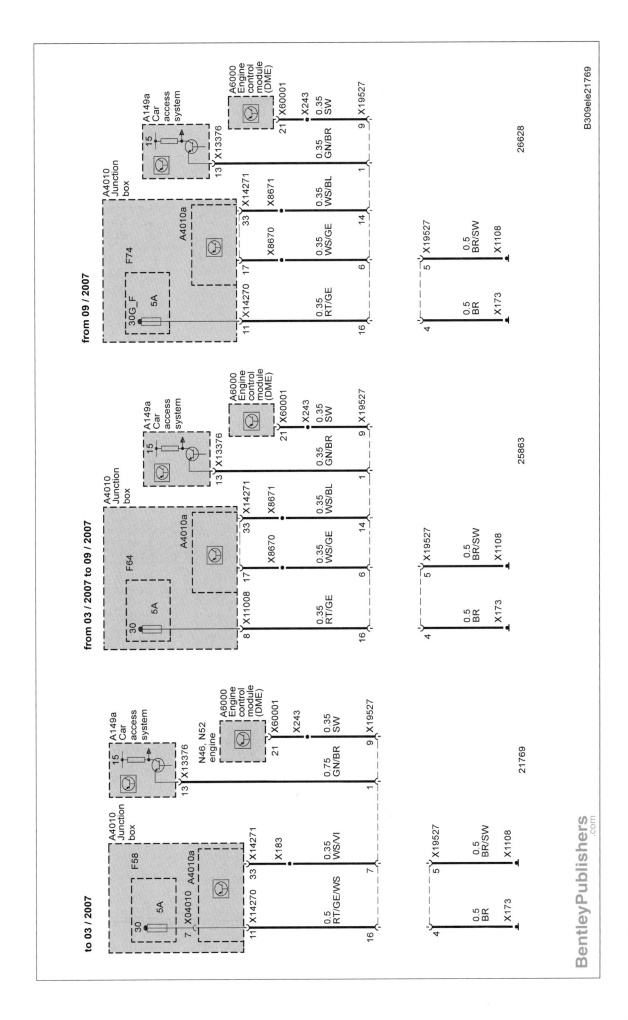

B309ele21769

# Exhaust flap

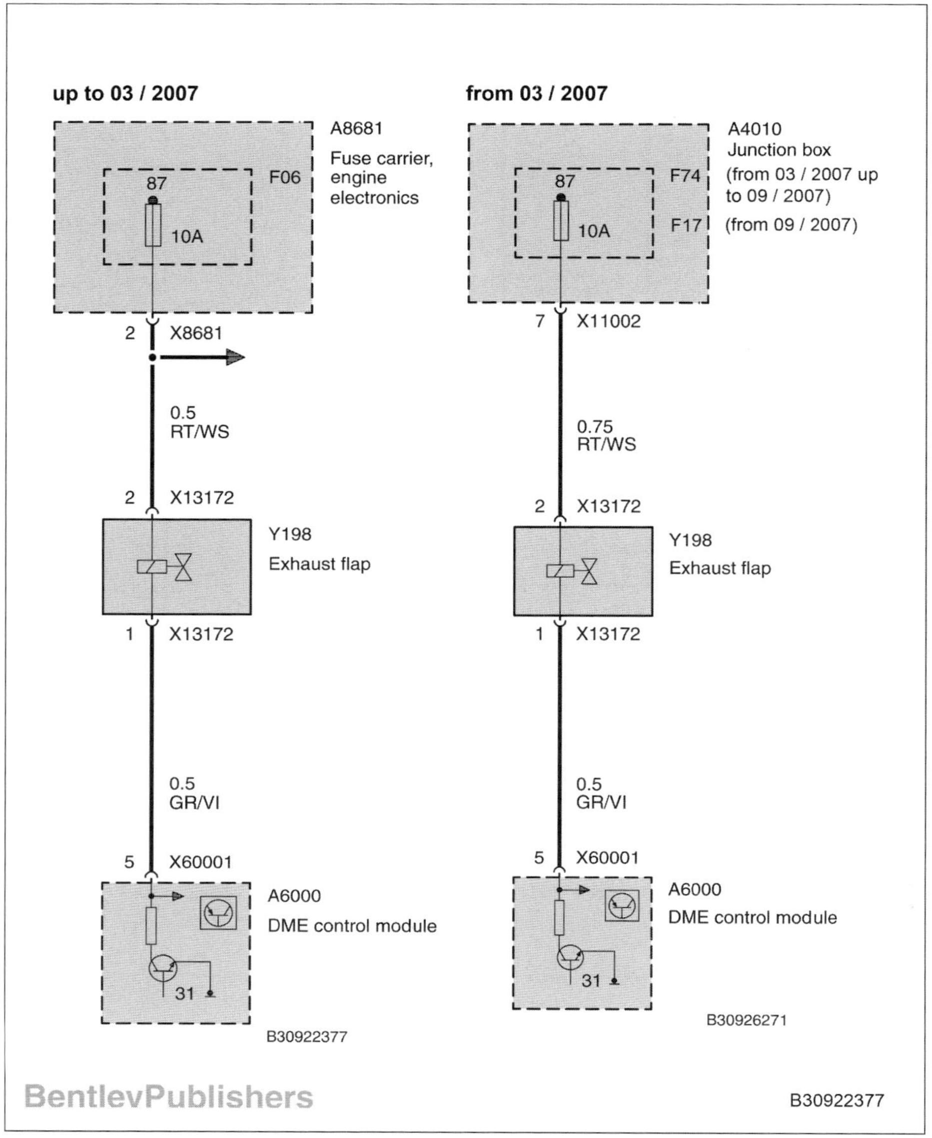
up to 03 / 2007
A8681
Fuse carrier, engine electronics
F06
87
10A
2
X8681
0.5
RT/WS
2
X13172
Y198
Exhaust flap
1
X13172
0.5
GR/VI
5
X60001
A6000
DME control module
31
B30922377
from 03 / 2007
A4010
Junction box
F74
(from 03 / 2007 up to 09 / 2007)
F17
(from 09 / 2007)
87
10A
7
X11002
0.75
RT/WS
2
X13172
Y198
Exhaust flap
1
X13172
0.5
GR/VI
5
X60001
A6000
DME control module
31
B30926271
BentleyPublishers
B30922377

**Oxygen sensors**

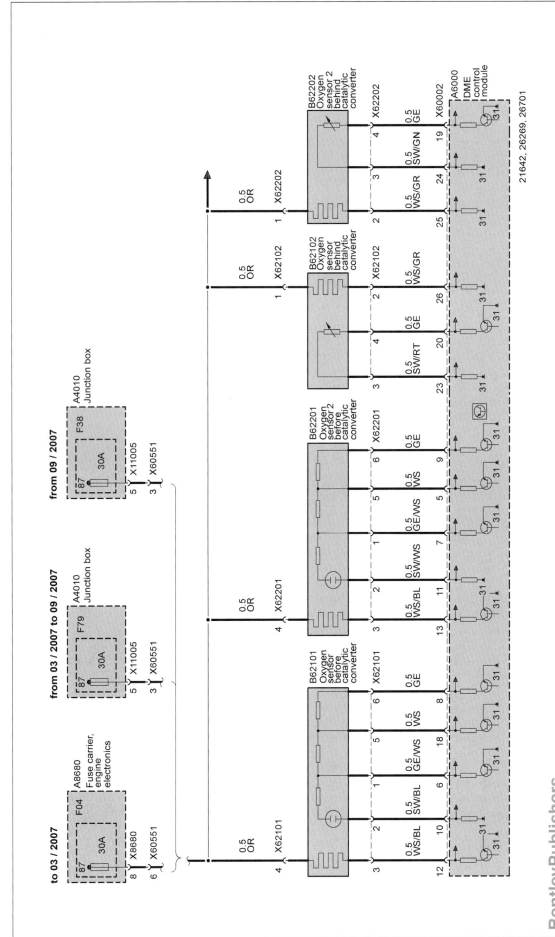

B309ele21642

**Crankshaft position sensor
N54 engine**

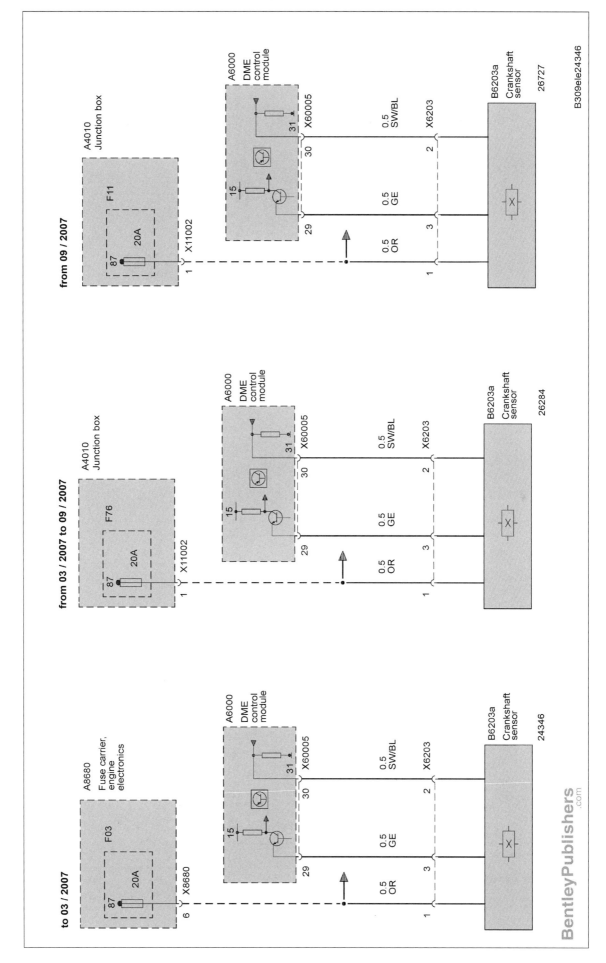

B309ele24346

BentleyPublishers
.com

## Valve gear, Camshaft position sensors, VANOS solenoids
## N54 engine

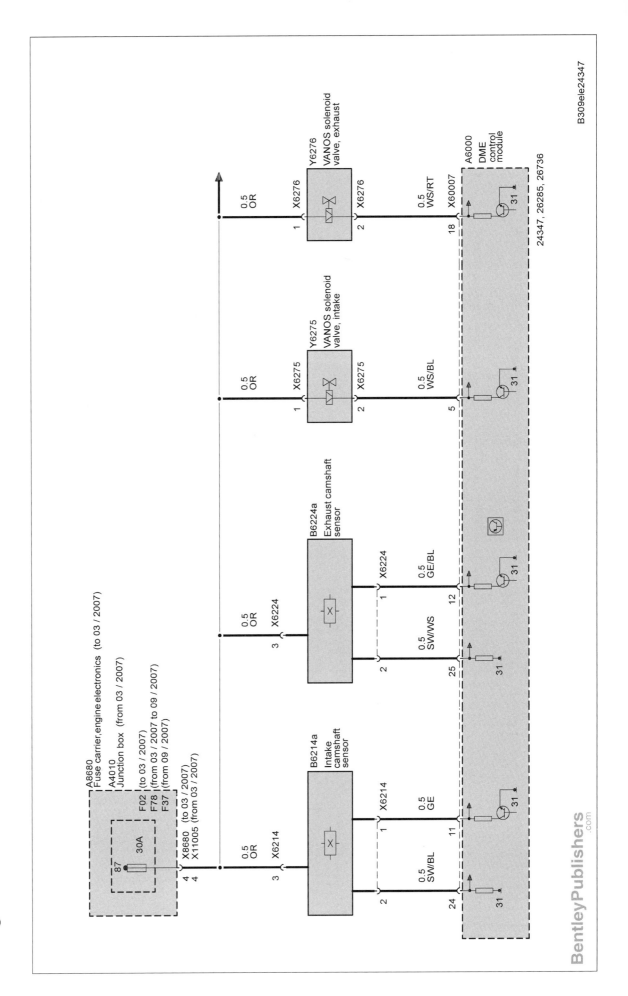

B309ele24347

# Valve gear, VANOS solenoids, Valvetronic (VVT)
# Crankshaft position sensor
# N52 and N51 engines (page 1 of 2)

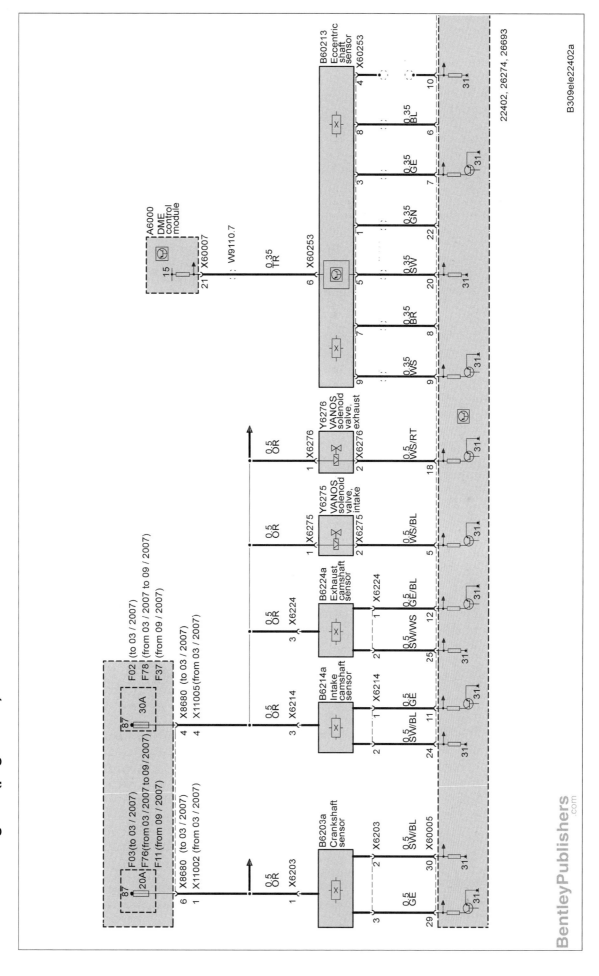

B309ele22402a

22402, 26274, 26693

**Valve gear, VANOS solenoids, Valvetronic (VVT)**
**Crankshaft position sensor**
**N52 and N51 engines (page 2 of 2)**

**E-box fan**

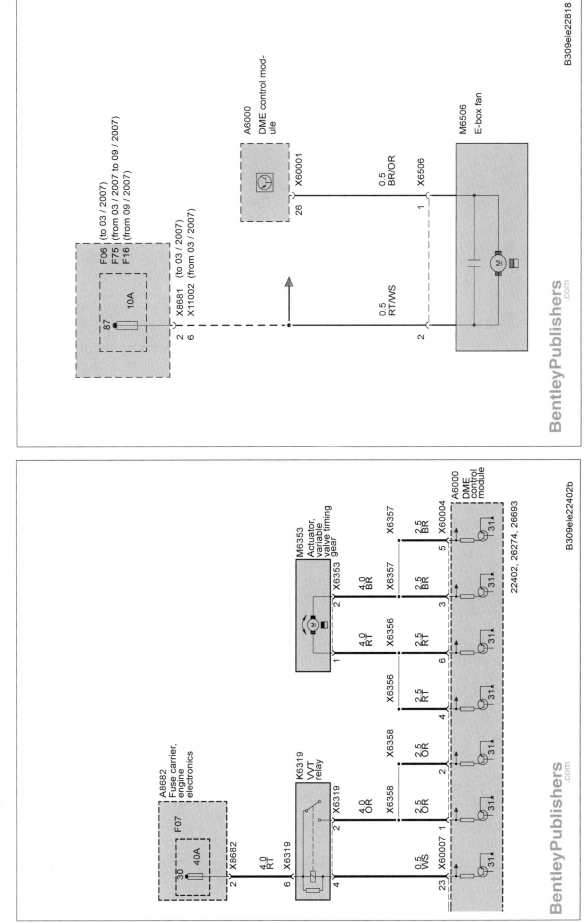

B309ele22818

B309ele22402b

**Accelerator pedal module, brake light switch**
**Clutch switch module**
**N54 engine**

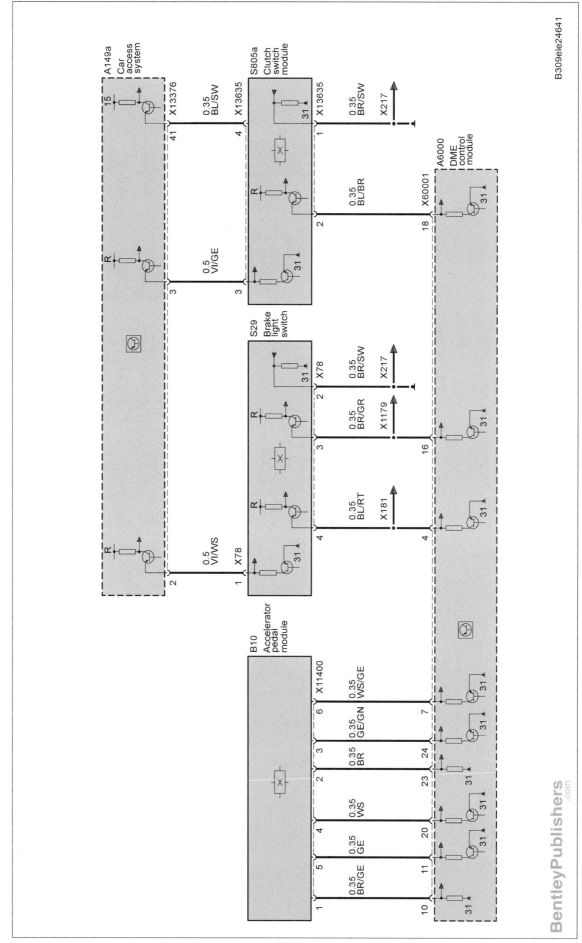

B309ele24641

**Brake light switch
N52 and N51 engines**

**Accelerator pedal module
N52 and N51 engines**

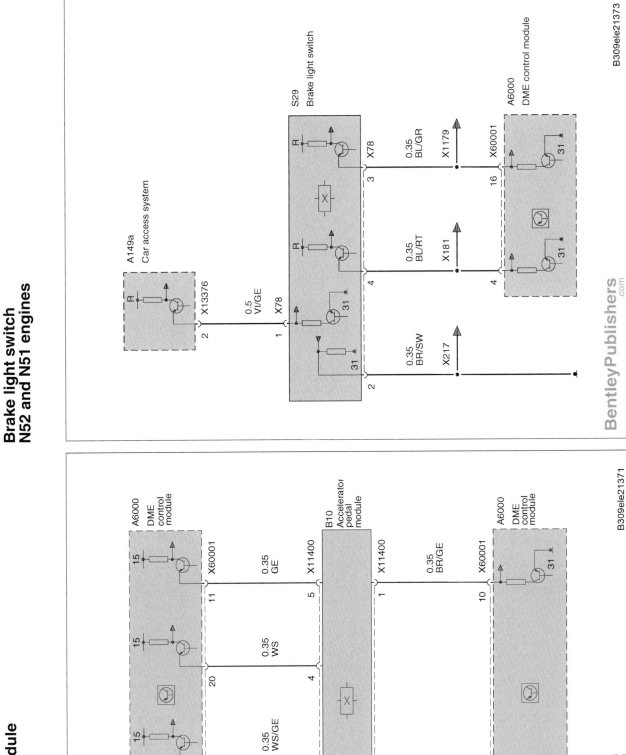

B309ele21373

B309ele21371

**Knock sensor**

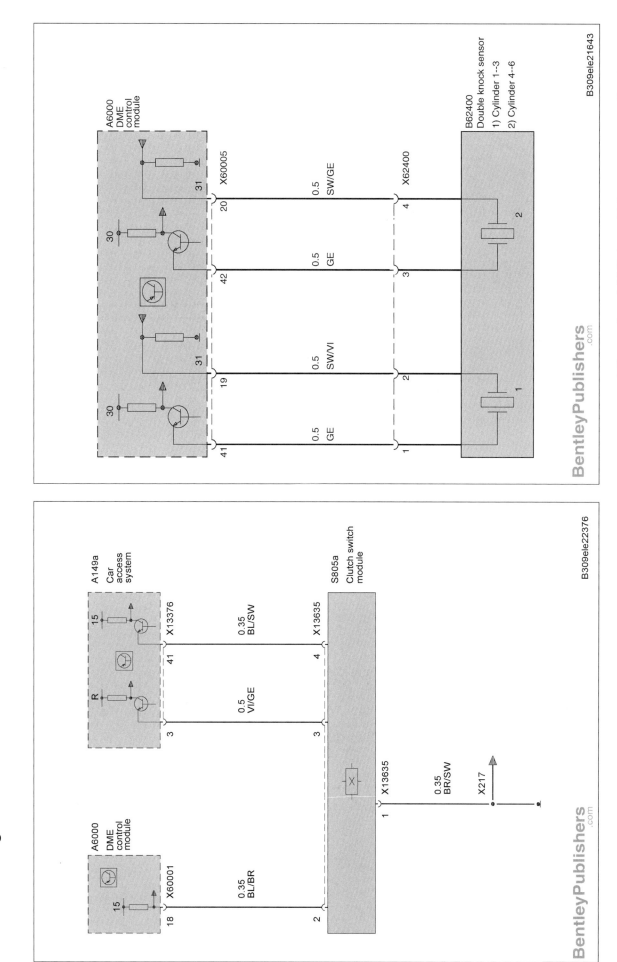

**Clutch switch module
N52 and N51 engines**

Electrical Wiring Diagrams   ELE-135

B309ele21643

B309ele22376

BentleyPublishers.com

BentleyPublishers.com

**Fuel injectors**
**N54 engine**

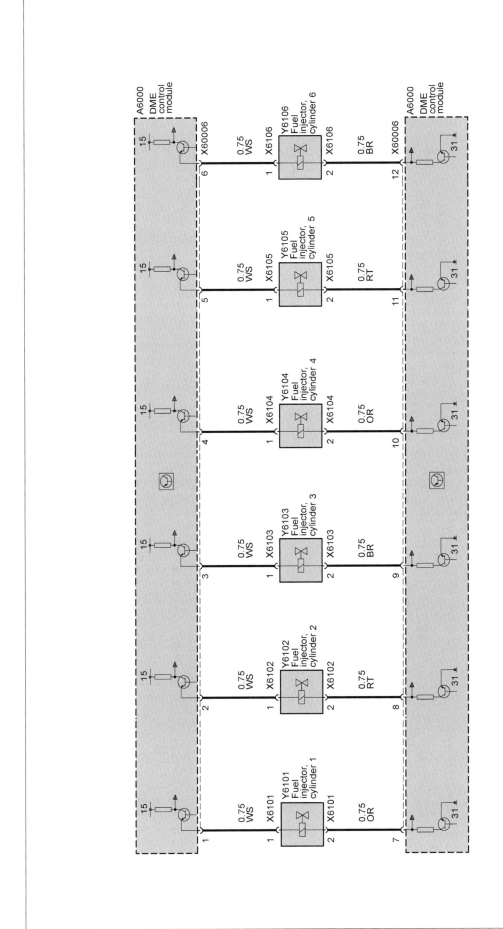

B309ele24342

**Fuel injectors**
**N52 and N51 engines**
**(to 03 / 2007)**

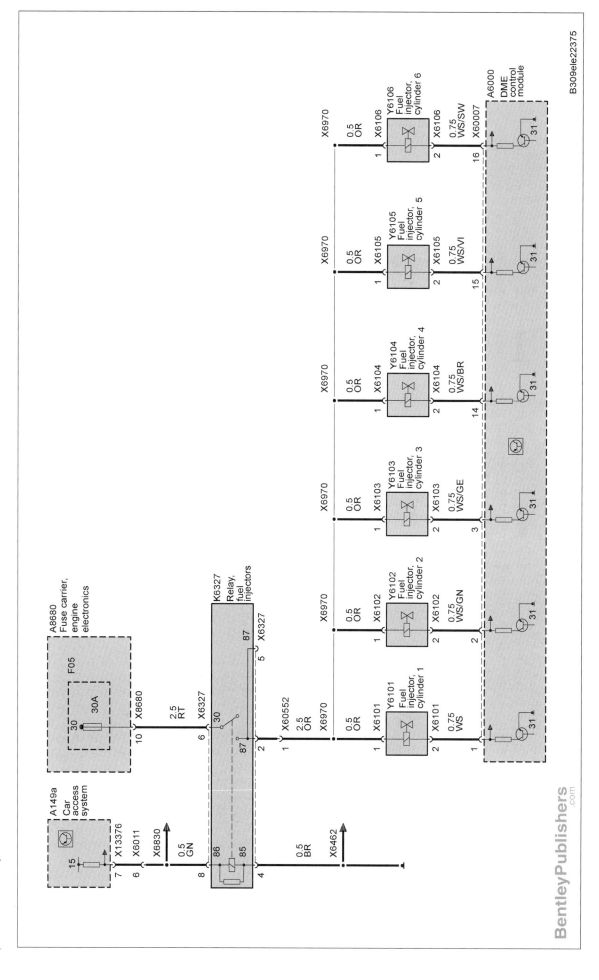

B309ele22375

BentleyPublishers
.com

**Fuel injectors**
**N52 and N51 engines**
**(from 03 / 2007)**

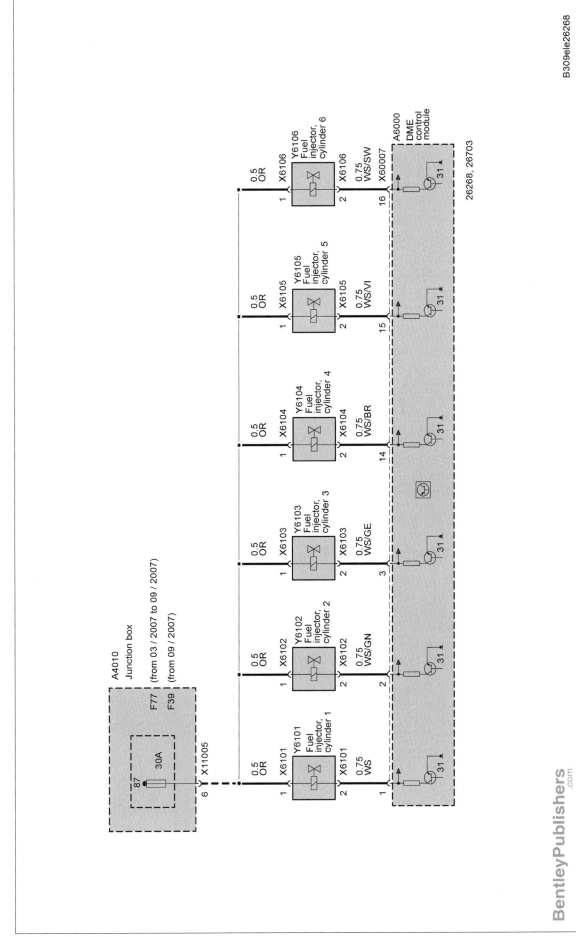

B309ele26268

**High pressure fuel system**
**N54 engine**

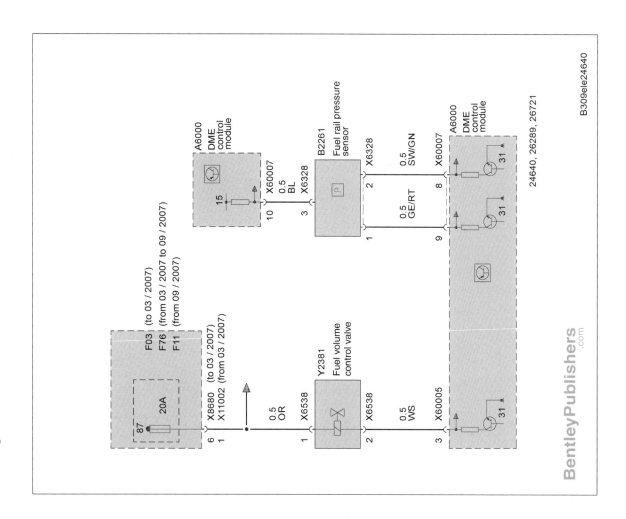

F03  (to 03 / 2007)
F76  (from 03 / 2007 to 09 / 2007)
F11  (from 09 / 2007)

A6000
DME control module

A6000
DME control module

B2261
Fuel rail pressure sensor

Y2381
Fuel volume control valve

A6000
DME control module

20A

X8680  (to 03 / 2007)
X11002 (from 03 / 2007)

0.5
OR

0.5
BL

0.5
GE/RT

0.5
SW/GN

0.5
WS

X6538

X6328

X60007

X60005

24640, 26289, 26721

B309ele24640

**Low pressure fuel system**
**N54 engine**

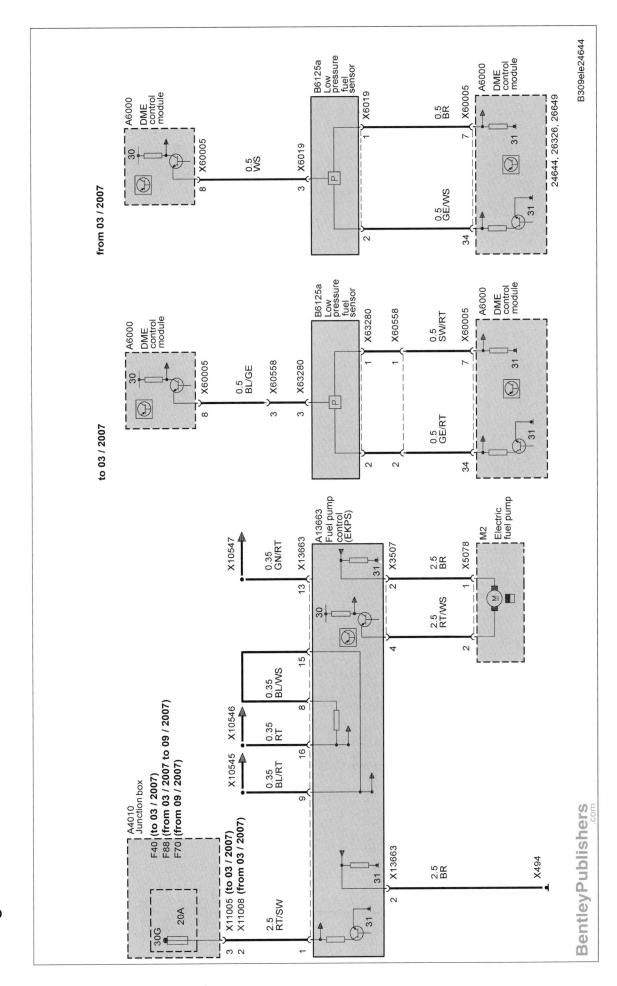

**Fuel pump, electronically controlled
N52 and N51 engines**

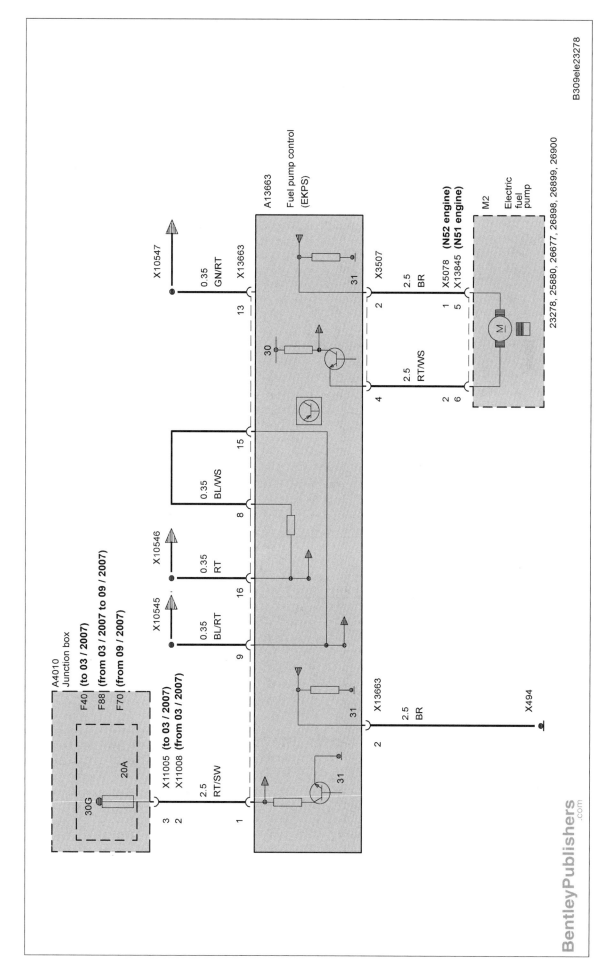

B309ele23278

BentleyPublishers
.com

**Air supply, electric throttle valve actuator, turbocharger
N54 engine**

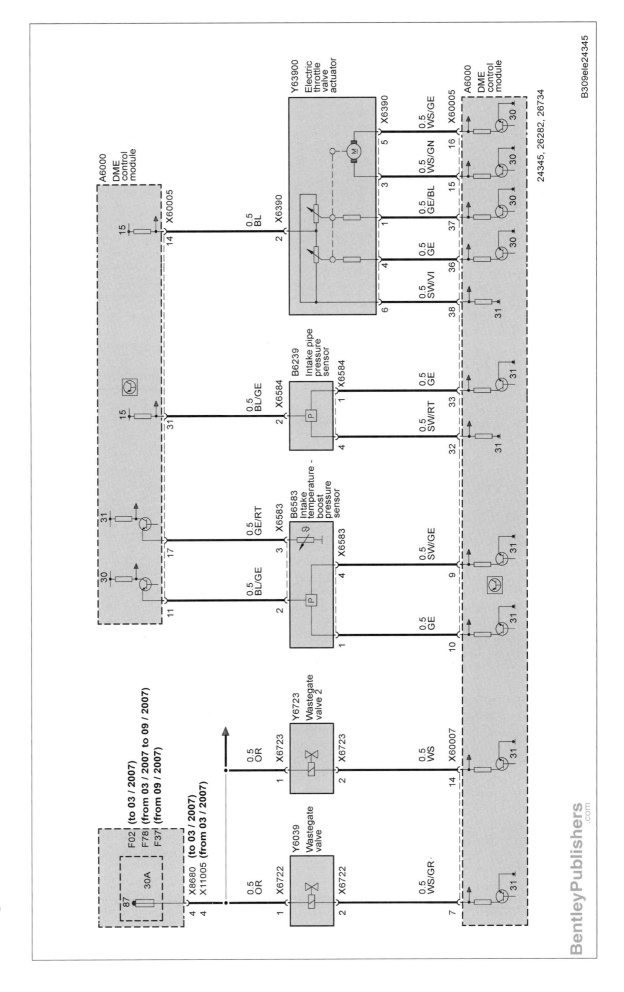

B309ele24345

BentleyPublishers.com

**Air supply, DISA, mass air flow sensor**
**Electric throttle valve actuator**
**N52 and N51 engines (to 03 / 2007)**

B309ele21644

**Air supply, DISA, mass air flow sensor**
**Electric throttle valve actuator**
**N52 and N51 engines (from 03 / 2007)**

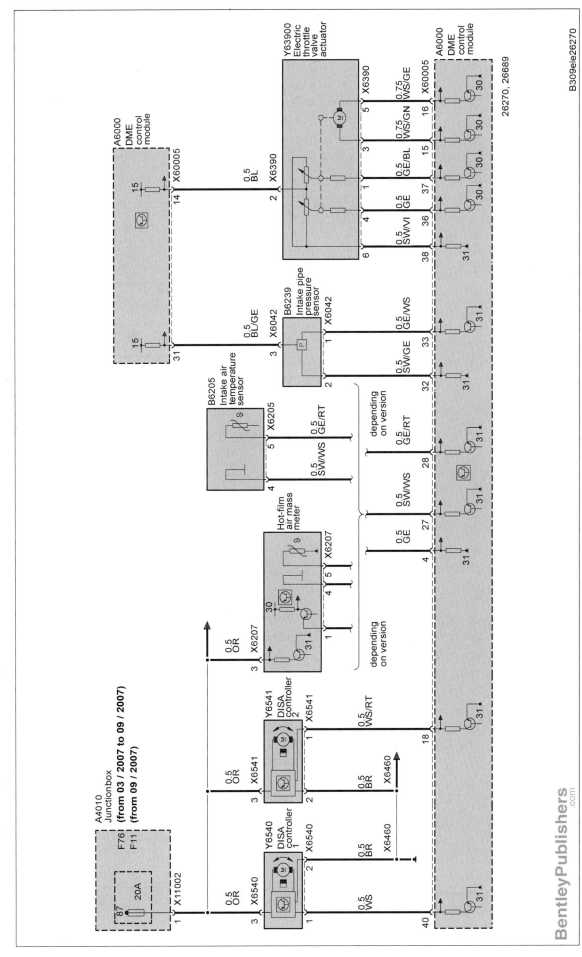

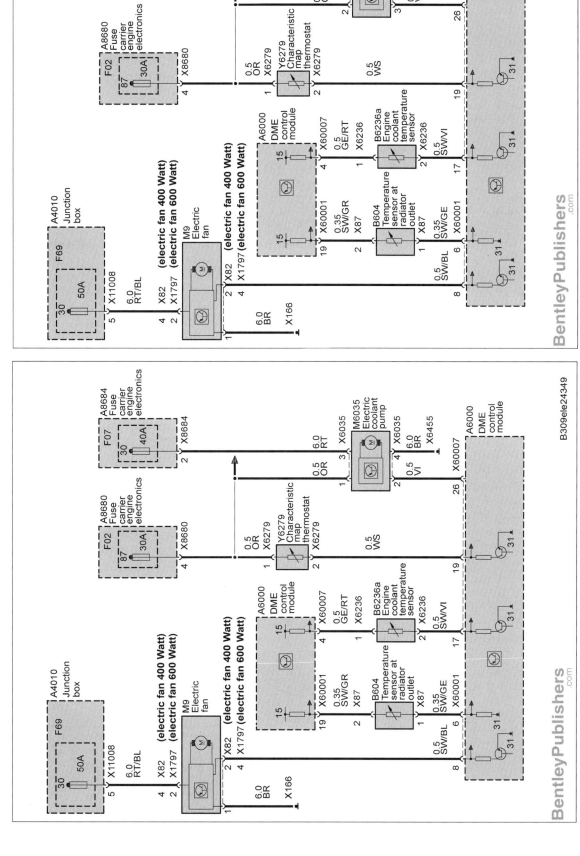

**Engine cooling system
N52 engine
(to 03 / 2007)**

**Engine cooling system
N54 engine
(to 03 / 2007)**

Electrical Wiring Diagrams  ELE-145

B309ele22378

B309ele24349

BentleyPublishers
.com

**Engine cooling system**
**N51 engine**
**(to 03 / 2007)**

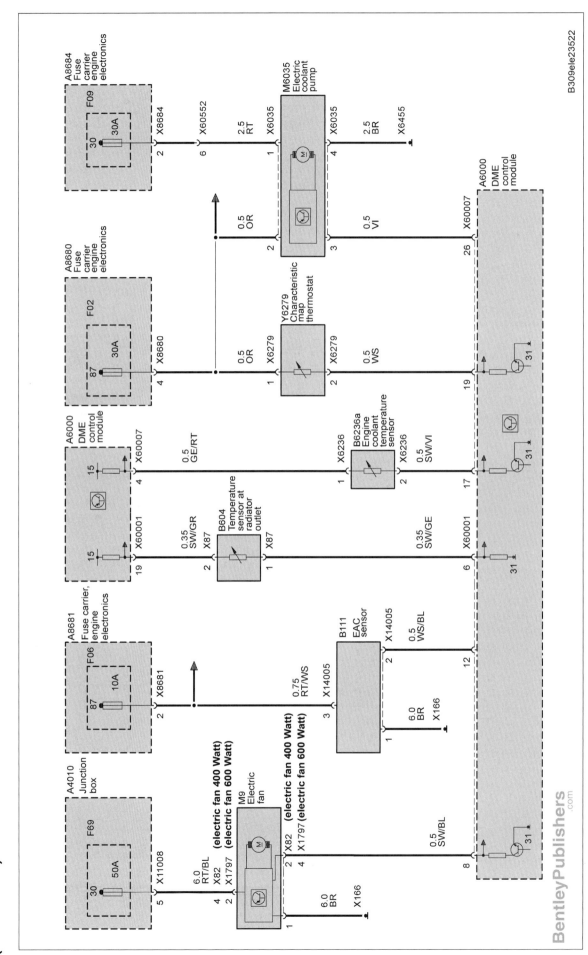

B309ele23522

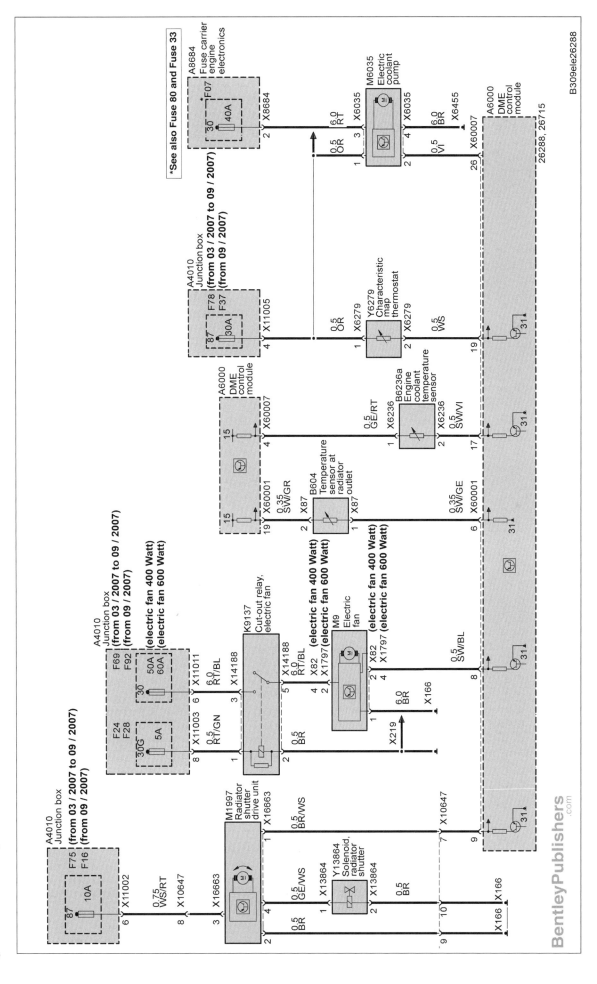

**Engine cooling system
N54 engine
(from 03 / 2007)**

B309ele26288

BentleyPublishers.com

**Engine cooling system
N52 engine
(from 03 / 2007)**

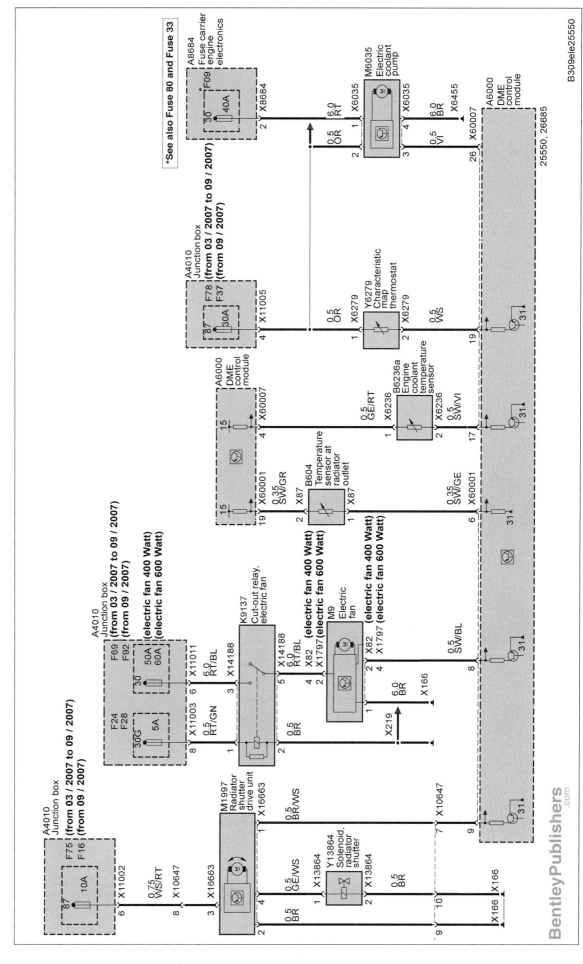

B309ele25550

**Engine cooling system
N51 engine
(from 03 / 2007)**

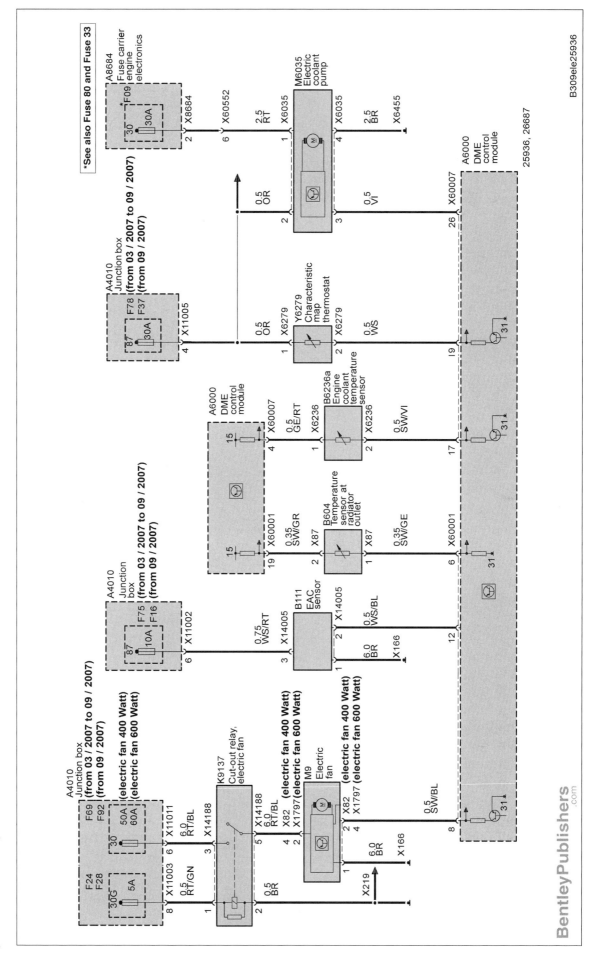

**Oil supply
N54 engine**

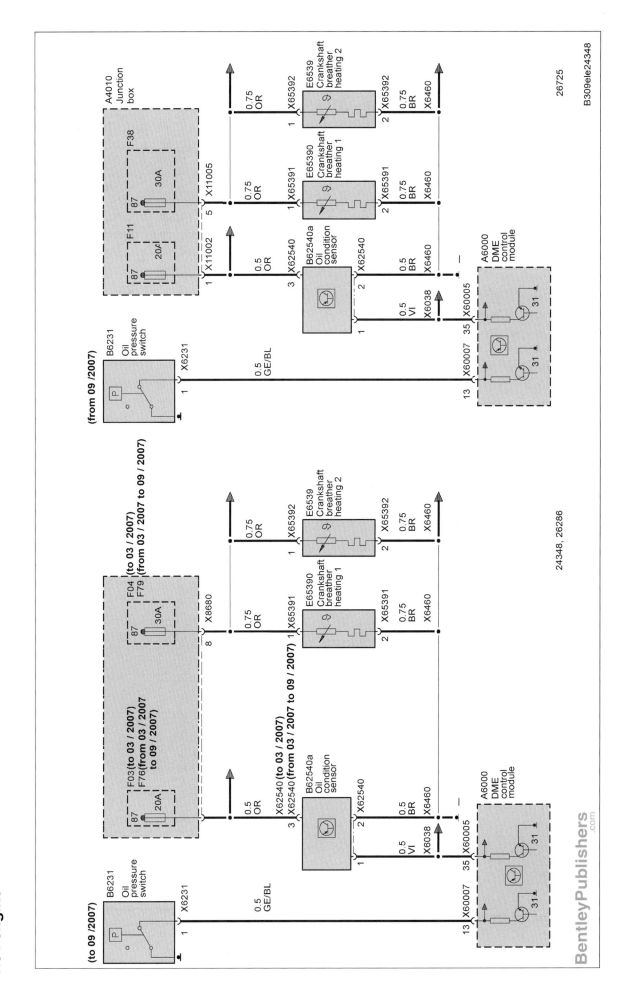

26725

B309ele24348

24348, 26286

**Oil supply
N52 and N51 engines**

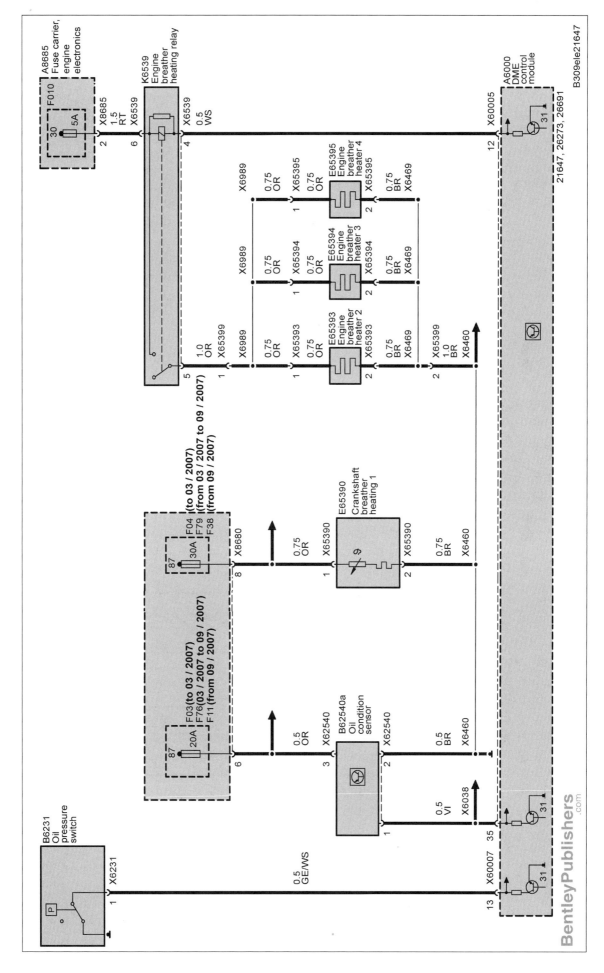

B309ele21647

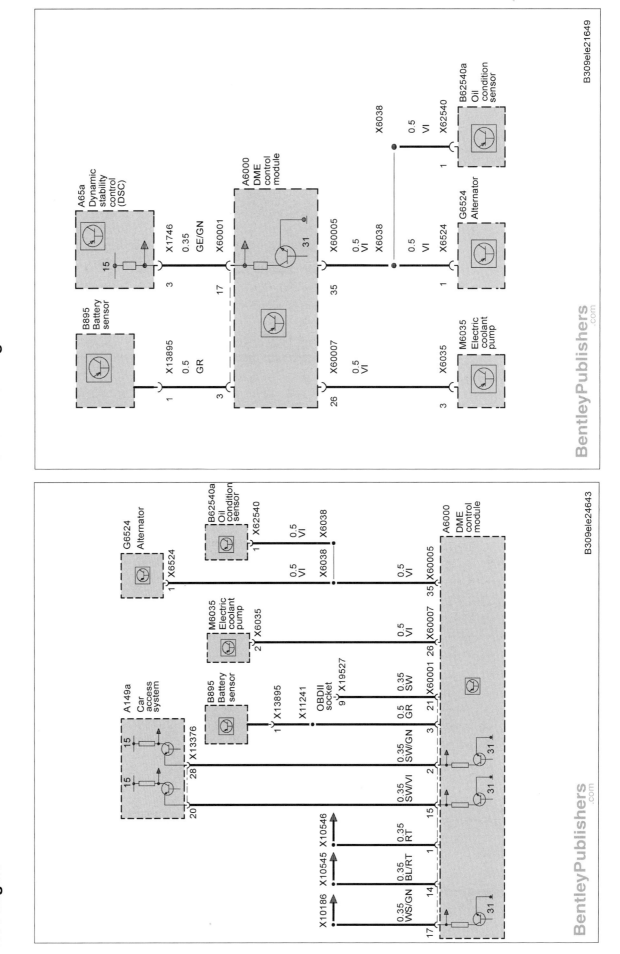

**BSD interface, battery sensor
N52 and N51 engines**

**Interface signals
N54 engine**

B309ele21649

B309ele24643

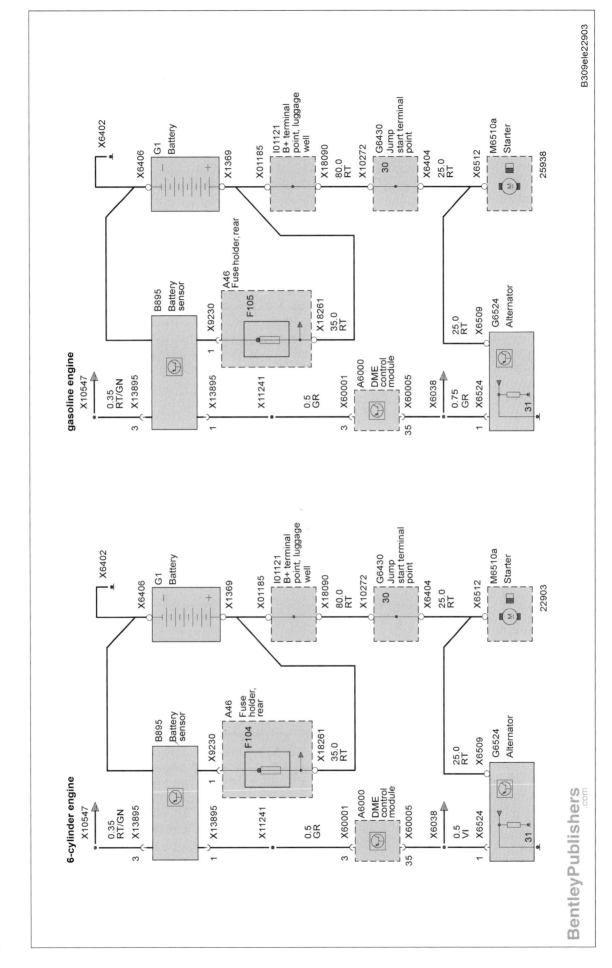

**Convenient start (with EWS 4)
(page 1 of 2)**

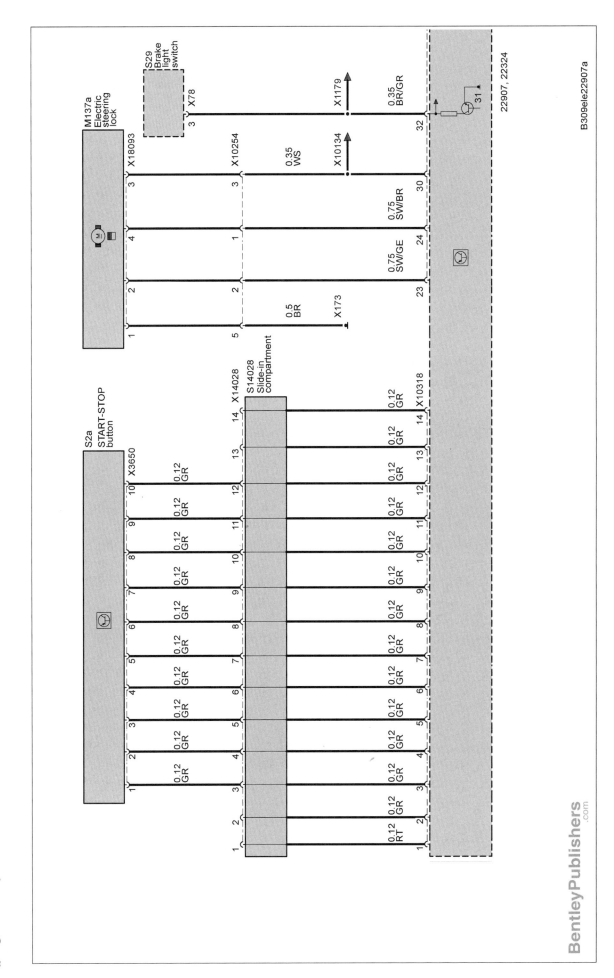

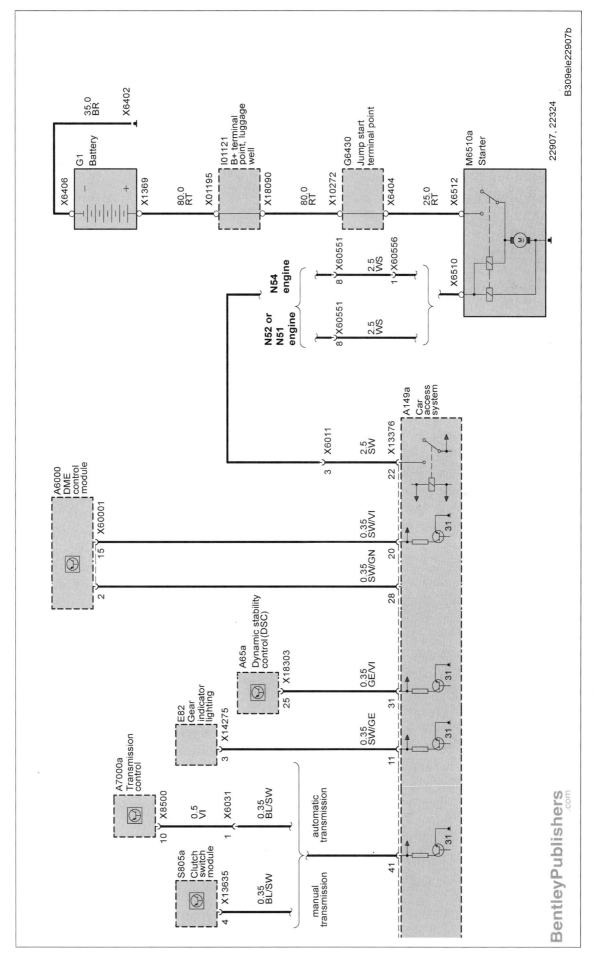

**Vehicle speed control**

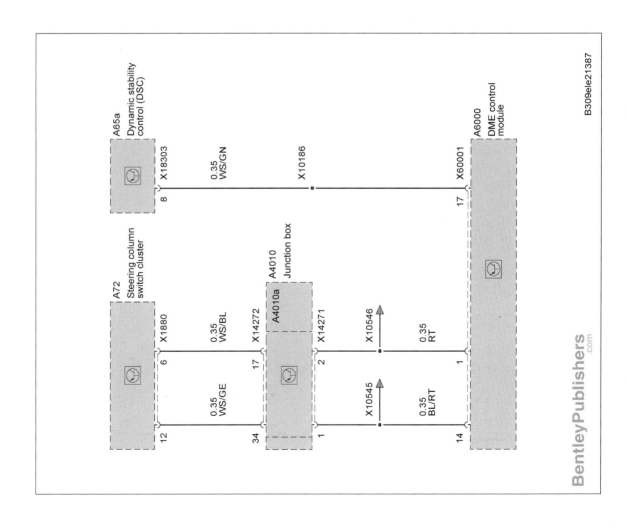

B309ele21387

**Secondary air system
(N51 engine)**

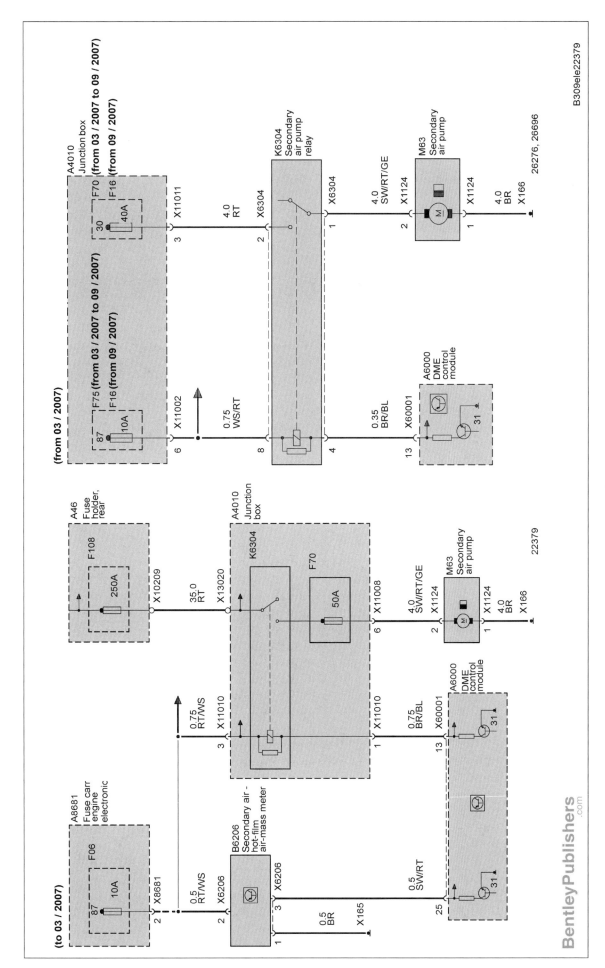

B309ele22379

BentleyPublishers
.com

**DME control module, voltage supply**
**N54 engine**
**(to 03 / 2007)**

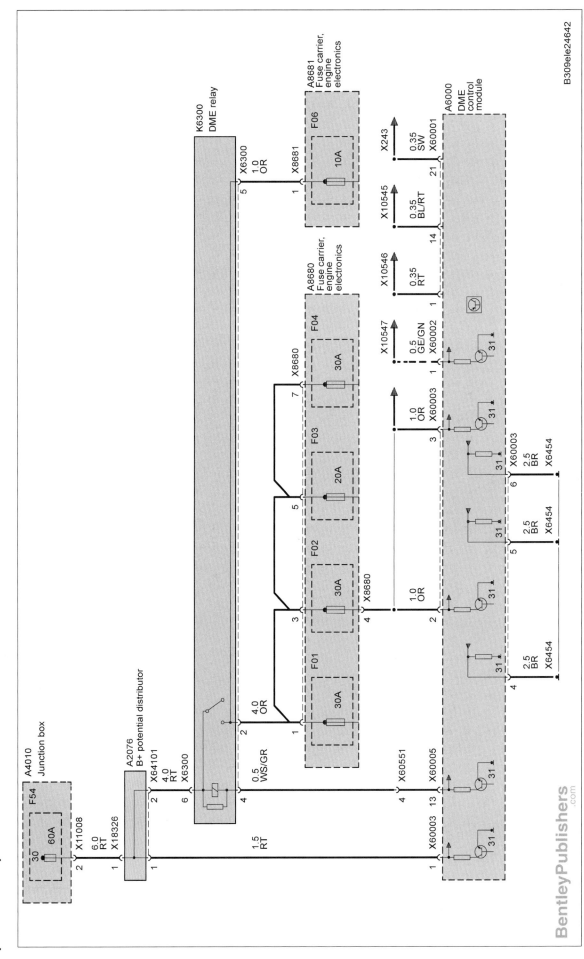

B309ele24642

**DME control module, voltage supply N52 and N51 engines (to 03 / 2007)**

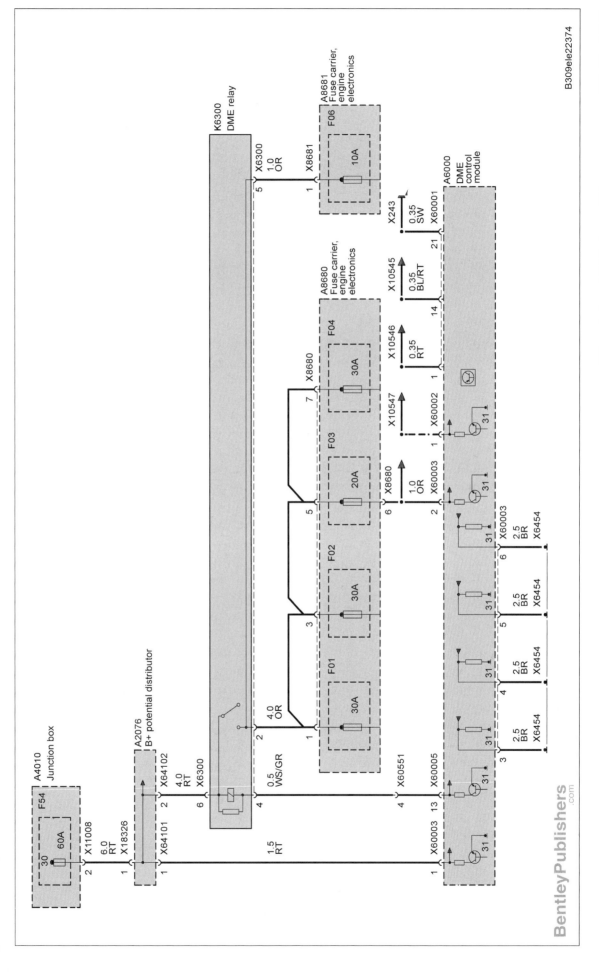

B309ele22374

BentleyPublishers.com

## DME control module, voltage supply
## N52 and N51 engines
## (from 03 / 2007)

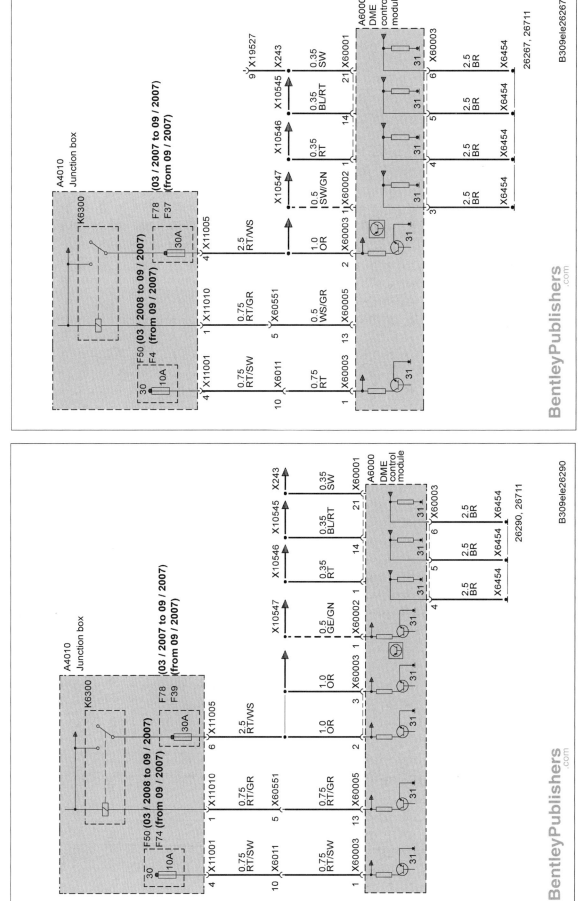

B309ele26267

26267, 26711

## DME control module, voltage supply
## N54 engine
## (from 03 / 2007)

B309ele26290

26290, 26711

# Fuel tank vent valve

## (to 03 / 2007)

A8680
Fuse carrier, engine electronics

F03

87 | 20A

6 | X8680

0.5
OR

1 | X6120

Y6120
Fuel tank vent valve

2 | X6120

0.5
WS/BL

23 | X60005

A6000
DME control module

31

21651

## (from 03 / 2007 to 09 / 2007)

A4010
Junction box

F76

87 | 20A

1 | X11002

0.5
OR

1 | X6120

Y6120
Fuel tank vent valve

2 | X6120

0.5
WS/BL

23 | X60005

A6000
DME control module

31

26275, 26291

## (from 09 / 2007)

A4010
Junction box

F11

87 | 20A

1 | X11002

0.5
OR

1 | X6120

Y6120
Fuel tank vent valve

2 | X6120

0.5
WS/BL

23 | X60005

A6000
DME control module

31

26719, 26694

Electrical Wiring Diagrams   ELE-161

B309ele21651

## Diagnostic module, fuel tank leak detection

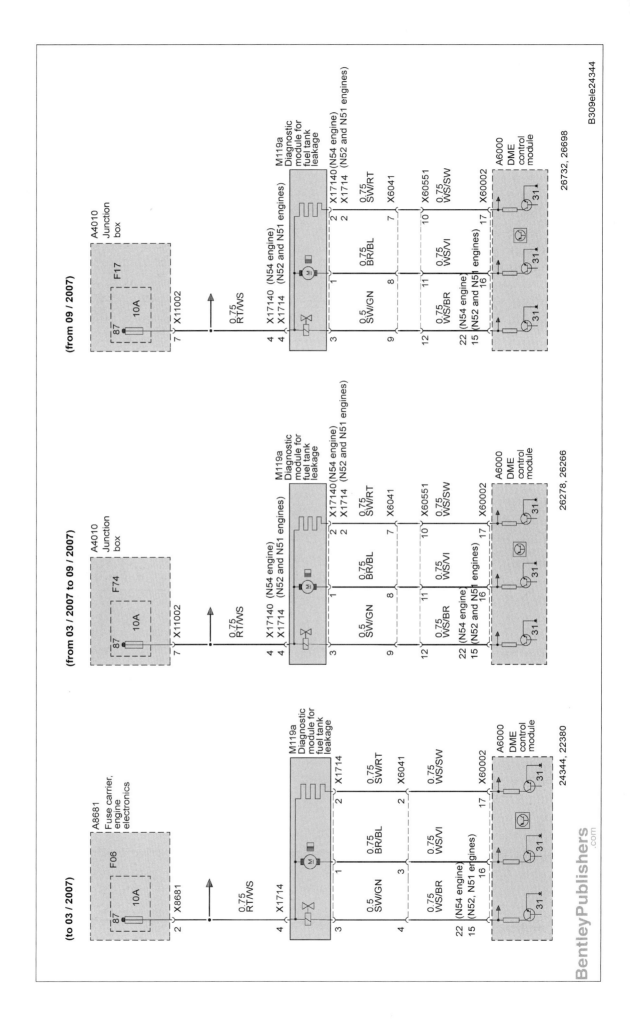

B309ele24344

BentleyPublishers.com

Electrical Wiring Diagrams   ELE-163

B309ele24343

**to 03 / 2007**

A8680
Fuse carrier, engine electronics

F01
30A
87

X8680

2

X60553
2.5
OR

8

**from 03 / 2007**

A4010
Junction box
F77 (from 03 / 2007 to 09 / 2007)
F39 (from 09 / 2007)

30A
87

X11005

6

1.0
RT/WS
I01046
Interference suppression capacitor for ignition coils

1.0
BR

X6171 (N54 engine)
X6176 (N52 and N51 engines)

T6156
Ignition coil, cylinder 6
4) Spark plug connection

X6156
1.0
OR

X6156

X6172 (N54 engine)
X6177 (N52 and N51 engines)

1.0
BR

X6156

1.0
WS/GR

3    4    2    1    6

X60004

T6155
Ignition coil, cylinder 5
4) Spark plug connection

X6155
1.0
OR

X6155

X6172 (N54 engine)
X6177 (N52 and N51 engines)

1.0
BR

X6155

1.0
WS/BL

3    4    2    1    5

T6154
Ignition coil, cylinder 4
4) Spark plug connection

X6154
1.0
OR

X6154

X6171 (N54 engine)
X6177 (N52 and N51 engines)

1.0
BR

X6154

1.0
WS

3    4    2    1    4

T6153
Ignition coil, cylinder 3
4) Spark plug connection

X6153
1.0
OR

X6153

X6171 (N54 engine)
X6176 (N52 and N51 engines)

1.0
BR

X6153

1.0
WS/GR

3    4    2    1    3

T6152
Ignition coil, cylinder 2
4) Spark plug connection

X6152
1.0
OR

X6152

X6170 (N54 engine)
X6176 (N52 and N51 engines)

1.0
BR

X6152

1.0
WS/BL

3    4    2    1    2

T6151
Ignition coil, cylinder 1
4) Spark plug connection

X6151
1.0
OR

X6151

X6170 (N54 engine)
X6176 (N52 and N51 engines)

1.0
BR

X6151

1.0
WS

3    4    2    1    1

A6000
DME control module

31    31    31    31    31    31

24343, 26280, 26738,
21646, 26272, 26705

BentleyPublishers
.com

## Car access system (CAS), voltage supply

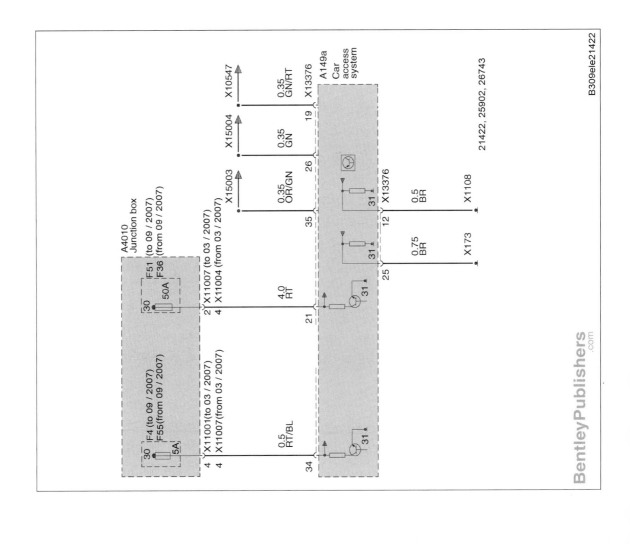

A4010
Junction box

F51 (to 09 / 2007)
F36 (from 09 / 2007)
50A

F4 (to 09 / 2007)
F55 (from 09 / 2007)
5A

X11001 (to 03 / 2007)
X11007 (from 03 / 2007)

X11007 (to 03 / 2007)
X11004 (from 03 / 2007)

0.5
RT/BL

4.0
RT

0.35
OR/GN

0.35
GN

0.35
GN/RT

X15003   X15004   X10547

X13376

A149a
Car access system

0.75
BR

0.5
BR

X173   X1108

X13376

B309ele21422

BentleyPublishers.com

21422, 25902, 26743

**Car access system (CAS), terminal voltage control**

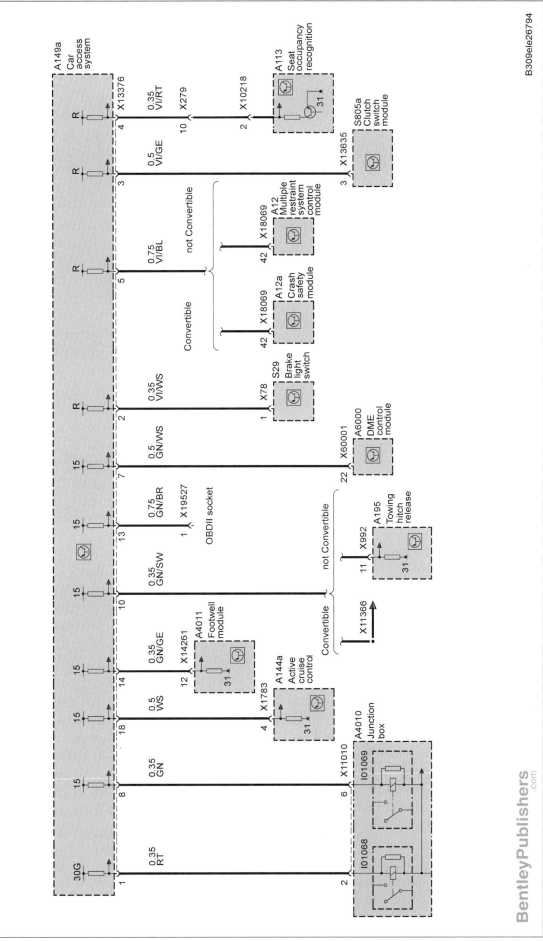

B309ele26794

## Dynamic stability control (DSC), power supply (without Bosch)

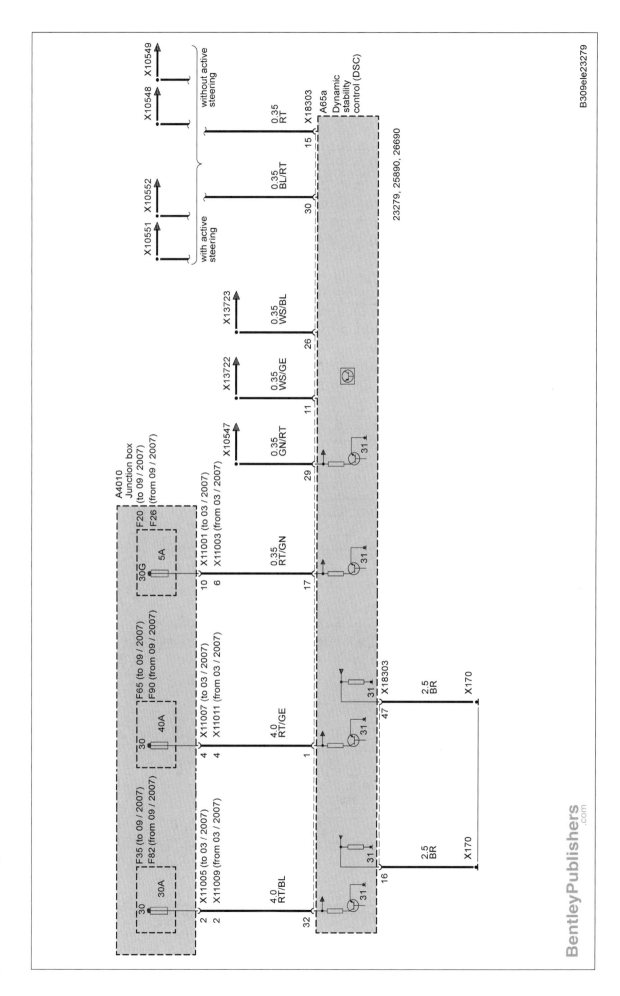

B309ele23279

# Dynamic stability control (DSC), power supply (Bosch)

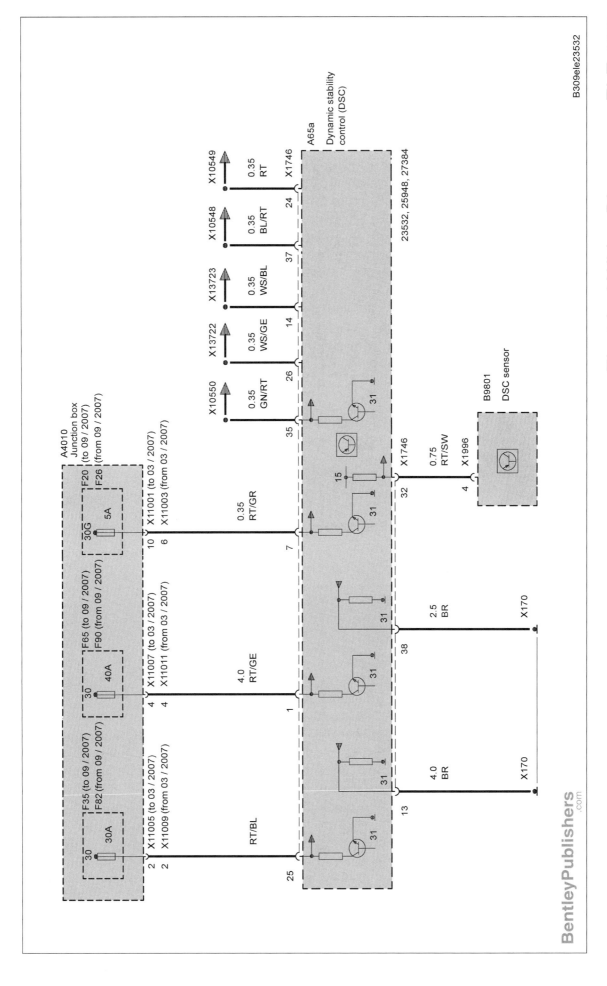

B309ele23532

**Dynamic stability control (DSC), switch functions (without Bosch)**

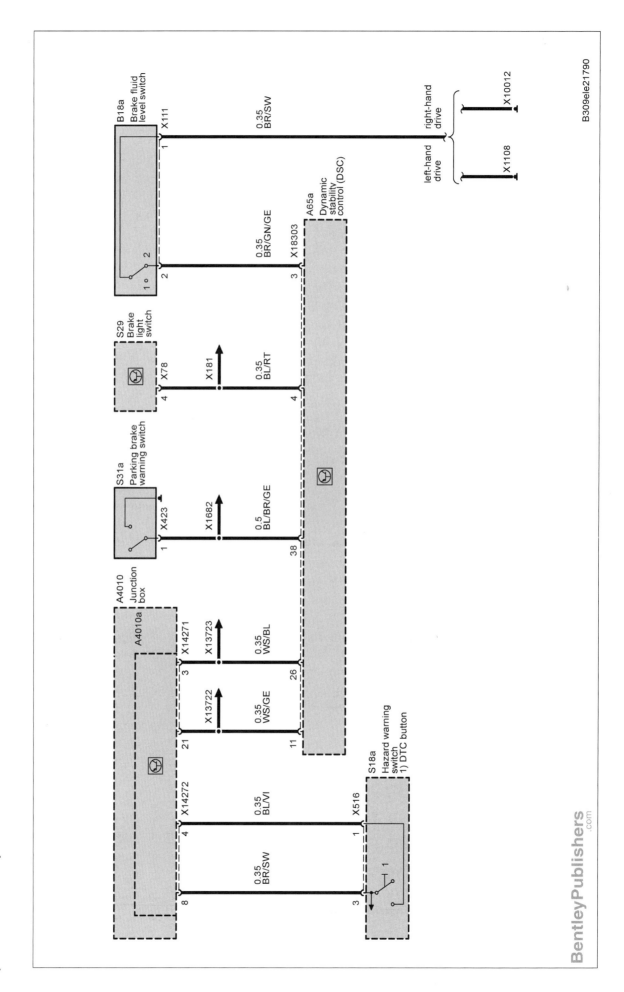

B309ele21790

# Dynamic stability control (DSC), switch functions (Bosch)

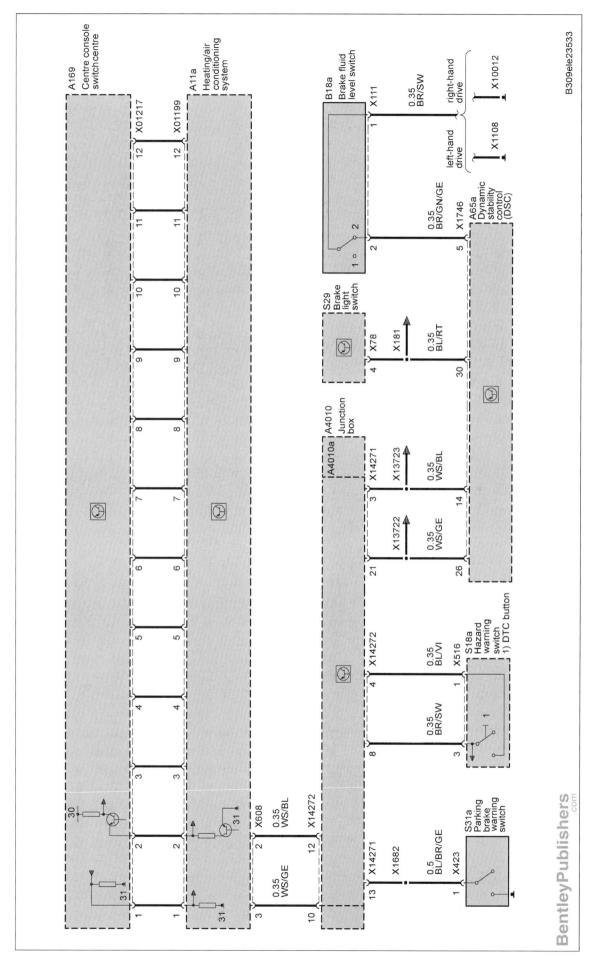

B309ele23533

**Dynamic stability control (DSC), sensor system
(without Bosch)
(page 1 of 2)**

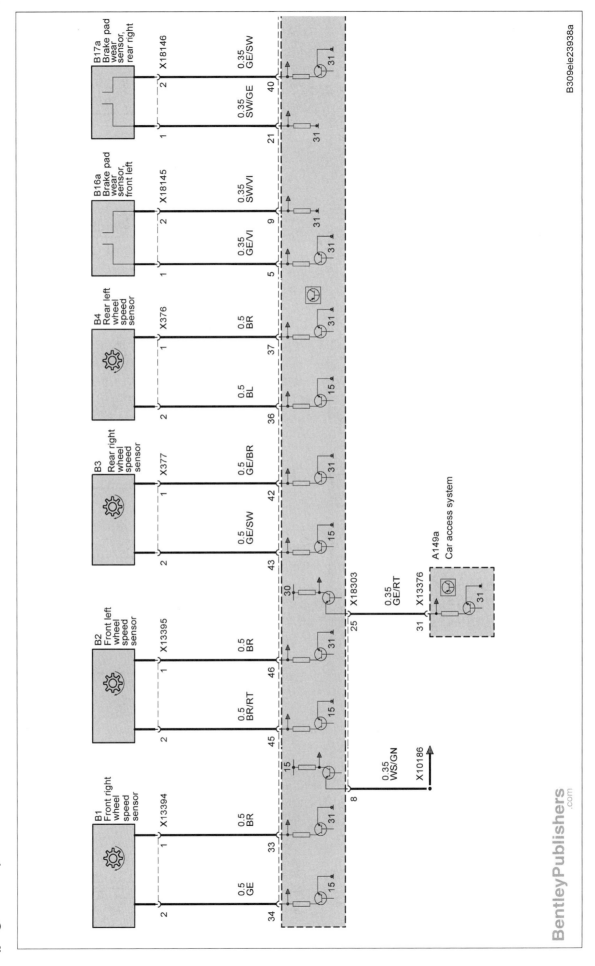

B309ele23938a

Dynamic stability control (DSC), sensor system
(without Bosch)
(page 2 of 2)

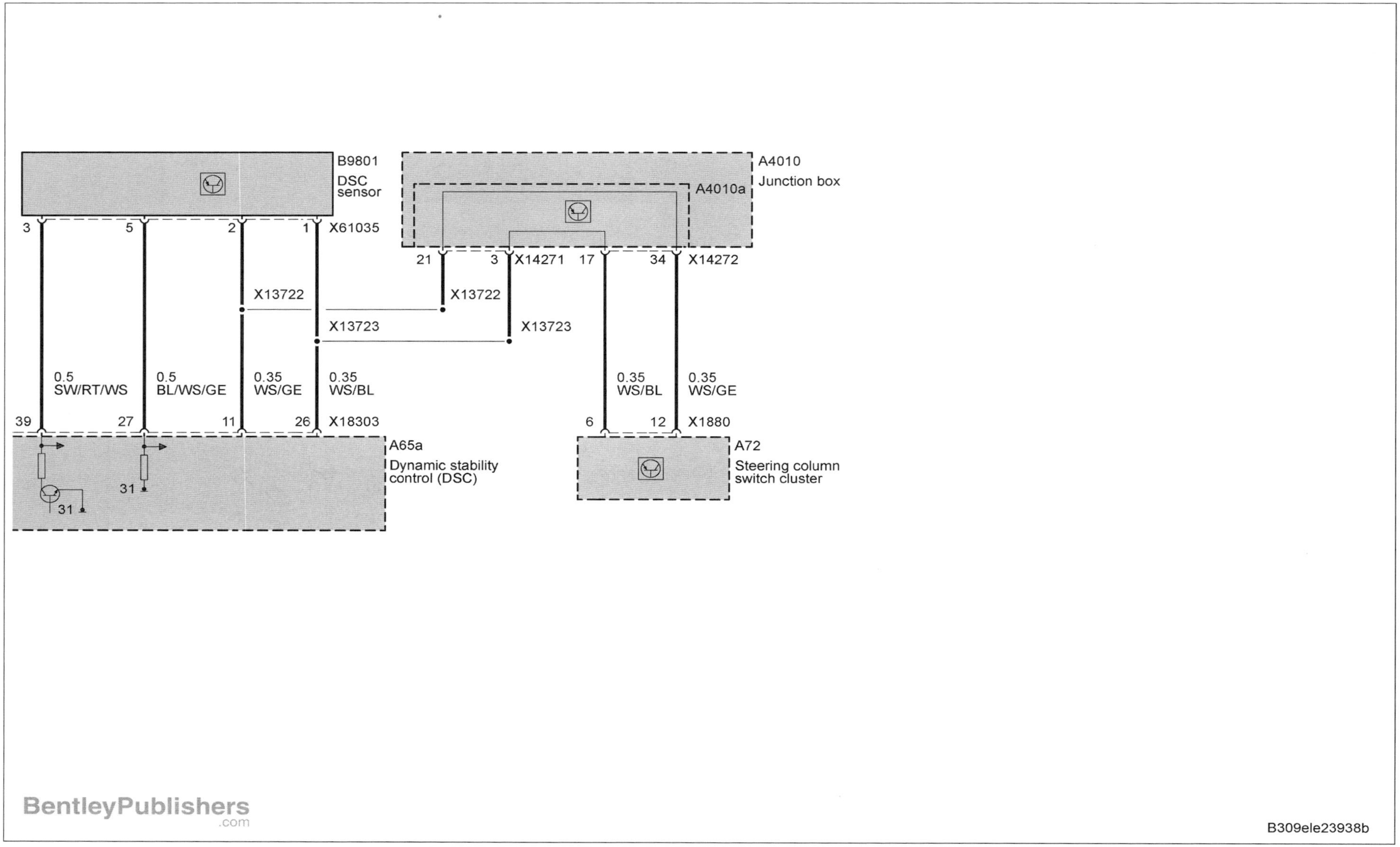

A4010
Junction box

A4010a

X14272

34    0.35
     WS/GE

17    0.35
     WS/BL

X14271

3
X13722

21

X13723

X18303

A72
Steering column
switch cluster

X1880

12    0.35
     WS/GE

6     0.35
     WS/BL

B9801
DSC
sensor

X61035

1    X13723    0.35     X18303
              WS/BL

X13722
2    0.35     26
     WS/GE

11

5    0.5      27
     BL/WS/GE

31

3    0.5      39
     SW/RT/WS

31

A65a
Dynamic stability
control (DSC)

**Dynamic stability control (DSC), sensor system (Bosch)**
**(page 1 of 2)**

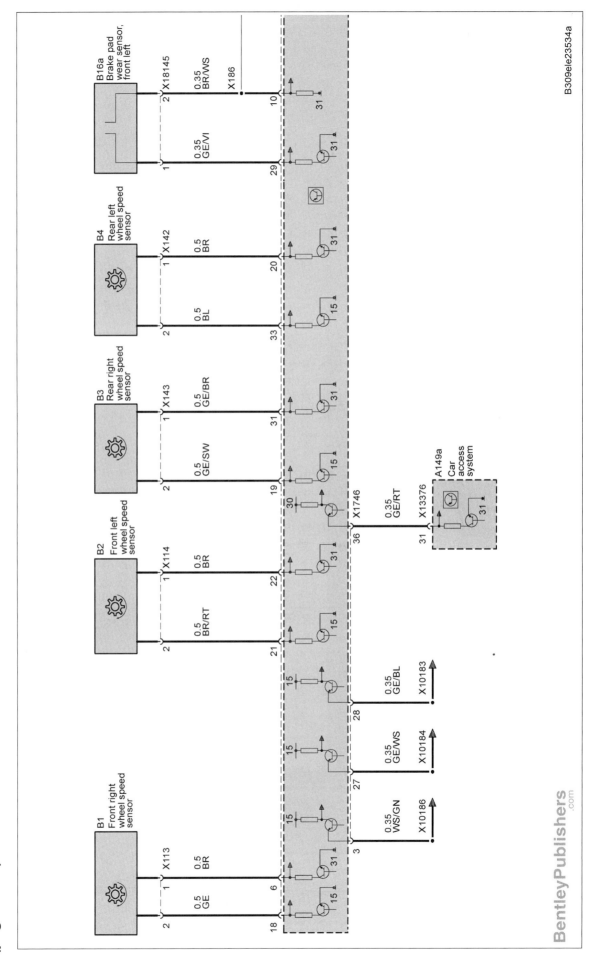

B309ele23534a

**Dynamic stability control (DSC), sensor system (Bosch)**
**(page 2 of 2)**

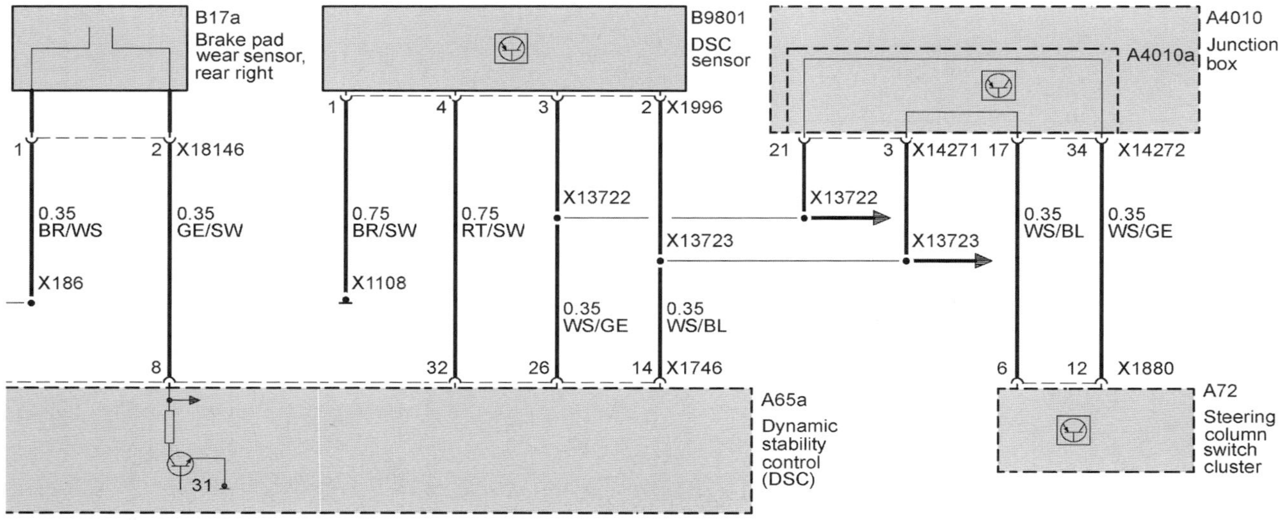

A4010
Junction box

A4010a

X14272

0.35
WS/GE

X1880

34

12

0.35
WS/BL

X14271  17

6

X13723

3

X13722

21

A72
Steering column switch cluster

B9801
DSC sensor

X1996

2

X13723

0.35
WS/BL

X1746

14

3

X13722

0.35
WS/GE

26

4

0.75
RT/SW

32

1

0.75
BR/SW

X1108

B17a
Brake pad wear sensor, rear right

X18146

2

0.35
GE/SW

8

A65a
Dynamic stability control (DSC)

31

1

0.35
BR/WS

X186

Steering column switch cluster (SZL)

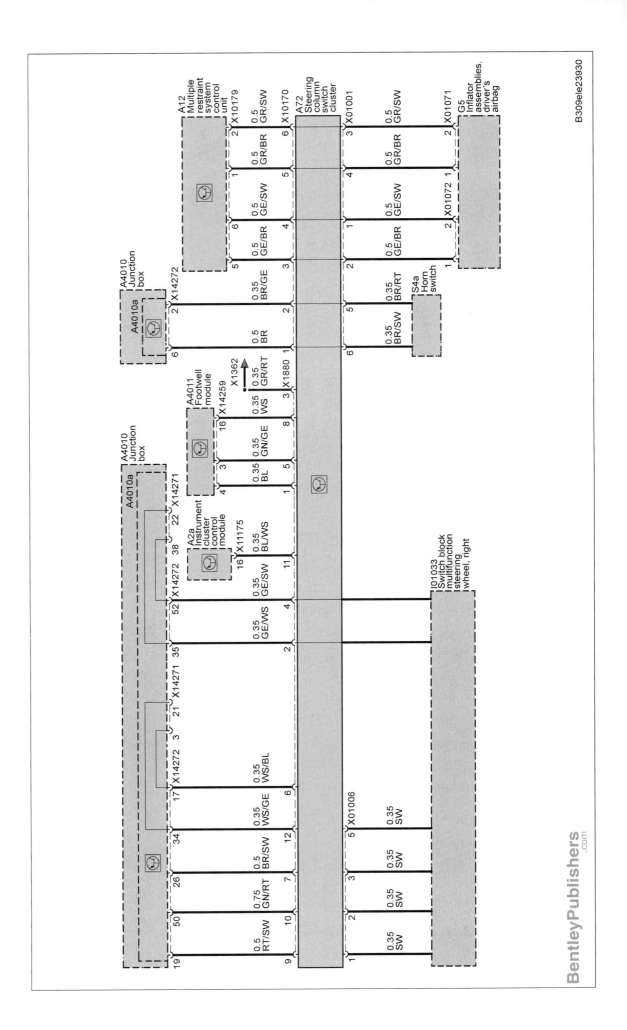

**Steering column switch cluster (SZL), power supply**

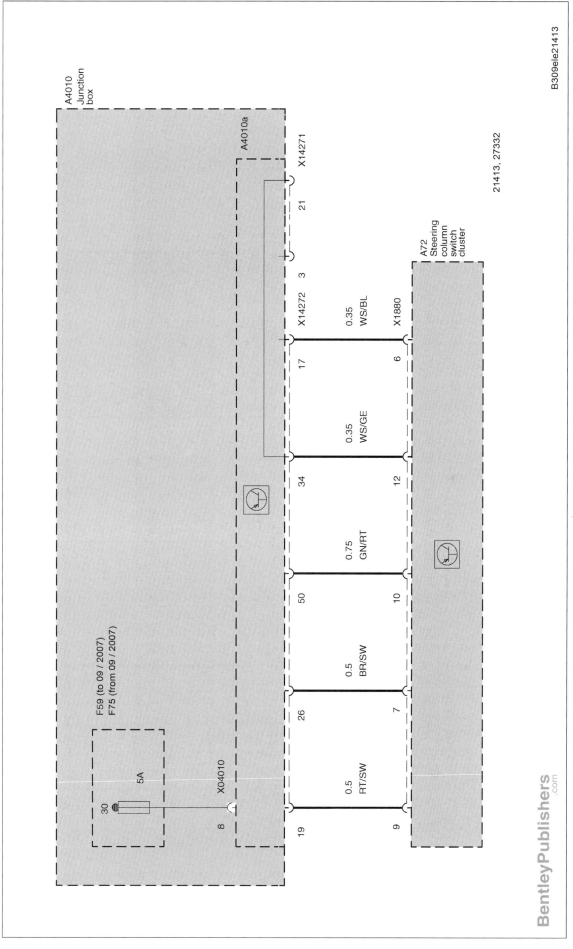

A4010
Junction box

A4010a

X14271

21

X14272   3

17

X14271

0.35
WS/BL

X1880

6

0.35
WS/GE

34

12

F59 (to 09 / 2007)
F75 (from 09 / 2007)

0.75
GN/RT

50

10

5A

X04010

0.5
BR/SW

26

7

30

8

0.5
RT/SW

19

9

A72
Steering
column
switch
cluster

21413, 27332

**Electric steering lock (ELV)**

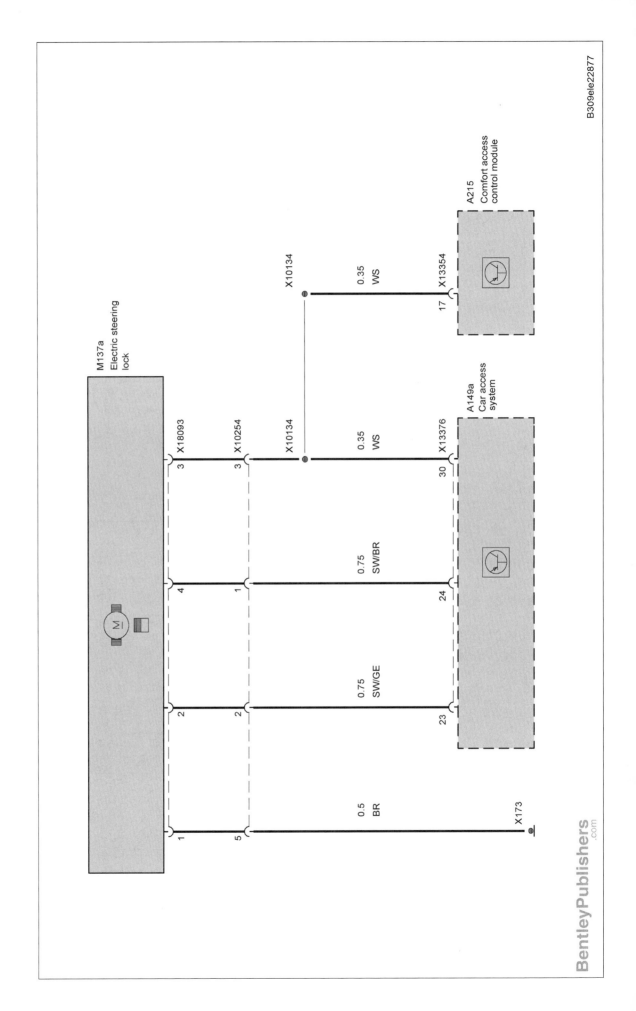

B309ele22877

**B44b**
Electronic
wheel
module
rear right

**B44a**
RDS
transmitter,
rear right

X18038

0.5
GR/BL

X18034

3 — 0.5 GR/BL — 10

2 — 0.5 SW/BL — 26

1 — 0.5 BR/BL — 25

**B45b**
Electronic
wheel
module
rear left

**B45a**
RDS
transmitter,
rear left

X18037

3 — 0.5 GR/GN — 8

2 — 0.5 SW/GN — 24

1 — 0.5 BR/GN — 9

**B46a**
RDC antenna

X18036

3 — 0.5 GR/GN — 

2 — 0.5 SW/GN — 27

1 — 0.5 BR/GN — 12

**B47b**
Electronic
wheel
module
front right

**B47a**
RDS
transmitter,
front right

X18041

3 — 0.5 GR/WS — 7

2 — 0.5 SW/WS — 23

1 — 0.5 BR/WS — 22

**B43b**
Electronic
wheel
module
front left

**B43a**
RDS
transmitter,
front left

X18040

3 — 0.5 GR/GE — 5

2 — 0.5 SW/GE — 21

1 — 0.5 BR/GE — 6

**A85a**
Tire
pressure
control
(RDC)

31 (multiple)

Electrical Wiring Diagrams   ELE-177

B309ele19403

## Tire pressure control (RDC)
(page 2 of 2)

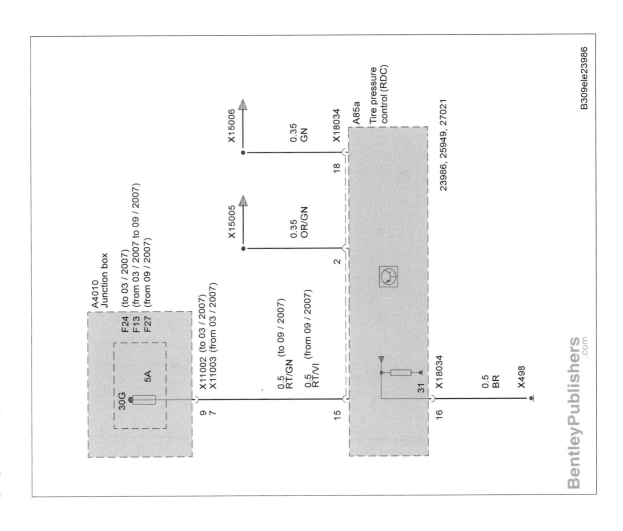

B309ele23986

**Car access system (to 03 / 2007)
(page 1 of 3)**

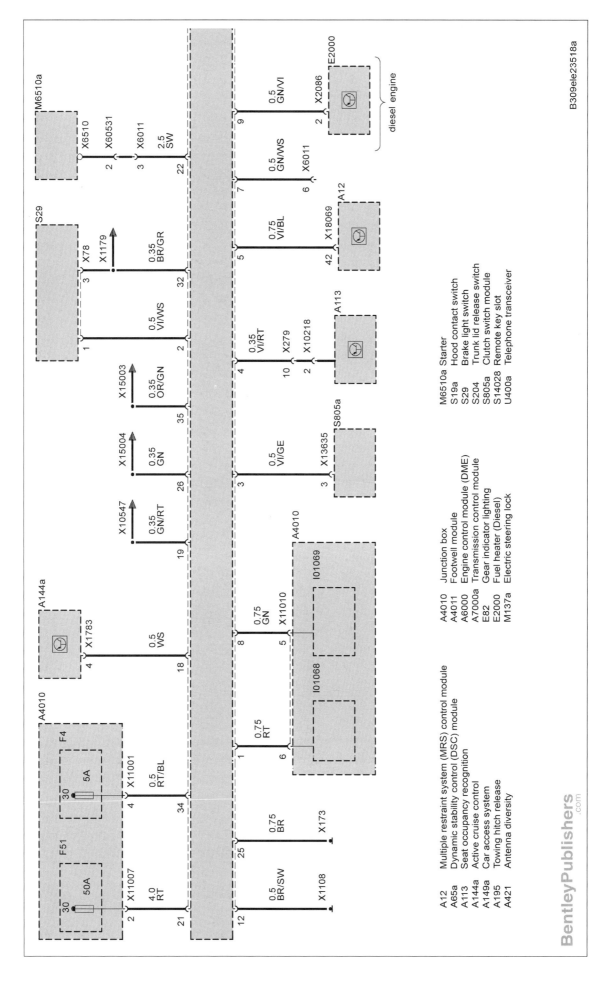

A12    Multiple restraint system (MRS) control module
A65a   Dynamic stability control (DSC) module
A113   Seat occupancy recognition
A144a  Active cruise control
A149a  Car access system
A195   Towing hitch release
A421   Antenna diversity

A4010  Junction box
A4011  Footwell module
A6000  Engine control module (DME)
A7000a Transmission control module
E82    Gear indicator lighting
E2000  Fuel heater (Diesel)
M137a  Electric steering lock

M6510a Starter
S19a   Hood contact switch
S29    Brake light switch
S204   Trunk lid release switch
S805a  Clutch switch module
S14028 Remote key slot
U400a  Telephone transceiver

B309ele23518a

**Car access system (to 03 / 2007)
(page 2 of 3)**

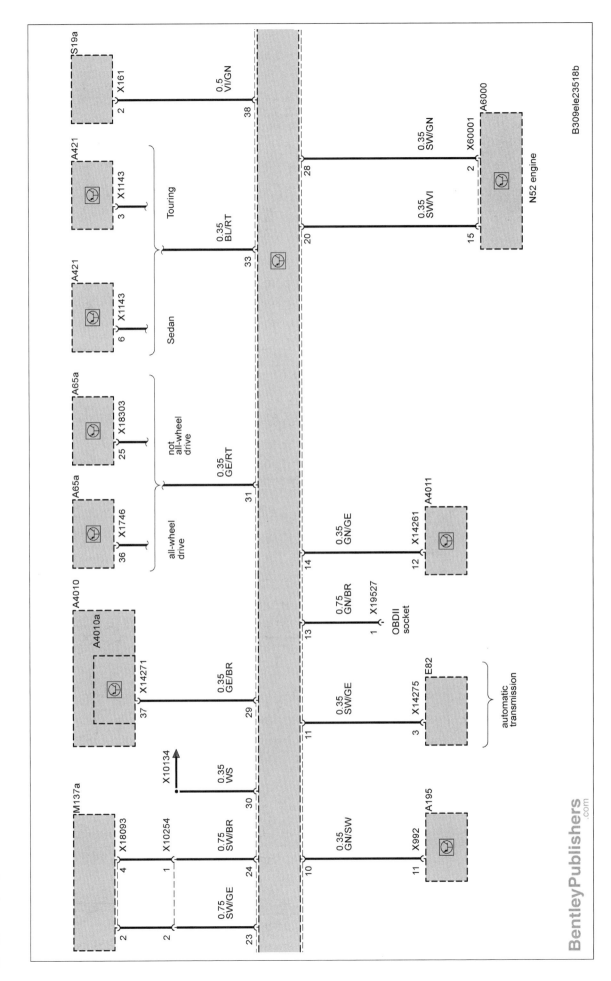

B309ele23518b

**Car access system (to 03 / 2007)**
**(page 3 of 3)**

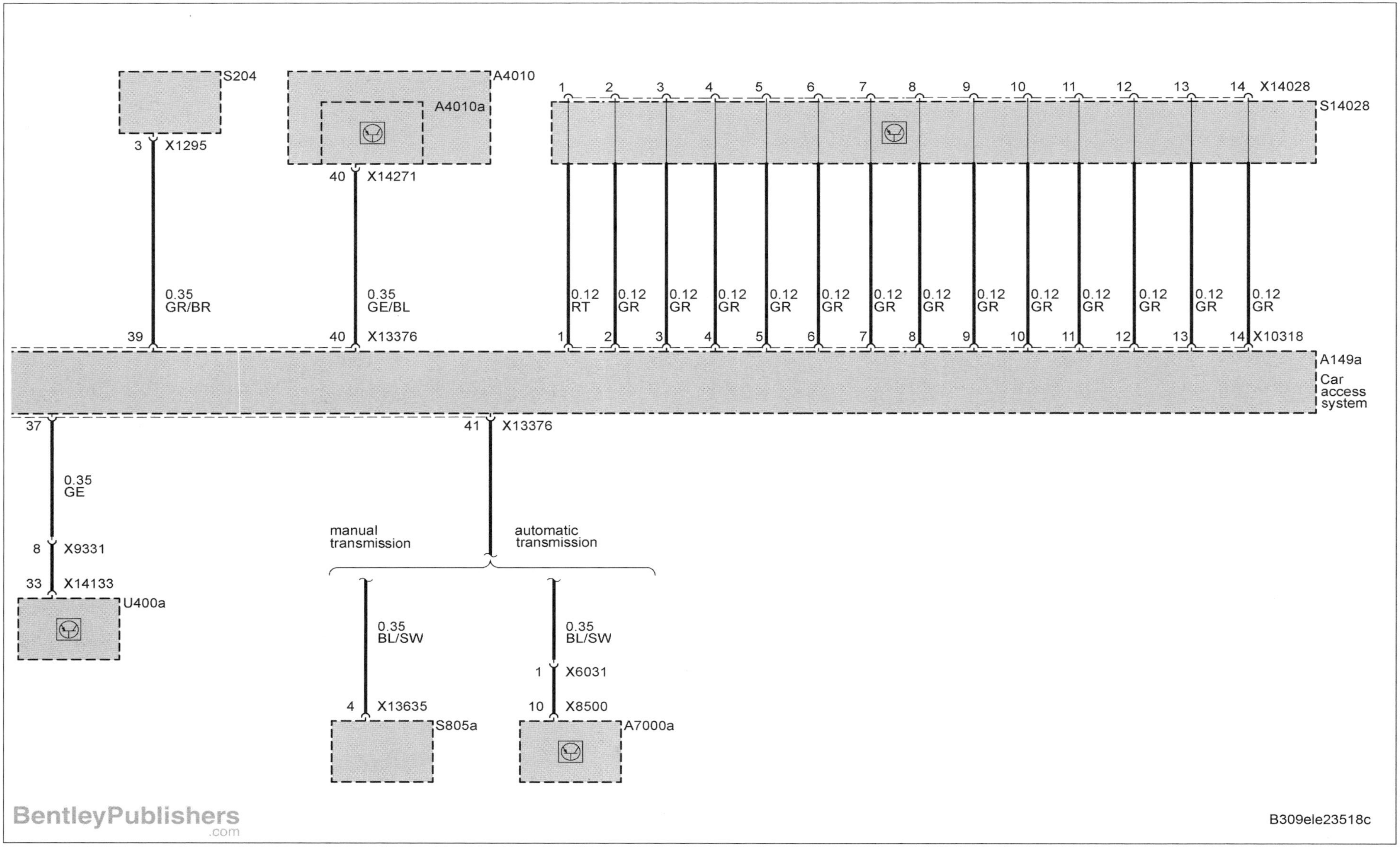

B309ele23518c

S14028
X14028
14 13 12 11 10 9 8 7 6 5 4 3 2 1

0.12 GR · 0.12 GR · 0.12 GR · 0.12 GR · 0.12 GR · 0.12 GR · 0.12 GR · 0.12 GR · 0.12 GR · 0.12 GR · 0.12 GR · 0.12 GR · 0.12 GR · 0.12 RT

X10318
14 13 12 11 10 9 8 7 6 5 4 3 2 1

A149a
Car access system

A4010
A4010a
X14271
40

0.35 GE/BL

X13376
40

S204
X1295
3

0.35 GR/BR

39

X13376
41

automatic transmission

0.35 BL/SW

X6031
1

X8500
10

A7000a

manual transmission

0.35 BL/SW

X13635
4

S805a

37

0.35 GE

X9331
8

X14133
33

U400a

**Car access system (from 03 / 2007)
(page 1 of 3)**

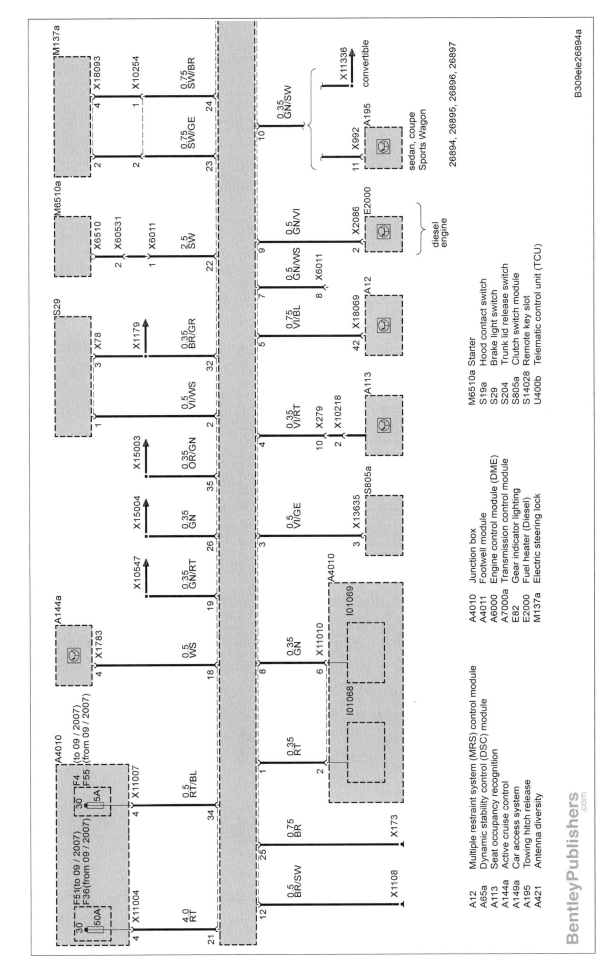

A12    Multiple restraint system (MRS) control module
A65a   Dynamic stability control (DSC) module
A113   Seat occupancy recognition
A144a  Active cruise control
A149a  Car access system
A195   Towing hitch release
A421   Antenna diversity

A4010  Junction box
A4011  Footwell module
A6000  Engine control module (DME)
A7000a Transmission control module
E82    Gear indicator lighting
E2000  Fuel heater (Diesel)
M137a  Electric steering lock

M6510a Starter
S19a   Hood contact switch
S29    Brake light switch
S204   Trunk lid release switch
S805a  Clutch switch module
S14028 Remote key slot
U400b  Telematic control unit (TCU)

26894, 26895, 26896, 26897

B309ele26894a

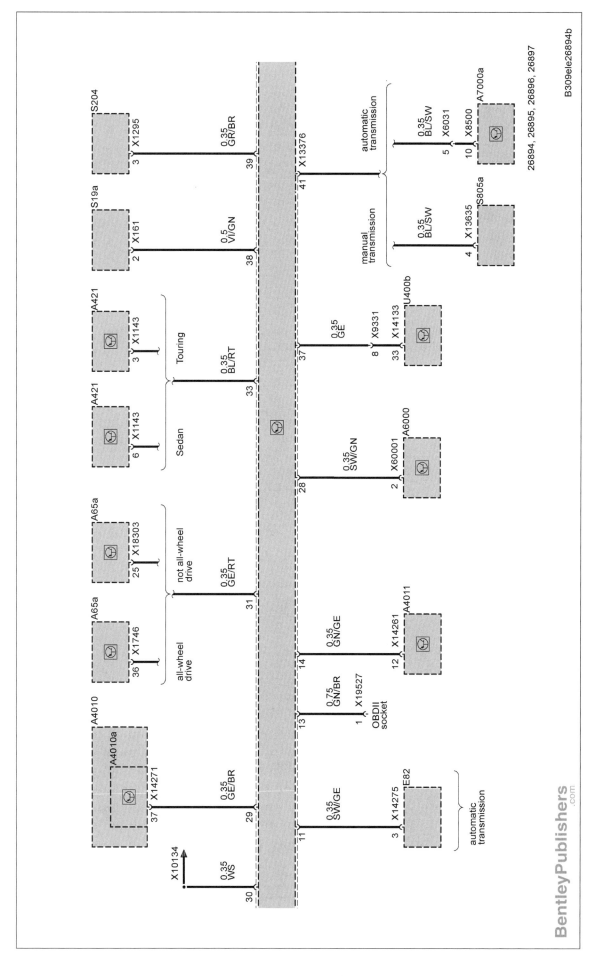

B309ele26894b

26894, 26895, 26896, 26897

**Car access system (from 03 / 2007)
(page 3 of 3)**

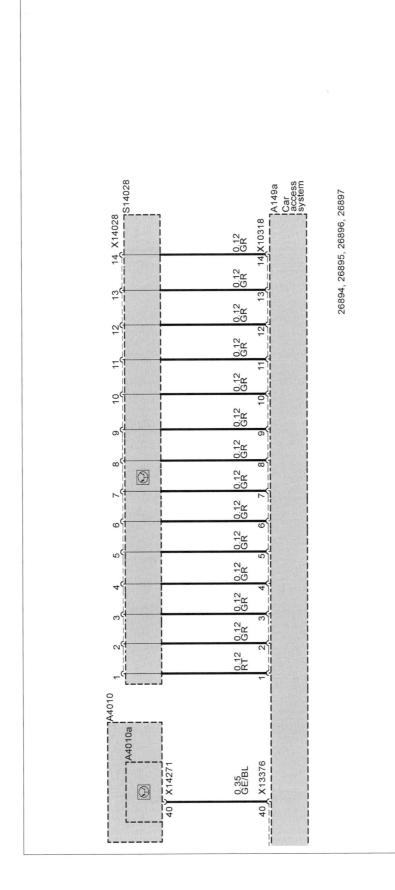

26894, 26895, 26896, 26897

B309ele26894c

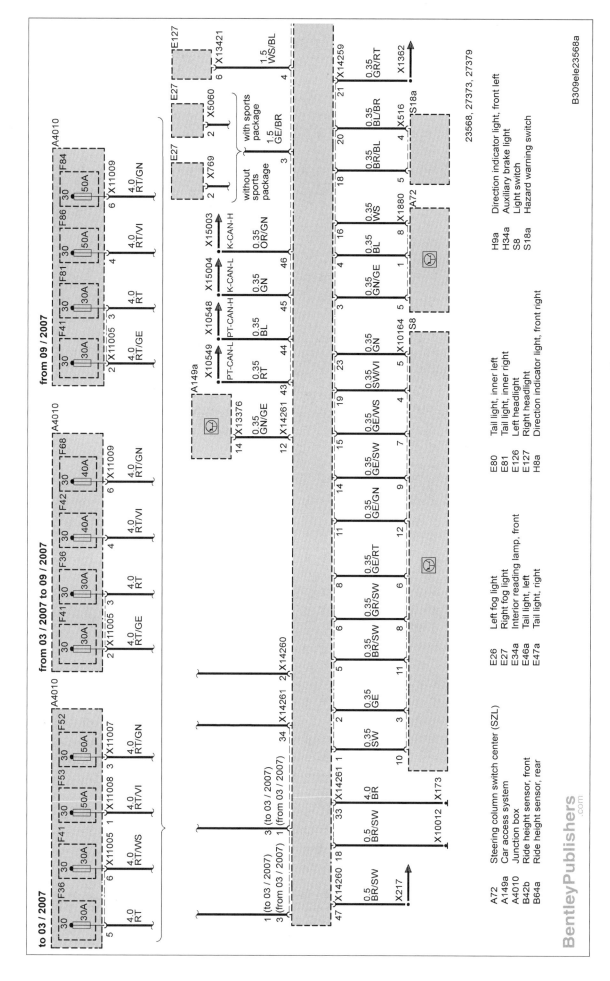

B309ele23568a

23568, 27373, 27379

| | | |
|---|---|---|
| A72 | Steering column switch center (SZL) | |
| A149a | Car access system | |
| A4010 | Junction box | |
| B42b | Ride height sensor, front | |
| B64a | Ride height sensor, rear | |

| | | |
|---|---|---|
| E26 | Left fog light | |
| E27 | Right fog light | |
| E34a | Interior reading lamp, front | |
| E46a | Tail light, left | |
| E47a | Tail light, right | |

| | | |
|---|---|---|
| E80 | Tail light, inner left | |
| E81 | Tail light, inner right | |
| E126 | Left headlight | |
| E127 | Right headlight | |
| H8a | Direction indicator light, front right | |

| | | |
|---|---|---|
| H9a | Direction indicator light, front left | |
| H34a | Auxiliary brake light | |
| S8 | Light switch | |
| S18a | Hazard warning switch | |

**Footwell module, Sedan and Sports Wagon
(page 2 of 4)**

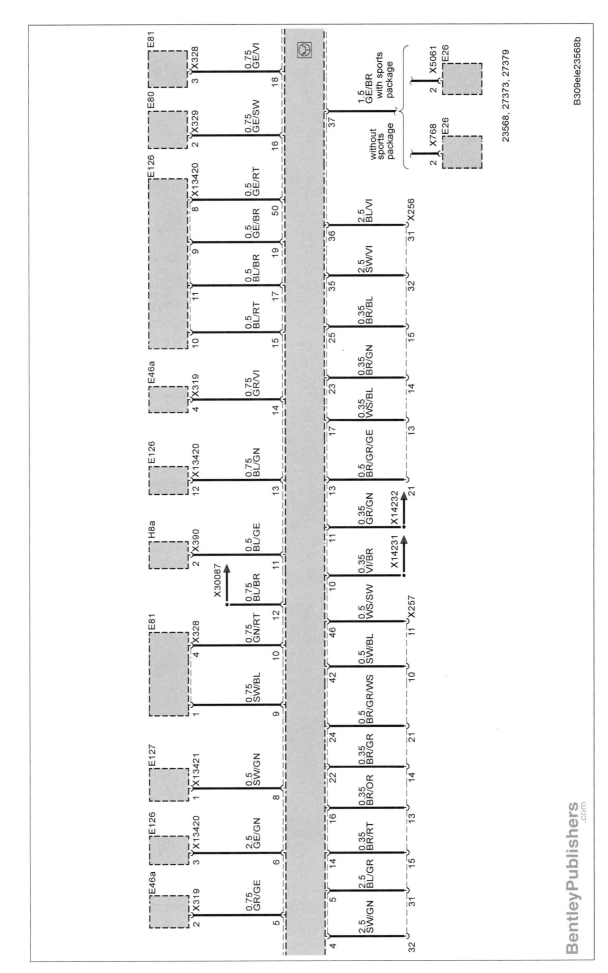

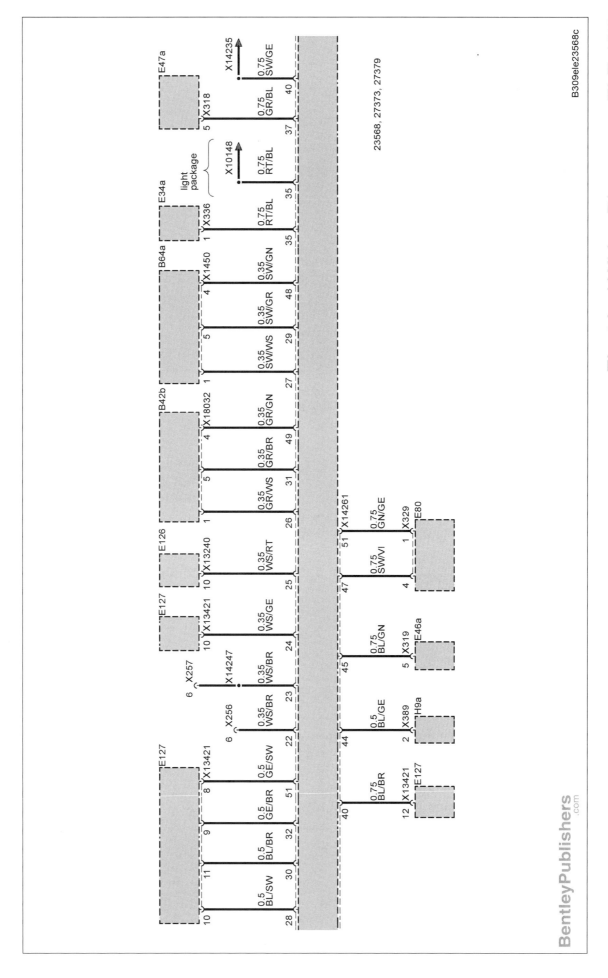

B309ele23568c

**Footwell module, Sedan and Sports Wagon
(page 4 of 4)**

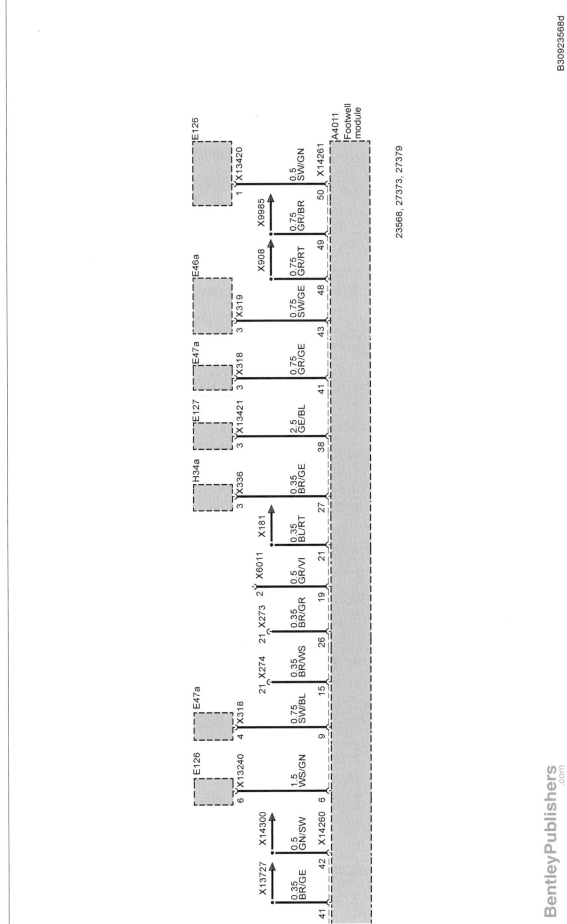

B30923568d

**Footwell module, Coupe (page 1 of 4)**

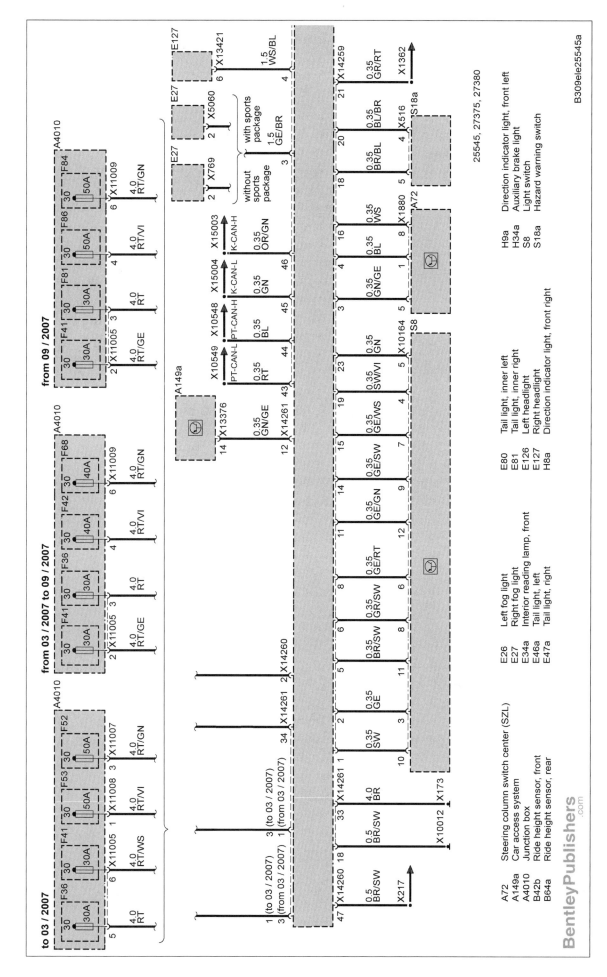

A72 Steering column switch center (SZL)
A149a Car access system
A4010 Junction box
B42b Ride height sensor, front
B64a Ride height sensor, rear

E26 Left fog light
E27 Right fog light
E34a Interior reading lamp, front
E46a Tail light, left
E47a Tail light, right

E80 Tail light, inner left
E81 Tail light, inner right
E126 Left headlight
E127 Right headlight
H8a Direction indicator light, front right

H9a Direction indicator light, front left
H34a Auxiliary brake light
S8 Light switch
S18a Hazard warning switch

25545, 27375, 27380

B309ele25545a

BentleyPublishers.com

**Footwell module, Coupe**
**(page 2 of 4)**

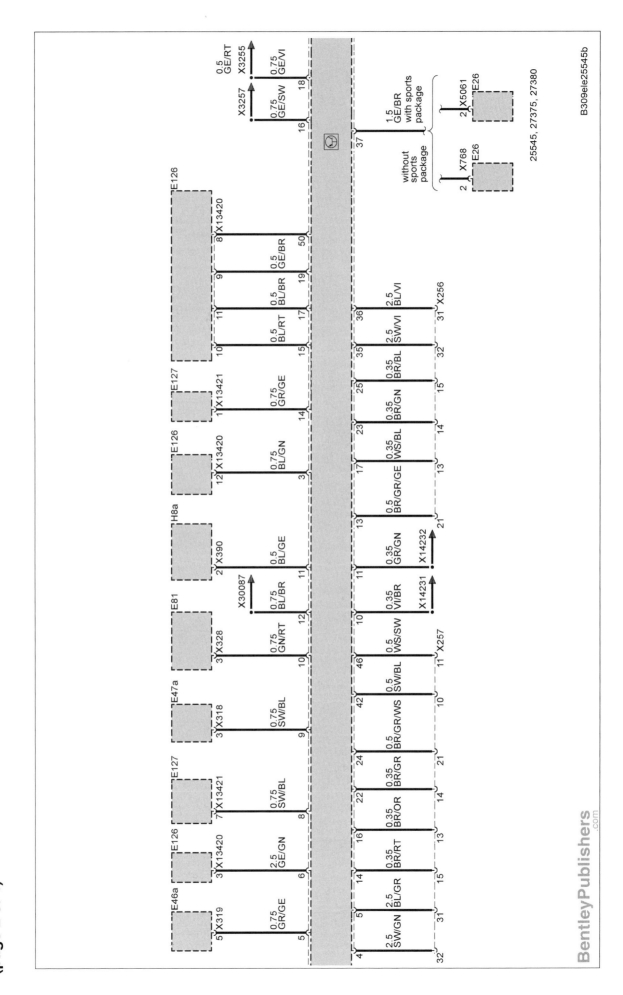

B309ele25545b

## Footwell module, Coupe
(page 3 of 4)

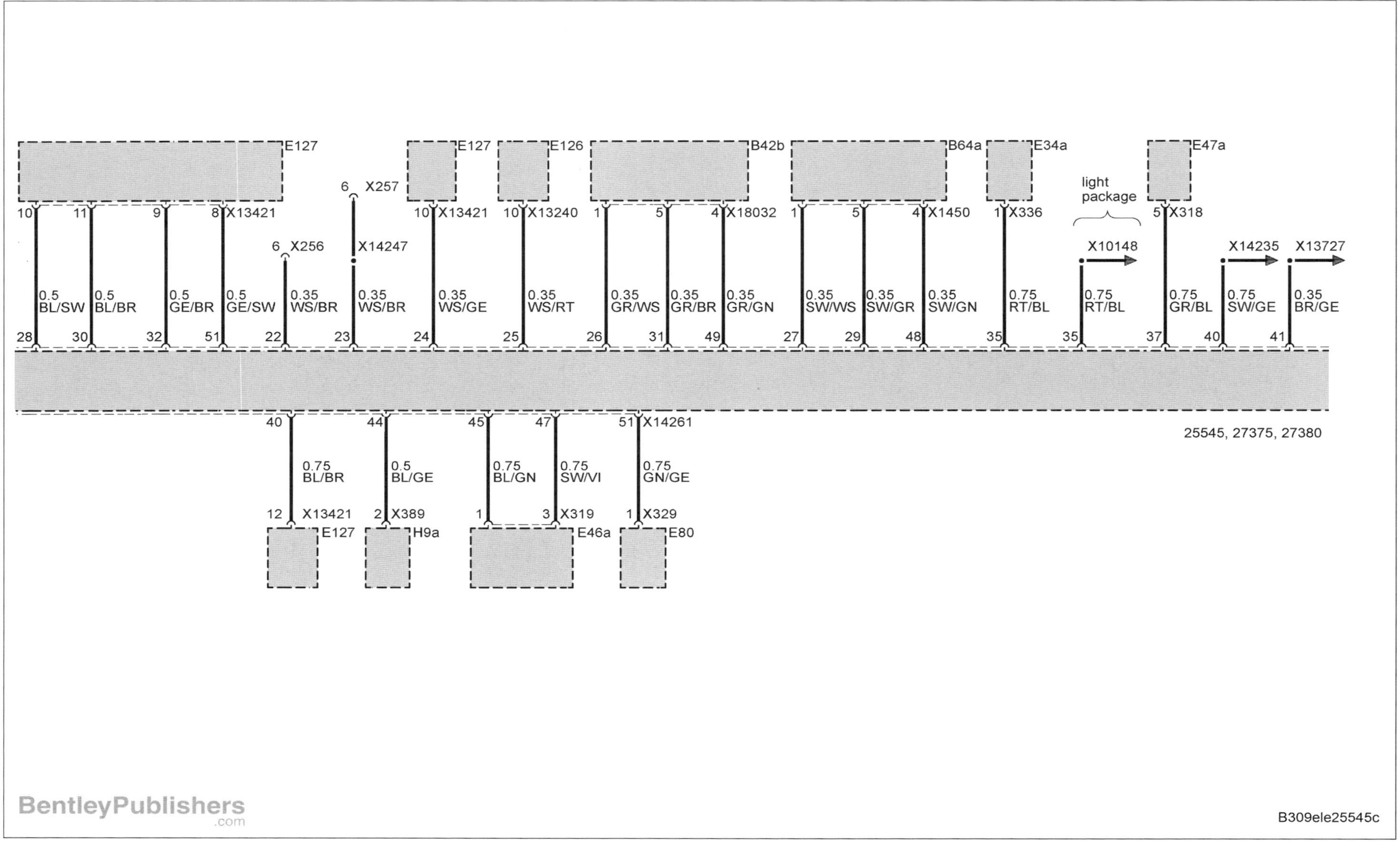

**Footwell module, Coupe
(page 4 of 4)**

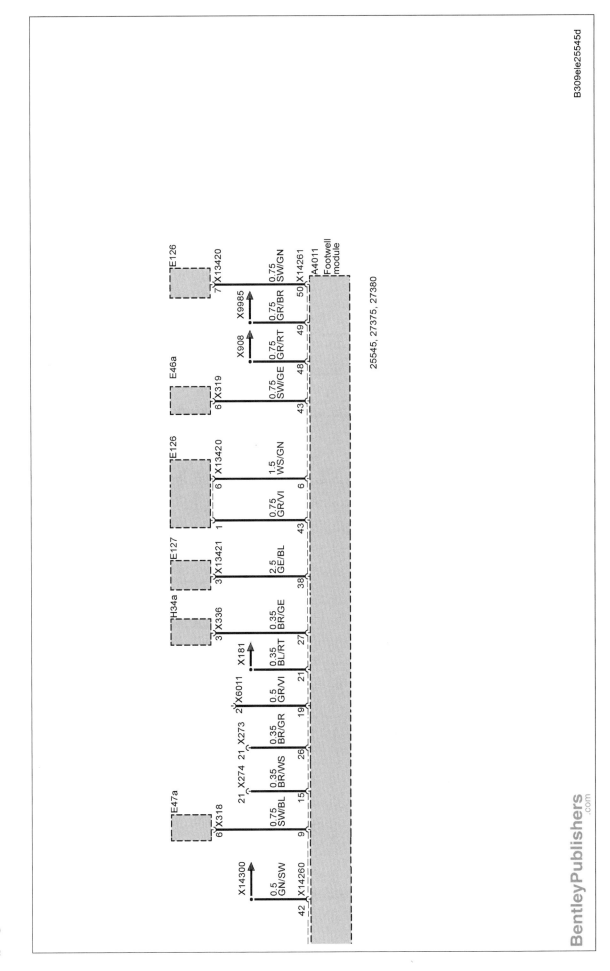

B309ele25545d

**Footwell module, Convertible (page 1 of 4)**

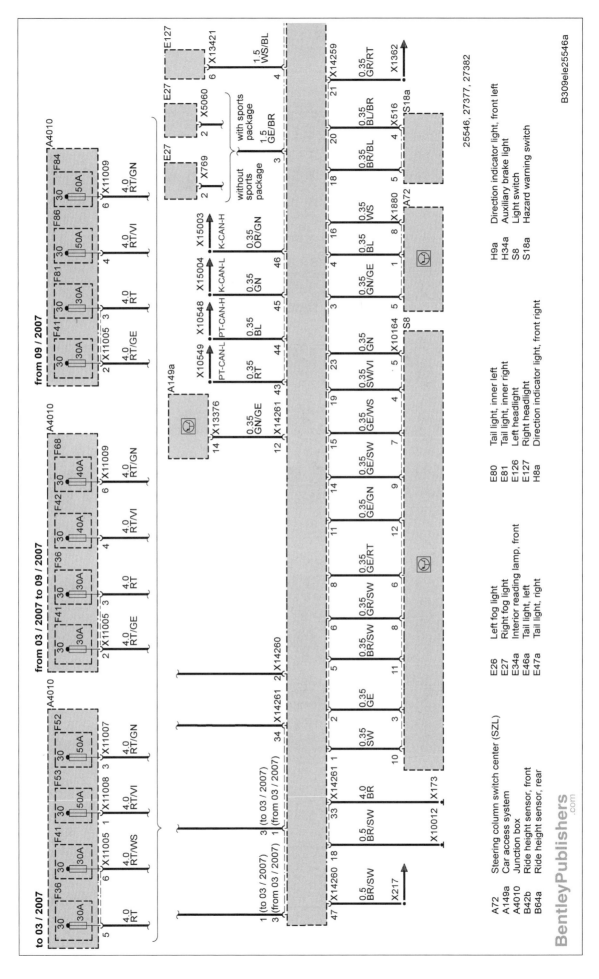

25546, 27377, 27382

A72    Steering column switch center (SZL)
A149a   Car access system
A4010   Junction box
B42b    Ride height sensor, front
B64a    Ride height sensor, rear

E26    Left fog light
E27    Right fog light
E34a   Interior reading lamp, front
E46a   Tail light, left
E47a   Tail light, right

E80    Tail light, inner left
E81    Tail light, inner right
E126   Left headlight
E127   Right headlight
H8a    Direction indicator light, front right

H9a    Direction indicator light, front left
H34a   Auxiliary brake light
S8     Light switch
S18a   Hazard warning switch

Electrical Wiring Diagrams    ELE-193

B309ele25546a

**Footwell module, Convertible
(page 2 of 4)**

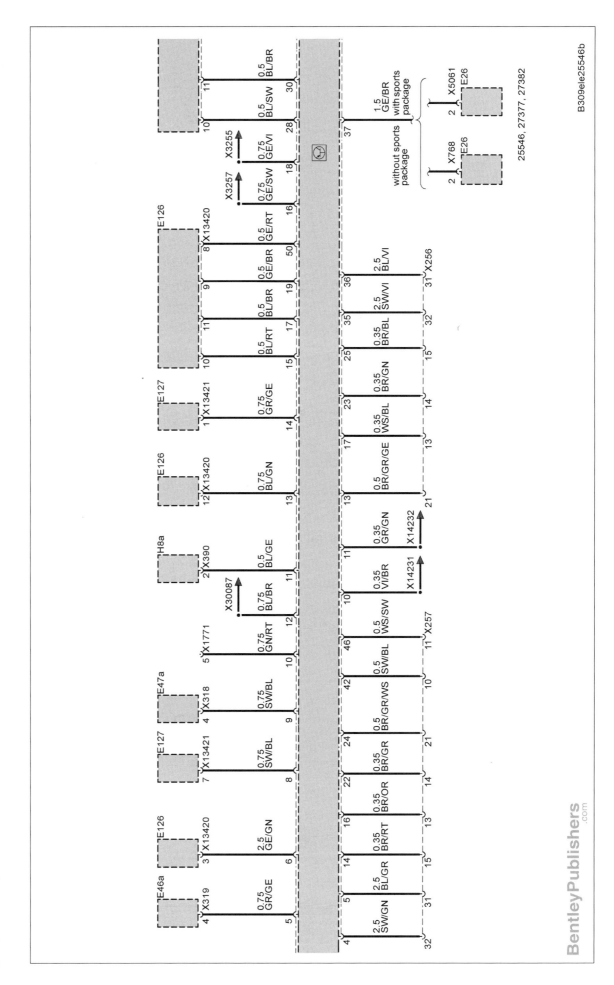

B309ele25546b

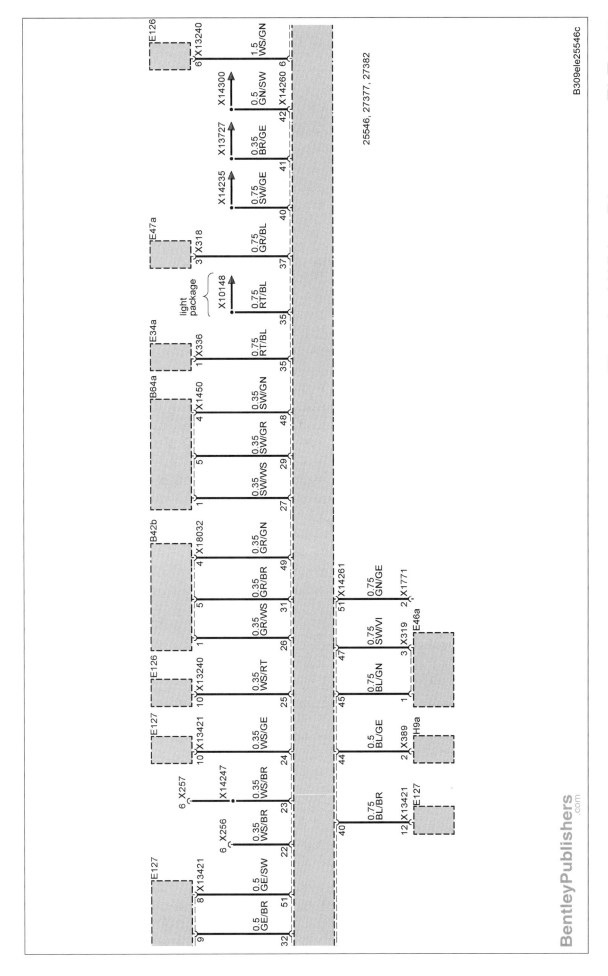

B309ele25546c

**Footwell module, Convertible
(page 4 of 4)**

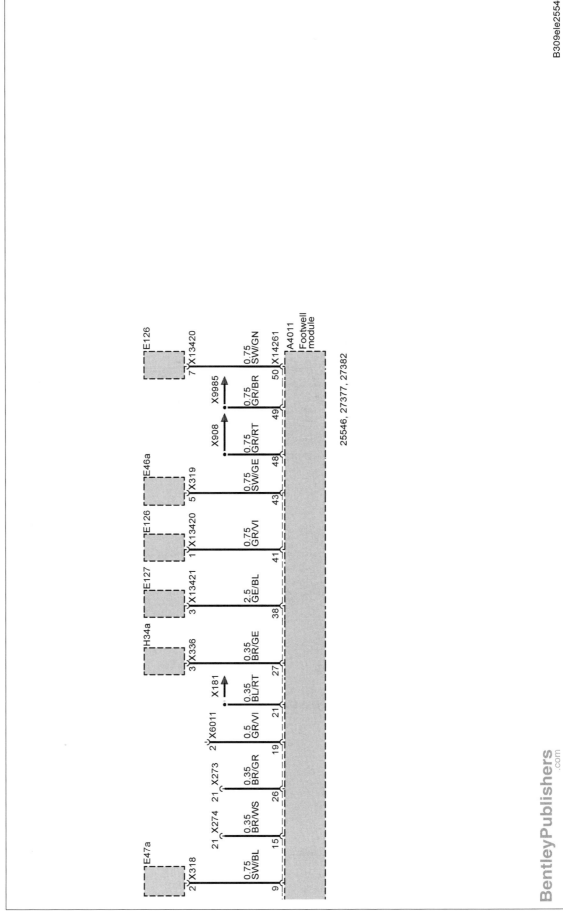

B309ele25546d

**Power window inputs**
**Sedan and Sports Wagon**
**(page 1 of 2)**

A4010 Junction box
A4010a

S42a Power window switch, rear passenger's side
S41a Power window switch, rear driver's side
S127 Power window switch, passenger's door

A4011 Footwell module
A23b Driver's switch cluster

A4010 Junction box
F21 (to 09 / 2007)
F66 (from 09 / 2007)
30G  7.5A

X11002 (to 03 / 2007)
X11008 (from 03 / 2007 to 09 / 2007)
X11002 (from 03 / 2007 to 09 / 2007)

0.5 GR/RT  X274  X647
0.5 WS/GE  X14271
0.5 BR  X835
0.5 GR/RT  X908  X273  X645
0.5 WS/GR
0.5 BR  X834
0.35 GR/RT  X908  X256  X324
0.35 GR/BL
0.35 BR  X891

0.35 WS/BR  X14260  X14247  X257  X10725
0.35 GR/RT  X908  X14261
0.35 BR  X849  X10725
0.75 RT/GR

21798, 26883, 26884

B309ele21798

**Power window outputs
Sedan and Sports Wagon
(page 2 of 2)**

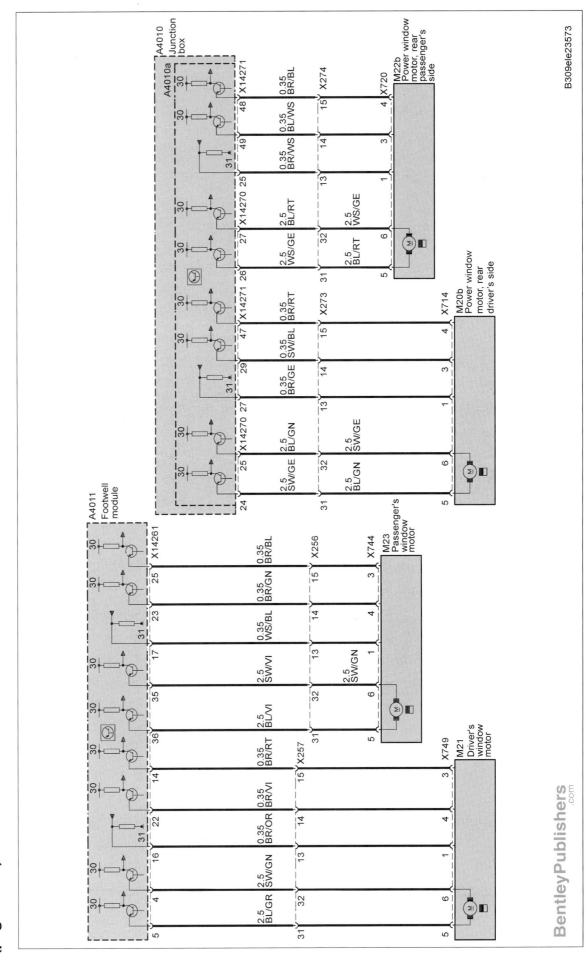

**Power window inputs**
**Coupe and Convertible**
**(page 1 of 2)**

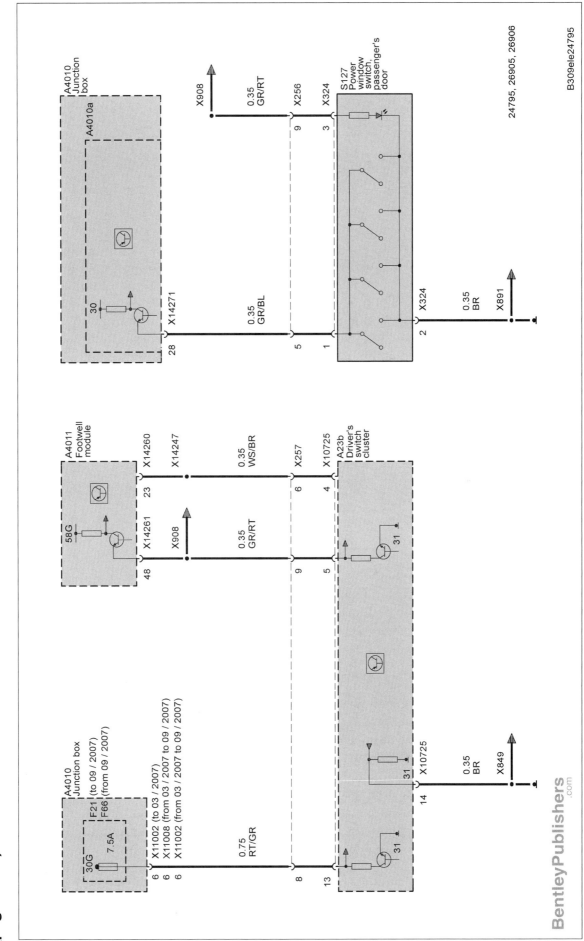

24795, 26905, 26906

B309ele24795

**Power window outputs
Coupe and Convertible
(page 2 of 2)**

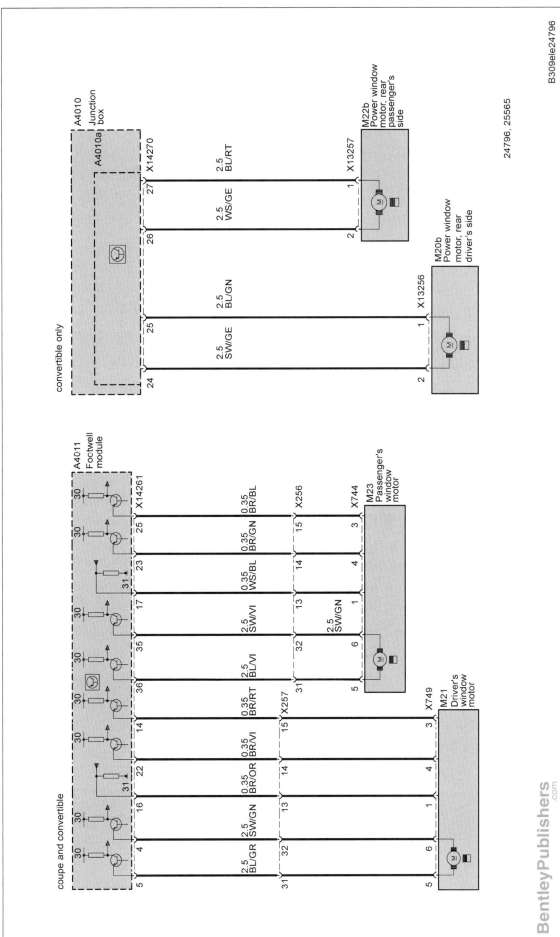

B309ele24796

24796, 25565

**Central locking system - inputs
(page 1 of 4)**

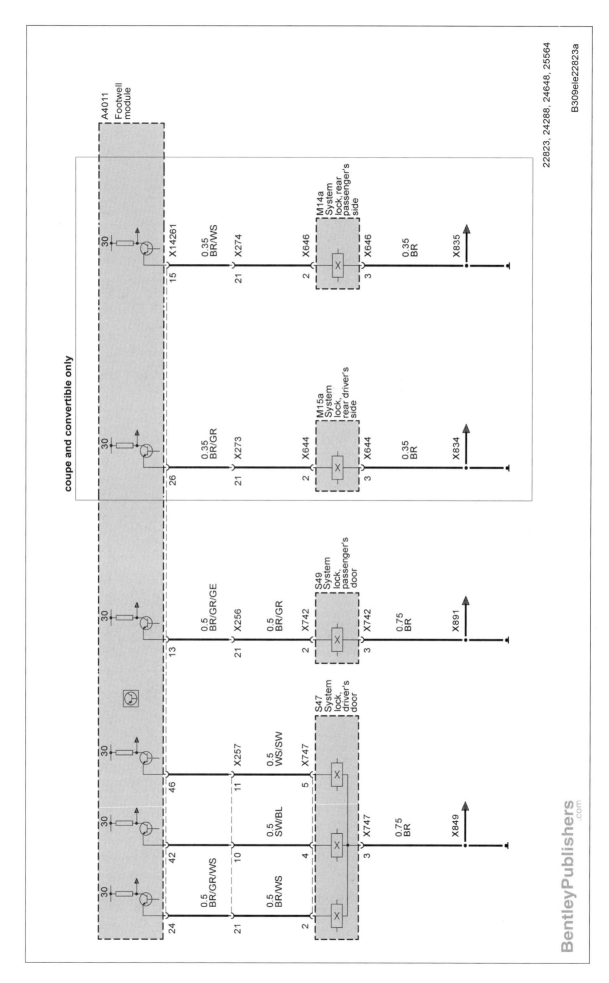

22823, 24288, 24648, 25564

B309ele22823a

Electrical Wiring Diagrams   ELE-201

**Central locking system - inputs
(page 2 of 4)**

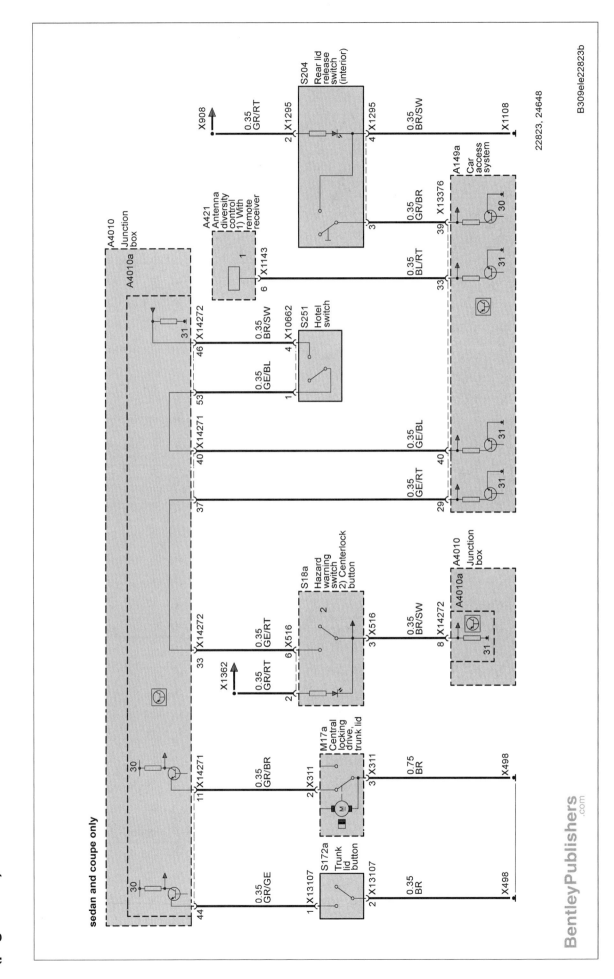

B309ele22823b

22823, 24648

**Central locking system - inputs (page 3 of 4)**

Sports Wagon only

X908

0.35 GR/RT · 2 · X1295 · S204 Rear lid release switch (interior) · 4 · X1295 · 0.35 BR/SW · X1108

A149a Car access system · 24288

A4010 Junction box · A4010a

A421 Antenna diversity control 1) With remote receiver · 1 · X1143 · 6

31 · X14272 · 46

0.35 BR/SW · X10662 · S251 Hotel switch · 4

0.35 GE/BL · 53 · 1

31 · 0.35 GR/BR · X13376 · 39 · 30

0.35 BL/RT · 33 · 31

X14271 · 40 · 0.35 GE/BL · 40 · 31

37 · 0.35 GE/RT · 29 · 31

X14272 · 33 · 0.35 GE/RT · 6 · X516 · S18a Hazard warning switch 2) Centerlock button · 2 · 3 · X516 · 0.35 BR/SW · 8 · X14272

X1362 · 0.35 GR/RT · 2 · 6 · A4010 Junction box · A4010a · 31

30 · X14271 · 50 · 0.5 BR/GE · 1 · X13059 · M96a Rear window lock · 3 · X13059 · 0.75 BR · X498

30 · 32 · 0.35 BR/RT · 1 · X30055 · A420 Wave trap · 3 · X30056 · 2 · X1265 · S147a Rear window button

30 · X14271 · 11 · 0.35 GR/BR · 2 · X311 · M17a Central locking drive, trunk lid · 3 · X311 · 0.75 BR · X498

30 · 44 · 0.35 GR/GE · 1 · X13107 · S172a Trunk lid button · 2 · X13107 · 0.35 BR · X498

BentleyPublishers.com

Electrical Wiring Diagrams ELE-203

B309ele22823c

**Central locking system - inputs
(page 4 of 4)**

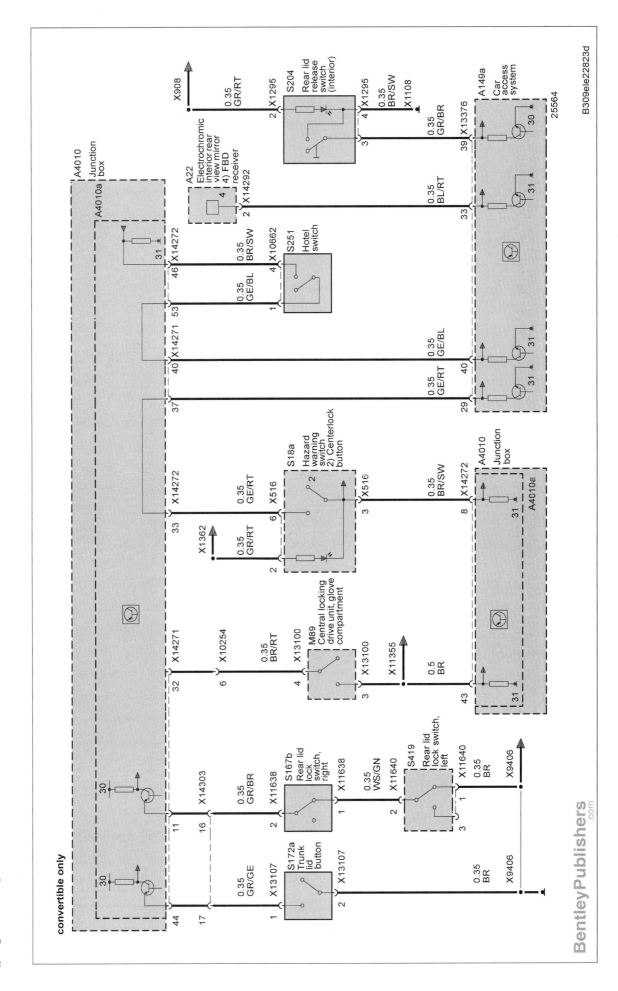

B309ele22823d

**Central locking system - outputs**
**Sedan**
**(page 1 of 4)**

A4010 Junction box

A4010a

X14270

20  0.75 BL  X312  M16 Central locking drive, fuel filler flap

16  0.75 SW  2

1

21793, 27340

12  0.5 GR/GN  X311  M17a Central locking drive, trunk lid

4  X311  3  0.75 BR  X498

44  X273  18  0.75 WS  X644  M15a System lock, rear driver's side

46  19  0.75 BL  6

42  20  0.75 SW  7

8

45  X274  18  0.75 WS  X646  M14a System lock, rear passenger's side

47  19  0.75 BL  6

43  20  0.75 SW  7

8

F57 (to 09 / 2007)
F73 (from 09 / 2007)

15A  X04010  5

17  X256  18  0.75 WS  X742  S49 System lock, passenger's door

19  19  0.75 BL  6

15  20  0.75 SW  7

8

F56 (to 09 / 2007)
F72 (from 09 / 2007)

15A  6

36  X257  18  0.75 WS  X747  S47 System lock, driver's door

18  19  0.75 BL  6

14  20  0.75 SW  7

8

B309ele21793

**Central locking system - outputs
Sports Wagon
(page 2 of 4)**

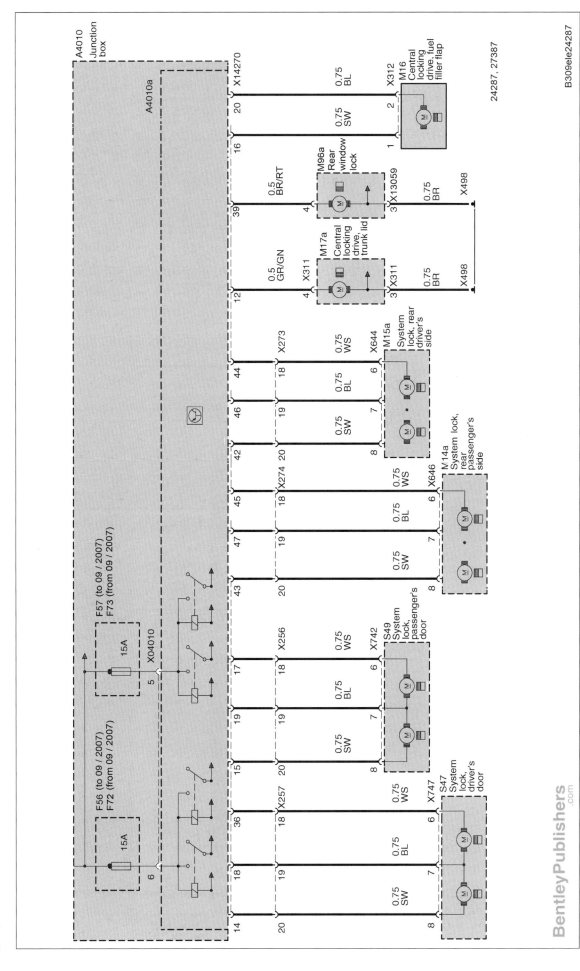

**Central locking system - outputs**
**Coupe**
**(page 3 of 4)**

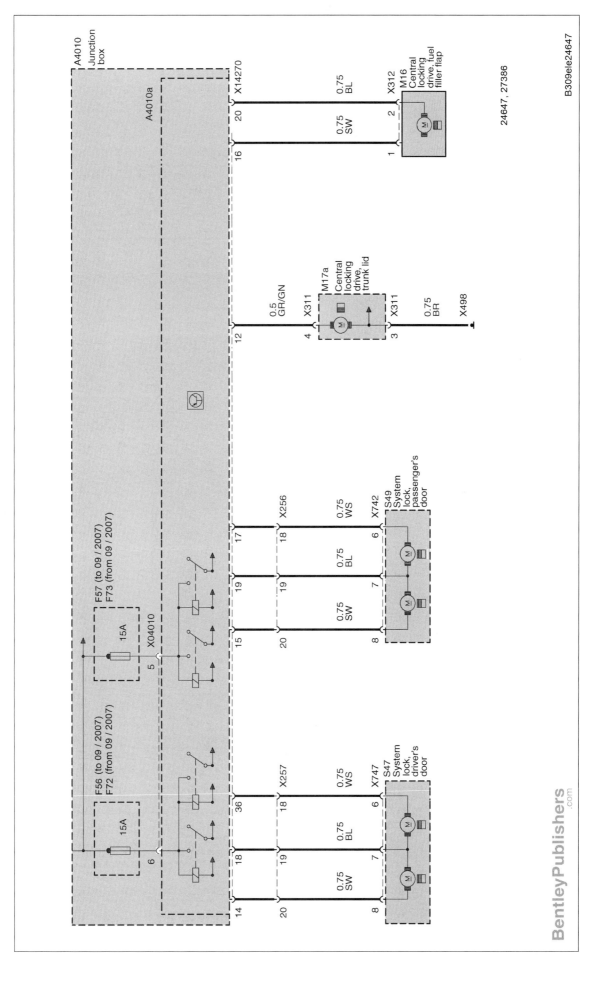

**Central locking system - outputs
Convertible
(page 4 of 4)**

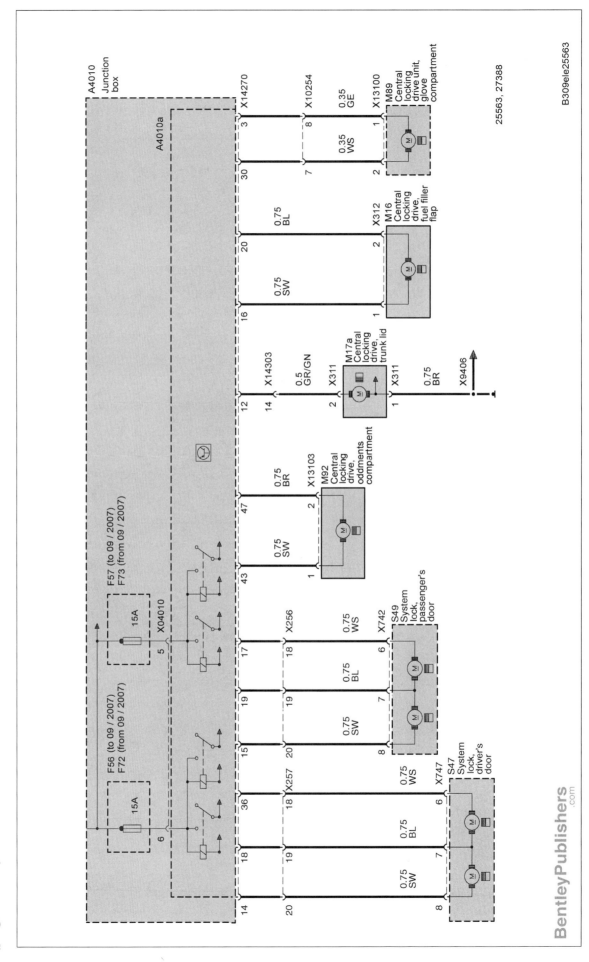

25563, 27388

B309ele25563

**Low beam / high beam
with xenon lights**

**Low beam / high beam
without xenon lights**

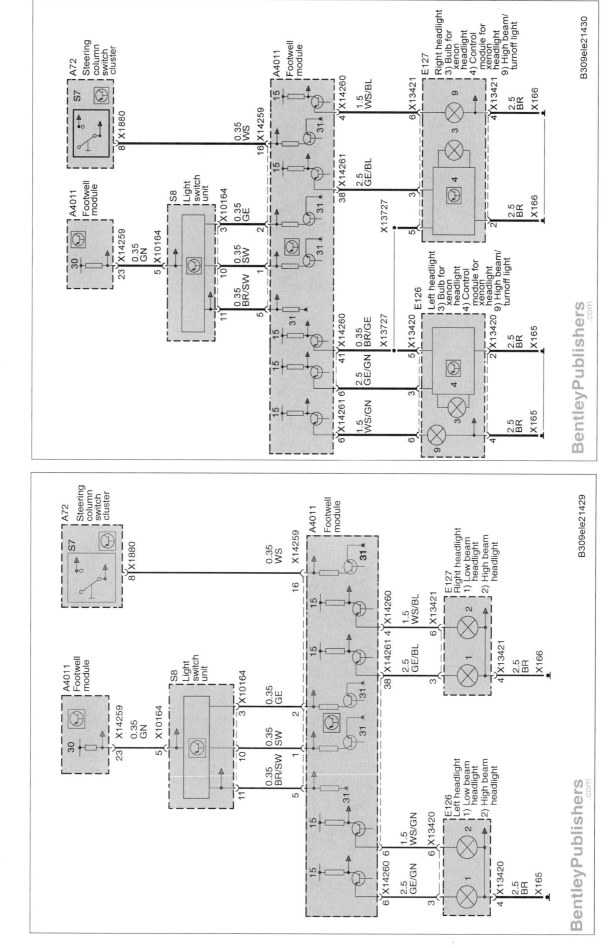

BentleyPublishers.com

**Side light, parking light**
**Sedan and Sports Wagon**

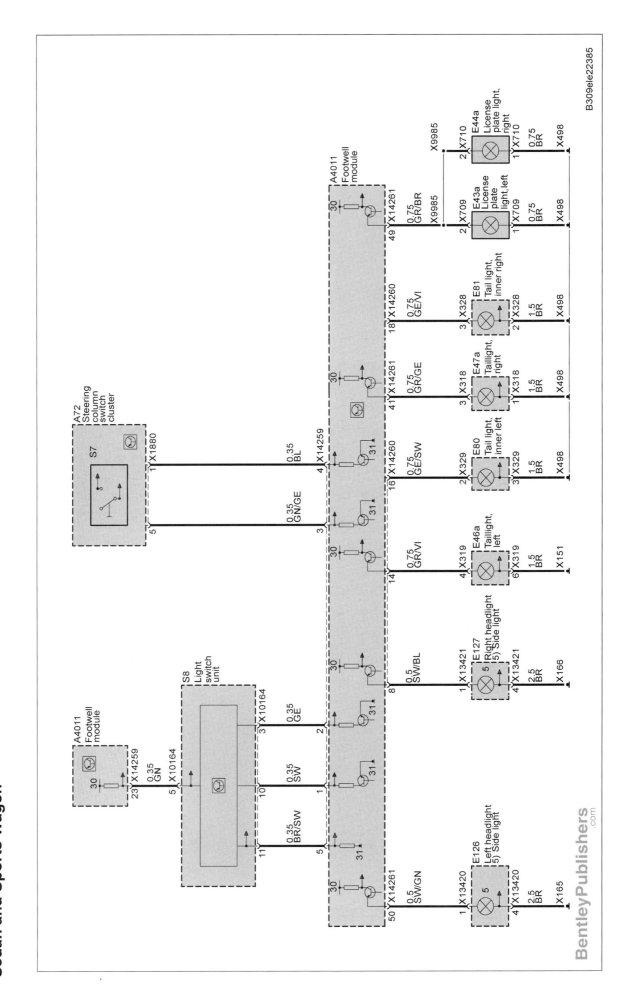

B309ele22385

**Side light, parking light**
**Coupe**

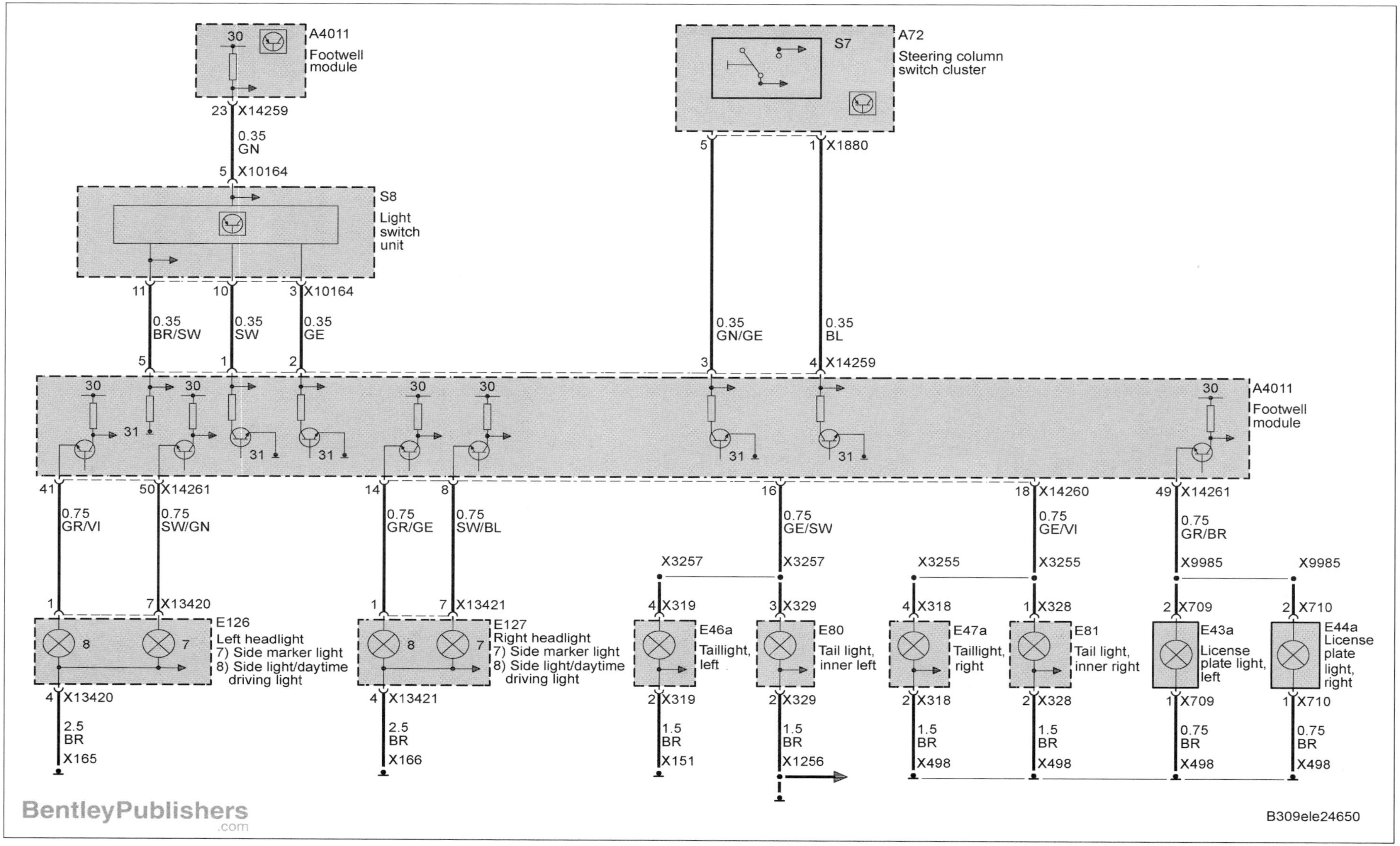

B309ele24650

BentleyPublishers.com

**Side light, parking light**
**Convertible**

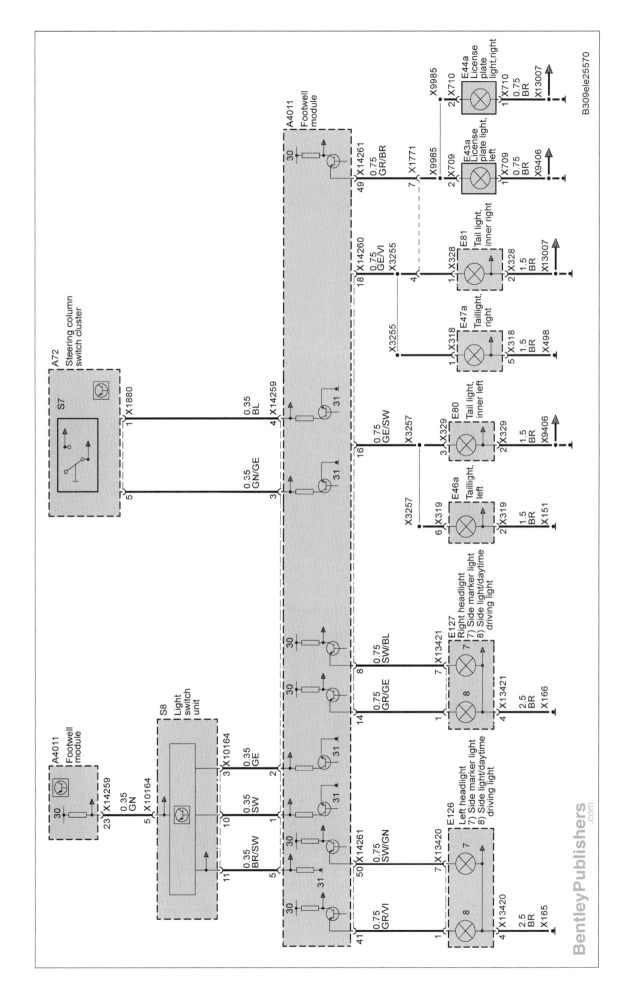

B309ele25570

**Turn signal indicator**
**Sedan and Sports Wagon**

A4011
Footwell module

A72
Steering column switch cluster

S7

30 | 4 X14259 | 0.35 BL | 1 X1880
30 | 3 | 0.35 GN/GE | 5

S18a
Hazard warning switch

30 | 20 | 0.35 BL/BR | 4 X516
30 | 18 | 0.35 BR/BL | 5

3 X516 | 0.35 BR/SW | 8 X14272

A4010
Junction box

A4010a

31

X30087 (from 03 / 2007)

E47a
Taillight, right

15 | 12 X14260 | 0.75 BL/BR | 2 X318 | 1 X318 | 1.5 BR | X498

E46a
Taillight, left

15 | 45 X14261 | 0.75 BL/GN | 5 X319 | 6 X319 | 1.5 BR | X151

H8a
Direction indicator light repeater, front right

15 | 11 X14260 | 0.5 BL/GE | 2 X390 | 1 X390 | 0.5 BR | X166

H9a
Direction indicator light repeater, front left

15 | 44 X14261 | 0.5 BL/GE | 2 X389 | 1 X389 | 0.5 BR | X165

E127
Right headlight
6) Direction indicator light

15 | 40 | 0.75 BL/BR | 12 X13421 | 6 | 4 X13421 | 2.5 BR | X166

E126
Left headlight
6) Direction indicator light

15 | 13 X14260 | 0.75 BL/GN | 12 X13420 | 6 | 4 X13420 | 2.5 BR | X165

BentleyPublishers.com

B309ele22389

22389, 24797

**Electrical Wiring Diagrams  ELE-213**

**Turn signal indicator**
**Coupe and Convertible**

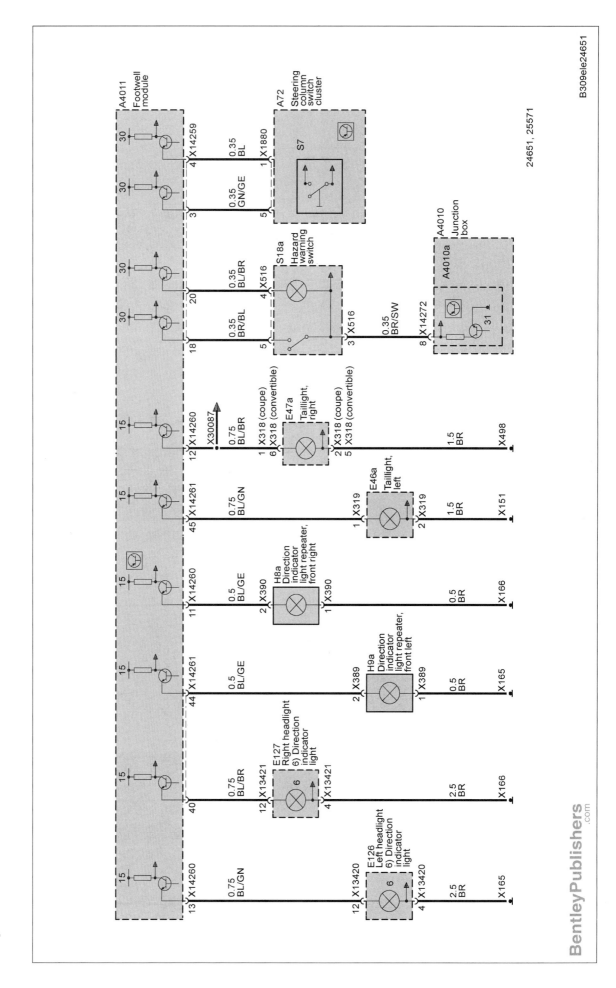

24651, 25571

B309ele24651

**Brake lights**
**Sedan and Sports Wagon**

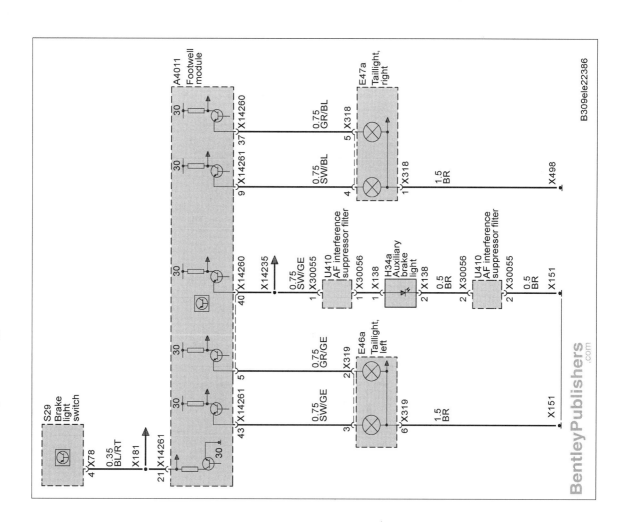

BentleyPublishers.com

B309ele22386

**Brake lights**
**Coupe**

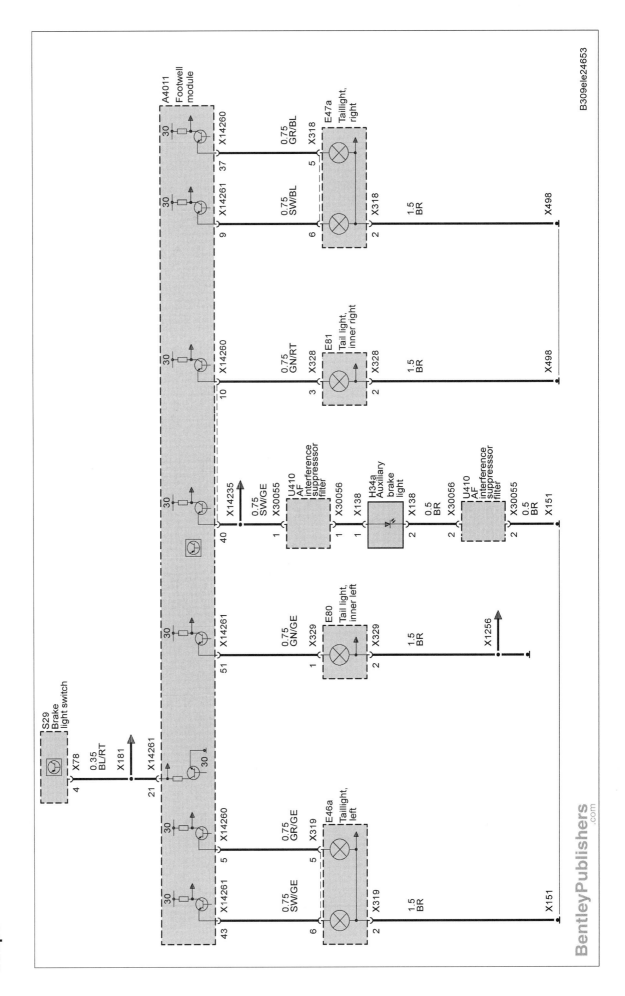

B309ele24653

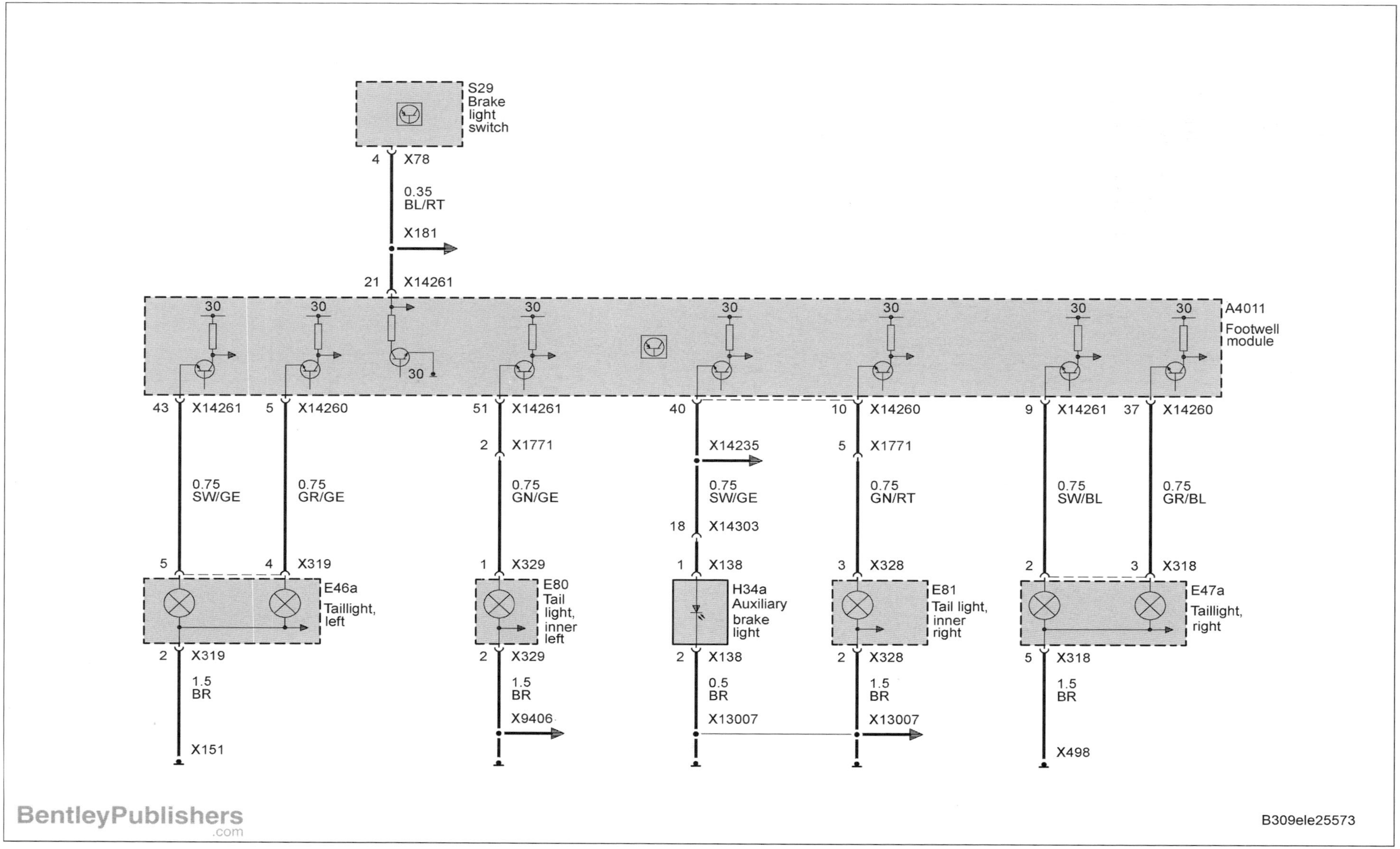

**Brake lights
Convertible**

B309ele25573

**Front and rear foglights**
**Sedan and Sports Wagon**
**(page 1 of 3)**

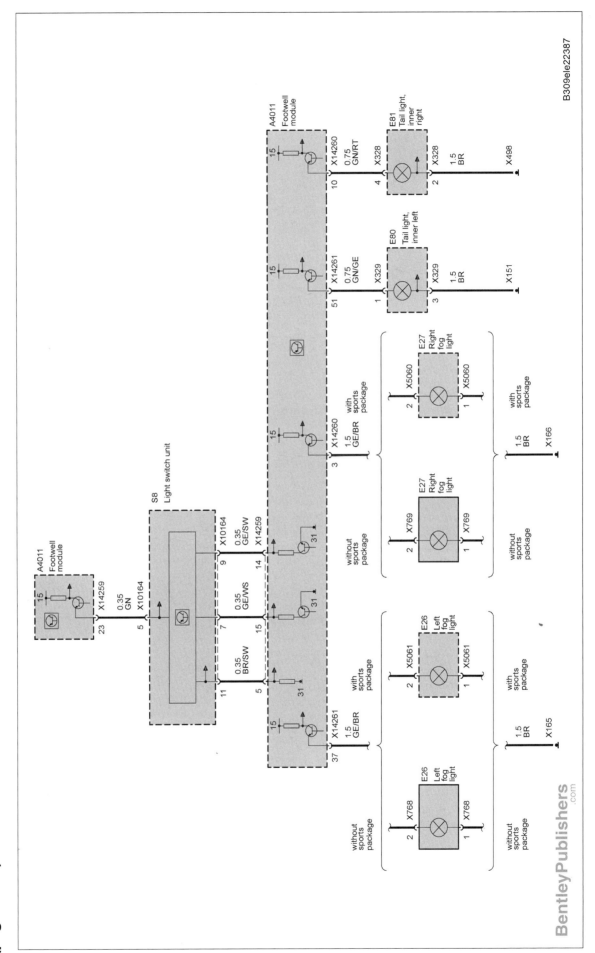

B309ele22387

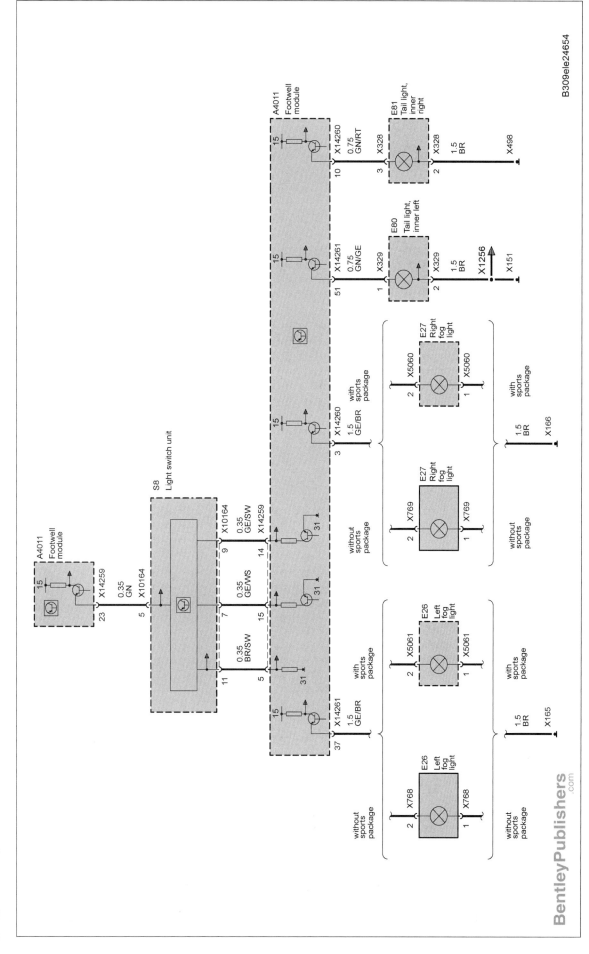

**Front and rear foglights**
**Convertible**
**(page 3 of 3)**

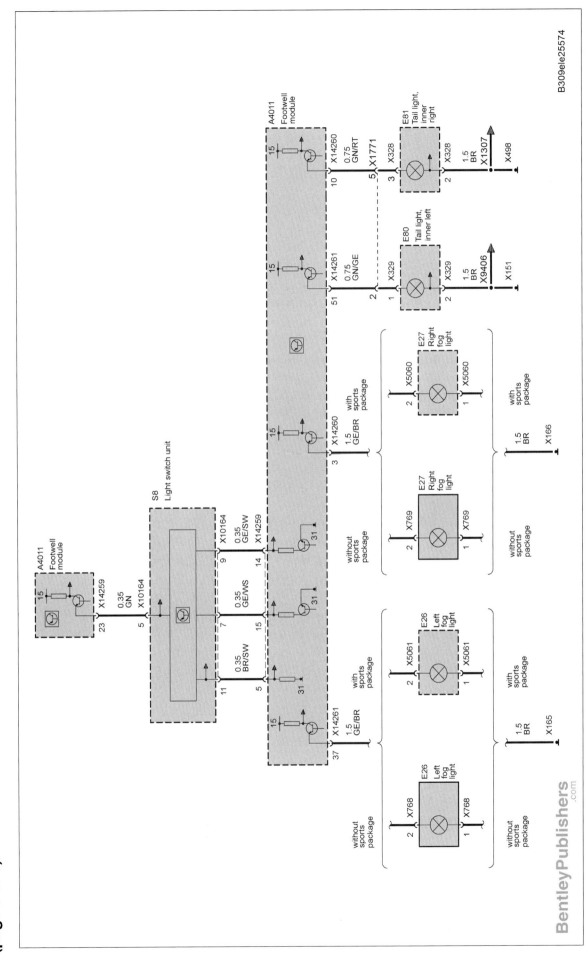

B309ele25574

**Backup lights**

automatic transmission

| X15003 | X15004 |
|---|---|
| 0.35 OR/GN | 0.35 GN |
| X14260 | |
| 46 | 45 |

A4011
Footwell module

15 — 15

| 9 | X14260 | 47 | X14261 |
|---|---|---|---|
| 0.75 SW/BL | | 0.75 SW/VI | |

coupe

30

| 19 | 0.5 GR/VI |
|---|---|

| 2 | X6011 (to 03 / 2007) |
| 9 | X6011 (from 03 / 2007) |

2 X8511

S8511
Reversing light switch

1 X8511

0.75 BR

X6462

convertible

| 3 X319 | 3 X318 |
|---|---|
| E46a Taillight, left | E47a Taillight, right |
| 2 X319 | 2 X318 |
| 1.5 BR | 1.5 BR |
| X498 | X498 |

coupe

| 3 X319 | 3 X318 |
|---|---|
| E46a Taillight, left | E47a Taillight, right |
| 2 X319 | 2 X318 |
| 1.5 BR | 1.5 BR |
| X498 | X498 |

sedan and Sports Wagon

| 4 X329 | 1 X328 |
|---|---|
| E80 Taillight, inner left | E81 Taillight, inner right |
| 3 X329 | 2 X328 |
| 1.5 BR | 1.5 BR |
| X498 | X498 |

22388, 24652, 25572, 25957, 25958, 25959

Electrical Wiring Diagrams   ELE-221

**Interior lights**
**without roof function center (FZD)**

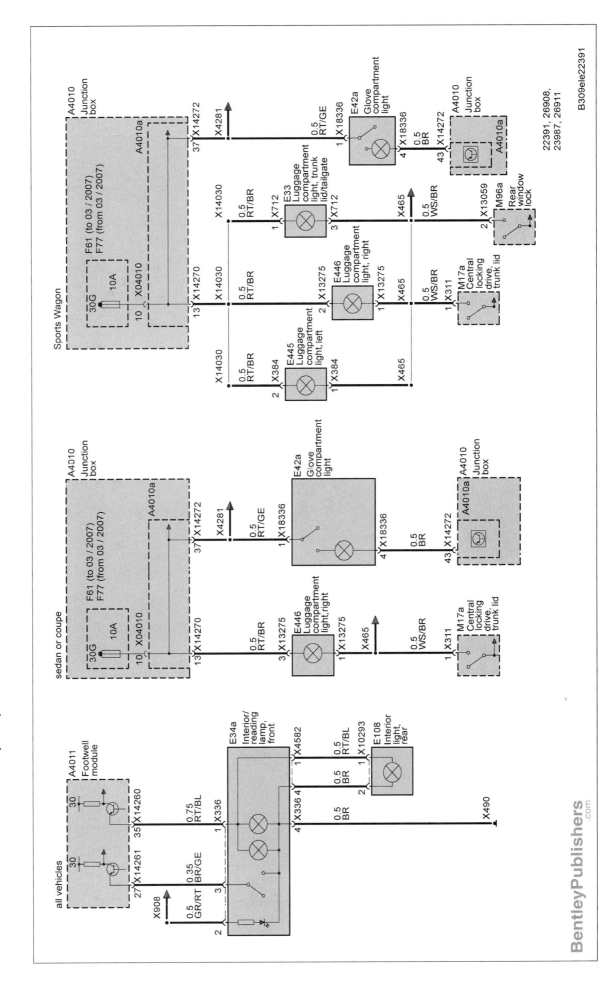

**Interior lights**
**Sedan with roof function center (FZD)**
**(page 1 of 2)**

A14286
Function control
centre, roof
1) Interior light,
front

A14286
Function control
centre, roof
1) Interior light,
front

58

30

30

30

30

30

30

30

30

17    16    18    15    20    19    14

X14289

0.35 GR/RT
0.35 SW/GN
0.5 BL/WS
0.35 SW/BL
0.5 RT/BL
0.5 BL/RT
0.35 SW/WS

X10293

4    7    8    5    3    1    2

E108
Interior light, rear
2) Map reading
   lights
3) Interior light
4) Top-light

2

3

6    X10293

22392, 26909,
22326, 26912

X14289

A14286
Function
control
centre,
roof

0.5 BR

13

31

30    30

4    6

0.5 RT/GE
0.5 RT/GE

2    X382    E36    2    X381    E35
Make-up          Make-up
mirror           mirror
light,           light,
front right      front left

1    X382    1    X381

0.5 GR/SW    0.5 GR/SW

1    X402    1    X401

S78              S77
Make-up          Make-up
mirror           mirror
switch,          switch,
front right      front left
0) OFF           0) OFF
1) ON            1) ON

3    X402    3    X401

0.5 BR    0.5 BR

3    5

31    31

BentleyPublishers.com

**Electrical Wiring Diagrams   ELE-223**

B309ele22392a

**Interior lights**
**Sedan with roof function center (FZD)**
**(page 2 of 2)**

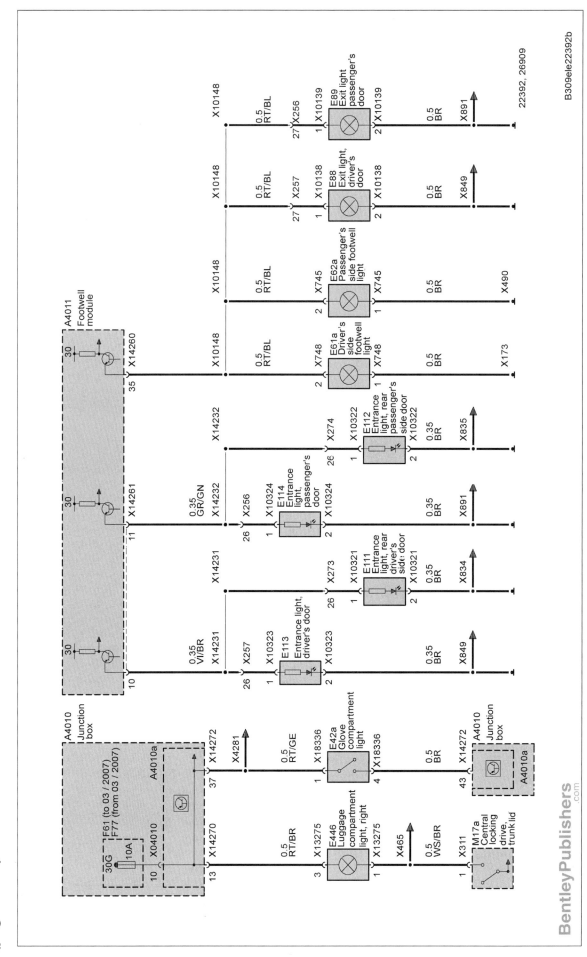

22392, 26909

B309ele22392b

**Interior lights**
**Coupe with roof function center (FZD)**
**(page 1 of 2)**

A14286
Function control centre, roof
1) Interior light, front

A14286
Function control centre, roof
1) Interior light, front

22392, 26909,
22326, 26912

E108
Interior light, rear
2) Map reading lights
3) Interior light
4) Top-light

58
30
30
30
30
30
30
30
30
30
30
30

X14289
17  0.35 GR/RT  X10293  4
16  0.35 SW/GN  7
18  0.5 BL/WS  8
15  0.35 SW/BL  5
20  0.5 RT/BL  3
19  0.5 BL/RT  1
14  0.35 SW/WS  2

X10293  6

A14286
Function control centre, roof
X14289  13  0.5 BR  31

E36
Make-up mirror light, front right
4  0.5 RT/GE  X382  2    1  X382  0.5 GR/SW  X402  1

S78
Make-up mirror switch, front right
0) OFF
1) ON
X402  3  0.5 BR  3  31

E35
Make-up mirror light, front left
6  0.5 RT/GE  X381  2    1  X381  0.5 GR/SW  X401  1

S77
Make-up mirror switch, front left
0) OFF
1) ON
X401  3  0.5 BR  5  31

B309ele22392a

**Interior lights**
**Coupe with roof function center (FZD)**
**(page 2 of 2)**

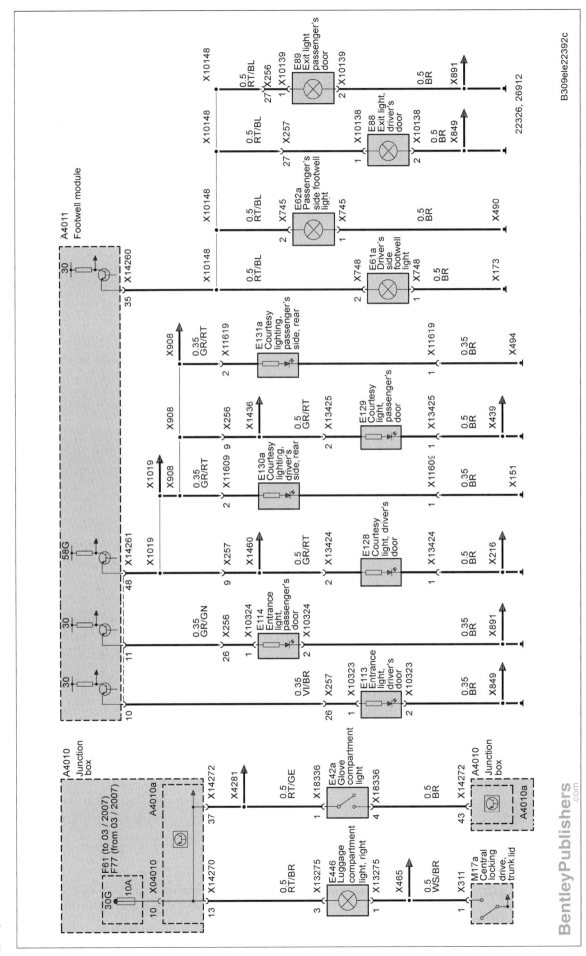

B309ele22392c

**Interior lights**
**Sports Wagon with roof function center (FZD)**
**(page 1 of 2)**

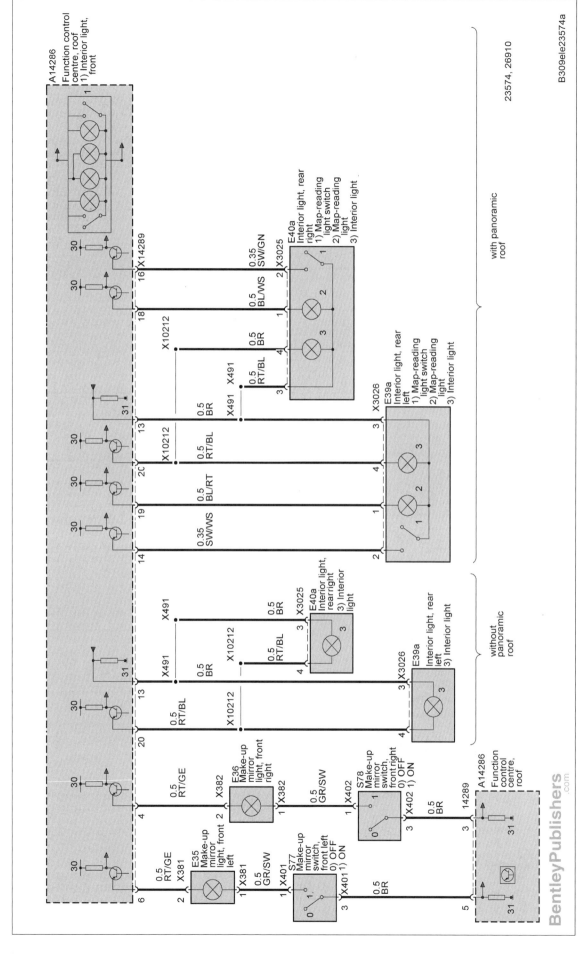

B309ele23574a

23574, 26910

BentleyPublishers
.com

**Interior lights**
**Sports Wagon with roof function center (FZD)**
**(page 2 of 2)**

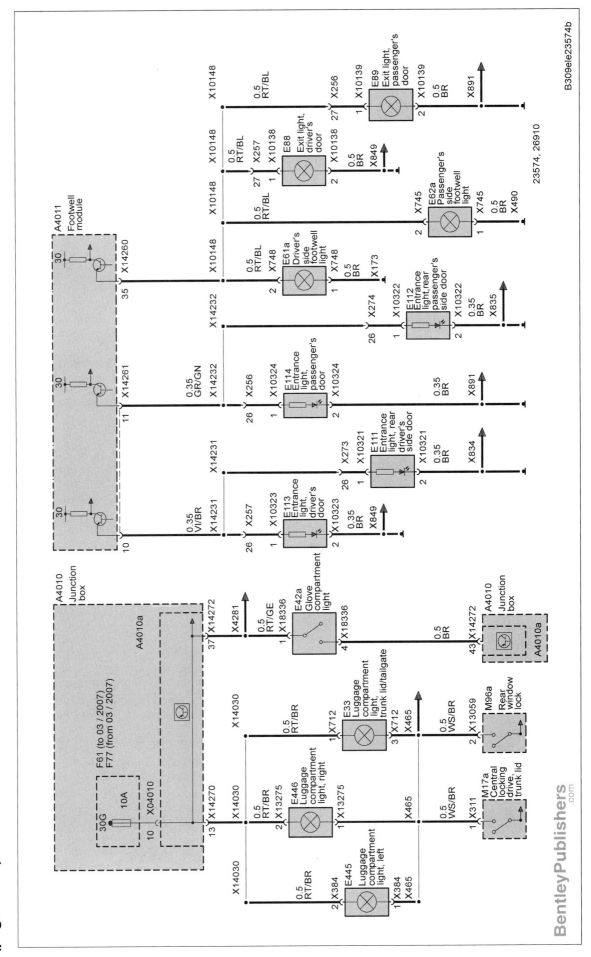

B309ele23574b

**Interior lights**
**Convertible with roof function center (FZD)**
**(page 1 of 2)**

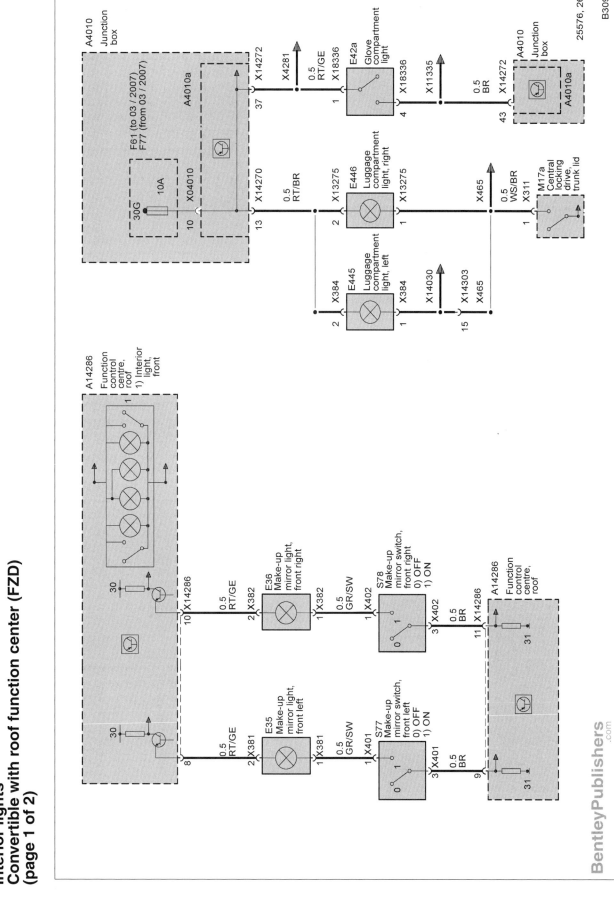

B309ele25576a

25576, 26913

**Interior lights**
**Convertible with roof function center (FZD)**
**(page 2 of 2)**

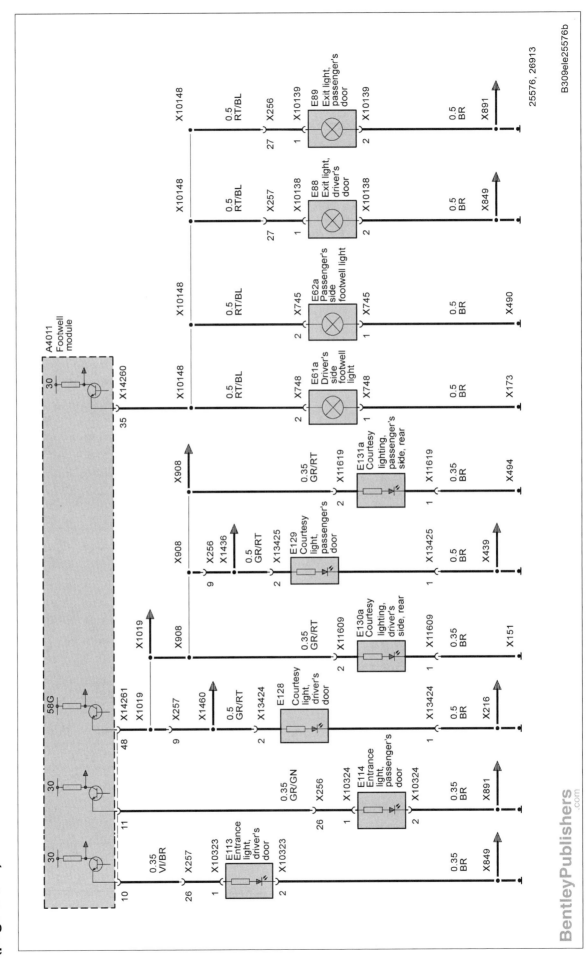

25576, 26913

B309ele25576b

**Roof function center (FZD), power supply**

convertible

A4010
Junction box

F5 (to 03 / 2007)
F40 (03 / 2007 to 09 / 2007)
F62 (from 09 / 2007)

F28 (to 09 / 2007)
F7 (from 09 / 2007)

30   7.5A
15   5A

X11001 (to 03 / 2007)
X11008 (from 03 / 2007)

X11003 (to 03 / 2007)
X11001 (from 03 / 2007)

0.75 (to 03 / 2007)
RT/GE
0.5 (from 03 / 2007)
RT/WS

0.35
GN/WS

X15002
X15001

0.35
GN

0.35
OR/GN

X14286

A14286
Function control centre, roof

0.75
BR

X490

31
31
31
31

1
2
3
4
8
7
5
10
12

25561, 26791, 26792

sedan, coupe, and
Sports Wagon

A4010
Junction box

F5 (to 03 / 2007)
F40 (03 / 2007 to 09 / 2007)
F62 (from 09 / 2007)

F12 (to 09 / 2007)
F25 (from 09 / 2007)

F28 (to 09 / 2007)
F7 (from 09 / 2007)

30   7.5A
30G   20A
15   5A

X11001 (to 03 / 2007)
X11008 (from 03 / 2007)

(to 03 / 2007)
X11003 (from 03 / 2007)

X11003 (to 03 / 2007)
X11001 (from 03 / 2007)

0.75 (to 03 / 2007)
RT/GE
0.5 (from 03 / 2007)
RT/WS

2.5
RT/GR

0.35
GN/WS

X15002
X15001

0.35
GN

0.35
OR/GN

X14286
X14287

A14286
Function control centre, roof

2.5
BR

X490

31
31
31
31

1
2
3
4
5
10
8
7

25950, 26789, 26790
21414, 25894, 26695

**Automatic headlight vertical aim control**

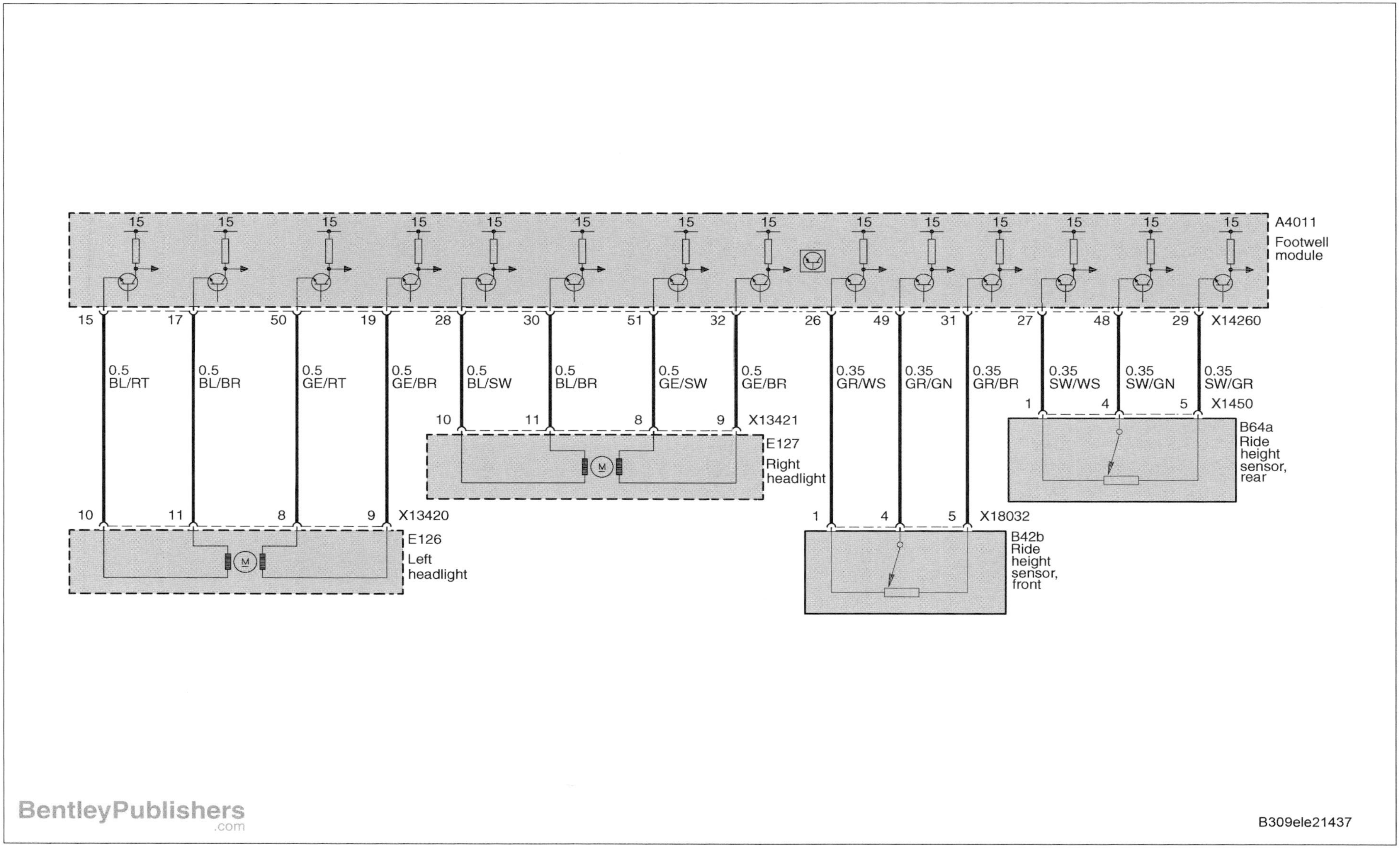

A4011
Footwell module

B64a
Ride height sensor, rear

B42b
Ride height sensor, front

E127
Right headlight

E126
Left headlight

X14260
X1450
X18032
X13421
X13420

0.35 SW/GR
0.35 SW/GN
0.35 SW/WS
0.35 GR/BR
0.35 GR/GN
0.35 GR/WS
0.5 GE/BR
0.5 GE/SW
0.5 BL/BR
0.5 BL/SW
0.5 GE/BR
0.5 GE/RT
0.5 BL/BR
0.5 BL/RT

B309ele21437

**Adaptive headlight**

B309ele22390

B64a
Ride height
sensor, rear

A4011
Footwell
module

E127
Right
headlight

B42b
Ride height
sensor, front

E126
Left
headlight

X1450

0.35
SW/WS

X14260

X14260

0.35
WS/GE

X13421

1

27

24

10

0.35
SW/GN

X14300

4

48

0.35
SW/GR

M

M

5

29

9

X13421

11

0.75
BR/SW

X10012

X18032

0.35
GR/WS

0.5
GN/SW

X14300

X13420

1

26

42

9

0.35
GR/GN

0.35
WS/RT

M

M

4

49

25

10

0.35
GR/BR

X13420

5

31

11

0.75
BR/SW

X1108

X181

0.35
BL/RT

21

**Automatic driving lights control**
**Sedan, Coupe and Sports Wagon without xenon headlights**

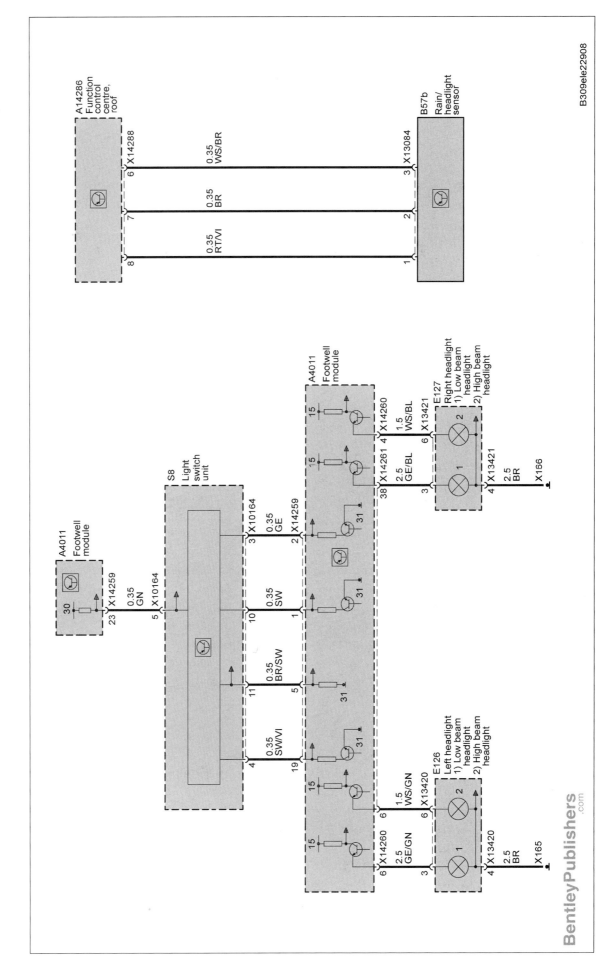

B309ele22908

BentleyPublishers.com

**Automatic driving lights control
Sedan, Coupe and Sports Wagon with xenon headlights**

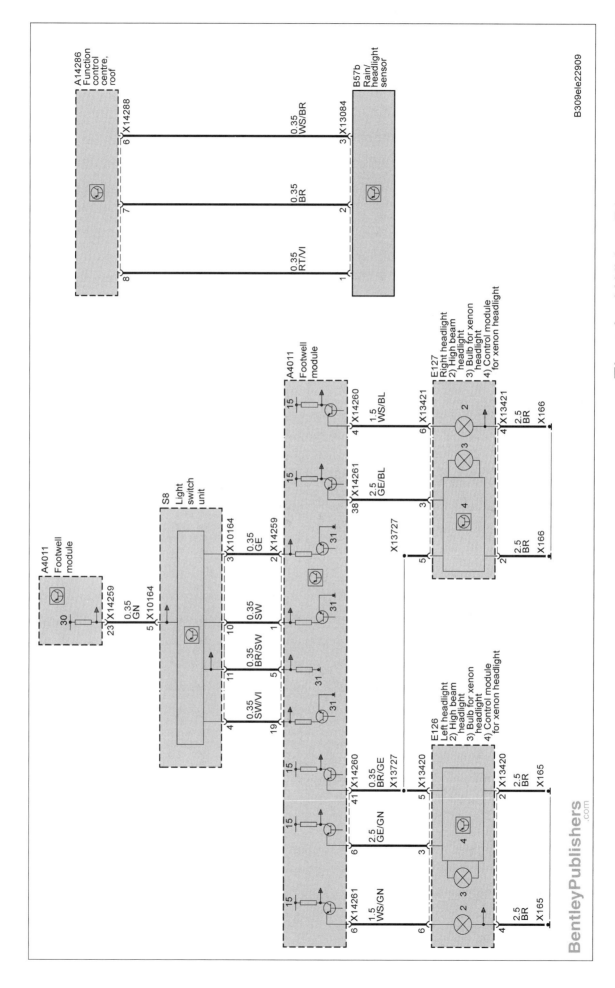

**Automatic driving lights control
Convertible**

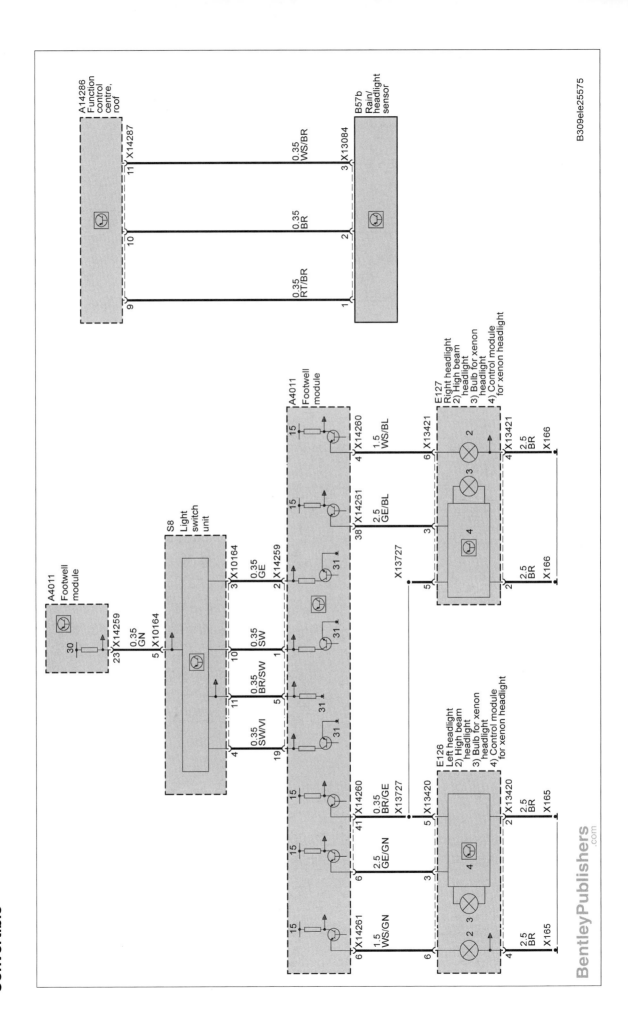

B309ele25575

# Trailer lighting

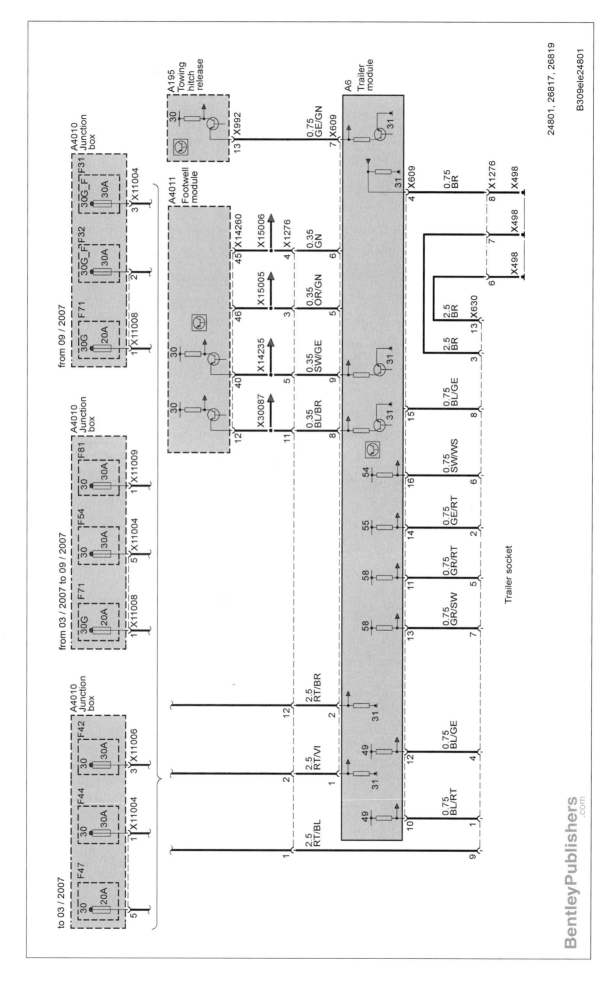

Electrical Wiring Diagrams   ELE-237

24801, 26817, 26819

B309ele24801

**Instrument lighting**
**Sedan and Sports Wagon**

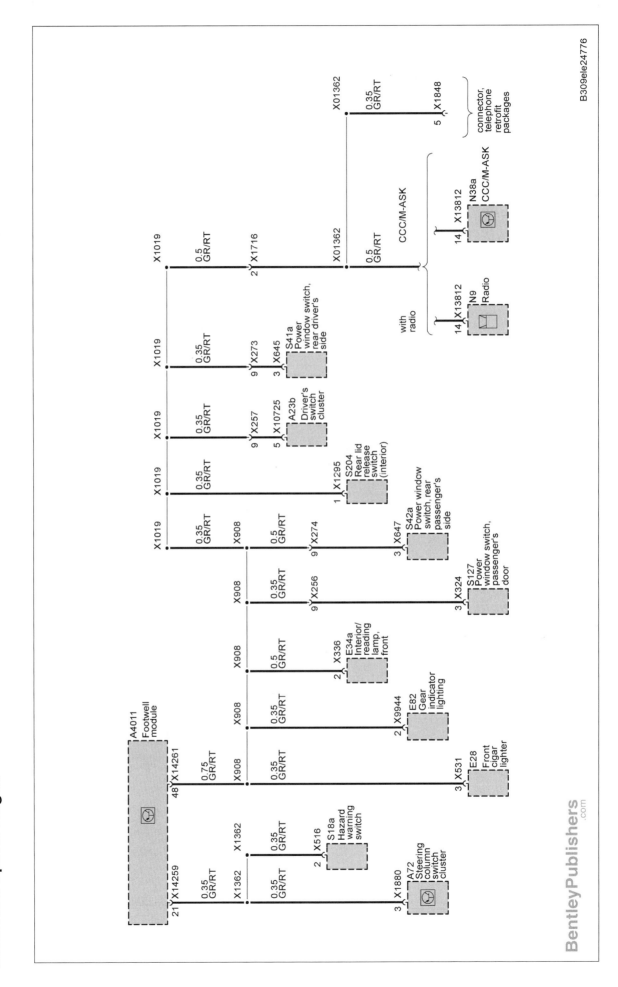

B309ele24776

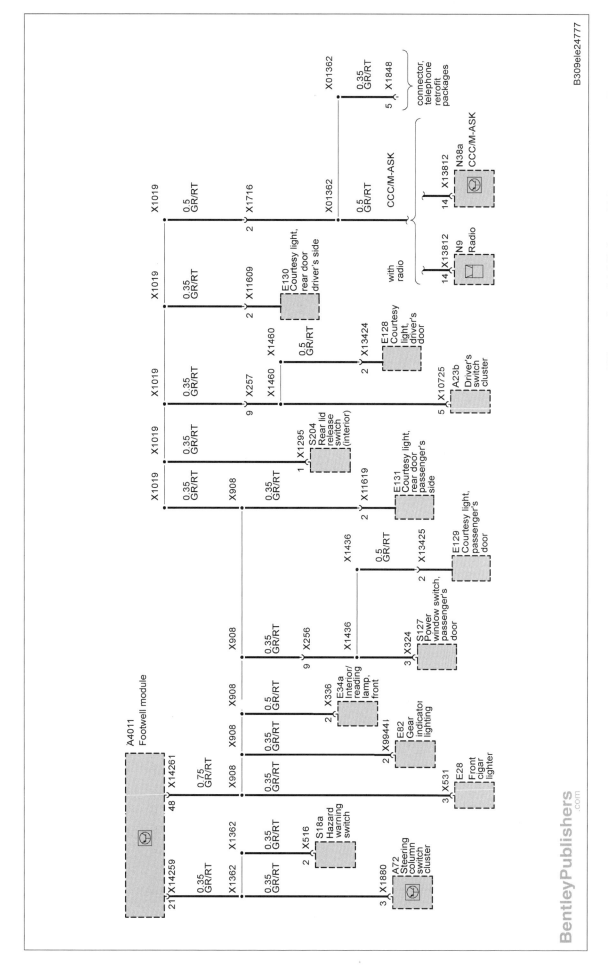

Instrument lighting
Coupe

B309ele24777

BentleyPublishers.com

**Instrument warning and indicator lights**

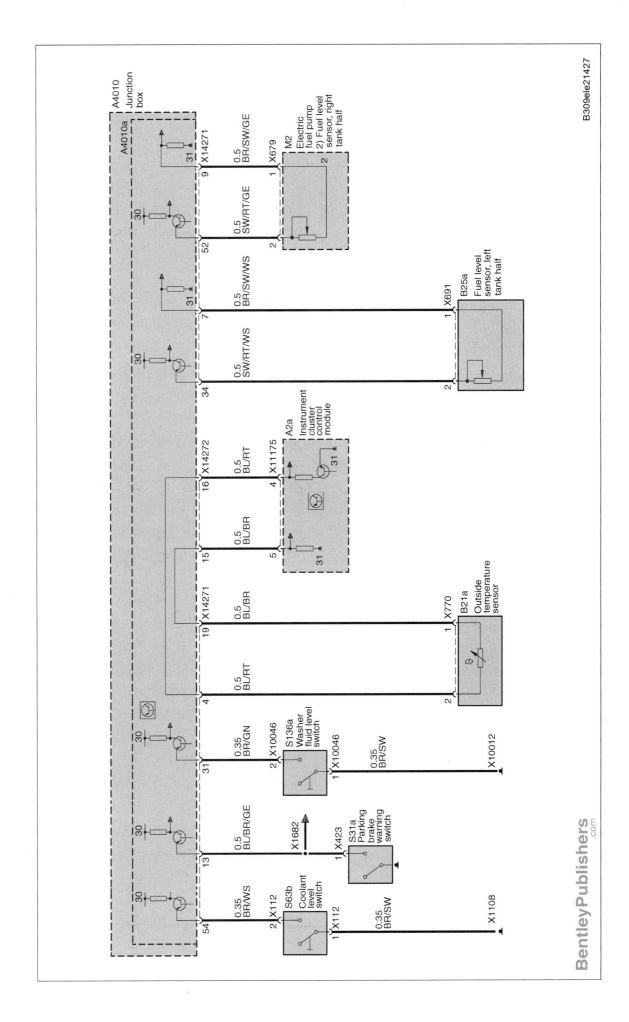

B309ele21427

**Electrochromic mirror
except Convertible**

A14286
Function
control
centre,
roof

30

X14288

16

0.35
BR/SW

X14292

5

30

15

0.35
GN/WS

4

30

14

0.35
GR/VI

1

15

20

0.35
GN/WS

3

30

19

0.35
RT/VI

8

31

31

31

31

X14292

31

10

0.35
BR/SW

X1108

left-hand drive

right-hand drive

X10012

with high beam
assistant

X15002

0.35
GN

X19594

2

X15001

0.35
OR/GN

1

A22
Electrochromic interior
rear view mirror
6) High beam assistant
sensor and control

6

BentleyPublishers
.com

Electrical Wiring Diagrams   ELE-241

B309ele24350

**Electrochromic mirror
Convertible**

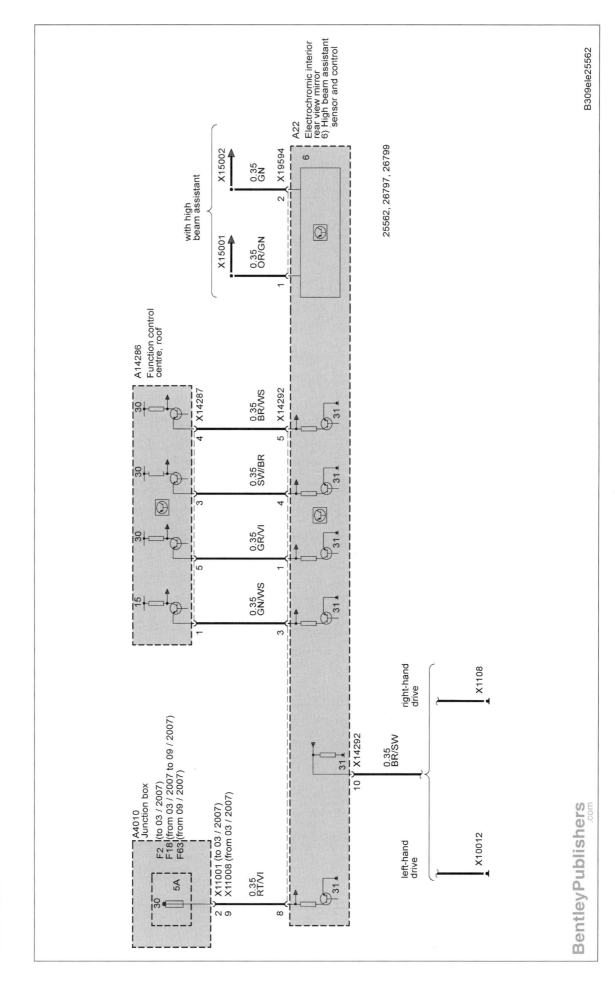

B309ele25562

# Heating and air-conditioning control module, power supply

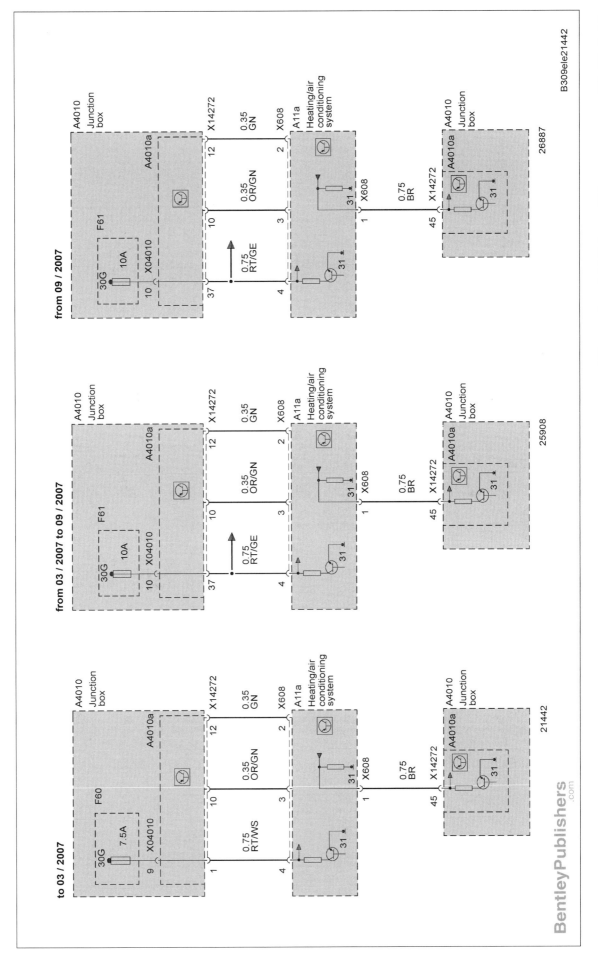

B309ele21442

**Heating and air-conditioning functions
(to 03 / 2007)
(page 1 of 3)**

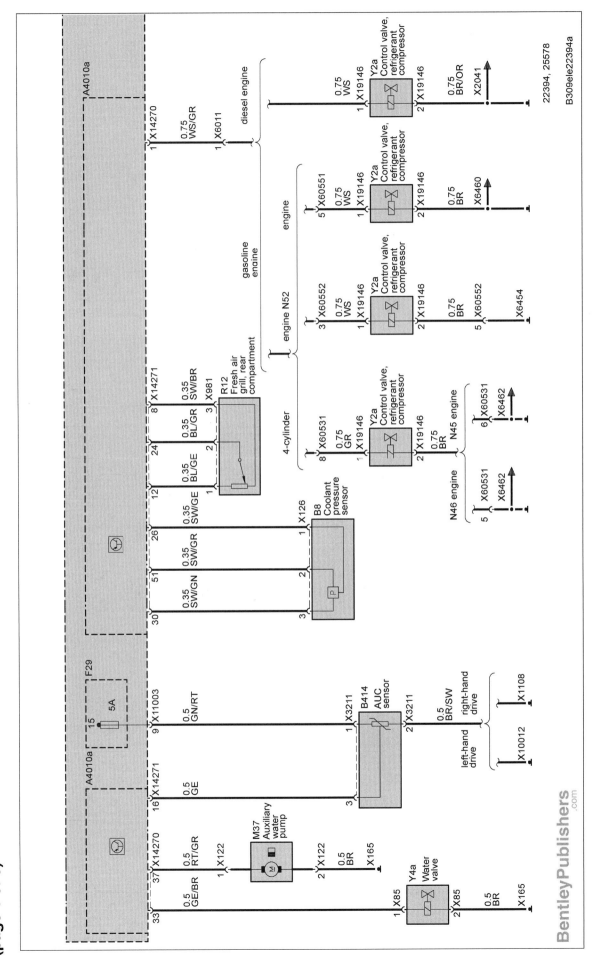

22394, 25578

B309ele22394b

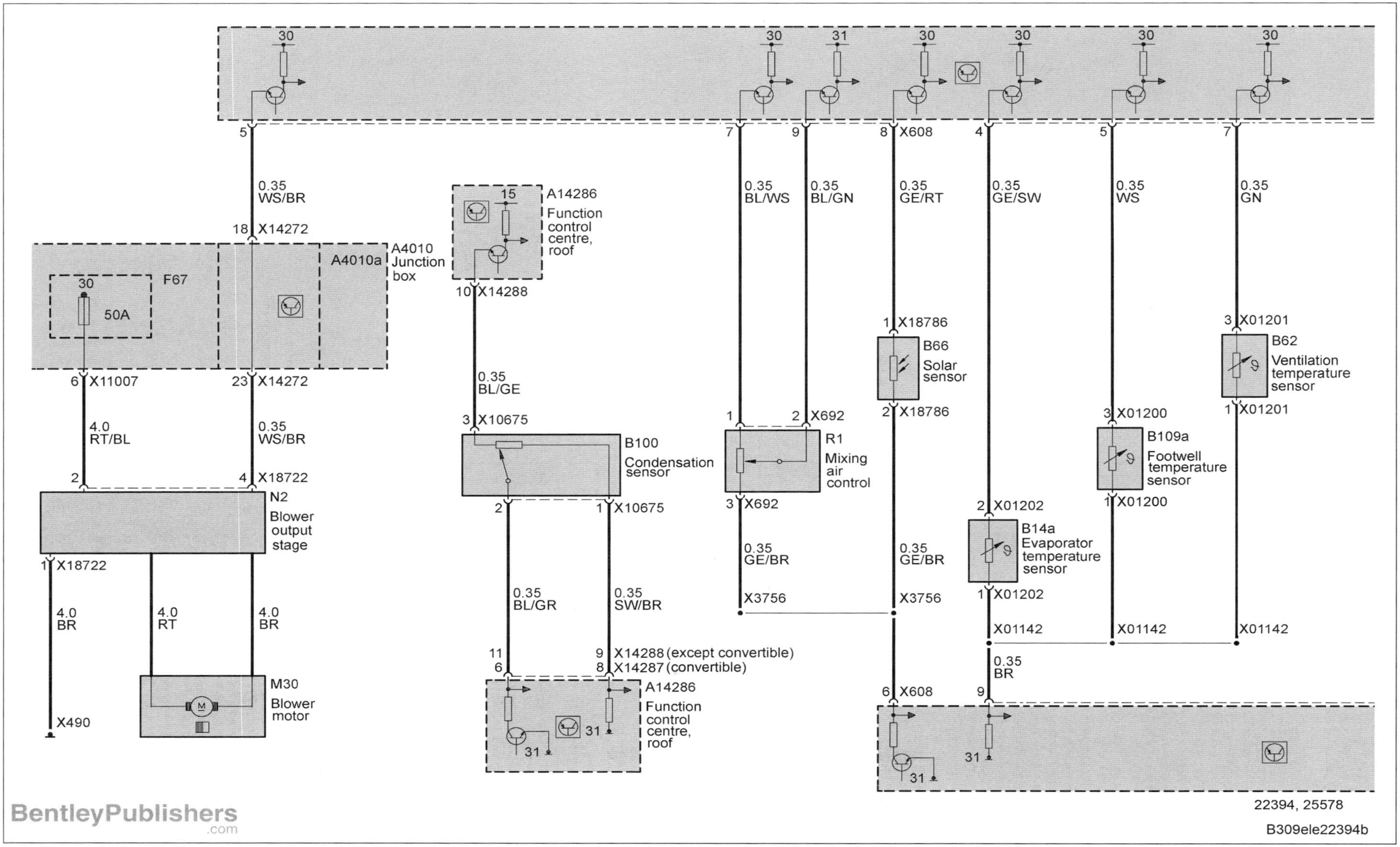

**Heating and air-conditioning functions
(to 03 / 2007)
(page 3 of 3)**

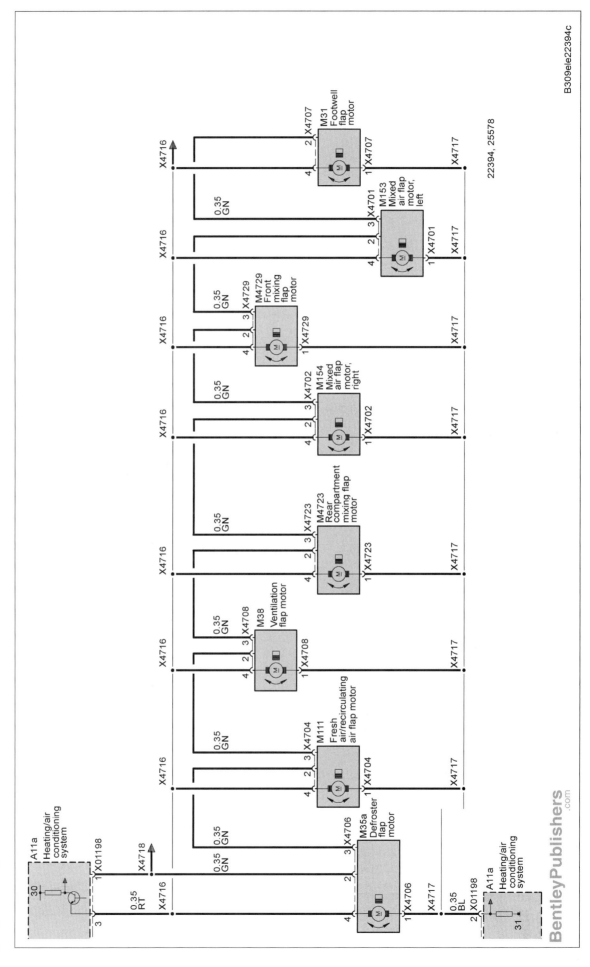

22394, 25578

B309ele22394c

**Heating and air-conditioning functions**
**(from 03 / 2007 to 09 / 2007)**
**(page 1 of 3)**

A4010 Junction box
A4010a

30

0.35 WS/BR    X14272

5    18 X14272

23 X14272    0.35 WS/BR    X18722

N2 Blower output stage

4    4.0 BR    M30 Blower motor

4.0 RT    X18722

F67    30    30A

2 X11011    4.0 RT/VI    2    1 X18722    4.0 BR    X490    diesel engine

7 X14270    0.75 WS/GN    X6011

0.75 WS/GR    7

1    6

Y2b Control valve in A/C compressor 1) Magnetic clutch
X1936    3    2 X1936    0.75 BR/OR    X2042
1

8 X14271    0.35 SW/BR    X981    3    R12 Fresh air grill, rear compartment

24    0.35 BL/GR    2

12    0.35 BL/GE    1

gasoline engine

Y2b Control valve in A/C compressor 1) Magnetic clutch
X1936    3    2 X1936    0.75 BR    X6454
1

26    0.35 SW/GE    1 X126    B8 Coolant pressure sensor

51    0.35 SW/GR    2

30    0.35 SW/GN    3

F15    15    5A

6 X11001    0.35 GN/RT    X3211    1    B414 AUC sensor    2 X3211    0.5 BR/SW    right-hand drive    X1108

X10012    left-hand drive

16 X14271    0.5 GE    3

37 X14270    0.5 RT/GR    X122    1    M37 Auxiliary water pump    2 X122    0.5 BR    X165

33    0.5 GE/BR    X85    1    Y4a Water valve    2 X85    0.5 BR    X165

A4010a

26299, 26300

B309ele26299a

**Heating and air-conditioning functions
(from 03 / 2007 to 09 / 2007)
(page 2 of 3)**

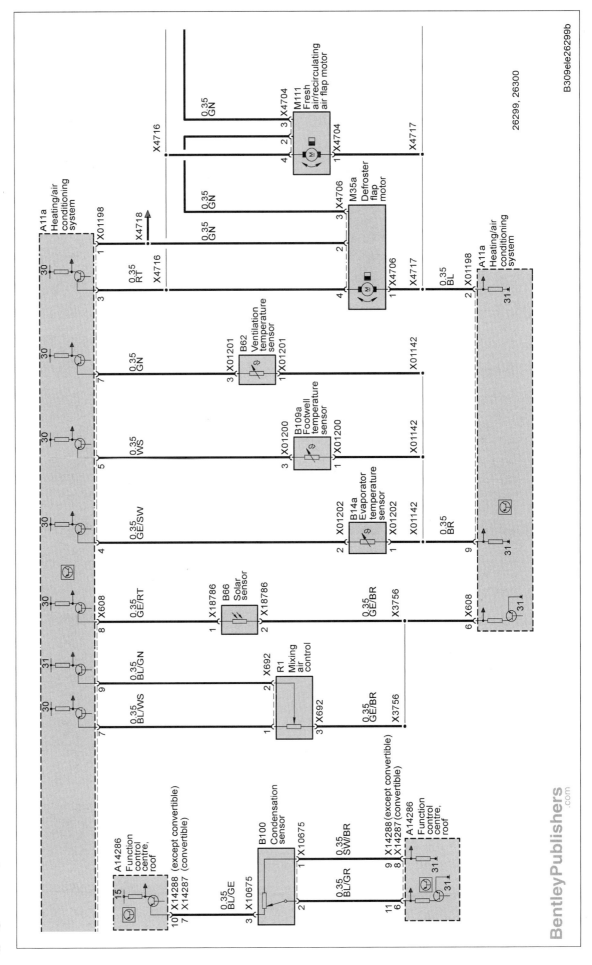

B309ele26299b

26299, 26300

## Heating and air-conditioning functions (from 03 / 2007 to 09 / 2007) (page 3 of 3)

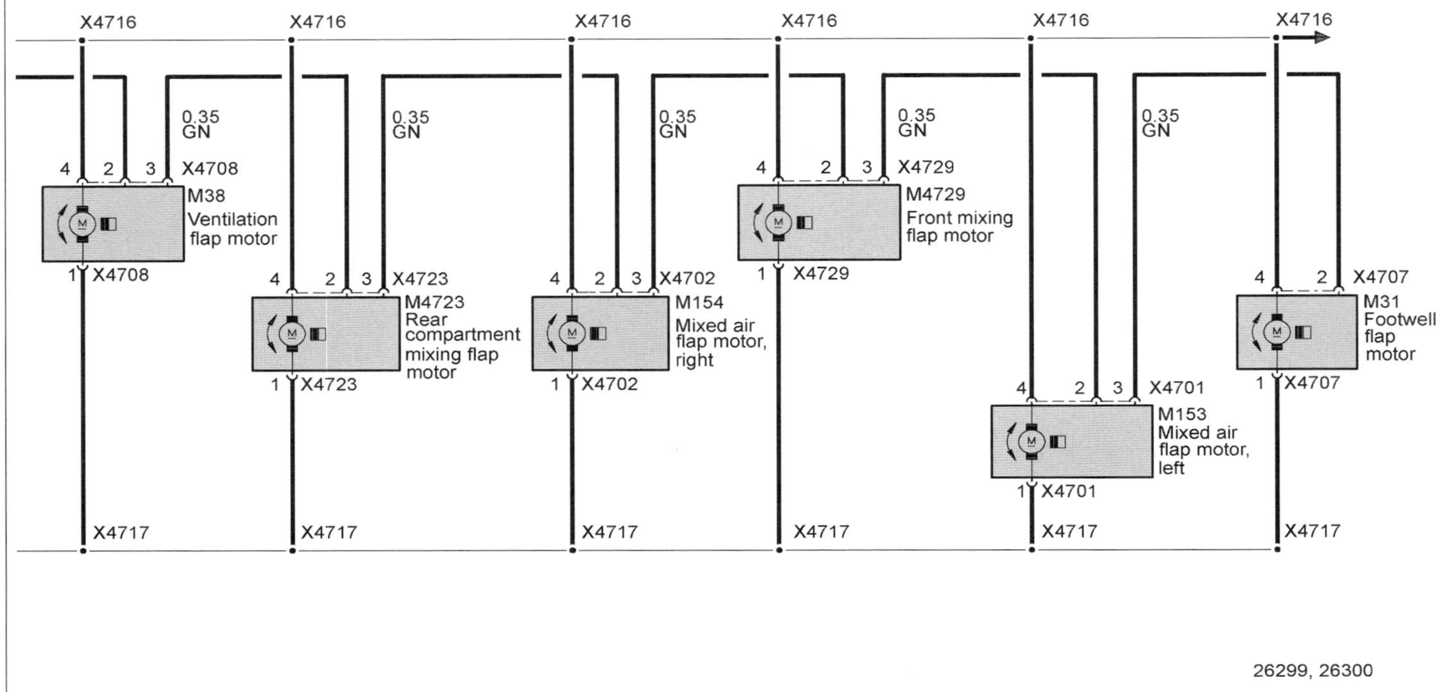
X4716
0.35 GN
4
2
3
X4708
M38
Ventilation flap motor
1
X4717
X4723
M4723
Rear compartment mixing flap motor
X4702
M154
Mixed air flap motor, right
X4729
M4729
Front mixing flap motor
X4701
M153
Mixed air flap motor, left
X4707
M31
Footwell flap motor
M
26299, 26300
BentleyPublishers.com
B309ele26299c

**Heating and air-conditioning functions
(from 09 / 2007)
(page 1 of 3)**

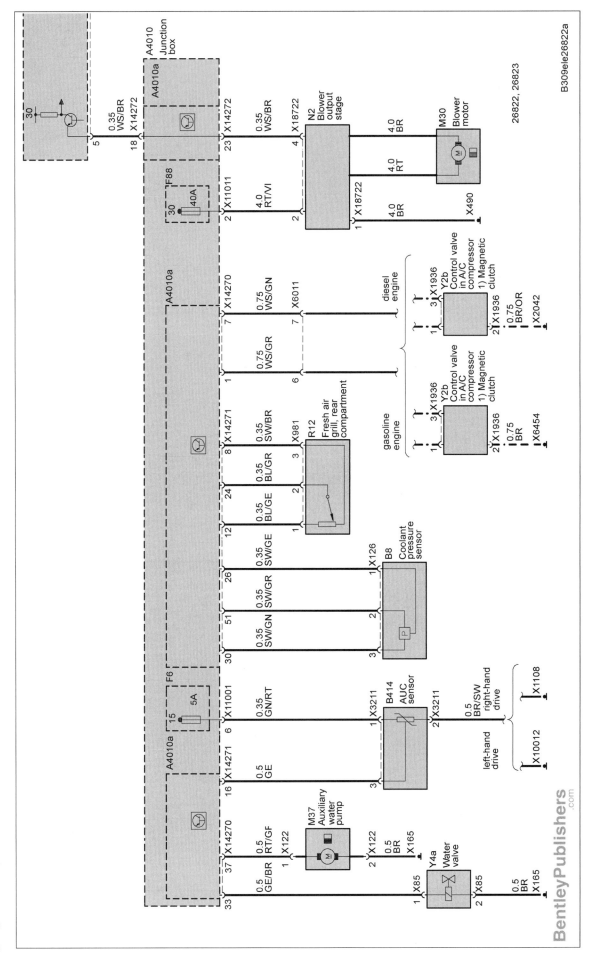

**Heating and air-conditioning functions
(from 09 / 2007)
(page 2 of 3)**

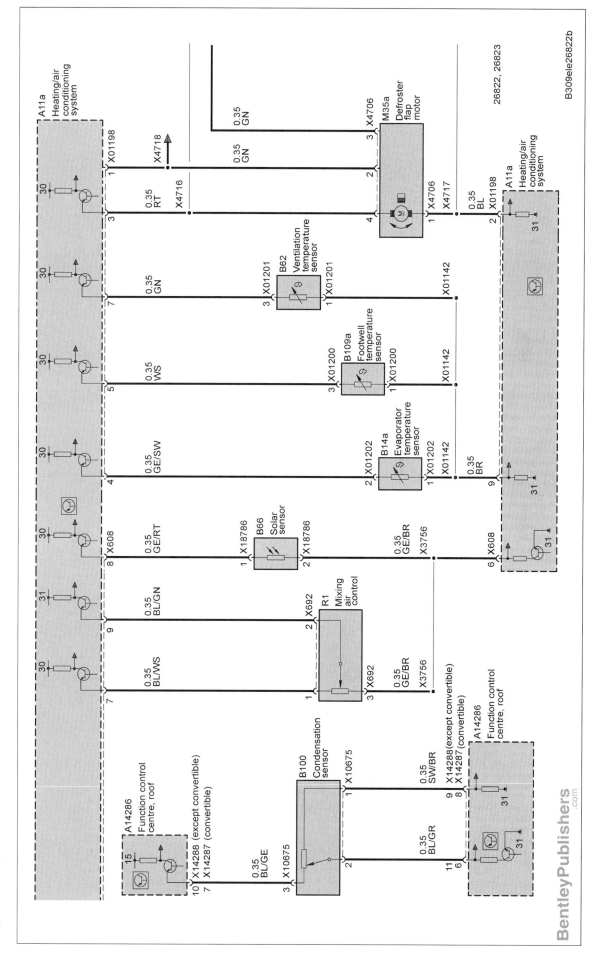

**Heating and air-conditioning functions
(from 09 / 2007)
(page 3 of 3)**

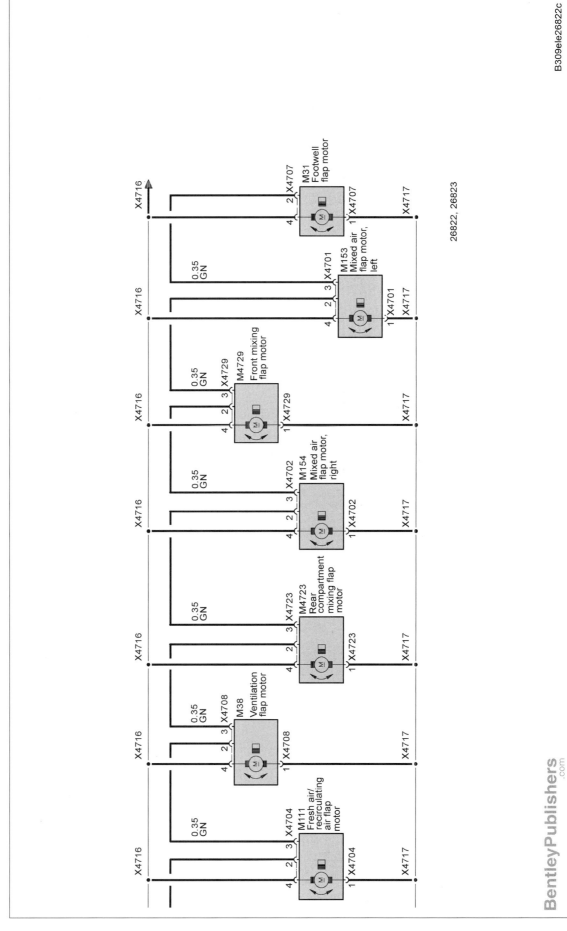

B309ele26822c

# Rear window defogger

## sedan and coupe

A4010
Junction box

K13

X04010  A4010a

F46 (to 09 / 2007)
F47 (from 09 / 2007)

30A

12

X14272

0.35
WS/BL

X608

A11a
Heating/air conditioning system

12

0.35
WS/GE

10

2

3

31

22841, 27394, 27397

X11004 (to 03 / 2007)
X11006 (from 03 / 2007)

2
6

4.0
SW

1

X18264

Z1
Lockout circuit for rear-window defroster (positive)

1

X01058

E9
Rear window defroster

1

X01059

Z2
Lockout circuit for rear-window defroster (ground)

1

X18265

2.5
BR

X151

## Sports Wagon

A4010
Junction box

K13

X04010  A4010a

F46 (to 09 / 2007)
F47 (from 09 / 2007)

30A

12

X14272

0.35
WS/BL

X608

A11a
Heating/air conditioning system

12

0.35
WS/GE

10

2

3

31

24357, 27395, 27398

X11004 (to 03 / 2007)
X11006 (from 03 / 2007)

2
6

2.5
SW

1

X14095

A420
Wave trap

1

X14096

X1265

E9
Rear window defroster

3

X1265

1

X14096

2

A420
Wave trap

2

X14095

2.5
BR

X151

## convertible

A4010
Junction box

K13

X04010  A4010a

F46 (to 09 / 2007)
F47 (from 09 / 2007)

30A

12

X14272

0.35
WS/BL

X608

A11a
Heating/air conditioning system

12

0.35
WS/GE

10

2

3

31

25577, 27396, 27399

X11004 (to 03 / 2007)
X11006 (from 03 / 2007)

2
6

4.0
SW

2

X13096

E9
Rear window defroster

1

X13096

2.5
BR

X498

B309ele22841

**Independent heating**
**(to 03 / 2007)**
**(page 1 of 2)**

A11a
Heating/air
conditioning
system

X608

11

0.35
WS/BL

X10254

4

A14
Control module,
independent/
auxiliary heating

2

5

0.5
BR/RT

X10131

M180
Metering
pump

X10151

1

0.5
SW

X997

1

M

2

X997

0.5
BR

X10151

2

X151

A4010
Junction
box

F7

30

20A

2

X11002

2.5
RT/GN

X10167

1

X10167

2

2.5
BR

X165

A4010a

X14270

37

0.5
RT/GR

X122

1

M37
Auxiliary
water
pump

M

2

X122

0.5
BR

X165

Y4a
Water
valve

X85

1

0.5
GE/BR

33

X85

2

0.5
BR

X165

B309ele22829

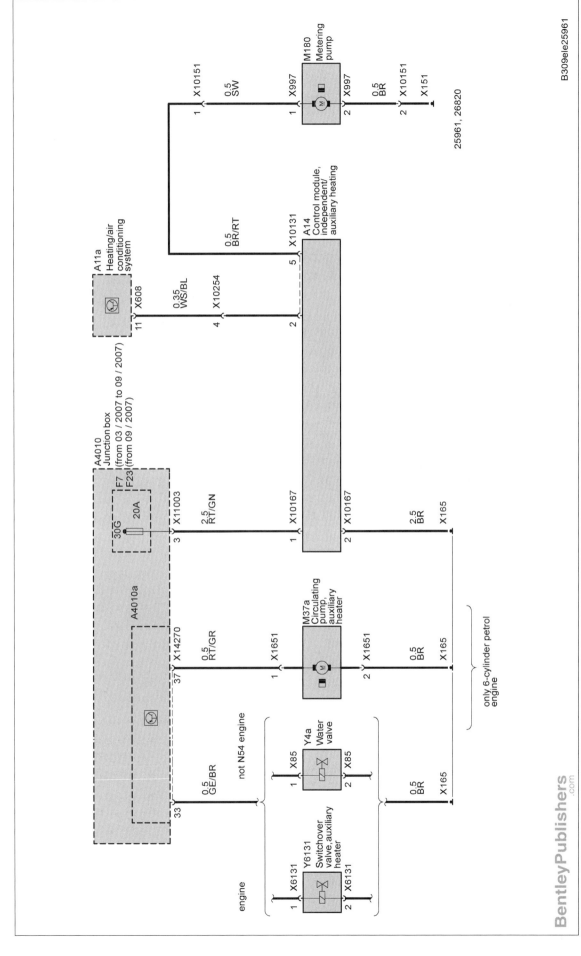

Electrical Wiring Diagrams   ELE-255

B309ele25961

## Convertible top module (CTM), power supply

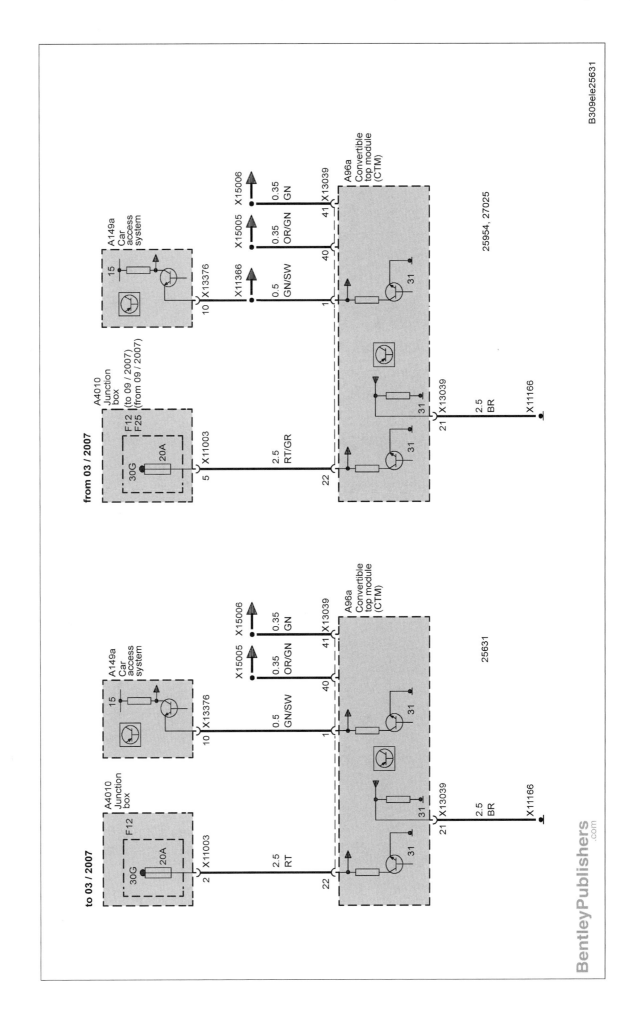

B309ele25631

**Convertible top, inputs
(page 1 of 2)**

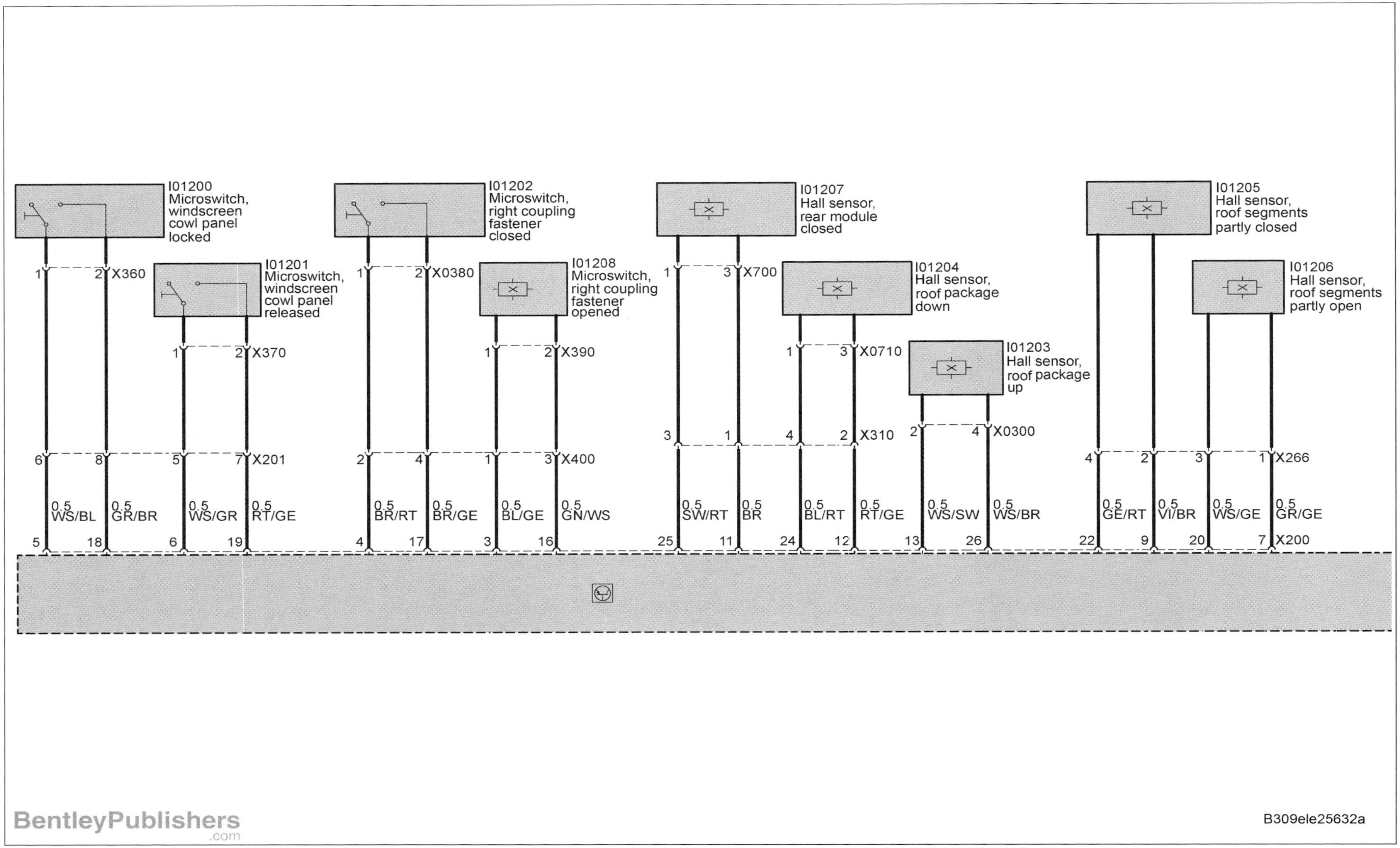

I01200 Microswitch, windscreen cowl panel locked

I01201 Microswitch, windscreen cowl panel released

I01202 Microswitch, right coupling fastener closed

I01208 Microswitch, right coupling fastener opened

I01207 Hall sensor, rear module closed

I01204 Hall sensor, roof package down

I01203 Hall sensor, roof package up

I01205 Hall sensor, roof segments partly closed

I01206 Hall sensor, roof segments partly open

X360 X370 X201 X0380 X390 X400 X700 X0710 X310 X0300 X266 X200

0.5 WS/BL 18
0.5 GR/BR 8
0.5 WS/GR 5
0.5 RT/GE 19
0.5 BR/RT 17
0.5 BR/GE 3
0.5 BL/GE 3
0.5 GN/WS 16
0.5 SW/RT 25
0.5 BR 24
0.5 BL/RT 12
0.5 RT/GE 13
0.5 WS/SW 26
0.5 WS/BR
0.5 GE/RT 22
0.5 VI/BR 9
0.5 WS/GE 20
0.5 GR/GE 7

5 6

**Convertible top, inputs
(page 2 of 2)**

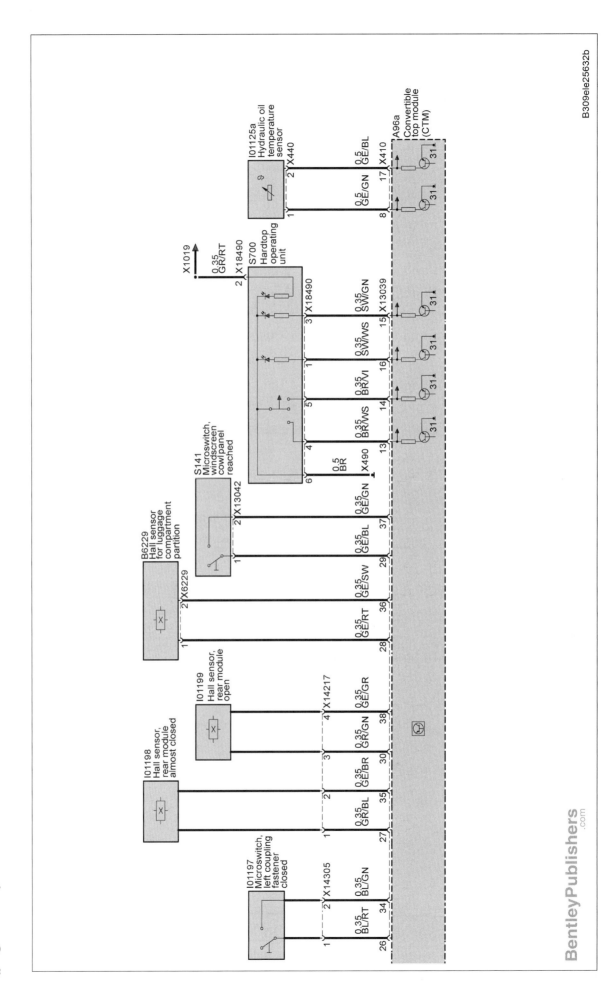

B309ele25632b

**Convertible top, outputs**

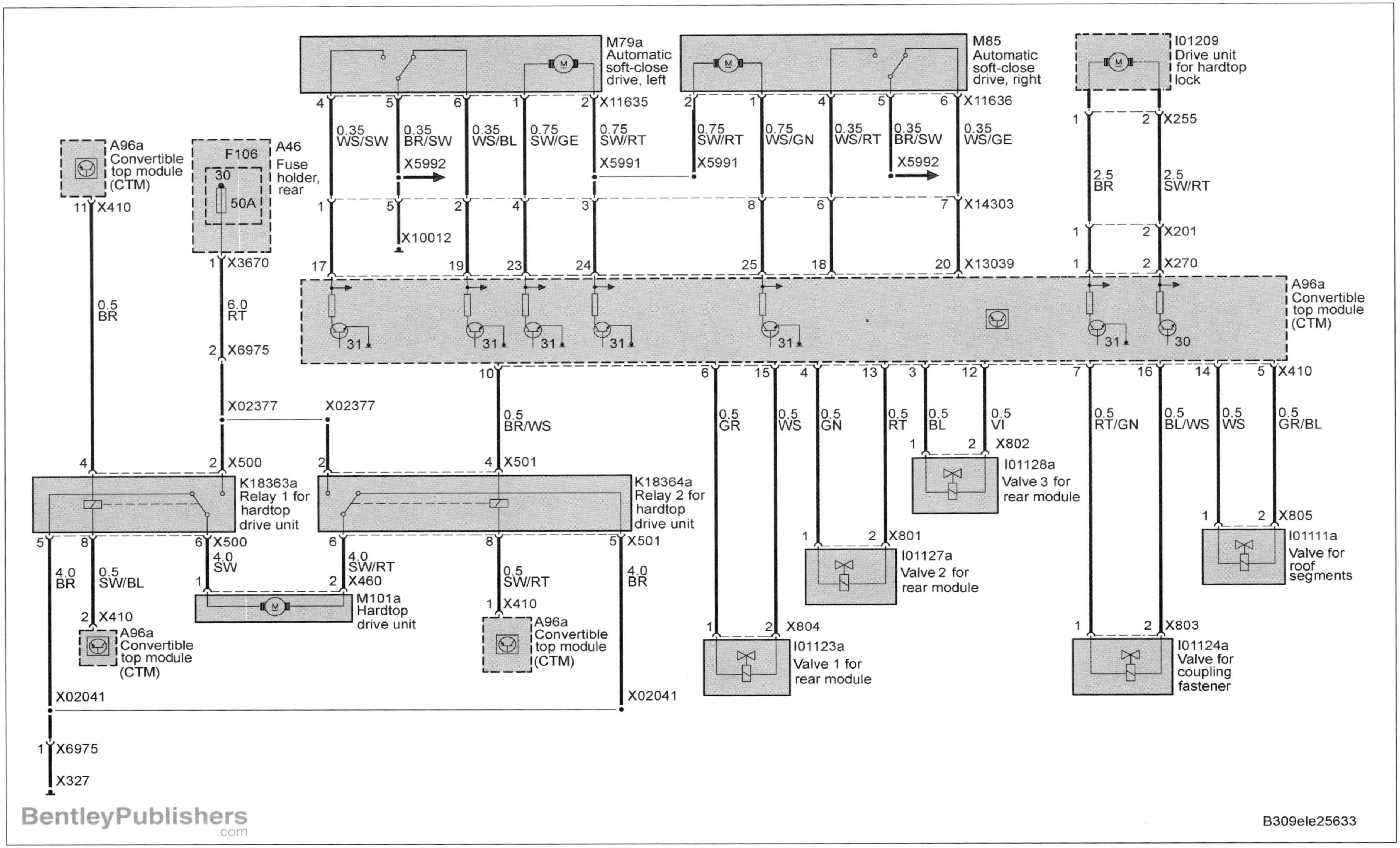

IO1209 Drive unit for hardtop lock

A96a Convertible top module (CTM)

IO1111a Valve for roof segments

IO1124a Valve for coupling fastener

M85 Automatic soft-close drive, right

IO1128a Valve 3 for rear module

IO1127a Valve 2 for rear module

IO1123a Valve 1 for rear module

M79a Automatic soft-close drive, left

K18364a Relay 2 for hardtop drive unit

A96a Convertible top module (CTM)

M101a Hardtop drive unit

A46 Fuse holder, rear

F106  30  50A

K18363a Relay 1 for hardtop drive unit

A96a Convertible top module (CTM)

A96a Convertible top module (CTM)

**Wiper-washer control
Sedan and Coupe (to 03 / 2007)
(page 1 of 2)**

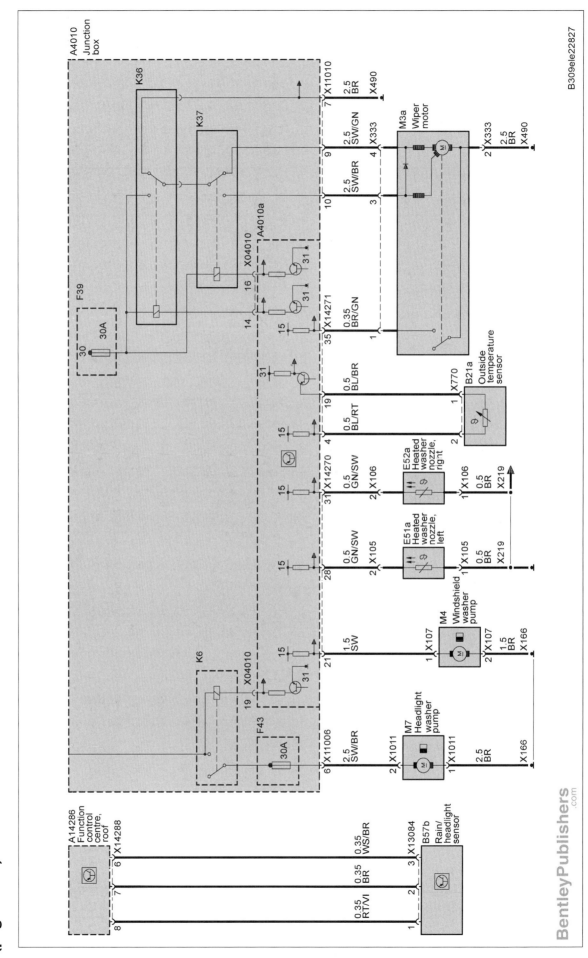

B309ele22827

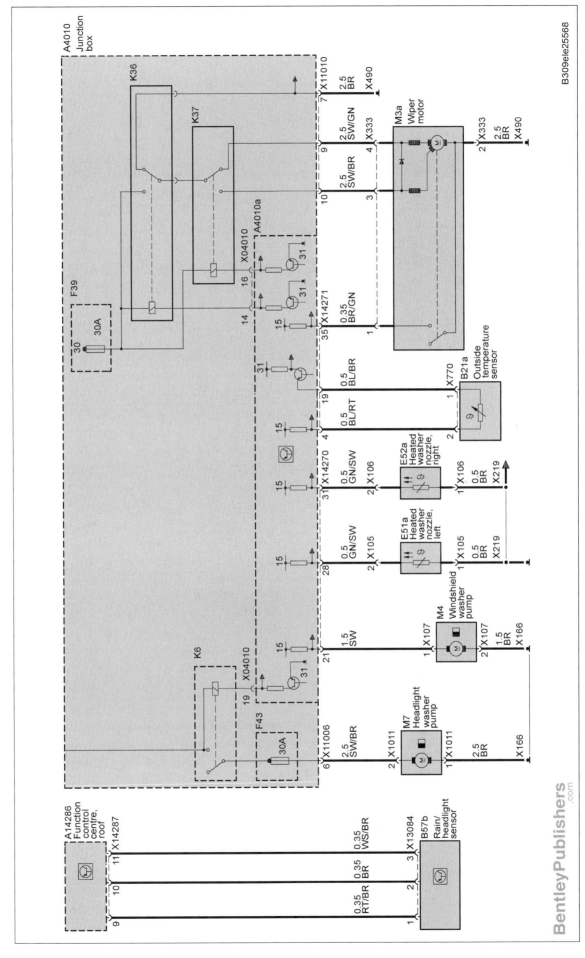

**Wiper-washer control
Convertible (to 03 / 2007)
(page 2 of 2)**

Electrical Wiring Diagrams  ELE-261

B309ele25568

BentleyPublishers.com

**Wiper-washer control
Sports Wagon
(page 1 of 2)**

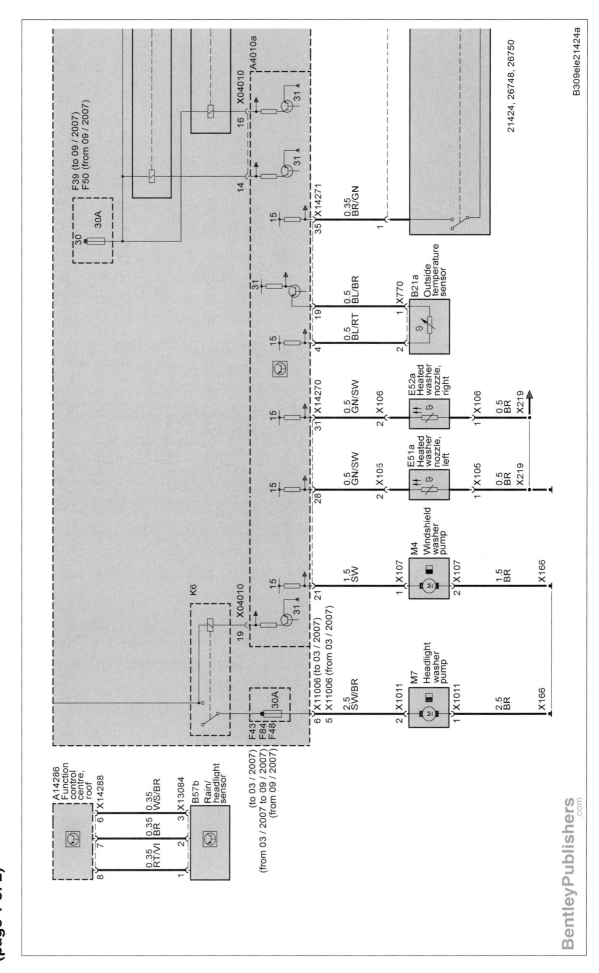

B309ele21424a

21424, 26748, 26750

**Wiper-washer control**
**Sports Wagon**
**(page 2 of 2)**

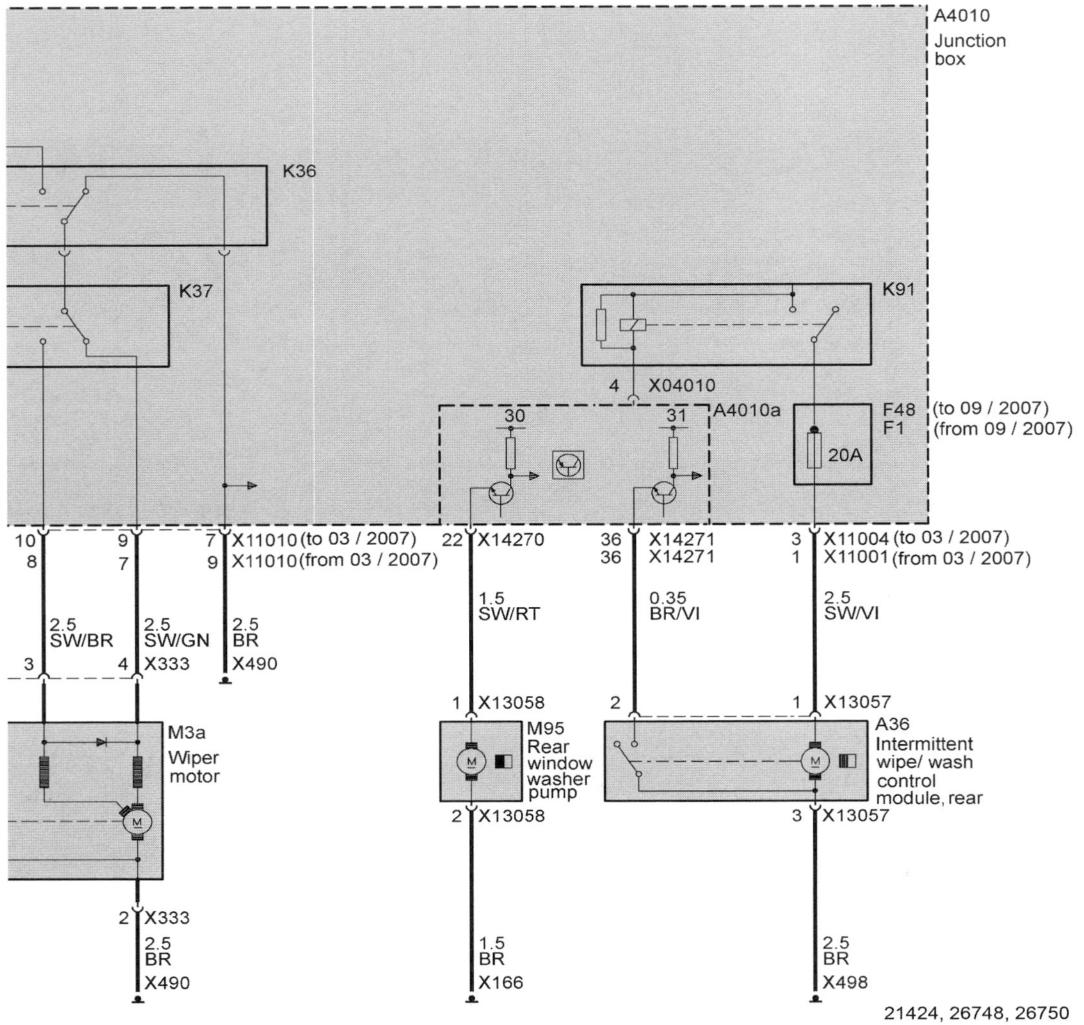

A4010
Junction
box

K91

F48 (to 09 / 2007)
F1 (from 09 / 2007)

20A

X11004 (to 03 / 2007)
X11001 (from 03 / 2007)

2,5
SW/VI

A36
Intermittent
wipe/ wash
control
module, rear

X13057

X13057

2,5
BR
X498

A4010a

X04010

31

X14271
X14271

0,35
BR/VI

30

X14270

1,5
SW/RT

M95
Rear
window
washer
pump

X13058

X13058

1,5
BR
X166

K36

K37

X11010 (to 03 / 2007)
X11010 (from 03 / 2007)

2,5
BR
X490

2,5
SW/GN
X333

M3a
Wiper
motor

X333

2,5
BR
X490

2,5
SW/BR
X333

21424, 26748, 26750

**Wiper-washer control
Sedan and Coupe (from 03 / 2007)
(page 1 of 2)**

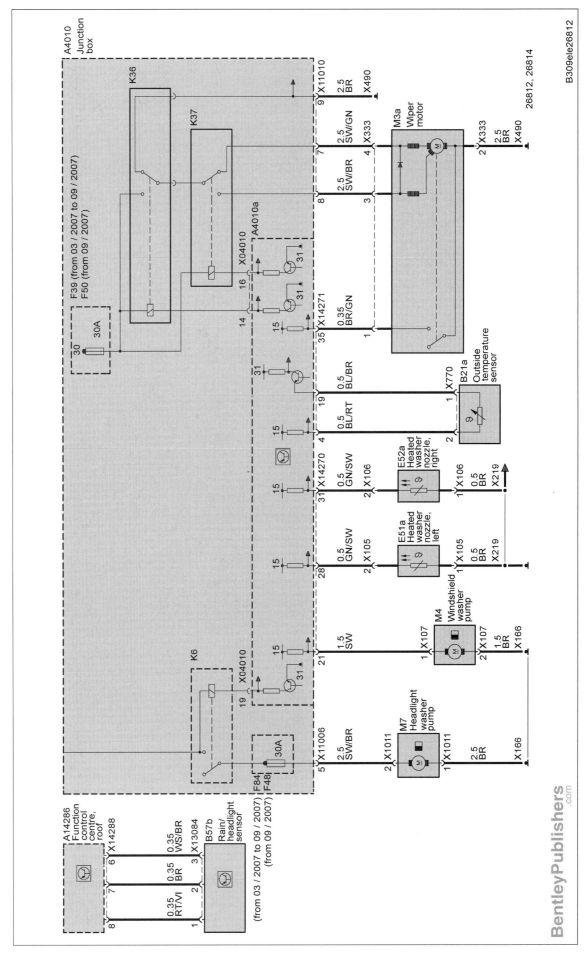

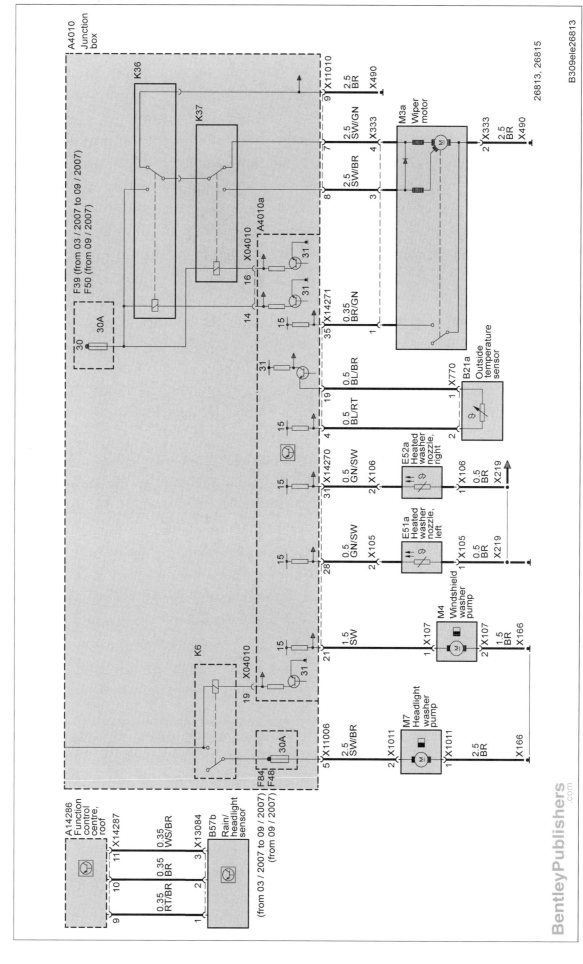

## Instrument cluster, power supply

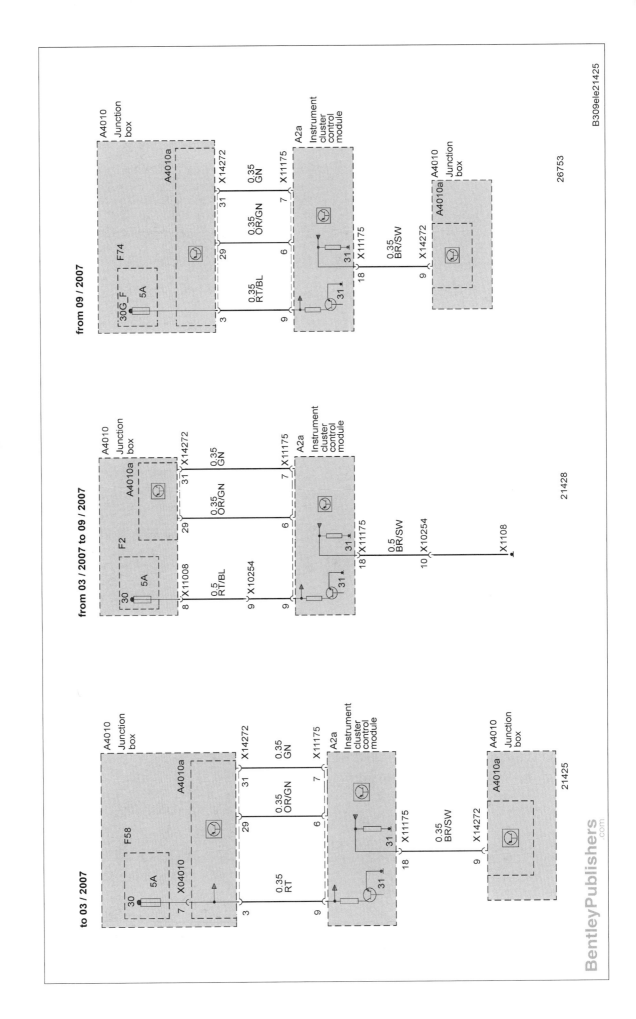

# OBD On-Board Diagnostics

## GENERAL

This chapter outlines the fundamentals and equipment requirements of On-Board Diagnostics II (OBD II) standards as they apply to BMW vehicles. Also covered here is a listing of BMW and OBD II diagnostic trouble codes (DTCs).

## ON-BOARD DIAGNOSTICS (OBD II)

OBD II standards were developed by the SAE (Society of Automotive Engineers) and CARB (California Air Resources Board). OBD II is the second generation of on-board self-diagnostic equipment requirements. These standards were originally mandated for California vehicles. Since 1996 they have been applied to all passenger vehicles sold in the United States.

On-board diagnostic capabilities are incorporated into the hardware and software of the engine control module (ECM) to monitor virtually every component that can affect vehicle emissions. The OBD II system works to ensure that emissions remain as clean as possible over the life of the vehicle.

Each emission-influencing component is checked by a diagnostic routine (called a monitor) to verify that it is functioning properly. If a problem or malfunction is detected, the **diagnostic executive** built into the OBD II system illuminates a malfunction indicator light (MIL) on the instrument panel.

The OBD II system also stores diagnostic trouble codes (DTCs) about the detected malfunction in the ECM so that a repair technician can accurately find and fix the problem. Specialized OBD II scan tool equipment is needed to access the fault memory and OBD II data.

OBD

The extra hardware needed to operate the OBD II system consists mainly of the following:

- Additional oxygen sensors downstream of the catalytic converters
- Fuel tank pressure sensor and device to pressurize fuel storage system
- Several engine and performance monitoring devices
- Standardized 16-pin OBD II connector under the dashboard
- Upgraded components for the federally required reliability mandate

## Malfunction indicator light (MIL)

OBD II software cause the malfunction indicator light (MIL) to illuminate when emission levels exceed 1.5 times Federal standards.

 For 3 Series vehicles covered by this manual, two MIL symbols are used.

MIL illuminates under the following conditions:

- Engine management system fault detected for **two** consecutive OBD II drive cycles. See **Drive cycle** in this repair group.
- Catalyst damaging fault detected.
- Component malfunction causes emissions to exceed 1.5 times OBD II standards.
- Manufacturer-defined specifications exceeded.
- Implausible input signal.
- Misfire faults.
- Leak in evaporative system.
- Oxygen sensors observe no purge flow from purge valve / evaporative system.
- ECM fails to enter closed-loop operation within specified time.
- ECM or automatic transmission control module (TCM) in "limp home" mode.
- Ignition key ON before cranking (bulb check function).

OBD II fault memory (including the MIL) can only be reset using a special scan tool. Removing the connector from the ECM or disconnecting the battery does not erase the fault memory.

### Additional MIL information:

- A fault code is stored within the ECM upon the first occurrence of a fault in the system being checked.
- Two **complete** consecutive drive cycles with the fault present illuminate the MIL. The exception to the two-fault requirement is a catalyst-damaging fault, which illuminates the MIL immediately.
- If the second drive cycle was not complete and the fault was not checked, the ECM counts the third drive cycle as the next consecutive drive cycle. The MIL illuminates if the system is checked and the fault is still present.
- Once the MIL is illuminated, it remains illuminated until the vehicle completes three consecutive drive cycles without detecting a fault.
- An existing fault code is cleared from memory automatically when the vehicle completes **40** consecutive drive cycles without the fault being detected.

In order to automatically clear a catalyst-damaging fault from memory, the condition under which the fault occurred must be evaluated for **80** consecutive drive cycles without the fault reoccurring.

A generic scan tool connected to the OBD II plug can display diagnostic trouble codes (DTCs), along with the conditions associated with the illumination of the MIL. Using a more advanced or BMW-dedicated scan tool, additional proprietary information is normally available.

## Scan tool and scan tool display

◄ The complexity of the OBD II system requires that all diagnostics begin by connecting a scan tool to the 16-pin OBD II plug inside the vehicle.

OBD II standards require that the 16-pin OBD II plug be located within three (3) feet of the driver and not require any tools to access.

Professional diagnostic scan tools available at the time of this printing include the BMW factory tools (GT1, ISTA) and a small number of aftermarket BMW-specific tools. See **020 Maintenance**.

In addition to the professional line of scan tools, inexpensive generic OBD II scan tool software programs and handheld units are readily available. Though limited, they are nonetheless powerful diagnostic tools. These tools read live data streams and freeze frame data as well as a host of other valuable diagnostic data.

## Diagnostic monitors

Diagnostic monitors run tests and checks on specific emission control systems, components, and functions.

A complete drive cycle is required for the tests to be valid. See **Drive cycle** in this repair group. The diagnostic monitor signals the ECM of the loss or impairment of the signal or component and determines if a signal or sensor is faulty based on 3 conditions:

• Signal or component shorted to ground

• Signal or component shorted to B+

• Signal or component missing (open circuit)

The OBD II system monitors all emission control systems that are installed. Emission control systems vary by vehicle model and year. For example, a vehicle may not be equipped with secondary air injection, so no secondary air readiness code would be present.

OBD II software monitors the following:

• Oxygen sensors

• Catalysts

• Engine misfire

• Fuel tank evaporative control system

• Secondary air injection

• Fuel system

**OBD**

**Oxygen sensor monitoring**. When driving conditions allow, response rate and switching time of each oxygen sensor is monitored. The oxygen sensor heater function is also monitored. The OBD II system differentiates between precatalyst and post-catalyst oxygen sensors and reads each one individually. In order for the oxygen sensor to be effectively monitored, the system must be in closed loop operation.

**Catalyst monitoring**. This strategy monitors the two heated oxygen sensors per bank of cylinders. It compares the oxygen content going into the catalytic converter to the oxygen leaving the converter.

The diagnostic executive knows that most of the oxygen should be used up during the oxidation phase. If it sees higher than programmed values, a fault is set and the MIL illuminates.

**Misfire detection.** This strategy monitors crankshaft speed fluctuations and determines if an engine misfire occurs by monitoring variations in speed between each crankshaft sensor trigger point. This strategy is so finely tuned that it can determine the severity of the misfire.

The system determines if a misfire is occurring, as well as other pertinent misfire information such as:
• Specific cylinder(s)
• Severity of the misfire event
• Emissions relevant or catalyst damaging

Misfire detection is an on-going monitoring process that is only disabled under certain limited conditions.

**Secondary air injection monitoring**. Secondary air injection is used to reduce HC and CO emissions during engine warm up. Immediately following a cold engine start (-10° to 40°C), fresh air (and therefore oxygen) is pumped directly into the exhaust manifold. By injecting additional oxygen into the exhaust manifold, catalyst warm-up time is reduced.

Secondary air system components are:
• Electric air injection pump
• Electric pump relay
• Non-return valve
• Vacuum / vent valve
• Mini air mass meter

The secondary air system is monitored via the use of the pre-catalyst oxygen sensors and a mini air mass meter. The oxygen sensors monitor exhaust gas for a lean condition once the air pump is active and air is injected into the system.If the oxygen sensor signal does not change, a fault is set and the faulty bank(s) identified. If after completing the next cold start a fault is again present, the MIL illuminates. The mini air mass meter monitors the air supplied by the secondary air pump when commanded on. If the mini air mass meter detects no air mass or insufficient air mass, a fault is stored in the ECM and the malfunction indicator light (MIL) is activated.

**Fuel system monitoring**. This monitor looks at the fuel delivery needed (long / short term fuel trim) for proper engine operation based on programmed data. If too much or not enough fuel is delivered over a predetermined time, a DTC is set and the MIL is turned on.

Fuel trim refers to adjustments to base fuel schedule. Long-term fuel trim refers to gradual adjustments to the fuel calibration adjustment as compared to short term fuel trim. Long term fuel trim adjustments compensate for gradual changes that occur over time.

Fuel system monitoring monitors the calculated injection time (ti) in relation to engine speed, load, and precatalytic converter oxygen sensor(s) signals.

Using this data, the system optimizes fuel delivery for all engine operating conditions.

**Evaporative system monitoring**. This monitor checks the fuel storage system and related fuel lines for leaks. It can detect very small leaks anywhere in the system.

A leak detection unit (DMTL) is used to pressurize the EVAP system on a continuous basis (as the drive cycle allows) and to check system integrity.

## Drive cycle

The OBD II drive cycle is an important concept in understanding OBD II requirements. The purpose of the drive cycle is to run all of the emission-related on-board diagnostics over a broad range of driving conditions.

A drive cycle is considered complete when all of the diagnostic monitors have run their tests without interruption. For a drive cycle to be initiated, the vehicle must be started cold and brought up to 160°F and at least 40°F above its original starting temperature.

## Readiness codes

Inspection/maintenance (I/M) readiness codes are mandated as part of OBD II. The readiness code is stored after complete diagnostic monitoring of specified components and systems is carried out. The readiness code function was designed to prevent manipulating an I/M emission test procedure by clearing faults codes or disconnecting the ECM or battery.

Readiness codes indicate whether the OBD II system is actually ready to monitor the various emission control systems on the vehicle. The vehicle must complete a drive cycle to set readiness codes. The code is binary:

• 0 for ready

• 1 for not ready

**OBD**

*Readiness codes*

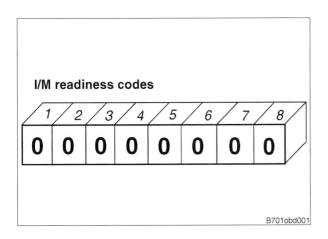

**I/M readiness codes**

| 1 | 2 | 3 | 4 | 5 | 6 | 7 | 8 |
|---|---|---|---|---|---|---|---|
| 0 | 0 | 0 | 0 | 0 | 0 | 0 | 0 |

B701obd001

The parameters which are monitored for readiness are:

1. Catalyst efficiency
2. Catalyst heating
3. Fuel tank evaporative control
4. Secondary air injection
5. A/C refrigerant
6. Oxygen sensors
7. Oxygen sensor heaters
8. Exhaust gas recirculation

When all zeros are displayed, the system has established readiness. Readiness codes can be displayed using BMW and aftermarket scan tools.

Readiness codes are set to 1 (not ready) in the following cases:

• The battery or ECM is disconnected.

• DTCs are erased after completion of repairs and a drive cycle is not completed.

## Diagnostic trouble codes (DTCs)

SAE standard J2012 mandates a 5-digit diagnostic trouble code (DTC) standard. Each digit represents a specific value. Emission related DTCs start with the letter P for power train. When the MIL illuminates it indicates that a DTC has been stored:

- DTCs are stored as soon as they occur, whether or not the MIL illuminates.
- DTCs store and display a time stamp.
- DTCs record the current fault status: Present, not currently present, or intermittent.

| DTC digit interpretation | |
|---|---|
| 1st digit<br>P<br>B<br>C | <br>powertrain<br>body<br>chassis |
| 2nd digit<br>0<br>1 | <br>SAE<br>BMW |
| 3rd digit<br>0<br>1<br>2<br>3<br>4<br>5<br>6<br>7 | <br>total system<br>air / fuel induction<br>fuel injection<br>ignition system or misfire<br>auxiliary emission control<br>vehicle speed & idle control<br>ECM inputs / outputs<br>transmission |
| 4th - 5th digits | individual circuits or components |

### DTC example: P 0 3 0 6

- **P:** A powertrain problem
- **0**: SAE sanctioned ('generic')
- **3:** Related to an ignition system / misfire
- **06** Misfire detected at cylinder #6

DTCs provide a freeze frame or snap-shot of a vehicle performance or emissions fault at the moment that the fault first occurs. This information is accessible through generic scan tools.

Freeze frame data contains, but isn't limited to, the following information:

- Engine load (calculated)
- Engine rpm
- Short and long-term fuel trim
- Vehicle speed
- Coolant temperature
- Intake manifold pressure
- Open / closed loop operation
- Fuel pressure (if available)

**OBD**

**Diagnostic trouble codes (DTCs)**

**Table a. Diagnostic trouble codes (DTCs)**

| P-code | BMW FC | Definition |
|--------|--------|------------|
| P00B2 | 2EEC | Radiator Coolant Temperature Sensor Circuit Range / Performance |
| P00B3 | 2EEA | Radiator Coolant Temperature Sensor Circuit Low |
| P00B4 | 2EEA | Radiator Coolant Temperature Sensor Circuit High |
| P0010 | 2A80 | 'A' Camshaft Position Actuator Circuit Open (Bank 1) |
| P0011 | | 'A' Camshaft Position Timing Over-Advanced or System Performance (Bank 1) |
| P0012 | 2A82 | 'A' Camshaft Position Timing Over-Retarded (Bank 1) |
| P0013 | 2A85 | 'B' Camshaft Position Actuator Circuit Open (Bank 1) |
| P0014 | | 'B' Camshaft Position Timing Over-Advanced or System Performance (Bank 1) |
| P0015 | 2A87 | 'B' Camshaft Position Timing Over-Retarded (Bank 1) |
| P0016 | 2AA4 | Camshaft Position Sensor Correlation) Bank 1 Sensor 'A') |
| P0017 | 2AA5 | Camshaft Position Sensor Correlation) Bank 1 Sensor 'B') |
| P0030 | 2C9C | HO2S Heater Control Circuit (Bank 1 Sensor 1) |
| P0031 | 2C9C | HO2S Heater Control Circuit Low (Bank 1 Sensor 1) |
| P0032 | 2C9C | HO2S Heater Control Circuit High (Bank 1 Sensor 1) |
| P0036 | 2C9E | HO2S Heater Control Circuit (Bank 1 Sensor 2) |
| P0037 | 2C9E | HO2S Heater Control Circuit Low (Bank 1 Sensor 2) |
| P0038 | 2C9E | HO2S Heater Control Circuit High (Bank 1 Sensor 2) |
| P0040 | 2C24 | HO2S Signals Swapped Bank 1 Sensor 1 / Bank 2 Sensor 1 |
| P0041 | 2C64 | HO2S Signals Swapped Bank 1 Sensor 2/ Bank 2 Sensor 2 |
| P0050 | 2C9D | HO2S Heater Control Circuit (Bank 2 Sensor 1) |
| P0051 | 2C9D | HO2S Heater Control Circuit Low (Bank 2 Sensor 1) |
| P0052 | 2C9D | HO2S Heater Control Circuit High (Bank 2 Sensor 1) |
| P0053 | 2CA6 | HO2S Heater Resistance (Bank 1 Sensor 1) |
| P0056 | 2C9F | HO2S Heater Control Circuit (Bank 2 Sensor 2) |
| P0057 | 2C9F | HO2S Heater Control Circuit Low (Bank 2 Sensor 2) |
| P0058 | 2C9F | HO2S Heater Control Circuit High (Bank 2 Sensor 2) |
| P0059 | 2CA7 | HO2S Heater Resistance (Bank 2 Sensor 1) |
| P0070 | 2F9A | Ambient Air Temperature Sensor Circuit |
| P0071 | 2F99 | Ambient Air Temperature Sensor Circuit Range / Performance |
| P0072 | 2F9A | Ambient Air Temperature Sensor Circuit Low |
| P0073 | 2F9A | Ambient Air Temperature Sensor Circuit High |
| P0090 | 2FBC | Fuel Pressure Regulator 1 Control Circuit Open |
| p0091 | 2FBC | Fuel Pressure Regulator 1 Control Circuit Low |
| P0092 | 2FBC | Fuel Pressure Regulator 1 Control Circuit High |
| P0A14 | 2FAB | Engine Mount 'A' Control Circuit Open |
| P0A15 | 2FAB | Engine Mount 'A' Control Circuit Low |

**Table a. Diagnostic trouble codes (DTCs) (continued)**

| P-code | BMW FC | Definition |
|--------|--------|------------|
| P0A16 | 2FAB | Engine Mount 'A' Control Circuit High |
| P0A3B | 2E97 | Generator Over Temperature |
| P0A3B | 2ECF | Generator Over Temperature |
| P0100 | 2D16 | Mass Air Flow or Volume 'A' Circuit |
| P0101 | 2D15 | Mass or Volume Air Flow Circuit Range/Performance |
| P0102 | | Mass or Volume Air Flow Circuit Low Input |
| P0103 | | Mass or Volume Air Flow Circuit High Input |
| P0107 | | Manifold Absolute Pressure/Barometric Pressure Circuit Low Input |
| P0108 | | Manifold Absolute Pressure/Barometric Pressure Circuit High Input |
| P0111 | 2F09 | Intake Temperature Sensor Bank 1 Temperature Range / Performance |
| P0112 | 2F08 | Intake Air Temperature Sensor 1 Circuit Low |
| P0113 | 2F08 | Intake Air Temperature Sensor 1 Circuit High |
| P0117 | 2EE0 | Engine Coolant Temperature Circuit Low |
| P0118 | 2EE0 | Engine Coolant Temperature Circuit High |
| P0121 | 2CF6 | Throttle/Pedal Position Sensor/Switch 'A' Circuit Range/Performance |
| P0122 | 2CF9 | Throttle/Pedal Position Sensor/Switch 'A' Circuit Low |
| P0123 | 2CF9 | Throttle/Pedal Position Sensor/Switch 'A' Circuit High |
| P0125 | | Insufficient Coolant Temperature for Closed Loop Fuel Control |
| P0128 | 2EF4 | Coolant Thermostat (Coolant Temperature Below Thermostat Regulating Temperature) |
| P0131 | 2C3F | O2 Sensor Circuit Low Voltage (Bank 1 Sensor 1) |
| P0132 | 2C3F | O2 Sensor Circuit High Voltage (Bank 1 Sensor 1) |
| P0133 | 2C39 | O2 Sensor Circuit Slow Response (Bank 1 Sensor 1) |
| P0134 | | O2 Sensor Circuit No Activity Detected (Bank 1 Sensor 1) |
| P0135 | 2CA6 | O2 Sensor Heater Circuit (Bank 1 Sensor 1) |
| P0137 | 2C75 | O2 Sensor Circuit Low Voltage (Bank 1 Sensor 2) |
| P0138 | 2C73 | O2 Sensor Circuit High Voltage (Bank 1 Sensor 2) |
| P0139 | 2C7B | O2 Sensor Circuit Slow Response (Bank 1 Sensor 2) |
| P0139 | | O2 Sensor Circuit Slow Response (Bank 1 Sensor 2) |
| P0140 | 2C77 | O2 Sensor Circuit No Activity Detected (Bank 1 Sensor 2) |
| P0141 | 2CA8 | O2 Sensor Heater Circuit (Bank 1 Sensor 2) |
| P0151 | 2C40 | O2 Sensor Circuit Low Voltage (Bank 2 Sensor 1) |
| P0152 | 2C40 | O2 Sensor Circuit High Voltage (Bank 2 Sensor 1) |
| P0153 | 2C3A | O2 Sensor Circuit Slow Response (Bank 2 Sensor 1) |
| P0154 | | O2 Sensor Circuit No Activity Detected (Bank 2 Sensor 1) |
| P0155 | 2CA7 | O2 Sensor Heater Circuit (Bank 2 Sensor 1) |
| P0157 | 2C76 | O2 Sensor Circuit Low Voltage (Bank 2 Sensor 2) |
| P0158 | 2C74 | O2 Sensor Circuit High Voltage (Bank 2 Sensor 2) |

**OBD**

**Table a. Diagnostic trouble codes (DTCs) (continued)**

| P-code | BMW FC | Definition |
|--------|--------|------------|
| P0159 | 2C7E | O2 Sensor Circuit Slow Response (Bank 2 Sensor 2) |
| P0159 | 2C7C | O2 Sensor Circuit Slow Response (Bank 2 Sensor 2) |
| P0160 | 2C78 | O2 Sensor Circuit No Activity Detected (Bank 2 Sensor 2) |
| P0161 | 2CA9 | O2 Sensor Heater Circuit (Bank 2 Sensor 2) |
| P0171 | 29E0 | System Too Lean (Bank 1) |
| P0171 | 2A2B | System Too Lean (Bank 1) |
| P0172 | 29E0 | System Too Rich (Bank 1) |
| P0172 | 2A2B | System Too Rich (Bank 1) |
| P0174 | 29E1 | System Too Lean (Bank 2) |
| P0174 | 2A2C | System Too Lean (Bank 2) |
| P0175 | 29E1 | System Too Rich (Bank 2) |
| P0175 | 2A2C | System Too Rich (Bank 2) |
| P0190 | 29E2 | Fuel Rail Pressure Sensor 'A' Circuit |
| P0192 | 29E2 | Fuel Rail Pressure Sensor 'A' Circuit Low |
| P0197 |  | Engine Oil Temperature Sensor Low |
| P0198 |  | Engine Oil Temperature Sensor High |
| P02AA | 3074 | Cylinder 5 Fuel Trim at Maximum Limit |
| P02AB | 3074 | Cylinder 5 Fuel Trim at Minimum Limit |
| P02AE | 3075 | Cylinder 6 Fuel Trim at Maximum Limit |
| P02AF | 3075 | Cylinder 6 Fuel Trim at Minimum Limit |
| P02A2 | 3072 | Cylinder 3 Fuel Trim at Maximum Limit |
| P02A3 | 3072 | Cylinder 3 Fuel Trim at Minimum Limit |
| P02A6 | 3073 | Cylinder 4 Fuel Trim at Maximum Limit |
| P02A7 | 3073 | Cylinder 4 Fuel Trim at Minimum Limit |
| P0201 | 2E30 | Injector Circuit/Open - Cylinder 1 |
| P0202 | 2E31 | Injector Circuit/Open - Cylinder 2 |
| P0203 | 2E32 | Injector Circuit/Open - Cylinder 3 |
| P0204 | 2E33 | Injector Circuit/Open - Cylinder 4 |
| P0205 | 2E34 | Injector Circuit/Open - Cylinder 5 |
| P0206 | 2E35 | Injector Circuit/Open - Cylinder 6 |
| P0221 | 2CF7 | Throttle/Pedal Position Sensor/Switch 'B' Circuit Range/Performance |
| P0222 | 2CFA | Throttle/Pedal Position Sensor/Switch 'B' Circuit Low |
| P0223 | 2CFA | Throttle/Pedal Position Sensor/Switch 'B' Circuit High |
| P0234 | 30FE | Turbocharger 'A' Overboost Condition |
| P0236 | 2ABD | Turbocharger Boost Sensor 'A' Circuit Range / Performance |
| P0237 | 2ABC | Turbocharger Boost Sensor 'A' Circuit Low |
| P0238 | 2ABD | Turbocharger Boost Sensor 'A' Circuit High |

**Table a. Diagnostic trouble codes (DTCs) (continued)**

| P-code | BMW FC | Definition |
|--------|--------|------------|
| P0243 | 30CF | Turbocharger Wastegate Solenoid 'A' |
| P0245 | 30CF | Turbocharger Wastegate Solenoid 'A' Low |
| P0246 | 30CF | Turbocharger Wastegate Solenoid 'A' High |
| P0247 | 30D0 | Turbocharger Wastegate Solenoid 'B' |
| P0249 | 30D0 | Turbocharger Wastegate Solenoid 'B' Low |
| P0250 | 30D0 | Turbocharger Wastegate Solenoid 'B' High |
| P0261 | 2E30 | Cylinder 1 Injector Circuit Low |
| P0262 | 2E30 | Cylinder 1 Injector Circuit High |
| P0264 | 2E31 | Cylinder 2 Injector Circuit Low |
| P0265 | 2E31 | Cylinder 2 Injector Circuit High |
| P0266 | 2E32 | Cylinder 3 Injector Circuit High |
| P0267 | 2E32 | Cylinder 3 Injector Circuit Low |
| P0268 | 2E32 | Cylinder 3 Injector Circuit High |
| P0270 | 2E33 | Cylinder 4 Injector Circuit Low |
| P0271 | 2E33 | Cylinder 4 Injector Circuit High |
| P0273 | 2E34 | Cylinder 5 Injector Circuit Low |
| P0274 | 2E34 | Cylinder 5 Injector Circuit High |
| P0276 | 2E35 | Cylinder 6 Injector Circuit Low |
| P0277 | 2E35 | Cylinder 6 Injector Circuit High |
| P029A | 3070 | Cylinder 1 Fuel Trim at Maximum Limit |
| P029B | 3070 | Cylinder 1 Fuel Trim at Minimum Limit |
| P029E | 3071 | Cylinder 2 Fuel Trim at Maximum Limit |
| P029F | 3071 | Cylinder 2 Fuel Trim at Minimum Limit |
| P0299 | 30FF | Turbocharger 'B' Overboost Condition |
| P0300 | 29CC | Cylinder Misfire, Several Cylinders |
| P0301 | 29CD | Cylinder 1 Misfire Detected |
| P0302 | 29CE | Cylinder 2 Misfire Detected |
| P0303 | 29CF | Cylinder 3 Misfire Detected |
| P0304 | 29D0 | Cylinder 4 Misfire Detected |
| P0305 | 29D1 | Cylinder 5 Misfire Detected |
| P0306 | 29D2 | Cylinder 6 Misfire Detected |
| P0313 | 29D9 | Misfire Detected with Low Fuel |
| P0326 | 2E68 | Knock Sensor 1 Circuit Range / Performance (Bank 1 or Single Sensor) |
| P0326 | 2CA6 | Knock Sensor 1 Circuit Range / Performance (Bank 1 or Single Sensor) |
| P0327 | 2E68 | Knock Sensor 1 Circuit Low (Bank 1 or Single Sensor) |
| P0328 | 2E68 | Knock Sensor 1 Circuit High (Bank 1 or Single Sensor) |
| P0332 |  | Knock Sensor 2 Circuit Low (Bank 2) |

**OBD**

*Diagnostic trouble codes (DTCs)*

**Table a. Diagnostic trouble codes (DTCs) (continued)**

| P-code | BMW FC | Definition |
|--------|--------|------------|
| P0335 | 2A94 | Crankshaft Position Sensor 'A' Circuit |
| P0339 | | Crankshaft Position Sensor 'A' Circuit Intermittent |
| P0340 | 2AA0 | Camshaft Position Sensor 'A' Circuit (Bank 1 or Single Sensor) |
| P0341 | 2A9A | Camshaft Position Sensor 'A' Performance (Bank 1) |
| P0344 | 2A9E | Camshaft Position Sensor 'A' Circuit Intermittent (Bank 1 or Single Sensor) |
| P0351 | 2E24 | Ignition Coil 'A' Primary / Secondary Circuit |
| P0352 | 2E25 | Ignition Coil 'B' Primary / Secondary Circuit |
| P0353 | 2E26 | Ignition Coil 'C' Primary / Secondary Circuit |
| P0354 | 2E27 | Ignition Coil 'D' Primary / Secondary Circuit |
| P0355 | 2E28 | Ignition Coil 'E' Primary / Secondary Circuit |
| P0356 | 2E29 | Ignition Coil 'F' Primary / Secondary Circuit |
| P0365 | 2AA1 | Camshaft Position Sensor 'B' Circuit (Bank 1) |
| P0366 | 2A9B | Camshaft Position Sensor 'B' Performance (Bank 1) |
| P0369 | 2A9F | Camshaft Position Sensor 'B' Circuit Intermittent (Bank 1) |
| P0370 | 29DB | Smooth Running Segment Timing |
| P0370 | 2A96 | Timing Reference High Signal 'A' Resolution |
| P0370 | 2A97 | Timing Reference High Signal 'A' Resolution |
| P0373 | 2A95 | Timing Reference High Signal 'A' Resolution Erratic |
| P0413 | | Secondary Air Injection System Switching Valve A Circuit Open |
| P0414 | | Secondary Air Injection System Switching Valve A Circuit Shorted |
| P0420 | 29F4 | Catalyst System Efficiency Below Threshold (Bank 1) |
| P0420 | 29F6 | Catalyst System Efficiency Below Threshold (Bank 1) |
| P0430 | 29F5 | Catalyst System Efficiency Below Threshold (Bank 2) |
| P0440 | 2A1A | Evaporative Emission System Incorrect Flow |
| P0441 | 2A1A | Evaporative Emission System Incorrect Purge Flow |
| P0442 | 2A15 | Evaporative Emission System Leak Detected (small leak) |
| P0443 | | Evaporative Emission System Purge Control Valve Circuit |
| P0444 | 2A19 | Evaporative Emission System Purge Control Valve Circuit Open |
| | 2A1A | Fuel Tank Venting Function Fault |
| P0445 | | Evaporative Emission System Purge Control Valve Circuit Shorted |
| P0455 | | Evaporative Emission System Leak Detected (large leak) |
| P0456 | 2A16 | Evaporative Emission System Leak Detected (very small leak) |
| P0457 | 2A1B | Evaporative Emission System Leak Detected (Fuel Filler Cap Loose) |
| P0458 | 2A19 | Evaporative Emission System Purge Control Valve Circuit Low |
| P0459 | 2A19 | Evaporative Emission System Purge Control Valve Circuit High |
| P0461 | 2A1C | Fuel Level Sensor A Performance |
| P0462 | 2DE2 | Fuel Level Sensor 'A' Circuit Low |

**Table a. Diagnostic trouble codes (DTCs) (continued)**

| P-code | BMW FC | Definition |
|--------|--------|------------|
| P0463 | 2DE2 | Fuel Level Sensor 'A' Circuit High |
| P0475 | 2F6C | Exhaust Pressure Control Valve |
| P0476 | 2F6C | Exhaust Pressure Control Valve Low |
| P0477 | 2F6C | Exhaust Pressure Control Valve Low |
| P0478 | 2F6C | Exhaust Pressure Control Valve High |
| P0480 | 2EFE | Fan 1 Control Circuit |
| P0491 | 2A00 | Secondary Air Injection System Insufficient Flow (Bank 1) |
| P0492 | 2A00 | Secondary Air Injection System Insufficient Flow (Bank 2) |
| P0500 | 2F4E | Vehicle Speed Sensor 'A' |
| P0503 | 2F4F | Vehicle Speed Sensor 'A' Intermittent / Erratic |
| P0505 | | Idle Air Control System |
| P0506 | 2ADF | Idle Air Control System Lower Than Expected |
| P0507 | 2ADF | Idle Air Control System Higher Than Expected |
| P0512 | 2F58 | Starter Request Circuit |
| P0520 | 2F7B | Engine Oil Pressure Switch Circuit |
| P0521 | 30C6 | Engine Oil Pressure Switch Range / Performance |
| P0522 | 30C3 | Engine Oil Pressure Switch Open |
| P0523 | 30C3 | Engine Oil Pressure Switch High |
| P0524 | 30C5 | Engine Oil Pressure Too Low |
| P053A | 2AE4 | Positive Crankcase Ventilation Heater Circuit Open |
| P053B | 2AE4 | Positive Crankcase Ventilation Heater Circuit Low |
| P053C | 2AE$ | Positive Crankcase Ventilation Heater Circuit High |
| P0545 | 2C87 | Exhaust Gas Temperature Sensor Circuit Low (Bank1 Sensor 1) |
| P0546 | 2C87 | Exhaust Gas Temperature Sensor Circuit High (Bank1 Sensor 1) |
| P0571 | 2F63 | Brake Switch 'A' Circuit |
| P0597 | 2EF5 | Thermostat Heater Control Circuit / Open |
| P0598 | 2EF5 | Thermostat Heater Control Circuit Low |
| P0599 | 2EF5 | Thermostat Heater Control Circuit High |
| P060C | 2D67 | Internal Control Module Internal Processor fault |
| P0600 | | Serial Communication Link |
| P0604 | 2AB2 | Internal Control Module Random Access Memory (RAM) Error |
| P0605 | 2D67 | Internal Control Module ROM |
| P0606 | 2D67 | ECM Processor |
| P062F | 2FA3 | Internal Control Module EEPROM Error |
| P0620 | 2ECD | Generator Control Circuit |
| P0620 | 2E97 | Generator Control Circuit |
| P0645 | 2F12 | A/C Clutch Relay Control Circuit |

**OBD**

**Table a. Diagnostic trouble codes (DTCs) (continued)**

| P-code | BMW FC | Definition |
|--------|--------|------------|
| P0646 | 2F12 | A/C Clutch Relay Control Circuit Low |
| P0647 | 2F12 | A/C Clutch Relay Control Circuit High |
| P0668 | 2F85 | ECM / TCM Internal Temperature Sensor Circuit Low |
| P0669 | 2F85 | ECM / TCM Internal Temperature Sensor Circuit High |
| P0686 | 2ACB | ECM Power Relay Control Circuit Low |
| P0687 | 2ACB | ECM Power Relay Control Circuit High |
| P0691 | 2EFE | Fan 1 Control Circuit Low |
| P0692 | 2EFE | Fan 1 Control Circuit High |
| P0700 | 2AD0 | Transmission Control System MIL Request |
| P0703 | 2F64 | Brake Switch 'B' Circuit |
| P0831 | 2F67 | Clutch Pedal Switch 'A' Circuit Low |
| P0832 | 2F67 | Clutch Pedal Switch 'A' Circuit High |
| P101A | 2A39 | VVT Self Learning Function Stops Not Learned |
| P101A | 2A46 | VVT Self Learning Function Stops Not Learned |
| P102C | 2A34 | VVT Eccentric Shaft Sensor Diagnostic Error |
| P103A | 2A45 | VVT System Temperature Too High |
| P104E | 2F0A | Turbocharger Intake Air Temperature Sensor 1 Circuit High or Open |
| P104F | 2F0A | Turbocharger Intake Air Temperature Sensor 1 Circuit Input Low |
| P105A | 2A77 | Internal Control Module Fault VVT Current Too High |
| P105B | 2A77 | Internal Control Module Fault VVT Current Too Low |
| P107A | 2A43 | VVT Overload Protection Current Too High (Bank 1) |
| P107B | 2A43 | VVT Overload Protection (Bank 1) |
| P107C | 2A43 | VVT Overload Protection Current Too High (Bank 1) |
|  | 2A44 | Valvetronic Power Limitation |
| P1004 | 2A35 | VVT Guiding Sensor Solenoid Loss (Bank 1) |
| P1006 | 2A31 | VVT Eccentric Shaft Sensor Parity Error (Bank 1) |
| P1012 | 2A36 | VVT Guiding Sensor Solenoid Loss (Bank 1) |
| P1014 | 2A32 | VVT Eccentric Shaft Sensor Parity Error (Bank 1) |
| P1017 | 2A37 | VVT Guiding Sensor Plausibility (Bank 1) |
| P1019 | 2A30 | VVT Eccentric Shaft Sensor Circuit Low |
| P102B | 2A33 | VVT Guiding Sensor Diagnostic Error (Bank 1) |
| P102C | 2A34 | VVT Reference Sensor Diagnostic Error (Bank 1) |
| P1020 | 2A30 | VVT Eccentric Shaft Sensor Circuit High |
| P1023 | 2A39 | VVT Self Learning Function Faulty Adjustment Range (Bank 1) |
| P1024 | 2A39 | VVT Self Learning Function Faulty Lower Learning Range (Bank 1) |
| P1030 | 2A38 | VVT Control Motor Position Control Deviation (Bank1) |
| P1041 | 2A3A | Internal VVT Module EEPROM Error |

**Table a. Diagnostic trouble codes (DTCs) (continued)**

| P-code | BMW FC | Definition |
|--------|--------|------------|
| P1047 | 2A3D | VVT Control Circuit High (Bank 1) |
| P1048 | 2A3D | VVT Control Circuit Low (Bank 1) |
| P1049 | 2A3D | VVT Control Circuit Short (Bank 1) |
| P1055 | 2A3F | VVT Control Circuit High (Bank 1) |
| P1056 | 2A3F | VVT Control Circuit High (Bank 1) |
| P1057 | 2A3C | VVT Motor Supply Voltage (Bank 1) |
| P1062 | 2A44 | VVT Limp Home Request Full Stroke Position Reached (Bank 1) |
| P1064 | 2A42 | VVT Value Comparison Starting / Parking Position Plausibility |
| P1075 | 2A41 | VVT Overload Protection (Bank 1) |
| P1076 | 2A40 | VVT Overload Protection ECM temperature (Bank 1) |
| P1078 | 2A3E | VVT Overload Protection Current Too High (Bank 1) |
| P1083 |  | Fuel Control Limit Mixture Too Lean (Bank 1 Sensor 1) |
| P1084 |  | Fuel Control Limit Mixture Too Rich (Bank 1 Sensor 1) |
| P1085 |  | Fuel Control Limit Mixture Too Lean (Bank 2 Sensor 1) |
| P1086 |  | Fuel Control Limit Mixture Too Rich (Bank 2 Sensor 1) |
| P1087 |  | O2 Sensor Circuit Slow Response in Lean Control Range (Bank 1 Sensor 1) |
| P1088 |  | O2 Sensor Circuit Slow Response in Rich Control Range (Bank 1 Sensor 1) |
| P1089 |  | O2 Sensor Circuit Slow Response in Lean Control Range (Bank 1 Sensor 2) |
| P1090 |  | Pre Catalyst Fuel Trim System Too Lean (Bank 1) |
| P1091 |  | Pre Catalyst Fuel Trim System Too Lean (Bank 2) |
| P1092 |  | Pre Catalyst Fuel Trim System Too Rich (Bank 1) |
| P1093 |  | Pre Catalyst Fuel Trim System Too Rich (Bank 2) |
| P1094 |  | O2 Sensor Circuit Slow Response in Rich Control Range (Bank 2 Sensor 1) |
| P110D | 2D07 | Throttle Position Sensor 'A' and 'B' Range / Performance |
| P110D | 2D61 | Throttle Position Sensor 'A' and 'B' Range / Performance |
| P1104 | 2D29 | Differential Pressure Sensor Intake Manifold Pressure Too Low Bank 1 |
| P1105 | 2D29 | Differential Pressure Sensor Intake Manifold Pressure Too High Bank 1 |
| P111E | 2F09 | Intake Temperature Sensor Bank 1 Maximum Temperature Implausible |
| P111F | 2F09 | Intake Temperature Sensor Bank 1 Temperature Implausible |
| P1111 |  | Engine Coolant Temperature Sensor Radiator Outlet Low Input |
| P1112 |  | Engine Coolant Temperature Sensor Radiator Outlet High Input |
| P112C | 2C3D | O2 Sensor Negative Current or Positive Current Control Circuit Open (Bank 1 Sensor 1) |
| P112D | 2C3E | O2 Sensor Negative Current or Positive Current Control Circuit Open (Bank 2 Sensor 1) |
| P112F | 2D2E | Manifold Absolute Pressure to Throttle Angle - Too High |
| P1120 |  | Pedal Position Sensor Circuit |
| P1121 |  | Pedal Position Sensor 1 Range/Performance Problem |
| P1122 |  | Pedal Position Sensor 1 Low Input |

**OBD**

**Table a. Diagnostic trouble codes (DTCs) (continued)**

| P-code | BMW FC | Definition |
|---|---|---|
| P1123 | | Pedal Position Sensor 1 High Input |
| P1124 | 2D2A | Differential Pressure Sensor Intake Manifold Pressure Offset Bank 1 |
| P1130 | 2C6D | O2 Sensor Circuit Dynamic Test (Bank 1 Sensor 2) |
| P1131 | 2C6E | O2 Sensor Circuit Dynamic Test (Bank 2 Sensor 2) |
| P1134 | | O2 Sensor Heater Circuit Signal Intermittent (Bank 1 Sensor 1) |
| P1135 | | O2 Sensor Heater Circuit Low Voltage (Bank 1 Sensor 1) |
| P1136 | | O2 Sensor Heater Circuit High Voltage (Bank 1 Sensor 1) |
| P1137 | | O2 Sensor Heater Circuit Signal Intermittent (Bank 1 Sensor 2) |
| P1138 | | O2 Sensor Heater Circuit Low Voltage (Bank 1 Sensor 2) |
| P1139 | | O2 Sensor Heater Circuit High Voltage (Bank 1 Sensor 2) |
| P114A | 2C7E | Post Catalyst Fuel Trim Too Rich Bank 1 |
| P114B | 2C7E | Post Catalyst Fuel Trim Too Lean Bank 1 |
| P114C | 2C7F | Post Catalyst Fuel Trim Too Rich Bank 2 |
| P114D | 2C7F | Post Catalyst Fuel Trim Too Lean Bank 2 |
| P114F | 2D16 | Air Mass Flow Sensor Defective |
| P1143 | | O2 Sensor Activity Check Signal Too High (Bank 1 Sensor 2) |
| P1144 | | O2 Sensor Activity Check Signal Too Low (Bank 1 Sensor 2) |
| P1149 | | O2 Sensor Activity Check Signal Too High (Bank 2 Sensor 2) |
| P115A | 2D15 | Mass or Volume Air Flow 'A' Maximum Exceeded |
| P115E | 2F0C | Turbocharger Intake Air Temperature Sensor 1 Gradient Implausible |
| P1150 | | O2 Sensor Activity Check Signal Too Low (Bank 2 Sensor 2) |
| P1151 | | O2 Sensor Heater Circuit Signal Intermittent (Bank 2 Sensor 1) |
| P1152 | | O2 Sensor Heater Circuit Low Voltage (Bank 2 Sensor 1) |
| P1153 | | O2 Sensor Heater Circuit High Voltage (Bank 2 Sensor 1) |
| P1155 | | O2 Sensor Heater Circuit Signal Intermittent (Bank 2 Sensor 2) |
| P1156 | | O2 Sensor Heater Circuit Low Voltage (Bank 2 Sensor 2) |
| P1157 | | O2 Sensor Heater Circuit High Voltage (Bank 2 Sensor 2) |
| P116C | 2D0F | Air Mass Flow Sensor Signal Range |
| P116E | 2D0F | Air Mass Flow Sensor Signal Electrical |
| P1171 | | Ambient Pressure Sensor Variant Recognition Value in Boot Range Implausible |
| P1172 | | Ambient Pressure Sensor Variant Recognition Error Value Stored in Boot Range |
| P1173 | | Ambient Pressure Sensor Variant Recognition Learning Failed |
| P119A | 2D33 | Manifold Absolute Pressure Sensor High (Bank 1) |
| P119B | 2D33 | Manifold Absolute Pressure Sensor Low (Bank 1) |
| P119D | 2E74 | Fuel Trim, Injector Aging Long Term Adaptation Too High (Bank 1) |
| P119E | 2E75 | Fuel Trim, Injector Aging Long Term Adaptation Too High (Bank 2) |
| P1190 | | Pre Catalyst Fuel Trim System (Bank 1) |

**Table a. Diagnostic trouble codes (DTCs) (continued)**

| P-code | BMW FC | Definition |
|--------|--------|------------|
| P1191 | | Pre Catalyst Fuel Trim System (Bank 2) |
| P1192 | | Post Catalyst Fuel Trim System (Bank 1) |
| P1193 | | Post Catalyst Fuel Trim System (Bank 2) |
| P1197 | 2D28 | Differential Pressure Sensor Intake Manifold High Input Bank 1 |
| P1198 | 2D28 | Differential Pressure Sensor Intake Manifold Low Input Bank 1 |
| P121C | 2AF0 | NOx Sensor Heater Control Circuit Shorted (Bank 1) |
| P121E | 2AF2 | NOx Sensor Heater Control Circuit Open (Bank 1) |
| P121F | 2AF2 | NOx Sensor Circuit Shorted (Bank 1) |
| P1214 | 2AAE | Fuel Pump Speed Too High |
| P1215 | 2AAE | Fuel Pump Speed Too Low |
| P1216 | 2AAE | Fuel Pump Emergency Operation |
| P1217 | 2AAE | Fuel Pump Over temperature Condition |
| P122E | 2AF6 | NOx Sensor Binary Oxygen Sensor Signal Control Circuit Open (Bank 1) |
| P122F | 2AF6 | NOx Sensor Binary Oxygen Sensor Signal Control Circuit Shorted (Bank 1) |
| P1222 | | Pedal Position Sensor 2 Low Input |
| P1223 | | Pedal Position Sensor 2 High Input |
| P1230 | 2F94 | Fuel Pump Relay Circuit |
| P1234 | 2F94 | Fuel Pump Relay Circuit Low |
| P1236 | 2F94 | Fuel Pump Relay Circuit High |
| P1244 | 2AAD | Fuel Pump Emergency Cut Off |
| P126F | 30E2 | NOx Sensor Linear Oxygen Sensor Signal Too Rich During Deceleration Test (Bank 1) |
| P127A | 30E2 | NOx Sensor Signal Too Low During Deceleration Test (Bank 1) |
| P127B | 30E2 | NOx Sensor Signal Too High During Deceleration Test (Bank 1) |
| P129B | 2D2B | Manifold Absolute Pressure Sensor Diagnosis Performance |
| P1298 | 2EAF | Serial Communication NOx Sensor (Bank 1) |
| P1299 | 2EAF | Serial Communication NOx Sensor (Bank 2) |
| P130A | 2AA3 | Camshaft Position Sensor 'B' Segment Timing Error (Bank 1) |
| P1300 | 2AA2 | Camshaft Position Sensor 'A' Segment Timing Error (Bank 1) |
| P1301 | 2E18 | Ignition Monitoring Cylinder 1 Spark Duration Too Short |
| P1302 | 2E19 | Ignition Monitoring Cylinder 2 Spark Duration Too Short |
| P1303 | 2E1A | Ignition Monitoring Cylinder 3 Spark Duration Too Short |
| P1304 | 2E1B | Ignition Monitoring Cylinder 3 Spark Duration Too Short |
| P1305 | 2E1C | Ignition Monitoring Cylinder 5 Spark Duration Too Short |
| P1306 | 2E1D | Ignition Monitoring Cylinder 6 Spark Duration Too Short |
| P1314 | | Fuel Mixture Deviation Detected with Low Fuel |
| P1327 | 2E69 | Knock Sensor 2 Circuit Low (Bank 1 or Single Sensor) |
| P1328 | 2E69 | Knock Sensor 2 Circuit Range / Performance (Bank 1 or Single Sensor) |

**OBD**

**Table a. Diagnostic trouble codes (DTCs) (continued)**

| P-code | BMW FC | Definition |
|--------|--------|------------|
| P1342 |  | Misfire During Start Cylinder 1 |
| P1343 |  | Misfire Cylinder 1 with Fuel Cut-Off |
| P1344 |  | Misfire During Start Cylinder 2 |
| P1345 |  | Misfire Cylinder 2 with Fuel Cut-Off |
| P1346 |  | Misfire During Start Cylinder 3 |
| P1347 |  | Misfire Cylinder 3 with Fuel Cut-Off |
| P1348 |  | Misfire During Start Cylinder 4 |
| P1349 |  | Misfire Cylinder 4 with Fuel Cut-Off |
| P135B | 2E69 | Knock Sensor 2 Circuit Range / Performance (Bank 1 or Single Sensor) |
| P1350 |  | Misfire during Start Cylinder 5 |
| P1351 |  | Misfire Cylinder 5 with Fuel Cut-Off |
| P1352 |  | Misfire during Start Cylinder 6 |
| P1353 |  | Misfire Cylinder 6 with Fuel Cut-Off |
| P1383 | 2E77 | Ignition Monitoring Malfunction |
| P1396 | 29DA | Crankshaft Position Sensor Segment Timing Plausibility |
| P140A | 2A00 | Secondary Air Injection System Flow Bank 1 and Bank 2 |
| P140E | 29DC | Cylinder Injection Cut Off, Fuel Level Too Low |
| P14C0 | 2EFF | Fan Mechanical Hardware Defect |
| P14C1 | 2F0F | Radiator Shutter Mechanical hardware Defect |
| P14C2 | 2AAB | DISA (Differentiated Intake Manifold) Actuator 1 Fault |
| P14C3 | 2AAC | DISA (Differentiated Intake Manifold) Actuator 2 Fault |
| P14C4 | 2F11 | Upper Radiator Shutter Mechanical fault |
| P14C5 | 2F11 | Upper Radiator Shutter Electrical fault |
| P14C6 | 2F10 | Lower Radiator Shutter Electrical fault |
| P140E | 29DC | Cylinder Injection Cut Off, Fuel Level Too Low |
| P1413 | 2A03 | Secondary Air Injection Pump Relay Control Circuit Signal Low |
| P1414 | 2A03 | Secondary Air Injection Pump Relay Control Circuit Signal High |
| P1407 | 2DE2 | Fuel Level Signal 1 |
| P1408 | 2DE1 | Fuel Level Signal 2 |
| P1415 | 2D06 | Mass or Volume Air Flow Too Low |
| P1417 | 2D06 | Throttle Control Incorrect Air Supply |
| P1417 | 2D09 | Throttle Control Incorrect Air Supply |
| P142A | 2AE4 | Crankcase Ventilation Heater Relay Circuit Input High |
| P142B | 2AE4 | Crankcase Ventilation Heater Relay Circuit Input Low |
| P142C | 2AE4 | Crankcase Ventilation Heater Relay Circuit Input Open |
| P142E | 29DC | Cylinder Injection Cut Off, Pressure Too Low (High Pressure Fuel System) |
| P142F | 29DC | Cylinder Injection Cut Off, Pressure Too Low (Low Pressure Fuel System) |

**Table a. Diagnostic trouble codes (DTCs) (continued)**

| P-code | BMW FC | Definition |
|--------|--------|------------|
| P1424 | 2D06 | Mass or Volume Air Flow Too High |
| P1429 | 2A18 | DMTL Heater |
| P143B | 2AD9 | Direct Ozone Reduction Catalyst Temperature Sensor Wrong Code |
| P143C | 2AD8 | Direct Ozone Reduction Catalyst Temperature / Radiator Temperature Correlation |
| P143E | 2AD8 | Direct Ozone Reduction Catalyst Temperature Sensor Gradient Too Low |
| P1430 | 2A18 | DMTL Heater Circuit Low |
| P1431 | 2A18 | DMTL Heater Circuit High |
| P1434 | 2A17 | DMTL Tank Leakage |
| P1444 | | Diagnostic Module Tank Leakage (DMTL) Pump Control Open Circuit |
| P1445 | | Diagnostic Module Tank Leakage (DMTL) Pump Control Circuit Signal Low |
| P1446 | | Diagnostic Module Tank Leakage (DMTL) Pump Control Circuit Signal High |
| P1447 | 2A17 | Diagnostic Module Tank Leakage (DMTL) Pump Current Too High during Switching Solenoid Test |
| P1448 | 2A17 | Diagnostic Module Tank Leakage (DMTL) Pump Current Too Low |
| P1449 | 2A17 | Diagnostic Module Tank Leakage (DMTL) Pump Current Too High |
| P1451 | | Diagnostic Module Tank Leakage (DMTL) Switching Solenoid Control Circuit Signal Low |
| P1452 | | Diagnostic Module Tank Leakage (DMTL) Switching Solenoid Control Circuit Signal High |
| P1453 | 2A03 | Secondary Air Injection Pump Relay Control Circuit Fault |
| P15AA | 30FC | Turbocharger Leak in System |
| P15A1 | 30C4 | Engine Oil Pressure Mechanical Valve Stuck in De-energized Position |
| P15A2 | 30C4 | Engine Oil Pressure Mechanical Valve Stuck in Fully Energized Position |
| P15A3 | 30C5 | Engine Oil Pressure Too High |
| P15A6 | 30C6 | Engine Oil Pressure Too High Before Start |
| P15A7 | 30C6 | Engine Oil Pressure Too Low Before Start |
| P15A9 | 2FC7 | Energy Saving Mode - Transportation Mode |
| P15B0 | 2DC3 | Terminal 15 Sense Circuit Input High |
| P15B1 | 2DC3 | Terminal 15 Sense Circuit Input Low |
| P15B2 | 2DC3 | Terminal 15 Sense Circuit CAS Error |
| P15B3 | 2DC3 | Terminal 15 Sense Circuit Range / Performance |
| P150A | 2E8B | Battery Sensor Extended Communication Circuit |
| P150B | 2E8B | Battery Sensor Serial Data Interface |
| P150C | 2E8B | Battery Sensor Firmware Implausible |
| P150D | 2E8B | Battery Sensor Temperature Error |
| P150E | 2E8C | Battery Sensor Voltage Error |
| P150F | 28EC | Battery Sensor Current Error |
| P1500 | | Idle-Speed Control Valve Stuck Open |
| P1501 | | Idle-Speed Control Valve Stuck Closed |
| P1502 | | Idle-Speed Control Valve Closing Solenoid Control Circuit Signal High |

**OBD**

**Table a. Diagnostic trouble codes (DTCs) (continued)**

| P-code | BMW FC | Definition |
|--------|--------|------------|
| P1503 | | Idle-Speed Control Valve Closing Solenoid Control Circuit Signal Low |
| P1504 | | Idle-Speed Control Valve Closing Solenoid Control Open Circuit |
| P1506 | | Idle-Speed Control Valve Opening Solenoid Control Circuit Signal High |
| P1507 | | Idle-Speed Control Valve Opening Solenoid Control Circuit Signal Low |
| P1508 | | Idle-Speed Control Valve Opening Solenoid Control Open Circuit |
| P151A | 2E8D | Battery Sensor Terminal 15 / 30 Wakeup Circuit |
| P151B | 2E8D | Battery Sensor Wakeup Circuit |
| P151C | 2E8D | Battery Sensor System Error |
| P1511 | 2AA8 | DISA (Differentiated Intake Manifold) Control Circuit |
| P1511 | 2AA9 | DISA (Differentiated Intake Manifold) Control Circuit |
| | 2AAA | Variable Intake System Plausibility |
| P1512 | 2AA8 | DISA (Differentiated Intake Manifold) Control Circuit Signal Low |
| P1512 | 2AA9 | DISA (Differentiated Intake Manifold) Control Circuit Signal Low |
| P1513 | 2AA8 | DISA (Differentiated Intake Manifold) Control Circuit Signal High |
| P1513 | 2AA9 | DISA (Differentiated Intake Manifold) Control Circuit Signal High |
| P1515 | 2F80 | Engine OFF Timer Plausibility |
| P1521 | 2E9F | Engine Oil Quality Sensor Temperature Communication Error |
| P1523 | | 'A' Camshaft Position Actuator Signal Low (Bank 1) |
| P1524 | | 'A' Camshaft Position Actuator Control Circuit Signal High (Bank 1) |
| P1525 | | 'A' Camshaft Position Actuator Control Open Circuit (Bank 1) |
| P1529 | | 'B' Camshaft Position Actuator Control Circuit Signal Low (Bank 1) |
| P1530 | | 'B' Camshaft Position Actuator Control Circuit Signal High (Bank 1) |
| P1531 | | 'B' Camshaft Position Actuator Control Open Circuit (Bank 1) |
| P1540 | 2AC6 | Driving Dynamics Switch Input High |
| P1541 | 2AC6 | Driving Dynamics Switch Input Low |
| P155A | 2DB7 | Multifunction Steering Wheel Toggle-Bit Fault |
| P1551 | 2F80 | Engine OFF Timer Time-out |
| P1553 | 2A99 | Engine Position System 'B' Performance (Bank 1) |
| P1554 | 2A98 | Engine Position System 'A' Performance (Bank 1) |
| P1561 | 2AE0 | Cold Start Idle RPM Lower Than Expected |
| P1562 | 2AE0 | Cold Start Idle RPM Higher Than Expected |
| P1563 | 2DB6 | Multifunction Steering Wheel Rocker Switch Defective |
| P1565 | 2DB5 | Multifunction Steering Wheel Rocker Switch + / - Pressed Simultaneously |
| P1567 | 2DB7 | Multifunction Steering Wheel Toggle Bit Error |
| | 2DBE | Adaptive Cruise Control Blocked for Driving Cycle |
| | 2DC0 | No Message From LDM |
| | 2DC3 | Monitoring Terminal 15 |

| Table a. Diagnostic trouble codes (DTCs) (continued) | | |
|---|---|---|
| P-code | BMW FC | Definition |
| P1576 | 2DB5 | Multifunction Steering Wheel Interface Error |
| P1582 | 30C2 | Oil Pump Circuit High |
| P1583 | 30C2 | Oil Pump Circuit Low |
| P1584 | 30C2 | Oil Pump Circuit Open |
| P1586 | 2E9F | Engine Oil Quality Sensor Temperature Measurement |
| P1587 | 2E9F | Engine Oil Quality Sensor Temperature Level Measurement |
| P1588 | 2E9F | Engine Oil Quality Sensor Temperature Permeability Measurement |
| P16A0 | 2AB3 | Internal Control Module Checksum Fault |
| P16A1 | 2AB3 | Internal Control Module Application Software Checksum Fault |
| P16A2 | 2AB3 | Internal Control Module Checksum Fault in Data |
| P16A3 | 2AB4 | Internal Control Module Checksum Fault in Non-Volatile Memory |
| P16A4 | 2AB5 | Time-out Control Module Knock Sensor SPI-Bus |
| P16A5 | 2AB6 | Time-out Control Module Multiple Output Stage SPI-Bus |
| P16A6 | 2D50 | Control Module Self test / Cruise Control Monitoring |
| P16A7 | 2D51 | Control Module Self Test Hot Film Air Mass Meter Monitoring |
| P16A8 | 2D51 | Control Module Self Test Throttle Position Monitoring |
| P16A9 | 2D52 | Control Module Self Test Speed Monitoring Reset |
| P16B1 | 2D56 | Control Module Self Test Idle Air Control System Plausibility |
| P16B2 | 2D56 | Control Module Self Test Idle Air Control System Component Plausibility |
| P16B3 | 2D57 | Control Module Self Test Engine Drag Torque |
| P16B4 | 2D50 | Control Module Self Test Dynamic Cruise Control Monitoring |
| P16B5 | 2D57 | Control Module Self Test Automatic Manual Transmission |
| P16B6 | 2D57 | Control Module Self Test ETC Monitoring |
| P16B7 | 2D58 | Control Module Self Test Clutch Torque Monitoring Maximum value Plausibility |
| P16B8 | 2D58 | Control Module Self Test Clutch Torque Monitoring |
| P16B9 | 2D58 | Control Module Self Test Torque Loss Monitoring |
| P16C0 | 2D58 | Control Module Self Test Driving Dynamics Control Switch Monitoring |
|  | 2D5A | Monitoring Engine Torque Limiting |
| P16C1 | 2D59 | Control Module Self Test Torque Monitoring Current Indicated value Plausibility |
| P16C2 | 2D53 | Control Module Self Test Speed Limitation Monitoring |
| P16C3 | 2D54 | Control Module Self Test Speed Limitation Reset |
| P16C5 | 2AAC | DME Main Relay Switching Delay |
| P16C6 | 2E7C | CAN Time-out Bit Serial Data Interface |
| P16C8 | 2DE0 | Serial Communication Link EKP (Electronic Fuel Pump) |
| P164C | 2D1D | Pedal Position Sensor Potentiometer Supply Channel 1 Electrical |
| P16B0 | 2D55 | Control Module Self Test Pedal Position Monitoring |
| P160A | 2DEC | Powermanagement Exhaustive Discharge |

OBD

**Table a. Diagnostic trouble codes (DTCs) (continued)**

| P-code | BMW FC | Definition |
|--------|--------|------------|
| P160B | 2DEC | Powermanagement Defective |
| P160C | 2DEB | Powermanagement Overvoltage |
| P160D | 2DEB | Powermanagement Undervolatge |
| P160E | 2DEB | Powermanagement Operation Without Battery |
| P160F | 2DED | Powermanagement No Load Current Error |
| P165F | 2CA6 | Internal Control Module Measurement Error O2 Sensor Heating (Bank 1 Sensor 1) |
| P1602 |  | Control Module Self-Test, Control Module Defective |
| P1603 |  | Control Module Self-Test, Torque Monitoring |
| P1604 |  | Control Module Self-Test, Speed Monitoring |
| P1611 | 2DC8 | Serial Communication Link TCM |
| P1612 | 2DD0 | Serial Communication Link Instrument Panel |
| P1613 | 2DCC | Serial Communication Link ASC |
| P1613 | 2DCD | Serial Communication Link ASC |
| P1613 | 2DCE | Serial Communication Link ASC |
| P1618 | 2D5C | Control Module Self Test AD-Converter Monitoring |
| P1619 |  | Map Cooling Thermostat Control Circuit Signal Low |
| P1620 |  | Map Cooling Thermostat Control Circuit Signal High |
| P1624 | 2D1D | Pedal Position Sensor Potentiometer Supply Channel 1 Electrical (M52: Coolant Thermostat (Coolant Temperature Below Thermostat Regulating Temperature)) |
| P1625 | 2D1E | Pedal Position Sensor Potentiometer Supply Channel 2 Electrical |
| P1632 | 2CFB | Throttle Valve Adaptation Conditions Not Met |
| P1633 | 2CFB | Throttle Valve Adaptation Limp-Home Position Unknown |
| P1634 |  | Throttle Valve Adaptation Spring Test Failed |
| P1634 | 2CFC | Throttle Valve Adaptation Spring Test Failed |
| P1635 | 2CFE | Throttle Valve Adaptation Lower Mechanical Stop not Adapted |
| P1636 | 2CEF | Throttle Valve Control Circuit |
| P1637 | 2CEE | Throttle Valve Position Control, Control Deviation |
| P1638 | 2CEC | Throttle Valve Position Control Throttle Stuck Temporarily |
| P1639 | 2CED | Throttle Valve Position Control Throttle Stuck Permanently |
| P164E | 2D0C | Throttle Deicing Stuck in Closed Direction |
| P164F | 2D0C | Throttle Deicing Stuck in Open Direction |
| P1644 | 2CFB | Throttle Valve Adaptation Relearning Lower Mechanical Stop |
| P166A | 2D50 | Control Module Self Test, Hot Film Air Mass Meter Monitoring |
| P166B | 2DC0 | Longitudinal Dynamics Module Torque Request Inspite of Brake Signal |
| P166C | 2DC0 | Longitudinal Dynamics Module Request Implausible |
| P166F | 2CA7 | Internal Control Module Measurement Error O2 Sensor Heating (Bank 2 Sensor 1) |
| P166F | 2CAB | Internal Control Module Measurement Error O2 Sensor Heating (Bank 2 Sensor 1) |

**Table a. Diagnostic trouble codes (DTCs) (continued)**

| P-code | BMW FC | Definition |
|--------|--------|------------|
| P1660 | 2F4A | EWS Telegram Error |
| P1661 | 2F4A | Time-out EWS Telegram |
| P165A | 2F4A | EWS Interface to ECM Error |
| P165B | 2F4A | EWS Interface to ECM Checksum Error |
| P165C | 2F4B | EWS Data, No Available Storage Possible |
| P165D | 2F4B | EWS Data, Faulty Release Code |
| P165E | 2F4B | EWS Data Checksum Error |
| P1667 | 2F49 | EWS Start Value not yet Programmed |
| P1668 | 2F4B | EWS Start Value Destroyed |
| P167C | 2D08 | Throttle Heating Relay Circuit Input Low |
| P167D | 2D08 | Throttle Heating Relay Circuit |
| P1675 | 2CFD | Throttle Valve Actuator Start Test Re-Adaptation Required |
| P169A | 2CFC | Throttle Valve Actuator Start Test Failed Limp Home Position |
| P1694 | 2CFB | Throttle Valve Actuator Start Test Spring Test and Limp-Home Position Failed |
| P1794 | 2DD3 | TCM Checksum Error |
| P2067 | 2DE1 | Fuel Level Sensor 'B' Circuit Low |
| P2068 | 2DE1 | Fuel Level Sensor 'B' Circuit High |
| P2088 | 2A80 | 'A' Camshaft Position Actuator Control Circuit Low (Bank 1) |
| P2089 | 2A80 | 'A' Camshaft Position Actuator Control Circuit High (Bank 1) |
| P2090 | 2A85 | 'B' Camshaft Position Actuator Control Circuit Low (Bank 1) |
| P2091 | 2A85 | 'B' Camshaft Position Actuator Control Circuit High (Bank 1) |
| P2096 | 2C31 | Post Catalyst Fuel Trim System Too Lean (Bank 1) |
| P2097 | 2C31 | Post Catalyst Fuel Trim System Too Rich (Bank 1) |
| P2098 | 2C32 | Post Catalyst Fuel Trim System Too Lean (Bank 2) |
| P2099 | 2C32 | Post Catalyst Fuel Trim System Too Rich (Bank 2) |
| P213F | 2AAD | Fuel Pump System Fault Engine Shut Down |
| P2120 | 2D1F | Throttle / Pedal Position Sensor 'D' Circuit |
| P2122 | 2D1B | Throttle Pedal Position Sensor 'D' Circuit Low |
| P2123 | 2D1B | Throttle Pedal Position Sensor 'D' Circuit High |
| P2127 | 2D1C | Throttle Pedal Position Sensor 'E' Circuit Low |
| P2128 | 2D1C | Throttle Pedal Position Sensor 'E' Circuit High |
| P213F | 2AAD | Fuel Pump Emergency Cut Off |
| P2138 | 2D20 | Throttle / Pedal Position Sensor 'D' 'E' Voltage Correlation |
| P2183 | 2EEC | Engine Coolant Temperature Sensor 2 Circuit Range / Performance |
| P2184 | 2EEA | Engine Coolant Temperate Sensor 2 Circuit Low |
| P2185 | 2EEA | Engine Coolant Temperate Sensor 2 Circuit High |
| P2187 | 29E0 | System Too Lean at Idle (Bank 1) |

**OBD**

**Table a. Diagnostic trouble codes (DTCs) (continued)**

| P-code | BMW FC | Definition |
|--------|--------|------------|
| P2188 | 29E0 | System Too Rich at Idle (Bank 1) |
| P2189 | 29E1 | System Too Lean at Idle (Bank 2) |
| P2190 | 29E1 | System Too Rich at Idle (Bank 2) |
| P2191 | 29E5 | System Too Lean, Higher Load (Bank 1) |
| P2192 | 29E5 | System Too Rich, Higher Load (Bank 1) |
| P2193 | 2E96 | System Too Lean, Higher Load (Bank 2) |
| P2194 | 2E96 | System Too Rich, Higher Load (Bank 2) |
| P2195 | 2C27 | O2 Sensor Signal Stuck Lean (Bank 1 Sensor 1) |
| P2196 | 2C27 | O2 Sensor Signal Stuck Rich (Bank 1 Sensor 1) |
| P2196 | 2C2B | O2 Sensor Signal Stuck Rich (Bank 1 Sensor 1) |
| P2196 | 2C2C | O2 Sensor Signal Stuck Rich (Bank 1 Sensor 1) |
| P2197 | 2C28 | O2 Sensor Signal Stuck Lean (Bank 2 Sensor 1) |
| P2198 | 2C2C | O2 Sensor Signal Stuck Rich (Bank 2 Sensor 1) |
| P2200 | 2AF4 | NOx Sensor Circuit (Bank 1) |
| P2205 | 2AF0 | NOx Sensor Heater Control Circuit Open (Bank 1) |
| P2228 | 2F76 | Barometric Pressure Circuit Low |
| P2229 | 2F76 | Barometric Pressure Circuit High |
| P2243 | 2C3D | O2 Sensor reference Voltage Circuit Open (Bank 1 Sensor 1) |
| P2247 | 2C3E | O2 Sensor Reference Voltage Circuit Open (Bank 2 Sensor 1) |
| P2270 | 2C6B | O2 Sensor Signal Stuck Lean (Bank 1 Sensor 2) |
| P2271 | 2C6B | O2 Sensor Signal Stuck Lean (Bank 1 Sensor 2) |
| P2272 | 2C6C | O2 Sensor Signal Stuck Lean (Bank 2 Sensor 2) |
| P2273 | 2C6C | O2 Sensor Signal Stuck Lean (Bank 2 Sensor 2) |
| P2297 | 2C2D | O2 Sensor Signal Out Of Range During Decel (Bank 1 Sensor 1) |
| P2298 | 2C2E | O2 Sensor Signal Out Of Range During Decel (Bank 2 Sensor 1) |
| P2299 | 2F8F | Brake Pedal Position / Accelerator Pedal Position Incompatible |
| P2301 | 30A0 | Ignition Coil Primary 'A' Circuit High |
| P2304 | 30A1 | Ignition Coil Primary 'B' Circuit High |
| P2307 | 30A2 | Ignition Coil Primary 'C' Circuit High |
| P2310 | 30A3 | Ignition Coil Primary 'D' Circuit High |
| P2313 | 30A4 | Ignition Coil Primary 'E' Circuit High |
| P2316 | 30A5 | Ignition Coil Primary 'F' Circuit High |
| P240A | 2A18 | DMTL Pump Heater Circuit Open |
| P240B | 2A18 | DMTL Pump Heater Circuit Low |
| P240C | 2A18 | DMTL Pump Heater Circuit High |
| P2400 | 2A13 | DMTL Activation Control Circuit Open |
| P2401 | 2A13 | DMTL Activation Control Circuit Low |

**Table a. Diagnostic trouble codes (DTCs) (continued)**

| P-code | BMW FC | Definition |
| --- | --- | --- |
| P2402 | 2A13 | DMTL Activation Control Circuit High |
| P2414 | 2C3B | O2 Sensor Oxygen Sample Error (Bank 1 Sensor 1) |
| P2415 | 2C3C | O2 Sensor Oxygen Sample Error (Bank 2 Sensor 1) |
| P2418 | 2A12 | DMTL Solenoid Control Circuit Open |
| P2419 | 2A12 | DMTL Solenoid Control Circuit Low |
| P2420 | 2A12 | Evaporative Emission System Switching Valve Control Circuit High |
| P250A | 2F9E | Engine Oil Level Sensor Circuit |
| P250B | 2F9E | Engine Oil Level Sensor Range / Performance |
| P250F | 2F9E | Engine Oil Level Too Low |
| P252A | 2EA1 | Engine Oil Quality Sensor Circuit |
| P2420 | 2A12 | DMTL Solenoid Control Circuit High |
| P2541 | 29F3 | Low Pressure Fuel System Sensor Circuit Low |
| P2542 | 29F3 | Low Pressure Fuel System Sensor Circuit High |
| P2568 | 2ADA | Direct Ozone Reduction Catalyst Temperature Sensor Performance |
| P2569 | 2ADA | Direct Ozone Reduction Catalyst Temperature Sensor Circuit Low |
| P2570 | 2ADA | Direct Ozone Reduction Catalyst Temperature Sensor Circuit High |
| P2626 | 2C3D | O2 Sensor Pumping Current Circuit Open (Bank 1 Sensor 1) |
| P2629 | 2C3E | O2 Sensor Pumping Current Circuit Open (Bank 2 Sensor 1) |
| P300A | 2F0D | Controlled Air Guiding Circuit High |
| P300B | 2F0D | Controlled Air Guiding Circuit Low |
| P300C | 2F0D | Controlled Air Guiding Circuit |
| P3003 | 29F2 | Fuel Rail Pressure Flow Rate Controlled, Pressure Too High |
| P3004 | 29F2 | Fuel Rail Pressure Flow Rate Controlled, Maximum Pressure Exceeded |
| P3022 | 2C41 | O2 Sensor Disturbed SPI WRAF-IC (Bank 1 Sensor 1) |
| P3023 | 2C42 | O2 Sensor Disturbed SPI WRAF-IC (Bank 2 Sensor 1) |
| P3024 | 2C41 | O2 Sensor Initialization Error WRAF-IC (Bank 1 Sensor 1) |
| P3025 | 2C42 | O2 Sensor Initialization Error WRAF-IC (Bank 1 Sensor 1) |
| P3026 | 2CAA | O2 Sensor Operating Temperature Not Reached (Bank 1 Sensor 1) |
| P3027 | 2CAA | O2 Sensor Operating Temperature Not Reached (Bank 2 Sensor 1) |
| P3041 | | O2 Sensor Lean and Rich Voltage Thresholds not Reached (Bank 2 Sensor 2) |
| P3090 | 29F2 | Fuel Rail Pressure Flow Rate Controlled, Fallen Below Minimum Pressure |
| P3094 | 2A2D | Fuel Low Pressure System Pressure Too High |
| P3095 | 2A2D | Fuel Low Pressure System Pressure Maximum Pressure Exceeded |
| P3096 | 2A2D | Fuel Low Pressure System Pressure Minimum Pressure Fallen Below |
| P310B | 2E30 | Cylinder 1 High Pressure Injector Low Side / High Side Electrical |
| P310E | 2E31 | Cylinder 2 High Pressure Injector Low Side / High Side Electrical |
| P3101 | 30AC | Cylinder 1 High Pressure Injector Low Side Circuit Low |

**OBD**

**Table a. Diagnostic trouble codes (DTCs) (continued)**

| P-code | BMW FC | Definition |
|--------|--------|------------|
| P3102 | 30AC | Cylinder 1 High Pressure Injector Low Side Circuit High |
| P3105 | 30AD | Cylinder 2 High Pressure Injector Low Side Circuit Low |
| P3106 | 30AD | Cylinder 2 High Pressure Injector Low Side Circuit high |
| P3109 | 30AE | Cylinder 3 High Pressure Injector Low Side Circuit Low |
| P311B | 2E32 | Cylinder 3 High Pressure Injector Low Side / High Side Electrical |
| P311E | 2E33 | Cylinder 4 High Pressure Injector Low Side / High Side Electrical |
| P3110 | 30AE | Cylinder 3 High Pressure Injector Low Side Circuit High |
| P3113 | 30AF | Cylinder 4 High Pressure Injector Low Side Circuit Low |
| P3114 | 30AF | Cylinder 4 High Pressure Injector Low Side Circuit High |
| P3117 | 30B0 | Cylinder 5 High Pressure Injector Low Side Circuit Low |
| P3118 | 30B0 | Cylinder 5 High Pressure Injector Low Side Circuit High |
| P312B | 2E34 | Cylinder 5 High Pressure Injector Low Side / High Side Electrical |
| P312E | 2E35 | Cylinder 6 High Pressure Injector Low Side / High Side Electrical |
| P3121 | 30B1 | Cylinder 6 High Pressure Injector Low Side Circuit Low |
| P3122 | 30B1 | Cylinder 6 High Pressure Injector Low Side Circuit High |
| P3149 | 30AC | Cylinder 1 High Pressure Injector High Side Circuit Low |
| P3150 | 30AC | Cylinder 1 High Pressure Injector High Side Circuit High |
| P3152 | 30AC | Cylinder 2 High Pressure Injector High Side Circuit Low |
| P3153 | 30AD | Cylinder 2 High Pressure Injector High Side Circuit High |
| P3155 | 30AD | Cylinder 3 High Pressure Injector High Side Circuit Low |
| P3156 | 30AE | Cylinder 3 High Pressure Injector High Side Circuit High |
| P3158 | 30AF | Cylinder 4 High Pressure Injector High Side Circuit Low |
| P3159 | 30AF | Cylinder 4 High Pressure Injector High Side Circuit High |
| P316A | 2EE6 | Engine Coolant Temperature Signal Stuck High |
| P3161 | 30B0 | Cylinder 5 High Pressure Injector High Side Circuit Low |
| P3162 | 30B0 | Cylinder 5 High Pressure Injector High Side Circuit High |
| P3164 | 30B1 | Cylinder 6 High Pressure Injector High Side Circuit Low |
| P3165 | 30B1 | Cylinder 6 High Pressure Injector High Side Circuit High |
|  | 2FBF | Fuel Supply Pressure Low During Release of Injection |
|  | 2FC0 | Fuel Rail Pressure Management Range |
| P319A | 2FBD | Fuel Pressure Control Minimum Characteristic Curve Operation 1 Out of Range |
| P3194 | 2FBD | Fuel Pressure Control Basic Characteristic Curve Operation 1 Out of Range |
| P3196 | 2EEC | Radiator Coolant Temperature Sensor High |
| P3197 | 2EEB | Radiator Coolant Temperature Gradient Too High |
| P3198 | 2EE3 | Engine Coolant Temperature Gradient Too High |
| P3199 | 2EE2 | Engine Coolant Temperature Signal Stuck |
| P3202 | CD87 | Powertrain CAN Chip Cut-Off |

**Table a. Diagnostic trouble codes (DTCs) (continued)**

| P-code | BMW FC | Definition |
|--------|--------|------------|
| P3205 | CD8B | Local CAN Chip Cut-Off |
| P321E | 2F77 | Ambient Pressure Sensor Maximum Pressure Implausible |
| P321F | 2F77 | Ambient Pressure Sensor Minimum Pressure Implausible |
| P3213 | 2DD3 | CAN Message Monitoring ETC Alive Check |
| P3223 | 2E97 | Generator Mechanical |
| P2332 | 2ED1 | Generator Mechanical |
| P3226 | 27F1 | E-box Control Fan High Input |
| P3227 | 27F1 | E-box Control Fan Low Input |
| P3228 | 27F1 | E-box Control Fan Open Circuit |
| P323F | 2D60 | Control Module Monitoring Fuel Volume, Air Mass Injected Fuel Volume Correlation |
| P3235 | 2FA4 | Control Module Monitoring Version Coding Plausibility |
| P3238 |  | Control Module Monitoring TPU Chip Defective |
| P324A | 2E97 | Generator Type Implausible |
| P324A | 2ED3 | Generator Type Implausible |
| P324C | 2ED0 | Generator Over Temperature Calculated |
| P324E | 2ED2 | Generator Regulator Type Implausible |
| P325A | 2ECE | Generator Electrical Error Calculated |
| P3255 | 2E96 | Generator Voltage In Starting Above Threshold |
| P3256 | 2DD2 | CAN Time-out Steering Angle Sensor |
| P3259 | 2D60 | Control Module Monitoring Fuel Volume, Lambda Implausible to Operating Mode |
| P3283 | 29F1 | Fuel Pressure Control Adaptive Fuel Volume Out of Range (Bank 1) |
| P3284 | 29F1 | Fuel Pressure Control Adaptive Fuel Volume Implausible (Bank 1) |

**OBD**

# 2  INDEX

**Engine**
applications 100-2
basic settings 130-5
belt 020-35
compartment 020-22, ECL-33
cooling system 100-8
  *see also* Cooling system
covers 020-25
crankcase 100-3
crankshaft seals 119-6
electrical system 121-1
grounds 130-6, ECL-29
hood 410-4
identification guide, non-turbo 113-2, 117-2
lubrication 119-1
management 100-2, 120-4, 130-4
N51 010-15
N52 010-12, 100-3
N54 010-16, 100-9
oil 020-39, 119-1
on-board diagnostics 130-6, OBD-1
pulley 117-5, 117-6
removal / installation 110-2
serial number 020-17, 100-1
specifications 100-2
troubleshooting 170-5
*see also* DME (digital motor electronics)
*see also* ECM (Engine control module)

**Engine control module**
*see* ECM (engine control module)

**Engine coolant temperature (ECT) sensor**
non-turbo 130-25
turbo 130-64
*see also* Cooling system

**Engine cooling fan**
170-2, 170-11

**Engine electronics fuse carrier**
ECL-25

**Engine hood**
410-4
service position 410-6

**Engine management**
*see* DME (digital motor electronics)

**Evaporative control system**
160-6
carbon canister, activated 160-3, 160-4, 160-6, 160-7, 160-27
DMTL 160-3, 160-4, 160-6, 160-28
monitoring OBD-5

**Evaporator**
temperature sensor 640-6

**EWS (electronic immobilizer)**
515-23

**Exhaust manifold**
non-turbo 180-5
turbo 180-6

**Exhaust system**
020-46, 180-1
diagrams 180-20
*see also* Catalytic converter
*see also* Oxygen sensor

**Expansion tank**
020-33, 170-2, 170-12

**Expansion valve**
640-22

**Exterior**
cleaning 020-49
washing 020-48

**F**

**Fan**
*see* Cooling system
*see also* IHKA, blower

**Fasteners**
020-12
aluminum 020-13

**Fault code**
*see* DTC (diagnostic trouble code)

**Fault memory**
OBD-2

**F-CAN**
600-6

**Fender**
front 410-2

**Filters**
air 020-27
cabin microfilter 020-32, 640-10, 640-19
fuel 020-42
oil 020-41

**Final drive**
*see* Differential

**Firing order**
120-2

**Flat tire indication**
020-19

**Flex-disc, rear driveshaft**
260-2, 260-13

**Flywheel**
210-14, 240-19

**Foglight**
630-26

**Footwell module (FRM)**
010-30, 512-1, 512-2, 515-4, 600-10, 630-4, 630-14

**Freeze-frame data**
OBD-3, OBD-7

**Fresh air microfilter**
020-32, 640-10, 640-19

**FRM (footwell module)**
010-30, 512-1, 512-2, 515-4, 600-10, 630-4, 630-14

**Front centering sleeve**
260-14

**Front end reinforcement**
310-2

**Front suspension**
010-20, 300-3, 310-2
aluminum components 300-2
arms 300-3, 310-9
ride height 320-18
  sensor 630-11
stabilizer bar 300-3, 310-18
struts / springs 300-1, 300-2, 300-3, 310-2, 310-4
subframe 300-3
wheel bearing 310-13
tension strut 300-3, 310-2, 310-11
thrust arm 300-3

**Fuel filler emergency release**
515-2

**Fuel filter**
020-42, 160-27

**Fuel injection**
*see* DME (digital motor electronics)
*see also* Fuel injector
*see also* Ignition system

**Fuel injector**
non-turbo 130-10, 130-18
turbo 130-47

**Fuel level sender**
160-15, 160-21

**Fuel pressure**
regulator 160-13
testing 160-13

**Fuel pump**
160-2, 160-15
fuse 160-8
high pressure 100-10, 160-22
module (EKP) 160-2, 160-3, 160-4, 160-8, 160-27
*see also* Fuel system

**Fuel rail**
non-turbo 130-18
turbo 130-56

**Fuel system**
160-3, 160-4
monitoring OBD-5
schematic 160-3, 160-4
troubleshooting 160-8

> **WARNING**
>
> *Your common sense, good judgement and general alertness are crucial to safe and successful service work. Before attempting any work on your BMW, be sure to read* **001 Warnings and Cautions** *and the copyright page at the front of the manual. Review these warnings and cautions each time you prepare to work on your car. Please also read any warnings and cautions that accompany the procedures in the manual.*

# Selected Books and Repair Information From Bentley Publishers

## Motorsports

**Alex Zanardi: My Sweetest Victory**
*Alex Zanardi and Gianluca Gasparini*
ISBN 978-0-8376-1249-2

**The Unfair Advantage** *Mark Donohue and Paul van Valkenburgh*
ISBN 978-0-8376-0069-7

**The Racing Driver: The Theory and Practice of Fast Driving** *Denis Jenkinson*
ISBN 978-0-8376-0201-1

**The Technique of Motor Racing**
*Piero Taruffi*
ISBN 978-0-8376-0228-8

**A French Kiss with Death: Steve McQueen and the Making of Le Mans**
*Michael Keyser*
ISBN 978-0-8376-0234-9

**Equations of Motion - Adventure, Risk and Innovation**
*William F. Milliken*
ISBN 978-0-8376-1570-7

## Engineering

**Bosch Fuel Injection and Engine Management** *Charles O. Probst, SAE*
ISBN 978-0-8376-0300-1

**Maximum Boost: Designing, Testing, and Installing Turbocharger Systems**
*Corky Bell* ISBN 978-0-8376-0160-1

**Supercharged! Design, Testing and Installation of Supercharger Systems**
*Corky Bell* ISBN 978-0-8376-0168-7

**Race Car Aerodynamics** *Joseph Katz*
ISBN 978-0-8376-0142-7

**Scientific Design of Exhaust and Intake Systems** *Phillip H. Smith & John C. Morrison* ISBN 978-0-8376-0309-4

## Audi Repair Manuals

**Audi A4 Service Manual: 1996-2001, 1.8L Turbo, 2.8L, including Avant and quattro** *Bentley Publishers*
ISBN 978-0-8376-1675-9

**Audi TT Service Manual: 2000-2006, 1.8L turbo, 3.2 L, including Roadster and quattro** *Bentley Publishers*
ISBN 978-0-8376-1625-4

**Audi A6, S6: 2005-2007 Repair Manual on DVD-ROM** *Audi of American*
ISBN 978-0-8376-1362-8

**Audi A6 (C5 platform) Service Manual: 1998-2004, includes A6, allroad quattro, S6, RS6** *Bentley Publishers*
ISBN 978-0-8376-1670-4

## BMW

**Unbeatable BMW** *Jeremy Walton*
ISBN 978-0-8376-1614-8

**BMW Enthusiast's Companion: Owner's Insights on Driving, Performance and Service** *BMW Car Club of America* ISBN 978-0-8376-0321-6

**BMW 6 Series Enthusiast's Companion** *Jeremy Walton*
ISBN 978-0-8376-0193-2

**BMW X5 (E53) Service Manual: 2000-2006** *Bentley Publishers*
ISBN 978-0-8376-1643-8

**BMW 3 Series (E46) Service Manual: 1999-2005** *Bentley Publishers*
ISBN 978-0-8376-1657-5

**BMW Z3 (E36/7) Service Manual: 1996-2002** *Bentley Publishers*
ISBN 978-0-8376-1617-9

**BMW 5 Series (E39) Service Manual: 1997-2003** *Bentley Publishers*
ISBN 978-0-8376-1672-8

**BMW 3 Series (E36) Service Manual: 1992-1998** *Bentley Publishers*
ISBN 978-0-8376-0326-1

**BMW 7 Series (E38) Service Manual: 1995-2001** *Bentley Publishers*
ISBN 978-0-8376-1618-6

**BMW 7 Series (E32) Service Manual: 1988-1994** *Bentley Publishers*
ISBN 978-0-8376-1619-3

**BMW 3 Series (E30) Service Manual: 1984-1990** *Bentley Publishers*
ISBN 978-0-8376-1647-6

**BMW 5 Series (E28) Service Manual: 1982-1988** *Bentley Publishers*
ISBN 978-0-8376-0318-6

**BMW 5 Series (E34) Service Manual: 1989-1995** *Bentley Publishers*
ISBN 978-0-8376-0319-3

**BMW 5 Series (E60, E61) Service Manual: 2004-2010** *Bentley Publishers*
ISBN 978-0-8376-1621-6

## Porsche

**Porsche Boxster Service Manual: 1997-2004** *Bentley Publishers*
ISBN 978-0-8376-1645-2

**Porsche 911 Carrera Service Manual: 1984-1989** *Bentley Publishers*
ISBN 978-0-8376-0291-2

**Ferdinand Porsche: Genesis of Genius**
*Karl Ludvigsen* ISBN 978-0-8376-1557-8

**Porsche: Excellence Was Expected**
*Karl Ludvigsen* ISBN 978-0-8376-0235-6

## Volkswagen

**Volkswagen Jetta Service Manual: 2006-2010** *Bentley Publishers*
ISBN 978-0-8376-1616-2

**Volkswagen Jetta, Golf, GTI Service Manual: 1999-2005** *Bentley Publishers*
ISBN 978-0-8376-1251-5

**Volkswagen Passat Service Manual: 1998-2005** *Bentley Publishers*
ISBN 978-0-8376-1669-8

**Volkswagen Rabbit, GTI Service Manual: 2006-2009** *Bentley Publishers*
ISBN 978-0-8376-1664-3

**Volkswagen Jetta, Golf, GTI: 1993-1999, Cabrio: 1995-2002 Service Manual** *Bentley Publishers*
ISBN 978-0-8376-1660-5

**Volkswagen GTI, Golf, Jetta Service Manual: 1985-1992** *Bentley Publishers*
ISBN 978-0-8376-1637-7

## MINI Repair Manuals

**MINI Cooper Service Manual: 2002-2006** *Bentley Publishers*
ISBN 978-0-8376-1639-1

**MINI Cooper Diagnosis Without Guesswork: 2002-2006**
*Bentley Publishers*
ISBN 978-0-8376-1571-4

## Mercedes-Benz

**Mercedes-Benz C-Class (W202) Service Manual 1994-2000**
*Bentley Publishers*
ISBN 978-0-8376-1572-1

**Mercedes Benz E-Class (W124) Owner's Bible: 1986-1995**
*Bentley Publishers*
ISBN 978-0-8376-0230-1

**Mercedes-Benz Technical Companion**
*Staff of The Star and members of Mercedes-Benz Club of America*
ISBN 978-0-8376-1033-7